JAVA

AN INTRODUCTION TO COMPUTER SCIENCE AND PROGRAMMING

SECOND EDITION

Walter Savitch

An Alan R. Apt Book

Prentice Hall
Upper Saddle River, New Jersey 07458

Library of Congress Cataloging-in-Publication Data on File

Publisher: Alan Apt
Vice-President and Editorial Director: Marcia Horton
Vice-President of Production and Manufacturing: David Riccardi
Director of Creative Services: Paul Belfanti
Associate Creative Director: Carole Anson
Art Director: Heather Scott
Executive Managing Editor: Vince O'Brien
Managing Editor: David A. George
Developmental Editor: Jerry Ralya
Production Supervision: Scott Disanno
Assistant to Art Director: John Christiana
Manufacturing Buyer: Dawn Murrin

© 2001 by Prentice Hall
Prentice-Hall Inc.
Upper Saddle River, NJ 07458

The author and publisher of this book have used their best efforts in preparing this book. These efforts include research, development, and testing of the theory and programs in this book to determine their effectiveness. The author and publisher make no warranty of any kind, expressed or implied, with regard to these programs or the documentation contained in this book. The author and publisher shall not be liable in any even for incidental or consequential damages in connection with, or arising out of, the furnishing, performance, or use of these programs

Printed in the United States of America
10 9 8 7 6 5 4 3 2

ISBN   0-13-031697-0

Prentice-Hall International (UK) Limited, London
Prentice-Hall of Australia Pty. Limited, Sydney
Prentice-Hall Canada Inc., Toronto
Prentice-Hall Hispanoamericana, S.A., Mexico
Prentice-Hall of India Private Limited, New Delhi
Prentice-Hall of Japan, Inc., Tokyo
Prentice-Hall P.TE Ltd., Singapore
Editora Prentice-Hall do Brasil, Ltda., Rio de Janeiro

TRADEMARK INFORMATION
ANSI is a registered trademark of American National Standards Institute
CodeWarrior is a registered trademark of Metrowerks, Inc.
Java, Duke, and all Java based trademarks and logos are trademarks or registered trademarks of Sun Microsystems, Inc. in the United States and other countries.
JBuilder and JBuilder Foundation are trademarks of Inprise/Borland.
Mac, Macintosh, and MacOS are trademarks of Apple Computer, Inc.
Netscape and Netscape Navigator are trademarks of Netscape Communications, Inc.
TextPad is a trademark of Helios Software Solutions.
UNIX is a trademark of UNIX System Laboratories.
Windows, WindowsNT, and Internet Explorer are trademarks or registered trademarks of Microsoft Corporation.

To
Christina

PREFACE FOR STUDENTS

This book is designed to teach you the Java programming language, and even more importantly, to teach you basic programming techniques. This book requires no previous programming experience and no mathematics other than some very simple high school algebra. However, to get the full benefit of the book, you should have a version of Java available on your computer, so that you can practice with the examples and techniques given in the book. You should have a version of Java called Java 2 (or some number higher than 2). If you have a version number of the form 1.1.x or 1.2.x, then the version number should be 1.2.x or higher. (The exact number that is filled in for the x is not critical. The x need not even be present. If it says only "version 1.2," that is fine.)

If You Have Programmed Before

You need not have any previous programming experience to use this book. This book was designed for beginners. However, the book can still be used to learn Java if you happen to have had experience with some other programming languages, but allow me to give you a few words of advice. If you have programmed before, do not assume that Java is the same as the programming language(s) you are used to using. All languages are different. And the differences, even if small, are large enough to give you problems. Read at least the boxed sections of Section 1.4 in Chapter 1 and all the boxed sections of Chapters 2 and 3. By the time you reach Chapter 4, it would be wise to read the entire chapter.

If you have programmed before in either C or C++, the transition to Java can be troublesome. While Java is very different from C and C++, at first glance it looks as if it is the same as C++. Appendix 11 has a comparison of Java and C++ that will help you see the differences between Java and C++ (or Java and C).

Copies of the Programs from the Text

This book contains a CD that includes all the programs and other software examples in the book, so that you can practice with these examples without having to type them into your computer.

Obtaining a Copy of Java

How and what version of Java you use depends somewhat on what operating system you are using. Be sure to consult the subsection below that corresponds to your operating system.

Microsoft Windows

Alternative 1:
The CD that comes with this book includes a version of JBuilder 3.5 Foundation, a complete Java integrated environment from Inprise/Borland. JBuilder includes an

editor and other utilities in addition to the Java language. This has everything you need to write and run Java programs. This is a professional strength environment, which can be a bit complex for novices, so we also have an alternative that gives you an easier environment.

Alternative 2:
This is a bit more complicated to initially set up, but easier to use once you do set up things. Download a free Java compile over the Internet from Sun Microsystems. Install that Java compiler and the TextPad environment, which is provided on the CD that comes with this book. The TextPad environment provides an editor and other tools to use when writing Java programs.

   At the time this book went to press, the site for the Java compiler download from Sun Microsystems was:

```
http://java.sun.com/products/jdk/1.2/
```

Mac Operating System

There is a version of Java for the Mac that can be downloaded from the Sun Micro-systems website. Unfortunately, users have not been happy with the Mac version of Java provided at this site, and indeed, it may not do all things discussed in this book.

   If you are using the Mac operating system, one good alternative is to purchase a version of CodeWarrior from Metrowerks, Inc. It works well with the Mac operating system.

   A version of JBuilder for the Mac is due out soon and promises be an excellent alternative for Mac users. You may want to check the following website to see if it is available. If it is, you can download it from there.

```
http://www.borland.com/jbuilder/foundation/download/
```

UNIX Operating System

Alternative 1:
The CD that comes with this book includes a version of JBuilder 3.5 Foundation, a complete Java integrated environment from Inprise/Borland. JBuilder includes an editor and other utilities in addition to the Java language. This has all the software you need in order to write and run Java programs. JBuilder has versions for both the Solaris and Linux operating systems.

Alternative 2:
You can down load a free Java compiler over the Internet from Sun Microsystems. At the time this book went to press, the site for the Java download from Sun Microsystems was:

```
http://java.sun.com/products/jdk/1.2/
```

We do not have an editor/environment (other than JBuilder) that we recommend for use with this compiler. You can use your favorite editor to write programs and then run your Java programs from the command line as described in Chapter 1. (Or you may find an environment you like and can use it.)

Self-Test Questions

Each chapter contains numerous self-test questions. Complete answers for all the self-test questions are given at the end of each chapter. One of the best ways to practice what you are learning is to do the self-test questions *without looking at the answers*. Only look at the answers after you have answered the self-test questions.

This Text Is Also a Reference Book

In addition to using this book as a textbook, you can and should use it as a reference. When you need to check a particular point that you may have forgotten or that you hear mentioned by somebody but have not yet learned yourself, just look in the index. Many index entries give a page number for "quick reference." Turn to this quick reference page. It will contain a short entry, usually set off in a box, that gives all the essential points on that topic. This can be done to check details of the Java language, as well as details on programming techniques.

    Boxed sections in every chapter give you a quick summary of the main points in that chapter. You can use these boxes to review the chapter, preview the chapter, or check details of the Java language.

Updates and Corrections

Any updates or corrections will be listed on the author's website for this book

```
http://www.cse.ucsd.edu/users/savitch/books/cs1.java/
```

We Want Your Opinions

This book was written for you, and I would like to hear any comments you have on the book. You can contact me via electronic mail at the following address:

```
wsavitch@ucsd.edu
```

    Unfortunately, I cannot provide you with answers to the programming exercises. Only instructors who adopt the book can receive (selected) answers from the publisher. For help on the programming exercises, you will have to contact your instructor. (Even if you are not enrolled in a class we still cannot provide answers to programming exercises.) But, remember that there are answers to all the self-test questions at the end of each chapter.

Walter Savitch
```
http://www.cse.ucsd.edu/users/savitch
```

PREFACE FOR INSTRUCTORS

This book was designed to be used in a first course in programming and computer science. It covers programming techniques, as well as the basics of the Java programming language. It is suitable for courses as short as one quarter or as long as one full academic year. It requires no previous programming experience and no mathematics other than a little high school algebra. This book can also be used for a course designed to teach Java to students who have already had another programming course, in which case, the first few chapters can be assigned as outside reading. (If students have had previous programming experience in C or C++, then there is also an appendix that explains some differences between Java and C or C++.) All the code in the book has been tested using Java 2 of Sun Microsystems. The coverage of Java was carefully arrived at by class testing and is a concise, accessible introduction for beginners.

Changes in this Edition

If you have not used the first edition of this text, you can skip this subsection. If you have used the first edition, this subsection will tell you how this second edition differs from the first edition.

For instructors, the transition from the first edition of this text to this edition is easy. You can teach the same course with basically the same topics presented in the same order. Some chapters have changed numbers, but you can still cover those chapters in the order you are currently using. The biggest change was to move the arrays chapter forward to Chapter 6. However, you can cover arrays later if you prefer with no loss of continuity in reading the text. The only significant change you will need to contend with is that this edition uses the Swing library instead of using only the AWT library as the first edition did. However, there have been changes and additions that you may find helpful.

This edition adds coverage of the Swing Libraries, the Graphics class, and linked data structures to the topics covered in the first edition. In addition, the entire book has been rewritten to make the material clearer and more complete. There are many more Self-Test Questions and many more Programming Exercises in this edition.

In response to requests from users of the first edition, we have adopted the policy of listing instance variables first in class definitions (as opposed to last, as in the first edition).

This book also contains some early, optional material on applets and another GUI class named JOptionPane. This allows instructors to introduce GUI interfaces early if they wish, or wait to introduce them later (or not at all) if that is preferred.

Java 2 Coverage

The first edition of this book was already fully compatible with Java 2. This edition adds coverage of Swing and other Java 2 details to provide more complete coverage of Java 2.

Flexible

If you are an instructor, this book adapts to the way you teach, rather than making you adapt to the book. This book does not tightly prescribe the order in which your course must cover topics. Neither does it prescribe the specialized libraries that must be used in your course. You can easily change the order in which chapters and sections are covered. The details about rearranging material are explained in a chart at the end of this preface and in more details in a prerequisite section at the start of each chapter.

Since Java does not include any simple console input, most texts, even more advanced texts, provide some added class library for console input. This book requires that you add as little nonstandard software as possible, since only one simple class is added (for console input). Even that one console input class, which is included early in the book, becomes an understandable programming example for students well before the end of the book. All the remaining software is from standard Java libraries that should be part of any Java installation.

Coverage of Problem Solving and Programming Techniques

This book is designed to teach students basic problem-solving and programming techniques and is not simply a Java syntax book. The book contains numerous case studies and programming tips, as well as many other sections that explain important problem-solving and programming techniques, such as loop design techniques, debugging techniques, style techniques, abstract data types, basic object-oriented programming including event-driven programming, and other computer science topics.

Object-Oriented and Traditional Techniques

Any course that really teaches Java must teach classes early, since almost everything in Java involves classes. The behavior of parameters depends on whether they are class parameters. Even the behavior of the equals operator (==) depends on whether it is comparing objects or simpler data items. Classes cannot be avoided, except by means of absurdly long and complicated "magic formulas." This book introduces classes fairly early. Some exposure to using classes is introduced in Chapters 1 and 2. Defining classes is covered in Chapter 4. Moreover, all the basic information about classes, including inheritance, is presented by the end of Chapter 7 (and this can be done omitting Chapter 6). However, some topics on classes, including inheritance, can be postponed to later in a course.

Although this is an early classes book, it does not neglect traditional programming techniques, such as top-down design and loop design techniques. These older topics may no longer be glamorous, but they are information that all beginning students need.

Swing, Applets, and Other GUIs

Starting with Java 2, Java comes with an improved GUI library known as Swing that allows programmers to design portability GUIs (graphical user interfaces). This book uses Swing to teach students to produce professional looking windowing interfaces. In the process, students learn event-driven programming, as well as receiving a lot of practice with object-oriented programming.

As this material was class-tested and views of instructors were gathered, we found that Swing was a more accessible way to teach students object-oriented programming than applets. Thus, we place greater emphasis on Swing. This makes sense, since almost all advanced applets tools are really Swing tools. However, for those who do want to cover applets early, Chapter 1 has an optional section that previews applets. Chapter 13 covers applets in detail and may be covered much earlier than the chapter number suggests. You may choose to introduce GUIs early, late, or not at all.

With the introduction of the Swing libraries, there is a new class named `JOptionPane` that allows an easier introduction to GUIs than applets provide. This book covers `JOptionPane` in an optional section of Chapter 2. You have the choice of introducing either or both applets and `JOptionPane` either late or early (or not at all).

In addition to this optional GUI material in Chapters 1 and 2, this book includes three full chapters on GUIs, which gives thorough coverage of Swing, applets, and the `Graphics` class for simple two-dimensional graphics.

Language Details and Sample Code

This book teaches programming technique and does not simply teach the Java language. However, neither students nor instructors would be satisfied with an introductory programming course that did not also teach the programming language. Until you calm a student's fears about language details, it is often impossible to get her or his attention to discuss bigger issues. For this reason, this book gives complete explanations of Java language features and lots of sample code. Programs are given in their entirety along with sample input and output. In many cases, there are even extra complete examples on the CD, in addition to the complete examples in the text.

Self-Test Questions

Self-test questions are spread throughout each chapter. These questions have a wide range of difficulty levels. Some require only a one-word answer, whereas others require the reader to write an entire, nontrivial program. Complete answers for all the self-test questions, including those requiring full programs, are given at the end of each chapter.

Class Tested

The material in this book has been fully class tested. Much of the material and methods of presentation were revised in response to this class testing.

Support Material

The support materials described below can be obtained from the publisher, obtained over the Internet, or are included with the book.

CD-ROM

Each book contains a CD that includes all the programs and classes in the book. The CD also includes a version of JBuilder 3.5 Foundation, a complete Java integrated environment from Inprise/Borland. JBuilder includes an editor and other utilities in addition to the Java language. The CD includes versions of JBuilder for Windows, Solaris, and Linux operating systems. The CD also includes a copy of TextPad, a very nice integrated environment that runs under Windows and that is a suitable environment for use with Sun's Java 2.

Free Software

You have a wide choice of free software to use with this book. As already noted the CD that comes with this book includes JBuilder and TextPad.

JBuilder works under Windows, Solaris, and Linux operating systems. At the time this book went to press a version of JBuilder for the Mac was not available, but was due out soon. You may want to check the following website to see if it is available. If it is, you can download it from there.

```
http://www.borland.com/jbuilder/foundation/download/
```

Another very good alternative is to download a version of Java-2 from Sun Microsystems website. At the time this book went to press, the URL for the website was:

```
http://java.sun.com/products/jdk/1.2/
```

Java-2 is the main version of Java that we used in developing this text. The TextPad environment (which comes on the CD that accompanies this book) is a good environment to use with Sun's Java-2, provided you are using a Windows operating system. TextPad only runs under Windows.

Instructor's Resource Guide and Companion Website

Instructor tools include a chapter-by-chapter Instructor's Resource Guide that contains numerous teaching hints, quiz questions with solutions, and solutions to many programming exercises. The Companion Website includes code, PowerPoint slides, and other teaching resources. Instructors should contact their Prentice Hall sales representative to obtain a copy of the Instructor's Resource Guide and receive information on how to access the Companion Website. For the name and number of your sales representative, please call Prentice Hall Faculty Services at 1-800-526-0485. Additional information on this book and other Prentice Hall products can be found on Prentice Hall's website at

```
http://www.prenhall.com/
```

Updates and Corrections

Any updates or corrections will be listed on the author's website for this book

```
http://www.cse.ucsd.edu/users/savitch/books/cs1.java/
```

Acknowledgments

I thank the Computer Science and Engineering Department of the University of California, San Diego (UCSD), which is my home department and the place that I tested much of this material. Many students in my classes were kind enough to help correct preliminary versions of this text. These student comments and the comments of instructors who class tested this book were a tremendous help in shaping the final book. In particular, I extend a special thanks to Carole McNamee of California State University, Sacramento and to both Paul Kube and Susan Marx of UCSD; their feedback and class testing of earlier editions or drafts of the book was a great help to me in producing this edition.

I thank all the reviewers who took the time to read drafts of this or the previous edition of this book. They provided invaluable detailed comments and suggestions. In alphabetical order within each group, they are

Reviewers for this second edition:

Jim Buffenbarger—Idaho State
Martin Chetlen—Moorpark C.C.
Tom Cortina—SUNY, Stony Brook
Prasun Dewan—University of North Carolina
Laird Dornan—Sun Microsystems
H.E. Dunsmore—Purdue, Lafayette
Adel Elmaghraby—University of Louisville
Gopal Gupta—New Mexico State
Ric Heishman—North Virginia C.C.
Rob Kelly—SUNY, Stony Brook
Dr. Le Gruenwald—University of Oklahoma
Blayne Mayfield—Oklahoma State
Alan Saleski—Loyola, Chicago

Reviewers for the first edition:

Michael Clancy—University of California, Berkeley
Michael Godfrey—Cornell University
Robert Herrmann—Sun Microsystems, Java Soft

Robert Holloway—University of Wisconsin, Madison
Lily Hou—Carnegie-Mellon University
John Motil—California State University, Northridge
James Roberts—Carnegie-Mellon University
Nan C. Schaller—Rochester Institute of Technology
Ryan Shoemaker—Sun Microsystems, Inc.
Donald E. Smith—Rutgers University

I also thank all the individuals at Prentice Hall who organized the reviewing and production of this book. In particular, I thank Jake Warde for a masterful job of coordinating the entire processes including the reviews, Jerry Ralya my developmental editor for his excellent work in all aspects of the writing on this edition, Toni Holm for her work in coordinating things between offices, and to Gail Cocker, Heather Scott, and especially Scott Disanno for work on the design and production of the book. All these wonderful people cheerfully did a great job. I extend a special thanks to my publisher Alan Apt for his invaluable support and advice throughout the writing and production process.

I thank Lew Rakocy for his excellent work on the programming exercises added to this edition. I thank Brian Durney for his fine work on the instructor's support material.

I thank Sun Microsystems for allowing me to use the Duke icon in a number of my GUI examples.

Finally, I give an extra special thanks to Christina for putting up with me while I worked late on this book and for even going so far as to proofread some sections of the book for me.

Walter Savitch
wsavitch@ucsd.edu
http://www.cse.ucsd.edu/users/savitch

DEPENDENCY CHART

If there is a line between two boxes, then the material in the higher box should be done before the material in the lower box. Minor variations to this chart are discussed in the prerequisites section at the start of each chapter. These variations usually provide more, rather than less, flexibility.

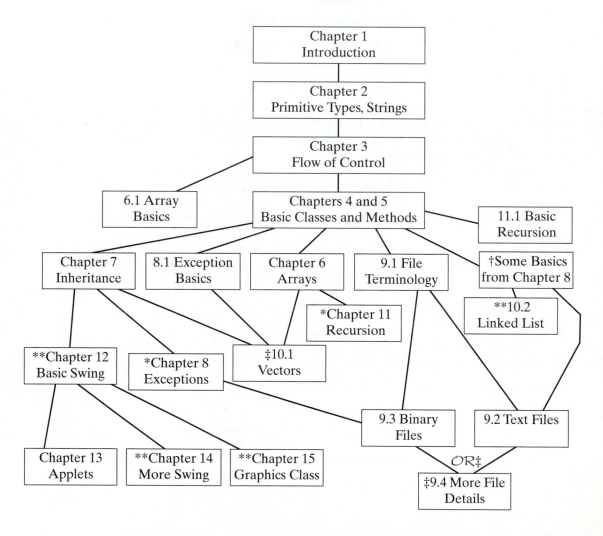

* Note that some sections of these chapters can be covered sooner. Those sections are given in this chart.

**See the chapter prerequisites section for full details.

† Section 8.1 and the subsection ***Declaring Exceptions*** of Section 8.3.

‡ 9.4 requires either text file or binary files, but not both.

Most of 10.1 (vectors) can be covered before covering inheritance.

BRIEF TABLE OF CONTENTS

CHAPTER 1	INTRODUCTION TO COMPUTERS AND JAVA OBJECTS 1	
CHAPTER 2	PRIMITIVE TYPES, STRINGS, AND INTERACTIVE I/O 51	
CHAPTER 3	FLOW OF CONTROL 127	
CHAPTER 4	DEFINING CLASSES AND METHODS 209	
CHAPTER 5	MORE ABOUT OBJECTS AND METHODS 295	
CHAPTER 6	ARRAYS 379	
CHAPTER 7	INHERITANCE 457	
CHAPTER 8	EXCEPTION HANDLING 511	
CHAPTER 9	STREAMS AND FILE I/O 577	
CHAPTER 10	DYNAMIC DATA STRUCTURES 663	
CHAPTER 11	RECURSION 721	
CHAPTER 12	WINDOW INTERFACES USING SWING OBJECTS 757	
CHAPTER 13	APPLETS AND HTML 845	
CHAPTER 14	MORE SWING OBJECTS 873	
CHAPTER 15	GRAPHICS OBJECTS 949	
APPENDIX 1	RESERVED WORDS 990	
APPENDIX 2	PRECEDENCE RULES 991	
APPENDIX 3	UNICODE CHARACTER SET 992	
APPENDIX 4	SAVITCHIN 993	
APPENDIX 5	PROTECTED AND PACKAGE MODIFIERS 1008	
APPENDIX 6	DecimalFormat CLASS 1009	
APPENDIX 7	INTERFACES 1012	
APPENDIX 8	THE Iterator INTERFACE 1015	
APPENDIX 9	CLONING 1017	
APPENDIX 10	JAVADOC 1020	
APPENDIX 11	DIFFERENCES BETWEEN C++ AND JAVA 1023	
APPENDIX 12	USING JBUILDER 1027	
INDEX	1031	

xv

TABLE OF CONTENTS

CHAPTER 1   INTRODUCTION TO COMPUTERS AND JAVA OBJECTS 1

Objectives 2
Prerequisites 2

1.1 | Computer Basics 3
A Short History of Computers 3
Hardware and Memory 5
Programs 8
Programming Languages and Compilers 9
Java Byte-Code 10
Linking 13
? Self-Test Questions 13

1.2 | Internet Basics 13
The Internet and The World Wide Web 14
History of The Internet 14
Privacy on The Internet 15

1.3 | Designing Programs 16
Object-Oriented Programming 17
Encapsulation 18
Polymorphism 19
Inheritance 20
If You Know Some Other Programming Language 20
Algorithms 21
? Self-Test Questions 22
Reusable Components 23
Testing and Debugging 23

Gotcha
Coping with "Gotchas" 24
Gotcha
Hidden Errors 24
? Self-Test Questions 25

1.4 | A Taste of Java 25
History of the Java Language 25
Applets and the Internet 26
A First Java Application Program 26
? Self-Test Questions 31
Java Spelling Rules 33

Java Tip
Java is Case Sensitive 34
Compiling a Java Program or Class 34

Running a Java Program 36

? Self-Test Questions 37

Preview Examples of Applets *(Optional)* 37

CHAPTER SUMMARY 40

GLOSSARY 41

ANSWERS to Self-Test Questions 46

PROGRAMMING EXERCISES 48

CHAPTER 2   PRIMITIVE TYPES, STRINGS, AND INTERACTIVE I/O 51

Objectives 52
Prerequisites 52

2.1 | Primitive Types and Expressions 53

Variables 53
Primitive Types 57
Assignment Statements 58
Specialized Assignment Operators 60
Simple Input and Output 61
Number Constants 62
Assignment Compatibilities 63
Type Casting 64

Java Tip
Type Casting a Character to an Integer 66

Programming Tip
Initialize Variables 67

Gotcha
Imprecision in Floating-Point Numbers 67

? Self-Test Questions 68

Arithmetic Operators 69
Parentheses and Precedence Rules 71

Case Study
Vending Machine Change 73

? Self-Test Questions 77

Increment and Decrement Operators 77
More About Increment and Decrement Operators 78
? Self-Test Questions 79

2.2 | The Class String 79

String Constants and Variables 80
Concatenation of Strings 80
String Methods 81
String Processing 85
Escape Characters 86

The Unicode Character Set 88
? Self-Test Questions 88

2.3 | Keyboard and Screen I/O 89

Screen Output 89
Input Using `SavitchIn` 91
More Input Methods 94

Gotcha
`readInt` **and** `readDouble` 96

Programming Tip
Echo Input 96
? Self-Test Questions 97

2.4 | Documentation and Style 98

Programming Tip
Use Meaningful Names for Variables 98

Documentation and Comments 99
Indenting 100
Named Constants 102
? Self-Test Questions 105

2.5 | Windowing I/O with `JOptionPane` *(Optional)* 105

A Simple Windowing Program 106

Gotcha
Users Who Enter Inappropriate Input 110

Gotcha
Forgetting `System.exit(0);` 112

Gotcha
Outputting Just a Number 113
? Self-Test Questions 113
Inputting Other Numeric Types 114

Java Tip
Multi-Line Output Windows 115
? Self-Test Questions 118

CHAPTER SUMMARY 118
ANSWERS to Self-Test Questions 119
PROGRAMMING EXERCISES 123

CHAPTER 3   FLOW OF CONTROL 127

Objectives 128
Prerequisites 128

3.1 | **Branching Statements 128**

The *if-else*-Statement 129

Introduction to Boolean Expressions **131**

Gotcha
Using == with Strings 135

Programming Tip
Alphabetical Order 136

? Self-Test Questions 139

Nested Statements and Compound Statements 140

Java Tip
Matching *else*'s and *if*'s 141

Multibranch *if-else*-Statements *143*

? Self-Test Questions 147

The *switch*-statement 148

Gotcha
Omitting a *break*-Statement 150

The Conditional Operator *(Optional)* 152

? Self-Test Questions 153

3.2 | **Java Loop Statements 154**

while-Statements 155

Java Tip
A *while*-Loop Can Perform Zero Iterations 157

The *do-while*-Statement 159

Gotcha
Infinite Loops 165

? Self-Test Questions 166

The *for*-Statement 167

The Comma in *for*-Statements *(Optional)* 168

Gotcha
Extra Semicolon in a Loop Statement 172

? Self-Test Questions 174

Java Tip
Choosing a Loop Statement 174

The *break*-Statement in Loops 175

Gotcha
Misuse of *break*-Statements 175

The *exit* Method 177

? Self-Test Questions 177

3.3 | **Programming with Loops 178**

The Loop Body 179

Initializing Statements 180

Ending a Loop 181

> *Programming Tip*
> **Do Not Declare Variables in a Loop Body 183**

? Self-Test Questions 183
Loop Bugs 186
Tracing Variables **188**
? Self-Test Questions 189

3.4 | The Type *boolean 189*
Boolean Expressions and Boolean Variables 190

> *Programming Tip*
> **Naming Boolean Variables 191**

Precedence Rules 191
Input and Output of Boolean Values 195

> *Case Study*
> **Using a Boolean Variable to End a Loop 196**

? Self-Test Questions 197

CHAPTER SUMMARY 199
ANSWERS to Self-Test Questions 200
PROGRAMMING EXERCISES 204

CHAPTER 4   DEFINING CLASSES AND METHODS 209

Objectives 210
Prerequisites 210

4.1 | Class and Method Definitions 211
Class Files and Separate Compilation 212
Instance Variables 213
Using Methods 215
void -Method Definitions 219
Methods that Return a Value 222

> *Java Tip*
> **Use of *return* in *void*-Methods 225**

The *this* Parameter 225

? Self-Test Questions 228
Local Variables 229
Blocks 231

> *Gotcha*
> **Variables Declared in a Block 232**

> *Java Tip*
> **Declaring Variables in a *for* -Statement 232**

Parameters of a Primitive Type 232

Gotcha
Use of the Terms "Parameter" and "Argument" 238

Summary of Class and Method Definition Syntax 239

? Self-Test Questions 240

4.2 | Information Hiding and Encapsulation 241

Information Hiding 241

Programming Tip
Formal Parameter Names Are Local to the Method 243

Precondition and Postcondition Comments 243
The *public* and *private* Modifiers 244

Programming Tip
Instance Variables Should Be Private 247

? Self-Test Questions 248
Encapsulation 252

Case Study
Changing the Implementation of an Encapsulated Class 259

Automatic Documentation with javadoc 263

? Self-Test Questions 264

4.3 | Objects and Reference 264

Variables of a Class Type and Objects 265

Gotcha
Use of = and == with Variables of a Class Type 270

Java Tip
Define an equals Method for Your Classes 270

Boolean-Valued Methods 275

? Self-Test Questions 278
Class Parameters 279
Comparing Class Parameters and Primitive-Type Parameters 281

? Self-Test Questions 283

CHAPTER SUMMARY 286
ANSWERS to Self-Test Questions 287
PROGRAMMING EXERCISES 292

CHAPTER 5   MORE ABOUT OBJECTS AND METHODS 295

Objectives 296
Prerequisites 297

5.1 | Programming with Methods 297

Methods Calling Methods 297

Programming Tip
Write Toy Programs 303

Programming Tip
Make Helping Methods Private 303

Java Tip
Make the Compiler Happy 304

Gotcha
"Null Pointer Exception" Message 305

? Self-Test Questions 305

5.2 | Static Methods and Static Variables 306
Static Methods 306

Gotcha
Invoking a Nonstatic Method within a Static Method 308

Java Tip
You Can Put A `main` **in Any Class** 311

? Self-Test Questions 312
Static Variables 314

? Self-Test Questions 316
The `Math` Class 316

? Self-Test Questions 319
`Integer`, `Double`, and Other Wrapper Classes 319

Gotcha
Assigning A Primitive Value to A Wrapper Class 323

? Self-Test Questions 323

5.3 | Designing Methods 324

Case Study
Formatting Output 324

Top–Down Design 329
Testing Methods 331
? Self-Test Questions 332

5.4 | Overloading 333
Overloading Basics 333

Gotcha
Overloading and Automatic Type Conversion 336

Gotcha
You Cannot Overload Based on The Returned Type 341

? Self-Test Questions 342
? Self-Test Questions 348

5.5 | Constructors 350
Defining Constructors 350

Programming Tip
You Can Use Other Methods in a Constructor 355

Gotcha
Omitting the Default Constructor 358

? Self-Test Questions 359

5.6 | Information Hiding Revisited 360

Gotcha
Privacy Leaks 360

? Self-Test Questions 362

5.7 | Packages 364

Packages and Importing 364
Package Names and Directories 365

? Self-Test Questions 367

5.8 | Inner Classes *(Optional)* 367

CHAPTER SUMMARY 369
ANSWERS to Self-Test Questions 370
PROGRAMMING EXERCISES 376

CHAPTER 6   ARRAYS **379**

Objectives 380
Prerequisites 380

6.1 | Array Basics 381

Creating and Accessing Arrays 382
Array Details 383

Programming Tip
Use Singular Array Names 386

The `length` Instance Variable 388

Java Tip
Array Indexes Start with Zero 388

Programming Tip
Use a `for`-**Loop to Step Through an Array 390**

Gotcha
Array Index Out of Bounds 390

Initializing Arrays 391

? Self-Test Questions 392

6.2 | Arrays in Classes and Methods 392

Case Study
Sales Report 393

? Self-Test Questions 400

Indexed Variables as Method Arguments 400
Entire Arrays as Method Arguments 403
Arguments for The Method main *(Optional)* 403

Gotcha
Use of = and == with Arrays 405

Methods That Return Arrays 409
? Self-Test Questions 411

6.3 | Programming with Arrays and Classes 412

Partially Filled Arrays 416
Searching an Array 420

Gotcha
Returning an Array Instance Variable 420

? Self-Test Questions 422

6.4 | Sorting Arrays 423

Selection Sort 423

Programming Tip
Correctness versus Efficiency 428

? Self-Test Questions 429

6.5 | Multidimensional Arrays 429

Multidimensional-Array Basics 430

Gotcha
Reversing Two Array Indexes 434

Multidimensional-Array Parameters and Returned Values 434
Implementation of Multidimensional Arrays 435
Ragged Arrays *(Optional)* 438
? Self-Test Questions 446

CHAPTER SUMMARY 447
ANSWERS to Self-Test Questions 448
PROGRAMMING EXERCISES 453

CHAPTER 7   INHERITANCE 457

Objectives 458
Prerequisites 458

7.1 | Inheritance Basics 458

Derived Classes 461
Overriding Method Definitions 465
Overriding Versus Overloading 466
The *final* Modifier 466

Gotcha
Use of Private Instance Variables from the Base Class 466

Gotcha
Private Methods Are Not Inherited 468

? Self-Test Questions 468

7.2 | Programming with Inheritance 469

Constructors in Derived Classes 469
The *this* Method *(Optional)* 470
Call to an Overridden Method 471
A Subtle Point About Overloading and Overriding *(Optional)* 475

Java Tip
You Cannot Use Multiple *super*s 476

Programming Tip
An Object of a Derived Class Has More than One Type 476

Programming Tip
"Is a" and "Has a" 479

? Self-Test Questions 479
Methods Inherited from the Class Object 480

? Self-Test Questions 481

Case Study
Character Graphics 482

? Self-Test Questions 494
Abstract Classes *(Optional)* 494

7.3 | Dynamic Binding and Polymorphism 496

Dynamic Binding 496
Type Checking and Dynamic Binding 498
Dynamic Binding with toString *(Optional)* 499
Polymorphism 500

? Self-Test Questions 500

CHAPTER SUMMARY 501
ANSWERS to Self-Test Questions 502
PROGRAMMING EXERCISES 507

CHAPTER 8   EXCEPTION HANDLING 511

Objectives 512
Prerequisites 512

8.1 | Basic Exception Handling 512

Exceptions in Java 513
? Self-Test Questions 524
Predefined Exception Classes 526

`ArrayIndexOutOfBoundsException` *(Alternative Ordering) 527*

? Self-Test Questions 527

8.2 | **Defining Exception Classes 528**

Defining Your Own Exception Classes 528

Java Tip
Preserve `getMessage` When You Define Exception Classes 533

? Self-Test Questions 535

Programming Tip
When to Define an Exception Class 537

8.3 | **Using Exception Classes 538**

Declaring Exceptions (Passing the Buck) 538
Exceptions That Do Not Need to Be Caught 542
Multiple Throws and Catches 543

Java Tip
Catch the More Specific Exception First 543

Programming Tip
Exception Handling and Information Hiding 547

? Self-Test Questions 547

Gotcha
Overuse of Exceptions 549

Programming Tip
When to Throw an Exception 549

Gotcha
Nested `try-catch`-Blocks 551

The `finally` Block *(Optional) 551*
Rethrowing an Exception *(Optional) 552*

? Self-Test Questions 552

Case Study
A Line-Oriented Calculator *553*

? Self-Test Questions 562

CHAPTER SUMMARY 568
ANSWERS to Self-Test Questions 569
PROGRAMMING EXERCISES 572

CHAPTER 9   **STREAMS AND FILE I/O 577**

Objectives 578
Prerequisites 578

9.1 | **An Overview of Streams and File I/O 579**

The Concept of a Stream 579

Why Use Files for I/O? 579
Differences Between Text Files and Binary Files 580
File Handling in Java 581
? Self-Test Questions 581

9.2 | Text File I/O 581

Text File Output with `PrintWriter` 581

Gotcha
A `try`-Block Is a Block 585

Gotcha
Overwriting a File 587

Java Tip
Appending to a Text File 588

? Self-Test Questions 590
Text File Input with `BufferedReader` 590
? Self-Test Questions 594
The `StringTokenizer` Class *(Optional)* 597

Java Tip
Testing for the End of a Text File 599

? Self-Test Questions 599
The Classes `FileReader` and `FileOutputStream` 599

? Self-Test Questions 602
Unwrapping the Class `SavitchIn` *(Optional) 603*

9.3 | Binary File I/O 604

Output to Files Using `DataOutputStream` 605
Some Details About `writeUTF` *(Optional) 612*

Gotcha
Overwriting a File 613

Java Tip
Appending to a Binary File 614

? Self-Test Questions   615
Reading Input from a File Using `DataInputStream` 615

Gotcha
Using `DataInputStream` with a Text File 618

? Self-Test Questions 619

Gotcha
Defining a Method to Open a Stream 619

? Self-Test Questions 623
Catching `IOExceptions` 623
The `EOFException` Class 625

Java Tip
Checking for the End of a Binary File 625

Gotcha
Forgetting to Check for the End of a File 628

Gotcha
Checking for the End of a File in the Wrong Way *(Alternative Ordering) 628*

The Classes `FileInputStream` and `FileOutputStream` 629

Programming Tip
Objects Should Do Their Own I/O 631

? Self-Test Questions 634

Case Study
Writing and Reading a File of Records 638

? Self-Test Questions 643

9.4 | File Objects and File Names 648

Using the `File` Class 648

Java Tip
Using Path Names 651

? Self-Test Questions 653

CHAPTER SUMMARY 653
ANSWERS to Self-Test Questions 654
PROGRAMMING EXERCISES 659

CHAPTER 10   DYNAMIC DATA STRUCTURES 663

Objectives 664
Prerequisites 664

10.1 | Vectors 665

Using Vectors 666

Programming Tip
Adding to a Vector 672

? Self-Test Questions 672

Gotcha
Vector Elements Are of Type `Object` 674

Comparing Vectors and Arrays 674

Gotcha
Using `capacity` Instead of `size` 676

Java Tip
Use `trimToSize` to Save Memory 677

Gotcha
Using the Method `clone` 677

? Self-Test Questions 679

10.2 | Linked Data Structures 679

Linked Lists 679

Gotcha
Null Pointer Exception 689

? Self-Test Questions 689

Gotcha
Privacy Leaks 689

Node Inner Classes 690
Iterators 691

Programming Tip
Internal and External Iterators 696

? Self-Test Questions 697
Exception Handling with Linked Lists 697
? Self-Test Questions 706
Variations on a Linked List 708
Other Linked Data Structures 709

CHAPTER SUMMARY 710
ANSWERS to Self-Test Questions 711
PROGRAMMING EXERCISES 717

CHAPTER 11   RECURSION 721

Objectives 722
Prerequisites 722

11.1 | The Basics of Recursion. 722

Case Study
Digits to Words 723

How Recursion Works 727

Gotcha
Infinite Recursion 729

? Self-Test Questions 732
Recursive versus Iterative Definitions 734
Recursive Methods That Return a Value 734
? Self-Test Questions 738

11.2 | Programming with Recursion 739

? Self-Test Questions 741

Case Study
Binary Search 741

Programming Tip
Generalize the Problem 749

? Self-Test Questions 749

CHAPTER SUMMARY 749
ANSWERS to Self-Test Questions 750

PROGRAMMING EXERCISES 752

CHAPTER 12 WINDOW INTERFACES USING SWING OBJECTS 757

Objectives 759
Prerequisites 759

12.1 | Background 759

GUIs—Graphical User Interfaces 759
Event-Driven Programming 760

? Self-Test Questions 761

12.2 | Basic Swing Details 761

Gotcha
Save All Your Work Before Running a Swing Program 762

Java Tip
Ending a Swing Program 767

Gotcha
Forgetting to Program the Close-Window Button 767

Gotcha
Forgetting to Use `getContentPane` 768

More About Window Listeners 768
Size Units for Screen Objects 769
More on `setVisible` 770

? Self-Test Questions 772
Some Methods of the Class `JFrame` 781

? Self-Test Questions 781
Layout Managers 783

Programming Tip
Copy Other Programmers' Code 789

? Self-Test Questions 789

12.3 | Buttons and Action Listeners 790

Buttons 791
Action Listeners and Action Events 792

Gotcha
Changing The Parameter List for `actionPerformed` 797

Programming Tip
Code Look and Actions Separately 800

Java Tip
Use the Method `setActionCommand` 800

? Self-Test Questions 801

12.4 | Container Classes 802

The `JPanel` Class 803

The Container Class 807

Java Tip
Guide for Creating Simple Window Interfaces 809

? Self-Test Questions 811

12.5 | Text I/O for GUIs 812

Text Areas and Text Fields 812

? Self-Test Questions 818
Inputting and Outputting Numbers 818

? Self-Test Questions 823

Case Study
A GUI Adding Machine 823

? Self-Test Questions 829
Catching a NumberFormatException *(Optional)* 830

CHAPTER SUMMARY 834
ANSWERS to Self-Test Questions 835
PROGRAMMING EXERCISES 841

CHAPTER 13   APPLETS AND HTML 845

Objectives 846
Prerequisites 846

13.1 | HTML 847

HTML Basics 847

Programming Tip
A Simple HTML Document Outline 849

Inserting Hyperlinks 850

Gotcha
Not Using Your Reload (Refresh) Button 853

Displaying a Picture 854

? Self-Test Questions 854

13.2 | Applets 855

Applet Basics 855
Running an Applet 858
Placing an Applet in an HTML Document 861

Java Tip
Converting a Swing Application to an Applet 861

? Self-Test Questions 864
Adding Icons to an Applet 864

Gotcha
Using an Old Web Browser 867

The Older `Applet` Class *(Optional)* 867
Applets and Security 868

? Self-Test Questions 869

CHAPTER SUMMARY 869
ANSWERS to Self-Test Questions 869
PROGRAMMING EXERCISES 870

CHAPTER 14   MORE SWING OBJECTS 873

Objectives 874
Prerequisites 874

14.1 | Menus 875

Menu Bars, Menus, and Menu Items 875
Nested Menus 880

? Self-Test Questions 880

14.2 | Making GUIs Pretty (and More Functional) 882

Adding Icons 882

Gotcha
Resizing Buttons 886

? Self-Test Questions 890
The `JScrollPane` Class for Scroll Bars 890

? Self-Test Questions 892
Adding Borders 893

Gotcha
Forgetting to Import `javax.swing.border` 900

Changing the Look and Feel 900
Lightweight and Heavyweight Components *(Optional)* 904

? Self-Test Questions 907

14.3 | More Layout Managers 907

The `BoxLayout` Manager Class 908
Struts and Glue 912

? Self-Test Questions 913

Gotcha
Using Struts and Glue with Other Layout Managers 914

The `Box` Container Class 914

? Self-Test Questions 917
The `CardLayout` Manager 917

? Self-Test Questions 922

14.4 | Inner Classes 923

Helping Classes 923

14.5 | More on Events and Listeners 925

The `WindowListener` Interface 925

? Self-Test Questions 927

Java Tip
Programming the Close-Window Button 930

? Self-Test Questions 934

? Self-Test Questions 938
Some More Details on Updating a GUI 938

14.6 | Another Look at the Swing Class Hierarchy 939

Buttons, Menus, and Abstract Buttons 939

Java Tip
More Methods for the Class `JMenuItem` 940

Java Tip
There are a Lot More Swing Classes and Methods 941

? Self-Test Questions 941

CHAPTER SUMMARY 941
ANSWERS to Self-Test Questions 942
PROGRAMMING EXERCISES 946

CHAPTER 15   GRAPHICS OBJECTS 949

Objectives 950
Prerequisites 950

15.1 | Basic Figures 951

Size and Coordinate System for Screen Objects 951
The `Graphics` Class and the Method `paint` 952
Drawing Lines, Rectangles, and Ovals 953
Drawing Arcs 956

? Self-Test Questions 958

Programming Tip
Use Defined Constants 960

Round Rectangles 960
Polygons *(Alternative Ordering)* 960

Java Tip
Use `paintComponent` **for Panels 961**

Action Drawings and `repaint` 962
`repaint` and `paint` 969

15.2 | Colors 970

Specifying a Drawing Color 970
Defining Colors 970

Gotcha
Using *doubles* **to Define a Color 972**
Dynamically Changing Colors 976
The JColorChooser Dialog 976
? Self-Test Questions 979

15.3 | Fonts and Other Text Details 979

The drawString Method 980
Fonts 980
? Self-Test Questions 983

CHAPTER SUMMARY 985
ANSWERS to Self-Test Questions 985
PROGRAMMING EXERCISES 988

APPENDIX 1   RESERVED WORDS 990

APPENDIX 2   PRECEDENCE RULES 991

APPENDIX 3   UNICODE CHARACTER SET 992

APPENDIX 4   SAVITCHIN 993

APPENDIX 5   PROTECTED AND PACKAGE MODIFIERS 1008

APPENDIX 6   DecimalFormat CLASS 1009

APPENDIX 7   INTERFACES 1012

APPENDIX 8   THE Iterator INTERFACE 1015

APPENDIX 9   CLONING 1017

APPENDIX 10   JAVADOC 1020

APPENDIX 11   DIFFERENCES BETWEEN C++ AND JAVA 1023

APPENDIX 12   USING JBUILDER 1027

INDEX   1031

CHAPTER 1

INTRODUCTION TO COMPUTERS AND JAVA OBJECTS

1.1   COMPUTER BASICS 3
A Short History of Computers 3
Hardware and Memory 5
Programs 8
Programming Languages and
     Compilers 9
Java Byte-Code 10
Linking 13

1.2   INTERNET BASICS 13
The Internet and The World Wide
     Web 14
History of The Internet 14
Privacy on The Internet 15

1.3   DESIGNING PROGRAMS 16
Object-Oriented Programming 17
Encapsulation 18
Polymorphism 19
Inheritance 20
If You Know Some Other
     Programming Language 20
Algorithms 21

Reusable Components 23
Testing and Debugging 23
Gotcha Coping with "Gotchas" 24
Gotcha Hidden Errors 24

1.4   A TASTE OF JAVA 25
History of the Java Language 25
Applets and the Internet 26
A First Java Application
     Program 26
Java Spelling Rules 33
Java Tip Java is Case Sensitive 34
Compiling a Java Program or
     Class 34
Running a Java Program 36
Preview Examples of Applets
     (Optional) 37

Chapter Summary 40
Glossary 41
Answers to Self-Test Questions 46
Programming Exercises 48

INTRODUCTION TO COMPUTERS AND JAVA

> *It is by no means hopeless to expect to make a machine for really very difficult mathematical problems. But you would have to proceed step-by-step. I think electricity would be the best thing to rely on.*
>
> **Charles Sanders Peirce (1839-1914)**

In this chapter, we give you a brief overview of computer hardware and software. Our discussion of software will include a description of a methodology for designing programs known as *object-oriented programming*. Much of this introductory material applies to programming in any language, not just to programming in Java. In Section 1.4, we specialize this introduction to the Java language and explain two simple Java programs. An optional section at the end of this chapter gives some sample applets, a kind of Java program that can be run from an Internet website.

Objectives

Give you a brief overview of computer hardware and software.

Introduce you to the basic techniques of program design in general and Object-oriented programming in particular.

Give you an overview of the Java programming language.

Prerequisites

When reading this book, you can easily make some changes to the ordering of chapters and sections. Each chapter has a section like this one that tells you what parts of the book you should read before reading each section of the chapter.

This first chapter does *not* assume that you have had any previous programming experience, but does assume that you have access to a computer. To get the full value from this chapter, and the rest of this book, you should have a computer that has the Java language installed so that you can try out the things you learn as you learn them. The preface discusses some ways to obtain a free copy of the Java language for your computer.

If you prefer, you may intersperse the reading of this first chapter with your reading of the next five chapters of the book. However, you should read at least Section 1.4 before moving on to Chapter 2. You can read Section 1.4 before reading Sections 1.1, 1.2, and 1.3. (In fact, you can read the sections 1.1, 1.2, 1.3, and 1.4 in any order.) One other good possibility is to skim Sections 1.1, 1.2, and 1.3, read Section 1.4 carefully, and then return to Sections 1.1 through 1.3 after reading Chapters 2 through 4. Of course, another good possibility is to just read this entire chapter carefully in the order in which it is written.

1.1 | Computer Basics

> *The Analytical Engine has no pretensions whatever to originate anything. It can do whatever we know how to order it to perform. It can follow analysis; but it has no power of anticipating any analytical relations or truths. Its province is to assist us in making available what we are already acquainted with.*
>
> **Ada Augusta, Countess of Lovelace**

Computer systems consist of **hardware** and **software**. The hardware is the physical computer machine. A set of instructions for the computer is called a **program**. All the different kinds of programs that are used to give instructions to the computer are referred to as software. In this book, we will be discussing software, but in order to understand the software, it does help to know a few basic things about computer hardware. We start with a bit of history to put things in perspective.

hardware
software
program

A Short History of Computers

A dictionary might define a computer as "a programmable electronic device that can store, retrieve, and process data." Let's back up a little, though, to see what came first, before electronics entered the picture.

Mechanical computing aids go way back in history. The abacus, a device with beads that are moved along rods on a wooden frame to represent numbers, and to perform calculations using the numbers, has been used for thousands of years. The abacus can still be seen in use in shops and marketplaces in many parts of the world today.

In the 1600s, Blaise Pascal, a French mathematician and philosopher, invented the first mechanical calculating device, which could add and subtract. Shortly thereafter, Gottfried von Leibniz, a German mathematician and philosopher, invented another device that could also multiply and divide. (In those days, mathematics, physics, philosophy, and theology were all interrelated and the combination "mathematician and philosopher" was common.)

Pascal

Leibniz

In the early and mid-1800s, two more elaborate calculating machines were designed by Charles Babbage, an English mathematician and physical scientist. Babbage's "difference engine" could automatically perform more complex calculations such as squaring numbers, and could even print the results. He built a prototype, but apart from that prototype, the device was never produced. His second machine, the "analytical engine"—although it remained at the blueprint stage—would, in fact, have been the first truly programmable computer. It was to have a central processing unit ("the mill") to do calculations, and main memory ("the store") to hold data. The analytical engine also was programmable, with instructions fed to the machine on punched cards. (The concept of using holes punched

Babbage

into cards to program a machine had already been invented by a weaver, Joseph Jacquard, in the early 1800s. The cards programmed a loom to produce patterns in cloth). Curiously (to us), Babbage's analytical engine, if built, would have been powered by steam like a locomotive. Most of what the world knows about Babbage's work comes from the writings of his colleague Ada Augusta, Countess of Lovelace. Ada Augusta is generally known as the first computer programmer, and probably deserves the title at least as much as anybody. (As a side human interest note, you might be interested in knowing that Ada Augusta was the daughter of the poet Byron.)

Ada Augusta Lovelace

Babbage was ahead of his time, and his computers or "engines" never saw use. But the punched card idea marched on, with Herman Hollerith designing a punched-card tabulating machine to help with the U.S. Census of 1890. Data were punched as holes into the cards, and the cards were tallied by electromechanical machines. Hollerith founded the Tabulating Machine Company, which later became I.B.M. These tabulating machines performed useful data summaries for decades.

Hollerith and punched cards

Tabulating machines summarized data, but didn't compute in all of the ways that modern computers do. The first electromechanical computer that could do general purpose calculations was the Mark I, built jointly by I.B.M. and Howard Aiken of Harvard, and completed in 1944.

Mark I

Other all-electronic computers soon followed, in particular the ENIAC (short for Electronic Numerical Integrator and Calculator) in 1946. It contained 18,000 vacuum tubes, weighed some 30 tons, and according to legend, dimmed the lights in downtown Philadelphia when it got down to serious work. Programming of machines like the Mark I and ENIAC was done slowly and cumbersomely by setting switches by hand and changing wires on plugboards.

ENIAC

The figure who marked the dawn of the modern era in computer design was John von Neumann, a mathematician and physicist of legendary intellectual abilities. Von Neumann was born in Budapest, Hungary and did most of the work we discuss here in the United States, where he spent much of his adult life. In a famous paper he analyzed the ENIAC computer and gave the design rules that led to computers as we know them today. He thought of computers as performing logical operations that could be conceptualized without any reference to the underlying physical implementation. Although that sounds like a theoretician's avoidance of hard practical problems, this view proved to be the critical change in thinking that lead to the modern design of computers. Von Neumann was known for both theoretical and applied work, and he knew how to place each at the service of the other. In the time before von Neumann, the lessons of Babbage seemed to be lost as researchers concentrated on the electrical engineering problems that were essential to the building of powerful computers. Von Neumann reintroduced the world to the abstract computer of Babbage.[1] Von Neumann conceptualized a computer as a logical processor and a memory that holds both program and data. Our analysis of modern computers, which we present in the next few sections follows von Neu-

Von Neumann

---

1. Von Neumann's inspiration seems to have come from the work of Alan Turing rather than that of Babbage, but the basic conceptual point is the same.

mann's outline, not because we took it from von Neumann's paper, but because computers are still structured that way.

The first computer build following von Neumann's plan was the EDSAC (Electronic Delay Storage Automatic Computer), built at Cambridge University in 1949. The EDSAC could read in different programs and store them internally, rather than using hand set switches for the program. EDSAC

With EDSAC, computers as we know them today had essentially arrived: They read in and stored their programs as well as their data, they were completely electronic, and they could be used for many different purposes. These computers were also huge, very slow, and extremely expensive by today's standards. They cost millions of dollars, and only large institutions or businesses could afford them. Further refinement for the next half century brought a succession of ever-more-amazing hardware discoveries—transistors to replace the vacuum tubes, then silicon chips to replace many transistorized circuits with a single chip. Among other advantages of miniaturization, the miniaturization of computer chips helped to increase the speed of computers. The speed of a computer is ultimately limited by the speed of its electric signals (186,000 miles per second, the same as the speed of light). This is because the electric signal must pass repeatedly through the circuitry of an electronic computer in order to perform a calculation—and so making circuits smaller, and packing them closer together, greatly increased speed. It also decreased the size of computers, and the cost has continued to plummet as well. Now computer designs change on an almost daily basis and you can read about recent developments for computer technology in the business press and other popular publications.

Hardware and Memory

Most of computers available today have the same basic components, configured in basically the same way. They all have input devices, such as a keyboard and a mouse. They all have output devices, such as a display screen and a printer. And, they have two or three other basic components usually housed in some sort of cabinet so that they are not so obvious. These other components are a *processor* and two kinds of *memory*, known as *main memory* and *auxiliary memory*.

The **processor** is the device inside your computer that follows a program's instructions. (The processor is also called the **CPU**, which is an abbreviation of **central processing unit**.) If you buy a PC, you will be told what kind of *chip* it has. The **chip** is the processor. Currently, one of the better known chips is the Pentium processor. One of the reasons it is called a chip is that it is not very large. You can easily hold the chip for a modern PC in your hand. In fact, you could hold several of them. The processor follows the instructions in a program but it can only carry out very simple instructions, such as moving numbers or other items around from one place in memory to another place in memory and performing some simple arithmetic operations like addition and subtraction. The power of a computer comes from its speed and the intricacies of its programs. The basic design of the hardware is relatively simple. processor
CPU
chip

A computer's memory holds data for the computer to process, and it holds the result of the computer's intermediate calculations. The way that you program in a language like Java is determined in large part by the nature of a computer's memory, so you need to know something about how a computer's memory is organized. The computer has two basic kinds of memory known as *main memory* and *auxiliary memory*. All of the various kinds of disk drives, diskettes, and compact discs that are used with computers are types of auxiliary memory. They are the (more or less) permanent memory. The working memory that your program uses for intermediate calculations (and for holding the program currently being followed) is called the **main memory**. It is the character of the main memory that you most need to be aware of when you are writing programs. Main memory holds the current program and much of the data that the program is manipulating. To make this more concrete, you may have heard PC computers (personal computers) described as having say, 128 megabytes of RAM and a ten gigabyte hard drive (or some other numbers for RAM and hard drive storage). RAM (short for random access memory) is the main memory and the hard drive is the principal (but not the only) form of auxiliary memory. A byte is a quantity of memory. So a 128 megabyte RAM has approximately 128 million bytes of memory, and a ten gigabyte hard drive has approximately 10 billion bytes of memory. So what is a byte? Read on.

> main memory

A **bit** is a digit that can assume only the two values 0 and 1. (Actually, any two values will do, but the two values are typically written as 0 and 1.) A **byte** is 8 bits of memory, that is a quantity of memory capable of holding 8 digits, each either 0 or 1. Both main memory and secondary memory are measured in bytes. In main memory the organization of the bytes is very important. The computer's main memory consists of a long list of numbered locations, each of which can hold one **byte** of information. The bytes on this list are numbered and the number of a byte is called its **address**. A piece of data, such as a number or a keyboard character, can be stored in one of these bytes. When the computer later needs to recover the data, the address of the byte is used to find the data item.

> bit

> byte

> main memory

> address

Data of various kinds, such as keyboard characters, numbers, and strings of text, are encoded as strings of zeros and ones and placed in the computer's memory. As it turns out, one byte is just large enough to store a single keyboard character. This is one of the reasons that a computer's memory is divided in these eight-bit bytes, instead of being divided into pieces of some other size. However, in order to store a large number or a string of text, the computer needs more than a single byte. When the computer needs to store a piece of data that cannot be coded so that it fits into a single byte, the computer uses a number of adjacent bytes. These adjacent bytes are then considered to be a single, larger **memory location** and the address of the first byte is used as the address of the entire larger memory location. Display 1.1 shows how a typical computer's main memory might be divided into memory locations. The boundaries between these locations are not fixed by the hardware. The size and location of the boundaries will be different when different programs are run.

> memory location

Recall that main memory is only used when the computer is running a program. Auxiliary memory is used to hold data in a more or less permanent form. Auxiliary memory is also divided into bytes, but these bytes are then grouped into much larger units known as **files**. A file may contain (in an encoded form) a program, a letter, a list of numbers, a picture, or almost any sort of data. The important charac-

> file

Display 1.1   Main Memory

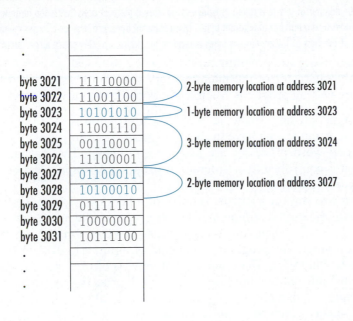

teristics of a file are that it has a name and that it can hold data. When you write a Java program, you will store the program in a file. The file is stored in auxiliary memory (typically some kind of disk storage), and when you want to run the program, the program is copied from auxiliary memory to main memory. These files are often organized into groups of files known as **directories** or **folders.** Folder and directory are two names for the same thing. Some computer systems use the name *directory* and some use the name *folder.* It would be a good idea to familiarize yourself with how your computer system names and organizes directories (folders). This will help you to organize your own work into coherent groups of files.

directory
folder

Why Just Zeros and Ones?

Computers use zeros and ones because it is easy to make a physical device that has only two stable states. However, when you are programming you normally need not be concerned about how data is encoded as zeros and ones. You can program as if the computer directly stored numbers, letters, or strings in memory, and you need not worry about zeros and ones.

There is nothing special about the digits zero and one. We could equally well use any two names, such as *A* and *B* or *true* and *false*, instead of *zero* and *one*. The important thing is that the underlying physical device has two stable states, such as on versus off, or high versus low voltage. Calling these two states *zero* and *one* is simply a convention, but a convention that is almost universally followed.

Bytes and Memory Locations

A byte is a memory location that can hold eight digits, each either zero or one. A computer's main memory is divided into numbered **bytes.** The number of a byte is called its **address.** To store a piece of data that is too large to fit in a single byte, the computer uses a number of adjacent bytes. These adjacent bytes are used as a larger memory location and the address of the first of these adjacent bytes is used as the address of this entire larger memory location.

■

Programs

You probably have some, possibly vague, idea of what a program is. You use programs all the time. For example, you have probably used a text editor or word processor. Text editors and word processor are programs. A bank ATM machine is really a computer that is controlled by a program. A **program** is simply a set of instructions for a computer to follow.

program

Display 1.2 shows two ways to view the running of a program. To see the first way, forget the box with the dotted outline. What's left is what really happens when you run a program. Note that, when you run a program, there (normally) are two kinds of input to a computer. The program is one kind of input; it has the instructions that the computer will follow. The other kind of input is often called the **data**

data

for the program. It is the information that the computer will process. For example, if the program is a simple spelling check program, the data would be the text that needs to be checked. As far as the computer is concerned, both these data and the program itself are input. The output is the result (or results) produced when the computer follows the instructions in the program. If the program is a simple spelling check program, then the output might be a list of words that are misspelled. When you give the computer a program and some data and tell the computer to follow the

Co

Display 1.2 *Running a Program*

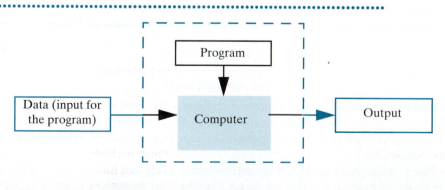

instructions in the program, that is called **running** the program on the data, and the computer is said to **execute** the program on the data.

That first view of running a program is what really happens when you run a program on some data, but that is not always the way we think about running a program. The data are often thought of as the input to the program and in this view the computer and the program are considered to be one unit that takes the data as input and produces the output. If you take this view, then the combined program/computer unit is indicated by the box with the dotted outline. When we take this view, we think of the data as input to the program and the output as output from the program, and although the computer is understood to be there, it is presumed to just be something that assists the program. Programmers find this second view to be more useful when designing a program, and so they think in this way, even though it is not a completely accurate reflection of the way the computer works.

There are more programs on your computer than you might think when first using your computer. Much of what you think of as "the computer" is actually a program rather than hardware. When you first turn on a computer, you are already running and interacting with a program. That program is called the **operating system**. The operating system is a kind of supervisory program that oversees the entire operation of the computer. If you want to run a program, you tell the operating system that you want to run the program. The operating system then retrieves the program and starts the program running. The program you run might be an editor, or a program to surf the World Wide Web, or some program that you wrote using the Java language. The way that you tell the operating system to run the program might be by clicking an icon with your mouse, or by choosing a menu item, or by typing in some simple command. What you probably think of as "the computer" is really the operating system. The operating system is a program that normally is run automatically when you turn on the computer. Some common operating systems are *DOS, Microsoft Windows*, Apple's (*Macintosh) MacOS, Linux*, and *UNIX*.

Software

The word **software** simply means programs. Thus, a software company is a company that produces programs. The software on your computer is just the collection of programs on your computer. ∎

Programming Languages and Compilers

Most modern programming languages are designed to be (relatively) easy for people to write and for people to understand. These kinds of programming languages that are designed for people are called **high-level languages**. Java is a high-level language. Most of the programming languages you are likely to have heard of, such as Pascal, FORTRAN, C, C++, BASIC, and Visual Basic, are also high-level languages. Unfortunately, computer hardware does not understand these high-level languages. So, a program written in a high-level language must be translated into a language that the computer can understand. The languages that the computer can (more directly) understand are called **low-level languages**. The translation of a program from a high-level language, like Java, to a language that the computer can understand is done by another program known as a **compiler**.

machine
language

These low-level languages that the computer can directly understand are usually referred to as **machine languages** or **assembly languages**. The language that the computer can directly understand is called machine language. Assembly language is almost the same thing as machine language, but it does need an additional, very simple translation before the computer can understand it. If a compiler translates your high-level language program to some low-level language program that is not exactly machine language, then it will need some small additional translation before it is run on the computer, but normally this is done automatically for you and need not concern you. In practice, it will look like you are running the program produced by the compiler.

compile

When you run a high-level language program, such as a Java program, you are actually running a translation of that program into a low-level language. Thus, before you run a high-level language program, you must first run the compiler on the program. When you run a compiler on your program, you are said to **compile** the program.

One disadvantage of the translation process we just described for high-level languages is that you need a different compiler for each make of computer and each operating system. If you want to run your high-level language program on three different makes of computers, then you need to use three different compilers and must compile your program three different times. Moreover, if a manufacturer comes out with a new make of computer, the manufacturer must hire a team of programmers to write a new compiler for that computer. This is a problem because compilers are very large programs that are expensive and time-consuming to produce. Despite this cost, this is the way most high-level language compilers work. Java, however, uses a slightly different and much more versatile approach to compiling. We discuss the Java approach to compiling in the next subsection.

source code
object code

code

When you use a compiler, the terminology can get a bit confusing, because with a compiler, both the input to the compiler program and the output from the compiler program are also programs. Everything in sight is a program of some kind or other. To help avoid confusion, the input program, which in our case will be a Java program, is called the **source program**, or **source code**. The translated low-level language program that is produced by the compiler is often called the **object program**, or **object code**. The word **code** just means a program or a part of a program.

Compiler

A **compiler** is a program that translates a high-level language program, such as a Java program, into a program in a simpler language that the computer can more or less directly understand.

Java Byte-Code

byte-code

Java Virtual
Machine

The Java compiler does not translate your program into the machine language for your particular computer. Instead, the Java compiler translates your Java program into a language called **byte-code**. Byte-code is not the machine language for any particular computer. Byte-code is the machine language for a hypothetical computer that is something like the average of all computers. This hypothetical computer is called the **Java Virtual Machine**. The Java Virtual Machine is not exactly like any

Byte-Code

The Java compiler translates your Java program into a language called **byte-code**. This byte-code is not the machine language for any particular computer, but is a language that is very similar to the machine language of most common computers and that is very easy to translate into the machine language of any particular computer. Each computer will have its own translator (called an *interpreter*) that translates from byte-code instructions to machine-language instructions for that particular computer.

particular computer, but it is very similar to all typical computers. Thus, it is very easy to translate from a program written in byte-code to a program in the machine language for any particular computer. The program that does this translation is called an **interpreter**. The interpreter works by translating each instruction of byte-code into instructions expressed in your computer's machine language and then executing those instructions on your computer. Thus, an interpreter translates and executes the instructions in the byte-code one after the other, rather than translating the entire byte-code program all at once. However, the only detail that we really need to know is that the interpreter somehow allows your computer to run Java byte-code.[1]

interpreter

In order to run your Java program on your particular computer, you would proceed as follows. First, you use the compiler to translate your Java program into byte-code. Then you use the byte-code interpreter for your computer in order to translate and run each byte-code instruction. The whole process is diagrammed in Display 1.3.

It sounds like Java byte-code just adds an extra step in the process. Why not write compilers that translate directly from Java to the machine language for your particular computer? That could be done. That is what is done for most other languages. Moreover, that would produce machine-language programs that typically run faster. However, Java byte-code does give Java one important advantage, namely, portability. After you compile your Java program into byte-code, you can use that byte-code on any computer. When you go to another computer, you do not need to recompile your program. This means you can send your byte-code over the Internet to another computer and have it easily run on that other computer. This is one of the reasons Java is good for Internet applications.

Portability has other advantages. When a manufacturer comes out with a new computer, the manufacturer does not have to design a new Java compiler. One Java compiler works on every computer. This means that Java can be added to a new computer very quickly and very economically. Of course, every computer must have its own byte-code interpreter in order to translate byte-code instructions into machine-language instructions for that particular computer, but these interpreters are simple programs when compared to a compiler.

(There can still be some differences between compilers, or at least between the compiler environments, from one computer to another, so you may not be able to simply move a Java compiler from one machine to another with absolutely no changes. However, the core of the compiler is the same or should be the same on

1. Sometimes people use the term *Java Virtual Machine* to refer to the Java byte-code interpreter (as well as using the term to refer to the underlying hypothetical machine that the interpreter is based on).

Display 1.3   Compiling and Running a Java Program

Java Program   Data for
                                Java Program

Java Compiler

Byte-Code
Program

Byte-Code Interpreter

Machine-
Language

Computer Execution
of Machine-Language Instructions

Output of
Java Program

different machines. And, you can move the byte-code of one compiler on one computer to another computer and run the byte-code on the other computer.)

It is important to know about Java byte-code, but in the day-to-day business of programming, you are not even aware of the fact that there is byte-code for your program. You normally give two commands, one to compile your program (into byte-code) and one to *run* your program. The **run command** executes the Java byte-code interpreter on the byte-code. This run command might be called "run" or something else, but is unlikely to be called "interpreter." You will come to think of the run command as running whatever the compiler produces and not even think about whether or not that is byte-code.

run command

> ### Why Is It Called "Byte-Code"?
>
> Low-level languages, such as byte-code and machine-language code, consist of instructions, each of which can be stored in a few bytes of memory. This is presumably why byte-code was given its name. To the designers of Java, byte-code must have looked like "a bunch of bytes."

Linking

A Java program is very seldom written as one piece all in one file. A Java program typically consists of different pieces, often written by different people, and each of these pieces is compiled separately. Thus, each piece is translated into a different piece of byte-code. In order to run your program, these pieces need to be connected together. The process of connecting these pieces is called **linking** and the program that does this linking is called a **linker**. Even the simplest of Java programs will use some standard pieces of byte-code written by somebody else, and so will need the linker. These standard pieces of byte-code come with the Java system. On the bright side, this linking is typically done automatically, so you usually need not be concerned with it.

linking

? Self-Test Questions

Every chapter has answers to these Self-Test Questions at the end of the chapter.

1. What are the two kinds of memory in a computer?
2. What is software?
3. What would be the data for a program that computes the average of all the quizzes you have taken in a course?
4. What is the difference between a machine-language program, a high-level language program, and a program expressed in Java byte-code?
5. What is a compiler?
6. What is a source program?
7. What do you call a program that translates Java byte-code instructions into machine-language instructions?

1.2 | Internet Basics

> *The web of our life is of a mingled yarn,*
> *good and ill together.*
>
> **William Shakespeare, All's Well That Ends Well**

The popularity of the Java language stems, in part, from its connection to the Internet—the network that connects computers all over the world for web surfing and electronic mail. In this book, we will have a little bit to say about Java's connection to the internet. Later in this chapter, in the subsections *Applets and the Internet* and

Preview Examples of Applets (Optional) we will discuss Applets, a form of Java program designed to run over the Internet. However, our main focus on Java is as a general purpose programming language to get you started on programming in general and Java in particular. Although we will not say a lot about Java and the Internet, knowing about the Internet is part of knowing about computers, and so we have include some basic information about this popular topic.

The Internet and The World Wide Web

Internet

The **Internet** is a network connecting computers all over the word. This network allows users of one computer to contact another computer on the network. Among other things, the Internet is used for e-mail and for viewing websites with a web browser. When you "surf the net," the Internet is the net you are surfing.

World Wide Web

The World Wide Web is intimately related to the Internet but it is not the same thing. The **World Wide Web** is a collection of addresses that tell how to get from one website (one location) on the Internet to another such website. You can think of the World Wide Web as imaginary links that connect websites. The World Wide Web uses the Internet as its physical connection from website to website. The World Wide Web is different from the Internet, but for many purposes so closely related to the Internet that people sometimes use the words interchangeably. To move around the World Wide Web you use a web browser.

A web browser is a software utility that allows you to view documents and programs on the **World Wide Web**. A web browser lets you move from one website to another website anywhere on the globe with just a click of your mouse. The most commonly uses web browsers are Netscape Navigator and Microsoft's Internet Explorer.

History of The Internet

To many people today, the Internet seems brand new, the wave of the future. It may in fact prove to be a wave of the future, but the Internet has already been around for a third of a century, and has dramatically changed course several times during that period.

ARPANET

In 1969, the U.S. Department of Defense's Advanced Research Planning Agency (ARPA) created the ARPANET. The purpose was to link together computer centers at several military and government agencies so that they could share computing power and data. There were only four computers on the original network! Soon after its creation, the ARPANET was joined to some colleges and other organizations outside of the government. The computers linked together were multimillion-dollar mainframe computers. These mainframe computers are large computers that are used simultaneously by many different users. To use the ARPANET, people sat at terminals connected to these mainframes. The terminals did nothing other than send the keyboard input to the mainframe. The mainframe did everything. Many of today's PCs are as powerful as some of these large, expensive mainframes.

An unintended use of ARPANET that soon became apparent was to send messages, not just data. The network became popular for exchanging ideas among colleagues at different locations, or simply chatting electronically without the fuss or expense of a long-distance phone call. This kind of communication would eventually become known as e-mail.

With the invention of microcomputers (PCs and other desk-top computers), individuals began to connect to what was now called the Internet. E-mail and chat rooms were the main use that people made of the Internet, as well as research for writing term papers and the like using distant resources. During the 1980s and 1990s, as microcomputer prices fell constantly and the number of homes that had microcomputers increased to many millions, so did the number of people hooked up to the Internet. As a way to help users uncomfortable with figuring out what text to type, web browsers with graphical user interfaces were introduced. These require some typing but mostly just mouse clicks. The web browsers made it much easier to move from site to site on the Internet, and to receive and send nontext including photographs, film or video segments, music, and radio programs.

With millions of people all over the world connected to the Internet, and access fairly easy through the World Wide Web, the Internet as we know it today was almost in place. The next and most recent major change in the Internet occurred in the mid-1990s, when one of the National Science Foundation-related organizations in charge of overseeing the Internet (MERIT, located in Ann Arbor) decided to permit businesses to sell their products over the Internet. Until then, the Internet was not used for commercial purposes. But soon after, corporate America leapt on the bandwagon. Today it is probably impossible to find a company that does not ask you to "visit its website" or that does not at least give its Web address. And of course, many firms (the "dot-coms") have recently emerged specifically to sell goods or services over the Internet, and have transformed the American economy.

The Internet still performs all of the functions it was designed for: serious research, talking with friends, getting information, sending pictures, and selling things. No one owns the Internet, and everyone has equal rights to use it.

Privacy on The Internet

On the Internet, your privacy is violated on a daily basis. Your e-mail program's in-box fills up with *spam*, your Web usage is tracked by giant companies you've never even heard of, *cookies* on your hard drive are reporting back to their secret masters, and if you're really unlucky someone is reading your private e-mail. In order to protect your privacy, begin by knowing what threats are out there, and how you can keep them from affecting you.

The most innocuous threat to your privacy is **spam**, or unsolicited e-mail. It clogs your mailbox with junk messages, but it's not hard to spot if you know what to look for. Because spam is advertising, its message title usually reads like ad copy, and because you probably didn't ask to receive it, spam always comes from an unfamiliar e-mail address. A good general rule: If it looks like spam, it probably is.

The prospect of having your private e-mail opened and read by a third party is a much nastier one—made all the more so by the inherent insecurity of e-mail. In its path from your computer to its destination your e-mail is routed through a number of other servers (computers), many of which store a copy of your message in the process—and these messages can be read by anyone with access to those servers. On top of that, the actual packets of information containing your e-mail can be

spam

intercepted along the way and opened by a third party. Does this mean you shouldn't use e-mail? Not at all—just don't use it to send sensitive information, such as credit card numbers.

cookie

A more subtle threat to your privacy is posed by **cookies**. Cookies are files with information about you that are left on your computer when you visit a web site. Normally, a cookie can only be read by the website that leaves the cookie. The information in a cookie is provided by you and your web browser, so it is not secrete information. However, it can be used by a web site to keep a profile on you. For example, an on line clothing store might keep a record of your purchases and clothes sizes in a cookie on your computer. You can delete these cookies from your hard drive or configure your Web browser to not accept any cookies or to only accept certain categories of cookies. However, if you turn cookies off entirely, many commercial websites will become inaccessible to you.

How can you protect your privacy? The first step is choosing good passwords. A good password should be hopefully impossible to guess. It should contain a mix of letters (uppercase and lowercase), numbers, and special symbols. The easiest way for someone else to figure out your password is to try everything they think you might have used, like your birthday, or the name of a family member. The second easiest is called a dictionary attack, and involves trying every word in the dictionary until your password is found. By mixing in uppercase characters and numbers and using unusual words, you can secure your password against a dictionary attack-and make it almost impossible to guess.

Another way to protect your privacy is to encrypt your sensitive files and sensitive e-mail messages. Free encryption software can be downloaded over the Internet.

It is also a good idea to protect yourself against viruses. Viruses can compromise your privacy, and even more likely, they can destroy your data. The simplest way to protect yourself from viruses is to be careful what files you download, as well as what e-mail attachments you open. Better yet, use a virus scanning program to run regular checks on your hard drive-and also to check downloaded files before you open or run them. By following these two guidelines, you will do a pretty good job of protecting your data and your privaicy.

1.3 | Designing Programs

> '*The time has come.*' *the Walrus said,*
> '*To talk of many things:*
>   *Of shoes–and ships–and sealing wax–*
> *Of cabbages–and–kings...*'
>
> **Lewis Carroll, Through the Looking Glass**

Programming is a creative process. We cannot tell you exactly how to write a program to solve whatever task you may want your program to solve. However, we can give you some techniques that experienced programmers have found to be extremely helpful for designing programs. In this section, we discuss some of these techniques. The techniques are applicable to programming in almost any programming language and are not particular to the Java programming language.

Object-Oriented Programming

Java was designed to do **object-oriented programming**, abbreviated **OOP**. What is OOP? It is a programming technique that uses objects. So, what are *objects*? The world around us consists of objects, such as people, automobiles, buildings, trees, shoes, ships, sealing wax, cabbages, kings, and so forth. Each of these objects has the ability to perform certain actions, and each of these actions has some effect on some of the other objects in the world. Object-oriented programming is a programming methodology that views a program as this sort of world consisting of objects that interact with each other by means of actions.

OOP

This is easier to understand if the program simulates something in the real world. For example, consider a program that simulates a highway interchange in order to see how it handles traffic flow. The program would have an object to simulate each of the automobiles that enter the interchange, perhaps other objects to simulate each lane of the highway, and so forth.

Object-oriented programming comes with its own terminology. The objects are called, appropriately enough, **objects**. The actions that an object can take are called **methods**. Objects of the same kind are said to have the same *type* or more often said to be in the same **class**. For example, in a simulation program, all the simulated automobiles might belong to the same class, probably called the `Automobile` class. All objects within a class have the same methods. Thus, in a simulation program, all automobiles have the same methods (or possible actions) such as moving forward, moving backwards, accelerating, and so forth. This does not mean that all simulated automobiles are identical. They can have different characteristics, which are indicated in the program by associating some data (that is, some information) with each particular automobile object. For example, the data associated with an automobile object might be a word telling the make of the automobile and a number indicating its current speed. All this will become clearer when you start to define classes yourself using the Java programming language.

object

method
class

Objects, Methods, and Classes

An **object** is a program construction that has data (that is, information) associated with it and that can perform certain actions. When the program is run, the objects interact with one another in order to accomplish whatever the program is designed to do. The actions performed by objects are called **method**s. A **class** is a type or kind of object. All objects in the same class have the same kinds of data and the same methods.

◼

As we will see, this same object-oriented methodology can be applied to any sort of computer program and is not limited to simulation programs. Object-oriented programming is not a new methodology, but its use in applications outside of simulation programs did not become popular until the early 1990s.

Object-oriented programming uses class and objects, but it does not simply use them in just any old way. It uses them while following certain design principles. Three of the main design principles of object-oriented programming are:

Encapsulation,

Polymorphism, and

Inheritance.

We will briefly discuss each of these principles in this chapter and more fully at appropriate places later in the book.

Encapsulation

encapsulation **Encapsulation** sounds like it means putting things into a capsule, or to rephrase it, packaging things up. This intuition is correct as far as it goes. But the most important part of encapsulation is not simply that things are put into a capsule, but that only part of what is in the capsule is visible. Let's look at an example.

Suppose you want to drive an automobile?. What is the most useful description of the automobile? It clearly is not a description of how many cylinders the automobile has and how they go through a cycle of taking in air and gasoline, igniting the gasoline/air mixture, and expelling exhaust. Such details are not needed to learning how to drive an automobile. Indeed, knowing those details would be of no real help to somebody who wants to learn to drive an automobile.

To a person who wants to learn to drive an automobile, the most useful description of an automobile consists of information such as the following:

If you press your foot on the accelerator peddle, the automobile will move faster.

If you press your foot on the brake peddle, the automobile will slow down and eventually stop.

If you turn the steering wheel to the right, the automobile will turn to the right.

If you turn the steering wheel to the left, the automobile will turn to the left.

There are other details to describe, but these are perhaps the main ones and are enough to illustrate the concept of encapsulation.

The principle of encapsulation says that an automobile should be described in the way we illustrated in the previous list of details for somebody who wants to learn to drive a car. In the context of programming, encapsulation means the same thing. It means that when you produce a piece of software, you should describe it in a way that tells some other programmer how to use your piece of software, but that spares the programmer all the details of how your piece of software works. So just as you need not tell somebody who wants to drive a car, how many cylinders the car has, you similarly need not tell somebody who uses a piece of software you wrote all the fine details of how you wrote the software. In particular, if your piece of software is ten pages long, then the description given to another programmer who use the software should be much shorter than ten pages, perhaps only a half page long. Of course, this is only possible if you write your software in such a way that it lends itself to this sort of short description.

Note that encapsulation hides the fine detail of what is inside the "capsule." For this reason encapsulation is often called **information hiding**.

information hiding

Another analogy that may help is that an automobile has certain things visible, like peddles and a steering wheel, and other things hidden under the hood. The automobile is encapsulated so that the details are hidden under the hood, and only the controls needed to drive the automobile are visible. Similarly, a piece of software should be encapsulated so that details are hidden and only the necessary controls are visible

Encapsulation is important because it simplifies the job of the programmer who uses the encapsulated software to write more software. As a result, software is produced more quickly and with fewer errors.

Encapsulation

Encapsulation is the process of hiding all the details of how a piece of software was written and telling only what is necessary to understanding how the software is used. Put another way, encapsulation is the process of describing a class or object by giving only enough information to allow a programmer to use the class or object. ▫

Polymorphism

Polymorphism comes from a Greek word meaning many forms. The basic idea of polymorphism is that it allows the same program instruction to mean different things in different contexts. Polymorphism commonly occurs in English and its use in a programming language make the programming language more like a human language. For example, the English instruction "Go play your favorite sport." means different things to different people. To one person it means go play baseball. To another person it means go play soccer.

polymorphism

In a programming language, such as Java, **polymorphism** means that one method name, used as an instruction, can cause different actions depending on what kind of objects perform the action. For example there can be a method named output that will output the data in an object. But, what data and how much data it outputs depends on what kind of object carries out the action. There is a bit more to explain about polymorphism, but this brief introduction will give you the general idea of what it is. We will explain polymorphism more fully in Chapter 6.

If polymorphism is an everyday occurrence in languages like English, why do they make a big deal of it in programming languages? The reason is that early programming languages had very little polymorphism. So, when it was introduced into programming languages, it was a big deal because it made programs easier to read and understand.

Polymorphism

In a programming language, such as Java, **polymorphism** means that one method name, used as an instruction, can cause different actions depending on what kind of objects performs the action. ▫

Inheritance

inheritance

Inheritance refers to a way of organizing classes. The name comes from the notion of inheritance of traits like eye color, hair color, and so forth, but it is perhaps clearer to think in terms of a classification system rather than a system of inherited traits. Such a classification system is shown in Display 1.4. Note that at each level the classifications become more specialized. The class of Vehicles includes the classes of Automobiles, Motorcycles, and Buses. The class of Automobiles includes the classes of Family Cars and Sports Cars.

The class of Vehicles has certain properties, like possessing wheels. The classes Automobile, Motorcycle, and Bus "inherit" the property of having wheels, but add more properties or restrictions. For example, an Automobile has four wheels, a motorcycle has two wheels, and a Bus has at least four wheels.

Note that as you go higher in the diagram the classes are more inclusive. A School Bus is a Bus. Since it is a Bus, a School Bus is also a Vehicle. However, a Vehicle is not necessarily a School Bus. A Sports Car is an Automobile, and is also a Vehicle, but a Vehicle is not necessarily a Sports Car.

In programming languages like Java, inheritance is used to organize classes in this way. This has the advantage of allowing the programmer to avoid repeating the same piece of programming instructions. For example, everything that is true of all Vehicles, such as "Has a motor," is only described once, and it is inherited by the classes Automobile, Motorcycle, and Bus. Without inheritance, descriptions like "Has a motor" would have to be repeated for each of the classes, Automobile, Motorcycle, Bus, School Bus, Luxury Bus, and so forth.

Inheritance is very important to object-oriented programming and to the Java language. However, it is a bit difficult to understand without concrete programming examples. We will discuss inheritance in the Java language in Chapter 7. At that point, we will explain the notion of inheritance more fully and more clearly.

Inheritance

In a programming language, such as Java, **inheritance** is a way or organizing classes so that classes with properties in common can be grouped so that their common properties need only be defined once for all the classes. ◻

Object Oriented Programming

Object-oriented programming (OOP) is a programming methodology that views a program as consisting of objects that interact with each other by means of actions (known as methods). Object-oriented programming uses objects, but it does not simply use them in just any old way. It uses them while following certain design principles. The main design principles of object-oriented programming are Encapsulation, Polymorphism, and Inheritance. ◻

If You Know Some Other Programming Language

If Java is your first programming language, then you should skip this subsection. If you know some other programming language, then this paragraph will try to explain objects in terms of things you may already know about. If you are already familiar

Display 1.4   An Inheritance Hierarchy

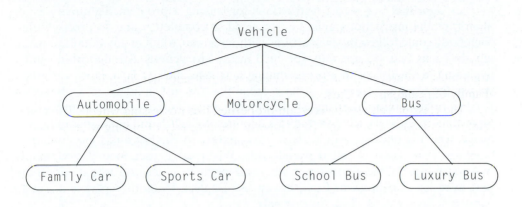

with some other object-oriented programming languages such as C++, Smalltalk, or Borland's Turbo Pascal or Delphi, then you already have a good idea of what objects, methods, and classes are. They are basically the same in all object-oriented programming languages, although some other languages use the word *function* or *procedure* to mean the same thing as *method*. If you are familiar with an older form of programming language that does not have anything called objects or classes, then objects can be described in terms of other, older programming constructs. If you have heard of variables and functions, then you can think of an object as a variable that has multiple pieces of data and that has its own functions. Methods are really the same thing as what are called *procedures* or *functions* in older programming languages.

Algorithms

Objects interact with one another by performing actions (called methods). You as a programmer need to design these actions by giving instruction for how the action is carried out. The hardest part of designing these actions is not figuring out how to express your solution in Java (or whatever programming language you are using). The hardest part is coming up with a plan or strategy for carrying out the action. For example, if you could come up with a strategy that would allow an object to predict the direction of the stock market on a daily basis, then you could sell this strategy for a huge amount of money. On the other hand, the programmer who writes the Java method to implement this strategy, while well paid, would not get nearly the same amount of money as you would get for designing the basic strategy. Of course, money paid is not necessarily an indication of difficulty, but in this case it does pretty much indicate the difference in difficulty. In less dramatic settings, such as completing a basic programming assignment or designing a method for balancing your checkbook,

algorithm

the same rule applies. The hard part is coming up with the strategy for the solution. This strategy is often expressed as something called an *algorithm.*

An **algorithm** is a set of instructions for solving a problem. To qualify as an algorithm, the instructions must be expressed so completely and so precisely that somebody could follow the instructions without having to fill in any details or make any decisions that are not fully specified in the instructions. An algorithm can be expressed in English or in a programming language, such as Java. However, when we use the word *algorithm,* we usually mean that the instructions are expressed in English or something like English. In practice, programmers do not express their algorithms in ordinary English, but in a mixture of English and a programming language, which in our case will be Java. This mixture of English and a programming language (like Java) is called **pseudocode**. When using pseudocode, you simply write each piece of the algorithm in whatever language is easiest for that part. If the part is easier to express in English, you use English. If another part is easier to express in Java, you use Java for that part.

pseudocode

An example may help to clarify the notion of an algorithm. Our first sample algorithm determines the total cost for a list of items. For example, the list of items might be a shopping list that includes the price of each item. The algorithm would then determine the total cost of all the items on the list. The algorithm is as follows:

Algorithm that determines the total cost of a list of items:

1. Write the number 0 on the blackboard.
2. Do the following for each item on the list:
   Add the cost of the item to the number on the blackboard.
   Replace the old number on the blackboard by the result of this addition.
3. Announce that the answer is the number written on the blackboard.

This algorithm uses a blackboard to store intermediate results. Most algorithms need to store some intermediate results. If the algorithm is written in the Java language and run on a computer, then these intermediate results are stored in the computer's main memory.

Algorithm

An **algorithm** is a set of instructions for solving a problem. To qualify as an algorithm, the instructions must be expressed so completely and precisely that somebody could follow the instructions without having to fill in any details or make any decisions that are not fully specified in the instructions. ◻

Pseudocode

Pseudocode is a mixture of English and a programming language (in our case Java). Algorithms are usually written in pseudocode and later translated into a programming language, such as Java. ◻

? Self-Test Questions

8. What is a method?

9. What is the relationship between classes and objects?
10. Do all objects of the same class have the same methods?
11. What is *encapsulation*?
12. What is *information hiding*?
13. What is *polymorphism*?
14. What is an algorithm?
15. What is pseudocode?

Reusable Components

When you first start to write programs, you can easily get the impression that each program that is produced is a completely separate project that is designed from scratch. That is not the way good software is produced. Most programs are created by combining already existing components. That saves time and money. Also, since the same software has been used many times, it is likely to be better tested and so be more reliable.

For example, a highway simulation program might include a new highway object to model a new highway design, but would probably model automobiles by using an automobile class that was already designed for some other program. In order to ensure that the classes you use in your programs are easily reusable, you must design them to be reusable. You must specify exactly how objects of that class interact with other objects. This is the principle of encapsulation that we discussed in a previous subsection. But encapsulation is not the only principle that you must follow. You must design your class so that the objects are general and not designed in an ad hoc way for one particular program. For example, if your program requires that all simulated automobiles only move forward, you should still include a reverse in your automobile class. Some other simulation may require automobiles to back up. We will return to the topic of reusability after we learn some details about the Java language and have some examples to work with.

Testing and Debugging

The way to write a correct program is to carefully design the objects your program needs, to carefully design the algorithms for the methods the objects will use, and finally to carefully translate all this into Java code (or code in whatever programming language you are using). Unless you proceed carefully, you will probably never get all of the errors out of your program. However, even a very carefully designed program might contain some errors. When you finish writing a program, you should test the program to see whether or not it performs correctly, and if it does not perform correctly fix any errors in the program.

A mistake in a program is called a **bug**. For this reason, the process of eliminating mistakes in your program is called **debugging**. There are three commonly recognized types of bugs or errors, and they are known as *syntax errors, run-time errors,* and *logic errors*. Let's consider them in order.

A **syntax error** is a grammatical mistake in your program. There are very strict grammar rules for how you write a program. If you violate one of these rules, for

bug
debugging

syntax error

example, by omitting a required punctuation, that is a syntax error. The compiler will catch syntax errors and output an error message telling you that it has found the error and what it thinks the error is. If the compiler says you have a syntax error, you probably do have an error. However, the compiler is only guessing at what the error is, and so it could be incorrect in what it says the error is.

Syntax

The rules for the correct way to write a program or part of a program (the grammar rules for a programming language) are called the **syntax** of the language.

---

run-time error

An error that is detected when your program is run is called a **run-time error.** If your program contains a run-time error, then the computer will output an error message when your program is run. The error message may or may not be easy to understand, but at least it lets you know that something is wrong, and sometimes it can tell you exactly what is wrong.

If there is some mistake in the underlying algorithm for your program or if you write something in Java that is incorrect but still legal, then your program will compile and run without any error message. You have written a valid Java program, but you have not written the program you want. The program runs and gives output, but gives incorrect output. In this case, your program contains a **logic error.** For example, if you were to mistakenly use the addition sign in place of the subtraction sign, that would be a logic error. You could compile and run your program with no error messages, but the program would give the wrong output. Logic errors are the hardest kind of error to locate, because the computer does not give you any error messages.

logic error

■ Gotcha
Coping with "Gotchas"

gotcha

Any programming language has details that can trip you up in ways that are surprising or that are hard to deal with. These sorts of problems are often called *pitfalls*, but a more colorful and more commonly used term is *gotchas*. The term stems from the fact that these problems, or pitfalls, or *gotchas* are like traps waiting to catch you. When you get caught in the trap, the trap has "got you," or as it is more commonly pronounced "gotcha."

In this book, we have sections, with headings like this section, that warn you about many of the most common *gotchas* and tell you how to avoid them or how to cope with them.

■ Gotcha
Hidden Errors

Just because your program compiles and runs without any errors and even gives "reasonable looking" output, that does not mean your program is correct. You should always run your program with some test data for which you know what the output is supposed to be. To do this, choose some data for which you can compute the correct output with pencil and paper, or by looking up the answer, or by some other means. Even this testing does not guarantee that your program is correct, but the more testing you do, the more confidence you can have in your program.

? Self-Test Questions

16. What is a syntax error?

17. What kinds of errors are likely to produce error messages that will alert you to the fact that your program contains an error?

18. Suppose you write a program that is supposed to compute which day of the week (Sunday, Monday, and so forth) a given date (like December 1, 2001) will fall on. Now, suppose you forget to account for leap years. Your program will then contain an error. What kind of program error is it?

1.4 | A Taste of Java

> *Java. An Island of Indonesia, 48,842 square miles in area, lying between the Indian Ocean and the Java Sea.*
> *java* **n.** *Informal. Brewed coffee. [From Java.]*
> **The American Heritage Dictionary of the English Language, First Edition**

In this section, we describe some of the characteristics of the Java language and examine a simple Java program.

History of the Java Language

Java is widely viewed as a programming language to design applications for the Internet. However, this book, and many other books and people, view Java as a general-purpose programming language that can be used without any reference to the Internet. At its birth, Java was neither of these things, but it did eventually evolve into both of these things.

The history of Java goes back to 1991 when James Gosling and his team at Sun Microsystems began designing the first version of Java (which was not yet called *Java*). The first version of Java was intended to be a programming language for programming home appliances, like toasters and TVs. That sounds like a humble engineering task, but in fact, it's a very challenging one. Home appliances are controlled by a wide variety of computer processors (chips). The language that Gosling and his team were designing needed to work on all these different processors. Moreover, a home appliance is typically an inexpensive item, so the manufacturer will not be willing to invest large amounts of time and money into developing complicated compilers. (A compiler is a program that translate the appliance language program into a language the processor can understand.) In this appliance language that the team was designing, and now in the Java language that it evolved into, programs are first translated into an **intermediate language** that is the same for all appliances (or all computers), then a small, easy-to-write, and hence inexpensive, program trans-

intermediate language

byte-code

lates this intermediate language into the machine language for a particular appliance or computer. This intermediate language is called **Java byte-code** or simply **byte-code**. The plan for programming appliances with this first version of Java never caught on with appliance manufactures, but that was not the end of the story.

In 1994, Gosling realized that his language would be ideal for developing a web browser (a program for finding and viewing sites on the Internet.) The web browser was produced by Patrick Naughton and Jonathan Payne at Sun Microsystems and has evolved into the browser that is today known as HotJava. This was the start of Java's connection to the Internet. In the fall of 1995, Netscape Incorporated decided to make the next release of its Netscape (Internet) browser capable of running Java programs. Other companies associated with the Internet have followed suit and have software that accommodates Java programs.

Why Is the Language Named "Java"?

This question does not have a very interesting answer. The current custom is to name programming languages pretty much the same way that parents name their children. The creator of the programming language simply chooses any name that sounds good to her or him. The original name of the language was "Oak", but it was later realized that there already was a computer language named Oak, so they needed another name for the language and "Java" was chosen. One hears conflicting explanations of the original of the name "Java". One traditional, and perhaps believable, story about where the name "Java" came from is that the name was thought of when, after a fruitless meeting trying to come up with a new name for the language, the development team went out for coffee, and the rest is, as they say, history.

Applets and the Internet

applet
application

There are two kinds of Java programs, **applets** and **applications** (that is, applets and regular programs). An *applet* sounds like a little apple, but the name is meant to convey the idea of a *little application*, not a little apple. Applets and applications are almost identical. The difference is that applications are meant to be run on your computer like any other program, whereas an applet is meant to be sent to another location on the Internet and run there.

Once you know how to design and write one of either applets or applications, it is easy to learn to write the other of these two kinds of programs. This book emphasizes applications rather than applets. The reason for this is that you need to know a number of things about the World Wide Web and websites (on the Internet) in order to use applets in the way applets were intended to be used, and we do not want to stop to discuss that whole other topic. However, if you do want to write applets, some sample applets are given later in this chapter in the subsection *Preview Examples of Applets (Optional)* and applets are covered in detail in Chapter 13 of this book.

A First Java Application Program

user

Our first Java program is shown in Display 1.5. Below the program we show two screen displays that might be produced when a *user* runs and interacts with this program. The person who interacts with a program is called the **user**. The text typed in by the user is shown in boldface. If you run this program (and you should do so), then

Display 1.5   A Sample Java Program

```java
public class FirstProgram
{
    public static void main(String[] args)
    {
        System.out.println("Hello out there.");
        System.out.println("Want to talk some more?");
        System.out.println("Answer y for yes or n for no.");

        char answerLetter;
        answerLetter = SavitchIn.readLineNonwhiteChar();
        if (answerLetter == 'y')
            System.out.println("Nice weather we are having.");

        System.out.println("Good-bye.");

        System.out.println("Press enter key to end program.");
        String junk;
        junk = SavitchIn.readLine();
    }
}
```

Sample Screen Dialogue 1

```
Hello out there.
Want to talk some more?
Answer y for yes or n for no.
y
Nice weather we are having.
Good-bye.
Press enter key to end program.
```

In order to run this program you must have both of the files FirstProgram.java and SavitchIn.java in the same directory (folder) and must compile both of these. Read the subsection **Compiling a Java Program or Class** later in this chapter.

Sample Screen Dialogue 2

```
Hello out there.
Want to talk some more?
Answer y for yes or n for no.
n
Good-bye.
Press enter key to end program.
```

both texts would look alike on your computer screen. The user may or may not be the person who wrote the program. In a programming class, they very often are the same person, but in a real world application, they are usually different people.

programmer

The person who writes the program is called the **programmer.** This book is teaching you to be the programmer and one of the first things you need to learn is that the user of your program cannot be expected to know what you want her or him to do, and so your program must give the user understandable instructions, as we have done in the sample screen dialogs.

In this subsection, we just want to give you a feel for the Java language by giving you a brief, informal description of the sample program shown in Display 1.5. In Chapters 2 and 3, we will explain the details of the Java features used in that program. *Do not worry if some of the details of this program are not completely clear on this first reading.* They will be clarified in Chapters 2 and 3. This is just a preview of things to come.

For now, ignore the following few lines that come at the start of the program. They set up a context for the program, but we need not worry about them yet.

```
public class FirstProgram
{
    public static void main(String[] args)
    {
```

You can think of these opening lines as being a hard-to-spell way of writing "Begin the program named `FirstProgram`."

The next three lines, shown in what follows, are the first things the program does. Let's discuss these three lines first.

output

```
System.out.println("Hello out there.");
System.out.println("Want to talk some more?");
System.out.println("Answer y for yes or n for no.");
```

Each of these lines begin with `System.out.println`. Each one causes the quoted string given within the parentheses to be output to the screen. For example, consider

```
System.out.println("Hello out there.");
```

This causes the line

```
Hello out there.
```

to be written to the screen.

For now, you can consider these lines that begin with `System.out.println` to be a funny way of saying "output what is shown in parentheses". However, we can tell you a little about what is going on here.

**System.out-
println**

Java programs work by having things called *objects* perform actions. The actions performed by an object are called *methods*. `System.out` is an object used for sending output to the screen; `println` is the method (that is, the action) that this object carries out in order to send what is in parentheses to the screen. When-

invoking

ever an object performs an action using a method, that is called **invoking** the method. In a Java program you write such a method invocation by writing the

dot

object followed by a period (called a **dot** in computer jargon), followed by the method name, and some parentheses that may or may not have something inside them. The thing (or things) inside of the parentheses is called an **argument** and provides the information needed by the method in order to carry out its action. In each of these first three lines, the method is `println`. The method `println` writes something to the screen, and the argument (a string in quotes) tells it what it should write.

argument

Classes, Objects, and Methods

A Java program works by having things called **objects** perform actions. The actions are known as **methods**. All objects of the same kind are said to be in the same class. So, a **class** is a category of objects. (If you want to know more details about classes and objects, read the subsection entitled ***Object-Oriented Programming*** that begins on page 17.) When the object perform the action for a given method, that is called **invoking the method**.

In some special cases a class can serve the same role as an object, that is, the class can perform the action (invoke the method), but that level of detail need not worry you yet. Just note that things called *objects* and things called *classes* both can perform actions, and the actions are called *methods*.

The next line of the program, shown in what follows, says that `answerLetter` is the name of a variable.

```
char answerLetter;
```

A **variable** is something that can store a piece of data. The `char` says that the data must be a single character; `char` is an abbreviation for *character*.

variable
char

The next line reads a character that is typed in at the keyboard and stores this character in the variable `answerLetter`:

```
answerLetter = SavitchIn.readLineNonwhiteChar();
```

`SavitchIn` is a class designed for users of this text. The class `SavitchIn` is used for obtaining input from the keyboard and `readlineNonwhiteChar` is a method that reads a single nonblank character from the keyboard. If the user types in some input on a single line and presses the enter key (also called the return key), then this method will read the first nonblank character on that line and discard everything else on that line of keyboard input. The expression

SavitchIn

```
SavitchIn.readLineNonwhiteChar();
```

is another kind of method invocation. This method invocation simply reads the first nonblank character, which in the first dialog is `'y'`, and dumps the character at the location of the invocation. The rest of that line tells what is to happen to this character `'y'`. The rest of the line, highlighted in what follows, says to make this character the value of the variable `answerLetter`.

```
answerLetter = SavitchIn.readLineNonwhiteChar();
```

The equal sign is used differently in Java than it is in everyday mathematics. In the preceding program line, the equal sign does not mean that `answerLetter` *is equal to* `SavitchIn.readLineNonwhiteChar()`. Instead, it is an instruction to the computer to *make* `answerLetter` *equal to* `SavitchIn.readLineNonwhiteChar()`; that is, to store the character read from the keyboard in the variable `answerLetter`.

equal sign

As it turns out, `SavitchIn` is not really an object, but is a class. However, in this context, we are using the class `SavitchIn` as if it were an object. For some special methods, you can use the name of a class rather than the name of an object when you invoke the method. In Chapter 5, we explain the significance of this distinction, but those details need not concern us until we get to Chapter 5. At this point, you could even consider the following as a peculiarly spelled instruction that tells the computer to read one character and store that character in the variable `answerLetter`:

```
answerLetter = SavitchIn.readLineNonwhiteChar();
```

As we will explain more fully later, `SavitchIn` is not something that automatically comes with the Java language. The programmer must define the class `SavitchIn` (or some similar class), but to get you started we have defined it for you and placed it on the CD that comes with this text.

double equal sign

The next two lines of the program makes a decision to do or not do something based on what the user types in at the keyboard. They perform a test for equality using the double equal sign. Java uses the double equal sign for what you might think of as ordinary equals. The following two program lines first check to see if the character stored in the variable `answerLetter` is equal to the character `'y'`. If it is, then `"Nice weather we are having."` is written to the screen.

```
if (answerLetter == 'y')
    System.out.println("Nice weather we are having.");
```

If the character stored in `answerLetter` is anything other than `'y'`, then these two lines cause no output to the screen.

Notice that one sample dialog outputs the string `"Nice weather we are having."` and one does not. That is because, in the first run of the program, the character `'y'` is stored in the variable `answerLetter`, and in the second run of the program, the character `'n'` is stored in `answerLetter`.

The following three lines at the end of the program are there to stop the screen output from going away before you can read it. Some systems will erase the screen as soon as the program ends. These three lines make the program, and the screen, wait for you to press the enter key (also called the return key):

```
System.out.println("Press enter key to end program.");
String junk;
junk = SavitchIn.readLine();
```

If pressing the enter key one time does not end the program, just press it a second time. This detail can vary a little from one system to another. Although you can use these three lines without understanding them, we can explain a bit more about these three lines.

The line

```
String junk;
```

declares a variable named `junk`. The type `String` means that `junk` can hold an entire string of characters. If the user enters a line of text and ends the line with the enter (return) key, then the following will read the entire line of text and make it the value of `junk`:

```
junk = SavitchIn.readLine();
```

If the user simply presses the enter (return) key, then this will still read the blank line of input, so all that the user needs to do is press the return key. The variable is named `junk`, because the value stored in the variable is not used for anything.

The method `readLine` is similar to the method `readLineNonwhiteChar`, except that `readLine` reads in an entire line of input rather than a single character. You could end the program in Display 1.5 by typing in the words

```
So long for now.
```

all on one line and ended by pressing the enter key. The entire line of text would be stored in the variable `junk`. However, all we really need the user to do is to press the enter key.

The only things left to explain in this first program are the final semicolons on each line and the curly brackets } at the end of the program. The semicolon acts as ending punctuation like a period in an English sentence. A semicolon ends an instruction to the computer. These instructions are called **statements**. The curly brackets } at the end simply says "This is the end of the program."

Of course, there are very precise rules for how you write each part of a Java program. These rules form the grammar for the Java language, just like there are rules for the grammar of the English language, but the Java rules are more precise. The grammar rules for a programming language (or any language) are called the **syntax** of the language.

statements

syntax

? Self-Test Questions

19. If the following statement were used in a Java program, it would cause something to be written on the screen. What would it cause to be written on the screen?

    ```
    System.out.println("Java is great!");
    ```

20. Give a statement or statements that can be used in a Java program to write the following on the screen:

    ```
    Java for one.
    Java for all.
    ```

21. Suppose `mary` is an object of a class named `Person` and suppose `increaseAge` is a method for the class `Person` that uses one argument that is an integer. How do you write an invocation of the method `increaseAge` for the object `mary` using the argument 5? The method `increaseAge` will change the data in `mary` so that it simulates `mary` aging by 5 years.

Method Invocation

A **method** is an action that an object is capable of performing. When you ask an object to perform the action of a method, that is called **invoking** the method. (Another term used to mean the same thing as *invoking a method* is **calling a method.**) In a Java program, a method invocation is specified by writing the object name (or in some special cases the class name instead of an object name), followed by a period (called a **dot**), followed by the method name, and followed by the *arguments* enclosed in parentheses. The **arguments** are information given to the method. (Another term that is often used to mean the same thing as arguments is *parameters*.)

Syntax:

> *Object_Name_Or_Class_Name* . *Method_Name* (*Arguments*)

(In this chapter the *Object_Name_Or_Class_Name* is usually a class name. However, it is more common for this first item to an object of the class. You will see that this is true as soon as you start defining your own class.)

Examples:

```
System.out.println("Hello out there.");
answerLetter = SavitchIn.readLineNonwhiteChar();
```

In the first example, `System.out` is the object, `println` is the method, and `"Hello out there"` is the argument. If there is more than one argument, the arguments are separated by commas.

In the second example, `SavitchIn` serves the same role as an object, the method is `readLineNon-whiteChar`, and there are no arguments. In some cases, such as the methods of the class `SavitchIn`, you can use a class name in place of an object name when you write a method invocation.

In a program, these method invocations are typically followed by a semicolon.

OOP Terminology: Messages

When a program contains an invocation of an object's method, such as the following, some programmers say that the object is **sent a message**.

```
System.out.println("Hello out there.");
```

In this case, the object `System.out` is sent the message `println("Hello out there.")`. When you take this view, you think of objects as performing actions in response to messages. In this case, the action taken by the object `System.out` in response to the message `println("Hello out there.")` is to output the string `"Hello out there."` to the screen. In this book, we will, however, use the terms *method invocation* and *method call* rather than phrases like *send a message to the object*.

22. What is the meaning of the following line, which appears in the program in Display 1.5/page 27:

```
answerLetter = SavitchIn.readLineNonwhiteChar();
```

23. Write a complete Java program that uses `System.out.println` to output the following to the screen when run:

```
Hello World!
```

Your program does nothing else, except that, if the output goes away before you get a chance to read it, then you should add the following to the end of your program:

```
System.out.println("Press enter key to end program.");
String junk;
junk = SavitchIn.readLine();
```

Note that you do not need to fully understand all the details of the program in order to write the program. You can simply follow the model of the program in Display 1.5/page 27. (You do want to eventually understand all the details, but that may take a few more chapters.)

Java Spelling Rules

identifier

The technical term for a name in a programming language is an **identifier**. The Java language has precise rules for what is allowed as an identifier (that is, as the name of something in a Java program), such as a class or a variable. An identifier (a name) must consist entirely of letters, digits (0 through 9), and the underscore character _, but the first character in a name cannot be a digit.[1] In particular, no name can contain a space or any other character such as a period or an *. There is no limit to the length of a name. (Well, in practice, there is always a limit, but there is no official limit and Java will accept even absurdly long names.) Java is **case-sensitive**. That means that uppercase and lowercase letters are considered to be different characters. For example, mystuff, myStuff, and MyStuff are considered to be three different names and you could have three different variables (or other items) with these three names. Of course, it is very poor programming practice to have two names that differ only in that one has uppercase letters where the other has the same letters in lowercase, but the Java compiler would be happy with them. Java uses a character set, called *Unicode*, that also includes characters that are used in other languages, but that do not exist in English. Java does allow you to use these extra letters in names. (However, most keyboards you are likely to use do not have them, and many people would not recognize them if you did use them). Within these spelling rules, you can use any name you want for a variable or for a class that you define or for an object of that class. But, we will give you some style guidelines for choosing names, so that your programs will be easier to read.

case-sensitive
upper- and
lowercase

The peculiar use of uppercase and lowercase letters, such as answerLetter, that we have used in our sample program deserves some explanation. It would be perfectly legal to use AnswerLetter or answer_letter instead of answerLetter, but there are some well-established conventions about how you should use uppercase and lowercase letters. By convention, we write names using only letters and digits. We "punctuate" multiword names using uppercase letters (since we cannot use spaces). So, the following are all legal names that also follow this well-established convention:

```
inputStream    YourClass    CarWash    hotCar    theTimeOfDay
```

---

1. Java does allow the dollar sign symbol $ to appear in an identifier, but these identifiers have a special meaning and you should not use the $ symbol in your identifiers.

The following are all illegal names in Java, and the compiler will complain if you use any of them:

```
My.Class    netscape.com    go-team    7eleven
```

The first three contain illegal characters, either a dot or the dash symbol. The last name is illegal because it starts with a digit.

Notice that some of the legal names start with an uppercase letter and others, such as `hotCar`, start with a lowercase letter, which may look a little strange at first. We will always follow the convention that the names of classes start with an uppercase letter, and the names of variables, objects, and methods start with a lowercase letter.

reserved word

Of course, there are words in a Java program, such as the word `if`, that do not name a variable, a class, or an object. Some words, such as `if`, are called **reserved words** or **keywords**. These reserved words have a special predefined meaning in the Java language and cannot be used as the names of classes or objects or anything else other than their intended meaning. A full list of reserved words for Java is given in Appendix 1, but it is easier to learn them by usage. From now on, we will show reserved words in italic, like so: *if*. Some other words, such as `String`, have a predefined meaning but are not reserved words. That means you can change their meaning, but it is a bad idea to do so, because it could easily confuse you or somebody else reading your program.

■ Java Tip

Java is Case Sensitive

Do not forget that Java is case sensitive. If you use an identifier, like `myNumber`, and then in another part of your program spell the identifier `MyNumber`, then Java will not recognize them as the same identifier. To be the same identifier they must have the same pattern of upper- and lower-case letters.

Names (Identifiers)

The name of something in a Java program, such as a variable, class, method, or object name, must not start with a digit and must consist entirely of letters, digits (0 through 9), and the underscore character _. Uppercase and lowercase letters are considered to be different characters. (The symbol $ is also allowed, but it is reserved for special purposes, and so you should not use $ in a Java name.)

Names in a program are often called **identifiers**.

Although it is not required by the Java language, the common practice, and the one followed in this book, is to start the names of classes with uppercase letters and to start the names of variables, objects, and methods with lowercase letters. These names are usually spelled using only letters and digits.

◻

Compiling a Java Program or Class

A Java program is divided into smaller parts called *classes*, and normally each class definition is in a separate file. Before you can run a Java program you must translate these classes into a language that the computer can understand. This translation process is called *compiling*. (There is more information on classes in the subsection *Ob-*

ject-Oriented Programming on page 17. There is more information on compiling in the subsection entitled *Programming Languages and Compilers* on page 9.)

A Java program can consist of any number of class definitions. The program in Display 1.5/page 27 consists of two classes. The first is the class named `FirstProgram`, which is shown in Display 1.5. Every program in Java is a class as well as a program. The other class used in this first program is the class `SavitchIn`, which has already been defined for you. At this point, you would not understand the definition of the class `SavitchIn`, but you can still obtain a copy of the class `SavitchIn`, compile it, and use it. A copy of the class `SavitchIn` is provided on the CD that accompanies this book along with the other classes defined in this book.

There are in fact two other classes used in the program in Display 1.5, the classes named `System` and `String`. However, these two classes are automatically provided for you by Java, and you need not worry about compiling either of them. As a rule, you do not need to compile the classes that are provided for you as part of Java. You normally need only compile the classes that you yourself write. So, why do you have to compile the class `SavitchIn`? The reason is that *you* are supposed to write the definition of the class `SavitchIn`. `SavitchIn` is not provided as part of Java. However, to make things easier for you, we have written the definition of the class `SavitchIn` for you. By the time you finish most of this text, you will be fully capable of writing the definition of classes such as `SavitchIn`.

Before you can compile a Java program, each class definition used in the program (and written by you the programmer) should be in a separate file. Moreover, the name of the file should be the same as the name of the class, except that the file name has `.java` added to the end. The program in Display 1.5/page 27 is a class called `FirstProgram` and so it should be in a file named `FirstProgram.java`. The program in Display 1.5 uses the class `SavitchIn`. The class definition of `SavitchIn` should be in a file named `SavitchIn.java`.

`.java` **files**

Before you can run the program in Display 1.5, you must compile both the class `SavitchIn`, which is in the file `SavitchIn.java`, and the class `FirstProgram`, which is in the file `FirstProgram.java`. (If you are in a course, then your instructor may have configured the system so that `SavitchIn` is already compiled for you, but later on when you define your own classes, you will need to compile them.)

If you are on a system that has a special environment for Java, you will have a menu command that can be used to compile a Java class or Java program. (You use the same command to compile and kind of Java file.) You will have to check your local documentation to see exactly what this command is, but it is bound to be very simple. (In the TextPad environment, which is provided on the CD that comes with this text, the command is "Compile Java" on the "File" menu.)

If your operating system expects you to type in a one-line command, that is easy to do. We will describe the commands for the Java system distributed by Sun Microsystems (usually called "the JDK" or "the SDK" or "Java 2"). If you have some other version of Java, these commands might be different.

`javac`

Suppose you want to compile a class named `MyClass`. It will be in a file named `MyClass.java`. To compile it, you simply give the following command to the operating system:

```
javac MyClass.java
```

To compile a Java class, the command is `javac` followed by the name of the file containing the class.

Thus, to compile all the classes needed to run the program in Display 1.5, you would give the following two commands (on two separate lines):

```
javac SavitchIn.java
javac FirstProgram.java
```

Remember, if you have an environment that lets you compile with a menu command, you will find it easier to use the menu command rather than the preceding commands.

.class **files**

When you compile a Java class, the translated version of the program, produced by the compiler, is called *byte-code*. When you compile a Java class, the resulting byte-code for that class is placed in a file of the same name, except that the ending is changed from `.java` to `.class`. So, when you compile a class named `MyClass` in the file `MyClass.java`, the resulting byte-code is stored in a file named `MyClass.class`. When you compile the class file named `SavitchIn.java`, the resulting byte-code is stored in a file named `SavitchIn.class`. And, of course, when you compile the class file named `FirstProgram.java`, the resulting byte-code is stored in a file named `FirstProgram.class`. (There is more information on byte-code in the subsection ***Java Byte-Code*** on page 10.)

running a Java program

Running a Java Program

A Java program can involve any number of classes, but when you run a Java program, you only run the class that you think of as the program. You can recognize this class because it will contain words identical to or similar to

```
public static void main(String[] args)
```

These words will probably (but not necessarily) be someplace near the beginning of the file. The critical words to look for are `public static void main`; the remaining portion of the line might be spelled slightly differently in some cases.

If you are on a system that has a special environment for Java, you will have a menu command that can be used to run a Java program. You will have to check your local documentation to see exactly what this command is. (In the TextPad environment, which is provided on the CD that comes with this text, the command is "Run Java Application" on the "File" menu.)

If your operating system expects you to type in a one-line command, then (on most systems) you can run a Java program by giving the command `java` followed by the name of the class you think of as the program. For example, for the program in Display 1.5, you would give the following one-line command:

```
java FirstProgram
```

Note that when you run a program, you use the class name, such as `FirstProgram` without any `.java` or `.class` ending. And remember that if you have a menu command for running a Java program, then that is an easier way to run your Java program.

(When you run a Java program, you are actually running the Java byte-code interpreter on the compiled version of your program. When you run your program, the system will automatically link in any classes you need and run the byte-code interpreter on these classes as well.)

In the preceding discussion, we were assuming that the Java compiler and other system software was already set up for you. We were also assuming that all the files were in one directory. (Directories are also called *folders*.) If you need to set up the Java compiler and system software, consult the manuals that came with the software. If you wish to spread your class definitions across multiple directories, that is possible and not difficult, but we will not concern ourselves with that detail now.

? Self-Test Questions

24. Are the following identifiers considered to be different or the same in Java?

    number   Number   NUMBER

25. Suppose you define a class named `SuperClass` in a file. What name should the file have?

26. Suppose you compile the class `SuperClass`. What will be the name of the file with the resulting byte-code?

27. Is the class `SavitchIn` part of the Java language (or does the programmer have to define the class)?

Preview Examples of Applets *(Optional)*

applet

An **applet** is special kind of Java program that can be displayed as part of an Internet site so that it can be send across the Internet to another user's computer and run on the user's computer. Applets have windowing interfaces so they are typically more flashy than the kind of programs we did in Display 1.5/page 27. In this section we will give you a brief look at two Java applets. This is just a preview. We will not be able to fully explain the applets we show you. We discuss applets in detail in Chapter 13. In this subsection we just give you a hint of how applets are written.

Display 1.6 shows a simple applet program and the window display that it produces. Let's look at the details.

The line

Swing

    import javax.swing.*;

says that this program uses the Swing library (package). Applets use software in the Swing library.

`PreviewApplet1` is the name of this applet, and the words *extends* `JApplet` say that this is an applet.

The part that begins

init

    public void init()

is the part that specifies the way the applet looks. The words *public void* will have to remain a mystery for now, but they are required. The word `init` is an abbreviation for "initialization" and indicates that this part describes how the applet is initialized.

Display 1.6   A Sample Java Applet

```java
import javax.swing.*;

public class PreviewApplet1 extends JApplet
{
    public void init()
    {
        JLabel myFirstLabel = new JLabel("Hello out there!");
        getContentPane().add(myFirstLabel);
    }
}
```

Click here with your mouse and the applet display will end.

Resulting GUI

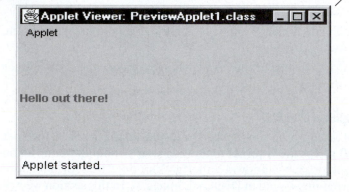

The line

```java
JLabel myFirstLabel = new JLabel("Hello out there!");
```

label

creates a label named myFirstLabel. A **label** is simply some text that can be added to the applet window. In this case the text says "Hello out there!". The next line, shown in what follows, adds the label myFirstLabel to the applet window.

```java
getContentPane().add(myFirstLabel);
```

The portion getContentPane() produces the inside of the applet window and so this line says to add the label myFirstLabel to (the inside of) the applet window.

Below the applet code in Display 1.6 is a view of what the applet display looks like when the applet is run. The term **GUI** stands for *graphical user interface*, which

GUI

Display 1.7   A Applet with an Icon Picture

```java
import javax.swing.*;

public class PreviewApplet2 extends JApplet
{
    public void init()
    {
        JLabel niceLabel = new JLabel("Java is fun!");
        ImageIcon dukeIcon = new ImageIcon("duke_waving.gif");
        niceLabel.setIcon(dukeIcon);
        getContentPane().add(niceLabel);
    }
}
```

Resulting GUI [1]

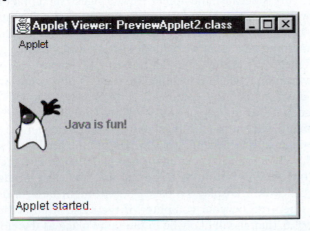

1. Java, Duke and all Java based trademarks and logos are trademarks or registered trademarks of Sun Microsystems, Inc. in the United States and other countries. (Duke is the figure waving.)

is a term used for windowing interfaces and so the applet window displayed is called a GUI.

Applets can contain pictures. The applet in Display 1.7 is similar to the one in Display 1.6 which you already saw, but there is one small difference and one significant difference. The label in Display 1.7 has the text `"Java is fun!"` instead of `"Hello out there!"`. The thing that is really new to this second applet is the addition of a picture, which is done with the following lines:

```java
ImageIcon dukeIcon = new ImageIcon("duke_waving.gif");
niceLabel.setIcon(dukeIcon);
```

icon

The first line creates an **icon** (a small picture) out of the picture file `duke_waving.gif`. This file `duke_waving.gif` contains a digital version of a picture of Duke, the guy waving in the GUI shown in Display 1.7. The second of the previous two lines adds this icon to the label named `niceLabel`. (Duke is a trademark of Sun Microsystems and serves as a mascot for the Java programming language.)

running an applet

These two applets simply display something for the user. They do not interact with the user. Other applets that we will consider in Chapter 13 will interact with the user, but these two will do as an introduction to applets.

An applet is compiled in the same way as any other Java program, but it is run in a different way.

applet viewer

An applet is designed to run from a website, but you need not know how to embed an applet in a website in order to run an applet. There are ways to run applets directly. You can run the applet by using an **applet viewer**. The one line command for an applet viewer is:

```
appletviewer PreviewApplet2.html
```

Note the ending `.html`. This is because the applet viewer places the applet in what is know as a HTML document, which is the kind of document that you read with a web browser. (This is probably all you need to do to run the applet, but in some cases you may need to do something more that we will not discuss until Chapter 13.)

An even easier and nicer way to run an applet is to run it from an environment, such as the TextPad environment, which is included on the CD that comes with this text. (In the TextPad environment the command is "Run Java Applet" on the "Tools" menu. If a window pops up asking you to "Choose a file", answer "No". This environment command will automatically invoke an applet viewier.)

ending an applet

The way that you end an applet depends on how you run the applets. If you run the applet with an applet viewer (or from an environment), then to end the applet display, you click the close window button with your mouse. The close window button will probably be as shown in Display 1.6/page 38, but might be at a different location on the applet when run on your computer. If the close window button is not as shown in Display 1.6, then it will likely be in the same place as the close window button on other windows on your computer. If the applet is run from a website, then the applet stays until the page it is on is taken off display.

- A computer's **main memory** holds the program that is currently being executed and it holds much of the data that the program is manipulating. A computer's main memory is divided into a series of numbered locations called **bytes.**

- A computer's **auxiliary memory** is used to hold data in a more or less permanent way.

- A **compiler** is a program that translates a program written in a high-level language like Java into a program written in a low-level language. The Java compiler translates your Java program into a program in the byte-code language. When you give the command to run your Java program, this byte-code program is translated into machine-language instructions and the machine-language instructions are carried out by the computer.

- An **object** is something that has data associated with it and that can perform certain actions. The actions performed by objects are called **methods**. A **class** defines a type of object. All objects in the same class have the same methods.

- Three of the main principles of object-oriented programming are encapsulation, polymorphism, and inheritance.

- An **algorithm** is a set of instructions for solving a problem. To qualify as an algorithm, the instructions must be expressed so completely and precisely that somebody could follow the instructions without having to fill in any details or make any decisions that are not fully specified in the instructions.

- In a Java program, a method invocation is specified by writing the object name (or class name), followed by a period (called a dot), followed by the method name, and followed by the arguments in parentheses.

Glossary

Below is a glossary of some terms related to the Java language and to program design techniques. You can use this as a reference to look up words you may have heard and wondered what they meant or to look up words we have discussed and whose definition you may have forgotten. Many of these terms have more detailed and more technical definitions later in this book.

Abstraction: In programming design *abstraction* means hiding details so that only what is needed to use the software is shown. *Abstraction, information hiding,* and *encapsulation* all mean the same thing.

Algorithm: A set of instructions for solving a problem. To qualify as an algorithm, the instructions must be expressed so completely and precisely that somebody could follow the instructions without having to fill in any details or make any decisions that are not fully specified in the instructions.

API: Abbreviation for *Application Programming Interface.* An API for a piece of software tells the programer who uses the software how to use it. see *Encapsulation.*

Applet: A special kind of Java program that can be displayed as part of an Internet site so that it can be send across the Internet to a user's computer and run on the user's computer. Applets have a windowing interface.

Application (Program): In Java an application program is any program that is not an applet.

Argument: see *Method Invocation.* Arguments are discussed in detail in Chapter 4.

AWT: A library of Java classes used to write programs for GUIs. The AWT library was produced earlier than the Swing library. This book uses the more recent Swing library. However, the Swing library does not replace the AWT. It builds on the AWT. So, a programmer usually needs to use both the AWT and the Swing libraries, when programming with Swing. see *GUI.*

Bit: A digit (or portion of memory) that can assume only two values. The two values are usually denoted by the digits 0 and 1.

Browser: see *Web Browser*

Byte: A computer's memory is divided into pieces each of size 8 bits. These 8 bit pieces are called *bytes.*

Byte-Code: A translated version of a Java program that is produced by a Java compiler or the language in which such a translated program is expressed. Byte-code is the machine language for a hypothetical computer known as the *Java Virtual Machine.* When the byte-code program is run, an interpreter translates each instruction of byte-code into instructions for the computer on which it is running.

Calling Object: Objects perform actions known as *methods.* The object that performs a method action is called *the calling object.*

Class: A category of objects. All objects in the same class have the same kinds of data and the same methods.

Code: When discussing programs, *code* means a program or part of a program.

Compiler: A program that translates a high-level language program, such as a Java program, into a low-level language program such as a machine-language program or a Java byte-code program. See *Byte-Code.*

Cookie: A file (typically with information about you) left on your computer by a website when you visit the website with your browser. When you next visit the same web site, this information is available to the web-site.

Data Hiding: Another term for *Information Hiding.*

Encapsulation: In programming design *encapsulation* means hiding details so that only what is needed to use the software is shown. *Abstraction, information hiding,* and *encapsulation* all mean the same thing.

Giga-: A prefix meaning one billion. For example, 20 gigabytes is 20 billion bytes.

GUI: Short for *Graphical User Interface*. A program or program interface that uses graphical elements such as windows, buttons, and menus.

Hardware: The physical parts of a computer machine, as opposed to software. see *Software*.

High-Level Language: A programming language designed to be easy for humans to read and write. Java is a high-level language. See *Compiler* and *Low-Level Language*.

HotJava: A web browser written using Java. It was of historical importance in that it showed that websites could be animated. It was important for showing the power of Java and helped to popularize Java. It is no longer widely used.

HTML: A language for writing documents that can be viewed on a web browser. Applets, among other things, can be included in an HTML document.

Information Hiding: In programming design *information hiding* means hiding details so that only what is needed to use the software is shown. *Abstraction, information hiding,* and *encapsulation* all mean the same thing.

Inheritance: a way or organizing classes so that classes with properties in common can be grouped so that their common properties need only be defined once for all the classes. Inheritance is described more precisely in Chapter 7.

Internet: A network connecting computers all over the word that allows users of one computer to contact another computer on the network. Among other things, the Internet is used for e-mail and for viewing websites with a web browser. See *World Wide Web*.

Interpreter: A program that translates a program (especially a program in byte-code) into instructions expressed in a computer's machine language and executes those instructions on the computer. An interpreter translates and executes statements in the source language one after the other, as opposed to a compiler, which translates the entire program before the program is executed.

Java 2: A family of Java products from Sun Microsystems that includes the SDK. see *SDK*.

Java Beans: This is a project (architecture) which includes a specification for reusable software components and software for designing and testing reusable software components. The components that meet the specification are called *Java Beans*. Java Beans can be written in the Java language, but they can also be written in other programming languages. Java Beans software is included with some Java compiler and environment packages.

JavaScript: A scripting language (simplified programming language) that can be used to program some things for a website on the Internet. JavaScript has nothing to do with the Java language.

Java Virtual Machine: A Java compiler produces a translation of a Java program into the machine language of a hypothetical computer. (A program for this hypothetical computer is called *byte-code*.) This hypothetical computer is known as the *Java Virtual Machine*. The interpreter that translates Java byte-code into another computer's machine language is also called the *Java Virtual Machine*. See *Byte-Code*.

JDK: Short for *Java Development Kit*. An environment distributed by Sun Microsystems that includes the Java compiler. The name has been replaced by the term *SDK*. see *SDK*.

Kilo-: A prefix meaning one thousand. For example, ten kilobytes is ten thousand bites. (In computer usage *kilo-* often means the power of two that is nearest to one thousand, since computers typically group by twos. This is still approximately one thousand.)

Linker: A program that connects different pieces of software so that they can be run as one program. A Java program is always linked this way. If the program is in only one piece it still needs to be linked to standard pieces of software that are part of Java.

Low-Level Language: A language that either is, or is very similar to, machine language. Java byte-code is a low-level language.

Machine Language: The language that a computer can directly execute without any need for translation or other processing.

Mega-: A prefix meaning one million. For example, a two megabytes is two million bytes.

Method Call: another term for *Method Invocation*.

Method Invocation: Whenever an object performs an action using a method, that is called *invoking* the method. In a Java program you write such a *method invocation* by writing the object name followed by a period (dot), followed by the method name, and some parentheses that may or may not have something extra information to use in the method invocation. This information in parentheses is known as *arguments* or *parameters*. Arguments and parameters are discussed more fully in Chapter 4.

Net Browser: another term for *Web Browser*.

Object: An object is a programming construct that has data and can take actions (known as methods). see also *Class*.

Object Code (Program): The low-level language program that a compiler outputs as the translation of a high-level language program. When you compile a Java program, the resulting byte-code is the object code from the compiler. The term "object code" has nothing directly to do with objects of a class.

Parameter: See *Method Invocation*. Parameters are discussed in detail in Chapter 4.

Polymorphism: *Polymorphism* means that one method name, used as an instruction, can cause different actions depending on what kind of objects performs the action. Polymorphism is discussed in more detail in Chapter 5.

SDK: Short for Software Development Kit. An environment distributed by Sun Microsystems that includes the Java compiler. SDK used to be called *JDK*, and you will still see the term *JDK* used. SDK is part of the *Java 2* Product Family. For readers of this book, the terms *JDK*, *SDK*, and *Java 2* all mean essentially the same thing. The SDK has different versions. Readers of this book should have version 1.2 or higher, such as SDK 1.2.2 or SDK 1.3. Earlier versions of SDK are called *JDK*, so if it is called *SDK* or *Java 2* you are fine. If it is called *JDK*, you need to check the version number.

Software: A program or collection of programs.

Source Code (Program): The high-level language program that a compiler translates. When you compile a Java program, your Java program is the source code for the compiler.

Swing: A library of Java classes used to write programs for GUIs, including applet programs. see *GUI*.

URL: The name (or location) of a document on the Internet is called a *URL*, which is an abbreviation for *Uniform Resource Locator*.

Tera-: A prefix meaning one trillion. For example five terabytes is five trillion bytes.

Virtual Machine: see *Java Virtual Machine*.

Virus: A program that infects other programs. Viruses are typically written by vandals to cause harm to computers. they are typically transmitted by e-mail or other software transferred from one computer to another.

Web Browser: A program that allows you to view documents and programs over the Internet. It can also view documents written in the HTML language that are on your computer,

Website (or Web Page): A location on the Internet or the documents (typically HTML documents) located there. The location is on some computer, typically has a URL, and can be accessed over the Internet. see *HTML* and *World Wide Web*.

World Wide Web: This is really just a collection of addresses (URLs and other addresses) that tell how to get from one website on the Internet to another such website. You can think of it as the imaginary links that connect websites. It is different from the *Internet*, but for many purposes so closely related to the Internet that people sometimes use the words interchangeably. The World Wide Web uses the Internet (and other connections) as its physical connection from website to website. see *Internet* and *Website*.

? ANSWERS to Self-Test Questions

1. Main memory and auxiliary memory.

2. Software is just another name for programs.

3. All the grades on all the quizzes that you have taken in the course.

4. A machine-language program is written in a form the computer can execute directly. A high-level language program is written in a form that is easy for a human being to write and read. A high-level language program must be translated into a machine-language program before the computer can execute it. Java byte-code is a low-level language that is very similar to the machine language of most common computers. It is relatively easy to translate a program expressed in Java byte-code into the machine language of almost any computer.

5. A compiler translates a high-level language program into a low-level language program such as a machine-language program or a Java byte-code program. When you compile a Java program, the compiler translates your Java program into a program expressed in Java byte-code.

6. The high-level language program that is input to a compiler is called the source program.

7. A program that translates Java byte-code instructions to machine-language instructions is called an *interpreter*.

8. A method is an action that an object is capable of taking. (In some other programming languages, methods are called *functions* or *procedures*.)

9. A class is a category of objects. All objects in the same class have the same kind of data and the same methods.

10. Yes, all objects of the same class have the same methods.

11. **Encapsulation** is the process of hiding all the details of an object that are not necessary to understanding how the object is used. Put another way, encapsulation is the process of describing a class or object by giving only enough information to allow a programmer to use the class or object.

12. **Information hiding** is another term for encapsulation.

13. In a programming language, such as Java, **polymorphism** means that one method name, used as an instruction, can cause different actions depending on what kind of objects performs the action.

14. An algorithm is a set of instructions for solving a problem. To qualify as an algorithm, the instructions must be expressed so completely and precisely that somebody could follow the instructions without having to fill in

any details or make any decisions that are not fully specified in the instructions.

15. Pseudocode is a mixture of English and a programming language (in our case, Java). Algorithms are usually written in pseudocode and later translated into a programming language, such as Java.

16. A syntax error is a grammatical mistake in your program. There are very strict grammar rules for how you write a program. If you violate one of these rules, for example, by omitting a required punctuation, that is a syntax error.

17. Syntax errors and run-time errors.

18. A logic error.

19. `Java is great!`

20.

```
System.out.println("Java for one.");
System.out.println("Java for all.");
```

21. `mary.increaseAge(5);`

22. This statement skips over blank spaces until it reaches the first nonblank character, and then it reads that nonblank character (in the sample dialogs 'y' or 'n') and stores that character in the variable `answerLetter`.

23.
```
public class ExerciseProgram1
{
    public static void main(String[] args)
    {
        System.out.println("Hello World!");
        System.out.println("Press enter key to end program.");
        String junk;
        junk = SavitchIn.readLine();
    }
}
```

Some details, such as identifier names, may be different in your program. Be sure you compile and run your program.

24. `number`, `Number`, and `NUMBER` are three different identifiers in Java.

25. The file with the class named `SuperClass` should be named `SuperClass.java`.

26. `SuperClass.class`

27. The class `SavitchIn` not part of the Java language. The programmer (like you) is supposed to define the class `SavitchIn`. To get you started we have defined it for you, but think of it as a class that you defined.

? PROGRAMMING EXERCISES

1. Obtain a copy of the file `SavitchIn.java` that contains the definition of the class `SavitchIn`. (It is on the CD provided with this book. In a course, your instructor may provide you with a copy. It is also in Appendix 4, but it would be a pain to copy the whole thing from there.) Compile the class `SavitchIn` so that you get no compiler errors. Next, obtain a copy of the Java program shown in Display 1.5/page 27. (That program is also on the CD that comes with this book.) Name the file `FirstProgram.java`. Compile the program so that you receive no compiler error messages. Finally, run the program in `FirstProgram.java`. If you are in a class and your instructor has already compiled the class `SavitchIn` for you, then you can skip that part.

2. Modify the Java program that you entered in Programming Exercise 1 so that if the user types in the letter n in response to the question

   ```
   Want to talk some more?
   ```

   then the program will output the phrase

   ```
   Too bad. You seem like such a nice person.
   ```

   The program should behave the same as in Display 1.5/page 27 if the user enters y instead of n. Compile and run the modified program. *Hint:* Include a second statement that begins with `if` and that tests whether `answerLetter` is equal to `'n'`.

3. Modify the Java program that you wrote in Programming Exercise 2 to include a third option to the question:

   ```
   Want to talk some more?
   ```

   In addition to the responses to y and n, if the user enters m for maybe, the program will output the phrase

   ```
   Sorry, but I can't wait for your decision.

   totalNumberOfClams = numberOfApples * clamsPerApple;
   ```

4. Both your eyes and color monitors use just three colors, red, blue and green, to create all other colors. In particular, yellow is made by combining red and green, magenta (a shade of purple) by combining red and blue, and cyan by combining green and blue. Write a program that asks the user which of the three colors, yellow, magenta or cyan, to break down into its two components. If the user enters the letter y for yellow it will display the message

   ```
   Yellow is made by combining red and green.
   ```

   Similarly, if the letter m is entered for magenta it will display the message

   ```
   Magenta is made by combining red and blue.
   ```

   and if the letter c is entered for cyan it will display the message

```
Cyan is made by combining green and blue.
```

5. Write a complete Java program that will ask the user for the initials of the user's first and last name, and then output a greeting that says "Hello" followed by the users initials and an exclamation mark. For example, if the user's initials are J and B, then the output greeting would be:

```
Hello J B!
```

If the user's initials are stored in the two variables `FirstInitial` and `LastInitial`, both of type *char*, then the above output can be produced by the following statement:

```
System.out.println("Hello " + FirstInitial + ' ' + LastInitial + '!');
```

Be sure to note that the blank symbol is output after `FirstInitial`. The use of the plus sign in this way is discussed in Chapter 2, but you do not need to read those details before doing this exercise.

CHAPTER 2

PRIMITIVE TYPES, STRINGS, AND INTERACTIVE I/O

2.1 PRIMITIVE TYPES AND EXPRESSIONS 53
Variables 53
Primitive Types 57
Assignment Statements 58
Specialized Assignment
    Operators 60
Simple Input and Output 61
Number Constants 62
Assignment Compatibilities 63
Type Casting 64

Java Tip Type Casting a Character to
    an Integer 66

Programming Tip Initialize Variables 67

Gotcha Imprecision in Floating-Point
    Numbers 67
Arithmetic Operators 69
Parentheses and Precedence
    Rules 71

Case Study Vending Machine
    Change 73

Increment and Decrement
    Operators 77
More About Increment and
    Decrement Operators 78

2.2 THE CLASS String 79
String Constants and Variables 80
Concatenation of Strings 80
String Methods 81
String Processing 85
Escape Characters 86
The Unicode Character Set 88

2.3 KEYBOARD AND SCREEN I/O 89
Screen Output 89
Input Using SavitchIn 91
More Input Methods 94

Gotcha readInt and
    readDouble 96

Programming Tip Echo Input 96

2.4 DOCUMENTATION AND STYLE 98

Programming Tip Use Meaningful
    Names for Variables 98
Documentation and Comments 99
Indenting 100
Named Constants 101

2.5 WINDOWING I/O WITH JOptionPane (Optional) 105
A Simple Windowing Program 106

Gotcha Users Who Enter
    Inappropriate Input 110

Gotcha Forgetting
    System.exit(0); 112

Gotcha Outputting Just a Number 113
Inputting Other Numeric Types 114

Java Tip Multi-Line Output
    Windows 115

Programming Example Another Program
    with I/O Windows 115

Chapter Summary 116
Answers to Self-Test Questions 119
Programming Exercises 123

PRIMITIVE TYPES, STRINGS, AND INTERACTIVE I/O

> *primitive* **adj. 1.** *Not derived from something else; primary or basic.*
> *string* **n. 1.** *A cord usually made of fiber, used for fastening, tying or lacing.*
> . . .
> **6.** *Computer Science. A set of consecutive characters treated by a computer as a single item.*
> **The American Heritage Dictionary of the English Language, Third Edition**

In this chapter, we explain enough about the Java language to allow you to write simple Java programs. You do not need to have done any programming to understand this chapter. On the other hand, if you are already familiar with some other programming language, such as C, C++, Pascal, BASIC, or FORTRAN, then much of what is in Section 2.1 will already be familiar to you. However, even if you know the concepts, you should learn the Java way of expressing these concepts.

Objectives

Become familiar with the Java data types used for numbers, characters, and similar simple data. These types are called primitive types.

Learn about the assignment statement and expressions.

Find out about the Java data type used for strings of characters and learn how to do simple string processing.

Learn about simple keyboard input and screen output.

Learn one way to do input and output using a windowing system. This final material is optional.

Prerequisites

If you have not read Chapter 1, you should at least familiarize yourself with Display 1.5/page 27 in that chapter before reading any of this chapter.

As with all optional sections, you do *not* need to cover the subsection of Chapter 1 entitled ***Preview Examples of Applets (Optional)*** before reading this chapter or any chapter of this book.

2.1 | Primitive Types and Expressions

> *Memory is necessary*
> *for all the operations of reason.*
>
> **Blaise Pascal**

In this section, we explain how simple variables and arithmetic expressions are used in Java programs.

Variables

Variables in a program are used to store data such as numbers and letters. Variables can be thought of as containers of a sort, but containers that hold things like numbers and letters. The number, letter, or other data item in a variable is called its **value.** This value can be changed, so that at one time the variable contains, say 6, and at another time after the program has run for a while, the variable contains a different value, such as 4. In the program in Display 2.1, `numberOfBaskets`, `eggsPerBasket`, and `totalEggs` are variables. For example, when this program is run with the input shown in the sample dialog, `eggsPerBasket` has its value set equal to the number 6 with the following statement, which reads a number from the keyboard.

variables

value of a variable

```
eggsPerBasket = SavitchIn.readLineInt();
```

Later, the value of the variable `eggsPerBasket` is changed to 4 when the program executes the following statement.

```
eggsPerBasket = eggsPerBasket - 2;
```

We will explain these two statements in more detail shortly. For now, simply note that the first one reads in a number that is typed at the keyboard and makes that the value of the variable `eggsPerBasket`, and that the second one changes the value of this variable by subtracting 2 from its value.

In Java, variables are implemented as memory locations. In Chapter 1, we discussed memory locations. Each variable is assigned one such memory location. When the variable is given a value, this value (encoded as a string of zeros and ones) is placed in the memory location assigned to that variable.

variables in memory

The rules for naming variables are given in the box entitled ***Variable Names***. Besides following those rules, you should also choose variable names that are helpful. Variable names should suggest their use or suggest the kind of data they will hold. For example, if a variable is used to count something, you might name the variable `count`. If the variable is used to hold the speed of an automobile, you might call the variable `speed`. You should almost never use single-letter variable names like `x` and `y`. Somebody reading the following would have no idea of what the program is really adding:

```
x = y + z;
```

In order to run your program, the computer must be given some basic information about each variable in your program. It needs to know the name of the vari-

variable declarations

Display 2.1   A Simple Java Program

```java
public class EggBasket
{
    public static void main(String[] args)
    {
        int numberOfBaskets, eggsPerBasket, totalEggs;

        System.out.println("Enter the number of eggs in each basket:");
        eggsPerBasket = SavitchIn.readLineInt();
        System.out.println("Enter the number of baskets:");
        numberOfBaskets = SavitchIn.readLineInt();

        totalEggs = numberOfBaskets * eggsPerBasket;

        System.out.println(eggsPerBasket + " eggs per basket.");
        System.out.println(numberOfBaskets + " baskets.");
        System.out.println("Total number of eggs is " + totalEggs);

        eggsPerBasket = eggsPerBasket − 2;
        totalEggs = numberOfBaskets * eggsPerBasket;

        System.out.println("Now we take two eggs out of each basket.");
        System.out.println(eggsPerBasket + " eggs per basket.");
        System.out.println(numberOfBaskets + " baskets.");
        System.out.println("Total number of eggs is " + totalEggs);

        System.out.println("Press enter key to end program.");
        String junk;
        junk = SavitchIn.readLine();
    }
}
```

Sample Screen Dialogue

```
Enter the number of eggs in each basket:
6
Enter the number of baskets:
10
6 eggs per basket.
10 baskets.
Total number of eggs is 60
Now we take two eggs out of each basket.
4 eggs per basket.
10 baskets.
Total number of eggs is 40
Press enter key to end program.
```

Variable Names (Identifiers)

Variable names (and all other names) must satisfy the spelling rules for names that we gave in Chapter 1. The name of a variable, like any other name in a Java program, must *not* start with a digit and must consist entirely of letters, digits (0 through 9), and the underscore character _. Uppercase and lowercase letter are considered to be different characters. (The symbol $ is also allowed, but it is reserved for special purposes, and so you should not use $ in a Java name.)

Although it is not required by the Java language, the common practice, and the one followed in this book, is to start the name of a variable with a lowercase letter.

---

able, how much computer memory to reserve for the variable, and how the data item in the variable is to be coded as strings of zeros and ones. All this information can be obtained provided the compiler (and so ultimately the computer) is told the name of the variable and what type of data are stored in the variable. You give this information by **declaring** the variable. Every variable in a Java program must be **declared** before it is used. For example, the following line from Display 2.1 declares the three variables `numberOfBaskets`, `eggsPerBasket`, and `totalEggs` to be variables of type `int`:

declare

```
int numberOfBaskets, eggsPerBasket, totalEggs;
```

A variable declaration consists of a type name, followed by a list of variable names separated by commas, and then all that is ended with a semicolon. All the variables named in the list are declared to have the type given at the start of the declaration.

The type `int` is the most commonly used type for variables that hold whole numbers, such as 42, −99, 0, and 2001. The word `int` is an abbreviation of *integer*. Java uses the reserved word `int` instead of the longer word *integer*.

int

A variable's **type** determines what kind of value the variable can hold. If the type is `int`, the variable can hold whole numbers. If the type is `double`, the variable can hold numbers with a decimal point and a fractional part after the decimal point. If the type is `char`, the variables can hold any one character from the computer keyboard.

type

A variable declaration tells the computer what type of data the variable will hold. Different types of data are stored in the computer's memory in different ways and so the computer must know the type of a variable in order to know how to store and retrieve the value of the variable from the computer's memory.

Variable Declarations

In a Java program, a variable must be declared before it can be used. Variables are declared as follows:

Syntax:

Type Variable_1, Variable_2, . . . ;

Examples:

```
int styleNumber, numberOfChecks, numberOfDeposits;
char answer;
double amount, interestRate;
```

class type
primitive type

There are two main kinds of types in Java, *class types* and *primitive types*. As the name implies, a **class type** is a type for a class, that is, a type for objects with both data and methods. A primitive type is a simpler type. Values of a **primitive type** are not complex items but simple, indecomposable values, such as a single number or a single letter. The type `SavitchIn` is a class type. `String` is another class type. The types `int`, `double`, and `char` are primitive types. By convention, primitive type names begin with a lowercase letter and class type names begin with and uppercase letter, but variable names of either class or primitive types begin with a lowercase letter. Variable names for class and primitive types are declared in the same way, but there is a different mechanism for storing values in the variables of class types and in variables of primitive types. In this chapter, we will mostly confine our attention to primitive types. We will occasionally use variables of a class type, but only in contexts where they behave pretty much the same as variables of a primitive type. In Chapters 3 and 4, we will explain what is different about variables of a class type.

location of
declarations

Every variable in a Java program must be declared before the variable can be used. Normally, a variable is declared either just before it is used or at the start of a method definition. In the simple programs we have seen so far, there is only one method, which is called `main`, so variables are declared either just before they are used or at the start of the program. However, as we will see, it is possible for a class to have many methods, and to declare variables inside of any or all of these methods.

Syntax

The rules for the correct way to write a program or part of a program (the grammar rules for a programming language) are called the **syntax** of the language.

Many of the boxes in this text describe Java syntax using **syntactic variables**. For example, in the box entitled ***Variable Declarations*** on page 55 we used the following:

Syntax:

> *Type Variable_1, Variable_2, . . . ;*

The words *Type*, *Variable_1*, and *Variable_2* are examples of syntactic variables. They are written in a different font and using underscore symbols so it will be easy for you to recognize them. Syntactic variables are not meant to be words that might appear in a Java program. **Syntactic variables** are a kind of blank that is meant to be filled in by a Java word of the kind described by the syntactic variable. *Type* can be replaced by any Java type. For example, *Type* can be replaced by `int`. *Variable_1* and *Variable_2* can each be replaced by any variable name. For example, *Variable_1* can be replaced by `styleNumber`, *Variable_2* can be replaced by `numberOfChecks`, and the ... indicates that the list of variables can be of any length. Thus,

> *Type Variable_1, Variable_2, . . . ;*

can be replaced by

> `int styleNumber, numberOfChecks, numberOfDeposits;`

to obtain a valid variable declaration that can be used in a Java program. To help clarify these syntax expression, they are usually followed by one or more examples of the Java item they specify. For an example, look at the box entitled ***Variable Declarations***.

Primitive Types

All the Java primitive types are given in Display 2.2. Notice that there are four types for integers: namely, *byte*, *short*, *int*, and *long*. The only difference between the various integer types is the range of integers they can store and the amount of computer memory they use. If you cannot decide which integer type to use, use the type *int*. It has a large enough range for most purposes and does not use as much memory as the type *long*.

 A whole number, such as 0, 1, –1, 2, or –2, is called an **integer**. A number with a fractional part, such as 9.99, 3.14159, –5.63, or 5.0 is called a **floating- point number**. Notice that 5.0 is a floating-point number, not an integer. If we ask the computer to include a fractional part and that fractional part happens to be zero, that does not change the type of the number. If it has a fractional part, even if the fractional part

integer

floating-point
number

Display 2.2 Primitive Types

Type Name	Kind of Value	Memory Used	Size Range
byte	integer	1 byte	−128 to 127
short	integer	2 bytes	−32768 to 32767
int	integer	4 bytes	−2147483648 to 2147483647
long	integer	8 bytes	−9223372036854775808 to 9223372036854775807
float	floating-point number	4 bytes	$\pm 3.40282347 \times 10^{+38}$ to $\pm 1.40239846 \times 10^{-45}$
double	floating-point number	8 bytes	$\pm 1.76769313486231570 \times 10^{+308}$ to $\pm 4.94065645841246544 \times 10^{-324}$
char	single character (Unicode)	2 bytes	all Unicode characters
boolean	*true* **or** *false*	1 bit	not applicable

is zero, then it is a floating-point number. As shown in Display 2.2, Java has two types for floating-point numbers, *float* and *double*. For example, the following declares two variables, one of type *float* and one of type *double:*

```
float cost;
double capacity;
```

If you cannot decide between the types *float* and *double*, use *double*. It allows a wider range of values and is used as a default type for floating-point numbers.

The primitive type *char* is used for single characters, such as letters or the percent sign. For example, the following declares the variable symbol to be of type *char*, stores the character for uppercase A in symbol, and then writes out that value to the screen so that an A would appear on the screen:

```
char symbol;
symbol = 'A';
System.out.println(symbol);
```

single quotes

Notice that when we give a character in a Java program, like 'A', we enclose the character in single quotes. Also note that there is only one single-quote symbol. The same quote symbol is used on both sides of the character. That one symbol serves as both the left and the right quote symbol. Finally, note that uppercase and lowercase letters are different characters. For example, 'a' and 'A' are two different characters.

The last primitive type we have to discuss is the type *boolean*. There are two values of type *boolean*, namely, *true* and *false*. This means we can use a variable of type *boolean* to store the answer to a true/false question such as "Is myTime less than yourTime?" We will have more to say about the type *boolean* in the next chapter.

Assignment Statements

assignment statement

If you know what value you want to give to a variable, you can use an assignment statement to give the variable that value. For example, if answer is a variable of type *int* and you want to give it the value 42, you would use the following **assignment statement**:

```
answer = 42;
```

assignment operator

The equal sign, =, is called the **assignment operator** when it is used in an assignment statement such as the preceding statement. It does not mean what the equal sign means in other contexts. The assignment statement is an order to the computer telling it to change the value stored in the variable on the left-hand side of the assignment operator, that is, on the left-hand side of the =. An assignment statement always consists of a single variable on the left-hand side of an assignment operator (equal sign) and an expression on the right-hand side. The assignment statement has a semicolon at the end. So, assignment statements take the form:

Variable = *Expression*;

The expression can be another variable, a number, or a more complicated expression made up by using arithmetic operators, such as + and *, to combine variables and numbers.

For example, the following are all examples of assignment statements:

```
amount = 3.99;
firstInitial = 'B';
score = numberOfCards + handicap;
eggsPerBasket = eggsPerBasket - 2;
```

(All the names, such as amount, score, and numberOfCards, are variables. We are assuming that the variable amount is of type *double*, firstInitial is of type *char*, and the rest of the variables are of type *int*.)

When the assignment statement is executed, the computer first evaluates the expression on the right-hand side of the expression to get the value of the expression. Then it uses that value to set the value of the variable on the left-hand side of the assignment operator (equal sign). You can think of the assignment operator (=) as saying, "make the value of the variable equal to what follows."

For example, if the variable numberOfCards has the value 7 and handicap has the value 2, then the following makes 9 the value of the variable score:

```
score = numberOfCards + handicap;
```

The following line from the program in Display 2.1/page 54 is another example of an assignment statement:

```
totalEggs = numberOfBaskets * eggsPerBasket;
```

This assignment statement tells the computer to set the value of totalEggs equal to the number in the variable numberOfBaskets multiplied by the number in the variable eggsPerBasket. The asterisk character '*' is the symbol used for multiplication in Java.

* is multiply

Note that a variable can meaningfully occur on both sides of the assignment operator, =, and can do so in ways that may at first seem a little strange. For example, consider

same variable
both sides of =

```
count = count + 10;
```

This does not mean that the value of count is equal to the value of count plus 10, which of course could not be true. This tells the computer to add 10 to the old value of count, and then make that the new value of count, which means that this statement will increase the value of count by 10. When an assignment statement is executed, the computer first evaluates the expression on the right-hand side of the assignment operator (that is, the right-hand side of the equal sign), and then it makes that value the new value of the variable on the left-hand side of the assignment operator. As another example, consider the following assignment statement from Display 2.1:

```
eggsPerBasket = eggsPerBasket - 2;
```

This assignment statement will decrease the value of eggsPerBasket by 2.

The number 2 in the preceding assignment statement is called a **constant**. It is called a *constant* because, unlike a variable such as eggsPerBasket, the value of 2

constant

cannot change. (Constants are sometimes also called **literals**.) Constants need not be numbers. The characters 'A', 'B', and '$' are three constants of type *char*. They cannot change their own value, but they can be used in an assignment statement to change the value of a variables of type *char*. For example, the following changes the value of the variable firstInitial to 'B':

```
firstInitial = 'B';
```

In the preceding assignment statement, the variable firstInitial would normally be of type *char*.

Similarly, the following changes the value of the variable price to 9.99:

```
price = 9.99;
```

In the preceding assignment statement, the variable price would normally be of type *double*. It cannot be of type *int* or *char*. As the saying goes, "You can't put a square peg in a round hole," and you can't put a *double* value in a variable of type *int*.

Assignment Statements with Primitive Types

An assignment statement with a variable of a primitive type on the left-hand side of the equal sign causes the following action: First, the expression on the right-hand side of the equal sign is evaluated, and then the variable on the left-hand side of the equal sign is set equal to this value.

Syntax:

  Variable = *Expression*;

Example:

```
score = goals - errors;
interest = rate * balance;
number = number + 5;
```

Specialized Assignment Operators

You can combine the simple assignment operator (=) with an arithmetic operator, such as +, to produce a kind of special-purpose assignment operator. For example, the following will increase the value of the variable amount by 5:

```
amount += 5;
```

This is really just a shorthand for

```
amount = amount + 5;
```

This is hardly a big deal, but it can sometimes be handy.

You can do the same thing with any of the other arithmetic operators −, *, /, and %. For example, consider the following line:

```
amount = amount*25;
```

This line could be replaced by the following equivalent line:

```
amount *= 25;
```

Simple Input and Output

The program in Display 2.1/page 54 uses the same kind of simple input and output as we used in the program we discussed in Chapter 1 (Display 1.5/page 27). In this subsection, we will give you a brief overview of input and output, so you can write and understand programs like the one in Display 2.1. In Section 2.3, we will continue the discussion of input and output that we start here.

As we noted in Chapter 1, `System.out` is an object and `println` is a method of this object that sends output to the screen. So,

```
System.out.println(eggsPerBasket + " eggs per basket.");
```

outputs the value of the variable `eggsPerBasket` (to the screen) followed by the phrase `" eggs per basket."` Be sure to notice that the + sign is not being used for arithmetic here. It is a kind of "and." You can read the preceding output statement as saying output the value of the variable `eggsPerBasket` *and* then output the string `" eggs per basket."`

Next, we consider input. In particular, consider the following line from Display 2.1:

```
numberOfBaskets = SavitchIn.readLineInt();
```

This is an assignment statement that sets the value of the variable `numberOfBaskets` equal to the value returned by the expression

```
SavitchIn.readLineInt()
```

This is an invocation of the method `readLineInt()` of the class `SavitchIn`. As we said in Chapter 1, a method is an action, and an invocation of a method causes that action to take place. The action performed by the method `readLineInt` is to read a single integer from a line of input and deliver that value to the program. In this case, the value becomes the new value of the variable `numberOfBaskets`.

There are a few technical details to note about invocations of the method `readLineInt`. First, note that there should be a pair of empty parentheses after the name `readLineInt`. Second, note that the user must input the integer on a line by itself with nothing, except possibly blank space, before or after the number. The value produced by an invocation of the method `readLineInt` (or any similar method) is usually referred to as the **value returned** by the method invocation.

The following line from Display 1.5 in Chapter 1 is similar to the invocation of `readLineInt` that we just discussed:

```
answerLetter = SavitchIn.readLineNonwhiteChar();
```

The class `SavitchIn` has a number of different methods for reading different kinds of data. The method `readLineNonwhiteChar` reads a single nonblank keyboard character, whereas the method `readLineInt` reads a single integer. Otherwise, the two methods `readLineInt` and `readLineNonwhiteChar` are very similar. There is also a method named `readLineDouble` that can be used to read a value of type *double*, that is, to read a number that contains a decimal point.

We will say more about this kind of input and output in Section 2.3 of this chapter.

readLineInt

value returned

readLine-NonwhiteChar

Returned Value

An expression like `numberOfBaskets * eggsPerBasket` produces a value. If `numberOfBaskets` has the value 2 and `eggsPerBasket` has the value 10, then the number produced is 20. In computer parlance, this is called the **value returned**. So, we would not say the "the number produced is 20." We would instead say, "the value returned is 20."

The same terminology is used with method invocations. If a method produces a value, we say that the method *returns* the value. For example, in the last of the following program statements, the method invocation `SavitchIn.readLineInt()` produces a value, namely, the value read from the keyboard. This value is called the value *returned* by the method invocation `SavitchIn.readLineInt()`.

```
int myNumber;
System.out.println("Enter an integer:");
myNumber = SavitchIn.readLineInt();
```

If the Screen Display Goes Away Too Quickly

Some systems make your program output go away as soon as the program ends. Because computers are fast, this means that the screen dialog can disappear before you get a chance to study it. If this happens on your system, you can add the following (or something very similar) to your programs, and then the screen display will remain visible until the user presses the enter key (also known as the return key):

```
System.out.println("Press enter key to end program.");
String junk;
junk = SavitchIn.readLine();
```

You insert these three lines at the end of your program. This is what we did in Display 1.5/page 27 and Display 2.1/page 54. However, we will not add these three lines to programs in the rest of this book. Your program may, or may not, need these lines, depending on your particular Java environment.

Number Constants

constant

A variable can have its value changed. That is why it is called a *variable*. Its value *varies*. A literal number like 2 cannot change. It is always 2. It is never 3. Literal values like 2 or 3.7 are called **constants**, because their values do not change. Literal expressions of type other than number types are also called *constant*. So, for example, 'Y' is a constant of type `char`. There is essentially only one way to write constants of type `char`, namely, placing the character in single quotes. On the other hand, some of the rules for writing number constants are more complicated.

integer
constant

Constants of integer types are written the way you would expect them to be written, like 2, 3, 0, −3, or 752. An integer constant can be prefaced with a plus or minus sign, as in +12 and −72. Number constants may not contain commas. The expression 1,000 is *not* correct in Java. Integer constants may not contain a decimal point. Numbers with a decimal point are floating-point numbers.

floating-point
constant

Floating-point constant numbers may be written in either of two forms. The simple form is like the everyday way of writing numbers with digits after the decimal point. The other, slightly more complicated, form is similar to a kind of notation commonly used in the physical sciences.

The more complicated notation for floating-point constants is frequently called **e notation**, **scientific notation**, or **floating-point notation**. For instance, consider the number 865000000.0, which can be expressed more clearly in the following form that is used in mathematics and physics but is not Java notation:

$$8.65 \times 10^8$$

scientific (e) notation

Java has a similar notation, but because keyboards have no way of writing exponents, the 10 is omitted and both the multiplication sign and the 10 are replaced by the letter e. So, in Java 8.65×10^8 is written as 8.65e8 (or in the less convenient form 865000000.0). The two forms, 8.65e8 and 865000000.0, are equivalent in a Java program.

Similarly, the number 4.83×10^{-4}, which is equal to 0.000483, could be written as 4.83e−4 in Java. The e stands for *exponent*, since it is followed by a number that is thought of as an exponent of 10.

Because multiplying by 10 is the same as moving the decimal point in a number, you can think of the number after the e as telling you to move the decimal point that many digits to the right. If the number after the e is negative, you move the decimal point that many digits to the left. For example, 2.48e4 is the same number as 24800.0, and 2.48e−2 is the same number as 0.0248.

The number before the e may be a number with or without a decimal point. The number after the e cannot contain a decimal point

In Java, no integer or floating-point number constant may contain a comma. For example, 5,000 is expressed as 5000 without any comma.

What Is "Floating" in a Floating-Point Number?

Floating-point numbers got their name because, with the e notation we described in this subsection, the decimal point can be made to "float" to a new location by adjusting the exponent. The decimal point in 0.000483 can be made to float to after the 4 by expressing this number as the equivalent expression 4.83e−4. Computer language implementers use this trick to store each floating-point number as a number with exactly one digit before the decimal point (and some suitable exponent). Because the implementation always floats the decimal point in these numbers, they are called *floating-point numbers*. (The numbers are actually stored in base 2, rather than as the base 10 numerals we used in our example, but the principle is the same.)

Assignment Compatibilities

You cannot put a square peg in a round hole, and similarly you cannot put a value of one type in a variable of another type. You cannot put an *int* value like 42 in a variable of type *char*. You cannot put a *double* value like 3.5 in a variable of type *int*. You cannot even put the *double* value 3.0 in a variable of type *int*. You cannot store a value of one type in a variable of another type unless the value is somehow converted to match the type of the variable. However, when dealing with numbers, this conversion will sometimes (but not always) be performed automatically for you. You can always assign a value of an integer type to a variable of a floating-point type, such as

```
double doubleVariable;
doubleVariable = 7;
```

Slightly more subtle assignments such as the following are also allowed:

```
int intVariable;
intVariable = 7;
double doubleVariable;
doubleVariable = intVariable;
```

More generally, you can assign a value of any type on the following list to a variable of any type that appears further down on the list:

```
byte-->short-->int-->long-->float-->double
```

For example, you can assign a value of type *long* to a variable of type *float* or to a variable of type *double* (or of course to a variable of type *long*). (Note that this is not an arbitrary ordering of the types. As you move down the list from left to right, the types become more complex, either because they allow larger values or because they allow decimal points in the numbers.)

You can assign a value of type *char* to a variable of type *int* or to any of the numeric types that follow *int* in our list of type. However, we do not advise doing so, because the result could be confusing.[1]

If you want to assign a value of type *double* to a variable of type *int*, then you must change the type of the value using a *type cast*, as explained in the next subsection.

Assignment Compatibilities

You can assign a value of any type on the following list to a variable of any type that appears further down on the list:

```
byte-->short-->int-->long-->float-->double
```

In particular, note that you can assign a value of any integer type to a variable of any floating-point type. ◻

Type Casting

The title of this subsection has nothing to do with the Hollywood notion of *type casting*. In fact, it is almost the opposite. In Java (and most programming languages), a **type cast** is the changing of the type of a value from its normal type to some other type, such as changing the type of 2.0 from *double* to *int*. In the previous subsection, we described when you could assign a value of one type to a variable of another

type cast

---

1. Readers who have used certain other languages, such as C or C++, may be surprised to learn that you cannot assign a value of type *char* to a variable of type *byte*. This is because Java uses the Unicode character set rather than the ASCII character set, and so Java reserves two bytes of memory for each value of type *char*, but naturally only reserves one byte of memory for values of type *byte*. This is one of the few cases where you might notice that Java uses the Unicode character set. Indeed, if you convert from an *int* to a *char* or vice versa, you can expect to get the usual correspondence of ASCII numbers and characters.

type. In all other cases, if you want to assign a value of one type to a variable of another type, you must perform a type cast. So, let's discuss how this is done in Java.

For example, suppose we have the following:

```
double distance;
distance = 9.0;
int points;
points = distance;
```

This is an illegal assignment.

As the note indicates, the last statement is illegal in Java. You cannot assign a value of type *double* to a variable of type *int*, even if the value of type *double* happens to have all zeros after the decimal point and so is conceptually a "whole number."

In order to assign a value of type *double* to a value of type *int*, you must place (*int*) in front of the value or the variable holding the value. For example, the preceding illegal assignment can be replaced by the following and you will get a legal assignment:

This is a legal assignment.

```
points = (int)distance;
```

The expression (*int*)distance is called a type cast. This does not change the value stored in the variable distance, but it does change the value returned by the expression. Thus, in the assignment

```
points = (int)distance;
```

neither distance nor the value stored in distance is changed in any way. But, the value stored in points is the "*int* version" of the value stored in distance. If the value of distance is 9.0, then the value of distance remains 9.0, but 9 is used to set the value of points.

It is important to note that a type cast does not really change any value of variable. An expression like (*int*)25.36 or (*int*)distance is an expression that *produces* an *int* value. So, the value of (*int*)25.36 is 25 but the 25.36 is still there and still has a "point three six" in it. The situation is analogous to computing the number of (whole) dollars you have in an amount of money. If you have $25.36, then the number of dollars you have is 25, but the $25.36 has not changed, it has merely been used to produce the whole number 25. For example, consider the following code

```
double dinnerBill;
dinnerBill = 25.36;
dinnerBillPlusTip = (int)dinnerBill + 5;
System.out.println(
        "The value of dinnerBillPlusTip is " + dinnerBillPlusTip);
```

The expression (*int*)dinnerBill produces the value 25, so the output of this code would be

```
The value of dinnerBillPlusTip is 30
```

But, the variable dinnerBill still contains the value 25.36.

Be sure to note that when you type cast from a *double* to an *int* (or from any floating-point type to any integer type), the amount is not rounded. The part after

truncating

the decimal point is simple discarded. This is know as **truncating**. For example, consider the following:

```
double dinnerBill;
dinnerBill = 26.99;
int numberOfDollars;
numberOfDollars = (int)dinnerBill;
```

This does not set `numberOfDollars` to 27. It sets `numberOfDollars` to 26. In the case of a floating-point value, like `26.99`, when you convert the value to an integer value with a type cast, the result is the whole number obtained by discarding the part after the decimal point. So, `26.99` yields the `int` value 26 as a result of the type cast, not the value 27. The result is *not rounded*.

When you assign an integer value to a variable of a floating-point type (such as a variable of type `double`), the integer is type cast to the type of the variable, but in this case the type cast is done automatically for you. For example, consider

```
double point;
point = 7;
```

the preceding assignment statement is equivalent to

```
point = (double)7;
```

The type cast `(double)` is really there in both versions of the assignment, but if you omit the `(double)`, then Java acts as if the `(double)` were there.

Type Casting

In many situations, you are not allowed to store a value of one type in a variable of another type. In these situations, you must use a **type cast** that converts the value to an "equivalent" value of the target type.

Syntax:

(*Type_Name*) *Expression*

Example:

```
double guess;
guess = 7.8;
int answer;
answer = (int)guess;
```

The value stored in `answer` will be 7. Note that the value is truncated, *not rounded*. Also note that the variable `guess` is not changed in any way. This only effects the value stored in `answer`.

■ **Java Tip**
Type Casting a Character to an Integer

Java sometimes treats values of type *char* as integers, but the assignment of integers to characters has no connection to the meaning of the characters. For example, the following type cast will output the *int* value corresponding to the character '7':

```
char symbol;
symbol = '7';
System.out.println((int)symbol);
```

You might expect the preceding to output 7 to the screen, but it does not. It outputs the number 55. The *int* value corresponding to '7' is 55. The reason for this is that the *int* values corresponding to *char* values are used for all characters and not just for digits. So, there is nothing special about digits, and so no effort was made to have digits correspond to their intuitive values.

■ Programming Tip
Initialize Variables

A variable that has been declared but that has not yet been given a value by some means, such as an assignment statement or being given a value from the keyboard, is said to be **uninitialized**. If the variable is a class variable, it literally has no value. If the variable is a variable of a primitive type, then it may have some default value. However, it makes your program clearer to explicitly give the variable a value, even if you are simply reassigning it the default value. (The exact details on default values have been known to change and should not be counted on.)

uninitialized variable

One easy way to ensure that you do not have an uninitialized variable is to initialize it within the declaration. Simply combine the declaration and an assignment statement, as in the following examples:

```
int count = 0;
double taxRate = 0.075;
char grade = 'A';
int balance = 1000, newBalance;
```

Note that you can initialize some variables and not initialize other variables in a declaration.

Sometimes the compiler may complain saying that you have failed to initialize a variable. In most cases, you will indeed have failed to initialize the variable. Occasionally, the compiler is mistaken in giving this advice. However, the compiler will not compile your program until you convince it that the variable in question is initialized. To make the compiler happy, initialize the variable when it is declared, even if the variable will be given a different value before the variable is used for anything. In such cases, you cannot argue with the compiler.

■ Gotcha
Imprecision in Floating-Point Numbers

Floating-point numbers are stored with a limited amount of accuracy and so are, for all practical purposes, only approximate quantities. For example, the floating-point number 1.0/3.0 is equal to

```
0.3333333...
```

where the three dots indicate that the 3's go on forever. The computer stores numbers something like the decimal representation on the previously displayed line, but

---

Combining a Variable Declaration and an Assignment

You can combine the declaration of a variable with an assignment statement that gives the variable a value.

Syntax:

Type Variable_1 = Expression__1,
      Variable_2 = Expression__2, . . . ;

Example:

```
int numberSeen = 0, increment = 5;
double height = 12.34, prize = 7.3 + increment;
char answer = 'y';
```

---

the computer only has room for a limited number of digits. If that number is 10 digits after the decimal, then 1.0/3.0 is stored as

0.3333333333 (and no more 3's)

So, 1.0/3.0 is stored as a number slightly smaller than one-third. In other words, the value stored as 1.0/3.0 is only approximately equal to one-third. In reality, the computer stores numbers in binary notation, rather than as numbers in base 10, but the principles are the same and the same sort of things happen. Some numbers lose accuracy when they are stored in the computer.

Floating-point numbers (like numbers of type *double*) and integers (like numbers of type *int*) are stored differently. As we indicated in the previous paragraph, floating-point numbers are, in effect, stored as approximate quantities. Integers, on the other hand, are stored as exact quantities. This difference sometimes can be subtle. For example, the numbers 5 and 5.0 are conceptually the same number. But Java considers them to be different. The whole number 5 is of type *int* and is an exact quantity. The number 5.0 is of type *double*, because it contains a fraction part (even though the fraction is 0), and so 5.0 is stored with only a limited amount of accuracy.

? Self-Test Questions

1. Give the declaration for a variable called count of type *int*. The variable should be initialized to zero in the declaration.

2. Give the declaration for two variables of type *double*. The variables are to be named rate and time. Both variables should be initialized to zero in the declaration.

3. Write the declaration for two variables called miles and flowRate. Declare the variable miles to be of type *int* and initialize it to zero in the declaration. Declare the variable flowRate to be of type *double* and initialize it to 50.56 in the declaration.

4. Write a Java assignment statement that will set the value of the variable interest to the value of the variable balance multiplied by 0.05. The variables are of type *double*.

5. Give a Java assignment statement that will set the value of the variable `interest` to the value of the variable `balance` multiplied by the value of the variable `rate`. The variables are of type *double*.

6. Give a Java assignment statement that will increase the value of the variable `count` by 3. The variable is of type *int*.

7. What is the output produced by the following lines of program code?

```
char a, b;
a = 'b';
System.out.println(a);
b = 'c';
System.out.println(b);
a = b;
System.out.println(a);
```

8. In the section entitled *Java Tip* **Type Casting a Character to an Integer,** we saw that the following does not output the integer 7:

```
char symbol;
symbol = '7';
System.out.println((int)symbol);
```

Thus, (*int*)symbol does not produce the number corresponding to the digit in `symbol`. Can you give an expression that will work to produce the integer that intuitively corresponds to the digit in `symbol` (assuming that `symbol` contains one of the 10 digits '0', '1', ..., '9')? *Hint*: The digits do correspond to consecutive integers, so if (*int*)'7' is 55, then (*int*)'8' is 56.

Arithmetic Operators

In Java you can form arithmetic expressions involving addition (+), subtraction (−), multiplication (*), and division (/) in basically the same way that you would form them in ordinary arithmetic or algebra. You can combine variables and/or numbers using the arithmetic operators +, −, *, and /. The meaning of such an expression is basically what you expect it to be, but there are some subtleties about the type of the result and occasionally even about the value of the result. All of the arithmetic operators can be used with numbers of any of the integer types, any of the floating-point types, and even with numbers of differing types. The type of the value produced depends on the types of the numbers being combined.

mixing types

Let's start our discussion with simple expressions that only combine two variables and/or numbers. If both operands (that is, both numbers and/or variables) are of the same type, then the result is of that type. If one of the operands is of a floating-point type and the other is of an integer type, then the result is of the floating-point type. For example, consider the expression

```
amount - adjustment
```

If the variables `amount` and `adjustment` are both of type *int*, then the result (the value returned) is of type *int*. If either `amount` or `adjustment`, or both, are of type *double*, then the result is of type *double*. If you replace the operator – with any of the operators +, *, or /, then the type of the result is determined in the same way.

Larger expressions using more than two operands can always be viewed as a series of steps each of which involve only two operands. For example, to evaluate the expressions

```
balance + (balance*rate)
```

you (or the computer) evaluate `balance*rate` and obtain a number, and then you combine that number with `balance` using addition. This means that the same rule that we used to determine the type of an expression with two operands can also be used for more complicated expressions: If all the items being combined are of the same type, then the result is of that type. If some of the items being combined are of integer type and some are of floating-point type, then the result is of a floating-point type.

Knowing whether the value produced is of an integer type or a floating-point type is typically all that you need to know. However, if you need to know the exact type of the value produced by an arithmetic expression, it can be determined as follows: The type of the value produced is one of the types used in the expression. Of all the types used in the expression, it is the last type (reading left to right) on the following list:

byte-->short-->int-->long-->float-->double

division

The division operator / deserves special attention, because the type of the result can affect the value produced in a dramatic way. When you combine two numbers with the division operator / and at least one of the numbers is of type *double* (or of some other floating-point type), then the result is what you would normally expect of a division. For example, 9.0/2 has one operand of type *double*,

integer division

namely, 9.0. Hence, the result is the type *double* number 4.5. However, when both operands are of an integer type, the result can be surprising. For example 9/2 has two operands of type *int*, and so it yields the type *int* result 4, not 4.5. The fraction after the decimal point is simply lost. Be sure to notice that when you divide two integers, the result *is not rounded*; the part after the decimal point is discarded no matter how large it is. So, 11/3 is 3 (not 3.6666...). If there is nothing but a zero after the decimal point, then that decimal point and zero after the decimal point are still lost, and even this seemingly trivial difference can be of some significance. For example, 8.0/2 evaluates to the type *double* value 4.0, which is only an approximate quantity. However, 8/2 evaluates to the *int* value 4, which is an exact quantity. The approximate nature of 4.0 can affect the accuracy of any further calculation that is performed with this result.

the % operator

The % **operator** can be used with operands of integer types to recover something equivalent to the fraction after the decimal point. When you divide one integer by another, you get a result (which some call a quotient) and a remainder. For example, 14 divided by 4 yields 3 with a remainder of 2. To rephrase it, 14 divided by 4 is 3 with 2 left over. The % operation gives the remainder, that is, the amount left over, after doing the division. So, 14/4 evaluates to 3 and 14%4 evaluates to 2, because 14 divided by 4 is 3 with 2 left over.

The % operator has more applications than you might at first suspect. It allows your program to count in 2's, 3's, or any other number. For example, if you want to do something to every other integer, you need to know if the integer is even or odd. Then, you can do it to every even integer (or alternatively every odd integer). An integer n is even if n%2 is equal to 0 and the integer is odd if n%2 is equal to 1. Similarly, if you want your program to do something to every third integer, then your program can step through all the integers using an *int* variable n to store the integer and can test n%3. In this case, your program might only do the action when n%3 is equal to 0.

Parentheses and Precedence Rules

Parentheses can be used to group things in an arithmetic expression in the same way as you use parentheses in algebra and arithmetic. With the aid of parentheses, you can tell the computer which operations are performed first, second, and so forth. For example, consider the following two expressions that differ only in the positioning of their parentheses:

parentheses

```
(cost + tax) * discount
cost + (tax * discount)
```

To evaluate the first expression, the computer first adds cost and tax and then multiplies the result by discount. To evaluate the second expression, it multiplies tax and discount and then adds the result to cost. If you use some numbers for the values of the variables and carry out the two evaluations, you will see that they produce different results.

If you omit parentheses, the computer will still evaluate the expression. For example, consider the following assignment statement:

```
total = cost + tax * discount;
```

This is equivalent to

```
total = cost + (tax * discount);
```

When parentheses are omitted, the computer performs multiplication before addition. More generally, when the order of operations are not determined by parentheses, the computer will perform the operations in an order determined by the **precedence rules** shown in Display 2.3. (Display 2.3 shows all the operators we will use in this chapter. More precedence rules will be given in Chapter 3, and an even more complete list of precedence rules is given in Appendix 2.) Operators that are listed higher on the list are said to have **higher precedence**. When the computer is deciding which of two operators to perform first and the order is not dictated by parentheses, then it does the operator of higher precedence before the operator of lower precedence. Some operators have equal precedence, in which case the order of operations is determined by the left-to-right order of the operators. Binary operators of equal precedence are performed in left-to-right order. Unary operators of equal precedence are performed in right-to-left order.

precedence rules

Display 2.3   Precedence Rules

Highest Precedence

```
First: the unary operators: +, −, ++, −−, and!
Second: the binary arithmetic operators: *, /, %
Third: the binary arithmetic operators: +, −
```

Lowest Precedence

unary operator   A **unary operator** is one that has only one argument (one thing it is applied to), like the operator − in the assignment statement

```
bankBalance = −cost;
```

binary operator   A **binary operator** has two arguments, like the operators + and * in

```
total = cost + (tax * discount);
```

Note that the same operator symbol, for examples − and +, can sometimes be used as both a unary and a binary operators.

These precedence rules are similar to rules used in algebra classes. However, except for some very standard cases, it is best to include the parentheses, even if the intended order of operations is the one indicated by the precedence rules. The parentheses make the expression clearer to a person reading the program code. One standard case where it is normal to omit parentheses is a multiplication within an addition. So,

```
balance = balance + (interestRate*balance);
```

would usually be written

```
balance = balance + interestRate*balance;
```

Both forms are acceptable and the two forms have the same meaning. We will discuss more precedence rules in Chapter 3.

spacing   When writing arithmetic expressions, you can insert spaces before and after operations or you can omit them. Similarly, you can insert or omit spaces around parentheses.

Display 2.4 shows some examples of how you write arithmetic expression in Java and indicates some of the parentheses that you would normally omit.

Display 2.4   Arithmetic Expression

Ordinary Mathematical Expression	Java Expression (preferred form)	Equivalent Fully Parenthesized Java Expression
$rate^2 + delta$	`rate*rate + delta`	`(rate*rate) + delta`
$2(salary + bonus)$	`2*(salary + bonus)`	`2*(salary + bonus)`
$\dfrac{1}{time + 3mass}$	`1/(time + 3*mass)`	`1/(time + (3*mass))`
$\dfrac{a-7}{t+9v}$	`(a - 7)/(t + 9*v)`	`(a - 7)/(t + (9*v))`

Case Study

Vending Machine Change

Vending machines often have small computers to control their operation. In this case study, you will write a program that performs one of the tasks that such a computer would need to do. In this case study, the input and output will be performed via the keyboard and screen. To integrate this into a vending machine computer, you would have to embed the code from this program into a larger program that takes its data from someplace other than the keyboard and send its results to someplace other than the screen, but that's another story. In this case study, the user enters an amount of change from 1 to 99 cents. The program responds by telling the user one combination of coins that equals that amount of change.

task specification

   For example, if the user enters 55 for 55 cents, then the program tells the user that 55 cents can be given as two quarters and one nickel (that is, two twenty five cent coins and one five cent coin). You decide that the dialog should read as in the following example, which you write out to see how it looks before coding the program:

```
Enter a whole number from 1 to 99.
I will output a combination of coins
that equal that amount of change.
87
87 cents in coins:
3 quarters
1 dime
0 nickels and
2 pennies
```

data

The program will need variables to store the amount of change and the number of each type of coin. So, it will need at least the following variables:

```
int amount, quarters, dimes, nickels, pennies;
```

That takes care of some routine matters, and now you are ready to tackle the heart of the problem. You need an algorithm to compute the number of each kind of coin. You come up with the following pseudocode:

pseudocode first try

Algorithm to determine the number of coins in `amount` cents:

Read the amount into the variable `amount`.
Set the variable `quarters` equal to the maximum number of quarters in `amount`.
Reset `amount` to the change left after giving out that many quarters.
Set the variable `dimes` equal to the maximum number of dimes in `amount`.
Reset `amount` to the change left after giving out that many dimes.
Set the variable `nickels` equal to the maximum number of nickels in `amount`.
Reset `amount` to the change left after giving out that many nickels.
`pennies = amount;`
Output the original amount and the numbers of each coin.

When you look at your pseudocode, you realize that the algorithm changes the value of `amount`, but at the end, you want the original amount, so you can output the original amount. So, you use one more variable, called `originalAmount`, to save the original amount. You modify the pseudocode as follows:

pseudocode revised

Algorithm to determine the number of coins in `amount` cents:

Read the amount into the variable `amount`.
`originalAmount = amount;`
Set the variable `quarters` equal to the maximum number of quarters in `amount`.
Reset `amount` to the change left after giving out that many quarters.
Set the variable `dimes` equal to the maximum number of dimes in `amount`.
Reset `amount` to the change left after giving out that many dimes.
Set the variable `nickels` equal to the maximum number of nickels in `amount`.
Reset `amount` to the change left after giving out that many nickels.
`pennies = amount;`
Output `originalAmount` and the numbers of each coin.

coding

You now need to produce Java code that does the same thing as your pseudocode. Much of it is routine. The first line of your pseudocode is a routine example of prompting the user and then reading input from the keyboard. You produce the following Java code for the first line of pseudocode:

```java
System.out.println("Enter a whole number from 1 to 99.");
System.out.println("I will output a combination of coins");
System.out.println("that equals that amount of change.");

amount = SavitchIn.readLineInt();
```

The next line of pseudocode, which sets the value of `originalAmount`, is already Java code. So, you need not do any translating.

Thus far, the `main` part of your program reads as follows:

```
public static void main(String[] args)
{
    int amount, originalAmount,
        quarters, dimes, nickels, pennies;

    System.out.println("Enter a whole number from 1 to 99.");
    System.out.println("I will output a combination of coins");
    System.out.println("that equals that amount of change.");

    amount = SavitchIn.readLineInt();
    originalAmount = amount;
```

Next, you need to translate the following to Java code:

Set the variable quarters **equal to the maximum number of quarters in** amount.
Reset amount **to the change left after giving out that many quarters.**

integer division
/ and %

You give this some thought and decide to try an example. For 55 cents, there are 2 quarters, because 55 divided by 25 is 2 with a remainder of 5. Ah ha! You realize that the operators / and % can be used for this kind of division. For example:

55/25 is 2 (the maximum number of 25's in 55)
55%25 is 5 (the remainder)

Replacing 55 with amount and changing to Java syntax, you produce the following:

```
quarters = amount/25;
amount = amount%25;
```

You realize that dimes and nickels are treated in a similar way, so you next produce the code:

```
dimes = amount/10;
amount = amount%10;
nickels = amount/5;
amount = amount%5;
```

The rest of the program coding is straightforward. You produce the program shown in Display 2.5 as your final program.

After producing your program, you need to test it on a number of different kinds of data. You decide to test it on each of the following inputs: 0 cents, 4 cents, 5 cents, 6 cents, 10 cents, 11 cents, 25 cents, 26 cents, 35 cents, 55 cents, 65 cents, and a number of other cases. This sounds like a lot of different inputs, but you want to try cases that give zero values for all possible coin values and want to test values near change points, like 25 and 26 cents, which changes from all quarters to quarters and another coin. All your tests are successful, but the grammar for the output is not exactly correct. For 26 cents, you get the output:

testing

```
26 cents in coins:
1 quarters
0 dimes
0 nickels and
1 pennies
```

Display 2.5   Change Program

••

```java
public class ChangeMaker
{
    public static void main(String[] args)
    {
        int amount, originalAmount,
            quarters, dimes, nickels, pennies;

        System.out.println("Enter a whole number from 1 to 99.");
        System.out.println("I will output a combination of coins");
        System.out.println("that equals that amount of change.");

        amount = SavitchIn.readLineInt();
        originalAmount = amount;

        quarters = amount/25;
        amount = amount%25;
        dimes = amount/10;
        amount = amount%10;
        nickels = amount/5;
        amount = amount%5;
        pennies = amount;

        System.out.println(originalAmount
                        + " cents in coins can be given as:");
        System.out.println(quarters + " quarters");
        System.out.println(dimes + " dimes");
        System.out.println(nickels + " nickels and");
        System.out.println(pennies + " pennies");
    }
}
```

> 25 goes into 87 three times with 12 left over.
> 87/25 is 3
> 87%25 is 12
> 87 cents is three quarters with 12 cents left over.

Sample Screen Dialogue

```
Enter a whole number from 1 to 99.
I will output a combination of coins
that equals that amount of change.
87
87 cents in coins can be given as:
3 quarters
1 dimes
0 nickels and
2 pennies
```

••

The output is correct but would read a lot nicer if it said 1 quarter instead of 1 quarters and 1 penny instead of 1 pennies. The techniques you need to produce this nicer looking output will be presented in the next chapter. For now, let's end this project here. The output is correct and understandable.

? Self-Test Questions

9. What is the output produced by the following lines of program code?

```java
int quotient, remainder;
quotient = 7/3;
remainder = 7%3;
System.out.println("quotient = " + quotient);
System.out.println("remainder = " + remainder);
```

10. What is the output produced by the following lines of program code?

```java
double result;
result = (1/2) * 2;
System.out.println("(1/2) * 2 equals " + result);
```

11. Consider the following statement from the program in Display 2.5/page 76:

```java
System.out.println(originalAmount
            + " cents in coins can be given as:");
```

Suppose that in that program, you change the preceding line to the following:

```java
System.out.println(amount
            + " cents in coins can be given as:");
```

How will this change the sample dialog in Display 2.5/page 76?

Increment and Decrement Operators

The increment and decrement operators can be used to increase or decrease the value of a variable by one. They are very specialized operators and you (and Java) could easily get along without them. But, they are sometimes handy and they are of cultural significance. Programmers use them. So, to be "in the club," you should learn how to use them. Even if you do not want to use them, you need to learn about them so you can understand them when you see them in other programmer's code.

The **increment operator** is written as two plus signs ++. For example, the following will increase the value of the variable count by one:

++ and ––

```java
count++;
```

This is a Java statement. If the variable count had the value 5 before this statement is executed, then count will have the value 6 after this statement is executed. You can use the increment operator with variables of any numeric type, but they are used most often with variables of integer type (such as the type *int*).

The **decrement operator** is similar, except that it subtracts one rather than add one to the value of the variable. The decrement operator is written as two minus signs – –. For example, the following will decrease the value of the variable count by one:

```
count− −;
```

If the variable count had the value 5 before this statement is executed, then count will have the value 4 after this statement is executed.

Note that

```
count++;
```

is equivalent to

```
count = count + 1;
```

and

```
count− −;
```

is equivalent to

```
count = count − 1;
```

So, the increment and decrement operators are really very specialized operators.

Why does Java have such very specialized operators? It inherited them from C++ (and C++ inherited them from C). In fact, this increment operator is where the ++ came from in the name of the C++ programming language. Why was it added to the C and C++ languages? Because adding or subtracting one is a very common thing to do when programming.

More About Increment and Decrement Operators

The increment and decrement operators can be used in expressions. When used in an expression, the increment operator both changes the value of the variable it is applied to, and it returns a value. Although we do not recommend using the increment and decrement operators in expressions, you should be familiar with them used in this way, because you are likely to see this use in other people's code.

In expressions, you can place the ++ or – – either before or after the variables, but the meaning is different depending on whether it is before or after the variable. For example, consider the code

```
int n = 3;
int m = 4;
int result;
result = n * (++m);
```

After this code is executed, the value of n is unchanged at 3, the value of m is 5, and the value of result is 15. Thus, ++m both changes the value of m and returns that changed value to be used in the arithmetic expression.

In the previous example, we placed the increment operator in front of the variables. If we place it after the variable m, then something slightly different happens. Consider the code

```
int n = 3;
int m = 4;
int result;
result = n * (m++);
```

In this case, after the code is executed, the value of n is 3 and the value of m is 5, just as in the previous case, but the value of result is 12, not 15. What is the story?

The two expressions n * (++m) and n * (m++) both increase the value of m by 1, but the first expression increases the value of m *before* it does the multiplication, whereas the second expression increases the value of m *after* it does the multiplication. Both ++m and m++ have the same effect on the final value of m, but when you use them as part of an arithmetic expression, they give a different value to the expression. If the ++ is *before* the m, then the value of m is increased *before* its value is used in the expression. If the ++ is *after* the m, then the value of m is increased *after* its value is used in the expression.

The − − operator works the same when it is used in an arithmetic expression. Both − −m and m− − have the same effect on the final value of m, but when you use them as part of an arithmetic expression, they give a different value to the expression. If the − − is *before* the m, then the value of m is decreased *before* its value is used in the expression. If the − − is *after* the m, then the value of m is decreased *after* its value is used in the expression.

The increment and decrement operators can be applied only to variables. They cannot be applied to constants or to entire, more complicated arithmetic expressions.

? Self-Test Questions

12. What is the output produced by the following lines of program code?

```
int n = 2;
n++;
System.out.println("n == " + n);
n--;
System.out.println("n == " + n);
```

2.2 | The Class String

> *Words, words, mere words, no matter from the heart.*
> **William Shakespeare, Troilus and Cressida**

Strings of characters, such as "Enter the amount:", are treated slightly differently from values of the primitive types. There is no primitive type for strings in Java. However, there is a class, called String, that can be used to store and process strings of characters. In this section we introduce you to the class String.

String

String Constants and Variables

You have already been using constants of type `String`. The quoted string

```
"Enter a whole number from 1 to 99."
```

which appears in the following statement from the program in Display 2.5/page 76, is a string constant:

```
System.out.println("Enter a whole number from 1 to 99.");
```

A value of type `String` is one of these quoted strings. That is, a value of type `String` is a sequence of characters treated as a single item. A variable of type `String` can name one of these string values.

The following declares `greeting` to be the name for a `String` variable:

```
String greeting;
```

The following sets the value of `greeting` to the `String` value `"Hello!"`:

```
greeting = "Hello!";
```

These two statements are often combined into one, as follows:

```
String greeting = "Hello!";
```

Once a `String` variable, such as `greeting`, has been given a value, you can write it out to the screen as follows:

```
System.out.println(greeting);
```

If the value of `greeting` has been set as we illustrated a bit earlier, then this will cause

```
Hello!
```

to be written on the screen

Concatenation of Strings

+ operator
concatenation

You can connect two strings using the + operator. Connecting ("pasting") two strings together to obtain a larger string is called **concatenation**. So, when it is used with strings, the + is sometimes called the **concatenation operator**. For example, consider the following:

```
String greeting = "Hello";
String sentence;
sentence = greeting + "my friend.";
System.out.println(sentence);
```

This will set the variable `sentence` to `"Hellomy friend."` and will write the following on the screen:

```
Hellomy friend.
```

Notice that no spaces are added when you concatenate two strings using the + operator. If you wanted `sentence` set to `"Hello my friend."`, then you should change the assignment statement to the following (or something that accomplishes the same thing):

```
sentence = greeting + " my friend.";
```

Notice the space before the word "my".

You can concatenate any number of String objects using the + operator. You can even connect a String object to any other type of object using the + operator. The result is always a String object. Java will figure out some way to express any object as a string when you connect it to a string with the + operator. For simple things like numbers, it does the obvious thing. For example:

```
String solution = "The answer is " + 42;
```

will set the String variable solution to "The answer is 42". This is so natural that it may seem like nothing special is happening, but this does require a real conversion from one type to another. The constant 42 is a number, whereas "42" is a string consisting of the two characters '4' followed by '2'. Java converts the number constant 42 to the string constant "42", and then concatenates the two strings "The answer is " and "42" to obtain the longer string "The answer is 42"..

Using the + Sign with Strings

You can concatenate two strings by connecting them with the + sign.

Example:

```
String name = "Neelix";
String greeting = "Hi " + name;
System.out.println(greeting);
```

This sets greeting to the string "Hi Neelix". So, it outputs the following to the screen:

```
Hi Neelix
```

Note that we needed to add a space at the end of "Hi ".

String Methods

A String variable is not just a simple variable, like a variable of type *int* is. A String variable is a variable of a class type. Something of a class type is an object with methods as well as a value. Thus, a String variable is an object,[1] and as an object, it has methods. These String methods can be used to manipulate string values. A few of these String methods are described in Display 2.6. As with any method, the method is called (is invoked) by writing a dot and the name of the method after the object name. In this section, the object name will always be a variable of type

---

1. When you declare a name, like greeting, to be of type String, greeting is not really an object of type String; greeting is merely a name for an object of type String. This sounds like so much double talk, and for what we are doing in this chapter is not a very important distinction. This distinction will turn out to be much more important when we study classes other than String, and we will discuss this distinction at that time.

Display 2.6   Methods in the Class `String`

Method	Description	Example
`length()`	Returns the length of the string object.	`String greeting = "Hello!";` `greeting.length()` returns 6.

`equals(Other_String)`	Returns *true* if the calling object string and the *Other_String* are equal. Otherwise, returns *false*.	`String greeting =`
		`        SavitchIn.readLine();`
		if `(greeting.equals("Hi"))`
		`    System.out.println(`
		`        "Informal Greeting.");`

`equalsIgnoreCase(`
`    Other_String)`
	Returns *true* if the calling object string and the *Other_String* are equal, considering uppercase and lowercase versions of a letter to be the same. Otherwise, returns *false*.	If a program contains,
		`String s1 = "mary!";`
		then after this assignment,
		`s1.equalsIgnoreCase("Mary!")`
		returns *true*.

`toLowerCase()`	Returns a string with the same characters as the string object, but with all characters converted to lowercase.	`String greeting = "Hi Mary!";`
		`greeting.toLowerCase()` returns
		`"hi mary!"`

`toUpperCase()`	Returns a string with the same characters as the string object, but with all characters converted to uppercase.	`String greeting = "Hi Mary!";`
		`greeting.toUpperCase()` returns
		`"HI MARY!"`

Display 2.6   Methods in the Class `String`

....

`trim()`	Returns a string with the same characters as the string object, but with leading and trailing whitespace removed.	`String pause = "   Hmm    ";` `pause.trim()` **returns** `"Hmm"`
`charAt(Position)`	Returns the character in the string at the *Position*. Positions are counted 0, 1, 2, etc.	`String greeting = "Hello!";` `greeting.charAt(0)` **returns** `'H'`. `greeting.charAt(1)` **returns** `'e'`.
`substring(Start)`	Returns the substring of the string object starting from *Start* through to the end of the string object. Positions are counted 0, 1, 2, etc.	`String sample = "AbcdefG";` `sample.substring(2)` **returns** `"cdefG"`.
`substring(Start, End)`	Returns the substring of the string object starting from position *Start* through, but not including, position *End* of the string object. Positions are counted 0, 1, 2, etc.	`String sample = "AbcdefG";` `sample.substring(2, 5)` **returns** `"cde"`.
`indexOf(A_String)`	Returns the position of the first occurrence of the string *A_String* in the string object. Positions are counted 0, 1, 2, etc. Returns −1 if *A_String* is not found.	`String greeting = "Hi Mary!";` `greeting.indexOf("Mary")` returns 3. `greeting.indexOf("Sally")` returns −1.

Display 2.6   Methods in the Class `String`

••

`indexOf(A_String, Start)`	Returns the position of the first occurrence of the string *A_String* in the string object that occurs at or after position *Start*. Positions are counted 0, 1, 2, etc. Returns −1 if *A_String* is not found.	`String name =` `"Mary, Mary quite contrary";` `name.indexOf("Mary", 1)` returns 6. The same value is returned if 1 is replaced by any number up to and including 6. `name.indexOf("Mary", 0)` returns 0. `name.indexOf("Mary", 8)` returns −1.
`lastIndexOf(A_String)`	Returns the position of the last occurrence of the string *A_String* in the string object. Positions are counted 0, 1, 2, etc. Returns −1, if *A_String* is not found.	`String name =` `"Mary, Mary, Mary quite so";` `name.lastIndexOf("Mary")` returns 12.
`compareTo(A_String)`	Compares the calling string object and the string argument to see which comes first in the lexicographic ordering. Lexicographic ordering is the same as alphabetical ordering when both strings are either all uppercase or all lowercase. If the calling string is first, it returns a negative value. If the two strings are equal, it returns zero. If the argument is first, it returns a positive number.	`String entry = "adventure";` `entry.compareTo("zoo")` **returns a negative number.** `entry.compareTo("adventure")` returns zero. `entry.compareTo("above")` returns a positive number.

`String`. Any arguments to the method are given in parentheses. Let's look at some examples.

length

The method `length` can be used to get the number of characters in a string. For example, suppose we declare `String` variables as follows:

```
String command = "Sit Fido!";
String answer = "bow-wow";
```

Then `command.length()` returns 9 and `answer.length()` returns 7. Notice that you must include a pair of parentheses, even though there are no arguments to the method `length`. Also notice that spaces, special symbols, and repeated characters are all counted in computing the length of a string. All characters are counted.

Display 2.7 String Indexes

The twelve characters in the string "Java is fun." have indexes 0 through 11. The index of each character is given below.

0	1	2	3	4	5	6	7	8	9	10	11
J	a	v	a		i	s		f	u	n	.

Note that the blanks and the period count as characters in the string.

You can use a call to the method `length` anywhere that you can use a value of type *int*. For example, all of the following are legal Java statements:

```
int count = command.length();
System.out.println("Length is " + command.length());
count = answer.length() + 3;
```

Many of the methods for the class `String` depend on counting **positions** in the string. Positions are counted starting with 0 not with 1. So, in the string "Hi Mom", 'H' is in position 0, 'i' is in position 1, the blank character is in position 2, and so forth. A position is usually referred to as an **index** in computer parlance. So it would be more normal to say: 'H' is at index 0, 'i' is at index 1, the blank character is at index 2, and so forth. Display 2.7 illustrates how index positions are numbered in a string.

position

index

The method `indexOf` will return the index of the substring given as its one argument. If the substring occurs more than once, `indexOf` returns the index of the first occurrence of its substring argument. For example, consider

```
String phrase = "Time flies like an arrow.";
```

After this declaration, the invocation `phrase.indexOf("flies")` will return 5 because the 'f' of "flies" is at index 5. (Remember, the first index is 0, not 1.)

String Processing

Many references on the Java language say objects of type `String` cannot be changed. There is a sense in which that is true, but it is a misleading statement. Notice that none of the methods in Display 2.6/page 82 changes the value of the String object. There are more `String` methods than those shown in Display 2.6, but none of them lets you write statements that say things like "Change the fifth character in the string object to `'z'`". This is not an accident. This was done intentionally in order to make the implementation of the `String` class more efficient; that is, in order to make the methods execute faster and use less computer memory. There is another string class that has methods for altering the string object. It is called `StringBuffer`, but we will not discuss it here because we do not need it.

Although there is no method that allows you to change the value of a `String` object, you can still write programs that change the value of a `String` variable, which is probably all you want anyway. To perform the change, you simply use an assignment statement, as in the following example:

```
String name = "Mulder";
name = "Fox " + name;
```

The assignment statement in the second line changes the value of the `name` variable so that the string it names changes from `"Mulder"` to `"Fox Mulder"`. Display 2.8 shows a sample program that demonstrates how to do some simple string processing that changes the value of a `String` variable. Part of that program is explained in the next subsection.

Escape Characters

quotes in quotes

Suppose you want to output a string with quotes inside of it. For example, suppose you want to output the following to the screen:

```
The word "Java" names a language, not just a drink!
```

The following will not work:

```
System.out.println("The word "Java" names a language, not just a drink!");
```

This will produce a compiler error message. The problem is that the compiler sees

```
"The word "
```

as a perfectly valid quoted string. Then the compiler sees `Java"`, which is not anything valid in the Java language (although the compiler might guess that it is a quoted string with one missing quote or guess that you forgot a + sign). The compiler has no way to know that you mean to include the `'"'` symbol as part of the quoted string,

**backslash **

unless you tell it that you mean to do so. You tell the compiler that you mean to include the quote in the string by placing a **backslash ** before the troublesome character, like so:

```
System.out.println("The word \"Java\" names a language, not just a drink!");
```

escape sequence

Some other special characters that are spelled using a backslash are listed in Display 2.9. These are often called **escape characters**, because they escape from the usual meaning of a character, such as the usual meaning of the double quote.

It is important to note that each escape sequence is a single character, even though it is spelled with two symbols. So, the string `"Say \"Hi\"!"` contains nine characters (`'S'`, `'a'`, `'y'`, the blank character, `'\"'`, `'H'`, `'i'`, `'\"'`, and `'!'`), not eleven characters.

Display 2.8 Using the String **Class**

••

```java
public class StringDemo
{
    public static void main(String[] args)
    {
        String sentence = "Text processing is hard!";
        int position;

        position = sentence.indexOf("hard");
        System.out.println(sentence);
        System.out.println("01234567890123456789012 3");
        System.out.println("The word \"hard\" starts at index "
                                    + position);

        sentence = sentence.substring(0, position) + "easy!";
        System.out.println("The changed string is:");
        System.out.println(sentence);
    }
}
```

The meaning of \" is discussed in the subsection entitled **Escape Characters.**

Sample Screen Dialogue

```
Text processing is hard!
01234567890123456789012 3
The word "hard" starts at index 19
The changed string is:
Text processing is easy!
```

••

Including a backslash in a quoted string is a little tricky. For example, the string `"abc\def"` is likely to produce the error message "Invalid escape character." To include a backslash in a string, you need to use two backslashes. The string `"abc\\def"`, if output to the screen, would produce

    abc\def

The escape sequence \n indicates that the string starts a new line at the \n. For example, the statement

    System.out.println("The motto is\nGo for it!");

Display 2.9   Escape Characters

```
\"  Double quote.
\'  Single quote.
\\  Backslash.
\n  New line. Go to the beginning of the next line.
\r  Carriage return. Go to the beginning of the current line.
\t  Tab. whitespace up to the next tab stop.
```

will write the following to the screen

```
The motto is
Go for it!
```

It may seem that there is no need for the escape sequence \', since it is perfectly valid to include a single quote inside a quoted string, such as "How's this?". But, you do need \' if you want to indicate the constant for the single-quote character, as in

```
char singleQuote = '\'';
```

The Unicode Character Set

ASCII

Unicode

Most other programming languages use the **ASCII** character set, which is given in Appendix 3. The ASCII character set is simply a list of all the characters normally used on an English-language keyboard together with a standard number assigned to each character. Java uses the **Unicode** character set instead. The Unicode character set includes all the ASCII character set plus many of the characters used in languages that have an alphabet different from English. As it turns out, this is not likely to be a big issue if you are using an English-language keyboard. Normally, you can just program as if Java were using the ASCII character set. The ASCII character set is a subset of the Unicode character set, and the subset you will use. Thus, Appendix 3 which list the ASCII character set i, in fact, listing the subset of the Unicode character set that you will use in Java. The advantage of the Unicode character set is that it makes it possible to easily handle languages other than English. The disadvantage of the Unicode character set is that it sometimes requires more computer memory to store each character than it would if Java used only the ASCII character set.

? Self-Test Questions

13. What is the output produced by the following?

```
String greeting = "How do you do";
System.out.println(greeting + "Seven of Nine.");
```

14. What is the output produced by the following?

```
String test = "abcdefg";
System.out.println(test.length());
System.out.println(test.charAt(1));
```

15. What is the output produced by the following?

```
String test = "abcdefg";
System.out.println(test.substring(3));
```

16. What is the output produced by the following?

```
System.out.println("abc\ndef");
```

2.3 | Keyboard and Screen I/O

> *Garbage in, garbage out.*
>
> ***Programmer's saying***

Input and output of program data are usually referred to as **I/O**. There are many different ways that a Java program can perform I/O. In this section, we present some very simple ways to handle simple text input typed in at the keyboard and simple text output sent to the screen. In future chapters (and in an optional section of this chapter), we will discuss more elaborate ways to do I/O.

I/O

In order to do I/O in Java, you almost always need to add some classes to the language. Sometimes these are classes that, although not part of the language proper, are nonetheless provided in all implementations of Java. Other times, these classes are not provided along with the language and you must write the classes yourself (or obtain them from whoever wrote the class definitions). In this section, we will do output using a class provided automatically along with the Java language. However, you cannot do simple keyboard input unless you add some class that is not automatically provided along with the Java language. So, we will do input using the class SavitchIn, which is not provided with the Java language but was written expressly for readers of this text.

Screen Output

We have been using simple output statements since the beginning of this book. This section will simply summarize and explain what we have already been doing. In Display 2.5/page 76, we used statements like the following to send output to the display screen:

System.out. println

```
System.out.println("Enter a whole number from 1 to 99.");
            . . .
System.out.println(quarters + " quarters");
```

System.out is an object that is part of the Java language. It may seem strange to spell an object name with a dot in it, but that need not concern us at this point.

This object, System.out, has println as one of its methods. So the preceding output statements are calls to the method println of the object System.out. Of course, you need not be aware of these details in order to use these output statements. You can consider `System.out.println` as one rather peculiarly spelled statement. However, you may as well get used to this dot notation and the notion of methods and objects.

In order to use output statements of this form, simply follow the expression `System.out.println` by what you want to output enclosed in parentheses, and then follow that with a semicolon. The things you can output are strings of text in double quotes, like `"Enter a whole number from 1 to 99."` or `" quarters"`, variables like `quarters`, numbers like 5 or 7.3, and almost any other object or value. If you want to output more than one thing, simply place an addition sign between the things you want to output. For example,

```
System.out.println("Lucky number = " + 13
                         + "Secret number = " + number);
```

If the value of `number` is 7, the output will be

```
Lucky number = 13Secret number = 7
```

Notice that no spaces are added. If you want a space between the 13 and the word `Secret` in the preceding output (and you probably do), then you should add a space to the string

```
"Secret number = "
```

so that it becomes

```
" Secret number = "
```

Notice that you use double quotes, not single quotes, and that the left and right quotes are the same symbol. Finally, notice that it is OK to place the statement on two lines if it is too long. However, you should indent the second line, and you should break the line before or after a + sign, not in the middle of a quoted string or a variable name.

You can also use the `println` method to output the value of a `String` variable, as illustrated by the following:

```
String greeting = "Hello Programmers!";
System.out.println(greeting);
```

This will cause the following to be written on the screen.

```
Hello Programmers!
```

Every invocation of `println` ends a line of output. For example, consider the following statements:

```
System.out.println("One, two, buckle my shoe.");
System.out.println("Three, four, shut the door.");
```

These two statements will cause the following output to appear on the screen:

```
One, two, buckle my shoe.
Three, four, shut the door.
```

print versus
println

If you want the output from two or more output statements to place all their output on a single line, then use `print` instead of `println`. For example:

```
System.out.print("One, two,");
System.out.print(" buckle my shoe.");
System.out.println(" Three, four,");
System.out.println(" shut the door.");
```

will produce the following output:

```
One, two, buckle my shoe. Three, four,
  shut the door.
```

Notice that a new line is not started until you use a `println`, rather than a `print`. Also notice that the new line starts *after* outputting the items specified in the `println`. This is the only difference between `print` and `println`.

`println` Output

You can output one line with `System.out.println`. The items output can be quoted strings, variables, constants such as numbers, or almost any object you can define in Java.

Syntax:

```
System.out.println(Output_1 + Output_2 + ... + Output_Last);
```

Example:

```
System.out.println("Hello out there!");
System.out.println("Area = " + theArea + " square inches");
```

That is all you need to know in order to write programs with this sort of output, but we can still explain a bit more about what is happening. Consider the following statement:

```
System.out.println("The answer is " + 42);
```

The expression inside the parentheses should look familiar:

```
"The answer is " + 42
```

In the section on the class `String`, we said that you could use the + operator to concatenate a string, like `"The answer is "`, and another item, like the number constant 42. The + operator inside these `System.out.println` statements is that same + operator that performs string concatenation. In the preceding `System.out.println` statement, Java converts the number constant 42 to the string `"42"` and then uses the + operator to obtain the string `"The answer is 42"`. Then the `System.out.println` statement outputs the string `"The answer is 42"`. The `println` method always outputs strings. Technically speaking, it never outputs numbers, even though it looks like it does.

Input Using `SavitchIn`

In order to do simple input in Java, you need to use some class that is defined for you (or defined by you). In this section, we will do input using the class `SavitchIn` which is in the file `SavitchIn.java` provided with this text. `SavitchIn` is an extremely

---

`println` versus `print`

`System.out.println` and `System.out.print` are almost the same method. The only difference is that with the `println` method, the *next* output goes on a new line, whereas with the `print` method, the *next* output will be placed on the same line.

Example:

```
System.out.print("one ");
System.out.print("two ");
System.out.println("three ");
System.out.print("four ");
```

will produce the following output

```
one two three
four
```

(The output would look the same whether the last line read `print` or `println`.)

---

simple class, and once you learn a little more Java, you will have no problem understanding the code for this class definition. However, in this section, we will not explain the definition of `SavitchIn`. We will only explain how to use the class `SavitchIn`.

It is very easy to obtain a copy of the class definition for `SavitchIn`. The definition is given in Appendix 4. However, there is no need to type in the definition. The definition is in the file `SavitchIn.java`, which is on the CD provided with this text. Just copy the file `SavitchIn.java` into the directory in which you keep your Java programs and compile the class `SavitchIn.java`. At this point, you need not even read the definition of the class `SavitchIn`. Although it may seem strange at first to use a class definition without reading it, this is a common thing to do. A class definition is just another piece of software, and you use all kinds of software without reading their code. For example, you use an editor without ever seeing the code for the editor, you use the Java compiler without ever seeing the code for the Java compiler, and you use the Java classes `String` and `System` (as in `System.out`) without reading their definitions.

The class `SavitchIn` has methods that read a piece of data from the keyboard and return that data. By placing one of these method invocations in an assignment statement, your program can read from the keyboard and place the data read into the variable on the left-hand side of the assignment operator. For example,

```
amount = SavitchIn.readLineInt();
```

The preceding statement from the program in Display 2.5/page 76 will read in one integer and make that integer the value of the variable `amount`. The method `read-LineInt` does not use any arguments. That is why there is nothing in the parentheses after the name `readLineInt`, but still you must include the parentheses.

`readLineInt`
The method `readLineInt` expects the user to input one integer (of type *int*) on a line by itself, possibly with space before or after it. If the user inputs anything else, then an error message will be output to the screen and the user will be asked to

reenter the input. Input is read only after the user starts a new line. So nothing happens until the user presses the enter key (also called the return key).

What if you want to read in a number of some type other than *int*? The methods `readLineLong`, `readLineFloat`, and `readLineDouble` work in the exact same way, except that they read in values of type *long*, *float*, and *double*, respectively. For example, the following will read a single number of type *double* and store that value in the variable `measurement`:

readLine-
Double

```
double measurement;
measurement = SavitchIn.readLineDouble();
```

You can use the method `readLineNonwhiteChar` to read in a single character on a line by itself (except possibly for whitespace before the character):

```
char symbol;
symbol = SavitchIn.readLineNonwhiteChar();
```

If there is more than one nonwhitespace character on the line, then `readLineNonwhiteChar` will read the first such character and discard the rest of the input line. **Whitespace** characters are all characters that print as whitespace if you output them to paper (or the screen). The only whitespace character you are likely to be concerned with at first is the blank space character. (The start of a new line and the tab symbol are also whitespace characters, but those details are not likely to concern you yet.)

whitespace

There is a slight difference between `readLineNonwhiteChar` and the methods that read a single number. For the methods `readLineInt` and `readLineDouble`, the input number must be on a line with nothing before or after the number, except possibly whitespace. The method `readLineNonwhiteChar` allows anything to be on the line after the first nonwhite character, but ignores the rest of the line. This way, when the user enters a word like yes, `readLineNonwhiteChar` can read the first letter, like 'y', and ignore the rest of the word yes.

If you want to read in an entire line, you would use the method `readLine` (without any `Int` or `Double` or such at the end). For example,

```
String sentence;
sentence = SavitchIn.readLine();
```

reads in one line of input and places that string in the variable `sentence`.

The class `SavitchIn` also has other methods, some of which are discussed in the next subsection.

The equal sign in a statement like the second of the two that follows is the assignment operator:

```
int number;
number = SavitchIn.readLineInt();
```

Earlier we pointed out that you can combine a declaration of a variable and an assignment of a value to that variable into one longer statement. So, the previous two lines of code can be expressed more compactly as the following:

```
int number = SavitchIn.readLineInt();
```

> ### `SavitchIn` Is Not Part of the Java Language
>
> The class `SavitchIn` is not part of the Java language and does not come with the Java language. You must add the class yourself. This class was defined by the author for readers of this book. That is why it is named `Savitch In`. That way you will know that it was written by Savitch and not think it is part of the Java language. The class `SavitchIn` is given in Appendix 4 and a copy is provided on the CD that accompanies this book. So, it is easy to obtain.
>
> Why do we use the class `SavitchIn`? Why don't we simply use the classes provided with the Java language? Unfortunately, the Java language does not provide any classes for simple keyboard input. If you want to do simple input from the keyboard, you must add some class or classes.

More Input Methods

All the methods in the class `SavitchIn` that begin with `readLine`, such as `readLine` and `readLineInt`, always read an entire line of text. That is why their names start with "read line." But, sometimes you do not want to read a whole line. For example, given the input

```
2 4 6
```

you might want to read these three numbers with three statements that put the numbers in three different variables. You can do this with the method `readInt`. For example, the following might appear in some program:

```
System.out.println("Enter 3 numbers on one line:");
int n1, n2, n3;
n1 = SavitchIn.readInt();
n2 = SavitchIn.readInt();
n3 = SavitchIn.readInt();
```

The user will be given the prompt:

```
Enter 3 numbers on one line:
```

Suppose that, in response to the prompt, the user enters the following, all on one line, and then presses the enter key:

```
2 4 6
```

Then n1 will be given the value 2, n2 will be given the value 4, and n3 will be given the value 6.

After an integer is read with `readInt`, the input continues on the same line (unless it just happens to have reached the end of the line). For example, if the user enters

```
10 20 30
```

then the following code

```
int n;
n = SavitchIn.readInt();
String theRest;
theRest = SavitchIn.readLine();
```

will set n equal to 10 and will set `theRest` equal to the string `"20 30"`.

Input Using `SavitchIn`

You use methods in the class `SavitchIn` to read values from the keyboard. When you invoke one of these methods, you use the class name `SavitchIn` as if it were the calling object. In other words, a typical method invocation has the form

Variable = `SavitchIn`.*Method_Name*();

Although there are other methods in `SavitchIn`, you should normally use the methods that include the word "`Line`.". These methods each read a single value, such as a number, on a line by itself. The value may have whitespace before and/or after it, but should not have other characters on the line. (The method `read-LineNonwhiteChar` is an exception and does allow nonwhitespace to follow the character that it reads.) There is a different method for each type of value you want to read from the keyboard. You need to use the method that matches the type of the value read, such as *int* for a whole number or *char* for a single character.

(The method invocation `SavitchIn`.`readLineInt`() returns an *int* value and can be used anyplace that an *int* value is allowed, such as in an arithmetic expression. The method invocation does not have to be used in a simple assignment statement as described below, but that is its most common usage. Similar remarks apply to the other methods, except that the type of the value returned is different for each method.)

Syntax:

Int_Variable = `SavitchIn.readLineInt()`;
Long_Variable = `SavitchIn.readLineLong()`;
Float_Variable = `SavitchIn.readLineFloat()`;
Double_Variable = `SavitchIn.readLineDouble()`;
Char_Variable = `SavitchIn.readLineNonwhiteChar()`;
String_Variable = `SavitchIn.readLine()`;

Example:

```
int count;
count = SavitchIn.readLineInt();
long bigOne;
bigOne = SavitchIn.readLineLong();
float increment;
increment = SavitchIn.readLineFloat();
double distance;
distance = SavitchIn.readLineDouble();
char letter;
letter = SavitchIn.readLineNonwhiteChar();
String wholeLine;
wholeLine = SavitchIn.readLine();
```

Two other similar methods in `SavitchIn` that read less than a whole line are `readDouble` and `readNonwhiteChar`. The only difference between these and `readInt` is that with `readDouble`, a value of type *double* is read, and with `read-NonwhiteChar`, a nonwhitespace character is read. **Whitespace** characters are blanks, tabs, and new lines. For the sort of simple things we will do, the only whitespace that will be relevant is the blank character.

whitespace

The methods `readInt`, `readDouble`, and `readNonwhiteChar` each require that the input items be separated by one or more blank spaces. Moreover, these methods do not prompt the user if the input format is incorrect. When using these methods, you need to be certain the input will be entered correctly the first time.

The last method from the class `SavitchIn` that we will consider here is `readChar`. The method `readChar` reads whatever single character is next in the input stream. For example, consider

```
char c1, c2, c3;
c1 = SavitchIn.readChar();
c2 = SavitchIn.readChar();
c3 = SavitchIn.readChar();
```

If the user enters

```
a b c d e f g h i
```

where `'a'` is the first thing on the line, then `c1` will be set to the value `'a'`, `c2` will have its value set to the blank character, and `c3` will have its value set to `'b'`. Any further reading would begin with the blank after the letter `'b'`.

As indicated in the next Gotcha section, it is safer to use the methods that begin with `readLine` and that read a whole line, and to only use the other methods sparingly and with caution.

■ Gotcha
`readInt` **and** `readDouble`

The methods `readLineInt` and `readLineDouble` in the class `SavitchIn` will prompt the user to re-enter the input if the user enters it in an incorrect format. The methods `readInt` and `readDouble`, on the other hand, have no such recovery mechanisms. If the user enters the input in an incorrect format, the program will crash. For this reason, you should try to use the methods `readLineInt` and `readLineDouble`, and avoid using the methods `readInt` and `readDouble`. The methods `readInt` and `readDouble` should be reserved for when you are certain that the input will be in the correct format. For most of our applications, you cannot count on the user entering the input in the correct format.

The methods `readChar` and `readNonwhiteChar` also do no checking for the format of the input, but they are less dangerous, because they will process almost any kind of input the user enters. After all, all input consists of characters of some sort. Even the input 178, which might be considered to be an integer, can be processed as the three-character input `'1'`, followed by `'7'`, followed by `'8'`.

■ Programming Tip
Echo Input

echoing input

You should write out all input so that the user can check that the input was entered correctly. This is called **echoing the input**. For example, the following two statements from the program in Display 2.1/page 54 echo the two input values that were read into the variables `eggsPerBasket` and `numberOfBaskets`:

Why Aren't `readInt` and `readDouble` Better?

Why don't `readInt` and `readDouble` prompt the user to correctly reenter input that is incorrect? They could easily be written that way, but they would confuse the user. The reason is that such prompts are likely to be in confusing places. The operating system always reads an entire line and then gives the entire line to Java. If the user enters four things on a line, and there is a format mistake in the second thing, then the operating system will read the whole line before Java notices anything wrong. So, the prompt to reenter would come after the fourth thing on the line, not after the second thing on the line where it applies. It would be possible to design `readInt` and `readDouble` so that they prompted for correctly reentering input and did so in an understandable way, but it would not be either simple to write or simple to understand. Moreover, many input methods in many languages behave like `readInt` and `readDouble`, so you should be made aware of such problems.

```
System.out.println(eggsPerBasket + " eggs per basket.");
System.out.println(numberOfBaskets + " baskets.");
```

It may seem that echoing input is not needed. After all, when the user enters input, it appears on the screen as it is entered. Why bother to write it to the screen a second time? There are several reasons for this. First, the input might be incorrect even though it looks correct. For example, the user might use a comma instead of a decimal point, or the letter "O" in place of a zero. Echoing the input will reveal such problems. Also, the echoed input gets the user's attention. Some users do not look at the screen as they type in input. In an ideal program, the user should even be given the opportunity to reenter the input if it is incorrect, but we do not yet have enough tools to do that. However, when something is wrong with the input, we do want the user to at least be aware that there is a problem.

? Self-Test Questions

17. Write Java statements that will cause the following to be written to the screen:

    ```
    Once upon a time,
    there were three little programmers.
    ```

18. What is the difference between `System.out.println` and `System.out.print`?

19. Write a Java statement that will set the value of the variable `amount` equal to the number typed in at the keyboard. Assume that `amount` is of type *double* and that the input is entered on a line by itself.

20. Write a Java statement that will set the value of the variable `answer` equal to the first nonwhitespace character typed in at the keyboard. The rest of the line of input is discarded. The variable `answer` is of type *char*.

21. What are the whitespace characters?

22. Is the class `SavitchIn` part of the Java language (or does the programmer have to define the class?)

2.4 | Documentation and Style

> *"Don't stand there chattering to yourself like that,"* Humpty Dumpty said,
> looking at her for the first time, *"but tell me your name and your business."*
>
> *"My* name *is Alice, but—"*
>
> *"It's a stupid name enough!"* Humpty Dumpty interrupted impatiently. *"What does it mean?"*
>
> *"Must a name mean something?"* Alice asked doubtfully.
>
> *"Of course it must,"* Humpty Dumpty said with a short laugh: *"my name means the shape I am—and a good handsome shape it is too. With a name like yours, you might be any shape, almost."*
>
> **Lewis Carroll, Through the Looking Glass**

A program that gives the correct output is not necessarily a good program. Obviously, you want your program to give the correct output, but that is not the whole story. Most programs are used many times and are changed to either fix bugs or to accommodate new demands by the user. If the program is not easy to read and understand, it will not be easy to change or might even be impossible to change with any realistic effort. Even if the program is going to be used only once, you should pay some attention to readability. After all, you will have to read the program in order to debug the program.

In this section, we discuss four techniques that can help make your program more readable: meaningful names, indenting, documentation, and defined constants.

■ Programming Tip

Use Meaningful Names for Variables

The names x and y are almost never good variable names. The name you give to a variable should be suggestive of what the variable is used for. If the variable holds a count of something, you might name it `count`. If the variable holds a tax rate, you might name it `taxRate`.

In addition to giving variables meaningful names and giving them names that the compiler will accept, you should also choose the names that follow the normal practice of programmers. That way it will be easier for others to read your code and to combine your code with their code, should you work on a project with more than one programmer. By convention, variable names are made up entirely of letters and digits. If the name consists of more than one word, "punctuate" it by using capital letters at the word boundaries, as in `taxRate`, `numberOfTries`, and `timeLeft`. Also, start each variable with a lowercase letter, as in the examples we just gave. This convention of starting with a lowercase letter may look strange at first, but it is a convention that is commonly used and you quickly get used to it. The reason we do not start variable names with an uppercase letter is because we use names that start with an uppercase letter for something else (namely, for class names like `String` and `SavitchIn`).

Documentation and Comments

The documentation for a program tells what the program does and how it does it. The best programs are **self-documenting**. That means that, thanks to a very clean style and very well-chosen variable names (and other names), what the program does and how it does it is obvious to any programmer who reads the program. You should strive for such self-documenting programs, but your programs will also need a bit of explanation to make them completely clear. This explanation can be given in the form of what are called *comments*.

self-documenting

Self-Documenting Code

A **self-documenting** program (or other piece of code) is one that uses well-chosen variable names (and other names) and has a style so clear that what the program does and how it does it is obvious to any programmer who reads the program, even if the program has no comments. To the extent that it is possible, you should strive to make your programs self-documenting. ☐

Comments are things written into your program that help a person understand the program, but that are ignored by the compiler. In Java, there are two ways of forming comments. Everything after the two symbols // through to the end of the line is a comment and is ignored by the compiler. These sorts of comments are handy for short comments, such as

// comments

```
String sentence; //Spanish version
```

If you want a comment of this form to span several lines, then each line must contain the symbols //.

/* */ comments

The second form of comments can more easily span multiple lines. Anything written between the matching symbol pairs /* and */ is a comment and is ignored by the compiler. For example,

```
/*This program should only
  be used on alternate Thursdays,
  except during leap years when it should
  only be used on alternate Tuesdays.*/
```

This is not a very likely comment, but it does illustrate the use of /* and */ to form comments. These sorts of comments are often formed into boxes by adding extra asterisks as follows:

```
/************************************
 *This program should only
 *be used on alternate Thursdays,
 *except during leap years when it should
 *only be used on alternate Tuesdays.
 ************************************/
```

In this book, we will write comments in italics, as illustrated just above. Many text editors automatically highlight comments in some way, such as showing them in color.

It is difficult to explain just when you should and when you should not put in a comment. Too many comments can be as bad as too few comments. With too many comments, the really important comments can be lost in a sea of comments that just state the obvious. As we show you more Java features, we will mention likely places for comments. For now, you should normally only need two kinds of comments.

First, every program file should have an explanatory comment at the beginning of the file. This comment should give all the important information about the file, what the program does, the name of the author, how to contact the author, the date that the file was last changed, and in a course, what the assignment is. This comment should be similar to the one shown at the top of Display 2.10.

The second kind of comment you need is a comment to explain any nonobvious details. For example, look at the program in Display 2.10. Note that there are two variables named `radius` and `area`. It is obvious that these two variables will hold the values for the radius and area of a circle, respectively. It would be a *mistake* to include comments like the following:

```
double radius; //holds the radius of a circle.
```

However, there is something that is not obvious. What units are used for the radius? Inches? Feet? Meters? Centimeters? So, you should add a comment that explains the units used, as follows:

```
double radius; //in inches
double area; //in square inches
```

These two comments are also shown in Display 2.10. In a well-written program, there should seldom be a need to explain such nonobvious detail, but occasionally such comments are needed.

Indenting

A program has a lot of structure. There are smaller parts within larger parts. For example, there is the part that starts with

```
public static void main(String[] args)
{
```

indenting

This part is ended with a closing curly bracket `}`. Within this part, there are statements, like assignment statements and `System.out.println` statements. In a simple program of the kinds we have seen thus far, there are basically three levels of nested structure as indicated by the vertical lines in Display 2.10. Each level of nesting should be indented to show the nesting more clearly. The outermost structure is not indented at all. The next level of nested structure is indented. The nested structure within that is double indented. This is illustrated in Display 2.10.

These levels of nesting are frequently indicated by **curly brackets** `{ }`, but whether or not there are any curly brackets, you should still indent each level of nesting.

If a statement does not fit on one line, you can write it on two or more lines. However, when you write a single statement on more than one line, indent the second (and third etc. if any) lines more than the first line.

We prefer to indent by four spaces for each level of indenting. Indenting more than that results in too little room left on the line. Indenting much less than that just does not show. Indenting two or three spaces would not be unreasonable, but we

Display 2.10 Comments and Indenting

```java
/*************************************
 *Program to determine area of a circle.
 *Author: Jane Q. Programmer.
 *E-mail Address: janeq@somemachine.etc.etc.
 *Programming Assignment 2.
 *Last Changed: October 7, 2001.
 *************************************/
public class CircleCalculation
{
    public static void main(String[] args)
    {
        double radius; //in inches
        double area; //in square inches

        System.out.println("Enter the radius of a circle in
                inches:");
        radius = SavitchIn.readLineDouble();

        area = 3.14159 * radius * radius;

        System.out.println("A circle of radius " + radius + " inches");
        System.out.println("has an area of " + area + " square inches.");
    }
}
```

The vertical lines indicate the indenting pattern

Later in this chapter, we will give an improved version of this program.

Sample Screen Dialogue

```
Enter the radius of a circle in inches:
2.5
A circle of radius 2.5 inches
has an area of 19.6349375 square inches.
```

find four spaces to be the clearest. If you are in a class, follow the rules on indenting given by your instructor. On a programming project, there is likely to be a style sheet that dictates the number of spaces you should indent. In any event, you should indent consistently within any one program.

Java Comments

There are two ways to add comments to a Java program (or piece of Java code).
1. Everything after the two symbols `//` through to the end of the line is a comment and is ignored by the compiler.
2. Anything written between the matching symbols pairs `/*` and `*/` is a comment and is ignored by the compiler.

Named Constants

Look again at the program in Display 2.10. You probably recognize the number `3.14159` as the approximate value of *pi*, the number that is used in many circle calculations and that is often written as π. However, you might not be sure that `3.14159` is *pi* and not some other number, and somebody other than you might have no idea of where the number `3.14159` came from. To avoid such confusions, you should always give a name to constants, such as `3.14159`, and use the name instead of writing out the number. For example, you might give the number `3.14159` the name `PI`. Then the assignment statement:

```
area = 3.14159 * radius * radius;
```

could be written more clearly as

```
area = PI * radius * radius;
```

How do you give a number, or other constant, a name like `PI`? You could use a variable named `PI` and initialize it to the desired value, like `3.14159`. But, you might then inadvertently change the value of this variable. Java provides a mechanism that allows you to define and initialize a variable and moreover fix the variable's value so it cannot have its value changed. The syntax is

```
public static final Type Variable = Constant;
```

For example, the name `PI` can be given to the constant `3.14159` as follows:

```
public static final double PI = 3.14159;
```

You can simply take this as a long, peculiarly spelled way of giving a name (like `PI`) to a constant (like `3.14159`), but we can explain most of what is on this line. The part

```
double PI = 3.14159;
```

simply declares `PI` as a variable and initializes it to `3.14159`. The words that precede this modify the variable `PI` in various ways. The word *public* says there are no restrictions on where you can use the name `PI`. The word *static* will have to wait until Chapter 5 for an explanation, but be sure to include it. The word *final* means the

---

Naming Constants

To define a name for a constant, such as a number, place the reserved words `public static final` in front of a variable declaration that includes the constant as the initializing value. Place this declaration within the class definition, but outside of the `main` method and outside of any other method definitions. (See Display 2.11/ page 104 for a complete example.)

Syntax:

```
public static final Type Variable = Constant;
```

Example:

```
public static final int MAX_STRIKES = 3;
public static final double MORTGAGE_INTEREST_RATE = 6.99;
public static final String MOTTO = "The customer is right!";
public static final char SCALE = 'K';
```

Although it is not required, it is the normal practice of programmers to spell named constants using all uppercase letters.

---

value `3.14159` is the *final* value assignment to `PI`, or to phrase it another way, it means that the program is not allowed to change the value of `PI`.

In Display 2.11, we have rewritten the program from Display 2.10/page 101 so that it uses the name `PI` as a defined name for the constant `3.14159`. Note that the definition of `PI` is placed outside of the `main` part of the program. As indicated there, defined names for constants need not be near the beginning of a file, but it is a good practice to place them near the beginning of the file. This is handy in case you need to change the definition of a named constant. You are not likely to want to change the definition of the named constant `PI`, but you may want to change the definition of some other named constant in some other program. For example, suppose you have a banking program that contains the defined constant

```
public static final double MORTGAGE_INTEREST_RATE = 6.99;
```

and suppose the interest rate changes to 8.5%. You can simply change the defined constants to

```
public static final double MORTGAGE_INTEREST_RATE = 8.5;
```

You would then need to recompile your program, but you need not change anything else in your program.

Note that a defined constant, like `MORTGAGE_INTEREST_RATE`, can save you a lot of work if the constant ever needs to be changed. In order to change the mortgage interest rate from 6.99% to 8.5%, you only needed to change one number. If the program did not use a defined constant, then you would have to look for every occurrence of `6.99` and change it to `8.5`. Moreover, even this might not be right. If some of the numbers `6.99` represented the mortgage interest rate and some of the numbers `6.99` represented some other kind of interest, then you would have to decide just what each `6.99` means, and that would surely produce confusion and probably introduce errors.

Notice that we have always spelled named constants using all uppercase letters

Display 2.11 Naming a Constant

```
/**************************************
 *Program to determine area of a circle.
 *Author: Jane Q. Programmer.
 *E-mail Address: janeq@somemachine.etc.etc.
 *Assignment Number: 2.
 *Last Changed: October 7, 2001.
 **************************************/
public class CircleCalculation2
{
    public static final double PI = 3.14159;

    public static void main(String[] args)
    {
        double radius; //in inches
        double area; //in square inches

        System.out.println("Enter the radius of a circle in
                inches:");
        radius = SavitchIn.readLineDouble();

        area = PI * radius * radius;

        System.out.println("A circle of radius "
                                   + radius + " inches");
        System.out.println("has an area of "
                                   + area + " square inches.");
    }

}
```

Although it would not be as clear, it is legal to place the definition of P I here instead.

Sample Screen Dialogue

```
Enter the radius of a circle in inches:
2.5
A circle of radius 2.5 inches
has an area of 19.6349375 square inches.
```

PI and `MORTGAGE_INTEREST_RATE`. This is not required by the definition of the Java language. However, this is a custom that is almost universally followed and one that it would pay for you to adopt. It helps when reading a program if you can easily tell what is a variable, what is a constant, and so forth.

? Self-Test Questions

23. What are the two kinds of comments in Java?

24. What is the output produced by the following Java code:

```
/*******************
 *Code for Exercise.
 *******************/
System.out.println("One");
//System.out.println("Two");
System.out.println("And hit it!");
```

25. Although it is kind of silly, state legislatures have been known to pass laws "changing" the value of *pi*. Suppose you live in a state where by law the value of *pi* is exactly 3.14. How must you change the program in Display 2.11/page 104 so as to make the program comply with the law on the value of *pi*?

2.5 | Windowing I/O with `JOptionPane` (Optional)

> *The game isn't over till it's over.*
>
> **Attributed to Yogi Berra**

The Java program we have seen so far in this chapter are, in at least one way, old fashioned program. When the program is run, the user enters simple text at the keyboard and simple, unadorned text is sent to the screen as output. Modern programs do not work this way. Modern programs use windowing interfaces with such features as menus and buttons that allow the user to make choices with a mouse. These modern windowing systems are called **GUIs**, which is short for Graphical User Interface. In the optional section of Chapter 1 entitled ***Preview Examples of Applets (Optional)*** we discussed applet programs, which are a kind of GUI program, but not every program that has a GUI interface is an applet. The programs we discuss in this section are not applets, but since they are GUIs, they have a number of elements in common with applets. However, you do not need to have covered the section ***Preview Examples of Applets (Optional)*** in order to cover this section.

GUI

In Chapters 12-14 you will learn to construct GUIs using a special library of classes called **Swing**. In this section we will show you just enough about Swing to let you create some very simple GUIs (windowing interfaces) for your Java application programs.

Swing

Display 2.12 A Java Program with A Windowing Interface *(Optional) (Part 1 of 2)*

```java
import javax.swing.*;

public class ASampleGUIProgram
{
    public static void main(String[] args)
    {
        String appleString;
        appleString =
            JOptionPane.showInputDialog("Enter number of apples:");
        int appleCount;
        appleCount = Integer.parseInt(appleString);

        String orangeString;
        orangeString =
            JOptionPane.showInputDialog("Enter number of oranges:");
        int orangeCount;
        orangeCount = Integer.parseInt(orangeString);

        int totalFruitCount;
        totalFruitCount = appleCount + orangeCount;

        JOptionPane.showMessageDialog(
            null, "The total number of fruits = " + totalFruitCount);

        System.exit(0);
    }
}
```

This entire section (from here to the chapter summary) is optional. The rest of this book does not depend on anything in this section.

A Simple Windowing Program

windows

Display 2.12 contains a very simple Java application program with a windowing interface. Below the program, we show the three windows produced by the program. The three windows are produced one at a time. The first window to appears is labeled Window 1 in Display 2.12. The user enters a number in the text field of the first window and then clicks the OK button with the mouse. When the user clicks the OK button, the first window goes away and the second window appears. The user handles the second window in a similar way. When the user clicks the OK button in the second

Display 2.12 A Java Program with A Windowing Interface *(Optional) (Part 2 of 2)*

Window 1

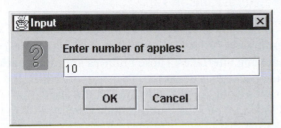

When the user clicks OK, the window goes away and the next window (if any) is displayed.

Window 2

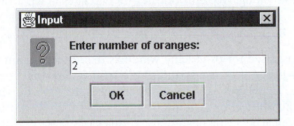

Window 3

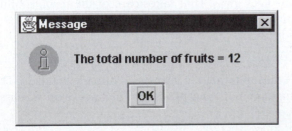

window, the second window goes away and the third window appears. Let's look at the details.

This program uses the class JOptionPane to construct the windows that interact with the user. The first line, shown next, tells the computer were to look for the definition of a class named JOptionPane:

```
import javax.swing.*;
```

You may recall that we mentioned a library called Swing which is the library of classes that we will use for windowing interfaces. These libraries are called **packages** and in a Java program, the Swing package is denoted javax.swing, with a lower case S. The previous line of code says to look for the definition of the class JOptionPane in the package named javax.swing. You must put this line at the start of any program file that uses the class JOptionPane.

The first program instruction for the computer is shown in what follows. It declares appleString to be a variable of type String.

```
String appleString;
```

The next two lines start the windowing action. The two lines are a single statement (instruction) and would normally be written on one line, except that it would make the line inconveniently long. We reproduce those two lines in what follows:

```
appleString =
    JOptionPane.showInputDialog("Enter number of apples:");
```

JOptionPane is a class used for producing windows that either obtain input or display output from your program. It is a standard predefined class that comes with every installation of Java. To make it available only requires the *import*-statement we discussed earlier in this subsection. The method showInputDialog produces a window for obtaining input. The string argument, in this case "Enter number of apples:", is written in the window to tell the user what to enter. You the programmer choose this string depending on what sort of input you want. This invocation of the method showInputDialog will produce the first window shown in Display 2.12. The user clicks her or his mouse in the text field and then types in some input. If the user does not like what she/he typed in, the user can use the backspace key to back up and retype the input. Once the user is happy with the input, the user clicks the OK button and the window goes away. That takes care of the responsibility of the user, but how does this input get to your program? Read on.

The method invocation

```
JOptionPane.showInputDialog("Enter number of apples:");
```

returns (that is, produces) the input that the user typed into the text field. The rest of the line tells where that input goes in your program. The line we are discussing:

```
appleCount = Integer.parseInt(appleString);
```

is an assignment statement that sets the value of the String variable appleCount to what is produced on the right hand side of the assignment sign (=). So, this assignment statement sets the variable appleCount so that it stores the input string that the user typed into the text field of the first window.

The following line is another variable declaration:

```
int appleCount;
```

The *int* says that the data stored in the variable `appleCount` must be an *integer*. This programer who wrote this program wants the user to enter an integer into that first input window and wants the program to store this integer in the variable `appleCount`. However, the program has recovered the input that the user types in as a string, not as a value of type *int*. Let's say the user types in 10, indicating that there are 10 apples. The user probably thinks that she/he has types in the number 10. However, what the user actually typed in was the character '1' followed by the character '0' to produce the string "10". After all, the user types in "10" using the same keyboard that the user would use to write the string "I love the numeral 10", and the 10 is typed in with the same two keys whether the 10 is meant to be part of a literal string or is meant to be what the user thinks of as a number. When using these input windows, you must be aware of the fact that all program input from the user (and all output to the user for that matter) consists of strings of characters. If you want your program to think of the input from an input window as a number, your program must convert the string, like "10", into the number, in this example 10. To computers "10" and 10 are very different thing. (In real life they are also different, but we usually ignore that difference.) "10" is a string consisting of two characters, while 10 is a number that can, for example, be added to or subtracted from another number. As we saw earlier, the string types in by the user (like "10") is stored in the variable `appleCount`. The program needs to convert the string stored in the variable `appleString` to an *int* and store the resulting *int* value in the variable `appleCount`. This is done with the next program line, which is reproduced next:

```
appleCount = Integer.parseInt(appleString);
```

Integer.
parseInt

Integer

`Integer` is a class. The part `parseInt` is a method of the class `Integer`. The method invocation `Integer.parseInt(appleString)` converts the string stored in the variable `appleString` into the corresponding integer number. For example, if the string stored in `appleString` were "10", then this method invocation would return the integer 10. The variable name, `appleCount`, and the equal sign say that this number 10 is stored in the variable `appleCount`.

The next few lines, shown in what follows, is only a very slight variation on what we have just discussed. They produce an input window that gets an input string from the user and store the corresponding integer in the variable `orangeCount`.

```
String orangeString;
orangeString =
    JOptionPane.showInputDialog("Enter number of oranges:");
int orangeCount;
orangeCount = Integer.parseInt(orangeString);
```

The window produced by the previous lines is shown as the second window in Display 2.12.

The next two lines of the program, shown in what follows, only use Java statements that you have already learned about:

```
int totalFruitCount;
totalFruitCount = appleCount + orangeCount;
```

The first of the previous two lines says that `totalFruitCount` is a variable of type `int` and the second line is an assignment statement that sets the value of `totalFruitCount` to the sum of the `int` values in the two variables `appleCount` and `orangeCount`.

output window

The program now should output the number stored in the variable `total-FruitCount`. This output is accomplished with the following:

```
JOptionPane.showMessageDialog(
    null, "The total number of fruits = " + totalFruitCount);
```

showMessage-Dialog

The part `showMessageDialog` is another method in the class `JOptionPane`. This method displays a window for showing some output. The method `JOptionPane` has two arguments, which are separated with a comma. For now the first argument will always be written as *null*. You will have to wait for an explanation of what this *null* is. Until then, you will not go too far wrong in thinking of *null* as a place holder that is being used because we do not need any "real" first argument. The second argument is easy to explain; it is the string that is written in the output window. So, the previous method invocation produces the third window shown in Display 2.12. This output window stays on the screen until the user click the OK button with the mouse, and then the window disappears.

null

Note that you can give the output string to a `JOptionPane` window in the same way that you give an output string as an argument to `System.out.println`. You can always use a variable name when we want the values stored in the variable. So, you can thing of `totalFruitCount` as standing for the integer value stored in `totalFruitCount`. Moreover, Java will automatically convert the integer value stored in `totalFruitCount` to the corresponding string. So the second argument to `showMessageDialog`, which, in the previous displayed line, is

```
"The total number of fruits = " + totalFruitCount
```

and this is a concatenation of strings. So, the second argument to `showMessageDialog` is, as it should be, a string.

System.exit

The last program statement, shown in what follows, simply says that the program should end.

```
System.exit(0);
```

`System` is a predefined Java class that is automatically provided by Java and `exit` is a method in the class `System`. The method `exit` ends the program as soon as it is invoked. In the programs that we will write, the integer argument 0 can be any integer, but by tradition we use 0, because 0 is used to indicate a normal ending of the program.

■ Gotcha

Users Who Enter Inappropriate Input

crash

A program is said to **crash** when it ends abnormally, usually because something went

JOptionPane For Windowing Input/Output *(Optional)*

You can use the methods `showInputDialog` and `showMessageDialog` to produce input and output windows for your Java programs. When using these methods, you must include the following at the start of the file that contains your program:

```
import javax.swing.*;
```

The syntax for input and output statement using these methods is given below:

Syntax: (Input)

String_Variable = JOptionPane.showInputDialog(*String_Expression*);

Example:

```
String orangeString;
orangeString = JOptionPane.showInputDialog(
                             "Enter number of oranges:");
```

The *String_Expression* is displayed in a window that has both a text field in which the user can enter input and a button labeled OK. When the user types in a string and clicks the OK button in the window, then the string that was typed in is returned by the method, and so the string typed in by the user is stored in the *String_Variable*. The window also disappears when the user clicks the OK button. Note that when input is done in this way, all input is string input. If you want the user to input, for example integers, then your program must convert the input string numeral to the equivalent number.

Syntax: (Output)

JOptionPane.showMessageDialog(*null*, *String_Expression*);

Example:

```
JOptionPane.showMessageDialog(
    null, "The total number of fruits = " + totalFruitCount);
```

The *String_Expression* is displayed in a window that has a button labeled OK. When the user clicks the OK button with the mouse, the window disappears.

wrong. When using the method JOptionPane.showInputDialog to do input (as in Display 2.12/page 106) the user must enter the input in the correct format, or else your program is likely to crash. If your program expects an integer to be entered and the user enters 2,000, then your program will crash, because, in Java, integer numerals cannot have a comma in them. (The user should enter 2000.) Later you will learn how to write more robust windowing programs that do not require that the user be so knowledgeable and careful. Until then, you have two simple alternatives to cope with input/output: Either tell the user to be very careful or else use the class SavitchIn for input. The methods in the class SavitchIn will detect if the input is in the wrong format and will ask the user to re-enter the input until the user enters it correctly.

■ Gotcha

Forgetting `System.exit(0);`

If you omit the last line

```
System.exit(0);
```

from the program in Display 2.12/page 106, then everything will work as we described. The user will give input using the input windows and the output window will show the output window. When the user clicks the `OK` button in the output window, the output window will go away, but the program will not end. The windows will all go away, but the "invisible" program is there. It will just hang there, using up computer resources and possibly keeping you from doing other things. So do not forget the `System.exit(0);` in all of your windowing programs.

But what do you do, if you forget the `System.exit(0);` and the program does not end by itself? The way that you end a program that does not end by itself depends on your particular operating system. On many systems (but not all), you can stop a program by typing control-C, which you type by holding down the control (Ctrl) key while pressing the C key.

When you write a program with a windowing interface, you always need to end the program with

```
System.exit(0);
```

If the program does not use a windowing interface, like the programs in sections 2.1 through 2.4, then you do not need the invocation `System.exit(0);`.

How Come Some Programs Need `System.exit` and Some Do Not?

A program with a windowing interface (as in Display 2.12/page 106) requires that the program end with the following method invocation:

```
System.exit(0);
```

A program that uses simple text input and output (as in the programs in sections 2.1 through 2.4) does not require this. What is the reason for this difference?

The reason that a program that uses simple text input and output *does not* need an invocation of the method `System.exit` is that Java can easily tell when the program should end; the program should end when all the statements have been executed.

The reason that a program with a windowing interface (as in Display 2.12) *does* require an invocation of the method `System.exit` is that Java cannot easily tell when a windowing program should end. Many windowing programs only end when certain buttons are clicked or certain other actions are taken, and those details are determined by the programmer not by the Java language. For the simple program we have seen so far, the program does happen to end when all the statements in the program have been executed, but for more complicated windowing programs, the end is not so easy to find, and so you must tell Java when the program ends by inserting a call to `System.exit` where the program should end.

■ Gotcha

Outputting Just a Number

In Display 2.12/page 106 the final program output was sent to an output window with the following:

```
JOptionPane.showMessageDialog(
        null,"The total number of fruits = "+totalFruitCount);
```

It is good style to always label any output. So, the string

```
"The total number of fruits = "
```

is very important to the style and understandability of the program. Moreover, the method invocation will not even compile unless you include a string in the output. For example, the following will not compile

```
JOptionPane.showMessageDialog(null, totalFruitCount);
```

The method showMessageDialog will not accept an *int* value (or any other primitive type) as its second argument. If you connect the variable or number to a string with the plus sign, then that converts the argument to a string, and so the argument will then be accepted.

? Self-Test Questions

26. In the following two lines, one identifier (word) names a class, one identifier names a method, and something is an argument. What is the class name? What is the method name? What is the argument?

```
appleString =
  JOptionPane.showInputDialog("Enter number of apples:");
```

27. Give a Java statement that will display a window on the screen with the message I Love You.

28. Give a Java statement that, when executed, will end the program.

29. What would happen if you omitted the following method invocation from the program in Display 2.12/page 106? Would the program compile? Would it run without problems?

```
System.exit(0);
```

30. Write a complete Java program that produces a window with the message Hello World!. Your program does nothing else.

31. Write a complete Java program that will do the following when run: the program displays an input window that asks the user to enter a whole number. When the user enters a whole number and clicks the OK button, the input window goes away and an output window appears. The output window simply tell the user what number she/he entered. (Hey, this is

only Chapter 2. The programs will get complicated soon enough.) When the user clicks the `OK` button in the output window, the program ends.

Inputting Other Numeric Types

You can use the method `JOptionPane.showInputDialog` to get input from the user of any of the numeric types. You use `JOptionPane.showInputDialog` in the exact same way as we used it to get whole numbers (that is, to get input of type *int*.), but if you want numbers of some type other than *int*, then you convert the input string to a number using a method other than `Integer.parseInt`. For example, the following code asks the user to input a value of type *double* and stores it in the variable decimalNumber of type *double*.

```
String numberString;
numberString = JOptionPane.showInputDialog(
                    "Enter a number with a decimal point:");
double decimalNumber;
decimalNumber = Double.parseDouble(numberString);
```

Display 2.13 lists the correct conversion method for each numeric type.

Display 2.13 Methods for Converting Strings to Numbers *(Optional)*

Type Name	Method for Converting
byte	Byte.parseByte(*String_To_Convert*)
short	Short.parseShort(*String_To_Convert*)
int	Integer.parseInt*String_To_Convert*)
long	Long.parseLong(*String_To_Convert*)
float	Float.parseFloat(*String_To_Convert*)
double	Double.parseDouble(*String_To_Convert*)

To convert a value of type `String` to a value of the type given in the first column, use the method given in the second column. Each of the methods in the second column returns a value of the type given in the first column. The *String_To_Convert* must be a correct string representation of a value of the type given in the first column. For example, to convert to an *int*, the *String_To_Convert* must be a whole number (in the range of the type *int*) that is written in the usual way without any decimal point.

Display 2.14   A Multi-Line Output Window *(Optional)*

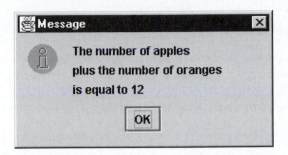

■ Java Tip

Multi-Line Output Windows

If you want to output multiple lines using the method JOptionPane.showMessa-geDialog, then you can insert the new line character '\n' into the string used as the second argument. If the string becomes too long, which it almost always does with multi-line output, then you can make each line into a separate string (ending with '\n') and connect the lines with the plus sign. If the lines are long or there are very many lines, then the window will be made larger so that it can hold all the output.

For example, consider

```
JOptionPane.showMessageDialog(null,
                    "The number of apples\n"
           + "plus the number of oranges\n"
           + "is equal to " + totalFruit);
```

The previous invocation of JOptionPane.showMessageDialog will produce the window shown in Display 2.14, provided totalFruit is a variable of type *int* whose value is 12.

Programming Example

Another Program with I/O Windows

The program in Display 2.15 uses a multi-line input window and a multi-line output window. Except for the input and output, the program is the same as the one in Display 2.5/page 76. If any of the details about calculating the numbers of coins is unclear, look back at the explanation of Display 2.5.

Display 2.15   Change Program with I/O Windows *(Optional) (Part 1 of 2)*

```java
import javax.swing.*;

public class ChangeMakerWindow
{
    public static void main(String[] args)
    {
        String amountString =
                JOptionPane.showInputDialog(
                    "Enter a whole number from 1 to 99.\n"
                  + "I will output a combination of coins\n"
                  + "that equals that amount of change.");

        int amount, originalAmount,
            quarters, dimes, nickels, pennies;

        amount = Integer.parseInt(amountString);
        originalAmount = amount;

        quarters = amount/25;
        amount = amount%25;
        dimes = amount/10;
        amount = amount%10;
        nickels = amount/5;
        amount = amount%5;
        pennies = amount;

        JOptionPane.showMessageDialog(null,
                    originalAmount
                  + " cents in coins can be given as:\n"
                  + quarters + " quarters\n"
                  + dimes + " dimes\n"
                  + nickels + " nickels and\n"
                  + pennies + " pennies");

        System.exit(0);
    }
}
```

25 goes into 87 three times with 12 left over.
87/25 is 3
87%25 is 12
87 cents is three quarters with 12 cents left over.

Do not forget that you need `System.exit` *in a program with input or output windows.*

Display 2.15 Change Program with I/O Windows *(Optional) (Part 2 of 2)*

Input Window

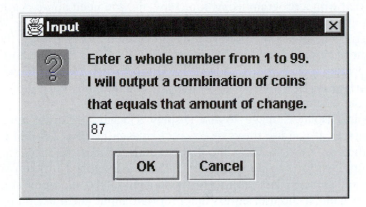

Output Window

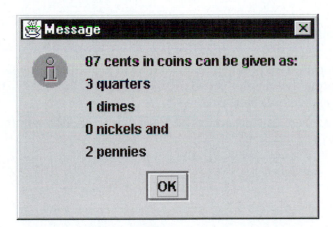

Be sure to note that both the input window and the output window display multiple lines of text.

Note that we did not forget the import statement

```
import javax.swing.*;
```

nor did we forget that with a program using `JOptionPane`, you need an invocation of the method `System.exit`. If you forget the import statement, the compiler will complain. However, if you omit the invocation of the method `System.exit`, then the compiler will not complain, but your program will not end, even after all the statements are executed and all the windows have disappeared. With windowing programs, *the game isn't over till it's over*. `System.exit` is what really ends the program, not running out of statements to execute.

The programs in Display 2.5/page 76 and Display 2.15 have different advantages and disadvantages. If you use the class `SavitchIn` as in Display 2.5, that has the disadvantage that you need to add a file that contains the class `SavitchIn`. If you use the class `JOptionPane` to do windowing I/O as in Display 2.15, then you need not explicitly add another class (although you do need to add an import statement). On the other hand, if the user enters inappropriate input (such as adding a comma to a numeral), then the program using `SavitchIn` will recover gracefully. However, the program using `JOptionPane` will crash if the user enters inappropriate input. (The program with `JOptionPane` can be made to recover gracefully from inappropriate input, but that requires some more advanced techniques that we will not get to until later in this book.)

? Self-Test Questions

32. Write a complete Java program that will read in two values of type *double* and output the sum of the two numbers. Use the class `JOptionPane` to do input and output using windows.

33. Write a Java statement that will cause a window to appear with the following text:

```
One two
Buckle my shoe.
Three four
Shut the door.
```

CHAPTER SUMMARY

- A **variable** can be used to hold values, like numbers. The type of the variable must match the type of the value stored in the variable.

CHAPTER SUMMARY

- Variables (and all other items in a program) should be given names that indicate how the variable is used.

- All variables should be initialized before the program uses their value.

- Parentheses in arithmetic expressions indicate the order in which the operations are performed.

- The methods in the class `SavitchIn` can be used to read keyboard input. The class `SavitchIn` is not part of the Java language, and so you must have a copy of `SavitchIn` in order to use it.

- Your program should output a prompt line when the user is expected to enter data from the keyboard.

- You can have variables and constants of type `String`. `String` is a class type that behaves very much like a primitive types.

- You can use the plus sign to concatenate two strings.

- There are methods in the class `String` that can be used for string processing.

- You should define names for number constants in a program and use these names rather than writing out the numbers within your program.

- Programs should be self-documenting to the extent possible. However, you should also insert comments to explain some points.

? ANSWERS to Self-Test Questions

1. `int count = 0;`
2. `double rate = 0.0, time = 0.0;`

    The following is also correct, because Java will automatically convert the *int* value 0 to the *double* value 0.0:

    `double rate = 0, time = 0;`

3.
```
int miles = 0;
double flowRate = 50.56;
```

4. `interest = 0.05 * balance;`

The following is also correct:

```
interest = balance * 0.05;
```

5. `interest = balance * rate;`

6. `count = count + 3;`

7.
```
b
c
c
```

The last output is c because the last assignment (shown in what follows) has no quotes:

```
a = b;
```

This last assignment sets the variable a equal to the value of the variable b, which is `'c'`.

8.
```
(int)symbol - (int)'0'
```

To see that this works, note that it works for `'0'`, and then see that it works for `'1'`, and then `'2'`, and so forth. You can use an actual number in place of `(int)'0'`, but this way, using `(int)'0'`, is a bit easier to understand.

9.
```
quotient = 2;
remainder = 1;
```

10. `(1/2) * 2 is equal to 0.0`

This is because `1/2` is integer division, which discards the part after the decimal point and produces `0`, instead of `0.5`.

11. The dialog would change to the following. (The only change is shown in color.)

```
Enter a whole number from 1 to 99
I will output a combination of coins
that equals that amount of change.
87
2 cents in coins can be given as:
3 quarters
1 dimes
0 nickels and
2 pennies
```

12.
```
n == 3
n == 2
```

13. How do you doSeven of Nine.
    Note that there is no space in doSeven.

14.
    ```
    7
    b
    ```

15. defg

16.
    ```
    abc
    def
    ```

17.
    ```
    System.out.println("Once upon a time,");
    System.out.println("there were three little programmers.");
    ```

    Since we did not specify where the next output goes, the following is also correct:

    ```
    System.out.println("Once upon a time,");
    System.out.print("there were three little programmers.");
    ```

18. With `System.out.println`, the next output goes on the next line. (By the next output, we mean the output that is produced by the first output statement after the `System.out.println` under discussion.) With `System.out.print`, the next output goes on the same line.

19. `amount = SavitchIn.readLineDouble();`

20. `answer = SavitchIn.readLineNonwhiteChar();`

21. The whitespace characters are the blank symbol, the tab symbol, and the new-line symbol `'\n'`. At this point you are likely to be concerned mostly with the blank symbol when discussing nonwhitespace characters.

22. The class `SavitchIn` not part of the Java language. The programmer (like you) is supposed to define the class `SavitchIn`. To get you started we have defined it for you, but think of it as a class that you defined.

23. The two kinds of comments are `//` comments and `/* */` comments. Everything following a `//` on the same line is a comment. Everything between a `/*` and a matching `*/` is a comment.

24.
    ```
    One
    And hit it!
    ```

25. Change the line

    ```
    public static final double PI = 3.14159;
    ```

    to

    ```
    public static final double PI = 3.14;
    ```

    Since values of type *double* are only stored with a limited amount of accuracy, you could argue that this is not "exactly" 3.14, but any legislator who is stupid enough to legislate the value of *pi* is unlikely to be aware of this subtlety.

26. JOptionPane is the class name, showInputDialog is the method name, and "Enter number of apples:" is the argument. The other identifier appleString is a variable name.

27. JOptionPane.showMessageDialog(*null*, "I Love You.");

28. System.exit(0);

29. The program would compile fine. The program would run and perform in the same way as if the statement were included. But, the program would hang and not end, even though all the statements had been executed.

30.

```
import javax.swing.*;

public class HelloWorldExercise
{
    public static void main(String[] args)
    {
        JOptionPane.showMessageDialog(null, "Hello World!");
        System.exit(0);
    }
}
```

31.

```
import javax.swing.*;

public class NumberExercise
{
    public static void main(String[] args)
    {
        String stringInput;
        stringInput =
            JOptionPane.showInputDialog("Enter a whole number:");

        int number;
        number = Integer.parseInt(stringInput);
        JOptionPane.showMessageDialog(
                        null, "You entered " + number);

        System.exit(0);
    }
}
```

Some details, such as identifier names, may be different in your program. Be sure you compile and run your program.

32.
```java
import javax.swing.*;

public class AddExercise
{
    public static void main(String[] args)
    {
        String numberString1 =
                JOptionPane.showInputDialog(
                    "Enter a number (decimal points OK):");
        String numberString2 =
                JOptionPane.showInputDialog(
                    "Enter another number (decimal points OK):");

        double number1 = Double.parseDouble(numberString1);
        double number2 = Double.parseDouble(numberString2);
        double sum = number1 + number2;

        JOptionPane.showMessageDialog(null, number1
                                    + " plus " + number2
                                    + " equals " + sum);

        System.exit(0);
    }
}
```

33.
```java
    JOptionPane.showMessageDialog(null, "One two\n"
                                + "Buckle my shoe.\n"
                                + "Three four\n"
                                + "Shut the door.");
```

? PROGRAMMING EXERCISES

1. Write a program that reads in three whole numbers and outputs the average of the three numbers.

2. Write a program that reads in the amount of a monthly mortgage payment, the outstanding balance (that is, the amount still owed), and that outputs the amount of the payment that goes to interest and the amount that goes to principal (that is, the amount that goes to reducing the debt). Assume the annual interest rate is 6.79%. Use a defined constant for the interest rate. Note that payments are made monthly, so the interest is only one-twelfth of the annual interest of 6.79%.

3. Write a program that reads in a four digit number (like 1998) and that outputs the number one digit per line, like so:

```
1
9
9
8
```

Your prompt should tell the user to enter a four-digit number and can then assume that the user follows directions. Your program will not read the number as a value of type *int*, but as four characters of type *char*.

4. Write a program that reads in a line of text and then outputs that line of text with the first occurrence of "hate" changed to "love". For example, a possible sample dialog might be

```
Enter a line of text.
I hate you.
I have rephrased that line to read:
I love you.
```

You can assume that the word "hate" occurs in the input. If the word "hate" occurs more than once in the line, then your program will only replace the first occurrence of "hate".

5. Write a program that will read a line of text as input and then output the line with the first word moved to the end of the line. For example, a possible sample dialog might be

```
Enter a line of text. No punctuation please.
Java is the language
I have rephrased that line to read:
Is the language Java
```

Assume that there is no space before the first word and that the end of the first word is indicated by a blank (not by a comma or other punctuation).

6. Write a program that will print out statistics for eight coin tosses. The user will input either an 'h' for heads or 't' for tails for eight tosses, then the program will print out the total number and percentages of heads and tails. Use the increment operator to count each 'h' and 't' input. For example, a possible sample dialog (with user input in bold) might be

```
For each coin toss enter either 'h' for heads
or 't' for tails.

First toss: h
Second toss: t
Third toss: t
Fourth toss: h
Fifth toss: t
Sixth toss: h
Seventh toss: t
Eighth toss: t

Number of heads: 3
Number of tails: 5
Percent heads: 37.5
Percent tails: 62.5
```

7. Write a program that asks the user to enter the first name of a friend or relative, a favorite color, a favorite food, and a favorite animal, then print the following two lines with the user's input replacing the items in italics:

I had a dream that *name* ate a *color animal*

and said it tasted like *food*!

For example, if the user entered Jake for the person's name, blue for the color, hamburger for the food, and dog for the animal, the output would be

```
I had a dream that Jake ate a blue dog
and said it tasted like hamburger!
```

Don't forget to put the exclamation mark at the end.

8. Write a program that converts degrees Celsius to Fahrenheit using the formula

degreesC = 5(*degreesF* − 32)/9

Prompt the user to enter a temperature in degrees Fahrenheit (just a whole number of degrees, without a fractional part) and print out the equivalent Celsius temperature including the fractional part to at least one decimal point. A possible dialog might be

```
Enter a temperature in degrees Fahrenheit: 72
72 degrees Fahrenheit = 22.2 degrees Celsius.
```

9. Write a program that determines the change to be dispensed from a vending machine. An item in the machine can cost anywhere between 25 cents and a dollar, in 5 cent increments (25, 30, 35, ..., 90, 95, or100), and accepts only a single dollar bill to pay for the item. For example, a possible sample dialog might be

```
Enter price of item
(from 25 cents to a dollar, in 5-cent increments): 45

You bought an item for 45 cents and gave me a dollar,
so your change is
2 quarters,
0 dimes, and
1 nickel.
```

10. Modify the program in Display 2.12/page 106 so that, in addition to the two input windows shown as the first two windows in Display 2.12, the program produces three output windows. One output window will tell the number of apples, a second output window tells the number of oranges, and the third output window is the same as the third window shown in Display 2.12.

11. Modify the Java program in Display 2.12/page 106 so that it has two input windows and one output window. One input window is for the number of apples and the other for the price per apple in clams, a fictional monetary unit in the comic strip "BC." The output window will display the total cost in clams by multiplying the number of apples by the cost per apple. Java uses the symbol * to indicate multiplication. For example, the following Java statement multiplies `appleCount` and `clamsPerApple` to get `totalNumberOfClams`:

```
totalNumberOfClams = appleCount * clamsPerApple;
```

12. Modify the program you wrote for Programming Exercise 11 so that it has four input windows and three output windows. Two input windows are the same: the number of apples and the cost per apple (in clams). Add two input windows for the number of oranges and the price per orange (in clams, too, of course). The first output window will be the same as in Programming Exercise 11: it will display the cost of the apples. The second output window will display the cost of the oranges (the product of the number of oranges and the cost per orange), and the third output window will display the total cost for both the apples and the oranges.

CHAPTER 3

FLOW OF CONTROL

3.1   BRANCHING STATEMENTS 128
The *if-else*-Statement 129
Introduction to Boolean
    Expressions 131
Gotcha Using == with Strings 135

Programming Tip Alphabetical
    Order 136
Nested Statements and Compound
    Statements 140
Java Tip Matching *else*'s and
    if's 141
Multibranch *if-else*-
    Statements 143
Programming Example Assigning Letter
    Grades 145
The *switch*-statement 148
Gotcha Omitting a *break*-
    Statement 150
The Conditional Operator
    (*Optional*) 152

3.2   JAVA LOOP STATEMENTS 154
while-Statements 155
Java Tip A *while*-Loop Can Perform
    Zero Iterations 157
The *do-while*-Statement 159
Programming Example
    Bug Infestation 161
Gotcha Infinite Loops 165
The *for*-Statement 167
The Comma in *for*-Statements
    (*Optional*) 168

Gotcha Extra Semicolon in a Loop
    Statement 172
Java Tip Choosing a Loop
    Statement 174
The *break*-Statement in Loops 175
Gotcha Misuse of *break*-
    Statements 175
The *exit* Method 176

3.3   PROGRAMMING WITH LOOPS 177
The Loop Body 179
Initializing Statements 180
Ending a Loop 181
Programming Tip Do Not Declare
    Variables in a Loop Body 183
Programming Example Nested Loops 183
Loop Bugs 186
Tracing Variables 188

3.4   THE TYPE *boolean* 189
Boolean Expressions and Boolean
    Variables 190
Programming Tip Naming Boolean
    Variables 191
Precedence Rules 191
Input and Output of Boolean
    Values 195
Case Study Using a Boolean Variable
    to End a Loop 196

Chapter Summary 199
Answers to Self-Test Questions 200
Programming Exercises 204

3

FLOW OF CONTROL

> *"Would you tell me, please, which*
> *way I ought to go from here?"*
> *"That depends a good deal on where*
> *you want to get to," said the Cat.*
>
> **Lewis Carroll, Alice in Wonderland**

flow of control

**branching
statement**

loop statement

Flow **of control** is the order in which a program performs actions. Until this chapter, that order has been simple. Actions were taken in the order in which they were written down. In this chapter, we show you how to write programs with a more complicated flow of control. Java, and most other programming languages, uses two kinds of statements to produce this more complicated flow of control: A **branching statement** chooses one action from a list of two or more possible actions. A **loop statement** repeats an action again and again until some stopping condition is met.

Objectives

Learn about Java branching statements.

Learn about loops.

Learn about the type `boolean`.

Prerequisites

You need to be familiar with all the material in Chapter 2, except for Section 2.4, before reading this chapter. You do not need to read Section 2.4 of Chapter 2, which covers windowing I/O, before reading this chapter.

3.1 | Branching Statements

> *When you come to a fork in the road, take it.*
>
> **Attributed to Yogi Berra**

The most basic branching statement in Java chooses between two possible alternative actions. We begin our discussion with this basic kind of Java statement.

The *if-else*-Statement

if-else

In programs, as in everyday life, things can sometimes go in one of two different ways. With some checking accounts, if you have money in your checking account, the bank will pay you a little interest. On the other hand, if you have overdrawn your checking account so your account balance is negative, then you will be charged a penalty that will make your balance more negative. This might be reflected in the bank's accounting program by the following Java statement, known as an *if-else*-statement:

```
if (balance >= 0)
    balance = balance + (INTEREST_RATE * balance)/12;
else
    balance = balance - OVERDRAWN_PENALTY;
```

The two symbols >= are used for greater-than-or-equal-to in Java, because the symbol $\geq$ is not on the keyboard.

The meaning of an *if-else*-statement is really just the meaning it would have if read as an English sentence. When your program executes an *if-else*-statement, it first checks the expression in parentheses after the *if*. This expression must be something that is either true or false. If it is true, then the statement before the *else* is executed. If the expression is false, then the statement after the *else* is executed. In the preceding example, if balance is positive (or zero), then the following action is taken. (The division by 12 is because this is for only one of twelve months.)

```
balance = balance + (INTEREST_RATE * balance)/12;
```

On the other hand, if the value of balance is negative, the following is done instead:

```
balance = balance - OVERDRAWN_PENALTY;
```

Display 3.1 shows this *if-else*-statement in a complete program.

If you want to include more than one statement in each branch, then simply enclose the statements in curly brackets, as in the following example:

```
if (balance >= 0)
{
    System.out.println("Good for you. You earned interest.");
    balance = balance + (INTEREST_RATE * balance)/12;
}
else
{
    System.out.println("You will be charged a penalty.");
    balance = balance - OVERDRAWN_PENALTY;
}
```

If you omit the *else* part, then when the expression after the *if* is false, nothing happens. For example, if your bank does not charge any overdraft penalty, then the statement in their program would be the following, instead of the preceding one:

else is optional

Display 3.1   A Program Using *if-else*

```
public class BankBalance
{
    public static final double OVERDRAWN_PENALTY = 8.00;
    public static final double INTEREST_RATE = 0.02;//2% annually

    public static void main(String[] args)
    {
        double balance;

        System.out.print("Enter your checking account balance: $");
        balance = SavitchIn.readLineDouble();
        System.out.println("Original balance $" + balance);

        if (balance >= 0)
            balance = balance + (INTEREST_RATE * balance)/12;
        else
            balance = balance - OVERDRAWN_PENALTY;

        System.out.println("After adjusting for one month");
        System.out.println("of interest and penalties,");
        System.out.println("your new balance is $" + balance);
    }
}
```

Sample Screen Dialogue 1

```
Enter your checking account balance: $505.67
Original balance $505.67
After adjusting for one month
of interest and penalties,
your new balance is $506.51278
```

Sample Screen Dialogue 2

```
Enter your checking account balance: $-15.53
Original balance $-15.53
After adjusting for one month
of interest and penalties,
your new balance is $-23.53
```

```
if (balance >= 0)
{
    System.out.println("Good for you. You earned interest.");
    balance = balance + (INTEREST_RATE * balance)/12;
}
```

To see how this statement works, let's give it a little more context by adding some additional statements, as shown in what follows:

```
System.out.print("Enter your balance $");
balance = SavitchIn.readLineDouble();
if (balance >= 0)
{
    System.out.println("Good for you. You earned interest.");
    balance = balance + (INTEREST_RATE * balance)/12;
}
System.out.println("Your new balance is $" + balance);
```

Now, suppose your checking account balance is $100.00. Then, the dialog would be

```
Enter your balance $100.00
Good for you. You earned interest.
Your new balance is $100.16
```

The expression after the *if* is true, so you earn a little interest. (We are using an interest rate of 2% per year as in Display 3.1, but all you need to note is that some interest was added. The exact amount is irrelevant to this example.)

Next, suppose your balance is $–50.00 (that is, minus 50 dollars). The dialog would then be as follows:

```
Enter your balance $–50.00
Your new balance is $–50.00
```

In this case, the expression after the *if* is false and there is no *else* part, so nothing happens, the balance is not changed, and the program simply goes on to the next statement, which is an output statement.

Introduction to Boolean Expressions

A **boolean expression** is simply an expression that is either true or false. The name *boolean* is derived from George Boole, a nineteenth-century English logician and mathematician whose work was related to these kinds of expressions.

boolean expression

We have already been using simple boolean expressions in *if-else*-statements. The simplest boolean expressions are comparisons of two things, such as numbers, variables, or other expressions, such as

```
time < limit
```

and

```
balance <= 0
```

if-else-Statements

The *Boolean_Expression* referred to in the following is an expression that is either true or false, such as `balance <= 0`.

Syntax Template (Basic Form):

```
if (Boolean_Expression)
    Statement_1
else
    Statement_2
```

If the *Boolean_Expression* is true, then *Statement_1* is executed; otherwise, *Statement_2* is executed.

Example:

```
if (time < limit)
    System.out.println("You made it");
else
    System.out.println("You missed the deadline.");
```

Syntax Template (Omitting the *else*-Part):

```
if (Boolean_Expression)
    Action_Statement
```

If the *Boolean_Expression* is true, then the *Action_Statement* is executed; otherwise, nothing happens and the program goes on to the next statement.

Example:

```
if (weight > ideal)
    calorieAllotment = calorieAllotment - 500;
```

Multistatement Alternatives:

If you want to include several statements as an alternative, then group the statements using curly brackets as in the following example:

```
if (balance >= 0)
{
    System.out.println("Good for you. You earned interest.");
    balance = balance + (INTEREST_RATE * balance)/12;
}
else
{
    System.out.println("You will be charged a penalty.");
    balance = balance - OVERDRAWN_PENALTY;
}
```

Note that a boolean expression need not be enclosed in parentheses to qualify as a boolean expression. However, within an *if-else*-statement, and with most other Java statements, a boolean expression does need to be enclosed in parentheses.

Display 3.2 shows the various Java comparison operators you can use to compare two expressions.

Display 3.2   Java Comparison Operators

Math Notation	Name	Java Notation	Java Examples
$=$	Equal to	$==$	balance == 0 answer == 'y'
$\neq$	Not equal to	!=	income != tax answer != 'y'
$>$	Greater than	$>$	expenses > income
$\geq$	Greater than or equal to	>=	points >= 60
$<$	Less than	$<$	pressure < max
$\leq$	Less than or equal to	<=	expenses <= income

Often, when you write an *if-else*-statement, you will want to use a boolean expression more complicated than a simple comparison. You can form more complicated boolean expressions from simpler ones, by joining the expression with the Java version of "and." The Java version of "and" is spelled &&. For example, consider the following:

&& for "and"

```
if ((pressure > min) && (pressure < max))
    System.out.println("Pressure is OK.");
else
    System.out.println("Warning: Pressure is out of range.");
```

If the value of pressure is greater than min, *and* the value of pressure is less than max, then the output will be

```
Pressure is OK.
```

Otherwise, the output is

```
Warning: Pressure is out of range.
```

Note that you *cannot* use a string of inequalities in Java, like the following

```
min < pressure < max
```

You must express each inequality separately and connect them with &&, as follows:

```
(pressure > min) && (pressure < max)
```

When you form a larger boolean expression by connecting two smaller expression with &&, the entire larger expression is true provided that both of the smaller expressions are true. If at least one of the smaller expressions is false, then the larger expression is false. For example,

```
(pressure > min) && (pressure < max)
```

is true provided that both (pressure > min) and (pressure < max) are true; otherwise, the expression is false.

Use && for "and"

The symbol pair && is the way that you spell "and" in Java. Using &&, you can form a larger boolean expression out of two smaller boolean expressions.

Syntax:

```
(Sub_Expression_1) && (Sub_Expression_2)
```

Example:

```
if ((pressure > min) && (pressure < max))
    System.out.println("Pressure is OK.");
else
    System.out.println("Warning: Pressure is out of range.");
```

|| for "or"

The Java way of spelling "or" is ||. The symbolism || is two vertical lines. (The symbol | prints with a break in the line on some systems.) You can form a larger boolean expression from smaller ones using || in the same way that you do using &&, but the meaning of the expression is different when you use ||. The meaning is essentially the same as the English word "or." For example, consider

```
if ((salary > expenses) || (savings > expenses))
    System.out.println("Solvent");
else
    System.out.println("Bankrupt");
```

If the value of salary is greater than the value of expenses or the value of savings is greater than the value of expenses (or both), then the output will be Solvent; otherwise, the output will be Bankrupt.

parentheses   The boolean expression in an *if-else*-statement must be enclosed in parentheses. An *if-else*-statement that uses the && operator is normally parenthesized as follows:

```java
if ((pressure > min) && (pressure < max))
    System.out.println("Pressure is OK.");
else
    System.out.println("Warning: Pressure is out of range.");
```

The parentheses in (pressure > min) and the parentheses in (pressure < max) are not required, but we will normally include them.

Parentheses are used in expressions using || in the same way as they are used with &&.

Use || for "or"

The symbol pair || is the way that you spell "or" in Java. Using ||, you can form a larger boolean expression out of two smaller boolean expressions.

Syntax::

(*Sub_Expression_1*) || (*Sub_Expression_2*)

Example:

```java
if ((salary > expenses) || (savings > expenses))
    System.out.println("Solvent");
else
    System.out.println("Bankrupt");
```

In Java, you can negate a boolean expression with !. For example,

```java
if (!(number >= min))
    System.out.println("Too small");
else
    System.out.println("OK");
```

This will output Too Small if number is not greater than or equal to min, and OK otherwise.

You normally can, and should, avoid using !. For example, the previous *if-else*-statement is equivalent to

```java
if (number < min)
    System.out.println("Too small");
else
    System.out.println("OK");
```

If you avoid using !, your programs will be easier to understand.

■ Gotcha
Using == with Strings

Although == does correctly test two values of a primitive type, such as two numbers, to see if they are equal, it has a different meaning when applied to objects.[1] Recall that an object is something that is a member of a class, such as a string. All strings are in the class String, and so == applied to two strings does not test to see whether the strings are equal. To test two strings (or any two objects) to see if they have equal values, you should use the method `equals` rather than `==`.

The program in Display 3.3 illustrates the use of the method `equals` as well as the `String` method `equalsIgnoreCase`. The notation may seem a bit awkward at first, because it is not symmetric between the two things being tested for equality. The two expressions

```
s1.equals(s2)
s2.equals(s1)
```

are equivalent.

The method `equalsIgnoreCase` behaves similarly to `equals`, except that with `equalsIgnoreCase` the upper- and lowercase versions of the same letter are considered the same. For example, `"Hello"` and `"hello"` are not equal because their first characters, `'H'` and `'h'`, are different characters. But they would be considered equal by the method `equalsIgnoreCase`. For example, the following will output `Equal`:

```
if ("Hello".equalsIgnoreCase("hello"))
    System.out.println("Equal");
```

Notice that it is perfectly legal to use a quoted string with a `String` method, such as the preceding use of `equalsIgnoreCase`. A quoted string is an object of type `String` and has all the methods that any other object of type `String` has.

For the kinds of applications we are looking at in this chapter, you could use `==` to test for equality of objects of type `String`, and it would deliver the correct answer. However, there are situations in which `==` does not correctly test strings for equality, and so you should get in the habit of using `equals` rather than `==` to test strings to see if they are equal.

■ Programming Tip
Alphabetical Order

Programs frequently need to compare two strings to determine which is alphabetically before the other. There is no built in Java comparison operator for alphabetic order, but it is easy to test for alphabetic order using the two `String` methods, `compareTo` and `toUpperCase`, which we described in Display 2.6/page 82.

lexicographic
ordering

The method `compareTo` will test two strings to determine their lexicographic order. **Lexicographic ordering** is similar to alphabetic ordering, and is sometimes, but not always, the same as alphabetic ordering. The easiest way to think about lexicographic ordering is to think of it as being the same as alphabetic ordering *but with the alphabet ordered differently.* Specifically, in lexicographic ordering, the letters and other characters are ordered as in the ASCII ordering, which is shown in Appendix 3. If you look at that appendix, you will see that *all* uppercase letters

---

1. When applied to two strings (or any two objects), `==` tests to see if they are stored in the same memory location, but we will not discuss that until Chapter 4. For now, we need only note that `==` does something other than test for the equality of two strings.

Display 3.3   Testing Strings for Equality

```java
public class StringEqualityDemo
{
    public static void main(String[] args)
    {
        String s1, s2;

        System.out.println("Enter two lines of text:");
        s1 = SavitchIn.readLine();
        s2 = SavitchIn.readLine();

        if (s1.equals(s2))
            System.out.println("The two lines are equal.");
        else
            System.out.println("The two lines are not equal.");

        if (s2.equals(s1))
            System.out.println("The two lines are equal.");
        else
            System.out.println("The two lines are not equal.");

        if (s1.equalsIgnoreCase(s2))
            System.out.println("But, the lines are equal ignoring case.");
        else
            System.out.println("Lines are not equal even ignoring case.");
    }
}
```

These two invocations of the method `equals` are equivalent.

Sample Screen Dialogue

```
Enter two lines of text:
The truth is out there.
The TRUTH is out THERE.
The two lines are not equal.
The two lines are not equal.
But, the lines are equal ignoring case.
```

The Methods equals and equalsIgnoreCase

When testing strings for equality, do not use ==. Instead, use either equals or equalsIgnoreCase.

Syntax:

String.equals(*Other_String*)

String.equalsIgnoreCase(*Other_String*)

Example:

```
String s1;
s1 = SavitchIn.readLine();
if ( s1.equals("Hello") )
    System.out.println("The string is Hello.");
else
    System.out.println("The string is not Hello.");
```

---

come before *all* lowercase letters. For example, 'Z' comes before 'a' in lexicographic order. So when comparing two strings consisting of a mix of lowercase and uppercase letters, lexicographic and alphabetic ordering are not the same. However, in Appendix 3 all the lowercase letters are in alphabetic order. So for any two strings of all lowercase letters, lexicographic order is the same as ordinary alphabetic order. Similarly in the ordering of Appendix 3, all the uppercase letters are in alphabetic order. So for any two strings of all uppercase letters, lexicographic order is the same as ordinary alphabetic order. Thus, to compare two strings of letters for (ordinary) alphabetic order, you need only convert the two strings to all uppercase letters (or to all lowercase letters) and then compare them for lexicographic ordering. Let's look at the Java details.

If s1 and s2 are two variables of type String that have been given String values, then

```
s1.compareTo(s2)
```

returns a negative number if s1 comes before s2 in lexicographic ordering, returns 0 if the two strings are equal, and returns a positive number if s2 comes before s2,
   Thus,

```
s1.compareTo(s2) < 0
```

returns true if s1 comes before s2 in lexicographic order, and returns false otherwise. For example, the following will produce correct output:

```
if (s1.compareTo(s2) < 0)
    System.out.println(
            s1 + " precedes " + s2 + " in lexicographic ordering");
else if (s1.compareTo(s2) > 0)
    System.out.println(
            s1 + " follows " + s2 + " in lexicographic ordering,");
else //s1.compareTo(s2) == 0
    System.out.println(s1 + " equals " + s2);
```

Lexicographic ordering is not always the same as alphabetic ordering, but it is the same provided both strings are all uppercase (or all lowercase). Thus, if the strings s1 and s2 consist entirely of letters, then one way to test them for alphabetic ordering is to convert them each to all uppercase letters and then use compareTo to test the uppercase versions of s1 and s2 for lexicographic ordering. Thus, the following will produce correct output:

```
String upperS1 = s1.toUpperCase();
String upperS2 = s2.toUpperCase();

if (upperS1.compareTo(upperS2) < 0)
    System.out.println(
        s1 + " precedes " + s2 + " in ALPHABETIC ordering");
else if (upperS1.compareTo(upperS2) > 0)
    System.out.println(
        s1 + " follows " + s2 + " in ALPHABETIC ordering,");
else //s1.compareTo(s2) == 0
    System.out.println(s1 + " equals " + s2 + " IGNORING CASE");
```

The above code will compile and produce results no matter what characters are in the strings s1 and s2. However, alphabetic order only makes sense, and the output only makes sense, if the two strings consist entirely of letters.

? Self-Test Questions

1. Suppose goals is a variable of type *int*. Write an *if-else*-statement that outputs the word Wow if the value of the variable goals is greater than 10 and the words Oh Well if the value of goals is at most 10.

2. Suppose goals and errors are variables of type *int*. Write an *if-else*-statement that outputs the word Wow if the value of the variable goals is greater than 10 and the value of errors is zero. Otherwise, the *if-else*-statement outputs the words Oh Well.

3. Suppose salary and deductions are variables of type *double* that have been given values. Write an *if-else*-statement that outputs OK and sets the variable net equal to salary minus deductions, provided that salary is at least as large as deductions. If, however, salary is less than deductions, the *if-else*-statement simply outputs the word Crazy, and does not change the value of any variables.

4. Suppose speed and visibility are variables of type *int*. Write an *if-else*-statement that sets the variable speed equal to 25 and outputs the word Caution, provided the value of speed is greater than 25 and the value of visibility is under 20. There is no *else* part.

5. Suppose salary and bonus are variables of type *double*. Write an *if-else*-statement that outputs the word OK provided salary is greater than or equal to MIN_SALARY or bonus is greater than or equal to MIN_BONUS and outputs Too low otherwise. MIN_SALARY and MIN_BONUS are named constants.

6. Assume `nextWord` is a `String` variable that has been given a `String` value consisting entirely of letters. Write some Java code that will output the message `"First half of the alphabet"`, provided `nextWord` precedes `"N"` in alphabetic ordering and will output `"Second half of the alphabet"`, if `nextWord` does not precedes `"N"` in alphabetic ordering. (Note that `"N"` uses double quotes to produce a `String` value, as opposed to using single quotes to produce a *char* value.)

Nested Statements and Compound Statements

Notice that an *if-else*-statement contains two smaller statements within it. For example, consider the statement

```
if (balance >= 0)
    balance = balance + (INTEREST_RATE * balance)/12;
else
    balance = balance - OVERDRAWN_PENALTY;
```

This statement contains within it the following two smaller statements:

```
balance = balance + (INTEREST_RATE * balance)/12;
balance = balance - OVERDRAWN_PENALTY;
```

indenting

Note that these smaller statements are indented one more level than the *if* and the *else*.

An *if-else*-statement can contain any sort of statements within it. In particular, you can use one *if-else*-statement within another *if-else*-statement, as illustrated by the following:

```
if (balance >= 0)
    if (INTEREST_RATE >= 0)
        balance = balance + (INTEREST_RATE * balance)/12;
    else
        System.out.println("Cannot have a negative interest.");
else
    balance = balance - OVERDRAWN_PENALTY;
```

If the value of `balance` is greater than or equal to 0, then the entire following *if-else*-statement is executed:

```
if (INTEREST_RATE >= 0)
    balance = balance + (INTEREST_RATE * balance)/12;
else
    System.out.println("Cannot have a negative interest.");
```

Later in this chapter, we will discuss the most common way of using *if-else*-statements nested within an *if-else*-statement.

Another simple but useful, way of nesting smaller statements within a larger statement is to place a list of statements in curly brackets { }. When you enclose a list of statements within curly brackets, they are considered to be one larger statement. So, the following is one large statement that has two smaller statements inside of it:

```
{
    System.out.println("Good for you. You earned interest.");
    balance = balance + (INTEREST_RATE * balance)/12;
}
```

These statements formed by enclosing a list of statements within curly brackets are called **compound statements**. They are seldom used by themselves, but are often used as substatements of larger statements such as *if-else*-statements. The preceding compound statement might occur in an *if-else*-statement such as the following:

compound statement

```
if (balance >= 0)
{
    System.out.println("Good for you. You earned interest.");
    balance = balance + (INTEREST_RATE * balance)/12;
}
else
{
    System.out.println("You will be charged a penalty.");
    balance = balance — OVERDRAWN_PENALTY;
}
```

Notice that compound statements can simplify our description of an *if-else*-statement. Once you know about compound statements, we can say that every *if-else*-statement is of the form

```
if (Boolean_Expression)
    Statement_1
else
    Statement_2
```

If you want one branch to contain several statements instead of just one statement, use a compound statement, as shown in the preceding example of an *if-else*-statement that deals with a bank balance That compound statement is technically speaking just one statement, so each branch of the *if-else*-statement is technically speaking a single statement. (This turns out to be a big help to compiler writers and others working with programming languages, because it simplifies the definition of the language.)

■ **Java Tip**

Matching *else*'s and *if*'s

When writing nested *if-else*-statements, you may sometimes become confused about which *if* goes with which *else*. To eliminate this confusion, you can use curly brackets like parentheses to group things.

For example, consider the following nested statement that we used earlier in this chapter:

```
if (balance >= 0)
    if (INTEREST_RATE >= 0)
        balance = balance + (INTEREST_RATE * balance)/12;
    else
        System.out.println("Cannot have a negative interest.");
else
    balance = balance - OVERDRAWN_PENALTY;
```

This statement can be made clearer with the addition of curly brackets as follows:

```
if (balance >= 0)
{
    if (INTEREST_RATE >= 0)
        balance = balance + (INTEREST_RATE * balance)/12;
    else
        System.out.println("Cannot have a negative interest.");
}
else
    balance = balance - OVERDRAWN_PENALTY;
```

In the previous case, the curly brackets were an aid to clarity but were not, strictly speaking, needed. In other cases, they are needed. If we omit an *else*, then things get a bit trickier. The following two statements differ only in that one has a pair of curly brackets, but they do not have the same meaning:

```
//First Version
if (balance >= 0)
{
    if (INTEREST_RATE >= 0)
        balance = balance + (INTEREST_RATE * balance)/12;
}
else
    balance = balance - OVERDRAWN_PENALTY;
```

and

```
//Second Version
if (balance >= 0)
    if (INTEREST_RATE >= 0)
        balance = balance + (INTEREST_RATE * balance)/12;
else
    balance = balance - OVERDRAWN_PENALTY;
```

In an *if-else*-statement, each *else* is paired with the nearest unmatched *if*. Thus, in the *Second Version* (the one without curly brackets), the *else* is paired with the second *if*, so the meaning is

```
//Equivalent to Second Version
if (balance >= 0)
{
    if (INTEREST_RATE >= 0)
        balance = balance + (INTEREST_RATE * balance)/12;
    else
        balance = balance - OVERDRAWN_PENALTY;
}
```

To clarify the difference a bit more, consider what happens when `balance` is greater than or equal to zero. In the *First Version*, this causes the following action:

```
if (INTEREST_RATE >= 0)
    balance = balance + (INTEREST_RATE * balance)/12;
```

If `balance` is not greater than or equal to zero in the *First Version*, then the following action is taken instead:

```
balance = balance - OVERDRAWN_PENALTY;
```

In the *Second Version*, if `balance` is greater than or equal to zero, then the following entire *if-else*-statement is executed:

```
if (INTEREST_RATE >= 0)
    balance = balance + (INTEREST_RATE * balance)/12;
else
    balance = balance - OVERDRAWN_PENALTY;
```

If `balance` is not greater than or equal to zero in the *Second Version*, then no action is taken.

Multibranch *if-else*-Statements

If you have the ability to branch two ways, then you have the ability to branch four ways. Just branch two ways and have each of those two outcomes branch two ways. Using this trick, you can use nested *if-else*-statements to produce multi-way branches that branch into any number of possibilities. There is a standard way of doing this. In fact, it has become so standard that it is treated as if it were a new kind of branching statement rather than just a nested statement made up of a lot of nested *if-else*-statements. Let's start with an example.

Suppose `balance` is a variable that holds your checking account balance and you want to know whether your balance is positive, negative (overdrawn), or zero. (To avoid any questions about accuracy, let's assume that `balance` is of type *int*. To be specific, let's say `balance` is the number of dollars in your account, with the cents ignored.) To find out if your balance is positive, negative, or zero, you could use the following nested *if-else*-statement:

```
if (balance > 0)
    System.out.println("Positive balance");
else if (balance < 0)
    System.out.println("Negative balance");
else if (balance == 0)
    System.out.println("Zero balance");
```

indenting

First, note the way we have indented this statement. This is the preferred way of indenting a multibranch *if-else*-statement. This is really an ordinary nested *if-else*-statement, but the way we have indented it reflects the way we think about these multibranch *if-else*-statements.

When a multibranch *if-else*-statement is executed, the computer tests the boolean expressions one after the other, starting from the top. When the first true boolean expression is found, the statement following that true boolean expression is executed. For example, if `balance` is greater than zero, then the preceding will output `"Positive balance"`. If `balance` is less than zero, then `"Negative balance"` will be output. If `balance` is equal to zero, then `"Zero balance"` will be output. Exactly one of the three possible outputs will be produced depending on the value of the variable `balance`.

In this first example, we had three possibilities, but you can have any number of possibilities; just add more *else-if*-parts if there are more possibilities.

In this first example, the possibilities were mutually exclusive. However, you can use any boolean expressions, even if they are not mutually exclusive. If more than one boolean expression is true, then only the action associated with the first boolean expression is executed. A multibranch *if-else*-statement never performs more than one action.

default case

If none of the boolean expressions are true, then nothing happens. However, it is a good practice to add an *else* clause (without any *if*) at the end, so that the *else* clause will be executed in case none of the boolean expressions is true. In fact, we can rewrite our original example (about a checking account balance) in this way. We know that if `balance` is neither positive nor negative, then it must be zero. So we do not need the test

```
if (balance == 0)
```

Our preceding multibranch *if-else*-statement is equivalent to the following:

```
if (balance > 0)
    System.out.println("Positive balance");
else if (balance < 0)
    System.out.println("Negative balance");
else
    System.out.println("Zero balance");
```

Multibranch `if-else`-Statement

Syntax:

```
if (Boolean_Expression_1)
    Action_1
else if (Boolean_Expression_2)
    Action_2
        .
        .
        .
else if (Boolean_Expression_n)
    Action_n
else
    Default_Action
```

Example:

```
if (number < 10)
    System.out.println("number < 10");
else if (number < 50)
    System.out.println("number >= 10 and number < 50");
else if (number < 100)
    System.out.println("number >= 50 and number < 100");
else
    System.out.println("number >= 100.");
```

The *Actions* are Java statements. The boolean expressions are tested one after the other starting from the top one. When the first true boolean expression is found, the action following that true boolean expression is executed. The *Default_Action* is executed if none of the boolean expressions are true.

Programming Example
Assigning Letter Grades

Display 3.4 contains a program that assigns letter grades according to the traditional rule that 90 or above is an A, 80 or above (up to 90) is a B, and so forth.

Note that, as with any multibranch `if-else`-statement, the boolean expressions are checked in order, and so the second boolean expression is not checked unless the first boolean expression is false. Thus, when and if the second boolean expression is checked, we know that the first boolean expression is false and so we know that `score` < 90. Thus, the multibranch `if-else`-statement would have the same meaning if we replaced

```
(score >= 80)
```

with

```
((score >= 80) && (score < 90))
```

Using the same sort of reasoning on each boolean expression, we see that the multibranch `if-else`-statement in Display 3.4 is equivalent to the following:

Display 3.4 Multibranch *if-else*-Statement

....

```
public class Grader
{
    public static void main(String[] args)
    {
        int score;
        char grade;

        System.out.println("Enter your score: ");
        score = SavitchIn.readLineInt();


        if (score >= 90)
            grade = 'A';
        else if (score >= 80)
            grade = 'B';
        else if (score >= 70)
            grade = 'C';
        else if (score >= 60)
            grade = 'D';
        else
            grade = 'F';


        System.out.println("Score = " + score);
        System.out.println("Grade = " + grade);
    }
}
```

Sample Screen Dialogue

```
Enter your score:
85
Score = 85
Grade = B
```

....

```
if (score >= 90)
    grade = 'A';
else if ((score >= 80) && (score < 90))
    grade = 'B';
else if ((score >= 70) && (score < 80))
    grade = 'C';
else if ((score >= 60) && (score < 70))
    grade = 'D';
else
    grade = 'F';
```

Most programmers would use the version in Display 3.4, because it is a bit more efficient, and it is more elegant, but either version is acceptable.

? Self-Test Questions

7. What output will be produced by the following code?

```
int time = 2, tide = 3;
if (time + tide > 6)
    System.out.println("Time and tide wait for no one.");
else
    System.out.println("Time and tide wait for me.");
```

8. What output will be Produced by the following code?

```
int time = 4, tide = 3;
if (time + tide > 6)
    System.out.println("Time and tide wait for no one.");
else
    System.out.println("Time and tide wait for me.");
```

9. What output will be produced by the following code?

```
int time = 2, tide = 3;
if (time + tide > 6)
    System.out.println("Time and tide wait for no one.");
else if (time + tide > 5)
    System.out.println("Time and tide wait for some one.");
else if (time + tide > 4)
    System.out.println("Time and tide wait for every one.");
else
    System.out.println("Time and tide wait for me.");
```

10. Suppose number is a variable of type *int* that has been given a value. Write a multibranch *If-else*-statement that outputs the word High if number is greater than 10, outputs Low if number is less than 5, and outputs So-so if number is anything else.

The *switch*-statement

The *Switch*-**statement** is a multi-way branch that makes its decision on which way to branch based on the value of an integer or character expression. Display 3.5 shows a sample *switch*-statement. The *switch*-statement begins with the word *switch* followed by an expression in parentheses. In Display 3.5, the expression is the variable numberOfBabies. This expression is called the **controlling expression**.

controlling expression

Below this is a list of cases, each case consisting of the reserved word *case* followed by a constant, then a colon, and then a list of statements, which are the actions for that case. The constant that is placed after the word *case* is called a **case label**. When the *switch*-statement is executed, the controlling expression, in this example, numberOfBabies, is evaluated. The list of alternatives is searched until a case label that matches the controlling expression (numberOfBabies in the example) is found, and the action associated with that label is executed. You are not allowed to have repeated case labels. That would produce an ambiguous situation. If no match is found, then the case labeled *default* is executed.

case label

default

The *default* case is optional. If there is no *default* case and no match is found to any of the cases, then no action takes place. Although the *default* case is optional, you are encouraged to always use it. If you think your cases cover all the possibilities without a *default* case, then you can insert an error message as the *default* case. You never know when you might have missed some obscure case.

Notice that the action for each case in Display 3.5 ends with the word *break*. This is a *break*-**statement** and it ends the case. The *break*-statement consists of the word *break* followed by a semicolon. If there is no *break*-statement, then the action just continues on into the next case until either a *break*-statement is encountered or the end of the *switch*-statement is reached.

break

Sometimes you do want a case without a *break*-statement. You cannot have multiple labels in one case, but you can list cases one after the other so that they all apply to the same action. For example, in Display 3.5, both the 4 and the 5 produce the same case action, because the 4 case has no *break*-statement (and, in fact, the 4 case has no action statements at all).

As another example, consider the following *switch*-statement:

```
switch (eggGrade)
{
    case 'A':
    case 'a':
        System.out.println("Grade A");
        break;
    case 'C':
    case 'c':
        System.out.println("Grade C");
        break;
    default:
        System.out.println("We only buy grade A and grade C.");
        break;
}
```

Display 3.5 A *switch*-Statement *(Part 1 of 2)*

```java
public class MultipleBirths
{
    public static void main(String[] args)
    {
        int numberOfBabies;
        System.out.print("Enter number of babies: ");
        numberOfBabies = SavitchIn.readLineInt();

        switch (numberOfBabies)
        {
            case 1:
                System.out.println("Congratulations.");
                break;
            case 2:
                System.out.println("Wow. Twins.");
                break;
            case 3:
                System.out.println("Wow. Triplets.");
                break;
            case 4:
            case 5:
                System.out.println("Unbelieveable.");
                System.out.println(numberOfBabies + " babies");
                break;
            default:
                System.out.println("I don't believe you.");
                break;
        }
    }
}
```

Sample Screen Dialogue 1

```
Enter number of babies: 1
Congratulations.
```

Sample Screen Dialogue 2

```
Enter number of babies: 3
Wow. Triplets.
```

Display 3.5   A *switch*-Statement *(Part 2 of 2)*

Sample Screen Dialogue 3

```
Enter number of babies: 4
Unbelievable.
4 babies
```

Sample Screen Dialogue 4

```
Enter number of babies: 6
I don't believe you.
```

In this example, the variable eggGrade would be of type *char*.

Note that the cases need not form any sort of range; you can have 'A' and 'C' and no 'B', as in the preceding example. Similarly, in a *switch*-statement with integer case labels, you could have integers 1 and 3, but no 2.

The controlling expression in a *switch*-statement need not be a single variable. It can be a more complicated expression involving +, *, and/or other things, but the expression must evaluate to something of type *int* or type *char*. (The types *byte* and *short* are also allowed, but the controlling expression cannot be of type *long* or any type other than *int*, *char*, *byte*, or *short*.)

The box labeled *switch*-**Statement** gives the syntax details for the *switch*-statement. Be sure to notice the colons after the case labels.

■ Gotcha
Omitting a *break*-Statement

If you test a program that contains a *switch*-statement and it executes two cases when you expect it to execute only one case, then you have probably forgotten to include a *break*-statement where one is needed.

switch-Statement

Syntax:

```
switch (Controlling_Expression)
{
    case Case_Label:
        Statement;
        Statement;
        . . .
        Statement;
        break;
    case Case_Label:
        Statement;
        Statement;
        . . .
        Statement;
        break;
```

Each Case_Label is a constant of the same type as the Controlling_Expression. Each case must have a different Case_Label. The Controlling_Expression must be of type char, int, short, or byte.

A break may be omitted. In that case, execution just continues to the next case.

<There can be any number of cases like the above. The following default case is optional:>

```
    default:
        Statement;
        Statement;
        . . .
        Statement;
        break;
}
```

Example:

```
int seatLocationCode;
    . . .
switch (seatLocationCode)
{
    case 1:
        System.out.println("Orchestra.");
        price = 40.00;
        break;
    case 2:
        System.out.println("Mezzanine.");
        price = 30.00;
        break;
    case 3:
        System.out.println("Balcony.");
        price = 15.00;
        break;
    default:
        System.out.println("Unknown ticket code.");
        break;
}
```

The Conditional Operator *(Optional)*

To allow compatibility with older programming styles, Java included a ternary operator which is a notational variant on certain forms of the *if-else*-statement. This variant is illustrated below. Consider the statement

```
if (n1 > n2)
    max = n1;
else
    max = n2;
```

conditional operator

This can be expressed using the *conditional operator* as follows:

```
max = (n1 > n2) ? n1 : n2;
```

The expression on the right-hand side of the assignment statement is the conditional expression

```
(n1 > n2) ? n1 : n2
```

The ? and : together form a ternary operator know as the **conditional operator** (or **ternary operator**). A **conditional operator expression** starts with a boolean expression followed by a ? and then followed by two expression separated with a colon. If the boolean expression is true, then the first of the two expressions is retuned; otherwise, the second of the two expression is returned.

As illustrated here, the most common use of the conditional operator is to set a variable to one of two different values depending on a boolean condition. Be sure to note that a condition expression always returns a value, and so is only equivalent to certain special kinds of *if-else*-statements. Another example may help to illustrate the conditional operator.

consider the following:

```
if (hoursWork <= 40)
    pay = hoursWorked*payRate;
else
    pay = hoursWorked*payRate + 1.5*(hoursWorked − 40)*payRate;
```

This says that an employee pay rate is the rate of pay multiplied by the hours worked, but if the employee works over 40 hours, then any time over 40 hours is paid at 1.5 times the usual pay rate. This can be expressed using the conditional operator as follows:

```
pay =
    (hoursWorked <= 40) ?
        (hoursWorked*payRate) :
        (hoursWorked*payRate + 1.5*(hoursWorked − 40)*payRate);
```

? Self-Test Questions

11. What is the output produced by the following code?

```
int code = 2;
switch (code)
{
    case 1:
        System.out.println("Hello.");
    case 3:
        System.out.println("Good-bye.");
        break;
    default:
        System.out.println("Till we meet again.");
        break;

}
```

12. Suppose you change the code in question 11 so that the first line is the following:

```
int code = 1;
```

What output would be produced?

13. What is the output produced by the following code?

```
char letter = 'B';
switch (letter)
{
    case 'A':
    case 'a':
        System.out.println("Some kind of A.");
    case 'B':
    case 'b':
        System.out.println("Some kind of B.");
        break;
    default:
        System.out.println("Something else.");
        break;
}
```

14. What output will be produced by the following code?

```
int key = 1;
switch (key + 1)
{
    case 1:
        System.out.println("Cake");
        break;
    case 2:
        System.out.println("Pie");
        break;
    case 3:
        System.out.println("Ice cream");
    case 4:
        System.out.println("Cookies");
        break;
    default:
        System.out.println("Diet time");
}
```

15. Suppose you change the code in question 14 so that the first line is the following:

```
int key = 3;
```

What output would be produced?

16. Suppose you change the code in question 14 so that the first line is the following:

```
int key = 5;
```

What output would be produced?

3.2 | Java Loop Statements

> *One more time.*
>
> **Count Basie, Recording of April in Paris**
>
> *Play it again, Sam.*
> **Reputed (incorrectly) to be in the movie Casablanca, which contains similar phrases such as Play it, Sam.**

Programs often need to repeat some action. For example, a grading program would contain some code that assigns a letter grade to a student based on the student's scores on assignments and exams. To assign grades to the entire class, the program would repeat this action for each student in the class. A portion of a program that repeats a statement or group of statements is called a **loop.** The statement (or group of statements) to be repeated in a loop is called the **body** of the loop. Each repetition of the loop body is called an **iteration** of the loop.

body

iteration

When you design a loop, you need to determine what action the body of the loop will take, and you need to determine a mechanism for deciding when the loop should stop repeating the loop body.

while-Statements

One way to construct a loop in Java is with a *while*-**statement**, which is also known as a *while*-**loop.** A *while*-statement repeats its action again and again until a controlling boolean expression becomes false. That is why it is called a *while* loop; the loop is repeated *while* the controlling boolean expression is true. For example, Display 3.6 contains a toy example of a *while*-statement. The statement starts with the reserved word *while* followed by a boolean expression in parentheses. That is the controlling boolean expression. The loop body (the part repeated) is repeated while that controlling boolean expression is true. The loop body is a statement, typically a compound statement enclosed in curly brackets { }. The loop body normally contains some action that can change the controlling boolean expression from true to false and so end the loop. Let's step through this sample *while*-loop.

while- **loop**

Consider the first sample dialog for the *while*-statement in Display 3.6. The user enters a 2 and this 2 becomes the value of the variable number. The controlling boolean expression is

```
(count <= number)
```

Since count is 1 and number is 2, this boolean expression is true, so the loop body, shown in what follows, is executed:

```
{
    System.out.println(count);
    count++;
}
```

The loop body writes out the value of count to the screen and then increase the value of count by one, so 1 is written to the screen, and the value of count becomes 2.

After iterating the loop body one time, the controlling boolean expression is checked again. Since count is 2 and number is 2, the boolean expression is still true. So, the loop body is executed one more time. The loop body again writes out the value of count to the screen and again increases the value of count by one, so 2 is written to the screen and the value of count becomes 3.

After iterating the loop body the second time, the controlling boolean expression is checked again. The value of count is now 3 and the value of number is still 2, and so, the controlling boolean expression, repeated in what follows, is now false.

```
(count <= number)
```

Because the controlling boolean expression is false, the *while*-loop ends and the program goes on to execute the two System.out.println-statements that follow the *while*-statement. The first System.out.println-statement ends the line of numbers output in the *while*-loop, and the second System.out.println-statement outputs "Buckle my shoe."

All *while*-statements are formed in a way similar to the sample shown in Display 3.6. The statement has the general form

Display 3.6 A *while*-Loop

```java
public class WhileDemo
{
    public static void main(String[] args)
    {
        int count, number;

        System.out.println("Enter a number");
        number = SavitchIn.readLineInt();

        count = 1;
        while (count <= number)
        {
            System.out.print(count + ", ");
            count++;
        }
        System.out.println();
        System.out.println("Buckle my shoe.");
    }
}
```

Sample Screen Dialogue 1

```
Enter a number:
2
1, 2,
Buckle my shoe.
```

Sample Screen Dialogue 2

```
Enter a number:
3
1, 2, 3,
Buckle my shoe.
```

Sample Screen Dialogue 3

```
Enter a number:
0

Buckle my shoe.
```

The loop body is iterated zero times.

```
while (Boolean_Expression)
    Body_Statement
```

The *Body_Statement* can be a simple statement, as in the following example:

```
while (next > 0)
    next = SavitchIn.readLineInt();
```

But it is much more likely that the *Body_Statement* is a compound statement, as in Display 3.6, so the most common form of a *while*-loop is

```
while (Boolean_Expression)
{
    First_Statement
    Second_Statement
        . . .
    Last_Statement
}
```

The semantics (meaning) of a *while*-loop is described in Display 3.7.

The *while*-Statement

Syntax:

```
while (Boolean_Expression)
    Body
```

The *Body* may be either a simple statement, or more likely, a compound statement consisting of a list of statements enclosed in curly brackets { }.

Example:

```
while (next > 0)
{
    next = SavitchIn.readLineInt();
    total = total + next;
}
```

■ **Java Tip**
A *while*-Loop Can Perform Zero Iterations

The body of a *while*-loop can be executed zero times. The first thing that happens when a *while*-loop is executed is that the controlling boolean expression is checked. If that boolean expression is false, then the loop body is not executed even one time. This may seem strange. After all, why write a loop if the body is never executed? The answer is that you may want a loop whose body is executed zero times or more than zero times, depending on input from the user. Perhaps the loop adds up the sum of all your bills for the day. If you did not go shopping one day, then you do not want the loop body to be executed at all. Sample Screen Dialog 3 of Display 3.6 shows a toy example of a *while*-loop that iterates its loop body zero times.

zero loop
iterations

Display 3.7   Semantics of the *while*-Statement

while (*Boolean_Expression*)
    *Body*¹

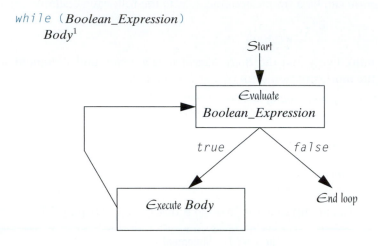

Example:
while (count <= number)
{
    System.out.print(count + ", ");
    count++;
}

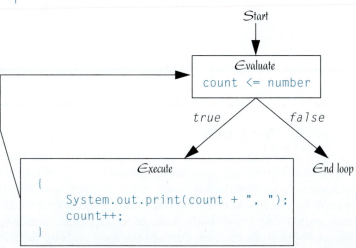

1. In a later subsection we discuss the *break*-statement used within loops. This semantics assumes that there is no *break*-statement in the body of the loop.

The *do-while*-Statement

do-while-
statement

The *do-while*-**statement** (also called a *do-while*-**loop**) is very similar to the *while*-statement. The main difference in how they behave is that, with a *do-while*-statement, the loop body is always executed at least once. As you will recall, with a *while*-loop, the loop body might be executed zero times. Display 3.8 contains a sample *do-while*-loop that is similar (but not identical) to the *while*-loop in Display 3.6/page 156. Note that with the *do-while*-loop, the loop body is always executed at least once even if the boolean expression starts out false, as in Sample Dialog 3.

The syntax for a *do-while*-statement is as follows:

```
do
        Body_Statement
while (Boolean_Expression);
```

The *Body_Statement* can be a simple statement, as in the following example:

```
do
        next = SavitchIn.readLineInt();
while (next > 0);
```

However, it is much more likely that the *Body_Statement* is a compound statement, as in Display 3.8, so the most common form of a *do-while*-loop is

```
do
{
        First_Statement
        Second_Statement
          . . .
        Last_Statement
}while (Boolean_Expression);
```

Be sure to notice the semicolon after the *Boolean_Expression* in parentheses.

(Note that we place the ending curly bracket } and the *while* on the same line. Some programmers prefer to place them on different lines. Either form is fine, but be consistent.)

When a *do-while*-loop is executed, the first thing that happens is that the loop body is executed. *After that,* a *do-while*-loop behaves exactly the same as a *while*-loop. The boolean expression is checked. If the boolean expression is true, then the loop body is executed one more time. If the boolean expression is false, the loop ends. This is done again and again as long as the boolean expression is true.

Although we do not recommend rewriting your *do-while*-loops this way, it may help you to understand a *do-while*-loop if you see the following rewriting done one time. The *do-while*-loop in Display 3.8 can be written as the following equivalent code that includes a *while*-loop:

Display 3.8   A *do-while*-Loop
....

```
public class DoWhileDemo
{
    public static void main(String[] args)
    {
        int count, number;

        System.out.println("Enter a number");
        number = SavitchIn.readLineInt();

        count = 1;
        do
        {
            System.out.print(count + ", ");
            count++;
        }while (count <= number);
        System.out.println();
        System.out.println("Buckle my shoe.");
    }
}
```

Sample Screen Dialogue 1

```
Enter a number:
2
1, 2,
Buckle my shoe.
```

Sample Screen Dialogue 2

```
Enter a number:
3
1, 2, 3,
Buckle my shoe.
```

Sample Screen Dialogue 3

```
Enter a number:
0
1,
Buckle my shoe.
```

The loop body is always iterated at least one time.

....

```
{
    System.out.print(count + ", ");
    count++;
}
while (count <= number)
{
    System.out.print(count + ", ");
    count++;
}
```

When viewed in this way, it is obvious that a *do-while*-loop differs from a *while*-loop in only one detail. With a *do-while*-loop, the loop body is always executed at least once. (Recall that, with a *while*-loop, the loop body may be executed zero times.)

The semantics (meaning) of a *do-while*-loop is shown in Display 3.9.   .

The *do-while*-Statement

With a *do-while*-statement, the loop body is always executed at least one time.

Syntax:

```
do
    Body
while (Boolean_Expression);
```

The *Body* may be either a simple statement, or more likely, a compound statement consisting of a list of statements enclosed in curly brackets { }. Be sure to notice the semicolon after the *Boolean_Expression* in parentheses.

Example:

```
do
{
    next = SavitchIn.readLineInt();
    total = total + next;
}while (next > 0);
```

Programming Example
Bug Infestation

Your hometown has been hit with an infestation of roaches. This is not the most pleasant topic, but fortunately a local company called Debugging Experts Inc. has a treatment that can eliminate roaches from a house. As the saying goes, "It's a dirty job, but somebody has to do it." The only problem is that the population is too complacent and may not exterminate the roaches before they get out of hand. So, the company has installed a computer at the local shopping mall in order to let people know how bad the problem is at their particular house. The program that is run on this computer is shown in Display 3.10.

The defined constants give the basic facts about this species of roach. The population grows relatively slowly for roaches, but that is still pretty bad. Left

Display 3.9   Semantics of the do-*while*-Statement

```
do
      Body¹
while (Boolean_Expression);
```

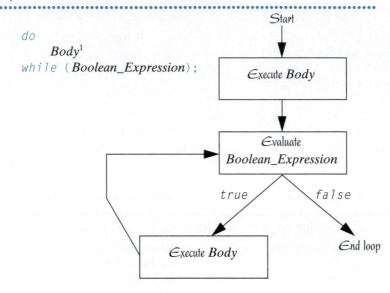

Example:
```
do
{
    System.out.print(count + ", ");
    count++;
}while (count <= number);
```

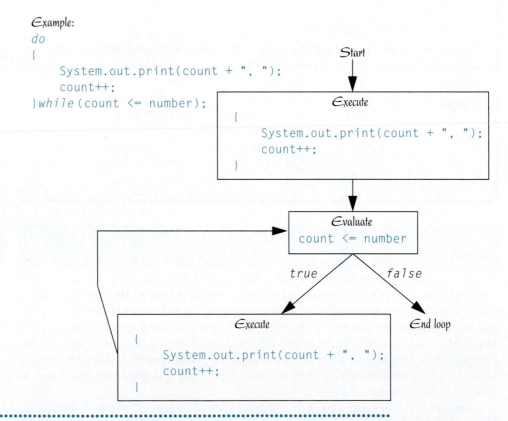

1. In a later subsection we discuss the *break*-statement used within loops. This
semantics assumes that there is no *break*-statement in the body of the loop.

Display 3.10   Roach Population Program *(Part 1 of 2)*

```
/**********************************************************
 *Program to calculate how long it will take a population of
 *roaches to completely fill a house from floor to ceiling.
 **********************************************************/
public class BugTrouble
{
    public static final double GROWTH_RATE = 0.95;//95% per week
    public static final double ONE_BUG_VOLUME = 0.002;//cubic feet

    public static void main(String[] args)
    {
        System.out.println("Enter the total volume of your house");
        System.out.print("in cubic feet: ");
        double houseVolume = SavitchIn.readLineDouble();

        System.out.println("Enter the estimated number of");
        System.out.print("roaches in your house:");
        int startPopulation = SavitchIn.readLineInt();
        int countWeeks = 0;
        double population = startPopulation;
        double totalBugVolume = population*ONE_BUG_VOLUME;

        while (totalBugVolume < houseVolume)
        {
            population = population + (GROWTH_RATE*population);
            totalBugVolume = population*ONE_BUG_VOLUME;
            countWeeks++;
        }

        System.out.println("Starting with a roach population of "
                                          + startPopulation);
        System.out.println("and a house with a volume of "
                             + houseVolume + " cubic feet,");
        System.out.println("after " + countWeeks + " weeks,");
        System.out.println("the house will be filled");
        System.out.println("floor to ceiling with roaches.");
        System.out.println("There will be " + (int)population
                                          + " roaches.");
        System.out.println("They will fill a volume of "
                        + (int)totalBugVolume + " cubic feet");
        System.out.println("Better call Debugging Experts Inc.");

    }

}
```

(`int`) is a type cast as discussed in Chapter 2.

Display 3.10 Roach Population Program *(Part 2 of 2)*

Sample Screen Dialogue

```
Enter the total volume of your house
in cubic feet: 20000
Enter the estimated number of
roaches in your house: 100
Starting with a roach population of 100
and a house with a volume of 20000.0 cubic
feet,
after 18 weeks,
the house will be filled
floor to ceiling with roaches.
There will be 16619693 roaches.
They will fill a volume of 33239 cubic feet
Better call Debugging Experts Inc.
```

unchecked, the population of roaches will almost double every week. If the population doubled every week, the growth rate would be 100% per week, but fortunately it is only 95% per week. These roaches are also pretty big. Expressed in cubic feet their average size is 0.002 cubic feet (which is just a bit smaller than 0.3 cubic inches). The program does make some simplifying assumptions. It assumes there is no furniture in the house, and it assumes that the roaches would fill the house with no space between them. The real situation would be even worse than that portrayed by this program with its simplifying assumptions.

In the following we reproduce the *while*-loop from the program in Display 3.10:

```
while (totalBugVolume < houseVolume)
{
    population = population + (GROWTH_RATE*population);
    totalBugVolume = population*ONE_BUG_VOLUME;
    countWeeks++;
}
```

This program simply updates the population of the roaches and the volume of roaches by the following statements, which show how the population and volume will change in one week:

```
population = population + (GROWTH_RATE*population);
totalBugVolume = population*ONE_BUG_VOLUME;
```

Because the growth rate and the volume of one bug are both positive, we know that the value of `population` and hence the value of `totalBugVolume` will increase on each loop iteration. So, eventually, the value of `totalBugVolume` will exceed the value of `houseVolume` and the controlling boolean expression, reproduced in what follows, will become false and end the `while`-loop:

```
(totalBugVolume < houseVolume)
```

The variable `countWeeks` starts out as zero and is increased by one on each loop iteration, and so, when the loop ends, the value of `countWeeks` is the total numbers of weeks it takes to make the volume of roaches exceed the volume of the house.

■ Gotcha
Infinite Loops

A common program bug is a loop that does not end, but that simply repeats its loop body again and again forever. (Well, conceptually forever.) A loop that iterates its body repeatedly without ever ending is called an **infinite loop.** Normally, some statement in the body of a `while`-loop or `do-while`-loop will change some variables so that the controlling boolean expression becomes false. If you do not get this variable change to happen in the right way, you can get an infinite loop. In order to see an example of an infinite loop, we need only make a slight change to a loop you have already seen.

infinite loop

Let's consider a slight variation of the program in Display 3.10. Suppose your town is hit by an infestation of roach-eating frogs. These frogs eat roaches so quickly that the roach population actually decreases, so that the roaches have a negative growth rate. To reflect this fact you could change the definition of one defined constant to the following, and recompile the program in Display 3.10:

```
public static final double GROWTH_RATE = −0.05;//−5% per week
```

If you make this change and run the program, the `while`-loop will be an infinite loop (provided the house starts out with a relatively small number of roaches). This is because the total number of roaches, and so the volume of roaches continually *decreases,* and hence the controlling boolean expression, shown again in what follows, is always true:

```
(totalBugVolume < houseVolume)
```

and so the loop never ends.

Some infinite loops will not really run forever, but will instead end your program in an abnormal state when some system resource is exhausted. However, some infinite loops will run forever if left alone. In order to end such a program with an infinite loop, you should learn how to force a program to stop running. The way to do this is different for different operating systems. On many systems (but not all), you can stop a program by typing control-C, which you type by holding down the control key while pressing the C key.

Sometimes a programmer might intentionally write an infinite loop. For example, an ATM machine would typically be controlled by a program with an infinite loop that handles deposits and withdrawals indefinitely. However, at this point in your programming, an infinite loop is likely to be an error.

? Self-Test Questions

17. What screen output will be produced by the following code?

```
int count = 0;
while (count < 5)
{
    System.out.println(count);
    count++;
}
System.out.println("count after loop = " + count);
```

18. Can a *while*-loop execute the body of the loop zero times? Can a *do-while*-loop execute the body of the loop zero times?

19. What screen output will be produced by the following code?

```
int count = 0;
do
{
    System.out.println(count);
    count++;
}while (count < 0);
System.out.println("count after loop = " + count);
```

20. Rewrite the following *do-while*-loop to obtain some equivalent code that does not contain a *do-while*-loop.

```
int number;
do
{
    System.out.println("Enter a whole number:");
    number = SavitchIn.readLineInt();
    System.out.println("You entered " + number);
}while (number > 0);
System.out.println("number after loop = " + number);
```

21. What screen output will be produced by the following code?

```
int count = 0;
while (count < 5)
{
    System.out.println(count);
    count--;
}
System.out.println("count after loop = " + count);
```

The *for*-Statement

The *for*-statement is a specialized loop statement that allows you to easily convert pseudocode such as the following into a Java loop:

```
Do the following for each value of count from 1 to 3:
    System.out.println(count);
System.out.println("Go");
```

This particular pseudocode can be expressed in Java as the following *for*-statement (followed by an output statement):

```
for (count = 1; count <= 3; count++)
    System.out.println(count);
System.out.println("Go");
```

The first two of the preceding lines are a *for*-statement that causes the output

```
1
2
3
```

After the *for*-statement ends, the last line outputs the word "Go".

In this first example of a *for*-statement, the loop body is the statement

```
System.out.println(count);
```

The iteration of the loop body is controlled by the line

```
for (count = 1; count <= 3; count++)
```

The first of the three expressions in parentheses, count = 1, tells what happens before the loop body is executed for the first time. The third expression, count++, is executed after each iteration of the loop body. The middle expression, count <= 3, is a boolean expression that determines when the loop will end, and that does so in the same way as the controlling boolean expression in a *while*-loop. Thus, the loop body is executed while count <= 3 is true. To rephrase what we just said, the *for*-statement

```
for (count = 1; count <= 3; count++)
    for-loop body
```

is equivalent to

```
count = 1;
while (count <= 3)
{
    for-loop body
    count++;
}
```

The syntax for a *for*-statement is as follows:

```
for (Initializing_Action; Boolean_Expression; Update_Action)
        Body_Statement
```

The *Body_Statement* can be a simple statement, as in the following example:

```
for (count = 1; count <= 3; count++)
    System.out.println(count);
```

However, it is more likely that the *Body_Statement* is a compound statement, as in Display 3.11, so the more common form of a `for`-loop can be described as follows:

> `for` (*Initializing_Action*; *Boolean_Expression*; *Update_Action*)
> {
>
>   *First_Statement*
>   *Second_Statement*
>   .
>   .
>   .
>   *Last_Statement*
>
> }

When it is executed, a `for`-statement of the preceding form is equivalent to the following:

> *Initializing_Action*;
> `while` (*Boolean_Expression*)
> {
>
>   *First_Statement*
>   *Second_Statement*
>   .
>   .
>   .
>   *Last_Statement*
>   *Update_Action*;
>
> }

Notice that a `for`-statement is basically another notation for a kind of `while`-loop. Thus, just like a `while`-loop, a `for`-statement might repeat its loop body zero times.

The semantics (meaning) of the `for`-loop is described in Display 3.12.

The Comma in `for`-Statements *(Optional)*

comma
operator

A `for`-loop can perform more than one initialization. To use a list of initialization actions, simply separate the actions with commas, as in the following example:

```
for (n = 1, product = 1; n <= 10; n++)
    product = product*n;
```

This `for`-loop will initialize n to 1 and will also initialize `product` to 1. Note that we use a comma, not a semicolon, to separate the initialization actions.

You cannot have multiple boolean expressions to test for ending a `for`-loop. However, you can string together multiple tests using the && operator to form one larger boolean expression.

You can have multiple update actions by stringing them together with commas. This can sometimes lead to a situation where the `for`-statement has an empty body and still does something useful. For example, the previous `for`-statement can be rewritten to the following equivalent version:

```
for (n = 1, product = 1; n <= 10; product = product*n, n++);
```

Display 3.11 A *for*-Statement

```java
public class ForDemo
{
    public static void main(String[] args)
    {

        int countDown;

        for (countDown = 3; countDown >= 0; countDown--)
        {
            System.out.println(countDown);
            System.out.println("and counting.");
        }

        System.out.println("Blast off!");
    }
}
```

Screen Output

```
3
and counting.
2
and counting.
1
and counting.
0
and counting.
Blast off!.
```

Display 3.12 Semantics of the *for*-Statement *(Part 1 of 2)*

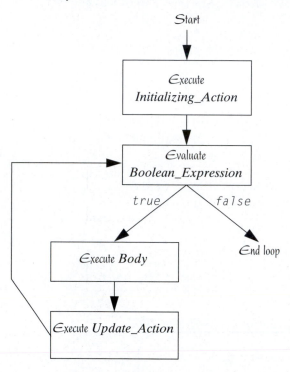

for (*Initializing_Action*; *Boolean_Expression*; *Update_Action*)
        Body

In effect, we have made the loop body part of the update action. It is a more readable style to use the update action only for variables that control the loop, as in the previous version of this *for*-loop. We do not advocate these *for*-loops with no body, but many programmers consider them "clever." As indicated in the section *Gotcha* **Extra Semicolon in a Loop Statement**, these *for*-loops with no body can also often occur as the result of a programer error.

    (If you have programmed in other programming languages that have a general-purpose comma operator, you need to be warned that, in Java, the comma operator can only be used in *for*-statements.)

Display 3.12 Semantics of the *for* **-Statement (Part 2 of 2)**

Example:
```java
for (countDown = 3; countDown >= 0; countDown--)
{
    System.out.println(countDown);
    System.out.println("and counting.");
}
```

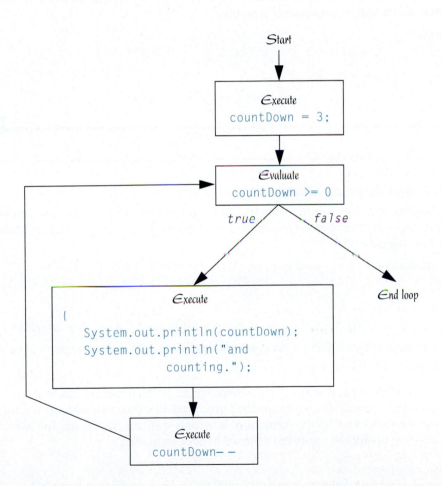

The *for*-Statement

Syntax:

```
for (Initializing_Action; Boolean_Expression; Update_Action)
       Body
```

The *Body* may be either a simple statement, or more likely, a compound statement consisting of a list of statements enclosed in curly brackets { }. Notice that the three things in parentheses are separated by two, not three, semicolons.

Our *for*-loops will always use only one variable in the three expressions in parentheses after the word *for*. However, you are allowed to use any Java expression and so can use more, or fewer than, one variable in the expressions, and moreover, the variables can be of any types.

Example:

```
for (next = 0; next <= 10; next = next + 2)
{
    sum = sum + next;
    System.out.println("sum now is " + sum);
}
```

■ Gotcha

Extra Semicolon in a Loop Statement

The following code looks quite ordinary. Moreover, it will compile and run with no error messages. It does, however, contain a mistake. See if you can find the mistake before reading on.

```
int product = 1, number;
for (number = 1; number <= 10; number++);
    product = product * number;
System.out.println(
            "Product of the numbers 1 through 10 is " + product);
```

If you include this code in a program and run the program, the output will be

```
Product of the numbers 1 through 10 is 11
```

Now do you know what is wrong? Try to explain the problem before reading on.

If you were testing the program that produced this puzzling output, it could leave you bewildered. Clearly, something is wrong with the *for*-loop, but what? The *for*-loop is suppose to set the value of product equal to

```
1 * 2 * 3 * 4 * 5 * 6 * 7 * 8 * 9 * 10
```

but instead, it sets the value of product equal to 11. How could that happen?

The problem is typographically very small. The *for*-statement has an extra semicolon at the end of the first line:

```
for (number = 1; number <= 10; number++(;)
    product = product * number;
```

What does this *for*-statement do? The semicolon at the end means that the body of the *for*-statement is empty. A semicolon by itself is considered a statement that does nothing. (This statement that does nothing is called the **empty statement** or the **null statement.**) This *for*-statement with the extra semicolon is equivalent to

empty statement

```
for (number = 1; number <= 10; number++)
{
    //Do nothing.
}
```

Thus, the body of the *for*-statement is in fact executed 10 times, but each time the loop does nothing, except that it does increment the variable number by one on each of the 10 loop iterations. That leaves number equal to 11 when the program reaches the statement

```
product = product * number;
```

(Remember, number starts out equal to 1 and is increased by one ten times, which adds 10 more to the initial 1, so the value becomes 11.)

Now let's look again at the entire piece of troublesome code:

```
int product = 1, number;
for (number = 1; number <= 10; number++);
    product = product * number;
System.out.println(
        "Product of the numbers 1 through 10 is " + product);
```

After executing the line that starts with *for*, the value of product is 1 and, as we have just seen, the value of number is 11. Then the following assignment statement is executed:

```
product = product * number;
```

This sets the value of product to 1 * 11, and so product ends up with the value 11, which is what the output says. To fix the problem, simply remove the extra semicolon at the end of the line that begins with *for*.

The same sort of problem can occur with a *while*-loop. The following *while*-loop has the same sort of problem as our troublesome *for*-loop, but the results are even worse:

```
int product = 1, number = 1;
while (number <= 10);
{
    product = product * number;
    number++;
}
System.out.println(
        "Product of the numbers 1 through 10 is " + product);
```

The extra semicolon ends the *while*-loop, so that the body of the *while*-loop is the empty statement. Because the body of the loop is the empty statement, nothing happens on each loop iteration. So, the value of `number` never changes and the condition

```
number <= 10
```

is always *true*. So the loop is an infinite loop that does nothing and does it forever!

? Self-Test Questions

22. What output is produced by the following Java code?

    ```
    int n;
    for (n = 1; n <= 4; n++)
        System.out.println(n);
    ```

23. What output is produced by the following Java code?

    ```
    int n;
    for (n = 1; n > 4; n++)
        System.out.println(n);
    ```

24. What output is produced by the following Java code?

    ```
    int n;
    for (n = 4; n > 0; n--)
        System.out.println(n);
    ```

25. What output is produced by the following Java code?

    ```
    double test;
    for (test = 0; test < 3; test = test + 0.5)
        System.out.println(test);
    ```

26. Write a *for*-statement that writes out the even numbers, 2, 4, 6, 8, and 10. The output should put each number on a separate line. Declare all the variables you use.

■ Java Tip
Choosing a Loop Statement

Suppose you decide that your program needs a loop. How do you decide whether to use a *while*-statement, *do-while*-statement, or *for*-statement? There are some general guidelines we can give you: You *cannot* use a *do-while*-statement unless you are certain that for all possible inputs to your program, you know the loop should be iterated at least one time. If you do know that your loop will always be iterated at least one time, then a *do-while*-statement is likely to be a good choice. However, more often than you might think, a loop requires the possibility of iterating the body zero times. In those cases, you must use either a *while*-statement or a *for*-statement. If it is a computation that changes some numeric quantity by some equal amount on each iteration, then consider a *for*-statement. If the *for*-statement does not work well, use a *while*-statement. The *while*-statement is always the safest choice. You can easily realize any sort of loop as a *while*-statement, but sometimes one of the other alternatives is nicer.

The *break*-Statement in Loops

As we have presented them so far, the *while*-, *do-while*-, and *for*-statements always complete their entire loop body on each iteration. Sometimes, you may want to end a loop in the middle of the loop body. You can do this using the *break*-statement. For example, the program in Display 3.13 reads a list of purchase amounts and totals them to see how much the user has spent. However, the user has a limit of $100, so as soon as the total reaches (or exceeds) $100, the program uses a *break*-statement to end the loop immediately. When a *break*-statement is executed, the immediately enclosing loop ends, and the remainder of the loop body is not executed. The *break*-statement can be used with a *while*-loop, a *do-while*-loop, or a *for*-loop.

break

This is the same *break*-statement that we used in *switch*-statements. If the loop is contained within a larger loop (or if the loop is inside of a *switch*-statement), then the *break*-statement ends only the innermost loop. Similarly, if the *break*-statement is within a *switch*-statement that is inside of a loop, then the *break*-statement ends the *switch*-statement but not the loop. The *break*-statement ends only the innermost loop or *switch*-statement that contains the *break*-statement.

■ Gotcha
Misuse of *break*-Statements

A loop *without* a *break*-statement has a simple, easy-to-understand structure. There is a test for ending the loop at the top (or bottom) of the loop, and every iteration will go to the end of the loop body. When you add a *break*-statement, this can make it more difficult to understand the loop. The loop might end because of the condition given at the start (or bottom) of the loop or because of the *break*-statement. Some loop iterations may go to the end of the loop body, but one loop iteration may end prematurely. Because of the complications they introduce, *break*-statements in loops should be avoided. Some authorities contend that a *break*-statement should never be used to end a loop, but virtually all programming authorities agree that they should be used at most sparingly.

The *break*-Statement in Loops

The *break*-statement can be used in a *switch*-statement or in any kind of loop statement. When the *break*-statement is executed, the immediately enclosing loop (or *switch*-statement) ends, and the remainder of the loop body is not executed.

■

Display 3.13 Ending a Loop with a *break* -Statement

```java
public class BreakDemo
{
    public static void main(String[] args)
    {
        int itemNumber;
        double amount, total;

        System.out.println("You may buy ten items, but");
        System.out.println("the total price must not exceed $100.");

        total = 0;
        for (itemNumber = 1; itemNumber <= 10; itemNumber++)
        {
            System.out.print("Enter cost of item #"
                                            + itemNumber + ": $");
            amount = SavitchIn.readLineDouble();
            total = total + amount;
            if (total >= 100)
            {
                System.out.println("You spent all your money.");
                break;
            }
            System.out.println("Your total so far is $" + total);
            System.out.println("You may purchase up to "
                        + (10 - itemNumber) + " more items.");
        }

        System.out.println("You spent $" + total);
    }
}
```

Sample Screen Dialogue

```
You may buy ten items, but
the total price must not exceed $100.
Enter cost of item #1: $90.93
Your total so far is $90.93
You may purchase up to 9 more items.
Enter cost of item #2: $10.50
You spent all your money.
You spent $101.43
```

The `exit` Method

Sometimes your program can encounter a situation that makes continuing with the program pointless. In these cases, you can end your program with a call to the `exit` method, as follows:

```
System.exit(0);
```

The preceding statement will end a Java program as soon as it is executed.

For example:

```
if (numberOfWinners == 0)
{
    System.out.println("Error: Dividing by zero.");
    System.exit(0);
}
else
{
    oneShare = payoff/numberOfWinners;
    System.out.println("Each winner will receive $" + oneShare);
}
```

This statement will normally output the share that each winner should receive. However, if the number of winners is zero, then that would produce a division by zero, which is an illegal operation. To avoid this division by zero, the program checks to see if the number of winners is zero, and if it is zero, it ends the program with a call to the `exit` method.

The number 0 given as the argument to `System.exit` is returned to the operating system. In many situations, you can use any number and the program will behave the same. But, most operating systems use 0 to indicate a normal termination of the program and 1 to indicate an abnormal termination of the program (just the opposite of what most people would guess). Thus, if your `System.exit` statement ends your program normally, the argument should be 0. In this case, *normal* means the program did not violate any system or other important constraints. It does not mean that the program did what you wanted it to do. So, you would almost always use a 0 as the argument.

The `exit` Method

An invocation of the `exit` method ends the program. The normal form for an `exit` method invocation is

```
System.exit(0);
```

? Self-Test Questions

27. What output is produced by the following Java code?

```
int n;
for (n = 1; n <= 5; n++)
{
    if (n == 3)
        break;
    System.out.println("Hello");
}
System.out.println("After the Loop.");
```

28. What output is produced by the following Java code?

```
int n;
for (n = 1; n <= 5; n++)
{
    if (n == 3)
        System.exit(0);
    System.out.println("Hello");
}
System.out.println("After the Loop.");
```

29. What output is produced by the following Java code?

```
int n;
for (n = 1; n <= 3; n++)
{

    switch (n)
    {
        case 1:
            System.out.println("One.");
            break;
        case 2:
            System.out.println("Two.");
            break;
        case 3:
            System.out.println("Three.");
            break;
        default:
            System.out.println("Default case.");
            break;
    }
}
System.out.println("After the Loop.");
```

3.3 | Programming with Loops

The cautious seldom err.

Confucius

In this section we give you some techniques to help you design loops. A loop is often broken into three parts: the initializing statements that must precede the loop, the loop body, and the mechanism for ending the loop. In this section we give you techniques for designing each of these loop constituents. Although the initializing statements come before the loop body, the loop body is naturally designed first, and so we will start our discussion with the loop body.

The Loop Body

One way to design a loop body is to write out the sequence of actions that you want your code to accomplish. For example, you might want your loop to perform the following actions:

> Output instructions to the user.
> Initialize variables.
> Read a number into the variable `next`.
> `sum = sum + next;`
> Output the number and the sum so far.
> Read another number into the variable `next`.
> `sum = sum + next;`
> Output the number and the sum so far.
> Read another number into the variable `next`.
> `sum = sum + next;`
> Output the number and the sum so far.
> Read another number into the variable `next`.
>   and so forth.

Then, look for a repeated pattern in the list of actions. In this case, a repeated pattern is

> Read another number into the variable `next`.
> `sum = sum + next;`
> Output the number and the sum so far.

So, the body of the loop, expressed in pseudocode, can be the preceding three actions. The entire pseudocode can be

> Output instructions to the user.
> Initialize variables.
> Do the following for the appropriate number of times:
> {
>
>   Read a number into the variable `next`.
>   `sum = sum + next;`
>   Output the number and the sum so far.
>
> }

Note that the pattern need not start with the first action. There may be some actions that need to be done before or after the loop is executed.

Pseudocode

In Chapter 1, we said that algorithms are usually written in pseudocode. **Pseudocode** is a mixture of English and Java. When using pseudocode, you simply write each piece of the algorithm in whatever language is easiest for that part. If the part is easier to express in English, you use English. If another part is easier to express in Java, you use Java for that part. The following simple algorithm (from the section entitled **The Loop Body**) is an example of pseudocode:

Read another number into the variable `next`.
```
sum = sum + next;
```
Output the number and the sum so far.

Initializing Statements

Consider the pseudocode we designed in the previous subsection. Notice that the variable `sum` is expected to have a value every time the following loop body statement is executed:

```
sum = sum + next;
```

In particular, this is true the first time the loop is iterated. So, `sum` must be initialized to some value before the loop starts. When trying to decide on the correct initializing value for `sum`, it helps to consider what you want to happen after one loop iteration. After one loop iteration, the value of `sum` should be set to the first value of `next`. The only way that `sum + next` can evaluate to `next` is if `sum` is 0. That means the value of `sum` must be initialized to 0. Thus, one of the variable initializations must be

```
sum = 0;
```

The only other variable used in the loop is `next`. The first statement performed with `next` is

Read a number into the variable `next`

This statement gives `next` a value, so `next` does not need to have a value before the loop is started. Thus, the only variable that needs to be initialized is `sum`, and we can rewrite the pseudocode to the following:

Output instructions to the user.
```
sum = 0;
```
Do the following the appropriate number of times:
{

    Read a number into the variable `next`
```
    sum = sum + next;
```
    Output the number and the sum so far.

}

Variables are not always initialized to zero. To see this, consider another example. Suppose your loop was computing the product of *n* numbers as follows:

```
for (count = 1; count <= n; count++)
{
    Read a number into the variable next
    product = product * next;
}
```

In this case, let's say that all variables are of type *int*.

If you initialize the variable `product` to zero, then no matter how many numbers are read in and multiplied, the value of `product` will still be zero. So, zero clearly is not the correct initialization value for `product`. The correct initializing value for `product` is 1. To see that 1 is the correct initial value, notice that the first time through the loop, you want `product` to be set equal to the first number read in. Initializing `product` to 1 will make this happen. Thus, the loop, with a correct initialization statement, is

```
product = 1;
for (count = 1; count <= n; count++)
{
    Read a number into the variable next
    product = product * next;
}
```

Ending a Loop

In this subsection, we discuss some standard techniques you can use to end a loop.

If you are lucky, your program may know exactly how many times the loop body must be repeated before the loops starts. In this simple case, you can use a *for*-loop to count the number of loop body iterations. For example, suppose `numberOfStudents` contains the number of students in a class and you want to know the average score on an exam in the course. The following will do nicely:

```
double next, average, sum = 0;
int count;
for (count = 1; count <= numberOfStudents; count++)
{
    next = SavitchIn.readLineDouble();
    sum = sum + next;
}
if (numberOfStudents > 0)
    average = sum/numberOfStudents;
else
    System.out.println("No scores to average.");
```

count-controlled loops

Be sure to notice that the variable `count` is not used in the loop body. The *for*-loop mechanism is simply being used to count from 1 to `numberOfStudents` and repeat the loop body that many times. Loops such as this one, that know the number of loop iterations before the loop starts, are called **count-controlled loops.** Count-controlled loops do not need to be implemented as *for*-loops, but that is the easiest way to implement a count-controlled loop. (Also note that we have allowed for the possibility of no students being in the class. In that case, the loop body is iterated zero times and the *if-else*-statement prevents division by zero.)

asking the user

The most straightforward way of ending a loop is to simply ask the user if it is time to end the loop. This works very well in situations where the total number of loop body iterations is expected to be fairly small. For example, the following would work nicely if each customer makes only a few purchases:

```
do
{
    System.out.println("Enter price $");
    price = SavitchIn.readLineDouble();
    System.out.print("Enter number purchased: ");
    number = SavitchIn.readLineInt();
    System.out.println(number + " items at $" + price);
    System.out.println("Total cost $" + price*number);
    System.out.println("Want to make another purchase?");
    System.out.println("Enter y for yes or n for no.");
    answer = SavitchIn.readLineNonwhiteChar();
}while ((answer == 'y') || (answer == 'Y'));
```

In some situations, this is best done with a *while*-loop. But if you know that each user will want at least one loop iteration, then a *do-while*-loop works fine.

sentinel value

For long input lists, you can sometimes use a **sentinel value**. A sentinel value is used for signaling the end of the input. It must be a value that is different from all possible real input values. For example, suppose you want some code to compute the highest and lowest scores on an exam, and suppose you know that there will be at least one exam score. If you know that nobody is ever given a negative score on the exam, then you can ask the user to mark the end of the list of scores with a negative number. The negative number is the sentinel value. It is not one of the exam scores. It is just an end marker. The code for computing the highest and lowest scores could be as follows:

```
System.out.println("Enter scores for all students");
System.out.println("Enter a negative number after");
System.out.println("you have entered all the scores.");
double max = SavitchIn.readLineDouble();
double min = max;//The max and min so far are the first score.
double next = SavitchIn.readLineDouble();
while (next >= 0)
{
    if (next > max)
        max = next;
    if (next < min)
        min = next;
    next = SavitchIn.readLineDouble();
}
System.out.println("The highest scores is " + max);
System.out.println("The lowest scores is " + min);
```

Be sure to notice that the last number is not used to determine the lowest score (or to determine the highest score). Suppose the user enters the scores as follows:

```
100
90
10
-1
```

then the output will be

```
The highest scores is 100
The lowest scores is 10
```

Be sure to note that the lowest score is 10, not −1. The −1 is just an end marker.
In Section3.4 we will discuss another method for ending a loop, but these three methods cover most situations you are likely to encounter.

Programming Example
Nested Loops

The body of a loop can contain any sort of statements. In particular, you can have a loop statement within the body of a larger loop statement. For example, the program in Display 3.14 computes the average of a list of scores using a *while*-loop. The program asks the user to enter a list of nonnegative scores with a negative sentinel value to mark the end of the list. This *while*-loop is then placed inside a *do-while*-loop, so that the user can repeat the entire process for another exam, and another, until the user wishes to end the program.

■ Programming Tip
Do Not Declare Variables in a Loop Body

Note that in Display 3.14, we have placed the declaration of all the variables at the beginning of the program so that they are outside of the body of the outer *do-while*-loop. If we had left some of the declarations inside the *do-while*-loop, then those declarations would be repeated on each execution of the body of the *do-while*-loop. Depending on how the compiler is written, this can be inefficient, because it may be recreating the variables on each loop iteration. There are times when it makes sense to declare a variable in a loop body, but if the variable declaration can easily be moved outside the loop, it is usually a good idea to do so.

? Self-Test Questions

30. Write a Java loop statement that will output the phrase `"One more time."` to the screen four times. Also, give any declarations or initializing statements that are needed.

31. Give a Java loop statement that will set the variable `result` equal to 2^5. Do this with a loop that starts out with the value of `result` equal to 1 and multiplies the value of `result` by 2 for each of 5 loop iterations. Also, give any declarations or initializing statements that are needed.

Display 3.14   Nested Loops *(Part 1 of 2)*

```
/************************************************************
 *Determines the average of a list of (nonnegative) exam scores.
 *Repeats for more exams, until the user says she/he is finished.
 ************************************************************/
public class ExamAverager
{
    public static void main(String[] args)
    {
        System.out.println("This program computes the average of");
        System.out.println("a list of (nonnegative) exam scores.");

        double sum;
        int numberOfStudents;
        double next;
        char answer;

        do
        {
            System.out.println();
            System.out.println("Enter all the scores to be averaged.");
            System.out.println("Enter a negative number after");
            System.out.println("you have entered all the scores.");
            sum = 0;
            numberOfStudents = 0;
            next = SavitchIn.readLineDouble();
            while (next >= 0)
            {
                sum = sum + next;
                numberOfStudents++;
                next = SavitchIn.readLineDouble();
            }
            if (numberOfStudents > 0)
                System.out.println("The average is "
                                + (sum/numberOfStudents));
            else
                System.out.println("No scores to average.");

            System.out.println("Want to average another exam?");
            System.out.println("Enter y for yes or n for no.");
            answer = SavitchIn.readLineNonwhiteChar();
        }while ((answer == 'y') || (answer == 'Y'));

    }
}
```

Display 3.14   Nested Loops *(Part 2 of 2)*

Sample Screen Dialogue

```
This program computes the average of
a list of (nonnegative) exam scores.

Enter all the scores to be averaged.
Enter a negative number after
you have entered all the scores.
100
90
100
90
-1
The average is 95.0
Want to average another exam?
Enter y for yes or n for no.
y

Enter all the scores to be averaged.
Enter a negative number after
you have entered all the scores.
90
70
80
-1
The average is 80.0
Want to average another exam?
Enter y for yes or n for no.
n
```

32. What output is produced by the following Java code:

```java
int count, innerCount;
for (count = 0; count <= 3; count++)
    for (innerCount = 0; innerCount < count; innerCount++)
        System.out.println(innerCount);
```

33. Give a Java loop statement that will read in a list of numbers of type *dou-ble* and then output their average. The numbers are all greater than or equal to 1.0. The list is ended with a sentinel value. You must specify the sentinel value. Also, give any declarations or initializing statements that are needed.

Loop Bugs

Programs with loops are more likely to contain mistakes than the programs you saw before you started using loops. Fortunately, there is a pattern to the kinds of mistakes you are most likely to make in designing a loop, so we can tell you what to look for. Moreover, there are some standard techniques you can use to locate and fix bugs in your loops.

The two most common kinds of loop errors are unintended infinite loops and *off-by-one errors*. Let's consider them in order.

infinite loops

We have already discussed infinite loops. There is, however, one subtlety about infinite loops that we need to emphasize. A loop might terminate for some input values but be an infinite loop for other values. Just because you tested your loop for some program input values and found that the loop ended, that does not mean that it will not be an infinite loop for some other input values. Let's consider an example.

You have a friend whose checking account balance is overdrawn. The bank charges a penalty each month that the balance is negative. Your friend wants a program that will tell her or him how long it will take to get the account balance to be nonnegative by making a fixed size deposit each month. You design the following code:

```java
count = 0;
while (balance < 0)
{
    balance = balance - penalty;
    balance = balance + deposit;
    count++;
}
System.out.println("You will have a nonnegative balance in "
                                    + count + " months.");
```

You place this code in a complete program and test the code with some reasonable values, like $15 for the penalty and $50 for the size of the deposit. The program runs fine. So you give it to your friend who runs it, and it then turns out to have an infinite loop. What happened? Your friend obviously does not have a head for numbers and decided to make small deposits. Your friend decided to deposit $10 per month. But, the bank charges a penalty of $15 a month when an account goes negative. So, the account simply gets a larger negative balance every month, even though your friend makes deposits.

It may seem that this could not happen. Your friend would not be so stupid. Don't count on it! It can happen even if your friend is not stupid. People are careless. One way to fix this bug is to add code that will test to see if the loop is infinite or not. For example, you might change the code to the following:

```java
if (payment <= penalty)
    System.out.println("payment is too small.");
else
{
    count = 0;
    while (balance < 0)
    {
        balance = balance - penalty;
        balance = balance + payment;
        count++;
    }
    System.out.println("You will have a nonnegative balance in "
                                        + count + " months.");
}
```

The other common kind of loop bug is an **off-by-one error**. This means that your loop repeats the loop body one too many times or one too few times. These sort of errors can result from carelessness in designing a controlling boolean expression. For example, if you use less-than when you should use less-than-or-equal, this can easily make your loop iterate the body the wrong number of times.

Another common problem with the controlling boolean expression of a loop has to do with the use of == to test for equality. This sort of equality testing works satisfactorily for integers and characters, but is not reliable for floating-point numbers. This is because the floating-point numbers are approximate quantities and == test for exact equality. The result of such a test is unpredictable. When comparing floating-point numbers, always use something involving less-than or greater-than, such as <=; do not use == or !=. Using a == or != to test floating-point numbers can produce an off-by-one error or an unintended infinite loop or even some other type of error.

One big danger with off-by-one errors is that they can easily go unnoticed. If a loop is iterated one too many times, or one too few times, then the results might still look reasonable, but be off by enough to cause trouble later on. Always make a specific check for off-by-one errors by comparing your loop results to results you know to be true by some other means, such as a pencil-and-paper calculation of a simple case.

off-by-one error

Always Retest

Whenever you find a bug in a program and "fix it," always retest the program. There may be yet another bug, or your "fix" may have introduced a new bug.

Tracing Variables

If your program misbehaves but you cannot see what is wrong, then your best bet is to *trace* some key variables. **Tracing variables** means watching the variables change value while the program is running. A program typically does not output a variable's value every time it changes the value of the variable, but it can help you to debug your program if you can see all these variable changes.

Many systems have a built-in utility that lets you easily trace variables without making any changes to your program. These debugging systems vary from one installation to another. If you have such a debugging facility, it is worth learning how to use it. If you do not have such a debugging facility, you can trace variables by simply inserting some extra, temporary output statements in your program. For example, suppose you want to trace the variables in the following code (which does contain an error):

```
count = 0;
while (balance < 0)
{
    balance = balance + penalty;
    balance = balance - deposit;
    count++;
}
System.out.println("You will have a positive balance in "
                                    + count + " months.");
```

You can trace the variables by adding the following output statements:

```
count = 0;
System.out.println("count == " + count);//trace
System.out.println("balance == " + balance);//trace
System.out.println("penalty == " + penalty);//trace
System.out.println("deposit == " + deposit);//trace
while (balance < 0)
{
    balance = balance + penalty;
    System.out.println("balance + penalty == " + balance);//trace
    balance = balance - deposit;
    System.out.println("balance - deposit == " + balance);//trace
    count++;
    System.out.println("count == " + count);//trace
}
System.out.println("You will have a positive balance in "
                                    + count + " months.");
```

After you have discovered the error and fixed the bugs in the code, you can remove the trace statements.

It may seem like a lot of bother to insert all the trace statements in the preceding example, but it is not so very much work. If you wish, you can first try tracing only some of the variables to see if that gives you enough information to find the problem. However, it is usually fastest to just trace all, or almost all, of the variables right from the start.

? Self-Test Questions

34. Add some suitable output statements to the following code, so that all variables are traced.

```
int n, sum = 0;
for (n = 1; n < 10; n++)
    sum = sum + n;
System.out.println("1 + 2 + ...+ 9 + 10 == " + sum);
```

35. What is the bug in the following code? What do you call this kind of loop bug?

```
int n, sum = 0;
for (n = 1; n < 10; n++)
    sum = sum + n;
System.out.println("1 + 2 + ...+ 9 + 10 == " + sum);
```

3.4 | The Type *boolean*

> *The truth is out there.*
> **Included in the credits for the television program The X Files.**
>
> *He who would distinguish the true from the false must have an adequate idea of what is true and false.*
> **Benedict Spinoza, Ethics**

The type *boolean* is a primitive type, just like the types *int*, *double*, and *char*. Just like these other types, you can have expressions of type *boolean*, values of type *boolean*, constants of type *boolean*, and variables of type *boolean*. However, there are only two values of type *boolean*: true and false. The two values *true* and *false* can be used in a program, just like numeric constants such as 2, 3.45, and the character constant 'A'.

Boolean variables can be used, among other things, to make your program easier to read. For example, a program might contain the following statement, where systemsAreOK is a boolean variable that is *true* if in fact the launch systems are ready to go:

```
if (systemsAreOK)
    System.out.println("Initiate launch sequence.");
else
    System.out.println("Abort launching sequence.");
```

If you do not use something like a boolean variable, then the preceding code is likely to read something like the following:

```
if ((temperature <= 100) && (thrust >= 12000) && (cabinPressure > 30))
    System.out.println("Initiate launch sequence.");
else
    System.out.println("Abort launching sequence.");
```

Clearly, the first version with the boolean variable is easier for a human being to understand.

Of course, your program needs to set the value of the boolean variable `systemsAreOK` in some way. As we will see, that is easy to do.

Boolean Expressions and Boolean Variables

boolean expression

A **boolean expression** evaluates to one of the two values *true* or *false*. For example, the expression `number > 0` in the following is a boolean expression:

```
if (number > 0)
    System.out.println("The number is positive.");
else
    System.out.println("The number is negative or zero.");
```

If `number > 0` evaluates to *true*, then the output is `"The number is positive."` If, on the other hand, `number > 0` evaluates to *false*, then the output is `"The number is negative or zero."` The meaning of a a boolean expression like `number > 0` is a bit easier to understand within a context, such as an `if-else`-statement. However, when programming with boolean variables you need to think about a boolean expression more or less without a context. A boolean expression can be evaluated and can produce a value of *true* or *false* without reference to any `if-else`-statement, `while`-loop, or other context that you have seen before this section.

boolean variables in assignments

A boolean variable can be assigned the value of a boolean expression by using an assignment statement, in the same way that you use an assignment statement to set the value of an `int` variable or any other type of variable. For example, the following sets the value of the boolean variable `isPositive` to *false*.

```
int number = -5;
boolean isPositive;
isPositive = (number > 0);
```

If you prefer, you can combine the last two lines as follows:

```
boolean isPositive = (number > 0);
```

The parentheses are not needed, but they do make it a bit easier to read.

Once a boolean variable has a value, you can use a boolean variable just like any other boolean expression. For example,

```
boolean isPositive = (number > 0);
if (isPositive)
    System.out.println("The number is positive.");
else
    System.out.println("The number is negative or zero.");
```

is equivalent to

```
if (number > 0)
    System.out.println("The number is positive.");
else
    System.out.println("The number is negative or zero.");
```

Of course, this is just a toy example. It is unlikely that anybody would use the first of the preceding two examples, but you might use something like this if the value of number, and so the value of the boolean expression, might change, as in the following, which might be part of a program to evaluate lottery tickets (by some stretch of the imagination):

```
System.out.println("Enter your number:");
number = SavitchIn.readLineInt();
boolean isPositive = (number > 0);
while (number > 0);
{
    System.out.println("Wow!");
    number = number - 1000;
}
if (isPositive)
    System.out.println("Your number is positive.");
else
    System.out.println("Sorry, your number is not positive.");
System.out.println("Only positive numbers can win.");
```

More complicated boolean expressions can be used in the same way. For example, if systemsAreOK is a variable of type *boolean*, it can be given a value as follows:

```
systemsAreOK =
  (temperature <= 100) && (thrust >= 12000) && (cabinPressure > 30);
```

■ Programming Tip
Naming Boolean Variables

When naming a boolean variable choose a statement that will be true when the value of the boolean expression is true, such as isPositive, systemsAreOK, and so forth. This way you can easily tell the meaning of the boolean variable when it is used in a *while*-loop, *if-else*-statement or other control statement. Do not use names that do not tell the meaning of the variable value. Do not use names like number-Sign, systemStatus, and so forth.

Precedence Rules

Java evaluates boolean expressions using the same strategy that it uses to evaluate arithmetic expressions. Let's consider an example:

```
(score >= 80) && (score < 90)
```

Suppose the value of `score` is `95`. The first subexpression (`score >= 80`) evaluates to *true*. The second subexpression (`score < 90`) evaluates to *false*. So the entire expression is reduced to

```
true && false
```

truth tables

The computer combines the values of *true* and/or *false* according rules called **truth tables** that are given in Display 3.15. So, the preceding expression evaluates to *false*.

When writing boolean expressions or arithmetic expressions, it is usually best to indicate the order of operations with parentheses. However, if parentheses are omitted, then the computer will perform the operations in the order determined by the **precedence rules** shown in Display 3.16. (Display 3.16 shows all the operators you are likely to use for some time, but a more complete list of precedence rules are given in Appendix 2.) Operators listed higher on the list are said to have **higher precedence.** When the computer is deciding which of two operators to perform first and the order is not dictated by parentheses, then it does the operator of higher precedence before the operator of lower precedence. Some operators have equal precedence, and then the order of operations is determined by the left-to-right order of the operators. Binary operators of equal precedence are performed in left-to-right order. Unary operators of equal precedence are performed in right-to-left order. Let's consider an example. (Recall that a unary operator is one that has only one argument (one thing it is applied to). A binary operator has two arguments.)

precedence
rules

The following is rather poor style, but the computer has no problem with it and it will be a good exercise to evaluate it using the precedence rules:

```
score < min/2 - 10 || score > 90
```

Of all the operators in the expression, the division operator has the highest precedence, and so is done first:

```
score < (min/2) - 10 || score > 90
```

Of the remaining operators in the expression, the subtraction operator has the highest precedence, and so is done next:

```
score < ((min/2) - 10) || score > 90
```

Of the remaining operators in the expression the > and < operators have the highest precedence and so they are done next. Because the > and < operators have equal precedence, they are done in left-to-right order:

```
(score < ((min/2) - 10)) || (score > 90)
```

Thus, we have produced a fully parenthesized version of the expression by using the precedence rules. To the computer, the two expressions are equivalent.

You should include most parentheses in order to make your arithmetic and boolean expressions easier to understand. However, one place where parentheses can be safely omitted is a simple string of &&'s or ||'s (but not a mixture of the two). For example, the following is good style even though a few parentheses are omitted:

```
(temperature > 95) || (rainFall > 20) || (humidity >= 60)
```

Display 3.15 **Truth Tables for Boolean Operators**

&& *(and)*

Value of A	Value of B	Resulting value of A && B
true	true	true
true	false	false
false	true	false
false	false	false

|| *(or)*

Value of A	Value of B	Resulting value of A || B
true	true	true
true	false	true
false	true	true
false	false	false

! *(not)*

Value of A	Resulting value of !(A)
true	false
false	true

Display 3.16 Precedence Rules

....

Highest Precedence

First: the unary operators: +, −, ++, − −, and !

Second: the binary arithmetic operators: *, /, %

Third: the binary arithmetic operators: +, −

Fourth: the boolean operators: <, >, <=, >=

Fifth: the boolean operators: ==, !=

Sixth: the boolean operator &

Seventh: the boolean operator |

Eighth: the boolean operator &&

Ninth: the boolean operator ||

Lowest Precedence

....

short-circuit evaluation

The way that Java handles || and && is just a bit more complicated than what we have said so far. Consider the following boolean expression:

```
(score > 90) || (assignmentsDone > 8)
```

Now, suppose that the value of score is 95. In this case we know that the boolean expression evaluates to *true*, no matter what the value of assignmentsDone is. This is because *true* || *true* and *true* || *false* both evaluate to *true*. So, it does not matter whether assignmentsDone > 8 evaluates to *true* or *false*. The value of the whole expression is bound to be *true*. Java evaluates an expression connected with || or && in just this way. It evaluates the first subexpression, and if that is enough information to determine the value of the whole expression, then it does not evaluate the second subexpression. So, in this example, Java never bothers to evaluate the expression assignmentsDone > 8. This way of evaluating only as much of an expression as it needs is called **short-circuit evaluation** and is the kind of evaluation that is done by Java with && and ||. (Short-circuit evaluation is also sometimes called **lazy evaluation**.)

Now, let's look at an example using && and let's give the boolean expression some context by placing it in an *if-else*-statement:

```
if ((assignmentsDone > 0) && ((totalScore/assignmentsDone) > 60))
    System.out.println("Good work.");
else
        System.out.println("Work harder.");
```

Suppose AssignmentsDone has a value of 0. Then the first subexpression is *false*. Now, both *false && true* and *false && false* evaluate to *false*. No matter whether the second expression is *true* or *false*, the entire boolean expression is *false*. So, Java does not bother to evaluate the second subexpression:

```
(totalScore/assignmentsDone) > 60
```

In this case, not evaluating the second subexpression does make a big difference, because the second subexpression includes a division by zero. If Java had tried to evaluate the second subexpression, that would have produced a run-time error. By using short-circuit evaluation Java has prevented a run-time error.

Java also allows you to ask for **complete evaluation**. In complete evaluation, when two expressions are joined by an "and" or an "or," *both* subexpressions are *always evaluated* and then the truth tables are used to obtain the value of the final expression. To obtain complete evaluation in Java, you use & rather than && for "and" and use | in place of || for "or."

complete evaluation

In most situations, short-circuit evaluation and complete evaluation give the same result, but as we have seen, there are some cases in which short-circuit evaluation can avoid a run-time error. There are some situations where complete evaluation is preferred, but we will not use those techniques in this book, and so we will always use && and || so as to obtain short-circuit evaluation.

Input and Output of Boolean Values

The values *true* and *false* of the type *boolean* can be input and output in the same way as values of the other primitive types, such as *int* and *double*. For example, consider the following fragment from a Java program:

```
boolean booleanVar = false;
System.out.println(booleanVar);
System.out.println("Enter a boolean value:");
booleanVar = SavitchIn.readLineBoolean();
System.out.println("You entered " + booleanVar);
```

This code could produce the following dialog:

```
false
Enter a boolean value:
true
You entered true
```

As you can see from this example, the class SavitchIn has a method named readLineBoolean that will read a single *boolean* value on a line by itself. For this method, you may spell *true*, and *false*, with either upper- or lowercase letters; you also may use a single letter t or f (upper- or lowercase) for *true* and *false*. These spelling variations of *true* and *false* apply only to input and only when using the method readLineBoolean. In a Java program, the spelling must always be either *true* or *false*, spelled out and in all lowercase.

T and F

Case Study

Using a Boolean Variable to End a Loop

In this case study, you will not solve a complete problem, but you will design a loop for a commonly occurring subtask and place it in a demonstration program. This will allow you to get used to one of the most common uses of boolean variables.

task
specification

In this case study, you want to design a loop to read in a list of numbers and compute the sum of all the numbers on the list. You know that the numbers are all nonnegative. For example, the numbers might be a list of the number of hours worked for each person on a programming team. Because nobody works a negative number of hours, you know the numbers are all nonnegative and so you can use a negative number as a sentinel value to mark the end of the list of numbers. For this task, you know the numbers will all be integers, but the same technique would work for other kinds of numbers and even for reading in nonnumeric data.

You will get a better grasp of the problem and possible solutions if you first design the loop in pseudocode. So, you design the following pseudocode:

```
int sum = 0;
Do the following for each number on the list:
        if (the number is negative)
                Make this the last loop iteration.
        else
                sum = sum + the number;
```

Because you know that there is a negative number marking the end of the list, you refine the pseudocode to the following:

```
int next, sum = 0;
while (There are numbers left to read.)
{
        next = SavitchIn.readLineInt();
        if (next < 0)
                Make this the last loop iteration.
        else
                sum = sum + next;
}
```

There are a number of different ways to finish converting this pseudocode to Java code. You have just learned about boolean variables, so let's say you decide to try them (and that will turn out to be a good decision). One nice thing about a boolean variable is that it can read just like an English sentence. So you decide to try a boolean variable named thereAreNumbersLeftToRead. Simply declaring this boolean variable and substituting it for the phrase "There are numbers left to read." yields the following:

```
int next, sum = 0;
boolean thereAreNumbersLeftToRead;
Initialize the variable thereAreNumbersLeftToRead.
while (thereAreNumbersLeftToRead)
{
    next = SavitchIn.readLineInt();
    if (next < 0)
        Make this the last loop iteration.
    else
        sum = sum + next;
}
```

Now it is straightforward to complete this loop to produce working Java code. The phrase "Make this the last loop iteration." can be translated in one obvious way. The loop ends when the boolean variable thereAreNumbersLeftToRead has a value of *false*. So, the way to end the loop is to set thereAreNumbersLeftToRead equal to *false*. So, "Make this the last loop iteration." will translate into

```
thereAreNumbersLeftToRead = false;
```

All that is left to do is to determine the initial value for the boolean variable thereAreNumbersLeftToRead. You know that even if the list of numbers is empty, there will at least be the sentinel value to read, so you know the loop body must be iterated at least once. Thus, in order for the loop to get started, thereAreNumbersLeftToRead must be *true*. So, you know that thereAreNumbersLeftToRead must be initialized to *true*. Thus, you come up with the following code:

```
int next, sum = 0;
boolean thereAreNumbersLeftToRead = true;
while (thereAreNumbersLeftToRead)
{
    next = SavitchIn.readLineInt();
    if (next < 0)
        thereAreNumbersLeftToRead = false;
    else
        sum = sum + next;
}
```

When the loop ends, the variable sum contains the sum of the numbers on the input list (not including the sentinel value).

All that is left is to put the loop into a program. You decide that the variable name thereAreNumbersLeftToRead is a bit too long and so you shorten it to numbersLeft and produce the program shown in Display 3.17.

? Self-Test Questions

36. What is the output produced by the following statements?

Display 3.17 Use of a Boolean Variable to End a Loop

```
//Illustrates the use of a boolean variable to control loop ending.
public class BooleanDemo
{
    public static void main(String[] args)
    {
        System.out.println("Enter nonnegative numbers, one per
                line.");
        System.out.println("Place a negative number at the end");
        System.out.println("to serve as an end marker.");

        int next, sum = 0;
        boolean numbersLeft = true;
        while (numbersLeft)
        {
            next = SavitchIn.readLineInt();
            if (next < 0)
                numbersLeft = false;
            else
                sum = sum + next;
        }

        System.out.println("The sum of the numbers is " + sum);
    }
}
```

Sample Screen Dialogue

```
Enter nonnegative numbers, one per line.
Place a negative number at the end
to serve as an end marker.
1
2
3
-1
The sum of the numbers is 6
```

```
int number = 7;
boolean isPositive = (number > 0);
if (number > 0);
    number = -100;
if (isPositive)
    System.out.println("Positive.");
else
    System.out.println("Not positive.");
```

37. What is the output produced by the following statements?

```
System.out.println(false);
System.out.println(7 < 0);
System.out.println(7 > 0);
int n = 7;
System.out.println(n > 0);
```

CHAPTER SUMMARY

- A statement that chooses one of a number of actions to perform is called a **branch**. The *if-else-* and *switch*-statements are branch statements.

- Java has two forms of multi-way branches: the *switch*-statement and the multibranch *if-else*-statement.

- A **loop** is a programming construct that repeats an action some number of times. The part that is repeated is called the **body** of the loop. Every repetition of the loop body is called a loop **iteration**.

- Java has three kinds of loop statements: *while*-statements, *do-while*-statements, and *for*-statements.

- One way to end an input loop is to place a sentinel value at the end of the input list and have your loop check for the sentinel value.

- The most common kinds of loop bugs are unintended infinite loops and off-by-one errors.

- Tracing a variable means that the value of the variable is output every time the variable is changed. This can be done with special debugging utilities or by inserting temporary output statements. (Sometimes you do not output every change but just selected changes.)

CHAPTER SUMMARY

■ The value of a boolean expression can be stored in a variable of type *boolean*. The variable of type *boolean* can then be used to control an *if-else*-statement, a *while*-statement, or anyplace else that a boolean expression is allowed.

? ANSWERS to Self-Test Questions

1.
```
if (goals > 10)
    System.out.println("Wow");
else
    System.out.println("Oh Well");
```

2.
```
if ((goals > 10) && (errors == 0))
    System.out.println("Wow");
else
    System.out.println("Oh Well");
```

3.
```
if (salary >= deductions)
{
    System.out.println("OK");
    net = salary - deductions;
}
else
{
    System.out.println("Crazy.");
}
```

It is also acceptable to omit the curly brackets in the *else*-part.

4.
```
if ((speed > 25) && (visibility < 20))
{
    speed = 25;
    System.out.println("Caution");
}
```

5.
```
if ((salary >= MIN_SALARY) || (bonus >= MIN_BONUS))
    System.out.println("OK");
else
    System.out.println("Too low");
```

6.

```
String upperWord = nextWord.toUpperCase();
if (upperWord.compareTo("N") < 0)
    System.out.println("First half of the alphabet");
else
    System.out.println("Second half of the alphabet");
```

7. Time and tide wait for me.

8. Time and tide wait for no one.

9. Time and tide wait for every one.

10.

```
if (number > 10)
    System.out.println("High");
else if (number < 5)
    System.out.println("Low");
else
    System.out.println("So-so");
```

11. Till we meet again.

12.

```
Hello
Good-bye
```

13. Some kind of B.

14. Pie

15. Cookies

16. Diet time:

17.

```
0
1
2
3
4
count after loop = 5
```

18. Yes, a *while*-loop can execute the body of the loop zero times. No, a *do-while*-loop cannot execute the body of the loop zero times.

19.

```
0
count after loop = 1
```

20.
```
int number;
{
        System.out.println("Enter a whole number:");
        number = SavitchIn.readLineInt();
        System.out.println("You entered " + number);
}
while (number > 0)
{
        System.out.println("Enter a whole number:");
        number = SavitchIn.readLineInt();
        System.out.println("You entered " + number);
}
System.out.println("number after loop = " + number);
```

21. This is an infinite loop. The `println`-statement after the loop will never be executed. The output begins
```
0
-1
-2
-3
.
.
.
```

22.
```
1
2
3
4
```

23. This loop causes no output. The boolean expression n > 4 is not satisfied the first time through the loop, so the loop ends without iterating its body.

24.
```
4
3
2
1
```

25.
```
0.0
0.5
1.0
1.5
2.0
2.5
```

26.
```
int n;
for (n = 1; n <= 5; n++)
    System.out.println(2*n);
```

27.
```
Hello
Hello
After the Loop.
```

28.
```
Hello
Hello
```
Note that it does not output "`After the Loop.`", because the program ends.

29.
```
One
Two
Three
After the Loop.
```
Note that the *break*-statement ends the *switch*-statement but does not end the *for*-loop.

30.
```
int time;
for (time = 1; time <= 4; time++)
    System.out.println("One more time.");
```

31.
```
int result = 1;
int count;
for (count = 1; count <= 5; count++)
    result = 2*result;
```

32.
```
0
0
1
0
1
2
```

33. You can use any number less than 1.0 as a sentinel value, but to avoid any problems with the approximate nature of *double* values, it should be significantly less than 1.0.

```
double sum = 0, next;
System.out.println("Enter a list of numbers. All the");
System.out.println("numbers must be 1.0 or larger");
System.out.println("Place a zero at the end");
System.out.println("to mark the end of the list.");
next = SavitchIn.readLineDouble();
int count = 0;
while (next > 0.9)//next >=1.0 runs a risk of being inaccurate.
{
    sum = sum + next;
    count++;
    next = SavitchIn.readLineDouble();
}
if (count > 0)
    System.out.println("Average is " + (sum/count));
else
    System.out.println("No numbers to average.");
```

34.
```
int n, sum = 0;
System.out.println("sum == " + sum);
for (n = 1; n < 10; n++)
{
    sum = sum + n;
    System.out.println("n == " + n);
    System.out.println("sum == " + sum);
}
System.out.println("1 + 2 + ...+ 9 + 10 == " + sum);
```

35. The boolean expression should be n <= 10 not n < 10. This is an *off-by-one error*.

36. Positive

37. The output produced is
```
false
false
true
true
```

? PROGRAMMING EXERCISES

1. Write a program that takes a one-line sentence as input and then outputs the following response: If the sentence ends with the question mark '?'

and the input contains an even number of characters, then output the word "Yes". If the sentence ends with the question mark '?' and the input contains an odd number of characters, then output the word "No". If the sentence ends with an exclamation mark '!', then output the word "Wow". In all other cases, your program will output the string "You always say " followed by the input string enclosed in quotes. Your output should all be on one line. Be sure to note that in the last case, your output must include quotation marks around the echoed input string. In all other cases, there are no quotes in the output. Your program should have a loop that allows the user to repeat this until the user indicates that she/he wants to end the program. Your program does not have to check the input to see that the user entered a legitimate sentence.

2. Write a program that allows the user to convert either from degrees Celsius to Fahrenheit or degrees Fahrenheit to Celsius. Use the following formulas

$$degreesC = 5(degreesF - 32)/9$$
$$degreesF = (9(degreesC)/5) + 32$$

Prompt the user to enter a temperature and either a 'C' (or 'c') for Celsius or an 'F' (or 'f') for Fahrenheit: allow either upper or lower case, but if anything other than 'C', 'c', 'F', or 'f' is entered, print an error message and ask the user to reenter a valid selection (upper or lower case 'C' or 'F'). Convert the temperature to Fahrenheit if Celsius is entered, or to Celsius if Fahrenheit is entered, then ask the user to enter 'Q' or 'q' to quit or any other key to repeat the loop and perform another conversion.

3. Write a program to read in a list of nonnegative integers and output: the largest integer, the smallest integer, and the average of all the integers. The end of the input is indicated by the user entering a negative sentinel value. Note that the sentinel value is not used in finding the largest, smallest, or average. It is only an end marker. The average should be a value of type *double* so that the average is computed with a fractional part.

4. Write a program to read a list of exam scores (integer percent scores, in the range 0 to 100) and output the total number of grades and the number of grades in each letter-grade category (90 to 100 = A, 80 to 89 = B, 70 to 79 = C, 60 to 69 = D, and 0 to 59 = F). The end of the input is indicated by entering a negative score as a sentinel value (the negative value is used only to end the loop, so do not use it in the calculations). For example, if the input is

```
98
87
86
85
85
78
73
72
72
72
70
66
63
50
−1
```

the output would be

```
Total number of grades = 14
Number of A's = 1
Number of B's = 4
Number of C's = 6
Number of D's = 2
Number of F's = 1
```

5. Combine the programs from problems 3 and 4 to read in test scores (whole number percentages from 0 to 100) and print out the following statistics:

```
Total number of scores
Total number of each letter grade
Percent of total for each letter grade
Range of scores: lowest and highest
Average score
```

As before, enter a negative score as a sentinel value to end the data input and print out the statistics.

6. Write a program that takes as input a bank account balance and an interest rate and outputs the value of the account in 10 years. The output should show the value of the account for three different methods of compounding interest: annually, monthly, and daily. When compounded annually, the interest is added once per year at the end of the year. When compounded monthly the interest is added in 12 times per year. When computed daily, the interest is added 365 times per year. You do not have to worry about leap years. Assume all years have 365 days. On annual interest, you can assume that the interest is posted exactly one year from the date of deposit. In other words, you do not have to worry about interest being posted on a specific day of the year, like December 31. Similarly, you can assume monthly interest is posted exactly one month after it in entered. Since the account earns interest on the interest, the account should have a higher balance when interest is posted more frequently. Be

sure to adjust the interest rate for the time period of the interest. If the rate is 5%, then when posting monthly interest, you use (5/12)%. When posting daily interest, you use (5/365)%. Do your calculation using a loop that adds in the interest for each time period. (Do not use some sort of algebraic formula.) Your program should have an outer loop that allows the user to repeat this calculation for a new balance and interest rate. The calculation is repeated until the user indicates that she/he wants to end the program.

7. Modify problem 7 from Chapter 2 to include input checking. Print the change only if a valid price is entered (no less than 25 cents, no more than 100 cents, and an integer multiple of 5 cents). Otherwise print separate error messages for any of the following invalid inputs: a cost under 25 cents, a cost that is not an integer multiple of 5, and a cost that is more than a dollar.

8. Write a program that asks the user to enter the size of triangle to print out (an integer from 1 to 50, then print the triangle by printing a series of lines with asterisks. The first line will have one asterisk, the next two, etc., each line having one more asterisk than the previous line up to the number entered by the user; on the next line print one less asterisk and continue by decreasing the number of asterisks by one for each successive line until only one asterisk is printed. Hint: use nested for loops; the outside loop controls the number of lines to print and the inside loop controls the number of asterisks to print on a line. For example, if the user enters 5 the output would be

```
*
**
***
****
*****
****
***
**
*
```

CHAPTER 4

DEFINING CLASSES AND METHODS

4.1 CLASS AND METHOD DEFINITIONS 211
Class Files and Separate
  Compilation 212
Instance Variables 213
Using Methods 215
void-Method Definitions 219
Methods that Return a Value 222
Java Tip Use of *return* in *void*-
  Methods 225
The *this* Parameter 225
Local Variables 229
Blocks 231
Gotcha Variables Declared in a
  Block 232
Java Tip Declaring Variables in a
  for-Statement 232
Parameters of a Primitive Type 232
Gotcha Use of the Terms "Parame-
  ter" and "Argument" 238
Summary of Class and Method
  Definition Syntax 239

4.2 INFORMATION HIDING AND ENCAPSULATION 241
Information Hiding 241
Programming Tip Formal Parameter
  Names Are Local to the
  Method 243
Precondition and Postcondition
  Comments 243

The *public* and *private*
  Modifiers 244
Programming Tip Instance Variables
  Should Be Private 247
Encapsulation 252
Programming Example Purchase Class 252
Case Study Changing the Implementa-
  tion of an Encapsulated Class 259
Automatic Documentation with
  javadoc 263

4.3 OBJECTS AND REFERENCE 264
Variables of a Class Type and
  Objects 265
Gotcha Use of = and == with
  Variables of a Class Type 270
Java Tip Define an *equals* Method
  for Your Classes 270
Boolean-Valued Methods 275
Programming Example A Species Class 275
Class Parameters 279
Comparing Class Parameters and
  Primitive-Type Parameters 281

Chapter Summary 286
Answers to Self-Test Questions 287
Programming Exercises 292

DEFINING CLASSES AND METHODS

> *class* n. **1. a.** *A set, collection, group, or configuration containing members having or thought to have at least one attribute in common; kind; sort.*
> ...
>
> **The American Heritage Dictionary of the English Language, Third Edition**

Recall that an object is named by a variable of a class. Like variables of the primitive types (such as `int`), objects have data, but they also can take actions. The actions are called *methods*. You have already been using some objects. The type `String` is a class and values of type `String` are objects. For example, if `name` is an object of type `String`, then the method `length` can be used to determine the length of the string. The length of the string is the value returned by the expression `name.length()`. In this chapter, we will show you how to define your own simple classes and how to use objects and methods of those classes.

Objectives

Become familiar with the concepts of a *class* and an *object* that instantiates the class.

Learn how to define classes in Java.

Learn to define and use *methods* (object actions) in Java.

Learn to create objects in Java.

Find out how *parameters* work in Java.

Learn about *information hiding* and *encapsulation*.

Become familiar with the notion of *reference* so that you can understand class variable and class parameters.

Prerequisites

You need to be familiar with the material in Chapters 2 and 3 before reading this chapter.

Display 4.1   **Class as an Outline**

```
Class Name: Automobile

Data:
  amount of fuel_____
  speed _____
  license plate _____

Methods (actions):
  increaseSpeed:
    How: Press on gas pedal.
  stop:
    How: Press on brake pedal.
```

Class Definition

Instantiations of the Class Automobile:

First Instantiation:
Object name: patsCar

```
amount of fuel: 10 gallons
speed: 55 miles per hour
license plate: "135 XJK"
```

Second Instantiation:
Object name: suesCar

```
amount of fuel: 14 gallons
speed: 0 miles per hour
license plate: "SUES CAR"
```

Third Instantiation:
Object name: ronsCar

```
amount of fuel: 2 gallons
speed: 75 miles per hour
license plate: "351 WLF"
```

Objects that are instantiations of the class

4.1 | Class and Method Definitions

A Java program consists of objects, from various classes, interacting with one another. Before we go into the details of how you define and use classes and objects in Java, it will help to have a general idea of what classes and object are all about.

Objects can represent objects in the real word, like automobiles, houses, employee records, almost anything you want. A **class** is the definition of a kind of object. It is like an outline or a plan for constructing specific objects. For example, Display 4.1 describes a class called Automobile. The class is a general description of

object
class

what an automobile is and what it can do. Objects are particular automobiles. The figure shows three Automobile objects. An object that satisfies the class definition

instantiate

of an Automobile is said to **instantiate** the Automobile class. Thus, objects are the individual automobiles, while the Automobile class is a description of what an automobile is and does. This is, of course, a very simplified Automobile class, but it illustrates the basic idea of what a class is. Let's look at some details.

A class specifies the kind of data the objects of that class have. The Automobile class definition says that an Automobile objects has three pieces of data: A number telling how many gallons of fuel are in the fuel tank, another number telling how fast the automobile is moving, and a string that shows what is written on the license plate. The class definition has no data (that is, no numbers and no string). The individual objects have the data, but the class specifies what kind of data they have.

The class also specifies what action the objects can take and how they accomplish those actions. The Automobile class specifies two actions: increaseSpeed and stop. Thus, in a program that uses the class Automobile, the only actions an Automobile object can take are increaseSpeed and stop. These actions are called

method

methods. All objects of the class Automobile have the exact same methods. All objects of any one class have the same methods. As you can see in our sample Automobile class, the definitions of the methods (how the actions are performed) are given in the class definition. However, the method actions are performed by the objects.

Notice a few more things about a class and the objects that instantiate the class. Each object has a name. In Display 4.1, the names are patsCar, suesCar, and ronsCar. Among other things, a class is a data type. In a Java program, these object names (patsCar, suesCar, and ronsCar) would be variables of type Automobile. But, now we are getting down to the nitty gritty of Java code. So, it is almost time to define a simple class in Java. But before we define our first Java class, we will tell you about how you store classes in files and how you compile them. That way you can see the classes and objects in action on your computer.

Class Files and Separate Compilation

We are about to tell you how to define classes in Java. If you want to follow this discussion by running the programs, all the classes and programs in this book are available on the CD provided with this book. Whether you use a class we write in this book or a class that you yourself write, you need to know a few basic details about how a Java class definition is stored in a file. Each Java class definition should be in a file by itself.[1] Not only should each Java class definition be in a separate file, but the name of the file should be the same as the name of the class, and the file name should end in .java. So, if you write a definition for a class called Automobile, then it should be in a file named Automobile.java. If you write a definition for a class called MyClass, then it should be in a file named MyClass.java.

You can compile a Java class before you have any program in which to use it. The compiled byte code for the class will be stored in a file of the same name but

---

1. There are exceptions to this rule, but we will seldom encounter these exceptions, and we need not be concerned about them yet.

ending in .class rather than .java. So, if you compile the file Automobile.java, that will create a file called Automobile.class. Later, you can compile a program file with a main part that uses the class Automobile, and you will not need to recompile the class definition for Automobile. This naming requirement applies to full programs as well as classes. Notice that every program with a main has a class name at the start of the file; this is the name you need to use for the file that holds the program. For example, the program in Display 4.3/page 217 should be in a file named SpeciesFirstTryDemo.java. As long as all the classes you use in a program are in the same directory as the program file, you need not worry about directories. In Chapter 5, we will discuss how you can place files in more than one directory.

Instance Variables

Display 4.2 contains a simple class definition. We have simplified this class to make this first example easier to explain. Later in this chapter, we will give this same example in a better style. But, this example has all the essentials of a class definition. It will take several subsections to fully explain this class definition. So, let's get started.

The class name is SpeciesFirstTry and is designed to hold records of endangered species. (It's called FirstTry because we will later give an improved version of this class.) Each object of this class has three pieces of data: a name, a population size, and a growth rate. The objects have three methods: readInput, writeOutput, and populationIn10. Both the data items and the methods are sometimes called **members** of the object, because they belong to the object; they are also sometimes called **fields**. However, we will use different names. We will call the data items *instance variables* and we will call the methods *methods*. Let's discuss the data items (that is, the instance variables) first.

member

field

The following three lines from the start of the class definition define three **instance variables** (three data members):

instance
variable

```
public String name;
public int population;
public double growthRate;
```

The word *public* simply means that there are no restrictions on how these instance variables are used. Each of these lines declares one instance variable name. You can think of an object of the class as a complex item with instance variables inside of it. So, you can think of an instance variable as a smaller variable inside each object of the class. In this case, the instance variables are called name, population, and growthRate. Each object of the class will have three instance variables named name, population, and growthRate. Display 4.3 contains a program that demonstrates the use of this class definition. Let's see how it handles these instance variables.

The following line from Display 4.3 creates an object of type Species-FirstTry and attaches the name speciesOfTheMonth to this object:

```
SpeciesFirstTry speciesOfTheMonth = new SpeciesFirstTry();
```

Display 4.2   A Class Definition (Part 1 of 2)

```java
public class SpeciesFirstTry
{
    public String name;
    public int population;
    public double growthRate;

    public void readInput()
    {
        System.out.println("What is the species name?");
        name = SavitchIn.readLine();
        System.out.println("What is the population of the species?");
        population = SavitchIn.readLineInt();
        while (population < 0)
        {
            System.out.println("Population cannot be negative.");
            System.out.println("Reenter population:");
            population = SavitchIn.readLineInt();
        }
        System.out.println(
                    "Enter growth rate (percent increase per year):");
        growthRate = SavitchIn.readLineDouble();
    }

    public void writeOutput()
    {
        System.out.println("Name = " + name);
        System.out.println("Population = " + population);
        System.out.println("Growth rate = " + growthRate + "%");
    }
```

We will give a better version of this class later in this chapter.

Later in this chapter we will see that the modifier public should be replaced with private.

Like all objects of type `SpeciesFirstTry`, the object `speciesOfTheMonth` has three instance variables called `name`, `population`, and `growthRate`. You can refer to one of these instance variables by writing the object name followed by a dot and then the instance variable's name. For example,

```java
speciesOfTheMonth.name
```

denotes the `name` instance variable for the object `speciesOfTheMonth`. Look again at the three lines that define the instance variables (repeated in what follows).

Display 4.2 A Class Definition *(Part 2 of 2)*

```java
    public int populationIn10()
    {
        double populationAmount = population;
        int count = 10;
        while ((count > 0) && (populationAmount > 0))
        {
            populationAmount = (populationAmount +
                            (growthRate/100) * populationAmount);

            count--;
        }
        if (populationAmount > 0)
            return (int)populationAmount;
        else
            return 0;
    }
}
```

(`int`) is a type cast, as discussed in *Chapter 2* starting on page 64.

```java
    public String name;
    public int population;
    public double growthRate;
```

Notice that each instance variable has a type. For example, the instance variable name is of type `String`, so the instance variable `speciesOfTheMonth.name` is a variable of type `String` and it can be used anyplace that you can use a variable of type `String`. For example, all of the following are legal Java expressions:

```java
    speciesOfTheMonth.name = "Klingon ox.";
    System.out.println("Save the " + speciesOfTheMonth.name);
    String niceName = speciesOfTheMonth.name;
```

Each object of type `SpeciesFirstTry` has its own three instance variables. For example, suppose your program were to also contain

```java
    SpeciesFirstTry speciesOfLastMonth = new SpeciesFirstTry();
```

Then `speciesOfTheMonth.name` and `speciesOfLastMonth.name` are two different instance variables that might have different string values.

Using Methods

Methods are actions that can be taken by an object of a class. A method **invocation** is an order telling the object to perform the method action, and to do it with the data

invocation

Why Do You Need *new*?

When used in an expression such as the following, you can think of *new* as creating the instance variables of the object.

```
SpeciesFirstTry speciesOfLastMonth = new SpeciesFirstTry();
```

A variable of a primitive type, such as a variable of type *int* or *double*, is a simple variable. A variable of a class type, such as `speciesOfLastMonth`, is a more complex variable that can, in some sense, have smaller variables inside of it, namely, the instance variables of the object. The *new* places these instance variables inside of the object. We will explain this use of *new* more completely in Section 4.3 | .

---

in the object. Some other terms that are used to mean the same thing as invoke a method are to *call a method* and to *pass a message to the object*. You have already used method invocations. For example, you have used the method `readLineInt()` of the class `SavitchIn`. You have also used the method `println` with the object `System.out`, as in the following statement:

```
System.out.println("Enter data on the Species of the Month:");
```

There are two kinds of methods: (1) those that return a single value and (2) those that perform some action other than returning a single value. The method `readLineInt` is an example of a method that returns a single value. The method `readLineInt` returns a value of type *int*. The method `println` is an example of a method that performs some action other than returning a single value. These two different kinds of methods are used in slightly different ways.

Two Kinds of Methods

There are two kinds of methods: (1) those that return a single value and (2) those that perform some action other than return a value. Methods that perform some action other than returning a single value are called *void-* **methods.**

Let's first discuss how you invoke a method that returns a single value, using the method `readLineInt` as an example that should be familiar to you. Suppose you have the following declaration in a program:

```
int next;
```

The following is an example of an invocation of the method `readLineInt` for the class `SavitchIn`:

```
next = SavitchIn.readLineInt();
```

(If you want to see this in the context of a full program, see Display 3.17/page 198.) Let's look at this method invocation in more detail.

calling object   A method defined in a class is usually invoked using an object of that class. This object is known as the **calling object,** and it is the first item that you give when writing a method invocation. For certain special methods, you can use the name of the class instead of using an object of the class, and our first example will use the class name `SavitchIn` rather than an object of that class. The way that you invoke a

Display 4.3 Using Classes and Methods

```java
public class SpeciesFirstTryDemo
{
    public static void main(String[] args)
    {
        SpeciesFirstTry speciesOfTheMonth = new SpeciesFirstTry();
        int futurePopulation;

        System.out.println("Enter data on the Species of the Month:");
        speciesOfTheMonth.readInput();
        speciesOfTheMonth.writeOutput();

        futurePopulation = speciesOfTheMonth.populationIn10();
        System.out.println("In ten years the population will be "
                                            + futurePopulation);

        speciesOfTheMonth.name = "Klingon ox";
        speciesOfTheMonth.population = 10;
        speciesOfTheMonth.growthRate = 15;
        System.out.println("The new Species of the Month:");
        speciesOfTheMonth.writeOutput();
        System.out.println("In ten years the population will be "
                                    + speciesOfTheMonth.populationIn10());
    }
}
```

Sample Screen Dialogue

```
Enter data on the Species of the Month:
What is the species' name?
Ferengie fur ball
What is the population of the species?
1000
Enter growth rate (percent increase per year):
−20.5
Name = Ferengie fur ball
Population = 1000
Growth rate = −20.5%
In ten years the population will be 100
The new Species of the Month:
Name = Klingon ox
Population = 10
Growth rate = 15.0%
In ten years the population will be 40
```

method is to write the calling object name or the class name (such as `SavitchIn`), followed by a dot, and then the name of the method (such as `readLineInt`), and finally a set of parentheses that may (or may not) have information for the method.

value returned If the method is one that returns a single value, such as the method `readLineInt`, then you can use this method invocation anyplace that it is legal to use a value of the type returned by the method. The method `readLineInt` returns a value of type `int`, and so you can use the method invocation

```
SavitchIn.readLineInt()
```

anyplace that it is legal to use a value of type `int`; that is, you can use an invocation of the method `readLineInt` anyplace you can use an `int` value such as the value 6 or 937. A value of type `int`, such as 6, can be used in an assignment statement, like this:

```
next = 6;
```

and so the method invocation `SavitchIn.readLineInt()` can be used in the same way, like so:

```
next = SavitchIn.readLineInt();
```

When a method that returns a single value is invoked, it is as if the method invocation were replaced by the value returned. So, if `SavitchIn.readLineInt()` returns the value 3, then the assignment statement

```
next = SavitchIn.readLineInt();
```

produces the same effect as

```
next = 3;
```

not returning a value Methods that perform some action other than returning a single value are similar, except that they are used to produce Java statements rather than Java values. For example, the following statement from the program in Display 4.3/page 217 includes an invocation of the method `println` with the calling object `System.out`:

```
System.out.println("Enter data on the Species of the Month:");
```

This method call causes the string `"Enter data on the Species of the Month:"` to be written to the screen. The method `writeOutput` for the class `Species-FirstTry` (used in Display 4.3) is similar, except that you do not have to tell `writeOutput` what to output by putting something inside the parentheses. The method `writeOutput` gets the information to send to the screen from its calling object.

For example, the program in Display 4.3 (after doing some other things) sets the values of the instance variables of the object `speciesOfTheMonth` with the following three assignment statements:

```
speciesOfTheMonth.name = "Klingon ox";
speciesOfTheMonth.population = 10;
speciesOfTheMonth.growthRate = 15;
```

The program then uses the following statements to output these values:

```
System.out.println("The new Species of the Month:");
speciesOfTheMonth.writeOutput();
```

The second of the previous two lines of code contains an *invocation* of the method `writeOutput` with the calling object `speciesOfTheMonth`. This invocation produces the output

```
Name = Klingon ox
Population = 10
Growth rate = 15.0%
```

A method invocation is an order telling the object to perform the method action, and to do it with the data of the calling object. In this sample case, the method is `writeOutput`, and the action is to write something on the screen—specifically to write the values of the instance variables of the object `speciesOfThe-Month`.

Recall that, to **invoke** a method for an object, you write the calling object name (such as `speciesOfTheMonth`), followed by a dot, and then the name of the method (such as `writeOutput`), and finally a set of parentheses that may have information for the method. If, as is true in this case, the method invocation is one that produces some action other than returning a single value, then you make it into a Java statement by placing a semicolon after the method invocation. So the following is an invocation of the method `writeOutput` for the object `speciesOfTheMonth`:

invoke

```
speciesOfTheMonth.writeOutput();
```

This causes the method to perform whatever action is specified in the method definition, so let's look at method definitions.

Method Invocation (Calling a Method)

You **invoke** a method by writing down the calling object followed by a dot, then the name of the method, and finally a set of parentheses that may (or may not) have information for the method.

If the method invocation returns a value, then you can use the method invocation anyplace that you are allowed to write a value of the type returned by the method. For example, the following includes an invocation of the method `populationIn10` by the calling object `speciesOfTheMonth`:

```
futurePopulation = speciesOfTheMonth.populationIn10();
```

If the method invocation is one that performs some action other than returning a single value, then you place a semicolon after the method invocation, and that produces a Java statement. (These methods that perform actions are called *void*-methods.) For example, the following is an invocation of the method `readInput` with the calling object `speciesOfTheMonth`:

```
speciesOfTheMonth.readInput();
```

This method invocation causes the method to perform whatever action is specified in the method definition.

For certain special methods (like the methods in the class `SavitchIn`), you can use the class name rather than a calling object. These kinds of methods are discussed more fully in Chapter 5.

---

void-Method Definitions

The following is a method invocation from Display 4.3/page 217:

```
speciesOfTheMonth.writeOutput();
```

Let's look at the definition of this method writeOutput in order to see how method definitions are written. The definition is given in Display 4.2/page 214 and is repeated here:

```
public void writeOutput()    ◀——— Heading
{
    System.out.println("Name = " + name);
    System.out.println("Population = " + population);
    System.out.println("Growth rate = " + growthRate + "%");
}
```

Body ⟨ (bracket indicating the block above)

All method definitions belong to some class and all method definitions are given inside the definition of the class to which they belong. If you look at Display 4.2, you will see that this method definition is inside the definition of the class Species-FirstTry. This means that this method can only be used with objects of the class SpeciesFirstTry.

void-method

The definition of a method that does not return a value starts with the reserved words *public void*, followed by the name of the method and a pair of parentheses. The word *public* indicates that there are no special restrictions on the use of the method. Later in this chapter, we will see that the word *public* can sometimes be replaced with other modifiers to restrict the use of the method. The word *void* is a rather poor choice for use here, but it is what is used in Java and in other languages. The word *void* indicates that the method takes some action other than returning a single value. The word *void* is used to indicate that no value is returned. The parentheses enclose a description of any extra information that the method will need. In this case, no extra information is needed, and so there is nothing inside the parentheses. Later in the chapter, we will see examples of the sorts of things that might appear inside these parentheses (for other method definitions). This first part of the method definition is called the **heading** for the method. The heading is normally written on a single line; but if it is too long for one line, it can be broken into two (or more) lines. Because of the use of the word *void* in the method heading, these methods (that do not return a value) are called *void*-**methods**.

method heading

method body

After the heading comes the **body** of the method definition, and that completes the method definition. The body of the method definition is enclosed between curly brackets { }. Between the curly brackets, you can place any statement or declaration that you can place in the main part of a program. Any variable used in a method definition (other than an instance variable) should be declared within that method definition.

When a *void*-method is invoked, it is as if the method invocation were replaced by the body of the method definition, and the statements (and declarations) within the body are executed. There are some subtleties about this replacement process, but for the simple examples we will look at now, it is like a literal replacement of the method invocation by the method definition body. Eventually, you want to think of the method definition as defining an action to be taken, rather than thinking of it as a list of statements to substitute for the method invocation, but this substitution idea is correct and is a good way to start thinking about method invocations.

For example, the following method invocation occurs in the program in Display 4.3/page 217:

```
speciesOfTheMonth.writeOutput();
```

When this method invocation is executed, it is as if the line with the method invocation were replaced by the body of the method definition for the method `writeOutput`. In this case, it is as if the preceding method invocation were replaced with the following:

```
{
    System.out.println("Name = " + name);
    System.out.println("Population = " + population);
    System.out.println("Growth rate = " + growthRate + "%");
}
```

These lines of code are the body of the method definition for the method `writeOutput`, and we just copied them from Display 4.2/page 214. The instance variable names (`name`, `population`, and `growthRate`) refer to the instance variables of the calling object; so in this example, they refer to the instance variables of the object `speciesOfTheMonth`. To be more precise, the invocation is equivalent to the following:

```
{
    System.out.println("Name = " + speciesOfTheMonth.name);
    System.out.println("Population = " + speciesOfTheMonth.population);
    System.out.println("Growth rate = "
                       + speciesOfTheMonth.growthRate + "%");
}
```

To be very concrete, if `speciesOfTheMonth.name` has the value "Klingon ox", `speciesOfTheMonth.population` has the value 10, and `speciesOfTheMonth.growthRate` has the value 15, then the method invocation

```
speciesOfTheMonth.writeOutput();
```

will cause the following to be written to the computer screen:

```
Name = Klingon ox
Population = 10
Growth rate = 15.0%
```

which is why the sample dialog contains these three lines near the end of the dialog.

If you look at the program in Display 4.3/page 217, you will see that the program looks like a class definition that has no instance variables and only a single method that is named `main`. It is in fact true that `main` is a method. A program is nothing other than a class that has a method named `main`. All the programs that we have written so far have no instance variables and no methods other than the method `main`, but a program can have other methods and can have instance variables. When you run a program, you are simply invoking the *void*-method that is named `main`. Of course, this is a special kind of method invocation, but it is a method invocation. For now, those extra words like *static* and `String[] args` will remain a bit of a mystery. Just put them in and eventually we will explain them all.

main method

Methods that Return a Value

methods that
return a value

A method that returns a single value is defined in basically the same way that a *void*-method is defined, except that there is one added complication, namely, specifying the value returned. Let's consider the method populationIn10 from the class SpeciesFirstTry. The method is used in the following line of the program in Display 4.3/page 217:

```
futurePopulation = speciesOfTheMonth.populationIn10();
```

This sets the value of the *int* variable futurePopulation equal to the value returned by the method invocation

```
speciesOfTheMonth.populationIn10()
```

The definition of the method populationIn10 tells the computer how to compute this value returned. Let's look at that method definition.

In what follows, we have reproduced the definition of the method populationIn10() from Display 4.2/page 214:

```java
public int populationIn10()
{
    double populationAmount = population;
    int count = 10;
    while ((count > 0) && (populationAmount > 0))
    {
        populationAmount = (populationAmount +
                        (growthRate/100) * populationAmount);
        count--;
    }
    if (populationAmount > 0)
        return (int)populationAmount;
    else
        return 0;
}
```

(int) is a type cast, as discussed in Chapter 2.

As was true of a *void*-method definition, the definition of a method that returns a value can be divided into two parts: the *method heading* and the *method body*. The following is the method heading for the method populationIn10.

```java
public int populationIn10()
```

The description of a method heading for a method that returns a value is almost the same as that for the heading of a *void*-method. The only difference is that for a method that returns a value, there is a type name instead of the reserved word *void*. The heading for a method that returns a value begins with the reserved word *public*, followed by a type name (rather than the word *void*), followed by the name of the method and a pair of parentheses. The parentheses enclose a description of any extra information that the method will need. In this case, no extra information is needed, and so there is nothing inside the parentheses. Later in the chapter, we will see examples of the sort of things that might appear inside these parentheses. The reserved word *public* indicates that there are no special restrictions on the use of the method. Later in this chapter, we will see that the word *public* can be replaced with other modifiers to restrict the use of the method. The important new element is the use of a type name, in this example *int*, in the method heading. Let's consider that type name.

The heading of a method that returns a value includes a type name. The type name is the type of the value returned. Each method can return values of only one type. In different situations, a method may return different values, but they must all be values of the type specified in the method heading.

type returned

The body of a method definition that returns a value is just like the body of a *void*-method definition, except that it must contain the following in one or more places:

return-statement

> *return Expression*;

This is called a *return*-**statement**. The *Expression* can be any expression that produces a value of the type specified in the heading of the method definition. This statement says that the value returned by the method is the value of this expression. For example, in the definition of the method populationIn10, there are two *return*-statements:

> *return* (*int*)populationAmount;

and

> *return* 0;

When a method that returns a value is invoked, the statements in the body of the method definition are executed. For example, consider the following method invocation from Display 4.3/page 217:

```
futurePopulation = speciesOfTheMonth.populationIn10();
```

When this assignment statement is executed, the body of the method definition for populationIn10 is executed. That body follows:

```
{
    double populationAmount = population;
    int count = 10;
    while ((count > 0) && (populationAmount > 0))
    {
        populationAmount = (populationAmount +
                        (growthRate/100) * populationAmount);
        count--;
    }
    if (populationAmount > 0)
        return (int)populationAmount;
    else
        return 0;
}
```

> (*int*) is a type cast, as discussed in Chapter 2.

The instance variable population refers to the instance variable of the calling object, which in this case is speciesOfTheMonth. The value of population is copied into the variable populationAmount, and then the *while*-loop is executed. Each iteration of the loop increase the value of populationAmount by the amount that the population will change in one year, and the loop is iterated 10 times. So, when the *while*-loop ends, the value of populationAmount is the projected size of the population in 10 years. At that point, populationAmount has the value that we want the method to return. For now, let's assume that that number is positive (that is, that the species is not extinct). In that case, the following *return*-statement is executed, and it says that the value of (*int*)populationAmount is the value computed by (returned by) the method invocation:

```
return (int)populationAmount;
```

The (*int*) is a type cast that changes the *double* value to an *int* value so that you do not have a fraction of an animal. (Ugh!) It is as if the method invocation were replaced by (*int*)populationAmount. In this case, the method invocation speciesOfTheMonth.populationIn10() is in the following assignment statement

```
futurePopulation = speciesOfTheMonth.populationIn10();
```

so the variable futurePopulation is set to the value of (*int*)populationAmount.

If the populationAmount happens to be zero or negative, the following *return*-statement is executed instead:

```
return 0;
```

This is a minor detail that ensures that the projected population will not yield a negative population value. After all, in the real world, once a population reaches zero individuals, the population just stays at zero; it does not go negative.

When a *return*-statement is executed, the value returned by the method is determined by that *return*-statement. When a *return*-statement is executed, that also ends the method invocation. If there are more statements after the *return*-statement, they are not executed.

A method that returns a value may perform some action, such as reading a value from the keyboard, as well as returning a value, but it definitely must return a value.

Naming Methods

Java will let you use any legal identifier as the name for a method. But, if you choose clear, meaningful names, your code will be easier to read. A good rule to follow when naming methods is to (usually) use verbs to name *void*-methods and to (usually) use nouns to name methods that return a value. This is because, like a verb, a *void*-method names an action. On the other hand, a method that returns a value can be used like a value, and a value is a thing, and nouns are used to denote things.

The normal convention when naming classes and methods is to start all method names with a lowercase letter and to start all class names with an uppercase letter.

Functions

Methods that return a value are called *functions* in some other programming languages, and a method that returns a value does correspond to the mathematical notion of a function. However, in Java they are called *methods (that return a value)*. They are not called *functions*.

■ *Java Tip*
Use of *return* in *void*-Methods

A *void*-method returns no value and so it is not required to have any *return*-statement. However, there is a kind of *return*-statement that you may sometimes want to use in a *void*-method. A *return*-statement within a *void*-method has the form

> *return*;

It is just like the other *return*-statements we have seen, except that you do not include any expression for the value returned (because there is no value returned). When this *return*-statement is executed, the invocation of the *void*-method ends. This can be used to end a method invocation early, such as when the method discovers some sort of problem. For example, you might add the following method to the definition of the class SpeciesFirstTry:

```
public void showLandPortion()
{
    if (population == 0)
    {
        System.out.println("Population is zero.");
        return;//Ends here to avoid division by zero.
    }
    double fraction;
    fraction = 6.0/population;
    System.out.println("If the population were spread");
    System.out.println("over 6 continents, then each");
    System.out.println("individual would have a fraction of");
    System.out.println("its continent equal to " + fraction);
}
```

The method ends with a *return* if the rest of the method would involve a division by zero. (OK, it's not a very likely method, but it does illustrate the point.)

The *this* Parameter

Look back at the class definition of the class SpeciesFirstTry in Display 4.2/page 214 and look at the program in Display 4.3/page 217 that uses this class. Notice that instance variables are written differently depending on whether you are within the class definition or someplace outside the class definition, such as in a program that uses the class. Outside of the class definition, you name an instance variable by giving the name of an object of the class, followed by a dot and the name of the instance variable, as in the following reference to the instance variable name that appears in Display 4.3/page 217:

```
speciesOfTheMonth.name = "Klingon ox";
```

However, inside the definition of a method of that same class, you can simply use the instance variable name without any object name or dot. For example, the following

Method Definitions

Every method belongs to some class. The definition of a method is given in the definition of the class to which it belongs. The two most common forms for a method definition follow.

void-**Method Definition:**

```
public void Method_Name(Parameters)
{
        Statement_1
        Statement 2
            . . .
        Statement_Last

}
```

(So far we have not discussed *Parameters*, but we will do so shortly. If there are no *Parameters*, then the parentheses are empty.)

Example:

```
public void writeOutput()
{
        System.out.println("Name = " + name);
        System.out.println("Population = " + population);
        System.out.println("Growth rate = " + growthRate + "%");
}
```

Definition of a Method That Returns a Value:

```
public Type_Returned Method_Name(Parameters)
{
        <List of statements, at least one of which
            must contain a return-statement.>
}
```

(So far, we have not discussed *Parameters*, but we will do so shortly. If there are no *Parameters*, then the parentheses are empty.)

Example: (this could be added to the class in Display 4.2/page 214):

```
public int halfThePopulation()
{
        return (population/2);
}
```

---

return-Statements

Every method definition for a method that returns a value must have one or more *return*-statements. A *return*-statement specifies the value returned by the method and ends the method invocation.

Syntax:

```
return Expression;
```

Example:

```
public int halfThePopulation()
{
    return (population/2);
}
```

A *void*-method is not required to have a *return*-statement, but can have one if you want to end the method invocation before the end of the code. The form for a *return*-statement in a *void*-method is

```
return;
```

---

line occurs inside the definition of the method `readInput` of the class `SpeciesFirstTry` in Display 4.2/page 214:

```
name = SavitchIn.readLine();
```

Now, every instance variable is an instance variable of some object. So, this instance variable `name` must be the instance variable of some object. The instance variable `name` is an instance variable of an object that is understood to be there, but that usually is not written. However, you can write in this understood object if you want. This understood object has the somewhat unusual name of `this`. For example, the preceding assignment of the instance variable `name`, which we copied from the definition of the method `readInput` in Display 4.2, is equivalent to the following:

this

```
this.name = SavitchIn.readLine();
```

As another example, the following is a rewrite of the method definition for the method `writeOutput` from Display 4.2. This one is equivalent to the version used in Display 4.2.

```
public void writeOutput()
{
    System.out.println("Name = " + this.name);
    System.out.println("Population = " + this.population);
    System.out.println("Growth rate = " + this.growthRate + "%");
}
```

The reserved word *this* stands for the name of the calling object. For example, consider the following method invocation from Display 4.3:

```
speciesOfTheMonth.writeOutput();
```

The calling object is `speciesOfTheMonth`. So, this invocation of the method `writeOutput` is equivalent to

```
{
    System.out.println("Name = " + speciesOfTheMonth.name);
    System.out.println("Population = " + speciesOfTheMonth.population);
    System.out.println("Growth rate = " + speciesOfTheMonth.growthRate + "%");
}
```

which we got by replacing *this* with speciesOfTheMonth.

The reserved word *this* is like a blank waiting to be filled in by the object that invokes the method. Because you would be using *this* so often if it were required, Java lets you omit the *this* and the dot as an abbreviation, but the *this* and the dot are understood to be there implicitly. This is an abbreviation that is almost always used. Programmers seldom use the *this* parameter, but there are some situations where it is needed.

The *this* Parameter

When giving a method definition, you can use the reserved word *this* as a name for the calling object.

? Self-Test Questions

1. Consider the program in Display 4.3/page 217. Suppose you wanted to add another species object called speciesOfTheYear and suppose you wanted the user to give it data, specifically a name, population, and growth rate. What code do you need to add to the program? (*Hint:* It only requires three or four lines of code.)

2. Suppose Employee is a class with a *void*-method named readInput and dilbert is an object of the class Employee. So, dilbert was named and created by the following:

   ```
   Employee dilbert = new Employee();
   ```

   Write an invocation of the method readInput with dilbert as the calling object. The method readInput needs no information in parentheses.

3. Let's say you want to assign a number as well as a name to each species in the world, perhaps to make it easier to catalog them. Modify the definition of the class SpeciesFirstTry in Display 4.2/page 214 so that it allows for a number. The number is to be of type *int*. (*Hint:* You mostly have to just add stuff. Note, part of what you need to do is to change some methods by adding stuff.)

4. Suppose you live in an idealized world where every species has exactly the same number of male and female members in its population. Give the definition of a method, called femalePopulation, that you could add to the definition of the class SpeciesFirstTry in Display 4.2/page 214. The method femalePopulation returns the number of females in the population. If the population is an odd number, then you have one species mem-

ber left over after pairing; assume that member is a female. For example, if the population is 6, there are 3 males and 3 females. If the population is 7, there are 3 males and 4 females. Also give the definition of a method called `malePopulation` that similarly returns the number of males in the population. (*Hint:* The definitions are very short. The bodies of the two definitions are a little bit different.)

5. Rewrite the definition of the method `writeOutput` in Display 4.2/page 214 using the *this* parameter. Note that the meaning of the definition will not change at all. You will just write it slightly differently. (*Hint:* All that you need to do is add *this* and dots in certain places.)

6. Rewrite the definition of the method `readInput` in Display 4.2/page 214 using the *this* parameter.

Local Variables

Notice the definition of the method `populationIn10` given in Display 4.2/page 214. That method definition includes the declaration of variables called `populationAmount` and `count`. A variable declared within a method is called a **local variable**. It is called *local* because its meaning is local to, that is, confined to, the method definition. If you have two methods and each of them declares a variable of the same name, for example, both named `populationAmount`, then these are two different variables that just happen to have the same name. Any change that is made to the variable named `populationAmount` within one method will have no effect upon the variable named `populationAmount` that is in the other method. It is as if the two methods were executed on different computers. Alternatively, it is as if the computer changed the name of the variable named `populationAmount` in one of the two methods to `populationAmount2`.

local variable

Since the `main` part of a program is itself a method, all variables declared in `main` are local variables for the method `main`. If they happen to have the same name as some variable declared in some other method, then these are two different variables that just happen to have the same name. For example, look at the program and class definition in Display 4.4. First consider the program, which is shown in the lower half of the display. The method `main` in the program includes the declaration of a variable named `newAmount`. Now look at the class definition in the upper half of the display. The method `showNewBalance` in the class also declares a variable named `newAmount`. These are two different variables, both of which are named `newAmount`. The variable named `newAmount` in `main` is set equal to 800.00. After that, there is the following method invocation:

```
myAccount.showNewBalance();
```

If you look at the definition of the method `showNewBalance` and do a little arithmetic, you will see that, within that method, another variable named `newAmount` is set equal to 105.00. Yet, this has no effect on the other variable named `newAmount` that is in `main`. After that method invocation, the variable named `newAmount` in `main` is written out and its value is still 800.00. Changing the value of the variable `newAmount` in the method `showNewBalance` had no effect on the variable named `newA-`

Display 4.4   Local Variables

```
/**********************************************************
 *This class is used in the program LocalVariablesDemoProgram.
 **********************************************************/
public class BankAccount
{
    public void showNewBalance()
    {
        double newAmount = amount + (rate/100.0)*amount;
        System.out.println("With interest added the new amount is $"
                                    + newAmount);
    }

    public double amount;
    public double rate;
}
```

> This class definition goes in a file named BankAccount.java.

> Two different variables named newAmount.

> This program goes in a file named LocalVariableDemoProgram.java.

```
/**********************************************************
 *A toy program to illustrate how local variables behave.
 **********************************************************/
public class LocalVariablesDemoProgram
{
    public static void main(String[] args)
    {
        BankAccount myAccount = new BankAccount();
        myAccount.amount = 100.00;
        myAccount.rate = 5;

        double newAmount = 800.00;
        myAccount.showNewBalance();
        System.out.println("I wish my new amount were $" + newAmount);
    }
}
```

> This does not change the value of the variable newAmount in main.

Screen Output

```
With interest added the new amount is $105.0
I wish my new amount were $800.0
```

mount in main. In this case, the two variables with the same name are in different definitions in two different files. However, the situation would be the same if the two methods were in the same class definition and so in the same file.

Local Variable

A variable declared within a method definition is called a **local variable**. If two methods each have a local variable of the same name, then these are two different variables, even though they have the same name.

Global Variables

Thus far, we have discussed two kinds of variables: instance variables, whose meaning is confined to an object of a class, and local variables, whose meaning is confined to a method definition. Some programming languages have another kind of variable, called **global variables**, whose meaning is only confined to the program, which means it's not confined at all. Java does not have these global variables.

Blocks

The terms *block* and *compound statement* really mean the same thing, namely, a set of Java statements enclosed in curly brackets { }. However, the two terms tend to be used in different contexts. When you declare a variable within a compound statement, the compound statement is usually called a **block** (although it would not be incorrect to call it a *compound statement*.)

compound statement

block

If you declare a variable within a block (that is, within a compound statement), that variable is local to the block (that is, local to the compound statement). That means that when the compound statement ends, all variables declared within the compound statement disappear. In many programming languages, you can even use that variable's name to name some other variable outside of the block. However, *in Java, you cannot have two variables with the same name inside of a single method definition*.

Local variables within blocks can sometimes be a little troublesome in Java. In Java, you cannot reuse the local variable name outside the block for another variable. As a result, it is sometimes easier to declare the variable outside the block. If you declare a variable outside of a block, then you can use it in the block, and it will have the same meaning whether it is in the block or outside the block (but all within the same method definition).

Blocks

A **block** is a compound statement, that is, a list of statements enclosed in curly brackets. Although a block and compound statement are the same thing, we tend to use the term *block* when there is a variable declaration contained within the curly brackets. The variables declared in a block are local to the block and so these variables disappear when the execution of the block is completed. However, even though the variables are local to the block, their names cannot be used for anything else within the same method definition.

■ Gotcha
Variables Declared in a Block

When you declare a variable within a block, that is, within a pair of curly brackets {
}, that variable becomes a local variable for the block. This means that you cannot
use the variable outside of the block. If you want to use a variable outside of a block,
then you must declare it outside of the block. Declaring the variable outside of the
block will let you use the variable both outside and inside the block.

■ Java Tip
Declaring Variables in a *for*-Statement

You can declare a variable within the initialization part of a *for*-statement as in the
following example:

```
int sum = 0;
for (int n = 1; n <= 10; n++)
    sum = sum + n*n;
```

If you do this, then the variable, in this case n, will be **local to the** *for*-**loop**, and cannot be used outside of the *for*-loop. For example, the following use of n in the Sys-
tem.out.println-statement is not allowed.

```
for (int n = 1; n <= 10; n++)
    sum = sum + n*n;
System.out.println(n);
```

This can sometimes be more of a nuisance than a helpful feature. Moreover,
these variables declared in the initialization part of a *for*-loop are treated differently in different programming languages and even in different versions of Java. For
these reasons, we prefer not to use this feature, and to instead declare our variables
outside of the *for*-loop. However, you should be aware of this feature, since you
will see it in other programmers' code.

Parameters of a Primitive Type

Consider the method populationIn10 for the class SpeciesFirstTry defined in
Display 4.2/page 214. It returns the projected population of a species 10 years in the
future. But what if you want the projection for 5 years in the future or 50 years in the
future? It would be much more useful to have a method that starts with an integer
for some number of years and returns the projected population for that many years
into the future. In order to do this, we need some way of having something like a
blank in a method so that each call of the method can have the blank filled in with a
different value. For a method that computes projected population, the blank would
be filled in with some number of years. The things that serve as kinds of blanks for
parameter
methods are called **parameters**. They are a bit more complicated than simple blanks,
but you will not go too far wrong if you think of them as blanks or placeholders to
be filled in with some value when the method is invoked.

The class definition in Display 4.5 includes a method called `projectedPopula-tion` that has one formal parameter called `years`. When the method is called, you give the value that you want substituted in for the parameter `years`. For example, in our previous program in Display 4.3/page 217, we had the following method call:

```
futurePopulation = speciesOfTheMonth.populationIn10();
```

This sets the variable `futurePopulation` equal to the projected population of the species in 10 years. The new class `SpeciesSecondTry` (Display 4.5) does not have a method named `populationIn10`, but we could instead use the method `projected-Population` as follows:

```
futurePopulation = speciesOfTheMonth.projectedPopulation(10);
```

In Display 4.6, we have rewritten the program from Display 4.3/page 217 so that it uses the class `SpeciesSecondTry`, which has the method `projectedPopulation`. With this version of the class, we could project any number of years into the future by replacing the 10 by some other number. We could even use a variable for the number of years, as follows:

```
int projectedYears, futurePopulation;
System.out.println("Enter the projected number of years:");
projectedYears = SavitchIn.readLineInt();
futurePopulation =
        speciesOfTheMonth.projectedPopulation(projectedYears);
System.out.println("In " + projectedYears + " years, the");
System.out.println("population will be " + futurePopulation);
```

Let's look at the definition of the method `projectedPopulation` in some more detail. The heading, reproduced in what follows, has something new.

```
public int projectedPopulation(int years)
```

The word `years` is called a **formal parameter**. A formal parameter is used in the method definition as a stand-in for a value that will be plugged in when the method is called. The thing that is plugged in is called an **argument** or **actual parameter**. For example, in the following call, the value 10 is an argument:

formal parameter

argument

```
futurePopulation = speciesOfTheMonth.projectedPopulation(10);
```

When you have a method invocation, like the preceding, the argument (in this case 10) is plugged in for the formal parameter *every place that the formal parameter occurs in the method definition*. In this case, the argument 10 would be plugged in for the formal parameters `years` in the definition of the method `projectedPopulation` in Display 4.5. After that, the method invocation proceeds as in all previous method invocations you have seen. The statements in the body of the method definition are executed until they reach a *return*-statement. At that point, the value specified by the expression in the *return*-statement is returned as the value returned by the method call.

It is important to note that only the value of the argument is used in this substitution process. If the argument in a method invocation is a variable, then it is the value of the variable that is plugged in, not the variable name. For example, consider the

Display 4.5   A Method with A Parameter

```
public class SpeciesSecondTry
{
    public String name;
    public int population;
    public double growthRate;

    public void readInput()
    {
        <The definition of the method readInput is the same as in Display 4.2/page 214.>
    }

    public void writeOutput()
    {
        <The definition of the method writeOutput is the same as in Display 4.2.>
    }


    /*************************************************
     *Returns the projected population of the calling object
     *after the specified number of years.
     *************************************************/
    public int projectedPopulation(int years)
    {
        double populationAmount = population;
        int count = years;
        while ((count > 0) && (populationAmount > 0))
        {
            populationAmount = (populationAmount +
                        (growthRate/100) * populationAmount);
            count--;
        }
        if (populationAmount > 0)
            return (int)populationAmount;
        else
            return 0;
    }
}
```

Later in the chapter, we will see that the modifier public *should be replaced with* private.

We will give an even better version of the class later in the chapter.

Display 4.6   Using a Method with a Parameter

```
/***************************************************************
 *Demonstrates the use of a parameter with the method projectedPopulation.
 ***************************************************************/
public class SpeciesSecondTryDemo
{
    public static void main(String[] args)
    {
        SpeciesSecondTry speciesOfTheMonth = new SpeciesSecondTry();
        int futurePopulation;

        System.out.println("Enter data on the Species of the Month:");
        speciesOfTheMonth.readInput();
        speciesOfTheMonth.writeOutput();

        futurePopulation = speciesOfTheMonth.projectedPopulation(10);
        System.out.println("In ten years the population will be " +
                                               futurePopulation);

        speciesOfTheMonth.name = "Klingon ox";
        speciesOfTheMonth.population = 10;
        speciesOfTheMonth.growthRate = 15;
        System.out.println("The new Species of the Month:");
        speciesOfTheMonth.writeOutput();
        System.out.println("In ten years the population will be " +
                        speciesOfTheMonth.projectedPopulation(10));
    }
}
```

Sample Screen Dialogue

The dialog is exactly the same as in
Display 4.3 on page 217

following, which might occur in some program that uses the class SpeciesSecondTry defined in Display 4.5:

```
SpeciesSecondTry mySpecies = new SpeciesSecondTry();
int yearCount = 12;
int futurePopulation;
futurePopulation =
        mySpecies.projectedPopulation(yearCount);
```

In this case, it is the value 12 that is plugged in for the formal parameter years in the
definition of the method projectedPopulation (in Display 4.5). It is *not* the variable yearCount that is plugged in for years. Because it is only the value of the argument that is used, this method of plugging in arguments for parameter is known

call-by-value

as the **call-by-value** mechanism of parameter substitution. In Java, this is the only
method of substitution that is used with parameters of a primitive type, such as int,
double, and char. However, we will eventually see that parameters of a class type
use a somewhat different substitution mechanism, but for now, we are only concerned with parameters and arguments of primitive types, such as int, double, and
char.

parameters as
local variables

The exact details of this parameter substitution method are a bit more complicated than what we have said so far. Usually, you need not be concerned with this
extra detail, but occasionally, you need to know all the details of the substitution.
So, here are the exact technical details: *The formal parameter that occurs in the
method definition is a local variable that is initialized to the value of the argument.*
The argument is given in parentheses in the method invocation. For example, for
the method call:

```
futurePopulation =
        mySpecies.projectedPopulation(yearCount);
```

The formal parameter years of the method projectedPopulation in Display 4.5 is
a local variable of the method projectedPopulation, and in this method invocation, the local variable years is set equal to the value of the argument yearCount,
so the effect is the same as if the body of the method definition were changed to the
following:

```
{
    years = yearCount;
    double populationAmount = population;
    int count = years;
    while ((count > 0) && (populationAmount > 0))
    {
        populationAmount = (populationAmount +
                            (growthRate/100) * populationAmount);
        count--;
    }
    if (populationAmount > 0)
        return (int)populationAmount;
    else
        return 0;
}
```

This is the effect of plugging in the argument yearCount.

Finally, notice that the formal parameter in a method heading has a type, such as the type *int* before the formal parameter years, shown in what follows:

parameters have a type

```
public int projectedPopulation(int years)
```

Every formal parameter has a type, and the argument that is plugged in for the formal parameter in a method invocation must match the type of the formal parameter. Thus, for the method `projectedPopulation`, the argument given in parentheses in a method invocation must be of type *int*. This rule is not as strict in practice as what we have just said. In many cases, Java will perform an automatic type conversion (type cast) if you use an argument in a method call that does not match the type of the formal parameter. For example, if the type of the argument in a method call is *int* and the type of the formal parameter is *double*, then Java will convert the value of type *int* to the corresponding value of type *double*. The following list shows the type conversions that will be performed for you automatically. An argument in a method invocation that is of any of these types will be automatically converted to any of the types that appear to its right if that is needed to match a formal parameter:[1]

```
byte --> short --> int --> long --> float --> double
```

Note that this is exactly the same sort of automatic type casting that we discussed in Chapter 2 for storing values of one type in a variable of another type. You can store a value of any of the listed types in a variable of any type that occurs further down on the list. Thus, we can express both the automatic type casting for arguments and the automatic type casting for variables as one more general rule: You can use a value of any of the listed types anywhere that Java expects a value of a type further down on the list. For example, you can use an *int* value anywhere that Java expects a *double* value.

All of our examples so far have been methods that return a value, but everything we said about formal parameters and arguments applies equally well to *void*-methods; *void*-methods may have parameters and they are handled in exactly the same way as what we just described for methods that return a value.

It is possible, even common, to have more than one formal parameter in a method definition. In that case, each formal parameter is listed in the method heading, and each formal parameter is preceded by a type. For example, the following might be the heading of a method definition:

more than one parameter

```
public void doStuff(int n1, int n2, double cost, char code)
```

Note that each of the formal parameters must be preceded by a type name, even if there is more than one formal parameter of the same type.

When you have a method invocation, there must be exactly the same number of arguments in parentheses as there are formal parameters in the method defini-

---

1. An argument of type *char* will also be converted to a matching number type, if the formal parameter is of type *int* or any type to the right of *int* in our list of types. However, we do not advocate using this feature.

Parameters of a Primitive Type

Formal parameters are given in parentheses after the method name at the beginning of a method definition. A formal parameter of a primitive type, such as `int`, `double`, or `char`, is a local variable. When there is an invocation of the method, the parameter is initialized to the value of the corresponding argument in the method invocation. This mechanism is known as the **call-by-value** parameter mechanism. The argument in a method invocation can be a literal constant, like `2` or `'A'`, a variable, or any expression that yields a value of the appropriate type.

Note that if you use a variable of a primitive type as an argument in a method invocation, then the method invocation cannot change the value of this argument variable.

---

tion heading. For example, the following might be an invocation of our hypothetical method `doStuff`:

```
anObject.doStuff(42, 100, 9.99, 'Z');
```

As suggested by this example, the correspondence is one of order. The first argument in the method call is plugged in for the first formal parameter in the method definition heading, the second argument in the method call is plugged in for the second formal parameter in the heading of the method definition, and so forth. The argument must match its corresponding parameter in type, except for the automatic type conversions that we discussed earlier.

class
parameters

One word of warning: Parameters of a class type behave differently from parameters of a primitive type. We will discuss parameters of a class type later in this chapter.

Correspondence between Formal Parameters and Arguments

Formal parameters are given in parentheses after the method name at the beginning of a method definition. In a method invocation, **arguments** are given in parentheses after the method name. There must be exactly the same number of arguments in a method invocation as there are formal parameters in the corresponding method definition.

The arguments are plugged in for the formal parameters according to their position in the lists in parentheses. The first argument in the method invocation is plugged in for the first formal parameter in the method definition, the second argument in the method invocation is plugged in for the second formal parameter in the method definition, and so forth. Arguments should be of the same types as their corresponding formal parameter, although in some cases, Java will perform an automatic type conversion when the types do not match.

■ Gotcha

Use of the Terms "Parameter" and "Argument"

The use of the terms *formal parameter* and *argument* that we follow in this book is consistent with common usage, but people also often use the terms *parameter* and *argument* interchangeably. When you see the terms *parameter* and *argument*, you must determine their exact meaning from context. Many people use the term *parameter* for both what we call *formal parameters* and what we call *arguments*. Other people use the term *argument* both for what we call *formal parameters* and what we call *arguments*. Do not expect consistency in how people use these two terms.

Summary of Class and Method Definition Syntax

In basic outline, a class definition has the following form:

```
public class Class_Name
{

    Instance_Variable_Declaration_1
    Instance_Variable_Declaration_2
        . . .
    Instance_Variable_Declaration_Last

    Method_Definition_1
    Method_Definition_2
        . . .
    Method_Definition_Last
}
```

This is the form we will use most often, but you are allowed to intermix the method definitions and the instance variable declarations.

The instance variable declarations that we have seen thus far are of the form

```
public Type_Name Instance_Variable_Name;
```

such as

```
public String name;
public int population;
public double growthRate;
```

As we will see in the next section, it is preferable to use the modifier *private* in place of the modifier *public* when declaring instance variables, but the other details are typical.

A method definition consist of two parts, in the following order:

```
Method_Heading
Method_Body
```

The method headings we have seen thus far are all of the form

```
public Type_Name_Or_void Method_Name(Parameter_List)
```

The *Parameter_List* consists of a list of formal parameter names, each preceded by a type. If the list has more than one entry, the entries are separated by commas. There may be no parameters at all, in which case there is nothing inside the parentheses.

Here are some sample method headings:

```
public double Total(double price, double tax)
public void setValue(int count, char rating)
public void readInput()
public int projectedPopulation(int years)
```

The *Method_Body* consists of a list of Java statements enclosed in curly brackets {}. If the method returns a value, then the method definition must include one or more *return*-statements. Here is a sample method, which you have seen before. The first line is the method heading and the rest is the method body.

```
public int projectedPopulation(int years)
{
    double populationAmount = population;
    int count = years;
    while ((count > 0) && (populationAmount > 0))
    {
        populationAmount = (populationAmount +
                          (growthRate/100) * populationAmount);
        count--;
    }
    if (populationAmount > 0)
        return (int)populationAmount;
    else
        return 0;
}
```

To see complete examples of class definitions, see Display 4.2/page 214 and Display 4.5/page 234.

? Self-Test Questions

7. Define a method called density that could be added to the definition of the class SpeciesSecondTry in Display 4.5/page 234. The method density has one parameter of type *double* that is named area. The parameter area gives the area occupied by the species expressed in square miles. The method density returns a value of type *double* that is equal to the number of individuals per square mile of the species. You can assume that the area is always greater than zero. (*Hint:* The definition is very short.)

8. Define a method called fixPopulation that could be added to the definition of the class SpeciesSecondTry in Display 4.5/page 234. The method fixPopulation has one parameter of type *double* that is named area, which gives the area occupied by the species in square miles. The method fixPopulation changes the value of the instance variable population so that there will be one pair of individuals per square mile.

9. Define a method called changePopulation that could be added to the definition of the class SpeciesSecondTry in Display 4.5/page 234. The method changePopulation has two parameters. One parameter is of type *double*, is named area, and gives the area occupied by the species in square miles. The other parameter is of type *int*, is named numberPerMile, and gives the desired number of individuals per square mile. The method changePopulation changes the value of the instance variable population so that the number of individuals per square mile is (approximately) equal to numberPerMile.

4.2 | Information Hiding and Encapsulation

> *The cause is hidden, but the result is well known.*
>
> **Ovid**, *Metamorphoses*

Information hiding sounds like it could be a bad thing to do. What advantage could there be to hiding information (except for nefarious schemes)? As it turns out the term *information hiding* as it is used in Computer Science does indeed refer to a kind of genuine hiding of information, but it is considered a good programming technique. The basic idea is that, when certain kinds of information are hidden, the programmer's job becomes simpler and the programmer's code becomes easier to understand. It is basically a way to avoid "information overload."

A programmer who is using a method that you have defined does not need to know the details of the code in the body of the method definition in order to use the method. The programmer only needs to know what task the method accomplishes. For example, you can use the method `SavitchIn.readlineInt` without even looking at the definition of that method. It is not that the code contains some secret that is forbidden to you. If you really want to see the definition, it is in Appendix 4. The point is that viewing the code will not help you use the method, but will give you more things to keep track of, and that could distract you from your programming tasks. If a method (or other piece of software) is well written, then a programmer who uses the method need only know *what* the method accomplishes and need not worry about *how* the method accomplishes its task. This section is concerned with various kinds of information hiding.

If the word *information hiding* sounds too negative to you, you might use the term *abstraction*. The terms *information hiding* and *abstraction* mean the same thing in this context. This should not be a surprising use of the term *abstraction*. When you *abstract* something, you lose some information. For example, an abstract of a paper or a book is a brief description of the paper or book, as opposed to the entire book or paper.

abstraction

Information Hiding

If a method is well-designed, the programmer can use the method without knowing the details of how the method body is coded. All the programmer needs to know is that if she or he provides the method with appropriate arguments, then the method will somehow perform the appropriate action. Designing a method so that it can be used without any need to understand the fine detail of the code is called **information hiding** in order to emphasize the fact that the programmer acts as if the body of the method were hidden from view.

information hiding

Display 4.7 contains two definitions of the method `projectedPopulation`. Either definition could be used in the definition of the class `SpeciesSecondTry` in Display 4.5/page 234. The class definition can only contain one of these two definitions of `projectedPopulation`, but the point we are making is that it does not matter which definition is used. The method will return the same number no matter

Display 4.7   Equivalent Method Definitions

```
/**************************************************
 *Returns the projected population of the calling object
 *after the specified number of years.
 **************************************************/
public int projectedPopulation(int years)
{
    double populationAmount = population;
    int count = years;
    while ((count > 0) && (populationAmount > 0))
    {
        populationAmount = (populationAmount +
                        (growthRate/100) * populationAmount);
        count--;
    }
  if (populationAmount > 0)
      return (int)populationAmount;
  else
      return 0;
}
```

> The class SpeciesSecondTry will only have one of these two definitions of the method projectedPopulation, but the programmer who uses the class does not care which one it has.

```
/**************************************************
 *Returns the projected population of the calling object
 *after the specified number of years.
 **************************************************/
public int projectedPopulation(int years)
{
    double populationAmount = population;
    double growthFraction = growthRate/100.0;
    int count = years;
    while ((count > 0) && (populationAmount > 0))
    {
        populationAmount = (populationAmount +
                    growthFraction * populationAmount);
        count--;
    }
    if (populationAmount < 0)
        populationAmount = 0;
    return (int)populationAmount;
}
```

which of the two definitions is used. In order to use the method `projectedPopula-tion`, all the programmer needs to know is that it returns the projected population of the species for the number of years into the future that is given as the argument.

If you want to see the two method definitions in Display 4.14 in action see the two files `SpeciesSecondTryVersion2.java` and `SpeciesSecondTryVersion2-Demo.java` on the CD that comes with this book,

extra code on CD

■ Programming Tip
Formal Parameter Names Are Local to the Method

Methods should be self-contained units that are designed separately from the incidental details of other methods of the class and separately from any program that uses the class. One incidental detail is the name of the formal parameters. Fortunately, in Java the formal parameter names can be chosen without any concern that the name of a formal parameter will be the same as some other identifier used in some other method. This is because the formal parameters are really local variables, and so their meanings are confined to their respective method definitions. Among other things, this means that on programming projects, one programmer can be assigned the job of writing a method definition while another programmer writes another part of the program that uses that method, and the two programmers need not agree on what names are used for formal parameters. They can choose their identifier names completely independently without any concern that some, all, or none of their identifiers may be the same.

Precondition and Postcondition Comments

The programmer who uses a method should not need to look at the method definition. The method heading and a description of what the method does (as opposed to how it does it) should be all that the programmer needs to know. An efficient and standard way to describe what a method does is by means of specific kinds of comments known as *preconditions* and *postconditions*. The **precondition** for a method states the conditions that must be true before the method is invoked. The method should not be used, and cannot be expected to perform correctly, unless the precondition is satisfied.

precondition

The **postcondition** describes the effect of the method call. The postcondition tells what will be true after the method is executed in a situation in which the precondition holds. For a method that returns a value, the postcondition will describe the value returned by the method. For a *void*-method, the postcondition will, among other things, describe any changes to the calling object. In general, the postcondition describes all the effects produced by a method invocation.

postcondition

For example, the following shows some suitable precondition and postcondition comments for the method `writeOutput` shown in Display 4.2/page 214:

```
/*****************************************************
 *Precondition: The instance variables of the calling
 *object have values.
 *Postcondition: The data stored in (the instance variables
 *of) the calling object have been written to the screen.
 *****************************************************/
public void writeOutput()
```

The comment for the method `projectedPopulation` in Display 4.7/page 242 (either version) can be expressed as follows:

```
/*****************************************************
 *Precondition: years is a nonnegative number.
 *Postcondition: Returns the projected population of the
 *calling object after the specified number of years.
 *****************************************************/
public int projectedPopulation(int years)
```

If the only postcondition is a description of the value returned, programmers omit the word *Postcondition* (although it would not be incorrect to include the word *Postcondition*). The previous comment would typically be written in the following alternative way:

```
/*****************************************************
 *Precondition: years is a nonnegative number.
 *Returns the projected population of the calling object
 *after the specified number of years.
 *****************************************************/
public int projectedPopulation(int years)
```

Some design specifications may require preconditions and postconditions for all methods. Others omit explicit preconditions and postconditions from certain methods whose names make their action obvious. Names such as `readInput`, `writeOutput`, and `set` are often considered self-explanatory. However, the sound rule to follow is to adhere to whatever guidelines your instructor or supervisor give, and when in doubt, add preconditions and postconditions.

Some programmers prefer to not use the words *precondition* and *postcondition* in their comments. However, you (and those programmers) should always think in terms of preconditions and postcondition when writing method comments. The really important thing is not the words *precondition* and *postcondition*, but the concepts they name.

The `public` and `private` Modifiers

It is *not* considered good programming practice to make the instance variables of a class `public`. Normally, all instance variables are given the modifier `private`. In this subsection, we explain the differences between the modifiers `public` and `private`.

public

The modifier `public` means, as we already said, that any other class or program can directly access the instance variable and can directly change the instance variable. For example, the program in Display 4.6/page 235 contains the following three

lines, which set the values of the *public* instance variables for the object
speciesOfTheMonth:

```
speciesOfTheMonth.name = "Klingon ox";
speciesOfTheMonth.population = 10;
speciesOfTheMonth.growthRate = 15;
```

The object speciesOfTheMonth is an object of the class SpeciesSecondTry and the
definition for that class is given in Display 4.5/page 234. As you can see by looking at
that class definition, the instance variables name, population, and growthRate all
have the modifier *public*, and so the preceding three statements are perfectly legal.

Now suppose that the modifier *public* before the instance variable name in the
definition of the class SpeciesSecondTry in Display 4.5 were changed to *private*   *private*
so that the class definition begins as follows:

```
public class SpeciesSecondTry
{
    private String name;
    public int population;
    public double growthRate;
```

With this change, it is illegal to have the following statement in the program in Display 4.6:

```
speciesOfTheMonth.name = "Klingon ox"; //Illegal when private.
```

The following two statements remain legal, because we left the modifiers of population and growthRate as *public*:

```
speciesOfTheMonth.population = 10;
speciesOfTheMonth.growthRate = 15;
```

It is considered good programming practice to *make all instance variables private*, as illustrated in Display 4.8. Whenever you place the modifier *private* before
an instance variable, then that instance variable's *name* is not accessible outside of
the class definition. Within any method of the class definition, you can use the
instance variable name in any way you wish. In particular, you can directly change
the value of the instance variable. However, outside of the class definition, you cannot make any direct reference to the instance variable name.

For example, consider the class SpeciesThirdTry shown in Display 4.8.
Because the instance variables are all marked *private*, the last three of the following lines would all be illegal in any program (or any class method definition other
than methods of the class SpeciesThirdTry):

```
SpeciesThirdTry secretSpecies = new SpeciesThirdTry();//Legal
secretSpecies.readInput();//Legal
secretSpecies.name = "Aardvark";//Illegal. name is private.
System.out.println(secretSpecies.population);//Illegal
                    //population is private.
System.out.println(secretSpecies.growthRate);//Illegal.
                    //growthRate is private.
```

Display 4.8   A Class with Private Instance Variables

```
public class SpeciesThirdTry
{
    private String name;
    private int population;
    private double growthRate;

    public void readInput()
    {
        System.out.println("What is the species name?");
        name = SavitchIn.readLine();
        System.out.println("What is the population of the species?");
        population = SavitchIn.readLineInt();
        while (population < 0)
        {
            System.out.println("Population cannot be negative.");
            System.out.println("Reenter population:");
            population = SavitchIn.readLineInt();
        }
        System.out.println(
                    "Enter growth rate (percent increase per year):");
        growthRate = SavitchIn.readLineDouble();
    }

    public void writeOutput()
```

We will give an even better version of the class later in the chapter.

<The definition of the method `writeOutput` is the same as in Display 4.2/page 214.>

```
    /*************************************************
     *Precondition: years is a nonnegative number.
     *Returns the projected population of the calling object
     *after the specified number of years.
     *************************************************/
    public int projectedPopulation(int years)
```

<The definition of the method `projectedPopulation` can
                            be either of the definitions in Display 4.7/page 242.>

```
}
```

Notice that the invocation of the method `readInput` is legal. So, there is still a way to set the instance variables of an object, even though those instance variables are *private*. Making an instance variable *private* does not mean that there is no way to change it. It only means that you cannot use the *instance variable name* to directly refer to the variable (except within the class definition that includes the instance variable).

Within the definition of methods in the same class, you can access private instance variables in any way that you want. Notice the definition of the method `readInput`, which is shown in Display 4.8. It sets the value of instance variables with assignment statements such as the following:

```
name = SavitchIn.readLine();
```

and

```
population = SavitchIn.readLineInt();
```

Within any class method, you can access all the instance variables of that class in any way you want, even if the instance variables are marked *private*.

To see a demonstration of the effect of the *private* qualifiers in the class `SpeciesThirdTry`, look at the program `SpeciesThirdTryDemo.java` on the CD that comes with this book.

extra code on CD

Class methods can also be *private*. If a method is marked *private*, then it cannot be invoked outside of the class definition, but it can still be invoked within the definition of any other method in that same class. Most methods are marked *public*, but if you have a method whose only purpose is to be used within the definition of other methods of that class, then it makes sense to mark this *helping* method *private*.

private methods

The *public* and *private* Qualifiers

Within a class definition, each instance variable declaration and each method definition can be preceded with either *public* or *private*. If an instance variable is preceded with *private*, then it cannot be referred to by name anyplace except within the definitions of methods of the same class. If it is preceded by *public*, there are no restrictions on the use of the instance variable name. If a method definition is preceded with *private*, then the method cannot be invoked outside of the class definition. If the method is preceded by *public*, there are no restrictions on the method's use.

Normally, all instance variables are marked *private* and most or all methods are marked *public*.

◻

Programming Tip
Instance Variables Should Be Private

You should make all the instance variables in a class *private*. The reason for this is that it forces the programmer who uses the class (whether that is you or somebody else) to access the instance variables only via methods. This allows the class to control how a programmer accesses the instance variables.

accessor
method

Making all instance variables *private* does control access to them, but what if you have a legitimate reason to access an instance variable? For these cases, you should provide *accessor methods*. An **accessor method** is simply a method that allows you to read data contained in one or more instance variables. In Display 4.9, we have rewritten the class for a species yet another time. This version has accessor methods for obtaining values of each instance variable. They are the methods that start with the word `get`, as in `getName`.

mutator
method

Accessor methods allow you to read the data in a private instance variable. Other methods, known as **mutator methods**, allow you to change the data stored in private instance variables. Our class definition has a mutator method, called `set`, for setting the instance variables to new values. The program in Display 4.10 illustrates the use of the mutator method `set`. That program is similar to the one in Display 4.6/page 235, but because this version of our species class has *private* instance variables, we must use the mutator method `set` to reset the values of the instance variables.

It may seem that accessor methods and mutator methods defeat the purpose of making instance variables *private*, but there is a method to this madness. (No pun intended, I think.) When you use a mutator methods, the mutator method can check that any change is appropriate and warn the user if there is a problem. For example, the mutator method `set` checks to see if the program inadvertently sets the `population` equal to a negative number.

Accessor and Mutator Methods

A public method that reads and returns data from one or more private instance variables is called an **accessor method**. The names of accessor methods typically begin with `get`. A public method that changes the data stored in one or more private instance variables is called a **mutator method**. The names of mutator methods typically begin with `set`.

? Self-Test Questions

10. In Display 4.10/page 250, we set the data for the object `speciesOfThe-Month` as follows:

    ```
    speciesOfTheMonth.set("Klingon ox", 10, 15);
    ```

    Could we have used the following code instead?

    ```
    speciesOfTheMonth.name = "Klingon ox";
    speciesOfTheMonth.population = 10;
    speciesOfTheMonth.growthRate = 15;
    ```

    If we could have used this alternative code, why didn't we? If we could not use this alternative code, explain why we cannot use it.

11. Give preconditions and postconditions for the following method, which is intended to be added to the class `SpeciesFourthTry` in Display 4.9/page 249.

Display 4.9   A Class with Accessor and Mutator Methods

```java
public class SpeciesFourthTry
{
    private String name;
    private int population;
    private double growthRate;
```

Yes, we will define an even better version of this class later.

<The definition of the methods `readInput, writeOutput,` **and** `projectedPopulation`
         go here. They are the same as in Display 4.2/page 214 and Display 4.5/page 234.>

```java
    public void set(String newName,
                       int newPopulation, double newGrowthRate)
    {
        name = newName;
        if (newPopulation >= 0)
            population = newPopulation;
        else
        {
            System.out.println(
                          "ERROR: using a negative population.");
            System.exit(0);
        }
        growthRate = newGrowthRate;
    }

    public String getName()
    {
        return name;
    }

    public int getPopulation()
    {
        return population;
    }

    public double getGrowthRate()
    {
        return growthRate;
    }
}
```

Display 4.10 Using an Mutator Method *(Part 1 of 2)*

```
/******************************************
 *Demonstrates the use of mutator method set.
 ******************************************/
public class SpeciesFourthTryDemo
{
    public static void main(String[] args)
    {
        SpeciesFourthTry speciesOfTheMonth =
                                        new SpeciesFourthTry();
        int numberOfYears, futurePopulation;

        System.out.println("Enter number of years to project:");
        numberOfYears = SavitchIn.readLineInt();


        System.out.println("Enter data on the Species of the Month:");
        speciesOfTheMonth.readInput();
        speciesOfTheMonth.writeOutput();


        futurePopulation =
            speciesOfTheMonth.projectedPopulation(numberOfYears);
        System.out.println("In " + numberOfYears
                            + " years the population will be "
                            + futurePopulation);


        speciesOfTheMonth.set("Klingon ox", 10, 15);
        System.out.println("The new Species of the Month:");
        speciesOfTheMonth.writeOutput();
        System.out.println("In " + numberOfYears
            +" years the population will be "
            + speciesOfTheMonth.projectedPopulation(numberOfYears));
    }
}
```

Display 4.10 Using a Mutator Method *(Part 2 of 2)*

Sample Screen Dialogue

```
Enter number of years to project:
10
Enter data on the Species of the Month:
What is the species' name?
Ferengie fur ball
What is the population of the species?
1000
Enter growth rate (percent increase per year):
-20.5
Name = Ferengie fur ball
Population = 1000
Growth rate = -20.5%
In 10 years the population will be 100
The new Species of the Month:
Name = Klingon ox
Population = 10
Growth rate = 15.0%
In 10 years the population will be 40
```

```java
public void updatePopulation()
{
    population = (int)(population
                      + (growthRate/100)*population);
}
```

12. What is an *accessor method*? What is a *mutator method*?

13. Give the complete definition of a class called `Person` that has two instance variables, one for the person's name and the other for the person's age. Include accessor methods and mutator methods following the model in Display 4.9/page 249. Also include methods for input and output. There are no other methods.

Programming Example
Purchase Class

Display 4.11 contains a class for a single purchase, such as 12 apples or 2 quarts of milk. It is designed to be part of a program to be used at the checkout stand of a supermarket. Recall that supermarkets give prices not in unit costs, that is, not as the price for one, but as the price for some number, such as 5 for $1.25 or 3 for a $1.00. They hope that if they price apples at 5 for $1.25, then you will buy 5 apples instead of two apples. But, 5 for $1.25 is really $0.25 each and if you buy two apples, they still only charge you $0.50.

The instance variables are reproduced in what follows:

```
private String name;
private int groupCount;//Part of price, like the 2 in 2 for $1.99.
private double groupPrice;
                    //Part of price, like the $1.99 in 2 for $1.99.
private int numberBought;//Total number being purchased.
```

It is easiest to explain the meaning of these instance variables with an example. If you buy 12 apples at 5 for $1.25, then name has the value "apples", groupCount has the value 5, groupPrice has the value 1.25, and numberBought has the value 12. Note that the price of 5 for $1.25 is stored in the two instance variables groupCount (for the 5) and groupPrice (for the $1.25).

Thus, for example, consider the method getTotalCost. The total cost of the purchase is calculated as

```
(groupPrice/groupCount)*numberBought
```

Or to be very specific: if this purchase is 12 apples at 5 for $1.25, the total cost is

```
(1.25 / 5) * 12
```

Also notice the methods readInput, setPrice, and setNumberBought. All of these methods check for negative numbers, when it does not make sense to have a negative number, such as when the user enters the number purchased. A simple demonstration program that uses this class is given in Display 4.12.

Encapsulation

encapsulation

In Chapter 1, we said that **encapsulation** is the process of hiding all the details of a class definition that are not necessary to understanding how objects of the class are used. For encapsulation to be useful, the class definition must be given in such a way that the programmer is spared the bother of worrying about the internal details of the class definition. We have already discussed some of the techniques for doing this under the heading of *information hiding*. Encapsulation is a form of information hiding. Encapsulation, when done correctly, neatly divides a class definition into two parts, which we will call the *user interface*[1] and the *implementation*. The **user interface**

user interface

1. The word *interface* also has a technical meaning in the Java language. We are using the word slightly differently when we say *user interface*, although in spirit, the two uses of the word *interface* are the same.

Display 4.11 Purchase Class *(Part 1 of 3)*

```java
/**********************************************************
 *Class for the purchase of one kind of item, such as 3 oranges.
 *Prices are set supermarket style, such as 5 for $1.25.
 **********************************************************/
public class Purchase
{
    private String name;
    private int groupCount;//Part of price, like the 2 in 2 for $1.99.
    private double groupPrice;
                    //Part of price, like the $1.99 in 2 for $1.99.
    private int numberBought;//Total number being purchased.

    public void setName(String newName)
    {
        name = newName;
    }

    /**********************************************************
     *Sets price to groupCount pieces for $costForCount. E.g., 2 for $1.99.
     **********************************************************/
    public void setPrice(int groupCount, double costForCount)
    {
        if ((groupCount <= 0) || (costForCount <= 0))
        {
            System.out.println("Error: Bad parameter in setPrice.");
            System.exit(0);
        }
        else
        {
            groupCount = groupCount;
            groupPrice = costForCount;
        }
    }

    public void setNumberBought(int number)
    {
        if (number <= 0)
        {
            System.out.println("Error: Bad parameter in setNumberBought.");
            System.exit(0);
        }
        else
            numberBought = number;
    }
```

Display 4.11 Purchase Class *(Part 2 of 3)*

```java
/**********************************************
 *Gets price and number being purchased from keyboard.
 **********************************************/
public void readInput()
{
    System.out.println("Enter name of item you are purchasing:");
    name = SavitchIn.readLine();
    System.out.println("Enter price of item on two lines.");
    System.out.println("For example, 3 for $2.99 is entered as");
    System.out.println("3");
    System.out.println("2.99");
    System.out.println("Enter price of item on two lines, now:");
    groupCount = SavitchIn.readLineInt();
    groupPrice = SavitchIn.readLineDouble();

    while ((groupCount <= 0) || (groupPrice <= 0))
    {//Try again:
        System.out.println(
                "Both numbers must be positive. Try again.");
        System.out.println("Enter price of item on two lines.");
        System.out.println(
                        "For example, 3 for $2.99 is entered as");
        System.out.println("3");
        System.out.println("2.99");
        System.out.println(
                    "Enter price of item on two lines, now:");
        groupCount = SavitchIn.readLineInt();
        groupPrice = SavitchIn.readLineDouble();
    }

    System.out.println("Enter number of items purchased:");
    numberBought = SavitchIn.readLineInt();

    while (numberBought <= 0)
    {//Try again:
        System.out.println(
                "Number must be positive. Try again.");
        System.out.println("Enter number of items purchased:");
        numberBought = SavitchIn.readLineInt();
    }
}
```

Display 4.11 Purchase Class *(Part 3 of 3)*

```
    /*************************************************
     *Outputs price and number being purchased to screen.
     *************************************************/
    public void writeOutput()
    {
        System.out.println(numberBought + " " + name);
        System.out.println("at " + groupCount
                                  + " for $" + groupPrice);
    }


    public String getName()
    {
        return name;
    }


    public double getTotalCost()
    {
        return ((groupPrice/groupCount)*numberBought);
    }


    public double getUnitCost()
    {
        return (groupPrice/groupCount);
    }


    public int getNumberBought()
    {
        return numberBought;
    }

}
```

tells a programmer all that she or he needs to know in order to use the class. The user
interface consists of the headings for the public methods of the class along with the
comments that tell a programmer how to use these public methods and the public
defined constants of the class. The user interface part of the class definition should
be all you need to know in order to use the class in your program.

The **implementation** consists of all private elements of the class definition, prin-   *implementation*
cipally the private instance variables of the class, along with the definitions of both
the public and private methods. The user interface and implementation of a class
definition are not separated in your Java code. They are mixed together. For example, for the class Purchase in Display 4.11, the user interface is shown in color and

Display 4.12 **Use of the Purchase Class**

```java
public class PurchaseDemo
{
    public static void main(String[] args)
    {
        Purchase oneSale = new Purchase();

        oneSale.readInput();
        oneSale.writeOutput();
        System.out.println("Cost each $" + oneSale.getUnitCost());
        System.out.println("Total cost $" + oneSale.getTotalCost());
    }
}
```

Sample Screen Dialogue

```
Enter name of item you are purchasing:
grape fruit
Enter price of item on two lines.
For example, 3 for $2.99 is entered as
3
2.99
Enter price of item on two lines, now:
4
5.00
Enter number of items purchased:
0
Number must be positive. Try again.
Enter number of items purchased:
2

2 grape fruit
at 4 for $5.0
Cost each $1.25
Total cost $2.5
```

Display 4.13   Encapsulation

A Well-encapsulated Class Definition

Implementation:

Private instance variables.
Private constants.
Private methods.
Bodies of public and private
method definitions.

Interface:
Comments.
Headings of public methods.
Public defined constants.

*Programmer who
uses the class.*

*A well-encapsulated class definition has
no public instance variables.*

the implementation is shown in black text. Although you need the implementation in order to run a program that uses the class, you should not need to know anything about the implementation in order to write the code that uses the class.

When defining a class using the principle of encapsulation, you must define the class in such a way that the interface and implementation do indeed neatly separate so that the interface is a simplified and safe description of the class. One way to think of this is to imagine that there is a wall between the implementation and interface with well-regulated communication across the wall. This is shown graphically in Display 4.13. When a class is defined in this way, using encapsulation to neatly separate the implementation and user interface, we will say the class is **well-encapsulated**.

well-
encapsulated

Some of the most important guidelines for defining a well-encapsulated class are the following:

encapsulation
guidelines

1.   Place a comment before the class definition that describes how the programmer should think about the class data and methods. (Note that this need not be a list of instance variables. If the class describes an amount of money, the programmer should think in terms of dollars and cents and not in terms of an instance variable of type *double*, if that is what is

used to record the amount of money, nor should the programmer think in terms of two instance variables of type *int* for dollars and cents, if that is what is used to record the amount of money. In fact, the programmer using the class should not care whether the money is represented as an instance variable of type *double* or two instance variables of type *int*, or is represented in some other way.)

2. All the instance variables in the class should be marked *private*.

3. Provide *public* accessor and mutator methods to read and change the data in an object. Also, provide *public* methods for any other basic methods that a programmer needs in order to manipulate the data in the class; for example, you should provide input and output methods.

4. Fully specify how to use each public method with a comment placed before the method heading.

5. Make any helping methods *private*.

comments

When you comment a class definition, some of the comments are part of the user interface telling the user of the class how to use the class. These comments are usually placed before the class definition to describe general properties and before particular method definitions to explain how to use that particular method. Other comments are only needed to understand the implementation. A good rule to follow is to use the /**/ types of comments for user-interface comments and the // types of comments for implementation comments. In Display 4.11, the user-interface comments are shown in color and the implementation comments are shown in black text.

When you use encapsulation to define your class, you can go back and change the implementation details of the class definition and any program that uses the class will not need to be changed. This is a good way to test to see if you have written a well-encapsulated class definition. There are often very good reasons for changing the implementation details of a class definition. For example, you may come up with a more efficient way to implement a method so that the method invocations run faster. You may even decide to change some details of what the implementation does without changing the way the methods are invoked and the basic things they do. For example, if you have a class for bank account objects, you might change the amount of the penalty charged to an account when the account is overdrawn.

API

The term **API** is an abbreviate of *Application Programmer Interface*. The API for a class is essentially the same thing as what we described as the user interface for the class. You will often see the term *API* when reading the documentation for class libraries.

ADT

The term **ADT** is an abbreviation of *Abstract Data Type*. An ADT is a data type that is written using good information hiding techniques. Thus in Java, an ADT is basically the same thing as a well-encapsulated class definition

---

Encapsulation

Encapsulation is a term often heard when describing modern programming techniques. **Encapsulation** means that the data and the actions are combined into a single item (in our case, a class object) and that the details of the implementation are hidden. Thus, *information hiding, ADTs,* and *encapsulation* all refer to basically the same general idea: In very operational terms, the idea is to spare the programmer who uses your class from needing to read the details of how your class is implemented.

Case Study

Changing the Implementation of an Encapsulated Class

One sure test to see if you have defined a well-encapsulated class is to see if you can change the implementation and not have to change any code that uses the class. One reason you might want to change the implementation is to make it more efficient, that is, to make it work faster and/or use less storage. For example, after you have used the class Purchase (Display 4.11/page 253) for a while, you might discover that you can improve the code in a number of ways. Display 4.14 shows a rewritten definition of the class Purchase that you might write so as to get an improved implementation of the class. Note that this definition of Purchase has the same user interface, but an implementation that is different from the old definition of Purchase given in Display 4.11. In both definitions, the user interface is shown in color and those parts of the definitions are identical. The program in Display 4.12/page 256 could be run using either definition of the class Purchase and the program would produce the same input/output dialogs, except that the improved version asks the user to confirm the input. This shows that your definition of the class Purchase is well-encapsulated. To complete our discussion of this class, let's look at how these two implementations differ.

The revised definition of the class Purchase (Display 4.14) has one additional instance variable, named priceForOne, that holds the price for one item. This way, when an object of the class needs to know the unit cost or compute the price for a number of items (as in the methods getUnitCost and getTotalCost), the revised version of the Purchase class can simply use the value of priceForOne, whereas the old version of Purchase (Display 4.11) needs to recompute the price of one item as

        groupPrice/groupCount

and it must recompute this quantity every time it invokes the method getUnitCost or the method getTotalCost. The second definition computes this quantity only once and stores it in the instance variable priceForOne.

Display 4.14 Purchase Class Alternative Implementation *(Part 1 of 3)*

```
/*****************************************************
 *Class for the purchase of one kind of item, such as 3 oranges.
 *Prices are set supermarket style, such as 5 for $1.25.
 *****************************************************/
public class Purchase
{
    private String name;
    private int groupCount;//Part of price, like the 2 in 2 for $1.99.
    private double groupPrice;
                    //Part of price, like the $1.99 in 2 for $1.99.
    private int numberBought;//Total number being purchased.
    private double priceForOne;                           New

    public void setName(String newName)
    {
        name = newName;
    }

    /*****************************************************
     *Sets price to groupCount pieces for $costForCount. E.g., 2 for $1.99.
     *****************************************************/
    public void setPrice(int numberInGroup, double costForNumber)
    {
        if ((numberInGroup <= 0) || (costForNumber <= 0))
        {
            System.out.println("Error: Bad parameter in setPrice.");
            System.exit(0);
        }
        else
        {
            groupCount = numberInGroup;
            groupPrice = costForNumber;
            priceForOne = groupPrice/groupCount;          New
        }
    }

    public void setNumberBought(int number)
    {
        if (number <= 0)
        {
            System.out.println("Error: Bad parameter in setNumberBought.");
            System.exit(0);
        }
        else
            numberBought = number;
    }
```

Display 4.14 Purchase Class Alternative Implementation *(Part 2 of 3)*

```
/***********************************************
 *Gets price and number being purchased from keyboard.
 *Does not check with user to see that the data is OK.
 ***********************************************/

private void inputData()
{
    System.out.println("Enter name of item you are purchasing:");
    name = SavitchIn.readLine();
    System.out.println("Enter price of item on two lines.");
    System.out.println("For example, 3 for $2.99 is entered as");
    System.out.println("3");
    System.out.println("2.99");
    System.out.println("Enter price of item on two lines, now:");
    groupCount = SavitchIn.readLineInt();
    groupPrice = SavitchIn.readLineDouble();

    while ((groupCount <= 0) || (groupPrice <= 0))
    {//Try again:
        System.out.println(
                    "Both numbers must be positive. Try again.");
        System.out.println("Enter price of item on two lines.");
        System.out.println(
                    "For example, 3 for $2.99 is entered as");
        System.out.println("3");
        System.out.println("2.99");
        System.out.println(
                    "Enter price of item on two lines, now:");
        groupCount = SavitchIn.readLineInt();
        groupPrice = SavitchIn.readLineDouble();
    }

    priceForOne = groupPrice/groupCount;

    System.out.println("Enter number of items purchased:");
    numberBought = SavitchIn.readLineInt();

    while (numberBought <= 0)
    {//Try again:
        System.out.println(
                        "Number must be positive. Try again.");
        System.out.println("Enter number of items purchased:");
        numberBought = SavitchIn.readLineInt();
    }
}
```

Private methods are part of the implementation, not part of the user interface.

New

Display 4.14 Purchase Class Alternative Implementation *(Part 3 of 3)*

```
/*************************************************
*Gets price and number being purchased from keyboard.
*************************************************/
public void readInput()
{
    inputData();
    writeOutput();
    System.out.println("Is that correct?(y/n)");
    char ans = SavitchIn.readLineNonwhiteChar();
    while ((ans != 'y') && (ans != 'Y'))
    {//Try again:
        inputData();
        writeOutput();
        System.out.println("Is that correct?(y/n)");
        ans = SavitchIn.readLineNonwhiteChar();
    }
}

public void writeOutput()
{
    System.out.println(numberBought + " " + name);
    System.out.println("at " + groupCount
                              + " for $" + groupPrice);
}

public String getName()
{
    return name;
}

public double getTotalCost()
{
    return (priceForOne*numberBought);
}

public double getUnitCost()
{
    return priceForOne;
}

public int getNumberBought()
{
    return numberBought;
}
}
```

New

The new version of Purchase (Display 4.14) has an easier-to-understand and more robust definition of the method readInput. In this version, the method read-Input uses two helping methods: the method writeOutput and a new private method named inputData. Because inputData is a private method, it cannot be used anyplace except in the implementation of Purchase. So, this does not affect any program (or other code) that uses the class Purchase. As far as programs that use the class Purchase are concerned, the two definitions are interchangeable.

Note that the new implementation of the class Purchase can be used in any program that used the old version of the class Purchase and the program would not need to be changed. However, a program that uses the new version might behave in a slightly different way when the user enters incorrect data. With the method read-Input in the old definition of the class Purchase, if the user enters incorrect data, such as saying that apples cost 2 for $3 when the user meant to enter 3 for $2, then the program simply produces incorrect output. With the definition of the method readInput in the new definition of the class Purchase, the user gets a chance to reenter the data. Both versions work exactly the same when nothing goes wrong, but the new version recovers from more user mistakes.

To see this alternative implementation of the Purchase class in action, see the files PurchaseVersion2.java and PurchaseVersion2Demo.java on the accompanying CD.

extra code on CD

Most programmers would say that the definition of the class Purchase given in Display 4.14 is preferable to the definition in Display 4.11, but that is a secondary point. The point we want to emphasize is that you can separate the user interface and the implementation of a class definition.

Automatic Documentation with javadoc

If your copy of Java came from Sun Microsystems (or even from certain other places), it will come with a program named javadoc that will automatically generate documentation for the user interfaces to your classes. This documentation tells somebody who uses your program or class what she or he needs to know in order to use it. To get a more useful javadoc document, you must give your comments in a particular way. All the classes in this book have been commented for use with javadoc. (Although because of space constraints in the book, the comments are a little sparser than would be ideal.) If you comment your class definition correctly, such as the way the class in Display 4.14/page 260 is commented, then the program javadoc will take your class definition as input and produce a nicely formatted display of the user interface for your class as the output of the program javadoc. For example, if javadoc is run on the class definition in Display 4.14, then the output will look like the class with all the black text removed and only the colored text left. (It will also adjust spacing and line breaks and such.)

You do not need to use javadoc in order to understand this book. You do not need to use javadoc in order to write Java programs. Moreover, in order to read the documents produced by javadoc, you must use a Web browser (or other HTML viewer). However, if you are already using a Web browser, such as Netscape Navigator or Microsoft's Internet Explorer, then you are likely to find javadoc both easy to use and very useful. Appendix 10 covers javadoc.

? Self-Test Questions

14. What is a well-encapsulated class definition?

15. Why is the method `inputData` in Display 4.14/page 260 labeled *private* instead of *public*?

16. In a class definition, is anything labeled *private* ever part of the user interface?

17. In a class definition, is the body of any method definition ever part of the user interface?

4.3 | Objects and Reference

> "You are sad," the Knight said in anxious tone: "let me sing you a song to comfort you.
>
> "Is it very long?" Alice asked, for she had heard a good deal of poetry that day.
>
> "It's long," said the Knight, "but it's very, very beautiful. Everybody that hears me sing it—either it brings the tears into their eyes, or else—"
>
> "Or else what?" said Alice, for the Knight had made a sudden pause.
>
> "Or else it doesn't, you know. The name of the song is called 'Haddocks' Eyes.'"
>
> "Oh, that's the name of the song, is it?" Alice asked, trying to feel interested.
>
> "No, you don't understand," the Knight said, looking a little vexed. "That's what the name is called. The name really is 'The Aged Aged Man.'"
>
> "Then I ought to have said 'That's what the song is called'?" Alice corrected herself.
>
> "No, you oughtn't: that's quite another thing! The song is called 'Ways and Means': but that's only what it's called, you know!"
>
> "Well, what is the song, then?" said Alice, who was by this time completely bewildered.
>
> "I was coming to that," the Knight said. "The song really is 'A-sitting On A Gate': and the tune's my own invention."
>
> **Lewis Carroll, Through The Looking-Glass**

Variables of a class type, such as the variable `oneSale` in Display 4.12/page 256, behave very differently from variables of the primitive types, such a *int*, *double*, and *char*. Variables of a class type are names for objects of their class, but the objects are not the values of the variables in the same way as, say, the number 6 can be the value of a variable of type *int*. A variable of a class type can name an object, but the naming process is a bit subtle. In this section, we discuss how a variable of a class type names objects, and we also discuss the related topic of how method parameters of a class type behave in Java.

Variables of a Class Type and Objects

The following line from Display 4.10/page 250 creates an object of type Species-
FourthTry and attaches the name speciesOfTheMonth to this object:

```
SpeciesFourthTry speciesOfTheMonth = new SpeciesFourthTry();
```

This is really an abbreviation for the following two lines, which we could have used
instead in that program:

```
SpeciesFourthTry speciesOfTheMonth;
speciesOfTheMonth = new SpeciesFourthTry();
```

The first line declares a variable named speciesOfTheMonth and says that it is a
suitable name for an object of the class SpeciesFourthTry. This line does not create
the object itself. After this line is executed, you merely have a name. It is the second
line, the one with the *new*, that actually creates an object of type SpeciesFourthTry   *new*
and associates it with the name speciesOfTheMonth. You can think of the *new* as
creating the instance variables of the object.

    This may not seem like a big distinction, but it truly is. Variables of a class type
behave very differently from variables of a primitive type. Consider the following
lines of code that might begin the main part of a program:

```
SpeciesFourthTry klingonSpecies, earthSpecies;
klingonSpecies = new SpeciesFourthTry();
earthSpecies = new SpeciesFourthTry();
int n, m;
n = 42;
m = n;
```

As you would expect, there are two variables of type *int*: n and m. Both have a value
of 42, but if you change one, the other still has a value of 42. For example, if the program continues with

```
n = 99;
System.out.println(n + " and " + m);
```

then the output produced will be

```
99 and 42
```

    No surprises so far, but let's suppose the program continues as follows: *assignment
with variables
of a class type*

```
klingonSpecies.set("Klingon ox", 10, 15);
earthSpecies.set("Black rhino", 11, 2);
earthSpecies = klingonSpecies;
earthSpecies.set("Elephant", 100, 12);
System.out.println("earthSpecies:");
earthSpecies.writeOutput();
System.out.println("klingonSpecies:");
klingonSpecies.writeOutput();
```

You might think that the klingonSpecies is the Klingon ox and the earthSpecies
is the elephant, but the output produced may surprise you. It is the following:

Display 4.15 Class Variables *(Part 1 of 2)*

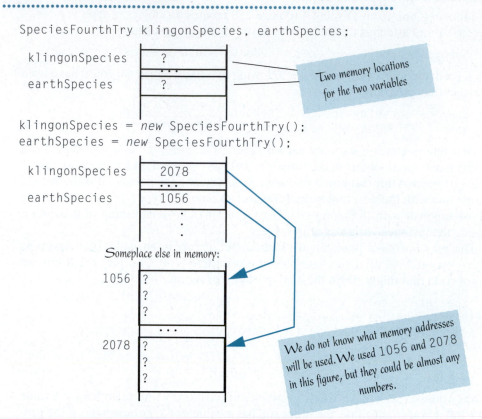

```
SpeciesFourthTry klingonSpecies, earthSpecies;
```

klingonSpecies   ?

earthSpecies   ?

Two memory locations for the two variables

```
klingonSpecies = new SpeciesFourthTry();
earthSpecies = new SpeciesFourthTry();
```

klingonSpecies   2078

earthSpecies   1056

Someplace else in memory:

1056   ? ? ?

2078   ? ? ?

We do not know what memory addresses will be used. We used 1056 and 2078 in this figure, but they could be almost any numbers.

```
klingonSpecies.set("Klingon ox", 10, 15);
earthSpecies.set("Black rhino", 11, 2);
```

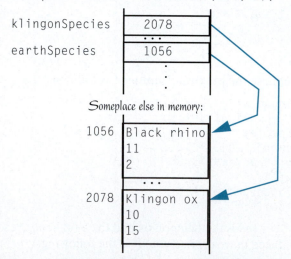

klingonSpecies   2078

earthSpecies   1056

Someplace else in memory:

1056   Black rhino 11 2

2078   Klingon ox 10 15

Display 4.15 Class Variables *(Part 2 of 2)*

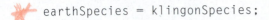

```
earthSpecies = klingonSpecies;
```

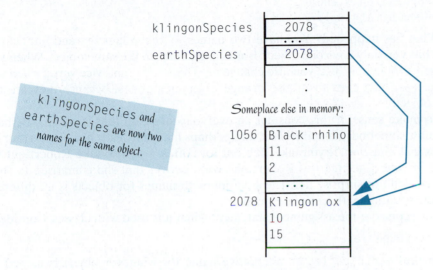

klingonSpecies   2078

earthSpecies   2078

klingonSpecies and earthSpecies are now two names for the same object.

Someplace else in memory:

1056 Black rhino
      11
      2

2078 Klingon ox
      10
      15

```
earthSpecies.set("Elephant", 100, 12);
```

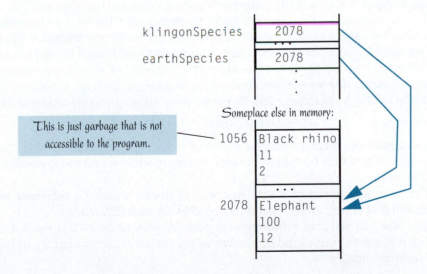

klingonSpecies   2078

earthSpecies   2078

This is just garbage that is not accessible to the program.

Someplace else in memory:

1056 Black rhino
      11
      2

2078 Elephant
      100
      12

```
earthSpecies:
Name = Elephant
Population = 100
Growth rate = 12%
klingonSpecies:
Name = Elephant
Population = 100
Growth rate = 12%
```

What has happened? You have two names, klingonSpecies and earthSpecies, but you only have one object. Both names refer to the same object. When you change klingonSpecies, you also change earthSpecies, and vice versa; when you change earthSpecies, you also change klingonSpecies, because they are the same object.

To make sense of this, consider an everyday situation that is similar. Perhaps you know somebody named *Robert*, and perhaps his family calls him *Robert*, but his friends call him *Bob*. If you take Bob out for coffee, you also take Robert out for coffee. If your sister marries Robert, she will discover that she is married to Bob, and that will not surprise her. The situation with names for objects is no different than the situation with names for people.

Let's consider the assignment statement when it is used with classes. Consider

    earthSpecies = klingonSpecies;

This makes earthSpecies an alternative name for whatever object is named by klingonSpecies. Now, that is a little hard to keep track of, so let's think of it another way. Let's think of it the way the computer thinks of it.

memory addresses   Each object is stored in the computer's memory in some location, and that location has an address. (If this does not make sense, reread Chapter 1.) The variables earthSpecies and klingonSpecies are really just ordinary variables (like the kind we use for *int* variables), but they store memory addresses for objects of the class SpeciesFourthTry. *When we say that a variable of a class type names an object, that means that the variable contains the memory address of that object.* This is illustrated in Display 4.15/page 266. When we have an assignment statement like

    earthSpecies = klingonSpecies;

this just copies the memory address in klingonSpecies into the variable earthSpecies, and now they both have the same memory address and so they both name the same object.

reference   The memory address of where an object is stored is called a **reference** to the object, and that is why this section is named ***Objects and Reference***.

One word of warning about memory addresses: A memory address is a number, but it is not the same kind of number as an *int* value. So, do not try to treat it as an ordinary integer .

Variables of a Class Type Store Memory Addresses

A variable of a primitive type stores a value of that type. Variables of a class type behave differently. *A variable of a class type does not store an object of that class.* A variable of a class type stores the memory address of where the object is located in the computer's memory. This does allow a variable of a class type to be used as a name for an object of that class.   However, some operations, such as = and ==, behave quite differently for variables of a class type than they do for variables of a primitive type.

Memory Addresses Are and Are Not Numbers

A variable of a class type stores a memory address. A memory address is a number. But, a variable of class type cannot be used like a variable that stores a number. This is not crazy. This is abstraction. The important property of a memory address is that it identifies a memory location. The fact that the implementors used numbers, rather than letters or colors or something else, to identify memory locations is just an accidental property. Java prevents you from using this accidental property. This prevents you from doing things you should not do, such as obtain access to restricted memory or otherwise screw up the computer. It also makes your code easier to understand.

Class Types and Reference Types

A variable of a class type does not actually hold an object of that class. A variable of a class type only holds the address of where that object is stored in memory. This memory address is often called a **reference** to the object in memory. For this reason, class types are often called *reference types*. A **reference type** is just a type whose variables hold references (that is, hold memory addresses), as opposed to actual values of objects. However, there are reference types other than class types, so we will use the term *class type* when referring to the name of a class. All class types are reference types, but as we will see in Chapter 6, there are reference types that are not class types.

What's *new*?

Variables of a class type work differently than variables of a primitive type. A variable of a primitive type holds a value of that type. A variable of a class type does not actually hold an object of that class. A variable of a class type only holds the address of where that object is stored in memory. The declaration

```
SpeciesFourthTry s;
```

creates a variable s that can hold a memory address. At this point, your program has a place to store a memory address, but no place to store the data in the instance variables of an object of type SpeciesFourthTry. To get a memory location to store the values of instance variables, your program needs to use *new*. The following assigns a memory location to an object of type SpeciesFourthTry and places the address of that memory location in the variable s. In a very informal sense, you can think of the *new* as creating the instance variables of the object.

```
s = new SpeciesFourthTry();
```

■ Gotcha

Use of = and == with Variables of a Class Type

In the previous subsection, we saw some of the surprises you can get when using the assignment operator with variables of a class type. The test for equality also behaves in what may seem like a peculiar way. Suppose the class SpeciesFourthTry is defined as in Display 4.9/page 249 and suppose you have the following in a program:

```
SpeciesFourthTry klingonSpecies = new SpeciesFourthTry();
SpeciesFourthTry earthSpecies = new SpeciesFourthTry();
klingonSpecies.set("Klingon ox", 10, 15);
earthSpecies.set("Klingon ox", 10, 15);
if (klingonSpecies == earthSpecies)
    System.out.println("They are EQUAL.");
else
    System.out.println("They are NOT equal.");
```

This will produce the output

```
They are NOT equal.
```

This is illustrated in Display 4.16.

But, the two species are equal in an intuitive sense. The problem is that a variable of a class type really contains only a memory address. There are two objects of type SpeciesFourthTry in memory. Both of them represent the same species in the real world, but they have different memory addresses and the == operator only checks to see if the memory addresses are equal. The == operator tests for a kind of equality, but not the kind of equality that you usually want. When defining a class, you should normally define a method for the class that is called equals and that tests objects to see if they are equal.

■ Java Tip

Define an equals Method for Your Classes

When you compare two objects using the == operator, you are checking to see if the two objects have the same address in memory. You are not testing for what you would intuitively call "being equal." To test for your intuitive notion of two objects being equal, you should define a method called equals to test two objects to see if they satisfy your idea of "being equal." In Display 4.17, we have redefined our definition of a class for species one last time. This time we have added a method called equals. This method equals is used with objects of the class Species in exactly the same way as we used the String method equals with objects of type String. For example, the program in Display 4.18 demonstrates use of the method equals.

Our definition of the method equals for the class Species uses the method equalsIgnoreCase of the class String. As we pointed out in Chapter 2, the method equalsIgnoreCase is a method of the class String and is automatically provided as part of the Java language. The method equalsIgnoreCase returns *true* if the two strings being compared are the same except that some letters differ

Display 4.16 Dangers of == with Objects

```
klingonSpecies = new SpeciesFourthTry();
earthSpecies = new SpeciesFourthTry();
```

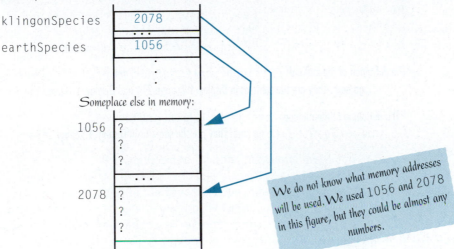

klingonSpecies   2078

earthSpecies   1056

Someplace else in memory:

1056   ? ? ?

2078   ? ? ?

We do not know what memory addresses will be used. We used 1056 and 2078 in this figure, but they could be almost any numbers.

```
klingonSpecies.set("Klingon ox", 10, 15);
earthSpecies.set("Klingon ox", 10, 15);
```

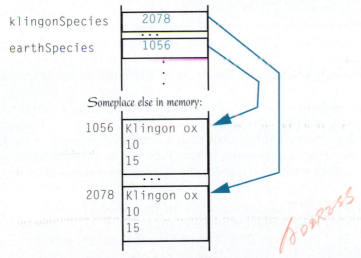

klingonSpecies   2078

earthSpecies   1056

Someplace else in memory:

1056   Klingon ox
       10
       15

2078   Klingon ox
       10
       15

```
if (klingonSpecies == earthSpecies)
    System.out.println("They are EQUAL.");
else
    System.out.println("They are NOT equal.");
```

The output is They are Not equal, because 2078 is not equal to 1056.

Display 4.17 Defining an `equals` Method

```java
public class Species
{
    private String name;
    private int population;
    private double growthRate;
```

<The definition of the methods `readInput`, `writeOutput`, and `projectedPopulation`
go here. They are the same as in Display 4.2/page 214 and Display 4.5/page 234.>

<The definition of the methods `set`, `getName`, `getPopulation`,
and `getGrowthRate` go here. They are the same as in Display 4.9/page 249.>

```java
    public boolean equals(Species otherObject)
    {
        return ((this.name.equalsIgnoreCase(otherObject.name))
                && (this.population == otherObject.population)
                && (this.growthRate == otherObject.growthRate));
    }
}
```

> `equalsIgnoreCase` is a method of the class `String` and is automatically provided as part of the Java language.

---

by being uppercase in one string and lowercase in the other string; otherwise, it returns *false*.

Notice that the method `equals` in Display 4.17 always returns either *true* or *false*, and so the type for the value returned is *boolean*. The *return*-statement may seen a bit strange, but is nothing other than a boolean expression of the kind you might use in an *if-else*-statement. It may help you to understand things if you note that the definition of `equals` in Display 4.17 can be expressed by the following pseudocode:

returning a
boolean
value

```
if ((this.name.equalsIgnoreCase(otherObject.name))
            && (this.population == otherObject.population)
            && (this.growthRate == otherObject.growthRate))
then return true
otherwise return false.
```

So, the following (from the program in Display 4.18):

```java
if (s1.equals(s2))
    System.out.println("Match with the method equals.");
else
    System.out.println("Do Not match with the method equals.");
```

Display 4.18 Demonstrating an equals Method

```java
public class SpeciesEqualsDemo
{
    public static void main(String[] args)
    {
        Species s1 = new Species(), s2 = new Species();

        s1.set("Klingon Ox", 10, 15);
        s2.set("Klingon Ox", 10, 15);

        if (s1 == s2)
            System.out.println("Match with ==.");
        else
            System.out.println("Do Not match with ==.");

        if (s1.equals(s2))
            System.out.println("Match with the method equals.");
        else
            System.out.println("Do Not match with the method equals.");

        System.out.println(
                    "Now we change one Klingon Ox to all lowercase.");
        s2.set("klingon ox", 10, 15);
        if (s1.equals(s2))
            System.out.println("Still match with the method equals.");
        else
            System.out.println("Do Not match with the method equals.");
    }
}
```

Screen Output

```
Do Not match with ==.
Match with the method equals.
Now we change one Klingon Ox to all lowercase.
Still match with the method equals.
```

is equivalent to the following pseudocode:

```
if "it is true that
        (s1.name.equalsIgnoreCase(s2.name))
            && (s1.population == s2.population)
            && (s1.growthRate == s2.growthRate), then"
    System.out.println("Match with the method equals.");
else
    System.out.println("Do Not match with the method equals.");
```

use of *this* **is optional**

We did not need to use the *this* parameter in the definition of equals in Display 4.17. The definition given there is equivalent to the following:

```
public boolean equals(Species otherObject)
{
    return ((name.equalsIgnoreCase(otherObject.name))
            && (population == otherObject.population)
            && (growthRate == otherObject.growthRate))
}
```

The instance variable population by itself always means the same as *this*.population. Similarly, any other instance variable by itself means the same as if it were preceded by a *this* and a dot.

We will say more about methods that return a value of type *boolean* in the subsection ***Boolean-Valued Methods*** a little later in this chapter.

There is no unique definition of equals that has been handed down by the gods for all time. The definition of equals that you give will depend on how you intend to use the class. The definition we gave in Display 4.17 says that two objects of the class Species are equal if they represent the same records, that is, the same species name, the same population size, and the same growth rate. In some other context, you might want to define equals to mean that two objects are equal if they have the same species name, but possibly different populations and/or different growth rates. This would correspond to considering two objects to be equal if they are records for the same species, even if they are records for the same species at different times.

You should always use the identifier equals for the name of your method to test two objects to see if they are equal. Do not use some other identifier, such as same; do not even use equal (without an s). This is because some other software that is part of Java depends on you using the exact name equals to test for equality of objects. This software invokes a method named equals, so your method had better be named equals.

If you do not define an equals method for your class, then Java will automatically create a default definition of equals, but it is unlikely to behave the way you want it to behave. So, it is best to define your own equals method.

The final version of our class for a species objects is given in Display 4.19. It is the same definition as the one in Display 4.17/page 272, but this time, we have included

Programming Example

A Species Class

all of the details so that you can see a complete example. We have also written the definition of the method `equals` without using the *this* parameter, since that is the form most programmers use. The definition of `equals` in Display 4.19 is completely equivalent to the definition in Display 4.17. It is only expressed using the abbreviation of leaving out the explicit writing of *this*.

Boolean-Valued Methods

Methods can return a value of type *boolean*. There is really nothing new about these methods: You just specify a return type of *boolean* and use a boolean expression in the *return*-statement. We have already seen one such method when we defined the `equals` method for the class `Species` from Display 4.19. In what follows, we reproduce the definition of the boolean-valued method `equals` from Display 4.19:

equals

```
public boolean equals(Species otherObject)
{
    return ((name.equalsIgnoreCase(otherObject.name))
               && (population == otherObject.population)
               && (growthRate == otherObject.growthRate));
}
```

The method simply evaluates the boolean expression, shown in color. That produces a value of *true* or *false*. That value of *true* or *false* is the value returned by the method `equals`.

As we have already been doing, you can use an invocation of the method `equals` in an *if-else*-statement, *while*-statement, or other statement that requires a boolean expression. You can also store the value returned by the method `equals`, or any other boolean-valued method, in a variable of type *boolean*. For example:

```
Species s1 = new Species(), s2 = new Species();
<Some code to set the values of s1 and s2.>
boolean areEqual;
areEqual = s1.equals(s2);
<Some more code.>
if (areEqual)
    System.out.println("They are equal.");
else
    System.out.println("They are not equal.");
```

As another example, you might add the following method to the definition of the class `Species` from Display 4.19:

examples

Display 4.19 A Complete Species Class *(Part 1 of 2)*

```
/**********************************
 *Class for data on endangered species.
 **********************************/
public class Species
{
    private String name;
    private int population;
    private double growthRate;

    public void readInput()
    {
        System.out.println("What is the species' name?");
        name = SavitchIn.readLine();
        System.out.println(
                    "What is the population of the species?");
        population = SavitchIn.readLineInt();
        while (population < 0)
        {
            System.out.println("Population cannot be negative.");
            System.out.println("Reenter population:");
            population = SavitchIn.readLineInt();
        }
        System.out.println(
                    "Enter growth rate (percent increase per year):");
        growthRate = SavitchIn.readLineDouble();
    }

    public void writeOutput()
    {
        System.out.println("Name = " + name);
        System.out.println("Population = " + population);
        System.out.println("Growth rate = " + growthRate + "%");
    }

    /*************************************************
     *Precondition: years is a nonnegative number.
     *Returns the projected population of the calling object
     *after the specified number of years.
     *************************************************/
    public int projectedPopulation(int years)
    {
        double populationAmount = population;
        int count = years;
```

This is the same class definition as in Display 4.17/page 272, but with all the details shown.

<Definition of projectedPopulation **continued on next page.>**

Display 4.19 A Complete Species Class *(Part 2 of 2)*

```
        while ((count > 0) && (populationAmount > 0))
        {
            populationAmount = (populationAmount +
                        (growthRate/100) * populationAmount);
            count--;
        }
        if (populationAmount > 0)
            return (int)populationAmount;
        else
            return 0;
    }

    public void set(String newName, int newPopulation, double newGrowthRate)
    {
        name = newName;
        if (newPopulation >= 0)
            population = newPopulation;
        else
        {
            System.out.println("ERROR: using a negative population.");
            System.exit(0);
        }
        growthRate = newGrowthRate;
    }

    public String getName()
    {
        return name;
    }

    public int getPopulation()
    {
        return population;
    }

    public double getGrowthRate()
    {
        return growthRate;
    }

    public boolean equals(Species otherObject)
    {
        return ((name.equalsIgnoreCase(otherObject.name))
                && (population == otherObject.population)
                && (growthRate == otherObject.growthRate));
    }
}
```

This version of equals *is equivalent to the version in* Display 4.17/page 272. *In* Display 4.17, *we explicitly used the* this *parameter. In this version, the* this *parameter is omitted but understood to be there implicitly.*

```
/***********************************************************
 *Precondition: The calling object and the argument otherSpecies
 *both have values for their population.
 *Returns true if the population of the calling object is greater
 *than the population of otherSpecies; otherwise, returns false.
 ***********************************************************/
public boolean largerPopulationThan(Species otherSpecies)
{
    return (population > otherSpecies.population);
}
```

You can then use the method `largerPopulationThan` in the same sorts of ways as you do the method `equals`. For example, the following might appear in some program:

```
Species s1 = new Species(), s2 = new Species();
<Some code to set the values of s1 and s2.>
if (s1.largerPopulationThan(s2))
    System.out.println(s1.speciesName()
                            + " has the larger population.");
else
    System.out.println(s2.speciesName()
                            + " has the larger population.");
```

As an additional example, you might also add the following method to the definition of the class `Species` from Display 4.19:

```
/***********************************************************
 *Precondition: The calling object has a value for its population.
 *Returns true if the population of the calling object is
 *zero; otherwise, returns false.
 ***********************************************************/
public boolean isExtinct()
{
    return (population == 0);
}
```

The following sample code might then appear in some program:

```
Species s1 = new Species();
<Some code to set the values of s1.>
if (s1.isExtinct())
    System.out.println(s1.speciesName() + " is extinct.");
else
    System.out.println(s1.getName() + " is still with us.");
```

? Self-Test Questions

18. What is a *reference type*? Are class types reference types? Are primitive types (like *int*) reference types?

19. When comparing two objects of a class type to see if they are "equal" or not, should you use == or the method `equals`?

20. Write a method definition for a method called `largerGrowthRateThan` that could be added to the class `Species` from Display 4.19/page 276. The method `largerGrowthRateThan` has one argument of type `Species`. The method returns *true* if the calling object has a larger growth rate than the growth rate of the one argument; otherwise, it returns *false*.

Class Parameters

Parameters of a class type are treated differently from parameters of a primitive type. In a sense, we have already discussed this difference when we discussed using the assignment operator with objects of a class type. Recall the following two points, which will help us describe how class parameters work:

1. First, recall how the assignment operator works with classes:

    When you use an assignment operator with objects of a class type, you are actually copying a memory address. Suppose `Species` is the class defined in Display 4.19/page 276 and consider the following code:

    ```
    Species species1 = new Species();
    Species species2 = new Species();
    species2.readInput();
    species1 = species2;
    ```

    As we discussed in the previous section, `species1` and `species2` are now two names for the same object.

2. Now consider how parameters *of a primitive type* work. For example, consider the following call to the method `projectedPopulation` that we used in Display 4.10/page 250:

    ```
    futurePopulation =
        speciesOfTheMonth.projectedPopulation(numberOfYears);
    ```

    The method definition for `projectedPopulation` is in Display 4.19. The definition begins as follows:

    ```
    public int projectedPopulation(int years)
    {
        double populationAmount = population;
        int count = years;
        while ((count > 0) && (populationAmount > 0))
        {
            .
            .
            .
    ```

    Recall that the formal parameter `years` is actually a local variable, and when the method `projectedPopulation` is invoked, this local variable `years` is initialized to the value of the argument `numberOfYears`. So when the method is called, it is as if the following assignment statement were temporarily inserted into the method definition:

```
years = numberOfYears;
```

So, it is as if the definition of the method projectedPopulation was, for the duration of this method invocation, changed as follows:

```
public int projectedPopulation(int years)
{
    years = numberOfYears;
    double populationAmount = population;
    int count = years;
    while ((count > 0) && (populationAmount > 0))
    {
        .
        .
        .
```

Wow, that's a long preamble; but if you understand those two points, it will be very easy to explain how parameters of a class type work. Parameters of a class type work the same as described in the preceding point 2 for parameters of a primitive type, *but because the assignment operator means something different for variables of a class type, the effect is very different!* [1]

Let's go through that explanation again with slightly different words (but the same message). Here is a rephrasing of how parameters of a class type are handled in Java: Consider the following call to the method equals that was used in Display 4.18/page 273:

```
if (s1.equals(s2))
    System.out.println("Match with the method equals.");
else
    System.out.println("Do Not match with the method equals.");
```

s2 is an argument of the class type Species defined in Display 4.19. In what follows, we reproduce the definition for the method equals: (This version of equals was given in Display 4.17/page 272 and is equivalent to the version in Display 4.19):

```
public boolean equals(Species otherObject)
{
    return ((this.name.equalsIgnoreCase(otherObject.name))
            && (this.population == otherObject.population)
            && (this.growthRate == otherObject.growthRate))
}
```

---

1. Some programmers refer to the parameter mechanism for class parameters as **call-by-reference** parameter passing. Others say that is incorrect terminology. The problem is that there is more than one commonly used definition of *call-by-reference*. One point is clear: class parameters in Java behave a bit differently from what is known as *call-by-reference* parameters in other languages. So, we will not use the term *call-by-reference*. In any event, the important thing is to understand how class parameters work, no matter what you call them.

When the method `equals` is called in `s1.equals(s2)`, it is as if the following assignment statement was temporarily inserted at the start of the method definition

```
otherObject = s2;
```

so that the method definition, for the duration of this call to `equals`, is equivalent to

```
public boolean equals(Species otherObject)
{
    otherObject = s2;//You cannot do this, but
                    //Java acts as if you could and did do this.
    return ((this.name.equalsIgnoreCase(otherObject.name))
            && (this.population == otherObject.population)
            && (this.growthRate == otherObject.growthRate))

}
```

But, recall that this assignment statement merely copies the memory address of `s2` into the variable `otherObject`, so `otherObject` just becomes another name for the object named by `s2`. Thus, anything done with the object named `otherObject` will in fact be done with the object named `s2`. Thus, it is as if the method performed the following action:

```
    return ((this.name.equalsIgnoreCase(s2.name))
            && (this.population == s2.population)
            && (this.growthRate == s2.growthRate))
```

Notice that with a parameter of a class type, whatever action is taken with the formal parameter (in this example, `otherObject`) is actually taken with the argument used in the method call (in this case, `s2`). So the argument used in the method call is actually acted upon and can be changed by the method call.

In the case of the method `equals`, the effect of this parameter-passing mechanism for parameters of a class type is not so different from what happens with parameters of a primitive type, but with some other methods, the difference is more dramatic. The next subsection gives a more dramatic example of how parameters of a class type differ from parameters of a primitive type.

Parameters of a Class Type

Formal parameters are given in parentheses after the method name at the beginning of a method definition. A formal parameter of a class type is a local variable that holds the memory address of an object of that class type. When there is an invocation of the method, the parameter is initialized to the address of the corresponding argument in the method invocation. In less technical terms, this means that the formal parameter will serve as an alternative name for the object given as the corresponding argument in a method invocation.

Note that this means that if you use an argument of a class type in a method invocation, then the method invocation can change the argument.

Comparing Class Parameters and Primitive-Type Parameters

Suppose we add a method named `makeEqual` to the class `Species` to form a new class called `DemoSpecies`, as shown in Display 4.20. This class is only for our demonstration, so do not worry about the rest of the class definition. Notice that the

Display 4.20 Just a Demonstration Class

```
/***********************************************************
 *This is a version of the class Species, but is only a toy example
 *designed to demonstrate the difference between parameters of
 *a class type and parameters of a primitive type.
 ***********************************************************/
public class DemoSpecies
{
    private String name;
    private int population;
    private double growthRate;

    /************************************************
     *Precondition: Calling object has been given values.
     *Postcondition: otherObject has the same data as the
     *calling object. The calling object is unchanged.
     ************************************************/
    public void makeEqual(DemoSpecies otherObject)
    {
        otherObject.name = this.name;
        otherObject.population = this.population;
        otherObject.growthRate = this.growthRate;
    }

    /************************************************
     *Tries to set intVariable equal to the population of
     *the calling object. But it cannot succeed, because
     *arguments of a primitive type cannot be changed.
     ************************************************/
    public void tryToMakeEqual(int intVariable)
    {
        intVariable = this.population;
    }

    public boolean equals(DemoSpecies otherObject)
```
<The rest of the class definition of the method `equals` is the same as in Display 4.19/page 276.>

<The rest of the class definition is the same as that of the class `Species` in Display 4.19.>
```
}
```

method `makeEqual` has formal parameters of type `DemoSpecies`, and that `make-Equal` changes the formal parameter. Now, let's play with this toy class.

Look at the demonstration program in Display 4.21 and look at the call to this method `makeEqual`, which has an argument `s2` of type `DemoSpecies`. Note that the change performed in the method body is actually performed on the argument named by `s2`. A method can actually change the value of an argument of a class type.

But, now look at the method named `tryToMakeEqual` also in Display 4.20. Notice that the method `tryToMakeEqual` has a formal parameter of the primitive type *int* and that `tryToMakeEqual` changes the formal parameter. Now, look again at the demonstration program in Display 4.21 and look at the call to this method `tryToMakeEqual`, which has an argument `aPopulation` of type *int*. Note that the change performed in the method body has no effect on the argument `aPopulation`. This is because, with arguments of a primitive type, Java uses the call-by-value parameter mechanism, and because variables of a primitive type hold actual values, not memory addresses. So, the parameter is a local variable that holds the value of the argument, and so any changes are made to this local variable and not to the argument.

Parameters of a class type are more versatile than parameters of a primitive type. Parameters of a primitive type can be used to give values to a method, but a method cannot change the value of any primitive-type variable that is given to it as an argument. On the other hand, parameters of a class type not only can be used to give information to a method, but the method can also change the object named by an argument of a class type.

Differences between Primitive and Class-Type Parameters

A method cannot change the value of a variable of a primitive type that is an argument to the method. On the other hand, a method can change the values of the instance variables of an argument of a class type.

? Self-Test Questions

21. What is wrong with a program that starts as follows? The class `Species` is defined in Display 4.19/page 276.

Display 4.21 Comparing Parameters of a Class and a Primitive Type

```java
public class ParametersDemo
{
    public static void main(String[] args)
    {
        DemoSpecies s1 = new DemoSpecies(),
                    s2 = new DemoSpecies();

        s1.set("Klingon Ox", 10, 15);
        s2.set("Ferengie Fur Ball", 90, 56);
        System.out.println("Value of s2 before call to method:");
        s2.writeOutput();
        s1.makeEqual(s2);
        System.out.println("Value of s2 after call to method:");
        s2.writeOutput();

        int aPopulation = 42;
        System.out.println(
                      "Value of aPopulation before call to method: "
                    + aPopulation);
        s1.tryToMakeEqual(aPopulation);
        System.out.println(
                      "Value of aPopulation after call to method: "
                    + aPopulation);
    }
}
```

Screen Output

```
Value of s2 before call to method:
Name = Ferengie Fur Ball
Population = 90
Growth Rate = 56.0%
Value of s2 after call to method:
Name = Klingon Ox
Population = 10
Growth Rate = 15.0%
Value of aPopulation before call to method: 42
Value of aPopulation after call to method: 42
```

An argument of a class type can change.

An argument of a primitive type cannot change.

```
public class SpeciesEqualsDemo
{
    public static void main(String[] args)
    {
        Species s1, s2;

        s1.set("Klingon Ox", 10, 15);
        s2.set("Klingon Ox", 10, 15);

        if (s1 == s2)
            System.out.println("Match with ==.");
        else
            System.out.println("Do Not match with ==.");
    }
}
```

22. What is the biggest difference between a parameter of a primitive type and a parameter of a class type?

23. What is the output produced by the following program? The class Species is defined in Display 4.19/page 276.

```
public class ExerciseProgram
{
    public static void main(String[] args)
    {
        Species s1 = new Species();
        ExerciseClass mysteryMaker = new ExerciseClass();
        int n = 0;
        s1.set("Hobbit", 100, 2);
        mysteryMaker.mystery(s1, n);
        s1.writeOutput();
        System.out.println("n = " + n);
    }
}
```

The class ExerciseClass is given below:

```
public class ExerciseClass
{
    public void mystery(Species s, int m)
    {
        s.set("Klingon Ox", 10, 15);
        m = 42;
    }
}
```

24. Redefine the class Person from Self-Test Question 13 so that it includes an equals method.

■ Classes have instance variables to store data and methods to perform actions.

■ All instance variables in a class should be declared to be *private*. When they are declared *private*, they cannot be accessed by name except within the definition of a method of the same class.

■ **Encapsulation** means that the data and the actions are combined into a single item (in our case, a class object) and that the *details of the implementation are hidden*. Making all instance variables private is part of the encapsulation process.

■ A variable of a class type is a **reference variable**. That means that a variable of a class type holds the memory address of where the object it names is stored in memory.

■ There are two kinds of methods: methods that return a value and *void*-methods.

■ Methods can have parameters of a primitive type and/or parameters of a class type, but they behave differently.

■ A parameter of a primitive type is a local variable that is initialized to the value of the corresponding argument when the method is called. This mechanism of substituting arguments for formal parameters is known as the **call-by-value** mechanism.

■ A parameter of a class type becomes another name for the corresponding argument in a method invocation. Thus, any change that is made to the parameter will be made to the corresponding argument.

■ The operators = and ==, when used on objects of a class, do not behave the same as they do on primitive types.

■ You usually want to define an `equals` method for the classes you define.

? ANSWERS to Self-Test Questions

1.
```
SpeciesFirstTry speciesOfTheYear = new SpeciesFirstTry();
System.out.println("Enter data for Species of the Year:");
speciesOfTheYear.readInput();
```

2. `dilbert.readInput();`

3.
```
public class SpeciesFirstTry
{
    public String name;
    public int number;
    public int population;
    public double growthRate;

    public void readInput()
    {
        System.out.println("What is the species' name?");
        name = SavitchIn.readLine();
        System.out.println("What is the species' number?");
        number = SavitchIn.readLineInt();
        while (number < 0)
        {
            System.out.println(
                      "Number cannot be negative.");
            System.out.println("Reenter number:");
            population = SavitchIn.readLineInt();
        }
        System.out.println(
                  "What is the population of the species?");
        population = SavitchIn.readLineInt();
        while (population < 0)
        {
            System.out.println("Population cannot be negative.");
            System.out.println("Reenter population:");
            population = SavitchIn.readLineInt();
        }
        System.out.println(
              "Enter growth rate (percent increase per year):");
        growthRate = SavitchIn.readLineDouble();
    }
```

```java
public void writeOutput()
{
    System.out.println("Name = " + name);
    System.out.println("Number = " + number);
    System.out.println("Population = " + population);
    System.out.println("Growth rate = " + growthRate + "%");
}


public int populationIn10()
<This method does not change.>
}
```

4.
```java
public int femalePopulation()
{
    return (population/2 + population%2);
}


public int malePopulation()
{
    return population/2;
}
```

5.
```java
public void writeOutput()
{
    System.out.println("Name = " + this.name);
    System.out.println("Population = " + this.population);
    System.out.println("Growth rate = "
                        + this.growthRate + "%");
}
```

6.
```java
public void readInput()
{
    System.out.println("What is the species' name?");
    this.name = SavitchIn.readLine();

    System.out.println(
                "What is the population of the species?");
    this.population = SavitchIn.readLineInt();
    while (this.population < 0)
    {
        System.out.println("Population cannot be negative.");
        System.out.println("Reenter population:");
        this.population = SavitchIn.readLineInt();
    }

    System.out.println(
            "Enter growth rate (percent increase per year):");
    this.growthRate = SavitchIn.readLineDouble();
}
```

7.

```java
public double density(double area)
{
    return population/area;
}
```

8.

```java
public void fixPopulation(double area)
{
    population = (int)(2*area);
}
```

9.

```java
public void changePopulation(double area, int
numberPerMile)
{
    population = (int)(numberPerMile*area);
}
```

10. We cannot use the alternative code because the instance variables are labeled *private* in the class definition and so cannot be accessed directly except within a method definition of the class SpeciesFourthTry.

11.

```java
/*******************************************************
*Precondition: Calling object's population and growth rate
*have been given values.
*Postcondition: Calling object's population was updated to
*reflect one year's change. Other data values are unchanged.
*******************************************************/
```

12. An accessor method is a public method that reads and returns data from one or more private instance variables. (The names of accessor methods typically begin with get.) A mutator method is a public method that changes the data stored in one or more private instance variables. (The names of mutator methods typically begin with set.)

13.

```java
public class Person
{
    private String name;
    private int age;
```

```java
public void readInput()
{
    System.out.println("What is the person's name?");
    name = SavitchIn.readLine();

    System.out.println("What is the person's age?");
    age = SavitchIn.readLineInt();
    while (age < 0)
    {
        System.out.println("Age cannot be negative.");
        System.out.println("Reenter age:");
        age = SavitchIn.readLineInt();
    }

}


public void writeOutput()
{
    System.out.println("Name = " + name);
    System.out.println("Age = " + age);
}


public void set(String newName, int newAge)
{
    name = newName;
    if (newAge >= 0)
        age = newAge;
    else
    {
        System.out.println("ERROR: Used a negative age.");
        System.exit(0);
    }
}


public String getName()
{
    return name;
}


public int getAge()
{
    return age;
}
}
```

14. A well-encapsulated class definition is one written so that it neatly separates into user interface and implementation, so that a programmer who

uses the class need only know about the user interface and need not be concerned with implementation details.

15. It is labeled *private* because it is only a helping method and so is not part of the public user interface, but is part of the private implementation.

16. No, it is part of the implementation.

17. No, it is part of the implementation.

18. A reference type is a type whose variables hold references (that is, hold memory addresses), as opposed to actual values of objects. Class types are reference types. (However, there are reference types other than class types, but we will not see any until later in this book.) Primitive types are not reference types.

19. Normally, you use the method equals when testing two objects to see if they are "equal" or not. (The only time you would use == is if you wanted to see if the objects were in the same place in memory, and it is unlikely that you will want to make such a test.)

20.
```
/************************************************************
*Precondition: The calling object and the argument otherSpecies
*both have values for their growth rates.
*Returns true if the growth rate of the calling object is greater
*than the growth rate of otherSpecies; otherwise, returns false.
************************************************************/
public boolean largerGrowthRateThan(Species otherSpecies)
{
    return (growthRate > otherSpecies.growthRate);
}
```

21. The variables s1 and s2 are names for object of type Species, but this program does not create any objects for them to name. They are just names, not yet objects. The program should begin as

```
public class SpeciesEqualsDemo
{
    public static void main(String[] args)
    {
        Species s1 = new Species(), s2 = new Species();
        <The rest of the code is OK.>
```

22. The biggest difference is how a method handles arguments that correspond to the different kinds of parameters. A method cannot change the value of a variable of a primitive type that is an argument to the method. On the other hand, a method can change the values of the instance variables of an object of a class type whose name is an argument to the method.

23.
```
Name = Klingon ox
Population = 10
Growth rate = 15.0%
n = 0
```

24. The class definition is the same as before except for the addition of the method `equals`. In what follows are two possible definitions of `equals`. The first corresponds to saying a person at one age is equal to the same person at another, later age. The second one corresponds to saying that a person at one age is not equal to what she or he will be at another age.

```
public boolean equals(Person otherObject)
{
    return (this.name.equalsIgnoreCase(otherObject.name));
}
```

```
public boolean equals(Person otherObject)
{
    return ((this.name.equalsIgnoreCase(otherObject.name))
            && (this.age == otherObject.age) );
}
```

They are also correct if you omit all the occurrences of *this* and the following dot.

? PROGRAMMING EXERCISES

1. Write a program to answer questions like the following: Suppose the species Klingon ox has a population of 100 and a growth rate of 15%, and the species elephant has a population of 10 and a growth rate of 35%. How many years will it take for the elephant population to exceed the Klingon ox population? Use the class `Species` in Display 4.19/page 276. Your program will ask for the data on both species and will respond by telling how many years it will take for the populations to change so that the species that starts with the lower population has a population that exceeds that of the species that starts with the higher population. The two species may be entered in any order. Note that it is possible that the species with the smaller population will never exceed that of the other species. In this case, your program should output a suitable message stating this fact.

2. Define a class called `Counter`. An object of this class is used to count things, so it records a count that is a nonnegative whole number. Include methods to set the counter to zero, to increase the count by 1, and to decrease the count by 1. Be sure that no method allows the value of the counter to become negative. Also, include an accessor method that returns the current count value. Also, include a method that outputs the count to the screen. There will be no input method. The only method that

can set the counter is the one that sets it to zero. Also, write a program to test your class definition. *Hint:* You only need one instance variable.

3. Write a grading program for a class with the following grading policies:

(a) There are two quizzes, each graded on the basis of 10 points.

(b) There is one midterm exam and one final exam, each graded on the basis of 100 points.

(c) The final exam counts for 50% of the grade, the midterm counts for 25%, and the two quizzes together count for a total of 25%. (Do not forget to normalize the quiz scores. They should be converted to a percent before they are averaged in.)

Any grade of 90 or more is an A, any grade of 80 or more (but less than 90) is a B, any grade of 70 or more (but less than 80) is a C, any grade of 60 or more (but less than 70) is a D, and any grade below 60 is an F. The program will read in the student's scores and output the student's record, which consists of two quiz and two exam scores as well as the student's overall numeric score for the entire course and final letter grade.

Define and use a class for the student record. The class should have instance variables for the quizzes, midterm, final, course overall numeric score, and course final letter grade. The overall numeric score is a number in the range 0 to 100, which represents the weighted average of the student's work. The class should have input and output methods. The input method should not ask for the final numeric grade nor should it ask for the final letter grade. The class should have methods to compute the overall numeric grade and the final letter grade. These last two methods will be *void*-methods that set the appropriate instance variables. Remember, one method can call another method. If you prefer, you can define a single method that sets both the overall numeric score and the final letter grade, but if you do this, use a helping method. Your program should use all the methods we discussed. Your class should have a reasonable set of accessor and mutator methods, whether or not your program uses them. You may add other methods if you wish.

4. Add methods to the Person class from Self-Test Question number 13 to set just the name attribute of a Person, to set just the age attribute of a Person, to test if two Persons are equal (have the same name and age), to test if two Persons have the same name, to test if two Persons are the same age, to test if one person is older than another, and to test if one person is younger than another. Write a driver (test) program that demonstrates each method with at least one true and one false case for each of the test methods.

5. Create a class that graphs the grade distribution (number of A's, B's, C's, D's, and F's) horizontally by printing lines with proportionate numbers of asterisks corresponding to the percentage of grades in each category. Write methods to set the number of each letter grade; read the number of

each letter grade, return the total number of grades, return the percent of each letter grade as a whole number between 0 and 100, inclusive; and draw the graph. Set it up so that 50 asterisks correspond to 100% (each one corresponds to 2%), include a scale on the horizontal axis indicating each 10% increment from 0 to 100%, and label each line with its letter grade. For example, if there are 1 A's, 4 B's, 6 C's, 2 D's, and 1 F, the total number of grades is 14, the percentage of A's is 7, percentage of B's is 29, percentage of C's is 43, percentage of D's is 14, and percentage of F's is 7. The A row would contain 4 asterisks (7% of 50 rounded to the nearest integer), the B row 14, the C row 21, the D row 7, and the F row 4, so the graph would look like this

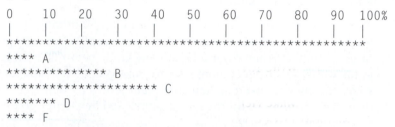

6. Write a program that uses the Purchase class (Display 4.11) to set the following prices:

Oranges: 10 for 2.99

Eggs: 12 for 1.69

Apples: 3 for 1.00

Watermelons: 4.39 each

Bagels: 6 for 3.50

and calculate the total bill and subtotals for each item for the following:

two dozen oranges,

three dozen eggs,

twenty apples,

two watermelons, and

a dozen bagels.

7. Write a program to answer questions like the following: Suppose the species Klingon ox has a population of 100, a growth rate of 15 %, and live in an area of 1500 square miles. How long would it take for the population density to exceed one per square mile? Use the class Species in Display 4.19/page 276 with the addition of the density method from Self-Test Question number 7.

CHAPTER 5

MORE ABOUT OBJECTS AND METHODS

5.1 PROGRAMMING WITH METHODS 297
Methods Calling Methods 297
Programming Tip Write Toy
    Programs 303
Programming Tip Make Helping
    Methods Private 303
Java Tip Make the Compiler
    Happy 304
Gotcha "Null Pointer Exception"
    Message 305

5.2 STATIC METHODS AND STATIC VARIABLES 306
Static Methods 306
Gotcha Invoking a Nonstatic Method
    within a Static Method 308
Java Tip You Can Put A main in Any
    Class 311
Static Variables 314
The Math Class 316
Integer, Double, and Other
    Wrapper Classes 319
Gotcha Assigning A Primitive Value to
    A Wrapper Class 323

5.3 DESIGNING METHODS 324
Case Study Formatting Output 324
Top–Down Design 329

Testing Methods 331

5.4 OVERLOADING 333
Overloading Basics 333
Gotcha Overloading and Automatic
    Type Conversion 336
Programming Example A Pet Class 336
Gotcha You Cannot Overload Based
    on The Returned Type 341
Programming Example A Class for
    Money 343

5.5 CONSTRUCTORS 350
Defining Constructors 350
Programming Tip You Can Use Other
    Methods in a Constructor 355
Gotcha Omitting the Default
    Constructor 358

5.6 INFORMATION HIDING REVISITED 360
Gotcha Privacy Leaks 360

5.7 PACKAGES 364
Packages and Importing 364
Package Names and Directories 365

5.8 INNER CLASSES (Optional) 367

Chapter Summary 369
Answers to Self-Test Questions 370
Programming Exercises 376

MORE ABOUT OBJECTS AND METHODS

> *A tourist stopped an elderly gentleman on the streets of New York City and asked him,*
> *"Please sir, could you tell me how I can get to Carnegie Hall?"*
> *"Practice, practice, practice," the old gentleman replied.*
>
> ***A very old joke***

In this chapter, we continue our discussion of how to define and use classes and their methods. We will discuss a technique called *overloading* that will allow you to have two or more methods with the same name and within the same class.

We also teach you how to define static methods. You have already used static methods. They are methods that can be invoked with the class name, rather than an object. All the methods in `SavitchIn` are static methods. Although you have used static methods before, we still need to show you how to define static methods.

We introduce *constructors*, which are methods used to automatically initialize a new object.

Our last (non-optional) topic is packages. Packages allow you to add classes to your environment so they can be conveniently used in any other class definition. Along the way, we also cover a number of techniques that will help you to write better method definitions.

This chapter also includes an optional section on inner classes, which are classes defined with another class definition.

Objectives

Become familiar with some more basic techniques for programming with classes and objects.

Learn about *overloading* a method name

Learn to define *constructor* methods in Java.

Learn about *static methods* and *static variables*.

Learn about *packages* and *import* statements in Java.

Optionally, you can also learn about *inner classes*.

Prerequisites

You must know the material in Chapter 4 before doing much in this chapter. As described in what follows, some of the sections in this chapter may be postponed until after you read some of the following chapters.

Section 5.6 discusses some subtle points about using instance variables of a class type. Strictly speaking, it is not required for the rest of the material in this book and so can be postponed. However, Section 5.6 does discuss fundamental issues that you should read at some point.

The material on packages in Section 5.7 requires a knowledge of directories (folders) and PATH variables. This material on packages is not required for any other material in this book, so you need not cover Section 5.7 until you are ready to do so, and you can read the rest of this book without reading Section 5.7.

The material in Section 5.8 covers inner classes. That material is repeated in Chapter 12, which covers windowing interfaces. If you plan to cover Chapter 12, you may wish to wait until then to cover inner classes, since that includes some of the most common uses of inner classes and so will have a number of good examples of inner classes. If you do not intend to cover Chapter 12, you can cover the Section 5.8 on inner classes now or at any later time.

5.1 | Programming with Methods

> *The greatest invention of the nineteenth century was the invention of the method of invention.*
> **Alfred North Whitehead, Science and the Modern World**

In this section, we describe a number of basic techniques to use for designing and testing methods.

Methods Calling Methods

A method body may contain a call to (that is, an invocation of) another method. The situation for these sorts of method calls is exactly the same as it would be if the method call had occurred in the `main` part of a program. However, if all the methods are in the same class, then there is an abbreviated notation that is usually used. Display 5.1 contains the definition of a class called `Oracle`. The method `dialog` of this class conducts a dialog with the user that answers a series of one-line questions that the user asks. (Of course, this is just a simple program, so the answers are actually obtained from the user herself/himself.) Notice that within the definition of the method `dialog`, there is a call to the method `answerOne`, which is also a method in the same class `Oracle`. If you look at the definition of the method `answerOne`, you will see that method in turn includes calls to the two other methods `seekAdvice` and `update`, both of which are also in the same class `Oracle`. Let's look at how these method invocations within method definitions are handled by Java.

Display 5.1   Methods Calling Another Methods
••

```java
public class Oracle
{
    private String oldAnswer = "The answer is in your heart.";
    private String newAnswer;
    private String question;

    public void dialog()
    {
        char ans;
        do
         {
            answerOne();
            System.out.println("Do you wish to ask another question? (y/n)");
            ans = SavitchIn.readLineNonwhiteChar();
         } while ((ans != 'n') && (ans != 'N'));

        System.out.println("The oracle will now rest.");
    }

    private void answerOne()
    {
        System.out.println("I am the oracle.");
        System.out.println("I will answer any one-line question.");
        System.out.println("What is your question?");
        question = SavitchIn.readLine();
        seekAdvice();
        System.out.println("You asked the question:");
        System.out.println(question);
        System.out.println("Now, here is my answer:");
        System.out.println(oldAnswer);
        update();
    }

    private void seekAdvice()
    {
        System.out.println("Hmm, I need some help on that.");
        System.out.println("Please give me one line of advice.");
        newAnswer = SavitchIn.readLine();
        System.out.println("Thank you. That helped a lot.");
    }

    private void update()
    {
        oldAnswer = newAnswer;
    }

}
```
••

Display 5.2   Oracle Demonstration Program

```
public class OracleDemo
{
    public static void main(String[] args)
    {
        Oracle delphi = new Oracle();
        delphi.dialog();
    }
}
```

Sample Screen Dialogue

```
I am the oracle.
I will answer any one-line question.
What is your question?
What time is it?
Hmm, I need some help on that.
Please give me one line of advice.
Seek and ye shall find the answer.
Thank you. That helped a lot.
You asked the question:
What time is it?
Now, here is my answer:
The answer is in your heart.
Do you wish to ask another question? (y/n)
yes
I am the oracle.
I will answer any one-line question.
What is your question?
What is the meaning of life?
Hmm, I need some help on that.
Please give me one line of advice.
Ask the car guys.
Thank you. That helped a lot.
You asked the question:
What is the meaning of life?
Now, here is my answer:
Seek and ye shall find the answer.
Do you wish to ask another question? (y/n)
no
The oracle will now rest.
```

Let's first consider the invocation of the method answerOne within the definition of the method dialog. Display 5.2/page 299 contains a demonstration program that creates an object named delphi of the class Oracle and then uses this object to invoke the method dialog. When this invocation takes place, the method dialog is executed using the object delphi. In what follows we reproduce the definition of the method dialog:

```
public void dialog()
{
    do
    {
        answerOne();
        System.out.println(
                "Do you wish to ask another question? (y/n)");
        ans = SavitchIn.readLineNonwhiteChar();
    } while ((ans != 'n') && (ans != 'N'));

    System.out.println("The oracle will now rest.");
}
```

Note that the method named answerOne is not preceded by an object and a dot. The calling object is understood to be the calling object of the method dialog. In the program in Display 5.2, the method dialog is invoked by the object delphi, as follows:

```
delphi.dialog();
```

So, for this invocation of dialog(), the invocation

```
answerOne();
```

in the definition of dialog, is understood to mean:

```
delphi.answerOne();
```

When you write the definition of a method like dialog, you do not know what the name of the calling object will be. It could be different at different times, such as

```
delphi.dialog();
```

in one program and

```
myObject.dialog();
```

in another program. Because you do not, in fact cannot, know the name of the calling object, you omit it. So, in the definition of the class Oracle in Display 5.1, when you write

```
answerOne();
```

within the definition of the method dialog, this means

```
The_Calling_Object.answerOne();
```

Because the *this* parameter just means *The_Calling_Object*, you can use the *this* parameter to name the calling object, so the following two calls to answerOne are equivalent:

```
answerOne();
```

and the equivalent

```
this.answerOne();
```

This omitting of the *this* and a dot when you refer to method in the same class is not really new. We have already been doing the exact same thing with instance variables.

This omitting of the calling object and dot only works with methods in the same class. If you call a method of one class within the definition of a method of another class, you must include an object and a dot.

Also, this omitting of the calling object only applies if the calling object can be expressed with the *this* parameter. If the calling object is some object declared and created with *new* within a method definition, then within that method definition, you must include the object name and dot. As a simple and sure test, remember that omitting the calling object and dot is only allowed if the call object is the *this* parameter. Now, let's continue with our discussion of method definitions in the class Oracle.

You can have methods that call other methods, that in turn call yet other methods in the same class. In the class Oracle, the definition of the method answerOne, in turn, includes calls to the two other methods seekAdvice and update, both of which are also in the same class Oracle. The methods named seekAdvice and update are not preceded by an object and a dot. However, as we just explained, when the calling object and dot are omitted, it has the same meaning as it would if the method invocation were proceeded by *this* and a dot. So, the invocation

methods calling methods calling other methods

```
seekAdvice();
```

is equivalent to

```
this.seekAdvice();
```

Similarly the invocation

```
update();
```

is equivalent to

```
this.update();
```

Now let's consider the following invocation from the program in Display 5.2:

```
delphi.dialog();
```

the definition of dialog includes the invocation

```
answerOne();
```

which is the equivalent to

```
this.answerOne();
```

Omitting the Calling Object

When the calling object in a method invocation is the *this* parameter, you can omit the *this* and the dot.

Example:
The following are equivalent:

```
public void answerOne()
{
        .
        .
        .
    this.seekAdvice();
        .
        .
        .
    this.update();
}
```

and

```
public void answerOne()
{
        .
        .
        .
    seekAdvice();
        .
        .
        .
    update();
}
```

But, because the calling object is delphi, this is equivalent to the invocation

```
delphi.answerOne();
```

The definition of answerOne, includes the invocations

```
seekAdvice();
```

and

```
update();
```

which are equivalent to

```
this.seekAdvice();
```

and

```
this.update();
```

But, in this case the calling object is delphi, so these are equivalent to

```
delphi.seekAdvice();
```

and

```
delphi.update();
```

You can have methods calling methods calling methods and so forth to any number of method calls. The details are always handled just as we described here.

Programming Tip

Write Toy Programs

The program in Display 5.1 is just a toy program. It is just a game. It does not do any engineering or business calculation. Moreover, it is not a very sophisticated game. Users are not likely to be fooled, but are certain to notice that they are providing their own answers. So why bother with such a useless program?

The answer is practice, practice, practice! The way to learn how to program is to practice each new technique and new program feature. Moreover, the first time you use a new feature, it pays to use it in a very simple context, so you are not distracted by having to design and debug a lot of things that are not directly relevant to what you are learning. If you look through more advanced programming books, you will see that the experts typically introduce a new feature with an example of just a few lines that may not do anything particularly useful and may not even be a complete program. This gives an uncluttered view of the feature being introduced.

Programming Tip

Make Helping Methods Private

Look again at Display 5.1/page 298. The methods `answerOne`, `seekAdvice` and `update` are labeled *private*, rather than *public*. Recall that if a method is labeled *private*, then it can only be used in the definitions of other methods of the same class. Thus, in some other class or program, the following invocation of the private method `answerOne` would be illegal and would produce a compiler error message:

```
Oracle myOracle = new Oracle();
myOracle.answerOne(); //Illegal: answerOne is private.
```

whereas the following call to the public method `dialog` would be perfectly legal:

```
myOracle.dialog(); //Legal.
```

The reason for making the methods `answerOne`, `seekAdvice`, and `update` private is that they are just helping methods. A user of the class `Oracle` is not expected to use these methods. The methods `answerOne`, `seekAdvice`, and `update` are only used in the definition of the method `dialog`. That means that the methods `answerOne`, `seekAdvice`, and `update` are part of the class implementation and not part of the user interface for the class. As we discussed in the subsection of Chapter 4 entitled *Encapsulation*, it is good programming practice to keep the implementation portion of a class private. Thus, we labeled some methods *private* because they are not intended to be seen by the outside world. They are part of the implementation (the inner workings) of the class, just like the private instance variables.

■ **Java Tip**

Make the Compiler Happy

The compiler will try to check to make sure you do certain necessary things, such as initializing variables and including a *return*-statement in the definition of a method that returns a value. Sometimes, you may find yourself in a situation where the compiler is asking you to do one of these things, and you are certain that either you have done it, or that you do not need to do it. In such cases, it does no good to argue with the compiler. You should just change something to make the compiler stop complaining. First of all, check to make sure the compiler is not correct. It usually is. If you cannot find a true error in your code, then change your code so that it is more obvious that you have done what the compiler is asking for.

For example, if you declare a variable `line` as follows

```
String line;
```

and the compiler insists that you initialize the variable `line`, then change the declaration to

```
String line = null;
```

The constant value *null* is a special constant that can be used to give a value to any variable of any class type.

As another example, suppose you have a method that returns a value of type *int* and the method definition ends with the following:

```
if (something > somethingElse)
    return something;
else
    return somethingElse;
```

In this case, every computation probably does end with a *return*-statement. If the compiler nonetheless complains saying you need a *return*-statement, change that last *if-else*-statement to the following

```
int answer;
if (something > somethingElse)
    answer = something;
else
    answer = somethingElse;
return answer;
```

This assumes the method returns a value of type *int*. For other types, just make the obvious adjustments.

---

null

null is a special constant that can be used to give a value to any variable of any class type. The constant *null* is not an object, but a sort of place holder for an object address. Because it is like an address, you use == and != rather than the method `equals` when you test to see if a variable is equal to *null*.

■

■ Gotcha
"Null Pointer Exception" Message

If the compiler asks you to initialize a class variable, you can always initialize the variable to *null*. However, *null* is not an object, and so you cannot invoke a method using a variable that is initialized to *null*. If you try you will get an error message that says "Null Pointer Exception." For example, the following would produce a "Null Pointer Exception," if the code is included in a program:

```
Species specialSpecies = null;
System.out.println("Enter data on special species:");
specialSpecies.readInput();
```

The class Species is defined in Display 4.19/page 276. However, there is no need to look at that class definition. These three lines of code will produce an error message no matter how the class Species is defined. The way to correct the problem is to use *new* to create an object of type Species, as follows:

```
Species specialSpecies = new Species()
System.out.println("Enter data on special species:");
specialSpecies.readInput();
```

Only use *null* to initialize a class variable when you know that, before the variable is used as a calling object for some method, your code will assign an object to the class variable using *new* (or some other technique). This means that you should only use null to initialize a class variable when it is conceptually unnecessary. However, the compiler will sometimes insist on an initialization even when it is not need. We discussed this situation in the preceding Programming Tip.

As you do more programming you will probably encounter other situations that produce a "Null Pointer Exception" message. In these cases look for an uninitialized class variable.

? Self-Test Questions

1. Can you invoke a method inside the definition of another method in the same class?

2. Suppose you changed the following line in the definition of the method answerOne in Display 5.1/page 298 from

   ```
   seekAdvice();
   ```

   to the following

   ```
   this.seekAdvice();
   ```

   What effect would this have?

3. What is wrong with a program that starts as follows? The class Species is defined in Display 4.19/page 276.

```
public class SpeciesDemo
{
    public static void main(String[] args)
    {
        Species s1 = null;
        Species s2 = null;

        s1.set("Klingon Ox", 10, 15);
        s2.set("Naked Mole Rat", 10000, 25);
```

5.2 | Static Methods and Static Variables

> *There is no there there.*
>
> **W. C. Fields**

Static methods and static variables are methods and variables that belong to a class as whole and that do not require any object. You have already been using static methods. All the methods in the class SavitchIn are static methods. In this section, we show you how to define your own static methods and static variables.

Static Methods

Sometimes you need a method that does not require an object of any kind. For example, you might need a method to compute the maximum of two integers, or a method to compute the square root of a number, or a method to convert a letter character from lowercase to uppercase. None of these methods has any obvious object to which they should belong. In these cases, you can define the method as *static*. When you define a method to be **static**, you still define the method in a class, so it is still a member of a class, but the method can be invoked without using any object. Instead of using an object name, you usually use the class name when invoking a static method. Static methods are also sometimes called **class methods**.

static method

class method

For example, Display 5.3 has the definition of a class named CircleFirstTry, which has two static method definitions. The methods may be called as in the following example:

```
double areaOfCircle = CircleFirstTry.area(12.7);
double circumOfCircle = CircleFirstTry.circumference(12.7);
```

Note that a static method is called by giving the name of the class, CircleFirstTry in this case, followed by a dot, and then the method name and parameters. So, the class name serves the same purpose as a calling object. (It would be legal to create an object of the class CircleFirstTry and use it to invoke the method area or the method circumference, but that is confusing style, so we usually use the class name when invoking a static method.) Another sample use of these static methods is given in Display 5.4.

Display 5.3 Static Methods

```
/**********************************************************
 *Class with static methods to perform calculations on circles.
 **********************************************************/
public class CircleFirstTry
{
    public static final double PI = 3.14159;

    public static double area(double radius)
    {
        return (PI*radius*radius);
    }

    public static double circumference(double radius)
    {
        return (PI*(radius + radius));
    }
}
```

Later in the chapter, we will give an alternate version of this class.

Note that when you define a static method, you define it the same way as you would define any other method, but you add the reserved word *static* to the heading, as shown in the examples in Display 5.3.

In the example of the class CircleFirstTry in Display 5.3, the class had no instance variables, but it is perfectly legal for a class to have both instance variable and static methods (and regular, nonstatic methods). However, if the class does have instance variables, then they cannot be referenced in the definition of any static method. Moreover, within the definition of any static method, you cannot invoke a nonstatic method of the class (unless you create a new object of the class and use this object as the calling object for the nonstatic method). This makes perfectly good sense, because a static method can be invoked without using any calling object and so can be invoked when there are no instance variables or calling object to refer to. This is explained more fully in the following Pitfall section.

The Methods in SavitchIn Are Static

The method readLineInt and all of the other input methods in the class SavitchIn are static methods, so they can be used with the class name in place of a calling object, as we have been doing all along. For example:

```
int n = SavitchIn.readLineInt();
```

Display 5.4 Using Static Methods

```
public class CircleDemo
{
    public static void main(String[] args)
    {
        double radius;

        System.out.println("Enter the radius of a circle in
                inches:");
        radius = SavitchIn.readLineDouble();

        System.out.println("A circle of radius "
                                        + radius + " inches");
        System.out.println("has an area of " +
            CircleFirstTry.area(radius) + " square inches,");
        System.out.println("and a circumference of " +
            CircleFirstTry.circumference(radius)+ " inches.");
    }
}
```

Sample Screen Dialogue

```
Enter the radius of a circle in inches:
2.3
A circle of radius 2.3 inches
has an area of 16.61901 square inches,
and a circumference of 14.45131 inches.
```

■ Gotcha
Invoking a Nonstatic Method within a Static Method

Display 5.5 shows the definition of another class to use in circle calculations. It is designed to be simple and yet have both static and nonstatic methods, so that you can see how the two kinds of methods can and cannot interact. The method `areaDialog` illustrates the only way that it is legal to invoke a nonstatic method from within a static method. The nonstatic methods `setDiameter` and `showArea` are invoked within the static method `areaDialog`. Let's look at the details more closely. We will concentrate on the method `showArea`. The details for the method `setDiameter` are similar.

Display 5.5   Mixing Static and Nonstatic Methods

```
public class PlayCircle
{
    public static final double PI = 3.14159;

    private double diameter;

    public void setDiameter(double newDiameter)
    {
        diameter = newDiameter;
    }

    public static double area(double radius)
    {
        return (PI*radius*radius);
    }

    public void showArea()
    {
        System.out.println("Area is " + area(diameter/2));
    }

    public static void areaDialog()
    {
        System.out.println("Enter diameter of circle:");
        double newDiameter = SavitchIn.readLineDouble();
        PlayCircle c = new PlayCircle();
        c.setDiameter(newDiameter);
        c.showArea();
    }
}
```

A static variable (used as a constant)

An instance variable

Because `areaDialog` is a static method, it can be invoked with only the class name, and without any object, as shown in the following line from Display 5.6:

```
PlayCircle.areaDialog();
```

The method `areaDialog`, in this invocation, has no object associated with it. Hence, if you want to invoke the nonstatic method `showArea` within the definition of `areaDialog`, then you must create an object and use the object to invoke the method `showArea`. This is what we did in the definition of the method `areaDialog`, which we reproduce in what follows:

```java
public static void areaDialog()
{
        System.out.println("Enter diameter of circle:");
        double newDiameter = SavitchIn.readLineDouble();
        PlayCircle c = new PlayCircle();
        c.setDiameter(newDiameter);
        c.showArea();
}
```

By contrast, suppose you delete the calling object c, so that the last line of the method definition reads as follows:

```java
showArea();
```

which looks like it is equivalent to

```java
this.showArea();
```

Display 5.6 Using Static and Nonstatic Methods
•••

```java
public class PlayCircleDemo
{
    public static void main(String[] args)
    {
        PlayCircle circle = new PlayCircle();
        circle.setDiameter(2);
        System.out.println("If circle has diameter 2,");
        circle.showArea();

        System.out.println("Now, you choose the diameter:");
        PlayCircle.areaDialog();
    }
}
```

Sample Screen Dialogue

```
If circle has diameter 2,
Area is 3.14159
Now, you choose the diameter:
Enter diameter of circle:
4
Area is 12.56636
```

•••

If you make this change to the definition of the method `areaDialog` and then re-compile the class definition for `PlayCircle` (which includes the definition of the method `areaDialog`), then you will get a compiler error. This is because any invocation of the method `showArea` must have data for the diameter of a circle, and within the definition of a static method, it cannot get that diameter data in any way except by having a calling object. Within the definition of a static method, like `areaDialog`, you have no instance variable available for any purpose whatsoever. Note that the problem is not that the class lacks instance variables. The class has a suitable instance variable named `diameter`. The problem is that the nonstatic method `showArea` is being invoked within the static method `areaDialog`.

You will often hear people say "You cannot invoke a nonstatic method within the definition of a static method." That is not quite true, when that phrase is taken literally. What they mean when they say that is the more precise, and correct, statement "You cannot invoke a nonstatic method within a static method, *unless you create and use a calling object for the nonstatic method*." Another way to phrase it is that, in the definition of a static method, you cannot use an instance variable or method that has an implicit or explicit *this* for a calling object. This is because a static method can be invoked without any calling object and so can be invoked when there is no meaning for *this*. As W. C. Fields might have said, in a static method, "there is no *this* there."

☆ Static Methods

If you place the reserved word *static* in the heading of the definition of a method, then the method can be invoked using the class name in place of a calling object.

Since it does not need a calling object, a static method cannot refer to a (nonstatic) instance variable of the class, nor can it invoke a nonstatic method of the class (unless it creates a new object of the class and uses this object as the calling object). Another way to phrase it is that, in the definition of a static method, you cannot use an instance variable or method that has an implicit or explicit *this* for a calling object.

Example (of invoking a static method):

```
int result = Math.max(n1, n2);
```

`Math` is a predefined class.

■ Java Tip
You Can Put A `main` in Any Class

So far, whenever we used a class in the `main` part of a program, that `main` method was by itself in another class definition within another file. However, sometimes it makes sense to have a `main` method within a regular class definition. The class can then be used for two purposes: It can be used to create objects in other classes or it can be run as a program. For example, you can combine the class definition `PlayCircle` in Display 5.5 with the program in Display 5.6 by placing the `main` method shown in Display 5.6 inside the definition of the class `PlayCircle` and so obtain the class definition shown in Display 5.7. With the class `PlayCircle` redefined in this way, it can be used in another program as an ordinary class to create objects of the class PlayCircle, but this redefined version of the class PlayCircle can also be run as a program. When it is run as a program, the main method is invoked and the rest of the class definition is ignored (except for its use in main). When it is used as an ordinary class to create objects, the main method is ignored.

Java requires that a program's main method be static. Thus, within a main method, you cannot invoke a nonstatic method of the same class, unless you create an object of the class and use it as a calling object for the nonstatic method. Notice the main in Display 5.7. It invokes the method showArea by first creating an object circle of the class PlayCircle and then using circle as the calling object. This is necessary, even though the main method is inside of the definition of the class PlayCircle. The situation with main is the same as that with any other static method: You cannot invoke a nonstatic method of the same class with main, unless you first create an object of that class and use the object as the calling object for the nonstatic method.

You will not want to place just any main method in a class definition that is to be used as a regular class to create object. However, one handy trick is to place a small diagnostic program in a main that is inside of your class definition. That way you can easily test the class definition, if you suspect something is wrong.

Every Class Can Have a main.

Every class can have a main method added to it. It can then be run as a program. If the class is not intended as a program, you still might want to include a main that is a test program for that class.

◼

? Self-Test Questions

4. Is the following legal? The class CircleFirstTry is defined in Display 5.3/page 307.

```
CircleFirstTry c = new CircleFirstTry();
double areaOfCircle = c.area(2.5);
```

5. Can a class contain both static and nonstatic (that is, regular) methods? Can it contain both instance variables and static methods?

6. Can you invoke a nonstatic method within a static method?

7. Can you invoke a static method within a nonstatic method?

8. Can you reference an instance variable within a static method? Why or why not?

9. Is the following legal (even though readLineInt is a static method and does not need a calling object)?

```
SavitchIn inputObject = new SavitchIn();
System.out.println("Enter an integer:");
int n = inputObject.readLineInt()
```

Display 5.7   Placing a main Method in a Class Definition

```java
public class PlayCircle
{
    public static final double PI = 3.14159;

    private double diameter;

    public static void main(String[] args)
    {
        PlayCircle circle = new PlayCircle();
        circle.setDiameter(2);
        System.out.println("If circle has diameter 2,");
        circle.showArea();

        System.out.println("Now, you choose the diameter:");
        PlayCircle.areaDialog();
    }
```

On the CD, this is PlayCircleV2.java.

Because this main is inside the definition of the class PlayCircle, you can omit this PlayCircle, if you wish.

```java
    public void setDiameter(double newDiameter)
    {
        diameter = newDiameter;
    }

    public static double area(double radius)
    {
        return (PI*radius*radius);
    }

    public void showArea()
    {
        System.out.println("Area is " + area(diameter/2));
    }

    public static void areaDialog()
    {
        System.out.println("Enter diameter of circle:");
        double newDiameter = SavitchIn.readLineDouble();
        PlayCircle c = new PlayCircle();
        c.setDiameter(newDiameter);
        c.showArea();
    }
}
```

10. Is the following legal? the class `PlayCircle` is defined in Display 5.5/page 309.

```
System.out.println("Enter the diameter of a circle:);
double newDiameter = SavitchIn.readLineDouble();
PlayCircle.setDiameter(newDiameter);
```

Static Variables

It is possible for a class to have variables that are static as well as methods that are static. We have already been using static variables in one special case, namely, the definition of constant values such as

```
public static final double PI = 3.14159;
```

static variable

There are also **static variables** that can change value. These are declared in the same way as defined constant values except that you do not use the word *final*. Thus, if the following occurred in a class definition, it would define a static variable that can change value:

```
public static double PI;
```

although this would be a poor choice for a static variable declaration, as explained in the next paragraph.

A static variable can be initialized or not, and can be public or private. However, like instance variables, static variables should normally be private and should be read or changed only via accessor and mutator methods. Thus, the following is a more likely example of a static (nonconstant) variable declaration:

```
private static int numberOfInvocations = 0;
```

This variable `numberOfInvocations` is initialized to 0. There is only one variable `numberOfInvocations`, and it can be accessed by every object of the class. So, objects could use this variable to communicate or perform some joint action. For example, in the class definition in Display 5.8, this static variable is used to keep track of how many invocations have been made by all objects of the class `StaticDemo` in the program. The program counts all invocations of the methods defined in Display 5.8, except for the method `main`.

extra code on CD

The class definition `StaticDemo2` on the accompanying CD gives a more common example of a way to use a static variable, but you will not understand it without the material in Section 5.5. You may wish to look at that example after reading Section 5.5.

There are cases where you want to use a static variable, but they are rare and we will not be using static variables in this text after we finish this discussion.

class variable

Static variables are also called **class variables**. Do not confuse the term *class variable* (which simply means a static variable within a class) with the notion of a variable of a class type (which means a variable whose type is a class, that is, a variable that is used to name objects of a class.)

Display 5.8   A Static Variable *(Part 1 of 2)*

object1 and *object2* use the same static variable *numberOfInvocations.*

```java
public class StaticDemo
{
    private static int numberOfInvocations = 0;

    public static void main(String[] args)
    {
        int i;
        StaticDemo object1 = new StaticDemo();
        for (i = 1; i <=10 ; i++)
            object1.outPutCountOfInvocations();

        StaticDemo object2 = new StaticDemo();
        for (i = 1; i <=10 ; i++)
            object2.justADemoMethod();

        System.out.println("Total number of invocations = "
                            + numberSoFar());
    }

    public void justADemoMethod()
    {
        numberOfInvocations++;
        //In a real example, more code would go here.
    }

    public void outPutCountOfInvocations()
    {
        numberOfInvocations++;
        System.out.println(numberOfInvocations);
    }

    public static int numberSoFar()
    {
        numberOfInvocations++;
        return numberOfInvocations;
    }
}
```

Sample Screen Dialogue

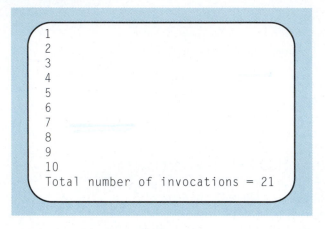

```
1
2
3
4
5
6
7
8
9
10
Total number of invocations = 21
```

? Self-Test Questions

11. What is the difference between a static variable and an instance variable?

12. Can you reference (by name) a *static variable* (without anything like a class name and dot) in the definition of a *static method*? Can you reference (by name) an *instance variable* (without anything like an object name and dot) in the definition of a *static method*?

13. Can you reference (by name) a *static variable* (without anything like a class name and dot) in the definition of a *nonstatic method*? Can you reference (by name) an *instance variable* (without anything like an object name and dot) in the definition of a *nonstatic method*?

The Math Class

Math **methods**

The predefined class Math provides you with a number of the standard mathematical methods. The class Math is automatically provided when you use the Java language. Some of the methods in the class Math are described in Display 5.9. All of these methods are static, which means that you do not need (and in fact have no real use for) an object of the class Math. You normally call these methods by using the class name, Math, in place of a calling object. For example, the following outputs the maximum of the two numbers 2 and 3.

Display 5.9 Static Methods in the Class Math

Name	Description	Type of Argument	Type of Value Returned	Example	Value Returned
pow	Powers	*double*	*double*	Math.pow(2.0,3.0)	8.0
abs	Absolute value	*int, long, float,* or *double*	Same as the type of the argument	Math.abs(−7) Math.abs(7) Math.abs(−3.5)	7 7 3.5
max	Maximum	*int, long, float,* or *double*	Same as the type of the arguments	Math.max(5, 6) Math.max(5.5, 5.3)	6 5.5
min	Minimum	*int, long, float,* or *double*	Same as the type of the arguments	Math.min(5, 6) Math.min(5.5, 5.3)	5 5.3
round	Rounding	*float* or *double*	*int* or *long,* respectively	Math.round(6.2) Math.round(6.8)	6 7
ceil	Ceiling	*double*	*double*	Math.ceil(3.2) Math.ceil(3.9)	4.0 4.0
floor	Floor	*double*	*double*	Math.floor(3.2) Math.floor(3.9)	3.0 3.0
sqrt	Square root	*double*	*double*	sqrt(4.0)	2.0

```
int ans;
ans = Math.max(2, 3);
System.out.println(ans);
```

It would also be legal to omit the variables ans and simply write

```
System.out.println("The maximum of 2 and 3 = " + Math.max(2, 3));
```

The class Math also has the two predefined constants E and PI. The constant PI (often written π in mathematical formulas) is used in calculations involving circles, spheres, and other geometric figures based on circles. PI is approximately 3.14159. The constant E is the base of the natural logarithm system (often written *e* in math-

Math constants

ematical formulas) and is approximately 2.72. (We do not use the predefined constant E in this text.) The constants PI and E are defined constants as described in Chapter 2. For example, the following computes the area of a circle, given its radius:

```
area = Math.PI * radius * radius;
```

Be sure to note that because the constants PI and E are defined in the class Math, they must have the class name Math and dot before them. For example, you could use these constants in the definition of the class CircleFirstTry in Display 5.3/page 307. In Display 5.10, we have rewritten the class in Display 5.3 so that it uses Math.PI.

If you look at the methods in the table in Display 5.9, you will find three similar, but not identical, methods named round, floor, and ceil. Some of these return a value of type *double*, but they all return a value that is intuitively a whole number that is close to the value of their arguments. The method round rounds a number to the nearest whole number, and (if the argument is a *double*) it returns that whole number as a value of type *long*. If you want that whole number as a value of type *int*, you must use a type cast as in the following:[1]

```
double start = 3.56;
int answer = (int)Math.round(start);
```

floor **and**
ceil

The methods floor and ceil are similar to round, but are just a bit different. Neither one really rounds, although they both yield a whole number that is close to their argument. They both return a whole number as a value of type *double* (not of type *int* or *long*). The method floor returns the nearest whole number that is less than or equal to its argument. So, Math.floor(3.9) returns 3.0, not 4.0. Math.floor(3.3) also returns 3.0.

The method ceil returns the nearest whole number that is greater than or equal to its argument. So, Math.ceil(3.1) returns 4.0, not 3.0. Of course, Math.ceil(3.9) also returns 4.0. (The word ceil is short for "ceiling," but you always use the short form ceil.)

If you want to store the value returned by either floor or ceil in a variable of type *int*, you must use a type cast as in the following example:

```
double start = 3.56;
int lowAnswer = (int)Math.floor(start);
int highAnswer = (int)Math.ceil(start);
```

In this example, Math.floor(start) returns the *double* value 3.0, and the variable lowAnswer received the *int* value 3. Math.ceil(start) returns the *double* value 4.0, and the variable highAnswer received the *int* value 4.

---

1. You cannot store a *long* value in a variable of type *int*, even if it is a value like 4 which could just as well have been an *int*. The value 4, for example, can be of type either *int* or *long* depending on how it was created.

Display 5.10 Predefined Constants

```
/***********************************************
 *Class with static methods to perform calculations on circles.
 ***********************************************/
public class Circle
{
    public static double area(double radius)
    {
        return (Math.PI*radius*radius);
    }

    public static double circumference(double radius)
    {
        return (Math.PI*(radius + radius));
    }
}
```

CircleDemo2.java on the CD is a demonstration program for this class.

This class behaves the same as the class CircleFirstTry in Display 5.3/page 307. This version differs only in that it uses the predefined constant Math.PI, rather than defining PI within the class.

? Self-Test Questions

14. What values are returned by each of the following:
    `Math.round(2.3)`, `Math.round(2.7)`, `Math.floor(2.3)`,
    `Math.floor(2.7)`, `Math.ceil(2.3)`, and `Math.ceil(2.7)`.

15. Suppose `speed` is a variable of type *double* and you want to assign
    `Math.round(speed)` to the variable `approxSpeed`, which is of type *int*.
    How do you write the assignment statement?

Integer, Double, and Other Wrapper Classes

Java makes a distinction between the primitive types, such as *int*, *double*, and *char*, and the class types, such as the class `String` and the programmer-defined classes. As we have seen, Java sometimes treats primitive and class types differently. For example, we saw in Chapter 4 that an argument to a method is treated differently depending on whether the argument is of a primitive or class type. In Chapter 4, we also saw that the assignment operator = behaves differently for primitive types and class types. To make things uniform, it would be handy sometimes to be able to convert a value of a primitive type, such as the *int* value 42, to an object of some class type that corresponds to the primitive type *int*.

In order to convert a value of a primitive type to an "equivalent" value of a class type, Java provides **wrapper classes** for each of the primitive classes. For example, the wrapper class for the primitive type *int* is the predefined class Integer. If you want to convert an *int* value, such as 42, to an object of type Integer, you can do so as follows:

Integer n = *new* Integer(42);

After the preceding, n names an object of the class Integer that corresponds to the *int* value 42. (The object n does in fact have the *int* value 42 stored in an instance variable of the object n.) To convert in the reverse direction, from an object of type Integer to an *int* value, you can do the following:

int i = n.intValue();*//n names an object of the class Integer.*

The method intValue() recovers the equivalent *int* value from an object of type Integer.

The wrapper classes for the primitive types *long*, *float*, *double*, and *char* are Long, Float, Double, and Character, respectively. And, of course, rather than the method intValue, the classes Long, Float, Double, and Character use the methods longValue, floatValue, doubleValue, and charValue, respectively.

Integer class (margin)

other wrapper classes (margin)

Wrapper Classes

Every primitive type has a wrapper class. Wrapper classes allow you to have something like a primitive type that is of a class type. Wrapper classes also contain a number of useful predefined constants and static methods.

This brief introduction to wrapper classes explains why they were created and explains why they are called *wrapper classes*, but for us, the main importance of these wrapper classes is not contained in this introduction. For our purposes, the importance of wrapper classes is that they contain a number of useful constants and static methods.

largest and smallest values (margin)

You can use the associated wrapper class to find the value of the largest and smallest values of any of the primitive number types. For example, the largest and smallest values of type *int* are

Integer.MAX_VALUE and Integer.MIN_VALUE

The largest and smallest values of type *double* are

Double.MAX_VALUE and Double.MIN_VALUE

strings to numbers (margin)

parse-Double (margin)

Wrapper classes have static methods that can be used to convert a string to the corresponding number of type *int*, *double*, *long*, or *float*. For example, suppose your program needs to convert the string "199.98" to a *double* value (which will turn out to be 199.98, of course). The static method parseDouble of the wrapper class Double will convert a string to a value of type *double*. So,

Double.parseDouble("199.98")

returns the *double* value 199.98: Of course, you knew that the number value is 199.98 and so it hardly seems worth all this effort. But, the same technique can be used to change the value of a string variable. For example, suppose theString is a variable of type `String` whose value is the string representation of a number of type *double*. Then, the following returns the *double* value corresponding to the string value of `theString`:

```
Double.parseDouble(theString)
```

If there is any possibility that the string named by `theString` has extra leading or trailing blanks, you should instead use

```
Double.parseDouble(theString.trim())
```

The method `trim` is a static method in the class `String` that trims off leading or trailing whitespace, such as blanks.

If the string is not a correctly formed numeral, then the invocation of `Double.parseDouble` will crash your program. The use of `trim` helps some in avoiding this problem.

This conversion of a string to a number can be done with any of the wrapper classes `Integer`, `Long`, and `Float`, as well as the wrapper class `Double`. Just use the static method `Integer.parseInt`, `Long.parseLong`, or `Float.parseFloat` instead of `Double.parseDouble`.

parseInt
parseLong

Each of the numeric wrapper classes also has a static method called `toString` that will convert in the other direction, that is, convert from a numeric value to a string representation of the numeric value. For example,

numbers to strings

```
Integer.toString(42)
```

returns the string value `"42"`. And

```
Double.toString(199.98)
```

returns the string value `"199.98"`.

`Character` is the wrapper class for the primitive type *char*. The following piece of code illustrates some of the basic methods for this class:

Character

```
Character c1 = new Character('a');
Character c2 = new Character('A');
if (c1.equals(c2))
    System.out.println(c1.charValue() +
                    " is the same as " + c2.charValue());
else
    System.out.println(c1.charValue() +
                    " is not the same as " + c2.charValue());
```

This outputs

```
a is not the same as A
```

The `equals` method checks for equality as characters, so uppercase and lowercase letters are considered different.

Some of the static methods in the class `Character` are give in Display 5.11.

There is also a wrapper class `Boolean`. It has names for two constants that we use: `Boolean.TRUE` and `Boolean.FALSE`. However, the Java reserved words *true* and *false* are names that are much easier to use for these constants. So, the constants in the class `Boolean` will not be of much help to us. The methods of the class

Boolean

Display 5.11 Static Methods in the Class Character

Name	Description	Type of Arguments	Type of Value Returned	Example	Value Returned
toUpper-Case	Convert to uppercase	char	char	Character.toUpper-Case('a') Character.toUpper-Case('A')	Both return 'A'
toLower-Case	Convert to lowercase	char	char	Character.toLower-Case('a') Character.toLower-Case('A')	Both return 'a'
isUpper-Case	Test for uppercase	char	boolean	Character.isUpper-Case('A') Character.isUpper-Case('a')	true false
isLower-Case	Test for lowercase	char	boolean	Character.isLower-Case('A') Character.isLower-Case('a')	false true
isWhitespace	Test for whitespace	char	boolean	Character.is-Whitespace(' ') Character.is-Whitespace('A')	true false
	Whitespace characters are those that print as white space, such as the blank, the tab character ('\t'), and the line break character ('\n').				
isLetter	Test for being a letter	char	boolean	Character.isLetter('A') Character.isLetter('%')	true false
isDigit	Test for being a digit	char	boolean	Character.isDigit('5') Character.isDigit('A')	true false

`Boolean` are also not used very often, and we will not discuss them here. Although the class `Boolean` is not useless, it will be of little use to us in this text and we will discuss it no further.

■ Gotcha

Assigning A Primitive Value to A Wrapper Class

The wrapper class `Integer` was designed to be something like a class version of the primitive type `int`. This may make it seem reasonable to think of assigning a value of type `int` to a variable of type `Integer`. However, this is not allowed in Java. The second of the following two assignment statements will produce a compiler error message:

```
Integer n = new Integer(42); //OK. This assigns an initial value.
n = 99; //ILLEGAL!
```

Similarly, you cannot assign a primitive value to a variable of any of the other wrapper classes.

The way to get the effect you are trying to get with the preceding illegal assignment of 99 to the `Integer` object n is

```
n = new Integer(99);
```

A Wrapper Classes Has Two Personalities

Each wrapper class has two related but distinct uses. For example, consider the wrapper class `Integer`. It can be used to produce objects of the class `Integer` that corresponds to values of type `int`, as in

```
Integer n = new Integer(42);
```

The wrapper class `Integer` also serves a library of useful static methods, such as the method `parseInt`, as in

```
String inputString = SavitchIn.readLineWord();
int number = Integer.parseInt(inputString);
```

Any one program can use both personalities of a wrapper class, but it is perhaps more likely that any given program will use only one of these personalities.

? Self-Test Questions

16. Which of the following are legal? If any are illegal, tell how to write a legal Java statement that does what the illegal statement "says" to do.

```
Integer n = new Integer(77);
int m = 77;
n = m;
m = n;
```

17. Write a Java expression to convert the number in the *double* variable x to a string. The expression returns a string that is the normal way of writing the value in x.

18. Write a Java expression to convert the string in the variable s to the corresponding value of type *int*. The variable s is of type String. Assume that s contains a string that is the normal way of writing some integer, such as "123".

19. How would you do Exercise 18, if the string might contain leading or trailing blanks, such as "   123   "?

20. Write Java code to output the largest and smallest values of type *double* that you can have in Java.

5.3 | Designing Methods

In this section we discuss some basic techniques that will help you to design and test methods. We start with a case study.

Case Study
Formatting Output

If you have a variable of type *double* that stores some amount of money, you would like your programs to output the amount in a nice format. However, if you just use System.out.println, you are likely to get output that looks like the following:

```
Your cost, including tax, is $19.98123576432
```

You would like the output to show only two digits for cents. You would like the output to look like the following:

```
Your cost, including tax, is $19.98
```

task
specification

In this case study, you will define a class called Dollars with two static methods named write and writeln that can be used to produce this kind of nicely formatted output. For example, if the amount of money is in a variable of type *double* that is named amount, then (after you finish with this case study) the output can be produced as follows:

```
System.out.print("Your cost, including tax, is ");
Dollars.writeln(amount);
```

Note that the method should add the dollar sign for you, and that the method should always output exactly two digits after the decimal point. So, it would output $2.10, not $2.1.

When the amount being written out has more than two digits after the decimal point, your must decide what to do with the extra digits. You decide to round the number to two digits after the decimal point. So, if the value to be output is 9.128, you would get an output of $9.13.

The difference between write and writeln will be the same as the difference between print and println. With write, the *next* output will go on the same line. With writeln, the *next* output will go on the next line.

In order to output an amount like 9.98, you have little choice but to break it into the pieces 9 and 98, and then output each piece separately.[1] So, you come up with the following pseudocode as an outline for the method write:

pseudocode

Algorithm to Output a *double* Amount as Dollars and Cents

(The Amount is in a variable named amount)

Determine the number of whole dollars in amount and store it in an *int* variable called dollars. Determine the number of cents in amount and store it in an *int* variable cents. Round if there are more than two digits after the decimal point.

```
System.out.print('$');
System.out.print(dollars);
System.out.print('.');
```
Output cents in the usual dollars and cents format.

You now need to convert each of these pseudocode instructions to Java code. Let's take them in order.

To obtain the number of whole dollars and the number of cents as two *int* values, you need to somehow get rid of the decimal point. One way to get rid of the decimal point is to convert the amount of money to all cents. To convert 10.95 dollars and cents to all cents, multiply by 100 to obtain 10.95*100, which is 1095.0. If there is a fraction of a penny, such as converting 10.9567 to 1095.67 (pennies), you can use the round method:

Math.round(1095.67) returns 1096, as a value of type *long*.

Note that you want the result of this rounding to be stored in the *int* variable for holding the total amount expressed as all cents (all pennies). However, Math.round returns a value of type *long*, and you cannot store a value of type *long* in a variable of type *int*, not even if it is a small integer. So, you need to perform a type cast to convert this *long* value to an *int* value as follows:

(*int*)(Math.round(1096)) returns 1096, as an *int* value.

Thus, your code will begin with something like

```
int allCents = (int)(Math.round(amount*100));
```

Now, you need to convert allCents to a dollar amount and a cents amount. There are 100 cents in a dollar, so you use integer division to obtain the number of dollars:

```
int dollars = allCents/100;
```

The number of cents is just the amount left over when you divide allCents by 100, so you can use the % operator to obtain the amount of cents:

```
int cents = allCents%100;
```

---

1. Java has classes that allow you to output numbers in any format that you wish. However, using these classes can get quite involved. It will be instructive, and perhaps even easier to program the details ourselves. If you want to know more about such formatting classes, look at Appendix 6 which has a brief discussion of the class DecimalFormat.

Thus, you have translated the first two steps in your pseudocode to the following Java code:

```java
int allCents = (int)(Math.round(amount*100));
int dollars = allCents/100;
int cents = allCents%100;
```

The next three instructions in your pseudocode are already expressed in Java, so all that is left to do is to translate the last instruction into Java code. That last instruction is

Output cents **in the usual dollars and cents format.**

This looks pretty easy. So, you try

```java
System.out.println(cents);
```

early testing

You then test your code and see output that looks like the following:

```
$10.95
```

which looks pretty good. So, you try some more examples and run into a problem with amounts less than 10. For example, one output you get is

```
$7.5
```

when you were expecting:

```
$7.05
```

This quick test makes you realize that you need to output a 0 before the amount of cents whenever the amount of cents is less than 10. So, you change your code for outputting the number of cents to

```java
if (cents < 10)
{
    System.out.print('0');
    System.out.print(cents);
}
else
    System.out.print(cents);
```

more testing

The full definition of the class you derived is shown in Display 5.12.

Now that you have a complete definition of the class, it is time for some serious testing. Display 5.13 shows the program you use to test the method write. These

driver program

sorts of programs are often called **driver programs** because they do nothing but exercise the method ("drive the method"). Any method can be tested in a program like this.

The testing goes quite well until you decide to try a negative number. After all, there is such a thing as a negative amount of money. It's called a *debt*. But, the amount −1.20 is output as $−1.0−20. Something is wrong with the way your method handles negative amounts.

It is easy to see what is wrong with negative amounts like −1.20. After outputting $−1., you want to output 20, not −20. There are a number of ways to fix this, but you hit on one clean and simple way. Since you have code that correctly outputs

Display 5.12 DollarsFirstTry

```java
public class DollarsFirstTry
{
    /********************************************************
     *Outputs amount in dollars and cents notation. Rounds after two
     *decimal points. Does not advance to the next line after output.
     *******************************************************/
    public static void write(double amount)
    {
        int allCents = (int)(Math.round(amount*100));
        int dollars = allCents/100;
        int cents = allCents%100;

        System.out.print('$');
        System.out.print(dollars);
        System.out.print('.');
        if (cents < 10)
        {
            System.out.print('0');
            System.out.print(cents);
        }
        else
            System.out.print(cents);
    }


    /********************************************************
     *Outputs amount in dollars and cents notation. Rounds after
     *two decimal points. Advances to the next line after output.
     *******************************************************/
    public static void writeln(double amount)
    {
        write(amount);
        System.out.println();
    }
}
```

Display 5.13 **Testing a Method**

```
public class DollarsFirstTryDriver
{
    public static void main(String[] args)
    {
        double amount;
        char ans;

        System.out.println("Testing DollarsFirstTry.write:");
        do
        {
            System.out.println("Enter a value of type double:");
            amount = SavitchIn.readLineDouble();
            DollarsFirstTry.write(amount);
            System.out.println();
            System.out.println("Test again?(y/n)");
            ans = SavitchIn.readLineNonwhiteChar();
        }while ((ans == 'y') || (ans == 'Y'));
        System.out.println("End of test.");
    }
}
```

> This kind of testing program is often called a **driver program**.

Sample Screen Dialogue

```
Testing DollarsFirstTry.write:
Enter a value of type double:
1.2345
$1.23
Test again?(y/n)
y
Enter a value of type double:
1.235
$1.24
Test again?(y/n)
y
Enter a value of type double:
9.02
$9.02
Test again?(y/n)
y
Enter a value of type double:
-1.20
$-1.0-20
Test again?(y/n)
n
```

OOPS.
A problem here.

nonnegative numbers, you can convert any negative number to a positive number and then output the positive number and insert the minus sign. The revised version of the class is shown in Display 5.14. Notice that the new method `writePositive` (Display 5.14) has a body that is almost the same as the old method `write` (Display 5.12). The only difference is that `writePositive` does not output the dollar sign. The dollar sign is output in the new version of the method `write`.

Every time you change the definition of a class or method, you should test it. So, you retest the class `Dollars` with a program similar to the one you used to test `DollarsFirstTry`. In this case, the test is successful.

retest

A driver program for the method `write` of the class `Dollars` is in the file `DollarsDriver.java` on the accompanying CD.

extra code on CD

Top–Down Design

In the last case study, we used the following pseudocode for our first attempt to design the method `write` of the class `Dollars` (Display 5.14/page 330):

> **Determine the number of whole dollars in** `amount` **and store it in an** *int* **variable called** `dollars`.
> **Determine the number of cents in** `amount` **and store it in an** *int* **variable** `cents`. **Round if there**
>   **are more than two digits after the decimal point.**
> ```
> System.out.print('$');
> System.out.print(dollars);
> System.out.print('.');
> ```
> **Output** `cents` **in the usual dollars and cents format.**

What we have done with this pseudocode is to decompose the task for outputting an amount of money into a number of subtasks, such as

> **Determine the number of whole dollars in** `amount` **and store it in an** *int* **variable called** `dollars`.

We then solved each of these subtasks separately and produced code for each subtask. After that, all we had to do to produce the final definition of the method was to combine the code for the subtasks.

As it turned out, we ended up using the code derived from the preceding pseudocode for the method `writePositive`, rather than the method `write`. But this was just a further illustration of using subtasks. The method `writePositive` solved a subtask that we used in the final definition of the method `write`.

Often, though not always, the solutions to subtasks are implemented as private helping methods. If the task is large, then to design these helping methods, you use the same technique: Divide the subtask into smaller subsubtasks and solve the subsubtasks separately. These subsubtasks may be further decomposed into smaller tasks, but eventually the tasks become small enough to be easy to design and code.

This technique of dividing the task to be performed by a method into subtasks is called **top–down design**. (Other terms that are used to mean the same thing as top–down design are **stepwise refinement** and **divide and conquer**.) This top–down design technique, although very simple in concept, is extremely powerful and can sometimes be the only way you can manage to write code for a method whose task is very large, or even only moderately large.

Display 5.14 Corrected Class Dollars **(Part 1 of 2)**

```
public class Dollars
{
    /**********************************************************
     *Outputs amount in dollars and cents notation.  Rounds after two
     *decimal points. Does not advance to the next line after output.
     **********************************************************/
    public static void write(double amount)
    {
        if (amount >= 0)
        {
            System.out.print('$');
            writePositive(amount);
        }
        else
        {
            double positiveAmount = -amount;
            System.out.print('$');
            System.out.print('-');
            writePositive(positiveAmount);
        }
    }

    //Precondition: amount >= 0;
    //Outputs amount in dollars and cents notation. Rounds
    //after two decimal points. Omits the dollar sign.
    private static void writePositive(double amount)
    {
        int allCents = (int)(Math.round(amount*100));
        int dollars = allCents/100;
        int cents = allCents%100;

        System.out.print(dollars);
        System.out.print('.');
        if (cents < 10)
        {
            System.out.print('0');
            System.out.print(cents);
        }
        else
            System.out.print(cents);
    }
```

Display 5.14 Corrected Class Dollars **(Part 2 of 2)**

```
/**********************************************************
 *Outputs amount in dollars and cents notation.  Rounds after
 *two decimal points.  Advances to the next line after output.
 **********************************************************/
public static void writeln(double amount)
{
    write(amount);
    System.out.println();
}

}
```

Testing Methods

One way to test a method is to use a driver program like the one in Display 5.13/page 328. Programs like that one are often called **driver programs** because they do nothing but exercise the method. These driver programs are just for your use and so they can be quite simple. They need not have any fancy output or anything else very fancy. All they have to do is to give the method some arguments and invoke the method. Any method can be tested in a similar driver program.

driver program

Every method you write for a class should be tested. Moreover, it should be tested in a program in which it is the only method that has not yet been fully tested. In that way, if you discover that something is wrong, you know which method contains the mistake. If you test more than one method in the same program, you can easily be fooled into thinking that the mistake is in one method, when in fact it is in some other method.

Test Methods Separately

Every method should be tested in a program in which it is the only untested method.

One way to test every method in a program in which it is the only untested program is a technique called **bottom–up testing**. With bottom–up testing, if method A uses method B, then method B is fully tested before you test method A.

bottom–up testing

Bottom–up testing is a good and safe method of testing, but sometimes it can become tedious, and there are other ways to find bugs quicker and less painfully. Sometimes you want to test a method before all the methods it uses are tested. However, you should still test the method in a program in which it is the only untested method. For example, you might want to test your general approach to the problem before even writing all the methods. Sometimes, you will find yourself in the situation where method A uses method B, and you want to test method A before you test method B (maybe even before you write method B). This presents a problem. If method A uses method B and method B is not yet tested, how can you test method A in a program in which it is the only untested method? The answer is to use a *stub* for method B.

stub

A **stub** is a simplified version of a method that is not good enough for the final class definition, but that is good enough for testing and that is simple enough for you to be sure it is correct (or as sure as one can be about correctness). For example, suppose you are testing the class Dollars in Display 5.14/page 330 and you want to test the method writeln before you test the method write. You can use a stub for the method write. The following is a stub for the method write:

```
public static void write(double amount)
{
    System.out.print("$99.12");
}
```

Now this is certainly not a correct definition of the class write. It always outputs $99.12, no matter what it gets as an argument. However, it is good enough to use in testing the method writeln. If you test the method writeln using this stub for the method write, and writeln outputs 99.12 in the correct way, then writeln is almost certain to be correct. Note that using this stub for write will let you test the method writeln before you even write either of the methods write or writePositive.

? Self-Test Questions

21. In this question, you will design a class to output values of type *double* (not necessarily for money amounts). The class will be called OutputFormat and it will have two static methods write and writeln, each of which take two arguments. The first argument gives a *double* value to be written to the screen. The second argument is an *int* value telling how many digits to show after the decimal point. Have your methods round any extra digits. This is very similar to the methods write and writeln in the class Dollars, and you can use the class Dollars as a model, but there are some differences between the methods in the two classes. As you would expect, output after write goes on the same line and output after writeln goes on the following line; otherwise, write and writeln do the same thing. The following is some sample output:

```
OutputFormat.writeln(9.1234667, 4);
OutputFormat.writeln(9.9999, 2);
OutputFormat.writeln(7.01234, 4);
```

It should produce the following output:

```
9.1235
10.00
7.0123
```

Do not forget to test your methods on numbers with zeros after the decimal point, like `1.023` and `1.0023`. *Hint:* You may find the static method `Math.pow` (Display 5.9/page 317) helpful as part of an expression to move a decimal point. This is a fairly difficult exercise, so allow yourself some time to complete it. If you do not succeed in writing this class, be sure that you at least understand the answer given at the end of the chapter. This is a very useful class.

22. In your definition of the class `OutputFormat` in Self-Test Question 21, would it be legal to use the names `print` and `println`, rather than `write` and `writeln`, or would this produce a name conflict with `System.out.println`?

23. Consider the variable `allCents` in the method `writePositive` in Display 5.14/page 330. It holds an amount of money as if it were all cents. So. for the amount $12.95, the *int* variable `allCents` would be set to 1295 (cents). This is somewhat limiting. The largest value of type *int* is `2147483647`. That means that the largest amount the method can handle is $21,474,836.47. That is more than 21 million dollars, a nice large sum, but we often need to consider larger sums, such as the sum for the national budget, a large company's budget, or even the salary for the CEO of a large company. How can you easily change the definition of the methods in the class `Dollars` so they handle larger amounts of money?

5.4 | Overloading

> *A good name is better than precious ointment...*
>
> ***Ecclesiastes 7:1***

We have seen that two (or more) different classes can have methods with the same name. For example, there are many classes that have a method named `readInput`. This is not so surprising. The type of the calling object allows Java to decide which definition of the method `readInput` to use. Java simply uses the definition in the class of the calling object. You may be more surprised to hear that you can also have two or more methods *in the same class* that have the same method name. How is this possible? Read on.

Overloading Basics

When you give two or more definitions of the same method name *within the same class* that is known as **overloading** the method name. To ensure that this works out, you must ensure that the different definitions of the method name have something different about there parameter lists. For example, in Display 5.15, we have written a very simple example of overloading.

overloading

The class `Statistician` (Display 5.15) has three different methods all named `average`. When there is an invocation of `Statistician.average`, how does Java know which definition of `average` to use? First, let's assume the arguments are all

Display 5.15 Overloading

```
/**********************************************
 *This is just a toy class to illustrate overloading.
 **********************************************/
public class Statistician
{
    public static void main(String[] args)
    {
        double average1 = Statistician.average(40.0, 50.0);
        double average2 = Statistician.average(1.0, 2.0, 3.0);
        char average3 = Statistician.average('a', 'c');

        System.out.println("average1 = " + average1);
        System.out.println("average2 = " + average2);
        System.out.println("average3 = " + average3);
    }

    public static double average(double first, double second)
    {
        return ((first + second)/2.0);
    }

    public static double average(double first,
                                 double second, double third)
    {
        return ((first + second + third)/3.0);
    }

    public static char average(char first, char second)
    {
        return (char)(((int)first + (int)second)/2);
    }
}
```

Sample Screen Dialogue

```
average1 = 45.0
average2 = 2.0
average3 = b
```

of type *double*. In that case, Java can tell which definition of average to use by the number of arguments. If there are two arguments of type *double*, then it uses the first definition of average. If there are three arguments, it uses the second definition of average.

Now, suppose there is an invocation of the method average that has two arguments of type *char*. Java knows that it should use the third definition of average because of the types of the arguments. There is only one definition that has two arguments of type *char*. (For now, don't worry about how this method averages two letters. That's a side issue that we will come back to shortly.)

Suppose you give more than one definition to the same method name within the same class definition. When there is an invocation of that method name for that class, Java determines which definition to use according to the number of arguments and the types of the arguments. If there is a definition of that method name that has the same number of parameters as there are arguments in the invocation, and if the types also match, that is, the first argument has the same type as the first parameter, the second argument has the same type as the second parameter, and so forth, then that is the definition of the method name that is used. If there is no such match, Java will try some simple type conversions of the kinds we discussed before, such as casting an *int* to a *double*, to see if that produces a match. If that fails, you will get an error message.

OK, now let's take a short side trip to explain how we average two characters. For this toy example, it does not matter if we use a crazy way of averaging two characters, but, in fact, the way we average characters in Display 5.15 is a very sensible way to average characters, or at least to average two letters. If the two letters are both lowercase, then the average computed will be the lowercase letter halfway between them in alphabetical order. (If there is no letter exactly halfway, it chooses one of the two that is as close to halfway as possible.) Similarly, if the two letters are both uppercase, then the average computed will be the uppercase letter halfway between them in alphabetical order. This works because the letters are assigned numbers in order. The number assigned to 'b' is one more than the number assigned to 'a', the number assigned to 'c' is one more than the number assigned to 'b', and so forth. So if you convert two letters to numbers, average the numbers, and then convert back to letters, you get the letter halfway in between.

averaging characters

As we will see, most class definitions have some overloading of method names. You have not seen any overloading until now because we carefully avoided it until we could explain it. Overloading can be applied to any kind of method. It can be applied to *void*-methods, to methods that return a value, to static methods, to non-static methods, or to any combination of these.

Note that you have already been using overloading, even though you may not have known the term before. In the previous section, many of the methods of the class Math use overloading. For example, the max method uses overloading based on the type of its arguments. If its two arguments are of type *int*, it returns a value of type *int*. If its two arguments are of type *double*, it returns a value of type *double*. Of course, this is not a very dramatic use of overloading, since the different definitions of max would be identical except for some type names. A more dramatic example is the division operator /, which we discussed in Chapter 2. If its arguments are of type *double*, it is defined to do floating-point division; so 5.0/2.0 returns 2.5. But, if both arguments are of type *int*, it is defined to perform integer division; so, 5/2 is 2.

Overloading

Within one class, you can have two (or more) definitions of a single method name. This is called **overloading** the method name. When you overload a method name, any two definitions of the same method name must either have different numbers of parameters or some parameter position must be of differing types in the two definitions. ◻

Programming Example
A Pet Class

Display 5.16 shows another simple class with overloading. In this case, we have overloaded the method name set. This is a class for a pet and the various set methods set different instance variables. There are four methods named set. One sets all three of name, age, and weight. The other three set only one each of these. There is a main method with a simple demonstration program. Notice that each invocation of the method set has either a different number of arguments or an argument whose type is different from the other invocations of set. Thus, each invocation of set uses a different definition of set.

■ Gotcha
Overloading and Automatic Type Conversion

In some situations, two friends are not better than one. Two good things can sometimes interact in a bad way. Overloading is a friend, or at least a helpful feature of the Java language. Automatic type conversion of arguments is also a helpful feature

automatic type conversion

of the Java language (such as converting an *int* like 2 to a *double* like 2.0 when a method wants a *double* as argument). But these two nice features can sometimes get in the way of each other.

For example, look at the main method in Display 5.16 and consider the following lines:

```
System.out.println("Changing weight.");
myDog.set(6.5);
```

This changes the weight of myDog to 6.5 pounds. But now suppose my dog does not weigh 6.5 pounds, but instead weighs only 6 pounds. In that case, I should change those two lines to

```
System.out.println("Changing weight.");
myDog.set(6.0);
```

This will change myDog's weight to 6 pounds. But, suppose that I forget the decimal point and the zero and write the following:

```
System.out.println("Changing weight.");
myDog.set(6);
```

Display 5.16   Pet Class *(Part 1 of 3)*

```
/**************************************
 *Class for basic pet records: name, age, and weight.
 **************************************/
public class Pet
{
    private String name;
    private int age;//in years
    private double weight;//in pounds

    /*************************************
     *This main is just a demonstration program.
     *************************************/
    public static void main(String[] args)
    {
        Pet myDog = new Pet();
        myDog.set("Fido", 2, 5.5);
        myDog.writeOutput();
        System.out.println("Changing name.");
        myDog.set("Rex");
        myDog.writeOutput();
        System.out.println("Changing weight.");
        myDog.set(6.5);
        myDog.writeOutput();
        System.out.println("Changing age.");
        myDog.set(3);
        myDog.writeOutput();
    }

    public void writeOutput()
    {
        System.out.println("Name: " + name);
        System.out.println("Age: " + age + " years");
        System.out.println("Weight: " + weight + " pounds");
    }

    public void set(String newName)
    {
        name = newName;
        //age and weight are unchanged.
    }
```

Display 5.16 Pet Class (Part 2 of 3)

```java
public void set(int newAge)
{
    if (newAge <= 0)
    {
        System.out.println("Error: illegal age.");
        System.exit(0);
    }
    else
        age = newAge;
    //name and weight are unchanged.
}

public void set(double newWeight)
{
    if (newWeight <= 0)
    {
        System.out.println("Error: illegal weight.");
        System.exit(0);
    }
    else
        weight = newWeight;
    //name and age are unchanged.
}

public void set(String newName, int newAge, double newWeight)
{
    name = newName;
    if ((newAge <= 0) || (newWeight <= 0))
    {
        System.out.println("Error: illegal age or weight.");
        System.exit(0);
    }
    else
    {
        age = newAge;
        weight = newWeight;
    }
}

public String getName()
{
    return name;
}
```

Display 5.16 Pet Class *(Part 3 of 3)*

```
public int getAge()
{
    return age;
}
 public double getWeight()
{
    return weight;
}
}
```

Sample Screen Dialogue

```
Name: Fido
Age: 2 years
Weight: 5.5 pounds
Changing name.
Name: Rex
Age: 2 years
Weight: 5.5 pounds
Changing weight.
Name: Rex
Age: 2 years
Weight: 6.5 pounds
Changing age.
Name: Rex
Age: 3 years
Weight: 6.5 pounds
```

I want this to change `myDog`'s weight to 6, but instead it will change `myDog`'s age to 6. This is because 6 is of type *int*, and the definition of `set` that has one parameter of type *int* will change the instance variable `age`, not the instance variable `weight`. If Java can find a definition of `set` that matches the number and types of arguments, it will not do any type conversion of *int*s to *double*s, or any other type conversions.

In the case we just went through, we needed a type conversion, but we did not get one. There are also cases where you do not want a type conversion and you do get one. For example, suppose I want to set `myDog`'s name to `"Cha Cha"`, weight to 2, and age to 3. I might try the following:

```
myDog.set("Cha Cha", 2, 3);
```

This will set `myDog`'s age to 2, not 3, and `myDog`'s `weight` to 3.0, not 2.0. The real problem, of course, is that I have reversed arguments 2 and 3, but let's look at it as Java does. Given the preceding invocation, Java looks for a definition of `set` with a heading of the following form:

```
public void set(String Name_1, int Name_2, int Name_3)
```

There is no such definition of `set`. So, there is no exact match to the invocation. So, Java tries to convert an *int* to a *double* to get a match. It notices that if it converts the 3 to 3.0, it will have a match to

```
public void set(String newName, int newAge, double newWeight)
```

and so it does the type conversion.

What went wrong (besides reversing two arguments)? I should have given the weight as 2.0, not 2. If I had used 2.0, or if Java had not done any automatic type conversions for me, then I would have received an error message. In this case, Java tried to help, but the help just got in the way.

There are situations in which a method invocation can be resolved in two different ways, depending on how overloading and type conversion interact. Such ambiguous method invocations are not allowed in Java and will produce a run time error message (or sometimes even a compiler error message). For example, you can overload a method name (`problemMethod`) so that it has the following two method headings in a `SampleClass`:

```
public class SampleClass
{
    public static void problemMethod(double n1, int n2)
        .
        .
        .
    public static void problemMethod(int n1, double n2)
        .
        .
        .
```

Such method definitions will compile. However an invocation such as the following will produce an error message, because Java cannot decide which overloaded definition of `problemMethod` to use:

```
SampleClass.problemMethod(5, 10);
```

Java cannot decide if it should convert the *int* value 5 to a *double* value and use the first definition of `problemMethod`, or if it should convert the *int* value 10 to a *double* value and use the second definition. In this situation, Java issues an error message saying the method invocation is ambiguous.

The following two method invocations are allowed:

```
SampleClass.problemMethod(5.0, 10);
SampleClass.problemMethod(5, 10.0);
```

However, such situations, while legal, are confusing and should be avoided. .

Overloading and Automatic Type Conversion

Java always tries to use overloading before it tries to use automatic type conversion. If Java can find a definition of a method that matches the types of the arguments, then Java will use that definition. Java will not do an automatic type conversion of a method's argument until after it has tried and failed to find a definition of the method name with parameter types that exactly match the arguments in the method invocation.

■ Gotcha

You Cannot Overload Based on The Returned Type

You cannot overload a method name by giving two definitions with headings that differ only in the type of the value returned. For example, consider the class `Pet` in Display 5.16/page 337. You might have wanted to add a method called `getWeight`, which returns a character telling if the pet is overweight or underweight; say, `'+'` for overweight, `'-'` for underweight, and `'*'` for just right. This would return a value of type `char`. If you did add this method `getWeight`, you would then have two methods with the following headings:

```
/*****************************
 *Returns the weight of the pet.
 *****************************/
public double getWeight()
```

> *You CANNOT have both of these methods within a single class.*

```
/*********************************
 *Returns '+' if overweight, '-' is
 *underweight and '*' if weight OK.
 *********************************/
public char getWeight()
```

Unfortunately this is illegal. In any class definition, any two definitions of the same method name must have different numbers of parameters or one or more parameters of differing types. You cannot overload based on the type returned.

If you think about it, it is not even possible to write the compiler so it overloads on the basis of the type returned. For example, suppose you have

```
Pet myFriend = new Pet();
     .
     .
     .
double value = myFriend.getWeight();
```

Now suppose that, contrary to actual fact, we allowed methods with both of the above headings and consider the job of the poor compiler. Although we have not made an issue of it, it is true that you can store a value of type *char* in a variable of type *double*. Java will perform an automatic type cast to change the *char* to a *double*. Thus, in this hypothetical scenario, the above variable `value` is happy with either a *double* or a *char*. So, there is no way to tell if the programmer who wrote this code meant getWeight to return a *char* or a *double*. The compiler would have to ask the programmer what she/he meant, and compilers are not allowed to ask the programmer questions.

? Self-Test Questions

24. Would the following be a legal method invocation to include in the program in Display 5.16/page 337?

```
myDog.set("Fido", 2, 7);
```

25. Can a class possibly contain both of the following method definitions?

```
/******************************************
 *Postcondition: Returns the number of people
 *in numberOfCouples couples.
 ******************************************/
public static int howMany(int numberOfCouples)
{
     return 2*numberOfCouples;
}


/******************************************
 *Postcondition: Returns the number of children
 *assuming that each couple has 2.3 children.
 ******************************************/
public static double howMany(int numberOfCouples)
{
     return 2.3*numberOfCouples;
}
```

26. Can a class possibly contain both of the following method definitions?

```
/************************************************************
 *Postcondition: Returns an int value approximately equivalent
 *to number. But, converts all negative numbers to zero.
 ************************************************************/
public static int convertedValue(double number)
{
     if (number > 0.0)
          return (int) number;
     return 0;
}
```

```
/*************************************************************
 *Postcondition: Returns a double value approximately equivalent
 *to number. But, converts all negative numbers to zero.
 ************************************************************/
public static double convertedValue(int number)
{
    if (number > 0)
        return (double) number;
    return 0.0;
}
```

27. Consider the class Species in Display 4.19/page 276 of Chapter 4. It has a method called set that sets the name, population, and growth rate of a species. Could this class have another method that is also named set, that only has one parameter for the name of the species, and that sets both the population and growth rate to zero? If so, give the definition of this other method named set.

Programming Example
A Class for Money

Display 5.17 contains a class, named Money, whose objects represent amounts of (U.S.) money, such as $9.99, $500.00, $0.50, and so forth. You may be inclined to think of money amounts as values of type *double*, but a user who does not know about programming (and many end users do not know about programming) would think of it as dollars and cents. To "the person on the street", $9.99 is not a value of type *double*. It turns out that "the person on the street" is correct. Sometimes, you can get away with using values of type *double* to represent amounts of money, but there is a problem with doing so. A value of type *double* is practically speaking an approximate quantity, and if you are writing an accounting program, approximate quantities are not always good enough. If a bank has account balances off by a few dollars or even a few cents, then that will produce dissatisfied customers and probably some sort of legal action by either customers or the government. The class Money is meant to hold data that represents money. To the programer who uses it or to the end user of any software product produced, the data is not thought of as values of type *double* or *int* or any other Java predefined type. They are values of type Money.

(In Display 5.14/page 330 we defined a class named Dollars which is concerned with treating amounts of money as values of type *double*. This programming example shows another approach to handling amounts of money and is not directly related to the class Dollars.)

Of course to implement the class Money, we must choose some sort of data representation. We want to represent money amounts as exact quantities so we will use an integer type. However, the type *int* cannot represent very large numbers and so cannot easily represent very large amounts of money. So, we will use the type *long*. An amount of money, like $3500.36 will be represented as the two integers 3500

Display 5.17   Money Class *(Part 1 of 3)*

```
/******************************************
 *Objects represent nonnegative amounts of money,
 *such as $100, $41.99, $0.05.
 ******************************************/
public class Money
{
    private long dollars;
    private long cents;

    public void set(long newDollars)
    {
        if (newDollars < 0)
        {
            System.out.println(
                "Error: Negative amounts of money are not allowed.");
            System.exit(0);
        }
        else
        {
            dollars = newDollars;
            cents = 0;
        }
    }

    public void set(double amount)
    {
        if (amount < 0)
        {
            System.out.println(
                "Error: Negative amounts of money are not allowed.");
            System.exit(0);
        }
        else
        {
            long allCents = Math.round(amount*100);
            dollars = allCents/100;
            cents = allCents%100;
        }
    }

    public void set(Money otherObject)
    {
        this.dollars = otherObject.dollars;
        this.cents = otherObject.cents;
    }
```

Display 5.17 **Money Class** *(Part 2 of 3)*

```
/********************************************************
*Precondition: The argument is an ordinary representation
*of an amount of money, with or without a dollar sign.
*Fractions of a cent are not allowed.
********************************************************/
public void set(String amountString)
{
    String dollarsString;
    String centsString;

    //Delete '$' if any:
    if (amountString.charAt(0) == '$')
        amountString = amountString.substring(1);
    amountString = amountString.trim();

    //Locate decimal point:
    int pointLocation = amountString.indexOf(".");

    if (pointLocation < 0) //If no decimal point
    {
        cents = 0;
        dollars = Long.parseLong(amountString);
    }
    else//String has a decimal point.
    {
        dollarsString =
                amountString.substring(0, pointLocation);
        centsString =
                amountString.substring(pointLocation + 1);
        if (centsString.length() <= 1)
        //if one digit meaning tenths of a dollar
            centsString = centsString + "0";

        dollars = Long.parseLong(dollarsString);
        cents = Long.parseLong(centsString);
        if ((dollars < 0) || (cents < 0) || (cents > 99))
        {
            System.out.println(
                "Error: Illegal representation of money amount.");
            System.exit(0);
        }
    }
}
```

Display 5.17 Money Class *(Part 3 of 3)*

```java
    public void readInput()
    {
        System.out.println("Enter amount on a line by itself:");
        String amount = SavitchIn.readLine();
        set(amount.trim());
    }

    /*************************************************
     *Does not go to the next line after outputting money.
     *************************************************/
    public void writeOutput()
    {
        System.out.print("$" + dollars);
        if (cents < 10)
            System.out.print(".0" + cents);
        else
            System.out.print("." + cents);
    }

    /********************************
     *Returns n times the calling object.
     ********************************/
    public Money times(int n)
    {
        Money product = new Money();
        product.cents = n*cents;
        long carryDollars = product.cents/100;
        product.cents = product.cents%100;
        product.dollars = n*dollars + carryDollars;
        return product;
    }

    /****************************************************
     *Returns the sum of the calling object and the argument.
     ****************************************************/
    public Money add(Money otherAmount)
    {
        Money sum = new Money();
        sum.cents = this.cents + otherAmount.cents;
        long carryDollars = sum.cents/100;
        sum.cents = sum.cents%100;
        sum.dollars = this.dollars
                        + otherAmount.dollars + carryDollars;
        return sum;
    }
}
```

and 36 stored in instance variables of type *long*. It certainly makes sense to have negative amounts of money and a final profession strength Money class would allow for negative amounts of money, but we want a fairly simple example for learning purposes, and so we will limit ourselves to nonnegative amounts of money.

Notice the overloaded method name set. The four methods named set allow a programmer to set an amount of money in any way that is convenient. The programmer can use a single integer values for an amount of dollars without any cents, a single value of type *double*, another object of type Money, or a string, such as "$9.98" or "9.98". The programmer does not, and should not, worry about what instance variables are used inside the class Money. The programmer who uses the class Money should think in terms of money amount and not in terms of any instance variables.

Let's look at some details in the definitions of the set methods. The set method with one parameters of type *long* is straight forward.

The set method with one parameter of type *double* works by converting the *double* value to a value that represents the amount of money as the number of pennies in the amount. This is done as follows:

```
long allCents = Math.round(amount*100);
```

The method Math.round eliminates any fractional part of a penny. The method Math.round returns a value of type *long* when its argument is of type *double*, as it is here. The integer division operators / and % are then used to convert the pennies to dollars and cents.

The set method with one parameter of type Money is also straightforward, but you should notice one important point. Note that the instance variables of the parameter, as in otherObject.dollars, can be directly accessed inside the class definition for the class Money. In the definition of a class, such as Money, you can directly access the instance variables of any object of the class, in this case any object of the class Money.

The set method with one parameter of type String is an exercise in string processing. It changes a string such as "$12.75" or "12.75" into the two integers 12 and 75. The main details are shown in color and we will review those colored lines. The rest of the definition has to do with special cases and checking for illegal arguements. First there is a check to see if there is a dollar sign or not as the first character in the string. this is done as follows:

```
if (amountString.charAt(0) == '$')
    amountString = amountString.substring(1);
```

The first character in the string amountString is produced by the string method invocation amountString.charAt(0). If this character is '$', then the string, which has index positions 0 through some last index, is replaced by the substring at indexes 1 through the end of the string, effectively removing the first character. This is done as follows:

```
amountString = amountString.substring(1);
```

trim

Since there may have been a blank (or blanks) between the character '$' and the number for the amount of money. Blanks are trimmed off with an invocation of the String method `trim`, as follows:

```
amountString = amountString.trim();
```

The string is then broken into the dollars substring and the cents substring, by locating the decimal point and breaking the string at the decimal point. The decimal point position is stored in the variable `pointLocation` as follows:

indexOf

```
int pointLocation = amountString.indexOf(".");
```

substring

The dollars and cents substrings are recovered as follows:

```
dollarsString =
    amountString.substring(0, pointLocation);
centsString =
    amountString.substring(pointLocation + 1);
```

You may want to review the descriptions of the `substring` methods given in Display 2.6/page 82.

parseLong

Finally, the dollars and cents substrings are converted to values of type *long* by using the static method `parseLong` in the wrapper class Long:

```
dollars = Long.parseLong(dollarsString);
cents = Long.parseLong(centsString);
```

If the methods `parseLong` sounds unfamiliar, check the subsection of this chapter entitled *Integer, Double, and Other Wrapper Classes* starting on page 319.

times **and**
add

The method `times`, is used to multiply an amount of money by an integer. The method `add` is used to add two objects of type Money. For example, suppose m1 and m2 are objects of type Money that both represent the amounts $2.00, then

`m1.times(3)` returns an object of the class Money that represents the amount $6.00, and

`m1.add(m2)` returns an objects of the class Money that represents the amount $4.00.

To understand the definition of the methods `times` and `add`, remember that there are 100 pennies in a dollar, so if `product.cents` might have a value of 100 cents or more, then the following will set the variable `carryDollars` equal to the number of whole dollars in that many cents.

```
long carryDollars = product.cents/100;
```

The number of cents left over after removing that many dollars is given by

```
product.cents%100
```

A demonstration program for the class Money is given in Display 5.18.

? Self-Test Questions

28. In Display 5.17/page 344, rewrite the method add so that it does not use the *this* parameter.

Display 5.18 Using the Money Class

```java
public class MoneyDemo
{
    public static void main(String[] args)
    {
        Money start = new Money();
        Money goal = new Money();

        System.out.println("Enter your current savings:");
        start.readInput();

        goal = start.times(2);
        System.out.print(
            "If you double that, you will have ");
        goal.writeOutput();

        System.out.println(", or better yet:");
        goal = start.add(goal);
        System.out.println(
            "If you triple that original amount, you will have:");
        goal.writeOutput();
        System.out.println();

        System.out.println(
                   "Remember: A penny saved");
        System.out.println("is a penny earned.");        }
    }
}
```

> Needed to end the line, because `writeOutput` does not end the line.

Sample Screen Dialogue

```
Enter your current savings:
$500.99
If you double that, you will have $1001.98, or better yet:
If you triple that original amount, you will have
$1502.97
Remember: A penny saved
is a penny earned.
```

29. In Display 5.17/page 344, the set method with a String parameter does not allow extra leading and trailing blanks in the string parameter. Rewrite it so that it ignores leading and trailing white space. For example, it should allow " $5.43 " as an argument.

5.5 | Constructors

> *First things first.*
>
> *Common saying*

When you create an object of a class, you often want certain initializing actions performed, such as giving values to the instance variables. A *constructor* is a special kind of method that is designed to perform such initializations. In this section, we tell you how to define and use constructors.

Defining Constructors

Until now, we created new objects as in the following example:

```
Pet goodScout = new Pet();
```

(The definition of the class Pet is in Display 5.16/page 337, but the point is independent of the details of this particular class.) For the classes we've seen thus far, this creates an object whose instance variables have no initial values (or have some default initial value that may not be what you want as the default). You may wish to have some or all instance variables automatically initialize to your specifications when an object is created. You can do this with a special kind of method called a *constructor*.

constructor   A **constructor** is a method that is called when a new object is created. A constructor can perform any action you write into its definition, but constructors were designed to perform initializing actions, such as initializing the values of instance variables. Constructors serve very much the same purpose as the methods named set in our definition of the class Pet in Display 5.16/page 337. But unlike the set methods, the constructors are called almost automatically whenever you create an object using the *new* operator.

One property of constructors that may seem strange at first is that constructors have the same name as the class. So, if the class is named Pet, then the constructors will be named Pet. If the class is named Species, then the constructors will be named Species. Although this may seem peculiar when you first hear this rule, it works out very well in practice.

As an example, in Display 5.19, we have rewritten our definition of the class for pet records so that it has constructor methods. As was true of our methods named set, constructors are normally overloaded so that there are multiple definitions of the constructor, each with different numbers or types of parameters. Display 5.19 and Display 5.16/page 337 are similar, but most of the differences between them are important. Let's look at those differences. <Text continues on page 354.>

Display 5.19 Pet Class with Constructors *(Part 1 of 3)*

```java
/**************************************************
 *Class for basic pet records: name, age, and weight.
 **************************************************/
public class PetRecord
{
    private String name;
    private int age;//in years
    private double weight;//in pounds

    public void writeOutput()
    {
        System.out.println("Name: " + name);
        System.out.println("Age: " + age + " years");
        System.out.println("Weight: " + weight + " pounds");
    }

    public PetRecord(String initialName, int initialAge,
                                        double initialWeight)
    {
        name = initialName;
        if ((initialAge < 0) || (initialWeight < 0))
        {
            System.out.println("Error: Negative age or weight.");
            System.exit(0);
        }
        else
        {
            age = initialAge;
            weight = initialWeight;
        }
    }

    public void set(String newName, int newAge, double newWeight)
    {
        name = newName;
        if ((newAge < 0) || (newWeight < 0))
        {
            System.out.println("Error: Negative age or weight.");
            System.exit(0);
        }
        else
        {
            age = newAge;
            weight = newWeight;
        }
    }
```

Constructors are only called when you create an object with new. *To change an already existing object, you need one or more methods like these* set *methods.*

Display 5.19 Pet Class with Constructors *(Part 2 of 3)*

```java
public PetRecord(String initialName)
{
    name = initialName;
    age = 0;
    weight = 0;
}

public void set(String newName)
{
    name = newName; //age and weight are unchanged.
}

public PetRecord(int initialAge)
{
    name = "No name yet.";
    weight = 0;
    if (initialAge < 0)
    {
        System.out.println("Error: Negative age.");
        System.exit(0);
    }
    else
        age = initialAge;
}

public void set(int newAge)
{
    if (newAge < 0)
    {
        System.out.println("Error: Negative age.");
        System.exit(0);
    }
    else
        age = newAge;
    //name and weight are unchanged.
}
```

Display 5.19 Pet Class with Constructors *(Part 3 of 3)*

```java
public PetRecord(double initialWeight)
{
    name = "No name yet";
    age = 0;
    if (initialWeight < 0)
    {
        System.out.println("Error: Negative weight.");
        System.exit(0);
    }
    else
        weight = initialWeight;
}

public void set(double newWeight)
{
    if (newWeight < 0)
    {
        System.out.println("Error: Negative weight.");
        System.exit(0);
    }
    else
        weight = newWeight; //name and age are unchanged.
}

public PetRecord()
{
    name = "No name yet.";
    age = 0;
    weight = 0;
}

public String getName()
{
    return name;
}

public int getAge()
{
    return age;
}

public double getWeight()
{
    return weight;
}
```

Default constructor

```java
}
```

1. There are some mundane changes to review before going on to the interesting changes. In Display 5.19, the class name is changed from `Pet` to `PetRecord`, because each class must have a different name. Also, in Display 5.19, we have deleted the method `main`, because it was just a toy demonstration program that we no longer need it. Now, on to the important differences.

2. We have added methods named `PetRecord`. These methods named `PetRecord` are constructors. Note that the headings of these constructors do not have the word *void* as the `set` methods do. When you define a constructor, you do not specify any return type. You do not even write *void* in place of a return type. These constructors are very much like the `set` methods. However, unlike some of the methods named `set`, the constructors give values to all the instance variables, even though there may not be an argument for each instance variable. The constructors would compile even if some of the instance variables were not given values, but it is normal practice to give values to all the instance variables when defining a constructor. As we will see, constructors and the `set` methods are used in related but different ways.

3. We have added a constructor, named `PetRecord`, that has no parameters. Whenever you define at least one constructor, you should be sure to include a constructor with zero parameters. A constructor with no parameters is called a **default constructor**.

default constructor

new calls a constructor

Constructors are called at the time that you use *new* to create an object. We have already been using constructors in statements such as the following, from the program in Display 5.16/page 337:

```
Pet myDog = new Pet();
```

This line defines `myDog` to be a name for an object of the class `Pet` and then creates a new object of the class `Pet`. The part that creates the new object is

```
new Pet()
```

The part `Pet()` is a call to a constructor for the class `Pet`. The parentheses are empty because this constructor takes no arguments.

automatically defined constructor

If you look at the definition of the class `Pet` (Display 5.16), you might object that the class definition includes no constructor definitions at all. However, whenever a class definition does not have a constructor definition, Java automatically creates one with zero parameters. This automatically created constructor does essentially nothing, but it does allow you to create objects of the class. However, once you add at least one constructor definition to a class, then you are in charge of constructors. *Once you add at least one constructor to a class, then no constructors are created automatically.* Thus, in Display 5.19, where we defined a class called `PetRecord` with constructors, we were careful to include a constructor with no parameters. A constructor with no parameters is called a **default constructor**. A complete program illustrating the use of constructors with the class `PetRecord` is given in Display 5.20.

    When you create a new object with the operator *new*, you must always include a call to a constructor after the operator *new*. As with any method invocation, you list any arguments in parentheses after the constructor name (which is the same as the class name). For example, suppose you want to use *new* to create a new object of the class `PetRecord` defined in Display 5.19. You might do so as follows:

constructor arguments

```
PetRecord fish = new PetRecord("Wanda", 2, 0.25);
```

The part `PetRecord("Wanda", 2, 0.25)` is a call to the constructor for the class `PetRecord` that takes three arguments: one of type `String`, one of type *int*, and the last of type *double*. This creates a new object to represent a pet named Wanda who is 2 years old and weighs 0.25 pound. Let's look at another example.

    Consider the following:

```
PetRecord newBorn = new PetRecord();
```

This creates a new object of the class `PetRecord` and calls the default constructor (that is, the constructor with zero parameters). If you look at the definition of the class `PetRecord` in Display 5.19, you will see that the constructor with zero parameters gives the object the name `"No name yet"`, and sets both the `age` and `weight` instance variables to zero. (A newborn pet does not weigh zero, of course. The value of 0 is just being used as a placeholder until the real weight can be determined; but anyway, that's biology not computer science.)

    A constructor can only be called when you create a new object with the operator *new*. Calls such as the following to objects of the class `PetRecord` are illegal:

resetting object values

```
newBorn.PetRecord("Fang", 1, 50.0); //Illegal!
```

Since you cannot call a constructor for an object after it is created, you need some other way to change the values of the instance variables of an object. That is the purpose of the `set` methods in Display 5.19. The way to accomplish what we tried with the preceding illegal invocations of the constructor `PetRecord` is to call `set` as follows:

```
newBorn.set("Fang", 1, 50.0);
```

You need not name these methods `set`; you can use any method name that is convenient. For example, you might prefer to call these methods `reset` or `giveNewValues`. However, it is traditional to name these methods `set` or some thing that includes "`set`".

■ Programming Tip
You Can Use Other Methods in a Constructor

A constructor is a method you use to create an object, and so it is the first method invoked with the object. However, this should not discourage you from using other methods of the same class in your definitions of constructors. For example, all of the constructors in the definition of the class `PetRecord` Display 5.19/page 351 can be

Display 5.20 Using Constructors and Reset Methods

```java
public class PetRecordDemo
{
    public static void main(String[] args)
    {
        PetRecord usersPet = new PetRecord("Jane Doe");
        System.out.println("My records on your pet are inaccurate.");
        System.out.println("Here is what they currently say:");
        usersPet.writeOutput();

        System.out.println("Please enter the correct pet name:");
        String correctName = SavitchIn.readLine();
        System.out.println("Please enter the correct pet age:");
        int correctAge = SavitchIn.readLineInt();
        System.out.println("Please enter the correct pet weight:");
        double correctWeight = SavitchIn.readLineDouble();
        usersPet.set(correctName, correctAge, correctWeight);
        System.out.println("My updated records now say:");
        usersPet.writeOutput();
    }
}
```

Sample Screen Dialogue

```
My records on your pet are inaccurate.
Here is what they currently say:
Name: Jane Doe
Age: 0
Weight: 0.0 pounds
Please enter the correct pet name:
Moon Child
Please enter the correct pet age:
5
Please enter the correct pet weight:
10.5
My updated records now say:
Name: Moon Child
Age: 5
Weight: 10.5 pounds
```

rewritten using the method `set`. Consider the following constructor definition from that class definition:

```
public PetRecord(String initialName, int initialAge,
                                    double initialWeight)
{
    name = Name;
    if ((initialAge < 0) || (initialWeight < 0))
    {
        System.out.println("Error: Negative age or weight.");
        System.exit(0);
    }
    else
    {
        age = initialAge;
        weight = initialWeight;
    }
}
```

If you prefer, you can use the following equivalent definition instead:

```
public PetRecord(String initialName, int initialAge,
                                    double initialWeight)
{
    set(initialName, initialAge, initialWeight);
}
```

The other constructors in that class definition can also be rewritten using the method `set`.

Many programmers would prefer the second definition using `set`. It is certainly shorter. Some programmers might prefer the first version, because it avoids any confusion about the order of arguments to `set` and it avoids the overhead of another method invocation. Either version is acceptable. Use whichever version your instructor or supervisor prefers.

Constructor

A **constructor** is a method that is called when an object of the class is created using *new*. Constructors are used to initialize objects. A constructor must have the same name as the class to which it belongs. Arguments for a constructor are given in parentheses after the class name, as in the following examples:

Examples:
```
PetRecord myDog = new PetRecord("Fido", 2, 4.5),
        yourDog = new PetRecord("Cha Cha", 3, 2.3);
```

A constructor is defined like any other method except that it does not have a type returned and does not even include a *void* in the method heading. See Display 5.19/page 351 for examples of constructor definitions.

Display 5.21 Constructor Returning a Reference

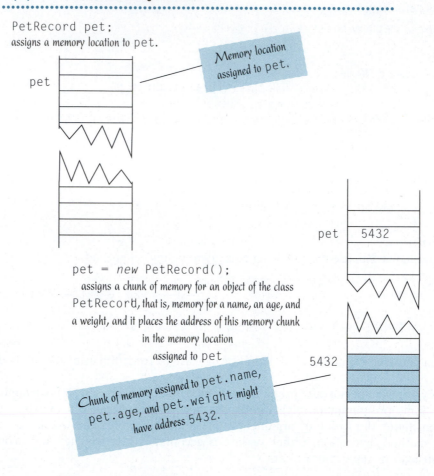

`PetRecord pet;`
assigns a memory location to `pet`.

pet

Memory location assigned to `pet`.

pet   5432

`pet = new PetRecord();`
    assigns a chunk of memory for an object of the class
    `PetRecord`, that is, memory for a name, an age, and
    a weight, and it places the address of this memory chunk
    in the memory location
    assigned to `pet`

5432

Chunk of memory assigned to `pet.name`, `pet.age`, and `pet.weight` might have address 5432.

■ **Gotcha**

Omitting the Default Constructor

Suppose we were to omit the constructor with zero parameters from the definition of the class `PetRecord` in Display 5.19/page 351; that is, suppose we *omitted* the following constructor definition:

```
public PetRecord()
{
    name = "No name yet";
    age = 0;
    weight = 0;
}
```

Constructors Return a Reference

A constructor invocation, such as *new* `PetRecord()`, returns a reference to an object, that is, it returns the memory address of an object.

Example:

If `PetRecord` is a class, then `PetRecord` is the name of a constructor for this class, *new* `PetRecord()` is an invocation of the constructor for the class `PetRecord`, and this constructor invocation returns a reference to (returns the memory address of) an object of the class `PetRecord`. If `pet` is a variable of type `PetRecord`, then the following assigns this reference to the variable `pet`:

```
pet = new PetRecord();
```

See Display 5.21/page 358 for a graphical illustration of this.

With this constructor omitted, the following would be illegal and would produce an error message:

```
PetRecord heinz57 = new PetRecord();
```

You might object that Java automatically provides a default constructor if none is defined and so this should be legal. However, the situation is slightly more complicated than that. If your class definition includes no constructors whatsoever, then Java will automatically provide a default constructor. However, if your class definition contains at least one constructor definition, then Java does not provide any constructors for you. *Once you start defining constructors, you are completely in charge of constructors and no constructors are generated other than the ones that you define.*

Because classes are often reused again and again, and because sooner or later you will probably want to create a new object without specifying parameters, as in

```
PetRecord heinz57 = new PetRecord();
```

So, you will avoid a lot of problems if you follow a policy of including a default constructor definition in every class you define.

Default Constructor

A constructor with no parameters is called the **default constructor.** Most of the classes you define should include a default constructor.

? Self-Test Questions

30. If a class is named `Student`, what name can you use for a constructor for this class?

31. When defining a constructor, what do you specify for the type of the value returned? A primitive type? A class type? *void*?

32. What is a default constructor?

33. Does every class in Java automatically have a default constructor? If not, when is a default constructor provided automatically by Java and when is it not provided?

5.6 | Information Hiding Revisited

The material in this section is not needed to understand most of the rest of this book, but it is very important material. You can safely postpone reading this material until you are more comfortable with classes, but do not postpone reading it indefinitely! When you start to write more complicated class definitions, you will need the material in this section in order to avoid certain kinds of subtle problems.

■ Gotcha
Privacy Leaks

A class can have instance variables of any type, including any class type. This can sometimes be a natural and handy thing to do. However, using instance variables of a class type takes special care, and we do not have the tools to handle them in the correct way. In this Gotcha section, we explain the problem and the general approach to the solution, but the full details of the solution are beyond the scope of this book. Some of the details are covered briefly in Appendix 9. After you become comfortable with using classes in simple cases, you may wish to read Appendix 9. If you do not wish to read this Gotcha section now but still want to avoid the problem, just note that the problem discussed here does not apply to any class you define provided that the class only has instance variables that are each either of a primitive type (such as *int*, *double*, *char*, and *boolean*) or of the type String. So, you can define lots of classes without being concerned with this problem.

The problem results from the fact that variables of a class type contain the memory address of where an object is stored in memory. For example, suppose goodGuy and badGuy are both variables of type PetRecord, a class we defined in Display 5.19/page 351. Now, suppose goodGuy names some object, and your program executes the following assignment statement:

```
badGuy = goodGuy;
```

After this assignment statement is executed, badGuy and goodGuy are two names for the same object. So, if you change badGuy, you will also change goodGuy. (There must be a moral lesson there someplace.) Let's give this assignment statement a bit more context to see the implications of this:

```
PetRecord goodGuy = new PetRecord();
goodGuy.set("Faithful Guard Dog", 5, 75);
PetRecord badGuy;
badGuy = goodGuy;
badGuy.set("Dominion Spy", 1200, 500);
goodGuy.writeOutput();
```

Because badGuy and goodGuy name the same object, this code will produce the following output:

Display 5.22   An Insecure Class

```
/*****************************************
*Example of a class that does NOT correctly
*hide its private instance variable.
*****************************************/
public class CadetClass
{
    private PetRecord pet;

    public CadetClass()
    {
        pet =
            new PetRecord("Faithful Guard Dog", 5, 75);
    }

    public void writeOutput()
    {
        System.out.println("Here's the pet:");
        pet.writeOutput();
    }

    public PetRecord getPet()
    {
        return pet;
    }
}
```

A realistic class would have more methods, but these are all we need for our demonstration.

```
Name: Dominion Spy
Age: 1200 years
Weight 500.0 pounds
```

The same thing can happen with instance variables and can cause some subtle problems. Let's look at an example.

Display 5.22 contains the definition of a class called CadetClass, which was written by a cadet programmer as a homework exercise. It does not have very many methods, but that is not the problem. (This is, after all, just an exercise.) The problem is that our cadet programmer mistakenly thinks that the data named by the instance variable pet cannot be changed by any program using the class PetRecord. This is an easy mistake for a cadet programmer to make. After all, our cadet made the instance variable pet private so it cannot be accessed by name. And just to be super safe, the cadet did not include any accessor methods that change the private instance variable pet. Our cadet will let anybody see the value of the object pet by using the public accessor method getPet, but our naive cadet thinks that no programmer can change the "Faithful Guard Dog". Our cadet is in for a rude awakening.

Look at the program in Display 5.23. That program has changed the values of the instance variables in the object named by the private instance variable pet! How could that be? The problem is that a variable of a class type stores a memory address, and as we saw at the beginning of this section, this means you can use the assignment operator to produce two names for the same object. That is what our hacker programmer who wrote the program in Display 5.23 did. Our hacker programmer had the accessor method getPet return "the value" of the private instance variable pet. But, that value was a memory address that was stored in the variable badGuy. So, badGuy is another name for pet. Our hacker cannot use the private name pet, but our hacker can use the equivalent name badGuy. All that our hacker needs to do is to use the name badGuy to invoke the method set of the class PetRecord, and because badGuy is another name for the object named by pet, our hacker has changed the object named by the private instance variable pet.

How can you write your class definitions to avoid this problem? It seems like it is impossible to have a private instance variable of a class type that is truly secure. A hacker can always get at it some other way, or so it seems. There are at least two ways around this problem: an easy way and a harder but better way.

The easy way around this problem is to only use instance variables of a primitive type or of the type String. The type String has no accessor methods that can change the String object's data, and so our hacker's trick will not work on them. Primitive types are not class types, and so the hacker's trick will not work on them either. This easy solution is the one we will take in this book. (You can also have private instance variables of class types other than String, provided these class types do not have methods that can change an object. However, the only class of this kind that we will encounter is the class String.)

clone

The harder solution is the better solution, but it is beyond the scope of this book, although we can give you a hint of it. There are methods that can produce an exact copy of an object. These exact copies are called **clones**. The harder solution is to never return an object named by a private instance variable of a class type that could be insecure, but to instead return a clone of the object. That way the hacker could do whatever she/he wanted with the clone and the private data would not be affected. There is a brief introduction to cloning in Appendix 9. After you become comfortable with classes, you may wish to look at that appendix.

Do not get the impression that instance variables of a class type are a bad idea. They are very natural and very useful. However, it does require more skill and care to deal with them effectively. Think of them the way you think of brain surgery: if you need it, it is very very good, but don't try it unless you know what you are doing.

? Self-Test Questions

34. Give the definition of three accessor methods that you can use in the definition of the class CadetClass (Display 5.22/page 361) instead of the sin-

Display 5.23 Changing Private Data in a Poorly Defined Class

```
/*********************************************************
 *Toy program to demonstrate how a programmer can access
 *and change private data in an object of the class CadetClass.
 *********************************************************/
public class Hacker
{
    public static void main(String[] args)
    {
        CadetClass starFleetOfficer = new CadetClass();
        System.out.println("starFleetOfficer contains:");
        starFleetOfficer.writeOutput();
        PetRecord badGuy;
        badGuy = starFleetOfficer.getPet();
        badGuy.set("Dominion Spy", 1200, 500);
        System.out.println("Looks like a security breach:");
        System.out.println("starFleetOfficer now contains:");
        starFleetOfficer.writeOutput();
        System.out.println("The pet wasn't so private!");
    }
}
```

Screen Output

```
starFleetOfficer contains:
Here's the pet:
Name: Faithful Guard Dog
Age: 5 years
Weight: 75.0 pounds
Looks like a security breach:
starFleetOfficer now contains:
Here's the pet:
Name: Dominion Spy
Age: 1200 years
Weight: 500.0 pounds
The pet wasn't so private!
```

This program has changed an object named by a private instance variable of the object starFleetOfficer.

gle access method `getPet`. These new accessor methods will not produce the problem described in the section *Gotcha* **Privacy Leaks**. These three methods will return all the data in an object of the class `CadetClass`, but will not return any object with accessor methods that can change anything. One method will return the pet's name, one will return the pet's age, and one will return the pet's weight.In the previous section, we gave two ways to avoid the problem in the Gotcha section. This question suggests a third way to avoid the problem.

5.7 | Packages

> *From mine own library with volumes that*
> *I prize above my dukedom.*
>
> **William Shakespeare, The Tempest**

Packages are a way of grouping and naming a collection of related classes so that they can serve as a library of classes that you can use in any program without having to place all those classes in the same directory as your program. Although this is an important and useful topic, it is nevertheless true that the rest of the material in this book does not use the material on packages presented here. So, you may cover this section at any time during your reading of this book.

In order to understand this material, you need to know about directories (which are called *folders* in some operating systems), you need to know about path names for directories (folders), and you need to know how your operating system uses a `PATH` variable. If you do not know about directories (folders), path names, or `PATH` variables, you may wish to skip this section until you have had some experience with these topics. Directories (folders), path names, and `PATH` variables are not Java topics. They are part of your operating system and the details depend on your particular operating system.

We will describe one typical way of using packages. There are other ways to set up the details of using packages, but that is beyond the scope of this book.

Packages and Importing

package

A **package** is nothing other than a collection of classes that have been grouped together and given a package name. The classes in the package are each placed in a separate file, and the file is named the same as the class, just as we have been doing all along. The only difference is that each file has the following as the *first line* in the file:

```
package Package_Name;
```

The *Package_Name* typically consists of all lowercase letters often punctuated with the dot symbol. For example, if you name the package `mystuff.utilities`, then each of the files in the package would have the following as its first line:

```
package mystuff.utilities;
```

The classes in the package are stored in a directory (folder[1]), and the package is named in a way we will describe shortly. Any program or class definition can then use all the classes in the package by placing a suitable *import* statement at the start of the file containing the program or class definition, and this is true even if the program or class definition is not in the same directory as the classes in the package. For example, if you want to use the classes in the package `mystuff.utilities`, you would place the following at the start of the file you are writing:

> *import* `mystuff.utilities.*;`

import

This use of packages allows you to define libraries (packages) of classes that you frequently use and store them away in a single directory. After that, you can use the classes in the package in any program or class you write no matter what directory the program or class is in. In effect, this lets you add classes to the Java language and so customize Java to your needs. Packages should, of course, consist of groups of related classes so that you can easily keep track of which classes are in which packages.

Package

A **package** is a collection of classes that have been grouped together and given a package name. The classes in the package are each placed in a separate file and the file is named the same as the class, just as we have been doing all along. The only difference is that each file has the following as the first line in the file:

Syntax:

> *package* *Package_Name*;

Examples:

> *package* `mystuff.utilities;`
> *package* `java.io;`

Package Names and Directories

A package name is not an arbitrary identifier. A package name tells the compiler where to find the classes in the package. In effect, the package name tells the compiler the path name for the directory containing the classes in the package. For example, suppose your classes were in the directory

directory

> `\myjavastuff\lib\math\stat`

then, provided your system is set up correctly for this, the package name can be

> `myjavastuff.lib.math.stat`

(Your operating system may use / instead of \, but it means the same thing.) A package name must be a path name for the directory that contains the classes in the pack-

---

1. Some operating systems used the word *folder* to mean the same thing as *directory*. We will use the word *directory*. If your operating system has things called *folders*, they are the same things as directories. Just read *folder* wherever you see *directory*.

---

import **Statement**

You can use all the classes in a package in any program or class definition by placing an *import* statement that names the package at the start of the file containing the program or class definition. The program or class need not be in the same directory as the classes in the package.

Syntax:

> *import* *Package_Name*;

Examples:

> *import* mystuff.utilities.*;
> *import* java.io.*;

The dot and the ∗ at the end mean that you are importing all the classes in this package. You can also import just a single class from a package by using the class name in place of the ∗, but that is seldom done.

Package Names

A package name must be a path name for the directory that contains the classes in the package, but the package name uses dots in place of \ or / (whichever one of \ or / that your operating system uses). When naming the package, you use a relative path name that starts from any directory named in the setting of the CLASSPATH environment variable.

Examples:

> mystuff.utilities
> java.io

---

age, but the package name uses dots in place of \ or / (whichever one of \ or / that your operating system uses) and a package name has no dot at the start of the name.

The path name for a package need not be a full path name, and almost never is a full path name. In fact, you may not even be able to get a full path name to work unless your system is set up for that.[1] However, you can use a relative path name that starts from any directory named in the setting of the CLASSPATH environment variable. The CLASSPATH environment variable is used just like the PATH environment variable, but it is used to locate classes in packages. For example, if the directory \myjavastuff\lib is named in your CLASSPATH variable setting, then you can use the simpler name math.stat as the package name instead of myjavastuff.lib.math.stat.

To find the directories in your CLASSPATH, look for some initializing file that includes something like *one* of the following lines:

```
CLASSPATH=c:\jdk\lib;c:\somename
SET CLASSPATH=c:\jdk\lib;c:\somename
CLASSPATH /usr/jdk/lib:/usr/somename
```

or

---

1. In order to use a full path name, the root directory must be listed in the setting of your CLASSPATH variable.

```
setenv CLASSPATH /usr/jdk/lib:/usr/somename
```

You are likely to find this in the same file that has your PATH variable setting. The exact things listed and the punctuation will depend on your particular operating system, but you should find the name CLASSPATH followed by a list of directories. These directories are the ones in your CLASSPATH. You can place a package in a subdirectory of any of these directories and name the package using a relative path name that starts at a directory in your CLASSPATH settings. You can also add a directory to the class path so that all (or some of) your packages are subdirectories of some directory that you set up.

? Self-Test Questions

35. Suppose you want to use classes in the package mypackages.library1 in a program you write. What do you need to put near the start of the file containing your program?

36. Suppose you want to make a class a member of the package named mypackages.library1. What do you need to put in the file containing the class definition? Where does this statement go in the file?

37. Can a package have any name you might want, or are there restrictions on what you can use for a class name? Explain any restrictions.

38. On your system, place the class SavitchIn into a package so that in any Java program, you can use the class SavitchIn by including a suitable import statement and need not move the class SavitchIn to the same directory (folder) as your program.

5.8 | Inner Classes *(Optional)*

Inner classes are classes defined within other classes. A full description of inner classes is beyond the scope of this book. However, some simple uses of inner classes can be both easy and helpful. In this section we will confine ourselves to one simple example of an inner class. In Chapter 12 we present other more realistic examples of the use of inner classes.

The ImprovedCadet class in Display 5.24/page 368 is an example of a class with an inner class inside of it. The class is similar to the class Cadet given in Display 5.22/page 361. That class Cadet was shown to be flawed by the program in Display 5.23/page 363. The Cadet class definition in Display 5.24 has a private instance variable of type PetRecord, but that private instance variable can be accessed outside of the class. The class in Display 5.24 avoids this problem by having the PetRecord class defined as an private inner class within the definition of the ImprovedCadet class. This way it does not even make sense to return an object of type PetRecord to the outside world, because the class definition PetRecord is not known outside of the class ImprovedCadet. Because the definition of the class PetRecord is a private definition inside of the class ImprovedCadet, the class PetRecord is local to the class ImprovedCadet. The program in Display 5.25/page 371 shows that

Display 5.24 An Inner Class *(Optional) (Part 1 of 2)*

```
/********************************************
 *Example of a class with a private inner class.
 *********************************************/
public class ImprovedCadet
{
    private String name;
    private PetRecord pet;
```

An inner class

```
    /************************************************
     *Class for basic pet records: name, age, and weight.
     *************************************************/
    private class PetRecord
    {
        private String name;
        private int age;//in years
        private double weight;//in pounds

        public PetRecord(String initialName, int initialAge,
                                        double initialWeight)
        {
            name = initialName;
            age = initialAge;
            weight = initialWeight;
        }

        public void writeOutput()
        {
            System.out.println("Name: " + name);
            System.out.println("Age: " + age);
            System.out.println("Weight: " + weight);
        }
    }


    public ImprovedCadet(String initialName)
    {
        name = initialName;
        pet =
            new PetRecord("Faithful Guard Dog", 5, 75);
    }
```

Display 5.24   An Inner Class *(Optional) (Part 2 of 2)*

```java
public void writeOutput()
{
    System.out.println("Cadet " + name);
    System.out.println("Here's the pet:");
    pet.writeOutput();
}

public String getPetName()
{
    return pet.name ;
}

public int getPetAge()
{
    return pet.age ;
}

public double getPetWeight()
{
    return pet.weight ;
}
}
```

Note that the outer class has direct access to the private instance variables of the inner class.

It would be legal include a method getPet *as in Display 5.22/page 361, but it would be of little or no use outside of the definition of the class* ImprovedCadet.

although the world outside of ImprovedCadet does not know about the class PetRecord, it can still know about the data kept in objects of the class PetRecord. (We are assuming there is not a definition of PetRecord outside of the definition of the ImprovedCadet class. This would be legal, but it would be a different PetRecord class and we do not wish to get into those subtleties now.)

CHAPTER SUMMARY

- A method definition can include a call to another method of the same class.

- If a method definition is labeled *static*, then that method can be invoked using the class name, rather than an object name. (It can also be invoked using an object name.)

CHAPTER SUMMARY

■ A **static variable** is a variable that is declared using the reserved word *static*. For each static variable name, there is only one variable of that name that is shared by all the objects of the class.

■ The top-down design method helps you to write method definitions by breaking the task to be accomplished by the method into subtasks.

■ Every method should be tested in a program in which it is the only untested method.

■ Each primitive type has a wrapper class that serves as a class version of that primitive type.

■ A method name can have two different definitions within the same class, provided the two definitions have different numbers of parameters or some parameters of differing types. This is called **overloading** the method name.

■ A constructor is a class method that is called when you create an object of the class using *new*. A constructor must have the same name as the class.

■ A constructor with no parameters is called a **default constructor**. Class definitions typically include a default constructor.

■ You can form a package of class definitions you use frequently. You can then use the classes in any program without needing to move them to the same directory (folder) as the program.

? ANSWERS to Self-Test Questions

1. Yes. See Display 5.1/page 298 for an example.

2. No effect at all. The following two lines are equivalent in this context:

   ```
   seekAdvice();
   ```

   and

   ```
   this.seekAdvice();
   ```

3. This will produce a "Null Pointer Exception" error message. The variables s1 and s2 do not name any objects. The lines

Display 5.25 Inner Class Demonstration *(Optional)*

```
/************************************
 *Program to demonstrate use of the class
 *ImprovedCadet, which has an inner class.
 ************************************/
public class InnerDemo
{
    public static void main(String[] args)
    {
        ImprovedCadet starFleetOfficer =
                    new ImprovedCadet("Wesley Crusher");
        System.out.println("starFleetOfficer contains:");
        starFleetOfficer.writeOutput();
    }
}
```

Screen Output

```
starFleetOfficer contains:
Cadet Wesley Crusher
Here's the pet:
Name: Faithful Guard Dog
Age: 5 years
Weight: 75.0 pounds
```

```
Species s1 = null;
Species s2 = null;
```

should be changed to

```
Species s1 = new Species();
Species s2 = new Species();
```

4. It is legal, but a more normal way of doing the same thing is

```
double areaOfCircle = CircleFirstTry.area(2.5);
```

5. Yes, you can have all these kinds of things together in one class.

6. You cannot invoke a nonstatic method within the definition of a static method, unless you create an object of the class and use that object as the calling object of the nonstatic method

7. Yes, you can invoke a static method within the definition of a nonstatic method. This requires nothing special.

8. No, you cannot reference an instance variable within the definition of a static method, because a static method can be invoked with no calling object, and if there is no calling object, there are no instance variables.

9. Yes it is legal, although it is not the normal way of invoking the method `readLineInt`. A more normal way of invoking `readLineInt` is:

```
int n = SavitchIn.readLineInt()
```

10. No, the following is illegal, because `setDiameter` is not a static method:

```
PlayCircle.setDiameter(newDiameter);
```

11. An *instance variable* is declared in a class *without* using the reserved word `static`. A *static variable* is declared in a class definition using the reserved word `static`. Every object of the class has its own *instance variables*. There is only one of each *static variable* for a class, and all objects share that static variable.

12. Yes, you can reference (by name) a *static variable* (without anything like a class name and dot) in the definition of a *static method*. An example is the static variable `numberOfInvocations` in the method `justADemoMethod` in Display 5.8/page 315. (There are also more examples in that class definition.) No you cannot reference (by name) an *instance variable* (without anything like an object name and dot) in the definition of a *static method*. This is because a static method can be used with the class name rather than a calling object, and with no calling object, there are no instance variables.

13. Yes, you can reference (by name) a *static variable* (without anything like a class name and dot) in the definition of a *nonstatic method*. Yes, you can reference (by name) an *instance variable* (without anything like an object name and dot) in the definition of a *nonstatic method*. Note that this means you can reference both kinds of variables in a nonstatic method.

14. 2, 3, 2.0, 2.0, 3.0, 3.0. Note that the first two values are of type `long`, while the last four values are of type `double`.

15. `approxSpeed = (int)Math.round(speed);`

16.
```
Integer n = new Integer(77); //Legal
int m = 77; //Legal
n = m; //Illegal, should be:
n = new Integer(m);
m = n;//Illegal, should be
m = n.intValue();
```

17. `Double.toString(x)`

18. `Integer.parseInt(s)`

19. If the string might contain leading or trailing blanks, you should use `Integer.parseInt(s.trim())`. In fact, it is always safest to use this version. You never know when leading or trailing blanks might appear.

20.
```
System.out.println("Largest double is " + Double.MAX_VALUE);
System.out.println("Smallest double is " + Double.MIN_VALUE);
```

21. The class `OutputFormat` is in the file `OutputFormat.java` included with the software on the CD that goes with this text and is given in what follows:

```
public class OutputFormat
{
    /*******************************************************
     *Writes out number with digitsAfterPoint digits after
     *the decimal point. Round any extra digits.
     *Does not advance to the next line after output.
     *******************************************************/
    private static void write(double number,
                                   int digitsAfterPoint)
    {
        if (number >= 0)
            writePositive(number, digitsAfterPoint);
        else
        {
            double positiveNumber = -number;
            System.out.print('-');
            writePositive(positiveNumber, digitsAfterPoint);
        }
    }

    //Precondition: number >= 0
    //Writes out number with digitsAfterPoint digits after the
    //decimal point. Rounds any extra digits.
    private static void writePositive(double number,
                                          int digitsAfterPoint)
    {
        int mover = (int)(Math.pow(10, digitsAfterPoint));
                   //1 followed by digitsAfterPoint zeros
        int allWhole;//number with the decimal point
                     //moved digitsAfterPoint places
        allWhole = (int)(Math.round(number*mover));
        int beforePoint = allWhole/mover;
        int afterPoint = allWhole%mover;

        System.out.print(beforePoint);
        System.out.print('.');
        writeFraction(afterPoint, digitsAfterPoint);
    }
```

```java
//Outputs the integer afterPoint with enough 0s
//in front to make it digitsAfterPoint digits long.
private static void writeFraction(int afterPoint,
                                      int digitsAfterPoint)
{
    int n = 1;
    while (n < digitsAfterPoint)
    {
        if (afterPoint < Math.pow(10, n))
            System.out.print('0');
        n = n + 1;
    }
    System.out.print(afterPoint);
}



/*************************************************
 *Writes out number with digitsAfterPoint digits after
 *the decimal point. Rounds any extra digits.
 *Advances to the next line after output.
 *************************************************/
public static void writeln(double number,
                                int digitsAfterPoint)
{
    write(number, digitsAfterPoint);
    System.out.println();
}
}
```

22. Yes, you could use the names `print` and `println`, rather than `write` and `writeln`, in the class `OutputFormat`. This would produce no name confusion with `System.out.println`, because when you invoke the method in `OutputFormat`, you specify the class name before the dot. (If you invoke the method with an object, instead of the class name, Java still knows the class name because it knows the type of the object.) However, the methods in `OutputFormat` behave a little differently from the method `System.out.println`, so it seems that a different name would be clearer.

23. Use variables of type `long`, rather than variables of type `int`. Note that, because the method `Math.round` returns a value of type `long` in the method `writePositive`, this will even save a type cast. For example,

    `int allCents = (int)(Math.round(amount*100));`

    would become

    `long allCents = (Math.round(amount*100));`

    The variables `dollars` and `cents` should also be changed to type `long`.

24. Yes, the `7` would be converted to `7.0` by Java, so that the types match the heading of one of the definitions of `set`.

25. No, you cannot overload a method name on the basis of the type returned.

26. Yes, they differ in the type of their parameter, so this is a legal overloading of the method name `convertValue`. (Note that the fact that they return values of different types does not affect whether or not both definitions can be used. It is only the types of the parameters that count in making overloading legal.)

27. Yes, it would be legal because no other method named `set` has the same number and types of parameters. The definition follows:

```
public void set(String newName)
{
    name = newName;
    population = 0;
    growthRate = 0;
}
```

28. Simply delete all occurrences of `this.` from the definition.

29. Simply add an invocation of the method `trim`. The rewritten version follows:

```
public void set(String amountString)
{
    String dollarsString;
    String centsString;

    amountString = amountString.trim();
```

<The rest of the method definition is the same as in Display 5.17.>

30. If a class is named `Student`, then every constructor for this class must also be named `Student`.

31. You specify no type returned for a constructor, not even *void*.

32. A default constructor is a constructor with no parameters.

33. No. Here are the details: If you give no constructor definition for a class, then Java will automatically provide a default constructor. If you provide one or more constructors of any sort, then Java does not provide any constructors beyond what you define. So, if you define one or more constructors and none of them is a default constructor, then the class has no default constructor.

34.

```
public String getPetName()
{
    return pet.getName();
}
```

```
public int getPetAge()
{
    return pet.getAge();
}

public double getPetWeight()
{
    return pet.getWeight();
}
```

35. `import mypackages.library1.*;`

36. You must make the following the first line in the file:

    `package mypackages.library1;`

37. A package name must be a path name for the directory that contains the classes in the package, but the package name uses dots in place of \ or / (whichever one of \ or / that your operating system uses). When naming the package, you use a relative path name that starts from any directory named in the setting of the CLASSPATH environment variable.

38. The way to do this depends a little on your operating system and on your personal preferences. Here is an outline of what you should do: Choose a package name and insert the following at the start of the file SavitchIn.java:

    `package Whatever_Package_Name_You_Choose;`

    Then, compile the modified file SavitchIn.java and move both of the files SavitchIn.java and SavitchIn.class to the directory corresponding to *Whatever_Package_Name_You_Choose*. (You really need only move the SavitchIn.class file but it will help you keep track of things to keep the SavitchIn.java and SavitchIn.class files together.)

? PROGRAMMING EXERCISES

1. Define a utility class for outputting values of type *double*. Call the class DoubleOut. Include all the methods from the class Dollars in Display 5.14/page 330, all the methods from the class OutputFormat of Self-Test Question 21/page 332 (answer on page 373), and a method called scienceWrite that outputs a value of type *double* in the e notation, such as 2.13e−12. (This e notation is also called *scientific notation*, which explains the method name.) When output in e notation, the number should always show exactly one (nonzero) digit before the decimal point (unless the number is exactly zero). The method scienceWrite will not advance to the next line. Also add a method called scienceWriteln that is the same as scienceWrite except that all future output goes on the next line. All but the last two method definitions can be simply copied from the text (or more easily from the files in the software that comes with this text). Note

that you will be overloading the method names write and writeln. Write a driver program to test your method scienceWriteln. This driver program should use a stub for the method scienceWrite. (Note that this means you can write and test scienceWriteln before you even write scienceWrite.) Then, write a driver program for the method science-Write. Then, write a program that is a sort of super driver program that takes a *double* value as input and then outputs it using the two writeln methods and the scienceWriteln method. Use the number 5 for the number of digits after the decimal point when you need to specify such a number. This super driver program should allow the user to repeat this testing with additional *double* numbers until the user is ready to end the program.

2. Modify the definition of the class Species in Display 4.19/page 276 by removing the method set and adding the following methods: (1) five constructors, one for each instance variable, one with three parameters for the three instance variables, and a default constructor; (2) four methods named set, which can reset values; one is the same as the method set in Display 4.19/page 276; the other three each reset one of the instance variables. Be sure that each constructor sets all of the instance variables. Then, write a test program to test all the methods you have added. Then, redo (or do for the first time) Programming Exercise 1/page 292 from Chapter 4. Be sure to use some constructor other than the default constructor when you define new objects in the class Species.

3. Redo (or do for the first time) Programming Exercise 3/page 293 of Chapter 4. This time, be sure your class definition contains suitable constructors and reset methods. Use at least one of the methods from the class OutputFormat of Self-Test Exercise 21/page 332.

4. Redo (or do for the first time) Exercise 4/page 293 of Chapter 4. This time, in addition to the reset and "test" methods (for the same name, same age, older, or younger), add the following four constructor methods: one for each instance variable, one with two parameters for the two instance variables, and a default constructor. Be sure that each constructor sets all of the instance variables. Write a test program to test each of the methods, including each of the four constructors, and at least one true and one false case for each of the test methods.

5. Write a new class TruncatedDollars that is the same as the class Dollars from Display 5.14/page 330, except that it truncates rather than rounding to obtain two digits after the decimal point. (When truncating all digits after the first two are discarded, so 1.229 becomes 1.22, not 1.23.) Use this class to redo (or do for the first time) Programming Exercise 3/page 175.

6. Write a program to read in data for five pets (use the PetRecord class from Display 5.19/page 351) and display the following data: name of smallest pet, name of largest pet, name of oldest pet, name of youngest pet, average weight of the five pets, and average age of the five pets.

7. Write a `Temperature` class that has two parameters, a temperature value (a floating point number) and type, either `'C'` for Celsius or `'F'` for Fahrenheit, and the following four constructor methods, one for each instance variable (assume 0 degrees if no value is specified and Celsius if no type is specified), one with two parameters for the two instance variables, and a default constructor (set to 0 degrees C). Include (1) two accessor methods to read the temperature (one to read the degrees C, the other to read the degrees F—use the formulas from Programming Exercise 2/page 205 to write two methods and round to the nearest tenth of a degree); (2) three reset methods (one to set the value, one to set the type, and to set both); (3) three comparison methods, one to test if two temperatures are equal, one to test if one temperature is greater than another, and one to test if one temperature is less than another. Then write a driver program that tests all the methods. Be sure to use each of the constructors, include at least one true and one false case for each of the comparison methods, and test at least the following temperature equalities: 0.0 degrees C = 32.0 degrees F, –40.0 degrees C = –40.0 degrees F, and 100.0 degrees C = 212.0 degrees F.

CHAPTER 6

ARRAYS

6.1 ARRAY BASICS 381
Creating and Accessing Arrays 382
Array Details 383

Programming Tip Use Singular Array
Names 386
The `length` Instance Variable 388

Java Tip Array Indexes Start with
Zero 388

Programming Tip Use a *for*-Loop to
Step Through an Array 390

Gotcha Array Index Out of
Bounds 390
Initializing Arrays 391

6.2 ARRAYS IN CLASSES AND METHODS 392
Case Study Sales Report 393
Indexed Variables as Method
Arguments 400
Entire Arrays as Method
Arguments 403
Arguments for The Method `main`
(Optional) 403

Gotcha Use of = and == with
Arrays 405
Methods That Return Arrays 409

6.3 PROGRAMMING WITH ARRAYS AND CLASSES 412
Programming Example A Specialized List
Class 412
Partially Filled Arrays 416
Searching an Array 420

Gotcha Returning an Array Instance
Variable 420

6.4 SORTING ARRAYS 423
Selection Sort 423

Programming Tip Correctness versus
Efficiency 428

6.5 MULTIDIMENSIONAL ARRAYS 429
Multidimensional-Array Basics 430

Gotcha Reversing Two Array
Indexes 434
Multidimensional-Array Parame-
ters and Returned Values 434
Implementation of Multidimen-
sional Arrays 435
Ragged Arrays *(Optional)* 438

Programming Example Employee Time
Records 440

Chapter Summary 447
Answers to Self-Test Questions 448
Programming Exercises 453

6

ARRAYS

An array is a special kind of object used to store a (possibly large) collection of
data. An array differs from the other objects we have seen in two ways:

1. All the data stored in an array must be of the same type. For example,
   you might use an array to store a list of values of type *double* that
   record rainfall readings in centimeters. You might use an array to store
   a list of objects of some class called Species that contain the records for
   various endangered species.

2. The only methods for an array object are a small number of predefined
   methods. Because arrays were used by programmers for many years before
   classes and objects (as we have used them) were invented, arrays use a special notation of their own to invoke those few predefined methods, and
   most people do not even call them methods.

In this chapter, we introduce you to arrays and show you how to use them in Java.

Objectives

Find out what an *array* is and how to use arrays in simple Java programs.

Learn how to use array parameters and how to define methods that return an array.

Learn the proper way to use an array as an instance variable in a class.

Introduce yourself to the topic of sorting an array.

Become familiar with *multidimensional arrays*.

Prerequisites

You can cover Section 6.1 with only the material in Chapters 1 through 3. You should
be familiar with the material in all previous five chapters before reading the rest of
this chapter (Sections 6.2, 6.3, 6.4, and 6.5).

This is the first point in this book where you have a significant choice of what to
read next. You need not read this chapter next. If you prefer, you can instead go on

in the book and return to this chapter at a later time. If you want to delay reading this chapter, you can read as much of Chapters 7, 8, and 9 as you wish before you read this chapter.

6.1 | Array Basics

> *And in such indexes, although small pricks*
> *To their subsequent volumes, there is seen*
> *The baby figure of the giant mass*
> *Of things to come.*
>
> **William Shakespeare, Troilus and Cressida**

Suppose you want to compute the average temperature for the seven days in a week. You might use the following code:

```
int count;
double next, sum, average;
System.out.println("Enter 7 temperatures:");
sum = 0;
for (count = 0; count < 7; count++)
{
    next = SavitchIn.readLineDouble();
    sum = sum + next;
}
average = sum/7;
```

This works fine if all you want to know is the average. But, let's say you also want to know which temperatures are above and which are below the average? Now, you have a problem. In order to compute the average, you must read in the seven temperatures, and you must do this before comparing each temperature to the average. Thus, in order to compare each temperature to the average, you must remember the seven temperatures. How can you do this? The obvious answer is to use seven variables of type *double*. This is a bit awkward, because seven is a lot of variables to declare, and in other situations, the problem can be even worse. Imagine doing the same thing for each day of the year instead of just each day of the week. Declaring 365 variables would be absurd. Arrays provide us with an elegant way to declare a collection of related variables.

An **array** is something like a list of variables, but it handles the naming of the variables in a nice, compact way. Our array for this particular problem of seven temperatures will turn out to be, among other things, an easy way to create seven variables with the names temperature[0], temperature[1], temperature[2], temperature[3], temperature[4], temperature[5], and temperature[6]. As you will see, an array can be viewed as a list of variables, each of which has a two-part name. One part of the name is an identifier, like temperature, and the other part is an integer enclosed in square brackets, like [5]. Because the identifier is the same for each of the variables on the list, this will give us a uniform way to refer to all the variables on the list.

array

Creating and Accessing Arrays

In Java, an array is a special kind of object, but it is often more useful to think of an array as a collection of variables all of the same type. For example, an array to serve as a collection of seven variables of type *double* can be created as follows:

```
double[] temperature = new double[7];
```

This is like declaring the following to be seven variables of type *double*:

```
temperature[0], temperature[1], temperature[2], temperature[3],
temperature[4], temperature[5], temperature[6]
```

Note that the numbering starts with 0, *not* 1. Each of these seven variables can be used just like any other variable of type *double*. For example, all of the following are allowed in Java:

```
temperature[3] = 32;
temperature[6] = temperature[3] + 5;
System.out.println(temperature[6]);
```

But, these seven variables are more than just seven plain old variables of type *double*. That number in square brackets allows you to actually compute the name of one of these variables. You need not write an integer constant in the square brackets. You can use any expression that evaluates to an integer that is at least 0 and at most 6. So, the following is allowed:

```
System.out.println("Enter day number (0-6):");
int index = SavitchIn.readLineInt();
System.out.println("Enter temperature for day " + index);
temperature[index] = SavitchIn.readLineDouble();
```

indexed variable

index

These variables with an integer expression in square brackets are referred to various ways. We will call them **indexed variables,** or **elements.** Some people call them **subscripted variables.** So, temperature[0], temperature[1], and so forth are indexed variables. The integer expression within the square brackets is called an **index** (or **subscript**). When we think of these indexed variables grouped together into one collective item, we will call them *an array*. So, we can refer to the *array* named temperature (without using any square brackets). As you will see, there are two different ways to view an array, like temperature:

1. You can view it as a collection of individual indexed variables like temperature[0], temperature[1], and so forth.

2. Alternatively, you can view it as one large composite object that has a number of different values all of the same type. In the case of our example array temperature, you can think of it as one object with seven values all of type *double*.

When programming with arrays, you need to be able to go back and forth between these two ways of viewing an array. We will discuss the first view now and will get to the second view later in the chapter when we discuss array parameters.

The program in Display 6.1 shows an example of using our sample array `temperature` as seven indexed variables all of type *double*.

Note that the program can compute the name of an indexed variable by using a variable as the index, as in the following *for*-loop:

```
for (index = 0; index < 7; index++)
{
    temperature[index] = SavitchIn.readLineDouble();
    sum = sum + temperature[index];
}
```

Array Details

An array is created like an object of a class type is created, but there are some small differences in the notation used. When creating an array of elements of type *Base_Type*, the syntax is as follows:

> *Base_Type*[ ] *Array_Name* = *new Base_Type*[*Length*];

For example, the following creates an array named `pressure` that is equivalent to 100 variables of type *int*:

```
int[] pressure = new int[100];
```

As you might guess, the preceding can be broken down into a two-step process:

```
int[] pressure;
pressure = new int[100];
```

The type for the elements, in this example *int*, is called the **base type** of the array. The number of elements in an array is called the **length** or the **size** of the array. So, this sample array `pressure` has length 100, which means it has indexed variables `pressure[0]` through `pressure[99]`. Note that because the indexes start at 0, an array of length 100, like `pressure`, will have *no* indexed variable `pressure[100]`.

The base type of an array can be any type. In particular it can be a class type. The following will create an array named `entry` that is equivalent to a collection of the three variables `entry[0]`, `entry[1]`, `entry[2]`, all of type Species (where Species is some class):

```
Species[] entry = new Species[3];
```

Do not confuse the three ways to use the square brackets [ ] with an array name. First, the square brackets can be used to create a type name, as in

```
int[] pressure;
```

Second, the square brackets can be used with an integer value as part of the special syntax Java uses to create a new array, as in

```
pressure = new int[100];
```

The third use of square brackets is to name an element (also called an indexed variable) of the array, such as `pressure[0]` or `pressure[3]`, as illustrated by the following two lines:

Margin notes: base type · length of an array · square brackets [ ]

Display 6.1   An Array Used in a Program *(Part 1 of 2)*

```java
public class ArrayOfTemperatures
{
    /*************************************************
    *Reads in 7 temperatures and shows which are above and
    *which are below the average of the 7 temperatures.
    *************************************************/
    public static void main(String[] args)
    {
        double[] temperature = new double[7];

        int index;
        double sum, average;
        System.out.println("Enter 7 temperatures:");
        sum = 0;
        for (index = 0; index < 7; index++)
        {
            temperature[index] = SavitchIn.readLineDouble();
            sum = sum + temperature[index];
        }
        average = sum/7;

        System.out.println("The average temperature is " + average);
        System.out.println("The temperatures are");
        for (index = 0; index < 7; index++)
        {
            if (temperature[index] < average)
                System.out.println(
                            temperature[index] + " below average.");
            else if (temperature[index] > average)
                System.out.println(
                            temperature[index] + " above average.");
            else //temperature[index] == average
                System.out.println(
                            temperature[index] + " the average.");
        }
        System.out.println("Have a nice week.");
    }
}
```

Display 6.1 **An Array Used in a Program** *(Part 2 of 2)*

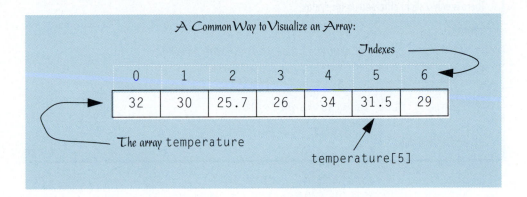

A *Common Way to Visualize an Array:*

Indexes

0	1	2	3	4	5	6
32	30	25.7	26	34	31.5	29

The array temperature

temperature[5]

Sample Screen Dialogue

```
Enter 7 temperatures:
32
30
25.7
26
34
31.5
29
The average temperature is 29.7428
The temperatures are
32.0 above average
30.0 above average
25.7 below average
26.0 below average
34.0 above average
31.5 above average
29.0 below average
Have a nice week.
```

Declaring and Creating an Array

You declare an array name and create an array in almost the same way that you create and name objects of classes. There is only a slight difference in the syntax.

Syntax:

Base_Type[ ] *Array_Name* = new *Base_Type*[*Length*];

Examples:

```
char[] symbol = new char[80];
double[] reading = new double[100];
Species[] specimen = new Species[80];
```

`Species` **is a class.**

```
pressure[3] = SavitchIn.readLineInt();
System.out.println("You entered " + pressure[3]);
```

The integer inside the square brackets does not have to be an integer constant, such as 100 or 3. It can be any expression that evaluates to an integer. For example, you can read in the length of an array from the keyboard, as follows:

reading an array length

```
System.out.println("How many temperatures will there be?");
int size = SavitchIn.readLineInt();
double[] temperature = new double[size];
```

A similar remark applies to the integer inside the square brackets in other situations. The integer can be given as any expression that evaluates to an appropriate integer, as in the following examples:

```
int point = 2;
temperature[point + 3] = 32;
System.out.println(
          "Temperature 5 is " + temperature[point + 3]);
```

Note that, in the preceding code, `temperature[point + 3]` and `tempera-ture[5]` are the same indexed variable, because `point + 3` evaluates to 5. The identity of an indexed variable, such as `temperature[point + 3]`, is determined by the value of its index expression, not by what the index expression looks like.

Display 6.2 illustrates some of most common terms used when referring to arrays. Notice that the word **element** has two meanings. An indexed variable is *element* sometimes called an element. The value of an indexed variable is also sometimes called an *element*.

■ Programming Tip
Use Singular Array Names

If you want an array to hold entries where each entry is an object of a class called `Species`, you might be tempted to use something like the following:

```
Species[] entries = new Species[20];//Legal but not nice.
```

Display 6.2 *Array Terminology*

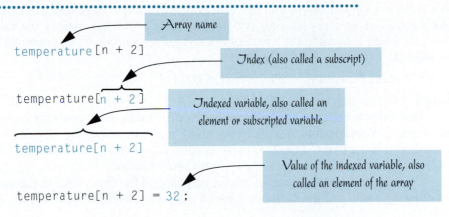

Using a plural, like `entries`, seems to make sense since the array holds more than one element. However, programmers find that it often makes their programs read nicer if they use a singular form, like the following:

```
Species[] entry = new Species[20];//Nicer.
```

The reason that the singular form works better here is that, when the array name is used in some sort of computation, the name refers to only one element. The expression `entry[2]` is a single element of the array, as in a statement such as

```
System.out.println("The second entry is " + entry[2]);
```

If you had used the plural name `entries`, this would not read as well. It would be one of the following, both of which are awkward:

```
System.out.println("The second entries is " + entries[2]);//ugly
```

or

```
System.out.println("The second entry is " + entries[2]);//ugly
```

The use of singular names for arrays is not an absolute rule. Sometimes it makes sense to use plural names. For example, if an array indexed variable contains the number of hours worked by employee number `n`, then the plural form `hours[n]` makes sense. The only sure test of whether to use a singular or plural name is to consider how an indexed variable would read in the context of your Java code.

The `length` Instance Variable

An array is a kind of object, and like other objects, it might have instance variables. As it turns out, an array has only one public instance variable, namely, the variable `length`, which is equal to the length of the array. For example, if you create an array as follows:

```
Species[] entry = new Species[20];
```

then `entry.length` has a value of 20.

The `length` instance variable can be used to make your program clearer by replacing a constant, like `20`, whose meaning may not always be obvious, with a meaningful name like `entry.length`. In Display 6.3 we have rewritten the program in Display 6.1/page 384 using the `length` instance variable.

The `length` instance variable cannot be changed by your program (other than by creating a new array with another use of *new*). For example, the following is illegal:

```
entry.length = 10;//Illegal!
```

■ *Java Tip*
Array Indexes Start with Zero

In Java, the indexes of an array always start with 0. They never start with 1 or any number other than 0. This means that the last index number is not the length of the array, but one less than the length of the array.

In a situation in which you normally think in terms of some other numbering scheme, you might need to adjust your code to reconcile the array indexes with the intuitive numbering. For example, you might want to think of the data stored in the array as being numbered starting with 1. For example, if employees are numbered starting with 1, then you might use code such as the following in a payroll program:

```
int[] hours = new int[100];
System.out.println("Enter hours worked for each employee:");
int index;
for (index = 0; index < hours.length; index++);
{
    System.out.println("Enter hours for employee " + (index + 1));
    hours[index] = SavitchIn.readLineInt();
}
```

With this code, employees are numbered 1 through 100, but their hours worked are stored in elements `hours[0]` through `hours[99]`.

Display 6.3 The `length` **Instance Variable**

```
public class ArrayOfTemperatures2
{
    /*************************************************
     *Reads in 7 temperatures and shows which are above and
     *which are below the average of the 7 temperatures.
     *************************************************/
    public static void main(String[] args)
    {
        double[] temperature = new double[7];

        int index;
        double sum, average;
        System.out.println("Enter " + temperature.length
                                    + " temperatures:");
        sum = 0;
        for (index = 0; index < temperature.length; index++)
        {
            temperature[index] = SavitchIn.readLineDouble();
            sum = sum + temperature[index];
        }
        average = sum/temperature.length;

        System.out.println("The average temperature is " + average);
        System.out.println("The temperatures are");
        for (index = 0; index < temperature.length; index++)
        {
            if (temperature[index] < average)
                System.out.println(
                        temperature[index] + " below average.");
            else if (temperature[index] > average)
                System.out.println(
                        temperature[index] + " above average.");
            else //temperature[index] == average
                System.out.println(
                        temperature[index] + " the average.");
        }
        System.out.println("Have a nice week.");
    }
}
```

The dialogue is the same as in Display 6.1/page 384.

■ Programming Tip
Use a *for*-Loop to Step Through an Array

The *for*-statement is the perfect mechanism for stepping through the elements of an array. For example, the following *for*-loop from Display 6.3 illustrates how you can step through an array:

```
for (index = 0; index < temperature.length; index++)
{
    temperature[index] = SavitchIn.readLineDouble();
    sum = sum + temperature[index];
}
```

■ Gotcha
Array Index Out of Bounds

A very easy mistake to make when programming with arrays is to use an indexed expression that evaluates to an illegal array index. For example, consider the following array declaration:

```
double[] entry = new double[5];
```

Every index for the array `entry` must evaluate to one of the five integers: 0, 1, 2, 3, or 4. For example, if your program contains the indexed variable `entry[n + 2]`, then the n + 2 must evaluate to one of the five integers 0, 1, 2, 3, or 4. If an index expression evaluates to some integer other than 0 through one less than the length of the array, then the index is said to be **out of bounds** or **illegal**. If your program uses an index expression that is out of bounds, then your program (or class) will compile without any error message for the illegal index, but Java will complain when you run your program.

index out of bounds

One common way that array indexes go out of bounds is when an array processing loop is iterated one too many times. This can happen with almost any kind of loop that deals with array indexes, but one very common example of this is a loop that fills an array. For example, when reading in a list of nonnegative numbers from the keyboard with a negative number as a sentinel value at the end, you might use the following:

```
System.out.println("Enter a list of nonnegative integers.");
System.out.println("Place a negative integer at the end.");
int[] a = new int[10];
int number = SavitchIn.readLineInt();
int i = 0;
while (number >= 0)
{
    a[i] = number;
    i++;
    number = SavitchIn.readLineInt();
}
```

If, however, the user enters more numbers than can fit in the array, this will produce an array index that is out of bounds. A better version of the preceding *while*-loop is the following:

```
while ( (i < a.length) && (number >= 0) )
{
    a[i] = number;
    i++;
    number = SavitchIn.readLineInt();
}
if (number >=0)
{
    System.out.println("Could not read in all the numbers.");
    System.out.println("Only read in " + a.length + " numbers.");
}
```

With this *while*-loop, the loop will end when the array is full.

Notice that in the second *while*-loop, we tested to see that the index i is strictly less than a.length. Because indexes start at 0, the last index is *not* a.length, but is one less than a.length. If you use <= instead of <, you may get an array index out-of-bounds error.

Initializing Arrays

An array can be initialized at the time that it is declared. To do this, you enclose the values for the individual indexed variables in curly brackets and place them after the assignment operator, as in the following example:

```
double[] reading = {3.3, 15.8, 9.7};
```

The array length (size) is set to the minimum that will hold the given values. So, this initializing declaration is equivalent to the following statements:

```
double[] reading = new double[3];
reading[0] = 3.3;
reading[1] = 15.8;
reading[2] = 9.7;
```

If you do not initialize the elements of an array, then they will automatically be initialized to a default value for the base type. For example, if you do not initialize an array of integers, then each element of the array will be initialized to 0. However, it is usually clearer to do your own explicit initialization. You can initialize either by using the curly brackets as we just described or by some other method, such as the following *for*-loop.

automatic initialization

```
int[] count = new int[100];
int i;
for (i = 0; i < count.length; i++)
    a[i] = 0;
```

? Self-Test Questions

1. What output will be produced by the following code?

```
int i;
int[] a = new int[10];
for (i = 0; i < a.length; i++)
    a[i] = 2*i;
for (i = 0; i < a.length; i++)
    System.out.print(a[i] + " ");
System.out.println();
```

2. What output will be produced by the following code?

```
char[] vowels = {'a', 'e', 'i', 'o', 'u'};
int index;
for (index = 0; index < vowels.length; index++)
    System.out.println(vowels[index]);
```

3. What is the output produced by the following code?

```
double tide[] = {12.2, -7.3, 14.2, 11.3};
System.out.println("Tide 1 is " + tide[1]);
System.out.println("Tide 2 is " + tide[2]);
```

4. What is wrong with the following code to initialize an array b?

```
int[] b = new int[10];
int i;
for (i = 1; i <= b.length; i++)
    b[i] = 5*i;
```

5. Write a complete Java program that will fill an array a with 20 values of type *double* read in from the keyboard, and that will output the numbers in the array as well as indicate how much each number differs from the last number in the input list. For example, if an array element is 2.0 and the last value in the input list is 5.0, the difference is 3.0. If an array element is 7.0 and the last value in the input list is 5.0, the difference is −2.0. Assume the users enter 20 numbers, one per line, from the keyboard. You need not give elaborate instructions to the user.

6.2 | Arrays in Classes and Methods

> *A little more than kin, and less than kind.*
>
> **William Shakespeare, Hamlet**

Arrays can be used as instance variables in classes. Both an indexed variable of an array and an entire array can be an argument to a method. Methods can return an array value. In short, arrays can be used with classes and methods just like other objects. We begin with a case study that uses an array as an instance variable in a class.

Case Study

Sales Report

In this case study, you will write a program to generate sales reports for a company's team of sales associates. The company wants to easily see which associate or associates have the highest sales and also wants to know how the sales of each associate compare to the average.

You know that you will need to record a name and the sales figures for each associate. So, you design a class for a single sales associate that holds these two data items, does input and output, and has a reasonable complement of accessor and mutator methods. The class you design is shown in Display 6.4. This class definition is routine.

Your program will use an array to keep track of the data on each sales associate. It will also need to record the average sales and the highest sales. So, you know you will need the following instance variables:

```
private double highest;
private double average;
private SalesAssociate[] record;
```

You realize that you need to know the number of associates. This will be the same as record.length, but it will be good to have a separate well-named variable for the number of associates. So, you decide to also include the following instance variable:

```
private int numberOfAssociates; //Same as record.length
```

The job of your program breaks down into three main subtasks:

Obtain the data.
Compute some figures (update the instance variables).
Display the results.

Thus, you know your program class will look like this

```
public class SalesReporter
{
    private double highest;
    private double average;
    private SalesAssociate[] record;
    private int numberOfAssociates; //Same as record.length

    public static void main(String[ ] arg)
    {
        SalesReporter clerk = new SalesReporter();
        clerk.getFigures();
        clerk.update();
        clerk.displayResults();
    }

    <More stuff needs to be added here.>
}
```

Display 6.4   Sales Associate Record Class *(Part 1 of 2)*

```
/*******************************
 *Class for sales associate records.
 *******************************/
public class SalesAssociate
{
    private String name;
    private double sales;

    public SalesAssociate()
    {
        name = "No record";
        sales = 0;
    }

    public SalesAssociate(String initialName,
                              double initialSales)
    {
        set(initialName, initialSales);
    }

    public void set(String newName, double newSales)
    {
        name = newName;
        sales = newSales;
    }

    public void readInput()
    {
        System.out.print("Enter name of sales associates: ");
        name = SavitchIn.readLine();
        System.out.print("Enter associate's sales: $");
        sales = SavitchIn.readLineDouble();
    }

    public void writeOutput()
    {
        System.out.println("Sales associates: " + name);
        System.out.println("Sales: $" + sales);
    }
```

Display 6.4 Sales Associate Record Class *(Part 2 of 2)*

```
    public String getName()
    {
        return name;
    }

    public double getSales()
    {
        return sales;
    }

}
```

All that remains is to design the three methods, getFigures, update, and displayResults (and to test and debug the program). You tackle the three methods in order.

The input method getFigures is relatively straightforward, especially since you have an input method for objects of the class SalesAssociate. However, there are a couple of subtle points to worry about. You design the following basic input loop:

getFigures

```
    int i;
    for (i = 0; i < numberOfAssociates; i++)
    {
        System.out.println("Enter data for associate number " + (i + 1));
        record[i].readInput();
    }
```

You handled one of the subtle points very nicely. The array indexes are numbered starting with 0 but the associates are numbered starting with 1, and so you have used record[i] for associate (i + 1). But another problem remains.

When you test this loop, you get an error message saying something about a "null pointer." This problem is due to the fact that the base type of the array record is a class type. To see the problem, consider another situation first. Suppose you had the following code:

```
    SalesAssociate a;
    a.readInput();
```

This code would produce the same error message talking about a "null pointer." The problem is that the variable a is just a name, but does not yet name any object of the class SalesAssociate. The preceding code omitted the usual use of *new*. The code should be

```
SalesAssociate a;
a = new SalesAssociate();
a.readInput();
```

The indexed variable `record[i]` is also a variable of a class type, and so it is also just a name. You need to use *new* before `record[i]` names an object that can be used with the method `readInput` (or any other method). Your code needs the following to be added:

```
record[i] = new SalesAssociate();
```

The complete definition of the method `getFigures` with this line inserted is shown in Display 6.5.

update

Next you turn your attention to the method `update`. You come up with the following code:

```
for (i = 0; i < numberOfAssociates; i++)
{
    sum = sum + record[i].getSales();
    if (record[i].getSales() > highest)
        highest = record[i].getSales();//highest sales figure so far.
}
average = sum/numberOfAssociates;
```

Now, this loop is basically OK, but you realize that the variables `sum` and `highest` must be initialized before the loop begins. You can initialize `sum` to 0, but what value do you use to initialize `highest`? Perhaps a negative number, since sales cannot be negative. However, you find out that sales can indeed be negative. If a customer returns goods, that is considered a negative sale. However, you do know that the company always has at least one sales associate, and so you initialize both `sum` and `highest` to the sales for the first associate. This takes one case outside of the loop and places it before the loop as follows:

```
highest = record[0].getSales();
double sum = record[0].getSales();
for (i = 1; i < numberOfAssociates; i++)
{
    sum = sum + record[i].getSales();
    if (record[i].getSales() > highest)
        highest = record[i].getSales();//highest sales figure so far.
}
average = sum/numberOfAssociates;
```

The preceding loop will work, but you realize that this code contains a repeated calculation. There are three identical method invocations of `record[i].get-Sales()`. You decide to only have one such invocation and store the result in a variables as follows:

Display 6.5   Sales Report (Part 1 of 3)

```
/********************************
 *Program to generate sales report.
 ********************************/
public class SalesReporter
{
    private double highest;
    private double average;
    private SalesAssociate[] record;//Array object created in getFigures.
    private int numberOfAssociates; //Same as record.length

    public void getFigures()
    {
        System.out.println("Enter number of sales associates:");
        numberOfAssociates = SavitchIn.readLineInt();
        record = new SalesAssociate[numberOfAssociates];
        int i;
        for (i = 0; i < numberOfAssociates; i++)
        {
            record[i] = new SalesAssociate();
            System.out.println("Enter data for associate " + (i+1));
            record[i].readInput();
            System.out.println();
        }
    }

    /*********************************************
     *Computes the average and highest sales figures.
     *Precondition: There is at least one salesAssociate.
     *********************************************/
    public void update()
    {
        int i;
        double nextSales = record[0].getSales();
        highest = nextSales;
        double sum = nextSales;
        for (i = 1; i < numberOfAssociates; i++)
        {
            nextSales = record[i].getSales();
            sum = sum + nextSales;
            if (nextSales > highest)
                highest = nextSales;//highest sales figure so far.
        }
        average = sum/numberOfAssociates;
    }
```

The main method is in Part 3 of the Display.

Array object created here.

SalesAssociate objects created here.

Already processed record[0], so the loop starts with record[1].

Display 6.5   **Sales Report** *(Part 2 of 3)*

```java
/******************************************
 *Displays sales report on console screen.
 ******************************************/
public void displayResults()
{
    System.out.println("Average sales per associate is $" + average);
    System.out.println("The highest sales figure is $" + highest);
    System.out.println();
    int i;
    System.out.println("The following had the highest sales:");
    for (i = 0; i < numberOfAssociates; i++)
    {
        double nextSales = record[i].getSales();
        if (nextSales == highest)
        {
            record[i].writeOutput();
            System.out.println("$" + (nextSales - average)
                                    + " above the average.");
            System.out.println();
        }
    }

    System.out.println("The rest performed as follows:");
    for (i = 0; i < numberOfAssociates; i++)
    {
        double nextSales = record[i].getSales();
        if (record[i].getSales() != highest)
        {
            record[i].writeOutput();
            if (nextSales >= average)
                System.out.println("$" + (nextSales - average)
                                        + " above the average.");
            else
                System.out.println("$" + (average - nextSales)
                                        + " below the average.");
            System.out.println();
        }
    }
}
```

Display 6.5 **Sales Report** *(Part 3 of 3)*

```
    public static void main(String[] arg)
    {
        SalesReporter clerk = new SalesReporter();
        clerk.getFigures();
        clerk.update();
        clerk.displayResults();
    }
}
```

Sample Screen Dialogue

```
Enter number of sales associates:
3
Enter data for associate number 1
Enter name of sales associates: Dusty Rhodes
Enter associate's sales: $3600

Enter data for associate number 2
Enter name of sales associates: Natalie Dressed
Enter associate's sales: $5000

Enter data for associate number 3
Enter name of sales associates: Sandy Hare
Enter associate's sales: $1000

Average sales per associate is $3200
The highest sales figure is $5000

The following had the highest sales:
Name: Natalie Dressed
Sales: $5000
$1800 above the average.

The rest performed as follows:
Name: Dusty Rhodes
Sales: $3600
$400 above the average.

Name: Sandy Hare
Sales: $1000
$2200 below the average.
```

```
int i;
double nextSales = record[0].getSales();
highest = nextSales;
double sum = nextSales;
for (i = 1; i < numberOfAssociates; i++)
{
    nextSales = record[i].getSales();
    sum = sum + nextSales;
    if (nextSales > highest)
        highest = nextSales;//highest sales figure so far.
}
average = sum/numberOfAssociates;
```

The complete final definition for the method update is given in Display 6.5.

The design of the final method displayResults only uses techniques that you have already seen, and so we will not go over the details. The final method definition is shown in Display 6.5.

? Self-Test Questions

6. Write some Java code that will declare an array named entry that has length 3, has SalesAssociate (Display 6.4/page 394) as its base type, and is filled with three identical records. The records use name "Jane Doe" and sales of $5000. Use a *for*-loop.

7. Rewrite the method displayResults of the program SalesReporter (Display 6.5/page 397) so that it uses the methods in the class Dollars (Display 5.14/page 330) to output the dollar amounts in the correct format for dollars and cents.

Indexed Variables as Method Arguments

An indexed variable for an array a, such as a[i], can be used anyplace that you can use any other variable of the base type of the array. So, an indexed variable for an array a, such as a[i], can be an argument to a method in exactly the same way that any other variable of the array's base type can be an argument. For example, the program in Display 6.6 contains a program that illustrates the use of an indexed variable as an argument to a method.

Consider the method average, which takes two arguments of type *int*. In the program Display 6.6, the array nextScore has base type *int*, so the program can use nextScore[i] as an argument to the method average, as in the following line from that program:

```
possibleAverage = average(firstScore, nextScore[i]);
```

The variable firstScore is an ordinary variable of type *int*. To help drive home the point that the indexed variable nextScore[i] can be used just like any other variable of type *int*, note that the program in Display 6.6 would behave exactly the same

Display 6.6   Indexed Variables as Arguments

```
/*********************************
 *A program to demonstrate the use of
 *indexed variables as arguments.
 *********************************/
public class ArgumentDemo
{
    public static void main(String[] arg)
    {
        System.out.println("Enter your score on exam 1:");
        int firstScore = SavitchIn.readLineInt();
        int[] nextScore = new int[3];
        int i;
        double possibleAverage;
        for (i = 0; i < nextScore.length; i++)
            nextScore[i] = 80 + 10*i;
        for (i = 0; i < nextScore.length; i++)
        {
            possibleAverage = average(firstScore, nextScore[i]);
            System.out.println("If your score on exam 2 is "
                                    + nextScore[i]);
            System.out.println("your average will be "
                                    + possibleAverage);
        }
    }

    public static double average(int n1, int n2)
    {
        return (n1 + n2)/2.0;
    }
}
```

Sample Screen Dialogue

```
Enter your score on exam 1:
80
If your score on exam 2 is 80
your average will be 80.0
If your score on exam 2 is 90
your average will be 85.0
If your score on exam 2 is 100
your average will be 90.0
```

if the two arguments to the method `average` were interchanged so that the preceding invocation of `average` were replaced with the following:

```
possibleAverage = average(nextScore[i], firstScore);
```

Also, note the definition of the method `average`. That definition contains no indication that its arguments can be indexed variables for an array of `int`. The method `average` accepts arguments of type `int` and neither knows nor cares about whether those `int`s came from an indexed variable, a regular `int` variable, or a constant `int` value.

evaluating indexes

There is one subtlety that applies to indexed variables used as method arguments. For example, again consider the method call:

```
possibleAverage = average(firstScore, nextScore[i]);
```

If the value of `i` is 2, then the argument is `nextScore[2]`. On the other hand, if the value of `i` is 0, then the argument is `nextScore[0]`. The indexed expression is evaluated in order to determine exactly which indexed variable to use as the argument.

Be sure to note that an indexed variable of an array a, such as a[i], is a variable of the base type of the array. When a[i] is used as an argument to a method, it is handled *exactly the same as any other variable of the base type of the array* a. In particular, if the base type of the array is a primitive type, such as `int`, `double`, or `char`, then the method cannot change the value of a[i]. On the other hand, if the base type of the array is a class type, then the method can change the object named by a[i]. This is nothing new. Just remember that an indexed variable, like a[i], is a variable of the base type of the array and is handled just like any other variable of the base type of the array.

Array Indexed Variables as Arguments

An array indexed variable can be used as an argument anyplace that a variable of the array base type can be used. For example, suppose you have

```
double[] a = new double[10];
```

Then, indexed variables such as a[3] and a[index] can be used as arguments to any method that accepts a *double* variable as an argument.

■

When Can a Method Change an Indexed Variable Argument?

Suppose a[i] is an indexed variable of an array a and a[i] is used as an argument in a method invocation such as

```
doStuff(a[i]);
```

Whether or not the method `doStuff` can change the array element a[i] depends on the base type of the array a. If the base type of the array a is a primitive type, such as `int`, `double`, or `char`, then as with any argument of a primitive type, the method `doStuff` cannot change the value of a[i]. However, if the base type of the array a is a class, then the method `doStuff` can change the object named by a[i]. Note that there is nothing new here. The indexed variable a[i] is treated just like any other variable of the base type of the array. (To review the details on method arguments, see Chapter 4.)

■

Entire Arrays as Method Arguments

We have already seen that an indexed variable of an array can be used as an argument to a method. An entire array can also be used as a single argument to a method. The way you specify an array parameter in a method definition is similar to the way you declare an array. For example, the method `incrementArrayBy2` (which follows) will accept any array of *double*s as its single argument:

```
public class SampleClass
{
    public static void incrementArrayBy2(double[] a)
    {
        int i;
        for (i = 0; i < a.length; i++)
            a[i] = a[i] + 2;
    }
    <The rest of the class definition goes here.>
}
```

To illustrate this, suppose you have the following in some method definition:

```
double[] a = new double[10];
double[] b = new double[30];
```

and suppose the elements of the arrays a and b have been given values, then the following are both legal method invocations:

```
SampleClass.incrementArrayBy2(a);
SampleClass.incrementArrayBy2(b);
```

There are a few things that we need to emphasize about array arguments. First, no square brackets are used when you give an entire array as an argument to a method. Second, a method can change the values in an array. This is illustrated by the preceding method `incrementArrayBy2`. Third, the same array parameter can be replaced with array arguments of different lengths. Note that the preceding method `incrementArrayBy2` can take any length array as an argument. When you specify a parameter as an array parameter, you specify the type of the array elements, but you do not specify the length of the array.

length of array arguments

Note that array arguments in method invocations are handled in basically the same way as class arguments in method invocations (although array parameters in method definitions have their own notation for specifying that the type of the parameter is an array type).

Arguments for The Method main *(Optional)*

The heading for the `main` method of a program is as follows:

```
public static void main(String[] args)
```

The part `String[] args` makes it look like `arg` is a parameter for an array of `String`s. Not only does it look like that, but it is in fact true that the method `main` does take an array of `String`s as an argument. But, we have never given `main` an ar-

Array Parameters and Array Arguments

An argument to a method may be an entire array. Array arguments are like objects of a class, in that the method can change the values in an array argument. A method with an array parameter is defined and invoked as illustrated by the following examples. (All the examples are assumed to be somewhere within a class definition.)

Examples: (of formal array parameters):

```java
public static void showArray(char[] a )
{
    int i;
    for (i = 0; i < a.length; i++)
        System.out.println(a[i]);
}

public static void reinitialize(int[] anArray)
{
    int i;
    for (i = 0; i < anArray.length; i++)
        anArray[i] = 0;
}
```

Examples: (of array arguments):

```java
char[] symbol = new char[10];
int[] a = new int[10];
int[] b = new int[20];
```

<Some code to fill the arrays goes here.>

Note that arrays a and b have different lengths. Also, note that no square brackets are used with array arguments.

```java
showArray(symbol );
reinitialize(a );
reinitialize(b );
```

ray argument, or any other kind of argument, when we ran any of our programs. What's the story?

As you know, an invocation of main is a very special sort of invocation. A default array of strings is automatically provided as a default argument to main when you run your program.

It is possible to provide additional "string arguments" when you run a program, and then those "string arguments" will automatically be made elements of the array argument that is automatically provided to main. This is normally done by running the program from the command line version of the operating system like so:

```
java TestProgram Sally Smith
```

This will set args[0] to "Sally" and args[1] to "Smith", and these two indexed variables can be used in the method main, as shown in the following sample program:

```
public class TestProgram
{
    public static void main(String[] args)
    {
        System.out.println("Hello " + args[0] + " " + args[1]);
    }
}
```

If the above program is compiled and then run with the one-line command

```
java TestProgram Josephine Student
```

The output produced by the program will be

```
Hello Josephine Student
```

Since the identifier `args` is a parameter, you can use any other (nonreserved word) identifier in place or `args`, and the meaning will be unchanged (as long as you change any occurrences of `args` that also occur in the body of `main`). However, it is traditional to use the identifier `args` for this parameter.

Finally, be sure to note that the argument to `main` is an array of *strings*. If you want numbers, you must convert the string representations of the numbers to values of a number type(s).

The Method ma i n Has an Array Parameter *(Optional)*

The heading for the `main` method of a program is as follows:

```
public static void main(String[] args)
```

The identifier `arg` is a parameter for an array of `Strings`. The details are explained in the text.

■ Gotcha
Use of = and == with Arrays

Arrays are objects, and so the assignment operator = and the equality operator == **assignment with arrays** behave (and perhaps misbehave) the same way with arrays as with the kinds of objects we saw before discussing arrays. To understand how this applies to arrays, you need to know a little bit about how arrays are stored in the computer's main memory. The important point for this discussion is that the entire array contents (that is, the contents of all the indexed variables) are stored together in one (possibly large) section of memory so that the location of the entire array contents can be specified by one memory address.

Now, recall that a variable for an object really contains the memory address of the object. The assignment operator copies this memory address. For example, consider the following code:

Display 6.7   Two Kinds of Equality *(Part 1 of 2)*

```
/************************************************************
 *This is just a demonstration program to see how equals and == work.
 ************************************************************/
public class TestEquals
{
    public static void main(String[] args)
    {
        int[] a = new int[3]; int[] b = new int[3]; int i;
        for (i = 0; i < a.length; i++)
            a[i] = i;
        for (i = 0; i < b.length; i++)
            b[i] = i;
        if (b == a)
            System.out.println("Equal by ==.");
        else
            System.out.println("Not equal by ==.");
        if (equals(b,a))
            System.out.println("Equal by the equals method.");
        else
            System.out.println("Not equal by the equals method.");
    }

    public static boolean equals(int[] a, int[] b)
    {
        boolean match;
        if (a.length != b.length)
            match = false;
        else
        {
            match = true; //tentatively
            int i = 0;
            while (match && (i < a.length))
            {
                if (a[i] != b[i])
                    match = false;
                i++;
            }
        }
        return match;
    }
}
```

> The arrays a and b contain the same integers in the same order.

```
int[] a = new int[3];
int[] b = new int[3];
int i;
for (i = 0; i < a.length; i++)
    a[i] = i;
b = a;
System.out.println("a[2] = " + a[2] + " b[2] = " + b[2]);
a[2] = 2001;
System.out.println("a[2] = " + a[2] + " b[2] = " + b[2]);
```

This will produce the following output:

```
a[2] = 2 b[2] = 2
a[2] = 2001 b[2] = 2001
```

The assignment statement b = a; (in the preceding code) gives the array variable b the same memory address as the array variable a. So, a and b are two different names for the same array. Thus, when we change the value of a[2], we are also changing the value of b[2].

Because of the complications we discussed in the previous paragraph, it is best to just not use the assignment operator = with arrays (and similarly not use == with arrays). If you want the arrays a and b in the preceding code to be different arrays with the same values, then instead of the assignment statement

```
b = a;
```

you must use something like the following:

```
int i;
for (i = 0; i < a.length; i++)
    b[i] = a[i];
```

Note that the preceding code assumes that the arrays a and b have the same length.

The equality operator == tests two arrays to see if they are stored in the same place in the computer's memory. For example, consider the following code:

== with arrays

Display 6.7   Two Kinds of Equality (Part 2 of 2)

Screen Output

```
Not equal by ==.
Equal by the equals method.
```

```
int[] a = new int[3];
int[] b = new int[3];
int i;
for (i = 0; i < a.length; i++)
    a[i] = i;
for (i = 0; i < a.length; i++)
    b[i] = i;

if (b == a)
    System.out.println("Equal by ==");
else
    System.out.println("Not equal by ==");
```

This produces the output

```
Not equal by ==
```

This is the output despite the fact that the arrays a and b contain the same integers in the same indexed variables. This happens because the arrays a and b are stored in different places in memory, and == tests for equal memory addresses.

If you want to test two arrays to see if they contain the same elements, then you can define an equals method for the arrays, just as you defined an equals method for a class. For example, Display 6.7/page 406 contains one possible definition of equals for arrays in a small demonstration class. There is not a uniquely correct definition of equals. The exact definition details depend on the application. Alternatively, you can simply write code to compare the two arrays element by element. For example, if the arrays a and b are arrays of *int*s of the same length, the following code could be used:

```
boolean match = true; //tentatively
int i = 0;
while (match && (i < a.length))
{
    if (a[i] != b[i])
        match = false;
    i++;
}
if (match)
    System.out.println("Arrays have the same contents");
else
    System.out.println("Arrays do not match");
```

Array Types Are Reference Types

A variable of an array type only holds the address of where the array is stored in memory. This memory address is often called a **reference** to the array object in memory. For this reason, array type are often called *reference types*. A **reference type** is any type whose variables hold references (that is, memory addresses), as opposed to the actual item named by the variable. Array types and class types are both reference types. Primitive types are not reference types.

Are Arrays Really Objects?

Arrays behave very much like objects. On the other hand, it is hard to come up with any commonly used name for the classes to which the arrays belong. There are also other features of objects that do not apply to arrays, such as inheritance (which we will discuss in Chapter 7). So, whether or not arrays should be considered objects is not 100% clear. However, that is primarily an academic debate. *In Java arrays are officially objects.* Whenever Java documentation says that something applies to all objects, then it also applies to arrays.

Methods That Return Arrays

In Java, a method may return an array. You specify the returned type for a method that returns an array in the same way that you specify a type for an array parameter. For example, Display 6.8 contains a slightly rewritten version of the program in Display 6.6/page 401. The program in Display 6.8 performs pretty much the same computation as the one in Display 6.6. However, in this new version (given in Display 6.8), the various possible average scores are computed by the method `averageArray` and returned as an array of scores (of type *double*).

Returning an Array

A method can return an array. The details are basically the same as for any other returned type.

Syntax (for a typical way of returning an array):

```
public static Base_Type[] Method_Name (Parameter_List )
{
    Base_Type[] temp = new Base_Type[Array_Size]
    Statements_To_Fill_temp
    return temp;
}
```

The method need not be static and need not be public. The following are some of the other acceptable method headings:

```
public Base_Type[] Method_Name (Parameter_List )

private static Base_Type[] Method_Name (Parameter_List )

private Base_Type[] Method_Name (Parameter_List )
```

Example: (Assumed to be in a class definition):

```
public static char[] vowels()
{
    char[] newArray = new char[5];
    newArray[0] = 'a';
    newArray[1] = 'e';
    newArray[2] = 'i';
    newArray[3] = 'o';
    newArray[4] = 'u';
    return newArray;
}
```

Display 6.8   A Method That Returns an Array

```
/****************************************************
 *A program to demonstrate a method returning an array.
 ****************************************************/
public class ReturnArrayDemo
{
    public static void main(String[] arg)
    {
        System.out.println("Enter your score on exam 1:");
        int firstScore = SavitchIn.readLineInt();
        int[] nextScore = new int[3];
        int i;
        for (i = 0; i < nextScore.length; i++)
            nextScore[i] = 80 + 10*i;
        double[] averageScore;
        averageScore = averageArray(firstScore, nextScore);
        for (i = 0; i < nextScore.length; i++)
        {
            System.out.println("If your score on exam 2 is "
                                + nextScore[i]);
            System.out.println("your average will be "
                                + averageScore[i]);
        }
    }

    public static double[] averageArray(int firstScore,
                                              int[] nextScore)
    {
        double[] temp = new double[nextScore.length];
        int i;
        for (i = 0; i < temp.length; i++)
            temp[i] = average(firstScore, nextScore[i]);
        return temp;
    }

    public static double average(int n1, int n2)
    {
        return (n1 + n2)/2.0;
    }
}
```

The sample screen dialogue is the same as in Display 6.6/page 401.

Notice that a new array is created and then the new array is returned, as follows:

```
double temp = new double[nextScore.length];
<Fill the array temp.>
return temp;
```

Spelling Type Names for Arrays

An array type name is always of the form

Base_Type[ ]

This is true when declaring an array variable, specifying the type for an array parameter, or specifying an array type as the type returned by a method.

Examples:

```
int[] n = new int[10];
Species[] s = new Species[20];
public static double[] halfAll(int[] arryToBeHalved);
{
              .
              .
              .
```

? Self-Test Questions

8. What output will be produced by the following code?

```
char[] a = new char[3];
char[] b;
int i;
for (i = 0; i < a.length; i++)
    a[i] = 'a';
b = a;
System.out.println("a[1] = " + a[1] + " b[1] = " + b[1]);
System.out.println("a[2] = " + a[2] + " b[2] = " + b[2]);
b[2] = 'b';
System.out.println("a[1] = " + a[1] + " b[1] = " + b[1]);
System.out.println("a[2] = " + a[2] + " b[2] = " + b[2]);
```

9. Give the definition of a method called showArray that has a single parameter for an array of *char*s and that writes a line of text to the screen consisting of the characters in the array argument written in order. Make it a static method. To test it, you can add it to any class, or better yet, write a class with a test program in the method main.

10. Give the definition of a method called halfArray that has a single parameter for an array of *double*s and that returns another array of *doubles* that has the same length and that has each element divided by 2.0. Make it a static method. To test it, you can add it to any class, or better yet, write a class with a test program in the method main.

11. What is wrong with the following method definition? It will compile, but does not work as you might hope.

```
public static void doubleSize(int[] a)
{
    a = new int[a.length * 2];
}
```

6.3 | Programming with Arrays and Classes

> *The Moving Finger writes; and, having writ,*
> *Moves on; nor all your Piety and Wit.*
> *Shall lure it back to cancel half a line.*
> *Nor all your Tears wash out a Word of it.*
> **Omar Khayyam, The Ruba'iyat (Fitzgerald translation)**

In this section, we present some additional techniques for working with arrays. In particular, we discuss using an array variable as an instance variable in a class. We begin with a programming example that illustrates some basic techniques.

Programming Example
A Specialized List Class

One way to use an array for a special purpose is to make the array an instance variable of a class and access it only through the class methods. This allows you to define classes whose objects are something like special-purpose arrays. The array is only accessed through the class methods, and so you can add any checks and automatic processing that you want. In this programming example, we present an example of one such class.

In this example, we will define a class whose objects can be used for keeping lists of items, such as a grocery list or a list of things to do. The class will have the rather long name OneWayNoRepeatsList. (Long names are traditional in Java, but we did not choose a long name just to be traditional. All the short names, like *List*, *Table*, and so forth, already have a technical meaning in computer science and it could be confusing to use these short names for something other than their usual meaning.)

The class OneWayNoRepeatsList will have a method for adding items to the list. An item on the list is a string, which in an application would say whatever you want the item to say, such as "Buy milk". This class has no method to change nor to delete a single item from the list. It does, however, have a method that lets you erase the entire list and start over again with a blank list. Each object of the class OneWayNoRepeatsList has a maximum number of items it can hold. At any time, the list might contain anywhere from zero to the maximum number of items.

An object of the class OneWayNoRepeatsList has an array of strings as an instance variable. This array holds the items on the list. However, you do not directly access the array. Instead, you use accessor and mutator methods. You can use *int* variables to hold a position in the list. One of these *int* variables is very much the same thing as an index, but positions are numbered starting with 1 rather than 0. For example, there is a method named getEntryAt that lets you recover the item at a given position. For example, if toDoList is an object of the class One-WayNoRepeatsList, then the following sets the string variable next to the entry at the second position:

```
String next = toDoList.getEntryAt(2);
```

There is no way to (directly) change an entry on the list. There is a method to add an entry to the end of the list and a method to erase the entire list, but those are the only ways that the list can be changed.

In Chapter 4 we discussed encapsulation. The class OneWayNoRepeatsList will be a good example of a well-encapsulated class. As we discussed in Chapter 4, a well-encapsulated class is defined so that the programmer who uses the class need not know the details of how the class is defined. If that is true of the class One-WayNoRepeatsList, then it makes sense to tell you how to use the class One-WayNoRepeatsList *before we give the definition of that class*. So, let's do that.

Display 6.9 contains a program that demonstrates how to use some of the methods for the class OneWayNoRepeatsList. Notice that there is a constructor that takes an integer argument. This integer specifies the maximum number of entries that can be placed in the list. Normally, the list will contain fewer than the maximum number of entries.

The method addItem adds a string to the list. For example, the following adds the string named by the variable next to the list toDoList.

```
toDoList.addItem(next);
```

If you look at the sample dialogue, you will see that "Buy milk." is added to the list twice, but that it only appears on the list once. If the item being added is already on the list, then the method addItem has no effect. This way the list has no repeats.

You can use an *int* variable to step through the list from beginning to end. The technique is illustrated in Display 6.9. The following initializes an *int* variable to the first position on the list:

stepping through a list

```
int position = toDoList.START_POSITION;
```

The defined constant toDoList.START_POSITION is simply another name for 1, but we use it because we are thinking of this as the start of the list, not as the number 1. You can recover the item at a given position with the method getEntryAt. For example, the following sets the string variable next equal to the string at the position (at the index) given by the variable position:

```
next = toDoList.getEntryAt(position);
```

To obtain the next item on the list, the program simply increments the value of position and repeats this sort of thing. The following code, taken from Display 6.9, illustrates stepping through the list:

Display 6.9   Using the Class OneWayNoRepeatsList *(Part 1 of 2)*

```java
public class ListDemo
{
    public static void main(String[] args)
    {
        OneWayNoRepeatsList toDoList =
                             new OneWayNoRepeatsList(3);

        System.out.println(
                    "Enter items for the list, when prompted.");
        boolean more = true;
        String next = null;
        char ans;

        while ( more && (! toDoList.full()))
        {
            System.out.println("Input an entry:");
            next = SavitchIn.readLine();
            toDoList.addItem(next);
            if (toDoList.full())
            {
                System.out.println("List if full.");
            }
            else
            {
                System.out.print(
                            "More items for the list?(y/n): ");
                ans = SavitchIn.readLineNonwhiteChar();
                if ((ans == 'n') || (ans == 'N'))
                    more = false;
            }
        }

        System.out.println("The list contains:");
        int position = toDoList.START_POSITION;
        next = toDoList.getEntryAt(position);
        while (next != null)
        {
            System.out.println(next);
            position++;
            next = toDoList.getEntryAt(position);
        }
    }
}
```

null indicates the end of the list.

Display 6.9   **Using the Class** OneWayNoRepeatsList *(Part 2 of 2)*

Sample Screen Dialogue

```
Enter items for the list, when prompted.
Input an entry:
Buy milk.
More items for the list?(y/n): y
Input an entry:
Walk dog.
More items for the list?(y/n): y
Input an entry:
Buy milk.
More items for the list?(y/n): y
Input an entry:
Write program.
The list is full.
The list contains:
Buy milk.
Walk dog.
Write program.
```

```java
int position = toDoList.START_POSITION;
next = toDoList.getEntryAt(position);
while (next != null)
{
    System.out.println(next);
    position++;
    next = toDoList.getEntryAt(position);
}
```

Once the value of position is incremented beyond the last position in the list, there is no entry at the position. So, we need some way to conveniently indicate that the end of the list has been reached, or we might access some "garbage value" in the unused portion of the array. To take care of this problem, we will define toDoList.getEntryAt(position) so that it returns the value *null* when there is no entry at the given position. Note that *null* is different from any real string, and so *null* is an item that will not appear on any list. Thus, your program can test for the

garbage values

end of the list by checking for the value *null*. Also, recall that to test for equality or inequality with *null*, you use == or !=; you do not use an equals method.

The complete definition of the class OneWayNoRepeatsList is given in Display 6.10. The entries in a list are kept in the instance variable entry, which is an array of Strings. Thus, the maximum number of entries that the list can hold is entry.length. However, the list will not normally be full, but will typically contain fewer than entry.length entries. In order to keep track of how much of the array entry is currently being used, the class has an instance variable called countOfEntries. The entries are kept in the indexed variables, entry[0], entry[1], entry[2], through entry[countOfEntries − 1]. The values of the elements with indexes countOfEntries or higher are just garbage values and do not represent entries on the list. Thus, when you want to step through the items on the list, you stop at entry[countOfEntries − 1].

For example, in the definition of the method onList, there is a *while*-loop that steps through the array, checking to see if the argument is equal to any of the entries on the list. The code only checks array elements with indexes less than countOfEntries. It does not check the entire array, because array entries at indexes greater than or equal to countOfEntries are not "on the list." So, the *while*-loop that checks to see whether item is on the list is

```
while ((! found) && (i < countOfEntries))
{
    if (item.equalsIgnoreCase(entry[i]))
        found = true;
    else
        i++;
}
```

The class OneWayNoRepeatsList has a few more methods than those we used in the demonstration program in Display 6.9. These extra methods are to make the class more useful for a wider variety of applications.

Note that although the array entry has indexes starting with 0, if you use an *int* variable as a position marker, such as the variable position in Display 6.9/page 414, then the numbering starts at 1, not 0. The class methods automatically adjust the indexes, so when you want the item at location position, it gives you entry[position − 1].

Partially Filled Arrays

The array entry in the class OneWayNoRepeatsList in Display 6.10/page 417 is being used as a partially filled array. In some situations, you need some, but not all, of the indexed variables in an array, such as when the array entry contains the entries on a list and the list is not yet full. In these situations, you need to keep track of how much of the array has been used and how much is not currently being used. This is normally done with an *int* variable, like the instance variable countOfEntries in the class OneWayNoRepeatsList in Display 6.10/page 417. For example, the instance variable countOfEntries tells the methods that the list consists of the array elements with indexes 0 through countOfEntries − 1. This is diagrammed in Dis-

Display 6.10   An Array Wrapped in a Class (Part 1 of 3)

```
/***************************************************************
 *An object of this class is a special kind of list. The list can only be
 *written from beginning to end. You can add to the end of the list, but
 *you cannot change individual entries. You can erase the entire list and
 *start over. No entry may appear more than once on the list. You can use
 *int variables as position markers into the list. Position markers are
 *similar to array indexes, but are numbered starting with 1.
 ***************************************************************/
public class OneWayNoRepeatsList
{
    public static int START_POSITION = 1;
    public static int DEFAULT_SIZE = 50;


    //entry.length is the total number of items you have room
    //for on the list. countOfEntries is the number of items
    //currently on the list.
    private int countOfEntries;//can be less than entry.length.
    private String[] entry;


    public OneWayNoRepeatsList(int maximumNumberOfEntries)
    {
        entry = new String[maximumNumberOfEntries];
        countOfEntries = 0;
    }



    /*************************************************
     *Creates an empty list with a capacity of DEFAULT_SIZE.
     *************************************************/
    public OneWayNoRepeatsList()
    {
        entry = new String[DEFAULT_SIZE];
        countOfEntries = 0;
    }
```

Display 6.10   An Array Wrapped in a Class *(Part 2 of 3)*

```
/****************************************************
 *Precondition: List is not full.
 *Postcondition:
 *If item was not on the list, it has been added to the list.
 ****************************************************/
public void addItem(String item)
{
    if (! onList(item))
    {
        if (countOfEntries == entry.length)
        {
            System.out.println("Adding to a full list!");
            System.exit(0);
        }
        else

        {
            entry[countOfEntries] = item;
            countOfEntries++;
        }
    }//else do nothing. Item is already on the list.
}

public boolean full()
{
    return (countOfEntries == entry.length);
}

public boolean empty()
{
    return (countOfEntries == 0);
}


/****************************************************
 *If the argument indicates a position on the list,
 *then the entry at that specified position is returned;
 *otherwise, null is returned.
 ****************************************************/
public String getEntryAt(int position)
{
    if ((1 <= position) && (position <= countOfEntries))
        return entry[position - 1];
    else
        return null;
}
```

Display 6.10   An Array Wrapped in a Class *(Part 3 of 3)*

```java
/*******************************************
 *Returns true if position is the index of the
 *last item on the list; otherwise, returns false.
 *******************************************/
public boolean atLastEntry(int position)
{
    return (position == countOfEntries);
}


/*******************************************
 *Returns true if item is on the list;
 *otherwise, returns false. Does not differentiate
 *between upper- and lowercase letters.
 *******************************************/
public boolean onList(String item)
{
    boolean found = false;
    int i = 0;
    while ((! found) && (i < countOfEntries))
    {
        if (item.equalsIgnoreCase(entry[i]))
            found = true;
        else
            i++;
    }

    return found;
}

public int maximumNumberOfEntries()
{
    return entry.length;
}

public int getNumberOfEntries()
{
    return countOfEntries;
}

public void eraseList()
{
    countOfEntries = 0;
}
}
```

Display 6.11 *A Partially Filled Array*

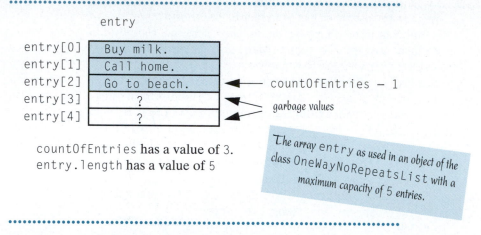

countOfEntries has a value of 3.
entry.length has a value of 5

The array entry *as used in an object of the class* OneWayNoRepeatsList *with a maximum capacity of 5 entries.*

play 6.11. It is very important to keep track of how much of the array is currently being used, because the other array entries contain garbage values that do not represent anything. When accessing a partially filled array, you only want to access those elements in the first part of the array that contain meaningful values, and you want to ignore the garbage values in the rest of the array. Of course, as you add or delete entries from a partially filled array, the borderline between meaningful values and garbage values can move, and this movement is recorded by changing the value of a suitable *int* variable, such as countOfEntries.

garbage values

Searching an Array

The method onList of the class OneWayNoRepeatsList (Display 6.10, part 3, page 419) searches the array entry to see if the parameter item is in the array entry. This is an example of a *sequential search* of an array. The **sequential search** algorithm is very simple and straightforward: Your code looks at the array elements in the order from first to last to see if the sought-after item is equal to any of the array elements. (If the array is a partially filled array, the search stops when it reaches the end of the meaningful values.)

**sequential
search**

■ Gotcha

Returning an Array Instance Variable

Consider the following accessor method that somebody might want to add to the class OneWayNoRepeatsList in Display 6.10:

```
public String[] getEntryArray()
{
    return entry;
}
```

Read the text to see what is wrong with this definition.

This definition looks innocent enough. It is pretty much like all the other accessor methods we have written for reading the data in a private instance variable. However, the fact that an array is returned, instead of a primitive type such as *int* or *double*, makes the situation very different. As we will see, the fact that this function returns an array and the fact that an array variable contains a reference (that is, a memory address) means that this method provides a way to get around the designation *private*. This method allows programmers to directly change the data in that private array instance variable named `entry`. Let's look at the details of the problem.

Suppose you add the method `getEntryArray` to the class `OneWayNoRepeatsList` and you define the method as we did at the beginning of this Gotcha section. Suppose further that a programmer creates an object of type `OneWayNoRepeatsList` as follows:

```
OneWayNoRepeatsList myList = new OneWayNoRepeatsList();
```

Now suppose the programmer wants direct access to the private array instance variable `entry` in the object `myList`. The programmer should not be able to get such access. The qualifier *private* before the declaration of `entry` (in the class definition) was designed expressly to prevent such access. However, all that this sneaky (or maybe just careless) programmer needs to do in order to get access to the private array variable `myList.entry` is the following:

```
String[] a = myList.getEntryArray();
```

After the preceding is executed, the array variable `a` contains the address of the array `myList.entry`. *So `a` is another name for the private array* `myList.entry`! Our sneaky programmer can do anything she or he wants to the private array `myList.entry` by simply using the array name `a`. For example, suppose the programmer wants to do the following:

```
myList.entry[2] = "Party tonight!";
```

Well, the programmer cannot do this, because the instance variable `myList.entry` is private, and so the programmer cannot use the name `entry`, and the preceding code will produce a compiler error message. But, if the programmer is sneaky, she/he can do the following, which means the exact same thing, because `a` is another name for `myList.entry`:

```
a[2] = "Party tonight!";
```

The arrays `myList.entry` and `a` are the exact same array!

Now, the preceding definition of the accessor method `getEntryArray` is not a suitable accessor method. So what should we do about providing an accessor method to the array `entry`? The first answer is that you do not need any accessor (or mutator) methods beyond those already in the class. The methods `getEntryAt`, `full`, `empty`, and so forth allow a programmer to do anything that legitimately needs to be done with a `OneWayNoRepeatsList`. It is, in fact, extremely unlikely that you would ever need an accessor method that returns an entire array instance variable. Unlikely, but not impossible.

Suppose that for some unusual reason you need to have the accessor method `getEntryArray`. The correct way to define the method is as follows:

```
public String[] getEntryArray()
{
    String[] temp = new String[entry.length];
    int i;
    for (i = 0; i < getNumberOfEntries(); i++)
        temp[i] = entry[i];
    return temp;
}
```

The array temp constructed in this method definition has the same entries as the array entry, but it is a different array. It is a copy of the array entry, but it is not the array entry itself. So, with this new definition of getEntryArray, the following is perfectly safe:

```
String[] a = myList.getEntryArray();
```

The programmer can change the array a, but that will have no effect on the array myList.entry. The array a is another name for the array temp constructed in the method definition; it is not a name for the array myList.entry. The array a is an identical copy of myList.entry, but is not the same array.[1]

If the array in question has a base type that is either a primitive type or the type String, this is pretty much the whole story, but if the base type of the array is a class type, then the problem does not go away that easily. If you have a private array instance variable with a class type as the base type, and you want an accessor method to return a safe copy of the array, you must not only copy the array, but must make a copy of each array entry. However, it is unlikely that you will need an accessor method that returns an entire array copy for a private instance variable whose base type is a class (other than the class String, which can be treated like a primitive type for this discussion.) So, we will not pursue this point any further. The problem is essentially the same as the problem we discussed in the subsection entitled *Gotcha* **Privacy Leaks** on page 360 of Chapter 5, and as we said there, these kinds of problems are beyond the scope of this book. However, remember that if the base type of the private array instance variable is a primitive type or the type String, then you can use the techniques we gave before this paragraph and that will produce a safe copy of the array instance variable.

? Self-Test Questions

12. Suppose a is an array of values of type *double*. Write some code to display all the elements in a to the screen, one per line.

13. Suppose a is an array of values of type *double*. Suppose a is being used as a partially filled array that contains meaningful values in only the first

---

1. You could argue that the arrays are not *identical* because we did not copy the garbage values at the end of the partially filled array entry. However, they are only garbage values. Moreover, if you really wanted to, you could also copy the garbage values, but there is no reason for that.

numberUsed elements. (numberUsed is a variable of type *int* that contains the number of elements that contain meaningful values.) Write some code to display all the meaningful values in the array a.

14. Consider the array a from question 13. Write some code that will add the number 42 to this partially filled array a. (*Hint:* You must update numberUsed. You can assume the array a is not full.)

15. Redo question 14, but this time assume that you do not know whether the array a is full. If the array a is full, your code should output an appropriate message to the screen.

6.4 | Sorting Arrays

> *A place for everything and everything in its place.*
> **Isabella Mary Beeton, The Book of Household Management**

Suppose you have an array of values. You might want the array values to be sorted in some way. For example, you might want to sort an array of numbers from lowest to highest or from highest to lowest, or you might want to sort an array of strings into alphabetical order. In this section, we will discuss a simple sorting algorithm and give a Java implementation of that algorithm. We will present this algorithm as an algorithm to sort an array of values of type *int*. However, with only minor, obvious changes, it can be adapted to sort arrays of values of any type that can be ordered, such as an array of objects that represents employee records and that needs to be sorted by social security number.

Selection Sort

In this subsection, we discuss one of the easiest of the sorting algorithms to understand, which is known as **selection sort**.

The algorithm will be implemented as a method that has an array of *int*s a as a parameter and that sorts the array a. The method will rearrange the values in the indexed variables of the array so that

```
a[0] <= a[1] <= a[2] <= ... <= a[a.length - 1]
```

The selection sort algorithm almost follows automatically from the specification of what we want the algorithm to do. We want the algorithm to sort an array named a. In other words, we want the algorithm to rearrange the values of the array so that a[0] is the smallest, a[1] the next smallest, and so forth. That specification leads to the following algorithm outline:

```
for (index = 0; index < a.length; index++)
```
   Place the indexth smallest element in a[index].

(In this case, we count starting with 0, so the smallest element is the 0th smallest element, the next smallest is the "1th smallest," and so forth.)

We will implement the details of this algorithm using only the one array a. This means that we have no extra locations to store any of the array elements we are

Display 6.12 Sorting by Swapping Values

a[0]	a[1]	a[2]	a[3]	a[4]	a[5]	a[6]	a[7]	a[8]	a[9]
7	6	11	17	3	15	5	19	30	14

7	6	11	17	3	15	5	19	30	14

3	6	11	17	7	15	5	19	30	14

3	6	11	17	7	15	5	19	30	14

3	5	11	17	7	15	6	19	30	14

3	5	6	7	11	14	15	17	19	30

moving. The only way we can move an array element, without losing the array elements, is to have the element swap places with another element of the array. Any sorting algorithm that uses this sort of swapping of values is called an **interchange sorting algorithm.** So, our selection sort algorithm will be an interchange sorting algorithm. Let's start with an example to see how the array elements are interchanged.

interchange sorting

Display 6.12 shows how an array is sorted by interchanging values. The first picture is the array with its starting values. The smallest value in the array is the 3 in a[4]. So the value in a[4] needs to be interchanged with the value in a[0]. After that interchange, the smallest value is in a[0] where it belongs. The next smallest value is the 5 in a[6]. So, the value in a[6] needs to be interchanged with the value in a[1]. After that, the values in a[0] and a[1] are the smallest and next smallest values, which is what they should be in the final sorted array. The algorithm then interchanges the next smallest element with a[2], and so forth until the entire array is sorted.

This analysis produces the following pseudocode version of the selection sort algorithm:

pseudocode

```
Selection Sort Algorithm to Sort an Array a

for (index = 0; index < a.length - 1; index++)
{//Place the correct value in a[index]:
    indexOfNextSmallest = the index of the smallest value among
                    a[index], a[index+1], ..., a[a.length-1];
    Interchange the values of a[index] and a[indexOfNextSmallest].
    //a[0] <= a[1] <=...<= a[index] and these are the
    //smallest of the original array elements.
    //The remaining positions contain the rest of
    //the original array elements.
}
```

Notice that the *for*-loop ends with the last value of index equal to a.length − 2, even though the last index is a.length − 1. This is OK because when there is only one element left to be switched into position (namely, a[a.length − 1]), then that element must already be in the correct place. To see this just, note that when the algorithm gets all the elements except a[a.length − 1] correctly sorted, then the correct value for a[a.length − 1] is the smallest value left to be moved, and the only value left to be moved is the value that is already in a[a.length − 1].

Display 6.13 contains a class with a static method named sort that implements this selection sort algorithm. The method sort uses two private helping methods named indexOfSmallest and interchange. Once you understand the methods indexOfSmallest and interchange, it is easy to see that the definition of the method sort is a direct translation of our pseudocode into Java code. So, let's discuss the methods indexOfSmallest and interchange.

The method indexOfSmallest searches the following array elements and returns the index of the smallest of the following:

indexOf-Smallest

```
a[startIndex], a[startIndex+1], ..., a[a.length-1]
```

Display 6.13   Selection Sort Class *(Part 1 of 2)*

```
/***************************************************
*Class for sorting an array of ints from smallest to largest.
***************************************************/
public class SelectionSort
{
    /*********************************************
     *Precondition:
     *Every indexed variable of the array a has a value.
     *Action: Sorts the array a so that
     *a[0] <= a[1] <= ... <= a[a.length – 1].
     *********************************************/
    public static void sort(int[] a)
    {
        int index, indexOfNextSmallest;
        for (index = 0; index < a.length – 1; index++)
        {//Place the correct value in a[index]:
            indexOfNextSmallest = indexOfSmallest(index, a);
            interchange(index,indexOfNextSmallest, a);
            //a[0] <= a[1] <=...<= a[index] and these are the
            //smallest of the original array elements.
            //The remaining positions contain the rest of
            //the original array elements.
        }
    }


    /****************************************************
     *Precondition: i and j are legal indexes for the array a.
     *Postcondition:
     *The values of a[i] and a[j] have been interchanged.
     ****************************************************/
    private static void interchange(int i, int j, int[] a)
    {
        int temp;
        temp = a[i];
        a[i] = a[j];
        a[j] = temp;//original value of a[i]
    }
```

Display 6.13 Selection Sort Class *(Part 2 of 2)*

```
/*********************************************
 *Returns the index of the smallest value among
 *a[startIndex], a[startIndex+1], ... a[a.length–1]
 *********************************************/
private static int indexOfSmallest(int startIndex, int[] a)
{
    int min = a[startIndex];
    int indexOfMin = startIndex;
    int index;
    for (index = startIndex + 1; index < a.length; index++)
        if (a[index] < min)
        {
            min = a[index];
            indexOfMin = index;
            //min is the smallest of a[startIndex] through a[index]
        }

    return indexOfMin;
    }
 }
```

The method does this using the two local variables min and indexOfMin. At any point in its search, min is equal to smallest array value found so far, and indexOfMin is the index of that value. Thus, among other things, a[indexOfMin] has the value min. Initially, min is set to a[startIndex], which is the first value considered for min, and indexOfMin is set to startIndex. Then, each array element is considered in turn to see if it is a new minimum. After all the candidate array elements are checked, the method returns the value of indexOfMin.

The method named interchange will interchange the values of a[i] and a[j]. There is one subtle point in this definition. If you execute the code

        a[i] = a[j];

then you will lose the value originally held in a[i]. So, before this is executed, the value of a[i] is saved in the local variable temp.

Display 6.14 contains a demonstration program that shows the selection sort class in action.

There are a number of well-known sorting algorithms, many of them more efficient (and more complicated) than selection sort. However, selection sort will suffice as an introduction to the general topic of sorting.

Display 6.14   Demonstration of the `SelectionSort` Class

• •

```java
public class SelectionSortDemo
{
    public static void main(String[] args)
    {
        int[] b = {7, 5, 11, 2, 16, 4, 18, 14, 12, 30};

        System.out.println("Array values before sorting:");
        int i;
        for (i = 0; i < b.length; i++)
            System.out.print(b[i] + " ");
        System.out.println();

        SelectionSort.sort(b);

        System.out.println("Array values after sorting:");
        for (i = 0; i < b.length; i++)
            System.out.print(b[i] + " ");
        System.out.println();
    }
}
```

Screen Output

```
Array values before sorting:
7 5 11 2 16 4 18 14 12 30
Array values after sorting:
2 4 5 7 11 12 14 16 18 30
```

• •

■ **Programming Tip**

Correctness versus Efficiency

The selection sort algorithm is not the most efficient sorting algorithm. In fact, it is significantly less efficient than a number of well-known sorting algorithms, but the selection sort algorithm is much simpler than these other algorithms. A simpler algorithm is less likely to have errors creep in when you code it. So, if you need to code a sorting algorithm in a hurry, it would be safer to use a selection sort (or some other simple algorithm).

On the other hand, if efficiency is a major issue, you may wish to use a more complicated and more efficient algorithm. But, be aware that the more complicated algorithm will take longer to code, test, and debug. Efficiency can be a subtle topic. Remember, getting the wrong result is always inefficient no matter how quickly your program can come up with the result.

? Self-Test Questions

16. How do you sort the following array using the class `SelectionSort`?

    `int[] myArray = {9, 22, 3, 2, 87, −17, 12, 14, 33, −2};`

17. How would you need to change the class `SelectionSort` so that it can sort an array of values of type *double* (rather than of type *int*)?

18. How would you need to change the class `SelectionSort` so that it can sort an array of values of type *int* into decreasing order, instead of increasing order?

19. If an array of *ints* has a value that occurs twice (like `b[0]` == 7 and `b[5]` == 7) and you sort the array using the method `SelectionSort.sort`, will there be one or two copies of the repeated value after the array is sorted?

6.5 | Multidimensional Arrays

> *Never trust to general impressions, my boy,*
> *but concentrate yourself upon details.*
>
> **Sir Arthur Conan Doyle,**
> **A Case of Identity (Sherlock Holmes)**

It is sometimes useful to have an array with more than one index. For example, suppose you wanted to store the figures in Display 6.15 in some sort of array. The shaded part is just labeling. The nonshaded portion shows the actual entries. There are 60 entries. If you use an array with one index, then the array will have length 60 and it would be almost impossible to keep track of which entry goes with which index number. On the other hand, if you allow yourself two indexes, you can use one index for the row and one index for the column. This is illustrated in Display 6.16. Note that, as was true for the simple arrays we have already seen, we begin numbering indexes with zero rather than one. The Java notation for array elements with multiple indexes is also illustrated in Display 6.16. If the array is named `table` and it has two indexes, then `table[3][2]` is the entry in row number 3 and column number 2. Arrays that have exactly two entries can be displayed on paper as a two-dimensional table, and are called **two-dimensional arrays**. By convention, we think of the first entry as

two-dimensional array

Display 6.15 A Table of Values

	Balances for Various Interest Rates Compounded Annually (Rounded to Whole Dollar Amounts)					
Year	**5.00%**	**5.50%**	**6.00%**	**6.50%**	**7.00%**	**7.50%**
1	$1050	$1055	$1060	$1065	$1070	$1075
2	$1103	$1113	$1124	$1134	$1145	$1156
3	$1158	$1174	$1191	$1208	$1225	$1242
4	$1216	$1239	$1262	$1286	$1311	$1335
5	$1276	$1307	$1338	$1370	$1403	$1436
6	$1340	$1379	$1419	$1459	$1501	$1543
7	$1407	$1455	$1504	$1554	$1606	$1659
8	$1477	$1535	$1594	$1655	$1718	$1783
9	$1551	$1619	$1689	$1763	$1838	$1917
10	$1629	$1708	$1791	$1877	$1967	$2061

n-dimensional array

denoting the row and the second as denoting the column. More generally, an array is said to be an *n*-**dimensional array** if it has *n* indexes. Thus, the ordinary one-index arrays that we used up to now are **one-dimensional arrays**.

Multidimensional-Array Basics

declarations

Arrays with multiple indexes are handled much like arrays with a single index. To illustrate the details, we will take you through a Java example program that displays an array like the one in Display 6.16. The program is shown in Display 6.17. The array is called table. The name table is declared, and the array is created, as follows:

```
int[][] table = new int[10][6];
```

As you might expect, this is equivalent to the two steps:

```
int[][] table;
table = new int[10][6];
```

Note that this is almost identical to the syntax you used for the one-dimensional case. The only difference is that we added a second pair of square brackets in two places, and we gave a number specifying the size of the second dimension (that is, the num-

Display 6.16 Row and Column Indexes for an Array Named `table`

Row Index 3

indexes	0	1	2	3	4	5
0	$1050	$1055	$1060	$1065	$1070	$1075
1	$1103	$1113	$1124	$1134	$1145	$1156
2	$1158	$1174	$1191	$1208	$1225	$1242
3	$1216	$1239	$1262	$1286	$1311	$1335
4	$1276	$1307	$1338	$1370	$1403	$1436
5	$1340	$1379	$1419	$1459	$1501	$1543
6	$1407	$1455	$1504	$1554	$1606	$1659
7	$1477	$1535	$1594	$1655	$1718	$1783
8	$1551	$1619	$1689	$1763	$1838	$1917
9	$1629	$1708	$1791	$1877	$1967	$2061

`table[3][2]` has a value of 1262

Column Index 2

ber of indexes in the second positions). You can have arrays with any number of indexes. To get more indexes, you just use more square brackets in the declaration.

Indexed variables for multidimensional arrays are just like indexed variables for one-dimensional arrays, except that they have multiple indexes, each enclosed in a pair of square brackets. This is illustrated by the following *for*-loop from Display 6.17:

indexed variables

```
for (row = 0; row < 10; row++)
    for (column = 0; column < 6; column++)
        table[row][column] =
            balance(1000.00, row + 1, (5 + 0.5*column));
```

Note that we used two *for*-loops, one nested within the other. This is a common way of stepping through all the indexed variables in a two-dimensional array. If there had been three indexes, then we would use three nested *for*-loops, and so forth for higher numbers of indexes. The illustration in Display 6.16 may help you to understand the meaning of the indexes in `table[row][column]` and the meaning of the nested *for*-loops.

Display 6.17 Using a Two-Dimensional Array *(Part 1 of 2)*

```
/*************************************************
 *Displays a two-dimensional table showing how interest
 *rates affect bank balances.
 *************************************************/
public class InterestTable
{
    public static void main(String[] args)
    {
        int[][] table = new int[10][6];
        int row, column;
        for (row = 0; row < 10; row++)
           for (column = 0; column < 6; column++)
              table[row][column] =
                   balance(1000.00, row + 1, (5 + 0.5*column));
        System.out.println("Balances for Various Interest Rates");
        System.out.println("Compounded Annually");
        System.out.println("(Rounded to Whole Dollar Amounts)");
        System.out.println("Years 5.00% 5.50% 6.00% 6.50% 7.00% 7.50%");
        System.out.println();
        for (row = 0; row < 10; row++)
        {
            System.out.print((row + 1) + "        ");
               for (column = 0; column < 6; column++)
                   System.out.print("$" + table[row][column] + "  ");
            System.out.println();
        }
    }

/*************************************************************
 *Returns the balance in an account that starts with startBalance
 *and is left for the indicated number of years with rate as the
 *interest rate.  Interest is compounded annually. The balance is
 *rounded to a whole number.
 *************************************************************/
public static int balance(double startBalance, int years, double rate)
{
    double runningBalance = startBalance;
    int count;
    for (count = 1; count <= years; count++)
       runningBalance = runningBalance*(1 + rate/100);
    return (int) (Math.round(runningBalance));
}
}
```

> A real application would do something more with the array `table`. This is just a demonstration program.

Display 6.17 Using a Two-Dimensional Array *(Part 2 of 2)*

Sample Screen Dialogue

```
Balances for Various Interest Rates
Compounded Annually
(Rounded to Whole Dollar Amounts)
Years   5.00%   5.50%   6.00%   6.50%   7.00%   7.50%

1       $1050   $1055   $1060   $1065   $1070   $1075
2       $1103   $1113   $1124   $1134   $1145   $1156
3       $1158   $1174   $1191   $1208   $1225   $1242
4       $1216   $1239   $1262   $1286   $1311   $1335
5       $1276   $1307   $1338   $1370   $1403   $1436
6       $1340   $1379   $1419   $1459   $1501   $1543
7       $1407   $1455   $1504   $1554   $1606   $1659
8       $1477   $1535   $1594   $1655   $1718   $1783
9       $1551   $1619   $1689   $1763   $1838   $1917
10       $1629   $1708   $1791   $1877   $1967   $2061
```

The last line is out of alignment because 10 has two digits. This is easy to fix, but that would clutter the discussion of arrays with extraneous concerns.

As was true of the indexed variables for one-dimensional arrays, indexed variables for multidimensional arrays are variables of the base type and can be used anyplace that a variable of the base type is allowed. For example, for the two-dimensional array `table` in Display 6.17, an indexed variable, such as `table[3][2]`, is a variable of type *int* and can be used anyplace that an ordinary *int* variable can be used.

Declaring and Creating a Multidimensional Array

You declare a multidimensional-array name and create a multidimensional array in basically the same way that you create and name a one-dimensional array. You simply use as many square brackets as there are indexes.

Syntax:

Base_Type[ ]...[ ] *Array_Name* = new *Base_Type*[*Length_1*]...[*Length_n*];

Examples:

```
char[][] page = new char[100][80];
int[][] table = new int[10][6];
double[][][] threeDPicture = new double[10][20][30];
SomeClass[][] entry = new SomeClass[100][80];
```

SomeClass is a class.

■ Gotcha

Reversing Two Array Indexes

Suppose you have a two-dimensional array named test such that test[i][j] holds the grade that student i received on test number j. Now suppose student 1 received a 100 on test 1 and test 2, and student number 2 received a 0 on tests 1 and 2. Then you have:

```
test[1][1] == 100
test[1][2] == 100
test[2][1] == 0
test[2][2] == 0
```

If you confuse the indexes, you would give test[1][2] and test[2][2] to student number 2. So, student number 2 gets one 100 and one 0, which is a good deal for student 2, since she/he really got two 0's. On the other hand, student 1 would get the grades test[1][1] and test[2][1]. So, student 1 would also get one 100 and one 0, which is a big injustice, since student 1 really got two 100's. In both cases, the program will give very incorrect results.

Naming the indexes will help in many ways, but it is no insurance against this problem. If studentNumber and testNumber are both integer variables, then

```
test[studentNumber][testNumber]
test[testNumber][studentNumber]
```

are both valid expressions, but only one is likely to be correct for the task at hand. In this sort of situation, it pays to take Sherlock Holmes's advice: *Never trust to general impressions, my boy* (or girl), *but concentrate yourself upon details.*

Multidimensional-Array Parameters and Returned Values

array
arguments

Methods may have multidimensional-array parameters and may return a multidimensional array as the value returned. Again, the situation is similar to that of the one-dimensional case except that you use more square brackets. A two-dimensional array parameter is illustrated in Display 6.18. That program is a slight rewrite of the program in Display 6.17. Note that the type for the array parameter is *int[][]*.

If you want to return a multidimensional array, then you use the same sort of type specification as you use for a multidimensional-array parameter. For example, the following method returns a two-dimensional array of *double*s:

returning an array

```
/*************************************************
 *Precondition: Each dimension of startArray is at least the
 *value of size.
 *The array returned is the same as the size-by-size
 *upper left corner of the array startArray.
 *************************************************/
public static double[][] corner(double[][] startArray, int size)
{
    double[][] temp = new double[size][size];
    int row, column;
    for (row = 0; row < size; row++)
        for (column = 0; column < size; column++)
            temp[row][column] = startArray[row][column];
    return temp;
}
```

Implementation of Multidimensional Arrays

In Java, multidimensional arrays are implemented using one-dimensional arrays. For example, consider the array

```
int[][] table = new int[10][6];
```

The array *table* is in fact a one-dimensional array of length 10 and its base type is the type *int[]*. In other words, multidimensional arrays are arrays of arrays.

arrays of arrays

Normally, you do not need to be concerned with the fact that multidimensional arrays are arrays of arrays. This detail is handled automatically by the compiler. However, there are a few occasions when you can profitably use your knowledge of this detail. For example, suppose you want to write a *for*-loop to fill a two-dimensional array with values. In the program in Display 6.18, we used the constants 6 and 10 to control the *for*-loops. It would be better style to use the *length* instance variable to control the *for*-loops. But when using the *length* instance variable, you need to think in terms of arrays of arrays. For example, the following is a rewrite of the nested *for*-loop in the *main* method in Display 6.18:

length

```
for (row = 0; row < table.length; row++)
    for (column = 0; column < table[row].length; column++)
        table[row][column] = balance(1000.00, row + 1, (5 + 0.5*column));
```

Let's analyze this nested *for*-loop in a bit more detail.

The array *table* is created with the following:

```
int[][] table = new int[10][6];
```

That means that *table* is actually a one-dimensional array of length 10, and each of the 10 indexed variables *table[0]* through *table[9]* is a one-dimensional

Display 6.18 A Multidimensional-Array Parameter

```
/***********************************************
 *Displays a two-dimensional table showing how interest
 *rates affect bank balances.
 ***********************************************/
public class InterestTable2
{
    public static void main(String[] args)
    {
        int[][] table = new int[10][6];
        int row, column;
        for (row = 0; row < 10; row++)
            for (column = 0; column < 6; column++)
                table[row][column] =
                    balance(1000.00, row + 1, (5 + 0.5*column));

        System.out.println("Balances for Various Interest Rates");
        System.out.println("Compounded Annually");
        System.out.println("(Rounded to Whole Dollar Amounts)");
        System.out.println("Years 5.00% 5.50% 6.00% 6.50% 7.00% 7.50%");
        System.out.println();
        showTable(table);
    }


    /***************************************************************
     *Precondition: The array displayArray has 10 rows and 6 columns.
     *Postcondition: The array contents are displayed with dollar signs.
     ***************************************************************/
    public static void showTable(int[][] displayArray)
    {
        int row, column;
        for (row = 0; row < 10; row++)
        {
            System.out.print((row + 1) + "         ");
            for (column = 0; column < 6; column++)
                System.out.print("$" + displayArray[row][column] + "   ");
            System.out.println();
        }
    }
```

> We will give a better definition of showTable later in the chapter.

> The output is the same as in Display 6.17/page 432.

```
    public static int balance(double startBalance, int years, double rate)
```
<The rest of the definition of balance is the same as in Display 6.17/page 432.>

```
}
```

Multidimensional-Array Parameters

An argument to a method may be an entire multidimensional array. The syntax is almost identical to that of one-dimensional array parameters, except that more square brackets [ ] are used.

Examples: (of multidimensional-array formal parameters):

```java
public static void showOneElement(char[][] a, int row, int column)
{
    System.out.print(a[row][column]);
}

public static void reinitialize(int[][] anArray)
{
    int row, column;
    for (row = 0; row < anArray.length; row++)
        for (column = 0; column < anArray[row].length; column++)
            anArray[row][column] = 0;
}
```

Examples: (of array arguments):

```java
char[][] page = new char[100][80];
int[][] a = new int[10][20];
int[][] b = new int[30][40];
    <Some code to fill the arrays goes here.>
showOneElement(page, 5, 10);
reinitialize(a);
reinitialize(b);
```

*length is explained in the subsection **Implementation of Multidimensional Arrays.***

Note that the arrays a and b have different dimensions. Also, note that no square brackets are used with array arguments.

(Preceding examples are in a method definition. All method definitions are assumed to be in the same class.)

Returning a Multidimensional Array

A method can return a multidimensional array value. The syntax is almost identical to that used to return one-dimensional arrays, except that more square brackets [ ] are used.

Syntax:

```java
public static Base_Type[]...[] Method_Name(Parameter_List)
Method_Body
```

You can use other modifiers instead of `public static`.

Example: (assumed to be in a class definition):

```java
public static char[][] blankPage(
                int numberOfLines, int charPerLine)
{
    char[][] newArray = new char[numberOfLines][charPerLine];
    int line, character;
    for (line = 0; line < numberOfLines; line++)
        for (character = 0; character < charPerLine; character++)
            newArray[line][character] = ' ';
    return newArray;
}
```

array of *int*s of length 6. That is why the first *for*-loop is terminated using `table.length`. For a two-dimensional array, like `table`, the value of `length` is the number of first indexes, or equivalently the number of rows, or in this case 10. Now let's consider the second *for*-loop.

The 0th row in the two-dimensional array `table` is the one-dimensional array `table[0]`, and it has `table[0].length` entries. More generally, `table[row]` is a one-dimensional array of *int*s and it has `table[row].length` entries. That is why the second *for*-loop is terminated using `table[row].length`. Of course, in this case, `table[0].length`, `table[1].length`, ... `table[9].length` all happen to equal 6.

You can use the fact that multidimensional arrays are arrays of arrays to rewrite the method `showTable` in Display 6.18. Notice that in Display 6.18, the method `showTable` assumes its array argument has 10 rows and 6 columns. That is fine for this particular program, but a nicer definition of `showTable` would work for an array of any two dimensions. In Display 6.19, we have redefined the method `showTable` so that its argument can be any two-dimensional array of *int*s with any number of rows and any number of columns.

Ragged Arrays *(Optional)*

Since a two-dimensional array in Java is an array of arrays, there is no need for each row to have the same number of entries. To phrase it slightly differently, different rows can have different numbers of columns. These sorts of arrays are called **ragged arrays**.

To illustrate what is involved, let's start with an ordinary, nonragged two dimensional array, created as follows:

```
int[][] a = new int[3][5];
```

This is equivalent to the following:

```
int[][] a;
a = new int[3][];
a[0] = new int[5];
a[1] = new int[5];
a[2] = new int[5];
```

The line

```
a = new int[3][];
```

makes `a` the name of an array of length 3, each entry of which is a name for an array of *int*s that can be of any length. The next three lines each create an array of *int*s of length 5 to be named by `a[0]`, `a[1]`, and `a[2]`. The net result is a two-dimensional array of *int*s with three rows and five columns.

The statements

```
a[0] = new int[5];
a[1] = new int[5];
a[2] = new int[5];
```

Display 6.19 The Method showTable **Redefined**

```
/************************************************************
 *The array displayArray can have any dimensions.
 *Postcondition: The array contents are displayed with dollar signs.
 *************************************************************/
public static void showTable(int[][] displayArray)
{
    int row, column;
    for (row = 0; row < displayArray.length; row++)
    {
        System.out.print((row + 1) + "      ");
        for (column = 0; column < displayArray[row].length; column++)
            System.out.print("$" + displayArray[row][column] + "  ");
        System.out.println();
    }
}
```

This version of showTable *will work for an array with any number of rows and any number of columns. In the program in Display 6.18/page 436, this version would behave the same as the version given in Display 6.18, but this version is more versatile and can be used in more different situations.*

The program InterestTable3 *on the accompanying CD uses this method in a complete program.*

invite the question: "Do all the lengths need to be 5?" The answer is *no*. In what follows, we define a similar (ragged) array b in which each row has a different length:

```
int[][] b;
b = new int[3][];
b[0] = new int[5];
b[1] = new int[7];
b[2] = new int[4];
```

It is worth noting that after you fill the preceding array b with values, you can display the array using the method showTable as defined in Display 6.19/page 439. However, you could not display b using showTable if you instead defined showTable as we did in Display 6.18/page 436.

There are situations where you can profitably use ragged arrays, but most applications do not require ragged arrays. However, if you understand ragged arrays, you will have a better understanding of how all multidimensional arrays work in Java.

Programming Example
Employee Time Records

In this programming example, a two-dimensional array named hours is used to store the number of hours worked by each employee of a company for each of the five days Monday through Friday. The first array index is used to designate a day of the week, and the second array index is used to designate an employee. The two-dimensional array is a private instance variable in a class named TimeBook in Display 6.20. The class includes a demonstration program in the method main that works for a small company with only three employees. The employees are numbered starting with 1, and the array indexes are numbered starting with 0, so an adjustment of minus one is sometimes needed when specifying and employee's array index. For example, the hours worked by employee number 3 on Tuesday is recorded in hours[1][2]. The first index denotes the second work day of the week (Tuesday), and the second index denotes the third employee. Days are numbered 0 for Monday, 1 for Tuesday, and so forth. Employees are numbered 1, 2, 3 but are stored in array index positions 0, 1, 2, and so you need to subtract one from the employee number to obtain the correct employee index.

The class TimeBook shown in Display 6.20 is not yet complete. It needs more methods to be a really useful class, but it has enough methods for the demonstration program in main. You can think of the definition in Display 6.20 as a first pass at writing the class definition. It even still has a stub for the definition of the method setHours. Recall that a stub is a definition of a method that can be used for testing, but which is not the final method definition. In one of the Programming Exercises, you are asked to complete this class definition, but at this stage, it is complete enough to illustrate the use of the two-dimensional array hours, which is an instance variable of the class.

The class TimeBook uses two ordinary one-dimensional arrays as instance variables, in addition to the two-dimensional array hours. The array weekHours is used to record the total hours worked in a week for each of the employees. The method computeWeekHours will set weekHours[0] equal to the total number of hours work by employee 1 in the week, weekHours[1] equal to the total number of hours work by employee 2 in the week, and so forth. The array dayHours will be used to record the total number of hours worked by all the employees on each day of the week. The method computeDayHours will set dayHours[0] equal to the total number of hours worked on Monday by all of the employees combined, will set dayHours[1] equal to the total number of hours worked on Tuesday by all of the employees, and so forth. Display 6.21 illustrates the relationships among the arrays hours, weekHours, and dayHours. In that display, we have shown some sample data for the array hours. These data, in turn, determine the values stored in weekHours and in dayHours.

Be sure to notice how the method computeWeekHours uses the array indexes of the two-dimensional array hours. There is a *for*-loop nested inside of a *for*-loop.

stub

Display 6.20   Time Keeping Program *(Part 1 of 4)*

```
/*************************************************
 *Class for a one-week record of the time worked by
 *each Employee. Uses a five-day week (Mon.-Fri.).
 *main has a sample application.
 ************************************************/
public class TimeBook
{
    private int numberOfEmployees;
    private int[][] hours;
        //hours[i][j] has the hours for employee j on day i.
    private int[] weekHours;
        //weekHours[i] has the week's hours work for employee i+1.
    private int[] dayHours;
        //dayHours[i] has the total hours worked by all employees.
        //on day i. Monday is 0, Tuesday 1, etc.,


    /***************************************************
     *Reads hours worked for each employee on each day of
     *the week into the two-dimensional array hours. (The method
     *for input is just a stub in this preliminary version.)
     *Computes the total weekly hours for each employee and
     *the total daily hours for all employees combined.
     **************************************************/
    public static void main(String[] args)
    {
        TimeBook book = new TimeBook(3);
        book.setHours();
        book.update();
        book.showTable();
    }
```

A real class would have more methods. We have only shown the methods used in main

```
    public TimeBook(int theNumberOfEmployees)
    {
        numberOfEmployees = theNumberOfEmployees;
        hours = new int[5][numberOfEmployees];
        //the 5 is for the 5 days Monday through Friday.
        weekHours = new int[numberOfEmployees];
        dayHours = new int[5];
    }
```

Display 6.20 Time Keeping Program *(Part 2 of 4)*

```java
public void setHours() //This is just a stub.
{
    hours[0][0] = 8;  hours[0][1] = 0;  hours[0][2] = 9;
    hours[1][0] = 8;  hours[1][1] = 0;  hours[1][2] = 9;
    hours[2][0] = 8;  hours[2][1] = 8;  hours[2][2] = 8;
    hours[3][0] = 8;  hours[3][1] = 8;  hours[3][2] = 4;
    hours[4][0] = 8;  hours[4][1] = 8;  hours[4][2] = 8;
}

public void update()
{
    computeWeekHours();
    computeDayHours();
}

private void computeWeekHours()
{
    int dayNumber, employeeNumber, sum;

    for (employeeNumber = 1;
         employeeNumber <= numberOfEmployees; employeeNumber++)
    {//Process one employee:
        sum = 0;
        for(dayNumber = 0; dayNumber < 5; dayNumber++)
            sum = sum + hours[dayNumber][employeeNumber - 1];
            //sum contains the sum of all the hours worked
            //in one week by employee with number employeeNumber.
        weekHours[employeeNumber - 1] = sum;
    }
}

private void computeDayHours()
{
    int dayNumber, employeeNumber, sum;

    for (dayNumber = 0; dayNumber < 5; dayNumber++)
    {//Process one day's (for all employees):
        sum = 0;
        for (employeeNumber = 1;
             employeeNumber <= numberOfEmployees; employeeNumber++)
            sum = sum + hours[dayNumber][employeeNumber - 1];
            //sum contains the sum of all hours worked by all
            //employees on day dayNumber.
        dayHours[dayNumber] = sum;
    }
}
```

Display 6.20 Time Keeping Program *(Part 3 of 4)*

```java
public void showTable()
{
    int row, column;
    System.out.print("Employee   ");
    for (column = 0; column < numberOfEmployees; column++)
        System.out.print((column + 1) + "     ");
    System.out.println("totals");
    System.out.println();

    for (row = 0; row < 5; row++)
    {
        System.out.print(day(row) + "  ");
        for (column = 0; column < hours[row].length; column++)
            System.out.print(hours[row][column] + "     ");
        System.out.println(dayHours[row]);
    }
    System.out.println();

    System.out.print("Total   =   ");
    for (column = 0; column < numberOfEmployees; column++)
        System.out.print(weekHours[column] + "   ");
    System.out.println();
}

//Converts 0 to "Monday", 1 to "Tuesday" etc.
//Blanks used to make all strings the same length.
private String day(int dayNumber)
{
    String dayName = null;
    switch (dayNumber)
    {
        case 0:
            dayName = "Monday   ";
            break;
        case 1:
            dayName = "Tuesday  ";
            break;
        case 2:
            dayName = "Wednesday";
            break;
```

> The method `showTable` can and should be made more robust. See Programming *Exercise 6.*

Display 6.20 Time Keeping Program *(Part 4 of 4)*

```
            case 3:
                dayName = "Thursday ";
                break;
            case 4:
                dayName = "Friday    ";
                break;
            default:
                System.out.println("Fatal Error.");
                System.exit(0);
                break;
        }

        return dayName;
    }

}
```

Sample Screen Dialogue

```
<In the final program, the stub setHours would be replaced with a
real method and there would then be an input dialog here that obtains the
numbers of hours worked by each employee on each day.>

Employee  1    2    3     totals

Monday    8    0    9     17
Tuesday   8    0    9     17
Wednesday 8    8    8     24
Thursday  8    8    4     20
Friday    8    8    8     24

Total  =  40   24   38
```

Display 6.21 Arrays for the Class `TimeBook`

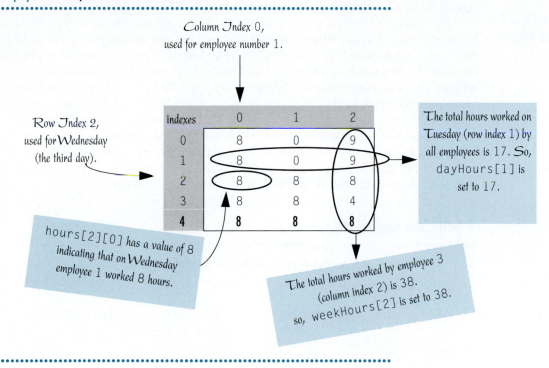

Column Index 0, used for employee number 1.

Row Index 2, used for Wednesday (the third day).

The total hours worked on Tuesday (row index 1) by all employees is 17. So, `dayHours[1]` is set to 17.

`hours[2][0]` has a value of 8 indicating that on Wednesday employee 1 worked 8 hours.

The total hours worked by employee 3 (column index 2) is 38. so, `weekHours[2]` is set to 38.

The outer *for*-loop cycles through all employees, and the inner *for*-loop is executed once for each day of the week. The five days of the week (Monday through Friday) are represented by the five numbers 0 through 4. The inner *for*-loop (together with an initialization of the variable `sum` and a following assignment statement) is reproduced in what follows:

```
sum = 0;
for(dayNumber = 0; dayNumber < 5; dayNumber++)
    sum = sum + hours[dayNumber][employeeNumber - 1];
    //sum contains the sum of all the hours worked
    //in one week by employee with number employeeNumber.
weekHours[employeeNumber - 1] = sum;
```

Note that when computing the sum of the hours for one employee, the second index, which represents the particular employee, is held constant. This inner *for*-loop goes through all values of the first index, and in this way cycles through all the days for the single employee represented by the second index.

The method `computeDayHours` works in a similar way to compute the total number of hours worked by all employees on each day of the week. However, in this case, the inner *for*-loop cycles through the second index while the first index is held constant. Or to phrase it another way, the roles of the employee index and the day of the week index are interchanged.

completing class definition

The class TimeBook is not yet a finished piece of software ready to be saved and reused again and again. What is there is correct, but not yet complete. The method setHours is just a stub and needs to be replaced by a more generally applicable method that obtains hours from the user at the keyboard. The method showTable will not give a display as neat as the one in Display 6.20 unless all the hours have the same number of digits. The method showTable needs to be made more robust so that it will neatly display any combination of hours worked. Finally, the class Time-Book should have more methods so it will be a class that is useful in a wide range of situations. In one of the Programming Exercises, you are asked to complete the definition of the class TimeBook in all of these ways. The version in Display 6.20 does, however, show all the essentials of using the two-dimensional array hours.

? Self-Test Questions

20. What is the output produced by the following code?

```
int[][] testArray = new int[4][4];
int index1, index2;
for (index1 = 0; index1 < testArray.length; index1++)
    for (index2 = 0; index2 < testArray[index1].length; index2++)
        testArray[index1][index2] = index2;
for (index1 = 0; index1 < testArray.length; index1++)
{
    for (index2 = 0; index2 < testArray[index1].length; index2++)
        System.out.print(testArray[index1][index2] + " ");
    System.out.println();
}
```

21. Write code that will fill the array a (declared in what follows) with numbers typed in at the keyboard. The numbers will be input five per line, on four lines (although your solution need not depend on how the input numbers are divided into lines):

```
int[][] a = new int [4][5];
```

22. Write a method definition for a *void* method called display such that the following invocation will display the contents of the array a in Self-Test Question 21, and will display it in the same format as we specified for the input there (that is, four lines of five numbers per line):

```
display(a);
```

Your method definition should also work for two-dimensional arrays that have sizes other than 4 by 5. Make your method a static method that can be added to a class.

CHAPTER SUMMARY

- An array can be thought of as a collection of variables all of the same type. An array can also be considered a single object with a large composite value consisting of all the elements of the array.

- Arrays are objects that are created with *new* just like the class objects we discussed before this chapter (although there is a slight difference in the syntax used).

- Array indexed variables are numbered starting with 0 and ending with the number one less than the length of the array. If a is an array, then a[i] is an indexed variable of the array a. The index i must have a value greater than or equal to 0 and strictly less than a.length. If i has any other value, that is called an **array index out of bounds error** and will cause an error message when you run your program.

- Array indexed variables are numbered starting with 0 and ending with the number one less than the length of the array. If a is an array, then a[i] is an indexed variable of the array a. The index i must have a value greater than or equal to 0 and strictly less than a.length. If i has any other value, that is called an **array index out of bounds error** and will cause an error message when you run your program.

- Array indexed variables are numbered starting with 0 and ending with the number one less than the length of the array. If a is an array, then a[i] is an indexed variable of the array a. The index i must have a value greater than or equal to 0 and strictly less than a.length. If i has any other value, that is called an **array index out of bounds error** and will cause an error message when you run your program.

- When an indexed variable is used as an argument to a method, it is treated just like any other argument of the base type. In particular, if the base type is a primitive type, then the method cannot change the value of the indexed variable, but if the base type is a class, then the method can change the element at the indexed variable.

- A method may return an array as the value returned by the method.

- When you only use part of an array, you normally store values in an initial segment of the array and use an *int* variable to keep track of how many values are stored in the array. This is called a partially filled array.

CHAPTER SUMMARY

■ An accessor method that returns an array corresponding to a private instance variable of an array type should be careful to return a copy of the array, and not to return the private instance variable itself.

■ The selection sort algorithm can be used to sort an array of values, such as numbers sorted into increasing order or numbers sorted into decreasing order.

■ You can have arrays with more than one index. These are known as multidimensional arrays.

■ A two-dimensional array can be thought of as a two-dimensional display with the first index giving the row and the second index giving the column.

■ Multidimensional arrays are implemented in Java as arrays of arrays.

? ANSWERS to Self-Test Questions

1. 0 2 4 6 8 10 12 14 16 18

2.
```
a
e
i
o
u
```

3.
```
Tide 1 is −7.3
Tide 2 is 14.2
```

4. The *for*-loop references elements b[1] through b[10], but there is no element indexed by 10. The array elements are b[0] through b[9]. If included in a complete class or program, the code will compile without any error messages, but when it is run, you will get an error message saying an array index is out of bounds.

5.

```java
public class Exercise
{
    public static void main(String[] args)
    {
        double[] a = new double[20];

        int index;
        System.out.println("Enter 20 numbers:");
        for (index = 0; index < a.length; index++)
            a[index] = SavitchIn.readLineDouble();

        System.out.println(
            "The numbers and differences from last number are:");
        for (index = 0; index < a.length; index++)
            System.out.println(a[index]
            + " differs from last by "
            + (a[a.length - 1] - a[index])));
    }
}
```

6.

```java
SalesAssociate[] entry = new SalesAssociate[3];
int i;
for (i = 0; i < entry.length; i++)
    entry[i] = new SalesAssociate("Jane Doe", 5000);
```

7. The lines that are changed are shown in color. Note that you should also change the definition of the method writeOutput in the class SalesAssociate. We have also shown it below. Remember that you must make the class Dollars available, either by placing it in the same directory or by putting it in a package and importing the package.

```java
/*******************************************
 *Displays sales report on console screen.
 ******************************************/
public void displayResults()
{
    System.out.println("Average sales per associate is $" + average);
    System.out.println("The highest sales figure is $" + highest);
    System.out.println();
    int i;
    System.out.println("The following had the highest sales:");
```

```
      for (i = 0; i < numberOfAssociates; i++)
      {
            double nextSales = record[i].getSales();
            if (nextSales == highest)
            {
                  record[i].writeOutput();
                  Dollars.write(nextSales - average);
                  System.out.println(" above the average.");
                  System.out.println();
            }
      }

      System.out.println("The rest performed as follows:");
      for (i = 0; i < numberOfAssociates; i++)
      {
            double nextSales = record[i].getSales();
            if (record[i].getSales() != highest)
            {
                  record[i].writeOutput();
                  if (nextSales >= average)
                  {
                        Dollars.write(nextSales - average);
                        System.out.println(" above the average.");
                  }
                  else
                  {
                        Dollars.write(average - nextSales);
                        System.out.println(" below the average.");
                  }

                  System.out.println();
            }
      }
}
```

Below is the rewritten version of the method `writeOutput` of the class `SalesAssociate`:

```
public void writeOutput()
{
      System.out.println("Sales associates: " + name);
      System.out.print("Sales: ");
      Dollars.writeln(sales);
}
```

8.
```
a[1] = a  b[1] = a
a[2] = a  b[2] = a
a[1] = a  b[1] = a
a[2] = b  b[2] = b
```

9.

```
public static void showArray(char[] a)
{
    int i;
    for (i = 0; i < a.length; i++)
        System.out.print(a[i]);
    System.out.println();//This line is optional.
}
```

10.

```
public static double[] halfArray(double[] a)
{
    double[] temp = new double[a.length];
    int i;
    for (i = 0; i < a.length; i++)
        temp[i] = a[i]/2.0;
    return temp;
}
```

11. If b is an array of size 10, then the invocation

```
doubleSize(b);
```

Will run with no error messages, but the size of b will not change. In fact nothing about b will change. The parameter a is a local variable that is initialized with a reference to b. The local variable a is changed so that it contains a reference to an array of twice the size of b, but that reference goes away as soon as the invocation ends.

12.

```
int i;
for (i = 0; i < a.length; i++)
    System.out.println(a[i]);
```

13.

```
int i;
for (i = 0; i < numberUsed; i++)
    System.out.println(a[i]);
```

14.

```
a[numberUsed] = 42;
numberUsed++;
```

15.

```
if (numberUsed == a.length)
    System.out.println("List is full. Cannot add 42.");
else
{
    a[numberUsed] = 42;
    numberUsed++;
}
```

16.

```
SelectionSort.sort(myArray);
```

17. Just change the types for the array elements to *double*. You can simply replace all occurrences of *int* by *double, except for those occurrences of int that give the type of an index*. For example, you would replace

    private static void interchange(*int* i, *int* j, *int[]* a)

    with

    private static void interchange(*int* i, *int* j, *double[]* a)

    Note that i and j are indexes and so they are still of type *int*.

18. All you need to do to make your code work for sorting into decreasing order is to replace the < with > in the following line of the definition of indexOfSmallest:

    if (a[index] < min)

    However, to make your code more readable, you should rename the method indexOfSmallest to something like indexOfLargest, rename the variable min to something like max, and rename the variable index-OfMin to something like indexOfMax. You should also rewrite some of the comments.

19. If an array of *int*s has a value that occurs twice and you sort the array using the method SelectionSort.sort, then there will be two copies of the repeated value after the array is sorted.

20.
    ```
    0 1 2 3
    0 1 2 3
    0 1 2 3
    0 1 2 3
    ```

21.
    ```
    int[][] a = new int [4][5];
    int row, column;

    System.out.println("Enter numbers:");
    for (row = 0; row < 4; row++)
        for (column = 0; column < 5; column++)
            a[row][column] = SavitchIn.readInt();
    ```

    Alternatively, you could use

    ```
    System.out.println("Enter numbers:");
    for (row = 0; row < a.length; row++)
        for (column = 0; column < a[row].length; column++)
            a[row][column] = SavitchIn.readInt();
    ```

22.
```
public static void display(int[][] anArray)
{
    int row, column;
    for (row = 0; row < anArray.length; row++)
    {
        for (column = 0; column < anArray[row].length;
                                           column++)
            System.out.print(anArray[row][column] + " ");
        System.out.println();
    }
}
```

? PROGRAMMING EXERCISES

1. Write a program that reads in a list of *int* values one per line and outputs their sum as well as all the numbers read in with each number annotated to say what percentage it contributes to the sum. Your program will ask the user how many integers there will be, create an array of that length, and then fill the array with the integers input. A possible dialogue is

```
How many numbers will you enter?
4
Enter 4 integers one per line:
2
1
1
2
The sum is 6.
The numbers are:
2 33.3333% of the sum.
1 16.6666% of the sum.
1 16.6666% of the sum.
2 33.3333% of the sum.
```

Use a method that takes the entire array as one argument and returns the sum of the numbers in the array.

2. Write a program that will read in a line of text and output a list of all the letters that occur in the text along with the number of times each letter occurs. End the line with a period that serves as a sentinel value. The letters should be listed in alphabetical order when they are output. Use an array of *ints* of length 26, so each indexed variable contains the count of how many letters there are. Array indexed variable 0 contains the number of a's, array indexed variable 1 contains the number of b's, and so forth. Allow both upper- and lowercase letters as input, but treat uppercase and lowercase versions of the same letter as being equal. *Hints:* You will want to use one of the functions toUpperCase or toLowerCase in the wrapper class Character described in Chapter 5. You will find it helpful to define

a method that takes a character as an argument and returns an *int* value that is the correct index for that character, such as 'a' returning 0, 'b' returning 1, and so forth. Note that you can use a type cast to change a *char* to an *int*, like (*int*)letter. Of course, this will not get the number you want, but if you subtract (*int*)'a', you will then get the right index. Allow the user to repeat this task until the user says she or he is through.

3. A **palindrome** is a string that reads the same forward and backwards, such as "warts n straw" or "radar". Write a program that will accept a string of characters terminated by a period and will determine whether or not the string (without the period) is a palindrome. You may assume that the input contains only letters and the blank symbol. You may also assume that the input word is at most 80 characters long. Disregard blanks when deciding if a string is a palindrome and consider upper- and lowercase version of the same letter to be equal, so the following will be considered a palindrome by your program:

"Able was I ere I saw Elba"

Your program need not check that the string is a correct English phrase or word. The string "xyzczyx" will be considered a palindrome by your program. Include a loop that allows the user to check additional strings until the user requests that the program end. For this exercise, you should define a static method called palindrome that begins as follows:

```
/*************************************************
 *Precondition: The array a contains letters and blanks in
 *positions a[0] through a[used - 1].
 *Returns true if the string is a palindrome and false otherwise.
 *************************************************/
public static boolean palindrome(char[] a, int used)
```

Your program will read the input string into an array with base type *char* and call the preceding method with the array and one other *int* variable. The other *int* variable keeps track of how much of the array is used as described in the subsection entitled **Partially Filled Arrays**.

4. Design a class called BubbleSort that is similar to the class Selection-Sort given in Display 6.13/page 426. The class BubbleSort will be used in exactly the same way as the class SelectionSort, but the class Bubble-Sort will use the bubble sort algorithm.

The bubble sort algorithm goes through all adjacent pairs of elements in the array from the beginning to the end and interchanges any two elements that are out of order. This brings the array closer to being sorted. This procedure is repeated until the array is sorted. The algorithm in pseudocode is as follows:

Bubble Sort Algorithm to Sort An Array a

Repeat the following until the array a is sorted:
```
for (index = 0; index < a.length - 1; index++)
    if (a[index] > a[index + 1])
        Interchange the values of a[index] and a[index + 1].
```

The bubble sort algorithm is very efficient for sorting an array that is "almost sorted." It is not competitive to other sorting methods for most other situations.

5. Design a class called `InsertionSort` that is similar to the class `Selec-tionSort` given in Display 6.13/page 426. The class `InsertionSort` will be used in exactly the same way as the class `SelectionSort`, but the class `InsertionSort` will use the insertion sort algorithm.

   The insertion sort algorithm uses an additional array and copies elements from the array to be sorted to the other array. As each element is copied, it is inserted into the correct position in the array. This will usually require moving a number of elements in the array receiving the new elements. The algorithm in pseudocode is as follows:

Insertion Sort Algorithm to Sort An Array a

```
for (index = 0; index < a.length; index++)
    insert the value of a[index] into the array temp so that
        all the elements so far copied into the array temp are sorted.
Copy all the elements from temp back to a.
```

The array `temp` will be a local variable in the method `sort`. The array `temp` will be a partially filled array. So, when it is only partly filled, all the values will be at the beginning of the array `temp`.

6. The class `TimeBook` in Display 6.20/page 441 is not really finished. Complete the definition of the class `TimeBook` in the way described on page 446. In particular, be sure to add a default constructor, accessor methods to recover and change each of the instance variables, and each indexed variable of each array instance variable. Be sure you replace the stub `setHours` with a method that obtains values from the keyboard. You should also define a private method with two *int* parameters that will output the first *int* parameter in the number of spaces given by a second parameter. The extra spaces not filled by the first *int* parameter are to be filled with blanks. This will let you, for example, write each array indexed element in exactly four spaces (or however many spaces you want), and so will allow you to output neat rectangular displays of array elements. Be sure the `main` in Display 6.20 works correctly with these new methods. Also, write a separate test program to test all the new methods. *Hint:* To output an *int* value *n* in a fixed number of spaces, use `Inte-ger.toString(n)` to covert the number to a string value and then work with the string value. This is discussed in the subsection *Integer, Dou-ble, and Other Wrapper Classes* on page 319 of Chapter 5.

7. Write a class definition for a class called `TicTacToe`. An object of type `TicTacToe` is a single game of `TicTacToe`. Store the game board as a single two-dimensional array of *char*s with three rows and three columns. Include methods to add a move, to display the board, to tell whose turn it is (X or O), to tell if there is a winner, to say who the winner is, and to reinitialize the game to the beginning. Write a `main` for the class that will allow the user to play the game at the terminal and keyboard. Both players will sit at the keyboard and enter their moves in turn.

CHAPTER 7

INHERITANCE

7.1   INHERITANCE BASICS 458
Programming Example A Person Class 459
Derived Classes 461
Overriding Method Definitions 465
Overriding Versus Overloading 466
The *final* Modifier 466
Gotcha Use of Private Instance Variables from the Base Class 466
Gotcha Private Methods Are Not Inherited 468

7.2   PROGRAMMING WITH INHERITANCE 469
Constructors in Derived Classes 469
The *this* Method (*Optional*) 470
Call to an Overridden Method 471
Programming Example MultiLevel Derived Classes 472
A Subtle Point About Overloading and Overriding (*Optional*) 475
Java Tip You Cannot Use Multiple *super*s 476

Programming Tip An Object of a Derived Class Has More than One Type 476
Programming Tip "Is a" and "Has a" 479
Methods Inherited from the Class *Object* 480
Case Study Character Graphics 482
Abstract Classes (*Optional*) 494

7.3   DYNAMIC BINDING AND POLYMORPHISM 496
Dynamic Binding 496
Type Checking and Dynamic Binding 498
Dynamic Binding with *toString* (*Optional*) 499
Polymorphism 500

Chapter Summary 501
Answers to Self-Test Questions 502
Programming Exercises 507

7

INHERITANCE

> *Like mother, like daughter.*
>
> **Common saying**

In this chapter, we cover *inheritance*, one of the key concepts in object-oriented programming, and one that is needed in order to use many of the libraries that come with the Java programming language. Inheritance will allow you to use an existing class to help you define new classes, making it easier to reuse software.

A related concept in object-oriented programming is *polymorphism*, which we also discuss in this chapter. Polymorphism is a way to use inheritance so different kinds of objects use different definitions (different actions) for the same method name.

Objectives

Become familiar with *inheritance* and *polymorphism* in general.

Learn how to use inheritance to define *derived classes* in Java.

Learn about *dynamic binding* in general and in Java.

Learn how to use *polymorphism* in Java.

Prerequisites

You need the material in Chapters 1 through 5 before you can understand this chapter. Chapter 6 is not needed for this chapter.

7.1 | Inheritance Basics

> *All men are mortal*
> *Socrates is a man.*
> *Therefore Socrates is mortal.*
>
> **Typical Syllogism**

inheritance

Inheritance is a major component of object-oriented programming. Inheritance will allow you to define a very general class, and then later define more specialized classes by simply adding some new details to the older more general class definition. This saves work, because the more specialized class *inherits* all the properties of the general class and you, the programmer, need only program the new features.

For example, you might define a class for vehicles that has instance variables to record the vehicle's number of wheels and maximum number of occupants. You might then define a class for automobiles, and let the automobile class *inherit* all the instance variables and methods of the class for vehicles. The class for automobiles would have added instance variables for such things as the amount of fuel in the fuel tank and the licence plate number, and would also have some added methods. (Some vehicles, such as a horse and wagon, have no fuel tank and normally no license plate, but an automobile is a vehicle that has these "added" items.) You would have to describe the added instance variables and added methods, but if you use Java's inheritance mechanism, you would get the instance variables and methods from the vehicle class automatically.

Before we construct an example of inheritance within Java, we first need to set the stage with the following Programming Example.

Programming Example
A Person Class

Display 7.1 contains a simple class called `Person`. This class is so simple that the only property it gives a person is a name. We will not have much use for the class `Person` by itself, but we will use the class `Person` in defining other classes. So, it is important to understand this class.

Most of the methods for the class `Person` are straightforward. Notice that the method `setName` and the constructor with one `String` parameter do the same thing. We need these two methods, even though they do the same thing, because only the constructor can be used after *new* when we create a new object of the class `Person`, but we need a different method, such as `setName`, to make changes to an object after the object is created.

The method `sameName` is similar to the `equals` methods we've seen, but since it uses a few techniques that you may not have completely digested yet, let's go over that definition, which we reproduce in what follows:

sameName

```
public boolean sameName(Person otherPerson)
{
    return (this.name.equalsIgnoreCase(otherPerson.name));
}
```

Recall that when the method `sameName` is used, there will be a calling object of the class `Person` and an argument of the class `Person`. The `sameName` method will tell whether the two objects have the same name. For example, here is some sample code that might appear in a program:

Display 7.1   A Base Class

```java
public class Person
{
    private String name;

    public Person()
    {
        name = "No name yet.";
    }

    public Person(String initialName)
    {
        name = initialName;
    }

    public void setName(String newName)
    {
        name = newName;
    }

    public String getName()
    {
        return name;
    }

    public void writeOutput()
    {
        System.out.println("Name: " + name);
    }

    public boolean sameName(Person otherPerson)
    {
        return (this.name.equalsIgnoreCase(otherPerson.name));
    }

}
```

```
Person p1 = new Person("Sam");
System.out.println("Enter the name of a person:");
String name = SavitchIn.readLine();
Person p2 = new Person(name);
if (p1.sameName(p2))
    System.out.println("They have the same name.");
else
    System.out.println("They have different names.");
```

Consider the call `p1.sameName(p2)`. When the method `sameName` is called, the `this` parameter is replaced with `p1`, and the formal parameter `otherPerson` is replaced with `p2`, so that the value of *true* or *false* that is returned is

```
p1.name.equalsIgnoreCase(p2.name)
```

Thus, the two objects are considered to have the same name (`sameName` will return *true*) provided the two objects have the same value for their `name` instance variables (ignoring any differences between uppercase and lowercase letters).

So, if the user enters `Sam` in response to the prompt

```
Enter the name of a person:
```

then the output will be

```
They have the same name.
```

If instead of `Sam`, the user enters `Mary`, then the output will be

```
They have different names.
```

Derived Classes

Suppose we are designing a college record-keeping program that has records for students, faculty, and (nonteaching) staff. There is a natural hierarchy for grouping these record types. They are all records of people. Students are one subclass of people. Another subclass is employees, which includes both faculty and staff. Students divide into two smaller subclasses: undergraduate students and graduate students. These subclasses my further subdivide into still smaller subclasses.

Display 7.2 diagrams a part of this hierarchical arrangement. Although your program may not need any class corresponding to people or employees, thinking in terms of such classes can be useful. For example, all people have names, and the methods of initializing, outputting, and changing a name will be the same for student, staff, and faculty records. In Java, you can define a class called `Person` that includes instance variables for the properties that belong to all subclasses of people, such as students, faculty, and staff. The class definition can also contain all the methods that manipulate the instance variables for the class `Person`. In fact, we have already defined such a `Person` class in Display 7.1.

Display 7.3 contains the definition of a class for students. A student is a person, so we define the class `Student` to be a *derived* class of the class `Person`. A **derived class** is a class defined by adding instance variables and methods to an existing class. The existing class that the derived class is built upon is called the **base class**. In our example, `Person` is the base class and `Student` is the derived class. The derived

derived class

base class

Display 7.2   A Class Hierarchy

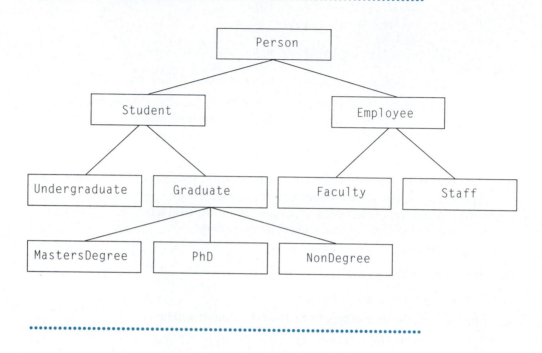

class has all the instance variables and methods of the base class, plus whatever added instance variables and methods you wish to add. If you look at Display 7.3, you will see that the way we indicate that Student is a derived class of Person is by including the phrase *extends* Person on the first line of the class definition, so that the class definition of Student begins

extends

```
public class Student extends Person
```

inheritance

When you define a derived class, you give only the added instance variables and the added methods. For example, the class Student has all the instance variables and all the methods of the class Person, but you do not mention them in the definition of Student. Every object of the class Student has an instance variable called name, but you do not specify the instance variable name in the definition of the class Student. The class Student (or any other derived class) is said to **inherit** the instance variables and methods of the base class that it extends.

For example, suppose you create a new object of the class Student as follows:

```
Student s = new Student();
```

There is an instance variable s.name. Because name is a private instance variable, it is not legal to write s.name (outside of the definition of the class Person), but the

Display 7.3   A Derived Class

```java
public class Student extends Person
{
    private int studentNumber;

    public Student()
    {
        super();
        studentNumber = 0;//Indicating no number yet
    }

    public Student(String initialName, int initialStudentNumber)
    {
        super(initialName);
        studentNumber = initialStudentNumber;
    }

    public void reset(String newName, int newStudentNumber)
    {
        setName(newName);
        studentNumber = newStudentNumber;
    }

    public int getStudentNumber()
    {
        return studentNumber;
    }
    public void setStudentNumber(int newStudentNumber)
    {
        studentNumber = newStudentNumber;
    }

    public void writeOutput()
    {
        System.out.println("Name: " + getName());
        System.out.println("Student Number : " + studentNumber);
    }

    public boolean equals(Student otherStudent)
    {
        return (this.sameName(otherStudent)
            && (this.studentNumber == otherStudent.studentNumber));
    }
}
```

super is explained in a later section. Do not worry about it until you reach the discussion of it in the text.

Display 7.4   Demonstrating Inheritance

```
public class InheritanceDemo
{
    public static void main(String[] args)
    {
        Student s = new Student();

        s.setName("Warren Peace");
        s.setStudentNumber(2001);
        s.writeOutput();

    }
}
```

setName is inherited from the class Person.

Screen Output

```
Name: Warren Peace
Student Number: 2001
```

instance variable is there, and it can be accessed and changed. Similarly, you can have the following method invocation:

```
        s.setName("Warren Peace");
```

The class Student inherits the method setName (and all the other methods of the class Person) from the base class Person.

A derived class, like Student, can also add some instance variables and/or methods to those it inherits from its base class. For example, Student adds the instance variable studentNumber and the methods reset, getStudentNumber, setStudentNumber, writeOutput, and equals, as well as some constructors. (But we will postpone the discussion of constructors until we finish explaining the other parts of these class definitions.)

Display 7.4 contains a very small demonstration program to illustrate inheritance. Notice that the object s can invoke the method setName, even though this is a method of its base class Person. The class Student inherits setName from the class Person. The class Student also adds new methods. In the sample program, the object s of the class Student invokes the method setStudentNumber. The method setStudentNumber was not in the class Person.

Derived Class

You define a **derived class** by starting with another already defined class and adding (and/or changing) methods and instance variables. The class you start with is called the **base class**. The derived class inherits all of the methods and instance variables from the base class and can add more instance variables and/or methods.

Syntax:

```
public class Derived_Class_Name extends Base_Class_Name
{
        Declarations_of_Added_Instance_Variables
        Definitions_of_Added__And_Overridden_Methods

}
```

Example:

See Display 7.3/page 463.

Overriding Method Definitions

In the definition of the class `Student`, we added a method called `writeOutput` that has no parameters (Display 7.3/page 463). But, the class `Person` also has a method called `writeOutput` that has no parameters. If the class `Student` were to inherit the method `writeOutput` from the base class `Person`, then `Student` would contain two methods with the name `writeOutput`, both of which have no parameters. Java has a rule to avoid this problem. If a derived class defines a method with the same name as a method in the base class and that *also has the same number and types of parameters as in the base class,* then the definition in the derived class is said to **override** the definition in the base class, and the definition in the derived class is the one that is used for objects of the derived class.

overriding a method

For example, in Display 7.4, the following invocation of the method `writeOutput` for the object `s` of the class `Student` will use the definition of `writeOutput` in the class `Student`, not the definition of the method `writeOutput` in the class `Person`:

```
s.writeOutput();
```

Although you can change the body of an overridden method definition to anything you wish, you cannot make any changes in the heading of the overridden method. In particular, when overriding a method definition, you cannot change the return type of the method.

Overriding Method Definitions

In a derived class, if you include a method definition that has the same name and the *exact* same number and types of parameters as a method already in the base class, then *for the derived class,* this new definition replaces the old definition of the method.

In such cases, the return type of the overridden method definition must be the same as the return type for the method in the base class. That is, when overriding a method definition you cannot change the return type of the method.

Overriding Versus Overloading

Do not confuse method overriding with method overloading. When you override a method definition, the new method definition given in the derived class has the exact same number and types of parameters. On the other hand, if the method in the derived class were to have a different number of parameters or a parameter of a different type from the method in the base class, then the derived class would have both methods. That would be overloading. For example, suppose we added the following method to the definition of the class `Student`:

```
public String getName(String title)
{
    return (title + getName());
}
```

In this case, the class `Student` would have two methods named `getName`: It would still inherit the method `getName` from the base class `Person` (Display 7.1/page 460), and it would also have the method named `getName` that we just defined. This is because these two methods called `getName` have different numbers of parameters.

If you get overloading and overriding confused, you do have one small consolation. They are both legal. So, it is more important to learn how to use them than it is to learn to distinguish between them. Nonetheless, you should learn the difference between them.

The *final* Modifier

If you want to specify that a method definition cannot be overridden with a new definition in a derived class, then you can do so by adding the *final* modifier to the method heading, as in the following sample heading:

```
public final void specialMethod()
{
       .
       .
       .
```

You are not very likely to need this modifier, but you are likely to see it in the specification of some methods in standard Java libraries.

If a method is declared to be final, then the compiler knows more about how it will be used, and so the compiler can generate more efficient code for the method. An entire class can be declared final, in which case you cannot use it as base class to derive any other class from it.

■ Gotcha

Use of Private Instance Variables from the Base Class

An object of the class `Student` (Display 7.3/page 463) inherits an instance variable called `name` from the class `Person` (Display 7.1/page 460). For example, the following would set the value of the instance variable `name` of the object `joe` to `"Josephine"`: (This also sets the instance variable `studentNumber` to 9891.)

```
Student joe = new Student("Josephine", 9891);
```

If you want to change `joe.name` (and `joe.studentNumber`), you can do so as follows:

```
joe.reset("Joesy", 9892);
```

But, you must be a bit careful about how you manipulate inherited instance variables such as `name`. The instance variable `name` of the class `Student` was inherited from the class `Person`, but the instance variable `name` is a private instance variable in the definition of the class `Person`. That means that `name` can only be directly accessed within the definition of a method in the class `Person`. An instance variable (or method) that is private in a base class is not accessible *by name* in the definition of a method for *any other class, not even in a method definition of a derived class*. Thus, although the class `Student` does have an instance variable named `name` (which was defined in the base class `Person`), it is illegal to directly access the instance variable `name` in the definition of any method in the class definition of `Student`!

For example, the following is the definition of the method `reset` from the definition of the class `Student`:

```
public void reset(String newName, int newStudentNumber)
{
    setName(newName);                                    Legal definition
    studentNumber = newStudentNumber;
}
```

You might have wondered why we needed to use the method `setName` to set the value of the `name` instance variable. You might be tempted to rewrite the method definition as follows:

```
public void reset(String newName, int newStudentNumber)
{
    name = newName;//ILLEGAL!                            Illegal definition
    studentNumber = newStudentNumber;
}
```

As the comment indicates, this will not work. The instance variable `name` is a private instance variable in the class `Person`, and although a derived class like `Student` inherits the variable `name`, it cannot access it directly. It must use some public mutator (or accessor) method to access the instance variable `name`. The correct way to accomplish the definition of `reset` in the class `Student` is the way we did it in Display 7.3 (which we reproduced as the first of the preceding two possible definitions of `reset`).

The fact that a private instance variable of a base class cannot be accessed in the definition of a method of a derived class often seems wrong to people. After all, if you are a student and you want to change your name, nobody says, "Sorry `name` is a private instance variable of the class `Person`." After all, if you are a student, you are also a person. In Java, this is also true; an object of the class `Student` is also an object of the class `Person`. However, the laws on the use of private instance variables and methods must be as we described, or else they would be pointless. If private instance variables of a class were accessible in method definitions of a derived class, then anytime you wanted to access a private instance variable, you could simply create a derived class and access it in a method of that class, and that would mean that all private instance variables would be accessible to anybody who wants to put in a little extra effort.

■ Gotcha

Private Methods Are Not Inherited

As we noted in the previous Gotcha section: An instance variable (or method) that is private in a base class is not directly accessible in the definition of a method for *any other class, not even in a method definition for a derived class.* Note that private methods are just like private variables in terms of not being directly available. But in the case of methods, the restriction is more dramatic. A private variable can be accessed indirectly via an accessor or mutator method. A private method is simply not available. It is just as if the private method were not inherited.

This should not be a problem. Private methods should just be used as helping functions, and so their use should be limited to the class in which they are defined. If you want a method to be used as a helping method in a number of inherited classes, then it is not *just* a helping method, and you should make the method public.

? Self-Test Questions

1. Suppose the class named `SportsCar` is a derived class of a class called `Automobile`. Suppose the class `Automobile` has instance variables named `speed`, `manufacturer`, and `numberOfCylinders`. Will an object of the class `SportsCar` have instance variables named `speed`, `manufacturer`, and `numberOfCylinders`?

2. Suppose the class named `SportsCar` is a derived class of a class called `Automobile`, and suppose the class `Automobile` has public methods named `accelerate` and `addGas`. Will an object of the class `SportsCar` have methods named `accelerate` and `addGas`? If so, do these methods have to perform the exact same actions in the class `SportsCar` as in the class `Automobile`?

3. If you are defining a derived class, can you directly access a private instance variable of the base class?

4. If you are defining a derived class, can you use a private method of the base class?

5. Give the complete definition of a class called `TitledPerson`. `TitledPerson` is to be a derived class of the class `Person` in Display 7.1/page 460. The class `TitledPerson` has one additional `String` instance variable for a title, such as `"Ms"`, `"Mr."`, or `"The Honorable"`. The class `TitledPerson` has two constructors, a default constructor and one that sets both the name and the title. It has an `writeOutput` method, a `reset` method, an `equals` method, an accessor method `getTitle` that returns the title, and a mutator method `setTitle` that changes the person's title. For two titled

people to be equal, they must have the same name and the same title. You may want to use the class `Student` in Display 7.3/page 463 as a model.

7.2 | Programming with Inheritance

Inheritance via derived classes is a powerful tool. It does, however, require that you learn some new techniques in order to use it productively. In this section, we discuss some of these techniques.

Constructors in Derived Classes

A derived class, such as the class `Student` in Display 7.3/page 463, has its own constructors. The base class from which it was derived, such as `Person`, also has its own constructors. When defining a constructor for the derived class, the typical first action is to call a constructor of the base class. For example, consider defining a constructor for the class `Student`. One of the things that need to be initialized is the student's name. This name initializing is normally done by the constructors for the base class `Person` (since the instance variable `name` was introduced in the definition of `Person`). Thus, a natural first action for a constructor for the class `Student` is a call to a constructor for its base class `Person`. For example, consider the following definition of a constructor for the derived class `Student` (from Display 7.3):

```
public Student(String initialName, int initialStudentNumber)
{
    super(initialName);
    studentNumber = initialStudentNumber;
}
```

The line

    `super(initialName);`

is a call to a constructor for the base class, in this case, a call to a constructor for the class `Person`. Notice that you use the reserved word *super* to call the constructor of   *super*
the base class.   You do not use the name of the constructor;   you do *not* use `Person(initialName)`.

There are some details to worry about with the use of *super*: It must always be the first action taken in a constructor definition. You cannot use it later in the definition of a constructor. In fact, if you do not include a call to the base-class constructor, then Java will automatically include a call to the default constructor of the base class as the first action of any constructor for a derived class.

Consider the following definition of a constructor for the class `Student` (Display 7.3):

```
public Student()
{
    super();
    studentNumber = 0;//Indicating no number yet
}
```

This definition is completely equivalent to the following:

```
public Student()
{
    studentNumber = 0;//Indicating no number yet
}
```

If there is no call to a constructor of the base class, then Java will automatically insert a call to the default constructor of the base class; that is, Java will automatically insert a call to *super()*. Some programmers prefer to explicitly write in such calls to a base-class default constructor, whether or not Java would call it automatically. That makes the code a bit clearer, because all actions are explicitly shown.

Call to a Base-Class Constructor

When defining a constructor for a derived class, you can use *super* as a name for the constructor of the base class. Any call to *super* must be the first action taken by the constructor.

Example:

```
public Student(String initialName, int initialStudentNumber)
{
    super(initialName);
    studentNumber = initialStudentNumber;
}
```

The *this* Method *(Optional)*

this as a method

When defining a constructor another common action is a call to one of the other constructors. You can use the reserved word *this* in a way similar to how you use *super*, but with *this*, the call is to a constructor of the same class and not a call to a constructor for the base class. For example, consider the following definition of a constructor that you might want to add to the class Student (from Display 7.3/page 463):

```
public Student(String initialName)
{
    this(initialName, 0);
}
```

The one statement in the body of this constructor definition is a call to the constructor whose definition begins

```
public Student(String initialName, int initialStudentNumber)
```

As with *super*, any use of *this* must be the first action in a constructor definition. Thus, a constructor definition cannot contain both a call using *super* and a call using *this*. What if you want a call with *super* and a call with *this*? In that case, use a call with *this*, and have the constructor that is called with *this* have *super* as its first action.

Call to Another Constructor in the Same Class *(Optional)*

When defining a constructor for a class, you can use *this* as a name for another constructor in the same class. Any call to *this* must be the first action taken by the constructor.

Example:

```
public Student(String initialName)
{
    this(initialName, 0);
}
```

Call to an Overridden Method

When you are defining a constructor for a derived class, you can use *super* as a name for the constructor of the base class. You can also use *super* to call a method of the base class that is overridden (redefined) in the derived class, but the way you do this is a bit different.

Call to An Overridden Method

Within the definition of a method of a derived class, you can call an overridden method of the base class by prefacing the method name with *super* and a dot.

Example:

```
public void writeOutput()
{
    super.writeOutput();
    System.out.println("Student Number: " + studentNumber);
}
```

For example, consider the method writeOutput for the class Student in Display 7.3/page 463. It uses the following to output the name of the Student:

```
System.out.println("Name: " + getName());
```

Alternatively, you could output the name by calling the method writeOutput *of the class* Person (Display 7.1/page 460), since the writeOutput method for the class Person will output the person's name. The only problem is that if you use the name writeOutput for a method in the class Student, it will mean the method named writeOutput in the class Student. What you need is a way to say "writeOutput() as it is defined in the base class." The way you say that is *super*.writeOutput(). So, an alternative definition of the writeOutput method for the class Student is the following:

```
    public void writeOutput()
    {
        super.writeOutput();
        System.out.println("Student Number: " + studentNumber);
    }
```

If you replace the definition of writeOutput in the definition of Student (Display 7.3/page 463) with the preceding, then the class Student will behave exactly the same as it did .before.

Programming Example
MultiLevel Derived Classes

You can form a derived class from a derived class. In fact, this is common. For example, in Display 7.5 we have defined the class Undergraduate, which is a derived class of the class Student (Display 7.3/page 463). This means that an object of the class Undergraduate has all the methods and instance variables of the class Student. But Student is already a derived class of Person (Display 7.1/page 460). So, this also means that an object of the class Undergraduate has all the methods and instance variables of the class Person. An object of the class Person has the instance variable name. An object of the class Student has the instance variables name and student-Number. An object of the class Undergraduate has the instance variables name, studentNumber, and the added instance variable level. An object of the class Undergraduate must use accessor and mutator methods to access and change the instance variables name and studentNumber, but it definitely has these instance variables.

Note that a chain of derived classes like this can produce a good deal of efficient reusing of code. Both the classes Undergraduate and Student (as well as any other classes derived from either of them), in effect, reuse the method code given in the definition of the class Person, because they inherit all the methods of the class Person.

super

Note the constructors for the class Undergraduate. They each begin with an invocation of *super*, which in this context stands for a constructor of the base class Student. But the constructors for the class Student also begin with an invocation of *super*, which in this case stands for a constructor of the base class Person. Thus, when a constructor for Undergraduate is invoked (using *new*), first a constructor for Person is invoked, then a constructor for Student is invoked, and then all the code following *super* in the constructor for Undergraduate is executed.

Notice the definition of the reset method in the class Undergraduate, which we reproduce in what follows:

```
    public void reset(String newName,
                            int newStudentNumber, int newLevel)
    {
        reset(newName, newStudentNumber);
        level = newLevel;
    }
```

Display 7.5   A Derived Class of a Derived Class

```java
public class Undergraduate extends Student
{
    private int level;//1 for freshman, 2 for sophomore, etc.

    public Undergraduate()
    {
        super();
        level = 1;
    }

    public Undergraduate(String initialName,
                    int initialStudentNumber, int initialLevel)
    {
        super(initialName, initialStudentNumber);
        level = initialLevel;
    }

    public void reset(String newName,
                        int newStudentNumber, int newLevel)
    {
        reset(newName, newStudentNumber);
        level = newLevel;
    }

    public int getLevel()
    {
        return level;
    }

    public void setLevel(int newLevel)
    {
        level = newLevel;
    }

    public void writeOutput()
    {
        super.writeOutput();
        System.out.println("Student Level: " + level);
    }

    public boolean equals(Undergraduate otherUndergraduate)
    {
        return (super.equals(otherUndergraduate)
            && (this.level == otherUndergraduate.level));
    }
}
```

Note that the method starts with an invocation of reset with only two arguments. This is an invocation of the method named reset in the base class Student. In the class Undergraduate, the method named reset is overloaded. In the class Undergraduate there are two definitions for the method name reset. One takes two arguments and the other takes three arguments. The one that takes two arguments is inherited from the class Student, but it is still a full-fledged method of the class Undergraduate.

In the three-argument version of reset (which is defined in the class Student and reproduced in the previous displayed code), the method reset of the base class Student resets the values of the instance variables name and studentNumber (to newName and newStudentNumber, respectively), with the invocation:

```
reset(newName, newStudentNumber);
```

Then, the new instance variable level is reset to newLevel with an assignment statement.

Remember that within the definition of the class Undergraduate, the private instance variables name and studentNumber (of base classes) cannot be referenced by name, and so a mutator method is need to change them. The reset method of the class Student is perfect for this purpose.

In contrast to the definition of the reset method in the class Undergraduate, notice the definition of the method writeOutput, which we reproduce in what follows:

```
public void writeOutput()
{
    super.writeOutput();
    System.out.println("Student Level: " + level);
}
```

The definition of reset gave us an example of over*loading*. The method writeOutput gives us an example of over*riding*.

With the method name reset, the version defined in the class Undergraduate has a different number of parameters than the one defined in the class Student. So, there is no conflict in having both versions of reset in the derived class Undergraduate. This is an example of overloading. By contrast to the method name reset, the method writeOutput defined in the derived class Undergraduate has exactly the same parameter list as the version in the base class Student. Thus, when writeOutput is invoked, Java must decide which definition of writeOutput to use. For an object of the derived class Undergraduate, it uses the version of writeOutput given in the definition of the class Undergraduate. This is an example of overriding the definition of a method name (writeOutput) in a derived class. However, the definition of the method writeOutput that was given in the base class Student is still inherited by the derived class Undergraduate. But, in order to invoke the version in the base class Student within the definition of the derived class Undergraduate, you must place super and dot in front of the method name writeOutput, as in the first line of the method definition of writeOutput, given in the definition of the derived class Undergraduate and displayed within the previous paragraph.

In Display 7.5 you can see a similar use of *super* in the method definitions of equals. Note that it is perfectly permissible, and indeed common, to redefine names like writeOutput, and equals in a derived class. The versions in the base class are still there and can be accessed by using the prefix *super* and a dot.

There is nothing unusual about how the class Undergraduate is used, but we have included a simple demonstration program for the class Undergraduate in the file UndergraduateDemo.java on the accompanying CD.

extra code on CD

Parent and Child Classes

When discussing derived classes, it is common to use terminology derived from family relationships. A base class is often called a **parent class**. A derived class is then called a **child class**. This makes the language of inheritance very smooth. For example, we can say that a child class inherits instance variables and methods from its parent class. This analogy is often carried one step further. A class that is a parent of a parent of a parent of another class (or some other number of "parent of" iterations) is often called an **ancestor class**. If class A is an ancestor of class B, then class B is often called a **descendent** of class A.

parent and child

ancestor and descendent

A Subtle Point About Overloading and Overriding *(Optional)*

Consider the method name equals in the classes Student and Undergraduate. They have different parameter lists. The one in the class Student has a parameter of type Student, while the one in the class Undergraduate has a parameter of type Undergraduate. They have the same number of parameters, namely one, but that one parameter is of different types in the two definitions. A difference in type is enough to qualify for overloading. To qualify as overloading, the two method definitions need to have a different number of parameters *or* a parameter position of different types in the two methods. So the second definitions of equals given in the derived class Undergraduate is, in some technical sense, overloading and not overriding.

Why, then, did we use *super* in the definition of equals, within the derived class Undergraduate? To help us analyze the situation, we reproduce the definition (used in the derived class Undergraduate) below:

```
public boolean equals(Undergraduate otherUndergraduate)
{
    return (super.equals(otherUndergraduate)
            && (this.level == otherUndergraduate.level));
}
```

Since the invocation *super*.equals is an invocation of an overloaded version of equals, why do we need the *super*? To see why, try omitting it, as follows:

```
return (equals(otherUndergraduate)
        && (this.level == otherUndergraduate.level));
```

The argument otherUndergraduate is of type Undergraduate, so Java would assume this refers to the definition of equals in the class Undergraduate. In order to force Java to use the definition of equals in the base class Student, we need to use the *super* and dot.

■ Java Tip
You Cannot Use Multiple *super*s

As we already noted, within the definition of a method of a derived class, you can call an overridden method of the base class by prefacing the method name with *super* and a dot. However, you cannot repeat the use of *super* to invoke a method from some ancestor class other than a direct parent. Suppose that the class Student is derived from the class Person, and the class Undergraduate is derived from the class Student. You might think that you can invoke a method of the class Person within the definition of the class Undergraduate, by using *super.super*, as in

```
super.super.writeOutput();//ILLEGAL!
```

You might hope that the previous statement would invoke the version of the method writeOutput that was defined in the class Person. However, as the comment indicates, it is illegal to have such a train of *super*'s in Java.

■ Programming Tip
An Object of a Derived Class Has More than One Type

Consider the class Undergraduate in Display 7.5/page 473. It is a derived class of the class Student. In the real world, every undergraduate is also a student. This relationship holds in Java as well. Every object of the class Undergraduate is also an object of the class Student. Thus, if you have a method that has a formal parameter of type Student, then the argument in an invocation of this method can be an object of type Undergraduate. In this case, the method could only use those instance variables and methods that belong to the class Student, but every object of the class Undergraduate has all these instance variables and methods so there are still lots of meaningful things that the method can do with an object of type Undergraduate.

parameters
types

For example, suppose that the classes Student and Undergraduate are defined as in Display 7.3/page 463 and Display 7.5/page 473 and consider the following method definition that might occur in some class:

```
public class SomeClass
{
    public static void compareNumbers(Student s1, Student s2)
    {
        if (s1.getStudentNumber() == s2.getStudentNumber())
            System.out.println(s1.getName()
                                    + " has the same number as "
                                    + s2.getName());
        else
            System.out.println(s1.getName()
                                    + " has a different number than "
                                + s2.getName());
    }
    ...
}
```

A program that uses this method might contain the following code:

```
Student studentObject = new Student("Jane Doe", 1234);
System.out.println("Enter name:");
String undergradName = SavitchIn.readLine();
System.out.println("Enter student number :");
int undergradStudentNumber = SavitchIn.readLineInt();
Undergraduate undergradObject =
    new Undergraduate(undergradName, undergradStudentNumber, 1);
SomeClass.compareNumbers(studentObject, undergradObject);
```

If you look at the heading for the method compareNumbers, you will see that both parameters are of type Student. However, the invocation

```
SomeClass.compareNumbers(studentObject, undergradObject);
```

uses one argument of type Student and one object that is of type Undergraduate. Why could we use an object of type Undergraduate where an argument of type Student is required? The answer is that every object of type Undergraduate is also of type Student. To make the point a little more dramatically, notice that you can reverse the two arguments and the method invocation will still be legal, as shown below:

```
SomeClass.compareNumbers(undergradObject, studentObject);
```

(Note that there is no automatic type casting here. An object of the class Undergraduate *is* a member of the class Student, and so it *is* of type Student. It need not be, and is not, type cast to an object of the class Student.)

An object can actually have more than two types as a result of inheritance. Recall that the class Undergraduate (Display 7.5/page 473) is a derived class of the class Student (Display 7.3/page 463), and Student is a derived class of the class Person (Display 7.1/page 460). This means that every object of the class Undergraduate is also an object of type Student and an object of type Person. Thus, everything that works for objects of the class Person also works for objects the class Undergraduate.

For example, suppose that the classes Person and Undergraduate are defined as in Displays 7.1 and 7.5 and consider the following code, which might occur in a program:

```
Person joePerson = new Person("Josephine Student");
System.out.println("Enter name:");
String newName = SavitchIn.readLine();
Undergraduate someUndergrad = new Undergraduate(newName, 222, 3);
if (joePerson.sameName(someUndergrad))
    System.out.println("Wow, same names!");
else
    System.out.println("Different names");
```

If you look at the heading for the method sameName in Display 7.1/page 460, you will see that it has one parameter and that parameter is of type Person. However, the call

```
joe.sameName(someUndergrad)
```

ancestor classes

two levels of derived classes

which is used in the preceding `if`-statement is perfectly legal, even though the argument `someUndergrad` is an object of the class `Undergraduate` (that is, is of type `Undergraduate`) and the argument is supposed to be of type `Person`. This is because every object of the class `Undergraduate` is also an object of the class `Person`. The object `someUndergrad` is of type `Undergraduate`, and it is also of type `Person`. This is one of the nice features of inheritance. Everything that works for objects of an ancestor class also works for objects of any descendant class.

An Object of a Derived Class Has More than One Type

An object of a derived class has the type of the derived class, and it also has the type of the base class, and more generally, has the type of every one of its ancestor classes.

---

ancestor classes

As we already saw, if A is a derived class of class B, and B is a derived class of class C, then an object of class A is of type A, it is also of type B, and it is also of type C. This works for any chain of derived classes no matter how long the chain is.

Object class

Java has an "Eve" class, that is, a class that is an ancestor of every class. In Java, every class is a derived class of a derived class of . . . (for some number of iterations of "a derived class of") of the class `Object`. So, every object of every class is of type `Object`, as well as being of the type of its class (and also of the types of all other ancestor classes). Even classes that you define yourself are descendent classes of the class `Object`. If you do not make your class a derived class of some class, then Java acts as if you made it a derived class of the class `Object`.

The Class `Object`

In Java, every class is a descendent of the predefined class `Object`. So, every object of every class is of type `Object`, as well as being of the type of its class (and probably also of the type of other ancestor classes as well).

---

assignments to variables

Because an object of a derived class has the types of all of its ancestor classes (as well as its "own" type), you can assign an object of a class to a variable of any ancestor type, but not the other way around. For example, if `Student` is a derived class of `Person`, and `Undergraduate` is a derived class of `Student`, then the following are all legal:

```
Person p1, p2;
p1 = new Student();
p2 = new Undergraduate();
```

However, the following are all illegal:

```
Student s = new Person(); //ILLEGAL!
Undergraduate ug = new Person(); //ILLEGAL!
Undergraduate ug2 = new Student(); //ILLEGAL!
```

"is a" relationship

This all makes perfectly good sense. For example, a `Student` *is a* `Person`, but a `Person` *is not necessarily* a `Student`. Some programers find the phrase "is a" to be useful in deciding what types an object can have and what assignments to variables are legal.

As another example, if `Employee` is a derived class of `Person`, then an `Employee` *is a* `Person`, So you can assign an `Employee` object to a variable of type `Person`. However, a `Person` is *not necessarily* an `Employee`, so you *cannot* assign an object created as just a plain `Person` to a variable of type `Employee`.

Assignment Compatibilities

You can assign an object of a derived class to a variable of any ancestor type, but not the other way around.

Programming Tip
"Is a" and "Has a"

As we noted in the previous subsection a `Student` is a `Person`, so we made the `Student` class a derived class of the `Person` class. This is an example of the "is a" relationship between classes. It is one way to make a more complex class out of a simpler class.

"has a"
relationship

Another way to make a more complex class out of a simpler class is know as the "has a" relationship. For example, if you have a class `Date` that records a date. Then you might add a date of enrollment to the `Student` class by adding an instance variable of type `Date` to the `Student` class. In this case we say a `Student` "has a" `Date`. As another example, if we have a class to simulate a `MechanicalArm` and we are defining a class to simulate a robot, then we can give the `Robot` class an instance variable of type `MechanicalArm`. In this case we say that a `Robot` "has a" `MechanicalArm`.

In most situations you can make your code work with either an "is a" relationship or a "has a" relationship. It seems silly (and it is silly) to make the `Robot` class a derived class of the `MechanicalArm` class, but it can be done and can be made to work (perhaps with difficulty). Fortunately, the best programming technique is usually to simply follow what sounds most natural in English. It makes more sense to say "A `Robot` has a `MechanicalArm`" than it is to say "A `Robot` is a `MechanicalArm`." So, it makes better programming sense to have a `MechanicalArm` as an instance variable of a `Robot` class. It makes little sense to make the `Robot` class a derived class of the `MechanicalArm` class.

You will often encounter these terms "is a" and "has a" in the literature on programming techniques.

? Self-Test Questions

6. Rewrite the definition of the method `writeOutput` for the class `Undergraduate` in Display 7.5/page 473 using `getName` and `getStudentNumber` instead of *super*.`writeOutput`. (Most programmers would use the version in Display 7.5, but you should be able to write either version.)

7. Rewrite the definition of the method reset for the class Undergraduate in Display 7.5/page 473 using setName and setStudentNumber instead of the overloaded reset method name. (Most programmers would use the version in Display 7.5, but you should be able to write either version.)

8. Can an object have more than one type?

9. What is the type or types of the object created in the following statement? (The definition of the class Undergraduate is given in Display 7.5/page 473.)

```
Undergraduate ug = new Undergraduate();
```

10. Which of the following lines are legal and which are illegal? (Student is a derived class of Person, and Undergraduate is a derived class of Student.)

```
Person p1 = new Student();
Person p2 = new Undergraduate();
Student s1 = new Person();
Student s2 = new Undergraduate();
Undergraduate ug1 = new Person();
Undergraduate ug2 = new Student();
Object ob = new Student();
Student s3 = new Object();
```

11. Describe two uses for the reserved word *super*.

12. (This question only applies to you if you read the optional section entitled **The *this* Method (Optional)**.) What is the difference between *this* and *super* when these words are used as the names of methods that are called in a constructor definition?

Methods Inherited from the Class Object

Every class is a descendent class of the class Object. So, there should be some methods that every class inherits from the class Object. There are such methods, and they are useful methods. For example, every object inherits the methods equals and toString from some ancestor class which either is the class Object or did itself inherit the methods ultimately from the class Object. However, the inherited methods equals and toString will not work correctly for (almost) any class you define. You need to override the inherited method definitions with new more appropriate definitions. Thus, whenever you defined the method equals for a class, you are technically speaking redefining the method equals.

toString

The inherited method toString takes no arguments. The method toString is suppose to return all the data in an object coded into a String. However, you will not automatically get a nice string representation of the data. The inherited version of toString is almost always useless, unless it is redefined. You need to override the definition of toString so it produces an appropriate String for the data in objects of the class being defined. .

For example, the following definition of toString could be added to the class Student (Display 7.3/page 463):

```
public String toString()
{
    return("Name: " + getName()
              + "\nStudent number: "
              + Integer.toString(studentNumber));
}
```

If this `toString` method were added to the class `Student`, then it can be used, among other things, to give output in the following way:

```
Student s = new Student("Joe Student", 2001);
System.out.println(s.toString());
```

The output produced would be

```
Name: Joe Student
Student number; 2001
```

(If the expression `Integer.toString(studentNumber)` seems puzzling, review the subsection *Integer, Double, and Other Wrapper Classes* starting on page 319 of Chapter 5.)

The version of the class `Student` on the accompanying CD includes this method `toString`. So, you can easily try out the method `toString`. **extra code on CD**

Another method inherited from the class `Object` is the method `clone`. The method `clone` takes no arguments and returns a copy of the calling object. The retuned object is supposed to have identical data to that of the calling object, but it is a different object (an identical twin or "a clone"). As with other methods inherited from the class `Object`, the method `clone` needs to be redefined (overridden) before it functions properly. However, in the case of the method `clone`, there are other things you must do as well. A thorough discussion of the method `clone` is beyond the scope is this text, but some discussion of the method `clone` is given in the subsection *Gotcha **Privacy Leaks*** (page 360) in Chapter 5 and in Appendix 9.

? Self-Test Questions

13. Consider the code below, which was discussed in the previous subsection:

    ```
    Student s = new Student("Joe Student", 2001);
    System.out.println(s.toString());
    ```

    Why is the output on two lines instead of being all on one line?

14. Consider the *return*-statement in the definition of `toString` given in the previous subsection. It includes the following method invocation as part od the *return*-statement:

    ```
    Integer.toString(studentNumber))
    ```

    This is an invocation of a static method named `toString` in the class `Integer`. Was this method inherited from the class `Object` (possibly via some chain of derived classes ending with the class `Integer`.)

Case Study

Character Graphics

Java has classes to draw graphics on your terminal screen. In Chapters 12-15, we will discuss some such classes. However, there are situations in which you have no graphics capability available on your screen or other output device. For example, some older terminals only allow for text output.

In this case study, you will design three simple classes to be used to produce simple graphics on a screen using only text output. These classes will produce their graphic figures by placing ordinary keyboard characters at certain places on each line, and will do this in such a way as to produce some simple pictures.

The origin of this case study is a request for graphics to be included in e-mail messages. The only thing you can be certain that you can include in an e-mail message so that the message can be handled by any mailer program, and so, understood by any person who receives the message, is plain text. So, this sort of character graphics is the only kind of graphics that will work for all people to whom you might send e-mail. In this case study, you will do this character graphics using the screen in order to have a demonstration prototype. The prototype will be used to demonstrate the graphics in the hope of obtaining a contract to create graphics that can be output to a file that can then be sent via e-mail. Although we have not yet covered output to files, it will turn out to be easy to modify these classes to send their output to a file rather than to the screen.

task specification

The exact details of what you will do in this case study are as follows: You will create two classes, one for a box and one for a triangle. You will then write a simple demonstration program that draws a pine tree using the triangle and box classes. If this prototype is successful with customers, you will then write more classes for figures, but these two are all you will do in this case study.

Each of the figures, the box and the triangle, will have an offset telling how far they are indented from the edge of the screen. Each figure will also have a size, although the size will be determined differently for a box and a triangle.

For a box, the size is given as the width and the height, *expressed in the number of characters*. Because characters are taller than they are wide, a box will look taller than you might expect when it is written on the screen. For example, a 5-by-5 box will not look square on the screen, but will look like what is shown in Display 7.6.

For a triangle, the size will be given by its base. The triangle will point up and the base will be at the bottom. The slope of a side of the triangle is limited to what you get by indenting one character per line (if you want it to be smooth). So, once the base is chosen, you have no choice in what the sides of the triangle will be. Display 7.6 shows a sample of both a box and a triangle.

base class

Figure

Because a box and a triangle are figures with many properties in common, you decide to design a base class named Figure. The classes Box and Triangle will then be derived classes of the class Figure. The class Figure will have instance variables for any properties that all figures have in common and will have methods

Display 7.6 Sample Boxes and Triangles

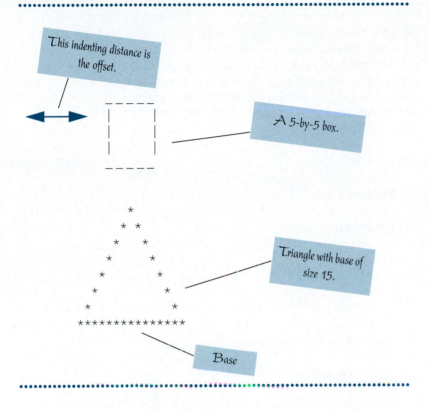

This indenting distance is the offset.

A 5-by-5 box.

Triangle with base of size 15.

Base

for the actions that all figures have. Your analysis produces the following list of properties and actions:

Properties. All figures have an offset, which is the number of spaces the figure is indented, so you decide to store the offset in an instance variable of type *int*. All figures will have a size, but the size of some figures is described by a single number and the size of other figures is determined by two or more numbers. For example, the size of the kind of triangle we will be using in this case study is given by one number, but the size of a box is given as two numbers, the height and the width. So, you decide not to specify size as part of the class Figure. Thus, you decide that the class Figure will have only the following instance variable:

> *private int* offset;

Actions. The only actions you need for all figures are to set the parameters for the figures and to draw the figures. Setting the parameters will be taken care of by constructors and reset methods. Display 7.7 contains the definition for the class Figure that you produce. The method drawHere will simply indent a number of

Display 7.7   The Figure Base Class (Part 1 of 2)

```java
/**********************************************************
*Class for simple character graphics figures to send to screen.
*This class can draw an asterisk on the screen as a test. But,
*it is not intended to be a figure used in graphics.
*It is intended to be used as a base class for the kinds
*of figures that will be used in graphics applications.
**********************************************************/
public class Figure
{
    private int offset;

    public Figure()
    {
        offset = 0;
    }

    public Figure(int theOffset)
    {
        offset = theOffset;
    }

    public void setOffset(int newOffset)
    {
        offset = newOffset;
    }

    public int getOffset()
    {
        return offset;
    }


    /*************************************
    *Draws the figure at lineNumber lines down
    *from the current line.
    *************************************/
    public void drawAt(int lineNumber)
    {
        int count;
        for (count = 0; count < lineNumber; count++)
            System.out.println();
        drawHere();
    }
```

Display 7.7 The `Figure` **Base Class** *(Part 2 of 2)*

```
/*********************************
 *Draws the figure at the current line.
 *********************************/
public void drawHere()
{
    int count;
    for (count = 0; count < offset; count++)
        System.out.print(' ');
    System.out.println('*');

}

}
```

spaces on the screen equal to the offset and then write an asterisk on the screen. This is just so you can have something to test. You do not intend to use this version of `drawHere` in any application. You will override the definition of `drawHere` when you define classes for boxes and triangles.

The method `drawAt` has one parameter of type *int*. The method `drawAt` inserts a number of blank lines equal to this parameter and then draws the figure by calling `drawHere`. Of course, in this case, that does not produce very much, but when we override `drawHere`, then `drawAt` will also produce more interesting figures.

Next you turn your attention to the class for drawing a box. The class, called `Box`, will be a derived class of the class `Figure`. You need to decide on the instance variables and methods that will be added to those in the class `Figure`. You also need to decide which if any method definitions in `Figure` will be overridden with a changed definition.

Box class

Properties. The class `Box` inherits the `offset` instance variables, but you need to add instance variables for the height and the width of the box, Thus, the class definition looks like the following:

```
public class Box extends Figure
{
    private int height;
    private int width;

    <Still needs method definitions.>
}
```

Note that you do not list the instance variable `offset`, which `Box` inherits from the base class `Figure`.

Actions. The class `Box` has the usual constructors and reset methods. It inherits both the method `drawAt` and the method `drawHere` from the class `Figure`. However, you need to override the definition of the method drawHere so that it does indeed draw a box. So, you put drawHere on your list of methods to define.

Next, you consider the method drawAt. Does it need to be overridden? When you look at the method drawAt (Display 7.7/page 484), you will see that, as long as drawHere is correctly defined, the method drawAt will work fine for a box or any other figure. Thus, you need not redefine the method drawAt. You only need to redefine the method drawHere.

Let's look first at a sample constructor. You will design one of the constructors so that it sets all instance variables to values given as arguments to the constructor. But, one instance variable, namely, offset, is a private instance variable of the base class Figure. Thus, you cannot access it directly, but must use a call to the base class constructor, *super*. Thus, the definition of this constructor is

```
public Box(int theOffset, int theHeight, int theWidth)
{
    super(theOffset);
    height = theHeight;
    width = theWidth;
}
```

The default constructor and reset method that you define are shown in Display 7.8. Note that the reset method needs to use an accessor method to reset the private instance variable offset, which is inherited from the base class Figure.

In your definition of the default constructor for the class Box, you could omit the call to the base-class constructor *super( )*, and it would be called automatically anyway, but you decide to leave it in for clarity.

Most of these definitions of constructors and accessor methods are similar to what they would be in any class definition. The definition of the method drawHere, however, depends heavily on the particulars of what figure it is drawing. You decide to define the method drawHere using the technique known as *top-down design*. The basic technique in top-down design is to break down the task to be done by the method into subtasks. You decide on the following subtasks:

drawHere

subtasks

```
To Draw a Box:
1. Draw the top line.
2. Draw the side lines.
3. Draw the bottom line.
```

Note that not every way of choosing subtasks will work. You might at first be tempted to have two subtasks, one for each side of the box. However, output must be produced one line after the other and you are not allowed to back up, so you must draw the two sides together (if you want them to be side by side as they should be).

Thus, the definition of the method drawHere is easy:

```
public void drawHere()
{
    drawHorizontalLine();
    drawSides();
    drawHorizontalLine();
}
```

Display 7.8   The Box Class *(Part 1 of 2)*

```java
/*****************************************************
 *Class for a rectangular box to be drawn on the screen.
 *Because each character is higher than it is wide, these
 *boxes will look higher than you might expect. Inherits
 *getOffset, setOffset, and drawAt from the class Figure.
 *****************************************************/
public class Box extends Figure
{
    private int height;
    private int width;

    public Box()
    {
        super();
        height = 0;
        width = 0;
    }

    public Box(int theOffset, int theHeight, int theWidth)
    {
        super(theOffset);
        height = theHeight;
        width = theWidth;
    }

    public void reset(int newOffset, int newHeight, int newWidth)
    {
        setOffset(newOffset);
        height = newHeight;
        width = newWidth;
    }

    /*********************************
     *Draws the figure at the current line.
     *********************************/
    public void drawHere()
    {
        drawHorizontalLine();
        drawSides();
        drawHorizontalLine();
    }
```

Display 7.8   The Box Class *(Part 2 of 2)*

```java
    private void drawHorizontalLine()
    {
        spaces(getOffset());
        int count;
        for (count = 0; count < width; count++)
            System.out.print('-');
        System.out.println();
    }

    private void drawSides()
    {
        int count;
        for (count = 0; count < (height - 2); count++)
            drawOneLineOfSides();
    }

    private void drawOneLineOfSides()
    {
        spaces(getOffset());
        System.out.print('|');
        spaces(width - 2);
        System.out.println('|');
    }

    //Writes the indicated number of spaces.
    private static void spaces(int number)
    {
        int count;
        for (count = 0; count < number; count++)
            System.out.print(' ');
    }
}
```

The method spaces was made static because it does not need a calling object. The class would work fine if spaces were not made static, but it is clearer if you make spaces static.

Although that was easy, it does postpone most of the work. You still need to define the methods `drawHorizontalLine` and `drawSides`. Because these are helping methods, they will be private methods.

You come up with the following pseudocode for `drawHorizontalLine`:

> Output `offset` blank spaces.
> Output `width` copies of the character `'–'`.
> `System.out.println();`

The final code for the method `drawHorizontalLine` is given in Display 7.8. Note that the task of writing a specified number of blanks is broken out as another helping method called `spaces`.

Next, you turn your attention to the method `drawSides`. This task is to draw a figure like the following:

```
|       |
|       |
|       |
|       |
```

Noticing that each line is identical, you decide to break out the writing of one of these lines as a subtask. So, the definition of the method `drawSides` is

```java
private void drawSides()
{
    int count;
    for (count = 0; count < (height - 2); count++)
        drawOneLineOfSides();
}
```

Note that you output two fewer lines than the height. The top and bottom horizontal lines account for those extra two units of height.

Just about all that there is left to do is to define the helping method `drawOneLineOfSides`. You design the following pseudocode for `drawOneLineOfSides`:

```java
spaces(getOffset());
System.out.print('|');
spaces(width - 2);
System.out.println('|');
```

Because you already have a method for the subtask of writing spaces, the pseudocode turns out to be Java code, and so the definition of `drawOneLineOfSides` is done. The complete class definition of `Box` is given in Display 7.8.

Although we will not stop to describe the testing process in this case study, all the methods in the class `Figure`, the class `Box`, and the class `Triangle` (which we have not yet discussed) need to be tested. Remember, each method should be tested in a program in which it is the only untested method.

Display 7.9 contains the definition of the class `Triangle`. You can design that class using the same techniques you used to design the class `Box`. We will only discuss one part of the method `drawHere` for which the technical details may not be clear at first reading. The method `drawHere` divides its task into two subtasks, draw the inverted V for the top of the triangle, and draw the horizontal line for the bot-

Display 7.9 The Triangle Class *(Part 1 of 2)*

```
/*************************************************************
 *Class for triangles to be drawn on screen. For this class,
 *a triangle points up and is completely determined by the size of
 *its base. (Screen character spacing determines the length of the
 *sides, given the base.)
 *Inherits getOffset, setOffset, and drawAt from Figure.
 *************************************************************/
public class Triangle extends Figure
{
    private int base;

    public Triangle()
    {
        super();
        base = 0;
    }


    public Triangle(int theOffset, int theBase)
    {
        super(theOffset);
        base = theBase;
    }


    public void reset(int newOffset, int newBase)
    {
        setOffset(newOffset);
        base = newBase;
    }


    /*****************************
     *Draws the figure at current line.
     *****************************/
    public void drawHere()
    {
        drawTop();
        drawBase();
    }
```

Display 7.9 The `Triangle` Class *(Part 2 of 2)*

```
private void drawBase()
{
    spaces(getOffset());
    int count;
    for (count = 0; count < base; count++)
        System.out.print('*');
    System.out.println();
}

private void drawTop()
{
    //startOfLine will be the number of spaces to the first '*' on a
    //line. Initially set to the number of spaces before the top '*'.
    int startOfLine = getOffset() + (base/2);
    spaces(startOfLine);
    System.out.println('*');//top '*'
    int count;
    int lineCount = (base/2) - 1;//height above base
    //insideWidth == number of spaces between the two '*'s on a line.
    int insideWidth = 1;
    for (count = 0; count < lineCount; count++)
    {
        //Down one line so the first '*' is one more space to the left.
        startOfLine--;
        spaces(startOfLine);
        System.out.print('*');
        spaces(insideWidth);
        System.out.println('*');
        //Down one line so the inside is 2 spaces wider.
        insideWidth = insideWidth + 2;
    }
}

private static void spaces(int number)
{
    int count;
    for (count = 0; count < number; count++)
        System.out.print(' ');
}
}
```

tom of the triangle. We will only discuss the method drawTop that draws the inverted V.

The method drawTop draws a figure like the following:

Note that there is an offset for the entire figure. The indenting for the wide bottom of the figure is exactly this offset. But going up from bottom to top, each line has a greater indentation. Alternatively, going down (as the computer must go), each line has a slightly smaller indentation. The indentation is smaller by one character each line. So if the indentation is given by the value of the *int* variable startOfLine, then the indentation can be performed by

```
spaces(startOfLine);
```

This can be made one line of a loop, and then the value of startOfLine will be decreased by one on each loop iteration. The size of the gap between the two asterisks on the same line increases by two as you go down one line. If this gap is given by the value of the *int* variable insideWidth, then the loop for drawing all of the inverted V except for the top asterisk can be

```
for (count = 0; count < lineCount; count++)
{
    spaces(startOfLine);
    System.out.print('*');
    spaces(insideWidth);
    System.out.println('*');
    insideWidth = insideWidth + 2;
    startOfLine--;//THIS LINE WILL MOVE.
}
```

The complete method definition of drawTop is given in Display 7.9. The preceding loop is given in color. Also, in order to accommodate the code that comes before the loop, the line

```
startOfLine--;
```

becomes the first line of the loop instead of the last, but it is still decremented once on each loop iteration.

application program   To complete this project you produce the sample application program shown in Display 7.10.

Display 7.10 Character Graphics Application

```java
public class GraphicsDemo
{
    public static final int indent = 5;
    public static final int topWidth = 21;
    public static final int bottomWidth = 4;
    public static final int bottomHeight = 4;

    public static void main(String[] args)
    {
        System.out.println("          Save the Redwoods!");

        Triangle top = new Triangle(indent, topWidth);
        Box base = new Box(indent + (topWidth/2) - (bottomWidth/2),
                                     bottomHeight, bottomWidth);
        top.drawAt(1);
        base.drawAt(0);
    }
}
```

Screen Output

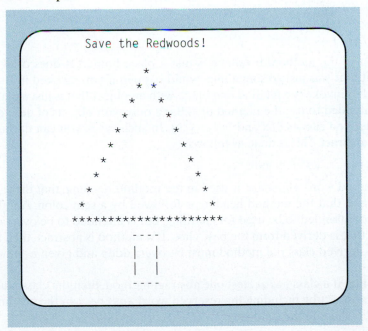

? Self-Test Questions

15. Define a class called `Diamond` that is a derived class of the class `Figure`. The class `Diamond` is similar to the class `Triangle`. However, when a `Diamond` is drawn, it has the same sort of top half as a `Triangle`, but it has a bottom half that is an inverted version of its top half.

Abstract Classes *(Optional)*

The class `Figure` defined in Display 7.7/page 484 was not intended to be used to create objects of the class `Figure`, but was designed to be used as a base class to derive other classes, such as the class `Box` (Display 7.8/page 487). Although, we did not really need to create objects of the class `Figure`, it is still legal to do so, as in the second of the following two statements

```
Figure figureVariable;
figureVariable = new Figure();
```

However, in order to make this legal, we needed to give a definition to the method `drawHere` in the class `Figure`. We repeat that class definition in what follows:

```
public void drawHere()
{
    int count;
    for (count = 0; count < offset; count++)
        System.out.print(' ');
    System.out.println('*');
}
```

This definition of the method `drawHere` is just a place holder. It does draw a single asterisk, but that was just so something would happen if you invoked it. But, we never intended to invoke the method `drawHere` with an object that is just a plain old `Figure`. We intended to use the method `drawHere` only with objects of derived classes (like the derived classes `Box` and `Triangle`). In such cases, you can declare the method to be **abstract**. This is done as follows:

abstract method

```
public abstract void drawHere();
```

Note that the reserved word *abstract* is used in the method heading, that there is no method body, and that the method heading is followed by a semicolon. An abstract method is not intended to be used for anything, but is intended to be overridden in every class that is derived from the base class. If a method is abstract, then in any (nonabstract) derived class the method must be overridden and given a "new" definition.

Java requires that if a class has at least one abstract method, then the class must be declared to be abstract by including the reserved word *abstract* in the heading of the class definition, like in the following:

```
public abstract class Figure
{
    . . .
```

Display 7.11 The F i g u r e Class Redone as An Abstract Class *(Optional)*

```
/**************************************************
 *Abstract class for simple character graphics figures to send to
 *screen. It is intended to be used as a base class for the kinds
 *of figures that will be used in graphics applications.
 **************************************************/
public abstract class Figure
{
    private int offset;

    public abstract void drawHere();
```

<All constructors and methods are *identical* to those in Display 7.7/page 484,
  except for the method d r a w H e r e. Methods other than d r a w H e r e do NOT use the
  reserved word *abstract* in their headings. Below we repeat one such method definition:>

```
    /************************************
     *Draws the figure at lineNumber lines down
     *from the current line.
     ************************************/
    public void drawAt(int lineNumber)
    {
        int count;
        for (count = 0; count < lineNumber; count++)
            System.out.println();
        drawHere();
    }
}
```

A class defined in this way is said to be an **abstract class**. If a class is abstract, you cannot have objects of that class (unless they are objects of a derived class). An abstract class can only be used as a base class to derive other classes.

In Display 7.11 we have redone the class F i g u r e as an abstract class. If we use this abstract version of the class F i g u r e, then all of our derived classes would work as before, but we could not create objects that were just plain old F i g u r e s.

Note that even though the class F i g u r e is abstract, not all of the methods are abstract. All the method definitions, except for the method d r a w H e r e, are exactly the same as in our original definition. They are full definitions (and do not use the reserved word *abstract*). When it makes sense to give a regular method definition

abstract class

in an abstract class, it should be given. This way as much detail as possible is pushed into the abstract class, so that such detail need not be repeated in derived classes.

Why have abstract classes? They simplify your thinking. We have already explained why we defined the class Figure. We defined the class Figure so we would only have to write the definitions of methods such as drawAt once for every kind of figure. An abstract class makes it easier to define classes like Figure by relieving you of the obligation to write useless method definitions. It says that if there is no point in defining some method, because it will always be overridden, then make it an abstract method (and so make the class abstract), and then you need not write the pointless method definition.

An abstract method serves a purpose, even though it is not given a full definition. An abstract method serves as a place holder for a method that must be defined in all (nonabstract) derived classes. Note that in Display 7.11 the method drawAt includes an invocation of the method drawHere. If the abstract method drawHere were omitted, then this invocation of drawHere would be illegal.

7.3 | Dynamic Binding and Polymorphism

In this section we discuss a very important feature of object-oriented programming (and of Java). We discuss one of the ways that different objects can have different definitions for the same method name, such as the method name drawAt. So, if b is a box object and t is a triangle object, then b and t use different definitions of drawAt, even though b and t may both be named by variables of the same type—in our example both objects will be named by variables of type Figure. (Hint: b and t are in more than one class, but now we are anticipating. So, let's get started.)

Dynamic Binding

Look at the definition of the method drawAt in the class Figure (Display 7.7/page 484). It makes a call to the method drawHere. If the only class around were Figure, this would not be anything exciting. But, we derived the class Box from the base class Figure. The class Box inherits the method drawAt from the class Figure, but the method Box overrides the definition of the method drawHere. "So what?" you may say. So plenty! Look at the poor compiler's job.

Consider the following:

```
Box b = new Box(1, 4, 4);
b.drawAt(2);
```

The method drawAt was defined in the class Figure, but it calls the method drawHere that was redefined in the method Box. The code for drawAt was compiled with the class Figure, and that class was compiled before the class Box was even written. So, this compiled code is using a definition of the method drawHere that was not even written at the time that drawAt was compiled. How can that be? When the code for drawAt is compiled, nothing is inserted for the call to drawHere except for an annotation that says, "use the currently applicable definition of drawHere." Then, when you invoke b.drawAt(2), the compiled code for drawAt reaches the annotation equivalent to "use the currently applicable definition of drawHere." This annotation is replaced by an invocation of the version of drawHere that goes with b. Because, in this case, b is of type Box, the version of drawHere will be the definition in the class Box.

It is important to note that the decision of which method definition to use depends on the object's place in the inheritance chain. *It is not determined by the type of the variable naming the object.* For example, consider the following code:

```
Box b = new Box(1, 4, 4);
Figure f = b;
f.drawAt(2);
```

As we noted earlier in this chapter, it is perfectly legal to assign an object of the class Box to a variable of type Figure. But, the object still remembers that it was created as a Box. In this case, f.drawAt(2) will use the definition of drawAt given in Box, not the definition of drawAt given in Figure. To determine which definition of drawAt to use, Java checks which class was used when the object was created using *new*.

(Java is so good at figuring out which definition of a method to use that even a type cast will not fool it. The meaning of b.drawAt(2) will always have the meaning defined in the method Box, even if you use a type cast to change the type of b to the type Figure such as the following:

```
Box b = new Box(1, 4, 4);
Figure f = (Figure)b;
f.drawAt(2);
```

In this case, f.drawAt(2) will use the definition of drawAt given in Box, not the definition of drawAt given in Figure.)

This way of handling an invocation of a method that may be overridden later is called **dynamic binding** or **late binding,** because the meaning of the method invocation is not bound to the location of the method invocation until you run the program. If Java did not use dynamic binding, then when you ran the preceding code, you would not see a triangle on the screen, but would only see what was drawn by the method drawHere of the class Figure (which happens to be a single asterisk).

Other languages do not automatically do dynamic binding as Java does. In many other languages, you must specify in advance what methods may need dynamic binding. This makes Java less efficient but easier to program and less prone to errors.

To see that dynamic binding really is a big deal, consider the following code:

```
Figure f;
Box b = new Box(1, 4, 4);
f = b;
f.drawAt(2);
Triangle t = new Triangle(1, 21);
f = t;
f.drawAt(2);
```

The two lines shown in color are *identical*, yet they use different method definitions for the name drawAt! The first draws a box and the second draws a triangle. An object remembers what method definitions it had when it was created with *new*. You can place the object in a variable of different (but ancestor) class type, but that has

dynamic (late) binding

no effect on which method definition the object uses for an overwritten method. Let's pursue this a bit more to see that it is even more dramatic than it may appear at first glance.

Note that objects of the classes Box and Triangle inherit the method drawAt from the class Figure. The method drawAt is not overridden in the definitions of either of the classes Box or Triangle. So, the text of the method definition is even the same for both Boxes and Triangles! It is the method drawHere, which is invoked within the definition of drawAt, that is (directly) overridden. In this situation you might say that the method name drawAt is **indirectly overridden** in the classes Box and Triangle.

indirectly overridden

Objects Know How They Are Supposed to Act

When an overridden method (or a method that uses an overridden method) is invoked, the action of that method is the one defined in the class used to create the object (with *new*). It is not determined by the type of the variable naming the object. A variable of any ancestor class can hold an object of a descendent class, but the object always remembers which method actions to use for every method name. The type of the variable does not matter. What matters is the class name when the object was created. This is because Java uses dynamic binding.

Type Checking and Dynamic Binding

You need to be aware of how dynamic binding interacts with the Java compiler's type checking. For example, if Employee is a derived class of the class Person, then you can assign an object of type Employee to a variable of type Person, as in

```
Person p = new Employee();
```

But, that is not the end of the story.

Although you can assign an object of type Employee to a variable of type Person, you can only invoke a method that is in the class Person when the calling object is the variable p (of type Person). However, if the method is overridden in the definition of the class Employee and the object named by the variable p is of type Employee, then it is the version of the method defined in Employee that will be used. *So, the variable determines what method names can be used, but the object determines which definition of the method name will be used.* If you want to use a method name that was first introduced in the class Employee with the object named by the variable p of type Person, then you must use a type cast. Something like the following will work: (Assume setEmployeeNumber was first defined in the class Employee.)

```
Employee e = (Employee)p;
e.setEmployeeNumber(5678);
```

Another example may help. Recall that Student (Display 7.3/page 463) is a derived class of Employee (Display 7.1/page 460). Now, suppose you have the following line in a program:

```
Person p = new Student("Joe", 1234);
```

The following is then legal:

```
p.setName("Josephine");
p.writeOutput();
```

And the second invocation will use the definition of `writeOutput` that was given in the class `Student`. *(The object, not the variable, determines which definition of a method name will be used.)*

On the other hand, the following is illegal, because `setStudentNumber` is not the name of a method in the class `Person`. *(The variable determines which method names can be used.)*

```
p.setStudentNumber(1234); //ILLEGAL
```

The variable p is of type `Person`, but the object in the variable p is still an object of type `Student`, and the object can still invoke the method `setStudentNumber`, but the compiler does not know this! To make the invocation legal you need a type cast, such as the following:

```
Student s = (Student)p;
s.setStudentNumber(1234); //Legal
```

You may think this is all just a silly exercise, because you would never assign an object of type `Student` to a variable of type `Person`. Not so. You may not often do the assignment directly, but you may very often do it without realizing it. Recall that you can "plug in" an argument of type `Student` for a method parameter of type `Person`. And, a parameter is a local variable that is assigned the value of the argument that is "plugged in" for it! In this case an object of type `Student` (the argument in the method invocation) is assigned to a variable of type `Person` (the parameter in the method definition).

(Yes, it is really the object reference, that is, the memory address of the object, that is assigned to the variable, but that is a side issue and not relevant to the point at hand. Hey, this is complicated enough as is!)

Dynamic Binding with `toString` *(Optional)*

In the subsection ***Methods Inherited from the Class*** `Object` (page 480), we noted that, if you add an appropriate `toString` method to the class `Student`, then you can give output to the screen using the `toString` method, as illustrated by the following:

```
Student s = new Student("Joe Student", 2001);
System.out.println(s.toString());
```

Thanks to dynamic binding, you do not even need to use the method `toString` in your invocation of `System.out.println`. The following will work just as well and will produce the exact same output:

```
Student s = new Student("Joe Student", 2001);
System.out.println(s);
```

The method invocation `System.out.println(s)` is an invocation of the method `println` with the calling object `System.out`. One definition of the method `println` has a single argument of type `Object`. The definition is equivalent to the following:

```
public void println(Object theObject)
{
    System.out.println(theObject.toString()):
}
```

(The invocation of the method `println` inside the curly brackets is a different, overloaded, definition of the method `println`. That invocation inside the curly brackets uses a method `println` that has a parameter of type `String`, not a parameter of type `Object`.)

This definition of `println` was given before the class `Student` was defined. Yet in the invocation

```
System.out.println(s);
```

with an object `s` of type `Student` (and hence also of type `Object`), it is the definition of `toString` in the class `Student` that is used, not the definition of `toString` in the class `Object`. Dynamic binding is what makes this work.

Polymorphism

polymorphism

Polymorphism comes from a Greek word meaning many forms. Its root meaning (in Computer Science) is using different definitions of the same method name in different contexts. With that original meaning, such things as overloading were considered polymorphism. However, the modern usage of the term is much more specific. As the word is currently used, it refers to the dynamic binding mechanism that determines which method action will be used for a (directly or indirectly) overridden method name. Thus, in current usage, *polymorphism* is basically another term to refer to dynamic binding.

So why is the title of this section "Dynamic Binding and Polymorphism"? Isn't that like saying "Dynamic Binding and Dynamic Binding"? Well, yes, but the terms still have a different feel to them. Dynamic binding is thought of as a process carried out by the computer, and polymorphism is thought of as something the objects do. (I know the objects are really in the computer. I said a different *feel*, not a totally different *meaning*.)

object-oriented programming

Polymorphism is one of the key features of object-oriented programming. In fact object-oriented programming is usually defined by listing its main features, which most authors list as encapsulation, inheritance, and polymorphism. So, polymorphism is a central feature of the object-oriented programming philosophy.

Polymorphism

Polymorphism means using the process of dynamic binding to allow different objects to use different method actions for the same method name.

◻

? Self-Test Questions

16. What is the difference between overloading a method name and overriding a method name?

17. Is the definition of `drawHere` given inDisplay 7.8/page 487 an example of overloading or overriding?

18. Is the definition of `drawHere` given inDisplay 7.9/page 490 an example of overloading or overriding?

19. Are the two definitions of the constructors given in Display 7.9/page 490 an example of overloading or overriding?

20. What is polymorphism?

21. What is dynamic binding? What is late binding? Give an example of each.

22. Is overloading a method name an example of polymorphism?

23. What are the three main characteristics of object-oriented programming as described in the preceding subsection?

24. In the following code, will the two invocations of `drawHere` produce the same picture on the screen or not? (The classes are defined in the preceding section.)

```
Figure f;
f = new Box(1, 4, 4);
f.drawAt(2);
f = new Triangle(1, 21);
f.drawAt(2);
```

CHAPTER SUMMARY

- A derived class is obtained from a base class by adding addition instance variables and/or additional methods. The derived class inherits all the instance variables and methods that are in the base class.

- When defining a constructor for a derived class, the first thing that happens is a call to the constructor for the base class. If you do not make an explicit call, then Java will call the default constructor of the base class.

- You can redefine a method from a base class so that it has a different definition in the derived class. This is called *overriding* the method definition.

- When you override a method definition, the new method definition given in the derived class has the exact same number and types of parameters. If the method in the derived class has a different number of parameters or a parameter position of a different type from the method in the base class, that is overloading.

CHAPTER SUMMARY

■ Private instance variables and private methods of a base class cannot be accessed directly in a derived class.

■ If A is a derived class of class B, then an object of class A is a member of class A (of course), but it is also a member of class B.

■ **Polymorphism** means using the process of dynamic binding to allow different objects to use different method actions for the same method name.

? ANSWERS to Self-Test Questions

1. Yes, a derived class has all the instance variables that the base class has, and can add more instance variables besides.

2. Yes, it will have the methods. Yes, a derived class has all the public methods that the base class has, and also can add more methods. If the derived class does not redefine (override) a method definition, then it does exactly the same action in the derived class as in the base class. However, the base class can contain a new definition (an overriding definition) of the method and the new definition will replace the old definition (provided it has the same number and types of parameters).

3. No.

4. No.

5.

```java
public class TitledPerson extends Person
{
    private String title;

    public TitledPerson()
    {
        super();
        title = "no title yet";
    }

    public TitledPerson(String initialName, String initialTitle)
    {
        super(initialName);
        title = initialTitle;
    }
```

```java
public void reset(String newName, String newTitle)
{
    setName(newName);
    title = newTitle;
}

public String getTitle()
{
    return title;
}
public void setTitle(String newTitle)
{
    title = newTitle;
}

public void writeOutput()
{
    System.out.println("Name: " + getName());
    System.out.println("Title: " + title);
}

public boolean equals(TitledPerson otherPerson)
{
    return (this.sameName(otherPerson)) &&
           (this.title.equalsIgnoreCase(otherPerson.title));
}
}
```

6.
```java
public void writeOutput()
{
    System.out.println("Name: " + getName());
    System.out.println("Student Number: "
                            + getStudentNumber());
    System.out.println("Student Level: " + level);
}
```

7.
```java
public void reset(String newName,
                  int newStudentNumber, int newLevel)
{
    setName(newName);
    setStudentNumber(newStudentNumber);
    level = newLevel;
}
```

8. Yes, an object can have more than one type. If class A is derived from class B, then an object of class A is of type A and is also of type B.

9. The object has four types: `Undergraduate`, `Student`, `Person`, and `Object`.

10.

```
Person p1 = new Student();//Legal. A Student is a Person.
Person p2 = new Undergraduate();//Legal.
                             //An Undergraduate is a Person.
Student s1 = new Person(); //ILLEGAL!
Student s2 = new Undergraduate(); //Legal.
                             //An Undergraduate is a Student.
Undergraduate ug1 = new Person(); //ILLEGAL!
Undergraduate ug2 = new Student(); //ILLEGAL!
Object ob = new Student(); //Legal. A Student is an Object.
Student s3 = new Object();//ILLEGAL!
```

11. It is used as the name for a constructor of the base class. (See Display 7.3/ page 463). When used as a "calling object" as in

    `super.writeOutput();`

    it is used to indicate that the method of the given name in the base class should be used. In Display 7.6/page 483 this is used to indicate the method `writeOutput` of the base class `Student`, as opposed to the method `writeOutput` of the class `Undergraduate`.

12. The reserved word *this*, when used as a method name, names a constructor in the same class as the one being defined. The reserved word *super*, when used as a method name, names a constructor for the base class of the derived class being defined.

13. Because the value returned by `toString` includes the new line character `'\n'`.

14. No, this `toString` method takes one argument of type *int* and the inherited method `toString` takes no argument. (Also, this method is static and the inherited method is not static.)

15.

```
/**********************************************************
*Class for diamonds to be drawn on screen. For this class, a
*diamond is completely determined by its diameter.
*(Screen character spacing determines the rest of the figure.)
*Inherits getOffset, setOffset, and drawAt from Figure.
***********************************************************/
public class Diamond extends Figure
{
    private int diameter;
```

```
public Diamond()
{
    super();
    diameter = 0;
}

public Diamond(int theOffset, int theDiameter)
{
    super(theOffset);
    diameter = theDiameter;
}

public void reset(int newOffset, int newDiameter)
{
    setOffset(newOffset);
    diameter = newDiameter;
}
/**********************************
 *Draws the figure at the current line.
 **********************************/
public void drawHere()
{
    drawTop();
    drawBottom();
}

public void drawTop()
{
    int startOfLine = getOffset() + (diameter/2);
    spaces(startOfLine);
    System.out.println('*');
    int count;
    int lineCount = (diameter/2) - 1;
    int insideWidth = 1;
    for (count = 0; count < lineCount; count++)
    {
        startOfLine--;
        spaces(startOfLine);
        System.out.print('*');
        spaces(insideWidth);
        System.out.println('*');
        insideWidth = insideWidth + 2;
    }
}
```

```
public void drawBottom()
{
    int startOfLine = getOffset();
    int count;
    int lineCount = (diameter/2);
    int insideWidth = 2*lineCount - 1;
    for (count = 0; count < lineCount; count++)
    {

        spaces(startOfLine);
        System.out.print('*');
        spaces(insideWidth);
        System.out.println('*');
        insideWidth = insideWidth - 2;
        startOfLine++;
    }
    spaces(startOfLine);
    System.out.println('*');
}

private static void spaces(int number)
{
    <This definition is identical to that of the method named
        spaces in the class Triangle (Display 7.9/page 490).>
}
}
```

This question points out that an alternative good way to do these character graphics classes is to have a utility class with public static methods, like the method spaces and other methods that do things like draw horizontal lines, big V's, and inverted big V's.

16. *Overriding* refers to redefining a base class method name so it has a different definition in a derived class. *Overloading* refers to giving a method name two definitions that are resolved by having a different parameter list. Overloading can occur in any class whether or not you explicitly name a base class when defining the class. Here is how to tell them apart: When you *override* a method definition, the new method definition given in the derived class has the exact same number and types of parameters. On the other hand, if the method in the derived class were to have a different number of parameters or a parameter of a different type from the method in the base class, then the derived class would have both methods. That would be *overloading*. You can also overload without involving a base class, by giving two method definitions in a single class definition.

17. Overriding

18. Overriding

19. Overloading

20. *Polymorphism* means using the process of dynamic binding to allow different objects to use different method actions for the same method name.

21. *Dynamic binding* and *late binding* are two words for the same thing (so we will only give one definition and only give one example.) Dynamic binding (or late binding) is a way of handling an invocation of a method that may be overridden in a derived class. With dynamic binding the meaning of the method invocation is not bound to the location of the method invocation until you run the program. Less formally, when deciding which definition of an overridden method to use, the computer uses the definition in effect *when the object was created* (with *new*) and does *not* necessarily use the definition that applies to *the type of the variable* naming the object. (Java uses dynamic binding.) Display 7.10/page 493 contains an example of dynamic binding. If Java did not use dynamic binding, then both invocations of the method drawAt would use the definition of drawAt given in the definition of the class Figure (Display 7.7/page 484) and all that would appear on the screen would be two asterisks. (But, fortunately Java does use dynamic binding, so the program gives the output shown in the display.)

22. (This question may not have a definitive answer. In the original definition of *polymorphism* overloading was considered an example of polymorphism and some books still use that old definition.) In current usage, and in this book, overloading a method name is *not* an example of polymorphism.

23. Most authors list encapsulation, inheritance, and polymorphism as the main characteristics of object-oriented programming.

24. No, they will produce different pictures. The first will draw a box. The second will draw a triangle. Neither will use the definition of drawAt that applies to the base class Figure.

? PROGRAMMING EXERCISES

1. Give the definition of a class named Employee whose objects are records for an employee. This class will be a derived class of the class Person given in Display 7.1/page 460. An employee record has an employee's name (inherited from the class Person), an annual salary represented as a single value of type *double*, a hired date that gives the year hired as a single value of type *int*, and a social security number, which is a value of type String. The social security number could be stored as an integer, but it might be too large an integer. So, use a string. (After all, a social security number is just an arbitrary identifier that does not use any numeric properties. Have you ever had to add two social security numbers? What could the result possible mean?) Be sure your class has a reasonable complement of constructors, accessor and mutator methods. Be sure your class has an equals method as well. Write a program to fully test your class definitions.

2. In this exercise, you will define two derived classes of the class Figure in Display 7.7/page 484. Your two classes will be called RightArrow and

LeftArrow. These classes will be like the classes Triangle and Box, but they will draw left- and right-pointing arrows that look like the following, which is a right-pointing arrow:

```
            *
          *  *
        *     *
************      *
        *     *
          *  *
        *
```

The size of the arrow is determined by two numbers, one for the size of the "tail," which is 12 in the preceding example, and one for the base of the arrow head, which is 7 in the preceding example. (If the size of the base is an even number, then the tail will not be exactly in the middle of the arrow head. That is OK.) Write a test program for each class that tests all the methods in the class. You can assume that the base of the arrow is 3 or more.

3. Give the definition of a class named Doctor whose objects are records for a clinic's doctors. This class will be a derived class of the class Person given in Display 7.1/page 460. A Doctor record has the doctor's name (inherited from the class Person), specialty (e.g. "Pediatrician," "Obstetrician," "General Practitioner," etc., so use type String), and office visit fee (use type *double*). Be sure your class has a reasonable complement of constructors and accessor methods, and an equals method as well. Write a driver program to test all your methods.

4. Give the definition of two classes, Patient and Billing, whose objects are records for a clinic. Patient will be derived from the class Person given in Display 7.1/page 460. A Patient record has the patient's name (inherited from the class Person) and social security number (use type String for the reasons described in Programming Exercise 1). A Billing object will contain a Patient object and a Doctor object (from Programming Exercise 3). Be sure your classes have a reasonable complement of constructors and accessor methods, and an equals method, as well. First write a driver program to test all your methods, then write a test program that creates at least two patients, at least two doctors, at least two Billing records, then prints out the total income from the Billing records.

5. Create a base class called Vehicle that has the manufacturer's name (type String), number of cylinder's in the engine (type *int*), and owner (type Person given in Display 7.1/page 460). Then create a class called Truck that is derived from Vehicle and has additional properties, the load capacity in tons (type *double* since it may contain a fractional part) and towing capacity in pounds (type *int*). Be sure your classes have a reasonable complement of constructors and accessor methods, and an equals method, as well. Write a driver program that tests all your methods.

6. Create three classes, RightTriangle and Rectangle, each of which is a derived class of the class Figure in Display 7.7/page 484. Then define a class Square that is a derived class of Rectangle. Each of these three classes will have two additional methods to calculate area and circumference, as well as the methods inherited. Do not forget to redefine the method drawHere. Be sure your classes have a reasonable complement of constructors and accessor methods. The Square class should include only one dimension, the side, and automatically set the height and width to the length of the side. You can use the dimensions of the character width and line spacing even though they are undoubtedly unequal, so a square will not look square (just like a Box as discussed in the chapter.) Note that the classes Square and Box produce the same figures but the two classes are produced in different ways. Write a driver program that tests all your methods.

7. Create a new class called Dog that is derived from the PetRecord class given in Display 5.19/page 351. The new class has the additional attributes of breed (type String) and boosterShot (type *boolean*, *true* if the pet has had its booster shot, *false* if it has not). Be sure your classes have a reasonable complement of constructors and accessor methods. Write a driver program to test all your methods, then write a program that reads in five pets of type Dog and print out the name and breed of all dogs that are over two years old and have not had their booster shots.

CHAPTER 8

EXCEPTION HANDLING

8.1   BASIC EXCEPTION HANDLING 512
Exceptions in Java 513
Predefined Exception Classes 526
ArrayIndexOutOfBounds-
    Exception *(Alternative
    Ordering)* 527

8.2   DEFINING EXCEPTION CLASSES 528
Defining Your Own Exception
    Classes 528
Java Tip Preserve getMessage When
    You Define Exception
    Classes 533
Programming Tip When to Define an
    Exception Class 537

8.3   USING EXCEPTION CLASSES 538
Declaring Exceptions (Passing the
    Buck) 538
Exceptions That Do Not Need to Be
    Caught 542

Multiple Throws and Catches 543
Java Tip Catch the More Specific
    Exception First 543
Programming Tip Exception Handling
    and Information Hiding 547
Gotcha Overuse of Exceptions 549
Programming Tip When to Throw an
    Exception 549
Gotcha Nested try-catch-
    Blocks 551
The finally Block *(Optional)* 551
Rethrowing an Exception
    (Optional) 552
Case Study A Line-Oriented
    Calculator 553

Chapter Summary 568
Answers to Self-Test Questions 569
Programming Exercises 572

EXCEPTION HANDLING

exception handling is the preferred way to handle certain kinds of special conditions in your program. Exception handling allows you to divide a program or method definition into separate sections for the normal case and for the exceptional case, thereby dividing one larger programming task into two smaller and more easily doable programming tasks.

Objectives

Become familiar with the notion of *exception handling.*

Learn Java syntax for exception handing.

Develop the ability to use exception handling effectively in your own classes and programs.

Prerequisites

Except for one subsection, this chapter requires only Chapters 1 through 5 and Chapter 7. The only subsection that requires more is entitled *ArrayIndexOutOf-BoundsException* **(Alternative Ordering)**, and that subsection can be considered optional. The subsection *ArrayIndexOutOfBoundsException* **(Alternative Ordering)** requires Chapter 6, which covers arrays.

Section 8.1 (except for the one subsection discussed in the previous paragraph) can be covered after Chapters 1 through 5. It does not require Chapters 6 or 7.

8.1 | Basic Exception Handling

One way to write a program is to first assume that nothing unusual or incorrect will happen. For example, if the program takes an entry off of a list, you might assume that the list is not empty. Once you have the program working for the core situation where things always go as planned, you can then add code to take care of the exceptional cases. In Java, there is a way to reflect this approach in your code. Basically, you write your code as if nothing very unusual happens. After that, you use the Java *exception-handling* facilities to add code for those unusual cases.

Perhaps the most important use of exceptions is to deal with methods that have some special case that is handled differently depending on how the method is used. Perhaps the method will be used in many programs and some will handle the special case in one way, while others will handle it in some other way. For example, if there is a division by zero in the method, then it may turn out that for some invocations of the method, the program should end, but for other invocations of the method something else should happen. You will see that such a method can be defined to throw an exception if the special case occurs, and let that special case be handled outside of the method. That way the special case can be handled differently for different invocations of the method.

In Java, **exception handling** proceeds as follows: Either the Java language itself, or your code, provides a mechanism that signals when something unusual happens. This is called **throwing an exception**. At another place in your program—in a separate class or method, or just in another part of the code for your program—you place the code that deals with the exceptional case. This is called **handling the exception**. This method of programming makes for cleaner code. Of course, we still need to explain the details of how you do this in Java.

exception handling

Exceptions in Java

Most short programs do not need very much, if any, exception handling, and what exception handling they do use is often not easy to see in the code. So, in order to get a simple example, we will use a toy program for our first example. First, we will do the program without using Java's exception-handling facilities, and then we will redo it using exception handling.

For this example, suppose that milk is such an important food in our culture that people almost never run out of it, but still we would like our programs to accommodate the very unlikely situation of running out of milk. The basic code, which assumes we do not run out of milk, might be as follows:

```
System.out.println("Enter number of donuts:");
donutCount = SavitchIn.readLineInt();

System.out.println("Enter number of glasses of milk:");
milkCount = SavitchIn.readLineInt();

donutsPerGlass = donutCount/(double)milkCount;
System.out.println(donutCount + " donuts.");
System.out.println(milkCount + " glasses of milk.");
System.out.println("You have " + donutsPerGlass
                    + " donuts for each glass of milk.");
```

If there is no milk, then this code will include a division by zero, which is an error. To take care of this special situation where we run out of milk, we can add a test for this unusual situation. The complete program with this added test for the special situation is shown in Display 8.1. Now, let's see how this program can be rewritten using Java's exception-handling facilities.

In Display 8.2, we have rewritten the program from Display 8.1 using an exception. This is only a toy example, and you would probably not use an exception in this case. However, it does give us a simple example. Although the program as a whole is not simpler, at least the part between the words *try* and *catch* is cleaner, and this hints at the advantage of using exceptions. Look at the code between the words *try* and *catch*. That code is basically the same as the code in Display 8.1, except that instead of the big *if-else*-statement (shown in color in Display 8.1) this new program has the following smaller *if*-statement:

```
if (milkCount < 1)
    throw new Exception("Exception: No Milk!");
```

This *if*-statement says that if there is no milk, then do something exceptional. That something exceptional is given after the word *catch*. The idea is that the normal situation is handled by the code following the word *try*, and that the code following the word *catch* is only used in exceptional circumstances. So we have separated the normal case from the exceptional case. In this toy example, that does not really buy us too much, but in other situations, it will prove to be very helpful. Let's look at the details.

try-block

The basic way of handling exceptions in Java consists of the *try-throw-catch* threesome. A ***try*-block** has the syntax

```
try
{
    Code_To_Try
}
```

This *try*-block contains the code for the basic algorithm that tells the computer what to do when everything goes smoothly. It is called a *try-block* because you are not 100% sure that all will go smoothly, but you want to "give it a try."

Now if something does go wrong, you want to throw an exception, which is a way of indicating that something went wrong. So the basic outline, when we add a *throw*, is as follows:

```
try
{
    Code_To_Try
    Possibly_Throw_An_Exception
    More_Code
}
```

An example of a *try*-block with a *throw*-statement included (copied from Display 8.2) is shown at the top of page 517:

Display 8.1   **One Way to Deal with a Problem Situation**

```java
public class GotMilk
{
    public static void main(String[] args)
    {
        int donutCount, milkCount;
        double donutsPerGlass;

        System.out.println("Enter number of donuts:");
        donutCount = SavitchIn.readLineInt();

        System.out.println("Enter number of glasses of milk:");
        milkCount = SavitchIn.readLineInt();

        if (milkCount < 1)
        {
            System.out.println("No Milk!");
            System.out.println("Go buy some milk.");
        }
        else
        {
            donutsPerGlass = donutCount/(double)milkCount;
            System.out.println(donutCount + " donuts.");
            System.out.println(milkCount + " glasses of milk.");
            System.out.println("You have " + donutsPerGlass
                        + " donuts for each glass of milk.");
        }
        System.out.println("End of program.");
    }
}
```

Sample Screen Dialogue

```
Enter number of donuts:
2
Enter number of glasses of milk:
0
No Milk!
Go buy some milk.
End of program.
```

Display 8.2   An Example of Exception Handling *(Part 1 of 2)*

```
public class ExceptionDemo
{
    public static void main(String[] args)
    {
        int donutCount, milkCount;
        double donutsPerGlass;

        try
        {
            System.out.println("Enter number of donuts:");
            donutCount = SavitchIn.readLineInt();

            System.out.println("Enter number of glasses of milk:");
            milkCount = SavitchIn.readLineInt();

            if (milkCount < 1)
                throw new Exception("Exception: No Milk!");

            donutsPerGlass = donutCount/(double)milkCount;
            System.out.println(donutCount + " donuts.");
            System.out.println(milkCount + " glasses of milk.");
            System.out.println("You have " + donutsPerGlass
                               + " donuts for each glass of milk.");
        }

        catch(Exception e)
        {
            System.out.println(e.getMessage());
            System.out.println("Go buy some milk.");
        }

        System.out.println("End of program.");
    }
}
```

This is just a toy example to learn the basic syntax for exception handling.

throw-statement

try-block

catch-block

```
try
{
    System.out.println("Enter number of donuts:");
    donutCount = SavitchIn.readLineInt();

    System.out.println("Enter number of glasses of milk:");
    milkCount = SavitchIn.readLineInt();

    if (milkCount < 1)
        throw new Exception("Exception: No Milk!");

    donutsPerGlass = donutCount/(double)milkCount;
    System.out.println(donutCount + " donuts.");
    System.out.println(milkCount + " glasses of milk.");
    System.out.println("You have " + donutsPerGlass
                          + " donuts for each glass of milk.");
}
```

Exception is a predefined class, and the following is called a *throw-*   *throw-statement*

Display 8.2   An Example of Exception Handling *(Part 2 of 2)*

Sample Screen Dialogue 1

```
Enter number of donuts:
3
Enter number of glasses of milk:
2
3 donuts.
2 glasses of milk.
You have 1.5 donuts for each glass of milk.
End of program.
```

Sample Screen Dialogue 2

```
Enter number of donuts:
2
Enter number of glasses of milk:
0
Exception: No Milk!
Go buy some milk.
End of program.
```

statement. A *throw*-statement creates a new object of the class Exception and *throws it:*

```
throw new Exception("Exception: No Milk!");
```

catch-block
When an exception is **thrown**, the code in the surrounding *try*-block stops executing and another portion of code, known as a *catch*-**block**, begins execution. This executing of the *catch*-block is called **catching the exception.** When an exception is thrown, it should ultimately be caught by some *catch*-block. In Display 8.2, the appropriate *catch*-block immediately follows the *try*-block. We repeat the *catch*-block in what follows:

```
catch(Exception e)
{
    System.out.println(e.getMessage());
    System.out.println("Go buy some milk.");
}
```

The *catch*-block looks a little like a method definition that has a parameter of a type Exception. *It is not a method definition*, but in some ways, a *catch*-block is like a method. It is a separate piece of code that is executed when your program encounters (and executes) the following (within the preceding *try*-block):

```
throw new Exception(Possibly_Some_Arguments);
```

So, this *throw*-statement is similar to a method call, but instead of calling a method, it calls the *catch*-block and says to execute the code in the *catch*-block.

---

throw-Statement

Syntax:

```
throw new Exception_Class_Name(Possibly_A_String);
```

When the *throw*-statement is executed, the program execution is stopped, and an exception is *thrown*. If the exception is caught in a *catch*-block, then the code in the *catch*-block is executed next. See the box entitled *try-throw-catch* later in the chapter for more details.

Example:

```
throw new Exception("Unexpected End of Input.");
```

What is that identifier e in the following line from a *catch*-block?

```
catch(Exception e)
```

catch-**block parameter**
That identifier e looks like a parameter, and acts very much like a parameter. So, we will call this e **the *catch*-block parameter**. (But remember, this does not mean that the *catch*-block is a method.) The *catch*-block parameter does two things:

1. The *catch*-block parameter is preceded by a class name that specifies what kind of exception the *catch*-block can catch.

2. The *catch*-block parameter gives you a name for the exception that is caught, so you can write code in the *catch*-block that does things with the exception object that is caught.

We will discuss these two functions of the *catch*-block parameter in reverse order. In this subsection, we will discuss using the *catch*-block parameter as a name for the exception object that is caught. In the subsection entitled **Multiple Throws and Catches,** later in this chapter, we will discuss which exception objects go to which *catch*-block. Our current example has only one *catch*-block, so in this simple example, there is no issue of which *catch*-block to use. The most common name for a *catch*-block parameter is e, but you can use any legal identifier in place of e.

Let's see how the *catch*-block in Display 8.2 works. In order to understand how it works, we need to also look at the *throw*-statement in the *try*-block. That is also in Display 8.2 and is reproduced here:

throw-
statement

```
throw new Exception("Exception: No Milk!");
```

This *throw*-statement is embedded in an *if*-statement, but for our purposes here, we do not need to know how it comes to be executed. We only want to show you what happens when it is executed. When this *throw*-statement is executed, a new object of the class Exception is created by the part

```
new Exception("Exception: No Milk!")
```

The string "Exception: No Milk!" is an argument for the constructor for the class Exception. The Exception object, created with the *new*, stores that string in an instance variable of the object, so that it can be recovered in the *catch*-block. The word *throw* indicates that this object created with the *new* is **thrown**. When an object is thrown, execution of the code in the *try*-block ends and control passes to the *catch*-block (or blocks) that are placed right after the *try*-block. The *catch*-block from Display 8.2 is reproduced here:

throwing

```
catch(Exception e)
{
    System.out.println(e.getMessage());
    System.out.println("Go buy some milk.");
}
```

When an exception is thrown, the exception must be of type Exception in order for this particular *catch*-block to apply; but as we will see, all exceptions are of type Exception, so this *catch*-block will catch any exception. The object thrown is plugged in for the *catch*-block parameter e, and the code in the *catch*-block is executed. So in this case, you can think of e as being the exception thrown by the following *throw*-statement:

```
throw new Exception("Exception: No Milk!");
```

Every exception has a method called getMessage, and unless you do something to change things, this method retrieves the string that was given to the exception object by its constructor (when it was thrown). So, in this case, e.getMessage() returns "Exception: No Milk!" Thus, when the *catch*-block in Display 8.2 is executed, it causes the following to be written to the screen:

getMessage

```
Exception: No Milk!
Go buy some milk.
```

catch-Block Parameter

The *catch*-block parameter is an identifier in the heading of a *catch*-block that serves as a placeholder for an exception that might be thrown. When a (suitable) exception is thrown in the preceding *try*-block, that exception is plugged in for the *catch*-block parameter. The identifier e is often used for *catch*-block parameters, but this is not required. You can use any legal (non-reserved-word) identifier for a *catch*-block parameter.

Syntax:

```
catch(Exception_Class_Name  Catch_Block_Parameter)
{
        <Code to be performed if an exception of the named exception class is thrown in the try-block.>
}
```

You may use any legal identifier for the *Catch_Block_Parameter*.

Example:

In the following, e is the *catch*-block parameter.

```
catch(Exception e)
{
    System.out.println(e.getMessage());
    System.out.println("Go buy some milk.");
}
```

The getMessage Method

Every exception has a String instance variable that contains some message, which typically identifies the reason for the exception. For example, if the exception is thrown as follows:

```
throw new Exception(Quoted_String_Argument);
```

then the quoted string given as an argument to the constructor Exception is used as the value of this String instance variable. If the object is called e, then the method call e.getMessage() returns this string.

Example:

Suppose the following *throw*-statement is executed in a *try*-block:

```
throw new Exception("Input must be positive.");
```

and suppose the following is a *catch*-block immediately following the *try*-block:

```
catch(Exception e)
{
    System.out.println(e.getMessage());
    System.out.println("Program aborted.");
    System.exit(0);
}
```

In this case, the method call e.getMessage() returns the string
"Input must be positive."

An Exception Is an Object

The following is a *throw*-statement:

```
throw new Exception("Illegal character on line 57.");
```

It is typically found embedded in a branching statement, but it is legal to use it as a simple statement. A *throw*-statement is not just some action that is taken and forgotten. A *throw*-statement creates an object that has a message (in this case the message is "Illegal character on line 57."). This object, and its message, is available to the *catch*-block, and so the effect of throwing an exception is more than just a transfer of control to the first statement of a *catch*-block.

To convince you that an object is really created in a *throw*-statement, note that the following, while unlikely to be used for anything, is legal:

```
Exception e = new Exception("Illegal character on line 57.");
```

The part *new* Exception("Illegal character on line 57.") is an invocation of a constructor for the class Exception, and it creates an object of the class Exception. In the above *throw*-statement, *new* Exception("Illegal character on line 57.") is also an invocation of a constructor for the class Exception, and it similarly creates an object of the class Exception.

The flow of control for the program in Display 8.2/page 516 is shown in Display 8.3. Part 1 of that display assumes that the user enters a positive number for the number of glasses of milk, and so *no exception is thrown* (as in the first dialog given in Display 8.2). Part 2 assumes that the user enters zero or a negative number for the number of glasses of milk, and so *an exception is thrown* (as shown in the second dialog given in Display 8.2).

One way to visualize the process is to think the statements in the *try*-block are people who stand one after the other. Each one does her or his thing and then taps the next one on the shoulder, and then the next one does her or his thing. When an exception is thrown (*throw new* Exception(...)), that person (statement) creates an exception, which you can think of as a rock with a note attached, and throws that rock (exception) at the first statement in the *catch*-block. The rock hits the first statement in the *catch*-block (gently) and wakes it up. The process then continues in the *catch*-block, with each statement doing its thing and starting the next statement. (The note is passed along in case any statement refers to the exception.) When the end of the *catch*-block is reached, the process keeps going and has the statements after the *catch*-block do their things. Note that the statement that throws the exception does not tap the next *try*-block statement on the shoulder, but instead wakes up the *catch*-block. So, the rest of the statements in the *try*-block are not executed.

If no exception is thrown, the process goes through the entire *try*-block. After the last statement in the *try*-block does its thing, that last statement runs around the *catch*-block, and if there are any statements after the *catch*-block, it wakes them up and gets them started (but it thus skips the *catch*-block. So the *catch*-block does nothing when no exception is thrown).

This makes it sound like a *try-throw-catch*-setup is equivalent to an *if-else*-statement. It almost is equivalent, except for the note attached to the rock.

comparison to
if-else

Display 8.3   Flow of Control with Exception Handling *(Part 1 of 2)*

```java
public class ExceptionDemo
{
    public static void main(String[] args)
    {
        int donutCount, milkCount;
        double donutsPerGlass;

        try
        {
            System.out.println("Enter number of donuts:");
            donutCount = SavitchIn.readLineInt();

            System.out.println("Enter number of glasses of milk:");
            milkCount = SavitchIn.readLineInt();

            if (milkCount < 1)
                throw new Exception("Exception: No Milk!");

            donutsPerGlass = donutCount/(double)milkCount;
            System.out.println(donutCount + " donuts.");
            System.out.println(milkCount + " glasses of milk.");
            System.out.println("You have " + donutsPerGlass
                        + " donuts for each glass of milk.");
        }

        catch(Exception e)
        {
            System.out.println(e.getMessage());
            System.out.println("Go buy some milk.");
        }

        System.out.println("End of program.");

    }
}
```

These arrows assume that the user inputs a positive number for the number of glasses of milk.

milkCount is positive, so an exception is NOT thrown here.

This code is NOT executed.

Display 8.3 **Flow of Control with Exception Handling** *(Part 2 of 2)*

```
public class ExceptionDemo
{
    public static void main(String[] args)
    {
        int donutCount, milkCount;
        double donutsPerGlass;

        try
        {
            System.out.println("Enter number of donuts:");
            donutCount = SavitchIn.readLineInt();

            System.out.println("Enter number of glasses of milk:");
            milkCount = SavitchIn.readLineInt();

            if (milkCount < 1)
                throw new Exception("Exception: No Milk!");

            donutsPerGlass = donutCount/(double)milkCount;
            System.out.println(donutCount + " donuts.");
            System.out.println(milkCount + " glasses of milk.");
            System.out.println("You have " + donutsPerGlass
                            + " donuts for each glass of milk.");
        }
        catch(Exception e)
        {
            System.out.println(e.getMessage());
            System.out.println("Go buy some milk.");
        }

        System.out.println("End of program.");
    }
}
```

These arrows assume that the user inputs zero or a negative number for the number of glasses of milk.

milkCount is zero or negative, so an exception is thrown here.

This code is NOT executed.

The rock and the note together represents the exception object that is thrown and that carries a message. Thus, a *try-throw-catch*-setup is equivalent to an *if-else*-statement *with the added ability to send a message to one of the branches.* This does not sound much different from an *if-else*-statement, but it will turn out that this exception object, with its message, gives the *try-throw-catch*-setup a lot more versatility than an *if-else*-statement.

To summarize in a more formal tone, a *try*-block contains some code that we are assuming includes a *throw*-statement. The *throw*-statement is normally executed only in exceptional circumstances, but when it is executed, it throws an exception of some exception class. (So far, Exception is the only exception class we know of, but there are others as well.) When an exception is thrown, that is the end of the *try*-block. All the rest of the code in the *try*-block is ignored and control passes to a suitable *catch*-block. A *catch*-block applies only to an immediately preceding *try*-block. If the exception is thrown, then that exception object is plugged in for the *catch*-block parameter, and the statements in the *catch*-block are executed. For example, if you look at the dialog in Display 8.2, you will see that as soon as the user enters a nonpositive number, the *try*-block stops and the *catch*-block is executed. For now, we will assume that every *try*-block is followed by an appropriate *catch*-block. We will later discuss what happens when there is no appropriate *catch*-block.

Next, we summarize what happens when no exception is thrown in a *try*-block. If no exception is thrown in the *try*-block, then after the *try*-block is completed, program execution continues with the code after the *catch*-block. In other words, if no exception is thrown, then the *catch*-block is ignored. Most of the time when the program is executed, the *throw*-statement will not be executed, and so in most cases, the code in the *try*-block will run to completion and the code in the *catch*-block will be ignored completely.

? Self-Test Questions

1. What output is produced by the following code?

```
int waitTime = 46;

try
{
    System.out.println("Try-block entered.");
    if (waitTime > 30)
        throw new Exception("Time Limit Exceeded.");
    System.out.println("Leaving try-block.");
}

catch(Exception e)
{
    System.out.println("Exception: " + e.getMessage());
}
System.out.println("After catch-block");
```

---

try-throw-catch

This is the basic mechanism for throwing and catching exceptions. The *throw*-**statement** throws the exception. The *catch*-**block** catches the exception. When the exception is thrown, the *try*-block ends and then the code in the *catch*-block is executed. After the *catch*-block is completed, the code after the *catch*-block(s) is executed (provided the *catch*-block has not ended the program or performed some other special action).

If no exception is thrown in the *try*-block, then after the *try*-block is completed, program execution continues with the code after the *catch*-block(s). (In other words, if no exception is thrown, then the *catch*-block(s) are ignored.)

Syntax:

```
try
{
    Some_Statements
    < Either some code with a throw-statement or a method invocation that might throw an exception.>
    Some_More_Statements
}
catch(Exception_Class_Name e)
{
    < Code to be performed if an exception of the named exception class is thrown in the try-block.>
}
```

You may use any legal identifier in place of e. The code in the *catch*-block may refer to e. If there is an explicit *throw*-statement, it is usually embedded in an *if*-statement or *if-else*-statement. There may be any number of *throw*-statements and/or any number of method invocations that may throw exceptions. Each *catch*-block can list only one exception, but there may be more than one *catch*-block.

Example:
See Display 8.2.

◻

2. What would be the output produced by the code in Self-Test Question 1 if we make the following change? Change the line

   ```
   int waitTime = 46;
   ```

   to

   ```
   int waitTime = 12;
   ```

3. What kind of thing is an exception? Is it an identifier? a variable? a method? an object? a class? or something else?

4. Is the following legal?

   ```
   Exception myException = new Exception("Hi Mom!");
   ```

5. In the code given in Self-Test Question 1, what is the *throw*-statement?

6. What happens when a *throw*-statement is executed? This is a general question. Tell what happens in general, not simply what happens in the code in Self-Test Question 1 or some other sample code.

7. In the code given in Self-Test Question 1, what is the *try*-block?

8. In the code given in Self-Test Question 1, what is the *catch*-block?

9. In the code given in Self-Test Question 1, what is the *catch*-block parameter?

10. Would the code given in Self-Test Question 1 perform any differently if the *catch*-block were changed to the following?

```
catch(Exception messenger)
{
    System.out.println("Exception: " +
messenger.getMessage());
}
```

11. Write a statement that will throw an exception if the value of the String variable named status is "bad". This would be inside a *try*-block, but you need not write the entire *try*-block. The exception is supposed to be a member of the class Exception, and the string recovered by get-Message should be "Exception thrown: Bad Status." You need not write the *catch*-block.

Predefined Exception Classes

When you learn about the methods of predefined classes, you will sometimes be told that they might throw certain types of exceptions. Usually, these are predefined exception classes. If you use one of these methods, you can put the method invocation in a *try*-block and follow it with a *catch*-block to catch the exception. The names of predefined exceptions are designed to be self-explanatory. Some sample predefined exceptions are

```
IOException,
ClassNotFoundException, and
FileNotFoundException.
```

When you catch an exception of one of these predefined exception classes, the string returned by the getMessage method will usually provide you with enough information to identify the source of the exception. Thus, if you have a class called Sample-Class and it has a method called doStuff, which throws exceptions of the class IOException, you might use the following:

```
SampleClass object = new SampleClass();
try
{
    <Possibly some code>
    object.doStuff();//may throw IOException
    <Possibly some more code>
}
catch(IOException e)
{
    <Code to handle the exception, probably including the following:>
    System.out.println(e.getMessage());
}
```

If you think the exception makes proceeding with the program infeasible, then the *catch*-block can end the program with a call to System.exit, as follows:

```
catch(IOException e)
{
    System.out.println(e.getmessage());
    System.out.println("Program aborted");
    System.exit(0);
}
```

You will hear about more predefined exception classes as you learn more about Java, but for now, the only predefined exception class you are likely to use is the class `Exception`. The class `Exception` is the root class of all exceptions. Every exception class is a descendent[1] of the class `Exception` (that is, it is directly derived from the class `Exception`, or it is derived from a class that is derived from the class `Exception`, or it arises from some longer chain of derivations ultimately starting with the class `Exception`). You can use the class `Exception` itself, just as we did in Display 8.2/page 516, but you are even more likely to use it to define a derived class[1] of the class `Exception`.

The Class `Exception`

Every exception class is a descendent class of the class `Exception`. You can use the class `Exception` itself in a class or program, but you are even more likely to use it to define a derived class[1] of the class `Exception`.

◼

`ArrayIndexOutOfBoundsException` *(Alternative Ordering)*

You should read some of Chapter 6, which covers arrays, before reading this short subsection. If you have covered some of Chapter 6, you should not consider this section optional.

If your program attempts to use an array index that is out of bounds, then an `ArrayIndexOutOfBoundsException` is thrown and your program ends, unless the exception is caught in a catch block. This is a special kind of exception that need not be caught or accounted for any way, and that normally is not caught in a *catch-* block. This sort of exception indicates that there is something wrong with your code, and what you need to do is to fix the mistake in your code. Thus, an `ArrayIndexOutOfBoundsException` normally functions more like a run time error announcement, rather than behaving like a regular exception.

? Self-Test Questions

....

12. Is the following legal?

    ```
    IOException sos = new IOException("Hello Houston!");
    ```

13. Is the following legal?

---

1. If you have not yet read Chapter 7, disregard all the references to *descendent classes* and *derived classes*.

```
IOException sos = new IOException("Hello Houston!");
throw sos;
```

8.2 | Defining Exception Classes

> *I'll make an exception this time.*
>
> **My mother**

In this section, we show you how to define your own exception classes and give you techniques for when and how to throw and catch exceptions.

Defining Your Own Exception Classes

You can define your own exception classes, but they must be derived classes of some already defined exception class. An exception class can be a derived class of any predefined exception class, or of any exception class that you have already successfully defined. Our examples will be derived classes of the class Exception, but you can use any existing exception class.

constructors   When defining an exception class, the constructors are the most important and often the only methods, other than those inherited from the base class. For example, in Display 8.4, we defined an exception class called DivideByZeroException, and the only methods we defined were a default constructor and a constructor with one String parameter. For our purposes, that is all we needed to define. However, the class does inherit all the methods of the class Exception.[1] In particular, the class DivideByZeroException inherits the method getMessage, which returns a string message. In the default constructor, this string message is set with the following, which is the first line in the default constructor definition:

```
super("Dividing by Zero!");
```

This is a call to a constructor of the base class Exception. As we have already noted, when you pass a string to the constructor for the class Exception, it sets the value of a String instance variable that can later be recovered with a call to getMessage. The class DivideByZeroException inherits this String instance variable as well as the method getMessage. For example, in Display 8.5, we give a sample program that uses this exception class. In Display 8.5, the exception is thrown using the default constructor as follows:

```
throw new DivideByZeroException();
```

---

1. Some programmers would prefer to make the DivideByZeroException class a derived class of the ArithmeticException class, but that would make it a kind of exception that you are not required to catch in your code, and so you would lose the help of the compiler in keeping track of uncaught exceptions. For more details, see the subsection ***Exceptions That Do Not Need to Be Caught*** later in this chapter. If this footnote does not make sense to you, you can safely ignore it. This footnote is primarily for any expert who might be looking over your, or my, shoulder.

Display 8.4   A Programmer-Defined Exception Class

```java
public class DivideByZeroException extends Exception
{
    public DivideByZeroException()
    {
        super("Dividing by Zero!");
    }

    public DivideByZeroException(String message)
    {
        super(message);
    }
}
```

You can do more in an exception constructor, but this form is common.

super is an invocation of the constructor for the base class Exception.

This exception is caught in the *catch*-block shown in Display 8.5. Consider the following line from that *catch*-block:

```java
System.out.println(e.getMessage());
```

This line produces the following output to the screen in Dialogs 2 and 3:

```
Dividing by Zero!
```

The definition of the class DivideByZeroException in Display 8.4 has a second constructor with one parameter of type String. This constructor allows you to choose any message you wish when you throw an exception. If the *throw*-statement in Display 8.5 had instead used the following string argument:

```java
throw new DivideByZeroException("Oops. Shouldn't Have Used Zero.");
```

then in Dialogs 2 and 3, the statement

```java
System.out.println(e.getMessage());
```

would have produced the following output to the screen:

```
Oops. Shouldn't Have Used Zero.
```

Notice that in Display 8.5, the *try*-block is the normal part of the program. If all goes normally, that is the only code that will be executed, and the dialog will be like the dialog shown in sample screen dialog 1. In the exceptional case, where the user enters a zero for a denominator, the exception is thrown and then caught in the *catch*-block. The *catch*-block outputs the message of the exception, and then calls the method secondChance. The method secondChance gives the user a

Display 8.5   Using a Programmer-Defined Exception Class *(Part 1 of 3)*

```java
public class DivideByZeroExceptionDemo
{
    private int numerator;
    private int denominator;
    private double quotient;

    public static void main(String[] args)
    {
        DivideByZeroExceptionDemo oneTime =
                              new DivideByZeroExceptionDemo();
        oneTime.doIt();
    }


    public void doIt()
    {
        try
        {
            System.out.println("Enter numerator:");
            numerator = SavitchIn.readLineInt();
            System.out.println("Enter denominator:");
            denominator = SavitchIn.readLineInt();
            if (denominator == 0)
                throw new DivideByZeroException();
            quotient = numerator/(double)denominator;
            System.out.println(numerator + "/"
                                + denominator
                                + " = " + quotient);
        }
        catch(DivideByZeroException e)
        {
            System.out.println(e.getMessage());
            secondChance();
        }
        System.out.println("End of Program.");
    }
```

We will present an improved version of this program later in this chapter.

```
public void secondChance()
{
    System.out.println("Try Again:");
    System.out.println("Enter numerator:");
    numerator = SavitchIn.readLineInt();
    System.out.println("Enter denominator:");
    System.out.println("Be sure the denominator is not zero.");
    denominator = SavitchIn.readLineInt();

    if (denominator == 0)
    {
        System.out.println("I cannot do division by zero.");
        System.out.println("Since I cannot do what you want,");
        System.out.println("the program will now end.");
        System.exit(0);
    }

    quotient = ((double)numerator)/denominator;
    System.out.println(numerator + "/"
                                    + denominator
                                    + " = " + quotient);

}

}
```

> *Sometimes it is better to handle an exceptional case without throwing an exception.*

Sample Screen Dialogue 1

```
Enter numerator:
5
Enter denominator:
10
5/10 = 0.5
End of Program.
```

Display 8.5 Using a Programmer-Defined Exception Class *(Part 3 of 3)*

Sample Screen Dialogue 2

```
Enter numerator:
5
Enter denominator:
0
Dividing by Zero!
Try again.
Enter numerator:
5
Enter denominator:
Be sure the denominator is not zero.
10
5/10 = 0.5
End of Program.
```

Sample Screen Dialogue 3

```
Enter numerator:
5
Enter denominator:
0
Dividing by Zero!
Try again.
Enter numerator:
5
Enter denominator:
Be sure the denominator is not zero.
0
I cannot do division by zero.
Since I cannot do what you want,
the program will now end.
```

second chance to enter the input correctly, and then carries out the calculation. (If the user tries a second time to divide by zero, the method ends the program.) The method `secondChance` is there only for this exceptional case. So, we have separated the code for the exceptional case of a division by zero into a separate method where it will not clutter the code for the normal case.

■ *Java Tip*
Preserve `getMessage` When You Define Exception Classes

For all predefined exception classes, `getMessage` will return the string that is passed as an argument to the constructor (or will return a default string if no argument is used with the constructor). For example, if the exception is thrown as follows:

```
throw new Exception("This is a big exception!");
```

then `"This is a big exception!"` is used as the value of the `String` instance variable. If the object is called e, then the method call `e.getMessage()` returns `"This is a big exception!"`

It is a good idea to preserve this behavior of the method `getMessage` in any exception class you define. For example, suppose you define an exception class called `MySpecialException` and an exception is thrown as follows:

```
throw new MySpecialException("Wow what an exception!");
```

If e is a name for the exception thrown, then `e.getMessage()` should return `"Wow what an exception!"` To ensure that the exception classes that you define behave this way, be sure to include a constructor with a string parameter that begins with a call to *super*, as illustrated by the following constructor:

```
public MySpecialException(String message)
{
    super(message);
    //There can be more code here, but often there is none.
}
```

The call to *super* is a call to a constructor of the base class. If the base class constructor handles the message correctly, then so will a class defined in this way.

You should also include a default constructor in each exception class, and this default constructor should set up a default value to be retrieved by `getMessage`. This default constructor should begin with a call to *super*, as illustrated by the following constructor:

```
public MySpecialException()
{
    super("MySpecialException thrown.");
    //There can be more code here, but often there is none.
}
```

If `getMessage` works as we described for the base class, then this sort of default constructor will work correctly for the new exception class being defined.

Exception Objects

The two most important things about an exception object are its type (the exception class) and a message it carries in an instance variable of type `String`. This string can be recovered with the method `getMessage`. This string allows your code to send a message along with an exception object, so that the `catch`-block can use the message. (The following subsections will explain why the type of an exception object is important.)

Programmer-Defined Exception Classes

You may define your own exception classes, but every such class must be a derived class of an already existing exception class (either predefined or successfully defined by you).

Guidelines:

- If you have no compelling reason to use any particular class as the base class, use the class `Exception` as the base class.

- You should define two (or more) constructors, as described in what follows. Your exception class inherits the method `getMessage`. Normally, you do not need to add any other methods, but it is legal to add other methods.

- You should start each constructor definition with a call to the constructor of the base class, such as the following sample:

      super("Tidal Wave Exception thrown!");

- You should include a default constructor, in which case the call to *super* should have a string argument that indicates what kind of exception it is. This string can then be recovered using the `getMessage` method.

- You should also include a constructor that takes a single string argument. In this case, that string should be an argument in the call to *super*. In this way, the string can be recovered with a call to `getMessage`.

Example:

```
public class TidalWaveException extends Exception
{
    public TidalWaveException()
    {
        super("Tidal Wave Exception thrown!");
    }

    public TidalWaveException(String message)
    {
        super(message);
    }
}
```

super is a call to the constructor for the base class `Exception`.

? Self-Test Questions

14. Define an exception class called `CoreBreachException`. The class should have a constructor with no parameters. If an exception is thrown with this zero argument constructor, then `getMessage` should return `"Core Breach! Evacuate Ship!"` The class should also have a constructor with a single parameter of type `String`. If an exception is thrown with this constructor, then `getMessage` returns the value that was used as an argument to the constructor.

15. Define an exception class called `MessageTooLongException`. The class should have a constructor with no parameters. If an exception is thrown with this zero argument constructor, then `getMessage` should return `"Message Too Long!"` The class should also have a constructor with a single parameter of type `String`. If an exception is thrown with this constructor, then `getMessage` returns the value that was used as an argument to the constructor.

16. Suppose the exception class `ExerciseException` is defined as follows:

```java
public class ExerciseException extends Exception
{
    public ExerciseException()
    {
        super("Exercise Exception thrown!");
        System.out.println("Exception thrown.");
    }

    public ExerciseException(String message)
    {
        super(message);
        System.out.println(
            "Exercise exception thrown with parameter.");
    }
}
```

What output would be produced by the following code (which is just an exercise and not likely to occur in a program)?

```java
ExerciseException e = new ExerciseException("Do Be Do");
System.out.println(e.getMessage());
```

17. Suppose the exception class `CrazyException` is defined as follows:

```java
public class CrazyException extends Exception
{
    public CrazyException()
    {
        super("Crazy Exception thrown!");
        System.out.println("Wow, Crazy exception thrown!!");
    }

    public CrazyException(String message)
    {
        super(message);
        System.out.println(
          "Wow, Crazy exception thrown with parameter!!");
    }

    public void crazyMethod()
    {
        System.out.println("Message is " + getMessage());
    }
}
```

What output would be produced by the following code (which is just an exercise and not likely to occur in a program)?

```java
CrazyException exceptionObject = new CrazyException();
System.out.println(exceptionObject.getMessage());
exceptionObject.crazyMethod();
```

18. Suppose the (unlikely) exception class `DoubleException` is defined as follows:

```java
public class DoubleException extends Exception
{
    public DoubleException()
    {
        super("Double Exception thrown!");
    }

    public DoubleException(String message)
    {
        super(message + message);
    }
}
```

What output would be produced by the following code (which is just an exercise and not likely to occur in a program)?

```
int number;
try
{
    System.out.println("try-block entered:");
    number = 42;
    if (number > 0)
        throw new DoubleException("Double Exception
thrown!");
    System.out.println("Leaving try-block.");
}

catch(DoubleException exceptionObject)
{
    System.out.println(exceptionObject.getMessage());
}
System.out.println("End of code.");
```

19. Suppose that in Self-Test Question 18 the `catch`-block were changed to the following. (The type `DoubleException` is replaced with `Exception`.) How would this effect the output?
```
catch(Exception exceptionObject)
{
    System.out.println(exceptionObject.getMessage());
}
```

20. Suppose that in Self-Test Question 18 the following line
```
    number = 42;
```
were changed to
```
    number = -99;
```
How would this effect the output?

■ **Programming Tip**
When to Define an Exception Class

As a general rule, if you are going to insert a `throw`-statement in your code, then it is probably best to define your own exception class. In that way, when your code catches an exception, your `catch`-blocks can tell the difference between your exceptions and exceptions thrown by methods in predefined classes. For example, in Display 8.5/page 530, we used the exception class `DivideByZeroException`, which we defined in Display 8.4/page 529.

Although it would not be a good idea, you might be tempted to throw the exception (in Display 8.5) using the predefined class `Exception`, as follows:
```
throw new Exception("Dividing by Zero!");
```
You could then catch this exception with the `catch`-block

```
catch(Exception e)
{
    System.out.println(e.getMessage());
    secondChance();
}
```

Although this will work for the program in Display 8.5, it is not the best technique. This is because that `catch`-block (displayed just before this paragraph) will catch any exception, such as an `IOException`. But an `IOException` might need a different action than `secondChance()`. Rather than using the class `Exception` to catch division by zero, it is better to use the more specialized programmer-defined class `DivideByZeroException`, as we did in Display 8.5.

8.3 | Using Exception Classes

> **buck** *n. small object placed before the dealer in poker.*
> *(Thus)* **pass the buck** *(means) shift responsibility (to).*
> **The Little Oxford Dictionary of Current English,**
> **Oxford University Press, 1986**
>
> *The buck stops here.*
> **Harry S. Truman (sign on Truman's desk while he was president)**

In this section, we discuss techniques for using exceptions in your programs and methods.

Declaring Exceptions (Passing the Buck)

Sometimes it makes sense to delay handling an exception. For example, you might have a method with code that throws an exception if there is an attempt to divide by zero, but you may not want to catch the exception in that method. Perhaps some programs that use that method should simply end if the exception is thrown, and other programs that use the method should do something else, so you would not know what to do about the exception if you caught it inside the method. In these cases, it makes sense to not catch the exception in the method definition, but instead to have any program (or other code) that uses the method place the method invocation in a `try`-block and catch the exception in a `catch`-block that follows that `try`-block.

However, if a method does not catch an exception, it must at least warn programmers that any invocation of the method might possibly throw an exception. This warning is called a **throws-clause**. For example, a method that might possibly throw a `DivideByZeroException` and that does not catch the exception would have a heading similar to the following:

```
public void sampleMethod() throws DivideByZeroException
```

The part `throws DivideByZeroException` is a `throws`-clause that says that an invocation of the method `sampleMethod` might throw a `DivideByZeroException`.

Most exceptions that might be thrown when a method is invoked must be accounted for in one of two ways:

1. The possible exception can be caught in a *catch*-block within the method definition.

2. The possible exception can be declared at the start of the method definition by placing the exception class name in a *throws*-clause (and letting whoever uses the method worry about how to handle the exception).

In any one method, you can mix these two alternatives catching some exceptions and declaring other exceptions in a *throws*-clause.

You already know about method 1, handling exceptions in a *catch*-block. Method 2 is a form of "passing the buck." For example, suppose methodA has a *throws*-clause as follows:

```
public void methodA() throws DivideByZeroException
```

In this case, methodA is absolved of the responsibility to catch any exceptions of type DivideByZeroException, which might occur when methodA is called. If, however, there is some methodB that includes an invocation of methodA, then methodB must handle the exception. When methodA adds the *throws*-clause, it is saying to methodB, "If you invoke me, you must handle any DivideByZeroException that I throw." In effect, methodA has passed the responsibility ("passed the buck") for any exceptions of type DivideByZeroException from itself to any method that calls it.

Of course, if methodA passes the buck to methodB by including a *throws*-clause such as

```
throws DivideByZeroException
```

then methodB may also pass the buck to whoever calls it by including the same *throws*-clause in its definition. But in a well-written program, every exception that is thrown should eventually be caught by a *catch*-block in some method that does not pass the buck.

Throwing an Exception Can End a Method

If a method throws an exception, and the exception is not caught inside the method, then the method invocation ends immediately after the exception is thrown.

In Display 8.6, we have rewritten the program from Display 8.5/page 530, so that the normal case is in a method called normal. The method main includes a call to the method normal and puts the call in a *try*-block. Because the method normal can throw a DivideByZeroException that is not caught in the method normal, we need to declare this in a *throws*-clause at the start of the definition of normal. If we set up our program in this way, the case where nothing goes wrong is completely isolated and easy to read. It is not even cluttered by *try*-blocks and *catch*-blocks.

A *throws*-clause can contain more than one exception type. In such cases, you separate the exception types with commas as follows:

```
public int superMethod() throws IOException, DivideByZeroException
```

Display 8.6 Passing the Buck with a *throws*-Clause *(Part 1 of 2)*

```java
public class DoDivision
{
    private int numerator;
    private int denominator;
    private double quotient;

    public static void main(String[] args)
    {
        DoDivision doIt = new DoDivision();

        try
        {
            doIt.normal();
        }
        catch(DivideByZeroException e)
        {
            System.out.println(e.getMessage());
            doIt.secondChance();
        }
        System.out.println("End of Program.");

    }


    public void normal() throws DivideByZeroException
    {
        System.out.println("Enter numerator:");
        numerator = SavitchIn.readLineInt();
        System.out.println("Enter denominator:");
        denominator = SavitchIn.readLineInt();
        if (denominator == 0)
            throw new DivideByZeroException();
        quotient = numerator/(double)denominator;
        System.out.println(numerator + "/"
                                    + denominator
                                    + " = " + quotient);
    }
```

```java
public void secondChance()
{
    System.out.println("Try Again:");
    System.out.println("Enter numerator:");
    numerator = SavitchIn.readLineInt();
    System.out.println("Enter denominator:");
    System.out.println("Be sure the denominator is not zero.");
    denominator = SavitchIn.readLineInt();
    if (denominator == 0)
    {
        System.out.println("I cannot do division by zero.");
        System.out.println("Since I cannot do what you want,");
        System.out.println("the program will now end.");
        System.exit(0);
    }
    quotient = ((double)numerator)/denominator;
    System.out.println(numerator + "/"
                                  + denominator
                                  + " = " + quotient);
}
```

}

Sample Screen Dialogue

The input/output dialogs are identical to those for the program in Display 8.5/page 530.

Uncaught Exceptions

If every method up to and including the `main` method simply includes a *throws*-clause for a particular class of exceptions, then it may turn out that an exception of that class is thrown but never caught. In such cases, when an exception is thrown but never caught, either the program ends or else its performance may become unreliable. For all the kinds of programs we have seen thus far, if an exception is thrown but never caught, then the program ends. (For GUI programs, programs with interactive windows of the kind we will discuss in Chapter 12, when an exception is thrown but never caught, the program will probably not end, but the program's behavior may be unreliable from then on.)

---

throws-Clause

If you define a method that might throw exceptions of some particular class, then normally either your method definition must include a *catch*-block that will catch the exception or else you must declare the exception class with a *throws*-clause, as described in what follows.

Syntax: (covers most common cases):

```
public Type_Or_void Method(Parameter_List) throws List_Of_Exceptions
Body_Of_Method
```

Example:

```
public void MyMethod(int n) throws IOException, MyExceptionClass
{
          .
          .
          .
}
```

Exceptions That Do Not Need to Be Caught

As we have presented exceptions so far, we said that, in most cases, an exception must either be caught in a *catch*-block or declared in a *throws*-clause. That is the basic rule, but there are exceptions to this rule. (An exception to a rule about exceptions! Seems reasonable enough.) There are some exceptional exceptions that you do not need to account for in this way. These are basically exceptions that result from errors of some sort. Normally, you do not write a *throw*-statement for these exceptions. Normally, they are thrown by predefined classes that you use.

Exceptions that are descendents of the class `Error` or of the class `RuntimeException` do not need to be accounted for in a *catch*-block or *throws*-clause. For example, one such exception is `NoSuchMethodError`. This means your code has used a method, but you have provided no definition for that method name. For all these sorts of exceptions, you should repair your code by fixing the bug in your code, not by adding a *catch*-block. Other exceptions that you do not need to catch or declare are exceptions that are more or less beyond your control. One such exception is `OutOfMemoryError`. If this is thrown, then your program has run out of memory, which means either you have an inefficient program or you need to buy more memory for your computer. Adding a *catch*-block will not help in this case, and it is not required. [1]

How do you know if an exception is one that you must account for by either catching or else declaring in a *throws*-clause? As a general rule, your code must either catch or declare in a *throws*-clause every exception that is explicitly thrown by your code, as in this example:

```
if (denominator == 0)
    throw new DivideByZeroException();
```

Also, if a method has a *throws*-clause for a type of exception and your code includes an invocation of that method, then your code must either catch the exception or declare it in a *throws*-clause.

However, you need not worry too much about which exceptions you do and do not need to declare in a *throws*-clause. If you fail to account for some exception that Java requires you to account for, then the compiler will tell you about the exception and you can either catch it or add it to a *throws*-clause.

Details on *throws*-Clauses in Derived Classes

If you redefine a method in a derived class, then the *throws*-clause for the redefined method cannot contain any exception classes that are not in the *throws*-clause of the same method in the base class. In other words, you cannot add exceptions to the *throws*-clause when you redefine a method. This, of course, means that you cannot throw any exceptions that are not either caught in a *catch*-block or already listed in the *throws*-clause of the same method in the base class. You can, however, declare fewer exceptions in the *throws*-clause of the redefined method.

Multiple Throws and Catches

A *try*-block can potentially throw any number of exceptions, and they can be of differing types. Each *catch*-block can only catch exceptions of one type, but you can catch exceptions of differing types by placing more than one *catch*-block after a *try*-block. For example, the program in Display 8.7 has two *catch*-blocks after its *try*-block. The class NegativeNumberException is defined in Display 8.8/page 546.)

■ *Java Tip*
Catch the More Specific Exception First

When catching multiple exceptions, the order of the *catch*-blocks can be important. When an exception is thrown in a *try*-block, the *catch*-blocks are tried in order, and the first one that matches the type of the exception thrown is the one that is executed. Thus, the following ordering of *catch*-blocks would not be good:

---

1. Technically speaking, the class Error and its descendent classes are not considered to be exception classes. They are not descendents of the class Exception. However, objects of these classes can be thrown and can be caught in a *catch*-block just like real exceptions. So, to us, they look like exceptions.

Display 8.7   Catching Multiple Exceptions *(Part 1 of 2)*

```java
public class TwoCatchesDemo
{
    public static void main(String[] args)
    {
        try
        {
            int jemHadar, klingons;
            double portion;

            System.out.println("Enter number of Jem Hadar warriors:");
            jemHadar = SavitchIn.readLineInt();
            if (jemHadar < 0)
                throw new NegativeNumberException("Jem Hadar");
            System.out.println("How many Klingon warriors do you have?");
            klingons = SavitchIn.readLineInt();
            if (klingons < 0)
                throw new NegativeNumberException("Klingons");

            portion = exceptionalDivision(jemHadar, klingons);
            System.out.println("Each Klingon must fight "
                                            + portion + " Jem Hadar.");
        }
        catch(DivideByZeroException e)
        {
            System.out.println("Today is a good day to die.");
        }
        catch(NegativeNumberException e)
        {
            System.out.println("Cannot have a negative number of "
                        + e.getMessage());
        }

        System.out.println("End of program.");
    }

    public static double exceptionalDivision(double numerator,
                    double denominator) throws DivideByZeroException
    {
        if (denominator == 0)
                throw new DivideByZeroException();
        return (numerator/denominator);
    }
}
```

This is just a toy example to learn the basic syntax for exception handling.

Display 8.7 Catching Multiple Exceptions *(Part 2 of 2)*

Sample Screen Dialogue 1

```
Enter number of Jem Hadar warriors:
1000
How many Klingon warriors do you have?
500
Each Klingon must fight 2.0 Jem Hadar.
End of program
```

Sample Screen Dialogue 2

```
Enter number of Jem Hadar warriors:
-10
Cannot have a negative number of Jem Hadar
End of program.
```

Sample Screen Dialogue 3

```
Enter number of Jem Hadar warriors:
1000
How many Klingon warriors do you have?
0
Today is a good day to die.
End of program.
```

```
catch (Exception e)
{
        .
        .
        .
}
catch(DivideByZeroExecption e)
{
        .            The second catch-block
        .            can never be reached.
        .
}
```

With this ordering, the *catch*-block for DivideByZeroException would never be used, because all exceptions are caught by the first *catch*-block. Fortunately, the compiler will probably warn you about this. The correct ordering is to reverse the *catch*-blocks so the more specific exception comes before its parent exception class, as shown in what follows:

```
catch(DivideByZeroException e)
{
        .
        .
        .
}
catch(Exception e)
{
        .
        .
        .
}
```

Display 8.8   NegativeNumberException

```java
public class NegativeNumberException extends Exception
{
    public NegativeNumberException()
    {
        super("Negative Number Exception!");
    }
    public NegativeNumberException(String message)
    {
        super(message);
    }
}
```

Exception Objects

The two most important thing about an exception object are its type (the exception class) and a message it carries in an instance variable of type `String`. The type of the exception object determines which `catch`-block will catch the exception. The importance of the string is explained in the text.

■ Programming Tip
Exception Handling and Information Hiding

A `throw`-statement is not the only kind of statement that can throw an exception. A method invocation is also a kind of statement that can throw an exception (specifically, one that is declared in the method's `throws`-clause). If an exception is thrown by any kind of statement, then it is handled in the exact same way, no matter what kind of statement threw the exception. It is either caught in a `catch`-block, or it is declared in a `throws`-clause. When analyzing a method invocation that might throw and exception, do not think about where the `throw`-statement is located "inside" of the method definition. It does not matter how the exception was thrown. All that matters is that the method invocation might throw an exception. The exception is handled in the same way no matter what happens "inside" the method. You should not clutter your thinking by worrying about the "inside" of the method.

? Self-Test Questions

21. Correct the following method definition by adding a suitable `throws`-clause:

    ```
    public void doStuff(int n)
    {
        if (n < 0)
            throw new Exception("Negative number.");
    }
    ```

22. What happens if an exception is thrown inside a method invocation but the exception is not caught inside the method?

23. Suppose there is an invocation of method A inside of method B, and an invocation of method B inside of method C. When there is an invocation of method C this leads to an invocation of method B, and that in turn leads to an invocation of method A. Now, suppose that method A throws an exception but does not catch it within A. Where might the exception be caught? In B? In C? Outside of C?

24. What output will be produced by the following code? (The definition of the class `NegativeNumberException` is given in the preceding material, but you do not even need to look at those definitions to answer this question.)

```
int n;
try
{
    n = 7;
    if (n > 0)
        throw new Exception();
    else if (n < 0)
        throw new NegativeNumberException();
    else
        System.out.println("Hello!");
}

catch(NegativeNumberException e)
{
    System.out.println("First catch.");
}
catch(Exception e)
{
    System.out.println("Second catch");
}
System.out.println("End of Code");
```

25. What would be the output produced by the code in Self-Test Question 24 if the line

    ```
    n = 7;
    ```

    were change to the following?

    ```
    n = -7;
    ```

26. What would be the output produced by the code in Self-Test Question 24 if the line

    ```
    n = 7;
    ```

    were change to the following?

    ```
    n = 0;
    ```

27. What is the output produced by the following program?

```
public class CatchDemo
{
    public static void main(String[] args)
    {
        CatchDemo object = new CatchDemo();
```

```
        try
        {
            System.out.println("Trying");
            object.sampleMethod();
            System.out.println("Trying after call.");
        }
        catch(Exception e)
        {
            System.out.println("Catching");
            System.out.println(e.getMessage());
        }
    }

    public void sampleMethod() throws Exception
    {
        System.out.println("Starting sampleMethod.");
        throw new
            Exception("From sampleMethod with love.");
    }
```

<There may be more methods and there may be instance variables,
but they are not needed to answer this question.>

```
}
```

Gotcha
Overuse of Exceptions

Exceptions allow you to write programs whose flow of control is so involved that it is almost impossible to understand the program. Moreover, this is not hard to do. Throwing an exception allows you to transfer flow of control from anyplace in your program to almost anyplace else in your program. In the early days of programming, this sort of unrestricted flow of control was allowed via a construct known as a *goto*. Programming experts now agree that such unrestricted flow of control is very poor programming style. Exceptions allow you to revert to these bad old days of unrestricted flow of control. Exceptions should be used sparingly and only in certain ways. In the next subsection, we discuss where it is good to use an exception. Another good rule is the following: If you are tempted to include a *throw*-statement, then think about how you might write your program or class definition without this *throw*-statement. If you think of an alternative that produces reasonable code, then you probably do not want to include the *throw*-statement.

Programming Tip
When to Throw an Exception

We have given some very simple code in order to illustrate the basic concepts of exception handling. However, our examples were sometimes unrealistically simple. A more complicated but better guideline is to separate throwing an exception and catching the exception into separate methods. In most cases, you should include any *throw*-statement within a method definition, declare the exception in a *throws*-clause in that method, and place the *catch*-clause in *a different method*. Thus, the preferred use of the *try-throw-catch* triple is as illustrated here:

```
public void methodA() throws MyException
{
        .
        .
        .
    throw new MyException("Bla Bla Bla");
        .
        .
        .
}
```

Then, in *some other method* (perhaps even some other method in some other class), you have

```
public void methodB()
{
        .
        .
        .
    try
    {
        .
        .
        .
        methodA();
        .
        .
        .
    }
    catch(MyException e)
    {
        Handle_Exception
    }
        .
        .
        .
}
```

Moreover, even this kind of use of a *throw*-statement should be reserved for cases where it is unavoidable. If you can easily handle a problem in some other way, do not throw an exception. Reserve *throw*-statements for situations in which the way the exceptional condition is handled depends on how and where the method is used. If the way that the exceptional condition is handled depends on how and where the method is invoked, then the best thing to do is to let the programmer who invokes the method handle the exception. In all other situations, it is preferable to avoid throwing exceptions.

The use of exceptions that we discussed in the previous paragraph is often used in predefined methods. When you learn of a predefined method, you may be told that it throws exceptions of certain kinds. You the programmer who uses the predefined method is then expected to handle any exception thrown by the method.

> ### When to Throw an Exception
>
> For the most part, *throw*-statements should be used within methods and declared in a *throws*-clause for the method. Moreover, they should be reserved for situations in which the way the exceptional condition is handled depends on how and where the method is used. If the way that the exceptional condition is handled depends on how and where the method is invoked, then the best thing to do is to let the programmer who invokes the method handle the exception. In all other situations, it is almost always preferable to avoid throwing an exception. ∎

■ Gotcha

Nested *try-catch*-Blocks

You can place a *try*-block and following *catch*-blocks inside a larger *try*-block or inside a larger *catch*-block. In rare cases this may be useful, but if you are tempted to do this, you should suspect that there is a nicer way to organize your program. It is almost always better to place the inner *try-catch*-blocks inside a method definition and place an invocation of the method in the outer *try*- or *catch*-block (or maybe just eliminate one or more *try*-blocks completely). In addition to poor style and confusing code, there are even other pitfalls associated with nesting *try*- and *catch*-blocks.

If you place a *try*-block and following *catch*-blocks inside a larger *catch*-block, then you will need to use different names for the *catch*-block parameters in the inner and outer blocks. This has to do with how Java handles nested blocks of any kind, but *try*-blocks and *catch*-blocks are blocks.

If you place a *try*-block and following *catch*-blocks inside a larger *try*-block, and an exception is thrown in the inner *try*-block but not caught in the inner *try-catch*-blocks, then the exception is thrown to the outer *try*-block for processing and might be caught there.

The *finally* Block *(Optional)*

You can add a *finally*-block after a *try*-block and its following *catch*-blocks. The code in the *finally*-block is executed whether or not an exception is thrown. The general syntax is as follows:

```
try-Block
catch-Block(s)
finally
{
     < Code to be executed whether or not an exception is thrown and/or caught.>
}
```

To see the significance and possible usefulness of a *finally*-block, suppose the *try-catch-finally*-blocks are inside a method definition. (After all, every set of *try-catch-finally*-blocks is inside of some method, even if it is only the method main.) There are three possibilities when the *try-catch-finally*-blocks code is run.

1. The *try*-block runs to the end and no exception is thrown. In this situ-

ation, the *finally*-block is executed after the *try*-block.

2. An exception is thrown in the *try*-block and caught in a matching *catch*-block positioned after the *try*-block. In this case, the *finally*-block is executed after the matching *catch*-block is executed.

3. An exception is thrown in the *try*-block and there is no matching *catch*-block in the method to catch the exception. In this case, the method invocation ends and the exception object is thrown to the enclosing method. In this case, the *finally*-block is executed before the method ends. Note that you cannot account for this third case by simply placing code after the string of *catch*-blocks.

At this stage of your programming, you may not have much need for a *finally*-block, but we include a description of it for completeness. At some point, you may find it useful.

Rethrowing an Exception *(Optional)*

It is legal to throw an exception within a *catch*-block. In rare cases you may want to catch an exception, and then, depending on the string produced by getMessage (or depending on something else), decide to throw the same or a different exception for handling farther up the chain of exception handling blocks.

? Self-Test Questions

28. Can you have a *try*-block and corresponding *catch*-blocks inside another larger *try*-block?

29. Can you have a *try*-block and corresponding *catch*-blocks inside another larger *catch*-block?

30. This exercise is for those who read the optional section **The *finally* Block (Optional)**. What is the output produced by the following program? What would the output be if the argument to sampleMethod were −99 instead of 99? What would it be if the argument were 0 instead of 99?

```java
public class FinallyDemo
{
    public static void main(String[] args)
    {
        try
        {
            sampleMethod(99);
        }
        catch(Exception e)
        {
            System.out.println("Caught in main.");
        }
    }
}
```

```
public static void sampleMethod(int n) throws Exception
{
    try
    {
        if (n > 0)
            throw new Exception();
        else if (n < 0)
            throw new NegativeNumberException();
        else
            System.out.println("No Exception.");
        System.out.println("Still in sampleMethod.");
    }
    catch(NegativeNumberException e)
    {
        System.out.println("Caught in sampleMethod.");
    }

    finally
    {
        System.out.println("In finally block.");
    }
    System.out.println("After finally block.");
}
}
```

Case Study

A Line-Oriented Calculator

You have been asked to write a program that can be used as a calculator, similar to a hand-held calculator. The calculator should do addition, subtraction, multiplication, and division. This program is going to be used with rather old equipment and so it cannot use a windowing interface, but must use simple line-by-line text input and text output (like the other programs in this chapter).

task specification

You need to be more specific about what the user interface will be. You propose that the user will be instructed to input operations and numbers as follows. Each operation and number is input on a line by itself as in the following example:

specification refinement

```
+ 3.4
```

It should not matter if there is or is not whitespace before or after either the operation, like +, or the number, like 3.4. As the user enters more operations and numbers, the program keeps track of the results of the operations performed so far, as in the following sample dialog. (The program assumes that the initial "result" is zero. The user's input is shown in bold. The other text is output from the program.)

```
result = 0
+ 80
result + 80 = 80
updated result = 80
−2
result − 2 = 78
updated result = 78
```

Notice that the input is echoed so that the user can see what the computer is doing. You further suggest that the user indicate the end of a calculation by entering the letter E (in either upper- or lowercase).

Your suggested interface is accepted and you begin the project design. You decide to design a class for a calculator. The class will have a main method that is a complete, simple calculator program that follows the specification you have refined. Later on, you might design a more elaborate interface for the calculator. So, the class will be a bit more powerful than what is needed for the method main.

data for class
The program keeps track of one number that serves the same purpose as the number displayed on a hand-held calculator. On the screen, it is shown as, for example:

```
updated result = 80
```

The user can, add, subtract, multiply, and divide with instructions such as

```
+3
```

result
The current result is kept in a private instance variable called result. The program always adds, subtract, multiplies, or divides the current result and the number entered. For instance, if the user enters

```
−9.5
```

and the current value of result is 80, then the value of result is changed to 70.5. When the user enters an 'e' or an 'E', that ends the program. If you look ahead to the sample screen dialog in Display 8.11 (part 5 on page 567), you can get an idea of how this calculator is used.

method actions
You decide that you need the class to have at least the following methods:

A method named reset to reset the value of result to zero.

A method to calculate the result of one operation. You decide to produce the result of one operation as a returned value, rather than immediately updating the instance variable result. This will make your class more versatile. You decide that the method should be approximately as follows

```
/*****************************************************
 *Returns n1 op n2, provided op is one of '+', '−', '*', or '/'.
 *****************************************************/
 public double evaluate(char op, double n1, double n2)
```

An accessor method getResult to recover the value of the instance variable result.

A mutator method called `setResult` to reset the value of `result` to any specified value.

A method `doCalculation` that includes a loop to do one series of operations producing a final result (with a call to `evaluate` on each loop iteration).

You decide to first write the code as if everything went smoothly, perhaps noting exceptions where they might occur, but you defer writing the exception handling until after the heart of the class actions is designed. The definitions of the methods `reset`, `setResult`, and `getResult` are routine, but the methods `evaluate` and `doCalculation` require a bit of thought. Let's consider `doCalculation` first.

unexceptional part

The heart of the calculator's action is performed by the method `doCalculation`. Until the user enters the letter `'e'` or an improper operator, the basic loop sequence should repeat the following again and again:

doCalculation

```
nextOp = SavitchIn.readNonwhiteChar();
nextNumber = SavitchIn.readLineDouble();
result = evaluate(nextOp, result, nextNumber);
```

Here `nextOp` is a variable of type *char*, `nextNumber` is one of type *double*, and `result` is the instance variable. When the user enters the letter `'e'` (in lowercase or uppercase), the loop ends and the calculation ends. You convert this to the following more complete Java loop:

```
boolean done = false;
while (! done)
{
    nextOp = SavitchIn.readNonwhiteChar();
    if ((nextOp == 'e') || (nextOp == 'E'))
        done = true;
    else
    {
        nextNumber = SavitchIn.readLineDouble();
        result = evaluate(nextOp, result, nextNumber);
        System.out.println("result " + nextOp + " "
                           + nextNumber + " = " + result);
        System.out.println("updated result = " + result);
    }
}
```

Note that `readLineDouble` reads the rest of the line after the method `readNonWhiteChar` has read a single character. The method `readLineDouble` does not have to start reading at the beginning of a line. If the user enters

```
+ 8.95
```

the method `readNonwhiteChar` reads the `'+'` and the `readLineDouble` reads the 8.95.

Next, you need to design the method `evaluate`, which you described as follows:

```
/***********************************************
* Returns n1 op n2, provided op is one of '+', '-', '*', or '/'.
***********************************************/
public double evaluate(char op, double n1, double n2)
```

The heart of the method `evaluate` can be a large *switch*-statement, something like the following:

```
switch (op)
{
    case '+':
        answer = n1 + n2;
        break;
    case '-':
        answer = n1 - n2;
        break;
    case '*':
        answer = n1 * n2;
        break;
    case '/':
        if (n2 == 0.0)
            throw new DivideByZeroException();
        answer = n1/n2;
        break;
}
return answer;
```

You decided to throw an exception if the user attempts to do a division by zero, and so the preceding case for division includes the following:

```
if (n2 == 0.0)
    throw new DivideByZeroException();
```

precision of floating-point numbers

This is conceptually fine, but there is one problem. The numbers involved are of type *double*. Floating-point numbers, such as numbers of type *double*, only represent approximate quantities, and so it does not make sense to use == to test them for exact equality. The value of n2 may be so close to zero that it behaves like division by zero and yet the test would say it is not equal to 0.0. You therefore decide to throw a DivideByZeroException whenever the denominator is very close to zero. However, you are not sure of what you should use as a definition of very close to zero. So, you decide that any quantity that is less than one ten-thousandth will be considered zero. However, since you are not sure this is the best choice, you decide to use an instance variable, named precision, that will tell how close a number must be to zero in order to be treated as if it were zero. The definition of precision is thus

```
private double precision = 0.0001;
```

The test for division by zero then becomes

```
if ( (-precision < n2) && (n2 < precision))
    throw new DivideByZeroException();
```

Thus, you rewrite the *switch*-statement to the following:

```
switch (op)
{
    case '+':
        answer = n1 + n2;
        break;
    case '-':
        answer = n1 - n2;
        break;
    case '*':
        answer = n1 * n2;
        break;
    case '/':
        if ( (-precision < n2) && (n2 < precision))
            throw new DivideByZeroException();
        answer = n1/n2;
        break;
}
```

But what if the user enters some character other than '+', '-', '*', or '/' for the op? You decide that that will be handled by throwing an exception. So the *switch*-statement now looks like

```
switch (op)
{
    case '+':
        answer = n1 + n2;
        break;
    case '-':
        answer = n1 - n2;
        break;
    case '*':
        answer = n1 * n2;
        break;
    case '/':
        if ( (-precision < n2) && (n2 < precision))
            throw new DivideByZeroException();
        answer = n1/n2;
        break;
    default:
        throw new UnknownOpException(op);
}
```

The DivideByZeroException class was defined in Display 8.4/page 529. UnknownOpException is a new exception class that you need to define. You also need to write code to catch and handle all exceptions.

The code for the UnknownOpException class is similar to the other exceptions we have written and is given in Display 8.9. Note that when the user enters an unknown operator, you want to tell the user that that particular operator is

UnknownOp-
Exception

Display 8.9   Unknown Operator Exception

```java
public class UnknownOpException extends Exception
{
    public UnknownOpException()
    {
        super("UnknownOpException");
    }

    public UnknownOpException(char op)
    {
        super(op + " is an unknown operator.");
    }

    public UnknownOpException(String message)
    {
        super(message);
    }
}
```

unknown, and so there is a constructor that takes an argument of type *char* that names the operator.

preliminary version

At this point, you have all of the program written except for the exception handling. This lets you produce a preliminary version of your program, as shown in Display 8.10. You can use this version to test and debug the unexceptional portion of your program. As long as the user does not enter an unknown operator or perform a division by zero, this version will run fine. This allows you to test and debug the unexceptional portions of your program before you write the exception-handling portion of your program.

exception handling

After you have debugged the preliminary version of your program that is shown in Display 8.10, you are then ready to add exception handling. The most significant exception is the UnknownOpException, and you consider it first. You have already given the definition of the class UnknownOpException, but you have not yet done anything with it other than declare it in a *throws*-clause. To make your program robust, you want to do something more serious and effective when an exception is thrown.

To make your program more robust, you use the *try-throw-catch* technique. The UnknownOpException will be thrown by the method evaluate. The method evaluate is invoked in the method doCalculation, and the method

Display 8.10 Unexceptional Cases (Part 1 of 3)

```
/*************************************************
 *PRELIMINARY VERSION without exception handling.
 *Simple line-oriented calculator program. The class
 *can also be used to create other calculator programs.
 *************************************************/
public class PrelimCalculator
{
    private double result;
    private double precision = 0.0001;
    //Numbers this close to zero are treated as if equal to zero.


    public static void main(String[] args)
                            throws DivideByZeroException,
                                   UnknownOpException

    {
        PrelimCalculator clerk = new PrelimCalculator();

        System.out.println("Calculator is on.");
        System.out.print("Format of each line: ");
        System.out.println("operator number");
        System.out.println("For example: + 3");
        System.out.println("To end, enter the letter e.");
        clerk.doCalculation();

        System.out.println("The final result is "
                                + clerk.resultValue());
        System.out.println("Calculator program ending.");
    }

    public PrelimCalculator()
    {
        result = 0;
    }

    public void reset()
    {
        result = 0;
    }
```

The definition of the main method will change before this case study ends.

Display 8.10   Unexceptional Cases (Part 2 of 3)

```
public void setResult(double newResult)
{
    result = newResult;
}

public double resultValue()
{
    return result;
}

public void doCalculation() throws DivideByZeroException,
                                     UnknownOpException
{
    char nextOp;
    double nextNumber;
    boolean done = false;
    result = 0;
    System.out.println("result = " + result);

    while (! done)
    {
        nextOp = SavitchIn.readNonwhiteChar();
        if ((nextOp == 'e') || (nextOp == 'E'))
            done = true;
        else
        {
            nextNumber = SavitchIn.readLineDouble();
            result = evaluate(nextOp, result, nextNumber);
            System.out.println("result " + nextOp + " "
                                + nextNumber + " = " + result);
            System.out.println("updated result = " + result);
        }
    }
}
```

This does not do exception handling and so is not yet complete. However, it does run and can be used for debugging.

Display 8.10 Unexceptional Cases *(Part 3 of 3)*

```
/*****************************************************
 *Returns n1 op n2, provided op is one of '+', '-', '*',or '/'.
 *Any other value of op throws UnknownOpException.
 *****************************************************/
public double evaluate(char op, double n1, double n2)
                               throws DivideByZeroException,
                                      UnknownOpException
{
    double answer;
    switch (op)
    {
        case '+':
            answer = n1 + n2;
            break;
        case '-':
            answer = n1 - n2;
            break;
        case '*':
            answer = n1 * n2;
            break;
        case '/':
            if ( (-precision < n2) && (n2 < precision))
                throw new DivideByZeroException();
            answer = n1/n2;
            break;
        default:
            throw new UnknownOpException(op);
    }

    return answer;
}

}
```

doCalculation is invoked in the method main. You have three normal ways of handling the exception:

1. Catch the exception in the method evaluate.

2. Declare the exception UnknownOpException in a *throws*-clause in the method evaluate and then catch the exception in the method doCalculation.

3. Declare the exception UnknownOpException in a *throws*-clause in both the method evaluate and the method doCalculation and then catch the exception in the method main.

Which approach you choose depends on what you want to happen when an exception is thrown. You would use method 1 or 2 if you want the user to reenter the operator. You would use method 3 if you want to restart the calculation.

You decide that the thing to do is to restart the calculation. So you decide to use method 3, which places the *try*- and *catch*-blocks in the method main. This leads you to rewrite main, as shown in Display 8.11. This has introduced two new methods, handleUnknownOpException and handleDivideByZeroException. All that is left to do is to define these two methods for handling exceptions.

handle-
UnknownOp-
Exception

If you look at the *catch*-block in the method main, you will see that when an UnknownOpException is thrown, it is handled by the method handleUnknownOpException. You design the method handleUnknownOpException so that it gives the user a second chance to do the calculation (starting from the beginning). If the user enters an unknown operator during this second chance, then again an UnknownOpException is thrown, but this time it is caught in the method handleUnknownOpException. To see this, look at the *catch*-block in the method handleUnknownOpException (Display 8.11, part 4). If there is such a second throwing of an UnknownOpException, then the program ends. (There are other good ways to handle an UnknownOpException, but this is one satisfactory way to handle the exception.)

Notice that in the definition of the method doCalculation (Display 8.11, part 2), you needed to include a *throws*-clause for the exception classes UnknownOpException and DivideByZeroException, even though the body of the method doCalculation does not include any *throw*-statements. This is because the method doCalculation includes a call to the method evaluate, and the method evaluate can throw an UnknownOpException or a DivideByZeroException.

handling division
by zero

You decide that if the user attempts to do a division by zero, you will simply end the program. (Perhaps you will do something more elaborate in a future version of this program, but this will do for now.) Thus, the method handleDivideByZeroException is very simple.

? Self-Test Questions

31. Write an accessor method called getPrecision that can be added to the class Calculator in Display 8.11 and that returns the value of the

Display 8.11 Complete Line-Oriented Calculator *(Part 1 of 5)*

```java
/***************************************************
 *Simple line-oriented calculator program. The class
 *can also be used to create other calculator programs.
 ***************************************************/
public class Calculator
{
    private double result;
    private double precision = 0.0001;
    //Numbers this close to zero are treated as if equal to zero.

    public static void main(String[] args)
    {
        Calculator clerk = new Calculator();

        try
        {
            System.out.println("Calculator is on.");
            System.out.print("Format of each line: ");
            System.out.println("operator number");
            System.out.println("For example: + 3");
            System.out.println("To end, enter the letter e.");
            clerk.doCalculation();
        }
        catch(UnknownOpException e)
        {
            clerk.handleUnknownOpException(e);
        }
        catch(DivideByZeroException e)
        {
            clerk.handleDivideByZeroException(e);
        }

        System.out.println("The final result is "
                                  + clerk.resultValue());
        System.out.println("Calculator program ending.");
    }

    public Calculator()
    {
        result = 0;
    }
```

Display 8.11 Complete Line-Oriented Calculator *(Part 2 of 5)*

```java
public void reset()
{
    result = 0;
}

public void setResult(double newResult)
{
    result = newResult;
}

public double resultValue()
{
    return result;
}

/*******************************************
 *The heart of a calculator.  This does not give
 *instructions.  Input errors throw exceptions.
 *******************************************/
public void doCalculation() throws DivideByZeroException,
                                    UnknownOpException
{
    char nextOp;
    double nextNumber;
    boolean done = false;
    result = 0;
    System.out.println("result = " + result);
    while (! done)
    {
        nextOp = SavitchIn.readNonwhiteChar();
        if ((nextOp == 'e') || (nextOp == 'E'))
            done = true;
        else
        {
            nextNumber = SavitchIn.readLineDouble();
            result = evaluate(nextOp, result, nextNumber);
            System.out.println("result " + nextOp + " "
                            + nextNumber + " = " + result);
            System.out.println("updated result = " + result);
        }
    }
}
```

reset, setResult, and getResult are not used in this program, but might be needed by some other application that uses this class.

Display 8.11 Complete Line-Oriented Calculator *(Part 3 of 5)*

```
/***************************************************
 *Returns n1 op n2, provided op is one of '+', '-', '*',or '/'.
 *Any other value of op throws UnknownOpException.
 ***************************************************/
public double evaluate(char op, double n1, double n2)
        throws DivideByZeroException, UnknownOpException
{
    double answer;
    switch (op)
    {
        case '+':
            answer = n1 + n2;
            break;
        case '-':
            answer = n1 - n2;
            break;
        case '*':
            answer = n1 * n2;
            break;
        case '/':
            if ( (-precision < n2) && (n2 < precision))
                throw new DivideByZeroException();
            answer = n1/n2;
            break;
        default:
            throw new UnknownOpException(op);
    }

    return answer;
}

public void
    handleDivideByZeroException(DivideByZeroException e)
{
    System.out.println("Dividing by zero.");
    System.out.println("Program aborted");
    System.exit(0);
}
```

Display 8.11 Complete Line-Oriented Calculator *(Part 4 of 5)*

```java
public void handleUnknownOpException(UnknownOpException e)
{
    System.out.println(e.getMessage());
    System.out.println("Try again from the beginning:");

    try
    {
        System.out.print("Format of each line: ");
        System.out.println("operator number");
        System.out.println("For example: +3");
        System.out.println("To end, enter the letter e.");
        doCalculation();
    }

    catch(UnknownOpException e2)
    {
        System.out.println(e2.getMessage());
        System.out.println("Try again at some other time.");
        System.out.println("Program ending.");
        System.exit(0);
    }

    catch(DivideByZeroException e3)
    {
        handleDivideByZeroException(e3);
    }
}

}
```

This block is done the first time `UnknownOpException` is thrown.

This block catches an `UnknownOpException` if it is thrown a second time.

Display 8.11 Complete Line Oriented Calculator *(Part 5 of 5)*

Sample Screen Dialogue

```
Calculator is on.
Format of each line: operator number
For example: + 3
To end, enter the letter e.
result = 0.0
+80
result + 80.0 = 80.0
updated result = 80.0
−2
result − 2.0 = 78.0
updated result = 78.0
%4
% is an unknown operator.
Try again from the beginning:
Format of each line is: operator number
For example: +3
To end, enter the letter e.
result = 0.0
+80
result + 80.0 = 80.0
updated result = 80.0
−2
result − 2.0 = 78.0
updated result = 78.0
* 0.04
result * 0.04 = 3.12
updated result = 3.12
e
The final result is 3.12
Calculator program ending.
```

instance variable `precision`. Also write a mutator method called `set-Precision` that changes the value of the instance variable `precision` to any specified value.

32. What would happen if you ran the program in Display 8.10/page 559 and the user used an unknown operator (such as % or # for which the program has no case to account for the operator)?

CHAPTER SUMMARY

■ An exception is an object of a class that is a descendent of the class `Exception`. (Descendents of the class `Error` are not exceptions, but behave like exceptions, and so we are also considering them to be exceptions.)

■ Exception handling allows you to design and code the normal case for your program separately from the code that handles exceptional situations.

■ There are predefined exception classes. You can also define your own exception classes.

■ Certain Java statements themselves might throw an exception. Methods from class libraries might throw exceptions. You can also explicitly throw an exception in your code by using a *throw*-statement.

■ An exception can be thrown in a *try*-block. Alternatively, an exception can be thrown in a method definition that does not include a *try*-block. In this case, an invocation of the method can be placed in a *try*-block.

■ When a method might throw an exception and not catch the exception, the exception class usually must be listed in a *throws*-clause for the method.

■ An exception is caught in a *catch*-block.

■ A *try*-block may be followed by more than one *catch*-block. In this case, always list the *catch*-block for a more specific exception class before the *catch*-block for a more general exception class.

■ Every exception has a `getMessage` method that can be used to recover a description of the exception caught.

■ Do not overuse exceptions.

? ANSWERS to Self-Test Questions

1.
```
Try-block entered.
Exception: Time Limit Exceeded.
After catch-block.
```

2.
```
Try-block entered.
Leaving try-block.
After catch-block.
```

3. An exception is an object. For example, in the following, `Exception` is a constructor for the class `Exception`:

    ```
    throw new Exception("Time Limit Exceeded.");
    ```

    and the following creates an exception object.

    ```
    new Exception("Time Limit Exceeded.");
    ```

4. Yes, it is perfectly legal, although it is unlikely that you would ever have a good reason to use it.

5.
    ```
    throw new Exception("Time Limit Exceeded.");
    ```

    Note that the following is an *if*-statement, not a *throw*-statement, even though it contains a *throw*-statement:

    ```
    if (waitTime > 30)
        throw new Exception("Time Limit Exceeded.");
    ```

6. When a *throw*-statement is executed, that is the end of the enclosing *try*-block. No other statements in the *try*-block are executed, and control passes to the following *catch*-block(s). When we say control passes to the following *catch*-block, we mean that the exception object that is thrown is plugged in for the *catch*-block parameter and the code in the *catch*-block is executed.

7.
    ```
    try
    {
        System.out.println("Try-block entered.");
        if (waitTime > 30)
            throw new Exception("Time Limit Exceeded.");
        System.out.println("Leaving try-block.");
    }
    ```

8.
    ```
    catch(Exception e)
    {
        System.out.println("Exception: " + e.getMessage());
    }
    ```

9. e is the *catch*-block parameter.

10. No. The *catch*-block parameter e is just a place holder and can be replaced by any other (non-reserved-word) identifier, like messenger.

11.
```
if (status.equals("bad"))
    throw new Exception("Exception thrown: Bad Status.");
```

12. Yes, it is perfectly legal, although it is unlikely that you would ever have a good reason to use it.

13. Yes, it is perfectly legal, although in almost any situation it would be preferable style to use the following instead:

```
throw new IOException("Hello Houston!");
```

In practice the above *throw*-statement would typically be included in some branching statement, such as an *if*-statement.

14.
```
public class CoreBreachException extends Exception
{
    public CoreBreachException()
    {
        super("Core Breach! Evacuate Ship!");
    }

    public CoreBreachException(String message)
    {
        super(message);
    }
}
```

15.
```
public class MessageTooLongException extends Exception
{
    public MessageTooLongException()
    {
        super("Message Too Long!");
    }

    public MessageTooLongException(String message)
    {
        super(message);
    }
}
```

16.
```
Exercise exception thrown with parameter.
Do Be Do
```

17.
```
Wow, Crazy exception thrown!!
Crazy exception thrown!
```

```
Message is Crazy exception thrown!
```

18.
```
try-block entered:
Double Exception thrown!Double Exception thrown!
End of code.
```

19. The output would not change at all. The modified program is completely equivalent to the original program.

20. The output would change to the following:
```
try-block entered:
Leaving try-block.
End of code.
```

21.
```
public void doStuff(int n) throws Exception
{
    if (n < 0)
        throw new Exception("Negative number.");
}
```

22. If a method throws an exception, and the exception is not caught inside the method, then the method invocation ends immediately after the exception is thrown. If the method invocation is inside a *try*-block, then the exception is thrown to a matching *catch*-block, if there is one. If there is no *catch*-block matching the exception, then you have an uncaught exception, and the method invocation ends as soon as that exception is thrown.

23. It might be caught in method B. If it is not caught in method B, it might be caught in method C. If it is not caught in method C, it might be caught outside of C.

24.
```
Second catch.
End of Code.
```

25.
```
First catch.
End of Code.
```

26.
```
Hello!
End of Code.
```

27.
```
Trying
Starting SampleMethod.
Catching
From sampleMethod with love.
```

28. Yes, you can have a *try*-block and corresponding *catch*-blocks inside another larger *try*-block. However, it would probably be better to place

the inner *try-* and *catch*-blocks in a method definition and place an invocation of the method in the larger *try*-block.

29. Yes, you can have a *try*-block and corresponding *catch*-blocks inside another larger *catch*-block. However, it would probably be better to place the inner *try-* and *catch*-blocks in a method definition and place an invocation of the method in the larger *catch*-block.

30. Output for argument 99 is
```
In finally Block.
Caught in main.
```

Output for argument −99 is
```
Caught in sampleMethod.
In finally block.
After finally block.
```

Output for argument 0 is
```
No Exception.
Still in sampleMethod.
In finally block.
After finally block.
```

31.
```
public double getPrecision()
{
    return precision;
}

public void setPrecision(double newPrecision)
{
    precision = newPrecision;
}
```

32. The program would end as soon as an `UnknownOpException` was thrown.

? PROGRAMMING EXERCISES

1. Write a program that converts from 24-hour time to 12-hour time. The following is a sample dialog:
```
Enter time in 24-hour notation:
13:07
That is the same as
1:07 PM
Again?(y/n)
y
```

```
Enter time in 24-hour notation:
10:15
That is the same as
10:15 AM
Again?(y/n)
y
Enter time in 24-hour notation:
10:65
There is no such time as 10:65
Try Again:
Enter time in 24-hour notation:
16:05
That is the same as
4:05 PM
Again?(y/n)
n
End of program
```

You will define an exception class called `TimeFormatException`. If the user enters an illegal time, like `10:65` or even gibberish like `8&*68`, then your program will throw and catch a `TimeFormatException`.

2. Write a program that uses the class `Calculator` in Display 8.11 to create a more powerful calculator. This calculator will allow you to save one result in memory and call the result back. Commands are

 e for end
 c for clear, sets result to 0
 m for save in memory, sets memory equal to `result`
 r for recall memory, displays the value of memory,
   but does not change `result`

You should define a derived class of the class `Calculator` that has one more instance variable for the memory, a new `main`, a redefinition of the method `handleUnknownOpException`, a `main` method that runs the improved calculator, and anything else new or redefined that you need. What a sample dialog should look like is shown in what follows. Your program need not produce an identical dialog, but it should be similar and just as nice or nicer.

```
Calculator on:
result = 0.0
+4
result + 4.0 = 4.0
updated result = 4.0
/2
result / 2.0 = 2.0
updated result = 2.0
m
result saved in memory
c
result = 0.0
+99
result + 99.0 = 99.0
updated result = 99.0
/3
result / 3.0 = 33.0
updated result = 33.0
r
memory recall
memory value = 2.0
result = 33.0
+2
result + 2.0 = 35.0
updated result = 35.0
e
End of Program
```

3. Use the exception class `MessageTooLongException` of Self-test Question 15/page 535 in a program that asks the user to input a line of text with no more than 20 characters. If the user enters an acceptable number of characters the program should print out the message "You entered x characters, which is an acceptable length." (with the letter x replaced by the actual number of characters). Otherwise a `MessageTooLongException` should be thrown. In either case the program should loop and ask if the user wants to enter another line or quit the program.

4. Write a program that converts dates from numerical month/day format to alphabetic month/day (e.g. 1/31 or 01/31 corresponds to January 31). The dialog should be similar to that in Programming Exercise 1. You will define two exception classes, one called `MonthException` and another called `DayException`. If the user enters anything other than a legal month number (integers from 1 to 12) then your program will throw and catch a `MonthException`. Similarly, if the user enters anything other than a valid day number (integers from 1 to either 29, 30, or 31, depending on the month), then your program will throw and catch a `DayException`. To keep things simple always allow 29 for February.

5. Define an exception class called `DimensionException` to use in the driver program from Programming Exercise 6 Chapter 7/page 509. Mod-

ify that driver program to throw and catch a `DimensionException`, if the user enters something less than or equal to zero for a dimension.

6. Modify the driver program from Programming Exercise 5 Chapter 7/ page 508 to use three exception classes called `CylinderException`, `LoadException`, and `TowingException`. The number of cylinders must be an integer from 1 to 12, the load capacity must be a number from 1 to 10 (possible with a fractional part), and the towing capacity must be an integer from 1000 to 10,000. Anything other than numbers in these ranges will throw and catch the appropriate exception. You also need to define the classes `CylinderException`, `LoadException`, and `TowingException`.

7. Write a program to input `Employee` data into an array (maximum: 100 employees, but your program should also work for any number of employees less than 100). Your program uses two exception class, one called `SSNLengthException` if the social security number (SSN) is not exactly nine characters and the other called `SSNCharacterException` if any character is not a digit (the SSN is to be entered with just the numbers and no dashes or spaces). When an exception is thrown, the user is told what she/he entered, why it is inappropriate, and asked to reenter the data. Your program will then output the records for all `Empolyee`s with an annotation telling if the employee's salary is above or below average. You will also need to define the classes `Employee`, `SSNLengthException` and `SSNCharacterException`. The class `Employee` will be a derived class of the class `Person` in Display 7.1/page 460 of Chapter 7. Among other things the class `Employee` should have input and output methods, as well as constructors, accessor and mutator methods. Every `Employee` object will record the `Empolyee`'s name, salary, and social security number (plus any other data you need or think is appropriate).

CHAPTER 9

STREAMS AND FILE I/O

9.1 **AN OVERVIEW OF STREAMS AND FILE I/O 579**
The Concept of a Stream 579
Why Use Files for I/O? 579
Differences Between Text Files and
Binary Files 580
File Handling in Java 581

9.2 **TEXT FILE I/O 581**
Text File Output with
`PrintWriter` 581

Gotcha A `try`-Block Is a Block 585

Gotcha Overwriting a File 587

Java Tip Appending to a Text File 588

Text File Input with
`BufferedReader` 590
Programming Example Reading a File
Name from the Keyboard 594
The `StringTokenizer` Class
(Optional) 597

Java Tip Testing for the End of a Text
File 599
The Classes `FileReader` and
`FileOutputStream` 599
Unwrapping the Class `SavitchIn`
(Optional) 603

9.3 **BINARY FILE I/O 604**
Output to Files Using
`DataOutputStream` 605
Some Details About `writeUTF`
(Optional) 612

Gotcha Overwriting a File 613

Java Tip Appending to a Binary
File 614

Reading Input from a File Using
`DataInputStream` 615
Gotcha Using `DataInputStream`
with a Text File 618
Gotcha Defining a Method to Open a
Stream 619
Programming Example Reading a File
Name from the Keyboard 619
Catching `IOExceptions` 623
The `EOFException` Class 625

Java Tip Checking for the End of a
Binary File 625

Gotcha Forgetting to Check for the
End of a File 628

Gotcha Checking for the End of a File
in the Wrong Way (Alternative
Ordering) 628
The Classes `FileInputStream`
and `FileOutputStream` 629
Programming Example Processing a File of
Data 630
Programming Tip Objects Should Do
Their Own I/O 631
Case Study Writing and Reading a File
of Records 638

9.4 **FILE OBJECTS AND FILE NAMES 648**
Using the `File` Class 648
Java Tip Using Path Names 651

Chapter Summary 653
Answers to Self-Test Questions 654
Programming Exercises 659

9

STREAMS AND FILE I/O

To a programmer, **I/O** refers to program input and output. Input can be taken from the keyboard or from a file. Similarly, output can be sent to the screen or to a file. In this chapter, we explain how you can write your programs to take input from a file and/or send output to another file. One advantage of files is that they give you a permanent copy of your data.

Input from a file and input from the keyboard are similar. We will develop enough general material on input that we can explain the code for the class `SavitchIn` in an optional section of this chapter.

Objectives

Become familiar with the concept of an *I/O stream*.

Find out the difference between binary files and text files.

Learn to save data in a file using a Java program.

Learn how to read data from a file using a Java program.

Prerequisites

You do not need Chapter 7 on inheritance, and only need some of Chapter 8 on exception handling in order to read this chapter.

You can cover either text files or binary files first. Section 9.1 is a general introduction to file handling that applies to both text files and binary files. Section 9.2 on text files and Section 9.3 on binary files may be covered in either order. Section 9.4, which covers the class `File` and path names, requires that you first cover either Section 9.2 on text files or Section 9.3 on binary files, but does not require that you cover both sections. The details are below.

Section	Prerequisite
Section 9.1	Chapters 1–5
Section 9.2 on text files.	Chapters 1–5, Section 8.1 of Chapter 8, and Section 9.1

Section 9.3 on binary files.	Chapters 1–5, Sections 8.1 and 8.2 of Chapter 8 Section 9.1. You do not need Section 9.2.
Sections 9.4 on the `File` class and file path names.	Chapters 1–5, Sections 8.1 of Chapter 8 and *either* Section 9.2 or Section 9.3

9.1 | An Overview of Streams and File I/O

> *Fish say, they have their stream and pond,*
> *But is there anything beyond?*
>
> **Rupert Brooke, Heaven**

In this section we give you a general introduction to file I/O. In particular, we explain the difference between text files and binary files. This organization will let you cover either text files or binary files first. The Java syntax for file I/O statements is given in the following sections.

The Concept of a Stream

You are already using files to store your Java classes and programs. You can also use files to store input for a program or to hold output from a program. In Java, file I/O, as well as simple keyboard/screen I/O, is handled by **streams.** A stream is an object that either delivers data to its destination, such as a file or the screen, or that takes data from a source, such as a file or the keyboard, and delivers the data to your program.

The object `System.out` is the only output stream we have used so far. The class `SavitchIn`, which we have been using for input, behaves like an input stream (and in fact, has an input stream embedded in its definition). In this chapter, we discuss streams that connect your program to files. If at first you do not completely understand the idea of a *stream*, do not be concerned. As long as you understand how to do file I/O in Java, understanding the stream concept will come with time and experience.

file

stream

Streams

A **stream** is a flow of data. The data might be characters, numbers, or bytes consisting of binary digits. If the data flows *into your program*, the stream is called an **input stream.** If the data flows *out of your program*, the stream is called an **output stream.** For example, if an input stream is connected to the keyboard, then the data flows from the keyboard into your program. If an input stream is connected to a file, then data flows from the file into your program. In Java, streams are implemented as objects of special stream classes. The object `System.out` is an example of an output stream. The class `SavitchIn` is an example of using an input stream.

input stream
output stream

Why Use Files for I/O?

The keyboard input and screen output we have used so far deal with temporary data. When the program ends, the data typed in at the keyboard, and the data left on the screen, go away. Files provide you with a way to store data permanently. The contents of a file remain until a person or program changes the file. If your program sends its output to a file, the output file will remain after the program has finished running.

An input file can be used over and over again by different programs without the need to type in the data separately for each program. Files also provide you with a convenient way to deal with large quantities of data. When your program takes its input from a large input file, your program receives a lot of data without making the user do a lot of typing

Differences Between Text Files and Binary Files

All data in any file are stored as binary digits (or bits), that is, as a (probably long) sequence of zero/one digits. However, in many situations, we do not think of a file's contents as a sequence of binary digits. We often think of a file's contents as consisting of a sequence of characters. Files that are thought of as a sequence of characters and that have streams and methods to make the binary digits look like characters to your program and your editor, are called **text files**. Files whose contents must be handled as sequences of binary digits are called **binary files**.

text files and binary files

Although it is not technically precise and correct, you can safely think of a text file as containing a sequence of characters, and think of a binary file as containing a sequence of binary digits. Your Java programs are stored in text files. Another way to phrase the distinction between binary files and text files is to note that text files are designed to be read by human beings, and binary files are designed to be read by programs.

One advantage of text files is that they are usually the same on all computers. So, you can move your text files from one computer to another with few or no problems. The implementation of binary files usually differs from one computer to another. So, your binary data files ordinarily must be read only on the same computer, and with the same programming language, as the program that created that file.

The advantage of binary files is that they are more efficient to process. Unlike other programming languages, Java gives its binary files some of the advantage of text files. In particular, the designers of Java made their binary files platform-independent; that is, with Java, you can move your binary files from one computer to another and your Java programs will still be able to read the binary files. This combines the portability of text files with the efficiency of binary files.

The one big advantage of text files is that a text editor can read and write them. With binary files, all the reading and writing must normally be done by a program. (Some editors may be able to read some of the information in some binary files.)

Text Files and Binary Files

Files that you write and read using an editor are called **text files**. Text files are sometimes also called *ASCII files* because they contain data encoded using the ASCII coding method (but, do not worry if you do not yet know what the ASCII encoding method is). There is another category of files called **binary files**. Binary files represent data in a way that is not convenient to read with a text editor, but that can be written to and read from a program in a very efficient way.

File Handling in Java

Java has classes for handling text files and classes for handling binary files. In the next two sections we discuss text file I/O and binary file I/O separately. You can cover the sections in the order you prefer, either doing text files first or doing binary files first.

Input and Output Terminology

To avoid confusion, remember that the word *input* means that data move *into your program* (not into the file). The word *output* means that data move *out of your program* (not out of the file).

? Self-Test Questions

1. Why would anybody write a program that sends its output to a file instead of to the screen?

2. When we discuss "input," which way is data moving: from the program to a file or from a file to the program?

3. What is the difference between a binary file and a text file?

9.2 | Text File I/O

> *Proper words in proper places,*
> *make the true definition of a style.*
> **Jonathan Swift, Letter to a young clergyman (January 9, 1720)**

Text files can be written to and read by people using a text editor. Java allows you to write programs that take input from a text file and/or send output to a text file. In this section, we will give a description of the most common ways to do text file I/O in Java.

Text File Output with `PrintWriter`

When you write a program to send output to a text file, you use a method named `println` that behaves the same as `System.out.println`, but that is a method in the class `PrintWriter`. The class `PrintWriter` is the preferred stream class for writing to a text file. Display 9.1 contains a simple program that writes data to a text file.

PrintWriter

Note that the program in Display 9.1 begins with the line:

```
import java.io.*;
```

import java.io.*

This tells the Java compiler (and linker) that you will be using the `java.io` library, which contains the definitions of the class `PrintWriter` and the other file I/O classes discussed in this chapter. Every program or class that does file I/O using any of the techniques given in this chapter must contain the preceding import statement near the beginning of the file.

Import Statement

Every program or class that does file I/O using any of the techniques given in this chapter must contain the following statement near the beginning of the file.

```
import java.io.*;
```

This tells the Java compiler (and linker) that your program will be using the `java.io` package (library), which contains the definitions of classes such as `PrintWriter` and the other file I/O classes discussed in this chapter.

The program in Display 9.1 creates a text file named `out.txt` that can be read using an editor or can be read by another Java program using the class `BufferedReader`, which we will discuss a little later. Notice how the file is *opened*.

```
outputStream =
         new PrintWriter(new FileOutputStream("out.txt"));
```

(The variable `outputStream` is of type `PrintWriter` and is declared outside the *try*-block.) The preceding two lines of code connect the stream named `outputStream` to the file named `out.txt`. This connecting is called **opening the file**. When you connect a file to a stream in this way, your program always starts with an empty file. If the file `out.txt` had already existed, the old contents of `out.txt` would be lost. If the file `out.txt` does not exist, then a new empty file named `out.txt` will be created.

opening a file

file name

Note that the name of the file, in this case `out.txt`, is given as a `String` value and so is given in quotes. You can think of the entire expression

```
Output_Stream_Name =
         new PrintWriter(new FileOutputStream(File_Name));
```

as one difficult-to-spell operation that takes a *File_Name* as an argument, produces an output stream in the class `PrintWriter`, and connects the stream to the named file so that your program can send output to the file.

The class `PrintWriter` has no constructor that takes a file name as its argument. So, we use the class `FileOutputStream` with the class `PrintWriter` in the way shown previously. However, you can simply view this as one difficult-to-spell operation and still write and understand Java programs.

When you open a text file as described in the previous paragraph, so that it is connected to a stream of type `PrintWriter`, that file opening can possibly throw a `FileNotFoundException`, and any such possible exception should be caught in a *catch*-block. (Actually it is the `FileOutputStream` constructor that might throw

---

A File Has Two Names

Every input and every output file used by your program has two names: (1) the real file name that is used by the operating system and (2) the name of the stream that is connected to the file. The stream name serves as a temporary name for the file that is used within your program. After you connect the file to the stream, your program always refers to the file by using the stream name.

Display 9.1   Output to a Text File

```java
import java.io.*;
public class TextFileOutputDemo
{
    public static void main(String[] args)
    {
        PrintWriter outputStream = null;
        try
        {
            outputStream =
                new PrintWriter(new FileOutputStream("out.txt"));
        }
        catch(FileNotFoundException e)
        {
            System.out.println("Error opening the file out.txt.");
            System.exit(0);
        }

        System.out.println("Enter three lines of text:");
        String line = null;
        int count;
        for (count = 1; count <= 3; count++)
        {
            line = SavitchIn.readLine();
            outputStream.println(count + " " + line);
        }
        outputStream.close();
        System.out.println("Those lines were written to out.txt.");
    }
}
```

Sample Screen Dialogue

```
Enter three lines of text:
A tall tree
in a short forest is like
a big fish in a small pond.
Those lines were written to out.txt.
```

File out.txt (after program is run with the given dialog)

```
1 A tall tree
2 in a short forest is like
3 a big fish in a small pond.
```

You can read this file using a text editor.

File Names

The rules for how you spell file names depend on your operating system. They do not depend on Java. When you give a file name to a Java constructor for a stream, you are not giving the constructor a Java identifier. You are giving the constructor a string corresponding to the file name. Most common operating systems allow you to use letters, digits, and the dot symbol when spelling file names. Many operating systems allow other characters as well, but letters, digits, and the dot symbol are enough for most purposes. A suffix, such as `.txt` in `output.txt`, has no special meaning to a Java program. We are using the suffix `.txt` to indicate a text file, but that is just a personal convention. It is not a rule you need to follow. You can use any file names that are allowed by your operating system.

the `FileNotFoundException`, but the net effect is that opening a file with the class `PrintWriter` in the way we have outlined can result in an `FileNotFoundException` being thrown.)

Notice that the *try*-block (in Display 9.1) encloses only the opening of the file. This is the only place an exception might be thrown. Also, note that the variable `outputStream` is declared outside of the *try*-block. This is so that the variable `outputStream` can be used outside of the *try*-block. Remember anything declared in a block (even in a *try*-block) is local to the block. This is explained more fully in the subsection entitled *Gotcha A **try-Block Is a Block***.

println

Notice that, as illustrated in Display 9.1, the method `println` of the class `PrintWriter` works the same for writing to a text file as the method `System.out.println` works for writing to the screen. The class `PrintWriter` also has the method `print` and it behaves just like `System.out.print` except that the out-

Connecting a Text File to a Stream for Writing
(Opening a Text File for Output)

You create a stream of the class `PrintWriter` and connect it to a text file for writing as follows.

Syntax:

```
PrintWriter Output_Stream_Name =
        new PrintWriter(new FileOutputStream(File_Name));
```

Example:

```
PrintWriter outputStream =
        new PrintWriter(new FileOutputStream("out.txt"));
```

In practice, you may want to separate the declaration of the stream variable and the invocation of the constructor (as shown in Display 9.1). After this, you can use the methods `println` and `print` to write to the file.

When used in this way, the `FileOutputStream` constructor, and so the `PrintWriter` constructor invocation, can throw a `FileNotFoundException`, which is a kind of `IOException`.

put goes to a text file. Display 9.2 describes some of the methods in the class `Print-Writer`.

When your program is finished writing to a file, it should **close** the stream connected to that file. In Display 9.1, the stream connected to the file `out.txt` is closed with the statement:

closing a file

```
outputStream.close();
```

The class `PrintWriter`, and every other class for file output or file input streams, has a method named `close`. When this method is invoked, the system releases any resources used to connect the stream to the file and does any other housekeeping that is needed. If your program does not close a file before the program ends, then Java will close it for you when the program ends, but it is safest to close the file with an explicit call to `close`.

Closing Text Files

When your program is finished writing to a file (or reading from a file), it should *close* the stream connected to that file by invoking the method named `close`.

Syntax:

Stream_Name`.close();`

Example:

```
outputStream.close();
```

■ Gotcha

A *try*-Block Is a Block

Look again at the program in Display 9.1/page 583. It is not an accident or a minor stylistic concern that caused us to declare the variable `outputStream` outside of the *try*-block. If you were to move that declaration inside the *try*-block, you would get a compiler error message. Let's look at the details.

Display 9.2   Some Methods in the Class `PrintWriter`

`PrintWriter(InputStream streamObject)`

   This is the only constructor you are likely to need, although it can be used in a number of ways, as explained below. There is no constructor that accepts a file name as an argument. If you want to create a stream using a file name, then you use

   new `PrintWriter(`*new* `FileOutputStream(`*File_Name*`))`

When used in this way, a blank file is created. If there already was a file named *File_Name*, then the old contents of the file are lost. If you want instead to append new text to the end of the old file contents, then use

   new `PrintWriter(`*new* `FileOutputStream(`*File_Name*`, `*true*`))`

(For an explanation of the argument *true*, read the subsection *Java Tip* **Appending to a Text File** .)

   When used in either of these ways, the `FileOutputStream` constructor, and so the `PrintWriter` constructor invocation, can throw a `FileNotFoundException`, which is a kind of `IOException` and so can be caught in a *catch*-block for `IOExceptions`.

   The `File` class will be covered in Section 9.4. We include the following so you will have a more complete reference in this display, but you can ignore the rest of this entry on the constructors until after you read Section 9.4:

   If you want to create a stream using an object of the class `File`, then use

   new `PrintWriter(`*new* `FileOutputStream(`*File_Object*`))`

   When used in this way, the `FileOutputStream` constructor, and so the `PrintWriter` constructor invocation, can throw a `FileNotFoundException`, which is a kind of `IOException`. Note that the append form with two arguments cannot be used with a `File` object.

public final void `println(Object outputStuff)`

   Arguments can be strings, characters, integers, floating-point numbers, boolean values, or any combination of these connected with + signs. The argument is output to the file connected to the stream. This also ends the line, and so the next output is sent to the next line.

public final void `print(Object outputStuff)`

   Arguments can be strings, characters, integers, floating-point numbers, boolean values, or any combination of these connected with + signs. The argument is output to the file connected to the stream. This does not end the line, and so the next output will be on the same line.

public void `close()`

   Closes the streams connection to a file. This method calls `flush` before closing the file.

public void `flush()`

   Flushes the output stream. This forces an actual physical write to the file of any data that have been buffered and not yet physically written to the file. Normally, you should not need to invoke `flush`.

Why Bother to Close a File?

If your program ends normally but without closing a file, the system will automatically close the file for you. So, why should you bother to close files with an explicit call to the method `close`? There are at least two reasons. First, if your program ends abnormally for some reason, then Java may not be able to close the file for you and the file could be left open with no program connected to it, and this can damage the file. The sooner you close a file, the less likely it is that this will happen. Second, if your program writes to a file and later reads from the same file, then it must close the file after it is through writing to the file and reopen the file for reading. (Java does have a class that allows a file to be opened for both reading and writing, but we will not cover that in this book.)

Suppose you replace

```
PrintWriter outputStream = null;
try
{
    outputStream =
        new PrintWriter(new FileOutputStream("out.txt"));
}
```

with the following in Display 9.1:

```
try
{
    PrintWriter outputStream =
        new PrintWriter(new FileOutputStream("out.txt"));
}
```

This looks innocent enough, but it makes the variable `outputStream` a variable that is local to the *try*-block, which would mean that you cannot use `outputStream` outside of the *try*-block. If you make this change and try to compile the changed program, you will get an error message saying that `outputStream` when used outside the *try*-block is an undefined variable.

Remember, a *try*-block is a block, and so any variable declared in a *try*-block will be local to the *try*-block.

final[a]

The reserved word *final* that appears in the description of many of the methods in Display 9.2/page 586 means that if you define a derived class, then you cannot redefine any of the methods that are marked *final*.

a. If you have not yet read Chapter 7 on inheritance, you can safely ignore any reference to *final*.

■ Gotcha
Overwriting a File

When you connect a stream to a text file using the class `PrintWriter` in the manner shown in what follows, you always produce an empty file.

```
PrintWriter outputStream =
        new PrintWriter(new FileOutputStream("out.txt"));
```

If there were no file named out.txt, then this would create an empty file named out.txt. If there already was a file named out.txt, then this would eliminate that file and create a new empty file named out.txt. So, if there were a file named out.txt before the preceding is executed, then all the data in that file would be eliminated. In Section 9.4, the subsection entitled **Using the File Class** tells you how to test to see if a file already exists so you can avoid accidentally overwriting a file. In the subsection *Java Tip* **Appending to a Text File**, we show you how to add data to a text file without losing the data already in the file.

■ Java Tip
Appending to a Text File

In Display 9.1/page 583, we used the following to create a stream object named outputStream of the class PrintWriter and connect the stream to the file out.txt so that we could write output to the file out.txt.

```
PrintWriter outputStream = null;
try
{
    outputStream =
        new PrintWriter(new FileOutputStream("out.txt"));
}
catch(FileNotFoundException e)
{
    System.out.println("Error opening the file out.txt.");
    System.exit(0);
}
```

appending

When you connect a file to a stream in this way, you always start with an empty file. If the file out.txt had already existed, the old contents of out.txt would be lost. Sometimes, that is not what you want. Sometimes you want to simply add the program output to the end of the file. This is called **appending to a file**. If you want to append program output to the file out.txt, you would connect the file to the stream outputStream as follows:

```
outputStream =
    new PrintWriter(new FileOutputStream("out.txt", true));
```

If the file out.txt does not already exist, Java will create an empty file of that name and append the output to the end of this empty file. (So, if there is no file named out.txt, the effect is the same as in Display 9.1.) However, if the file out.txt already exists, then the old file contents will remain, and the programs output will go after the old contents of the file.

When appending to a text file in this way, you would use the same *try*- and *catch*-blocks as in Display 9.1, but you may wish to change the error message in the *catch*-block as shown in what follows:

```
PrintWriter outputStream = null;
try
{
    outputStream =
        new PrintWriter(
            new FileOutputStream("out.txt", true));
}
catch(FileNotFoundException e)
{
    System.out.println("File out.txt does not exist.");
    System.out.println("and/or cannot be created.");
    System.exit(0);
}
```

Note that when opening a text file for program output (in any of the ways we have shown), a `FileNotFoundException` will not be thrown in every situation in which the file does not exist. If the file does not exist, but can be created, no `File-NotFoundException` exception will be thrown. A `FileNotFoundException` is thrown only if the file does not exist *and it cannot be created for some reason*, such as if the name is already in use as the name of a directory (folder).

File-
NotFound-
Exception

Connecting a Text File to a Stream for Appending
(Opening a Text File for Appending)

To create a stream of the class `PrintWriter` and connect it to a text file for appending text to the end of the text already in the file, proceed as follows.

Syntax:

```
PrintWriter Output_Stream_Name =
    new PrintWriter(
        new FileOutputStream(File_Name, True_Boolean_Expression));
```

Example:

```
PrintWriter outputStream =
    new PrintWriter(
        new FileOutputStream("out.txt", true));
```

In practice, you may want to separate the declaration of the stream variable and the invocation of the constructor (in a way similar to what we did in Display 9.1). After this, you can use the methods `println` and `print` to write to the file, and the new text will be written after the old text in the file.

When used in this way, the `FileOutputStream` constructor, and so the `PrintWriter` constructor invocation, can throw a `FileNotFoundException`, which is a kind of `IOException`.

OK, so what is the reason for using that second parameter *true*? Why the boolean constant *true*? Why not something like the string `"append"`? The reason is that this version of the constructor for the class `FileOutputStream` was designed to also allow you to use a boolean variable (or expression) to decide if you append to file or create a new file. For example, the following might be used in the previous *try*-block:

```
System.out.println("Enter A for append or N for a new file:");
char ans = SavitchIn.readLineNonwhiteChar();
boolean append = (ans == 'A' || ans == 'a');
outputStream =
        new PrintWriter(
            new FileOutputStream("out.txt", append));
```

From this point on, your program writes to the file in exactly the same way as inDisplay 9.1/page 583. If the user answered with an 'a' or 'A', then the old contents of the file will not be lost, and any input will be added after the old file contents. If the user answered with 'N' (or with anything other than an 'a' or 'A'), then any old contents of the file are lost.   A version of the program in Display 9.1 that uses the above way of opening the file out.txt is in the program AppendTextFile.java on the accompanying CD.

extra code on CD

? Self-Test Questions

4. Write some code that will create a stream named outStream that is a member of the class PrintWriter, and that connects the stream to a text file named sam so that your program can send output to the text file sam. Do this in a way such that, if the file sam already exists, then *the old contents of* sam *will be erase* and *the program will start with an empty file* named sam. (If the file sam does not exist, then of course the file will be created and will start off empty.)

5. As in question 4, write some code that will create a stream named outStream that is a member of the class PrintWriter, and that connects the stream to a text file named sam so that your program can send output to the text file sam. But this time, do this in such a way that, if the file sam already exists, then *the old contents of* sam *will not be lost*, and *the program output will be written after the old contents of the file*. (If the file sam does not exist, then of course the file will be created and will start off empty.)

6. What kind of exception might be thrown by the following, and what would it indicate if this exception were thrown?

```
PrintWriter outputStream =
    new PrintWriter(new FileOutputStream("out.txt"));
```

7. Does the class PrintWriter have a constructor that accepts a string (for a file name) as an argument, so that the following code would be legal?

```
PrintWriter outputStream =
    new PrintWriter("myFile.txt");
```

Text File Input with BufferedReader

Display 9.3 contains a simple program that reads data from a text file and writes them back to the screen. This is just a toy program to let you see how text file input

Display 9.3 Input from a Text file

```java
import java.io.*;
public class TextFileInputDemo
{
    public static void main(String[] args)
    {
        try
        {
            BufferedReader inputStream =
                new BufferedReader(new FileReader("data.txt"));

            String line = null;
            line = inputStream.readLine();
            System.out.println("The first line in data.txt is:");
            System.out.println(line);

            line = inputStream.readLine();
            System.out.println("The second line in data.txt is:");
            System.out.println(line);
            inputStream.close();
        }
        catch(FileNotFoundException e)
        {
            System.out.println("File data.txt was not found");
            System.out.println("or could not be opened.");
        }
        catch(IOException e)
        {
            System.out.println("Error reading from file data.txt.");
        }
    }
}
```

File `data.txt`

```
1 2
buckle my shoe.
3 4
shut the door.
```

This file could have been made with a text editor or made by another Java program.

Screen Output

```
The first line in data.txt is:
1 2
The second line in data.txt is:
buckle my shoe.
```

works. The file `data.txt` is a text file that could have been created with a text editor or could have been created by a Java program using the class `PrintWriter`.

Notice how the file is opened:

```
BufferedReader inputStream =
            new BufferedReader(new FileReader("data.txt"));
```

Buffered-Reader

The class `BufferedReader` is the preferred stream class for reading from a text file.

As was true of the class `PrintWriter`, the class `BufferedReader` has no constructor that takes a file name as its argument, so we need to use another class, in this case, the class `FileReader`, to help with opening the file. The class `FileReader` will accept a file name as a constructor argument and produce a stream that is a `Reader`. The constructor for `BufferedReader` will accept a `Reader` as an argument. `Reader` is an abstract class that includes all the streams with "Reader" in their name. However, rather than keep track of this rather complicated explanation, you can simply think of the following as one long, peculiarly spelled expression for connecting a text file to a stream of the class `BufferedReader` so that your program can read from the file:

```
BufferedReader Stream_Name =
            new BufferedReader(new FileReader(File_Name));
```

Notice that the program in Display 9.3 catches two kinds of exceptions, `FileNotFoundException` and `IOException`. The opening of the file may throw a `FileNotFoundException` and any of the invocations of `inputStream.readLine()` may throw an `IOException`. Because a `FileNotFoundException` is a kind of `IOException`, you could use only the *catch*-block for `IOException`. However, if you did this, then you would get less information if an exception is thrown. If you use only one *catch*-block and an exception is thrown, then you would not know if there was a problem with opening the file or a problem with reading from the file after it was opened.

Connecting a Text File to a Stream for Reading
(Opening a Text File for Reading)

You create a stream of the class `BufferedReader` and connect it to a text file for reading as follows.

Syntax:

```
BufferedReader Stream_Name =
            new BufferedReader(new FileReader(File_Name));
```

Example:

```
BufferedReader inputStream =
            new BufferedReader(new FileReader("data.txt"));
```

After this, you can use the methods `readLine` and `read` to read from the file.

When used in this way, the `FileReader` constructor, and so the `BufferedReader` constructor invocation, can throw a `FileNotFoundException`, which is a kind of `IOException`.

Display 9.4   Some Methods in the Class `BufferedReader`

`BufferedReader(Reader readerObject)`
This is the only constructor you are likely to need. There is no constructor that accepts a file name as an argument. If you want to create a stream using a file name, then you use

`new BufferedReader(new FileReader(File_Name))`

When used in this way, the `FileReader` constructor, and so the `BufferedReader` constructor invocation, can throw a `FileNotFoundException`, which is a kind of `IOException`.

The `File` class will be covered in Section 9.4. We include the following so you will have a more complete reference in this display, but you can ignore the rest of this entry on the constructors until after you read Section 9.4:
If you want to create a stream using an object of the class `File`, then you use

`new BufferedReader(new FileReader(File_Object))`

When used in this way, the `FileReader` constructor, and so the `BufferedReader` constructor invocation, can throw a `FileNotFoundException`, which is kind of `IOException`.

`public String readLine() throws IOException`
Reads a line of input from the input stream and returns that line. If the read goes beyond the end of the file, then *null* is returned. (Note that an `EOFException` is not thrown at the end of a file. The end of a file is signaled by returning *null*.)

`public int read() throws IOException`
Reads a single character from the input stream and returns that character as an *int* value. If the read goes beyond the end of the file, then −1 is returned. Note that the value is returned as an *int*. To obtain a *char*, you must perform a type cast on the value returned. The end of a file is signaled by returning −1. (All of the "real" characters return a positive integer.)

`public void close() throws IOException`
Closes the streams connection to a file.

Notice that the method `readLine` of the class `BufferedReader` works the same for reading from a text file as the method `readLine` of the class `SavitchIn` works for reading a line of text from the keyboard. However, the class `BufferedReader` does *not* have any of the other read methods that are in `SavitchIn`, such as `readLineInt`, `readLineDouble`, and `readLineNonwhiteChar`. Display 9.4 describes some of the methods in the class `BufferedReader`.

readLine

Because `BufferedReader` has no methods like `readInt` that can read a number, the only way that you can read a number from a text file using the class `BufferedReader` is to read it as a string and then convert the string to a number. Some techniques for converting strings to numbers are discussed in the subsection *The StringTokenizer Class (Optional)*, which comes a little later in this chapter.

reading numbers

The class `BufferedReader` does have a method, named simply `read`, that will read a single character. This method `read` is similar to the method `readChar` in the class `SavitchIn`. There is, however, one complication. The method `read` returns a value of type *int* that corresponds to the character read; it does not return the character itself. Thus, to get the character, you must use a type cast, as in:

```
char next = (char)(inputStream.read());
```

If `inputStream` is in the class `BufferedReader` and is connected to a text file, this will set `next` equal to the first character in the file that has not yet been read.

Programming Example
Reading a File Name from the Keyboard

Thus far, we have written the literal file names for our input and output text files into the code of our programs. We did this by giving the file name as the argument to a constructor when we connected the file to a stream. For example, we used the following in Display 9.3/page 591 to connect the file `data.txt` to the stream named `inputStream`:

```
BufferedReader inputStream =
                new BufferedReader(new FileReader("data.txt"));
```

However, you may not know what the file name will be when you write a program and so you may want to have the user enter the file name at the keyboard when the program is run. This is easy to do. Simply have the program read the file name into a variable of type `String` and use that `String` variable in place of the file name. This technique is illustrated in Display 9.5.

Notice that the program in Display 9.5 reads input from two different places. The class `SavitchIn` is used to read the file name from the keyboard. The stream named `inputStream` is connected to the file `data.txt` and reads its input from that file.

Use of Path Names

You can use a full or relative path name for a file whenever Java calls for a string that is the file name. Thus, you can use a path name as an argument to the constructor for any of the stream class constructors that accept a file name. However, the exact details on how you write the path name may (or may not) depend on the operating system you are using. We will give more details about path names in section of 9.4 under *Java Tip* **Using Path Names**.

? Self-Test Questions

8. Write some code that will create a stream named `textStream` that is a member of the class `PrintWriter` and that connects the stream to a text file named `dobedo` so that your program can send output to the text file `dobedo`.

Display 9.5   Reading a File Name *(Part 1 of 2)*

```java
import java.io.*;

public class TextFileInputDemo2
{
    public static void main(String[] args)
    {
        System.out.println("Enter file name:");
        String fileName = SavitchIn.readLineWord();

        try
        {
            BufferedReader inputStream =
                new BufferedReader(new FileReader(fileName));

            String line = null;
            line = inputStream.readLine();
            System.out.println("The first line in "
                                 + fileName + " is:");
            System.out.println(line);

            line = inputStream.readLine();
            System.out.println("The second line in "
                                 + fileName + " is:");
            System.out.println(line);
            inputStream.close();
        }
        catch(FileNotFoundException e)
        {
            System.out.println("File " + fileName + " not found.");
        }
        catch(IOException e)
        {
            System.out.println("Error reading from file " + fileName);
        }
    }
}
```

9. Suppose you run a program that writes to the text file dobedo using the stream defined in question 8. Give some code that will create a stream named inputStream that can be used to read from the text file dobedo in the ways we discussed in this section.

10. BufferedReader has a method named readLine that is essentially the same as the method readLine in the class SavitchIn, except that it takes its input from a text file. Does BufferedReader have any methods like readInt, readDouble, readWord, or readChar?

11. Might the methods read and/or readLine in the class BufferedReader throw an exception? If so, what type of exception?

12. Notice one difference between the *try*-blocks in Display 9.1/page 583 and Display 9.5/page 595. The *try*-block in Display 9.1 encloses only the opening of the file, but the *try*-block in Display 9.5 encloses most of the action in the program. Why is the *try*-block in Display 9.5 larger than the one in Display 9.1?

13. What is the type of a value returned by the method readLine in the class BufferedReader? What is the type of the value returned by the method read in the class BufferedReader?

Display 9.5   Reading a File Name *(Part 2 of 2)*
....

File data.txt

```
1 2
buckle my shoe.
3 4
shut the door.
```

This file could have been made with a text editor or made by another Java program.

Sample Screen Dialogue

```
Enter file name:
data.txt
The first line in data.txt is:
1 2
The second line in data.txt is:
buckle my shoe.
```

....

The `StringTokenizer` Class *(Optional)*

When using the class `BufferedReader` to read input from a text file, you can read either entire lines or single characters. Often you would like to read words, but `BufferedReader` has no method that reads a single word. You can usually realize something roughly equivalent to reading words by reading an entire line of text and then using the predefined class `StringTokenizer` to break the string into individual words.

You can use the class `StringTokenizer` to break down a string into the separate words contained in the string. The following example illustrates a simple, but typical, way that the class is used:

```
StringTokenizer wordFinder =
                    new StringTokenizer("We love you madly.");
while (wordFinder.hasMoreTokens())
{

    System.out.println(wordFinder.nextToken());
}
```

This will produce the output:

```
We
love
you
madly.
```

The constructor (the part after the *new*) produces a new object of the class `StringTokenizer`. This object can produce the individual words in the string used as the argument to the constructor. These individual words are called **tokens.**

tokens

The method `nextToken` returns the first token (word) when it is invoked for the first time, returns the second token when it is invoked the second time, and so forth. The method `hasMoreTokens` returns *true* as long as `nextToken` has not yet returned all the tokens in the string, and it returns *false* after the method `next-Token` has returned all the tokens in the string.

The class `StringTokenizer` is in the `java.util` (short for utility) package. So, any class or program that uses the class `StringTokenizer` must contain the following at the start of the file:

```
import java.util.*;
```

When the constructor for `StringTokenizer` is used with a single argument, as in the preceding example, then the tokens are substrings of nonwhitespace characters and the whitespace characters are used as the separators for the tokens. Any string of one or more whitespace characters is considered a separator. (Recall that whitespace characters are the blank, new line, and other symbols that print as whitespace if printed on paper.) Thus, in the preceding example, the last word is `"madly."`, including the period. This is because the period is not a whitespace character and so is not a separator. If you want to specify your own set of separator characters, rather than simply accept the default set consisting of the whitespace characters, then you give a second argument to the constructor when you set up the string tokenizer using *new*. The second argument is a string consisting of all the separator characters. Thus, if you want your separators to consist of the blank, new-line character, period, and comma, then you could proceed as in the following example:

```
StringTokenizer secondWordFinder =
            new StringTokenizer("Love you, madly.", " \n.,");
while (secondWordFinder.hasMoreTokens())
{
    System.out.println(secondWordFinder.nextToken());
}
```

This will produce the output:

```
Love
you
madly
```

Be sure to notice that the period and comma are not part of the tokens produced, because they are now token separators. Also, note that the string of tokens is the second argument to the constructor.

You can see another example of the use of the `StringTokenizer` class in the definition of the method `readLineWord` in the class `SavitchIn` given in Appendix 4. Some of the methods for the class `StringTokenizer` are summarized in what follows.

Some Methods in the Class `StringTokenizer`

public `StringTokenizer(String theString)`
Constructor for a tokenizer using whitespace characters to find tokens in `theString`.

public `StringTokenizer(String theString, String delimiters)`
Constructor for a tokenizer that will use the characters in the string `delimiters` as separators to find tokens in `theString`.

public boolean `hasMoreTokens()`
Tests if there are more tokens available from this tokenizer's string. When used in conjunction with `next-Token`, it returns *true* as long as `nextToken` has not yet returned all the tokens in the string; returns *false* otherwise.

public `String nextToken()`
Returns the next token from this string tokenizer. (Throws `NoSuchElementException` if there are no more tokens to return.)

public int `countTokens()`
Returns the number of tokens remaining to be returned by `nextToken`.

■ *Java Tip*
Testing for the End of a Text File

When using the class `BufferedReader`, if your program tries to read beyond the end of the file with either of the methods `readLine` or `read`, then the method returns a special value to signal that the end of the file has been reached. When `readLine` tries to read beyond the end of a file, it returns the value *null*. Thus, your program can test for the end of the file by testing to see if `readLine` returns *null*. This technique is illustrated in Display 9.6. When the method `read` tries to read beyond the end of a file, it returns the value −1. Because the *int* value corresponding to each ordinary character is positive, this can be used to test for the end of a file.

Checking for the End of a Text File

The method `readLine` of the class `BufferedReader` returns *null* when it tries to read beyond the end of a text file. The method `read` of the class `BufferedReader` returns −1 when it tries to read beyond the end of a text file. (Neither of these methods would throw an `EOFException`.) ■

? Self-Test Questions

14. What happens when the method `readLine` in the class `BufferedReader` attempts to read beyond the end of a file? How can you use this to test for the end of a file?

15. What is the type of value returned by the method `read` in the class `BufferedReader`?

16. What happens when the method `read` in the class `BufferedReader` attempts to read beyond the end of a file? How can you use this to test for the end of a file?

The Classes `FileReader` and `FileOutputStream`

We have used the stream class `FileReader` or `FileOutputStream` whenever we created a stream of the class `BufferedReader` or `PrintWriter`. For example, the following were used in Display 9.6:

```
BufferedReader inputStream =
            new BufferedReader(new FileReader("story.txt"));
PrintWriter outputStream =
        new PrintWriter(new FileOutputStream("storylines.txt"));
```

We used the classes `FileReader` and `FileOutputStream` because they accept a file name as a constructor argument, such as the arguments `"story.txt"` and `"storylines.txt"` in the preceding examples. Neither `BufferedReader` nor `PrintWriter` accepts a file name as an argument. Thus, when you connect a `BufferedReader` to a file using a string name, you must do so in two steps. First, you create an object of the class `FileReader` with, for example, *new*

Display 9.6   Checking for the End of a Text File *(Part 1 of 2)*

```java
import java.io.*;

/************************************************************
 *Makes storylines.txt the same as story.txt but with each line numbered.
 ************************************************************/
public class TextEOFDemo
{
    public static void main(String[] args)
    {
        try
        {
            BufferedReader inputStream =
                new BufferedReader(new FileReader("story.txt"));
            PrintWriter outputStream =
                new PrintWriter(new FileOutputStream("storylines.txt"));

            int count = 0;
            String line = inputStream.readLine();
            while (line != null)
            {
                count++;
                outputStream.println(count + " " + line);
                line = inputStream.readLine();
            }
            System.out.println(count
                            +" lines written to storylines.txt.");

            inputStream.close();
            outputStream.close();
        }
        catch(FileNotFoundException e)
        {
            System.out.println("File story.txt not found.");
        }
        catch(IOException e)
        {
            System.out.println("Error reading from file story.txt.");
        }
    }
}
```

`FileReader("story.txt")`, and then you use this object of the class `FileReader` to create an object of the class `BufferedReader` with

```
BufferedReader inputStream =
          new BufferedReader(new FileReader("story.txt"));
```

Similarly, we produce a `PrintWriter` from a file name in two steps using `FileOutputStream`.

Since *new* `FileReader("story.txt")` produces an input stream connected to the file named by the string in the variable `"story.txt"`, why didn't we just use that stream instead of going on to create a `BufferedReader`? The reason is that the class `FileReader` does not have the nice input methods we want to use, like `read`, and `readLine`. To get the nice methods in the class `BufferedReader`, we need to convert the `FileReader` to a `BufferedReader`. Whenever you chain streams together in this way, the resulting stream always has the methods of the last (that is, the leftmost) stream named. For example, in

```
BufferedReader inputStream =
          new BufferedReader(new FileReader("story.txt"));
```

the stream `inputStream` has all the methods of the class `BufferedReader`, but does not have the methods of the class `FileReader`.

Similar remarks apply to why we do not simply use the class `FileOutputStream`, but instead go on to form a `PrintWriter`.

Since we will only use the classes `FileReader` and `FileOutputStream` in arguments to constructors for stream classes such as `BufferedReader` and `Print-`

Display 9.6   Checking for the End of a Text File (Part 2 of 2)

File `story.txt`

```
Once upon a time
there were three little
auto mechanics: Click,
Clack, and Joe.
```

story.txt could have been made with a text editor or made by another Java program.

File `storylines.txt` (after the program is run)

```
1 Once upon a time
2 there were three little
3 auto mechanics: Click,
4 Clack, and Joe.
```

Do not be concerned if your version of storylines.txt has numbered blank lines after 4. That just means you had blank lines at the end of story.txt.

Writer, we do not really care what methods the classes FileReader and FileOutputStream may or may not have, except for their constructor methods. We do care what constructors these classes have, because it is the constructors that we use with *new* in the preceding examples and similar cases. In particular, you need to know that the classes FileReader and FileOutputStream each have a constructor that accepts a file name. .

When using FileReader and FileOutputStream in the ways we have described, it is important to note that the constructors for these classes can throw exceptions. The constructors for FileReader and FileOutputStream can throw an exception in the class FileNotFoundException. A FileNotFoundException is a kind of IOException, so a *catch*-block that catches IOExceptions will catch a FileNotFoundException.

FileReader and FileOutputStream

In this book, we will use the classes FileReader and FileOutputStream for their constructors and nothing else. Each of these two classes has a constructor that takes a file name as an argument . We use these constructors to produce arguments for the constructors for stream classes such as BufferedReader and PrintWriter, whose constructors do not take a file name as an argument. Below are samples of using FileReader and FileOutputStream:

```
PrintWriter outputStream =
        new PrintWriter(new FileOutputStream("stuff.txt"));

BufferedReader inputStream =
        new BufferedReader(new FileReader("story.txt"));
```

The constructors for FileReader and FileOutputStream can throw an exception in the class FileNotFoundException, which is a kind of IOException.

? Self-Test Questions

17. Which of the following classes have a constructor that accepts a file name as an argument? PrintWriter, BufferedReader, FileReader, FileOutputStream.

18. Is the following legal?

```
FileReader readerObject = new
FileReader("myFile.txt");

BufferedReader inputStream =
        new BufferedReader(readerObject);
```

Unwrapping the Class SavitchIn *(Optional)*

The class SavitchIn reads from the keyboard. It does not read from a text file. However, keyboard input is processed in the same way as text file input. You do not need to read the definition of the class SavitchIn to be able to read the rest of this book or to be able to learn the Java language. However, if you have read this chapter and a few of the optional subsections (listed below), then you know enough to understand the definition of the class SavitchIn. The definition for the class SavitchIn is given in Appendix 4. In this subsection, we point out a few points that will make it easier for you to understand the code given there.

The class SavitchIn uses System.in.read to define the method readChar. *readChar* System.in.read behaves the same as the method read in the class BufferedReader, except that System.in.read reads from the keyboard rather than reading from a text file. The code for the method readChar in SavitchIn is repeated in what follows:

```java
public static char readChar()
{
    int charAsInt = -1; //To keep the compiler happy
    try
    {
        charAsInt = System.in.read();
    }
    catch(IOException e)
    {
        System.out.println(e.getMessage());
        System.out.println("Fatal error. Ending Program.");
        System.exit(0);
    }

    return (char)charAsInt;
}
```

Note that System.in.read returns an *int*, not a *char*. To obtain a *char* value, the code needs to do a type cast as shown in the preceding code.

The class SavitchIn uses the method readChar in the definition of the method readLine. The method readLine in SavitchIn behaves very much like the *readLine* method readLine in the class BufferedReader. The code for the method readLine in SavitchIn is repeated in what follows:

```java
public static String readLine() throws IOException
{
    char nextChar;
    String result = "";
    boolean done = false;
```

```
while (!done)
{
    nextChar = readChar();
    if (nextChar == '\n')
        done = true;
    else if (nextChar == '\r')
    {
        //Do nothing. Next loop iteration will detect '\n'.
    }
    else
        result = result + nextChar;
}
return result;
}
```

The symbol '\r' is a special character called the **carriage return symbol**. You should already know about the next line symbol '\n'. Some systems simply use '\n' to denote the end of a line. Other systems use '\r' followed by '\n' to denote the end of a line. The method readLine checks for both possibilities.

The remaining methods use either readLine and/or readChar to do their reading from the keyboard. In order to understand these other methods, you should know how to convert strings to numbers, as discussed in the subsection **Inputting Other Numeric Types**, which is in Chapter 2 (in the optional section on JOption-Pane). You should also know about the StringTokenizer class, as described in the subsection **The StringTokenizer Class (Optional)** earlier in this chapter. You also need to know the basics of exception handling covered in Chapter 8. The exception class NumberFormatException is thrown when one of the methods for converting a string to a number fails because the string is not a correctly written numeral.

9.3 | Binary File I/O

> *The White Rabbit put on his spectacles. "Where shall I begin, please your Majesty?" he asked.*
> *"Begin at the beginning," the King said, very gravely, "And go on till you come to the end: then stop."*
>
> **Lewis Carroll, Alice in Wonderland**

Binary files store data in the same format as they are stored in the computer's main memory (which we described in Chapter 1). Each data item, such as an integer, is stored as a sequence of bytes. Your Java program reads these bytes in very much the same way that it reads a data item, like an integer, from the computer's main memory. This fact that binary files store data in the same format as in the computer's main memory is why binary files can be handled so efficiently by a program. Binary files created by a Java program can be moved from one computer to another and still be read by a Java program—but only by a Java program. They cannot normally be read with a text editor.

The most commonly used stream classes for processing binary files are `DataInputStream` and `DataOutputStream`. Each has methods to read or write data one byte at a time. These streams can also automatically convert numbers and characters to bytes that can be stored in a binary file. They allow your program to be written as if the data placed in the file, or read from the file, were not just bytes but were strings or items of any of Java's primitive data types, *int*, *char*, *double*, and so forth. If you do not need to access your files using an editor, then the easiest and most efficient way to read and write data to files is to use `DataOutputStream` to write to a binary file and `DataInputStream` to read from the binary file. The following subsections discuss these two stream classes in more detail.

Output to Files Using `DataOutputStream`

If you want to create a binary file to store either `String` values or values of any of the primitive data types, such as *char*, *int*, and *double*, then you can use the stream class `DataOutputStream`. Display 9.7 shows a program that writes integers to a binary file. Let's look at the details shown in that program.

connecting a stream to a file

Note that the substance of what goes on in the program is in a *try*-block. Any code that does binary file I/O in the ways we are describing can throw an `IOException`, which is usually a way of saying that something has gone wrong with your program I/O. Your programs can catch any `IOException` in a *catch*-block, so that if an `IOException` is thrown, you get an error message and the program ends normally. In a latter section we will discuss exception handling in more detail. Until then, we will simply put all our I/O code in a large *try*-block and follow it with a *catch*-block to catch any `IOException`.

The output stream for writing to the file `numbers.dat` is created and named with the following:

```
DataOutputStream outputStream =
    new DataOutputStream(new FileOutputStream("numbers.dat"));
```

If the file `numbers.dat` does not already exist, this will create an empty file named `numbers.dat`. If the file `numbers.dat` does already exist, then this will erase the contents of the files so that the files starts out empty.

The stream named `outputStream` is an object of the class `DataOutputStream`. It has some similarity to the stream `System.out` in that it has methods for handling program output. However `System.out` and objects of the class `DataOutputStream` have output methods that have different names and that behave somewhat differently. Objects of the class `DataOutputStream` do not have a method named `println`. However, as shown in Display 9.7, an object of the class `DataOutputStream` does have a method named `writeInt` that can write a single *int* value to a file, and it also has other output methods that we will discuss shortly. But first, we need to explain the details in the above two lines that create and name the stream object called `outputStream`.

The two lines

```
DataOutputStream outputStream =
    new DataOutputStream(new FileOutputStream("numbers.dat"));
```

Display 9.7   Using `DataOutputStream` to Write to a File *(Part 1 of 2)*

```java
import java.io.*;

public class DataOutputDemo
{
    public static void main(String[] args)
    {
        try
        {
            DataOutputStream outputStream =
                    new DataOutputStream(new FileOutputStream("numbers.dat"));
            int n;

            System.out.println("Enter nonnegative integers, one per line.");
            System.out.println("Place a negative number at the end.");

            do
            {
                n = SavitchIn.readLineInt();
                outputStream.writeInt(n);
            }while (n >= 0);

            System.out.println("Numbers and sentinel value");
            System.out.println("written to the file numbers.dat.");
            outputStream.close();
        }
        catch(IOException e)
        {
            System.out.println("Problem with output to file numbers.dat.");
        }
    }
}
```

.

Import Statement

Every program or class that does file I/O using any of the techniques given in this chapter must contain the following statement near the beginning of the file.

```java
import java.io.*;
```

This tells the Java compiler (and linker) that your program will be using the `java.io` package (library), which contains the definitions of classes such as `DataOutputStream` and the other file I/O classes discussed in this chapter.

Display 9.7   Using `DataOutputStream` to Write to a File *(Part 2 of 2)*

Sample Screen Dialogue

```
Enter nonnegative integers, one per line.
Place a negative number at the end.
1
2
3
-1
Numbers and sentinel value
written to the file numbers.dat.
```

File `numbers.dat` **(after program is run)**

```
1
2
3
-1
```

Notice that the −1 is in the file. It does not have to be in the file, but in this program, we want it there as a sentinel value.

This is a binary file. You cannot read this file with your text editor.

connect the stream named `outputStream` to the file named `numbers.dat`. This connecting is often called **opening the file**. Note that the name of the file, in this case `numbers.dat`, is given as a `String` value and so is given in quotes. We will explain the words *new* `FileOutputStream` shortly, but for the moment, just think of the entire expression

opening a file

```
DataOutputStream Output_Stream_Name =
    new DataOutputStream(new FileOutputStream(File_Name));
```

as one difficult-to-spell operation that takes a *File_Name* as an argument, produces an output stream in the class `DataOutputStream`, and connects the stream to the named file. You can take this as one difficult-to-spell operation and still write working programs, but it will be more satisfying and more useful to understand a few more details.

Constructors for the class `DataOutputStream` create new streams in the class `DataOutputStream`. However, the class `DataOutputStream` does not have a constructor that takes a file name as an argument. If you try the following, you will get a compiler error message:

```
DataOutputStream outputStream =
    new DataOutputStream("numbers.dat"); //This is ILLEGAL!
```

File Names

The rules for how you spell file names depend on your operating system. They do not depend on Java. When you give a file name to a Java constructor for a stream, you are not giving the constructor a Java identifier. You are giving the constructor a string corresponding to the file name. Most common operating systems allow you to use letters, digits, and the dot symbol when spelling file names. Many operating systems allow other characters as well, but letters, digits, and the dot symbol are enough for most purposes. A suffix, such as `.dat` in `numbers.dat`, has no special meaning to a Java program. We are using the suffix `.dat` to indicate that a binary file can be used as *data* for a Java program, but that is just a personal convention. It is not a rule you need to follow. You can use any file names that are allowed by your operating system.

Closing a File

When your program is finished writing to a file (or reading from a file), it should close the stream connected to that file by invoking the method named `close`.

Syntax:

  Stream_Name`.close();`

Example:

  `outputStream.close();`

 If your program does not close a file before the program ends, then Java will close it for you when the program ends, but it is safest to close the file with an explicit call to `close`.

The argument for the `DataOutputStream` constructor must be an output stream. It cannot be a string naming a file. Thus, when you connect a file to a stream of the class `DataOutputStream`, it must be a two-step process. First, you connect the file to another type of output stream that does work with a file name, and then you connect this other output stream to a stream in the class `DataOutputStream`. For example, the following two lines from Display 9.7 create the output stream named `output-Stream` and connect it to the file `numbers.dat`:

```
DataOutputStream outputStream =
        new DataOutputStream(new FileOutputStream("numbers.dat"));
```

FileOutput-
Stream

It may help to note that the previous code creating the stream `outputStream` is equivalent to

```
FileOutputStream middleman =
            new FileOutputStream("numbers.dat");
DataOutputStream outputStream =
            new DataOutputStream(middleman);
```

The only difference is that the first version does not bother to give the stream of type `FileOutputStream` the name `middleman`.

writeInt
  Once a stream in the class `DataOutputStream` is connected to a file, you can write integers to the file with the method `writeInt`, as in the following line from Display 9.7:

```
outputStream.writeInt(n);
```

Connecting a Binary File to a Stream for Writing
(Opening an Output File)

You create a stream of the class `DataOutputStream` and connect it to a binary file as follows:

Syntax:

```
DataOutputStream Output_Stream_Name =
    new DataOutputStream(new FileOutputStream(File_Name));
```

Examples:

```
DataOutputStream myOutputStream =
    new DataOutputStream(new FileOutputStream("myfile.dat"));
```

When used in this way, the `FileOutputStream` constructor, and so the `DataOutputStream` constructor invocation, can throw a `FileNotFoundException`, which is kind of `IOException`. After opening the file, you can use the methods of the class `DataOutputStream` to write to the file.

A File Has Two Names

Every input and every output file used by your program has two names: (1) the real file name that is used by the operating system and (2) the name of the stream that is connected to the file. The stream name serves as a temporary name for the file that is used within your program. After you connect the file to the stream, your program always refers to the file by using the stream name.

In Display 9.7, the preceding line writes the value of the *int* variable n to the file `numbers.dat`. If you look at Display 9.8, you will see that there are similar methods `writeLong`, `writeDouble`, and `writeFloat` that write numbers of other types to a file. Also note, that all of these methods can throw an `IOException`.   writeDouble

Notice that the program in Display 9.7 sends output to two different places by using two different output streams. The stream named `outputStream` is connected to the file `numbers.dat` and sends its output to that file. The other output stream is `System.out`. You are so used to using it that you might not think of `System.out` as an output stream, but it is an output stream that is connected to the screen. So output statements that use `System.out.println` send their output to the screen.

In Display 9.7, we made it look like the numbers in the file `numbers.dat` are written one per line in a human-readable form. That is not what happens. There are no lines or other separators between the numbers. Instead, the numbers are written in the file one immediately after the other, and they are encoded as a sequence of bytes in the same way that the numbers would be encoded in the computer's main memory. These coded *int* values cannot be read using your editor. Realistically, they can only be read by another Java program.

Display 9.8 contains a list of some of the methods in the class `DataOutput-Stream`.

That ends our description of the sample program in Display 9.7, but we still have not discussed all the methods of `DataOutputStream` listed in Display 9.8. We do that next.

Display 9.8   Some Methods in the Class `DataOutputStream`

●●●

public `DataOutputStream(OutputStream streamObject)`
    This is the only constructor. If you want to create a stream using a file name, then you use

    new `DataOutputStream(new FileOutputStream(`*File_Name*`))`

When used in this way, a blank file is created. If there already was a file named *File_Name*, then the old contents of the file are lost. If you want instead to append new text to the end of the old file contents, then use

    new `DataOutputStream(new FileOutputStream(`*File_Name*`, `*true*`))`

(For an explanation of the argument *true*, see the subsection *Java Tip* **Appending to a Binary File**.)
    The `FileOutputStream` constructor, and so the `DataOutputStream`
constructor invocation, can throw a `FileNotFoundException`, which is kind of `IOException`.

    The `File` class will be covered in Section 9.4. We include the following so you will have a more complete reference in this table, but you can ignore the rest of this entry on the constructors until after you read Section 9.4:
    If you want to create a stream using an object of the class `File`, then you use

    new `DataOutputStream(new FileOutputStream(`*File_Object*`))`

When used in this way, the `FileOutputStream` constructor, and so the `DataOutputStream`
constructor invocation, can throw a `FileNotFoundException`, which is kind of `IOException`.
Note that the append form with two arguments cannot be used with a `File` object.

---

public final void `writeInt(`*int* `n) `*throws* `IOException`
    Writes the *int* value n to the output stream.

---

public final void `writeLong(`*long* `n) `*throws* `IOException`
    Writes the *long* value n to the output stream.

---

public final void `writeDouble(`*double* `x) `*throws* `IOException`
    Writes the *double* value x to the output stream.

---

public final void `writeFloat(`*float* `x) `*throws* `IOException`
    Writes the *float* value x to the output stream.

---

public final void `writeChar(`*int* `n) `*throws* `IOException`
    Writes the *char* value n to the output stream. Note that it expects its argument to be an *int* value. You can use a type cast in order to convert *char* value to an *int* value. For example:
        `outputStream.writeChar((`*int*`)'A');`
In actual fact, you do not need the type cast to an *int*, because Java will automatically convert a *char* value to an *int* value for you. So, the following is equivalent to the above invocation of `writeChar`:
        `outputStream.writeChar('A');`

Display 9.8   Some Methods in the Class `DataOutputStream`
••

> `public final void writeBoolean(boolean b) throws IOException`
>   Writes the `boolean` value b to the output stream.

> `public final void writeUTF(String aString) throws IOException`
>   Writes the `String` value `aString` to the output stream. "UTF" refers to a particular method of en-
> coding the string. To read the string back from the file, you should use the method `readUTF` of the class
> `DataInputStream`.

> `public void close() throws IOException`
>   Closes the stream's connection to a file. This method calls `flush` before closing the file.

> `public void flush() throws IOException`
>   Flushes the output stream. This forces an actual physical write to the file of any data that have been buffered
> and not yet physically written to the file. Normally, you should not need to invoke `flush`.

> ### *final*[a]
>
> The reserved word *final* that appears in the description of many of the methods in Display 9.8/page 610 means
> that if you define a derived class, then you cannot redefine any of the methods that are marked *final*.

   a. If you have not yet read Chapter 7 on inheritance, you can safely ignore any reference to *final*.

You can use a stream from the class `DataOutputStream` to output values of any
primitive type and also to write data of the type `String`. Each primitive data type
has a corresponding write method in the class `DataOutputStream`. We have already   `writeChar`
mentioned the write methods for outputting numbers. The method `writeChar` can
be used to output a single character. The method `writeBoolean` can be used to output a single boolean value. For example, the following would output the character   `write-`
'A' followed by the boolean value *false* to the file connected to the stream named   `Boolean`
`outputStream`:

```
outputStream.writeChar((int)'A');
outputStream.writeBoolean(false);
```

The method `writeChar` has one possibly surprising property: It expects its
argument to be of type *int*. So if you start with a value of type *char*, the *char* value
must be type cast to an *int* before it is giving it to the method `writeChar`. For
example, to output the contents of a *char* variable named `symbol`, you can use

```
outputStream.writeChar((int)symbol);
```

In actual fact, you do not need to write in the type cast to an *int*, because Java will
automatically convert a *char* value to an *int* value for you, and this is one place

were it may make sense to take advantage of that automatic type casting. So, the following is equivalent to the above invocation of `writeChar`:

```
outputStream.writeChar(symbol);
```

That takes care of outputting the primitive types. To output a value of type `String`, you use the method `writeUTF`. For example, if `outputStream` is a stream of type `DataOutputStream`, then the following will write the string `"Hi Mom"` to the file connected to that stream:

(margin note: writeUTF for strings)

```
outputStream.writeUTF("Hi Mom");
```

Of course, with `writeUTF` or any of the write methods, you can use a variable of the appropriate type (in this case, the type `String`) as an argument to the method.

You may write output of different types to the same file. So, you may write a combination of, for example, `int`, `double`, and `String` values. However, mixing types in a file does require special care in order to make it possible to read them back out of the file. To read them back, you need to know the order in which the various types appear in the file, because, as you will see, a program that reads from the file will use a different method to read data of each different type.

Display 9.8 has one last method that we must discuss. Like all output streams that can be connected to a file, any stream object of the class `DataOutputStream` has a method named `flush`. We have not used `flush`, but you should be familiar with this important method. Like most programming languages, Java does not always send output immediately to its destination, such as a file, but sometimes it waits to send a larger package of data to the output destination. Thus, the output from a `writeInt` or a `writeUTF` may not be sent to the output file immediately. Instead, it might be saved and packaged with the output from the next write method invocation, and then the output from both write method invocations might be sent to the file at the same time. This technique is called **buffering** and is done for efficiency reasons. The `flush` method sends all the pending data to their output destination. When you call the method `close`, that automatically calls the method `flush`. So, for most simple applications, you do not need to explicitly call the method `flush`. However, if you continue to program, you will eventually encounter situations where you want to use `flush`. The syntax is illustrated by the following example:

(margin note: flush)

(margin note: buffering)

```
outputStream.flush();
```

Some Details About `writeUTF` *(Optional)*

The method `writeInt` writes integers into a file using the same number of bytes— that is, the same number of zeros and ones—to store any integer. Similarly, the method `writeLong` uses the same number of bytes to store each value of type `long`. (But the methods `writeInt` and `writeLong` use a different number of bytes from each other.) The situation is the same for all the other write methods, with the exception of `writeUTF`. All the write methods except for `writeUTF` write out the same number of bytes every time they write a value of their respective type. However, the method `writeUTF` uses differing numbers of bytes to store different strings in a file. Longer strings require more bytes than shorter strings. This can present a problem to Java,

---

What Does "UTF" Stand For?

To write an `int` (when using the class `DataOutputStream`), you use `writeInt`; to write a `double`, you use `writeDouble`; and so forth. However, to write a string, you do *not* use `writeString`. You use `writeUTF`. There is no method called `writeString` in `DataOutputStream`. Why this funny name `writeUTF`? *UTF* stands for *Unicode Text Format*. That is not a very descriptive name. Here is the full story:

Recall that Java uses the Unicode character set, a set of characters that includes many letters used in Asian languages and other languages whose character sets are very different from English. Most editors and most operating systems use the ASCII character set, which is the character set normally used for English and for typical Java programs. The ASCII character set is a subset of the Unicode character set, so the Unicode character set has a lot of characters you do not need. There is a standard Unicode way of coding all the Unicode characters, but for English-speaking countries, it is not a very efficient coding scheme. The UTF coding scheme is an alternative coding scheme that still codes all Unicode characters but that favors the ASCII character set. The UTF coding method gives short, efficient codes for ASCII characters. The price is that it gives long, inefficient codes to the other Unicode characters. However, because you probably do not use the other Unicode characters, this is a good deal. ∎

---

because there are no separators between data items in a binary file. The way that Java manages to make this work out is by writing some extra information at the start of each string. This extra information tells how many bytes are used to write the string, so `readUTF` knows how many bytes to read and convert. (`readUTF` will be discussed a little later in this chapter, but as you may have already guessed, it reads a `String` value.)

The situation with `writeUTF` is even a little more complicated than what we discussed in the previous paragraph. We made a point of saying that the information at the start of the string code in the file tells how many *bytes* to read, *not how many characters are in the string*. These two figures are not the same. With the UTF way of encoding, different characters are encoded in different numbers of bytes. However, all the ASCII characters are stored in just one byte, and you are undoubtedly using only ASCII characters, so this difference is more theoretical than real to you now. The box entitled ***What Does "UTF" Stand For?*** has some additional discussion of this variable length coding.

■ Gotcha
Overwriting a File

When you connect a stream to a file using the class `DataOutputStream` in the manner shown in what follows, you always produce an empty file.

```
DataOutputStream outputStream =
    new DataOutputStream(new FileOutputStream("numbers.dat"));
```

If there were no file named `numbers.dat`, then this would create an empty file named `numbers.dat`. If there already was a file named `numbers.dat`, then this would eliminate that file and create a new empty file named `numbers.dat`. So, if there were a file named `numbers.dat` before the preceding was executed, then all the data in that file would be eliminated. In Section 9.4, the subsection entitled ***Using the `File` Class*** tells you how to test to see if a file already exists so you can avoid accidentally overwriting a file. In the subsection *Java Tip* **Appending to a Binary File**, we show you how to add data to a file without losing the data already in the file.

■ Java Tip
Appending to a Binary File

In Display 9.7/page 606, we used the following to create a stream object named `outputStream` of the class `DataOutputStream` and connect the stream to the file `numbers.dat` so that we could write output to the file `numbers.dat`.

```
DataOutputStream outputStream =
        new DataOutputStream(new FileOutputStream("numbers.dat"));
```

When you connect a file to a stream in this way, you always start with an empty file. If the file `numbers.dat` had already existed, the old contents of `numbers.dat` would be lost. Sometimes that is not what you want. Sometimes you want to simply add the program output to the end of the file, so that the original file contents are not lost. This is called **appending to a file**. If you want your program to append output to the file `numbers.dat`, you would connect the file to the stream `outputStream` as follows:

appending

```
DataOutputStream outputStream =
    new DataOutputStream(
                    new FileOutputStream("numbers.dat", true));
```

If `numbers.dat` does not already exist, Java will create an empty file of that name and append the output to the end of this empty file. (So, if there is no file named `numbers.dat`, the effect is the same as in Display 9.7.)

Connecting a Binary File to a Stream for Appending
(Opening a Binary File for Appending)

If you want your code to create a stream of the class `DataOutputStream` and connect it to a binary file for appending data to the end of the data already in the file, then you do so as follows.

Syntax:

```
DataOutputStream Output_Stream_Name =
    new DataOutputStream(
        new FileOutputStream(File_Name, True_Boolean_Expression));
```

Example:

```
DataOutputStream outputStream =
    new DataOutputStream(
        new FileOutputStream("numbers.dat", true));
```

When used in this way, the `FileOutputStream` constructor, and so the `DataOutputStream` constructor invocation, can throw an `FileNotFoundException`, which is kind of `IOException`. After opening the file, you can use the methods of the class `DataOutputStream` to write to the file. ■

What is the reason for using that second parameter *true*? Why doesn't Java indicating appending with some other argument that sounds like it has something to do with appending? The reason is that this version of the constructor for the class `FileOutputStream` was designed to also allow you to use a boolean variable (or other boolean expression) to decide if you append to a file or create a new file. For example, the following might be used to open a binary file:

```
System.out.println("Enter A for append or N for a new file:");
char ans = SavitchIn.readLineNonwhiteChar();
boolean append = (ans == 'A' || ans == 'a');
DataOutputStream outputStream =
    new DataOutputStream(
            new FileOutputStream("numbers.dat", append));
```

A version of the program in Display 9.7 that uses the above way of opening the file `numbers.dat` is in the program `BinaryAppend.java` on the accompanying CD.

extra code on
CD

Use of Path Names

You can use a full or relative path name for a file whenever Java calls for a string that is the file name. However, the exact details on how you write the path name may (or may not) depend on the operating system you are using. The subsection **Using the** `File` **Class** in Section 9.4 has more information on using path names.

? Self-Test Questions

19. How do you create an output stream of type `DataOutputStream` that is named `toFile` and is connected to a binary file named `stuff.data`? Do it so your program adds its data to an empty file.

20. Give three statements that will write the values of the three *double* variables x1, x2, and x3 to the file `stuff.data`. Use the stream `toFile` that you created as the answer to question 19.

21. Give a statement that will close the stream `toFile` created as the answer to question 19.

22. How do you create an output stream of type `DataOutputStream` that is named `appendToFile` and is connected to a binary file named `records.data`? Do it so your program does not delete any of the data in the file `records.data`, but appends its data to the end of the file after the data already in the file.

23. What import statement do you use when doing I/O as described in this chapter?

Reading Input from a File Using `DataInputStream`

If you write to a file using `DataOutputStream`, you can read from that binary file using the stream class `DataInputStream`. Display 9.9 gives some of the most commonly used methods for the class `DataInputStream`. If you compare that table with the methods for `DataOutputStream` given in Display 9.8/page 610, you will see that corresponding to each output method for `DataOutputStream`, there is a corresponding input method in `DataInputStream`. For example, if you write an integer to

Display 9.9   Some Methods in the Class DataInputStream

```
DataInputStream(InputStream streamObject)
```
This is the only constructor. If you want to create a stream using a file name, then you use

```
new DataInputStream(new FileInputStream(File_Name))
```

When used in this way, the FileInputStream constructor, and so the DataInputStream constructor invocation, can throw a FileNotFoundException, which is a kind of IOException.

The File class will be covered in Section 9.4. We include the following so you will have a more complete reference in this table, but you can ignore the rest of this entry on the constructors until after you read Section 9.4:
If you want to create a stream using an object of the class File, then you use

```
new DataInputStream(new FileInputStream(File_Object))
```

When used in this way, the FileInputStream constructor, and so the DataInputStream constructor invocation, can throw a FileNotFoundException, which is a kind of IOException.

public final int readInt() *throws* IOException

Reads an *int* value from the input stream and returns that *int* value. If readInt tries to read a value from the file and that value was not written using the method writeInt of the class DataOutputStream (or written in some equivalent way), then the *int* value returned is a "garbage value" and further reading from the file is likely to be corrupted. If the read goes beyond the end of the file, then an EOFException is thrown.

public final long readLong() *throws* IOException

Reads a *long* value from the input stream and returns that *long* value. If readLong tries to read a value from the file and that value was not written using the method writeLong of the class DataOutputStream (or written in some equivalent way), then the *long* value returned is a "garbage value" and further reading from the file is likely to be corrupted. If the read goes beyond the end of the file, then an EOFException is thrown.

Note that it is not acceptable to write an integer with writeLong and later read the same integer with readInt, or to write an integer with writeInt and later read it with readLong.

public final double readDouble() *throws* IOException

Reads a *double* value from the input stream and returns that *double* value. If readDouble tries to read a value from the file and that value was not written using the method writeDouble of the class DataOutputStream (or written in some equivalent way), then the *double* value returned is a "garbage value" and further reading from the file is likely to be corrupted. If the read goes beyond the end of the file, then an EOFException is thrown.

Display 9.9   Some Methods in the Class `DataInputStream`

public final float `readFloat()` *throws* `IOException`
   Reads a *float* value from the input stream and returns that *float* value. If `readFloat` tries to read a value from the file and that value was not written using the method `writeFloat` of the class `DataOutputStream` (or written in some equivalent way), then the *float* value returned is a "garbage value" and further reading from the file is likely to be corrupted. If the read goes beyond the end of the file, then an `EOFException` is thrown.
   Note that it is not acceptable to write a floating-point number with `writeDouble` and later read the same number with `readFloat`, or to write a floating-point number with `writeFloat` and later read it with `readDouble`. Other type mismatches, such as writing with `writeInt` and reading with `readFloat` or `readDouble`, are also not acceptable.

public final char `readChar()` *throws* `IOException`
   Reads a *char* value from the input stream and returns that *char* value. If `readChar` tries to read a value from the file and that value was not written using the method `writeChar` of the class `DataOutputStream` (or written in some equivalent way), then the *char* value returned is a "garbage value" and further reading from the file is likely to be corrupted. If the read goes beyond the end of the file, then an `EOFException` is thrown.

public final boolean `readBoolean()` *throws* `IOException`
   Reads a *boolean* value from the input stream and returns that *boolean* value. If `readBoolean` tries to read a value from the file and that value was not written using the method `writeBoolean` of the class `DataOutputStream` (or written in some equivalent way), then the *boolean* value returned is a "garbage value" and further reading from the file is likely to be corrupted. If the read goes beyond the end of the file, then an `EOFException` is thrown.

public final String `readUTF()` *throws* `IOException`
   Reads a `String` value from the input stream and returns that `String` value. If `readUTF` tries to read a value from the file and that value was not written using the method `writeUTF` of the class `DataOutputStream` (or written in some equivalent way), then the `String` value returned is a "garbage value" and further reading from the file is likely to be corrupted. If the read goes beyond the end of the file, then an `EOFException` is thrown.

public void `close()` *throws* `IOException`
   Closes the streams connection to a file.

a file using the method `writeInt` of `DataOutputStream`, then you can read that integer back with the method `readInt` of `DataInputStream`. If you write a number to a file using the method `writeDouble` of `DataOutputStream`, then you can read that number back with the method `readDouble` of `DataInputStream`, and so forth. Display 9.10 gives an example of using `readInt` in this way.

   Note that a binary file is opened for reading with `DataInputStream` in a manner similar to what you have already seen for `DataOutputStream`. In Display 9.10, the file `numbers.dat` is opened and connected to a stream named `inputStream` as follows:

```
DataInputStream inputStream =
     new DataInputStream(new FileInputStream("numbers.dat"));
```

Note that this is identical to what we used with `DataOutputStream` in Display 9.7/ page 606, except that we use the class `DataInputStream` instead of `DataOutput-Stream` and we use the class `FileInputStream` instead of `FileOutputStream`. The reason for needing `FileInputStream` is the same as the reason we needed `File-OutputStream` with `DataOutputStream`.

close

Also note that when you are through reading from a file, you should close the file with an invocation of the method `close`. The syntax and the reasons for closing a file read with `DataInputStream` are the same as we discussed for `DataOutput-Stream`.

reading multiple types

Using `DataInputStream`, you may read input of different types from the same file. So, you may read a combinations of, for example, *int* values, *double* values, and `String` values. However, if the next data item in the file is not of the type expected by the reading method, then the result is likely to be a mess. For example, if your program writes an integer using `writeInt`, then any program that reads that integer should read it using `readInt`. If you instead use `readLong` or `readDouble`, then your program will misbehave. The case study **Writing and Reading a File of Records** shows a program that writes data of differing types to a file and it shows another program that reads the data.

Connecting a Binary File to a Stream for Reading
(Opening an Input File)

You create a stream of the class `DataInputStream` and connect it to a binary file as follows.

Syntax:

```
DataInputStream Input_Stream_Name =
     new DataInputStream(new FileInputStream(File_Name));
```

Examples:

```
DataInputStream myInputStream =
     new DataInputStream(new FileInputStream("myfile.dat"));
```

After this, you can use the methods of the class `DataInputStream` to read from the file.

■ Gotcha
Using `DataInputStream` with a Text File

Binary files and text files encode their data in different ways. Thus, a stream that expects to read a binary file, such as a stream in the class `DataInputStream`, will have problems reading a text file. If you attempt to read a text file with a stream in the class `DataInputStream`, then your program will either read "garbage values" or will encounter some other error condition.

? Self-Test Questions

24. How do you create an input stream of type `DataInputStream` that is named `fromFile` and is connected to a file named `stuff.data`?

25. Give three statements that will read three *double* numbers from the file `stuff.data`. Use the stream `fromFile` that you created as the answer to question 24. Declare three variables to hold the three numbers.

26. Give a statement that will close the stream `fromFile` created as the answer to question 24.

27. Can one program write a number to a file using `writeInt` and then have another program read that number using `readLong`? Can a program read that number using `readDouble`?

28. Can you use `readUTF` to read a string from a text file?

Programming Example
Reading a File Name from the Keyboard

Thus far, we have written the literal file names for our binary files into the code of our programs. We did this by giving the file name as the argument to a constructor when we connected the file to a stream. For example, we used the following in Display 9.10/page 620 to connect the file `numbers.dat` to the stream named `inputStream`:

```
DataInputStream inputStream =
        new DataInputStream(new FileInputStream("numbers.dat"));
```

However, you may not know what the file name will be when you write a program and so you may want to have the user enter the file name at the keyboard when the program is run. This is easy to do. Simply have the program read the file name into a variable of type `String`, and use that `String` variable in place of the file name. This technique is illustrated in the program in Display 9.11.

Notice that the program in Display 9.11 reads input from two different places. The class `SavitchIn` is used to read the file name from the keyboard. The stream named `inputStream` is connected to the file `numbers.dat` and reads its input from that file.

Gotcha
Defining a Method to Open a Stream

The following looks like a fairly reasonable method to include in some class, but it has a problem:

Display 9.10 Using DataInputStream **to Read from a File**

```java
import java.io.*;

public class DataInputDemo
{
    public static void main(String[] args)
    {
        try
        {
            DataInputStream inputStream =
                new DataInputStream(new FileInputStream("numbers.dat"));
            int n;
            System.out.println("Reading the nonnegative integers");
            System.out.println("in the file numbers.dat.");
            n = inputStream.readInt();
            while (n >= 0)
            {
                System.out.println(n);
                n = inputStream.readInt();
            }

            System.out.println("End of reading from file.");
            inputStream.close();
        }
        catch(IOException e)
        {
            System.out.println("Problem with input from file numbers.dat.");
        }
    }
}
```

Screen Output
(Assuming the program in Display 9.7/page 606 was already run with the dialog shown there.)

```
Reading the nonnegative integers
in the file numbers.dat.
1
2
3
End of reading from file.
```

Notice that the sentinel value −1 is read from the file, but is not output to the screen.

Display 9.11 Reading a File Name

```java
import java.io.*;

public class FileNameDemo
{
    public static void main(String[] args)
    {
        String fileName = null;
        try
        {
            System.out.println("Enter file name:");
            fileName = SavitchIn.readLineWord();
            DataInputStream inputStream =
                new DataInputStream(new FileInputStream(fileName));
            int n;
            System.out.println("Reading the nonnegative integers");
            System.out.println("in the file " + fileName);
            n = inputStream.readInt();
            while (n >= 0)
            {
                System.out.println(n);
                n = inputStream.readInt();
            }
            System.out.println("End of reading from file.");
            inputStream.close();
        }
        catch(IOException e)
        {
            System.out.println("Problem with output to file " + fileName);
        }

    }
}
```

Sample Screen Dialogue
(Assuming the program in Display 9.7/page 606 was run first, with the dialog shown there.)

```
Enter file name:
numbers.dat
Reading the nonnegative integers
in the file numbers.dat
1
2
3
End of reading from file.
```

```
//This method does do not what we want it to do.
public static void openFile(DataOutputStream streamName)
                                          throws IOException
{
    System.out.println("Enter file name:");
    String fileName = SavitchIn.readLineWord();
    streamName =
        new DataOutputStream(new FileOutputStream(fileName));
}
```

The method will compile fine and can be invoked, but it will not perform as you might hope. For example, consider the following. (Recall that *null* is a value that can be assigned to any variable of a class type. Although the exact details of what *null* is do not matter here, you can find more information about *null* in Chapter 4.)

```
DataOutputStream outputStream = null;
openFile(outputStream);
```

After this code is executed, the value of outputStream is still *null*. The file that was opened in the method openFile went away when the method was over. The problem is a bit subtle and is unlikely to arise in very many situations, but this is one of those situations.

The problem has to do with how Java handles arguments of a class type. These arguments are passed to the method as a *memory address that cannot be changed*. The memory address normally names something that can be changed, but the memory address itself cannot be changed. Another (equivalent) way to think about this is to recall that an object variable, like the preceding outputStream, is a name. A method can change the contents of the file named by outputStream. For example, it can send output to the stream and so change the file connected to the stream. However, a method cannot change the stream name, so that it names a different file. When you use *new*, you are changing outputStream so that it names a different file, and that is not allowed.

Be sure to note that this is a narrow restriction that applies only in very limited circumstances. Once a stream is connected to a file, you can pass the stream name as an argument to method and the method can change the file. Also note that this only applies to arguments to methods. If the stream name is a local variable or if the stream name is an instance variable, then you can open a file and connect it to a stream and this problem will not occur. (Of course, the local variable goes away when the method invocation ends, but that is to be expected with a local variable and should not be a problem.)

The best way to avoid this problem is to use a method that returns the stream object after the stream object is connected to the file. The following method has no problems:

```
public static DataOutputStream openFile() throws IOException
{
    DataOutputStream tempStreamName;
    System.out.println("Enter file name:");
    String fileName = SavitchIn.readLineWord();
    tempStreamName =
        new DataOutputStream(new FileOutputStream(fileName));
    return tempStreamName;
}
```

A simple program demonstrating the use of this method is in the file `OpenFile-Demo.java` on the accompanying CD.

extra code on CD

? Self-Test Questions

29. Write some Java code to create a stream of type `DataOutputStream`. Name the stream `writer`, and connect it to the binary file whose name is stored in the `String` variable `theFile`.

30. Give some Java code to create a stream of type `DataInputStream`. Name the stream `reader`, and connect it to the file whose name is stored in the `String` variable name `theFile`.

31. Write a complete Java program that will ask the user for a binary file name and output the first data item in that file to the screen. Assume that the first data item is a string that was written to the file with the method `writeUTF`.

Catching `IOExceptions`

`IOException` is a predefined exception class. Any code that does file I/O in the ways we are describing might throw an `IOException` when something goes wrong with the I/O processing. Such exceptions should not be ignored. You should not simply list `IOException` in a *throws*-clause of the method `main`, but you should instead catch any possible `IOException` in a *catch*-block, even if the *catch*-block simply issues an error message and ends the program.

IO-Exception

The program in Display 9.12 is a rewritten version of the program in Display 9.10/page 620. The only difference between this version and the one in Display 9.10 is that this version has a separate *catch*-block for exceptions in the class `FileNotFoundException`. The class `FileNotFoundException` is another predefined exception class. An object of that class is thrown when a file is opened for reading input from the file, but there is no file with the name specified. A `FileNotFoundException` is also thrown in certain other situations, as we discussed earlier in this chapter.

File-NotFound-Exception

The `FileNotFoundException` class is a derived class of the class `IOException`. So any *catch*-blocks that catch exceptions of the class `IOException` will also catch exceptions of the class `FileNotFoundException`. Thus, if we had omitted the *catch*-block for `FileNotFoundException`, then the program in Display 9.12

Display 9.12 Catching Exceptions with `DataInputStream`

```java
import java.io.*;

public class DataInputDemoImproved
{
    public static void main(String[] args)
    {
        try
        {
            DataInputStream inputStream = new DataInputStream(
                            new FileInputStream("numbers.dat"));
            int n;

            System.out.println("Reading the nonnegative integers");
            System.out.println("in the file numbers.dat.");
            n = inputStream.readInt();
            while (n >= 0)
            {
                System.out.println(n);
                n = inputStream.readInt();
            }

            System.out.println("End of reading from file.");
            inputStream.close();
        }
        catch(FileNotFoundException e)
        {
            System.out.println("Cannot find file numbers.dat.");
        }
        catch(IOException e)
        {
            System.out.println("Problem with input from file numbers.dat.");
        }
    }
}
```

This is an improved version of the program in Display 9.10/page 620.

Screen Output
(Assuming there is no file named `numbers.dat`.**)**

If nothing goes wrong, this program performs the same as the program in Display 9.10/page 620.

```
Cannot find file numbers.dat.
```

would still catch all exceptions, but we would not get as much information. By having a separate *catch*-block for the exception class FileNotFoundException, you ensure that you will get a message telling you when the named file is not found. If you only had the *catch*-block for IOException, then you would still get an error message if the named file was not found, but you would not know whether the error was due to the file not being found or to some other I/O problem.

FileNotFoundException **Class**

If your program attempts to open a file for reading and there is no such file, then a FileNotFoundException is thrown. (A FileNotFoundException is also thrown in certain other situations.)

The class FileNotFoundException is a derived class of the class IOException. So, every exception of type FileNotFoundException is also of type IOException. In particular, a *catch*-block that catches exceptions of the class IOException will also catch exceptions in the class FileNotFoundException.

The EOFException **Class**

Many, but not all, methods that read from a file will throw an exception of the class EOFException when they try to read beyond the end of a file. All of the DataInputStream methods shown in Display 9.9/page 616 throw an EOFException if they try to read beyond the end of a file.

As illustrated in Display 9.13, the class EOFException can be used to test for the end of a file when you are using DataInputStream. As illustrated in that sample program, the reading is placed in an "infinite loop," in this case, by using *true* as the boolean expression in the *while*-loop. The loop is not really infinite, because when the end of the file is reached, an exception is thrown, and that ends the entire *try*-block and passes control to the *catch*-block. It is instructive to compare the program in Display 9.13 with the similar program in Display 9.12/page 624. The one in Display 9.12 tests for the end of a file by testing for a negative number. This is fine, but this means that you cannot store negative numbers in the file (except as a sentinel value). The program in Display 9.13 uses EOFException to test for the end of a file, and so it can handle files that store any kind of integers including negative integers.

EOF-
Exception

■ Java Tip
Checking for the End of a Binary File

When reading a file, it is often the case that you want to read and process all the data in the file. The general outline of how your program might proceed is a loop of the form

> Repeat the following until you get to the end of the file:
> {
>   read some data.
>   process the data.
> }

Display 9.13 Using EOFException **(Part 1 of 2)**

```java
import java.io.*;

public class EOFExceptionDemo
{
    public static void main(String[] args)
    {
        try
        {
            DataInputStream inputStream =
                new DataInputStream(new FileInputStream("numbers.dat"));
            int n;

            System.out.println("Reading ALL the integers");
            System.out.println("in the file numbers.dat.");
            try
            {
                while ( true )
                {
                    n = inputStream.readInt();
                    System.out.println(n);
                }
            }
            catch(EOFException e)
            {
                System.out.println("End of reading from file.");
            }

            inputStream.close();
        }
        catch(FileNotFoundException e)
        {
            System.out.println("Cannot find file numbers.dat.");
        }
        catch(IOException e)
        {
            System.out.println("Problem with input from file numbers.dat.");
        }
    }
}
```

The loop ends when an exception is thrown.

In order to implement this pseudocode, you need some way to test for reaching the end of the file. In Java, there are a number of different ways to test for the end of a file, depending on what stream is connected to the file and what method you use for reading. The commonly used methods to test for the end of a file all use one of the following three basic techniques:

1. Set up the input file so that it ends with a special value to serve as a sentinel value. Then your program can stop reading when the sentinel value is read. For example, a file of nonnegative integers could use a negative integer at the end as a sentinel value. In the subsection **Ending a Loop** of Chapter 3, we discussed using this technique for input from the keyboard. The same technique works for input from a file. Display 9.12/page 624 shows a program that uses this technique.

2. Throwing and catching an exception of the class `EOFException`. This is the technique we used in the program in Display 9.13/page 626.

3. Many of the methods for reading from a file return a special value when they try to read beyond the end of a file. None of the `DataInputStream` methods shown in Display 9.9/page 616 behave this way. So, if you are using `DataInputStream` for file input, this third possibility cannot be used. This technique is often used when reading from a text file, as discussed in Section 9.2/page 581.

Display 9.13 Using `EOFException` *(Part 2 of 2)*

Screen Output
(Assuming the program in Display 9.7/page 606 was run with the dialog shown there.)

```
Reading ALL the integers
in the file numbers.dat.
1
2
3
-1
End of reading from file.
```

Notice that when you use `EOFException`, −1 is just like any other integer. `EOFException` allows you to have files that can contain any kind of integers.

EOFException **Class**

If your program is reading from a file using any of the methods listed in Display 9.9/page 616 for the class DataInputStream and your program attempts to read beyond the end of the file, then an EOFException is thrown. This can be used to end a loop that reads all the data in a file. Other methods in other classes may also throw an EOFException when they try to read beyond the end of a file, but this is not true of all methods for reading from a file. As a general rule, if your program is reading from a binary file, then your program will probably throw an EOFException when it tries to read beyond the end of a file, but if your program is reading from a text file, then it probably will not throw an EOFException (or any exception) when the program attempts to read beyond the end of the file. This general rule applies to the techniques discussed in this chapter. For classes and methods not discussed in this chapter, you must check the documentation for each method you use to see if it will throw an EOFException. The class EOFException is a derived class of the class IOException. So, every exception of type EOFException is also of type IOException.

■ Gotcha

Forgetting to Check for the End of a File

If your program makes no provisions for detecting the end of a file, then when the end of a file is reached, what happens will depend on the details of your program—but whatever happens, it will not be good. If your program tries to read beyond the end of a file, it may enter an infinite loop or it might end abnormally. Always be sure your program checks for the end of a file and does something appropriate when it reaches the end of the file. Even if you think your program will not read past the end of the file, you should provide for this eventuality just in case things do not go exactly as you planned.

■ Gotcha

Checking for the End of a File in the Wrong Way *(Alternative Ordering)*

This Gotcha is only relevant if you have covered both binary files and text files.

Different file-reading methods (usually in different classes) check for the end of a file in different ways. Some throw an exception in the class EOFException when they try to read beyond the end of a file. Others return a special value, such as *null*, when they try to read beyond the end of a file. When reading from a file, you must be careful to test for the end of a file in the correct way for the method you are using. If you test for the end of a file in the wrong way, then one of two things will probably happen: Either your program will go into an unintended infinite loop or your program will terminate abnormally.

How can you tell whether or not a method for reading a file will throw an EOFException at the end of the file, return *null*, or do something else? You must check the documentation or try a sample program. As a general rule, if your program is reading from a binary file, then you can expect an EOFException to be thrown when reading goes beyond the end of the file. If you are reading from a text file, you can except that some special value, such as *null*, will be returned when your program attempts to read beyond the end of the text file, and you can expect that no EOFException will be thrown with a text file.

The Classes `FileInputStream` and `FileOutputStream`

We have used the stream class `FileInputStream` or `FileOutputStream` whenever we created a stream of the class `DataInputStream` or `DataOutputStream`. For example, the following were used in Display 9.7/page 606 and Display 9.13/page 626, respectively:

```
DataOutputStream outputStream =
    new DataOutputStream(new FileOutputStream("numbers.dat"));

DataInputStream inputStream =
    new DataInputStream(new FileInputStream("numbers.dat"));
```

We used the classes `FileOutputStream` and `FileInputStream` because they accept a file name as a constructor argument, such as the argument `"numbers.dat"` in the preceding examples. Neither `DataInputStream` nor `DataOutputStream` accepts a file name as an argument. Thus, when you connect a `DataInputStream` to a file using a string name, you must do so in two steps. First, you create an object of the class `FileOutputStream` with, for example, `new FileOutputStream("numbers.dat")`. Then you use this object of the class `FileOutputStream` to create an object of the class `DataOutputStream` with

```
DataOutputStream outputStream =
    new DataOutputStream(new FileOutputStream("numbers.dat"));
```

Similarly, we produce a `DataInputStream` from a file name in two steps using `FileInputStream`.

Since `new FileOutputStream("numbers.dat")` produces an output stream connected to the file named by the string `"numbers.dat"`, why didn't we just use that stream instead of going on to create a `DataOutputStream`? The reason is that the class `FileOutputStream` does not have the nice output methods we want to use, like `writeInt`, `writeDouble`, and `writeUTF`. The class `FileOutputStream` does have methods for outputting raw bytes of data, but no methods that do the nice conversions from the Java types, such as *int*, *double*, and `String`. To get the nice methods in the class `DataOutputStream`, we need to convert the `FileOutputStream` to a `DataOutputStream`. Whenever you chain streams together in this way, the resulting stream always has the methods of the last (that is, leftmost) stream named. For example, in

```
DataOutputStream outputStream =
    new DataOutputStream(new FileOutputStream("numbers.dat"));
```

the stream `outputStream` has all the methods of the class `DataOutputStream`, but does not have the methods of the class `FileOutputStream`.

Similar remarks apply to why we do not simply use the class `FileInputStream`, but instead go on to form a `DataInputStream`.

Since we will only use the classes `FileInputStream` and `FileOutputStream` in arguments to constructors for stream classes such as `DataInputStream` and `DataOutputStream`, we do not really care what methods the classes `FileInput-`

Stream and `FileOutputStream` may or may not have, except for the constructor methods. We do care what constructors these classes have, because it is the constructors that we use with *new* in the preceding examples and similar cases. In particular, you need to know that the classes `FileInputStream` and `FileOutputStream` each have a constructor that accepts a file name.

When using `FileInputStream` and `FileOutputStream` in the ways we have described, it is important to note that the constructors for these classes can throw exceptions. The constructors for `FileInputStream` and `FileOutputStream` can throw an exception in the class `FileNotFoundException`. A `FileNotFoundExcep-tion` is a kind of `IOException`, and so can be caught in a *catch*-block for `IOEx-ceptions`.

FileInputStream and FileOutputStream

In this book, we use the classes `FileInputStream` and `FileOutputStream` for their constructors and nothing else. Each of these two classes has a constructor that takes a file name as an argument. We use these constructors to produce arguments for the constructors for stream classes such as `DataInputStream` and `DataOutputStream`, that do not take a file name as an argument. Below are samples of using `FileIn-putStream` and `FileOutputStream`:

```
DataOutputStream fileOutput =
        new DataOutputStream(new FileOutputStream("stuff.dat"));
DataInputStream fileInput =
            new DataInputStream(new FileInputStream(name));
```

The constructors for `FileInputStream` and `FileOutputStream` can throw an exception in the class `FileNotFoundException`. A `FileNotFoundException` is a kind of `IOException`.

Programming Example
Processing a File of Data

Display 9.14 contains a program that does some simple processing of data. It asks the user for two file names, and then copies all the numbers in one file into the other file, but multiplies each number by 2 so that the numbers in the output file are all double the values in the input file. This is not a very complicated programming task, but it does employ a lot of standard programming techniques for handling file I/O. In particular, note that the variables for stream objects connected to the files are instance variables, and note that the task is broken down into subtasks assigned to various methods.

Note that we have made the *try*-blocks small, so that when an exception is thrown, it is caught in a nearby *catch*-block. If we had fewer *try*-blocks, it would be harder to decide what part of the code threw an exception.

Display 9.14 Catching All Exceptions *(Part 1 of 3)*

```java
import java.io.*;

public class FileProcessor
{
    private DataInputStream inputStream = null;
    private DataOutputStream outputStream = null;

    /***********************************************************
     *Doubles the integers in one file and puts them in another file.
     ***********************************************************/
    public static void main(String[] args)
    {
        FileProcessor twoTimer = new FileProcessor();
        twoTimer.connectToInputFile();
        twoTimer.connectToOutputFile();
        twoTimer.timesTwo();
        twoTimer.closeFiles();
        System.out.println("Numbers from input file");
        System.out.println("doubled and copied to output file.");
    }
}
```

■ *Programming Tip*
Objects Should Do Their Own I/O

One of the principles of object-oriented programming is that objects are not simply passive collections of data, but are active things that should carry out whatever actions need to be performed with the data. Thus, when we define classes, we often define input and output methods for the class. Before this chapter, the only input methods we could define obtained input from the keyboard, and the only output methods we could define sent their output to the screen. Now that you have learned about file I/O, you should also include methods for file input and file output whenever you define a class whose objects might be written to or read from a file.

As an example, we have rewritten the definition of the class Species from Chapter 4 (Display 4.19/page 276) so that it includes a method to send output to a binary file and a method to obtain input from a binary file. The class definition is

Display 9.14 Catching All Exceptions *(Part 2 of 3)*

```java
public void connectToInputFile()
{
    String inputFileName = getFileName("Enter input file name:");
    try
    {
        inputStream =
            new DataInputStream(
                          new FileInputStream(inputFileName));
    }
    catch(FileNotFoundException e)
    {
        System.out.println("File " + inputFileName
                                    + " not found.");
        System.exit(0);
    }
}

public void connectToOutputFile()
{
    String outputFileName = getFileName("Enter output file name:");
    try
    {
        outputStream = new DataOutputStream(
                          new FileOutputStream(outputFileName));
    }
    catch(FileNotFoundException e)
    {
        System.out.println("Error opening output file "
                                        + outputFileName);
        System.out.println(e.getMessage());
        System.exit(0);
    }
}

private String getFileName(String prompt)
{
    String fileName = null;
    System.out.println(prompt);
    fileName = SavitchIn.readLineWord();
    return fileName;
}
```

Display 9.14 Catching All Exceptions *(Part 3 of 3)*

```java
public void timesTwo()
{
    int next;
    try
    {
        while (true)
        {
            next = inputStream.readInt();
            outputStream.writeInt(2*next);
        }
    }
    catch(EOFException e)
    {
        //Do nothing. This just ends the loop.
    }
    catch(IOException e)
    {
        System.out.println(
                "Error: reading or writing files.");
        System.out.println(e.getMessage());
        System.exit(0);
    }
}

public void closeFiles()
{
    try
    {
        inputStream.close();
        outputStream.close();
    }
    catch(IOException e)
    {
        System.out.println("Error closing files "
                                    + e.getMessage());
        System.exit(0);
    }
}
}
```

A real-life class might also have other methods that take data from the input file, transform the data in some way, and write the changed data to the output file.

shown in Display 9.15. (We have also taken this opportunity to add two constructors to the class definition. When we first defined the class Species, we had not yet
learned about constructors.)

overloading

Notice that in the new class Species, the two names readInput and write-
Output are overloaded. Java decides which of the two definitions of readInput to
use by checking the number of arguments. There is one definition that is used when
the method readInput is called with no arguments and another definition that is
used when the method readInput is called with an argument of type DataInput-
Stream. If the readInput method is called with no arguments, then the input is
taken from the keyboard. If the readInput method is called with an argument of
type DataInputStream, then the input is taken from the file connected to the input
stream. Java also decides which definition of writeOutput to use by checking the
arguments. If the writeOutput method is called with no arguments, then the output goes to the screen. If the writeOutput method is called with an argument of
type DataOutputStream, then the output goes to a binary file.

Notice that the methods readInput and writeOutput for writing to and reading from a file match in terms of the order of data types. The method writeOutput
writes data to the file with

```
outputStream.writeUTF(name);
outputStream.writeInt(population);
outputStream.writeDouble(growthRate);
```

This writes a string, followed by an *int*, followed by a *double*. In order to read this
data back out of the file, the data must be read as a string, followed by an *int*, followed by a *double*. This is exactly what the readInput method does. It reads a
record with the following:

```
name = inputStream.readUTF();
population = inputStream.readInt();
growthRate = inputStream.readDouble();
```

? Self-Test Questions

32. Suppose you want to create an input stream and connect it to the binary
file named mydata.dat. Will the following work? If not, how can you
write something similar that does work?

```
DataInputStream inputStream =
                new DataInputStream("mydata.dat");
```

33. Does the class FileInputStream have a method named readInt? Does
it have one named readDouble? Does it have one named readUTF?

34. Does the class FileOutputStream have a constructor that accepts a file
name as an argument?

35. Does the class DataOutputStream have a constructor that accepts a file
name as an argument?

Display 9.15 Species Class with Binary File I/O *(Part 1 of 3)*

```java
import java.io.*;

/*****************************************************************
 *Class for data on endangered species. This is a new, improved definition
 *of the class Species, which replaces the definition in Chapter 4.
 *****************************************************************/
public class Species
{
    private String name;
    private int population;
    private double growthRate;

    public Species()
    {
        name = null;
        population = 0;
        growthRate = 0;
    }

    public Species(String initialName, int initialPopulation,
                                    double initialGrowthRate)
    {
        name = initialName;
        if (initialPopulation >= 0)
            population = initialPopulation;
        else
        {
            System.out.println("ERROR: Negative population.");
            System.exit(0);
        }
        growthRate = initialGrowthRate;
    }

    public void set(String newName, int newPopulation,
                                    double newGrowthRate)
    {
        name = newName;
        if (newPopulation >= 0)
            population = newPopulation;
        else
        {
            System.out.println("ERROR: Negative population.");
            System.exit(0);
        }
        growthRate = newGrowthRate;
    }
```

Display 9.15 Species Class with Binary File I/O *(Part 2 of 3)*

< The methods `getName`, `getPopulation`, `getGrowthRate`, `equals`, and `projectedPopulation` are the same as in Display 4.19/page 276. >

The method name `writeOutput` is overloaded. With no arguments, it sends output to the screen. With an argument of type `DataOutputStream`, it sends output to a binary file.

```java
/*************************
*Sends output to the screen.
*************************/
public void writeOutput()
{
    System.out.println("Name = " + name);
    System.out.println("Population = " + population);
    System.out.println("Growth rate = " + growthRate + "%");
}



/*********************************************************
*Precondition: The stream outputStream has been connected
*to a file.
*Action: A record of the species is written to the file
*that is connected to outputStream. The record is written
*as three items, IN THIS ORDER: a String for the name, an
*int for the population, and a double for the growth rate.
*********************************************************/
public void writeOutput(DataOutputStream outputStream)
                                        throws IOException
{
    outputStream.writeUTF(name);
    outputStream.writeInt(population);
    outputStream.writeDouble(growthRate);
}
```

Display 9.15 Species Class with Binary File I/O *(Part 3 of 3)*

> The method name `readInput` is overloaded. With no argument, it reads its input from the keyboard. With an argument of type `DataInputStream`, it takes input from a binary file.

```java
/****************************
 *Takes input from the keyboard.
 ***************************/
public void readInput()
{
    System.out.println("What is the species' name?");
    name = SavitchIn.readLine();
    System.out.println("What is the population of the species?");
    population = SavitchIn.readLineInt();
    System.out.println("Enter growth rate (percent increase per
        year):");
    growthRate = SavitchIn.readLineDouble();
}


/*********************************************************
 *Precondition: The stream inputStream is connected to a file.
 *Each species record appears in the file as three items,
 *IN THIS ORDER: a String for the name, an int for the
 *population, and a double for the growth rate.
 *Action: Reads a record from the stream and resets the data
 *for the calling object. An attempt to read past the end
 *of the file will throw an EOFException.
 *********************************************************/
public void readInput(DataInputStream inputStream)
                                        throws IOException
{
    name = inputStream.readUTF();
    population = inputStream.readInt();
    growthRate = inputStream.readDouble();
}

}
```

> The method `readInput` throws an `EOFException` when it tries to read past the end of a file because `readUTF`, `readInt`, and `readDouble` each throw an `EOFException` when they try to read past the end of a file.

36. When opening a binary file for output in the ways discussed in this chapter, might an exception be thrown? What kind of exception? When opening a binary file for input in the ways discussed in this chapter, might an exception be thrown? What kind of exception?

37. Suppose a binary file contains three numbers written to the file with the method `writeDouble` of the class `DataOutputStream`. Suppose further that your program reads all three numbers with three invocations of the method `readDouble` of the class `DataInputStream`. If your program invokes `readDouble` to try to read a fourth number from the file, what will happen?

Case Study

Writing and Reading a File of Records

task specification

You have been hired by an international conservation group to write software to keep track of its records on endangered species. The group wants you to write software to store species records in a file and to display all the records for a specified file on a terminal screen.

file type and class for data

You decide that the records should be stored in a binary file, since that is the most efficient kind of file to use.

You decide to structure your software by using two classes, as well as the application program that will use these classes. One class is `Species`, which we defined in Display 9.15/page 635. This gives you a structure for the species records and a method to read and write species records to a binary file. The second class is a class with a method to create a file of records, a method to read a file of records and display them on the screen, and any auxiliary methods needed for these two tasks. You decide to call this class `SpeciesFiler`. The final program can then consist of an interface that invokes methods of the class `SpeciesFiler`.

data

You decide that the class `SpeciesFiler` should have the following instance variables to hold data:

> `fileName`: An instance variable of type `String` to hold a file name.
>
> `inputStream`: An instance variable of type `DataInputStream` to connect to files for reading input from a file.
>
> `outputStream`: An instance variable of type `DataOutputStream` to connect to files for writing output to a file.

actions

You decide that the class `SpeciesFiler` should have at least the following methods:

> `buildAFile`: A method that will ask the user for a file name and then fill the file with records read from the keyboard.
>
> `viewAFile`: A method that will ask the user for a file name and display the records in the named file to the screen.

You notice that both these methods have a common subtask, namely, obtaining a file name from the user. So, you decide to include a method for obtaining a file name from the user. Because this is just a helping method, you decide to make it a private method, so its definition will begin

getFileName

```
private String getFileName(String prompt)
```

The code for `getFileName` is similar to other code we have seen and can be easily filled in. The class outline, as you have developed it so far, is shown in Display 9.16. Since it is routine, you fill in the code for the method `getFileName`.

Display 9.16 Outline of the Class `SpeciesFiler`

```
public class SpeciesFiler
{
    private String fileName = null;
    private DataInputStream inputStream = null;
    private DataOutputStream outputStream = null;

    /*********************************************
     *Obtains a file name from the user and fills the
     *file with species records.
     *********************************************/
    public void buildAFile()
            <You still must complete the definition of buildAFile.>

    /**********************************************
     *Obtains a file name from the user and displays the
     *file content to the screen.
     *Precondition: The file must be a binary file of
     *the kind created by buildAFile.
     **********************************************/
    public void viewAFile()
                <You still must complete the definition of viewAFile.>

    private String getFileName(String prompt)
    {
        String nameString = null;
        System.out.println(prompt);
        nameString = SavitchIn.readLineWord();
        return nameString;
    }

}
```

Next you consider the method buildAFile. The class Species has a full complement of input and output methods, so buildAFile can use an object of the class
Species to obtain a record from the user and store it in the file. You thus write the
following pseudocode for the method buildAFile:

buildAFile

```
fileName = getFileName("Enter name of file to hold records:");
outputStream =
          new DataOutputStream(new FileOutputStream(fileName));
Species oneSpecies = new Species();
Do the following while there are still records to be placed in the file:
{
    oneSpecies.readInput();
    oneSpecies.writeOutput(outputStream);
}
outputStream.close();
```

It is fairly routine to convert this pseudocode to Java code. The resulting definition
is shown in Display 9.17. You realize that the user might overwrite a file if she or he
gives the name of an existing file. So, you also add a warning to the user.

viewAFile

Next you turn your attention to the method viewAFile. You decide to separate
the ordinary case from the exceptional cases. One important exceptional case is
when the user enters the name of a file that does not exist. You decide that if you
process the ordinary case as if this would not happen, then if the user does enter the
name of a nonexistent file, Java will throw a FileNotFoundException. So, you
decide to write a method, called viewAFileNoProblems, and to invoke this method
in a *try*-block. Thus, the method viewAFile can be defined as follows:

```
public void viewAFile()
{
    try
    {
        viewAFileNoProblems();
    }
    catch(FileNotFoundException e)
    {
        System.out.println("Cannot find a file named "
                                        + fileName);
    }
    catch(IOException e)
    {
        System.out.println("Error reading from file "
                                        + fileName);
    }
}
```

Even though you have not yet defined the method viewAFileNoProblems, you
know that if the named file is not found, then it will throw a FileNotFoundException, and if something else goes wrong it might throw an IOException.

viewAFile-
NoProblems

You now turn your attention to the method viewAFileNoProblems. Obtaining
the file name and connecting the file to a stream named by the instance variable
inputStream is all routine. The part of the method definition that requires more

Display 9.17 **The Method** `buildAFile` **of the Class** `SpeciesFiler`

```java
/***************************************************************
 *Obtains a file name from the user and fills the file with species records.
 ***************************************************************/
public void buildAFile()
{
    System.out.println("This program will record the species records");
    System.out.println("you enter and store them in a file.");
    fileName = getFileName("Enter name of file to hold records:");
    System.out.println("If there already exists a file");
    System.out.println("with that name, the data will be lost.");
    System.out.println("OK to continue with the file "
                        + fileName + "? (y/n)");
    char ans = SavitchIn.readLineNonwhiteChar();
    if ((ans == 'n') && (ans == 'N'))
        System.out.println("File " + fileName + " not changed.");
    else
    {
        try
        {
            outputStream =
                new DataOutputStream(new FileOutputStream(fileName));

            Species oneSpecies = new Species();
            System.out.println("Ready to start entering?(y/n)");
            ans = SavitchIn.readLineNonwhiteChar();
            while ((ans == 'y') || (ans == 'Y'))
            {
                oneSpecies.readInput();
                oneSpecies.writeOutput(outputStream);
                System.out.println("Enter another species?(y/n)");
                ans = SavitchIn.readLineNonwhiteChar();
            }
            outputStream.close();
            System.out.println("Species records written to the file "
                                + fileName);
        }
        catch(FileNotFoundException e)
        {
            System.out.println("Error opening file " + fileName);
        }
        catch(IOException e)
        {
            System.out.println("Error writing to file " + fileName);
        }
    }
}
```

attention is the input/output loop. That loop will continually read a record from the file and write it to the screen.

The heart of the loop body for reading one record from the file and writing it to the screen can be as follows (where oneSpecies is an object of the class Species):

```
oneSpecies.readInput(inputStream);
oneSpecies.writeOutput();
```

loop design

Whenever you design a loop, there are two main things that you need to consider: (1) the loop body and (2) a mechanism for ending the loop. You have already designed the heart of the loop body, but you still need a mechanism to determine how the loop will end. The pseudocode for the entire loop can be

Do the following until all records in the file have been read:

```
{

        oneSpecies.readInput(inputStream);
        oneSpecies.writeOutput();

}
```

checking for end of file

To complete the Java code for this loop, you need some mechanism to determine when the end of the file is reached. In this case, you know that when the end of the file is reached, the method invocation oneSpecies.readInput(input-Stream) will throw an exception in the class EOFException (because that is how we defined the method readInput of the class Species in Display 9.15/page 635). So you terminate the loop when an EOFException is thrown. To do this, you write a loop that looks like an infinite loop, but you place it in a *try*-block to end the loop gracefully when an EOFException is thrown. So, your loop now looks like the following:

```
try
{
    while (true)
    {

        oneSpecies.readInput(inputStream);
        oneSpecies.writeOutput();
    }
}
catch(EOFException e)
{
    System.out.println("No more records in the file "
                                        + fileName");
}
```

slowing down the output

When you try out this loop in a test program, you see that there are some problems in how it displays data on the screen. If there are more records than can fit on one screen, they will go by so fast that the user can't read them. You need some way to stop the screen after each record is displayed. One easy way to stop the screen is to ask for some input after each record is displayed. But what input should you ask for? None is needed. The simplest thing to do is to ask the user to press the enter key (return key) when she or he is ready to read the next record. That simple input, of pressing the enter key, can be read as follows:

```
String junk = SavitchIn.readLine();
```

Thus, you can slow down the screen by using the following loop:

```
try
{
    while (true)
    {
        oneSpecies.readInput(inputStream);
        oneSpecies.writeOutput();
        System.out.println("Press Enter to see more.");
        String junk = SavitchIn.readLine();
    }
}
catch(EOFException e)
{
    System.out.println("No more records in the file "
                                        + fileName);
}
```

The string read into the variable `junk` will be the empty string, but you really do not care what string it is, because it is just discarded. The complete method definition for the method `viewAFileNoProblems` is shown in Display 9.18. That display also has the complete final definition of the class `SpeciesFiler`.

So far, you have simply developed a lot of tools. You have not even begun to write the application program that you contracted to write. However, with all these tools, it will be very easy to write the application program. All you need to do in the application program is present the user with a menu that chooses between an invocation of `buildAFile`, `viewAFile`, and quitting the program. So, you quickly (but carefully) write the program shown in Display 9.19.

application program

? Self-Test Questions

38. The following appears in the program in Display 9.13/page 626:

```
try
{
    while (true)
    {
        n = inputStream.readInt();
        System.out.println(n);
    }
}
catch(EOFException e)
{
    System.out.println("End of reading from file.");
}
```

< Exercise continued on page 648.>

Display 9.18 A File-Handling Class *(Part 1 of 2)*

```java
import java.io.*;

/****************************************************
*A class to build files of species records and to display
*the file contents on the screen. Uses the class Species.
****************************************************/
public class SpeciesFiler
{
    private String fileName = null;
    private DataInputStream inputStream = null;
    private DataOutputStream outputStream = null;

    /***********************************************************
    *Obtains a file name from the user and fills the file with species records.
    ***********************************************************/
    public void buildAFile()
            <The rest of the method definition is the same as in Display 9.17/page 641.>

    //Throws a FileNotFoundException if there is no file with the given name.
    private void viewAFileNoProblems() throws IOException
    {
        System.out.println("This program will display all the species");
        System.out.println("records contained in the file you specify.");
        fileName = getFileName("Enter name of file with records:");
        inputStream = new DataInputStream(new FileInputStream(fileName));
        Species oneSpecies = new Species();
        System.out.println("Records from the file " + fileName + ":");
        try
        {
            while (true)
            {
                oneSpecies.readInput(inputStream);
                oneSpecies.writeOutput();
                System.out.println("Press Enter to see more.");
                String junk = SavitchIn.readLine();
            }
        }
        catch(EOFException e)
        {
            System.out.println("No more records in the file "
                                                    + fileName);
        }
        inputStream.close();
        System.out.println("File " + fileName + " put away.");
    }
```

Display 9.18   A File-Handling Class (Part 2 of 2)

```
/*************************************************
 *Obtains a file name from the user and displays the
 *file contents to the screen.
 *Precondition: The file must be a binary file of
 *the kind created by buildAFile.
 *************************************************/
public void viewAFile()
{

    try
    {
        viewAFileNoProblems();
    }
    catch(FileNotFoundException e)
    {
        System.out.println("Cannot find a file named "
                                            + fileName);
    }
    catch(IOException e)
    {
        System.out.println("Error reading from file "
                                            + fileName);
    }

}



private String getFileName(String prompt)
    <The rest of the method definition is the same as in Display 9.16/page 639.>




}
```

Display 9.19   Application Program for Files of Species Records *(Part 1 of 2)*

```java
import java.io.*;

/************************************************************
 *Program to store species records in a file and/or display all
 *the records in a file on a terminal screen.
 ************************************************************/
public class FileServer
{
    public static void main(String[] args)
    {
        SpeciesFiler filer = new SpeciesFiler();
        System.out.print("This program can build and");
        System.out.println(" display files of species records.");

        char ans;
        boolean done = false;
        do
        {
            System.out.print("Enter choice: ");
            System.out.println(
                "B to build a file. V to view a file. Q to quit.");
            ans = SavitchIn.readLineNonwhiteChar();
            switch (ans)
            {
                case 'B':
                case 'b':
                    filer.buildAFile();
                    break;
                case 'V':
                case 'v':
                    filer.viewAFile();
                    break;
                case 'Q':
                case 'q':
                    done = true;
                    break;
                default:
                    System.out.println("That is not a valid choice.");
                    break;
            }
        }while ( ! done);
        System.out.println("File service closing down.");
    }
}
```

Display 9.19 Application Program for Files of Species Records *(Part 2 of 2)*

Sample Screen Dialogue

```
This program can build and display files of species records.
Enter choice: B to build a file. V to view a file. Q to quit.
B
This program will record the species records
you enter and store them in a file.
Enter name of file to hold records:
species.dat
If there already exists a file named species.dat
then all the data in that file will be lost.
OK to continue with the file species.dat? (y/n)
y
Ready to start entering records?(y/n)
y
What is the species name?
California Condor
What is the population of the species?
40
Enter growth rate (percent increase per year):
5
Enter another species?(y/n)
y
What is the species name?
Black Rhino
What is the population of the species?
100
Enter growth rate (percent increase per year):
2
Enter another species?(y/n)
n
Species records written to the file species.dat
Enter choice: B to build a file. V to view a file. Q to quit.
Q
File service closing down.
```

Why isn't this an infinite loop?

39. The method to input records from a file that we gave in Display 9.15/page 635 throws an exception in the class `EOFException` whenever it tries to read past the end of a file, but the method definition begins

```
public void readInput(DataInputStream inputStream)
                                       throws IOException
```

Why doesn't it say *throws* `EOFException`?

40. Write a complete Java program that will read all the numbers in a binary file named `temperatures` and will write the numbers to the screen, one per line. Assume the file consists entirely of numbers written to it with the method `writeDouble`.

9.4 | File Objects and File Names

> *An ounce of prevention is worth a pound of cure.*
>
> **Common saying**

In this section, we describe the class `File`, which is not an I/O stream class but is very useful when doing file I/O. This is followed by a subsection that discusses how Java handles path names for files. If you do not know about file path names, you can skim that subsection. However, you should eventually learn about path names and should eventually give that subsection a careful reading. The details of file path names depend on the operating system you are using. They are not part of the Java language.

Using the `File` Class

You can use the class named `File` to check properties of files. You can check things like whether or nor there is a file with a specified name, and whether or not the file is readable. Display 9.20 gives a sample program using the class `File` when reading a *binary* file. Display 9.21 gives a sample program using the class `File` when reading a *text* file. If you have only covered one of the two kinds of files (text files or binary files), then you need only read the sample that applies to you. (Both programs illustrate the same point.)

The `File` class is like a wrapper class for file names. A string like `"treasure.dat"` may be a file name, but only has string properties. It has no file-name properties. The object

```
new File("treasure.dat")
```

is not simply a string. It is an object that knows it is supposed to name a file.

Suppose you create a `File` object and name the object `fileObject` with the following code:

```
File fileObject = new File("treasure.dat");
```

exists   You can then use the method named `exists`, of the class `File`, to test whether there is any file with the name `treasure.dat`. For example,

Display 9.20 Using the File Class when Handling Binary Files

```
/**************************************************
 *Demonstrates use of the class File with binary files.
 **************************************************/
import java.io.*;

public class FileClassDemo1
{
    public static void main(String[] args)
    {
        String name = null;
        File fileObject = null;

        System.out.println("I will show you the first string");
        System.out.println("in a binary file you name.");
        System.out.println("The first data item in the file");
        System.out.println("must be a string.");

        System.out.println("Enter file name:");
        name = SavitchIn.readLineWord();
        fileObject = new File(name);
        while ((!fileObject.exists()) || (!fileObject.canRead()))
        {
            if ( ! fileObject.exists())
                System.out.println("No such file");
            else if ( ! fileObject.canRead())
                System.out.println("That file is not readable.");
            System.out.println("Enter file name again:");
            name = SavitchIn.readLineWord();
            fileObject = new File(name);
        }

        try
        {
            DataInputStream fileInput =
                    new DataInputStream(new FileInputStream(name));
            System.out.println("The first string in the file is:");
            String firstString = fileInput.readUTF();
            System.out.println(firstString);

            fileInput.close();
        }
        catch(IOException e)
        {
            System.out.println("Problem reading from file.");
        }
    }
}
```

If you have not yet covered binary files, you can skip this display, but should study Display 9.21/page 650, which does a similar thing with a text file.

If you wish, you can use fileObject instead of name as the argument to FileInputStream.

Display 9.21   Using the File Class when Handling Text Files

```
/***********************************************
 *Demonstrates use of the class File with text files.
 ***********************************************/
import java.io.*;

public class FileClassDemo2
{
    public static void main(String[] args)
    {
        String name = null;
        File fileObject = null;

        System.out.println("I will show you the first line");
        System.out.println("in a text file you name.");
        System.out.println("The file must contain one or more lines.");

        System.out.println("Enter file name:");
        name = SavitchIn.readLineWord();
        fileObject = new File(name);
        while ((!fileObject.exists()) || (!fileObject.canRead()))
        {
            if ( ! fileObject.exists())
                System.out.println("No such file");
            else if ( ! fileObject.canRead())
                System.out.println("That file is not readable.");
            System.out.println("Enter file name again:");
            name = SavitchIn.readLineWord();
            fileObject = new File(name);
        }

        try
        {
            BufferedReader fileInput =
                    new BufferedReader(new FileReader(name));
            System.out.println("The first line in the file is:");
            String firstLine = fileInput.readLine();
            System.out.println(firstLine);
            fileInput.close();
        }
        catch(IOException e)
        {
            System.out.println("Problem reading from file.");
        }
    }
}
```

> If you have not yet covered text files, you can skip this display, but should study Display 9.20/page 649, which does a similar thing with a binary file.

> If you wish, you can use fileObject instead of name as the argument to FileReader.

```
if ( ! fileObject.exists())
    System.out.println("No file by that name.");
```

If there is a file with that name, you can tell if the operating system will let you read from the file with the method canRead. For example,

canRead

```
if ( ! fileObject.canRead())
    System.out.println("Not allowed to read from that file.");
```

Most operating systems let you designate some files as not readable or as only readable by certain people. This is a good way to check whether you or somebody else has inadvertently (or intentionally) made a file nonreadable.

Notice the annotation in Display 9.20/page 649 and/or Display 9.21/page 650. It says that you can use the file object as an argument for a certain stream constructor in place of a file name argument. You can usually (but not always) use an object of type File as an argument for a stream constructor whenever you can use a file name as the argument. In particular the classes FileInputStream, FileOutput-Stream, and FileReader each accept a File object as an argument.[1]

Display 9.22 lists some of the methods in the class File.

■ **Java Tip**
Using Path Names

When giving a file name as an argument to a constructor for the class File (or any-place else you need a file name), you may use a simple file name, in which case it is assumed that the file is in the same directory (folder) as the one in which the program is run. You can also use a full or relative path name. A **path name** gives not only the name of the file, but also tells what directory (folder) the file is in. A **full path name**, as the name suggests, give a complete path name. A **relative path name**, gives the path to the file starting in the directory that your program is in. Path names have to do with your operating system rather than the Java language. The way that you give path names depends on your particular operating system, and we will not go into all the details here.

path names

A typical UNIX path name is

```
/user/smith/home.work/java/FileClassDemo.java
```

To create a File object from this and name the object programFile, you use

```
File programFile =
    new File("/user/smith/home.work/java/FileClassDemo.java");
```

and this will work even if the program is run on a computer with an operating system that uses a different syntax for path names (such as a Windows operating system).

A typical Windows path name is

```
D:\Work\Java\Programs\FileClassDemo.java
```

---

1. If you have not yet read about binary files (Section 9.3), you may not know about the class FileInputStream. If you have not yet read about text files (Section 9.2), you may not know about the class FileReader. If you do not know about either of these files, just ignore the reference to that class.

To create a `File` object from this and name the object `programFile`, you use

```
File programFile = new File(
               "D:\\Work\\Java\\Programs\\FileClassDemo.java");
```

Note that you need to use \\ in place of \, since otherwise Java will interpret expressions such as \W as escape characters. Although you must worry about a backslash \ in a quoted string, this problem does not occur with names read in from the keyboard. Suppose you run a program like the one in Display 9.20/page 649 or Display 9.21/page 650, and suppose part of the dialog is as follows, where the second line is input from the user:

```
Enter file name:
D:\Work\Java\Programs\FileClassDemo.java
```

This will be understood. The user need not type in

```
D:\\Work\\Java\\Programs\\FileClassDemo.java
```

Display 9.22 Some Methods in the Class `File`

```
public boolean exists()
```
Tests whether there is a file with the name used to create the `File` object.

```
public boolean canRead()
```
Tests if the program can read from the file.

```
public boolean canWrite()
```
Tests if the program can write to the file.

```
public boolean delete()
```
Tries to delete the file. Returns *true* if it was able to delete the file. Returns *false* if it was unable to delete the file.

```
public long length()
```
Returns the length of the file in bytes.

```
public String getName()
```
Returns the name of the file. (Note this is not a path name, just the simple name.)

```
public String getPath()
```
Returns the path name of the file.

and in fact, the use of \\ in input might (or might not) produce an incorrect reading of the file name. When the user enters input, Java knows that \J must be the backslash character followed by a J and is not an escape character. It knows this because everything the user types in is a character.

One way to avoid these escape character problems altogether is to use UNIX conventions when writing path names. A Java program will except a path name written in either Windows or UNIX format, even if it is run on a computer with an operating system that does not match the syntax. Thus, an alternate way to create the File object programFile is

```
File programFile = new File(
            "D:/Work/Java/Programs/FileClassDemo.java");
```

and this will work for a Java program when run on a computer with a Windows operating system, a UNIX operating system, or any other operating system.

? Self-Test Questions

41. Write a complete Java program that will ask the user for a file name, test if the file exists, and if the file exists, will ask the user if it should be deleted or not, and then delete it or not as the user requests.

CHAPTER SUMMARY

■ Files that are considered to be strings of characters and that look like characters to your program and your editor are called *text files*. Files whose contents must be handled as strings of binary digits are called *binary files*.

■ Your program can use the class PrintWriter to write to a text file and can use the class BufferedReader to read from a text file.

■ Your program can use the class DataOutputStream to write to a binary file and can use the class DataInputStream to read from a binary file.

■ When reading from a file, you should always check for the end of a file and do something appropriate if the end of the file is reached. The way that you test for the end of a file depends on the method you are using to read from the file.

■ You can read a file name from the keyboard into a variable of type String and use that variable in place of a file name.

CHAPTER SUMMARY

- The class `File` can be used to check to see if there is a file with a given name. It can also check to see if your program is allowed to read the file and/or allowed to write to the file.

? ANSWERS to Self-Test Questions

1. If a program sends its output to the screen, the output goes away when (or soon after) the program ends. A program that sends its output to a file has made a (more or less) permanent copy of its output. Files provide you with a way to store data permanently. The contents of a file remain until a person or program changes the file. If your program sends its output to a file, the output file will remain after the program has finished running.

2. From a file to the program.

3. Text files are the kind of files you write and read using an editor. Text files can be thought of as containing characters. Binary files represent data in a way that is not convenient to read with a text editor, but binary files can be written to and read from a program in a very efficient way. Binary files represent data using the same format as the one used to store the data in the computer's main memory.

4.
```
PrintWriter outStream =
        new PrintWriter(new FileOutputStream("sam"));
```

5.
```
PrintWriter outStream =
        new PrintWriter(new FileOutputStream("sam", true));
```

6. A `FileNotFoundException` would be thrown if the file does not exist *and* cannot be created, for example because there is a directory (folder) named `out.txt`. Note that if the file does not exist, but can be created, then no exception is thrown. If you answered `IOException`, you are not wrong, because a `FileNotFoundException` is an `IOException`. However, the better answer is the more specific exception class, namely `File-NotFoundException`.

7. No. That is why we use an object of the class `FileOutputStream` as an argument. So, the correct way to express the code displayed in the questions is as follows:
```
PrintWriter outputStream =
        new PrintWriter(new FileOutputStream("myFile.txt"));
```

8.
```
PrintWriter textStream =
        new PrintWriter(new FileOutputStream("dobedo"));
```

9.
```
BufferedReader inputStream =
            new BufferedReader(new FileReader("dobedo"));
```

10. No, but the method `read` in the class `BufferedReader` can be used to read a single character, and so is approximately equivalent to the method `readChar` in the class `SavitchIn`. However, the method `read` in the class `BufferedReader` returns its character as an *int* value and needs a type cast to make it into a *char* value.

11. Both `read` and/or `readLine` in the class `BufferedReader` might throw an `IOException`.

12. The *try*-block in Display 9.5 is larger so that it includes the invocations of the method `readLine`, which might throw an `IOException`. The methods `println` in Display 9.1 does not throw any exceptions.

13. The method `readLine` returns a value of type `String`. The method `read` reads a single *character*, but it returns it as a value of type *int*. To get the value of type *char*, you need to do a type cast.

14. When the method `readLine` tries to read beyond the end of a file, it returns the value *null*. Thus, you can test for the end of a file by testing for *null*.

15. The method `read` reads a single *character*, but it returns it as a value of type *int*. To get the value of type *char*, you need to do a type cast.

16. When the method `read` tries to read beyond the end of a file, it returns the value −1. Thus, you can test for the end of a file by testing for the value −1. This works because all true characters return a positive *int* value.

17. The classes `FileReader` and `FileOutputStream` have constructors that take a file name as an argument. The classes `PrintWriter` and `BufferedReader` do not have constructors that take a file name as an argument.

18. Yes, it is equivalent to the following (except that, in the following, the object `readerObject` is not given a name):

```
BufferedReader inputStream =
        new BufferedReader(new FileReader("myFile.txt"));
```

19.
```
DataOutputStream toFile =
    new DataOutputStream(new FileOutputStream("stuff.data"));
```

20.
```
toFile.writeDouble(x1);
toFile.writeDouble(x2);
toFile.writeDouble(x3);
```

21. `toFile.close();`

22.
```
DataOutputStream appendToFile =
        new DataOutputStream(
                new FileOutputStream("records.data", true));
```

23. `import java.io.*;`

24.
```
DataInputStream fromFile =
        new DataInputStream(new FileInputStream("stuff.data"));
```

25.
```
double x1, x2, x3;
x1 = fromFile.readDouble();
x2 = fromFile.readDouble();
x3 = fromFile.readDouble();
```

26. `fromFile.close();`

27. If a number is written to a file with `writeInt`, then it should only be read with `readInt`. If you use `readLong` or `readDouble` to read the number, something will go wrong.

28. You should not use `readUTF` to read a string from a text file. You should only use `readUTF` to read a string from a binary file. Moreover, the string should have been written to that file using `writeUFT` (or something equivalent).

29.
```
DataOutputStream writer =
        new DataOutputStream(new FileOutputStream(theFile));
```

30.
```
DataInputStream reader =
        new DataInputStream(new FileInputStream(theFile));
```

31.
```
import java.io.*;

public class FileNameExercise
{
    public static void main(String[] args)
    {
        String fileName = null;//to use fileName in catch-block,
                               //must declare it outside of try-block.
        try
        {
            System.out.println("Enter file name:");
            fileName = SavitchIn.readLineWord();
            DataInputStream inputStream =
                new DataInputStream(new FileInputStream(fileName));
```

```
         System.out.println("The first thing in the file");
         System.out.println(fileName + " is");
         String first = inputStream.readUTF();
         System.out.println(first);
         inputStream.close();
      }
   catch(IOException e)
      {
         System.out.println("Problem with input from file "
                                      + fileName);
      }
    }
}
```

32. It will not work because `DataInputStream` does not have a constructor with a parameter of type `String`. The correct way to accomplish the desired effect is

    ```
    DataInputStream inputStream =
          new DataInputStream(new FileInputStream("mydata.dat"));
    ```

33. The class `FileInputStream` does not have any of the methods `readInt`, `readDouble`, or `readUTF`.

34. Yes.

35. No.

36. When opening a binary file for either output or input in the ways discussed in this chapter, a `FileNotFoundException` might be thrown. If you answered `IOException`, you are not wrong, because a `FileNot-FoundException` is an `IOException`. However, the better answer is the more specific exception class, namely `FileNotFoundException`.

37. An `EOFException` will be thrown.

38. Because when the end of the file is reached, an exception will be thrown, and that will end the entire *try*-block.

39. Because `EOFException` is a derived class of `IOException`, every `EOFEx-ception` is also an `IOException`. So the *throws*-clause *throws* `IOEx-ception` accounts for any exceptions of type `EOFException`.

40.
```
import java.io.*;

public class TemperatureShow
{
    public static void main(String[] args)
    {
```

```java
        try
        {
            DataInputStream inputStream =
                    new DataInputStream(new FileInputStream(
                                            "temperatures")));
            double t;

            System.out.println(
                        "Numbers from the file temperatures:");

            try
            {
                while (true)
                {
                    t = inputStream.readDouble();
                    System.out.println(t);
                }
            }
            catch(EOFException e)
            {
                //Do nothing
            }

            System.out.println("End of reading from file.");
            inputStream.close();
        }
        catch(IOException e)
        {
            System.out.println("Problem reading from file.");
        }
    }
}
```

41.

```java
import java.io.*;

public class FileClassExercise
{
    public static void main(String[] args)
    {
        String name = null;
        File fileObject = null;

        System.out.print("Enter a file name and I will ");
        System.out.println("tell you if it exists.");
        name = SavitchIn.readLineWord();
        fileObject = new File(name);
```

```java
if (fileObject.exists())
{
    System.out.println("I found the file " + name);
    System.out.println("Delete the file? (y/n)");
    char ans = SavitchIn.readLineNonwhiteChar();

    if ((ans == 'y') || (ans == 'Y'))
    {
        System.out.println(
                    "If you delete the file " + name);
        System.out.println(
                    "all data in the file will");
        System.out.println("be lost. Delete? (y/n)");
        ans = SavitchIn.readLineNonwhiteChar();

        if ((ans == 'y') || (ans == 'Y'))
        {
            if (fileObject.delete())
                System.out.println("File deleted.");
            else
                System.out.println(
                                "Cannot delete file.");
        }
        else
            System.out.println("File not deleted.");
    }
    else
        System.out.println("File not deleted.");
}
else
    System.out.println("I cannot find " + name);
    }
}
```

? PROGRAMMING EXERCISES

1. Write a program that searches a file of numbers and outputs, the largest number in the file, the smallest number in the file, and the average of all the numbers in the file. The output should go to the screen. Do not assume that the numbers in the file are in any special order. Your program should obtain the file name from the user. Text file version: the file should be a text file with one number per line. Binary file version: the file should be a binary file that consists entirely of numbers of type *double* that were written using `writeDouble`.

2. Write a program that reads a file of numbers of type *int* and outputs all the numbers to another file, but without any repeated numbers. Assume that the input file is sorted from smallest first to largest last. After the program is run, the new file will contain all the numbers in the original file but no number will appear more than once in the file. The numbers in the

output file should also be sorted from smallest to largest. Your program should obtain both file names from the user. Text file version: the file should be a text file with one number per line. Binary file version: the file should be a binary file that consists entirely of numbers of type *int* that were written using `writeInt`.

3. Write a program that will check a text file for a number of format and punctuation matters. The program will ask for an input file name and an output file name and will then copy all the text from the input file to the output file but with the following two changes: (1) Any string of two or more blanks symbols is replaced by a single blanks. (2) All sentences start with an uppercase letter. Define a sentence as beginning after a period, question mark, or exclamation mark followed by one or more whitespace characters.

4. Display 9.19/page 646 allows you to write records of endangered species to a file. Write another program that can search a file created by the program in Display 9.19 and show the user any requested record. The user gives the file name. The user then enters the name of the species and the program displays the entire record for that species or else it gives a message saying it has no record on that species. Allow the user to enter additional species names until the user says she or he is finished.

5. Display 9.19/page 646 allows you to write records of endangered species to a file. Write another program that reads from a file created by the program in Display 9.19 and outputs the following information to the screen: the record of the species with the smallest population and the record of the species with the largest population. Do not assume that the records in the file are in any particular order. The user gives the file name. Use the version of the class for species given in Display 9.15/page 635 and use the input method in that species class definition.

6. Display 9.19/page 646 allows you to write records of endangered species to a file. Write another program that reads from the file created by the program in Display 9.19 and outputs the records to another file. However, the records in the output file should not show the same population figure as in the input file, but should instead give the population as what it would be in 100 years given that species growth rate. You will want to use the method `projectedPopulation` of the class `Species`.

7. Write a program similar to `FileServer` in Display 9.19/page 646 that allows you to write and read records of type `PetRecord` (Display 5.19/page 351) to a file. The program asks the user if the user wants to write to a file or read from a file. In either case. the program next asks for the file name. If the user asked to write to a file, the user is then allowed to enter as many records as the user wants. If the user is asked to read from a file, then the user is shown all records in the file. Be sure the records do not go by so quickly that the user cannot read the records.

8. Write a program that reads `PetRecords` from a file (created by the program from Programming Exercise 6) and outputs the following informa-

tion to the screen: the name and weight of the largest pet, the name and weight of smallest pet, the name and age of the youngest pet, and the name and age of the oldest pet.

CHAPTER 10

DYNAMIC DATA STRUCTURES

10.1 VECTORS 665

Using Vectors 666

Programming Tip Adding to a Vector 672

Gotcha Vector Elements Are of Type
Object 674

Comparing Vectors and Arrays 674

Gotcha Using capacity Instead of
size 676

Java Tip Use `trimToSize` to Save
Memory 677

Gotcha Using the Method clone 677

10.2 LINKED DATA STRUCTURES 679

Linked Lists 679

Gotcha Null Pointer Exception 689

Gotcha Privacy Leaks 689

Node Inner Classes 690
Iterators 691

Programming Tip Internal and External
Iterators 696

Exception Handling with Linked
Lists 697
Variations on a Linked List 708
Other Linked Data Structures 709

Chapter Summary 710
Answers to Self-Test Questions 711
Programming Exercises 717

DYNAMIC DATA STRUCTURES

> *All is in flux, nothing stays still*
>
> **Heraclitus**

A **data structure** is a construct used to organize data in a specific way. For example, an array is a kind of data structure. Each data structure organizes data in its own particular way. In this chapter we discuss two kinds of data structures that can grow (and shrink) in size while your program is running: vectors and linked data structures. Vectors are similar to arrays but offer more flexibility in some situations. Linked data structures are a general group of data structures that can grow and shrink in a wide variety of ways. Although there are many different kinds of linked data structures, we will emphasize one simple but useful linked data structure know as a *linked list*.

Objectives

Become familiar with vectors and how they are used in Java.

Learn what a linked data structure is and how it can be realized in Java.

Find out how to manipulate linked lists.

Learn what iterators are and how to create and use them.

Prerequisites

Sections 10.1 on vectors and 10.2 on linked data structures may be read in either order.

You need to read Chapters 1 through 6 in order to fully understand this chapter. You also need some familiarity with basic inheritance and basic exception handling. The details are as follows:

Section	Prerequisite
Section 10.1 on vectors	Chapters 1–6 and Section 7.1 of Chapter 7, and Section 8.1 of Chapter 8
	.

Sections 10.2 on linked data structures (omitting the subsection **Exception Handling with Linked Lists**.)	Chapters 1–6, and some knowledge of inner classes to do the last few sections.
The subsection of Sections 10.2 entitled *Exception Handling with Linked Lists.*	Chapters 1–6 and Chapter 8

The last parts of Section 10.2 require material on inner classes covered in an optional section of Chapter 5. The beginning of Section 10.2 can be covered without knowing anything about inner classes. But the last parts of that section, starting with the subsection entitled *Node Inner Classes*, does require a knowledge of inner classes. Inner classes are covered in Section 5.8 of Chapter 5 (*Inner Classes (Optional)*) and in Section 14.4 of Chapter 14 (*Inner Classes (Optional)*). You need to have read only one of these two subsections on inner classes in order to understand the last parts of Section 10.2.

10.1 | Vectors

> *"Well, I'll eat it," said Alice, "and if it makes me grow larger, I can reach the key; and if it makes me grow smaller, I can creep under the door; so either way I'll get into the garden. . . ."*
>
> **Lewis Carroll, Alice's Adventures in Wonderland**

Vectors can be thought of as arrays that can grow (and shrink) in length while your program is running. In Java, you can read in the length of an array when the program is run, but once your program creates an array of that length, it cannot change the length of the array. For example, suppose you write a program to record customer orders for a mailorder house, and suppose you store all the orders for one customer in an array of objects of some class called `OrderItem`. You could ask the user how many items she or he will order, store the number in a variable called `numberOfItems`, and then create the array `item` with the following:

compared to arrays

```
OrderItem[] item = new OrderItem[numberOfItems];
```

But, suppose the customer enters `numberOfItems` items and then decides to order another item? There is no way to increase the size of the array `item`. There are ways around this problem with arrays, but they are all rather complicated and all require creating a new array. Vectors serve the same purpose as arrays except that they can change length while the program is running. So, a vector could handle the customer's extra order without any problems.

If vectors are like arrays but have the nice added feature of being able to change length, then why don't we just always use vectors instead of arrays? It often seems that every silver lining has a cloud, and that is true of vectors as well. There are two main problems with vectors: (1) They are less efficient than arrays, and (2) The elements in a vector must be objects; they cannot be values of a primitive type, such as *int*, *double*, or *char*. For example, if you want a vector of *int*s, you must

which to use?

simulate this with a vector of `Integers`, where `Integer` is a wrapper class whose objects simulate *int* values. Thus, it is best to use arrays whenever you know that the length of the array does not need to change, and to use vectors when the capacity of the vector will change often and by unpredictable amounts.

Using Vectors

Vectors are used much like arrays, but there are some important differences. First, the definition of the class `Vector` is not provided automatically. The definition is in the package `jave.util`, and so any code that uses the class `Vector` must contain the following, normally at the start of the file:

java.util.*

```
import java.util.*;
```

A vector is created and named in the same way as objects of any class. For example,

```
Vector v = new Vector(20);
```

capacity

This makes `v` the name of a vector that has an *initial* **capacity** of 20 items. When we say that a vector has a certain capacity, we mean that it has been allocated memory for that many items, but if it needs to hold more items, the system will automatically allocate more memory. By carefully choosing the capacity of a vector, you can (often) make your code more efficient, but it has no effect on what you can do with the vector. If you choose your capacity to be large enough, then the system will not need to reallocate memory too often, and so your program should run faster. On the other hand, if you make your capacity too large, you will waste storage. However, no matter what capacity you choose, you can still do anything you want with the vector. Other constructors, as well as most of the other methods for the class `Vector`, are described in Display 10.1. Which constructor you use can effect efficiency, but has no other effect on how the vector can be used.

Creating and Naming a Vector

An object of the class `Vector` is created and named in the same way as any other object.

Examples:

```
Vector v = new Vector();
Vector v2 = new Vector(30);
```

When a number is given as an argument to the constructor, that number determines the initial capacity of the vector.

---

no square
brackets

Vectors can be used like arrays, but they do not have the array square bracket notation. If you would use the following for an array of strings a,

```
a[index] = "Hi Mom!";
```

then to do the analogous thing for a vector v, you would use

set-
ElementAt

```
v.setElementAt("Hi Mom!", index);
```

Constructors

public `Vector(`*int* `initialCapacity,` *int* `capacityIncrement)`
 Constructs an empty vector with the specified initial capacity and capacity increment. When the vector needs to grow, it will add room for `capacityIncrement` more items.

public `Vector(`*int* `initialCapacity)`
 Creates an empty vector with the specified initial capacity. When the vector needs to increase its capacity, the capacity doubles.

public `Vector()`
 Creates an empty vector with an initial capacity of `10`. When the vector needs to increase its capacity, the capacity doubles.

Array-like Methods

public *void* `setElementAt(Object newElement,` *int* `index)`
 Sets the element at the specified `index` to `newElement`. The element previously at that position is discarded. If you draw an analogy between the vector and an array a, then this is analogous to setting a`[index]` to the value `newElement`. The `index` must be a value greater than or equal to `0` and less than the current size of the vector. Throws `ArrayIndexOutOfBoundsException` if the `index` is not in this range.

public `Object elementAt(`*int* `index)`
 Returns the element at the specified index. This is analogous to returning a`[index]` for an array a. The `index` must be a value greater than or equal to `0` and less than the current size of the vector. Throws `ArrayIndexOutOfBoundsException` if the `index` is not in this range.

Methods to Add Elements

public *void* `addElement(Object newElement)`
 Adds the specified element to the end of the calling vector and increases its size by one. The capacity of the vector is increased if that is required.

Display 10.1 Some Methods in the Class `Vector`

● ●

public void `insertElementAt(Object newElement, int index)`
  Inserts `newElement` as an element in the calling vector at the specified index. Each element in the vector with an index greater or equal to `index` is shifted upward to have an index one greater than the value it had previously. The `index` must be a value greater than or equal to 0, and less than *or equal to* the current size of the vector. Throws `ArrayIndexOutOfBoundsException` if the index is not in this range. Note that you can use this method to add an element after the last current element. The capacity of the vector is increased if that is required.

Methods to Remove Elements

public void `removeElementAt(int index)`
  Deletes the element at the specified index. Each element in the vector with an index greater than or equal to `index` is decreased to have an index one less than the value it had previously. The `index` must be a value greater than or equal to 0 and less than the current size of the vector. Throws `ArrayIndexOutOf-Bounds-Exception` if the `index` is not in this range.

public boolean `removeElement(Object theElement)`
  Removes the first occurrence of `theElement` from the calling vector. If `theElement` is found in the vector, then each element in the vector with an index greater than or equal to the `theElement`'s index is decreased to have an index one less than the value it had previously. Returns *true* if `theElement` was found (and removed). Returns *false* if `theElement` was not found in the calling vector.

public void `removeAllElements()`
  Removes all elements from the calling vector and sets its size to zero.

Search Methods

public boolean `contains(Object target)`
  Returns *true* if `target` is an element of the calling vector; otherwise, returns *false*.

public int `indexOf(Object target)`
  Returns the index of the first element that is equal to `target`. Uses the method `equals` of the object `target` to test for equality. Returns −1 if `target` is not found.

Display 10.1 Some Methods in the Class `Vector`

public int `indexOf(Object target, int startIndex)`
  Returns the index of the first element that is equal to `target`, but only considers indexes that are greater than or equal to `startIndex`. Uses the method `equals` of the object `target` to test for equality. Returns −1 if `target` is not found.

public int `lastIndexOf(Object target)`
  Returns the index of the last element that is equal to `target`. Uses the method `equals` of the object `target` to test for equality. Returns −1 if `target` is not found.

public Object `firstElement()`
  Returns the first element of the calling vector. Throws `NoSuchElementException` if the vector is empty.

public Object `lastElement()`
  Returns the last element of the calling vector. Throws `NoSuchElementException` if the vector is empty.

Memory Management (Size and Capacity)

public boolean `isEmpty()`
  Returns *true* if the calling vector is empty (that is, has size 0); otherwise, returns *false*.

public int `size()`
  Returns the number of elements in the calling vector.

public int `capacity()`
  Returns the current capacity of the calling vector.

public void `ensureCapacity(int newCapacity)`
  Increases the capacity of the calling vector to ensure that it can hold at least `newCapacity` elements. Using `ensureCapacity` can sometimes increase efficiency, but its use is not needed for any other reason.

public void `trimToSize()`
  Trims the capacity of the calling vector to be the vector's current size. This is used to save storage.

public void `setSize(int newSize)`
  Sets the size of the calling vector to `newSize`. If `newSize` is greater than the current size, the new elements receive the value *null*. If `newSize` is less than the current size, all elements at index `newSize` and greater are discarded. Throws an `ArrayIndexOutOfBoundsException` if `newSize` is negative.

Display 10.1   Some Methods in the Class `Vector`

Make a Copy

> *public* Object clone()
> Returns a clone of the calling vector. The clone is an identical copy of the calling vector.

If you would use the following for an array of strings `a`,

```
String temp = a[index];
```

then to do the analogous thing for a vector `v`, you would use

```
String temp = (String)v.elementAt(index);
```

The type cast `(String)` is needed because the base type of all vectors is `Object`. This point is discussed in more detail later in this chapter. The two methods `set-ElementAt` and `elementAt` give vectors approximately the same functionality that square brackets give to arrays. However, there is one important point that needs to be noted. The method invocation

```
v.setElementAt("Hi Mom!", index);
```

is *not* always completely analogous to

```
a[index] = "Hi Mom!";
```

setElement
restrictions

The method `setElementAt` can replace any existing element, but unlike an array, you cannot use `setElementAt` to put an element at just any index. The method `set-ElementAt` is used to change elements, not to set them for the first time. To set an el-

addElement

ement for the first time, you usually use the method `addElement`. The method `addElement` adds elements at index position 0, position 1, position 2, and so forth in that order. This means that vectors must always be filled in the order position 0, 1, 2, and so forth. But your code can then go back and change any individual element, just as in an array.

size

You can find out how many indexes already have elements by using the method `size`. If `v` is a vector, `v.size()` returns the size of the vector, which is the number

> ### Accessing at an Index
>
> If `v` is a vector, then elements can be accessed as follows:
>
> **Examples:**
>
> ```
> v.setElementAt("Here", index);//Sets the element
>                                 //at index to "Here".
> String temp = (String)v.elementAt(index);//The expression
>     //v.elementAt(index) returns the element at position index.
> ```
>
> The `index` must be greater than or equal to 0 and *less than the current size of the vector* `v`.

---

addElement

Elements can be added to a vector using the method `addElement`. The elements are added to index positions 0, then 1, then 2, and so forth.

Examples:

```
v.addElement("Zero");
v.addElement("One");
v.addElement("Two");
```

The object `v` is a vector.

---

of elements stored in it. The indexes of these elements go from 0 to one less than `v.size()`.

With arrays, the square brackets and the instance variable `length` are the only tools automatically provided for you the programmer. If you want to use arrays for other things, you must write code to manipulate the arrays. Vectors, on the other hand, come with a large selection of powerful methods that can do many of the things you would need to write code to do with arrays. For example, the class `Vector` has a method to insert a new element between two elements in the vector. Most of these methods are described in Display 10.1.

The base type of an array can be any type whatsoever. On the other hand, all vectors have the base type `Object`. In other words, in order to store an item in a vector, it must be of type `Object`. As you will recall, every class is a descendent class of the class `Object`. Thus, every object of every class type is also of type `Object`. So, you can add elements of any class type to a vector. In fact, you can even add elements of different class types to the same vector, but this can be a dangerous thing to do. On the other hand, you cannot add elements of any primitive type, such as `int`, `double`, or `char`, to a vector.

base type

primitive types

If you want to do something equivalent to having a vector of elements of some primitive type, such as the type `int`, then you must use the corresponding wrapper class, in this case `Integer`. You can have a vector of elements that are of type `Integer`. Wrapper classes are discussed in Chapter 5.

The Method `size`

The method `size` returns the number of elements in a vector.

Example:

```
for (index = 0; index < v.size(); index++)
    System.out.println(v.elementAt(index));
```

`v` is a vector and `index` is of type `int`.

■ Programming Tip
Adding to a Vector

To place an element in a vector position (at a vector index) for the first time, you usually use the method `addElement`. The method `addElement` adds elements at index positions 0, 1, 2, and so forth, in that order. This means that vectors must always be filled in the order position 0, position 1, position 2, and so forth. But your code can then go back and change any individual element using `setElementAt`. However, `setElementAt` can only reset the element at an index that already has an element. You cannot use `setElementAt` to add an element to a vector at a previously unused index position.

You can also add elements to a vector using `insertElementAt`. For example to insert the string `"Do Be Do"` at index position 3 of a vector named `v`, you can use the following:

```
v.insertElementAt("Do Be Do", 3);
```

If 3 is greater than `v.size()`, then when this code is run, you will get an error message saying `ArrayIndexOutOfBoundsException`. The error message (exception) mentions arrays, but in this case, it applies to vectors. Note that this is a run time error message and not a compiler error message.

More generally, in order for the following to be valid

```
v.insertElementAt(elementToInsert, index);
```

the value of `index` must be less than or equal to `v.size()`. Since the last index position used is `v.size() − 1`, this means that you can insert an elements at the first unused index position (as well as at any used index positions), but you cannot insert an element at any higher index position. This insures that the elements in a vector are always in positions 0, 1, and for forth to some last index, with no gaps.

When you use the method `insertElementAt` to insert a new element at an index position, then all the elements that were at that index position or higher have their index increased by one, so that there is room to insert the new element without losing any of the older elements. Unlike when you insert into an array, this all happens automatically and you need not write any extra code to move elements,

? Self-Test Questions

1. Suppose v is a vector. How do you add the string `"Hello"` to the vector v?

2. Suppose `instruction` is a vector with the string `"Stop"` at index position 5. How do you change the string at index position 5 to `"Go"`?

3. Can you use the method `setElementAt` to place an element in a vector at any index you want?

4. Can you use the method `insertElementAt` to place an element in a vector at any index you want? Can you use the method `insertElementAt` to insert an element at any position (any index) for which you cannot use `setElementAt`?

5. If you create a vector with the following, can the vector contain more than 20 elements?

   ```
   Vector v = new Vector(20);
   ```

6. Give code that will output all the elements in a vector v to the screen. Assume that the elements are of type `String`.

7. Write a class for sorting strings into lexicographic order that follows the outline of the class `SelectionSort` in Display 6.13/page 426. Your definition, however, will use a vector of elements (all of which happen to be strings), rather than an array of elements of type `int`. For words, lexicographic order reduces to alphabetic order if all the words are in lowercase letters (or if all the words are in uppercase). You can compare two strings to see which is lexicographically first by using the `String` method `compareTo`. For strings s1 and s2, s1.compareTo(s2) returns a negative number if s1 is lexicographically before s2, returns 0 if s1 equals s2, and returns a positive number if s1 is lexicographically after s2. Call your class `StringSelectionSort`. *Hint:* Vector elements are of type `Object`, so if you want to use a `String` method, such as `compareTo`, with an element of the vector, you will need to do a type cast to a `String`. A test program you can use to test your class follows:

```java
import java.util.*;

public class StringSelectionSortDemo
{
    public static void main(String[] args)
    {
        Vector b = new Vector();
        b.addElement("time");
        b.addElement("tide");
        b.addElement("clouds");
        b.addElement("rain");

        System.out.println("Vector values before sorting:");
        int i;
        for (i = 0; i < b.size(); i++)
            System.out.print(b.elementAt(i) + " ");
        System.out.println();

        StringSelectionSort.sort(b);
        System.out.println("Vector values after sorting:");
        for (i = 0; i < b.size(); i++)
            System.out.print(b.elementAt(i) + " ");
        System.out.println();
    }
}
```

■ Gotcha

Vector Elements Are of Type Object

The fact that an element added to a vector must be an Object has more consequences than you might at first think. Consider the following:

```
Vector v = new Vector();
String greeting = "Hi Mom!";
v.addElement(greeting);
System.out.println("Length is " + (v.elementAt(0)).length());
```

Read text to see what is wrong with this.

Although this may look fine, it will produce an error message telling you that the class Object does not have a method named length.

You might protest, v.elementAt(0) is of type String and so it does have a method named length. You are right, but Java acts as if it does not know that v.elementAt(0) is of type String. It only knows it is an element of a vector, and all it admits to knowing about elements of a vector is that they are of type Object. You need to tell Java that v.elementAt(0) is of type String by using a type cast as follows:

```
(String)(v.elementAt(0))
```

So, the troublesome output statement needs to be rewritten to the following, which will work fine:

```
System.out.println("Length is " +
                        ((String)(v.elementAt(0))).length());
```

Base Type of a Vector

All vectors have base type Object, but all classes are descendent classes of the class Object. This means that an element of a vector can be an object of any class, but you cannot have vector elements of a primitive type such as *int*, *double*, or *char*.

■

Comparing Vectors and Arrays

Vectors are used for the same sorts of applications as arrays. So, how do you decide whether to use a vector or an array? Each has its advantages and disadvantages. The advantage of vectors is that they have many built-in features. For example, a vector is automatically a partially filled vector. The method size keeps track of how much of the vector is filled with meaningful elements. This is illustrated in the sample program in Display 10.2. Vectors also have built-in methods to accomplish many of the common tasks that would require you to design your own code if you were using arrays. For example, with vectors, you have a method to insert an element at any specified point in the vector, a method to delete an element from any place in the vector, and a method to test if an element is in the vector or not.

Perhaps the biggest advantage of vectors over arrays is that vectors automatically increase their capacity should your program need room for more elements.

Display 10.2   Vector Demonstration *(Part 1 of 2)*

```java
import java.util.*;


public class VectorDemo
{
    public static void main(String[] args)
    {
        Vector toDoList = new Vector(10);


        System.out.println(
                "Enter items for the list, when prompted.");
        boolean done = false;
        String next = null;
        char ans;
        while (! done)
        {
            System.out.println("Input an entry:");
            next = SavitchIn.readLine();
            toDoList.addElement(next);
            System.out.print("More items for the list?(y/n): ");
            ans = SavitchIn.readLineNonwhiteChar();
            if ((ans == 'n') || (ans == 'N'))
                    done = true;
        }


        System.out.println("The list contains:");
        int position;
        int vectorSize = toDoList.size();
        for (position = 0; position < vectorSize; position++)
        System.out.println(
                    (String)(toDoList.elementAt(position)));
    }


}
```

Display 10.2 Vector Demonstration *(Part 2 of 2)*

Sample Screen Dialogue

```
Enter items for the list, when prompted.
Input an entry
Buy milk.
More items for the list?(y/n): y
Input an entry
Wash car.
More items for the list?(y/n): y
Input an entry
Do assignment.
More items for the list?(y/n): n
The list contains:
Buy milk.
Wash car.
Do assignment.
```

Your program can determine the size of an array when the program is run, but once the array is created, the size cannot be changed. The size of a vector can change.

The advantage of arrays is that they are more efficient, that they have a very nice notation that uses the square brackets, and perhaps most importantly, the base type of an array can be of any type. The base type of a vector is always the type `Object`. This is not much of a disadvantage if you want to store objects of some class, but if you want to store values of a primitive type in a vector, then you need to use a wrapper class for the primitive type. With an array, you can simply make the primitive type the base type of the array.

■ Gotcha

Using `capacity` **Instead of** `size`

In Display 10.2, we used the following code to print out the list of all strings in the vector `toDoList`:

```
int vectorSize = toDoList.size();
for (position = 0; position < vectorSize; position++)
    System.out.println(
                  (String)(toDoList.elementAt(position)));
```

If we had mistakenly used the method `capacity` instead of `size`, we would be trying to write out garbage values. In this case, we are likely to find the error, because if we use `capacity` instead of `size`, then the program will end with a message saying it has thrown an `ArrayIndexOutOfBoundsException` (unless by coincidence the size and the capacity are equal).

■ *Java Tip*
Use `trimToSize` to Save Memory

Vectors automatically increase their capacity when your program needs them to have additional capacity. However, it may increase the capacity more than what your program requires. Also, when your program needs less capacity in a vector, the vector does not automatically shrink. If your vector has a large amount of excess capacity, you can save memory by using the methods `setSize` and `trimToSize` to shrink the capacity of a vector. If `v` is a vector, then an invocation of `v.setSize(n)` will set the size of `v` to `n` and discard any elements in positions `n` or higher. The invocation `v.trimToSize()` will shrink the capacity of the vector `v` down to the size of `v`, so that there is no unused capacity in `v`. Normally, you should only use `trimSize` when you know the vector will not later need its extra capacity.

■ *Gotcha*
Using the Method `clone`

As was true of objects for other classes, and for arrays, you cannot make a copy of a vector using the assignment statement. For example, consider the following code:

```
Vector v = new Vector(10);
<Some code to fill the vector v.>
Vector otherV;
otherV = v;
```

This code simply makes `otherV` another name for the vector `v`, so you have two names but only one vector. If you want to make `otherV` an identical, but different, copy of `v`, you use the method `clone` as follows:

```
Vector otherV = (Vector)v.clone();
```

Be sure to notice the type cast to the type `Vector` in the preceding line of code. That type cast is needed. Because the method `clone` returns a value of type `Object`, the following will produce an error message:

```
Vector otherV = v.clone();//Incorrect form
```

The reason that `clone` returns a value of type `Object` has to do with language features other than vectors and is a bit too complicated to explain here, but the way to cope with this inconvenience is clear and simple: just insert a type cast as shown in the preceding example.

A class can have a private instance variable of type `Vector`. However, private instance variables of type `Vector` have complications similar to those we discussed for private instance variables of an array type. Suppose you have a class with a private instance variable of an array type. In the subsection *Gotcha* **Returning an Array Instance Variable** on page 420 of Chapter 6, we noted that to keep programmers from having direct access to the private array instance variables, your accessor methods should return a copy of the array. The exact same lesson applies to private instance variables of type `Vector`. An accessor method should not return the private instance vector itself, but should return a copy of the vector. To produce a copy of a vector you can use the vector method `clone` to produce a clone (a copy) of the private instance vector and return the clone.

Using the method `clone`, however, can be a bit complicated and produces a few pitfalls. First of all, the return type of the method `clone` is `Object`; it is not `Vector`. To see the problems that this can produce, suppose you have a private instance variable named v declared as follows:

```
public class SampleClass
{
    private Vector v;
        .
        .
        .
}
```

The following accessor method will produce a compiler error message when added to the class `SampleClass`:

```
public Vector getVector()
{
    return v.clone();
}
```

The problem is that `v.clone` is of type `Object` and needs a type cast to make it match the specified return value of `Vector`. One way to avoid the compiler error message is to write this accessor method as follows:

```
public Vector getVector()
{
    return (Vector)v.clone();
}
```

One other problem is a general problem frequently encountered with the use of the method `clone` with most classes, not just with the class `Vector`. If the objects stored in the vector do not themselves have a well-behaved `clone` method, then the clone of the vector will simply copy the memory addresses of the elements in the vector and not make copies of the elements in the vector. This can still allow for access of private data. The situation is similar to what we described for arrays of class in the subsection *Gotcha* **Returning an Array Instance Variable** on page 420 of Chapter 6. Even if the other classes being used all have well-behaved `clone` methods, you may still need to do some extra work to get the accessor method in `SampleClass` to work correctly. The exact details are beyond the scope of this book, but you have at least been warned of the potential problems.

? Self-Test Questions

8. What is the base type of a vector?

9. Can you store a value of type *int* in a vector?

10. Suppose v is a vector. What is the difference between v.capacity() and v.size()?

10.2 | Linked Data Structures

> *Do not mistake the pointing finger for the moon.*
>
> **Zen Saying**

A **linked data structure** is a collection of objects (known as *nodes*) each of which contains data and a reference to another node. There are many popular linked structures, but the concept is best explained by a simple example. So, we will confine most of our discussion of linked data structures to a simple (but widely used) kind of linked data structure known as *linked lists*.

The beginning of this section can be covered without knowing anything about inner classes. But the last parts of this section, starting with the subsection entitled ***Node Inner Classes***, does require a knowledge of inner classes. Inner classes are covered in Section 5.8 of Chapter 5 and in Section 14.4 of Chapter 14. You need to have read only one of these two sections on inner classes in order to understand the last parts of this section.

Linked Lists

There is a predefined LinkedList class that comes with Java. It is in the java.util package. It makes sense to use this predefined class, since it was defined by experts, is well tested, and will save you a lot of work. However, it will not teach you how you can implement linked data structures in Java. To do that you need to see a simple example of building at least one linked data structure. A linked list is both a simple and typical linked data structure. So, we will construct our own simplified example of a linked list, in order to let you see how this sort of thing is done.

A **linked list** is shown in diagrammatic form in Display 10.3. A linked list, or any linked data structure, consist of objects known as nodes. In the display the nodes are the boxes that are divided in half with a vertical line. Each node has a place for some data and a place to hold a link to another node. The **links** are shown as arrows that point to the node they "link to." In Java, the links will be implemented as references to a node, and in practice will be instance variables of the node type. However, for your first look at a linked list, you can simply think of the links as "arrows." In a linked list, each node contains only one link, and the nodes are arranged one after the other so as to form a list, as in Display 10.3. In an intuitive sense, you, or more properly your code, moves from node to node following the

linked list

link

Display 10.3   A Linked List

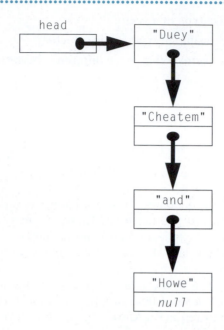

links. The link marked head is not on the list of nodes, and is not even a node, but is a link that gets you to the first node. (In implementations, head will contain a reference to a node. So, in practice head is a variable of the node type.) Your code can easily move through the list in order from the first node to the last node, but it is extremely difficult to move from some node to some other randomly chosen node. Now, let's see exactly how we can realize a linked list in Java.

Linked List

A **linked list** is a data structure consisting of objects known as **nodes**, such that each node can contain both data and a reference to one other node so that the entire linked list forms a list, as illustrated in Display 10.3. The first node in the list is known as the **head node**.

In Java, each node is an object of a class that has two instance variables, one for the data and one for the link. Display 10.4 gives the definition of a Java class that can serve as the node class for linked lists like the one shown in Display 10.3. In this case, the data in each node consist of a single String value.[1] (As noted in Display 10.4, we will later give a better definition of this node class and its accompanying linked list class. But many programmers use this first version just as it is, and it is sufficient to learn the basic techniques you need for linked data structures.)

Notice that the `link` instance variable of the class `ListNode` in Display 10.4 is of type `ListNode`. This sounds circular, and in a sense, is perhaps circular. However, this kind of class definition is perfectly legal in Java. Recall that a variable of a class type holds a reference to an object of that class. So, the `link` instance variable of an object of the `ListNode` class will contain a reference to another object of the class `ListNode`. Thus, the arrows shown in the diagram in Display 10.3 are realized as references in Java. Each node object of a linked list contains (in its `link` instance variable) a reference to another object of the class `ListNode`, and this other object contains a reference to another object of the class `ListNode`, and so on until the end of the linked list.

`ListNode`

When dealing with a linked list, your code needs to be able to "get to" the first node, and you need some way to detect when the last node is reached. To get your code to the first node, you use a variable of type `ListNode` that contains a reference to the first node. In Display 10.3/page 680, the variable with a reference to the first node is named `head` and is represented by the box labeled `head`. The first node in a linked list is called the **head node**, and it is common to use the name `head` for a variable that contains a reference to this first node.

head node

In Java, you indicate the end of a linked list by setting the `link` instance variable of a node object to *null*, as shown in Display 10.3. That way your code can test whether or not a node is the last node in a linked list. To test to see if a node is the last node, your code tests to see whether or not its `link` instance variable contains *null*. In Display 10.3 and in the Java node definition in Display 10.4, the `data` instance variable is of type `String`, and so you normally check two such `String` instance variables for equality by using the `equals` method. However, remember that you check for a `link` being "equal" to *null* by using `==`.

Most Nodes Have No Name

The variable `head` contains a reference to the first node in a linked list. So, `head` can be used as a name for the first node. However, the other nodes in the linked list have no named variable that contains a reference to any of them, and so the rest of the nodes in the linked list are usually nameless. The only way to name one of them is via some indirect reference, like `head.link.link`, or by using another variable of type `ListNode`, such as the local variable `position` in the method `showList` (Display 10.5/page 683). ■

Display 10.5/page 683 contains a definition of a linked list class that uses the node class definition given in Display 10.4/page 682. Note that there is only one instance variable and it is named `head`. This `head` instance variable contains a reference to the first node in the linked list, or it contains *null* if the linked list if empty (that is, if the linked list contains no nodes). The one constructor sets this `head` instance variable to *null*, indicating an empty list.

empty list

---

1. Technically speaking, the node does not contain the string, but only contains a reference to the strung, as would be true of any variable of type `String`. However, for our purposes here we can think of the node as containing the string, since we never use this string reference as an "arrow.".

Display 10.4   A Node Class

```
public class ListNode
{
    private String data;
    private ListNode link;

    public ListNode()
    {
        link = null;
        data = null;
    }

    public ListNode(String newData, ListNode linkValue)
    {
        data = newData;
        link = linkValue;
    }

    public void setData(String newData)
    {
        data = newData;
    }

    public String getData()
    {
        return data;
    }

    public void setLink(ListNode newLink)
    {
        link = newLink;
    }

    public ListNode getLink()
    {
        return link;
    }
}
```

We will give a better definition of this class later in this chapter.

This method works but has a problem. We will discuss the problem later and provide a better alternative.

Display 10.5 A Linked List Class *(Part 1 of 2)*

```java
public class StringLinkedList
{
    private ListNode head;

    public StringLinkedList()
    {
        head = null;
    }

    /**************************************
     *Returns the number of nodes in the list.
     **************************************/
    public int length()
    {
        int count = 0;
        ListNode position = head;
        while (position != null)
        {
            count++;
            position = position.getLink();
        }
        return count;
    }

    /*****************************************************************
     *Adds a node at the start of the list. The added node has addData
     *as its data. The added node will be the first node in the list.
     *****************************************************************/
    public void addANodeToStart(String addData)
    {
        head = new ListNode(addData, head);
    }

    public void deleteHeadNode()
    {
        if (head != null)
        {
            head = head.getLink();
        }
        else
        {
            System.out.println("Deleting from an empty list.");
            System.exit(0);
        }
    }
}
```

We will give a better definition of this class later in this chapter.

Display 10.5 A Linked List Class *(Part 2 of 2)*

```java
public boolean onList(String target)
{
    return (Find(target) != null);
}



/************************************************************
 *Finds the first node containing the target data, and returns a
 *reference to that node.  If target is not in the list, null is returned
 ************************************************************/
private ListNode Find(String target)
{
    ListNode position;
    position = head;
    String dataAtPosition;
    while (position != null)
    {
        dataAtPosition = position.getData();
        if (dataAtPosition.equals(target))
            return position;
        position = position.getLink();
    }
    return null;
}


public void showList()
{
    ListNode position;
    position = head;
    while (position != null)
    {
        System.out.println(position.getData());
        position = position.getLink();
    }
}
```

Use *null* for the Empty List

Let's say the variable head is supposed to contain a reference to the first node in a linked list. Linked lists usually start out empty. What value do you give head until the first node is added? Give head the value *null* to indicate the empty list. This is traditional and it works out nicely for many linked list manipulation algorithms.

Before we go on to discuss how nodes are added and removed from a linked list, let's suppose that the linked list already has a few nodes, and that you want to write out the contents of all the nodes to the screen. You can do this with the method showList (Display 10.5) whose code is reproduced in what follows:

stepping through a list

```
ListNode position = head;
ListNode dataAtPosition;
while (position != null)
{
    System.out.println(position.getData());
    position = position.getLink();
}
```

The method uses a local instance variable named position that contains a reference to one node. The variable position starts out with the same reference as the head instance variable. So position starts out positioned at the first node. The position variable has its position moved from one node to the next with the assignment:

```
position = position.getLink();
```

This is illustrated in Display 10.6. To see that this assignment "moves" the position variable to the next node, note that the position variable contains a reference to the node pointed to by the position arrow in Display 10.6. So, position is a name for that node, and position.link is a name for the link out of that node. The value of link is produced with the accessor method getLink. So the reference to the next node in the linked list is position.getLink(). Finally you "move" the position variable by giving it the value of position.getLink().

The method showList continues to move the position variable down the linked list and outputs the data in each node as it goes along. When position reaches the last node, it outputs the data in the last node, and then again executes

```
position = position.getLink();
```

If you study Display 10.6/page 686 you will see that when position is at the last node, this sets the value of position to *null*. So, when the value of position is *null*, we want to stop the loop. So we iterate the loop *while* (position != null).

Next let's consider how the method addANodeToStart adds a node to the start of the linked list, so that the new node becomes the first node in the list. It does with with the single statement

adding a node

```
head = new ListNode(addData, head);
```

The new node is created with *new* ListNode(addData, head), which returns a reference to this new node. So the variable head is set equal to a reference to this new node. That is fine, because it makes the new node the first node in the linked list, but we need to add the other nodes on after this new node. To add on the entire old linked list, we need only set the `link` instance variable of the new node equal to a reference to the *old first node*. But, `head` used to point to the old first node, and so if we use the name *head* on the *right-hand side of an assignment operator*, `head` will denote a references to the *old first node*. So, the new node produced by *new* `List-Node(addData, head)` does produce a node pointing to the *old first node*. So, everything works out as it should. This is illustrated in Display 10.7.

Note that we always add a node at the start of the linked list. We will later discuss adding nodes at other places in a linked list, but the easiest place to add a node is at the start of the list. Similarly, the easiest place to delete a node is at the start of the linked list.

removing a node

The method `deleteHeadNode` removes the first node from the linked list and leaves the `head` variable containing a reference to the old second node (which is now the first node) in the linked list. We will leave it to you to figure out that the following assignment correctly accomplishes this deletion:

```
head = head.getLink();
```

Display 10.6   Moving Down a Linked List

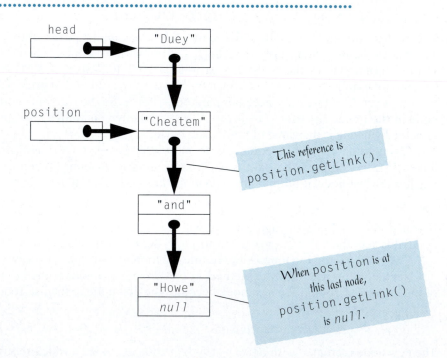

Display 10.7 Adding a Node at the Start

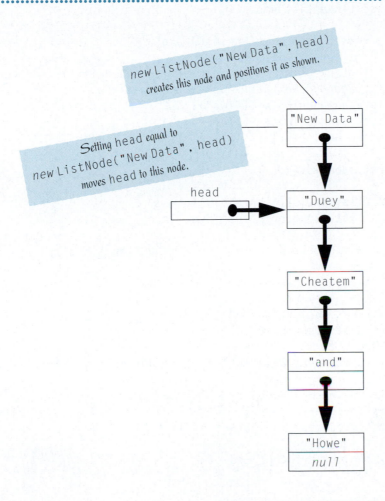

new `ListNode("New Data", head)` *creates this node and positions it as shown.*

`"New Data"`

Setting head equal to `new ListNode("New Data", head)` *moves head to this node.*

head

`"Duey"`

`"Cheatem"`

`"and"`

`"Howe"`

null

It is easy to see that this removes the first node from the linked list and leaves the linked list one node shorter, but you may wonder what happens to this deleted node. You need not worry about this deleted node, Java automatically collects any nodes that are no longer accessible and recycles the memory they occupy. This is known as **automatic garbage collection**.

garbage collection

Display 10.8 contains a simple program that demonstrates how some of the methods in the class `StringLinkedList` behave.

Display 10.8   A Linked List Demo

```java
public class LinkedListDemo
{
    public static void main(String[] args)
    {
        StringLinkedList list = new StringLinkedList();
        list.addANodeToStart("One");
        list.addANodeToStart("Two");
        list.addANodeToStart("Three");
        System.out.println("List has " + list.length()
                                 + " entries.");
        list.showList();

        if (list.onList("Three"))
            System.out.println("Three is on list.");
        else
            System.out.println("Three is NOT on list.");

        list.deleteHeadNode();

        if (list.onList("Three"))
            System.out.println("Three is on list.");
        else
            System.out.println("Three is NOT on list.");

        list.deleteHeadNode();
        list.deleteHeadNode();
        System.out.println("Start of list:");
        list.showList();
        System.out.println("End of list.");
    }
}
```

Screen Output

```
List has 3 entries.
Three
Two
One
Three is on list.
Three is NOT on list.
Start of list:
End of list.
```

■ Gotcha
Null Pointer Exception

You have undoubtedly received the message `NullPointerException` at some time when you ran a program. (If you have not received the message, congratulations. You are an exceptionally careful programmer.) The message `NullPointerException` indicates that your code tried to access some member of a class variable (some instance variable, method, or such) and the class variable names no object, that is, does not contain a reference to any object. This message may seem more sensible to you now. In our nodes, we used *null* to indicate that a link instance variable contains no reference. Java does the same sort of thing with class variables that contain no reference to an object. So a value of *null* indicates no object reference, and that is why the exception is called `NullPointerException`.

A `NullPointerException` is one of the exceptions that do not need to either be caught in a *catch*-block or declared in a *throws* clause. It indicates that you need to fix your code, not add a *catch*-block.

? Self-Test Questions
••

11. Define a method named `empty` that can be added to the class `StringLinkedList` (Display 10.5/page 683) The method `empty` returns a *boolean* value. It returns *true* if the list is empty (no nodes) and *false* if the list has at least one node in it.

12. What output is produced by the following code?

```
StringLinkedList list = new StringLinkedList();
list.addANodeToStart("A");
list.addANodeToStart("B");
list.addANodeToStart("C");
list.showList();
```

■ Gotcha
Privacy Leaks

The point that is made in this Gotcha section is important, but a bit subtle. It would help you to understand this section, if you first review the Gotcha section of the same name in Chapter 5 (page 360).

Consider the method `getLink` in the class `ListNode` (Display 10.4/page 682). It returns a value of type `ListNode`. To be very specific it returns a reference to a `ListNode`. In Chapter 5 (*Gotcha* **Privacy Leaks**, page 360), we said that if a method (such as `getLink`) returns a reference to an instance variable of a class type, then (except for certain classes such as `String`) the *private* restriction on the instance variable can easily be defeated. The privacy leak results from the fact that getting a reference to an object may allow a programmer to change the private instance variables of the object. In this case the problem may be a bit confusing, since the instance variable is of the same type as the object, but it can still result in an improper changing of the data in the object named by the instance variable. There are a number of ways to fix this, the most straightforward is to make the class `ListNode` a private inner class in the method `StringLinkedList`, as discussed in the section ***Node Inner Classes***. (Another, and similar, solution is to place both of the classes `ListNode` and `StringLinkedList` into a package, change the private instance variable restriction to the package restriction as discussed in Appendix 5, and omitting the accessor method `getLink`. Of course, that does require that you read Appendix 5.)

Note that this privacy problem can arise in any situation in which a method returns a reference to a private instance variable of a class type. The method `getData()` of the class `ListNode` comes very close to having this problem. In this case, the method `getData` causes no privacy leak, only because the class `String` has no methods that will allow the user to change the value of the string (without changing the reference). The class `String` is a special case. If the data were of most other class types, then you would get a problem like the one described in Chapter 5 (*Gotcha* **Privacy Leaks**, page 360). In particular, you would have this problem if the data instance variable were of the type `CadetClass` described in that section (*Gotcha* **Privacy Leaks**) of Chapter 5.

In this particular case (namely, the `ListNode` class), the privacy leak is not a problem, *provided* the class `ListNode` is only used in the definition of the class `StringLinkedList` (and very similar classes). This is because no public method in the class `StringLinkedList` returns a reference to a node. Note that the method `Find` returns a reference to a `ListNode`, but the method `Find` is a *private* method. If the method `Find` were *public*, that would produce a privacy leak. So, that *private* in the definition of the method `Find` is not simply a minor style point.

Although there is no problem with the class definition of `ListNode` provided it is only used in a class definition like `StringLinkedList`, there is no way to guarantee that the class `ListNode` will not be used elsewhere unless you do something similar to making the class `ListNode` a private inner class in the class `StringLinkedList`. (see the subsection ***Node Inner Classes***)

Node Inner Classes

You can make data structures like `StringLinkedList` self-contained by making the node class an inner class. In particular, you can make the class `StringLinkedList` more self-contained by making `ListNode` an inner class of the class `StringLinkedList`; this can be done as follows:

```
public class StringLinkedList
{
    private ListNode head;
    <The methods in Display 10.5/page 683 are inserted here.>

    private class ListNode
    {
        <The rest of the definition of ListNode is the same as in Display 10.4/page 682.>
    }
}
```

Note that we made the class `ListNode` a private inner class. If the class `ListNode` is not intended to be used elsewhere, the inner class `ListNode` should be made private.

Making `ListNode` a private inner class is also safer, because it hides the method `getLink` from the world outside the `StringLinkedList` definition. As we noted in subsection *Gotcha* **Privacy Leaks**, it can be dangerous for a publicly available method to return a reference to a class instance variable.

If you are going to make the class `ListNode` a private inner class in the definition of `StringLinkedList`, then you can safely simplify the definition of `ListNode` by eliminating the accessor and mutator methods (the `set` and `get` methods). In Display 10.9, we have rewritten the class `StringLinkedList` in this way. This version, named `StringLinkedListSelfcontained`, is equivalent to the class `String-LinkedList` in Display 10.3/page 680 in that it has the same methods that perform the same actions. In particular, if you run the program `LinkedListDemo` in Display 10.8/page 688 with the class `StringLinkedList` replaced by `StringLinkedList-Selfcontained`, then the sample dialog will not change (The Program `String-LinkedListSelfcontainedDemo` on the accompanying CD does just that).

extra code on CD

Node Inner Class

You can make a linked list (or other linked data structure) self-contained by making the node class an inner class of the linked list class.

■

Iterators

When you have a collection of objects, such as the nodes of a linked list, you often need to step through all the objects in the collection and perform some action on each object, such as writing it out to the screen, or in some way editing the data in each object. An **iterator** is any object that allows you to step through the list in this way.

iterator

An array is a collection of objects (or values of a primitive type). An iterator for an array is an `int` variable. If the array is named `a` and the `int` variable is named `index`, then you can step through all the objects in the array as follows:

```
for (index = 0; index < a.length; index++)
    process a[index];
```

The `int` variable `index` is the iterator. You can **iterate**—that is, go to the next object—with the action `index++;`

to iterate

Display 10.9   A Linked List with Node as Inner Class *(Part 1 of 3)*

```java
public class StringLinkedListSelfcontained
{
    private ListNode head;

    public StringLinkedListSelfcontained()
    {
        head = null;
    }

    /**********************************
     *Returns the number of nodes in the list.
     **********************************/
    public int length()
    {
        int count = 0;
        ListNode position = head;
        while (position != null)
        {
            count++;
            position = position.link;
        }
        return count;
    }

    /**************************************************************
     *Adds a node at the start of the list. The added node has addData
     *as its data. The added node will be the first node in the list.
     **************************************************************/
    public void addANodeToStart(String addData)
    {
        head = new ListNode(addData, head);
    }

    public void deleteHeadNode()
    {
        if (head != null)
        {
            head = head.link;
        }
        else
        {
            System.out.println("Deleting from an empty list.");
            System.exit(0);
        }
    }
```

Display 10.9 A Linked List with Node as Inner Class *(Part 2 of 3)*

```java
public boolean onList(String target)
{
    return (Find(target) != null);
}


/******************************************************
 *Finds the first node containing the target data, and returns a
 *reference to that node. If key is not in the list, null is returned.
 ******************************************************/
private ListNode Find(String target)
{
    ListNode position;
    position = head;
    String dataAtPosition;
    while (position != null)
    {
        dataAtPosition = position.data;
        if (dataAtPosition.equals(target))
            return position;
        position = position.link;
    }
    return null;
}

public void showList()
{
    ListNode position;
    position = head;
    ListNode dataAtPosition;
    while (position != null)
    {
        System.out.println(position.data);
        position = position.link;
    }
}
```

Display 10.9 A Linked List with Node as Inner Class *(Part 3 of 3)*

```java
        private class ListNode
        {
            private String data;
            private ListNode link;

            public ListNode()
            {
                link = null;
                data = null;
            }

            public ListNode(String newData, ListNode linkValue)
            {
                data = newData;
                link = linkValue;
            }

        }
    }
```

If you place all the data objects in a linked list into an array, then you can iterate through the array, and that is equivalent to iterating through the linked list, provided you do not want to change the data in the linked list but only look at it. For this reason, it is common to have a method in a list class that places all the data in the linked list into an array. Such a method is shown in Display 10.10. This method, named `arrayCopy`, can be added to the linked list in Display 10.9/page 692. (This has been done in the file `StringLinkedListSelfcontained.java` on the accompanying CD.)

extra code on CD

Iterators

Suppose you have a collection of data items, such as an array or a linked list. Any object that allows you to step through the collection one item at a time in a reasonable way is called an **iterator**. By "a reasonable way" we mean that each item is visited exactly once in one full cycle of iterations, and each item can have its data read and, if the data items allow it, can have the data changed.

For example, an int variable that holds an index value can serve as an iterator for an array. To go to the next item in the collection (in the array), your code need only increase the value of the int variable by one.

If you want an iterator that will move through the linked list and allow you to do any operations, such as change the data at a node or even insert or delete a node, an array that contains the linked list data will not suffice. However, you can take a hint from the idea of an array and an iterator for an array. Just as an index specifies

Display 10.10 Placing the Linked List Data in an Array

```java
public String[] arrayCopy()
{
    String[] a = new String[length()];

    ListNode position;
    position = head;
    int i = 0;
    while (position != null)
    {
        a[i] = position.data;
        i++;
        position = position.link;
    }

    return a;
}
```

an array element, a reference for a node specifies a node. Thus, if you add an instance variable, perhaps named current, to the linked list class String-LinkedListSelfcontained given in Display 10.9/page 692, you can use this instance variable as an iterator. We have done this in Display 10.11 and have renamed the class StringLinkedListWithIterator. As you can see, we have added a number of methods to manipulate the instance variable current. The variable named current is the iterator, but because it is marked private, we need methods in order to manipulate it. We have also added methods for adding and deleting a node anyplace in the linked list. The iterator makes it easier to express these methods for adding and deleting nodes, because the iterator gives us a way to name a arbitrary node. Let's go over the details.

In addition to the instance variables head and current, we have added an instance variable named previous. The idea is that as the reference current moves down the linked list, the reference previous follows behind by one node. This gives us a way to refer to the node before the node named by current. Since the links in the linked list all move in one direction, we need the node previous to do something equivalent to backing-up one node.

previous

The method resetIteration starts current at the beginning of the linked list by giving it a reference to the first (head) node, as follows:

reset-Iterator

```java
current = head;
```

goToNext

Because the instance variable `previous` has no previous node to reference, it is simply given the value *null* by the `resetIteration` method.

The method `goToNext` moves the iterator to the next node, as follows:

```
previous = current;
current = current.link;
```

This is illustrated in Display 10.12. In the `goToNext` method, the last two clauses of the multibranch *if-else*-statement simply produces an error message when the method `goToNext` is used in a situation where it does not make sense to use it.

moreTo-
Iterate

The method `moreToIterate` returns *true* as long as `current` is not equal to *null*, that is, as long as `current` contains a reference to some node. This makes obvious sense most of the time, but you may wonder why it returns *true* when `current` contains a reference to the last node. When `current` contains a reference to the last node, your program does not know that `current` is at the last node. It cannot tell that `current` is at the last node until it invokes `goToNext` one more time. If you study Display 10.12 or the definition of `goToNext`, you will realize that if your program invokes `goToNext` when the iterator contains a reference to the last node, then `current` will be set to *null*, and that indicates that the entire list has been iterated through. So, when `current` is equal to *null*, `moreToIterate` returns *false*.

Now that your linked list has an iterator, your code has a way to refer to any node in the linked list. You can refer to the node **at the iterator**. The `current` instance variable can hold a reference (a link) to any one node; that one node is known as *the node at the iterator*. The method `insertAfterIterator` inserts a new node after the node at the iterator (at `current`). This is illustrated in Display 10.13. The method `deleteCurrentNode` deletes the node at the iterator. This is illustrated in Display 10.14.

inserting and
deleting inside
a list

The methods in the class `StringLinkedListWithIterator` (Display 10.11/page 698) that we have not discussed are fairly straightforward and we will leave it up to you to read their definitions and see how they work on your own.

What Happens to a Deleted Node?

When your code deletes a node from a linked list (as in Display 10.14/page 704) your code removes the linked list's reference to that node. So, as far as the linked list is concerned, the node is no longer on the linked list. But, we gave no command to destroy the node, so it must be someplace in the computer's memory. If there is no other reference to the deleted node, then the storage that is occupied by that deleted node should be made available for other uses (since your code has no way to use the node). In many programming languages, you the programmer must keep track of items such as deleted nodes and must give explicit commands to return their memory for recycling to other uses. This is called **garbage collecting**. In Java this is done for you automatically, or as it is ordinarily phrased: Java has **automatic garbage collection**.

◻

■ Programming Tip

Internal and External Iterators

The class `StringLinkedListWithIterator` (Display 10.11/page 698) used an instance variable of type `ListNode` (named `current`) as an iterator to step through

---

A Linked List Can Be Its Own Iterator

For the linked list class in Display 10.11/page 698 we said that the instance variable `current` was the iterator for the linked list. That is fine if you are speaking informally, but often you want the iterator for a linked list to be an object of some sort. If you want the iterator to be an object, then you can use the same linked list object as both the linked list and the iterator.

---

the linked list one node after the other. An iterator defined within the linked list class, like this, is known as an **internal iterator**.

internal iterator

If you write out the values in a linked list to an array using the method `copy-ToArray`, then you can use a variable of type `int` as an iterator on the array (and hence on the linked list, provided it does not change). The `int` variable holds one index of the array and so specifies one element of the array (and so one data item of the linked list). If the `int` variable is named `position` and the array is named `a`, the the iterator `position`, specifies the element `a[position]`. To move to the next item, simply increase the value of `position` by one (for example, with `position++;`). An iterator that is defined outside of the linked list, such as the `int` variable `position`, is known as an **external iterator** (for the linked list and/or the array). Note that the important thing is not that the array is outside of the linked list, but that the `int` variable `position`, which is the iterator, is outside the linked list. To emphasize this point, note that the `int` variable `position` is also an external iterator for the array. You can define external iterators that work directly with the linked list, rather than working with an array of linked list data. However, that is a bit more complicated and we will not go into that in this text.

external iterator

? Self-Test Questions

13. Why does the definition of the inner class `ListNode` in Display 10.9/page 692 not have the accessor and mutator methods `getLink`, `setLink`, `get-Data`, and `setData`, like the class definition `ListNode` in Display 10.4/page 682?

14. What is an *iterator* for a collection of items, such as an array or a linked list?

Exception Handling with Linked Lists

As you may well guess, you need to have read Chapter 8 on exception handling before reading this subsection. Consider the class `StringLinkedListWithIterator` in Display 10.11/page 698. We defined the methods such that whenever something went wrong, the method sent an error message to the screen and ended the program. However, it may not always be necessary to end the program when something unusual happens. To allow the programmer to provide an action in these usual situations, it would make more sense to throw an exception and let the programmer decide how to handle the situation. The programmer can still decide to end the pro-

Display 10.11 Linked List with Iterator *(Part 1 of 4)*

```
/************************************************************
 *Linked list with a notion of "current node." The current node
 *can be changed to the next node with then method goToNext. At
 *any time after iteration is initialized, one node is the current
 *node, until iteration has moved beyond the end of the list.
 ************************************************************/
public class StringLinkedListWithIterator
{
    private ListNode head;
    private ListNode current;
    private ListNode previous;

    public StringLinkedListWithIterator()
    {
        head = null;
        current = null;
        previous = null;
    }

    /***********************************
     *Returns the number of nodes in the list.
     ***********************************/
    public int length()
    <The rest of the definition is the same as in Display 10.9/page 692.>

    public void addANodeToStart(String addData)
    {
        head = new ListNode(addData, head);
        if (current == head.link && current != null)
        //if current is at old start node
            previous = head;
    }

    public boolean onList(String target)
    <The rest of the definition is the same as in Display 10.9/page 692.>

    /************************************************************
     *Finds the first node containing the target data, and returns a
     *reference to that node. If key is not in the list, null is returned
     ************************************************************/
    private ListNode Find(String target)
    <The rest of the definition is the same as in Display 10.9/page 692.>

    public void showList()
    <The rest of the definition is the same as in Display 10.9/page 692.>
```

Display 10.11 Linked List with Iterator *(Part 2 of 4)*

```java
    public String[] arrayCopy()
    <The rest of the definition is the same as in Display 10.10/page 695.>

    public void resetIteration()
    {
        current = head;
        previous = null;
    }

    public void goToNext()
    {
        if (current != null)
        {
            previous = current;
            current = current.link;
        }
        else if (head != null)
        {
            System.out.println(
                "Iterated too many times or uninitialized iteration.");
            System.exit(0);
        }
        else
        {
            System.out.println("Iterating with an empty list");
            System.exit(0);
        }
    }
    public boolean moreToIterate()
    {
        return (current != null);
    }
    public String getDataAtCurrent()
    {
        if (current != null)
            return (current.data);
        else
        {
            System.out.println(
                    "Getting data when current is not at any node.");
            System.exit(0);
        }
        return null;//to keep the compiler happy
    }
```

Display 10.11 Linked List with Iterator *(Part 3 of 4)*

```java
public void resetDataAtCurrent(String newData)
{
    if (current != null)
    {
        current.data = newData;
    }
    else
    {
        System.out.println(
            "Setting data when current is not at any node.");
        System.exit(0);
    }
}

/*************************************************************
*Inserts node with newData after the current node. The current
*node is the same after invocation as it is before invocation.
*Should not be used with an empty list. Should not be
*used when the current node has iterated past entire list.
*************************************************************/
public void insertNodeAfterCurrent(String newData)
{
    ListNode newNode = new ListNode();
    newNode.data = newData;
    if (current != null)
    {
        newNode.link = current.link;
        current.link = newNode;
    }
    else if (head != null)
    {
        System.out.println(
                "Inserting when iterator is past all "
            + "nodes or uninitialized iterator.");
        System.exit(0);
    }
    else
    {
        System.out.println(
            "Using insertNodeAfterCurrent with empty list");
        System.exit(0);
    }
}
```

Display 10.11 Linked List with Iterator *(Part 4 of 4)*

```
/*********************************************
 *Deletes current node. After the invocation,
 *the current node is the node after the
 *deleted node or null if there is no next node.
 *********************************************/
public void deleteCurrentNode()
{
    if ((current != null) && (previous != null))
    {
        previous.link = current.link;
        current = current.link;
    }
    else if( (current != null) && (previous == null))
    {//At head node
        head = current.link;
        current = head;
    }
    else //current == null
    {
        System.out.println(
          "Deleting with uninitialized current or an empty list");
        System.exit(0);
    }
}

private class ListNode
{
    private String data;
    private ListNode link;

    public ListNode()
    {
        link = null;
        data = null;
    }

    public ListNode(String newData, ListNode linkValue)
    {
        data = newData;
        link = linkValue;
    }
}
}
```

deleteHeadNode is no longer needed, since you have deleteCurrentNode, but if you want deleteHeadNode it must be redefined to account for current and previous.

Display 10.12 goToNext

```
list.gotoNext();
```
(list *names the linked list.*)

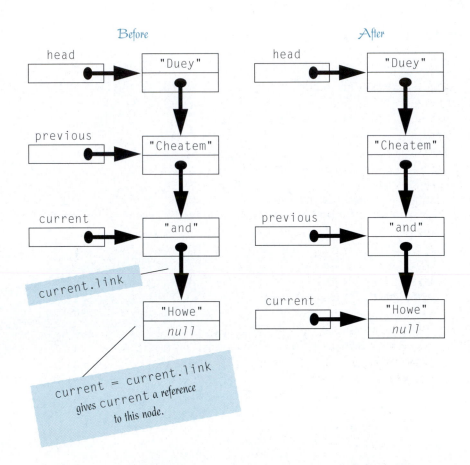

Before

head → "Duey"

previous → "Cheatem"

current → "and"

current.link

"Howe"
null

current = current.link
gives current *a reference to this node.*

After

head → "Duey"

"Cheatem"

previous → "and"

current → "Howe"
null

Display 10.13 Adding a Node

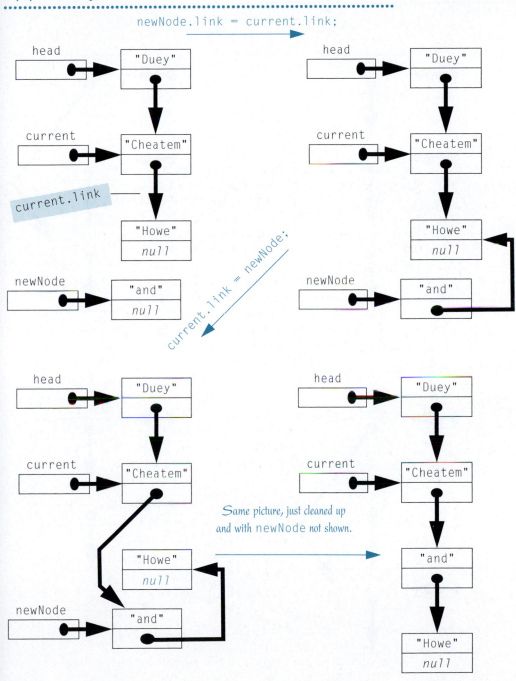

newNode.link = current.link;

current.link

current.link = newNode;

Same picture, just cleaned up
and with newNode not shown.

Display 10.14 Deleting a Node

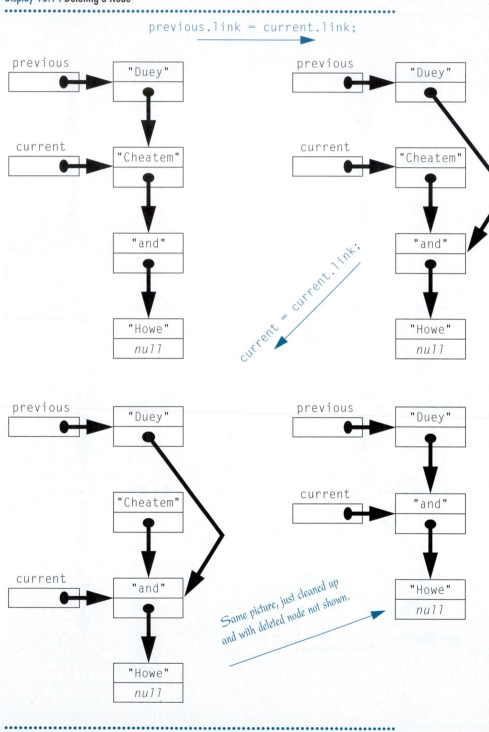

Display 10.15 LinkedListException **Class**

••

```java
public class LinkedListException extends Exception
{
    public LinkedListException()
    {
        super("Linked List Exception");
    }

    public LinkedListException(String message)
    {
        super(message);
    }
}
```

••

gram in such situations, but also has the option of doing something else, For example, you could rewrite the method gotoNext as follows:

```java
public void goToNext() throws LinkedListException
{
    if (current != null)
    {
        previous = current;
        current = current.link;
    }
    else if (head != null)
            throw new LinkedListException("Iterated too many times"
                            + " or uninitialized iteration.");
    else
        throw new LinkedListException(
                        "Iterating with an empty list");
}
```

In this version we have replaced each of the branches that end the program with a branch that throws an exception. The exception class LinkedListException can be a routine exception class as shown in Display 10.15.

Suppose the version of StringLinkedListWithIterator that throws exceptions (as we showed for goToNext) is named StringLinkedListWithIterator2. A programmer who uses this revised class StringLinkedListWithIterator2 could use the thrown exception for a number of different purposes. One possibility is to use the exception to check for the end of a linked list. For example, the following code removes all nodes that contain a specified BadString from the linked list:

```
StringLinkedListWithIterator2 list =
            new StringLinkedListWithIterator2();
String BadString;
<Some code to construct the linked list and set the BadString.>
list.resetIteration();
try
{
    while (list.length() >= 0)
    {
        if (BadString.equals(list.getDataAtCurrent()))
            list.deleteCurrentNode();
        else
            list.goToNext();
    }
}
catch(LinkedListException e)
{
    if(e.getMessage().equals("Iterating with an empty list"))
    {//This should never happen, but the catch clause is compulsory.
        System.out.println("Fatal Error.");
        System.exit(0);
    }
    //else Finished list when you get here.
}
System.out.println("List cleaned of bad strings.");
```

This use of exceptions to test for the end of a list may seem a bit strange at first, but Java requires something like this when checking for the end of a binary file. So, similar uses of exceptions do occur in Java programming, and of course there are many other uses for `LinkedListExceptions`.

The Self-Test Questions ask you to rewrite more of the methods in `StringLinkedListWithIterator` so that they throw exceptions in unusual or error situations.

The Java `Iterator` Interface

Java has an interface named `Iterator` that specifies how Java would like an iterator to behave. It is in the package `java.util` (and so requires that you import this package). Our iterators do not satisfy this interface, but it is easy to define classes that use our iterators and that do satisfy this interface. The iterator interface uses exception handling, but is not difficult to understand. In Self-Test Question 19 you are asked to define a linked list class that satisfies the iterator interface. (The `Iterator` interface is given in Appendix 8.).

? Self-Test Questions

15. Redefine the method `getDataAtCurrent` in `StringLinkedListWithIterator` (Display 10.11/page 698) so that it throws an exception instead of ending the program when something unusual happens (i.e., when the definition in Display 10.11 would end the program).

16. Redefine the method `resetDataAtCurrent` in `StringLinkedListWith-Iterator` (Display 10.11/page 698) so that it throws an exception instead of ending the program when something unusual happens (that is, when the definition in Display 10.11 would end the program).

17. Redefine the method `insertNodeAfterCurrent` in `String-LinkedListWithIterator` (Display 10.11/page 698) so that it throws an exception instead of ending the program when something unusual happens (that is, when the definition in Display 10.11 would end the program).

18. Redefine the method `deleteCurrentNode` in `StringLinkedListWith-Iterator` (Display 10.11/page 698) so that it throws an exception instead of ending the program when something unusual happens (that is, when the definition in Display 10.11 would end the program).

19. The class `StringLinkedListWithIterator` (Display 10.11/page 698 is its own iterator, but does not quite implement the Java `Iterator` interface. (If you follow the instructions carefully, you do not need to know what an interface is, although knowing what it is may make you feel more comfortable.) The `Iterator` interface requires methods `next`, `remove`, and `hasNext`, as described below. Redefine the class `String-LinkedListWithIterator` so that it implements the Java `Iterator` interface. To do so you begin the class definition with

```java
import java.util.*;

public class StringLinkedListWithIterator2 implements Iterator
{
    private ListNode head;
    private ListNode current;
    private ListNode previous; //follows current
    private ListNode twoBack; //follows previous
    private boolean removeSinceNext;//true if removed has been
                //called since the last invocation of next.
                //Also true if next has not been called at all.


    public StringLinkedListWithIterator2()
    {
        head = null;
        current = null;
        previous = null;
        twoBack = null;
        removeSinceNext = true;
    }
```

The rest of the definition is the same as in Display 10.11/page 698, except that you add the method definitions given below and delete the methods `deleteCurrentNode`, `deleteHeadNode`, `goToNext`, and `moreToIterate`, which become redundant. There is also a small change to the method `resetIterator` so that `twoBack` is reset.

```
/*********************************************
*Returns the next element (String) in the list.
*Throws a NoSuchElementException if there is
*no next element to return.
*********************************************/
public Object next() throws NoSuchElementException


/*********************************************
*Removes the last element that was returned by next.
*Throws an IllegalStateException, if the next method has
*not yet been called or if the remove method has already
*been called after the last call to the next method.
*********************************************/
public void remove() throws IllegalStateException



/*********************************************
*Returns true if there is at least one more element
*for next to return. Otherwise, returns false.
*********************************************/
public boolean hasNext()
```

HINTS:

(1.) Despite its pretentious sounding details, this is a fairly easy exercise. The three method definitions you need to add are very easy to implement using the methods we have.

(2.) Note that the method `hasNext` and the method `moreToIterate` in Display 10.11/page 698 are not exactly the same.

(3.) The exception classes mentioned are all predefined and you should not define them. All the exception classes are of the kind that do not require exceptions to be caught or declared in a *throws*-clause.

(The Iterator interface says that the method `remove` throws an `UnsupportedOperationException` if the remove method is not supported. However, your method `remove` has no need to ever throw this exception.)

Variations on a Linked List

tail

Sometimes it is handy to have a reference to the last node in a linked list. This last node is often called the **tail** of the list, so the linked list definition might begin as follows:

```
public class StringLinkedListWithTail
{
    private ListNode head;
    private ListNode tail;
    private ListNode current;
    private ListNode previous;
```

The constructors and methods must be modified to accommodate this new reference `tail`, but the details are routine.

You can have a linked list of any kind of data. To do so, just replace the type `String` in the definition of the node class (and other corresponding places) with the data type you want to use. You can even have a linked list of objects of different kinds, by replacing the type `String` in the node definition (and other corresponding places) with the type `Object`, as shown in what follows:

other kinds of data

```
private class ListNode
{
    private Object data;
    private ListNode link;

    public ListNode()
    {
        link = null;
        data = null;
    }

    public ListNode(Object newData, ListNode linkValue)
    {
        data = newData;
        link = linkValue;
    }
}
```

Because an object of any class type is also of type `Object`, you can store any kinds of objects in a linked list with nodes of this kind. (If you have read Section 10.1 on vectors, you will realize that this is similar to how vectors can store data of multiple types.)

An ordinary linked list only allows you to move down the list in one direction (following the links). A **doubly linked list** has one link that has a reference to the next node and one that has a reference to the previous node. Diagrammatically a doubly linked list looks like the following:

doubly linked list

The node class for a doubly linked list can begin as follows:

```
private class ListNode
{
    private Object data;
    private ListNode next;
    private ListNode previous;
```

The constructors for the node class need not change, but some of the methods in the doubly linked list class will have changes (from the singly linked case) in their definitions to accommodate the extra links.

Other Linked Data Structures

We have given a few examples of linked lists as examples of linked data structures. The study of data structures is a large topic with many good books on the subject. In this book we want to introduce you to all aspects of programming and cannot go into subtopics in exhaustive detail. So we will not present any more linked data structures in detail, but will give you just an informal introduction to a few more important linked data structures.

stack

A **stack** is not necessarily a linked data structure, but it can be implemented as a linked list. A stack is a data structure that removes items in the reverse order to which they are inserted. So, if you insert "one", then "two", and then "three" into a stack and then remove them, they will come out in the order "three", then "two", and finally "one". Stacks are discussed in more details in Chapter 11. A linked list that only inserts and deletes at the head of the list (such as the one in Display 10.5/page 683) is in fact a stack.

tree

binary tree

A very common and powerful data structure is a **tree**. A tree has each node leading to multiple other nodes. The most common form of tree is a **binary tree**, in which each node has links to at most two other nodes. A binary tree has the same kind of nodes as a doubly linked list, but they are used in a very different way. A binary tree can be represented diagramatically as follows:

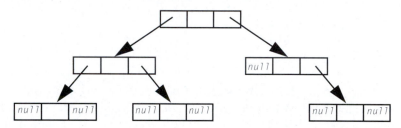

It is not an accident that we have no references leading back up the tree in our diagram of a binary tree. In a tree, the nodes must be arranged without any loops, as in the diagram displayed.

root node

The top node in a binary tree (where top is as in our diagram) is known as the **root node**, and there is normally a reference to this root node, just as there is a reference to the head (start) node in a linked list. Every node can be reached from the root node by following suitable links.

CHAPTER SUMMARY

■ Vectors can be thought of as arrays that can grow in length.

■ The base type of all vectors is Object. Thus, the elements of a vector may be of any class type, but they cannot be of a primitive type.

■ A **linked list** is a data structure consisting of objects known as nodes, such that each node can contain data and such that each node has a reference to one other node so that the entire linked list forms a list.

CHAPTER SUMMARY

- You can make a linked list (or other linked data structure) self-contained by making the node class an inner class of the linked list class.

- You can use an iterator to step through the elements of a collection, such as the elements in a linked list.

? ANSWERS to Self-Test Questions

1. `v.addElement("Hello");`

2. `v.setElementAt("Go", 5);`

3. No. The index for `setElementAt` must be greater than or equal to 0 and less than the size of the vector. Thus, you can replace any existing element, but you cannot place the element at any higher index. This is unlike an array. If an array is partially filled to index 10, then you can add an element at index 20, as long as the array is that large. With a vector, you cannot add an element beyond the last-used index.

4. No. The index for `insertElementAt` must be greater than or equal to 0 and less than or equal to the size of the vector. Thus, you can insert at any index that is currently holding an element, but you cannot insert an element at any higher index, except that you can insert an element in the first available unfilled position. Note that if the vector is named `v`, then you can use `insertElementAt` to insert an element at any index position that is less than or equal to `v.size()`, but with `setElementAt` the index position must be less than or equal to `v.size() - 1`.

5. Yes. The vector can contain more than 20 elements. The number 20 used as an argument to the constructor merely gives the initial memory allocation for the vector. More memory is automatically allocated when it is needed.

6.
```
int index;
for (index = 0; index < v.size(); index++)
    System.out.println(v.elementAt(index));
```

7.

```java
import java.util.*;

/****************************************************
*Class for sorting a vector of Strings lexicographically
*(approximately alphabetically).
****************************************************/
public class StringSelectionSort
{

    /****************************************************
    *Sorts the vector a so that a.elementAt(0), a.elementAt(1),...,
    *a.elementAt(a.size()- 1) are in lexicographic order.
    ****************************************************/
    public static void sort(Vector a)
    {
        int index, indexOfNextSmallest;
        for (index = 0; index < a.size() - 1; index++)
        {//Place the correct value in position index:
            indexOfNextSmallest =
                            indexOfSmallest(index, a);
            interchange(index,indexOfNextSmallest, a);
            //a.elementAt(0), a.elementAt(1),...,
          //a.elementAt(index) are sorted. The rest of
            //the elements are in the remaining positions.
        }
    }

    /****************************************************
    *Precondition: i and j are legal indexes for the vector a.
    *Postcondition: The values of a.elementAt(i) and
    *a.elementAt(j) have been interchanged.
    ****************************************************/
    private static void interchange(int i, int j, Vector a)
    {
        Object temp;
        temp = a.elementAt(i);
        a.setElementAt(a.elementAt(j), i);
        a.setElementAt(temp, j);
    }

    /****************************************************
    *Returns the index of the lexicographically first value among
    *a.elementAt(startIndex), a.elementAt(startIndex+1),...,
    *a.elementAt(a.size() - 1)
    ****************************************************/
    private static int indexOfSmallest(int startIndex, Vector a)
```

```
{
    String min = (String)a.elementAt(startIndex);
    int indexOfMin = startIndex;
    int index;
    for (index = startIndex + 1; index < a.size(); index++)
    if (((String)(a.elementAt(index))).compareTo(min) < 0)
    {
        min = (String)a.elementAt(index);
        indexOfMin = index;
    }
    return indexOfMin;
}
}
```

8. Object. (Every object of every class is of type Object.)

9. No, you can only store objects of a class type in a vector. You cannot store values of any primitive type.

10. The method invocation v.size() returns the number of elements in the vector v. The method invocation v.capacity() returns the number of elements for which the vector currently has memory allocated.

11.
```
public boolean empty()
{
    return (length() == 0);
}
```

12.
```
C
B
A
```

13. They are not needed, because the methods in the linked list class have access to the instance variables data and link of the nodes. This is one of the advantages of using an inner class.

14. Any object that allows you to step through the collection one item at a time in a reasonable way is called an *iterator*. By "a reasonable way" we mean that each item is visited exactly once in one full iteration cycle, and each item can have its data read and, if the data items allow it, can have the data changed. For example, an *int* variable that holds an index value can serve as an iterator for an array. To go to the next item in the collection (in the array), your code need only increase the value of the *int* variable by one. An iterator can be a different object than the collection object, or the collection object can serve as its own iterator,

15.

```java
public String getDataAtCurrent()
                                throws LinkedListException
{
    if (current != null)
        return (current.data);
    else
        throw new LinkedListException(
            "Getting data when current is not at any node.");
}
```

16.

```java
public void resetDataAtCurrent(String newData)
                                throws LinkedListException
{
    if (current != null)
        current.data = newData;
    else
        throw new LinkedListException(
            "Setting data when current is not at any node.");
}
```

17.

```java
/************************************************************
 *Inserts node with newData after the current node. The current
 *node is the same after invocation as it is before invocation.
 *Should not be used with an empty list. Should not be
 *used when the current node has iterated past entire list.
 ************************************************************/
public void insertNodeAfterCurrent(String newData)
                                throws LinkedListException
{
    ListNode newNode = new ListNode();
    newNode.data = newData;
    if (current != null)
    {
        newNode.link = current.link;
        current.link = newNode;
    }
    else if (head != null)
    {
        throw new LinkedListException(
                    "Inserting when iterator is past all"
                + " nodes or uninitialized iterator.");
    }
    else
    {
        throw new LinkedListException(
            "Using insertNodeAfterCurrent with empty list");
    }
}
```

18.

```
/********************************************
 *Deletes current node. After the invocation,
 *the current node is the node after the
 *deleted node, or null if there is no next node.
 ********************************************/
public void deleteCurrentNode() throws LinkedListException
{
    if ((current != null) && (previous != null))
    {
        previous.link = current.link;
        current = current.link;
    }
    else if( (current != null) && (previous == null))
    {//At head node
        head = current.link;
        current = head;
    }
    else //current == null
    {
        throw new LinkedListException(
                    "Deleting with uninitialized current"
                + " or an empty list");
    }
}
```

19.

```
import java.util.*;

public class StringLinkedListWithIterator2 implements Iterator
{
    private ListNode head;
    private ListNode current;
    private ListNode previous; //follows current
    private ListNode twoBack; //follows previous
    private boolean removeSinceNext;//true if removed has been
                //called since the last invocation of next.
                //Also true if next has not been called at all.

    public StringLinkedListWithIterator2()
    {
        head = null;
        current = null;
        previous = null;
        twoBack = null;
        removeSinceNext = true;
    }
```

```
/***********************************************
 *Returns the next element (String) in the list.
 *Throws a NoSuchElementException if there is
 *no next element to return. You should invoke
 *resetIteration before the first invocation of next().
 ***********************************************/
public Object next()
{
    if (current != null)
    {
        twoBack = previous;
        previous = current;
        current = current.link;
        removeSinceNext = false;
        return (previous.data);
    }
    else
    {
        throw new NoSuchElementException();
    }
}

/***********************************************
 *Removes the last element that was returned by next.
 *Throws an IllegalStateException, if the next method has
 *not yet been called or if the remove method has already
 *been called after the last call to the next method.
 ***********************************************/
public void remove()
{
    if ((previous != null) && (twoBack != null)
        && (!removeSinceNext))
    {//remove node at previous
        twoBack.link = previous.link;
        previous = twoBack;
        removeSinceNext = true;
        //twoBack not updated until next invocation of next()
    }
    else if( (previous != null) && (twoBack == null)
        && (!removeSinceNext))
    {//previous at head node and current
     //at head node after deletion
        head = current;
        previous = null;
        twoBack = null;
        removeSinceNext = true;
    }
```

```
        else
        {
            throw new IllegalStateException();
        }
    }

    /*************************************************
     *Returns true if there is at least one more element
     *for next to return. Otherwise, returns false.
     *************************************************/
    public boolean hasNext()
    {
        return (current != null);
    }

    public void resetIteration()
    {
        current = head;
        previous = null;
        twoBack = null;
        removeSinceNext = true;
    }
```

<The rest of the definition is the same as in Display 10.11/page 698, except for the deleted methods. The complete definition is given in the file `StringLinkedListWithIterator2.java` on the accompanying CD. That class also includes methods from Self-Test Exercises 15-17.>

extra code on
CD

? PROGRAMMING EXERCISES

1. Do Programming Exercise 4 in Chapter 6 (page 454), except that in this exercise the class will sort a vector rather than an array. Assume the elements in the vector are all `Strings`. (*Hint:* Check out Self-Test Question 7/page 673.)

2. Do Programming Exercise 5 in Chapter 6 (page 455), except that in this exercise, the class will sort a vector rather than an array. Assume the elements in the vector are all `Strings`. (*Hint:* Check out Self-Test Question 7/page 673.)

3. Write a program that reads in a list of `PetRecords` from the keyboard into a vector, sorts the vector into alphabetic order by pet name, and finally writes the records from the vector to the screen. Be sure the screen output does not go by too quickly for the user to see the records. The class `PetRecord` is given in Chapter 5, Display 5.19/page 351.

4. Write a program that reads `Species` records from a file into a vector, sorts the vector alphabetically by `Species` name, and then writes the sorted records to both the screen and a file. All file names are to be provided by the user. Be sure the screen output does not go by too quickly for the user to see the records. You can use the `FileServer` program (Display 9.19/page 646) to create a file of `Species` records. (If you have

not yet covered the binary files sections of Chapter 9, then read the `Species` records from the keyboard and send output only to the keyboard.)

5. Write a program that reads in a list of `PetRecords` from the keyboard into a vector, sorts the records in the vector by pet weight, and finally writes the records from the vector to the screen (sorted by pet weight) followed by the number and percentage of pets under 5 pounds, the number and percentage of pets that are 5 to 10 pounds, and the number and percentage of pets over 10 pounds. Be sure the screen output does not go by too quickly for the user to see the records. the class `PetRecord` is given in Chapter 5, Display 5.19/page 351. (If you have covered some of Chapter 9, then take the input from a file and send the output to another file. If you have covered binary files, use binary files, otherwise use text files. The file names are obtained from the user.)

6. Write a program that uses `StringLinkedListSelfcontained` from Display 10.9/page 692 to create a linked list of `Species`, then asks the user to enter a `Species` name, then searches the linked list and displays one of the following messages, depending on whether or not the name is on the list:

Species *Species_Name* is one of the *number_of_Species_names_on_list* Species on the list.

or

There are *number_of_Species_names_on_list* Species on the list, but *Species_Name* is not one of them.

The user is allowed to enter more `Species` names until the user indicates that she/he wants to end the program. Of course the appropriate `Species` name and number of names on the list should be inserted in place of *Species_Name* and *number_of_Species_names_on_list*.

The class `Species` is given in Chapter 4, Display 4.19/page 276.

If you have covered some of Chapter 9, then read the `Species` records from a file. If you have not covered any of Chapter 9, read the `Species` records from the keyboard.

7. Write a program that uses `StringLinkedListSelfcontained` from Display 10.9/page 692 to create a linked list of `Employees`, then asks the user to enter an `Employee`'s Social Security Number, then searches the linked list and displays the employee record with that Social Security Number, provided that there is such a record; otherwise it displays a message saying that it could not find the requested social security number.

The user is allowed to enter more Social Security Numbers until the user indicates that she/he wants to end the program.

The class `Employee` was defined as part of Programming Exercise 7 of Chapter 8. If you have not already done that exercise, then you will need to define the class `Employee`. Follow the instructions for the class `Employee` given in Programming Exercise 7 of Chapter 8 on page 575.

If you have covered some of Chapter 9, then read the `Employee` records from a file. If you have not covered any of Chapter 9, read the `Employee` records from the keyboard.

CHAPTER 11

RECURSION

11.1 THE BASICS OF RECURSION. 722

Case Study Digits to Words 723

How Recursion Works 727

Gotcha Infinite Recursion 729

Recursive versus Iterative
   Definitions 734
Recursive Methods That Return a
   Value 734

11.2 PROGRAMMING WITH RECURSION 739

Case Study Binary Search 741

Programming Example Ask Until the User
   Gets It Right 741

Programming Tip Generalize the
   Problem 749

Chapter Summary 749
Answers to Self-Test Questions 750
Programming Exercises 752

RECURSION

> *There are two kinds of people in the world, those who divide the world into two kinds of people and those who do not.*
>
> ***Anonymous***

Many people believe that you should never define anything in terms of itself. That would be a kind of circularity, they say. However, there are situations in which it is both possible and useful to define a method in terms of itself. If you do it correctly, it need not even be circular (although that may take a little explaining).

Java permits you to, in some sense, define a method in terms of itself. More precisely, a Java method definition may contain an invocation of the very method being defined. When a method definition contains an invocation of itself, the method is said to be **recursive**, and the general topic of these recursive methods is called **recursion.** In this chapter, we tell you about recursion.

Objectives

Become familiar with the idea of recursion.

Learn to use recursion as a programming tool.

Become familiar with the binary search algorithm.

Prerequisites

The bulk of this chapter can be read after reading only Chapters 1 through 5. Only one case study requires any additional material. The case study **Binary Search**, at the end of this chapter, requires that you know about arrays, which are covered in Chapter 6.

11.1 | The Basics of Recursion

> *This statement is false.*
>
> ***Paraphrasing of an ancient paradox***

It often turns out that a natural way to design an algorithm involves using the same algorithm on one or more subcases. For example, here is an outline of an algorithm to search for a name in a phone book: Open the phone book to the middle of the book. If the name is on that page you are done. If the name is alphabetically before that page, then search the first half of the book. If the name is alphabetically after that page, then search the second half of the book. Searching half of the phone book is a smaller version of the original task of searching the entire phone book.

As we will see, this sort of algorithm can be realized as a recursive Java method. More generally, whenever an algorithm has one subtask that is a smaller version of the entire algorithm's task, you can realize the algorithm as a Java recursive method. Of course, you must do this in the right way, or your Java code will produce problems, but the goal of this chapter is to show you that right way. We begin with a simple example to illustrate recursion in Java.

Recursive Call

If a method definition contains an invocation of the very method being defined, then that invocation is called a **recursive call** or **recursive invocation**.

Case Study

Digits to Words

In this case study, you will write the definition of a method that takes a single integer as an argument, and that writes out the digits in that integer as words. For example, if the argument is the number 223, then the method should output

```
two two three
```

The heading of your method will be

```
/*************************************************
*Precondition: numeral >= 0
*Action: The digits in numeral are written out in words.
**************************************************/
public static void inWords(int numeral)
```

algorithm design

If the number is only a single digit, then you can use a long *switch*-statement to decide which word to use for a given digit. The method digitWord in Display 11.1 uses just such a *switch*-statement, so that digitWord(0) returns "zero", digitWord(1) returns "one", and so forth. But, we still must consider the case of a number with more than one digit.

We now consider a number with more than one digit. There are lots of different ways to break this task down into subtasks. Some of them lend themselves to a solution using recursion and some do not. You will quickly learn which is which, but for this your first try, we will tell you one suitable decomposition into subtasks. One good way to decompose this task into two subtasks, so that you can immediately solve one of the subtasks (and so that the other lends itself to the use of recursion), is

Output all but the last digit as words.
Output the word for the last digit.

Display 11.1 Demonstrating Recursion *(Part 1 of 2)*

```java
public class RecursionDemo
{
    public static void main(String[] args)
    {
        System.out.println("Enter an integer:");
        int numeral = SavitchIn.readLineInt();
        System.out.println("The digits in that number are:");
        inWords(numeral);
        System.out.println();

        System.out.println("If you add ten to that number, ");
        System.out.println("the digits in the new number are:");
        numeral = numeral + 10;
        inWords(numeral);
        System.out.println();
    }

    /*****************************************************
     *Precondition: numeral >= 0
     *Action: The digits in numeral are written out in words.
     *****************************************************/
    public static void inWords(int numeral)
    {
        if (numeral < 10)
            System.out.print(digitWord(numeral) + " ");
        else //numeral has two or more digits
        {
            inWords(numeral/10);
            System.out.print(digitWord(numeral%10) + " ");
        }
    }

    /***********************************
     *Precondition: 0 <= digit <= 9
     *Returns the word for the argument digit.
     ***********************************/
    private static String digitWord(int digit)
    {
        String result = null;

        switch (digit)
        {
            case 0:
                result = "zero";
                break;
```

Recursive call

Display 11.1 Demonstrating Recursion *(Part 2 of 2)*

```
            case 1:
                result = "one";
                break;
            case 2:
                result = "two";
                break;
            case 3:
                result = "three";
                break;
            case 4:
                result = "four";
                break;
            case 5:
                result = "five";
                break;
            case 6:
                result = "six";
                break;
            case 7:
                result = "seven";
                break;
            case 8:
                result = "eight";
                break;
            case 9:
                result = "nine";
                break;
            default:
                System.out.println("Fatal Error.");
                System.exit(0);
                break;
        }
        return result;
    }
}
```

Sample Screen Dialogue

```
Enter an integer:
987
The digits in that number are:
nine eight seven
If you add ten to that number,
the digits in the new number are:
nine nine seven
```

The second subtask can be accomplished with a call to the method digitWord. The first subtask is a smaller version of the original problem. It is, in fact, the exact same problem as the one with which we started, except that the number in question is smaller. That means that the first subtask can be accomplished by a recursive call of the very method we are defining. (This must be done with some care, but as you will see, it can be done this way.) This leads you to the following outline for an algorithm to use for the method inWords:

recursive
subtasks

Algorithm for inWords(numeral)
```
inWords(numeral with the last digit deleted);
System.out.print(digitWord(last digit of numeral) + " ");
```

Now, consider a number with more than one digit, like 534. You want to divide 534 into the two numbers 53 and 4. As it turns out, you can accomplish this by doing integer division by 10. For example, 534/10 is 53 and 534%10 is 4. So, you can refine your algorithm to the following Java code:

```
inWords(numeral/10);
System.out.print(digitWord(numeral%10) + " ");
```

Well, it looks like you are done. It looks as if the following definition will work:

```
public static void inWords(int numeral)//Not quite right
{
    inWords(numeral/10);
    System.out.print(digitWord(numeral%10) + " ");
}
```

As the comment indicates, this will not quite work. It includes the right basic idea, but it has one big problem: The preceding definition assumes that the argument numeral is more than one digit long. You need to make a special case of numbers that are only one digit long. As we will see, unless this simple case is made to work correctly, no other case will work correctly. This leads you to rewrite the method definition as follows:

```
public static void inWords(int numeral)
{
    if (numeral < 10)
        System.out.print(digitWord(numeral) + " ");
    else //numeral has two or more digits
    {
        inWords(numeral/10);
        System.out.print(digitWord(numeral%10) + " ");
    }
}
```

The definition of the method inWords is now complete. Display 11.1/page 724 shows the method embedded in a demonstration program. However, before we leave this case study, let's discuss the method inWords a bit more.

The following recursive call of the method `inWords` occurs in the definition of the method `inWords`:

```
inWords(numeral/10);
```

Note that the argument `numeral/10` used in the recursive call is smaller than the parameter `numeral` that is used for the entire method definition. A recursive call solves a version of the original problem, but it is important that the problem solved by the recursive call be a "smaller" version of the original problem (in some intuitive notion of "smaller," which we will make clearer before this chapter ends.)

As you will see in the next subsection, the successful execution of a recursively defined method, such as `inWords`, requires that the simplest case be handled in a way that does not involve a recursive call. In the definition of `inWords`, this simplest case is handled as follows:

```
if (numeral < 10)
    System.out.print(digitWord(numeral) + " ");
```

Note that if the argument `numeral` is only one digit in length, then no recursive call is used.

How Recursion Works

Exactly how does the computer handle a recursive call? To see the details, consider the following invocation of the method `inWords` from Display 11.1/page 724.

```
inWords(987);
```

Although the definition of `inWords` contains a recursive call, the computer does nothing special to handle this or any other invocation of `inWords`. The computer plugs in the argument 987 into the method definition and executes the resulting code. Plugging in 987 for the parameter `numeral` in the method definition produces code equivalent to the following:

```
{//Code for invocation of inWords(987)
    if (987 < 10)
        System.out.print(digitWord(987) + " ");
    else //987 has two or more digits
    {
        inWords(987/10);
        System.out.print(digitWord(987%10) + " ");
    }
}
```

Just as with any other method invocation, the computer executes the above code with the argument 987 plugged in for the parameter `numeral`. The computer first checks the boolean expression after the `if`. The boolean expression evaluates to `false`, because 987 is not less than 10. Because the boolean expression evaluates to `false`, the compound statement after the `else` is executed. Now, the compound statement after the `else` starts with the following recursive call:

```
inWords(987/10);
```

The rest of the computation cannot proceed until this recursive call is completed. The computer must stop what it is doing and make a side excursion to handle this new recursive call. So, the execution of the code for inWords(987) is suspended, and the computer works on the new recursive call inWords(987/10). After the computer completes the recursive call inWords(987/10), it will return to complete the interrupted computation of inWords(987).

The new recursive invocation, inWords(987/10), is handled just like any other method invocation: The argument 987/10 is plugged in for the parameter numeral in the method definition, and the resulting code is executed. Since 987/10 evaluates to 98, the computer plugs in 98 for the parameter numeral, resulting in code equivalent to the following:

```
{//Code for invocation of inWords(98)
    if (98 < 10)
        System.out.print(digitWord(98) + " ");
    else //98 has two or more digits
    {

        inWords(98/10);
        System.out.print(digitWord(98%10) + " ");
    }

}
```

While executing this new code, the computer once again encounters a recursive call, specifically the recursive call inWords(98/10);. At that point, the preceding computation is suspended, and the computer proceeds to the recursive call inWords(98/10);. Since 98/10 is equal to 9, 9 is plugged in for the parameter numeral in the definition of inWords, and the following code is executed:

```
{//Code for invocation of inWords(9)
    if (9 < 10)
        System.out.print(digitWord(9) + " ");
    else //9 has two or more digits
    {

        inWords(9/10);
        System.out.print(digitWord(9%10) + " ");
    }

}
```

Because 9 is indeed less than 10, the first part of the if-else-statement is executed. So, only the following is executed:

```
System.out.print(digitWord(9) + " ");
```

stopping case

This is a **stopping case**, that is, a case with no recursive calls. A quick look at the definition of the method digitWord shows that the preceding System.out.println causes the string "nine " to be written to the screen. The invocation of inWords(98/10) is now completed. At this point, the suspended computation, shown in what follows, can resume:

```
{//Code for invocation of inWords(98)
    if (98 < 10)
        System.out.print(digitWord(98) + " ");
    else //98 has two or more digits
    {
        inWords(98/10); ◄────────────────
        System.out.print(digitWord(98%10) + " ");
    }
}
```

The computation resumes after the position indicated with the arrow, so the following is executed:

```
System.out.print(digitWord(98%10) + " ");
```

This causes the string "eight " to be output to the screen and this ends the invocation of the recursive call inWords(98);.

Stay with us, dear reader! The process is almost over. Once the invocation of inWords(98); is completed, there is one suspended computation waiting to be completed, and it is shown in what follows:

```
{//Code for invocation of inWords(987)
    if (987 < 10)
        System.out.print(digitWord(987) + " ");
    else //987 has two or more digits
    {
        inWords(987/10); ◄────────────────
        System.out.print(digitWord(987%10) + " ");
    }
}
```

The computation resumes after the position indicated by the arrow, and the following code is executed:

```
System.out.print(digitWord(987%10) + " ");
```

This causes "seven " to be written to the screen, and the entire process ends. The sequence of recursive calls is illustrated in Display 11.2.

Note that the computer does nothing special when it encounters a recursive method call. It simply plugs in arguments for parameters and executes the code in the method definition, just as it does with any method invocation.

■ Gotcha
Infinite Recursion

Consider the method inWords defined in Display 11.1. Suppose we had been careless and had defined it as follows:

```
public static void inWords(int numeral)//Not quite right
{
    inWords(numeral/10);
    System.out.print(digitWord(numeral%10) + " ");
}
```

In fact, we almost did define it this way, until we noticed an omitted case. But, suppose we did not notice the omitted case and had used this shorter definition. If you go through the recursive call inWords(987); as we did in the previous subsection, you will see that the process never ends. Let's quickly trace the computation of this incorrect recursive method definition.

The method invocation inWords(987); (among other things) produces the recursive call inWords(987/10); which in turn is equivalent to inWords(98);. The invocation of inWords(98); produces the recursive call inWords(98/10); which is equivalent to inWords(9);. Because our incorrect version of inWords has no special case for one-digit numbers, the invocation of inWords(9); produces the recursive call inWords(9/10); which is equivalent to inWords(0);. Now the problem becomes apparent. The invocation of inWords(0); produces the recursive call inWords(0/10); which is equivalent to inWords(0);. So, the invocation of inWords(0); produces another invocation of inWords(0); which produces yet another invocation of inWords(0); and so forth forever (or until your computer runs out of resources). This is called **infinite recursion.**

infinite recursion

The preceding shorter and incorrect definition of inWords is incorrect in the sense that it performs the wrong computation. However, it is not illegal. The Java compiler will accept this definition of inWords (and any similar recursive method definition that does not have a case to stop the series of recursive calls). However, unless your recursive definition is defined in such a way as to ensure that you do not get an unending chain of recursive calls, then when the method is invoked, you will get an infinite chain of recursive calls, causing your program to either run forever or to end abnormally.

stopping case base case

In order for a recursive method definition to work correctly and not produce an infinite chain of recursive calls, there must be one or more cases that for certain values of the parameter(s) will end without producing any recursive call. These cases are called **base cases,** or **stopping cases.** The correct definition of inWords, given in Display 11.1/page 724, has one stopping case which is highlighted below:

Display 11.2 What Happens with a Recursive Call

`inWords(987);` **is equivalent to executing:**

```
{//Code for invocation of inWords(987)
    if (987 < 10)
        System.out.print(digitWord(987) + " ");
    else //987 has two or more digits
    {
        inWords(987/10);
        System.out.print(digitWord(987%10) + " ");
    }
}
```

Computation waits here for the completion of the recursive call.

`inWords(987/10);` **is equivalent to** `inWords(98);` **which is equivalent to executing:**

```
{//Code for invocation of inWords(98)
    if (98 < 10)
        System.out.print(digitWord(98) + " ");
    else //98 has two or more digits
    {
        inWords(98/10);
        System.out.print(digitWord(98%10) + " ");
    }
}
```

Computation waits here for the completion of the recursive call.

`inWords(98/10);` **is equivalent to** `inWords(9);` **which is equivalent to executing:**

```
{//Code for invocation of inWords(9)
    if (9 < 10)
        System.out.print(digitWord(9) + " ");
    else //9 has two or more digits
    {
        inWords(9/10);
        System.out.print(digitWord(9%10) + " ");
    }
}
```

This invocation does not cause another recursive call to be executed.

```
public static void inWords(int numeral)
{
    if (numeral < 10)
        System.out.print(digitWord(numeral) + " ");
    else //numeral has two or more digits
    {
        inWords(numeral/10);
        System.out.print(digitWord(numeral%10) + " ");
    }
}
```

Stopping case

These stopping cases must be designed so that they terminate every chain of recursive calls. A method invocation can produce a recursive invocation of the same method, and that invocation may produce another recursive invocation, and so forth for some number of recursive calls, but every such chain must eventually lead to a stopping case that ends with no recursive invocation. Otherwise, an invocation of the method might never end (or not end until the computer runs out of resources.)

A typical recursive method definition includes an *if-else*-statement or other branching statement that chooses between one or more cases that each include a recursive call of the method and one or more cases that each end the method invocation without any recursive invocation. Every chain of recursive calls must eventually lead to one of those stopping cases that do not involve any recursive calls.

The most common way to ensure that a stopping case is always reached is to make all the recursive invocations of the method use a "smaller" argument (in some intuitive sense of "smaller"). For example, consider the correct definition of inWords given in Display 11.1/page 724 and reproduced a few paragraphs back. The parameter to inWords is numeral. The parameter to the recursive invocation of inWords is the smaller value numeral/10. In this way the recursive invocations in a chain of recursive calls each have a smaller argument. Because the correct definition of inWords has a stopping case for all "small" arguments, we know that eventually a stopping case is always reached.

Stack Overflow

When a method invocation leads to infinite recursion, your program is likely to end with an error message that refers to a "stack overflow." The term **stack** refers to a data structure that is used to keep track of recursive calls (and other things as well). Intuitively, a record of each recursive call is stored on something analogous to a piece of paper. These pieces of paper are intuitively stacked one on top of the other. When this "stack" becomes too large for the computer to handle, that is called a **stack overflow**.

□

? Self-Test Questions

1. What is the output produced by the following program?

```java
public class RecursionExercise
{
    public static void main(String[] args)
    {
        methodA(3);
    }

    public static void methodA(int n)
    {
        if (n < 1)
            System.out.println('B');
        else
        {
            methodA(n - 1);
            System.out.println('R');
        }
    }
}
```

2. What is the output produced by the following program?

```java
public class RecursionExercise2
{
    public static void main(String[] args)
    {
        methodB(3);
    }

    public static void methodB(int n)
    {
        if (n < 1)
            System.out.println('B');
        else
        {
            //The following two lines are the reverse of
            //what they are in Self-Test Question 1.
            System.out.println('R');
            methodB(n - 1);
        }
    }
}
```

3. Write a recursive method definition for the following method:

```java
/**********************************************
 *Precondition: n >= 1.
 *Action: Writes out n of the symbol '#' on one line
 *and advances to the next line.
 **********************************************/
public static void sharp(int n)
```

Note that the output advances to the next line after outputting the last '#'. So,

```
sharp(3);
```

is equivalent to

```
System.out.println("###");
```

If you have trouble with this one, then first do it so that it does not advance to the next line. For that simpler case, you need not worry about the distinction between `print` and `println`. In the simpler case, you only use `print` and never use `println`. After doing the simpler case, try to do the exercise as stated.

Recursive versus Iterative Definitions

Any method definition that includes a recursive call can be rewritten so that it accomplishes the same task and does not use recursion. For example, Display 11.3 contains a rewritten version of the program in Display 11.1/page 724, but this version has a definition of `inWords` that does not use recursion. Both versions of `inWords` perform the exact same action, that is, the same output to the screen. As is true in this case, the nonrecursive version of a method definition typically involves a loop in place of recursion and so it is called an **iterative version**.

iterative version

A recursive version of a method definition is usually less efficient (that is, runs slower and/or uses more storage) than an iterative definition of the same method. This is because of the overhead to the computer that results from keeping track of the recursive calls and suspended computations. Hence, you should confine your use of recursion to cases where it makes your code easier to understand. But, there are indeed cases where recursion can be a big aid to clarity.

Recursive Methods That Return a Value

Any kind of method may involve recursion. A recursive method can be a *void*-method or it can be a method that returns a value. You design a recursive method that returns a value in basically the same way as what we described for *void*-methods. The basic technique for defining a well-behaved recursive method definition that returns a value is as follows:

- The heart of the method definition can be an *if-else*-statement or some other branching statement that leads to different cases depending on some property of a parameter to the method being defined.

- One or more of the branches leads to cases in which the value returned is computed in terms of calls to the same method (that is, using recursive calls). The arguments for the recursive calls should intuitively be "smaller."

stopping case
base case

- One or more of the branches lead to cases in which the value returned is computed without the use of any recursive calls. These cases without any recursive calls are called **base cases** or **stopping cases**. (Every chain of recursive calls should always end in one of these stopping cases.)

Display 11.3 Iterative Version of `inWords`

```java
public class IterativeDemo
{
    public static void main(String[] args)
    <The rest of main is the same as in Display 11.1/page 724.>


    /********************************************************
     *Precondition: numeral >= 0
     *Action: The digits in numeral are written out in words.
     ********************************************************/
    public static void inWords(int numeral)
    {
        int divisor = powerOfTen(numeral);
        int next = numeral;
        while (divisor >= 10)
        {
            System.out.print(digitWord(next/divisor) + " ");
            next = next%divisor;
            divisor = divisor/10;
        }

        System.out.print(digitWord(next/divisor) + " ");
    }

    /********************************************************
     *Precondition: n >= 0. Returns the number of the form one
     *followed by all zeros that is the same length as n.
     ********************************************************/
    private static int powerOfTen(int n)
    {
        int result = 1;
        while(n >= 10)
        {
            result = result*10;
            n = n/10;
        }

        return result;
    }

    private static String digitWord(int digit)
    <The rest of digitWord is the same as in Display 11.1/page 724.>
}
```

The dialog is exactly the same as in Display 11.1/page 724

This technique is illustrated by the method numberOfZeros defined in Display 11.4. The method numberOfZeros takes a single *int* argument and returns the number of zeros in the number (when written in the usual way). For example, numberOfZeros(2030) returns 2 because 2030 contains two zero digits. Let's look at how the method numberOfZeros works.

The definition of the method numberOfZeros uses the following simple fact:

> **If n is two or more digits long, then the number of zero digits in n is (the number of zeros in n with the last digit removed) plus one more, if that last digit is zero.**

For example, the number of zeros in 20030 is the number of zeros in 2003 plus one for that last zero. The number of zeros in 20031 is the number of zeros in 2003 without adding anything, because the extra digit is not zero. With this in mind, let's go through a simple computation using numberOfZeros.

First, consider the simple expression:

```
numberOfZeros(0)
```

(which might occur as the right-hand side of some assignment statement). When the method is called, the value of the parameter n is set equal to 0 and the code in the body of the method definition is executed. Because the value of n is equal to zero, the first case of the multiway *if-else*-statement applies; so the value returned is 1.

Next consider another simple expression:

```
numberOfZeros(5)
```

When the method is called, the value of the parameter n is set equal to 5 and the code in the body of the method definition is executed. Since the value of n is not equal to zero, the first case of the multiway *if-else*-statement does not apply. The value of n is, however, less than 10, so the second branch of the multiway *if-else*-statement applies and the value returned is 0. So, that's two simple cases that work out right.

Now let's look at an example that involves a recursive call. Consider the expression

```
numberOfZeros(50)
```

When the method is called, the value of n is set equal to 50, and the code in the body of the method definition is executed. Since this value of n is not equal to 0 and is not less than 10, neither of the first two branches of the multiway *if-else*-statement applies. However, n%10 (that is, 50%10) is 0 and so the third branch applies. So, the value returned is

```
numberOfZeros(n/10) + 1
```

which in this case is equivalent to

```
numberOfZeros(50/10) + 1
```

which, in turn, is equivalent to

```
numberOfZeros(5) + 1
```

Display 11.4 **A Recursive Method That Returns a Value**

```java
public class RecursionDemo2
{
    public static void main(String[] args)
    {
        System.out.println("Enter a nonnegative number:");
        int number = SavitchIn.readLineInt();
        System.out.println(number + " contains "
                            + numberOfZeros(number) + " zeros.");
    }

    /*************************************
     *Precondition: n >= 0
     *Returns the number of zero digits in n.
     *************************************/
    public static int numberOfZeros(int n)
    {
        if (n == 0)
            return 1;
        else if (n < 10)//and not 0
            return 0;//0 for no zeros
        else if (n%10 == 0)
            return(numberOfZeros(n/10) + 1);
        else //n%10 != 0
            return(numberOfZeros(n/10));
    }
}
```

Sample Screen Dialogue

```
Enter a nonnegative number:
2001
2001 contains 2 zeros.
```

But, we already decided that `numberOfZeros(5)` returns 0, so the value returned by `numberOfZeros(50)` is

```
0 + 1
```

(which is 1 and which is the correct value).

Larger numbers will produce longer chains of recursive calls. For example, consider the expression

```
numberOfZeros(2001)
```

The value of `numberOfZeros(2001)` is calculated as follows:

```
numberOfZeros(2001) is numberOfZeros(200) plus nothing
   numberOfZeros(200) is numberOfZeros(20) + 1
     numberOfZeros(20) is numberOfZeros(2) + 1
       numberOfZeros(2) is 0 (a stopping case)
```

When the computer reaches the stopping case `numberOfZeros(2)`, there are three suspended computations. After calculating the value returned for the stopping case, it resumes the most recently suspended computations to determine the value of `numberOfZeros(20)`. After that, the computer completes each of the other suspended computations, using each value computed as a value to plug into another suspended computation, until it reaches and completes the computation for the original invocation `numberOfZeros(2001)`. The suspended computations are completed as follows (which is like evaluating the preceding list of suspended computation *bottom to top*):

```
       numberOfZeros(2) is 0 (a stopping case)
     numberOfZeros(20) is numberOfZeros(2) + 1, which is 0 + 1 == 1
   numberOfZeros(200) is numberOfZeros(20) + 1, which is 1 + 1 == 2
numberOfZeros(2001) is numberOfZeros(200) plus nothing,
                                which is 2 plus nothing == 2
```

Thus, the final value returned by the invocation `numberOfZeros(2001)` is 2, which is correct because 2001 has two zero digits.

Recursion and Overloading

Do not confuse recursion and overloading. When you overload a method name, you are giving two different methods the same name. If the definition of one of these two methods includes a call to the other, that is not recursion. In a recursive method definition, the definition of the method includes a call to the exact same method with the exact same definition, including the same number and types of parameters.

? Self-Test Questions

4. What is the output of the following program?

```
public class RecursionExercise4
{
    public static void main(String[] args)
    {
        System.out.println(mysteryValue(3));
    }

    public static int mysteryValue(int n)
    {
        if (n <= 1)
            return 1;
        else
            return (mysteryValue(n - 1) + n);
    }
}
```

5. Complete the definition of the following method. Your definition should be recursive. *Hint:* 10^n is $10^{n-1} *$ 10 for $n > 1$.

```
/**************************
 *Precondition: n >= 0
 *Returns 10 to the power n.
 ***********************/
public static int tenToThe(int n)
```

6. Complete the definition of the following method definition. Your definition should be recursive. It should use the same technique you used for question 5 and should also have one more recursive case for negative exponents. *Hints:* 10^n is $1/10^{-n}$ for negative values of n. Also, if n is negative, then $-n$ is positive. This one differs from Question 5 in that it also allows negative numbers as arguments.

```
/********************************
 *Precondition: n can be any int.
 *Returns 10 to the power n.
 ******************************/
public static double tenToThe(int n)
```

11.2 | Programming with Recursion

> *All short statements about programming techniques are false.*
>
> **Anonymous**

In this section we do a programming example and a case studies both of which use recursion. The case study does binary search, a well know and important search technique.

Display 11.5 **Recursion for Starting Over**

```java
public class CountDown
{
    private int count;

    public static void main(String[] args)
    {
        CountDown countDowner = new CountDown();
        countDowner.getCount();
        countDowner.showCountDown();
    }

    public void getCount()
    {
        System.out.println("Enter a positive number:");
        count = SavitchIn.readLineInt();
        if (count <= 0)
        {
            System.out.println("Input must be positive.");
            System.out.println("Try again.");
            getCount();//start over
        }
    }

    public void showCountDown()
    {
        int left;
        System.out.println("Counting down:");
        for (left = count; left >= 0; left--)
            System.out.print(left + ", ");
        System.out.println("Blast Off!");
    }
}
```

Sample Screen Dialog

```
Enter a positive number:
0
Input must be positive.
Try again.
Enter a positive number:
3
Counting down:
3, 2, 1, 0, Blast Off!
```

Programming Example
Ask Until the User Gets It Right

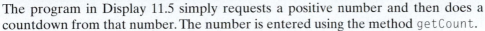

The program in Display 11.5 simply requests a positive number and then does a countdown from that number. The number is entered using the method `getCount`.

Notice that if the user enters a nonpositive number, the method `getCount` makes a recursive call to itself. This starts the input process all over again from the beginning. Thus, if the user enters another incorrect input, there will be another recursive call and the input will start yet again. This is repeated until the user enters a positive integer. Of course, in practice, a recursive call would seldom take place, but it will take place as often as is needed.

? Self-Test Questions

7. (To do this exercise, you need to know about exception handling, which is covered in Chapter 8. If you have not yet read Chapter 8, you should skip this exercise.) Sometimes a recursive call is not signaled by the boolean expression of an *if*-statement, but is signaled by throwing an exception. Look at the code for the method `readLineInt` of the class `SavitchIn` (Appendix 4 and also on the CD that comes with this book). It uses a loop to do something similar to what we did in Display 11.5. Rewrite the method `readLineInt` so that it uses recursion instead of a loop. (One reason we did not do this in the original definition of `readLineInt` is so that the code could be understood by students who had not yet covered recursion.) Hint: the recursive call will be in a *catch*-block for the exception class `NumberFormatException`.

Case Study
Binary Search

This case study requires that you have already covered the basics about arrays given in Chapter 6.

In this case study, you will design a recursive method that tells you whether or not a given number is in an array of integers. If the sought-after number is in the array, the method will also tell you the index of where the number is in the array. For example, the array may contain a list of winning lottery tickets, and you might want to search the list to see if you are a winner. In Chapter 6, we discussed a method for searching an array by simply checking every array position. (See subsection **Searching an Array** on page 420 of Chapter 6.) The method you developed in this section will be much faster than that simple serial search we saw in Chapter 6. However, for this faster method to work, the array must be sorted.

task specification

We will assume that the array is sorted and completely filled. So, if the array is named `a`, then we know

```
a[0] <= a[1] <= a[2] <= ... <= a[a.length − 1]
```

Often you want to know more than just whether or not an element is in an array. If the element is in the array, you often want to also know where it is in the array. For example, if you are searching for a winning lottery number, then the array index may serve as a record number. Another array indexed by these same indexes may hold phone numbers to call and arrange to claim your winnings. Hence, if the sought-after value is in the array, you will want your method to tell where it is in the array. Thus, you design your method to return an integer that gives the index of the sought-after number. If the number is not in the array, the method will return −1 to indicate that it is not in the array. Before you worry about the exact setup of the class and methods and connecting the method to an array, you first design some pseudocode to solve the search problem.

algorithm design

The algorithm you design will make use of the fact that the numbers in the array are sorted. Notice that, because the array is sorted, you can sometimes rule out whole sections of the array that could not possibly contain the number you are looking for. For example, if you are looking for the number 7 and you know that a[5] is equal to 9, then, of course, you know that 7 is not equal to a[5], but you know much more; you know that 7 is not equal to a[i] for any value of i that is greater than or equal to 5. Because the array is sorted, you know that

7 < a[5] <= a[i] whenever i is greater than or equal to 5.

So all the elements a[i] for i greater than or equal to 5 need not be searched. You know that the sought-after value 7 is not among them, without needing to check them.

Similarly, if the sought-after number 7 were instead greater than a[5] (for example, if a[5] were 3 instead of 9), then you could rule out all the elements a[i] with i less than or equal to 5.

Replacing 5 (in the preceding examples) with whatever index is in the middle of the array leads you to your first draft of an algorithm:

```
mid = approximate midpoint between 0 and (a.length − 1);
if (target == a[mid])
    return mid;
else if (target < a[mid])
    return the result of searching a[0] through a[mid − 1].
else if (target > a[mid])
    return the result of searching a[mid + 1] through a[a.length − 1].
```

Notice that searching a subsegment of the array (as in each of the two *else-if* cases) is a smaller version of the very task you are designing. Thus, the subsegments of the array can be searched with recursive calls to the algorithm itself.

The two pieces of pseudocode that correspond to recursive calls are

```
return the result of searching a[0] through a[mid − 1].
```
and
```
return the result of searching a[mid + 1] through a[a.length − 1]
```

There is, however, one complication. (Isn't there always?) In order to implement these recursive calls, you need more parameters. These recursive calls specify that a subrange of the array is to be searched. In the first case, it is the elements indexed by 0 through mid − 1. In the second case, it is the elements indexed by mid + 1 through `a.length − 1`. Thus, you need two extra parameters to specify the first and last indexes of the subrange of the array that is to be search. You call these extra parameters `first` and `last`. Using these parameters to specify the subrange to be searched, we can express the pseudocode more precisely as follows:

preliminary
pseudocode

> **Algorithm to search** `a[first]` **through** `a[last]`:
> `mid` = approximate midpoint between `first` and `last`;
> `if (target == a[mid])`
>   `return mid;`
> `else if (target < a[mid])`
>   return the result of searching `a[first]` through `a[mid − 1]`.
> `else if (target > a[mid])`
>   return the result of searching `a[mid + 1]` through `a[last]`.

If you want to search the entire array, you set `first` set equal to 0 and `last` equal to `a.length − 1`. Each recursive call will use some other values for `first` and `last`. For example, the first recursive call would set `first` equal to 0 and `last` equal to `mid − 1`.

You should always check that any recursive algorithm you write will not produce infinite recursion. Let's check whether every possible invocation of the algorithm will lead to a stopping case. Consider the three cases in the nested `if-else-`statement. In the first case, the sought-after number is found on the list, and there is no recursive call, and the process terminates. In each of the other two cases, a smaller subrange of the array is searched by a recursive call. If the sought-after number is in the array, the algorithm will narrow the range down smaller and smaller until it finds the number. But, what if the number is not anywhere in the array? Will the resulting series of recursive calls eventually lead to a stopping case if the number is not in the array? Well, unfortunately not, but that is not hard to fix.

Note that in each recursive call, the value of `first` is increased or the value of `last` is decreased. If they ever pass each other and `first` actually becomes larger than `last`, then we will know that there are no more indexes left to check, and that the number `target` is not in the array. If we add this test to our pseudocode, we get the following more complete pseudocode:

complete
pseudocode

> **Algorithm to search** `a[first]` **through** `a[last]`:
> `mid` = approximate midpoint between `first` and `last`;
> `if (first > last)`
>   `return −1;`
> `else if (target == a[mid])`
>   `return mid;`
> `else if (target < a[mid])`
>   return the result of searching `a[first]` through `a[mid − 1]`.
> `else if (target > a[mid])`
>   return the result of searching `a[mid + 1]` through `a[last]`.

Next you need to translate this pseudocode algorithm into Java code. You decide that the method will be called `search` and it will be in a class called `Array-Searcher`. The class will have an instance variable to name the array and the array to be searched will be given that name by the constructor. The final code is shown

coding

Display 11.6 Binary Search Class *(Part 1 of 2)*

```
/**************************************************
 *Class for searching an already sorted array of ints.
 *To search the sorted and completely filled array b,
 *use the following:
 *ArraySearcher bSearcher = new ArraySearcher(b);
 *int index = bSearcher.find(target);
 *index will be given an index of where target is located
 *index will be set to -1 if target is not in the array.
 **************************************************/
public class ArraySearcher
{
    private int[] a;

    /******************************************
     *Precondition: theArray is full and is sorted
     *from lowest to highest.
     ******************************************/
    public ArraySearcher(int[] theArray)
    {
        a = theArray;//a is now another name for theArray.
    }

    /***********************************************************
     *If target is in the array, returns the index of an occurrence
     *of target. Returns -1 if target is not in the array.
     ***********************************************************/
    public int find(int target)
    {
        return search(target, 0, a.length - 1);
    }

    //Uses binary search to search for target in a[first] through
    //a[last] inclusive. Returns the index of target if target
    //is found. Returns -1 if target is not found.
    private int search(int target, int first, int last)
    {
        int result = -1;//to keep the compiler happy.
        int mid;
        if (first > last)
            result = -1;
        else
```

Display 11.6 Binary Search Class *(Part 2 of 2)*

```
        {
            mid = (first + last)/2;

            if (target == a[mid])
                result = mid;
            else if (target < a[mid])
                result = search(target, first, mid - 1);
            else //(target > a[mid])
                result = search(target, mid + 1, last);

        }

        return result;
    }
}
```

in Display 11.6. A diagram of how the method performs on a sample array is given in Display 11.7/page 746.

You realize that the method `search` has extra parameters that the user would always have to set equal to 0 and `a.length` − 1 to specify that the entire array is searched. You do not want the user to worry about this detail, so you add the method `find`, which allows the user to simply specify the `target` value and not worry about indexes. The method `find` simply calls the method `search`, but this saves the user a lot of bother. Since the method `search` is now just a helping method, you make it a private method.

find **versus** search

A simple program that demonstrates how the class `ArraySearcher` works is given in Display 11.8/page 747.

The binary search algorithm is extremely fast. In the binary search algorithm, you eliminate about half the array from consideration right at the start. You then eliminate another quarter, and then an other eighth of the array, and so forth. That means that most of the array need not be searched at all, and that saves a lot of time. For example, to search an array with 1000 elements, the binary search will only need to compare about 10 array elements to the target value. By comparison, a simple serial search could compare as many as all 1000 array elements to the target, and on the average will compare about 500 array elements to the target.

efficiency

Display 11.7 Binary Search Example

••

`target` **is** 33

Eliminate half of the array:

Array contains:

↓

`a[0]=5 a[1]=7 a[2]=9 a[3]=13 a[4]=32 a[5]=33 a[6]=42 a[7]=54 a[8]=56 a[9]=88`

`mid = (0 + 9)/2` **(which is** 4**).**
`33 > a[mid]` **(that is,** `33 > a[4]`**)**

So, if 33 **is in the array, then** 33 **is one of**
`a[5]=33 a[6]=42 a[7]=54 a[8]=56 a[9]=88`

Eliminate half of the remaining array elements:

If 33 **is in the array,**
then 33 **is one of**   ↓
`a[5]=33 a[6]=42 a[7]=54 a[8]=56 a[9]=88`

`mid = (5 + 9)/2` **(which is** 7**)**
`33 < a[mid]` **(that is,** `33 < a[7]`**)**

So, if 33 **is in the array, then** 33 **is one of**
`a[5]=33 a[6]=42`

Eliminate half of the remaining array elements:

If 33 **is in the array, then** 33 **is one of**
`a[5]=33 a[6]=42`

↑

`mid = (5 + 6)/2` **(which is** 5**)**
`33 == a[mid]` **So, we found** 33 **at index** 5.

33 found in `a[5]`.

••

```java
public class ArraySearcherDemo
{
    public static void main(String[] args)
    {
        int [] a = new int[10];
        System.out.println("Enter 10 integers in increasing order.");
        System.out.println("One per line.");
        int i;
        for (i = 0; i < 10; i++)
            a[i] = SavitchIn.readLineInt();

        System.out.println();
        for (i = 0; i < 10; i++)
            System.out.print("a[" + i + "]=" + a[i] + " ");
        System.out.println();
        System.out.println();

        ArraySearcher finder = new ArraySearcher(a);

        char ans;
        do
        {
            System.out.println("Enter a value to search for:");
            int target = SavitchIn.readLineInt();
            int result = finder.find(target);

            if (result < 0)
                System.out.println(
                        target + " is not in the array.");
            else
                System.out.println(
                        target + " is at index " + result);

            System.out.println("Again?(y/n)");
            ans = SavitchIn.readLineNonwhiteChar();
        }while ((ans == 'y') || (ans == 'Y'));

        System.out.println(
                "May you find what you're searching for.");
    }
}
```

Sample Screen Dialogue

```
Enter 10 integers in increasing order.
One per line.
0
2
4
6
8
10
12
14
16
18

a[0]=0 a[1]=2 a[2]=4 a[3]=6 a[4]=8 a[5]=10 a[6]=12 a[7]=14 a[8]=16
a[9]=18

Enter a value to search for:
14
14 is at index 7
Again?(y/n)
y
Enter a value to search for:
0
0 is at index 0
Again?(y/n)
y
Enter a value to search for:
2
2 is at index 1
Again?(y/n)
y
Enter a value to search for:
13
13 is not in the array.
Again?(y/n)
n
May you find what you're searching for.
```

■ *Programming Tip*
Generalize the Problem

When designing a recursive algorithm, you often need to solve a more general problem than the one you set out to solve. For example, consider the method `search`, which you designed to search an entire array in the previous case study. You needed to design it so that it could not only search the entire array, but so that it could search any subrange of the array. This was necessary in order to be able to express the recursive subcases. It is very often true that when you are designing a recursive algorithm, you must make the problem a bit more general so that you can easily express the recursive subcases.

? Self-Test Questions

8. Will the binary search algorithm work if the array is not sorted?

9. Do the values in the array used with the constructor for `ArraySearcher` have to be all different, or is it OK to have repeated values?

10. Suppose you want the class `ArraySearcher` to work for arrays whose values are sorted from largest down to smallest instead of from smallest up to largest. How do you need to change the definition of `ArraySearcher`?

CHAPTER SUMMARY

■ If a method definition includes an invocation of the very method being defined, that is called a **recursive call**. Recursive calls are legal in Java and can sometimes make a method definition clearer.

■ Whenever an algorithm has one subtask that is a smaller version of the entire algorithm's task, you can realize the algorithm as a Java recursive method.

■ In order to avoid infinite recursion, a recursive method definition should contain two kinds of cases: one or more cases that include recursive call(s) and one or more stopping cases that do not involve any recursive calls.

? ANSWERS to Self-Test Questions

1.
```
B
R
R
R
```
Note that the 'B' is the first output not the last output.

2.
```
R
R
R
B
```
Note that the 'B' is the last output.

3.
```java
/***********************************************
 *Precondition: n >= 1.
 *Action: Writes out n of the symbol '#' on one line
 *and advances to the next line.
 ***********************************************/
public static void sharp(int n)
{
    if (n <= 1)
        System.out.println('#');
    else
    {
        System.out.print('#');
        sharp(n - 1);
    }
}
```

4. 6

5.
```java
/************************
 *Precondition: n >= 0
 *Returns 10 to the power n.
 ************************/
public static int tenToThe(int n)
{
    if (n <= 0)
        return 1;
    else
        return ( tenToThe(n - 1)*10 );
}
```

6.

```
/*****************************
 *Precondition: n can be any int.
 *Returns 10 to the power n.
 ****************************/
public static double tenToThe(int n)
{
    if (n == 0)
        return 1;
    else if (n > 0)
        return (tenToThe(n - 1)*10 );
    else //n < 0
        return (1/tenToThe(-n));

}
```

7.

```
/*********************************************************************
 *Precondition: The user has entered a whole number of type int on a line by
 *itself, except that there may be white space before and/or after the number.
 *Action: Reads and returns the number as a value of type int. The rest
 *of the line is discarded. If the input is not entered correctly, then
 *in most cases, the user will be asked to reenter the input. In particular,
 *this applies to incorrect number formats and blank lines.
 *******************************************************************/
public static int readLineInt()
{
    String inputString = null;
    int number = 0;//To keep the compiler happy.

    try
    {
        inputString = readLine();
        inputString = inputString.trim();
        number = Integer.parseInt(inputString);
    }
    catch (NumberFormatException e)
    {
        System.out.println(
            "Your input number is not correct. Your input number must be");
        System.out.println(
            "a whole number written as an ordinary numeral, such as 42");
        System.out.println(
            "Please, try again. Enter a whole number:");
        number = readLineInt();
    }

    return number;
}
```

8. No.

9. It is OK to have repeated values, as long as the array is sorted.

10. The multiway `if-else`-statement in the method `search` needs to have two comparison operators changed so that it reads as shown in what follows. No other changes are needed, but the comments should change to reflect the fact that the array is sorted largest to smallest.

```
if (target == a[mid])
    result = mid;
else if (target > a[mid])//Changed from < to >
    result = search(target, first, mid − 1);
else if (target < a[mid])//Changed from > to <
    result = search(target, mid + 1, last);
```

? PROGRAMMING EXERCISES

1. Write a static recursive method definition for a method that has one argument of type *int* and returns the length of its argument (when written in the usual way). This will be a static method. You must allow for both positive and negative arguments. For negative arguments, the sign does not count as part of the length. So, −123 has length 3. Embed the method in a program and test it.

2. Write a static recursive method definition for a method that has one parameter for an array of *int*s and that returns the sum of the elements in the array (that is, the sum of the integers in the array). You can assume that every indexed variable of the array has a value. Embed the method in a test program.

3. One of the most common examples of recursion is one algorithm to calculate the **factorial** of an integer. The notation $n!$ is used for the factorial of the integer n and is defined as follows:

```
0! is equal to 1
1! is equal to 1
2! is equal to 2*1 = 2
3! is equal to 3*2*1 = 6
4! is equal to 4*3*2*1 = 24
        .
        .
        .
n! is equal to n*(n−1)*(n−2)*...*3*2*1
```

An alternate way to describe the calculation of $n!$ is the recursive formula $n*(n-1)!$ plus a stopping case of 0! being defined as 1. Write a static method that implements this recursive formula for factorial. Place the method in a test program that allows the user to compute $n!$ (with and invocation of your static method). Your program should allow the user to repeat the calculation for additional inputted values of n until the user says she/he wants to end the program.

4. A common example of a recursive formula is one to compute the sum of the first n integers, $1 + 2 + 3 + \ldots + n$. The recursive formula can be expressed as

$$1 + 2 + 3 + \ldots + n = n + (1 + 2 + 3 + \ldots + (n-1))$$

Write a static method that implements this recursive formula to compute the sum of the first n integer. Place the method in a test program that allows the user to compute the sum of the first n integer (with and invocation of your static method). Your program should allow the user to repeat the calculation for inputted values of n until the user says she/he wants to end the program. Note: Your method definition should not use a loop to add the first n integer. That would not be a recursive method, or at least not a nice recursive method.

5. Write a static recursive method definition for a method that has one parameter of type `String` and returns a *boolean* value. The method returns *true* if the argument is a palindrome and returns *false* otherwise. A **palindrome** is a string that reads the same forward and backward, such as `"radar"`. Disregard spaces and punctuations and consider upper- and lowercase versions of the same letter to be equal. So, for example, the following would be considered a palindrome by your method:

`"Straw? No, too stupid a fad, I put soot on warts."`

Your method need not check that the string is a correct English phrase or word. The string `"xyzczyx"` will be considered a palindrome by your method. Embed the method in a program and test it.

6. Two common progressions are the **geometric progression**, defined as the product of the first n integers, and the **harmonic progression**, defined as the sum of the inverses of the first n integers. The mathematical notation for them is

`Geometric(n)` is equal to $\displaystyle\prod_{i=1}^{n} i$

where this notation means multiply the integers from 1 to n.

`Harmonic(n)` is equal to $\displaystyle\prod_{i=1}^{n} \frac{1}{i}$

Both have the equivalent recursive definition:

$$\prod_{i=1}^{n} i \;\; == \;\; n \times \prod_{i=1}^{n-1} i \quad \text{for a geometric progression.}$$

$$\prod_{i=1}^{n} \frac{1}{i} \;\; == \;\; \frac{1}{n} \times \prod_{i=1}^{n-1} \frac{1}{i} \quad \text{for a harmonic progression.}$$

Write static methods that implement these recursive formulas to compute `Geometric(n)` and `Harmonic(n)`. Do not forget to include a stopping case, which is not given in the formulas we just gave, but which you must determine. Place the methods in a test program that allows the user to compute both `Geometric(n)` and `Harmonic(n)` for an input integer n (with invocations of your static methods). Your program should allow the user to repeat the calculation for inputted values of n until the user says she/he wants to end the program. Note: Neither of your methods should use a loop to multiply n numbers. That would not be a recursive method, or at least not a nice recursive method.

7. The **Fibonacci** series occurs frequently in nature as the growth rate for certain idealized animal populations. The series begins with 0 and 1, and each successive Fibonacci number is the sum of the two previous Fibonacci numbers. Hence, the third number in the series is $0 + 1 == 1$, the fourth number is $1 + 1 == 2$, the fifth number is $1 + 2$, etc. Continuing in a similar way, the first ten Fibonacci numbers are 0, 1, 1, 2, 3, 5, 8, 13, 21, 34. This series occurs in nature in may contexts besides population growth (for example the series can be used to describes the form of a spiral) and the ratio of the last number to the next last number in the series converges to a constant, approximately 1.618, which is called the "golden mean." Humans find the ratio so pleasing that it is often used for such things as the length and width ratios of rooms and postcards. Use a recursive formula to define a static method to compute the nth Fibonacci number, given n as an argument. (Your method should not use a loop to compute all the Fibonacci numbers up to the desired one, but should be a nice simple recursive method.) Place this static recursive method in a program that demonstrates how the ratio of Fibonacci numbers converges. Your program will ask the user to specify the number of Fibonacci numbers to calculate and then display the Fibonacci numbers, one per line, and, after the first two lines, also display the ratio of the current and previous Fibonacci number on each line. (The ratio does not make sense for the first two lines of Fibonacci numbers.) The output should look something like the following if the user enters 5:

CHAPTER 12

WINDOW INTERFACES USING SWING OBJECTS

12.1 BACKGROUND 759

GUIs—Graphical User
Interfaces 759
Event-Driven Programming 760

12.2 BASIC SWING DETAILS 761

Gotcha Save All Your Work Before
Running a Swing Program 762
Programming Example A Simple
Window 762
Java Tip Ending a Swing Program 767
Gotcha Forgetting to Program the
Close-Window Button 767
Gotcha Forgetting to Use
getContentPane 768
More About Window Listeners 768
Size Units for Screen Objects 769
More on setVisible 770
Programming Example A Better Version
of Our First Swing Program 772
Programming Example A Window with
Color 776
Some Methods of the Class
JFrame 781
Layout Managers 783
Programming Tip Copy Other
Programmers' Code 789

12.3 BUTTONS AND ACTION LISTENERS 790

Buttons 791
Programming Example Adding
Buttons 791
Action Listeners and Action
Events 792
Gotcha Changing The Parameter List
for actionPerformed 797
Programming Tip Code Look and
Actions Separately 800
Java Tip Use the Method setAction-
Command 800

12.4 CONTAINER CLASSES 802

The JPanel Class 803
The Container Class 807
Java Tip Guide for Creating Simple
Window Interfaces 809

12.5 TEXT I/O FOR GUIs 812

Text Areas and Text Fields 812
Programming Example Labeling a Text
Field 817
Inputting and Outputting
Numbers 818
Case Study A GUI Adding Machine 823
Catching a NumberFormat-
Exception (Optional) 830

Chapter Summary 834
Answers to Self-Test Questions 835
Programming Exercises 841

12

Window Interfaces Using Swing Objects

> *"What is the use of a book," thought Alice,*
> *"without pictures or conversations?"*
> ***Lewis Carroll, Alice's Adventures in Wonderland***

So far, almost all your programs have used the simplest form of input. The user enters simple text at the keyboard, and simple, unadorned text is sent to the screen as output. We have kept the input and output simple to concentrate on other basic features of programming and the Java language. But, modern programs do not use such simple input and output.

Modern programs use windowing interfaces with such features as menus and buttons that allow the user to make choices with a mouse. In this chapter and Chapter 14, you will learn how to write Java programs that create such modern windowing interfaces for input and output using a special library of classes called **Swing**. Swing is a standard library that comes with all versions of Java 2 (also known as JDK 1.2 and as SDK 1.2). (Higher numbered versions should also include the Swing library.) Entire books have been written on Swing, and so we will not have room to give you a complete description of Swing in two chapters. However, in this chapter we will teach you enough to allow you to write simple windowing interfaces, and in Chapter 14 we will give you some more advanced details about designing windowing systems with Swing.

Swing

Swing is part of a larger collection of classes known as the **Java Foundation Classes**, or **JFC**. For what we are doing here, you do not need to be aware of anything about the JFC other than what we will tell you about Swing. However, if you hear about the JFC, you should be aware that you know something about the JFC, namely whatever you learn about Swing.

JFC

There is another, older library of classes for writing windowing interfaces. This older library is known as the **Abstract Windows Toolkit**, or **AWT** for short. Swing can be viewed as an improved version of the AWT. However, Swing did not replace the AWT. Swing added to the AWT to produce a richer collection of classes, and the AWT remains as a necessary complement to the Swing library. We will use classes from both Swing and the AWT. However, you will not go too far wrong if you think of them as all part of a single (larger) Swing library.

AWT

(If you are already familiar with the AWT, you will find that programming for Swing is very similar to programming with the AWT. In fact, in many situations the only difference is the spelling of some class names. If you are not familiar with the AWT, do not worry. We assume no knowledge of the AWT.)

Objectives

Learn the basics of event driven programming.

Learn to design and code a simple GUI including buttons and text. (Menus are covered in Chapter 14.)

Along the way you will learn about the Swing (or Swing related) classes: `BorderLayout`, `Color`, `Container`, `FlowLayout`, `GridLayout`, `JButton`, `JComponent`, `JFrame`, `JLabel`, `JPanel`, `JTextArea`, `JTextField`, `Window-Adapter`, and others.

Prerequisites

Before covering this chapter (and the next two chapters on Applets and more Swing), you need to have covered Chapters 1 through 5 and Chapter 7, which covers inheritance. Except for one optional section, you need not read any of the other chapters that precede this chapter before reading this chapter.

In order to cover the section **Catching a** `NumberFormatException` **(Optional)**, you need to first read Chapter 8. If you have not yet read Chapter 8, you can skip that section.

12.1 | Background

> *event* **n. 1.** *An occurrence, incident, or experience, especially one of some significance.*
> **The American Heritage Dictionary of the English Language, First Edition**

Let's begin with some general background about the elements in any windowing interface, and about a programming technique known as *event-driven programming*, which is used when writing windowing interfaces.

GUIs—Graphical User Interfaces

Windowing systems that interact with the user are often called *GUIs*. **GUI** is pronounced "gooey" and stands for **graphical user interface**. The words are pretty much self-explanatory. It's called *graphical* because it uses graphical elements such as windows, buttons, and menus. It's called a *user interface* because it is the part of a program that interfaces with (that is, interacts with) the user. A GUI obtains information from the user and gives it to the program for processing. When the program is finished processing the information, the GUI gives the results to the user, usually in some sort of window.

GUI

Let's just briefly list the terms used for some basic elements that make up a GUI. Although you have undoubtedly used all these elements before, you may not

window

menu

button

have given them the same names we will use. A **window** is a portion of the user's screen that serves as a smaller screen within the screen. A window usually has a border defining its outside edges and a title of some sort giving the window a name. Inside a window you may have smaller window-like objects. Some of these smaller window-like objects are *menus*. A **menu** is a list of alternatives offered to the user, usually by offering a list of names. The user chooses one of these alternatives, usually by clicking it with a mouse. A **button** is very similar to an entry in a menu. A button is simply something that looks like a button to be pushed and that typically has a label. To "push" the button, you use your mouse to click on the button. These elements will have more precise definitions within Swing, but these are the basic properties they have within any windowing system.

GUI

Windowing systems that interact with the user are often called **GUI**s. *GUI* is pronounced "gooey" and stands for **graphical user interface**.

Event-Driven Programming

event

firing an event

listener

event handler

Swing programs and most other graphical user interface (GUI) programs use *events* and *event handlers*. An **event** in a graphical user interface is an object that represents some action such as clicking a mouse, dragging the mouse, pressing a key on the keyboard, clicking the close-window button on a window, or any other action that is expected to elicit a response. Actually, events are more general than just the events of a graphical user interface. For example, a message from a printer to the operating system saying that the printer is ready to print another document can be considered an event. However, in this chapter, the only events that we will be concerned with are those generated within a graphical user interface.

When an object generates an event, that is called **firing** the event. In Swing, every object that can fire events, such as a button that might be clicked, can have one or more **listener objects**. You the programmer specify what objects are the listener objects for any given object that might fire an event. For example, if you click a button, that fires an event, and if the button has a listener object associated with it, then the event is automatically sent to this listener object. A listener object has methods that specify what will happen when events of various kinds are sent to the listener. These methods that handle events are called **event handlers**. You the programmer will define (or redefine) these event-handler methods.

Notice that event-driven programming is very different from the sort of programming we've seen before now. All our previous programs consisted of a list of statements executed in some order. There were some variations on this theme of performing a list of statements: Loops repeat statements, branches choose one of a list of statements to do next, and a method invocation brings in a different list of statements to be executed. However, at some level, all the programs we have seen so far were designed to be performed by one agent (the computer) following a simple set of instructions of the form "first do this, then do that, then do something else, and so forth."

Event-driven programming is a very different game. In event-driven programming, you create objects that can fire events and you create listener objects to react to the events. For the most part, your program does not determine the order in which things happen. The events determine that order. When an event-driven program is running, the next thing that happens depends on the next event.

Listener objects are almost like people sitting around a room waiting for phone calls. Each person has her or his own phone. When the phone rings, the person with that phone answers and does whatever the phone call says to do. Maybe the message says, "Joe this is your mother calling, I want you to close the window in your room." Then, Joe goes home and closes the window in her or his room. In a graphical user interface, the message is something like "close the window" or "The 'A' key has been pressed" or "The mouse was dragged" from someplace to someplace else. When an event is fired, it is automatically sent to the listener object(s) for the particular object that fired the event. The listener object then calls the appropriate event-handling method to handle the event.

If you have never done event-driven programming before, one aspect of event-driven programming may seem strange to you: *You will be writing definitions for methods that you will never invoke in any program.* This may seem strange, because a method is of no value unless it is invoked. So somebody or something other than you the programmer must be invoking these methods. That is exactly what does happen. The Swing system automatically invokes certain methods when an event signals that the method needs to be called.

The event-driven programming that we will be doing with the Swing library makes extensive use of inheritance. The classes that you define will be derived classes of some basic predefined classes that are in the Swing library. When you define these classes, they will inherit methods from their parent class. Some of these inherited methods will work fine just as they were written for the parent class (base class). However, often it will be necessary to override a method definition to provide a new definition that is appropriate to the derived class.

? Self-Test Questions

1. How does event-driven programming differ from the sort of programming we did in previous chapters?
2. How is *GUI* pronounced? What do the letters stand for?

12.2 | Basic Swing Details

> *It don't mean a thing (if it ain't got that swing!)*
>
> **Song Title, Duke Ellington**

A **window** is a portion of the user's screen that serves as a smaller screen within the screen. A window has a border defining its outside edges and a title, usually given within the top border. In this section, we will tell you how to create simple windows using Swing.

There are lots of things you can put in a window when designing a GUI interface. We will start with some simple, but very useful, elements and show you how to build windows with these elements. The window elements we will introduce in this section are a way to close (that is, end) the window, a way to put text in the window, a way to color the window, and way to put a title on the window. This may not seem like much to do with a window, but this will introduce you to the basic methods for doing all kinds of programming with Swing. In future sections, we will use the techniques you learn here to introduce more sophisticated window features you can build with Swing.

This section has essentially one demonstration program, although we develop more than one version of the program. In this section we are primarily interested in introducing you to some Swing details, so when we first present the program we deliberately oversimplify it. At the end of this section we rewrite this program in the style that you should follow when writing Swing programs.

■ Gotcha
Save All Your Work Before Running a Swing Program

Programs that use Swing can take control of your computer screen, mouse, and keyboard. If they go awry, and they often do, then the usual ways of communicating with the computer may be shut down. On a PC, this may require that you reboot your computer. On any system, this may require that you, in some sense, "restart the whole thing." If you are editing a file, or performing some other task, do not simply stop doing the editing but actually close the file before running any Swing program that you have not yet fully debugged. If the Swing program causes you to restart your computer, any open files may be damaged.

Programming Example
A Simple Window

Display 12.1 contains a Java program that produces a simple window using Swing. Below it is a picture of what the screen will look like when you run this program. This window does not do very much. It simply appears on the screen and contains the text

close-window button

`"Please, don't click that button!"` Just about the only other thing it can do is disappear. If you click the close-window button, the program will end and the window will disappear. The picture shown is a typical example of the kind of window produced. The window may look slightly different on your system. Now, let's look at the code for this first GUI program.

The first line, repeated in what follows, says that the program uses the Swing library. Any program using the Swing library should contain this line at the beginning of the file containing the program (possibly along with other `import` state-

java.swing. ments).

```
import javax.swing.*;
```

Display 12.1 A Very Simple Swing Demonstration Program

```java
import javax.swing.*;

/****************************************************
 *A simple demonstration of a window constructed with Swing.
 ***************************************************/
public class FirstSwingDemo
{
    public static final int WIDTH = 300;
    public static final int HEIGHT = 200;

    public static void main(String[] args)
    {
        JFrame myWindow = new JFrame();
        myWindow.setSize(WIDTH, HEIGHT);
        JLabel myLabel = new JLabel("Please don't click that button!");
        myWindow.getContentPane().add(myLabel);

        WindowDestroyer myListener = new WindowDestroyer();
        myWindow.addWindowListener(myListener);

        myWindow.setVisible(true);
    }
}
```

This is just a simple demo program and is not typical of the style we will use in Swing programs.

Resulting GUI

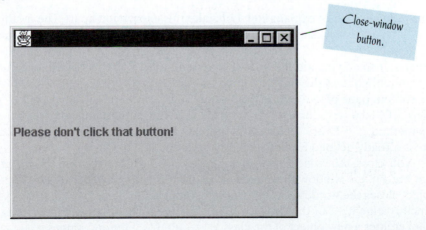

Close-window button.

Please don't click that button!

The rest of the program is a simple class definition with only a `main` method. Let's look at the code in this `main` method. The first line creates an object of the class `JFrame`. That line is reproduced below:

```
JFrame myWindow = new JFrame();
```

JFrame

The name `myWindow` is chosen by you the programmer. The object `myWindow` is an object of the class `JFrame`. A `JFrame` in Swing is what you probably think of as a window. A `JFrame` is a very simple window, but among other things, it does have a border, a place for a title, and the close-window button that you expect to find on any window. (No title is used in this program.) Soon you will see that we do not normally use simple `JFrame` objects, but instead define a derived class of the class `JFrame` and use objects of the derived class. However, for this very first demonstration program we will use `JFrame` directly.

setSize

The next line, reproduced below, sets the size of the `JFrame` window:

```
myWindow.setSize(WIDTH, HEIGHT);
```

The method `setSize` is a method of the class `JFrame` and sets the size of the window. Swing size units are discussed in a later subsection of this chapter. For now, simply note that this says the window is `WIDTH` units wide and `HEIGHT` units tall, and do not yet worry about what those units are.

JLabel

The next line creates an object of class `JLabel` and names the object `myLabel`:

```
JLabel myLabel = new JLabel("Please don't click that button!");
```

label

The name `myLabel` is chosen by you the programmer. An object of the class `JLabel` is usually simply called a **label** and is a special kind of text that can be added to a `JFrame` (or to any of a number of other kinds of objects). The string for the label is given as an argument to the constructor for the `JLabel` class, so in this case the string of text for the label is `"Please don't click that button!"`.

getContent-
Pane

The next line of the program, given below, adds the label `myLabel` to the `JFrame` named `myWindow`:

```
myWindow.getContentPane().add(myLabel);
```

content pane

add

This requires a bit of explanation. Lets take this expression apart. The method `getContentPane` is a method of the class `JFrame` that produces the **content pane** of the `JFrame`. Every `JFrame` has a content pane. You do not add things directly to the `JFrame`. Instead you add things to the content pane of the `JFrame`. You can think of the content pane as the "inside" of the `JFrame`. So, `myWindow.getContentPane()` is the content pane of `myWindow` (the "inside" of `myWindow`). The label `myLabel` is added to `myWindow.getContentPane()` (that is, to the content pane of `myWindow`) using the method `add`. Every `JFrame` content pane has a method named `add`. The method `add` is already defined for you; you do not define it.

Window-
Destroyer

You close this window by clicking the close-window button. When you click that button, the window fires an event and sends it to a listener object. The listener object closes the window. In this program, the listener object is named `myListener`, which is a member of the class `WindowDestroyer`. The following line from the program creates a new object of the class `WindowDestroyer` and names it `myListener`:

```
WindowDestroyer myListener = new WindowDestroyer();
```

The `JLabel` Class

An object of the class `JLabel` is little more than one line of text that can be added to a `JFrame` (or certain other objects).

Example:

```
JFrame myWindow = new JFrame();
JLabel myLabel = new JLabel("Please don't click that button!");
myWindow.getContentPane().add(myLabel);
```

Note that you use `getContentPane().add` to add a `JLabel` to a `JFrame`, as illustrated above.

You the programmer choose the name `myListener`. The next line, shown in what follows, associates the object `myListener` with the object (the window) `myWindow`, so that `myListener` will receive any event fired by the object `myWindow`:

```
myWindow.addWindowListener(myListener);
```

An object, like `myListener`, that receives events from an object is called a **listener**. A listener that listens to events from a window, such as clicking the close-window button, is known as a **window listener**. Associating the listener with the object it is listening to is called **registering the listener**.

registering a listener

An object of the class `WindowDestroyer` will close the window `myWindow` when `myWindow` fires an appropriate event. We need to define the class `WindowDestroyer`, but let's postpone that for a bit, and for now, just assume that the class `WindowDestroyer` has been defined so that, when the user clicks the close-window button of `myWindow`, the object `myListener` will close `myWindow` and end the program.

The last statement in `main` is a call to the method `setVisible`:

set-Visible

```
myWindow.setVisible(true);
```

This call to `setVisible` makes the window named `myWindow` visible on the screen. The method `setVisible` is a method of the class `JFrame` (and also a method in many other swing classes). With the argument `true`, as in Display 12.1, the object is displayed. If the argument `false` were to be used instead, then the object would not be shown.

That's the end of the code for `main`, but not the end of the program. The window just sits on the screen looking pretty until the user clicks the close-window button. At that point, an event `e` is fired by the object `myWindow`. The event `e` is sent to the listener object called `myListener`. The object `myListener` recognizes `e` as an event signaling that the object `myWindow` should be closed, and `myListener` then closes the window and ends the program.

The object `myListener` is a member of the class `WindowDestroyer`. We have been assuming that the class `WindowDestroyer` has already been defined, but you need to define it and compile it before you can really run the program in Display 12.1. So, let's define the class `WindowDestroyer`.

The listener class `WindowDestroyer` is defined in Display 12.2. A window listener class for a GUI that involves windows (more precisely, that involves an object

Display 12.2 A Listener Class for Window Events

```java
import java.awt.*;
import java.awt.event.*;

/**********************************************************
 *If you register an object of this class as a listener to any
 *object of the class JFrame, then if the user clicks the
 *close-window button in the JFrame, the object of this class
 *will end the program and close the JFrame.
 **********************************************************/
public class WindowDestroyer extends WindowAdapter
{
    public void windowClosing(WindowEvent e)
    {
        System.exit(0);
    }
}
```

> The class WindowDestroyer is not in Swing. This is a class that you, the programmer, must define.

WindowAdapter of the class JFrame) will often be a derived class of the class WindowAdapter. This is indicated by the phrase *extends* WindowAdapter on the first line of the class definition. A derived class of the class WindowAdapter, such as our class WindowDestroyer, inherits all its methods from WindowAdapter. Each of these methods automatically respond to a different kind of event. Normally, no new methods are added, because there already is a method for each kind of event. However, the way the event is handled is up to you and should depend on the window you are defining. So, normally, you would redefine (override) one or more of the method definitions that your class inherits from WindowAdapter.

The class WindowAdapter has a number of different methods, each of which processes a different kind of event. All these methods are inherited by the class WindowDestroyer. These inherited methods determine the names of the methods, but you need to determine what the methods do by redefining the methods. However, you only need to define (actually redefine) those methods that your window will use. For this application, the only kind of event that we need our listener class to respond to is an event that signals that the window should close. The method that handles those events is named windowClosing. So, we have only redefined the method windowClosing. The method definition is very simple, it simply executes the one command

```java
System.exit(0);
```

and as we explain in the following programming tip, this ends the program and so closes the window.

In order to run the program in Display 12.1, you must define and compile both the class `FirstWindow` in Display 12.1 and the class `WindowDestroyer` in Display 12.2. Note that the class `WindowDestroyer` is not a Swing class. It is a class that you the programmer must define. In this case we have defined it for you, but you should think of it as a class that you define.

Note that the import statements for the class `WindowDestroyer` are as follows:

```
import java.awt.*;
import java.awt.event.*;
```

When you are defining a listener class, you must have these two import statements. These import statements simply tell the compiler where the definitions for `Window-Adapter` and for event handling are located. (You may recall that we said the AWT was a precursor of the Swing library. The class `WindowAdapter` and the event handling model are in the AWT and that is why you see the name `awt` in the import statements.)

■ Java Tip
Ending a Swing Program

A GUI program is normally based on an kind of infinite loop. There may or may not be a Java loop statement in the program, but, normally, the GUI program still need not ever end. The windowing system normally stays on the screen until the user indicates that it should go away (for example, by clicking a close-window button). If the user never asked the system to go away, it would never go away. When you write a GUI program (using Swing), you need some way to say "End the program now." The following statement will end a Java program as soon as this statement is executed:

```
System.exit(0);
```

`System.exit`

This will end any Java program. A Java program that uses `System.exit` does not have to use Swing, but we will often use this statement in Swing programs.

The number 0 given as the argument to `System.exit` is returned to the operating system. In many situations, you can use any number and the program will behave the same. But most operating systems use 0 to indicate a normal termination of the program and 1 to indicate an abnormal termination of the program (just the opposite of what most people would guess). Thus, if your `System.exit` statement ends your program normally, the argument should be 0. An example of using this `System.exit` statement can be found in the definition of the method `window-Closing` in Display 12.2/page 766.

■ Gotcha
Forgetting to Program the Close-Window Button

The following lines from Display 12.1/page 763 ensure that when the user clicks the close-window button, the program will end and the window will go away:

```
WindowDestroyer myListener = new WindowDestroyer();
myWindow.addWindowListener(myListener);
```

You need not use these exact lines to program the action of the close-window button. For example, you may define a class of your own in place of `WindowDestroyer`. However, you do need to do some programming to ensure that when the user clicks the close-window button, the GUI will do what you want it to. If you do not program the close-window button, then when the user clicks the close-window button, the window will disappear, but the program will not end. If your GUI has only one window, that will mean that you have no easy way to end the program. There is also the added confusion that, even though the program is still running, it looks like the program has ended because the window has disappeared.

■ Gotcha

Forgetting to Use `getContentPane`

Recall that in Display 12.1 we added the label `myLabel` to the `JFrame` named `myWindow` as follows:

```
myWindow.getContentPane().add(myLabel);
```

Because you are "adding `myLabel` to `myWindow`" you might be tempted to use the following instead:

```
myWindow.add(myLabel);
```

If you omit `getContentPane()`, as we did above, then your program will not work correctly. Moreover, the compiler will probably not warn you about this mistake and so you must be very careful to avoid this mistake.

More About Window Listeners

WindowAdapter

As with our window listener class named `WindowDestroyer` in Display 12.2, any window listener class is typically a derived class of the class `WindowAdapter`. The class `WindowAdapter` has a number of different methods, each of which is automatically invoked when the listener object is sent an event that matches that method. The methods and corresponding events are given in the table in Display 12.3. When you define a derived class of the class `WindowAdapter`, you only define those methods that you need. The class `WindowDestroyer` is only needed to close windows, and so when we defined `WindowDestroyer`, we only defined the method `windowClosing`. We will not need any of these methods except `windowClosing`, but Display 12.3 lists all the methods for completeness.

In discussing our definition of the class `WindowDestroyer` in Display 12.2, it would be more proper for us to say that we *redefined* the method `windowClosing` rather than saying we *defined* it. This is because we are changing the definition of `windowClosing`. If in the definition of a derived class of the class `WindowAdapter` you give no definition for a method (from Display 12.3), then the class inherits the definition from the class `WindowAdapter`. However, when a method is inherited without being redefined, the method seldom does what you want. The methods are only useful if they are overridden in some derived class, such as the class `WindowDestroyer`. The class `WindowAdapter` is a special kind of class known as an **abstract class**, which means that you cannot create an object of the class `WindowAdapter`

abstract class

using *new* `WindowAdapter()`. You can only use `WindowAdapter` as a base class when defining other classes.

Display 12.3 Methods in the Class `WindowAdapter`

● ●

public void `windowOpened(WindowEvent e)`
    Invoked when a window has been opened.

public void `windowClosing(WindowEvent e)`
    Invoked when a window is in the process of being closed. Clicking the close-window button causes an invocation of this method.

public void `windowClosed(WindowEvent e)`
    Invoked when a window has been closed.

public void `windowIconified(WindowEvent e)`
    Invoked when a window is iconified.

public void `windowDeiconified(WindowEvent e)`
    Invoked when a window is deiconified.

public void `windowActivated(WindowEvent e)`
    Invoked when a window is activated.

public void `windowDeactivated(WindowEvent e)`
    Invoked when a window is deactivated.

Size Units for Screen Objects

When using Swing, the size of an object on the screen is measured in *pixels*. A **pixel** is the smallest unit of space on which your screen can write. Think of a pixel as a small rectangle that can have one of a small fixed number of colors and think of your screen as being paved with these little pixels. (It may help to think in terms of a simple black-and-white screen where a pixel is either black or white, even though most screens now offer more colors than just black and white.) The more pixels you have on your screen, the greater the resolution on your screen. That is, the more pixels you have, the more fine detail you can see.

    The size of a pixel depends on the size of your screen and the resolution of your screen. Although Swing uses pixels as if they were units of length, they do not represent any fixed length. The length of a pixel will vary from one screen to another. On a screen with high resolution (lots of pixels), an object of size 300 by 200 will look very small. On a screen with low resolution (not many pixels), an object of size

pixel

300 by 200 will look very large. For example, consider the following statement from Display 12.1/page 763:

```
myWindow.setSize(WIDTH, HEIGHT);
```

which is equivalent to

```
myWindow.setSize(300, 200);
```

This says that the object `myWindow` (which happens to be a kind of window) will be 300 pixels wide and 200 pixels high, but the actual size will depend on the resolution of the screen you are using when you run the program.

Notice that, although Java and Swing are portable and the code you write with Swing will run on any system that supports Java, the exact size of what you produce on the screen will vary from one screen to another. This is one feature of Java that is not as portable as would be ideal. To get the desired size for a window, you may need to change the dimensions to suit your particular screen size and screen resolution. However, it is only the absolute size that will vary. At least the relative size of things will be the same no matter where you run your Swing application. Moreover, for most window-like objects on most systems, after the window is displayed, the user can resize the window using the mouse.

Pixels

A **pixel** is the smallest unit of space on which your screen can write. The more pixels you have on a screen, the greater the screen resolution. With Swing, both size and position of objects on the screen are measured in pixels. Thus, a screen object will look smaller on a screen with high resolution and larger on a screen with low resolution.

Resolution versus Size

The relationship of resolution and size can seem confusing at first. A high-resolution screen is a screen of better quality than a low-resolution screen, so why does an object look smaller on a high-resolution screen? Isn't bigger better? It's not quite that simple. You have to think of counting pixels if you want a complete explanation, but here's one way to make it seem more sensible: If a screen has low resolution, you cannot see smaller things. Thus, when a screen has low resolution, the only way it can display a small object is to make it larger.

More on `setVisible`

setVisible

Consider the method `setVisible`, which is called in the program in Display 12.1/page 763. The particular line from Display 12.1 is the following:

```
myWindow.setVisible(true);
```

Every Swing object that can be displayed on the screen has a `setVisible` method.

The method `setVisible` takes one argument of type *boolean*. In other words, the argument to `setVisible` is either *true* or *false*. If w is an object, such as a window that can be displayed on the screen, then the call

```
w.setVisible(true);
```

will make w visible and the call

```
    w.setVisible(false);
```

will make w invisible.

You might think that displaying an object on the screen should happen auto-matically. After all, why would you define a window display unless you want it to be displayed on the screen? The answer is that you may not want it to be displayed at all times. You have undoubtedly worked with windowing systems where some win-dows come and go, either because they are no longer needed (like a pull-down menu after you make a choice) or because the window is covered by other windows. Swing cannot read the programmer's mind to determine when the window (or other GUI object) should be displayed and so the programmer must tell the system when to display the window. The programmer tells the system when to display the window by inserting a call to the method setVisible. If you rerun the program from Display 12.1 but omit the invocation of setVisible, then you will see nothing on the screen. The window will be constructed, but will not be displayed. (But be warned, if you eliminate the call to setVisible and then run the program in Display 12.1, you will then have no close-window button and so no way to end the program!)

The setVisible Method

Every Swing object that can be displayed on the screen will have a setVisible method.

The setVisible method takes one argument of type *boolean*. If w is an object, such as a window, that can be displayed on the screen, then the call

```
    w.setVisible(true);
```

will make w visible. The call

```
    w.setVisible(false);
```

will hide w, that is, will make w invisible.

Syntax: (for an invocation of the setVisible method):

Object_For_Screen.setVisible(*true_or_false*);

Example: (from Display 12.1/page 763):

```
    public static void main(String[] args)
    {
        JFrame myWindow = new JFrame();
            .
            .
            .
        myWindow.setVisible(true);
    }
```

? Self-Test Questions

3. How would you change the program in Display 12.1/page 763 so that the text in the window reads "I love you!" instead of "Please, don't click that button!"?

4. What units of measure are used in the following call to `setSize` that appeared in the `main` method of the program in Display 12.1/page 763? In other words, 300 of what? Inches? Feet? Centimeters? And similarly, 200 of what?

   ```
   myWindow.setSize(WIDTH, HEIGHT);
   ```

   which is equivalent to

   ```
   myWindow.setSize(300, 200);
   ```

5. What Swing class do you normally use to define a window? Any window class that you define would normally be an object of this class.

6. Give a Java statement that, when executed, will immediately end the program.

7. Give a Java statement that will add the label `superLabel` to the `JFrame` named `myGUI`.

Programming Example
A Better Version of Our First Swing Program

Display 12.4 and Display 12.5 together are a rewriting of the demonstration program in Display 12.1/page 763. This new version does essentially the same thing, except that it shows two rather than just one window. However, the new version (Display 12.4 and Display 12.5) is done in the style you should follow in writing your own GUI interfaces and programs. Notice that the definition of the window (Display 12.4) is in a class by itself (no pun intended). The window is then displayed in a program that uses the class (Display 12.5). A window class like `FirstWindow` in Display 12.4 is typically a class for an input/output interface that can be used in any of a number of programs. Let's look more carefully at the class `FirstWindow` in Display 12.4.

derived class   Observe that `FirstWindow` is a derived class of the class `JFrame`. This is the normal way to define a windowing interface. The base class `JFrame` gives some basic window facilities, and then the derived class adds whatever additional features you want in your windowing interface.

Note that the constructor in Display 12.4 starts by calling the constructor for the parent class `JFrame` with the line

```
super();
```

This ensures that any initialization that is normally done for all objects of type `JFrame` in fact will be done. When defining classes by inheritance from Swing classes, this is always safe and, in some other situations, absolutely necessary. There is one

Display 12.4 A Swing Window Class

```java
import javax.swing.*;

/*********************
 *A simple window class.
 *********************/
public class FirstWindow extends JFrame
{
    public static final int WIDTH = 300;
    public static final int HEIGHT = 200;

    public FirstWindow()
    {
        super();

        setSize(WIDTH, HEIGHT);
        JLabel myLabel = new JLabel("Please don't click that button!");
        getContentPane().add(myLabel);

        WindowDestroyer listener = new WindowDestroyer();
        addWindowListener(listener);
    }
}
```

case where it is not necessary, and Display 12.4 is an example of that case. *If the base-class constructor you call has no arguments,* then it will be called automatically whether or not you put in *super( )*; so, you could have omitted the invocation of *super( )* in Display 12.4. However, if the base class constructor needs an argument, as it may in some other situations, then you must include a call to the base class constructor, *super.*

Note that almost all the initializing for the window `FirstWindow` in Display 12.4 is placed in the constructor for the class. That is as it should be. The initializations, such as setting the initial window size, should be part of the class definition and not actions performed by objects of the class (as they were in Display 12.1/page 763). All the initializing methods, such as `setSize`, `getContentPane`, and `addWindowListener`, are inherited from the class `JFrame`. Because they are invoked in the constructor for the window, the window itself is the calling object. In other words, a method invocation such as

constructor

```java
setSize(WIDTH, HEIGHT);
```

is equivalent to

```java
this.setSize(WIDTH, HEIGHT);
```

Display 12.5   A Program that Uses the Class FirstWindow

```java
import javax.swing.*;

/****************************************************
 *A simple demonstration of using a window class. To see
 *both windows you will probably have to move the top window.
 ****************************************************/
public class FirstWindowDemo
{
    public static void main(String[] args)
    {
        FirstWindow window1 = new FirstWindow();
        window1.setVisible(true);

        FirstWindow window2 = new FirstWindow();
        window2.setVisible(true);
    }
}
```

Resulting GUI

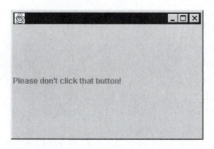

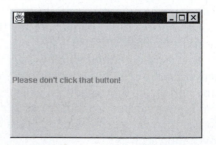

If it looks like you have only one window when you run this, move the window. The windows may be one on top of the other.

Similarly, the method invocation

```
getContentPane().add(myLabel);
```

is equivalent to

```
this.getContentPane().add(myLabel);
```

Aside from the fact that they are done in the constructor for a derived class, the details in the definition of `FirstWindow` in Display 12.4 are essentially the same as those details in Display 12.1/page 763.

Adding Items to a JFrame

You can add a `JLabel` to a `JFrame` as follows. (Later we will see that you can add other items in the same way.)

Syntax: (inside of a constructor):

```
getContentPane().add(JLabel);
```

Example: (within a constructor for a class called FirstWindow):

```
public FirstWindow()
{
        .
        .
        .
    JLabel myLabel =
            new JLabel("Please don't click that button!");
    getContentPane().add(myLabel);
        .
        .
        .
}
```

Let's next consider the program, Display 12.5, that uses the class `FirstWindow` in Display 12.4. All this program does is display two (identical) objects of the class `FirstWindow`. These two windows will probably be placed one exactly on top of the other. So, when you run it, it may look like only one window is displayed. However, if you use your mouse to move the top window, you will see a second window underneath it. If the class `FirstWindow` had been more complicated or more versatile, the program might have done more than just display the windows, but for a window class as simple as `FirstWindow` there is not much else you can do with the window. (This is after all our first example of a windowing interface, and as such, is very simple.)

Note that almost all of the initializations for the windows in Display 12.5 have been moved to the constructor for the class `FirstWindow`. However, we have placed the invocations of the method `setVisible` in the application program that uses the window class `FirstWindow`. We could have placed an invocation of `setVisible` in the constructor for `FirstWindow` and omitted the invocation of `setVisible` from the application program (Display 12.5); we would have gotten the same results when we ran the application program. However, in normal situations, the application program knows when the window should be displayed, and so it is normal to put the invocation of the method `setVisible` in the application program. The programmer who gave the definition of the class `FirstWindow` cannot anticipate when a programmer who use the window will want to make it visible (or invisible)

JFrame **Classes**

When we say that a class is a **JFrame class**, that means the class is a descendant class of the class `JFrame`. For example, the class `FirstWindow` in Display 12.4/page 773 is a `JFrame` class. ∎

Programming Example
A Window with Color

Display 12.6 contains a slight variant of the class shown in Display 12.4/page 773. This version has two constructors. The default constructor is the same as that in Display 12.4 but with four new elements added. The new elements are the title "Second Window", a local variable named `contentPane` to hold the content pane of the `JFrame`, a background color (blue), and a new way to add the window listener. Let's consider these four new elements one at a time. For the moment we are only considering the default constructor (the one with no arguments).

setTitle We have given the window a title with the following method invocation

```
setTitle("Second Window");
```

The method `setTitle` is inherited from the class `JFrame`. (Recall that the class for our window is a derived class of the class `JFrame`.) The method `setTitle` takes one string argument and writes that string in the title bar of the window. There is no calling object for this invocation because it is in a constructor and the calling object is an implicit *this*. The preceding invocation is equivalent to

```
this.setTitle("Second Window");
```

Other method invocations in the constructor also have an implicit *this*.

Note the following line from the first constructor in Display 12.6:

```
Container contentPane = getContentPane();
```

This gives us a name, `contentPane`, for the content pane of the `JFrame` windowing GUI we are defining. Thus, an invocation of the method `add` can be written in the simpler form:

```
contentPane.add(label);
```

instead of the slightly more complex (and slightly less efficient) expression

```
getContentPane().add(label);
```

The important thing to note here is that the method `getContentPane` produces an object of type `Container`. We will say a bit more about the class `Container` later in this chapter. For now, all you need to know about the class `Container` is that it is the type to use for the object returned by the method `getContentPane` (that is, for the content pane of the `JFrame`).

Display 12.6 Another Simple Window Constructed with Swing

```java
import javax.swing.*;
import java.awt.*;//needed for the Color class

public class SecondWindow extends JFrame
{
    public static final int WIDTH = 200;
    public static final int HEIGHT = 200;

    public SecondWindow()
    {
        super();

        setSize(WIDTH, HEIGHT);

        Container contentPane = getContentPane();
        JLabel label = new JLabel("Now available in color!");
        contentPane.add(label);

        setTitle("Second Window");
        contentPane.setBackground(Color.blue);

        addWindowListener(new WindowDestroyer());
    }

    public SecondWindow(Color customColor)
    {
        super();

        setSize(WIDTH, HEIGHT);

        Container contentPane = getContentPane();
        JLabel label = new JLabel("Now available in color!");
        contentPane.add(label);

        setTitle("Second Window");
        contentPane.setBackground(customColor);

        addWindowListener(new WindowDestroyer());
    }
}
```

If you prefer, you can omit this call to super. Because it is the default constructor, it will be called automatically anyway.

If you prefer, you can omit this call to super.

> ## Why Do JFrames Have a Content Pane?
>
> Unfortunately, this question does not have an easy answer. It has to do with ways of using a JFrame object which we will not go into in this book. If it seems to you that there is no need for a content pane, take comfort in the fact that your observation is well taken. It is not needed for what we are doing in this book. In fact, the precursor class of the class JFrame did not have a content pane. However, a JFrame object does have a content pane and you must deal with the content pane or you programs will not work correctly.

In Display 12.6, we have also given the window a background color with the method call

set-
Background

```
contentPane.setBackground(Color.blue);
```

The method setBackground is another method that is inherited from the class JFrame. The method setBackground takes one argument, which is a color. The class Color contains constants for many of the common colors. Color.blue is a pre-defined constant that stands for the color blue. The color constants you have available are listed in Display 12.7. To see what each of these colors looks like, replace the constant Color.blue in Display 12.6 with the color you want to see, compile, and then run the modified program. You can also define your own colors with the class Color, but we will not go into that topic until Chapter 15. Because the Color class is in the AWT package (library), the following import statement is needed when a class or program uses the Color class:

```
import java.awt.*;//needed for the Color class
```

(As we pointed out earlier the AWT library is a precursor of the Swing library, but some of the classes in the AWT are need when you program in Swing.)

Display 12.7 The Color Constants

```
Color.black          Color.magenta
Color.blue           Color.orange
Color.cyan           Color.pink
Color.darkGray       Color.red
Color.gray           Color.white
Color.green          Color.yellow
Color.lightGray
```

The class Color is in the AWT package (library). So, when using these colors, you need the following import statement:

```
import java.awt.*;
```

What Kind of Color is Cyan?

You might wonder why the designers of the Java libraries chose to have defined constants for some of the colors in Display 12.7. Certainly colors like black, white, red, green, and most of the others are common colors, but why did they pick the colors cyan and magenta? The answer is that one of the common ways of making colors is to mix the four colors black, yellow, cyan, and magenta. So, cyan and magenta are indeed "basic colors" in some sense of the words.

Cyan is kind of very light blue. Magenta is a kind of purple. The other common way of mixing colors is to mix red, green, and blue. Your TV uses red, green, and blue. Books printed in color use black, yellow, cyan, and magenta.

---

new in arguments

At the end of the first constructor definition we added a listener for our window with the following invocation of the method `addWindowListener`:

```
addWindowListener(new WindowDestroyer());
```

Certain methods, such as `addWindowListener`, need objects as arguments, but once the object is given as an argument to the method, you never need to refer to it again in your programming. That means that you do not need a name for the argument. An argument such as `new WindowDestroyer()` in the preceding invocation of the method `addWindowListener` is a way to create an object and pass it as an argument to the method `addWindowListener`, and yet not have to give the argument a name. The invocation

```
addWindowListener(new WindowDestroyer());
```

is equivalent to the following:

```
WindowDestroyer listener = new WindowDestroyer();
addWindowListener(listener):
```

The only difference between the preceding two ways of adding a window listener is that in the first form, we do not bother to use a name for the object of type `WindowDestroyer`, and in the second, two-line version, we give the listener object the name `listener`.

Using *new* as Part of a Method Argument

You can create an object and pass it as an argument to a method without bothering to give the object a name. You do this by using *new* and the class name as the argument. In these cases, the class name is being used as the name of the constructor for the class.

Syntax:

Method_Name (*new* *Class_Name_As_Constructor* (*Possibly_Parameters*)) ;

Example:

```
addWindowListener(new WindowDestroyer());
```

anonymous arguments

The argument *new* `WindowDestroyer()` is often called an **anonymous object**, because it has no name.

Display 12.8 A Demonstration Program for SecondWindow

```
import java.awt.*;//for the class Color used in an argument.

public class SecondWindowDemo
{
    /*********************************************************
    *Creates and displays two windows of the class SecondWindow.
    *********************************************************/
    public static void main(String[] args)
    {
        SecondWindow window1 = new SecondWindow();
        window1.setVisible(true);

        SecondWindow window2 = new SecondWindow(Color.pink);
        window2.setVisible(true);
    }
}
```

Resulting GUI

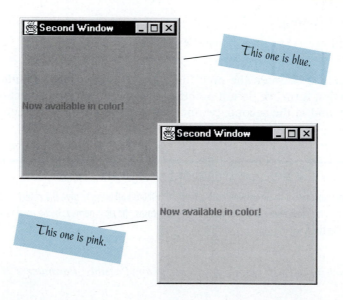

Now let's consider the second constructor. The second constructor is almost the same as the default constructor except for how it handles the background color. This second constructor has one parameter of type `Color` and sets the background color to this one parameter. You can easily see the difference between these two constructors by looking at the demonstration program in Display 12.8. The two windows produced are identical except that one has a blue background and one has a pink background. (As with the previous example, when you run the program in Display 12.8 one window will probably be on top of the other, so that it looks like you have only one window. Just use your mouse to move the top window, and you will see the other window.)

Some Methods of the Class `JFrame`

Display 12.9 contains some of the methods for the class `JFrame`. You will recall that `JFrame` is the basic class out of which you normally build windows. A window class is normally a derived class of the class `JFrame`, and so the window class inherit all these methods.

What Import Statements to Use

It is rather difficult to keep track of which import statement you need for a Swing class definition or Swing program. The following import statements will suffice for most Swing window interfaces:

```
import javax.swing.*;
import java.awt.*;
import java.awt.event.*;
```

The loss of efficiency for including an extra import statement is minimal, so there is no need to be obsessive in keeping them to a minimum. However, in order to give you more information, the class definitions in this text use only those import statement that are needed.

■

? Self-Test Questions

8. How would you modify the class definition in Display 12.6/page 777 so that the window produced by the default constructor is yellow instead of blue.

9. How do you set the title of a window you create with Swing?

10. Suppose you declared and created a window object of the class `MyWindowClass` with the following code:

```
MyWindowClass gui = new MyWindowClass();
```

The window `gui` is not yet visible on the screen. Give a program statement that will make it visible.

11. Rewrite the following without using a name for the object `listener`:

```
WindowDestroyer listener = new WindowDestroyer();
addWindowListener(listener);
```

Display 12.9 Some Methods in the Class `JFrame`

Method	Description
`JFrame()`	Constructor for creating a new `JFrame`.
`JFrame(String title)`	Constructor for creating a new `JFrame` with the specified `title`.
`add`	`JFrame` has a method `add`, but it should not be used. (It is basically a useless inheritance from an ancestor class). To add something to a `JFrame` use `getContentPane().add(` *Item_Added*`)`
void `addWindowListener(` `    WindowListener ear)`	Registers `ear` as a listener for events fired by the `JFrame`.
`Container getContentPane()`	Returns the content pane object of the `JFrame`. Note that the content pane that is returned is of type `Container`.
void `setBackground(Color c)`	Sets the background color to `c`.
void `setForeground(Color c)`	Sets the foreground color to `c`.
void `setSize(int width, int height)`	Resizes the window to the specified width and height.
void `setTitle(String title)`	Writes the `title` on the title bar of the window.
void `setVisible(boolean b)`	Makes the window visible if the argument is *true*. Makes it invisible if the argument is *false*.

12. Suppose `myWindowGUI` is a windowing interface whose class was defined as a derived class of the class `JFrame`. Suppose `myLabel` is an object of the class `JLabel`, and you want to add the label `myLabel` to `myWindowGUI`. Will the following work correctly? If not, what should be used instead?

```
myWindowGUI.add(myLabel);
```

Layout Managers

We have seen that you can add a `JLabel` to a `JFrame` by using the method `getContentPane` to get the content pane of the `JFrame`, and then using the method `add` to add the `JLabel` to the content pane. For an example, look at Display 12.6/page 777. If you only add one label, it seems like there is no question of where the label goes, but what if you add two or more labels? How are they arranged? One on top of the other? One next to the other? Which is first, which is second, and so forth? That arranging is done by a special kind of object known as a **layout manager**. The layout manager arranges the items you add according to certain rules. Different layout managers follow different rules, and so you will have a good deal of control over how things are arranged in a windowing interface (that is, in a `JFrame` or similar GUI). The next example adds three labels to a `JFrame` and uses a layout manager to arrange the three labels.

layout manager

Display 12.10 contains an example of a class used to create a window with three labels. A layout manager is used to place the labels one below the other on three lines, rather than in some other arrangement such as all on one line. Let's look at the details.

First note one minor point that we have not seen before in our discussion of Swing (although we have seen it in other kinds of classes, for example Display 5.7/page 313). We have placed a demonstration `main` method in the class definition. Normally, a Swing GUI class is used to create and display a GUI in a `main` (or other method) in some other class. However, it is perfectly legal and sometimes convenient to place a `main` method in the GUI class definition so that it is easy to display a sample of the GUI. Note that the `main` that is given in the class itself is written in the same way as a `main` that is in some other class. In particular, you need to construct an object of the class, as in the following line from the `main` in Display 12.10:

```
BorderLayoutDemo gui = new BorderLayoutDemo();
```

Now let's move on to the things that are truly new in Display 12.10.

A layout manager is added to the GUI in Display 12.10 with the following line:

```
content.setLayout(new BorderLayout());
```

setLayout

`BorderLayout` is a layout manager class, and so `new BorderLayout()` produces a new object of the class `BorderLayout`. This `BorderLayout` object is given the task of arranging components (in this case, labels) that are added to the GUI. The way you specify that this object (namely, `new BorderLayout()`) is given the task of arranging components is by making it an argument to the method `setLayout`. It may help to note that the above invocation of `setLayout` is equivalent to the following:

Display 12.10 Using The BorderLayout Manager *(Part 1 of 2)*

```java
import javax.swing.*;
import java.awt.*;

/************************************************************
 *Simple demonstration of using a layout manager to arrange labels.
 ************************************************************/
public class BorderLayoutDemo extends JFrame
{
    public static final int WIDTH = 300;
    public static final int HEIGHT = 200;

    /**********************************************************
     *Creates and displays a window of the class BorderLayoutDemo.
     **********************************************************/
    public static void main(String[] args)
    {
        BorderLayoutDemo gui = new BorderLayoutDemo();
        gui.setVisible(true);
    }

    public BorderLayoutDemo()
    {
        setSize(WIDTH, HEIGHT);
        addWindowListener(new WindowDestroyer());
        setTitle("Layout Demonstration");
        Container content = getContentPane();

        content.setLayout(new BorderLayout());

        JLabel label1 = new JLabel("First label here.");
        content.add(label1, BorderLayout.NORTH);

        JLabel label2 = new JLabel("Second label there.");
        content.add(label2, BorderLayout.SOUTH);

        JLabel label3 = new JLabel("Third label anywhere.");
        content.add(label3, BorderLayout.CENTER);
    }
}
```

```
BorderLayout manager = new BorderLayout();
content.setLayout(manager);
```

Note that the method setLayout is invoked not by the JFrame itself, but by the content pane of the JFrame, which in this case is named content. This is because we actually add the labels to the content pane and not (directly) to the JFrame. In general, the invocation of setLayout should be made with the same object that you use to invoke add (and so far that has always been the content pane of a JFrame).

A BorderLayout manager places labels (or other components) into the five regions: BorderLayout.NORTH, BorderLayout.SOUTH, BorderLayout.EAST, BorderLayout.WEST, and BorderLayout.CENTER. The five regions are arranged as follows:

BorderLayout

BorderLayout.NORTH		
BorderLayout. WEST	BorderLayout.CENTER	BorderLayout. EAST
BorderLayout.SOUTH		

In the above diagram, the outside dark edge represents the content pane (or other container to which you will add things). The five regions are divided by finer lines on

Display 12.10 Using The BorderLayout Manager *(Part 2 of 2)*

Resulting GUI

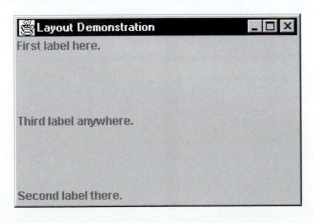

the inside of the diagram. The fine lines will not be visible unless you do something to make them visible. We drew them in to show you where each region is located. Let's look at our example from Display 12.10. We added labels as follows:

```
JLabel label1 = new JLabel("First label here.");
content.add(label1, BorderLayout.NORTH);

JLabel label2 = new JLabel("Second label there.");
content.add(label2, BorderLayout.SOUTH);

JLabel label3 = new JLabel("Third label anywhere.");
content.add(label3, BorderLayout.CENTER);
```

BorderLayout.NORTH, BorderLayout.SOUTH, BorderLayout.EAST, Border-Layout.WEST, and BorderLayout.CENTER are five constants defined in the class BorderLayout, although you do not have to think of them as anything more than five things that you now know how to spell and that specify the five regions for a border layout manager. Note that when you use a border layout manager, you give the region as a second argument to the method add, as in:

```
content.add(label1, BorderLayout.NORTH);
```

Note that the labels (or other components to be added) need not be added in any particular order, because the second argument completely specifies where the label is placed.

That seems to conclude our discussion of Display 12.10, except for one point. What became of the regions BorderLayout.EAST and BorderLayout.WEST? The answer is simple. They were not used. You need not use all five regions. If some regions are not used, then any extra space is given to the BorderLayout.CENTER region.

Layout Managers

The objects that you add to a container class are arranged by an object known as a **layout manager**. You add a layout manager with the method setLayout, which is a method of every container class, such as the content pane of a JFrame or an object of some other container classes that we will introduce later in this chapter. If you do not add a layout manager, then a default layout manager will be provided for you.

Syntax:

```
Container_Object.setLayout(new Layout_Manager_Class());
```

Example: (within a constructor for a class called FlowLayoutDemo):

```
public FlowLayoutDemo()
{
        ...
    Container contentPane = getContentPane();
    contentPane.setLayout(new FlowLayout());

    JLabel label1 = new JLabel("Labels are good.");
    contentPane.add(label1);
        ...
}
```

Specifying The BorderLayout Region

We have specified the region in which to place a button (or other component) using the five constants `Border-Layout.NORTH`, `BorderLayout.SOUTH`, `BorderLayout.EAST`, `BorderLay-out.WEST`, and `BorderLayout.CENTER`. If you prefer, you can instead use the five strings `"North"`, `"South"`, `"East"`, `"West"`, and `"Center"`. For example, the following rewrites some code from Display 12.10/page 784 using these strings:

Example:

```
JLabel label1 = new JLabel("First label here.");
content.add(label1, "North");

JLabel label2 = new JLabel("Second label there.");
content.add(label2, "South");

JLabel label3 = new JLabel("Third label anywhere.");
content.add(label3, "Center");
```

Using the strings `"North"`, `"South"`, and so forth saves typing. However, a region is not a string, and so some programmers prefer to use the constants, such as `BorderLayout.NORTH`, for philosophical and stylistic reasons. Either approach is reasonable.

From our discussion it sounds like you can place only one item in each region, but later in this chapter we will see that there is a way to group items so that more than one item can (in effect) be placed in each region.

There are some standard predefined layout managers and you can also define your own layout managers. However, for most purpose, the predefined layout managers are all that you need, and we will not discuss how you can create your own layout manager classes. We will discuss the three most commonly used predefined layout managers: the border layout manager, which you have already seen, and the two layout managers we discuss next. (One additional layout manager called the *box layout manager* will be introduced in Chapter 14.)

The simplest layout manager is the **flow layout manager**. An object of the class `FlowLayout` is a layout manager that arranges the components you add to a class in the most obvious way. The components are arranged one after the other going from left to right. The components are laid out in the order in which you add them to the class using the method `add`. For example, if the class in Display 12.10 had used the flow layout manager, then it would use the following code:

`FlowLayout`

```
content.setLayout(new FlowLayout());

JLabel label1 = new JLabel("First label here.");
content.add(label1);

JLabel label2 = new JLabel("Second label there.");
content.add(label2);

JLabel label3 = new JLabel("Third label anywhere.");
content.add(label3);
```

Note that if we had used the flow layout manager, as in the above code, then the `add` method has only one argument. Also note that, with a flow layout manager, the items are displayed in the order they are added, so that labels would be displayed all on one line as follows:

```
First label here.Second label there.Third label anywhere.
```

Extra code on CD

(If you want to see the full program, look at the file `FlowLayoutDemo.java` on the accompanying CD.) You will see a number of examples of the GUIs that use the `FlowLayout` manager class later in this chapter.

GridLayout

A `GridLayout` **manager** arranges components in rows and columns with each entry being the same size. For example, the following says to use the a `GridLayout` manager with `aContainer` (which can be a content pane or other container).

```
aContainer.setLayout(new GridLayout(2, 3));
```

The two numbers given as arguments to the constructor `GridLayout` specify the number of rows and columns. This would produce the following sort of layout.

The lines will not be visible unless you do something special to make them visible. They are just to show you the region boundaries.

When using the `GridLayout` class, the method `add` has only one argument. The items are placed in the grid from left to right first filling the top row, then the second row, and so forth. You are not allowed to skip any grid position (although we will later see that you can add something that does not show and so gives the illusion of skipping a grid position).

Extra code on CD

If you want to see the class `GridLayout` in action, look at the class `GridLayoutDemo.java` on the accompanying CD.

The three layout managers are summarized in Display 12.11.

Display 12.11 Some Layout Managers

Layout Manager	Description
`FlowLayout`	Displays components left to right in the same fashion that you normally write things on a piece of paper.
`BorderLayout`	Displays the components in five areas: north, south, east, west, and center. You specify which area a component goes into in a second argument of the `add` method.
`GridLayout`	Lays components out in a grid with each component stretched to fill its box in the grid.

Default Layout Managers

If you do not add a layout manager, then a default layout manager will be provided for you. For example, in Display 12.6/page 777 we did not specify any layout manager, but we could still add a label because there was a default layout manager provided automatically. The default layout manager class for the content pane of a `JFrame` is the `BorderLayout` class. (If you are using the `BorderLayout` class and use `add` with no second argument, then it is the same as if you gave `BorderLayout.CENTER` as a second argument. We relied on this detail for our first few programs, but now that we know about layout managers, we will always use a second argument when adding to a container with a `BorderLayout` manager.)

Until we learned about layout managers, we simply left things to the default layout manger. However, it is preferable to always specify a layout manger. This makes your code clearer and more likely to survive any future changes to new versions of the Swing classes. From now on we will always use an explicit layout manager.

■ *Programming Tip*
Copy Other Programmers' Code

Before I get in trouble with any instructors, let me clarify what the title of this section does not mean. It does not mean that you should have somebody else do your assignments. What this means is that one very good way to learn how to program, and to produce good programs in a hurry, is to start out with a program that does something similar to what you want and then change it to do exactly what you want. For example, if you want to write a program for a window that has something written in it, you can start with the program in Display 12.10/page 784 and change the details. Code for Swing GUIs can be pretty complicated, and it is not easy to learn all the details of all the various predefined classes and methods. Sometimes, the best way to learn these details is to copy and change code until the details become routine.

? Self-Test Questions

13. How would you modify the class definition in Display 12.10/page 784 so that the three labels are displayed as follows?

    ```
    First label here.
    Second label there.
    Third label anywhere.
    ```

    (There may be space between each of the above lines.)

14. How would you modify the class definition in Display 12.10/page 784 so that the three labels are displayed as follows?

    ```
    First label here.
                                    Second label there.
    Third label anywhere.
    ```

    (There may be space between each of the above lines.)

15. The following occurs in the definition of the constructor in Display 12.10/ page 784. What is the meaning of the *new*? What kind of argument is being used?

    ```
    contentPane.setLayout(new BorderLayout());
    ```

16. Suppose you are defining a windowing GUI class in the usual way, as a derived class of the class `JFrame`, and suppose that the constructor obtains the content pane as follows:

    ```
    contentPane = getContentPane();
    ```

    Now suppose you want to specify a layout manager for `contentPane` so as to produce the following sort of layout:

    What should the argument to `setLayout` be?

17. Suppose the situation is as described in Self-Test Question 16, except that you want the following sort of layout:

    What should the argument to `setLayout` be?

12.3 | Buttons and Action Listeners

> *I claim not to have controlled events, but confess plainly*
> *that events have controlled me.*
> **Abraham Lincoln, Letter to A. G. Hodges (April 4, 1864)**

So far the GUIs we have produced using Swing have included no actions. They just sat there and displayed some text. The only action they took was to go away in response to clicking the close-window button. In this section we start to show you how to design GUIs that do things, like changing color, changing text, or some more complicated actions. A button is simply a component in a GUI that looks like a button and that does something when you click it with your mouse. You create buttons in a way that is very similar to how you create labels. You add buttons to a `JFrame` in the same way that you add labels to a `JFrame`, but there is also something very new about buttons. You can associate an action with a button, so that when the user clicks the button with a mouse, the GUI performs some action. An example should make the details clear.

Programming Example
Adding Buttons

Display 12.12 contains a program that creates a window with two buttons, labeled `"Red"` and `"Green"`. When the program is run, the window shown in Display 12.12 is displayed. If you click the button marked `"Red"` with your mouse, the color of the window changes from blue (or whatever color it is) to red. If you click the button labeled `"Green,"` the color of the window changes to green. That is all the program does (but as you can see, you are gradually learning to build more complicated windowing interfaces). To end the program and make the window disappear, you click the close-window button.

Much of what appears in Display 12.12 is already familiar to you. The class `ButtonDemo` is a derived class of the class `JFrame` and so it is a window interface similar to the ones we have already seen in this chapter. A window listener of the class `WindowDestroyer` is added with the method `addWindowListener` as in previous examples. The size is set, and the content pane is obtained, with `getContentPane` as in previous examples. We use a layout manager as we did in the previous example (Display 12.10/page 784), although this time we use the `FlowLayout` manager class.

What is new in Display 12.12 is the use of button objects of the class `JButton` and a new kind of listener class. We will discuss buttons and the new listener class in the next few subsections.

Buttons

A button is a GUI component that looks like a button and that can do something when you click it with your mouse. In this subsection we tell you how to add buttons to your GUI. In the next subsection we tell you how to specify what happens when the button is clicked.

A button object is created in the same way that any other object is created, but you use the class `JButton` when you want buttons. For example, the following example from Display 12.12 creates a button:

adding buttons

```
JButton stopButton = new JButton("Red");
```

The argument to the construct, in this case `"Red"`, is a string that will be written on the button when the button is displayed. The string argument to the constructor, in this example `"Red"`, specifies the string that will appear on the button when it is displayed on the screen. If you look at the GUI in Display 12.12, you will see that the two buttons are labeled `"Red"` and `"Green"`.

The button is added to the content pane with the following:

```
contentPane.add(stopButton);
```

There is no second argument to the method add because we are using the FlowLay-out manager class. If we had instead used the BorderLayout manger class, then we would have used some second argument, such as BorderLayout.NORTH.

In the next subsection we explain the lines from Display 12.12 involving the method addActionListener.

The JButton Class

An object of the class JButton is displayed in a GUI as a component that looks like a button. You click the button with your mouse instead of actually pushing it. When creating an object of the class JButton using *new*, you can give a string argument to the constructor and the string will be displayed on the button.

You can add objects of the class JButton to the content pane of a JFrame using the method add. We will later see that you can also add buttons to other GUI objects in a similar way.

Example: (within a constructor for a class called ButtonDemo**):**

```
public ButtonDemo()
{
        .
        .
        .
    Container contentPane = getContentPane();
        .
        .
        .
    contentPane.setLayout(new FlowLayout());
        .
        .
        .
    JButton stopButton = new JButton("Red");
        .
        .
        .
    contentPane.add(stopButton);
        .
        .
        .
        .
}
```

The Close-Window Button is Not in the Class JButton

The buttons that you add to a GUI are all objects of the class JButton. The close-window button (which you get automatically in any derived class of the class JFrame) is not an object of the class JButton. That close-window button is part of the JFrame object.

Action Listeners and Action Events

When you click a button with your mouse (or activate some other item in a GUI), that creates an object known as an **event** and sends the object to another object (or objects) known as the **listener**. This is called **firing** the event. The listener then performs some action. When we say that the event is "sent" to the listener object, what we really mean is that some method in the listener object is invoked with the event object as the argument. This invocation happens automatically. Your Swing GUI class definition will not normally contain an invocation of this method. However,

Display 12.12 A GUI with Buttons Added *(Part 1 of 2)*

```java
import javax.swing.*;
import java.awt.*;
import java.awt.event.*;

/***********************************************
 *Simple demonstration of putting buttons in a JFrame.
 ********************************************/
public class ButtonDemo extends JFrame implements ActionListener
{
    public static final int WIDTH = 300;
    public static final int HEIGHT = 200;

    /***************************************************
     *Creates and displays a window of the class ButtonDemo.
     ****************************************************/
    public static void main(String[] args)
    {
        ButtonDemo buttonGui = new ButtonDemo();
        buttonGui.setVisible(true);
    }

    public ButtonDemo()
    {

        setSize(WIDTH, HEIGHT);

        addWindowListener(new WindowDestroyer());
        setTitle("Button Demo");
        Container contentPane = getContentPane();
        contentPane.setBackground(Color.blue);

        contentPane.setLayout(new FlowLayout());

        JButton stopButton = new JButton("Red");
        stopButton.addActionListener(this);
        contentPane.add(stopButton);

        JButton goButton = new JButton("Green");
        goButton.addActionListener(this);
        contentPane.add(goButton);
    }
```

It will take several subsections to fully explain this program. The explanation does not end until the end of the subsection entitled **Action Listeners and Action Events.**

Display 12.12 A GUI with Buttons Added *(Part 2 of 2)*

```java
public void actionPerformed(ActionEvent e)
{
    Container contentPane = getContentPane();

    if (e.getActionCommand().equals("Red"))
        contentPane.setBackground(Color.red);
    else if (e.getActionCommand().equals("Green"))
        contentPane.setBackground(Color.green);
    else
        System.out.println("Error in button interface.");
}
}
```

Resulting GUI

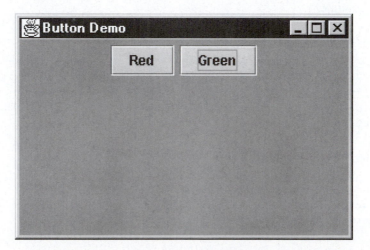

Why Do So Many Class Names Start with "J"?

"J" for "Java." Right? Well yes, but that is not the whole story. Why not name the classes `Frame`, `Label`, `Button`, and so forth, instead of names like `JFrame`, `JLabel`, and `JButton`? The answer is that the AWT, the precursor of Swing, already has classes named `Frame`, `Label`, `Button`, and so forth. Since Swing does not completely replace the AWT library, you must use the AWT together with Swing (although you may not always be aware of this) and so Swing class names should be different from AWT class names. Because the AWT already has classes named `Frame`, `Label`, `Button`, and so forth, Swing named the corresponding Swing classes `JFrame`, `JLabel`, `JButton`, and so forth.

---

your Swing GUI class definition does need to do two things: First for each button, it needs to specify what object(s) are listeners that will respond to events fired by that button; this is called **registering** the listener. Second, your GUI class definition(s) must also define the method(s) that will be invoked when the event is sent to the listener. Note that these methods will be defined by you, but in normal circumstances, you will never write an invocation of these methods. The invocations will take place automatically.

The following line from Display 12.12

```
stopButton.addActionListener(this);
```

registers *this* as a listener to receive events from the button named `stopButton`. A similar statement also registers *this* as a listener to receive events from the button named `goButton`. Because the argument is *this*, that means that *this* (the class `ButtonDemo` itself) is the listener class. Recall that within the definition of a class, an object of that class is called *this*. The class `ButtonDemo` is itself the listener class for the buttons inside of `ButtonDemo`. (To be a bit more precise, this means that each object of the class `ButtonDemo` is the listener for the buttons in that object.) Next we explain how to make a class, such as `ButtonDemo`, into a listener class for events fired by buttons.

Different kinds of components require different kinds of listener classes to handle the events they fire. A button fires events known as **action events,** which are handled by listeners known as **action listeners**.

An action listener is an object of type `ActionListener`. `ActionListener` is not a class, but is a property that you can give to any class you define. (These properties, such as `ActionListener`, are known as **interfaces.**) To make a class into an `ActionListener`, you need to do two things:

1. You add the phrase *implements* `ActionListener` to the beginning of the class definition, normally at the end of the first line.
2. You define a method named `actionPerformed`.

In Display 12.12, we made the `JFrame` class named `ButtonDemo` into an `ActionListener` in just this way. In what follows, we reproduce an outline of the definition of the class `ButtonDemo` (with the omitted sections indicated by three dots):

registering a listener

addAction_
Command

action event
action listener

Action-
Listener

action-
Performed

```
public class ButtonDemo extends JFrame implements ActionListener
{
          .
          .
          .
    public void actionPerformed(ActionEvent e)
    {
          .
          .
          .
    }
          .
          .
          .
}
```

We could have defined a separate class that did nothing but handle button events, but it's more convenient to make the window class ButtonDemo into the Action-Listener that will handle button events. This is convenient because the button events are supposed to change the window, and the easiest way to change a window is by a method within the window itself.

Now, suppose we create an object, buttonGui, of the class ButtonDemo as follows:

```
ButtonDemo buttonGui = new ButtonDemo();
```

action-
Performed

Then the *this* parameter in the definition of the class ButtonDemo refers to button-Gui. So buttonGui is the action listener for the two buttons inside of buttonGui. So when a button is clicked, the method actionPerformed will be automatically invoked with the event fired by the button as the argument to actionPerformed. All that is left to explain is how the method actionPerformed works. Let's continue with our object buttonGui of the class ButtonDemo.

If you click one of the buttons inside of buttonGui with your mouse, that sends an action event to the action listener for that button. But, buttonGui is the action listener for the buttons in buttonGui, so the action event goes to buttonGui. When an action listener receives an action event, the event is automatically passed to the method actionPerformed. The method actionPerformed is typically a branching statement that determines what kind of action event was fired and then performs some appropriate action. Let's look at the code for the method actionPerformed in the class ButtonDemo in Display 12.12. For convenience, we reproduce the definition in what follows:

```
public void actionPerformed(ActionEvent e)
{
    Container contentPane = getContentPane();

    if (e.getActionCommand().equals("Red"))
        contentPane.setBackground(Color.red);
    else if (e.getActionCommand().equals("Green"))
        contentPane.setBackground(Color.green);
    else
        System.out.println("Error in button interface.");
}
```

In this case, the method `actionPerformed` needs to know whether the action event came from the button labeled `"Red"` or the button labeled `"Green"`. If e is an action event that was fired by clicking a button, then `e.getActionCommand()` returns the string written on the button; in this case it returns either `"Red"` or `"Green"`. So, all that the method `actionPerformed` needs to do is to see if `e.getActionCommand()` is `"Red"` or `"Green"` and perform the appropriate action for that button. Note that `e.getActionCommand()` is an object of the class `String`. The class `String` has a method `equals` that can be used to check to see if `e.getActionCommand()` is equal to `"Red"` or `"Green"` (or any other string). The method invocation

getAction-
Command

    e.getActionCommand().equals(*String_Argument*)

returns *true* if `e.getActionCommand()` is equal to the *String_Argument*, and returns *false* otherwise. Thus, the following code tests to see if `e.getActionCommand()` is equal to `"Red"` or `"Green"` and changes the color of the GUI accordingly:

```
if (e.getActionCommand().equals("Red"))
    contentPane.setBackground(Color.red);
else if (e.getActionCommand().equals("Green"))
    contentPane.setBackground(Color.green);
else
    System.out.println("Error in button interface.");
```

The final *else* clause should never need to be executed. It is just there so that we would get a warning, if we made some unnoticed mistake in the code.

■ Gotcha

Changing The Parameter List for `actionPerformed`

When you make a class into an action listener, the header for the method `action-Performed` is determined for you. It must have exactly one parameter and that parameter must be of type `ActionEvent`, as in the following:

```
public void actionPerformed(ActionEvent e)
```

If you change the type of the parameter or if you add (or subtract) a parameter, you will not have given a correct definition of an action listener.[1] The only thing you can change is the name of the parameter e, since it is just a "place holder." So, the following change is acceptable:

```
public void actionPerformed(ActionEvent theEvent)
```

Of course, if you make this change, then inside the body of the method `actionPer-formed`, you will use the identifier `theEvent` in place of the identifier `e`.

---

1. Although it would be rather questionable style, you can overload the method name `actionPerformed` so you have multiple versions of the method `actionPerformed`, each with a different parameter list. But, only the one shown above has anything to do with making a class into an action listener.

Action Events and Action Listeners

Buttons, and certain other components, fire events in the class `ActionEvent`. These events are know as **action events** and must be handled by an action listener. Any class can be an action listener class. The details in outline form are as follows:

1. Make some class (maybe a window class) into an `ActionListener` by adding the phrase

    implements `ActionListener`

to the heading of the class definition and adding a definition for a method named `actionPerformed`. The `ActionListener` can be any class. In particular, the class may serve some other function besides being an `ActionListener`.

2. Register the `ActionListener` object with the button (or other component that will fire the action event). To do this, you use the method `addActionListener`. A button or other component may register more than (or less than) one listener.

Example: (The complete details are in Display 12.12/page 793):

```
public class ButtonDemo extends JFrame implements ActionListener
{
        .
        .
        .
    public ButtonDemo()
    {
        .
        .
        .
        Container contentPane = getContentPane();
        .
        .
        JButton stopButton = new JButton("Red");
        stopButton.addActionListener(this);
        contentPane.add(stopButton);
        .
        .
        .
    }

    public void actionPerformed(ActionEvent e)
    {
        .
        .
        .
    }
}
```

The `actionPerformed` Method

In order to be an `ActionListener` a class must, among other things, have a method named `action-Performed` that has one parameter of type `ActionEvent`. This is the only method required by the `ActionListener` interface.

Syntax:

```java
public void actionPerformed(ActionEvent e)
{
    Code_for_Actions_Performed
}
```

The *Code_for_Actions_Performed* is typically a branching statement depending on some property of `e`. Often the branching depends on `e.getActionCommand()`. If `e` is an event fired by clicking a button, then `e.getActionCommand()` is a string known as the **action command**. The action command is the string written on the button, unless you specify a different action command.

(You can specify a different action command with the method `setActionCommand`. For details, see the subsection entitled *Java Tip* **Use the Method** *setActionCommand* on page 800.)

Example:

```java
public void actionPerformed(ActionEvent e)
{
    Container contentPane = getContentPane();

    if (e.getActionCommand().equals("Red"))
        contentPane.setBackground(Color.red);
    else if (e.getActionCommand().equals("Green"))
        contentPane.setBackground(Color.green);
    else
        System.out.println("Error in button interface.");
}
```

Interfaces

Look again at Display 12.12/page 793. We want the class `ButtonDemo` to be both a `Frame` and an `ActionListener`. But, `ButtonDemo` can only be a derived class of one base class, so we made it a derived class of the class `JFrame`. That means that `ActionListener` must serve a similar but different function from that of the base class `JFrame`. This `ActionListener` thing is not a class but is an *interface*. An **interface** is a property of a class that says what methods it must have. A class such as `ButtonDemo` that satisfies an interface is said to **implement the interface**. In order to implement an interface, a class must include the phrase *implements* `ActionListener` (or whatever the name of the interface is) and it must define all the methods specified in the interface. (The particular interface `ActionListener` specifies only the one method `actionPerformed`.)

Although and interface is not a class, it is a type. For example, a method can have a parameter of type `ActionListener`. Then, any class that implements the `ActionListener` interface can be an argument to that method.

■ Programming Tip
Code Look and Actions Separately

You can simplify writing the code for a Swing GUI into two major parts: coding what the GUI looks like on the screen and coding the actions of the GUI. For example consider the program in Display 12.12/page 793. Your first version of this program might use the following definition of the method `actionPerformed`:

```
public void actionPerformed(ActionEvent e)
{}
```

With this "do nothing" version of the method `actionPerformed`, your program will run and will show a display on the screen just as shown in Display 12.12. If you press either of the two color change buttons nothing will happen, but you can use this phase of coding to adjust details, such as which button is listed first. (Note that the close-window button does, however, work.)

After you get the GUI to look like you want it to look, you can then define the action parts of the GUI, typically the method `actionPerformed`. This breaks the task of coding the Swing GUI into two smaller tasks: coding the appearance of the GUI and coding the actions of the GUI. In this case that may not seem like a big deal, but on a complicated Swing GUI, each of these two tasks can be formidable, but reasonable, while coding the entire GUI as one piece can be maddeningly difficult. In such cases, this dividing into two parts can be a great help.

If you include the phrase *implements* `ActionListener` at the start of your `JFrame` definition, then you must include some definition of the method `action-Performed`. A "do nothing" or "do little" method definition, such as

```
public void actionPerformed(ActionEvent e)
{}
```

stub

is often called a **stub**. Using stubs is a good programming technique in many contexts not just in Swing programs.

Alternatively when doing your first version of a Swing GUI like the one in Display 12.12, you could omit the definition of the method `actionPerformed` completely, *provided you also omit the phrase* implements `ActionListener` *and omit the invocations of* `addActionListener`.

■ Java Tip
Use the Method `setActionCommand`

When you click a button with your mouse, that fires an event e known as an *action event*. The event e normally goes to the method `actionPerformed` of the action listener(s) for that button. The method `actionPerformed` needs to find out what button was clicked when it gets the event e. When discussing the class `ButtonDemo` in Display 12.12/page 793 we said that the method invocation `e.getActionCommand()`

action
command

returns the string written on the button. That was a slightly simplified explanation. The invocation `e.getActionCommand()` returns a string known as the **action command** for the button. The default action command is the string written on the button, but if you want to, you can specify that a different string be the action command for a button.

For example, in Display 12.12 we created the `stopButton` as follows:

```
JButton stopButton = new JButton("Red");
```

setAction-Command

If we do nothing more, the action command for the `stopButton` will be `"Red"`. However, if you want you can change the action command to some other string, such as `"Stop"`. You would do so as follows:

```
stopButton.setActionCommand("Stop");
```

The method `actionPerformed` would then check for the string `"Stop"` rather than the string `"Red"`. A rewritten version of the class `ButtonDemo` that uses `setAction-Command` can be found in the file `SetActionCommandDemo.java` on the accompanying CD.

Extra code on CD

You may eventually find yourself in a situation where you want the same string written on two different buttons. In such a case, you can distinguish the two buttons by using `setActionCommand` to give them different action commands.

`setActionCommand` **and** `getActionCommand`

Every button (and every other object that fires action events) has a string associated with it that is known as the **action command** for that button. When the button is clicked, that fires an action event e. The following invocation returns the action command for the button that fired e:

```
e.getActionCommand()
```

The method `actionPerformed` typically uses this action command string to decide which button was clicked.

The default action command for a button is the string written on the button, but if you want, you can change the action command with an invocation of the method `setActionCommand`. For example, the following will write the string `"Red"` on the `JButton` named `stopButton`, but will make the string `"Stop"` the action command for the button `stopButton`:

Example:

```
JButton stopButton = new JButton("Red");
stopButton.setActionCommand("Stop");
```

? Self-Test Questions

18. What kind of listener do you need for a button component? How do you create such a listener?

19. Consider the following code from Display 12.12/page 793:

```
contentPane.setLayout(new FlowLayout());

JButton stopButton = new JButton("Red");
stopButton.addActionListener(this);
contentPane.add(stopButton);

JButton goButton = new JButton("Green");
goButton.addActionListener(this);
```

```
contentPane.add(goButton);
```

Can you replace this code with the following and have it mean the same thing?

```
contentPane.setLayout(new FlowLayout());

JButton b = new JButton("Red");
b.addActionListener(this);
contentPane.add(b);

b = new JButton("Green");
b.addActionListener(this);
contentPane.add(b);
```

In other words, can you use only the one named b, even though there are two buttons?

20. The method `actionPerformed` in Display 12.12/page 793 contains the following line:

```
Container contentPane = getContentPane();
```

Does the content pane have to be name `contentPane` or could it be named something else, such as in the following:

```
Container insideOfJFrame = getContentPane();
```

21. What does it mean when we say that an event is "sent" to a listener object?

22. What effect would it have on the program in Display 12.12/page 793 if we replaced the e with the identifier `buttonEvent` as follows:

```
public void actionPerformed(ActionEvent buttonEvent)
{
    Container contentPane = getContentPane();

    if (buttonEvent.getActionCommand().equals("Red"))
        contentPane.setBackground(Color.red);
    else if (buttonEvent.getActionCommand().equals("Green"))
        contentPane.setBackground(Color.green);
    else
        System.out.println("Error in button interface.");
}
```

12.4 | Container Classes

> *Fill all the glasses there, for why*
> *Should every creature drink but I,*
> *Why, man of mortals, tell me why?*
>
> **Abraham Cowley, Anacreon**

When you use Swing to make a GUI such as the windows we have been defining, you build new classes for the GUI out of already existing classes. There are two principal ways to build new GUI classes out of old classes. You can use inheritance. For example, to build a window interface, you normally use the Swing class `JFrame` and make your window a derived class of `JFrame`. The second way to make new classes out of old classes is to use one of the Swing classes as a *container* and to place components in the container.[1] For example, in the class `ButtonDemo` (Display 12.12/page 793) we added a button to the window as follows:

container

```
    JButton stopButton = new JButton("Red");
        . . .
    contentPane.add(stopButton);
```

You do not choose between these two ways of building a GUI. In almost all cases, you use both of these techniques when you define a GUI class.

In this section we will look at the class `JPanel` which is often used to define subparts of a window. We then go on to discuss the general properties of container classes such as `JPanel` and the content pane of `JFrame`.

The `JPanel` Class

A GUI is often organized in a hierarchical fashion, with window-like containers inside of other window-like containers. In this section, we introduce a new class that facilitates this organization: The class `JPanel` is a very simple container class that does little more than group objects. It is one of the simplest of container classes, but one you will use frequently. A `JPanel` object is little more than an area of the screen into which you put other objects, such as buttons and labels. The `JPanel` object may then be put in the content pane of a `JFrame`. Thus, one of the main functions of `JPanel` objects is to subdivide a `JFrame` into different areas. These `JPanel` object are usually simply called **panels** when we want a shorter, less formal term. The judicious use of panels can affect the arrangement of components in a window as much as the choice of a layout manager. For example, suppose you use a `BorderLayout` manager, then you can place components in each of the five locations: `BorderLayout.NORTH`, `BorderLayout.SOUTH`, `BorderLayout.EAST`, `BorderLayout.WEST`, and `BorderLayout.CENTER`. But what if you want to put two components at the bottom of the screen, in the `BorderLayout.SOUTH` position? To get two components in the `BorderLayout.SOUTH` position, you put the two components in a panel and then place the panel in the `BorderLayout.SOUTH` position.

JPanel

panel

Display 12.13 contains a slight variation of the program in Display 12.12/page 793. In Display 12.13, we have placed the buttons in a panel, called `buttonPanel`, so that the portion of the window with the buttons does not change color when the rest of the window changes color. As was true for the program in Display 12.12, when you click the `"Red"` button in the GUI in Display 12.13, the window's color

---

1. Technically speaking, adding components to a container class does not necessarily make it a new class. However, the way that we advocate adding components is in the class constructor; so for all practical purposes it will produce a new class. In any event, this is a technical detail that need not concern you when first learning about Swing. For our purposes, we will think of adding components as producing a new class.

Display 12.13 Putting the Buttons in a Panel *(Part 1 of 2)*

```java
import javax.swing.*;
import java.awt.*;
import java.awt.event.*;

/************************************************
 *Simple demonstration of putting buttons in a panel.
 ***********************************************/
public class PanelDemo extends JFrame implements ActionListener
{
    public static final int WIDTH = 300;
    public static final int HEIGHT = 200;

    public static void main(String[] args)
    {
        PanelDemo guiWithPanel = new PanelDemo();
        guiWithPanel.setVisible(true);
    }

    public PanelDemo()
    {
        setSize(WIDTH, HEIGHT);
        addWindowListener(new WindowDestroyer());
        setTitle("Panel Demonstration");
        Container contentPane = getContentPane();
        contentPane.setBackground(Color.blue);
        contentPane.setLayout(new BorderLayout());

        JPanel buttonPanel = new JPanel();
        buttonPanel.setBackground(Color.white);

        buttonPanel.setLayout(new FlowLayout());

        JButton stopButton = new JButton("Red");
        stopButton.setBackground(Color.red);
        stopButton.addActionListener(this);
        buttonPanel.add(stopButton);

        JButton goButton = new JButton("Green");
        goButton.setBackground(Color.green);
        goButton.addActionListener(this);
        buttonPanel.add(goButton);

        contentPane.add(buttonPanel, BorderLayout.SOUTH);
    }
```

```java
    public void actionPerformed(ActionEvent e)
    {
        Container contentPane = getContentPane();

        if (e.getActionCommand().equals("Red"))
            contentPane.setBackground(Color.red);
        else if (e.getActionCommand().equals("Green"))
            contentPane.setBackground(Color.green);
        else
            System.out.println("Error in button interface.");
    }
}
```

Resulting GUI

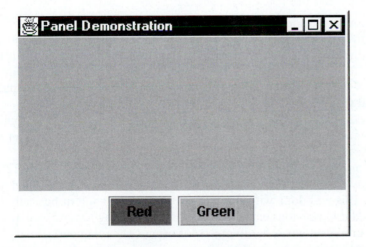

changes to red, and, similarly, the color changes to green when you click the
"Green" button. But in Display 12.13, the buttons are in a separate panel that is
white and that does not change color. As you can see, you use a layout manager and
the method add with a JPanel object in exactly the same way that you do for the
content pane of a JFrame. The buttons are placed in the panel with add as in the following example:

```
buttonPanel.add(stopButton);
```

and then the JPanel is placed in the JFrame with add as follows:

```
contentPane.add(buttonPanel, BorderLayout.SOUTH);
```

Note that the content pane (contentPane) and the panel (buttonPanel) each have
their own layout manager.

Be sure to notice that you add things to a JFrame and JPanel in slightly different ways. With a JFrame, you first get the content pane with getContentPane and
then use the method add with the content pane. With a JPanel, you use the method
add directly with the JPanel object. There is no content pane to worry about with a
JPanel.

Notice how the action listeners are set up. Each button registers the *this*
parameter as a listener, as in the following line:

```
stopButton.addActionListener(this);
```

Because the line appears inside of the constructor for the class PanelDemo, the *this*
parameter refers to PanelDemo, which is the entire window interface. Thus, the entire window container is the listener, not the JPanel. (Remember PanelDemo is the
window with the JPanel. It is not itself the JPanel.) So, when you click the button
labeled "Red", it is the background of the bigger window that turns red. The panel
with the buttons always stays white.

Note that, because it is the PanelDemo class that is the listener for button clicking events, it is PanelDemo that implements ActionListener and has the method
actionPerformed.

There is also one other small, but new technique, introduced in Display 12.13.
In that class we gave each button a color, as well as giving colors to the panel and
the content pane. This was done with the method setBackground in basically the
same way that we did in previous examples. The only new thing to note, is that you
can give a button or almost any other item a color using setBackground.

hierarchies of panels

You can add one JPanel to another JPanel using the method add, and each
JPanel can have a different layout manager. With a hierarchy of panels build it this
way, you can create almost any sort of arrangement of components inside of a GUI.

The JPanel Class

A JPanel object is little more than an area of the screen into which you can add other objects, such as buttons
and labels. The JPanel object is then, typically, added to the content pane of a JFrame (or to another
JPanel). Thus, one of the main functions of JPanel objects is to subdivide a JFrame into different areas.

◻

The `Container` Class

There is a predefined class called `Container`. Any descendent class of the class `Container` can have components added to it (or more precisely can have components added to objects of the class). The class `JFrame` is a descendent class of the class `Container`, so any descendent class of the class `JFrame` can serve as a container to hold labels, buttons, panels, or other components.

Container

Similarly, the class `JPanel` is a descendent of the class `Container`, any object of the class `JPanel` can serve as a container to hold labels, buttons, other panels, or other components. Display 12.14 shows a portion of the Swing hierarchy as well as some of the classes in the AWT library. Note that the `Container` class is in the AWT library and not in the Swing library. This is not a major issue, but does mean that you need to import the awt package when using the `Container` class. So any class definition that contains a reference to the class `Container` must contain the following import statement:

```
import java.awt.*;
```

A **container class** is any descendent class of the class `Container`. Any descendent class of the class `JComponent` is called a `JComponent`, or sometimes more simply a **component**. You can add any `JComponent` object to any container class object.

container class
component

Note that the class `JComponent` is derived from the class `Container` and so you can add a `JComponent` to another `JComponent`. Sometimes, this will turn out to be a good idea and sometimes it is something to avoid. We will discuss the different cases as we go along. The classes `Component`, `Frame`, and `Window` are AWT classes that some readers may have heard of. We include them for reference value, but we will have no need for these classes. We will eventually discuss all the other classes shown in Display 12.14.

Container Classes

A **container class** is any descendent class of the class `Container`. In particular, this means that any descendent class of the class `JFrame` is a container class and that `JPanel` is a container class. Every container class can have items added to it, such as labels, buttons, panels, and so forth. The items are added in one of two ways, depending on the particular container class:

1. For a `JFrame` object, by using the method `getContentPane` to obtain the content pane and then using `add` with the content pane as the calling object, or

2. For all other container classes discussed in this book, by simply using the `add` method directly with an object of the container class.

The `add` Method

Every Swing container class has a method called `add`. You can use the method `add` to add any `JComponent` object, whether predefined or defined by you, to the container class. In the case of a `JFrame`, you must first use the method `getContentPane` to obtain the content pane and use the method `add` with the content pane as the calling object.

> ### Abstract Classes
>
> If you look at Display 12.14/page 810, you will see that some of the classes are *abstract classes*. An **abstract class** is a kind of class that is used solely to simplify your thinking. You do not, in fact you cannot, directly create objects of an abstract class. So, what do you do with an abstract class? You derive new classes using the abstract class as the base class. The abstract class is a way of grouping together classes that are similar. For example, `Abstract-Button` is an abstract class. Both of the classes `JButton` and `JMenuItem` are derived from the class `AbstractButton`. That means that the classes `JButton` and `JMenuItem` share all the properties of the class `AbstractButton`, and as we will see in Chapter 14, that means that `JButton`s and `JMenuItem`s behave very similarly. (Menus are covered in Chapter 14.)
>
> An analogy to an abstract class taken from everyday life is the class of all automobiles. It is an abstract class. You can have Fords, Toyotas, Hondas, BMWs, and so forth. But you cannot have just a plain old automobile. It must be some specific kind of automobile. Similarly, you cannot have just a plain old `AbstractButton`. It must be some specific kind of `AbstractButton`, such as a `JButton` or a `JMenuItem`.
>
> It is possible to define your own abstract classes, but we will not cover that topic in this book. ∎

content pane

There are two ways that you can add a `JComponent` to a container. One way is the way we added components to a `JFrame`: You first obtain the content pane of the `JFrame` using the method `getContentPane`. Then, you add components to the content pane using the method `add`. Another way is the way we add items to a `JPanel`: With a `JPanel`, you directly use the method `add` with the `JPanel`. With a `JPanel`, there is no content pane to worry about. How do you decide which of these two approaches (with or without `getContentPane`) you need to use? For each container class you must either memorize which approach to use or look it up.[1] If you only use the classes discussed in this text, then it is easy to decide. With objects of the class `JFrame` (including objects of any derived class of `JFrame`), you use `getContentPane`. None of the other container classes discussed in this chapter use `getContentPane`.

layout manager

When you are dealing with a Swing container class, you have three kinds of objects to deal with: The container class itself (probably some sort of window-like object), the components you add to the container (like labels, buttons, and panels), and a **layout manager,** which is an object that positions the components inside the container. We have seen examples of these three kinds of objects in almost every `JFrame` class we have defined. Almost every complete GUI interface you build, and many subparts of the GUIs you build, will be made up of these three kinds of objects.

---

1. Some who are more familiar with Swing might contend that there is an "easier" way to determine whether or not you use `getContentPane` with a container classes. They would say that you use `getContentPane` with a container, whenever the container class implement the `RootPaneContainer` interface. That is correct as far as it goes, but to find out if the class implements the `RootPaneContainer` class, you must either memorize that fact or look it up. (Other than this footnote, we will not discuss the `RootPaneContainer` interface in this book.)

When Do You Need to Use `getContentPane`?

With a `JFrame` you add things with a combination of `getContentPane` and `add`, as in the following

```
Container contentPane = getContentPane();
JLabel label = new JLabel("Please don't click that button!");
contentPane.add(label);
```

However, with a `JPanel`, you do not use `getContentPane`, but instead use the method `add` directly with the `JPanel` object, as illustrated below:

```
JPanel buttonPanel = new JPanel();
    . . .
JButton stopButton = new JButton("Red");
    . . .
buttonPanel.add(stopButton);
```

With `JFrame` objects (and certain other objects not discussed in this text) you need to use the method `get-ContentPane` to get the content pane of the `JFrame` object and then use the method `add` with the content pane as the calling object. With all other container classes discussed in this text, you use the method `add` directly with an object of the container class and do not use a content pane. ☐

Java Tip
Guide for Creating Simple Window Interfaces

Most simple windowing GUIs follow a pattern that is easy to learn and that will get you started with Swing. Here is an outline of some of the main points we've seen so far:

1. A typical GUI consists of some windowing object that is derived from the class `JFrame` and that contains a number of components, such as labels and buttons.

2. When the user clicks the close-window button, the window should close, but this will not happen correctly unless your program registers a window listener to close the window. One way to accomplish this is to add the following to the GUI class definition within a constructor definition:

   ```
   addWindowListener(new WindowDestroyer());
   ```

   You can use the definition of `WindowDestroyer` given in Display 12.2/ page 766

3. You can group components together by placing the components in a `JPanel` and adding the `JPanel` to the GUI.

4. The GUI (that is, the `JFrame`) and each `JPanel` in the GUI should be given a layout manager using the method `setLayout`.

5. If any of the components, such as a button, generate action events, then you need to make the GUI (or some other class) an action listener. Every component that generates an action event should have an action

Display 12.14 **Hierarchy of Swing Classes**

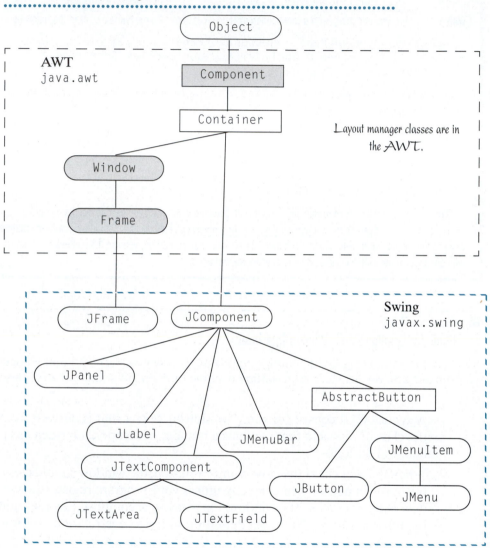

If there is a line between two classes, then the lower class is a derived class of the higher class. Shaded classes are not used in this text but are included for reference. If you have not heard of them, you can safely ignore them.

listener registered with it. You register an action listener with the method `addActionListener`.

6. In order to make your windowing GUI (or other class) into an action listener, you need to add the following to the beginning of the class definition:

   implements `ActionListener`

   You also need to add a definition of the method `actionPerformed` to the class.

This is not the only way to create a GUI window class, but it shows a simple and common way to do it, and it is basically the only way we know of so far.

? Self-Test Questions

23. When adding components to a `JFrame`, do you need to use `getContentPane`? When adding components to a `JPanel`, do you need to use `getContentPane`?

24. What kind of listener do you need for a `JButton` component? How do you create such a listener?

25. What do the classes `WindowDestroyer` (Display 12.2/page 766 and the class `ButtonDemo` (Display 12.12/page 793) have in common?

26. What is the type for the object returned when you invoke `getContentPane` with a `JFrame` object?

27. What import statement do you need in a class definition that refers to the class `Container`?

28. Is an object of the class `JPanel` a container class? Is it a component class?

29. How does a `FlowLayout` manager arrange components in a container?

30. How does a `BorderLayout` manager arrange components in a container?

31. Suppose you are using a `BorderLayout` manager and you want to put two buttons in the region `BorderLayout.NORTH`. How do you do this?

32. How does a `GridLayout` manager arrange components in a container?

33. With a grid layout manger you cannot leave any grid element empty, but you can do something that will make a grid element look empty to the user. What can you do?

34. You are used to defining derived classes of the Swing class `JFrame`. You can also define derived classes of other Swing classes. Define a derived class of the class `JPanel` that is called `PinkJPanel`. An object of the class `PinkJPanel` can be used just like we used objects of the class `JPanel`, but an object of the class `PinkJPanel` is pink in color (unless you explicitly change its color). The class `PinkJPanel` will only have one constructor, namely the default constructor. (Hint: This is very easy.)

12.5 | Text I/O for GUIs

> Polonius: *What do you read my lord?*
> Hamlet: *Words, words, words.*
>
> ***William Shakespeare, Hamlet***

So far we have made pretty window displays, but we do not yet have very versatile techniques for program input and output via GUIs, and input/output is the reason programmers want GUIs. As a programmer, you will want to use a GUI as the input/output part of your programs. Buttons give you some input and labels give you some output, but they are not as versatile as text input and output. In this section we show you how to add text input and text output to your Swing GUIs.

Text Areas and Text Fields

The GUI in Display 12.10/page 784 has some text in the window but it is static text. Neither the user nor the program can change the text. If we are going to have text input from the user as part of a GUI, then we need some way for the user to enter text into the GUI. Display 12.15 contains a program that produces a GUI with a text area in which the user can write any text she or he wishes. That text is then saved as a memo that can be recalled later. In this simple example, the user is only allowed two memos, but that is good enough to illustrate how a text area is created and used. The area in the center, colored white, is an object of the class JTextArea. The user can type any sort of text into this JTextArea. If the user clicks the "Save Memo 1" button, the text is saved as memo 1. If the user clicks the "Save Memo 2" button, the text is saved as memo 2. Either memo can be called back up to the JTextArea by clicking one of the buttons "Get Memo 1" or "Get Memo 2". The JTextArea can be cleared by clicking the "Clear" button. Now, let's look at how the program does this.

TextArea

The buttons in Display 12.15 are put in a JPanel and then that JPanel is put in the JFrame just as they were in Display 12.13/page 804. The TextArea is set up with the following code, which appears in the constructor definition in Display 12.15:

```
JPanel textPanel = new JPanel();
textPanel.setBackground(Color.blue);
theText = new JTextArea(LINES, CHAR_PER_LINE);
theText.setBackground(Color.white);
textPanel.add(theText);
contentPane.add(textPanel, BorderLayout.CENTER);
```

The object theText is a member of the class JTextArea. Note the arguments in the constructor for JTextArea . The arguments LINES, which is a defined constant for 10, and CHAR_PER_LINE, which is a defined constant for 40, say that the text area will be 10 lines from top to bottom and will allow at least 40 characters per line. If you type in more text than will fit in a text area of the size specified by the two arguments to the constructor, then what happens can sometimes be unpredictable. So, it is best to make these numbers large enough to accommodate the largest

Display 12.15 GUI with Text Area (Part 1 of 2)

> There is a demonstration ma i n in part 2 of this display.

```
import javax.swing.*;
import java.awt.*;
import java.awt.event.*;

public class MemoSaver extends JFrame implements ActionListener
{
    public static final int WIDTH = 600;
    public static final int HEIGHT = 300;
    public static final int LINES = 10;
    public static final int CHAR_PER_LINE = 40;

    private JTextArea theText;
    private String memo1 = "No Memo 1.";
    private String memo2 = "No Memo 2.";

    public MemoSaver()
    {
        setSize(WIDTH, HEIGHT);
        addWindowListener(new WindowDestroyer());
        setTitle("Memo Saver");
        Container contentPane = getContentPane();
        contentPane.setLayout(new BorderLayout());

        JPanel buttonPanel = new JPanel();
        buttonPanel.setBackground(Color.white);
        buttonPanel.setLayout(new FlowLayout());
        JButton memo1Button = new JButton("Save Memo 1");
        memo1Button.addActionListener(this);
        buttonPanel.add(memo1Button);
        JButton memo2Button = new JButton("Save Memo 2");
        memo2Button.addActionListener(this);
        buttonPanel.add(memo2Button);
        JButton clearButton = new JButton("Clear");
        clearButton.addActionListener(this);
        buttonPanel.add(clearButton);
        JButton get1Button = new JButton("Get Memo 1");
        get1Button.addActionListener(this);
        buttonPanel.add(get1Button);
        JButton get2Button = new JButton("Get Memo 2");
        get2Button.addActionListener(this);
        buttonPanel.add(get2Button);
        contentPane.add(buttonPanel, BorderLayout.SOUTH);

        JPanel textPanel = new JPanel();
        textPanel.setBackground(Color.blue);
```

> If you get memo 1 before you set memo 1, you get the message "No Memo 1."

Display 12.15 GUI with Text Area *(Part 2 of 2)*

```
                    theText = new JTextArea(LINES, CHAR_PER_LINE);
                    theText.setBackground(Color.white);
                    textPanel.add(theText);
                    contentPane.add(textPanel, BorderLayout.CENTER);
        }

        public void actionPerformed(ActionEvent e)
        {
                    String actionCommand = e.getActionCommand();
                    if (actionCommand.equals("Save Memo 1"))
                        memo1 = theText.getText();
                    else if (actionCommand.equals("Save Memo 2"))
                        memo2 = theText.getText();
                    else if (actionCommand.equals("Clear"))
                        theText.setText("");
                    else if (actionCommand.equals("Get Memo 1"))
                        theText.setText(memo1);
                    else if (actionCommand.equals("Get Memo 2"))
                        theText.setText(memo2);
                    else
                        theText.setText("Error in memo interface");
        }

        public static void main(String[] args)
        {
                    MemoSaver guiMemo = new MemoSaver();
                    guiMemo.setVisible(true);
        }
}
```

> *theText is an instance variable.*

Resulting GUI

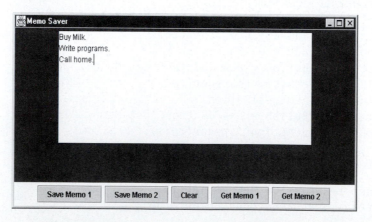

expected text. (Problems of too much text can be handled by using the method `setLineWrap`, as described in the box at the end of this section, and/or using scroll bars, as described in Chapter 14.)

We are using a `BorderLayout` manager. The `textPanel` is added to the `JFrame` in the `BorderLayout.CENTER` position. The `BorderLayout.CENTER` position always takes up all the `JFrame` room that is left. This much of our program sets up the look of the GUI, but we still need to discuss how writing in the text area is handled by the GUI.

The two memos are stored in the two instance variables `memo1` and `memo2`, both of type `String`. When the user clicks the `"Save Memo 1"` button, the text in the text area is saved as the value of the instance variable `memo1`. This is done by the following code, which is the first three lines in the definition of the `actionPerformed` method:

getText

```
String actionCommand = e.getActionCommand();
if (actionCommand.equals("Save Memo 1"))
    memo1 = theText.getText();
```

Recall that the `getActionCommand` method returns the label of the button that is clicked. So, this says that when the button with label `"Save Memo 1"` is clicked, the following happens:

```
memo1 = theText.getText();
```

The method `getText()` returns the text that is written in the object `theText` of the class `JTextArea`. In other words, it returns what the user typed into the text area. If you read further in the definition of the method `actionPerformed`, you see that the second memo is stored in a similar way.

The memos are displayed in the text area and the text area is cleared with the following clauses from the definition of the method `actionPerformed`:

setText

```
else if (actionCommand.equals("Clear"))
    theText.setText("");
else if (actionCommand.equals("Get Memo 1"))
    theText.setText(memo1);
else if (actionCommand.equals("Get Memo 2"))
    theText.setText(memo2);
```

The method `setText` of the class `JTextArea` changes the text in the text area into what is given as the argument to `setText`. Two quotes with nothing in between are given as the argument to `setText` in the second line of the preceding code. These two quotes denote the empty string and so produce a blank text area.

empty string

The class `JTextField` (which is not used in Display 12.15) is very similar to the class `JTextArea` except that it displays only one line of text. It is useful for interfaces where the user gives only a few characters of text, like a single number, the name of a file, or the name of a person. The constructor for `JTextField` takes one argument, which is the number of characters visible in the text field. You can enter more characters, but only the specified number will be shown. So, be sure to make the text field one or two characters longer than the longest string you expect to have entered into the text field.

JTextField

The Classes `JTextArea` and `JTextField`

The classes `JTextArea` and `JTextField` can be used to add areas for changeable text to a GUI. An object of the class `JTextArea` has a size consisting of a specified number of lines and a specified number of characters per line. An object of the class `JTextField` has only one line that contains some specified number of characters. More text can be typed into a `JTextArea` or `JTextField` than is specified in its size, but the extra text is not visible.

Example: (using `JTextArea`):

```
JPanel aPanel = new JPanel();
JTextArea someText = new JTextArea(10, 30);
aPanel.add(someText);
```

Example: (using `JTextField`):

```
JPanel anotherPanel = new JPanel();
JTextField name = new JTextField(30);
anotherPanel.add(name);
```

Size of `JTextField` and `JTextArea`

When you create an object of either of the classes `JTextArea` or `JTextField`, you specify the number of characters, or number of characters per line, that will be displayed, as in the following examples:

```
JTextField someText = new JTextField(40);
JTextArea someMoreText = new JTextArea(10, 40);
```

The number 40, in either of the above lines, is not the size of just any 40 characters. That 40 represents 40 m-spaces. An **m-space** is the space need to hold one letter m, which is the widest letter in the alphabet. So, a line that is 40 wide, as above, will always be able to hold 40 characters, but depending on the particular characters, it may be able to hold more than 40 characters. (The above 10 does represent 10 lines. There is nothing to explain about that number.)

`getText` and `setText`

The classes `JTextArea` and `JTextField` both contain methods called `getText` and `setText`. The method `getText` can be used to retrieve the text written in the text area or text field. The method `setText` can be used to change the text written in the text area or text field.

**Example: (`theText` can be an object of the class `JTextArea`
or an object of the class `JTextField`):**

```
memo1 = theText.getText();
theText.setText("Hi Mom!");
```

Both the classes `JTextArea` and `JTextField` can have some initial text contents specified when you create an object using *new*. The initial text is a string given as the first argument to the constructor. For example,

initializing text

```
JTextField inputOutputField = new JTextField("Hello User.", 20);
```

The text field `inputOutputField` will have room for 20 visible characters and will start out containing the text `"Hello User."`

Both the classes `JTextArea` and `JTextField` have a constructor with no argument that sets the various parameters to some default values. .

Line Wrapping in Text Areas

You can set the line wrapping policy for a `JTextArea` using the method `setLineWrap`. The method takes one argument of type *boolean*. If the argument is *true*, then at the end of a line, any additional characters for that line will appear on the following line of the text area. If the argument is *false*, the extra characters will be on the same line and will not be visible.

Example:
If you add the following invocation of `setLineWrap` to the constructor in Display 12.15/page 813, then when the user types in more characters that can fit on a line, the extra characters will appear on the following line:

```
public MemoSaver()
{
    ...
    theText.setLineWrap(true);
```

Read Only Text Components

You can specify that a `TextField` or `TextArea` cannot be written in by the user. To do so use the method `setEditable`, which is a method in both the `TextField` and `TextArea` classes. If `theText` names an object in either of the classes `TextField` or `TextArea`, then

```
theText.setEditable(false);
```

Will set `theText` so that your GUI program can change the text in the text component `theText`, but the user cannot change the text. After this invocation of `setEditable`, if the user clicks the mouse in the text component `theText` and then types at the keyboard, that will not change the text in `theText`.

To reverse things and make `theText` so that the user can edit the text in the text component, use *true* in place of *false*, as follows:

```
theText.setEditable(true);
```

If no invocation of `setEditable` is made, then the user *can* change the text in the text component.

Programming Example
Labeling a Text Field

Sometimes you want a label for a text field. For example, suppose the GUI asks for a name and an identification number and expects the user to enter these in two text fields. In this case, the GUI needs to label the two text fields so that the user knows in which field to write the name and in which field to write the number. You can use an object of the class JLabel to label a text field or any other component in an Swing GUI.

Display 12.16 contains a program that shows how you can attach a label to a text field (or any other component). You put both the text field and the label in a panel. You can then add the entire panel to a container. In Display 12.16 the code shown in color does just that.

The program in Display 12.16 is just a demonstration program and does not do very much. If the user enters a name in the text field and clicks the "Test" button, then the GUI gives an evaluation of the name. However, all names receive the same evaluation, namely, "A very good name!" So, if the user enters a name and then clicks the "Test" button, the display will look like the GUI shown in Display 12.16.

? Self-Test Questions

35. What is the difference between an object of the class JTextArea and an object of the class JTextField?

36. How would you change the program in Display 12.15/page 813 so that the buttons appear above the text area instead of below the text area?

37. Write a statement that will create a text field called name that has room for 30 visible characters and that starts out with text "Your name here."

38. Change the definition of the method actionPerformed in Display 12.15/ page 813 so that when the user saves the text as memo 1, the text area changes so that it says "Memo 1 saved." and so that when memo 2 is saved, it changes to "Memo 2 saved."

39. In Display 12.15/page 813, the instance variables memo1 and memo2 are of type String. An object of type String is a single string of characters. But, the user can enter text that consists of multiple lines. Is something wrong? How can you get multiple lines in one String object?

inputting numbers

Inputting and Outputting Numbers

When you want to input numbers using a GUI, your GUI must convert input text to numbers. For example, when you input the number 42 in a JTextArea or JText-Field, your program will receive the string "42", not the number 42. Your program must convert the input string value "42" to the integer value 42. When you want to output numbers using a GUI constructed with Swing, you must convert numbers to a string and then output that string. For example, if you want to output the number 43, your program would convert the integer value 43 to the string value "43". With Swing, all typed input is string input and all written output is string output.

Let's consider inputting numbers. Your program will need to convert a string, such as "42", to a number. The static method parseInt in the class Integer can accomplish the conversion. For example,

```
Integer.parseInt("42")
```

Display 12.16 Labeling a Text Field *(Part 1 of 2)*

```java
import javax.swing.*;
import java.awt.*;
import java.awt.event.*;

/****************************************************
 *Class to demonstrate placing a label on a text field.
 ***************************************************/
public class LabelDemo extends JFrame implements ActionListener
{
    public static final int WIDTH = 300;
    public static final int HEIGHT = 200;

    private JTextField name;

    public LabelDemo()
    {
        setTitle("Name Tester");
        setSize(WIDTH, HEIGHT);
        addWindowListener(new WindowDestroyer());
        Container content = getContentPane();
        content.setLayout(new GridLayout(2, 1));

        JPanel namePanel = new JPanel();
        namePanel.setLayout(new BorderLayout());
        namePanel.setBackground(Color.lightGray);

        name = new JTextField(20);
        namePanel.add(name, BorderLayout.SOUTH);
        JLabel nameLabel = new JLabel("Enter your name here:");
        namePanel.add(nameLabel, BorderLayout.CENTER);

        content.add(namePanel);

        JPanel buttonPanel = new JPanel();
        buttonPanel.setLayout(new FlowLayout());
        JButton b = new JButton("Test");
        b.addActionListener(this);
        buttonPanel.add(b);
        b = new JButton("Clear");
        b.addActionListener(this);
        buttonPanel.add(b);

        content.add(buttonPanel);
    }
```

Display 12.16 Labeling a Text Field *(Part 2 of 2)*

```java
public void actionPerformed(ActionEvent e)
{
    if (e.getActionCommand().equals("Test"))
        name.setText("A very good name!");
    else if (e.getActionCommand().equals("Clear"))
        name.setText("");
    else
        name.setText("Error in window interface.");
}


public static void main(String[] args)
{
    LabelDemo w = new LabelDemo();
    w.setVisible(true);
}


}
```

Resulting GUI

A label.

returns the integer 42. If these details do not make sense to you, you should review the section *Integer, Double, and Other Wrapper Classes* in Chapter 5.

If the number were written in a JTextField named inputOutputField, then you can recover the input string with the method getText. So inputOutput-Field.getText() would produce the input string. To change the input string to a number, you can use the following expression:

```
Integer.parseInt(inputOutputField.getText())
```

If there is any chance that the user might add extra white space before or after the input, you should add an invocation of the method trim to the string object inputOutputField.getText(). Thus, a more robust way to obtain the number that was input would be the following (which adds an invocation of the method trim):

trim

```
Integer.parseInt(inputOutputField.getText().trim())
```

Once your program has this number, it can use it just like any other number. For example, to store this number in an *int* variable named n, the following assignment statement will work fine:

```
int n =
    Integer.parseInt(inputOutputField.getText().trim());
```

If you want to input numbers of type *double*, just use the class Double in place of the class Integer and the method parseDouble in place of the method parseInt. For example, to store the number in inputOutputField in a *double* variable named x, the following assignment statement will work fine:

```
double x =
        Double.parseDouble(inputOutputField.getText().trim());
```

You can also do the analogous thing with the classes Long and Float.

You should be able to understand and even write long expressions like

```
Integer.parseInt(stringObject.trim())
```

However, your code will be easier to read and easier to write if you define a method to express this as a simple method invocation. Here is one such method:

stringTo-Int **method**

```
private static int stringToInt(String stringObject)
{
    return Integer.parseInt(stringObject.trim());
}
```

Then an expression like

```
n = Integer.parseInt(inputOutputField.getText().trim());
```

can be expressed more clearly as

```
n = stringToInt(inputOutputField.getText());
```

If the method is to be merely a tool in some GUI class, then it should be declared as private, because it has no use outside of the class. Alternatively, it could be part of a utility class with a number of different useful functions. In that case, it would make more sense to make it public.

Inputting Numbers With a GUI

You can design a GUI using Swing so that input can consist of a number typed into a text field (or text area). The following will return the number of type *int* that is typed into the text field. This assumes that nothing other than the number and white space are typed into the text fields.

Syntax:

```
Integer.parseInt(Name_Of_Text_Field.getText().trim())
```

Example: (that stores an *int* value in a variable n):

```
int n =
    Integer.parseInt(inputOutputField.getText().trim());
```

You can do the same things for numbers of the types *double*, *float*, and *long*. Just use the class Double, Float, or Long in place of the class Integer, and use the method parseDouble, parseFloat, or parseLong in place of the method parseInt.

Example: (that stores a *double* value in a variable x):

```
double x =
    Double.parseDouble(inputOutputField.getText().trim());
```

Example:

You can also package these sorts of long formulas into methods such as

```
private static double stringToDouble(String stringObject)
{
    return Double.parseDouble(stringObject.trim());
}
```

(Depending on where this method is defined and used, it might be either *public* or *private*.) You can use this method to shorten the previous example to:

```
double x =
    stringToDouble(inputOutputField.getText());
```

---

outputting numbers

To send an output number to a JTextField or JTextArea of a GUI, you use the static method toString. For example, suppose you have the number 43 stored in the *int* variable sum. You can convert this 43 to the string "43" as follows:

```
Integer.toString(sum)
```

We used the class Integer when invoking toString because we were dealing with integers. If on the other hand, you have a variable total of type *double* and you want to convert the number in total to a string, you would use

```
Double.toString(total)
```

If you want the number in the *int* variable sum to appear in the JTextField named inputOutputField, then you use setText as follows:

```
inputOutputField.setText(Integer.toString(sum));
```

This produces the string for the integer. If you wanted a string for the value in the variable `total` of type *double*, you would instead use

```
inputOutputField.setText(Double.toString(total));
```

These techniques for inputting and outputting numbers are illustrated in the next case study.

Outputting Numbers With a GUI

You can design a GUI using Swing so that output consisting of a number (or numbers) is displayed in a text field (or text area). The following will take a number in a variable and display the number in the text field. (The details are the same if you are working with a `TextArea` rather than a `TextField`.)

Syntax:

Name_Of_Text_Field`.setText(`*Wrapper_Class*`.toString(`*Variable*`));`

Examples:

```
inputOutputField.setText(Integer.toString(sum));
inputOutputField.setText(Double.toString(area));
```

You can do the same things for numbers of the types *float* and *long*. Just use the class `Float` or `Long` in place of the class `Integer` or `Double`.

? Self-Test Questions

40. Write an expression to convert the *double* value `7.77` to the string `"7.77"`. Include it in an assignment statement that stores that string in the variable `s` of type `String`. (Use the techniques in the preceding subsection.)

41. Write an expression to convert the string `"3.14159"` to the *double* value `3.14159`. Include it in an assignment statement that stores that value in the variable `x` of type *double*. (Use the techniques in the preceding subsection.)

42. Suppose the `String` object `s` has the value `"   3.14159   "`. Write an expression that starts with the `String` object `s` and returns the *double* value `3.14159`. Include it in an assignment statement that stores that value in the variable `x` of type *double*. (Use the techniques in the preceding subsection.)

Case Study

A GUI Adding Machine

In this case study, you will design a program that uses Swing to produce an adding machine program. The required interface is illustrated in Display 12.17. The white text field initially contains the text `"Numbers go here."` The user can enter a number by dragging the mouse over the text in the white text field and then typing in the

task
specification

Display 12.17 GUI Interface for an Adding Machine

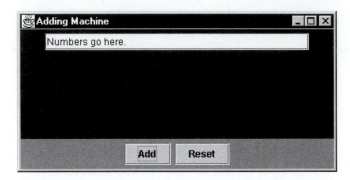

number so that the number typed in becomes the contents of the text field. When the user clicks the "Add" button, the number is added to a running total and the new total is displayed in the text field. The user can continue to add in more numbers for as long as she or he wants. To start over, the user clicks the "Reset" button, which makes the running sum equal to zero.

Adder class   You decide that the adding machine will be an object of a class named Adder. You begin by making a list of the data needed to accomplish the adding machine computation and the Swing objects you will need to construct your class Adder. The user will enter a number in a text field, so you will need one instance variable of type JTextField. You also need a number to keep a running sum of the numbers entered so far. Because these numbers might contain a decimal point, you make this an instance variable of type *double*. Thus, you come up with the following instance variables for your class:

data
```
private JTextField inputOutputField;
private double sum = 0;
```

You next make the following list of additional objects needed to construct an object of the class Adder:

objects
As always, you need to be able to close the window and end your program. So, you decide to use an object of the class WindowDestroyer in the usual way.

textPanel: A panel to hold the text field inputOutputField.

addButton and resetButton: The two buttons.

buttonPanel: A panel to hold the two buttons.

A layout manager to arrange the buttons in their panel. You decide that this should be a `FlowLayout` manager.

A layout manager to place the text field in its panel. You decide that this should also be a `FlowLayout` manager.

A layout manager to arrange the panels in the window. You decide that this should be a `BorderLayout` manager

You need listeners to listen to the buttons. You decide to use the window itself as the only listener and have it respond to button events.

The class `Adder` itself will be a window class and so will be a derived class of the class `JFrame`. So, you know the class definition begins like the following:

base class
`JFrame`

```
public class Adder extends JFrame
```

When listing the objects you need, you decided that the window itself would be the listener for the button events. Button events are action events, so you need to make the window (that is, any object of the class `Adder`) an action listener. You do that as follows:

Action-Listener

```
public class Adder extends JFrame implements ActionListener
```

Placing components in containers and initializing the components, colors, and such is best done in the constructor. So, you begin by doing the default constructor, which will be the only constructor. First, there are the routine details, namely, setting up the mechanisms for closing the window and placing a title in the title bar and setting the initial size of the window. So, you know the constructor starts something like

```
setTitle("Adding Machine");
addWindowListener(new WindowDestroyer());
setSize(WIDTH, HEIGHT);
```

You add the buttons to a button panel in the usual way:

components in containers

```
JPanel buttonPanel = new JPanel();
buttonPanel.setBackground(Color.gray);
buttonPanel.setLayout(new FlowLayout());
JButton addButton = new JButton("Add");
addButton.addActionListener(this);
buttonPanel.add(addButton);
JButton resetButton = new JButton("Reset");
resetButton.addActionListener(this);
buttonPanel.add(resetButton);
```

The window itself is the listener.

In your outline of objects, you said that the window containing this panel would use the `BorderLayout` manager, and the specifications for the GUI say the buttons go on the bottom of the window, so you add the button panel as follows:

adding a panel

```
contentPane.add(buttonPanel, BorderLayout.SOUTH);
```

In order to add a panel in this way, you need to give the content pane a `BorderLayout` manager as follows:

```
contentPane.setLayout(new BorderLayout());
```

Display 12.18 An Addition GUI *(Part 1 of 2)*

```java
import javax.swing.*;
import java.awt.*;
import java.awt.event.*;

/***************************************
 *GUI for totaling a series of numbers.
 ***************************************/
public class Adder extends JFrame implements ActionListener
{
    public static final int WIDTH = 400;
    public static final int HEIGHT = 200;

    private JTextField inputOutputField;
    private double sum = 0;

    public static void main(String[] args)
    {
        Adder guiAdder = new Adder();
        guiAdder.setVisible(true);
    }

    public Adder()
    {
        setTitle("Adding Machine");
        addWindowListener(new WindowDestroyer());
        setSize(WIDTH, HEIGHT);
        Container contentPane = getContentPane();
        contentPane.setLayout(new BorderLayout());

        JPanel buttonPanel = new JPanel();
        buttonPanel.setBackground(Color.gray);
        buttonPanel.setLayout(new FlowLayout());
        JButton addButton = new JButton("Add");
        addButton.addActionListener(this);
        buttonPanel.add(addButton);
        JButton resetButton = new JButton("Reset");
        resetButton.addActionListener(this);
        buttonPanel.add(resetButton);
        contentPane.add(buttonPanel, BorderLayout.SOUTH);

        JPanel textPanel = new JPanel();
        textPanel.setBackground(Color.blue);
        textPanel.setLayout(new FlowLayout());
```

*The **GUI** display produced by this program is shown in Display 12.17/page 824.*

This should be executed before any components are added. So, you decide to place this line near the start of the constructor definition along with the other actions that set things like the initial size of the window.

You are tempted to add the text field directly to the content pane, but you try it and find that the text field is much larger than you would like. You then recall that with a border layout manger, a component is stretched to fill the entire region. So you decide to instead place the text field in a panel, and then place the panel in the content pane.

panel for text field

The text field is inserted into its panel in a manner similar to the way you added buttons to the button panel, and then the panel with the text field is inserted in the content pane. The only differences from the button case are that the text panel goes in the BorderLayout.CENTER and you need to decide how many characters you will

adding a text field

Display 12.18 An Addition GUI *(Part 2 of 2)*

```
        inputOutputField = new JTextField("Numbers go here.", 30);
        inputOutputField.setBackground(Color.white);
        textPanel.add(inputOutputField);
        contentPane.add(textPanel, BorderLayout.CENTER);
    }

    public void actionPerformed(ActionEvent e)
    {
        if (e.getActionCommand().equals("Add"))
        {
            sum = sum +
                stringToDouble(inputOutputField.getText());
            inputOutputField.setText(Double.toString(sum));
        }
        else if (e.getActionCommand().equals("Reset"))
        {
            sum = 0;
            inputOutputField.setText("0.0");
        }
        else
            inputOutputField.setText("Error in adder code.");
    }

    private static double stringToDouble(String stringObject)
    {
        return Double.parseDouble(stringObject.trim());
    }
}
```

allow in the text field. Thirty characters seem plenty long enough for a number and some extra white space. So, you produce the following code:

```java
JPanel textPanel = new JPanel();
textPanel.setBackground(Color.blue);
textPanel.setLayout(new FlowLayout());
inputOutputField = new JTextField("Numbers go here.", 30);
inputOutputField.setBackground(Color.white);
textPanel.add(inputOutputField);
contentPane.add(textPanel, BorderLayout.CENTER);
```

This completes your definition of the default constructor. The full definition is given in Display 12.18/page 826.

use a picture

As you can see from your work on the constructor, placing components in containers is fairly routine. If you start with a picture like the one in Display 12.17/page 824, you can almost read the code from the picture. The only subtle part is deciding what will be the listener objects. Often, the best choice is the window itself, which is what you decided to do this time.

handling events

Handling events is not as routine as adding components to containers, but it does follow from a careful analysis of the problem specification (and perhaps a bit of inspiration). For this GUI, there are four basic things that can happen:

1. The user can click the close-window button to end the program.
2. The user can write a number in the text field.
3. The user can push the add button.
4. The user can push the reset button.

Closing the window by clicking the close-window button is handled by an object of the class WindowDestroyer, as in all our examples. That is routine.

When the user types some number in the text field, no action is required. In fact, you do not want any action as a result of just writing a number. After all, the user may decide the input was entered incorrectly and change it. You do not want any action until one of the two buttons is pushed. So, the two button-pushing events are the only events that still need to be handled.

actionPerformed

Pushing a button is an action event, and an action event is handled by the method actionPerformed of the ActionListener. The window itself is the ActionListener, so the method actionPerformed is a method of the class Adder. The header of the method actionPerformed is determined for you:

public void actionPerformed(ActionEvent e)

pseudocode

You have no choice on the header, but you must decide what the method does. You produce the following pseudocode for the method actionPerformed:

```
if (e.getActionCommand().equals("Add"))
{
      sum = sum + the number written in inputOutputField.
      Display the value of sum in inputOutputField.
}
else if (e.getActionCommand().equals("Reset"))
{
      sum = 0;
      Display "0.0" in inputOutputField.
}
```

You decide to use a private method to convert strings to numbers. You use the method stringToDouble given in the box entitled ***Inputting Numbers With a GUI*** on page 822. That means the method stringToDouble will be a private helping method, and the pseudocode for the method actionPerformed can be refined to the following:

stringTo-Double

```
if (e.getActionCommand().equals("Add"))
{
      sum = sum +
                  stringToDouble(inputOutputField.getText());
      Display the value of sum in inputOutputField.
}
else if (e.getActionCommand().equals("Reset"))
{
      sum = 0;
      Display "0.0" in inputOutputField.
}
```

The rest of the translation from pseudocode to Java is straightforward. You decide to add a final *else*-clause to the nested *if-else*-statement, just in case of an unexpected error. The final code you produce and the final definition of the class Adder is given in Display 12.18.

This is only a very simple adding machine, but it has the elements you need to create a GUI for a display equivalent to a complete hand-held calculator. One of the Programming Exercises at the end of this chapter asks you to produce just such a calculator GUI. The program for that Programming Exercise will be longer than the one in Display 12.18, but each of the GUI features that you need to add are only slight variants of features that already appear in Display 12.18.

? Self-Test Questions

43. What would happen if the user running the GUI in Display 12.18/page 826 were to type the number 10 into the text field and then click the "Add" button three times? Explain your answer.

44. In the GUI in Display 12.18/page 826, how come we made the text field inputOutputField an instance variable, but we did not make either of the buttons (addButton and resetButton) instance variables?

45. Suppose you change the `main` method in Display 12.18/page 826 to the following:

```
public static void main(String[] args)
{
    Adder guiAdder1 = new Adder();
    guiAdder1.setVisible(true);

    Adder guiAdder2 = new Adder();
    guiAdder2.setVisible(true);
}
```

You will then get two adder windows displayed. (If one is on top of the other, you can use your mouse to move the top one.) If you add numbers in one of these adders, will anything change in the other adder? The best thing to do is to try it out, but the answer is in the back of the chapter if you are still unsure after trying it.

46. Suppose you change the `main` method in Display 12.18/page 826 as we described in Self-Test Exercise 45. You will then get two adder windows displayed. If you click the close-window button in one of the windows, will one window go away or will both windows go away?

47. Suppose that in the GUI of Display 12.18/page 826 you want a third button that will clear the text field, but will *not* reset the running total. Suppose you want the button to have `"Clear"` written on it. For example, if the running sum is 10 and you click the `"Clear"` button, the text field becomes blank. if you then type in the number 5 and click the `"Add"` button, then the running sum is changed to 15 and `"15"` is displayed in the text field. How do you need to change the definition of the class `Adder` to accomplish this?

Catching a `NumberFormatException` *(Optional)*

This subsection uses material from Chapter 8 on exception handling. If you have not yet covered exception handling, you should skip this programming example until after you cover Chapter 8. If you have already covered some of Chapter 8, this section is not especially difficult and there is no need to skip it.

The GUI in Display 12.18/page 826 serves as an adding machine with the user entering numbers and adding them into a total. There is, however, one problem with that GUI. If the user enters a number in an incorrect format, such as placing a comma in a number, then one of the methods throws a `NumberFormatException`. In a Swing program, throwing an uncaught exception does not end the GUI, but it does leave it in an unpredictable state. On some systems, the user might be able to reenter the number, but you cannot count on that, and even if it is true, the user may not know that she/he should and could reenter the last number. Display 12.19 contains a slight modification of the GUI class given in Display 12.18. When the user tries to add in an incorrectly formatted number, a `NumberFormatException` is thrown, but in this version the exception is caught and the user is given a message

Display 12.19 A GUI with Exception Handling *(Part 1 of 2) (Optional)*

```java
import javax.swing.*;
import java.awt.*;
import java.awt.event.*;

/***********************************************
 *GUI for totaling a series of numbers. If the user
 *tries to add in a number in an incorrect format,
 *such as 2,000 with a comma, then an error message is
 *generated and the user can restart the computation.
 ***********************************************/
public class ImprovedAdder extends JFrame
                            implements ActionListener
{
    public static final int WIDTH = 400;
    public static final int HEIGHT = 200;

    private JTextField inputOutputField;
    private double sum = 0;

    public static void main(String[] args)
    {
        ImprovedAdder guiAdder = new ImprovedAdder();
        guiAdder.setVisible(true);
    }

    public ImprovedAdder()
        <The rest of the definition is the same as the constructor
                Adder in Display 12.18/page 826 .>

    public void actionPerformed(ActionEvent e)
    {
        try
        {
            tryingCorrectNumberFormats(e);
        }
        catch (NumberFormatException e2)
        {
            inputOutputField.setText("Error: Reenter Number.");
        }
    }
```

This class is identical to the classes Adder in Display 12.18/page 826, except that the name of the class is changed and the method actionPerformed is changed.

Display 12.19 A GUI with Exception Handling *(Part 2 of 2) (Optional)*

> `NumberFormatExceptions` *do not need to be declared in a* `throws`*-clause, but they can be caught like other exceptions.*

```
//This method can throw NumberFormatExceptions.
public void tryingCorrectNumberFormats(ActionEvent e)
{
    if (e.getActionCommand().equals("Add"))
    {
        sum = sum +
            stringToDouble(inputOutputField.getText());
        inputOutputField.setText(Double.toString(sum));
    }
    else if (e.getActionCommand().equals("Reset"))
    {
        sum = 0;
        inputOutputField.setText("0.0");
    }
    else
        inputOutputField.setText("Error in adder code.");
}

//This method can throw NumberFormatExceptions.
private static double stringToDouble(String stringObject)
{
    return Double.parseDouble(stringObject.trim());
}
}
```

Resulting GUI

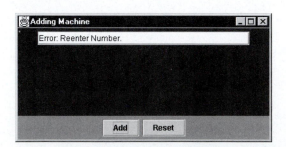

> As long as the user enters correctly formatted numbers, this **GUI** behaves exactly the same as the one in Display 12.18/page 826.
>
> If the user tries to add in an incorrectly written number, such as a number with a comma, then the **GUI** looks like this.

telling her/him to reenter the number (as shown in the GUI display in Display 12.19).

When the user clicks one of the buttons in the GUI in Display 12.19, that fires an action event `e`. The method `actionPerformed` is then automatically invoked with this action event `e` as the argument. The method `actionPerformed` invokes the method `tryingCorrectNumberFormats` using the action event `e` as an argument. The method `tryingCorrectNumberFormats` then processes the event just as it was processed in the previous version (Display 12.18). If the user enters all numbers in the correct format, then everything behaves as in the previous version (Display 12.18). But, if the user tries to add in an incorrectly formatted number, such as `2,000` with a comma instead of `2000` without a comma, then something different happens.

If the user tries to add in a number with an incorrectly formatted number, such as `2,000` instead of `2000`, then the method `tryingCorrectNumberFormats` makes an invocation of the method `stringToDouble` with the alleged number string `"2,000"` as an argument. Then, `stringToDouble` calls `Double.parseDouble`, but `Double.parseDouble` cannot convert `"2,000"` to a number, because no Java number string can contain a comma. So the method `Double.parseDouble` throws a `NumberFormatException`. Since this happens within an invocation of `stringToDouble`, `stringToDouble` throws a `NumberFormatException`. The invocation of `stringToDouble` takes place inside the invocation of `tryingCorrectNumberFormats`. So, `tryingCorrectNumberFormats` throws the `NumberFormatException` that it received from the invocation of `stringToDouble`. However, the invocation of `tryingCorrectNumberFormats` is inside of a *try-catch* block (shown in color in Display 12.19). The exception is caught in the *catch*-block. At that point, the `TextField` (named `inputOutputField`) is set to the error message `"Error: Reenter Number."` so that the GUI looks like the picture in Display 12.19.

Whenever you have numeric input in a Swing GUI, your code must convert the string input, like `"2000"`, to a number like `2000`. If the user enters a string that is not in the correct format for a number of the appropriate type, then a `NumberFormatException` will be thrown. It is a good idea to catch any such `NumberFormatException` so that the GUI can do something graceful, such as giving an error message, instead of entering some unfortunate state.

Notice that if a `NumberFormatException` is thrown, then the value of the instance variable `sum` is not changed. `NumberFormatException` is possibly thrown by an invocation of `stringToDouble` in the following line of code from the method `tryingCorrectNumberFormats`:

```
sum = sum +
      stringToDouble(inputOutputField.getText());
```

If an exception is thrown because an incorrectly written number was entered, then the execution of the method ends as soon as the exception is thrown. The exception is thrown by the method `stringToDouble` and so the exception is thrown before the above addition is performed. Thus, if an exception is thrown, the addition that would change the value of `sum` is not performed. So, `sum` is unchanged, and the user can re-enter the last number and proceed with the GUI as if that incorrect number were never entered.

Notice that none of the methods in Display 12.19 has a *throws* -clause of the form

```
throws NumberFormatException
```

That is because `NumberFormatException` is a descendent of the class `RuntimeException`, and Java does not require you to declare a `RuntimeException` in a *throws* -clause. However, you can still catch a `NumberFormatException`, just like any of the other exceptions we have seen.

CHAPTER SUMMARY

- GUIs (graphical user interfaces) are programmed using *event-driven programming*. In **event-driven programming,** a user action, like a mouse click, generates an event and that event is automatically passed to an event-handling method that performs the appropriate action.

- There are two main ways of building up a GUI using Swing. You can use inheritance to create a derived class of one of the predefined Swing classes or you can build up a GUI by adding components to a container class or you can do both in defining a single class.

- The class `JFrame` is the Swing class that you use to create a windowing GUI. A windowing GUI is defined as a derived class of the class `JFrame`.

- A button is an object of the class `JButton`.

- When adding components to an object of a container class, such as adding a button to a window, you use the method `add`. The components in a container are arranged by an object called a layout manager.

- For an object of the class `JFrame`, you do not use the method `add` with the object. Instead, you use the method `getContentPane` to produce the content pane of the object and you then use the `add` method with the content pane.

- A panel is a container object that is used to group components inside of a larger container. Panels are objects in the class `JPanel`.

- Text fields (objects of the class `JTextField`) and text areas (objects of the class `JTextArea`) are used for text input and output in a GUI constructed with Swing.

? ANSWERS to Self-Test Questions

1. All the programs we have seen before this chapter were designed to be performed by one agent (the computer) following a simple set of instructions of the form "first do this, then do that, then do something else, and so forth." In event-driven programming, you create a number of objects and let them interact via events. Each object simply waits around for some event to happen and then, if appropriate, it reacts to it. So the next thing that happens depends on the next event.

2. *GUI* is pronounced "gooey" and stands for *graphical user interface*.

3. Change the creation of the label from

```
JLabel myLabel = new JLabel("Please don't click that button!");
```

to the following:

```
JLabel myLabel = new JLabel("I love you");
```

4. Sizes in Swing are measured in pixels.

5. The `JFrame` class.

6. `System.exit(0);`

7. `myGUI.getContentPane().add(superLabel);`

8. Change the following line in the constructor in Display 12.6 from

```
setBackground(Color.blue);
```

to

```
setBackground(Color.yellow);
```

9. You use the `setTitle` method, which is inherited from the class `JFrame`. For example, the following line from the constructor in Display 12.6/page 777 sets the window title to `"Second Window"`.

```
setTitle("Second Window");
```

10. Use the `setVisible` method, which is inherited from the class `JFrame`. The following will display the window

```
gui.setVisible(true);
```

To make the window invisible, you use

```
gui.setVisible(false);
```

11. `addWindowListener(new WindowDestroyer());`

12. The following will not work correctly (and the compiler may not warn you that there is a problem).

```
myWindowGUI.add(myLabel);
```

You should instead use the following (or something equivalent):

```
myWindowGUI.getContentPane().add(myLabel);
```

13. You need to change the add statements as in the following rewritten section of code:

```
JLabel label1 = new JLabel("First label here.");
content.add(label1, BorderLayout.NORTH);

JLabel label2 = new JLabel("Second label there.");
content.add(label2, BorderLayout.CENTER);

JLabel label3 = new JLabel("Third label anywhere.");
content.add(label3, BorderLayout.SOUTH);
```

14. You need to change the add statements as in the following rewritten section of code:

```
JLabel label1 = new JLabel("First label here.");
content.add(label1, BorderLayout.NORTH);

JLabel label2 = new JLabel("Second label there.");
content.add(label2, BorderLayout.EAST);

JLabel label3 = new JLabel("Third label anywhere.");
content.add(label3, BorderLayout.SOUTH);
```

15. The argument *new* BorderLayout() creates a new object of the class BorderLayout and passes this argument to the method setLayout. This use of *new* is a way to create an argument without having to give the argument a name.

16. setLayout(*new* GridLayout(1, 3));
It is also possible to do something similar with BorderLayout, but a grid layout manager will work nicer here.

17. setLayout(*new* GridLayout(3, 1));
It is also possible to do something similar with BorderLayout, but a grid layout manager will work nicer here.

18. You need an action listener. You make a class into an action listener by adding *implements* ActionListener at the end of the class heading (after *extends* JFrame if it is a window object). You also must add a definition of the method actionPerformed to the class. Every component that generates an action event normally should have one or more action listeners registered with it. You do this with the method addActionListener.

19. Yes. The two pieces of code are equivalent. Some people think each button must have its own name, but that is not needed in this case. In the alternative piece of code, the name b is used for one button, and then, *after* the button is set up and added to the GUI, the name b is reused for the second button. This second way of writing the code is, in fact, the way most experienced programmers would write it, but we used the first way, with two names, to avoid confusion, and that is also OK.

20. You may name the content pane anything you wish (other than a reserved word). So, the following is perfectly legal:

```
Container insideOfJFrame = getContentPane();
```

(Of course, if you make this change, then `contentPane` will need to be replaced by `insideOfJFrame` where ever else it occurs in the method `actionPerformed`.)

21. When we say that an event is "sent" to a listener object, what we really mean is that some method in the listener object is invoked with the event object as the argument. This invocation happens automatically. Your Swing GUI class definition will not normally contain an invocation of this method.

22. It would have no effect on the program. The `e` is a parameter for the method `actionPerformed`, and we can use any (non-reserved-word) identifier as the parameter.

23. When adding components to a `JFrame`, you need to use `getContentPane` to get the content pane and then add components to the content pane. When adding components to a `JPanel`, there is no content pane and no need to use `getContentPane`.

24. Events from a `JButton` go to action listeners. Buttons, and certain other components, fire events in the class `ActionEvent`. These events are know as *action events* and must be handled by an action listener. Any class can be an action listener class. The details in outline form are as follows:

    1. Make some class (maybe a window class) into an `ActionListener` by adding the phrase

    implements `ActionListener`

    to the heading of the class definition and adding a definition for a method named `actionPerformed`. The `ActionListener` can be any class. In particular, the class may serve some other function besides being an `Action-Listener`.

    2. Register the `ActionListener` object with the button (or other component that will fire the action event). To do this, you use the method `add-ActionListener`. A button or other component may register more than (or less than) one listener.

25. They have a number of trivial things in common, but the commonality we were looking for in this question is that they are both listener classes. `WindowDestroyer` is a window listener class, and `ButtonDemo` is an action listener class.

26. `Container`.

27. *import* `java.awt.*;`
    (Plus probably other import statements, but this is the one you need to account for the class `Container`.)

28. Yes to both. An object of the class `JPanel` is both a container class and a component class?

29. A `FlowLayout` manager arranges the components you add to a container one after the other going from left to right. The components are laid out in the order in which you add them to the container using the method `add`.

30. A `BorderLayout` manager places components into the five regions `BorderLayout.NORTH`, `BorderLayout.SOUTH`, `BorderLayout.EAST`, `BorderLayout.WEST`, and `BorderLayout.CENTER`. The five regions are arranged as follows:

BorderLayout.NORTH		
BorderLayout. WEST	BorderLayout.CENTER	BorderLayout. EAST
BorderLayout.SOUTH		

31. Put the two buttons in a `JPanel` object and add the `JPanel` object to the region `BorderLayout.NORTH`.

32. A `GridLayout` manager arranges components in rows and columns with each entry being the same size. For example, the following says to use the a `GridLayout` manager with `aContainer` (which can be a content pane or other container).

```
aContainer.setlayout(new GridLayout(2, 3));
```

The two numbers given as arguments to the constructor `GridLayout` specify the number of rows and columns. This would produce the following sort of layout.

When using the `GridLayout` class, the method `add` has only one argument. The items are placed in the grid from left to right first filling the top row, then the second row, and so forth. You are not allowed to skip any grid position.

33. To make it look like you have an empty grid elements, add an empty panel to the grid element.

34.

```java
import javax.swing.*;
import java.awt.*;

public class PinkJPanel extends JPanel
{
    public PinkJPanel()
    {
        setBackground(Color.pink);
    }
}
```

Extra Code on CD

Look at the program `PinkJPanelDemo.java` on the accompanying CD to see that you use a `PinkJPanel` the same way that you use a ordinary `JPanel`.

35. A text field displays only a single line. A text area can display more than one line of text.

36. Change the following line in the constructor

```java
contentPane.add(buttonPanel, BorderLayout.SOUTH);
```

to

```java
contentPane.add(buttonPanel, BorderLayout.NORTH);
```

37. `TextField name = new TextField("Your name here.", 30);`

38. The portions in color are changed from Display 12.15.

```java
public void actionPerformed(ActionEvent e)
{
    String actionCommand = e.getActionCommand();
    if (actionCommand.equals("Save Memo 1"))
    {
        memo1 = theText.getText();
        theText.setText("Memo 1 saved.");
    }
    else if (actionCommand.equals("Save Memo 2"))
    {
        memo2 = theText.getText();
        theText.setText("Memo 2 saved.");
    }
    else if (actionCommand.equals("Clear"))
        theText.setText("");
    else if (actionCommand.equals("Get Memo 1"))
        theText.setText(memo1);
    else if (actionCommand.equals("Get Memo 2"))
        theText.setText(memo2);
    else
        theText.setText("Error in memo interface");
}
```

39. To get multiple lines in one `String` object, just insert the character `'\n'` at the line breaks. This happens automatically when `getText` returns the text in the `TextArea`.

40. `s = Double.toString(7.77);`

41. `x = Double.parseDouble("3.14159");`
alternatively, you could add the method `stringToDouble` (box entitled ***Inputting Numbers With a GUI*** on page 822) to the class and use
`x = stringToDouble("3.14159");`

42. `x = Double.parseDouble(s.trim());`
alternatively, you could add the method `stringToDouble` (box entitled ***Inputting Numbers With a GUI*** on page 822) to the class and use
`x = stringToDouble(s);`
(The `trim` is in the method `stringToDouble`.)

43. Every time the user clicks the `"Add"` button, the following clause from the method `actionPerformed` applies:

```
if (e.getActionCommand().equals("Add"))
{
    sum = sum +
            stringToDouble(inputOutputField.getText());
    inputOutputField.setText(Double.toString(sum));
}
```

The assignment to `sum` takes place every time the `"Add"` button event is generated. So, the number in the text field is added in as many times as the user clicks the `"Add"` button. Moreover, the last line updates the value in the text field, so that the number that is added in is the updated number. If the user clicks the `"Add"` button three times, the number *in the text field* will be added in three times. Let's say the user starts the GUI and types in 10. Now the user clicks the `"Add"` button. That adds in the 10, so the value of `sum` is 10 and 10 is displayed. Now the user clicks the `"Add"` button again. That adds in the 10, so the value of sum is 20 and 20 is displayed. Now the user clicks the `"Add"` button a third time. This time the 20 is added in, so the value of `sum` is 40 and 40 is displayed. Note that it is always the number in the text field that is added in.

44. We made the text field an instance variable because we needed to refer to it in the definition of the method `actionPerformed`, as in the following:

```
sum = sum
        + stringToDouble(inputOutputField.getText());
```

On the other hand, the only direct reference we had to the buttons was in the constructor. So, we only need names for the buttons in the constructor definition. (An object need not be named by an instance variable to be part of an Swing object, or any kind of object for that matter. Objects do not go away as long as they are being used and the buttons are being used by the object of the class `Adder`, so they stay around whether or not you have a permanent name for them.)

45. The two adder windows are completely independent in terms of numbers. The sum or the number added in to one adder has no effect on the other added.

46. If you click the close-window button in either adder window the entire program ends because of the invocation `System.exit(0);` and so both windows go away.

47. You need to add the "`Clear`" button by adding the following to the constructor:

```
JButton clearButton = new JButton("Clear");
clearButton.addActionListener(this);
buttonPanel.add(clearButton);
```

You also need to change the method `actionPerformed` to the following. (The additions are shown in color.)

```
public void actionPerformed(ActionEvent e)
{
    if (e.getActionCommand().equals("Add"))
    {
        sum = sum +
            stringToDouble(inputOutputField.getText());
        inputOutputField.setText(Double.toString(sum));
    }
    else if (e.getActionCommand().equals("Reset"))
    {
        sum = 0;
        inputOutputField.setText("0.0");
    }
    else if (e.getActionCommand().equals("Clear"))
        inputOutputField.setText("");
        //Note that sum is not changed.
    else
        inputOutputField.setText("Error in adder code.");
}
```

It would be a good idea to try these modification and run the changed program.

? PROGRAMMING EXERCISES

1. Rewrite the program in Display 12.13/page 804 so that the panel with the buttons changes to pink when the larger panel turns red, and the panel with the buttons changes to blue when the larger panel turns green. Also, add a label to the larger panel which says "`Watch this panel!`". Also, add a button to the button panel that is labeled "`Change`". When the "`Change`" button is clicked, the colors change (from pink and red to blue and green, or vice versa). The "`Change`" button has no effect in the initial configuration with the big panel blue and the button panel gray.

2. Rewrite the program in Display 12.15/page 813 so that it has all of the following changes:

   i. Change the class name to `MemoSaver2`.

   ii. There are six buttons instead of five and they are arranged as follows:

Save Memo 1	Save Memo 2	Clear
Get Memo 1	Get Memo 1	Exit

   The buttons are still at the bottom of the GUI with the text area above it. (Hint: use a grid layout manager on the button panel.)

   iii. When the user saves the text as memo 1, the text area changes so that it says `"Memo 1 saved."`, and when memo 2 is saved, it changes to `"Memo 2 saved."` (See Self-Test Exercise 38 on page 818 for a hint.)

   iv. When the `"Exit"` button is clicked, the program ends and the window goes away. The close-window button also ends the program. So, the `"Exit"` button and the close-window button perform the same action.

   v. In addition to the default constructor, there is also a constructor of the following form:

   ```
   public MemoSaver2(int lineCount, int charCount)
   ```

   When this constructor is used, it produces the same display except that the text area has dimensions of `lineCount` number of lines and `charCount` number of characters per line.

   vi. The text area has line wrap so that if more characters are entered than will fit on the line, then the extra characters automatically go on the next line.

   vii. The method `main` constructs two windows, one using the default constructor and one using the above constructor with parameters 5 and 60 in that order.

3. (You should do Programming Exercise 2 before doing this one.) Write a GUI using Swing that behaves as follows. When the program is run a window appears and asks the user how many lines and how many characters per line, she or he wants for a memo saver. If the user clicks the close-window button, the program ends. More typically, the users enters these two numbers in two text fields. There is a button with the string `"Continue"` on it. If the user clicks the `"Continue"` button, the window disappears and another window appears. This second window is just like the memo saver in Programming Exercise 2, except that the text area has the number of lines and characters per line specified by the user in the previous window.

4. (The Swing part of this exercise is quite straightforward, but you do need to know a little about how to convert numbers from one base to another.)

Write a program that converts numbers from base ten (ordinary decimal) notation to base two notation. The program uses Swing to do input and output via a windowing interface. The base ten numeral is entered in one text field, the user clicks a button with "Convert" written on it and the equivalent base two numeral appears in another text field. Be sure the two text fields are labeled. Include a "Clear" button that clears both text fields when clicks. Be sure the close-window button works correctly.

5. (It would probably help to do Programming Exercise 4 first.) Write a program that converts numbers from base two notation to base ten (normal) notation. The program uses Swing to do input and output via a windowing interface. The base two numeral is entered in one text field, the user clicks a button with "Convert" written on it and the equivalent base ten numeral appears in another text field. Be sure the two text fields are labeled. Include a "Clear" button that clears both text fields when clicks. Be sure the close-window button works correctly. (Hint: Include a private method that converts the string for a base two numeral to an equivalent *int* value.)

6. (It would probably help to do Programming Exercises 4 and 5 first.) Write a program that converts numbers from base two notation to base ten (normal) notation and vice versa. The program uses Swing to do input and output via a windowing interface. There are two text fields, one for base two numerals and one for base ten numeral. There are three buttons with the strings "To Base 10", "To Base 2", and "Clear". If the user enters a base two numeral in the base two text field and clicks the button with "To Base 10" written on it, then the equivalent base ten numeral appears in the base ten text field. Similarly, if the user enters a base ten numeral in the base ten text field and clicks the button with "To Base 2" written on it, then the equivalent base two numeral appears in the base two text field. Be sure the two text fields are labeled. Include a "Clear" button that clears both text fields when clicks. Be sure the close-window button works correctly.

7. Write a program that produces a GUI with the functionality and look of a hand-held calculator. Your calculator should allow for addition, subtraction, multiplication, and division. It should allow you to save and later recall two different values. Use the program in Display 12.18/page 826 as a model.

CHAPTER 13

APPLETS AND HTML

13.1   HTML 847

HTML Basics 847

Programming Tip A Simple HTML
    Document Outline 849

Inserting Hyperlinks 850

Gotcha Not Using Your Reload
    (Refresh) Button 853

Displaying a Picture 854

13.2   APPLETS 855

Applet Basics 855

Running an Applet 858

Programming Example
    An Adder Applet 858

Placing an Applet in an HTML
    Document 861

Java Tip Converting a Swing Application
    to an Applet 861

Adding Icons to an Applet 864

Gotcha Using an Old Web
    Browser 867

The Older Applet Class
    (Optional) 867

Applets and Security 868

Chapter Summary 869
Answers to Self-Test Questions 869
Programming Exercises 870

APPLETS AND HTML

All that has come before this chapter is important to learning how to program and to learning the Java language. However, we have not yet touched on the thing that initially made Java famous. Java became famous in large part due to its connection to the Internet.

In this chapter, we describe a version of Java programs that can be run across the Internet. The World Wide Web (Web for short) is the collection of locations on the Internet that you can view with a web browser. Applets are simply Java programs that are designed to run from a document (page) on the Web. HTML is a language used to create web documents. A Java applet runs from within an HTML document, so we will say a bit about HTML before we discuss applets.

Objectives

Learn to write a simple HTML document.

Find out how to write applets and how to embed an applet in an HTML document.

Prerequisites

Section	Prerequisite
Section 13.1	None
Section 13.2	Chapters 1–5, 7, and 12, as well as Section 13.1

web browser To really get much benefit from this chapter, you should know how to use a web browser such as the Netscape Navigator or Microsoft's Internet Explorer. All the constructs discussed in this chapter produce things to be viewed via a web browser. We will assume that you have used a web browser to read something on the Web, but will not assume that you know how to create things to be viewed on the Web. Most readers could get sufficient experience by simply playing with a web browser without any instruction or reading. To get the full benefit of this chapter, you should also understand how path names are used on your operating system so that you can name a file that is contained in a different directory (different folder).

13.1 | HTML

> *You shall see them on a beautiful quarto page, where a neat rivulet of text shall meander through a meadow of margin.*
> **Richard Brinsley Sheridan, The School for Scandal**

Documents designed to be read on the Web, or through a web browser whether or not they are on the Web, are typically written in a language called **HTML**. HTML stands for **Hypertext Markup Language. Hypertext** is simply text that contains items that you can click with your mouse to go to another document. These connections from document to document are called **links,** or **hyperlinks.** The documents themselves are often called **pages,** which is why a person's or a company's main location on the Web is called a **home page.** The terms **HTML document** and **HTML page** mean the same thing and simply refer to a hypertext document created with the HTML language.

hypertext

home page

HTML is not a full-blown programming language like Java. HTML is just a collection of simple commands that you can insert into a page of text to convert it to something that can be viewed on a web browser. The commands allow you to insert pictures and hyperlinks in the page. They also allow you to write editing commands that specify what is a main heading, what is a subheading, a paragraph beginning, and so forth. In short, most of HTML is simply a language for copy editing a manuscript so it can be viewed on the Web.

This is not a book on HTML programming, so we will only give you a small taste of the language. This will allow you to design some very simple documents for the Web (or just for your browser). If you want to become an expert in HTML, you should eventually go on to a book dedicated entirely to it.

HTML Basics

Most HTML commands are of the form

```
<Command>
Some text
</Command>
```

For example, the following makes the phrase "My Home Page" a number 1 heading, which is the largest standard heading.

```
<H1>
My Home Page
</H1>
```

`<H1>`

Notice that the notation `</Command>`, in this example `</H1>`, is used to mark the end of the text to which the command applies.

You can have smaller heads, called number 2 heads (command H2), and even smaller heads, called number 3 heads (command H3), and so forth.

`<H2>`

HTML Is Not Case Sensitive

We will write our HTML commands in uppercase letters. However, unlike Java, HTML does not distinguish between uppercase and lowercase letters in commands, and so the commands would behave the same if expressed in lowercase letters. (Any text to be displayed as text to be read by the person viewing the document will, of course, display uppercase letters in uppercase and lowercase letters in lowercase.)

Some commands do not require that they be closed with a command of the form </*Command*>. One such command is

```
<BR>
```

<P>

which is a command to begin a new line. Another is

```
<P>
```

which is a command to begin a new paragraph.

Commands in HTML are not absolute commands that determine the exact size of a portion of text, or even the exact line breaks. You give a command for a number 1 head and you can reasonably assume that it will be bigger than a number 2 head, but the browser will determine the exact size of the text. You can force a line break by inserting the **break command:**

break

```
<BR>
```

If you write a large piece of text (or even sometimes a small amount of text), the browser will insert line breaks where it determines it is necessary to fit on the screen and where it thinks it "looks good," and it will ignore your line breaks unless they are indicated with the <BR> command.

<CENTER>

You can make some layout specifications. For example, anything between the commands <CENTER> and </CENTER> will be centered on the page when it is displayed. So, the following will center the number 1 head we discussed earlier:

```
<H1>
<CENTER>
My Home Page
</CENTER>
</H1>
```

or, if you prefer, it can also be written

```
<CENTER>
<H1>
My Home Page
</H1>
</CENTER>
```

HTML File Names

An HTML file is a regular text file that you create and edit with a text editor, just the way you write a Java program. HTML files should end with .html, but otherwise can be named using the same rules as those for all other files on your system.

■ Programming Tip
A Simple HTML Document Outline

Display 13.1 contains an outline for a simple HTML document. That display also illustrates how you write comments in HTML. For example,

comments

```
<!--Beginning of HTML document-->
```

Display 13.1 Outline of a Simple HTML Document

```
<HTML> <!--Beginning of HTML document-->
<HEAD> <!--Begin the document head-->
<TITLE> <!--Begin document title. Used for browser "bookmarks"-->
Title of document.
</TITLE> <!--End document title-->
</HEAD> <!--End the document head-->
<BODY> <!--Stuff to appear on screen begins here-->
<H1>
First main heading.
</H1>
Maybe some text.
<H2>
First subheading.
</H2>
Probably some text.
<H2>
Second subheading.
</H2>
Probably some text.
<H1>
Second main heading.
</H1>
And then more of the same.
    . . .
</BODY> <!--Regular stuff ends here, but ADDRESS is displayed-->
<ADDRESS> <!--Optional, but normally used-->
The e-mail address of the person maintaining the page.
Also, the date of the last time the page was changed.
(You can actually put in whatever you want here, but the
 e-mail address and date are what people expect.)
</ADDRESS>
</HTML> <!--End of HTML Document-->
```

A real HTML document should not have this many comments.

is a comment. A comment begins with <!-- and ends with -->. We have used comments to explain the new HTML commands, but a real document would not have this many comments, nor would it explain basic HTML commands as we have done here.

<HTML>
<HEAD>

The beginning and end of the entire document is enclosed in the pair <HTML> and </HTML>. The head of the document is enclosed in <HEAD> and </HEAD>. The head is not displayed when the document is viewed, but does record information that is used by a browser. In our document, it only records a title (enclosed in

<TITLE>

<TITLE> and </TITLE>). The title is used as a name for the document. For example, a browser will let you set a bookmark at a document so you can return to the document at a later time. The bookmark will be named by this title. (Some browsers use the word "Favorites" instead of bookmarks.)

<BODY>

The part of the document that is displayed on the screen is divided into two parts. The **body** (enclosed in <BODY> and </BODY>) is the real content of the doc-

<ADDRESS>

ument. The other displayed part is enclosed in <ADDRESS> and </ADDRESS>, and is optional. It is used to give an e-mail address to contact the document's owner and usually includes the date that the document was last modified.

A very simple HTML document is shown in Display 13.2. The display that would be shown when this is viewed on a browser is shown in Display 13.3. Remember that the exact line breaks, size of letters, and other layout details are determined by the particular browser, and so might look a little different on your browser. The portion that discusses the Sun Microsystems website is explained in the next subsection.

Inserting Hyperlinks

Well this is all nice, but would hardly be worth the effort if an HTML document did not also contain some active elements. The key active element is a link that the person viewing the document can click to view another HTML document. The other document may be on the same computer, or thousands of miles away. These links are

hyperlink

called **hyperlinks,** or simply **links.**

The syntax for hyperlinks is as follows:

```
<A HREF="Path_To_Document">
Displayed_Text_To_Click
</A>
```

For example, a link to the author's home page would be as follows:

```
<A HREF="http://www-cse.ucsd.edu/users/savitch">
Walter Savitch
</A>
```

Be sure to include the quotation marks as shown. This link can be included in any text, and this part of the text will be underlined (or otherwise highlighted) by the browser. In this example, if the person viewing the document clicks the text Walter Savitch, then the browser will display the author's home page. You can insert this in any document in any part of the world, and it will take you to La Jolla, California with a click of your mouse.

Display 13.2 A Very Simple HTML Document

```
<HTML>
<HEAD>
<TITLE>
Java Club Home Page
</TITLE>
</HEAD>
<BODY>
<H1>
<CENTER>
Java Club
</CENTER>
</H1>

<H2>
Club Purpose
</H2>
<P>
A major goal of the club is to encourage
its members to become good programmers,
<P>
The club provides a setting where people who
like to program in the Java language can meet
and talk with other like-minded programmers.

<H2>
Meeting Times
</H2>
The first Wednesday of each month at 7 PM.
<H2>
Sun Microsystems Java Website
</H2>
<A HREF="http://java.sun.com">
Click here for the website
</A>
<P>
</BODY>

<ADDRESS>
javaclub.somemachine@someschool.edu
<BR>
January 1, 2001
</ADDRESS>
</HTML>
```

Blank lines are ignored when the document is displayed, but they can make your HTML code easier to read.

Text may have different line breaks when displayed on your browser.

A new paragraph will always produce a line break and some separation.

*This is explained in the subsection entitled **Inserting Hyperlinks**.*

Display 13.3 Browser View of Display 13.2

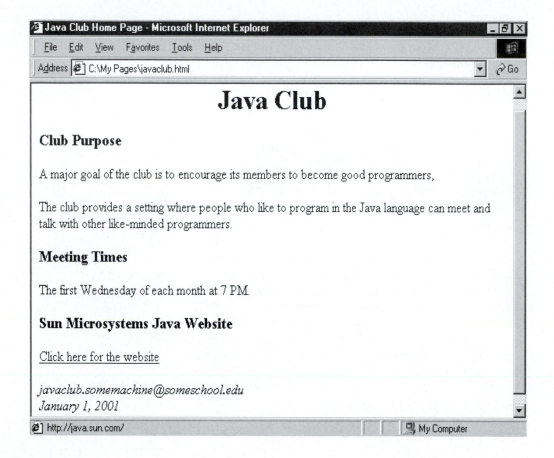

Display 13.2 shows an HTML document that includes a link to the Java website of Sun Microsystems. If you view this HTML document with a browser, it will look approximately like Display 13.3. If the user clicks the text that is underlined, the browser will display Sun Microsystems's Java website. (That is, it will display the HTML document on the company's computer that gives information about Java.)

Inserting a Hyperlink

The command for inserting a hyperlink is as follows. This may appear inside any text:

Syntax:

```
<A HREF="Path_To_Document">
Displayed_Text_To_Click
</A>
```

Example:

```
<A HREF="http://java.sun.com">
Sun Microsystems Java website
</A>
```

Either a full or relative path name or a link to any place on the Web may be used to name the document file with *Path_To_Document*. If the person viewing the document clicks the *Displayed_Text_To_Click*, then the document in the file *Path_To_Document* will be displayed.

URL

URL

The name of an HTML document on the Web is called a **URL,** which is an abbreviation for **Uniform Resource Locator.** The name is a kind of path name for the World Wide Web system, a system that covers the entire globe. The hyperlinks we described in this section are all URLs, such as

```
http://java.sun.com
```

URLs are absolute path names to documents that can be anywhere on the globe. You can also use relative path names for links to HTML documents on your own computer.

URLs often begin with `http`, which is the name of the protocol used to transfer and interpret the HTML document (but now we are getting beyond the scope of this book). Most browsers will allow you to omit the beginning part `http://` and will fill it in for you.

■ Gotcha

Not Using Your Reload (Refresh) Button

Most browser keep copies of the most recently used HTML pages. That way, if you want to go back to one of those pages, the browser can recover the pages very quickly. Usually, this is a good thing, since it makes your browser run faster. However, when you are designing and debugging an HTML page, this can be a problem.

Suppose you test an HTML page with your browser and notice something that needs to be fixed. If you change the HTML page to fix the problem and then again look at the page with your browser, you will probably see no change. This can be true even if you exit your browser, reenter the browser starting with some other page, and then jump to page being fixed. The problem is that, as we said, most browsers keep copies of the most recent pages that the browser has displayed. The browser reuses those copies instead of loading new copies of the pages.

To ensure that your browser is displaying the most current version of a page, click the button labeled "Reload," "Refresh," or something similar. This will cause the browser to reload the page and so give you the latest version.

Automatic Documentation with `javadoc`

The Java language comes with a program named `javadoc` that can automatically generate documentation for your Java classes. The documentation that is produced by `javadoc` is an HTML document that you read with a browser, just like any other HTML document. The program `javadoc` is described in Appendix 10.

Displaying a Picture

For what we are doing with HTML, we do not need pictures, but you might want to put a picture in your HTML document. The command to insert a picture is as follows:

```
<IMG SRC="File_With_Picture">
```

For example, suppose you have a digital version of a picture in the subdirectory `images`. To be concrete, suppose the picture file `mypicture.gif` is in the directory `images`, and `images` is a subdirectory of where the HTML page is. You could add the picture to your HTML document by inserting the following:

```
<IMG SRC="images/mypicture.gif">
```

The picture can be in any directory, but you must give a path that will lead to the picture file. Either a full or relative path name (from the HTML document) may be used to name the file with the encoded picture. Various picture-encoding formats are accepted.

? Self-Test Questions

1. What is the difference between the commands `<H2>` and `<h2>`?

2. How do you insert a link to the following home page?

   ```
   http://www.fool.com/
   ```

3. How will the following be displayed by a browser? (Where would the line breaks be? Where would it add space?)

   ```
   <P>
   A major goal of the club is to encourage
   its members to become good programmers,
   <P>
   The club provides a setting where people who
   like to program in the Java language can meet
   and talk with other like-minded programmers.
   ```

13.2 | Applets

> *An applet a day keeps the doctor away.*
>
> **Anonymous**

The word *applet* sounds like it refers to a small apple, but it is supposed to sound like a small application. Thus, applets are just "little Java programs," in some sense of the word *little*. However, the character of applets comes not from their size, but from how and where they are run. Applets are Java programs that can be embedded in an HTML document and can be run using a browser that views the document. An applet is very much like a Swing GUI, and if you understand some details about Swing, then you will find it very easy to write applets. In this section, we will assume that you are already familiar with the Swing material given in Chapter 12. We will show you how to write simple applets that do the same thing as the windowing systems we covered in Chapter 12. If you go on to learn more about Java, and Java graphics in particular, then you can add graphics to your applets.

Applet Basics

An applet is a derived class of the class `JApplet` (actually, any descendent class, but typically a directly derived class). The class `JApplet` is a class in the Swing library, so you need the following import statement when using the class `JApplet`:

```
import javax.swing.*;
```

import

When you are writing an applet, you may also need the AWT library, so your full list of import statements is likely to be the following:

```
import javax.swing.*;
import java.awt.*;
import java.awt.event.*;
```

Display 13.4 shows a part of the class hierarchy to help you put the class `JApplet` in context. Note that a `JApplet` is a `Container`. Thus, you can add things to an applet in the same way you add components to other containers, such as adding to a `JPanel`.

In Display 13.4 you might notice the class `Applet`. The class `Applet` is an older class than the class `JApplet`. The `Applet` class was used to create applets before the introduction of the class `JApplet`.

An applet class can be designed much the same way you design a windowing system using Swing. The main difference is that you derive an applet class from the class `JApplet` instead of the class `JFrame`. Other differences between an applet class and a Swing windowing class mostly consist of things that are omitted from the applet class definition.

Applets do not need the `setVisible` method. Applets are embedded in HTML documents, and it is the HTML document that displays the applet. For this reason, an applet also normally does not have a `main` method. A trivially simple

Display 13.4 Placing Applets in the Class Hierarchy

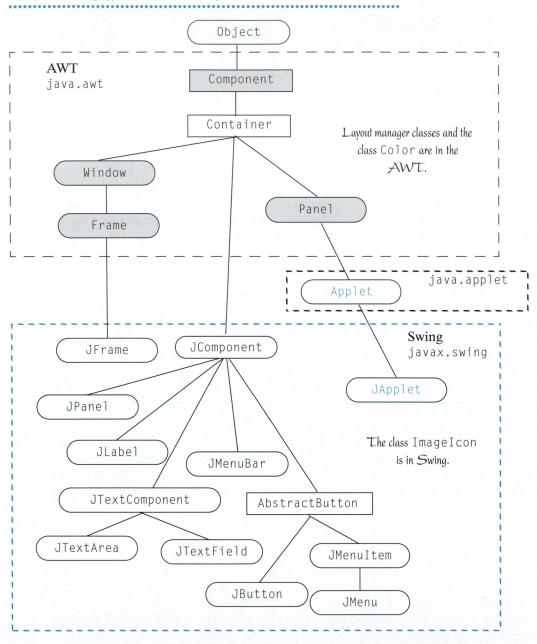

If there is a line between two classes, then the lower class is a derived class of the higher class.
Shaded classes are not used in this text but are included for reference. If you have not heard of them,
you can safely ignore them.

Display 13.5 A Trivial Applet

```
import javax.swing.*;
import java.awt.*;//For Container class

public class HelloApplet extends JApplet
{
    public void init()
    {
        Container contentPane = getContentPane();
        contentPane.setLayout(new FlowLayout());
        JLabel friendlyLabel = new JLabel("Hello out there!");
        contentPane.add(friendlyLabel);
    }
}
```

Resulting GUI (Using an Applet Viewer)

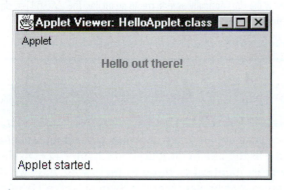

applet is shown in Display 13.5. When this applet is viewed (typically within an HTML document), it will simply display the text

```
Hello out there!
```

Note that a JApplet has a content pane just like a JFrame, and you add components to the content pane of the JApplet, rather than adding them directly to the JApplet. As illustrated in Display 13.5, you add a JLabel (or other component) to a JApplet,   JLabel just as you would add it to a JFrame.

Applets do not have titles, and so there is no need to use the setTitle method in an applet. This is because applets normally go into HTML documents, and you can insert the title in the HTML document that displays the applet. As we will see in the next subsection, the HTML document also takes care of sizing the applet, so you do not give any size instructions for an applet.

init

Applets do not normally use constructors, but they do use a method named init that serves a similar purpose. When defining an applet, you place all the initializing actions—such as setting colors, adding buttons, adding text fields, and so forth—in the method named init. The init method has no parameters.

Applets do not need to be closed with listeners, and so do not include an invocation of addWindowListener in their init methods. When the HTML document is closed, that will automatically close the applet.

(Other very simple examples of applets are given in Chapter 1. In Chapter 1, the applets have no layout manager specified. If a JApplet has no layout manager specified, then by default it has the BorderLayout manager. If a component is added without specifying a region, it goes in the region BorderLayout.CENTER. In Chapter 1 we did not use any layout manager, in order to keep the examples simple, but now that you understand layout managers, we suggest that you always use an explicit layout manager.)

The JApplet Class

The JApplet class is the class normally used to create an applet. The JApplet class is in the Swing library, and so, when using this class, you use the following import statement:

import javax.swing.*;

Programming Example
An Adder Applet

Display 13.6 contains an applet that will produce an adding machine window that is essentially the same as the one we produced in Chapter 12 (Display 12.18/page 826). The details are almost identical to those in the Swing class we defined in Display 12.18. To obtain this adder applet from the Swing class in Display 12.18, we simply did the following:

Replaced *extends* JFrame with *extends* JApplet.

Deleted the main method.

Replaced the constructor heading by the init method heading.

Deleted some lines not needed for an applet.

Running an Applet

applet viewer

The normal way to run an applet is from an HTML document, but if you want to test out an applet, you can run it using an *applet viewer*. An **applet viewer** is basically a program that automatically puts your applet in a simple HTML page and then runs it from there. However, an applet viewer makes it look like an applet is run just like any other program. If you are using an integrated environment that has a menu command called "Run Applet," "Run," or "Execute," or something similar, then you can probably run an applet just like you run an ordinary Java application program by

Display 13.6 An Applet Adding Machine *(Part 1 of 2)*

```java
import javax.swing.*;
import java.awt.*;
import java.awt.event.*;

public class AdderApplet extends JApplet
                         implements ActionListener
{
    private JTextField inputOutputField;
    private double sum = 0;


    public void init()
    {
        Container contentPane = getContentPane();
        contentPane.setLayout(new BorderLayout());

        JPanel buttonPanel = new JPanel();
        buttonPanel.setBackground(Color.gray);
        buttonPanel.setLayout(new FlowLayout());
        JButton addButton = new JButton("Add");
        addButton.addActionListener(this);
        buttonPanel.add(addButton);
        JButton resetButton = new JButton("Reset");
        resetButton.addActionListener(this);
        buttonPanel.add(resetButton);
        contentPane.add(buttonPanel, BorderLayout.SOUTH);

        JPanel textPanel = new JPanel();
        textPanel.setBackground(Color.blue);
        textPanel.setLayout(new FlowLayout());
        inputOutputField =
                    new JTextField("Numbers go here.", 30);
        inputOutputField.setBackground(Color.white);
        textPanel.add(inputOutputField);
        contentPane.add(textPanel, BorderLayout.CENTER);
    }
```

Display 13.6 An Applet Adding Machine *(Part 2 of 2)*

```
public void actionPerformed(ActionEvent e)
{
    if (e.getActionCommand().equals("Add"))
    {
        sum = sum +
            stringToDouble(inputOutputField.getText());
        inputOutputField.setText(Double.toString(sum));
    }
    else if (e.getActionCommand().equals("Reset"))
    {
        sum = 0;
        inputOutputField.setText("0.0");
    }
    else
        inputOutputField.setText("Error in adder code.");
}

private static double stringToDouble(String stringObject)
{
    return Double.parseDouble(stringObject.trim());
}
}
```

Resulting GUI (Using an Applet Viewer)

using one of these commands. (In the TextPad environment, which comes on the CD included in this book, the command is "Run Java Applet" on the "Tools" menu. If a window pops up asking you to "Choose a file", answer "No". This environment command will automatically invoke an applet viewier.)

If you cannot run an applet viewer from an environment, you can undoubtedly run an applet viewer as a one-line command. For example, the applet in Display 13.6 would be run as follows:

```
appletviewer AdderApplet.html
```

However, if you run an applet with a one-line command in this way, you may need to create an HTML document yourself (named `AdderApplet.html` in this example) and place the Applet in the HTML document. The details of placing an applet in an HTML document are described in the next subsection.

If you run the applet in Display 13.6 in an applet viewer, the result will look similar to the GUI shown in that display.

An applet is normally displayed from an HTML document as described in the next subsection, However, when you are debugging an applet, you normally test the applet with an applet viewer.

Placing an Applet in an HTML Document

If you place the following command in an HTML document, then the document will display the adder window created by the applet in Display 13.6/page 859:

```
<APPLET CODE="AdderApplet.class" WIDTH=400 HEIGHT=200>
</APPLET>
```

This assumes that the HTML file and the file `AdderApplet.class` are in the same directory (same folder). If they are not in the same directory (same folder), then you would use an absolute or relative path name for the class `AdderApplet.class`. An expression such as the one previously displayed is often called an **applet tag.**

applet tag

For example, Display 13.7 contains a sample HTML document that includes the applet given in Display 13.6/page 859. When displayed with a browser, this HTML document would look approximately as shown in Display 13.8.

Notice that when you place an applet in an HTML document, you give the name of the byte-code file that ends in `.class`, rather than the `.java` or other file name. Also, notice that you specify the width and height of the applet in this command and not within the applet class definition.

sizing an applet

■ Java Tip
Converting a Swing Application to an Applet

It is easy to convert a Swing application to an applet. In most cases, you simply follow these instructions:

1. Derive the class from the class `JApplet` instead of deriving it from the class `JFrame`. That is, replace *extends* `JFrame` with *extends* `JApplet` on the first line of the class definition.

Display 13.7 An HTML Document with an Applet

```
<HTML>
<HEAD>
<TITLE>
Budget Help
</TITLE>
</HEAD>

<BODY>
<H1>
The Budget Help Home Page
<BR>
Helpful Hints for a Balanced Budget
</H1>

<H2>
Pay off your credit cards every month.
</H2>

<H2>
Do not spend more than you earn.
</H2>

<H2>
Here is an adder to help you plan your budget:
</H2>
<APPLET CODE="AdderApplet.class" WIDTH=400 HEIGHT=200>
</APPLET>
<P>
</BODY>

<P>
<ADDRESS>
budgethelp@fleeceyou.com
<BR>
December 31, 2001
</ADDRESS>
</HTML>
```

2. Remove the `main` method. An applet does not need the things that are typically placed in `main`. An applet is automatically made visible and its size and location are determined by the HTML page from which it is run.

3. Replace the constructor with a method named `init`. The body of the `init` method can be the same as the body of the deleted constructor, but with some items removed, as described in the following steps.

4. Delete any invocation of `addWindowListener`. (When the HTML document is closed, that will automatically close the applet. So, you do not

Display 13.8 Browser View of Display 13.7

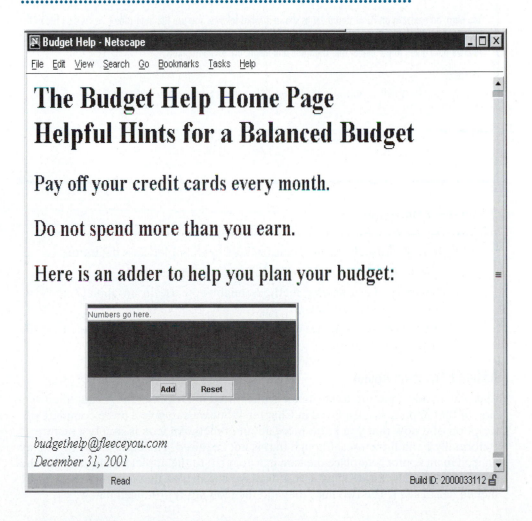

need any window listener object, such as an object of the class `Window-Destroyer` from Chapter 12.)

5. Delete any invocation of `setTitle`. (Applets have no titles, although you can put a title on the HTML page.)

6. Delete any invocation of `setSize`. (Sizing is done by the HTML page from which the applet is run.)

7. Make an HTML page with an `APPLET` tag that refers to the byte-code (`.class`) version of the applet.

For example, the applet in Display 13.6 was obtained from the Swing application in Display 12.18/page 826 by following these rules.

Applets in HTML Documents

You place an applet in an HTML document as shown in what follows. You use the byte-code (`.class`) file of the applet. If the file is not in the same directory (same folder) as the HTML document, you can use either a full or relative path name to the applet file. The width and height are given in pixels.

Syntax:

```
<APPLET CODE="Name_Of_.class_File" WIDTH=Integer HEIGHT=Integer>
</APPLET>
```

Example:

```
<APPLET CODE="AdderApplet.class" WIDTH=400 HEIGHT=200>
</APPLET>
```

? Self-Test Questions

4. Do you normally include constructors in an applet class definition?

5. Is it normal for an applet class to have a `main` method?

6. Which of the following methods might you use in an applet? `addWindowListener`, `getContentPane`, `setTitle`, `setSize`

7. When you list an applet in an HTML document, do you list the `.java` file or the `.class` file?

Adding Icons to an Applet

One way to add a picture to an applet is illustrated in Display 13.9. A simplified version of that applet was displayed in Chapter 1, but we can give a more complete description of it now that you know more about applets. An icon is simply a picture. It is normally a small picture, although that is not required. The easiest way to display an icon in an applet is to place the icon in a `JLabel`. In the applet in Display 13.9, the picture in the file `duke_waving.gif` is displayed as an icon that is part of the `JLabel` named `niceLabel`. The two lines that add the icon are reproduced below:

Display 13.9 An Applet with an Icon

```java
import javax.swing.*;
import java.awt.*;

public class DukeApplet extends JApplet
{
    public void init()
    {
        Container contentPane = getContentPane();
        contentPane.setLayout(new BorderLayout());

        JLabel spacer = new JLabel("                  ");
        contentPane.add(spacer, "West");
        JLabel niceLabel = new JLabel("Java is fun!");
        ImageIcon dukeIcon = new ImageIcon("duke_waving.gif");
        niceLabel.setIcon(dukeIcon);
        getContentPane().add(niceLabel, BorderLayout.CENTER);
    }
}
```

Resulting GUI [1] .

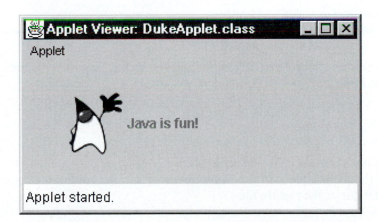

---

1. Java, Duke, and all Java-based trademarks and logos are trademarks or registered trademarks of Sun Microsystems, Inc. in the United States and other countries.

```
ImageIcon dukeIcon = new ImageIcon("duke_waving.gif");
niceLabel.setIcon(dukeIcon);
```

ImageIcon

ImageIcon is a class in the Swing library. The label niceLabel is a label created in the normal way that we described in Chapter 12:

```
JLabel niceLabel = new JLabel("Java is fun!");
```

The icon picture is a digital picture in one of the standard formats. The picture, in this case duke_waving.gif, must be converted to an ImageIcon before it can be added to a label. This is done as follows: new ImageIcon("duke_waving.gif"). So, the following creates an ImageIcon based on the picture duke_waving.gif and stores a reference to the icon in the variable dukeIcon:

```
ImageIcon dukeIcon = new ImageIcon("duke_waving.gif");
```

The method setIcon adds an icon to a label, as in the following:

```
niceLabel.setIcon(dukeIcon);
```

If you want only the icon and do not want the label to have any text, then simply use the default constructor when you create the JLabel. For example, if we used the following in Display 13.9

```
JLabel niceLabel = new JLabel();
```

instead of

```
JLabel niceLabel = new JLabel("Java is fun!");
```

then the string "Java is fun!" would not appear in the applet; only the icon would be displayed.

Chapter 14 contains more material on icons.

Icons and the Class ImageIcon

An **icon** is simply a small picture, although it is not really required to be small. The class ImageIcon is used to convert a picture file to a Swing icon.

Syntax:

```
ImageIcon Name_Of_ImageIcon =
        new ImageIcon(Picture_File_Name);
```

The *Picture_File_Name* is a string giving either a relative or absolute path name to the picture file. (So, if the picture file is in the same directory as your applet, then you need give only the name of the picture file.)

Example:

```
ImageIcon SmileyFaceIcon =
        new ImageIcon("smiley.gif");
```

Who is Duke?

Duke is shown in the Applet in Display 13.9/page 865. He has become a mascot for the Java language. The Duke icon is used here with permission from Sun Microsystems, Inc.

■ **Gotcha**

Using an Old Web Browser

Your web browser must be set up to run applets. The web browser does not use the same interpreter that is used to run an application. If you have an old web browser that is not set up for applets or that is only set up for applets from an earlier version of Java, then you may not be able to run applets from an HTML document, and this can be true even if Java applications run fine on your system. In such cases, all you can do is obtain a new browser,

Unfortunately, even obtaining a new browser does not always help, because the Java updates for browsers are typically made much later than the updates for the core Java language. Moreover, if you place an applet in an HTML document and you expect other people to view the applet over the Web, then the applet `.class` file will be sent to other people's browsers and run on their browsers. And of course, you cannot reasonably expect all these other people to have the most recent browser.

If you expect an applet to be widely viewed over the Web, then you should test it on a number of different browsers. Testing your applet on Netscape Navigator and Microsoft's Internet Explorer should be sufficient, but you should test it on older as well as the latest versions of these browsers. If you have trouble getting your applet to work on older browsers, consider using the older `Applet` class as described in the subsection *The Older* `Applet` *Class (Optional)*

Although you may have problems running your applets on a browser, you should have no such problem running the applets from the appletviewer, as long as you have a recent version of Java. So, you should be able to run and test your applets, even if you cannot run them from an HTML page. However, if they are not ultimately placed in HTML documents, you may as well use regular Swing GUIs derived from `JFrame`.

applet viewer

The Older `Applet` Class *(Optional)*

If you find that your applet does not work on a wide enough array of browsers, try using the older class `Applet` class instead of the `JApplet` class. This can usually be done by simply deleting all the `J`s, replacing `JApplet` with `Applet`, `JButton` with `Button`, `JLabel` with `Label`, and so forth. This will require adding the import statement:

Applet

```
import java.awt.*;
import Java.awt.event.*;
import java.applet.*;
```

And you may as well delete the import statement:

```
import javax.swing.*;
```

You need to do one more, slightly more complicated alteration. Unlike a `JApplet`, an `Applet` has no content pane. So you use `add` with the applet itself rather than using a content pane, and in general, whatever you would do to the content pane of a

`JApplet`, you do directly to an `Applet`. For example, if the method `init` contains the line

```
getContentPane().add(friendlyLabel);
```

in the `JApplet`, then in converting it to an `Applet`, you need to replace it with

```
add(friendlyLabel);
```

For most simple applets these changes will produce an applet that will run on older as well as newer browsers. However, the class `Applet` cannot easily accommodate icons, so your applets should not contain icons when you use the `Applet` class.

We have followed these rules to produce applets based on the `Applet` class instead of the `JApplet` class for the applets in Display 13.5/page 857 and Display 13.6/page 859. The results are in the files `OlderHelloApplet.java` and `OlderAdderApplet.java` on the accompanying CD.

extra code on
CD

The `Applet` Class *(Optional)*

The class `Applet` is an older applet class that was used to produce applets before the `JApplet` class came on the scene. The class `Applet` cannot produce applets with as many features as the class `JApplet` can produce. However, applets produced with the `Applet` class will work on a wider range of browsers. So, if you expect your applets to be viewed by a wide array of users, then it might be prudent to use the class `Applet`, rather than the class `JApplet`. For very simple applets, it is easy to convert a `JApplet` to an `Applet`. The details are given in the section ***The Older*** `Applet` ***Class (Optional)***. The `Applet` class requires the following import statement:

```
import java.applet.*;
```

Applets and Security

Suppose somebody on the Web reads your HTML page and that HTML page contains an applet. That applet's byte code is run on the reader's browser, which is on the reader's computer. So, your applet can be a program that runs on other people's computers, and more frightening, other people's applets can be programs that run on your computer! Moreover, you do not know that an HTML page contains an applet until you load it into your browser, and then it is too late to reject the applet. The applet is loaded on your computer.

Whenever somebody else's program runs on your computer, there are serious security concerns. Will the program leave a virus on your computer? Will the program read confidential information from your files? Will the program change and thus corrupt your operating system? Applets are designed so that they cannot (or at least cannot easily) do any of these things. Applets cannot run any of your programs. Applets cannot read or write to files on your computer (unless the applet originated on your computer). But be warned, there are programs, other than applets, that can be run through your browser and that can gain access to things on your computer; things that you may have thought were private.

? Self-Test Questions

8. How would you create a label with the picture `duke_waving.gif` but with no text?

9. What command would you add to the `init` method of a `JApplet` to display the `JLabel` you defined in question 8?

CHAPTER SUMMARY

■ Documents designed to be read across the World Wide Web or through a web browser are typically written in a language called HTML. HTML stands for Hypertext Markup Language.

■ Applets are Java programs designed to be placed in and run from an HTML document.

■ Applets are similar to Swing GUIs derived from the class `JFrame`.

■ An applet is normally a derived class of the class `JApplet`.

■ An applet normally has no `main` method and no constructors. However, the method `init` serves the same purpose as a constructor for an applet.

■ An applet's `init` method does not include any invocations of `addWindowListener`, `setTitle`, or `setSize`.

? ANSWERS to Self-Test Questions

1. None. HTML is not case-sensitive.

2.
```
<A HREF="http://www.fool.com/">
Anything you want to say goes here.
</A>
```

3. A line break and some extra space will be added at each `<P>`. The line breaks in the text will be ignored and the browser will insert line breaks where it needs to in order to fit the text in the browser window.

4. Applet classes do not usually use constructors. However, they do use a method named `init` that serves a similar purpose.

5. Applet classes do not normally have a `main` method.

6. You are very likely to use `getContentPane` when defining an applet. You would not normally use `addWindowListener`, `setTitle`, or `setSize`, because an applet does not have a title, and its size and closing are handled by the HTML document in which it is embedded. (It is possible to use them in certain kinds of components that might be added to an applet, but that is not what we are emphasizing in this question.)

7. The `.class` file.

8.
```
JLabel pictureOnly = new JLabel();
ImageIcon dukeIcon = new ImageIcon("duke_waving.gif");
pictureOnly.setIcon(dukeIcon);
```
There are also other ways to do this, but this is the way we discussed in this chapter.

9.
```
getContentPane().add(pictureOnly, BorderLayout.CENTER);
```
It need not go in the center position, and you could even use a different layout manager.

? PROGRAMMING EXERCISES

1. Design an HTML home page for yourself. Use your imagination to put in whatever you would like people to know about you or that you think they should know about you. Some possibilities are your name, your occupation or class schedule, where you go to school or work, your hobbies, your favorite quotation, how to reach you by e-mail, and/or anything you like. Note that your home page, as any home page, will consist of several files, each of which contains HTML documents. The hyperlinks allow the person viewing the document to move from one HTML document to another by clicking with a mouse. Variations: If you are in a class, ask your instructor whether or not you need to include an applet on your home page.

2. Convert the Swing application in Display 12.15/page 813 to an applet and place it in an HTML document.

3. Convert the `FileServer` program from Display 9.19/page 646 to an applet. In other words, add an applet interface to the program `FileServer` in Display 9.19/page 646.

4. Every first year electrical engineering student learns that two resistors (resistors are a common type of electrical component) can be connected in either of two configurations, series or parallel, and there are simple formulas to calculate the equivalent resistance of both configurations (the value of a single resistor that can replace the two). If $R1$ and $R2$ are the two resistor values, then

Series Resistance = $R1 + R2$, and

Parallel Resistance = *R*1 * *R*2 / (*R*1 + *R*2)

Write an applet that provides a windowing interface to let a user enter two resistor values and choose which configuration to calculate. Include two text fields (label them "Resistor 1" and "Resistor 2") to read in two values; two buttons (label them "Series" and "Parallel") to select the configuration; and another text field (label it "Equivalent Resistance") to display the calculated value and whichever configuration was selected. For example, if 100 is entered for *R*1, 50 for *R*2, and the "Series" button clicked, then the message would read "Series Equivalent = 150" and if the "Parallel" button is clicked, then the message would read "Parallel Equivalent = 33.3". Put the applet in a web page that explains the calculations.

5. Modify the GUI calculator program from Chapter 12 Programming Exercise 7/page 843 to run as an applet. If you have not already done Programming Exercise 7 in Chapter 12, then do it now but do it as an applet.

6. (The Swing part of this exercise is quite straightforward, but you do need to know a little about how to convert numbers from one base to another.) Write an applet that converts from base ten (normal) notation to base sixteen (hexadecimal notation). The program uses Swing to do input and output via an applet interface. The base ten integer numeral is entered in one text field, the user clicks a button labeled "Convert", and the equivalent hexadecimal numeral appears in another text field. Be sure the two fields are labeled. Include a "Clear" button that clears both text fields.

7. Rewrite the program in Display 12.15/page 813 (Chapter 12) so that it is an applet and so that it has all of the following changes:

i. Change the class name to MemoApplet.

ii. There are six buttons instead of five and they are arranged as follows:

Save Memo 1	Save Memo 2	Clear
Get Memo 1	Get Memo 1	Exit

The buttons are still at the bottom of the GUI with the text area above it. (Hint: use a grid layout manager on the button panel.)

iii. When the user saves the text as memo 1, the text area changes so that it says "Memo 1 saved.", and when memo 2 is saved, it changes to "Memo 2 saved." (See Self-Test Exercise 38 of Chapter 12, page 818 for a hint.)

iv. The text area has line wrap so that if more characters are entered than will fit on the line, then the extra characters automatically go on the next line.

CHAPTER 14

MORE SWING OBJECTS

14.1 MENUS 875
Menu Bars, Menus, and Menu
 Items 875
Programming Example A GUI with a
 Menu 875
Nested Menus 880

14.2 MAKING GUIS PRETTY (AND MORE FUNCTIONAL) 882
Adding Icons 882
Gotcha Resizing Buttons 886
The JScrollPane Class for Scroll
 Bars 890
Adding Borders 893
Gotcha Forgetting to Import
 javax.swing.border 900
Changing the Look and Feel 900
Lightweight and Heavyweight Com-
 ponents (Optional) 904

14.3 MORE LAYOUT MANAGERS 907
The BoxLayout Manager Class 908
Struts and Glue 912
Gotcha Using Struts and Glue with
 Other Layout Managers 914

The Box Container Class 914
The CardLayout Manager 917

14.4 INNER CLASSES 923
Helping Classes 923

14.5 MORE ON EVENTS AND LISTENERS 925
The WindowListener
 Interface 925
Java Tip Programming the Close-Window
 Button 930
Programming Example Components with
 Changing Visibility 935
Some More Details on Updating a
 GUI 938

14.6 ANOTHER LOOK AT THE SWING CLASS HIERARCHY 939
Buttons, Menus, and Abstract
 Buttons 939
Java Tip More Methods for the Class
 JMenuItem 940
Java Tip There are a Lot More Swing
 Classes and Methods 941

Chapter Summary 941
Answers to Self-Test Questions 942
Programming Exercises 946

MORE SWING OBJECTS

> *The more the merrier.*
>
> *John Heywood, Proverbs (1546)*

In this chapter we give you some additional information about Swing, so that you can create more profession looking GUIs. Section 14.1 introduces menus, which we have not discussed before. However, as you will see, much of what you learned about buttons will carry over to menus. So, Swing menus will not look completely new to you. The material in Sections 14.2 through 14.6 cover some enhancements of basic things you already are doing with Swing. In particular, Section 14.4 covers inner classes. Section 14.2 covers look and feel in Swing, a topic that is something of a hallmark for Swing.

Along the way you will learn about these Swing (or Swing-related) classes: `AbstractButton`, `Box`, `BoxLayout`, `BevelBorder`, `Dimension`, `EmptyBorder`, `EtchedBorder`, `ImageIcon`, `Inset`, `JMenu`, `JMenuBar`, `JMenuItem`, `JScrollPane`, `LineBorder`, `MatteBorder`, and others.

Objectives

Learn to add menus, icons, borders, and scroll bars to your GUIs.

Understand the `BoxLayout` manager and the `Box` class.

Find out how to change the look and feel of a Swing GUI.

Understand some uses and advantages of inner classes.

Learn about the `WindowListener` interface.

Find out how to create GUIs with components that change from visible to invisible and vice versa.

Prerequisites

Before covering this chapter, you need to have covered Chapter 12 which introduces you to Swing. You do not need to have covered Chapter 13 (Applets) before covering this chapter. For the subsection entitled *Changing the Look and Feel* in Section 14.2, you need to have read the beginning of Chapter 8 on exception handling.

The boxed subsection *Adding Icons to Menu Items (Alternative Ordering)* in Section 14.2 naturally requires that you first cover the subsection *Menu Bars, Menus, and Menu Items* in Section 14.1. Aside from that one clearly marked boxed

subsection, the sections 14.1 (menus), 14.2 (icons, look and feel, plus other good-
ies), 14.3 (Box containers) and 14.4 (inner classes) are independent of each other.
You can cover them in any order.

14.1 | Menus

Swing GUIs can have menus and you already learned most of what you need to
know about menus in Swing. You learned it when you learned about buttons in
Chapter 12. Menu items behave the same as buttons. An example will make this
clear.

Programming Example
A GUI with a Menu

Display 14.1 contains a program that constructs a GUI with a menu. This GUI does
the same thing as the GUI in Display 12.15/page 813, except that the GUI in Display
14.1 uses a pull-down menu and the GUI in Display 12.15 uses buttons to specify the
actions. The user writes memos in the text area just as in Display 12.15. When memos
are recalled, they appear in the text area just as in Display 12.15. But the GUI in Display 14.1 does not have any buttons. Instead, it has a menu bar at the top of the window. The menu bar lists the names of all the pull-down menus. This GUI has only one
pull-down menu, which is named "Memos". However, there could be more pull-down
menus in the same menu bar.

The user can pull down a menu by clicking the menu name in the menu bar.
Display 14.1 contains two pictures of the GUI. The first is what you see when the
GUI first appears. In that picture, the menu name "Memos" can be seen in the menu
bar, but you cannot see the menu. If you click the word "Memos" with your mouse,
the menu pulls down, as shown in the second picture of the GUI. If you click "Save
Memo 1", the text in the text area is saved. The other menu choices similarly behave
the same as the buttons in Display 12.15.

There is one new choice on this menu, namely, Exit. When the user clicks on
the entry Exit, the program ends and the window disappears. The exact same thing
happens if the user clicks her or his mouse on the close-window button. So, there
are two ways that a user can end this GUI.

In the next few sections, we go over the details of the program in Display 14.1.

Menu Bars, Menus, and Menu Items

When adding menus in the way we did in Display 14.1, you use the three Swing classes JMenuBar, JMenu, and JMenuItem. Entries on a menu are objects of the class

Display 14.1 A GUI with a Menu *(Part 1 of 3)*

```java
import javax.swing.*;
import java.awt.*;
import java.awt.event.*;

public class MemoGUI extends JFrame implements ActionListener
{
    public static final int WIDTH = 600;
    public static final int HEIGHT = 300;
    public static final int LINES = 10;
    public static final int CHAR_PER_LINE = 40;

    private JTextArea theText;
    private String memo1 = "No Memo 1.";
    private String memo2 = "No Memo 2.";

    public MemoGUI()
    {
        setSize(WIDTH, HEIGHT);
        addWindowListener(new WindowDestroyer());
        setTitle("Memo Saver");
        Container contentPane = getContentPane();
        contentPane.setLayout(new BorderLayout());

        JMenu memoMenu = new JMenu("Memos");
        JMenuItem m;

        m = new JMenuItem("Save Memo 1");
        m.addActionListener(this);
        memoMenu.add(m);

        m = new JMenuItem("Save Memo 2");
        m.addActionListener(this);
        memoMenu.add(m);

        m = new JMenuItem("Get Memo 1");
        m.addActionListener(this);
        memoMenu.add(m);

        m = new JMenuItem("Get Memo 2");
        m.addActionListener(this);
        memoMenu.add(m);

        m = new JMenuItem("Clear");
        m.addActionListener(this);
        memoMenu.add(m);
```

<Constructor MemoGUI continued in next part of display.>

Display 14.1   A GUI with a Menu *(Part 2 of 3)*

<*public* MemoGUI( ) **continued.**>

```java
        m = new JMenuItem("Exit");
        m.addActionListener(this);
        memoMenu.add(m);

        JMenuBar mBar = new JMenuBar();
        mBar.add(memoMenu);
        setJMenuBar(mBar);

        JPanel textPanel = new JPanel();
        textPanel.setBackground(Color.blue);
        theText = new JTextArea(LINES, CHAR_PER_LINE);
        theText.setBackground(Color.white);
        textPanel.add(theText);
        contentPane.add(textPanel, BorderLayout.CENTER);
    }

    public void actionPerformed(ActionEvent e)
    {
        String actionCommand = e.getActionCommand();
        if (actionCommand.equals("Save Memo 1"))
            memo1 = theText.getText();
        else if (actionCommand.equals("Save Memo 2"))
            memo2 = theText.getText();
        else if (actionCommand.equals("Clear"))
            theText.setText("");
        else if (actionCommand.equals("Get Memo 1"))
            theText.setText(memo1);
        else if (actionCommand.equals("Get Memo 2"))
            theText.setText(memo2);
        else if (actionCommand.equals("Exit"))
            System.exit(0);
        else
            theText.setText("Error in memo interface");
    }

    public static void main(String[] args)
    {
        MemoGUI gui = new MemoGUI();
        gui.setVisible(true);
    }
}
```

Resulting GUI

Resulting GUI (after clicking Memos in the menu bar)

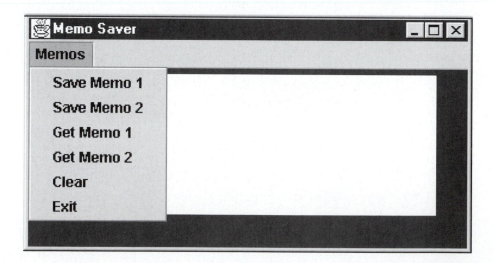

`JMenuItem`. These `JMenuItems` are placed in `JMenus`, and then the `JMenus` are typically placed in a `JMenuBar`. Let's look at the details.

    An object of the class `JMenuItem` is one of the choices on a menu. It is identified by the string that labels it, such as `"Save Memo 1"`. An object of the class `JMenu` is a menu such as the one shown in the GUI in Display 14.1. You can add as many `JMenuItems` as you wish to a menu. The menu lists the items in the order in which they are added. The following code, taken from the constructor in Display 14.1, creates a new `JMenu` object named `memoMenu`, and then adds a `JMenuItem` labeled `"Save Memo 1"`. Other menu items are added in a similar way.

JMenuItem

JMenu

```
JMenu memoMenu = new JMenu("Memos");
JMenuItem m;

m = new JMenuItem("Save Memo 1");
m.addActionListener(this);
memoMenu.add(m);
```

    Note that, just as we did for buttons, we have registered the *this* parameter as an `ActionListener`. Defining `ActionListeners` and registering listeners for menu items are done in the exact same way as for buttons. In fact, the syntax is even the same. If you compare Display 12.15 and Display 14.1/page 876, you will see that the method `actionPerformed` is defined in the same way in both cases. The only difference is that in Display 14.1, the method has one additional case for the new entry labeled `"Exit"`.

    You add a `JMenuItem` to an object of the class `JMenu` using the method `add` in exactly the same way that you add a component, such as a button, to a container object. Moreover, if you look at the preceding code, you will see that you specify a string for a `JMenuItem` in the same way that you specify a string label for a button. So, the syntax for adding menu items to a menu is really nothing new.

    A **menu bar** is a container for menus, typically placed near the top of a windowing interface. You add a menu to a menu bar using the method `add` in the same way as you just saw for adding menu items to a menu. The following code from the constructor in Display 14.1 creates a new menu bar named `mBar`, and then adds the menu named `memoMenu` to this menu bar:

menu bar

JMenuBar

```
JMenuBar mBar = new JMenuBar();
mBar.add(memoMenu);
```

    Thus, adding menu items to menus, and adding menus to a menu bar, are done with the method `add` in the same way as you saw for adding buttons and other items to a panel or other container.

    There are two different ways to add a menu bar to a `JFrame`. You can use the method `setJMenuBar`, as shown by the following code from Display 14.1:

```
setJMenuBar(mBar);
```

This sets an instance variable of type `JMenuBar` so that it names the menu bar `mBar`. Saying it less formally, this adds the menu bar `mBar` to the `JFrame` and places the menu bar at the top of the `JFrame`.

    Alternatively, you can add a menu bar to the content pane of a `JFrame` (or to any other `Container`), and you do so in the same way you add any other compo-

extra code on
CD

nent, such as labels or buttons. An example of using add to add a JMenuBar to the content pane of a JFrame is given in the file MenuAdd.java on the accompanying CD.

Menus and Menu Bars

A menu item is an object of the class JMenuItem. A menu is an object of the class JMenu, and a menu bar is an object of the class JMenuBar. A menu item is added to a menu using the method add. A menu is added to a menu bar using the method add. A menu bar can be added to a JFrame in two different ways. You can add a JMenuBar to the content pane of a JFrame (or to any other Container, for that matter) using the method add and any layout manager you wish. Alternatively and perhaps more typically, a menu bar can be added to a JFrame using the method setJMenuBar.

Events and listeners for menu items are handled exactly the same as they are for buttons.

Setting the Action Command for a Menu Item

As with buttons, the text for a JMenuItem is the default action command for the menu item. As with a button, you can set the action command for a menu item to some other string by using the method setActionCommand.

Syntax:

Menu_Item_Object.setActionCommand(*Action_Command_String*);

Example:

```
JMenuItem item = new JMenuItem("Click me!");
item.setActionCommand("From the click me item with love.");
```

.

Nested Menus

The class JMenu is a descendent of the JMenuItem class. So, every JMenu object is also a JMenuItem object. Thus, a JMenu can be a menu item in another menu. This means you can nest menus. For example, the outer menu might give you a list of menus. You can choose one of the menus on that list by clicking the name of the desired menu. You can then choose from that menu list using your mouse again. There is nothing new you need to know to create these nested menus. You simply add menus to menus just as you add other menu items. There is an example of nested menus in the file NestedMenus.java on the accompanying CD

extra code on
CD

? Self-Test Questions

1. What kind of event is fired when you click a JMenuItem? How does it differ from the kind of event fired when you click a JButton?

2. If you want to change the action command for a JButton, you use the method setActionCommand. What method do you use to change the action command for a JMenuItem?

Adding Menus to a `JFrame`

In this box, we assume that all additions take place inside a constructor for a (derived class of) `JFrame`. Otherwise, most method invocations would require an object name and dot before them. To see the following examples put together to produce a complete GUI, see the constructor in Display 14.1/page 876.

Creating Menu Items

A menu item is an object of the class `JMenuItem`. You create a new menu item in the usual way, as illustrated by the following example. The string in the argument position is the label of the menu item.

```
JMenuItem m;
m = new JMenuItem("Save Memo 1");
```

Menu Item Listeners

Events and listeners for menu items are handled in the same way as they are for buttons: Menu items fire action events that are received by objects of the class `ActionListener`.

Syntax:

```
JMenu_Item_Name.addActionListener(Action_Listener);
```

Example:

```
m.addActionListener(this);
```

Add Menu Items to a Menu

A menu is an object of the class `JMenu`. You use the method `add` to add menu items to a menu.

Syntax:

```
JMenu_Name.add(JMenu_Item);
```

Example: (`memoMenu` **is an object of the class** `JMenu`):

```
memoMenu.add(m);
```

Add the Menu to a Menu Bar

A menu bar is an object of the class `JMenuBar`. You add a menu to a menu bar as follows:

Syntax:

```
JMenu_Bar_Name.add(JMenu_Name);
```

Example: (`mBar` **is an object of the class** `JMenuBar`):

```
mBar.add(memoMenu);
```

Add the Menu Bar to the Frame

There are two different ways to add a menu bar to a `JFrame`. You can use the method `add` to add the menu bar to the content pane of the `JFrame` (or to any other `Container`). Another common way of adding a menu bar to a `JFrame` is to use the predefined method `setJMenuBar` as follows:

Syntax:

```
setJMenuBar(JMenu_Bar_Name);
```

Example:

```
setJMenuBar(mBar);
```

3. Is the following legal in Java?

```
AbstractButton b = new AbstractButton();
```

4. Is the following legal in Java?

```
JMenu myMenu = new JMenu();
    . . .
JMenu mySubMenu = new JMenu();
    . . .
myMenu.add(mySubMenu);
```

5. How many `JMenuBars` can you have in a `JFrame`?

6. Write code to create a new menu item named `mItem` that has the label `"Choose Me!"`

7. Suppose you build a GUI interface using Swing. If the user clicks a menu item, this fires an event. What kind of listener receives the event?

8. Suppose you are defining a class called `MenusGalor` that is a derived class of the class `JFrame`. Write code to add the menu item `mItem` to the menu `m` and then add `m` to the menu bar `mBar`, and then add the menu bar to the `JFrame MenusGalor`. Assume this all takes place inside a constructor for `MenusGalor`. Assume everything has already been constructed with *new*, and that all necessary listeners are registered. You just need to do the adding of things.

14.2 | Making GUIs Pretty (and More Functional)

> *In matters of grave importance,*
> *style, not sincerity, is the vital thing.*
> **Oscar Wilde, The Importance of Being Earnest**

In this section we describe a number of Swing facilities that can easily make your GUIs more attractive and professional looking. Some, such as changing the look and feel, have a purely esthetic purpose. Other, such as adding scroll bars to text areas, have a utilitarian purpose. Still others, such as icons, cannot be categorized as either purely esthetic or purely utilitarian in nature. Perhaps you could say icons are utilitarian as a result of their esthetic properties.

Adding Icons

icon

With Swing, labels, buttons, and menu items may have icons. An **icon** is simply a small picture, although they are not required to be small. The picture can be a picture of anything. Pictures are produced in a number of formats that can be displayed on a computer screen (such as `GIF` and `JPEG`). One of these pictures in most any standard format can be used as the basis for an icon. Swing will make one of these pictures into an icon, and you can then add it to a label, button, or other component. The label or button may have just a string displayed on it, just an icon on it, or both on it (or nothing at all on it, for that matter).

Icons and the Class `ImageIcon`

An **icon** is simply a small picture, although they are not really required to be small. The class `ImageIcon` is used to convert a picture file to a Swing icon.

Syntax:

```
ImageIcon Name_Of_ImageIcon =
        new ImageIcon(Picture_File_Name);
```

The *Picture_File_Name* is a string giving either a relative or absolute path name to the picture file. (So, if the picture file is in the same directory as your program, then you need give only the name of the picture file.)

Example:

```
ImageIcon smileyIcon =
        new ImageIcon("smiley.gif");
```

The class `ImageIcon` is used to convert a picture file to a Swing icon. For example, if you have a picture in a file named `duke_waving.gif`, then the following will use this file to produce an image icon named `dukeWavingIcon`:

ImageIcon

```
ImageIcon dukeWavingIcon =
        new ImageIcon("duke_waving.gif");
```

The file `duke_waving.gif` should be in the same directory as the class in which this code appears. Alternatively, you can use a complete or relative path name to specify the picture file. The picture file name is given as the argument to the constructor `ImageIcon`. Because the picture file is given as a string, you should have quotes around the name or use a variable or expression of type `String`. The file `duke_waving.gif` and other picture files we will use are all provided on the CD that accompanies this text.

You can add this image icon to a label by giving it as an argument to the `JLabel` constructor, as follows:

```
JLabel dukePicture = new JLabel(dukeWavingIcon);
```

You can then, add the label `dukePicture` to a `JFrame`, `JPanel`, or other container, and the label will display a picture instead of a string of text.

button with only an icon

You can produce a button with (just) an icon on it. That is done in a similar way:

```
JButton dukeButton = new JButton(dukeWavingIcon);
```

If you create a button in this way, you should use `setActionCommand` to explicitly give the button an action command, since there is no string on the button. (See the box entitled *setActionCommand* **and** *getActionCommand* in Chapter 12, if this sounds unfamiliar to you.)

So far we have put icons on labels and button and in Chapter 12 we put strings on labels and buttons. If you want, and you often do want this, you can place both an icon and string on a label or button. One way to do this is to make the string the argument to the constructor for the label or button, and to add the icon with the method `setIcon`. This is illustrated in the following code:

setIcon

Display 14.2 Using Icons *(Part 1 of 2)*

```
import javax.swing.*;
import java.awt.*;
import java.awt.event.*;

/***********************************************************
 *Simple demonstration of putting icons in buttons and labels.
 ***********************************************************/
public class IconDemo extends JFrame implements ActionListener
{
    public static final int WIDTH = 400;
    public static final int HEIGHT = 200;

    private JTextField message;

    public IconDemo()
    {
        setSize(WIDTH, HEIGHT);
        addWindowListener(new WindowDestroyer());
        setTitle("Icon Demonstration");
        Container content = getContentPane();
        content.setBackground(Color.white);
        content.setLayout(new BorderLayout());

        JLabel niceLabel = new JLabel("Nice day!");
        ImageIcon smileyIcon = new ImageIcon("smiley.gif");
        niceLabel.setIcon(smileyIcon);
        content.add(niceLabel, BorderLayout.NORTH);

        JPanel buttonPanel = new JPanel();
        buttonPanel.setLayout(new FlowLayout());
        JButton helloButton = new JButton("Hello");
        ImageIcon dukeWavingIcon = new ImageIcon("duke_waving.gif");
        helloButton.setIcon(dukeWavingIcon);
        helloButton.addActionListener(this);
        buttonPanel.add(helloButton);
        JButton byeButton = new JButton("Good bye");
        ImageIcon dukeStandingIcon =
                    new ImageIcon("duke_standing.gif");
        byeButton.setIcon(dukeStandingIcon);
        byeButton.addActionListener(this);
        buttonPanel.add(byeButton);
        content.add(buttonPanel, BorderLayout.SOUTH);

        message = new JTextField(30);
        content.add(message, BorderLayout.CENTER);
    }
```

Display 14.2 Using Icons *(Part 2 of 2)*

```
    public void actionPerformed(ActionEvent e)
    {
        if (e.getActionCommand().equals("Hello"))
            message.setText("Glad to meet you!");
        else if (e.getActionCommand().equals("Good bye"))
            message.setText(
                    "OK, click the upper right button. I'll miss you.");
        else
            System.out.println("Error in button interface.");
    }


    /*************************************************
     *Creates and displays a window of the class IconDemo.
     *************************************************/
    public static void main(String[] args)
    {
        IconDemo iconGui = new IconDemo();
        iconGui.setVisible(true);
    }
}
```

Resulting GUI [1]

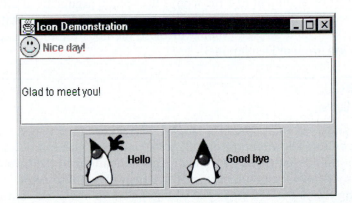

_____

1. Java, Duke, and all Java-based trademarks and logos are trademarks or registered trademarks of Sun Microsystems, Inc. in the United States and other countries.

```
JButton helloButton = new JButton("Hello");
ImageIcon dukeWavingIcon = new ImageIcon("duke_waving.gif");
helloButton.setIcon(dukeWavingIcon);
```

you can add both a string and an icon to a `JLabel` in the same way as we just discussed for adding them to a `JButton`.

Display 14.2/page 884 contains a program that illustrates the use of icons with labels and buttons. The text field is initially blank. When the user clicks the "Hello" button, the phrase

```
"Glad to meet you!"
```

appears in the text field as shown in Display 14.2. When the user clicks the "Good bye" button, the phrase

```
"OK, click the upper right button. I'll miss you."
```

appears in the text field. The program ends when the used clicks the close-window button.

Note that when a button is created in a way such as the following

```
JButton helloButton = new JButton("Hello");
```

then the action command is the string on the button, in this case "Hello", even though you may also add an icon to the button as in the following from Display 14.2.

```
helloButton.setIcon(dukeWavingIcon);
```

Aside from the addition of icons, there is nothing new in Display 14.2.

Both of the classes `JButton` and `JLabel` have constructors that let you specify text and an icon to appear on the button or label. The constructor can specify no text or icon, text only, icon only, or both text and icon. When listing text and icon, the text is the first argument and the icon is the second argument. If either or both text and/or icon are not given in the constructor, they can be added later with the methods `setText` and `setIcon`. Some of these methods for the classes `JButton` and `Jlabel` are given in Display 14.3.

setText

■ Gotcha
Resizing Buttons

If you look at the button methods in Display 14.3, you will see that you can change the size of a button. The methods for setting the preferred, maximum, and minimum size are a bit troublesome. They are only recommendations to the layout manager. There is no guarantee that your sizing instructions will be followed.

Changing the size of a button can change other things in the button, such as how the string in the button is displayed. Sometimes this problem can be fixed by setting the size of the margin between the contents of the button and the edge of the button. For example, if you want no margin in a button, b, you would use the following:

```
b.setMargin(new Insets(0, 0, 0, 0));
```

Yet another problem with button sizes is that: if the icon is too big to fit on the button, the image may be clipped. When resizing buttons, you can expect to do a lot of tuning to get the GUI to look good.

`setIcon` and `setText`

The method `setIcon` can be used to add an icon to a `JButton`, `JLabel`, or certain other components. The argument to `setIcon` must be an `ImageIcon` object.

Syntax:

> *Component*.`setIcon`(*ImageIcon_Object*);

The *Component* can be a `JButton`, `JLabel`, or certain other components.

Example:

```
JLabel helloLabel = new JLabel("Hello");
ImageIcon dukeWavingIcon = new ImageIcon("duke_waving.gif");
helloLabel.setIcon(dukeWavingIcon);
```

The method `setText` can be used to add text to a `JButton`, `JLabel`, or certain other components.

Syntax:

> *Component*.`setText`(*Text_String*);

The *Component* can be a `JButton`, `JLabel`, or certain other components.

Example:

```
ImageIcon dukeWavingIcon = new ImageIcon("duke_waving.gif");
JLabel helloLabel = new JLabel(dukeWavingIcon);
helloLabel.setText("Hello");
```

The two examples are equivalent.

Adding Icons to Menu Items *(Alternative Ordering)*

(This should only be skipped if you have not covered menus. If you have covered menus, this is easy.)

You can add an icon to a `JMenuItem` using the method `setIcon` in the exact same way that you add an icon to a `JButton`. An example is given in the file `MemoIconDemo.java` on the accompanying CD.

extra code on
CD

Display 14.3 Some Methods in the Classes `JButton` and `JLabel`
••

public `JButton()`
public `JLabel()`
 Creates a button or label with no text or icon on it. (Typically, you will later use `setText` and/or `setIcon` with the button or menu item.)

public `JButton(String text)`
public `JLabel(String text)`
 Creates a button or label with the `text` on it.

public `JButton(ImageIcon picture)`
public `JLabel(ImageIcon picture)`
 Creates a button or label with the icon `picture` on it.

public `JButton(String text, ImageIcon picture)`
public `JLabel(`
        `String text, ImageIcon picture, int horizontalAlignment)`
 Creates a button or label with both the `text` and the icon `picture` on it. `horizontalAlign-ment` is one of the constants `SwingConstants.LEFT`, `SwingConstants.CENTER`, `SwingConstants.RIGHT`, `SwingConstants.LEADING`, or
`SwingConstants.TRAILING`.

public void `setText(String text)`
 Makes `text` the only text on the button or label.

public void `setIcon(ImageIcon picture)`
 Makes `picture` the only icon on the button or label.

public void `setMargin(Insets margin)`
 `JButton` has the method `setMargin`, but `JLabel` does not.
 The method `setMargin` sets the size of the margin around the text and icon in the button. The following special case will work for most simple situations. The *int* values give the number of pixels from the edge of the button to the text and/or icon on it.
public void `setMargin(new Insets(`
                `int top, int left, int bottom, int right)`

Display 14.3 Some Methods in the Classes `JButton` and `JLabel`

public void `setPreferredSize(Dimension preferredSize)`

Sets the preferred size. Note, this is only a suggestion to the layout manager. The layout manager is not required to use the preferred size. The following special case will work for most simple situations. The *int* values give the width and height in pixels.

public void `setPreferredSize(new Dimension(int width, int height))`

public void `setMaximumSize(Dimension maximumSize)`

Sets the maximum size. Note, this is only a suggestion to the layout manager. The layout manager is not required to respect this maximum size. The following special case will work for most simple situations. The *int* values give the width and height in pixels.

public void `setMaximumSize(new Dimension(int width, int height))`

public void `setMinimumSize(Dimension minimumSize)`

Sets the minimum size. Note, this is only a suggestion to the layout manager. The layout manager is not required to respect this minimum size. The following special case will work for most simple situations. The *int* values give the width and height in pixels.

public void `setMinimumSize(new Dimension(int width, int height))`

public void `setVerticalTextPosition(int textPosition)`

Sets the vertical position of the text relative to the icon. The `textPosition` should be one of the constants `SwingConstants.TOP`, `SwingConstants.CENTER` (the default position) or `SwingConstants.BOTTOM`.

public void `setHorizontalTextPosition(int textPosition)`

Sets the horizontal position of the text relative to the icon. The `textPosition` should be one of the constants `SwingConstants.RIGHT`, `SwingConstants.LEFT`, `SwingConstants.CENTER`, or `SwingConstants.LEADING`, `SwingConstants.TRAILING`.

The Classes `Dimension` and `Inset`

Objects of these classes are used with buttons, labels, and other objects to specify a size. The parameters in the following constructors are pixels.

Constructors:

```
Insets(int top, int left, int bottom, int right)
Dimension(int width, int height)
```

Examples:

```
aButton.setMargin(new Insets(10, 20, 10, 20));
aLabel.setPreferredSize(new Dimension(20, 50));
```

? Self-Test Questions

● ●

9. Suppose you want to create a button that has on it both the text "Push Me" and the picture in the file `alice.gif`. How do you do it?

10. How would you to add the picture in the file `alice.gif` to the `JPanel` named `picturePanel`? Assume that `picturePanel` has a flow layout manager.

11. Suppose you wanted to create a button that has the picture in the file `alice.gif` on the button and no text on the button. Suppose further that you want the button to have the action command "Curiouser and curiouser!". How do you create the button and set up the action command?

The `JScrollPane` Class for Scroll Bars

When you create a text area, you specify the number of lines that are visible and the number of characters per line, as in the following example:

```
JTextArea theText = new JTextArea(10, 40);
```

The text area `theText` will have room for 10 lines of text, and each line will have room for at least 40 characters. It would be better to not have a firm limit on the number of lines or the number of characters per line that the user can type in and can see in some convenient way.

view port

In professionally produced GUIs you have worked with, you have undoubtedly seen text areas where you can type in any amount of text and the text is viewed in a "window" or **view port** that shows only part of the text. You can change the section of text that is viewable by using the scroll bars that are placed along the sides of the view port. In these professionally produced GUIs it is as if the text were written on an unbounded sheet of paper, but the paper is covered by another piece of paper that you cannot see through, except for a rectangular hole that lets you see a portion of the text. The rectangular hole is the view port. This is illustrated in Display 14.4. You then use the scroll bars to move the paper with the text so that different portions of the text are brought into view through this view port hole. Swing was meant to be used to produce professional style GUIs, and so it should come as no surprise that you can have this scroll bar arrangement for text areas in your Swing

`JScroll-Pane`

GUIs. You provide the scroll bars by using the class `JScrollPane`.

An object of the class `JScrollPane` is essentially a view port with scroll bars. When you create a `JScrollPane` you give the text area as an argument to the `JScrollPane` constructor. For example, if `theText` is an object of the class `JTextArea` (as created in the line of code at the start of this subsection), then you can place `theText` in a `JScrollPane` as follows:

```
JScrollPane scrolledText = new JScrollPane(theText);
```

The `JScrollPane` can then be added to a container, such as a `JPanel` of `JFrame`, as follows:

```
textPanel.add(scrolledText);
```

This is illustrated by the program in Display 14.5, which is the same as the one in Display 12.15/page 813, except that this version has scroll bars.

Note the following two lines in the constructor definition in Display 14.5: setting scroll bar policies

```
scrolledText.setHorizontalScrollBarPolicy(
            JScrollPane.HORIZONTAL_SCROLLBAR_ALWAYS);
scrolledText.setVerticalScrollBarPolicy(
            JScrollPane.VERTICAL_SCROLLBAR_ALWAYS);
```

Despite the imposing length of these two method invocations, they perform a very simple task. The first merely specifies that the horizontal scroll bar will always be present. The second specifies that the vertical scroll bar will always be present.

If you omit the invocation of the two methods `setHorizontalScrollBarPolicy` and `setVerticalScrollBarPolicy`, then the scroll bars will only be visible when you need them. If you omit these two method invocations and all the text fits in the view port, then no scroll bars will be visible. When you add enough text to

Display 14.4   View Port for A Text Area

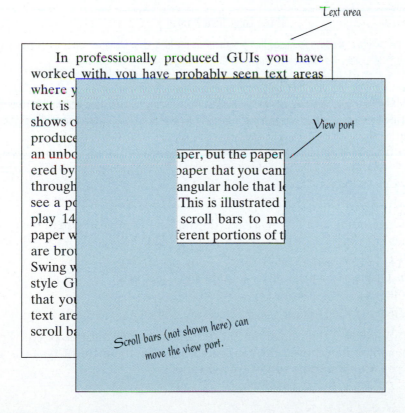

Text area

In professionally produced GUIs you have worked with, you have probably seen text areas where y...

View port

...per, but the paper...
...paper that you can...
...angular hole that le...
...This is illustrated...
...scroll bars to mo...
...ferent portions of t...

Scroll bars (not shown here) can move the view port.

need scroll bars, the needed scroll bars will appear automatically. Thus, you do not absolutely need the methods `setHorizontalScrollBarPolicy` and `setVerticalScrollBarPolicy`, but they are sometimes nice to have. In some situations, the user may find it reassuring to always see the scroll bars.

Display 14.6 summarizes what we have said about the class `JScrollPane`. We are only interested in using `JScrollPane` with text areas. However, as noted in the table, `JScrollPane` can be used with almost any sort of component.

JScrollPane

The class `JScrollPane` is used to add scroll bars to a `JTextArea` (and certain other components). The `JTextArea` object is given as an argument to the constructor that creates the `JScrollPane`.

Syntax:

```
JScrollPane Identifier = new JScrollPane(Text_Area_Object);
```

Examples:

```
JTextArea theText = new JTextArea(LINES, CHAR_PER_LINE);
JScrollPane scrolledText = new JScrollPane(theText);
textPanel.add(scrolledText);
contentPane.add(textPanel, BorderLayout.CENTER);
```

Those Long Java Names

It is part of the culture of the Java language that programmers use long, clear identifiers and do not use abbreviations for identifier names. However, some may think the following is getting a bit too long:

```
JScrollPane.HORIZONTAL_SCROLLBAR_AS_NEEDED
```

Whether you like these long names or not, you must admit they are easy to understand and easy to remember, even if a bit of a bother to type. Most programmers eventually get used to the long, clear names and even come to prefer them.

? Self-Test Questions

12. When setting up a `JScrollPane`, do you have to invoke both of the methods `setHorizontalScrollBarPolicy` and `setVerticalScrollBarPolicy`?

13. In Display 14.6/page 893 we listed the constructor for `JScrollPane` as follows:

    ```
    public JScrollPane(Component objectToBeScrolled)
    ```

    This indicates that the argument to the constructor must be of type `Component`. But, we used the constructor with an argument of type `JTextArea`. Isn't this some sort of type violation?

Display 14.6 Some Methods and Constants in the Class `JScrollPane`

```
public JScrollPane(Component objectToBeScrolled)
```
Creates a new `JScrollPane` for the `objectToBeScrolled`. Note, that the `objectToBe-Scrolled` need not be a `JTextArea`, although that is the only type of argument considered in this text.

```
public void setHorizontalScrollBarPolicy(int policy)
```
Sets the policy for showing the horizontal scroll bar. The `policy` should be one of
`JScrollPane.HORIZONTAL_SCROLLBAR_ALWAYS`,
`JScrollPane.HORIZONTAL_SCROLLBAR_NEVER`,
`JScrollPane.HORIZONTAL_SCROLLBAR_AS_NEEDED`.
(As indicated, these constants are defined in the class `JScrollPane`. You should not need to even be aware of the fact that they have `int` values. Think of them as policies not as `int`s.)

```
public void setVerticalScrollBarPolicy(int policy)
```
Sets the policy for showing the vertical scroll bar. The `policy` should be one of
`JScrollPane.VERTICAL_SCROLLBAR_ALWAYS`,
`JScrollPane.VERTICAL_SCROLLBAR_NEVER`,
`JScrollPane.VERTICAL_SCROLLBAR_AS_NEEDED`.
(As indicated, these constants are defined in the class `JScrollPane`. You should not need to even be aware of the fact that they have `int` values. Think of them as policies not as `int`s.)

```
JScrollPane.HORIZONTAL_SCROLLBAR_AS_NEEDED.
JScrollPane.VERTICAL_SCROLLBAR_AS_NEEDED.
```
Constants in the class `JScrollPane`. The phrase "AS_NEEDED" means the scroll bar is only shown when it is needed. This is explained more fully in the text. The meaning of the other policy constants are obvious from their names.

Adding Borders

You can add a border to any `JComponent`. A **border** is simply an area around the component that frames the component. As you will see, the border can have a variety of different appearances. A border can serve two purposes. First, it can make the component more attractive. Second, the border can provide a way to separate the component from other components; in other words, it can add space around the component.

border

If your program uses the border classes, then you need to include the following import statement:

```
import javax.swing.border.*;
```

import

Display 14.7 contains a program that does little more than display some borders. In terms of what it does, the GUI produced is identical to the GUI produced by the program in Display 12.16/page 819. However, the two GUIs look quite different esthetically. The GUI produced by the program in Display 14.7 may not look

Display 14.5   A Text Area with Scroll Bars *(Part 1 of 2)*

```
import javax.swing.*;
import java.awt.*;
import java.awt.event.*;

public class ScrollBarDemo extends JFrame implements ActionListener
{
    public static final int WIDTH = 600;
    public static final int HEIGHT = 300;
    public static final int LINES = 10;
    public static final int CHAR_PER_LINE = 40;

    private JTextArea theText;
    private String memo1 = "No Memo 1.";
    private String memo2 = "No Memo 2.";

    public ScrollBarDemo()
    {
        setSize(WIDTH, HEIGHT);
        addWindowListener(new WindowDestroyer());
        setTitle("Scrolling Memo Saver");
        Container contentPane = getContentPane();
                  .
                  .
                  .
        JPanel textPanel = new JPanel();
        textPanel.setBackground(Color.blue);
        theText = new JTextArea(LINES, CHAR_PER_LINE);
        theText.setBackground(Color.white);
        JScrollPane scrolledText = new JScrollPane(theText);
        scrolledText.setHorizontalScrollBarPolicy(
                    JScrollPane.HORIZONTAL_SCROLLBAR_ALWAYS);
        scrolledText.setVerticalScrollBarPolicy(
                    JScrollPane.VERTICAL_SCROLLBAR_ALWAYS);
        textPanel.add(scrolledText);
        contentPane.add(textPanel, BorderLayout.CENTER);
    }
```

The omitted statements are the same as in Display 12.15/page 813. In fact, this constructor is the same as that in Display 12.15, except that the name of the class is changed, and the above four statement shown in color have been added. All other methods are the same as in Display 12.15.

Display 14.5   A Text Area with Scroll Bars *(Part 2 of 2)*

```
    public void actionPerformed(ActionEvent e)
    {
        <This method is identical to the one in Display 12.15/page 813.>
    }

    public static void main(String[] args)
    {
        ScrollBarDemo guiMemo = new ScrollBarDemo();
        guiMemo.setVisible(true);
    }
}
```

Resulting GUI

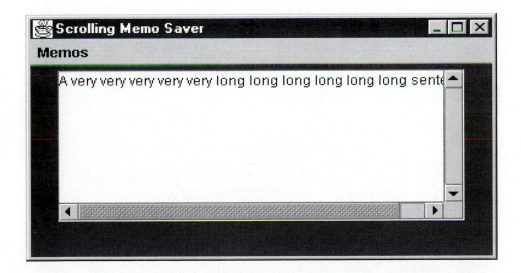

Display 14.7 Demonstration of Different Borders *(Part 1 of 2)*

```java
import javax.swing.*;
import java.awt.*;
import java.awt.event.*;
import javax.swing.border.*;

/***********************************************
 *Class to demonstrate adding borders to components.
 ***********************************************/
public class BorderDemo extends JFrame implements ActionListener
{
    public static final int WIDTH = 400;
    public static final int HEIGHT = 300;

    private JTextField name;

    public BorderDemo()
    {
        setTitle("Name Tester with Borders");
        setSize(WIDTH, HEIGHT);
        addWindowListener(new WindowDestroyer());
        Container content = getContentPane();
        content.setLayout(new GridLayout(2, 1));

        JPanel namePanel = new JPanel();
        namePanel.setLayout(new BorderLayout());
        namePanel.setBackground(Color.white);

        name = new JTextField(20);
        //The following border is not as dramatic as others,
        //but look closely and you will see it.
        name.setBorder(new EtchedBorder(Color.green, Color.blue));
        namePanel.add(name, BorderLayout.SOUTH);
        JLabel nameLabel = new JLabel("Enter your name here:");
        //The following does insert space around the label.
        //To see the difference, comment out the following line:
        nameLabel.setBorder(new EmptyBorder(20, 10, 0, 0));
        namePanel.add(nameLabel, BorderLayout.CENTER);

        namePanel.setBorder(new LineBorder(Color.black, 10));
        content.add(namePanel);

        JPanel buttonPanel = new JPanel();
        buttonPanel.setLayout(new FlowLayout());
        JButton testButton = new JButton("Test");
        testButton.addActionListener(this);
        testButton.setBorder(new BevelBorder(BevelBorder.LOWERED));
        buttonPanel.add(testButton);
```

Display 14.7 Demonstration of Different Borders *(Part 2 of 2)*

```java
        JButton clearButton = new JButton("Clear");
        clearButton.addActionListener(this);
        clearButton.setBorder(new BevelBorder(BevelBorder.RAISED));
        buttonPanel.add(clearButton);

        buttonPanel.setBorder(
                new MatteBorder(60, 40, 30, 20, Color.pink));
        content.add(buttonPanel);
    }

    public void actionPerformed(ActionEvent e)
    {
        if (e.getActionCommand().equals("Test"))
            name.setText("A very good name!");
        else if (e.getActionCommand().equals("Clear"))
            name.setText("");
        else
            name.setText("Error in window interface.");
    }

    public static void main(String[] args)
    {
        BorderDemo w = new BorderDemo();
        w.setVisible(true);
    }
}
```

Resulting GUI

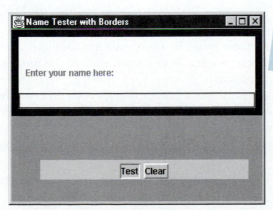

To get a really clear view of these borders, run the program.

all that esthetically pleasing to you, because it is a hodgepodge of different border styles. However, it does give you a good sample of the kinds of borders you can produce. These borders can be used with more restraint and a more artistic flair to improve the look of your Swing GUIs.

setBorder

You use the method `setBorder` to add a border to a component. For example, consider the following code from Display 14.7:

```
JButton testButton = new JButton("Test");
testButton.addActionListener(this);
testButton.setBorder(new BevelBorder(BevelBorder.LOWERED));
```

The last line gives the button `testButton` a `BevelBorder`. The general syntax is

JComponent.`setBorder`(*Border_Object*);

You can place a border around any `JComponent`, such as a `JButton`, `JLabel`, `JPanel`, or `JTextField`. The exact look of the border will depend on the *Border_Object* used as an argument to the method `setBorder`.

Bevel-
Border

There are a variety of border classes. Each border class produces a different looking border. Also, each border class constructor takes some arguments that make small adjustment to this look. For example, the `BevelBorder` class produces a border that makes the component look as if it either stands out from the plane of the GUI or is recessed into the plane of the GUI. The argument `BevelBorder.RAISED` makes it look as if it is raised out of the plane of the GUI. The argument `BevelBorder.LOWERED` makes it look as if it is recessed into the plane of the GUI. The `BevelBorder` class can be very effective when used with buttons. However, any border class can be used with any `JComponent`. So, you could have a `BevelBorder` around a `JPanel` or any other `JComponent`.

It is very common to use an anonymous arguments for border objects, as in:

```
testButton.setBorder(new BevelBorder(BevelBorder.LOWERED));
```

However, if you prefer, you can give a name to the border object. The previous line of code is equivalent to the following:

```
BevelBorder myBorder = new BevelBorder(BevelBorder.LOWERED);
testButton.setBorder(myBorder);
```

Some border classes and their possible arguments are summarized in Display 14.8. The best way to learn about borders is to try out each of the border classes to see what kind of borders it produces.

Each of the border classes produces a border that serves a different function, or at least has a different look from the other border types. An `EmptyBorder` object simply inserts space around the component. You can specify the amount of space (in pixels) for each of the four borders, as in the following from our sample program in Display 14.7:

Empty-
Border

```
JLabel nameLabel = new JLabel("Enter your name here:");
//The following does insert space around the label.
//To see the difference, comment out the following line:
nameLabel.setBorder(new EmptyBorder(20, 10, 0, 0));
```

Display 14.8 Some Border Classes

```
public BevelBorder(int bevelType)
```
Constructor for creating a new `BevelBorder` object. The argument `bevelType` should be one of the constants `BevelBorder.RAISED` or `BevelBorder.LOWERED`.

```
public EtchedBorder(int etchType, Color highlight, Color shadow)
```
Constructor for creating a new `EtchedBorder` object. An etched border is similar to a `BevelBorder`, except that you cannot set its size, and it has colored shadow properties with the specified highlight and shadow colors. The argument `etchType` should be one of the constants `EtchedBorder.RAISED` or `Etched.LOWERED`.

```
public EtchedBorder(Color highlight, Color shadow)
```
Constructor for creating a new lowered `EtchedBorder` object with the specified highlight and shadow colors.

```
public EmptyBorder(int top, int left, int bottom, int right)
```
Constructor for creating a new `EmptyBorder` object. An empty border is essentially space around the component. The arguments give the size in pixels of the four border areas.

```
public LineBorder(Color theColor, int thickness)
```
Constructor for creating a new `LineBorder` object. A line border is a colored border of given thickness. The thickness is given in pixels.

```
public MatteBorder(
        int top, int left, int bottom, int right, Color theColor)
```
Constructor for creating a new `MatteBorder` object. A `MatteBorder` is similar to a `LineBorder`, but you can specify the size (in pixels) of each of the four borders. (You should also read the box entitled **Icons in a `MatteBorder`.**)

The border in the preceding code adds 20 pixels of space above the label, 10 pixels of space to the left of the label, 0 pixels of space below the label, and 0 pixels of space after the label. Of course, the GUI itself may have extra space, and so there may actually be some space after the label even if you "add" no space after the label. A similar remark applies to the other borders.

The class `LineBorder` inserts a colored border of a specified size around the component, as in the following example that adds a black border that is 10 pixels wide all around the outside of a `JPanel` named `namePanel`. (The example is from Display 14.7.)

Line-
Border

```
namePanel.setBorder(new LineBorder(Color.black, 10));
```

Matte-
Border

A `MatteBorder` is similar to a `LineBorder`, but you can specify the size in pixels) of each of the four borders. The following example from Display 14.7 places a pink border around the `buttonPanel`. The border will be 60 pixels wide on top, 40 pixels wide on the left side, 30 pixel wide below, and 20 pixels wide on the right side:

```
buttonPanel.setBorder(
              new MatteBorder(60, 40, 30, 20, Color.pink));
```

Etched-
Border

An `EtchedBorder` is similar to a `BevelBorder`, but is always narrow and shows some colored shadows. You cannot set the width of an `EtchedBorder`. The best way to learn what an `EtchedBorder` is like is to play with the class producing various examples and looking at them.

The `setBorder` Method

You can use the `setBorder` method to add a border to any `JComponent`.

Syntax:

   JComponent.`setBorder(`*Border_Object*`);`

The *JComponent* can be any `JComponent` object, such as a `JButton`, `JLabel`, `JPanel`, or other `JComponent`. The *Border_Object* can any object of any of the border classes given in Display 14.8/page 899.

Example:

```
namePanel.setBorder(new LineBorder(Color.black, 10));
```

Icons in a `MatteBorder`

The class `MatteBorder` has a constructor that lets you specify an icon, instead of a color. The constructor is:

```
public MatteBorder(
        int top, int left, int bottom, int right, ImageIcon theIcon)
```

extra code on
CD

This constructor will create a new `MatteBorder` object which is tiled with copies of the `theIcon` (like a wallpaper pattern). A sample of a program using this constructor is in the file `BorderDemoWithIcon.java` on the accompanying CD.

■ Gotcha

Forgetting to Import `javax.swing.border`

If the compiler says it cannot find the border classes you are using, you have undoubtedly forgotten the following import statement, which you need when dealing with borders:

```
import javax.swing.border.*;
```

Changing the Look and Feel

look and feel

The **look and feel** of a GUI refers to the general appearance of the GUI. It includes such things as the shape and exact placement of buttons, default colors, and almost anything that effects the way a GUI looks without affecting what it does. For example, if you use one of the Windows operating systems, then the operating system produces windows to communicate with you, for example to give you error messages. Similar windows are used in the Mac operating system (or any other different operating system), but the windows will look a little bit different. With Swing you can choose the look and feel for your GUIs. It is even possible to define your own look and feel in Swing, but that is fairly complicated and not really needed for most purposes. So, we will not discuss defining your own look and feel in this book. We will confine ourselves to describing how you use some of the standard predefined look and feels.

Three standard looks and feels that come with most versions of Java:

> **Metal**, which is considered the standard Java look and feel

> **Motif**, which is often considered to be a Unix look and feel

> **Windows**, which looks like the windows you get in a Windows operating system

Metal

Motif

Windows look and feel

Samples of each of these three looks and feels are given in Display 14.9. As you can see, the same window with a different look and feel does not look that much different, and if you needed to, you could get along fine with just one look and feel. (Mac users may be happy to know there is also a Mac look and feel, but it is not as universally distributed.).

Look and Feel

The look and feel of a GUI refers to the general appearance of the GUI. It includes such things as the shape and exact placement of buttons, default colors, and almost anything that effects the way a GUI looks without affecting what it does.   ◻

If you look back at any of our previous Swing programs (in Chapter 12 or in this chapter), you will see that they contain nothing that specifies a look and feel. If no look and feel is specified, then the GUI will have the default look and feel for your system, which is usually the Metal look and feel. In this book we show GUIs with the Metal look and feel. You can ignore the question of look and feel and just settle for whatever default look and feel happens to be on your computer. However, if you want to specify the look and feel for a Swing GUI, you can easily do so.

To obtain a different look and feel for a `JFrame` simply insert the following in the constructor for the `JFrame` (or at some other suitable location):

default look and feel

changing the look and feel

```
try
{
    UIManager.setLookAndFeel(Look_And_Feel_Class_Name);
    SwingUtilities.updateComponentTreeUI(this);
}
catch (Exception e)
{//You might use a more explicit error message:
    System.out.println("Could not load the desired look and feel");
}
```

Display 14.9 Three Different Look and Feels

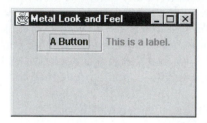

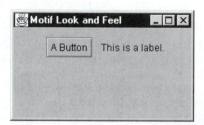

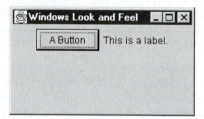

setLook-
AndFeel

The static method setLookAndFeel in the class UIManager sets the look and feel. The argument to setLookAndFeel should be a string that gives what is called *the fully qualified class name* for the look and feel class. (The method setLookAndFeel would also accept a look and feel object, but we will not discuss that here.) For example, to obtain the Motif look and feel the fully qualified name is

```
"com.sun.java.swing.plaf.motif.MotifLookAndFeel"
```

So, to display your GUI with the Motif look and feel, the code would be the following:

```
try
{
    UIManager.setLookAndFeel(
            "com.sun.java.swing.plaf.motif.MotifLookAndFeel");
    SwingUtilities.updateComponentTreeUI(this);
}
catch (Exception e)
{
    System.out.println("Could not load the Motif look and feel");
}
```

Display 14.10 gives the fully qualified class names for the three most standard looks and feels. A **fully qualified class name** is a name that completely specifies the directory (folder) path to the class using a standard Java notation.

fully qualified class name

Display 14.10 Class Names for Three Looks and Feels

Look and Feel	Fully Qualified Class Name (as a String).
Metal	`"javax.swing.plaf.metal.MetalLookAndFeel"`
Motif	`"com.sun.java.swing.plaf.motif.MotifLookAndFeel"`
Windows	`"com.sun.java.swing.plaf.windows.WindowsLookAndFeel"`

These are the arguments to `UIManager.setLookAndFeel`. Be sure to include the quotation marks, because the argument is of type `String`.

The statement

```
SwingUtilities.updateComponentTreeUI(this);
```

*updateCom-
ponentTreeUI*

updates the display of its argument. If this were outside of a constructor, then the argument `this` would be replaced by a name for the GUI being displayed. If this is omitted when the look and feel is changed, then the GUI might have the old look and feel or the default look and feel.

Note that the look and feel need not match your operating system. You can have a Unix (Motif) look and feel on a Windows computer, or a Windows look and feel on a Unix computer, or any other possible combination of operating system and look and feel.

Note that we use the class `Exception` in our catch block, rather than a more specific exception class. This is because the full list of exceptions that could be thrown is relatively long. You might prefer to have a catch block for each of these exceptions, although it would make for a long list of catch blocks. The method `UIManager.setLookAndFeel` can throw any of the following exceptions:

exceptions

> ClassNotFoundException, InstantiationException,
> IllegalAccessException, and UnsupportedLookAndFeelException

Each of these four exception classes would need a separate catch block, if we did not use a catch block with the more general class Exception.

Display 14.11 shows a class called LookNFeelSample whose objects really do nothing other than display a look and feel. Each object has a button that does nothing and a label that says nothing very interesting. However, you can set the look and feel by giving the fully qualified class name for the look and feel as the first argument to the constructor. The second argument gives the title.

For example, the following will display a GUI with the Metal look and feel and with the title "Metal Look and Feel":

```
LookNFeelSample metalGUI = new LookNFeelSample(
    "javax.swing.plaf.metal.MetalLookAndFeel",
    "Metal Look and Feel");
metalGUI.setVisible(true);
```

The above could be in any main. It need not be in the main for the class LookNFeelSample. However, in the main of the class LookNFeelSample we do use the preceding two statements and two similar pair of statements to display three different look and feels. If you run this program, it will display the three GUIs shown in Display 14.9/page 902. When you run the program, the three GUIs will probably be one on top of the other, but if you use your mouse to move the top two, you will see all three GUIs.

Changing The Default Look and Feel

There is a default look and feel for each system. If you do not specify a look and feel, then your Swing GUIs will have this default look and feel. It should be possible to easily set the default look and feel. However, when this book went to print, this facility was not yet available. Until that facility is available, if you want to change the look and feel, you must do it for each object you display.

Lightweight and Heavyweight Components *(Optional)*

When you read discussions of GUI libraries, such as Swing, you will often see references to *lightweight* and *heavyweight* components. For the things we are doing in this book, you do not need to know these two words, but the two concepts they name have a lot to do with how Swing GUIs look, and it will be good background information to know what these two words are about.

heavyweight

peer

A **heavyweight** component is one that is implemented using a similar corresponding component (known as a **peer**) that comes with the underlying operating system. For example, a heavyweight frame might be implemented using the standard utility for producing a window that comes with the host operating system, and so would look like other windows on the host operating system. When such a frame is moved to another operating system, it would use a different peer window constructing utility, and so would look different. A heavyweight component is easy for the library designers to produce, because the peer component does most of the work, and somebody else has already defined it.

Display 14.11 Showing Three Looks and Feels *(Part 1 of 2)*

```java
import javax.swing.*;
import java.awt.*;

/*****************************************
 *Used only to show samples of looks and feels.
 *****************************************/
public class LookNFeelSample extends JFrame
{
    public static final int WIDTH = 300;
    public static final int HEIGHT = 200;

    /*********************************************************
     *Object will have the look and feel of the first argument.
     *********************************************************/
    public LookNFeelSample(String lookNFeelClassName, String title)
    {
        setSize(WIDTH, HEIGHT);
        addWindowListener(new WindowDestroyer());
        setTitle(title);
        Container content = getContentPane();
        content.setLayout(new FlowLayout());

        JButton aButton = new JButton("A Button");
        content.add(aButton);

        JLabel aLabel = new JLabel("This is a label.");
        content.add(aLabel);

        try
        {
            UIManager.setLookAndFeel(lookNFeelClassName);
            SwingUtilities.updateComponentTreeUI(this);
        }
        catch (Exception e)
        {
            System.out.println("Look and feel problem.");
        }
    }
```

The GUI displayed is the one shown in Display 14.9/page 902.

Display 14.11 Showing Three Looks and Feels *(Part 2 of 2)*

```java
public static void main(String[] args)
{
    LookNFeelSample metalGUI = new LookNFeelSample(
        "javax.swing.plaf.metal.MetalLookAndFeel",
        "Metal Look and Feel");
    metalGUI.setVisible(true);

    LookNFeelSample motifGUI = new LookNFeelSample(
        "com.sun.java.swing.plaf.motif.MotifLookAndFeel",
        "Motif Look and Feel");
    motifGUI.setVisible(true);

    LookNFeelSample windowsGUI = new LookNFeelSample(
        "com.sun.java.swing.plaf.windows.WindowsLookAndFeel",
        "Windows Look and Feel");
    windowsGUI.setVisible(true);
}
}
```

lightweight

A **lightweight** component is implemented using only very basis low-level primitives, like lines and points. A lightweight component is harder for the library designers to produce but it can give the programmer using the component more freedom to change the detail of the component.

In Swing the basic containers, like frames, are heavyweight components or based on heavy weight components. (As you might guess, being heavyweight is not an all or nothing proposition. Some heavyweight components are "heavier" than others.) These heavyweight components are always rectangular in shape and opaque. In Swing most other components are lightweight, which means they can be transparent and can, in effect, have shapes other than rectangles. The fact that Swing uses lightweight components is one of the reasons it is easy to change the look and feel of a Swing GUI. If all components were heavyweight, then all GUIs produced would look like the standard windowing system for the host operating system.

? Self-Test Questions

....

14. In Display 14.11/page 905 we changed the look and feel of a Swing GUI with the following code:

```
try
{
    UIManager.setLookAndFeel(lookNFeelClassName);
    SwingUtilities.updateComponentTreeUI(this);
}
catch (Exception e)
{
    System.out.println("Look and feel problem.");
}
```

What is the purpose of the following which appears in the *try* block?

```
SwingUtilities.updateComponentTreeUI(this);
```

15. Suppose you have already defined Swing GUI object of a class called `MyGUI`? Suppose you want to display this GUI and want it to have the Motif look and feel. How do you do this (without changing the definition of the class `MyGUI`)?

14.3 | More Layout Managers

> ***box*** n. *1. A container typically constructed with four sides perpendicular to the base and often having a lid or cover. ....*
> **The American Heritage Dictionary of the English Language, third edition**

A kind of panel that is often needed for a GUI is one that is simply a horizontal or vertical array of items, such as an array of buttons. If it is a horizontal array that is needed, then using a `JPanel` with a flow layout manager will do. If it is a vertical array that is needed, then a `JPanel` with a grid layout manager with only a single column will do. The `BoxLayout` manager class and the `Box` container class allow you to do the same thing in a way that is perhaps simpler and that offers some very handy extra features. The extra features include good ways to create invisible components to separate other components so that you can, for example, add space between buttons. A `Box` container is essentially a panel-like class that uses the `BoxLayout` manager in a convenient way. We will first discuss a program that uses the `BoxLayout` manager with `JPanel`s, and then we will discuss a second program that does the same thing but that uses the `Box` container class to simplify and automate some of the programming. Both programs will produce the same GUI, which is shown in Display 14.12.

Display 14.12 A GUI Built with Box Layout Managers

Resulting GUI

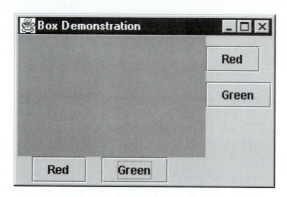

The GUI in Display 14.12 has buttons labeled "Red" and "Green" along the bottom and also has two other buttons labeled "Red" and "Green" along the right side of the GUI. The center is initially blue. If either "Red" button is clicked, the center panel turns red. Similarly, if either "Green" button is clicked, the center panel turns green. There is nothing very new here in terms of what the GUI does. This is meant as a sample of doing component layouts using a BoxLayout manager and/or the Box container class. We will focus on having a vertical array of components (in this case buttons) with some space before the first component and some space between successive components. Similarly, we will also focus in the same way on horizontal arrays of components. That is why this sample has both a vertical and a horizontal array of buttons.

The BoxLayout Manager Class

The program in Display 14.13/page 910 will produce the GUI in Display 14.12 when it is run. It uses the BoxLayout manager class. The code in the program is, in many ways, just more of what you have already seen. The content pane of the JFrame is divided into three sections by using three panels. The buttons are created and added to the panels as you have already seen. The method actionPerformed is almost identical to similar actionPerformed methods that you saw before in this chapter and in Chapter 12. In fact, all the code that is not in color uses only techniques you have seen before.

One minor point that you may not have seen before is that there are two buttons with `"Red"` written on them, and the methods `actionPerformed` does not care which one is clicked because they have the same action command, namely the string `"Red"`. And of course, the situation with the two `"Green"` buttons is similar.

The really new material in Display 14.13 is given by the code shown in color. The panel named `horizontalPanel` holds the buttons at the bottom of the screen. The panel uses a `BoxLayout` manager. the syntax for creating a `BoxLayout` manager is slightly different from what you have used for other layout managers, and is illustrated by the following statement from Display 14.13:

BoxLayout

```
horizontalPanel.setLayout(
        new BoxLayout(horizontalPanel, BoxLayout.X_AXIS));
```

Note that, unlike the layout manager classes you saw in Chapter 12, the `BoxLayout` manager constructor takes arguments, in fact two arguments. The first argument is the container for which it is the layout manager. This is clearly redundant, because when used this way it is the same as the calling object. But redundant or not, that first argument is required. The second argument must be one of the two constants `BoxLayout.X_AXIS` and `BoxLayout.Y_AXIS`. The constant specifies whether the layout will be vertical (`X_AXIS`) or horizontal (`Y_AXIS`).

X_AXIS and Y_AXIS

When the second argument to the `BoxLayout` constructor is `BoxLayout.X_AXIS`, the layout is a horizontal panel with components added left to right. Thus, the previously displayed layout manager is almost equivalent to:

```
horizontalPanel.setLayout(new FlowLayout());
```

At first, you might not notice any difference between these two layout managers (horizontal `BoxLayout` and `FlowLayout`). Thinking of the horizontal `BoxLayout` as being the same as the `FlowLayout` is a good first approximation to what a horizontal `BoxLayout` manager does. However, there are subtle but sometimes important distinctions between the two layout manager classes. As we will see, a horizontal `BoxLayout` manager does exactly what you tell it to do. If you say leave 15 pixels at the beginning of the panel, it will always leave exactly 15 pixels. On the other hand, a `FlowLayout` manager thinks it knows better than you do and may add extra pixels to make the display "look better."

Note that with a `BoxLayout` manager, components are added using the `add` method in the way you are used to for a `FlowLayout` manager. If the layout is horizontal, as we have been discussing, the components are laid out left to right in the order in which they are added. If the layout is vertical, which we will discuss next, then the components are laid out top to bottom in the order in which they are added.

Wow, that was a lot of work and a lot of explanation to get something that is only a little more than a `FlowLayout` manager! But, there is a payoff coming. The rest of the program in Display 14.13 shows some of the real power of the `BoxLayout` manager class.

We have just discussed how you can get a horizontal layout of components using the `BoxLayout` manager class. To get a vertical layout with a `BoxLayout` manager, you simply use `BoxLayout.Y_AXIS`, instead of `BoxLayout.X_AXIS`, as the second argument to the `BoxLayout` constructor. This is illustrated by the panel that

Display 14.13 The BoxLayout Manager *(Part 1 of 2)*

```
import javax.swing.*;
import java.awt.*;
import java.awt.event.*;

/**************************************************************
 *Simple demonstration of BoxLayout manager class and the use of
 *struts to separate components (in this case buttons). (For an
 *alternative implementation see BoxClassDemo in Display 14.14.)
 **************************************************************/
public class BoxLayoutDemo extends JFrame
                                implements ActionListener
{
    public static final int WIDTH = 300;
    public static final int HEIGHT = 200;
    public static final int HORIZONTAL_STRUT_SIZE = 15;
    public static final int VERTICAL_STRUT_SIZE = 10;

    private JPanel colorPanel;

    public BoxLayoutDemo()
    {
        setSize(WIDTH, HEIGHT);
        addWindowListener(new WindowDestroyer());
        setTitle("Box Demonstration");
        Container content = getContentPane();
        content.setLayout(new BorderLayout());

        colorPanel = new JPanel();
        colorPanel.setBackground(Color.blue);
        content.add(colorPanel, BorderLayout.CENTER);

        //Horizontal buttons at bottom of frame:
        JPanel horizontalPanel = new JPanel();
        horizontalPanel.setLayout(
                new BoxLayout(horizontalPanel, BoxLayout.X_AXIS));

        Component horizontalStrut =
                Box.createHorizontalStrut(HORIZONTAL_STRUT_SIZE);
        horizontalPanel.add(horizontalStrut);

        JButton hStopButton = new JButton("Red");
        hStopButton.addActionListener(this);
        horizontalPanel.add(hStopButton);

        Component horizontalStrut2 =
                Box.createHorizontalStrut(HORIZONTAL_STRUT_SIZE);
        horizontalPanel.add(horizontalStrut2);
```

Display 14.13 The `BoxLayout` **Manager** *(Part 2 of 2)*

```java
        JButton hGoButton = new JButton("Green");
        hGoButton.addActionListener(this);
        horizontalPanel.add(hGoButton);

        content.add(horizontalPanel, BorderLayout.SOUTH);

        //Vertical buttons on right side of frame:
        JPanel verticalPanel = new JPanel();
        verticalPanel.setLayout(
            new BoxLayout(verticalPanel, BoxLayout.Y_AXIS));

        Component verticalStrut =
            Box.createVerticalStrut(VERTICAL_STRUT_SIZE);
        verticalPanel.add(verticalStrut);

        JButton vStopButton = new JButton("Red");
        vStopButton.addActionListener(this);
        verticalPanel.add(vStopButton);

        Component verticalStrut2 =
            Box.createVerticalStrut(VERTICAL_STRUT_SIZE);
        verticalPanel.add(verticalStrut2);

        JButton vGoButton = new JButton("Green");
        vGoButton.addActionListener(this);
        verticalPanel.add(vGoButton);

        content.add(verticalPanel, BorderLayout.EAST);
    }

    public void actionPerformed(ActionEvent e)
    {
        if (e.getActionCommand().equals("Red"))
            colorPanel.setBackground(Color.red);
        else if (e.getActionCommand().equals("Green"))
            colorPanel.setBackground(Color.green);
        else
            System.out.println("Error in button interface.");
    }

    public static void main(String[] args)
    {
        BoxLayoutDemo gui = new BoxLayoutDemo();
        gui.setVisible(true);
    }
}
```

displays buttons along the right hand side of the GUI. The panel with buttons can be seen on the right side of the GUI in Display 14.12/page 908. The program in Display 14.13 specifies that the panel is a vertical panel with the following code:

```
verticalPanel.setLayout(
            new BoxLayout(verticalPanel, BoxLayout.Y_AXIS));
```

This layout manager will lay things out in a way analogous to what we discussed for buttons at the bottom of the GUI. However, in this case the buttons are laid out vertically from top to bottom, rather than horizontally from left to right.

Note that with a vertical layout, you cannot get any approximation to a Box-Layout manager by using a FlowLayout manager. You can get a rough approximation to a vertical BoxLayout manager with a GridLayout manager that has only one column, but the spacing will be different. With a BoxLayout manager, you have complete control over spacing. With other layout managers, you can only make suggestions to the layout manager, but you cannot count on the instructions being followed. For example, with a GridLayout manager, the components are always stretched so they have equal size and they are always placed right next to each other.

We said that a BoxLayout manager gives you complete control over spacing of components, but to realize this complete control you need to use invisible components know as *struts* and *glue components*. We discuss these kinds of components in the next subsection.

Struts and Glue

Part of the importance of the BoxLayout manager class comes from some of the static methods contained in the related class named Box. Some of these static methods can produce invisible components that can be added to a container. These sorts of invisible components can be used to add space between the visible components. For example, consider the following code from Display 14.13/page 910:

```
Component horizontalStrut =
            Box.createHorizontalStrut(HORIZONTAL_STRUT_SIZE);
horizontalBox.add(horizontalStrut);
```

strut

The method createHorizontalStrut is a static method in the class Box. It creates an object of type Component that is know as a *strut*. A **strut** is an invisible component that has a fixed horizontal size. For example, the method invocation:

```
Box.createHorizontalStrut(HORIZONTAL_STRUT_SIZE);
```

produces a strut whose horizontal size is HORIZONTAL_STRUT_SIZE pixels, which happens to be 15 pixels in the program in Display 14.13. A layout manager can change the vertical size of this strut but it cannot change the horizontal size (cannot change the width). The strut is always exactly 15 pixels wide, and so if the strut is added to a container with a BoxLayout manager, it will always produce a space of 15 pixels between components.

horizontal strut

There are two kinds of struts, *horizontal struts* and *vertical struts*. We have just discussed horizontal struts. A **horizontal strut** is created with the method createHorizontalStrut and has a fixed width that cannot be changed. The layout manager can change the height of the strut but not is width. A **vertical strut** is similar, except it is the height that is fixed. A vertical strut is created with the method `createVerticalStrut` and has a fixed height that cannot be changed. The layout manager can change the width of the strut but not its height. Think of a strut as a stick of a fixed length that is used to separate visible component. That is, in fact, the root meaning of the word *strut* and is why the designers of Swing used the word *strut* for these components.

vertical strut

Glue components are invisible component that are similar to struts, except that they are not rigid. They are used to separate visible components. The word "glue" is actually misleading and was a poor choice of term for these components. Glue components do not glue anything to anything else. The word *glue* is meant to convey the idea that they are not rigid like struts, but "squishy like glue." (Perhaps a better name would have been "goo," but we are stuck with the word "glue." No pun intended.)

glue components

The layout manager can make a glue components larger or smaller. There are both **horizontal** and **vertical glue** components. They are created with the static methods `createHorizontalGlue` and `createVerticalGlue`. Both of these methods are in the `Box` class. For example, the following creates a horizontal and vertical glue components:

horizontal and vertical glue

```
Component horizontalGlue = Box.createHorizontalGlue();
Component verticalGlue = Box.createVerticalGlue();
```

Glue components are added to a container using the method `add` in the same way that struts are added. There is an example of a program that uses glue components in the file `GlueDemo.java` on the accompanying CD.

extra code on CD

? Self-Test Questions

16. Suppose `myPanel` is a `JPanel`. How do you give `myPanel` a vertical `BoxLayout` manager?

17. What is the difference between setting a layout manager in the following two ways:

```
horizontalPanel.setLayout(
        new BoxLayout(horizontalPanel, BoxLayout.X_AXIS));
```

or

```
horizontalPanel.setLayout(new FlowLayout());
```

18. Give a statement that will create a horizontal strut named `horizontalSpace` that has a width of 20 pixels.

19. What is the difference between a strut component and a glue component?

■ Gotcha

Using Struts and Glue with Other Layout Managers

Struts and glue components are designed to be used with a `BoxLayout` manager. They can be used with other layout managers, but they usually do not realize their intended purpose when used with other layout managers. If a horizontal strut that is 15 pixels wide is added with some other layout manager, such as the `FlowLayout` manager, then its width is still technically 15 pixels, but the layout manager may add extra space around it. Because a strut is invisible, adding extra space is pretty much equivalent to changing the size of the strut. Problems also arise with glue components used with layout managers other than a `BoxLayout` manager.

In the next subsection we discuss `Box` containers. A container object of the `Box` class automatically comes with a `BoxLayout` manager. So, it is perfectly fine to add struts and glue components with a `Box` container.

The `Box` Container Class

Box container

We have already discussed the static functions `createHorizontalStrut`, `create-VerticalStrut`, `createHorizontalGlue`, and `createVerticalGlue`, which are in the class `Box`. In this subsection we discuss objects of the class `Box`. An object of the class `Box` behaves just like a panel that has a `BoxLayout` manager. The details are illustrated by the program in Display 14.14. That program will produce the same GUI as the one in Display 14.12/page 908. So the programs in Display 14.13/page 910 and the program in Display 14.14 are equivalent. However, the program in Display 14.14 uses the `Box` containers—that is, objects of the class `Box`— rather than `JPanel`s to hold the buttons. The details that involve new material are discussed in the rest of this subsection.

If you look at the programs in Display 14.14 and Display 14.13, you will see that the only difference is that the panel `horizontalPanel` in Display 14.13 is replaced by the `Box` object `horizontalBox` in Display 14.14, and the panel `verticalPanel` in Display 14.13 is replaced by the `Box` object `verticalBox` in Display 14.14.

*createHori-
zontalBox*

The object `horizontalBox` is created with the following statement from Display 14.14:

```
Box horizontalBox = Box.createHorizontalBox();
```

*createVer-
ticalBox*

Similarly, the object `verticalBox` is created with the following statement from Display 14.14:

```
Box verticalBox = Box.createVerticalBox();
```

Note that you create a box differently from what you might expect. To create an object of the class `Box`, you use the static methods `Box.createHorizontalBox` or the static method `Box.createVerticalBox`. The difference between these two methods is that the first creates a horizontal box and the second creates a vertical box.

Display 14.14 The Box Container Class *(Part 1 of 2)*

```java
import javax.swing.*;
import java.awt.*;
import java.awt.event.*;

/**************************************************************
 *Simple demonstration of Box container class and the use of struts
 *to separate components (in this case buttons). For an alternative
 *implementation see BoxLayoutDemo in Display 14.13/page 910.
 **************************************************************/
public class BoxClassDemo extends JFrame implements ActionListener
{
    public static final int WIDTH = 300;
    public static final int HEIGHT = 200;
    public static final int HORIZONTAL_STRUT_SIZE = 15;
    public static final int VERTICAL_STRUT_SIZE = 10;

    private JPanel colorPanel;

    public BoxClassDemo()
    {
        setSize(WIDTH, HEIGHT);
        addWindowListener(new WindowDestroyer());
        setTitle("Box Demonstration");
        Container content = getContentPane();
        content.setLayout(new BorderLayout());

        colorPanel = new JPanel();
        colorPanel.setBackground(Color.blue);
        content.add(colorPanel, BorderLayout.CENTER);

        //Horizontal buttons at bottom of frame:
        Box horizontalBox = Box.createHorizontalBox();

        Component horizontalStrut =
            Box.createHorizontalStrut(HORIZONTAL_STRUT_SIZE);
        horizontalBox.add(horizontalStrut);

        JButton hStopButton = new JButton("Red");
        hStopButton.addActionListener(this);
        horizontalBox.add(hStopButton);
        Component horizontalStrut2 =
            Box.createHorizontalStrut(HORIZONTAL_STRUT_SIZE);
        horizontalBox.add(horizontalStrut2);

        JButton hGoButton = new JButton("Green");
        hGoButton.addActionListener(this);
        horizontalBox.add(hGoButton);
```

Display 14.14 The Box **Container Class** *(Part 2 of 2)*

```
            content.add(horizontalBox, BorderLayout.SOUTH);

            //Vertical buttons on right side of frame:
            Box verticalBox = Box.createVerticalBox();

            Component verticalStrut =
                    Box.createVerticalStrut(VERTICAL_STRUT_SIZE);
            verticalBox.add(verticalStrut);

            JButton vStopButton = new JButton("Red");
            vStopButton.addActionListener(this);
            verticalBox.add(vStopButton);

            Component verticalStrut2 =
                    Box.createVerticalStrut(VERTICAL_STRUT_SIZE);
            verticalBox.add(verticalStrut2);

            JButton vGoButton = new JButton("Green");
            vGoButton.addActionListener(this);
            verticalBox.add(vGoButton);

            content.add(verticalBox, BorderLayout.EAST);
    }

    public void actionPerformed(ActionEvent e)
    {
        if (e.getActionCommand().equals("Red"))
            colorPanel.setBackground(Color.red);
        else if (e.getActionCommand().equals("Green"))
            colorPanel.setBackground(Color.green);
        else
            System.out.println("Error in button interface.");
    }

    public static void main(String[] args)
    {
        BoxClassDemo gui = new BoxClassDemo();
        gui.setVisible(true);
    }
}
```

You do not need to use the method `setLayout` to give a layout manager to a `Box` object. In fact, you should not use the method `setLayout` to give a layout manager to a `Box` object. An object of the class `Box` is automatically given a `BoxLayout` manager when it is created.

new `Box(...)`

If you prefer, you can create a `Box` object by an invocation of the constructor for the class `Box` using *new* in the usual way. For example, the following:

```
Box horizontalBox = new Box(BoxLayout.X_AXIS);
```

is equivalent to:

```
Box horizontalBox = Box.createHorizontalBox();
```

Similarly, the following:

```
Box verticalBox = new Box(BoxLayout.Y_AXIS);
```

is equivalent to:

```
Box verticalBox = Box.createVerticalBox();
```

Note that when you use the constructor for the class `Box` with *new*, you need to give the constructor an argument. If the argument is the constant `BoxLayout.X_AXIS`, then a horizontal `Box` container is created. If the argument is the constant `BoxLayout.Y_AXIS`, then a vertical `Box` container is created.

? Self-Test Questions

20. Give two ways to create a vertical `Box` container named `vBox`. (Hint: One way uses a method and one way uses a constructor.)

21. When coding for a Swing GUI that uses a `Box` container, should you use the `setLayout` method to specify a layout manager for the `Box` container?

The `CardLayout` Manager

`CardLayout` is a layout manager class that can add a dynamic element to your Swing GUIs. A `CardLayout` manager allows you to have a set of views that you can change, rather like a deck of cards that you flip through and view one at a time. With a `CardLayout` manager, you add any number of things to a container, but only one of those things is viewable at a line. You can go through the views in order or jump from a view to any other arbitrary view. So, this layout manager does more than simply arrange the components in the container. Let's look at an example.

Display 14.15 shows an example of a GUI that uses the CardLayout manager. The central portion of the GUI has three possible views, to move from one view to the other, the user clicks one of the buttons. An object of the `CardLayout` class is created, and a container is given the layout manager just as with any other layout manager class. This is shown in the following lines from Display 14.15 that gives the panel `deckPanel` a `CardLayout` manager.

Display 14.15 The `CardLayout` **Manager** *(Part 1 of 3)*

```java
import javax.swing.*;
import java.awt.*;
import java.awt.event.*;

public class CardLayoutDemo extends JFrame implements ActionListener
{
    public static final int WIDTH = 300;
    public static final int HEIGHT = 200;

    private CardLayout dealer;
    private JPanel deckPanel;

    public CardLayoutDemo()
    {
        setSize(WIDTH, HEIGHT);
        addWindowListener(new WindowDestroyer());
        setTitle("CardLayout Demonstration");
        Container contentPane = getContentPane();
        contentPane.setLayout(new BorderLayout());

        deckPanel = new JPanel();
        dealer = new CardLayout();
        deckPanel.setLayout(dealer);

        JPanel startCardPanel = new JPanel();
        startCardPanel.setLayout(new FlowLayout());
        startCardPanel.setBackground(Color.lightGray);
        JLabel startLabel = new JLabel("Hello");
        startCardPanel.add(startLabel);
        deckPanel.add("start", startCardPanel);

        JPanel greenCardPanel = new JPanel();
        greenCardPanel.setLayout(new FlowLayout());
        greenCardPanel.setBackground(Color.green);
        JLabel goLabel = new JLabel("Go");
        greenCardPanel.add(goLabel);
        deckPanel.add("green", greenCardPanel);

        JPanel redCardPanel = new JPanel();
        redCardPanel.setLayout(new FlowLayout());
        redCardPanel.setBackground(Color.red);
        JLabel stopLabel = new JLabel("Stop");
        redCardPanel.add(stopLabel);
        deckPanel.add("red", redCardPanel);
```

```java
            contentPane.add(deckPanel, BorderLayout.CENTER);

            JPanel buttonPanel = new JPanel();
            buttonPanel.setBackground(Color.white);
            buttonPanel.setLayout(new FlowLayout());
            JButton stopButton = new JButton("Red");
            stopButton.addActionListener(this);
            buttonPanel.add(stopButton);
            JButton goButton = new JButton("Green");
            goButton.addActionListener(this);
            buttonPanel.add(goButton);
            JButton resetButton = new JButton("Reset");
            resetButton.addActionListener(this);
            buttonPanel.add(resetButton);
            contentPane.add(buttonPanel, BorderLayout.SOUTH);
            dealer.first(deckPanel);//Optional
    }


    public void actionPerformed(ActionEvent e)
    {
        String actionCommand = e.getActionCommand();

        if (actionCommand.equals("Red"))
            dealer.show(deckPanel, "red");
        else if (actionCommand.equals("Green"))
            dealer.show(deckPanel, "green");
        else if (actionCommand.equals("Reset"))
            dealer.show(deckPanel, "start");
        else
            System.out.println("Error in CardLayout Demo.");
    }


    public static void main(String[] args)
    {
        CardLayoutDemo demoGui = new CardLayoutDemo();
        demoGui.setVisible(true);
    }
}
```

Display 14.15 The `CardLayout` Manager *(Part 3 of 3)*

First GUI Displayed

This is the view produced when the "Reset" button is clicked.

GUI Displayed When the "`Red`" Button is Clicked

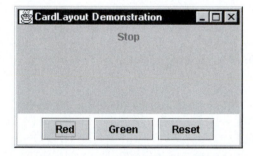

GUI Displayed When the "`Green`" Button is Clicked

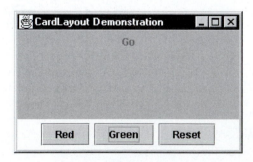

```
deckPanel = new JPanel();
dealer = new CardLayout();
deckPanel.setLayout(dealer);
```

Note that we did not use an anonymous `CardLayout` argument to the `setLayout` method. The following, while legal, is of little use:

```
deckPanel.setLayout(new CardLayout());//Do not use this!
```

We need a name (`dealer`) for the `CardLayout` manager so we can use it to change the "card" that is displayed. Moreover, we needed to refer to the `CardLayout` manager in more than one method, and so we made `dealer` an instance variable of type `CardLayout`.

As illustrated in our GUI code, when you add an element to a container that use a `CardLayout` manager, you give a string as the first argument and the component as the second argument. The string in the first argument serves as a name for the component.

```
deckPanel.add("start", startCardPanel);
    . . .
deckPanel.add("green", greenCardPanel);
    . . .
deckPanel.add("red", redCardPanel);
```

When the GUI is first displayed, the first component added is displayed. To go to another display, your code will use the method `show` or some similar method. For example, consider the following from the definition of `actionPerformed` in Display 14.15:

```
dealer.show(deckPanel, "red");
```
show

When this is executed, the view ("the card") currently displayed changes to the view named `"red"`. In the GUI in Display 14.15 this means that when the user clicks the button labeled `"Red"`, the panel named `redCardPanel` is displayed. Note that the container is given as the first argument to `show`. (After all, the layout manager can manage more than one container.)

Two other methods that you can use to go to a new view ("card") are `first` and `next`. The following, from the end of the constructor in Display 14.15, displays the first component added to the container:

```
dealer.first(deckPanel);//Optional
```
first

As indicated by the word *Optional*, the GUI will behave the same if you omit this particular invocation of `first`. This is because the container always starts with the first component on view. However, at some other place, this methods would change the display.

The method `next` goes to the next view ("next card"), the ordering is the order in which the component are added. After the last component, `next` goes back to the first component. The following is not used in Display 14.15, but if it were used, it would change the view from the current component to the next component.

```
dealer.next(deckPanel);
```
next

Some of the methods in the class `CardLayout` are summarized in Display 14.16.

The `CardLayout` Manager Class

A `CardLayout` manager displays components added to its container one at a time using the methods given in Display 14.16. Each component is assigned a string name when added to the component, as follows:

Syntax:

> *Container* . `add(`*String_Name*, *Component*`)`;

Example:

> `deckPanel.add("start", startCardPanel);`

Display 14.16 Some Methods in the `CardLayout` Manager Class

··

public void `first(Container theContainer)`
   Causes the first "card" in `theContainer` to be displayed.

public void `last(Container theContainer)`
   Causes the last "card" in `theContainer` to be displayed.

public void `next(Container theContainer)`
   Causes the next "card" in `theContainer` to be displayed. The next card is the one that was added after the currently displayed "card" was added.

public void `previous(Container theContainer)`
   Causes the previous "card" in `theContainer` to be displayed. The previous card is the one that was added before the currently displayed "card" was added

public void `show(Container theContainer, String cardName)`
   Displays the "card" that was added with the `String cardName` as its name.

? Self-Test Questions

···

22. In Display 14.15/page 918 we added the layout manager to the panel `deckPanel` as follows:

    ```
    dealer = new CardLayout();
    deckPanel.setLayout(dealer);
    ```

    Why didn't we add the layout manager as follows?

    ```
    deckPanel.setLayout(new CardLayout());
    ```

23. Write a Java code that will display the next "cards" in the `deckPanel` of Display 14.15/page 918

14.4 | Inner Classes

> *Something deeply hidden had to be behind things.*
> **Albert Einstein, Note quoted in New York Times Magazine (August 2, 1964)**

Inner classes are classes defined within other classes. Their use is not confined to programs and classes using Swing. However, they are often used when programming with Swing. A full description of inner classes is beyond the scope of this book. However, some simple uses of inner classes can be both easy and helpful. We will describe one of the most useful applications of inner classes, namely, inner classes used as helping classes.

Helping Classes

All of our Swing windows used the class `WindowDestroyer` (Display 12.2/page 766) for closing the window. Doing things as we have been doing them, we must always have this class `WindowDestroyer` around. Inner classes let us move the definition of a helping class, like `WindowDestroyer`, inside the class definition. For example, the class in Display 14.17 is a simple demonstration of an inner class used as a window listener. The GUI has essentially the same display as one of our very first Swing GUI classes (Display 12.4/page 773), but it uses the inner class `InnerDestroyer` rather than the class `WindowDestroyer`. Be sure to note that the definition of the class `InnerDestroyer` is inside the class `InnerClassDemo` (Display 14.17), so that the entire program is in one class definition (with another class definition inside of it).

There are two big advantages to inner classes. First, because they are defined within a class, they can be used to make the outer class self-contained or more self-contained than it would otherwise be. The second advantage was not used in Display 14.17, but can be very helpful. When you define an inner class, the methods in the inner class have access to all the instance variables and methods of the class in which it is defined, even if they are private. For this second reason inner classes are very useful helping classes, because they can do things more easily than a class defined outside of the class they are helping. Because of these convenient features, inner classes are frequently used as listeners to handle events fired from within the outer class or component of the outer class. For a longer example and one that uses more of the power of inner classes, see the program `InnerClassDemo2.java` on the accompanying CD.

Extra Code on
CD

There is yet one more advantage to inner classes. The name of the inner class is local to the class in which it is defined. You could have another class named `InnerDestroyer` that is not an inner class, and the program in Display 14.17 would completely ignore that other class named `InnerDestroyer`, and the other class named `InnerDestroyer` would completely ignore the inner class named `InnerDestroyer`.

We have made the inner class `InnerDestroyer` private because it is a helping class. It is possible to have a public inner class, but there are some subtleties involved in using public inner classes and we will not go into that topic in this book.

Display 14.17 An Inner Class

```java
import javax.swing.*;
import java.awt.*;
import java.awt.event.*;

public class InnerClassDemo extends JFrame
{
    public static final int WIDTH = 300;
    public static final int HEIGHT = 200;

    /*******************************************************
     *Creates and displays a window of the class InnerClassDemo.
     *******************************************************/
    public static void main(String[] args)
    {
        InnerClassDemo sampleGUI = new InnerClassDemo();
        sampleGUI.setVisible(true);
    }

    public InnerClassDemo()
    {
        setSize(WIDTH, HEIGHT);
        setTitle("Inner Class Demo");
        Container contentPane = getContentPane();
        contentPane.setLayout(new BorderLayout());

        JLabel label = new JLabel(
                        "Please don't click that button!");
        contentPane.add(label, BorderLayout.CENTER);

        addWindowListener(new InnerDestroyer());
    }

    //An inner class with the same functionality
    //as the class WindowDestroyer.
    private class InnerDestroyer extends WindowAdapter
    {
        public void windowClosing(WindowEvent e)
        {
            System.exit(0);
        }
    }
}
```

The **GUI** display produced by this program is the same as the one produced by the class in Display 12.4/page 773, except that this one has the title Inner Class Demo. (The **GUI** produced is shown in Display 12.1/page 763.)

> **Invoking A Method of The Outer Class**
>
> Java makes it easy to invoke a method of an outer class within the definition of an inner class. If there is a method invocation and the inner class has no method of that name, but the outer class does have a method of that name, then Java interprets this to be an invocation of the method for the outer object (that is, the calling object is the *this* of the outer class, not the *this* of the inner class.) An illustration of such invocations is given in the file `InnerClassDemo2.jave` on the accompanying CD.

Extra Code on CD

14.5 | More on Events and Listeners

> *A man may see how this world goes with no eyes.*
> *Look with thine ears....*
>
> **William Shakespeare, King Lear**

The `WindowListener` Interface

When we placed buttons in a window, we made the window itself the button listener class. On the other hand, when we wanted a window listener to respond to window-closing events, we made the window listener a separate class, named `WindowDestroyer` (or an inner class named `InnerDestroyer`). (See examples in Chapter 12, if this sounds unfamiliar.) In this subsection we show you how to make the window itself the window listener.

You have made a window itself a button listener by making it implement the interface named `ActionListener`. There is also an interface named `WindowListener` that is used in a similar way. For example, in Display 12.12/page 793, we made the window class `ButtonDemo` an `ActionListener` by adding *implements* `ActionListener` as follows:

```
public class ButtonDemo extends JFrame
                    implements ActionListener
```

If we wanted to make `ButtonDemo` a `WindowListener` instead of an `ActionListener`, the definition would begin

```
public class ButtonDemo extends JFrame
                    implements WindowListener
```

If, as is more likely, we wanted to make `ButtonDemo` both an `ActionListener` and a `WindowListener`, it would begin

```
public class ButtonDemo extends JFrame
                    implements ActionListener, WindowListener
```

Note that when a class implements more than one interface, we only use the reserved word *implements* one time, and we separate the interface names with commas.

The reason we tend to avoid making a window its own window listener is that when a class implements an interface, such as the `ActionListener` or the `WindowListener` interfaces, it must include definitions for *all* of the methods specified for the interface. The interface `ActionListener` has only the single method `actionPerformed`, so this is not an onerous requirement. The interface `Window-`

Display 14.18 Methods in the Interface `WindowListener`
....

> *public void* windowOpened(WindowEvent e)
> Invoked when a window has been opened.

> *public void* windowClosing(WindowEvent e)
> Invoked when a window is in the process of being closed. Clicking the close-window button causes an invocation of this method.

> *public void* windowClosed(WindowEvent e)
> Invoked when a window has been closed.

> *public void* windowIconified(WindowEvent e)
> Invoked when a window is iconified.

> *public void* windowDeiconified(WindowEvent e)
> Invoked when a window is deiconified.

> *public void* windowActivated(WindowEvent e)
> Invoked when a window is activated.

> *public void* windowDeactivated(WindowEvent e)
> Invoked when a window is deactivated.

Listener, however, has the same seven methods as the class `WindowAdapter`. The methods were given in Chapter 12 and are repeated in Display 14.18. If a class implements the `WindowListener` interface, it must have definitions for all seven of these methods. If you do not need all of these methods, then you can define the ones you do not need to have empty bodies, like this:

```
public void windowDeiconified(WindowEvent e)
{}
```

If you only need one or two methods in the `WindowListener` interface, this is a nuisance, although it is not difficult to do.

There are advantages to using the `WindowListener` interface. If you make the window class a derived class of the class `JFrame` and have it implement the `WindowListener` interface, then it is easy to call a method in the window class within the window listener class (because they are the same class).

For example, the program in Display 14.19 is a variant of a program we gave in Chapter 12 (Display 12.12/page 793). In Display 14.19, the GUI class is its own window listener. That allows it to have the following invocation in the method `window-Closing`:

> `this.dispose();`

The method `dispose` is a method in the class `JFrame` and the class `WindowListenerDemo` is a derived class of the class `JFrame`, so it inherits the method `dispose`. The method `dispose` releases any resources used by the window. In a program this simple, the call to `dispose` is not really needed because the resources are automatically released when the program ends, but if the program had several windows and was going to run longer and only eliminate this one window, then the call to `dispose` (without the call to `System.exit`) might prove useful. We only used `dispose` to have a simple example. (In the subsection entitled *Java Tip* **Programming the Close-Window Button** we present a more realistic use of the `dispose` method.)

Why bother to have both `WindowListener` and `WindowAdapter`? The reason is that `WindowAdapter` is a variant of `WindowListener` that is provided solely for the convenience of the programmer. `WindowAdapter` is a class that implements the interface `WindowListener` by giving every method an empty body. That way when you define a derived class of `WindowAdapter`, you do not have to put in those empty definitions. So, why not use `WindowAdapter` all the time? Often, you want a listener class to be a derived class of some class, such as `JFrame`, and to also be a window listener. A class cannot be a derived class of two classes, such as `JFrame` and `WindowAdapter`. So, in this situation, you cannot use `WindowAdapter`. In this situation, you make the class a derived class of the class `JFrame`, and you make it implement the `WindowListener` interface. A class can be a derived class of only one class, but it can also implement one or more interfaces.

The `dispose` Method

The class `JFrame` has a method named `dispose` that will dispose of the `JFrame` without ending the program. When `dispose` is invoked, the resources consumed by the `JFrame` are returned for reuse, so the `JFrame` is gone, but the program does not end. The method `dispose` is often used in a program with multiple windows to eliminate one window without ending the program.

Syntax:

> *JFrame_Object*`.dispose();`

The *JFrame_Object* is often an implicit `this`. A complete example of using `dispose` can be seen in Display 14.19/page 928.

? Self-Test Questions

24. When you define a class and make it implement the `WindowListener` interface what methods must you define? What do you do if there is no particular action that you want one of these methods to take?

Display 14.19 A WindowListener *(Part 1 of 2)*

```java
import javax.swing.*;
import java.awt.*;
import java.awt.event.*;

public class WindowListenerDemo extends JFrame
                    implements ActionListener, WindowListener
{
    public static final int WIDTH = 300;
    public static final int HEIGHT = 200;

    public static void main(String[] args)
    {
        WindowListenerDemo demoWindow = new WindowListenerDemo();
        demoWindow.setVisible(true);
    }

    public WindowListenerDemo()
    {
        setSize(WIDTH, HEIGHT);

        addWindowListener(this);
        setTitle("Window Listener Demonstration");
        Container content = getContentPane();
        content.setBackground(Color.blue);

        content.setLayout(new FlowLayout());

        JButton stopButton = new JButton("Red");
        stopButton.addActionListener(this);
        content.add(stopButton);

        JButton goButton = new JButton("Green");
        goButton.addActionListener(this);
        content.add(goButton);
    }

    public void actionPerformed(ActionEvent e)
    {
        Container content = getContentPane();
        if (e.getActionCommand().equals("Red"))
            content.setBackground(Color.red);
        else if (e.getActionCommand().equals("Green"))
            content.setBackground(Color.green);
        else
            System.out.println("Error in WindowListenerDemo.");
    }
```

This version does not need the class WindowDestroyer or any similar class.

Display 14.19 A WindowListener *(Part 2 of 2)*

```java
    public void windowOpened(WindowEvent e)
    {}

    public void windowClosing(WindowEvent e)
    {
        this.dispose();
        System.exit(0);
    }

    public void windowClosed(WindowEvent e)
    {}

    public void windowIconified(WindowEvent e)
    {}

    public void windowDeiconified(WindowEvent e)
    {}

    public void windowActivated(WindowEvent e)
    {}

    public void windowDeactivated(WindowEvent e)
    {}
}
```

The **GUI** produced is the same as in Display 12.12/page 793, except that the title is different.

The WindowListener Interface

Any class can be made a window listener by either making it a derived class of the class WindowAdapter, as discussed in Chapter 12, or by having it implement the WindowListener interface. One common example of a kind of class that implements the WindowListener interface are JFrame classes that are the window listener for their own close-window button. However, any kind of class can implement the WindowListener interface. The class need not be a JFrame.

In order for a class to implement the WindowListener interface, the class must have the following at the start of the class definition (after *extend* JFrame if the class is a JFrame class):

```java
    implements WindowListener
```

The class must also implement all the method interfaces given in Display 14.18/page 926.

25. Can a class be a derived class of more than one class?

26. Can a class implement more than one interface?

27. If you want a Swing program to end completely, you can invoke the methods System.exit. What if you want a window to go way, but do not want the program to end? What method can you invoke?

■ Java Tip
Programming the Close-Window Button

You can program the close-window button to end the program using the Window-Listener interface as we did in Display 14.19/page 928. Alternatively, you can use the methods WindowDestroyer as in the following line from Display 12.12/page 793 (or almost any of our Swing class definitions):

```
addWindowListener(new WindowDestroyer());
```

You need not use these exact lines to program the action of the close-window button. For example, you may define a class of your own in place of the class WindowDestroyer. However, you almost always need to do some programming to ensure that when the user clicks the close-window button, the GUI will do what you want it to. If you do not program the close-window button in any way, then when the user clicks the close-window button, the window will disappear, but the program will not end. If your GUI has only one window, that will mean that you have no easy way to end the program.

If you wish to program the close-window button of a JFrame class to do something other than going away and/or ending the program, then you should add the following invocation of the method setDefaultCloseOperation to the constructor:

setDefault-
Close-
Operation

```
setDefaultCloseOperation(WindowConstants.DO_NOTHING_ON_CLOSE);
```

For example, such an invocation is used in the class definition in Display 14.20. That class programs the close-window button so that when the user clicks the close-window button, a second window appears and asks the user if she/he wants to end the program. If the user clicks "No", the second window goes away but the first window remains. If the user clicks "Yes", then the program ends and both windows go away. Let's look at some of the details in the class definition in Display 14.20.

The method setDefaultCloseOperation does what its name implies. It sets the default behavior for what happens when the user clicks the close-window button. If you do not invoke setDefaultCloseOperation, the default behavior is that the window disappears but that the program does not end. Note that simply reprogramming the method windowClosing does not cancel the default action. So that if you simply reprogram windowClosing and do not invoke the method setDefaultCloseOperation, then when the user clicks the close-window button, the window will probably do what you programmed into the method windowClosing, but it will also go away. If you do not want the window to go away, you must first reset the default action with the method setDefaultCloseOperation.

Display 14.20 Programming the Close-Window Button *(Part 1 of 3)*

```java
import javax.swing.*;
import java.awt.*;
import java.awt.event.*;

/****************************************************
 *Demonstration of programming the close-window button.
 ***************************************************/
public class CloseWindowDemo extends JFrame
{
    public static final int WIDTH = 300;
    public static final int HEIGHT = 200;

    public static void main(String[] args)
    {
        CloseWindowDemo gui = new CloseWindowDemo();
        gui.setVisible(true);
    }

    public CloseWindowDemo()
    {
        setSize(WIDTH, HEIGHT);
        setDefaultCloseOperation(
                WindowConstants.DO_NOTHING_ON_CLOSE);
        addWindowListener(new InnerDestroyer());
        setTitle("Close Window Demo");
        Container contentPane = getContentPane();
        contentPane.setLayout(new BorderLayout());

        JLabel message = new JLabel(
                    "Please don't click that button.");
        contentPane.add(message, BorderLayout.CENTER);
    }
```

An inner class.

```java
    //Displays a window that checks if the user wants to exit.
    private class InnerDestroyer extends WindowAdapter
    {
        public void windowClosing(WindowEvent e)
        {
            ConfirmWindow askWindow = new ConfirmWindow();
            askWindow.setVisible(true);
        }
    }
}
```

Display 14.20 Programming the Close-Window Button *(Part 2 of 3)*

```
//Designed to be used with the inner class InnerDestroyer in
//the class CloseWindowDemo. Checks if the user wants to exit.
private class ConfirmWindow extends JFrame
                                implements ActionListener
{
    public static final int WIDTH = 200;
    public static final int HEIGHT = 100;

    public ConfirmWindow()
    {
        setSize(WIDTH, HEIGHT);
        Container confirmContent = getContentPane();
        confirmContent.setBackground(Color.white);
        confirmContent.setLayout(new BorderLayout());

        JLabel msgLabel = new JLabel(
                        "Are you sure you want to exit?");
        confirmContent.add(msgLabel, BorderLayout.CENTER);

        JPanel buttonPanel = new JPanel();
        buttonPanel.setLayout(new FlowLayout());

        JButton exitButton = new JButton("Yes");
        exitButton.addActionListener(this);
        buttonPanel.add(exitButton);

        JButton cancelButton = new JButton("No");
        cancelButton.addActionListener(this);
        buttonPanel.add(cancelButton);

        confirmContent.add(buttonPanel, BorderLayout.SOUTH);
    }

    public void actionPerformed(ActionEvent e)
    {
        if (e.getActionCommand().equals("Yes"))
            System.exit(0);
        else if (e.getActionCommand().equals("No"))
            dispose();//Destroys only the ConfirmWindow.
        else
            System.out.println("Error in Confirm Window.");
    }

}
}
```

Another inner class

Display 14.20 Programming the Close-Window Button *(Part 3 of 3)*

Resulting GUI

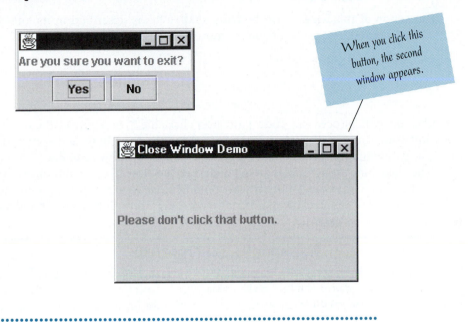

When you click this button, the second window appears.

The class `CloseWindowDemo` sets things up so its close-window button can be programmed to do anything you want by the following lines from the constructor:

```
setDefaultCloseOperation(
        WindowConstants.DO_NOTHING_ON_CLOSE);
```

The close-window button for the class `CloseWindowDemo` is programmed by registering the inner class `InnerDestroyer` as the window listener with the following line from the constructor for `CloseWindowDemo`:

```
addWindowListener(new InnerDestroyer());
```

To see what action is being programmed, you need to look at the definition of the method `windowClosing` in the inner class `InnerDestroyer`. That method definition is reproduced in what follows:

```
public void windowClosing(WindowEvent e)
{
    ConfirmWindow askWindow = new ConfirmWindow();
    askWindow.setVisible(true);
}
```

Note that when the close-window button of the outer class, `CloseWindowDemo`, is clicked, this method `windowClosing` will be invoked. This method then creates a window of the class `askWindow` and makes it visible, as shown in Part 3 of Display 14.20.

The action of this window of the class `askWindow` is described in its `action-Performed` method. The relevant code is reproduced in what follows:

```
if (e.getActionCommand().equals("Yes"))
    System.exit(0);
else if (e.getActionCommand().equals("No"))
    dispose();//Destroys only the ConfirmWindow.
```

As indicated in the proceeding code, if the user clicks the `"Yes"` button, the program ends and both windows disappear. If the user clicks, the `"No"` button, the invocation of `dispose`, eliminates the second window, but the first window remains.

(The class `ConfirmWindow` is an inner class of the class `CloseWindowDemo`. That makes the class `CloseWindowDemo` self contained. However, the program would behave exactly the same, if the class `ConfirmWindow` were defined as an independent class outside of the class `CloseWindowDemo`.)

Programming the Close-Window Button

If you want to program the close-window button of a `JFrame` to do anything other than either ending the program or making the window go away (such as with a call to `System.exit` or to `dispose`), then you need to add the following invocation to the constructor (or add it someplace that has the same effect as adding it to the constructor):

```
setDefaultCloseOperation(WindowConstants.DO_NOTHING_ON_CLOSE);
```

? Self-Test Questions

28. Suppose you define a windowing GUI and do absolutely nothing to specify what happens when the close-window button is clicked. What happens when the close-window button is clicked?

29. If you want to program the close-window button of a `JFrame` to do something other than go away or end the program, what method invocation do you add to the constructor?

30. Suppose you make a `JFrame` into a window listener so that it can be the listener for its own close-window button. And suppose you define the method `windowClosing` for the `JFrame` as follows:

```
public void windowClosing(WindowEvent e)
{
    dispose();
}
```

Should you add the invocation given as the answer to Self-Test Question 29 to the constructor for the JFrame?

31. What is `WindowConstants.DO_NOTHING_ON_CLOSE`? Is it a method invocation? A class? Something else? What?

Programming Example
Components with Changing Visibility

Display 14.21 gives an example of a Swing GUI that has components (in this case tables) that change from visible to invisible and back again. When a suitable button is clicked one label disappears and the other appears. When the button labeled "Up" is clicked, the label "Here I am up here" becomes visible at the top of the frame and the label "Here I am down here!" disappears. When the button labeled "Down" is clicked, the label "Here I am down here!" becomes visible at the bottom of the frame and the label "Here I am up here!" disappears.

The two labels are added and set to be invisible in the constructor. The relevant code from Display 14.21 is reproduced in what follows:

```
upLabel = new JLabel("Here I am up here!");
contentPane.add(upLabel, BorderLayout.NORTH);
upLabel.setVisible(false);
downLabel = new JLabel("Here I am down here!");
contentPane.add(downLabel, BorderLayout.SOUTH);
downLabel.setVisible(false);
```

Note that you can make a component invisible without making the entire GUI invisible. The labels upLabel and downLabel are private instance variables so they can be referenced in both the constructor and the method actionPerformed.

In this GUI a label becomes visible or invisible when a button is clicked. For example, the following code from the method actionPerformed in Display 14.21 determines what happens when the button with the text "Up" on it is clicked:

```
if (e.getActionCommand().equals("Up"))
{
    upLabel.setVisible(true);
    downLabel.setVisible(false);
    validate();
}
```

The two statements

```
upLabel.setVisible(true);
downLabel.setVisible(false);
```

make upLabel visible and downLabel invisible in the representation of the GUI inside the computer. However, to make this change show on the screen requires a call to the method validate.

validate

Every container class has the method validate. An invocation of validate causes the container to lay out its components again. It's a kind of "update" method that makes changes in the components actually happen on the screen. Simple

Display 14.21 Invisible Labels *(Part 1 of 2)*

```java
import javax.swing.*;
import java.awt.*;
import java.awt.event.*;

public class VisibilityDemo extends JFrame
                               implements ActionListener
{
    public static final int WIDTH = 300;
    public static final int HEIGHT = 200;

    private JLabel upLabel;
    private JLabel downLabel;

    public VisibilityDemo()
    {
        setSize(WIDTH, HEIGHT);
        addWindowListener(new WindowDestroyer());
        setTitle("Visibility Demonstration");
        Container contentPane = getContentPane();
        contentPane.setLayout(new BorderLayout());
        contentPane.setBackground(Color.white);

        upLabel = new JLabel("Here I am up here!");
        contentPane.add(upLabel, BorderLayout.NORTH);
        upLabel.setVisible(false);
        downLabel = new JLabel("Here I am down here!");
        contentPane.add(downLabel, BorderLayout.SOUTH);
        downLabel.setVisible(false);

        JPanel buttonPanel = new JPanel();
        buttonPanel.setBackground(Color.white);
        buttonPanel.setLayout(new FlowLayout());
        JButton upButton = new JButton("Up");
        upButton.addActionListener(this);
        buttonPanel.add(upButton);
        JButton downButton = new JButton("Down");
        downButton.addActionListener(this);
        buttonPanel.add(downButton);
        contentPane.add(buttonPanel, BorderLayout.CENTER);
    }
```

Display 14.21 Invisible Labels *(Part 2 of 2)*

```java
public void actionPerformed(ActionEvent e)
{
    if (e.getActionCommand().equals("Up"))
    {
        upLabel.setVisible(true);
        downLabel.setVisible(false);
        validate();
    }
    else if (e.getActionCommand().equals("Down"))
    {
        downLabel.setVisible(true);
        upLabel.setVisible(false);
        validate();
    }
    else
        System.out.println("Error in VisibilityDemo interface.");
}

public static void main(String[] args)
{
    VisibilityDemo demoGui = new VisibilityDemo();
    demoGui.setVisible(true);
}
}
```

Resulting GUI (Two views of the same GUI)

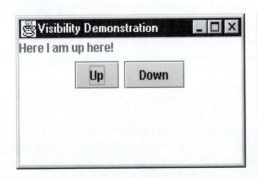
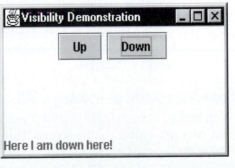

changes that are made to a Swing GUI, like changing color or changing the text in a text field, happen automatically. Other changes, such as the addition of components or changes in visibility require an invocation of `validate` (or some other "update" method.) Although it can make your program less efficient to invoke `validate` when it is not needed, it will have no other ill effects on your GUI if you mistakenly include an extra invocation of `validate`.

The `validate` Method

The class `Container`, and hence every container class, has a method named `validate`, which is a method for updating the container. An invocation of `validate` will cause the container to layout its components again. As discussed in the text, certain changes to a Swing GUI require an invocation of `validate` to update the screen and make the change show on the screen.

Syntax:

> *Container_Object*.validate();

The *Container_Object* is often an implicit *this*. A complete example of using `validate` can be seen in Display 14.21/page 936. ∎

? Self-Test Questions

32. In Display 14.21/page 936 we made text come and go by making labels visible and invisible. This required an invocation of the method `validate`. Suppose we had used an object of the class `TextField` instead of labels, and had changed the text in the text field in order to make it look like one word went away and other word appeared. Would we need an invocation of `validate` for the text field changes to show on the screen?

33. Rewrite the program in Display 14.21/page 936 so that when you click the `"Up"` button, the `"Up"` button becomes invisible and the `"Down"` button becomes visible, and similarly, when you click the `"Down"` button, the `"Down"` button becomes invisible and the `"Up"` button becomes visible. When the GUI is first displayed, both buttons are visible. (This one is long, but does not require that you add very much code to the program in Display 14.21.)

Some More Details on Updating a GUI

repaint manager

With Swing, most changes to a GUI windowing system are updated automatically so that they are visible on the screen. This is done by an object known as the **repaint manager**. The repaint manager works automatically and you need not even be aware of its presence . However, there are a few updates that the repaint manager will not do for you. You have already seen that you need to update the screen with an invocation of the method `validate` when your GUI changes the visibility of a component, as in Display 14.21/page 936.

pack

Two other updating methods that you will often see when looking at Swing code are `pack` and `repaint`. The method `pack` causes the window to be resized, usually to a smaller size, but more precisely to an approximation of a size known as the *preferred size*. (Yes, you can change the preferred size, but we do not have room to cover all of the Swing library in these two chapters.) The method `repaint`, repaints the window. The `repaint` method is discussed in Chapter 15.

repaint

We do not have room in this book to go into all the details of how a GUI is updated on the screen, but these few remarks may make some code you find in more advanced books a little less puzzling.

14.6 | Another Look at the Swing Class Hierarchy

> *All men are mortal.*
> *Aristotle is a man.*
> *Therefore, Aristotle is mortal.*
>
> **Common example of a syllogism**

Buttons, Menus, and Abstract Buttons

Display 14.22 shows a portion of the Swing class hierarchy. Note that the classes `JButton` and `JMenuItem` are both derived from the class `AbstractButton`. All of the basic properties and methods of the classes `JButton` and `JMenuItem` are inherited from the class `AbstractButton`. That is why objects of the class `JButton` and objects of the class `JMenuItem` are so similar. All of the methods (other than constructors) that are listed for the class `JButton` in Display 14.3/page 888 are inherited from the class `AbstractButton`. The class `JMenuItem` also inherits all these same methods from the class `AbstractButton`, and so a `JMenuItem` has all of the methods (other than constructors) that are listed for the class `JButton` in Display 14.3. (Some of these methods were inherited by the class `AbstractButton` from the class `JComponent`, so you may sometimes see some of the methods listed as "inherited from `JComponent`.")

Abstract-
Button.

The method `AbstractButton` is an abstract class. As we said in Chapter 12, you cannot, directly create objects of an abstract class. The only reason the class `AbstractButton` was defined was so that classes such as `JButton` and `JMenuItem` could be derived from the class `AbstractButton`. This provides for a unified view of `JButton`s and `JMenuItem`s, and it means that the designers of Swing did not have to write duplicate code, once for the class `JButton` and again for the class `JMenuItem`; they just wrote the code one time for the class `AbstractButton`.

abstract class

As we presented them, the classes `JLabel` and `JButton` are also very similar. However they are not as much alike as the classes `JButton` and `JMenuItem` are. These degrees of similarity are also reflected in the Swing class hierarchy shown in Display 14.22. All three classes are descendent classes of the class `JComponent`, but only `JButton` and `JMenuItem` are descendents of the class `AbstractButton`.

There are a number of other things that you can see in the hierarchy shown in Display 14.22. Note that `JMenu` is a derived from `JMenuItem`. That means a menu is also a menu item, and that is why you can add a `JMenu` to another `JMenu`, just as you add a more ordinary `JMenuItem` to a `JMenu`. This makes it possible to have nested menus.

Display 14.22 Portion of the Swing Class Hierarchy

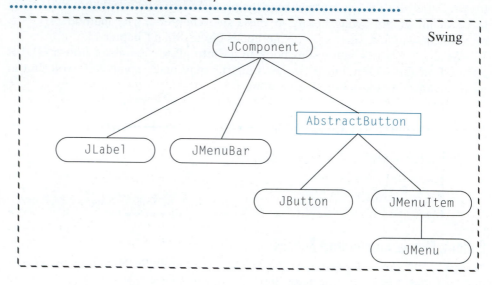

If there is a line between two classes, the lower class is a derived class of the higher class.

```
   Class

Abstract Class
```

Note also that the class JMenuBar is a derived class of the class JComponent. That means you can add a JMenuBar to a container, such as a panel or the content pane of a JFrame, just like you can add any other JComponent, such as a label or button. This means that, with a suitable layout manager, you can have as many JMenuBars as you want and you can place them almost anyplace in the container.

◼ Java Tip
More Methods for the Class JMenuItem

The class JMenuItem has all of the methods (other than constructors) that are listed for the class JButton in Display 14.3/page 888. (This is discussed in the section entitled ***Buttons, Menus, and Abstract Buttons.***) The class JMenuItem also has constructors similar to those listed for the class JButton in Display 14.3. We list those constructors below:

public JMenuItem( )
Creates a menu item with no text or icon. (Presumable, you will later use setText and/or setIcon with

the menu item.)

```
public JMenuItem(String text)
```
Creates a menu item with the `text` on it.

```
public JMenuItem(ImageIcon picture)
```
Creates a menu item with the icon `picture` on it.

```
public JMenuItem(String text, ImageIcon picture)
```
Creates a menu item with both the `text` and the icon `picture` on it.

■ *Java Tip*
There are a Lot More Swing Classes and Methods

In Chapters 12 and 14 you learned a good sample of Swing, enough of Swing to can do most of the basic things you might want to do with Swing. However, we cannot give you complete coverage of Swing. Swing is too large for that. A typical book on Swing for experienced Java programmers is longer than this entire book and usually is still not complete. If you feel that there is some method, class, or other facility that should be in Swing and that we have not covered in this book, there is a good chance that it is in Swing someplace. In most cases, we have given only the most important methods in a class, not all the methods for each class.

A good place to explore for new Swing classes and methods is the documentation that comes with the Java 2 (aka JDK 1. 2, aka SDK 1.2 or higher number). If you have down loaded Java 2, then you probably already have this documentation on your machine. If you do not have the documentation, you can get it from the Sun Java website. At the time this book was sent out for printing the web address was the one given below:

```
http://www.javasoft.com/products/jdk/1.2/download-docs.html
```

If that does not work, find Sun's Java website and follow the links to the documentation.

? Self-Test Questions

34. Is a `JButton` an `AbstractButton`? Is a `JLabel` an `AbstractButton`? Is a `JMenuItem` an `AbstractButton`? Is a `JMenu` an `AbstractButton`? (Hint: The last question is a little harder than the other three.)

CHAPTER SUMMARY

- A menu item is an object of the class `JMenuItem`. A menu is an object of the class `JMenu`, and a menu bar is an object of the class `JMenuBar`.

- You can add icons to `JButtons`, `JLabels`, and `JMenuItems`.

CHAPTER SUMMARY

- A `JMenuBar` can be added to a `JFrame` with the method `setJMenuBar`. It can also be added using the method `add`, just like any other component.

- Both buttons and menu items fire action events and so should have an `ActionListener` registered with them to respond to the events.

- You can use the class `JScrollPane` to add scroll bars to a text area.

- You can define a window listener class by having it implement the `WindowListener` interface.

- When you define a GUI using Swing, you can specify the look and feel for the GUI.

- You can reprogram the close-window button of a `JFrame` to do anything any other button can do. However, if you want to program it to do something other than close the window, you must use the method `setDefaultCloseOperation` as described in the chapter.

- If you change the visibility of a component (or do certain other changes), you should use the method `validate` to update the GUI.

? ANSWERS to Self-Test Questions

1. When you click a `JMenuItem` that fires an action event (that is, an object of the class `ActionEvent`). This is the same as with a `JButton`. There is no difference in this regard.

2. To change the action command for a `JMenuItem`, you use the method `setActionCommand`, just as you would for a `JButton`.

3. No, it is not legal. `AbstractButton` is an abstract class and you cannot directly create an object of an abstract class. If you want an `Abstract-Button` object, it must be an object of a more specific class such as `JButton` or `JMenuItem`.

4. Yes it is perfectly legal. It is, in fact, normal to add menus to menus. That is how you get nested menus.

5. As many as you want. Only one can be added with the method `setJMenuBar`, but any number more can be added to the content pane using the `add` method.

6. ```
JMenuItem mItem = new JMenuItem("Choose Me!");
```

or, equivalently,

```
JMenuItem mItem;
mItem = new JMenuItem("Choose Me!");
```

7. A menu item fires events of the class `ActionEvent`. Listeners for `ActionEvent` objects are in the class `ActionListener`. Note that this is the same as it is for objects of the class `JButton`.

8.

```
m.add(mItem);
mBar.add(m);
setJMenuBar(mBar);
```

You could use the following instead of using `setJMenuBar`:

```
getContentPane().add(mBar);
```

In case you are wondering why we did not mention the class `MenusGalor`, it is because it is named implicitly. This will all take place inside a constructor named `MenusGalor`.

9. We list three solutions. There are other solutions as well.

```
JButton myButton = new JButton("Push Me");
ImageIcon aliceIcon = new ImageIcon("alice.gif");
myButton.setIcon(aliceIcon);
```

The following will also work:

```
JButton myButton = new JButton("Push Me");
myButton.setIcon(new ImageIcon("alice.gif"));
```

The following will also work:

```
ImageIcon aliceIcon = new ImageIcon("alice.gif");
JButton myButton = new JButton(aliceIcon);
myButton.setText("Push Me");
```

10. We list two solutions. There are other solutions as well.

```
ImageIcon aliceIcon = new ImageIcon("alice.gif");
JLabel alicePicture = new JLabel(aliceIcon);
picturePanel.add(alicePicture);
```

The following will also work:

```
picturePanel.add(new JLabel(
                    new ImageIcon("alice.gif")));
```

11.

```
ImageIcon aliceIcon = new ImageIcon("alice.gif");
JButton aliceButton = new JButton(aliceIcon);
aliceButton.setActionCommand("Curiouser and curiouser!")
```

The following will also work:
```

```
JButton aliceButton = new JButton(new ImageIcon("alice.gif"));
aliceButton.setActionCommand("Curiouser and curiouser!")
```

12. No. You can invoke both methods, either one without the other, or invoke neither method.

13. No, there is no type violation. The class JTextArea is a descendent class of the class Component, so every JTextArea is also of type Component. If this is not clear, Display 12.14/page 810 and the accompanying text may help clarify things.

14. The statement

```
SwingUtilities.updateComponentTreeUI(this);
```

updates the screen display. If this is omitted, then the GUI might not have the look and feel specified in the invocation of setLookAndFeel.

15.

```
try
{
    UIManager.setLookAndFeel(
        "com.sun.java.swing.plaf.motif.MotifLookAndFeel");
    MyGUI motifGUI = new MyGUI();
    motifGUI.setVisible(true);
}
catch(Exception e)
{
    System.out.println("Look and Feel Problem.");
}
```

16.

```
myPanel.setLayout(
            new BoxLayout(myPanel, BoxLayout.Y_AXIS));
```

17. There is no difference in how components are added and no different in the ordering of components, but there is a difference in the spacing of components. With the BoxLayout manager a strut will not have extra space added around it, but with the FlowLayout manager it might have extra space added around it. Other differences in spacing and sizing components might also happen.

18.

```
Component horizontalSpace =
            Box.createHorizontalStrut(20);
```

19. A strut component has a fixed size in one dimension (either height or width) while a glue component can change size.

20.

```
Box vBox = new Box(BoxLayout.Y_AXIS);
```

and the equivalent

```
Box vBox = Box.createVerticalBox();
```

21. No. A `Box` container automatically gets a `BoxLayout` manager. However, you do specify what kind of `BoxLayout` manager it gets (either vertical or horizontal) when you create the `Box` container.

22. Because we needed a name for the layout manager so we could switch the "card" displayed, as in the following from the definition of the method `actionPerformed`:

    ```
    dealer.show(deckPanel, "red");
    ```

23. `dealer.next(deckPanel);`

24. You must define all of the methods given in Display 14.18/page 926. Moreover the number and type of the method parameter must be exactly as shown in Display 14.18. If you do not want to define a method to do anything special, you can give it an empty body, as follows:

    ```
    public void windowIconified(WindowEvent e)
    {}
    ```

25. No.

26. Yes, just list all of the interface names after the reserved word *imple-ments* and separate them with commas, as in the following example:

    ```
    public class WindowListenerDemo extends JFrame
                    implements ActionListener, WindowListener
    ```

    You also need to implement all the methods in all the interfaces.

27. You can invoke `dispose()` using the object you want to go away as the calling object.

28. The window goes away, but the program does not end. This is a problem if there are no other windows in the program, because then you have no nice way to end the program.

29.
    ```
    setDefaultCloseOperation(WindowConstants.DO_NOTHING_ON_CLOSE);
    ```

30. No, there is no need for it. (Although it would do no serious harm if you did add it.)

31. It is a constant named `DO_NOTHING_ON_CLOSE` that is defined in the class `WindowConstants`. You should be able to figure that out from the way it is written and the way it is used. (By the way, the class `WindowConstants` is in the package `javax.swing`. So the only import statement you need in order to use the class (and the constant) is:

    ```
    import javax.swing.*;
    ```

32. No. The method `setText`, that is used to set the text in a text field or text area, will automatically takes care of updating the GUI.

33. You need names for the buttons. So, add the following two instance variables:

    ```
    private JButton upButton;
    private JButton downButton;
    ```

The only changes in the constructor are to change

```
JButton upButton = new JButton("Up");
```

to

```
upButton = new JButton("Up");
```

and to change

```
JButton downButton = new JButton("Down");
```

to

```
downButton = new JButton("Down");
```

The only other change is to change the nested *if-then-else* in the method `actionPerformed` to the following:

```
if (e.getActionCommand().equals("Up"))
{
    upLabel.setVisible(true);
    downLabel.setVisible(false);
    upButton.setVisible(false);
    downButton.setVisible(true);
    validate();
}
else if (e.getActionCommand().equals("Down"))
{
    downLabel.setVisible(true);
    upLabel.setVisible(false);
    downButton.setVisible(false);
    upButton.setVisible(true);
    validate();
}
else
    System.out.println(
            "Error in VisibilityDemoExercise interface.");
```

extra code on CD

The complete program is on the CD that accompanies this text in the file `VisibilityDemoExercise.java`.

34. A `JButton` is an `AbstractButton`. A `JLabel` is not an `AbstractButton`. A `JMenuItem` is an `AbstractButton`. A `JMenu` is an `AbstractButton`. The first three answers are immediate from Display 14.22/page 940. To see that a `JMenu` is an `AbstractButton`, recall that a `JMenu` is a `JMenuItem` and a `JMenuItem` is an `AbstractButton`. However, it is not always practical to use all the methods of an `AbstractButton` with a `JMenu`. So, a `JMenu` is not a "typical" `AbstractButton`.

? PROGRAMMING EXERCISES

1. Write a GUI program that will let the user see three different looks and feels (Metal, Motif, and Windows). When run, it displays a GUI that

shows buttons and labels. Three of the buttons have the strings `"Metal"`, `"Motif"`, and `"Windows"` written on them. (One string per button, of course.) When the button is clicked the look and feel of the GUI is changed according to what is written on the button. Do this in the following way. You will define a Swing class that is a derived class of `JFrame`. The `JFrame` will implement the `ActionListener` interface and use the method `actionPerformed` to change the look and feel. The GUI will have three labels with the strings `"Metal Look and Feel"`, `"Motif Look and Feel"`, and `"Windows Look and Feel"`. Only one of these three labels, the one that corresponds to the current look and feel, will be visible. There will be one (or more) other labels that are always visible.

2. Write a GUI that will let the user sample icons. There is a menu named `Icons` that offers three choices: `Smiley Face`, `Duke Waving`, and `Duke Standing`. When the user chooses a menu item, the corresponding icon is displayed (and no other icons are displayed). When the GUI is first displayed no icons are visible. The picture files for these icons are on the accompanying CD.

3. Enhance the memo saver GUI in Display 14.1/page 876 in all of the following ways:

There is a menu called `View` that has two submenus. One named `Look and Feel` and one named `Scroll Bars`.

The submenu named `Look and Feel` lets the user change the look and feel of the GUI to any of the three look and feels: Metal, Motif, and Windows.

The submenu named `Scroll Bars` offer the user three choices: `Never`, `Always`, and `As Needed`. When the user makes a choice, the scroll bars are displayed according to the choice.

When the user clicks the close-window button another window pops up and asks the user if she/he is sure she/he wants to end the program, as in Display 14.19/page 928.

4. Enhance the program of Programming Exercise 7 Chapter 9/page 660 to have a GUI interface that allows the user to write and read records of type `PetRecord` (Display 5.19/page 351) to a file. Include a menu with options to create a new file, read an existing one, or exit. Create two `PetRecord` files, named `dogPetRecords` and `catPetRecords`, and list them in a submenu under the read option. Hint: You can use this program to create the files `dogPetRecords` and `catPetRecords`. This will require two testing phases, one before and one after adding `dogPetRecords` and `catPetRecords`, but that is not a major problem.

5. Write a GUI that will let the user sample borders. Include a menu named `Borders` that offers three options, bevel border, etched border, and line border and submenus with the following options:

Beveled Border Options: Raised and Lowered
Etched Border Options: Raised and Lowered
Line Border Options: Small, Medium, and Large
Each Line Border submenu should have a submenu with three color options, black, red, and blue.

Put the borders around a `JLabel` containing text that describes the border, such as. `"Raised Border"`, `"Lowered Etched Border"`, etc. Fix the highlight and shadow colors for the Etched Border options to whatever colors you like, and make the Small Line Border 1 pixel wide, the Medium one 5 pixels, and the Large one 10 pixels.

6. Redo or do for the first time Programming Exercise 4 (this chapter), but this time, use the `BoxLayout` manager (or the `Box` container class) to create the GUI and put two buttons, one to write a file, the other to read a file, vertically on the left.

7. Write a "skeleton" GUI program that implements the `WindowListener` interface. Write code for each of its seven methods (Display 14.18/page 926) that simply prints out a message identifying which event occurred. Printout the message in a text field. Note that your program will not end when the close-window button is clicked (but will instead simply send a message to the text field saying that the `windowClosing` method has been invoked). Include a button labeled `Exit` that the user can click to end the program.

GRAPHICS OBJECTS

15.1 BASIC FIGURES 951
Size and Coordinate System for
Screen Objects 951
The Graphics Class and the
Method paint 952
Programming Example A Happy Face 952
Drawing Lines, Rectangles, and
Ovals 953
Drawing Arcs 956

Programming Tip Use Defined
Constants 960
Round Rectangles 960
Polygons (Alternative Ordering) 960

Java Tip Use paintComponent for
Panels 961

Action Drawings and
repaint 962
repaint and paint 969

15.2 COLORS 970
Specifying a Drawing Color 970
Defining Colors 970

Gotcha Using doubles to Define a
Color 972
Dynamically Changing Colors 976
The JColorChooser Dialog 976

15.3 FONTS AND OTHER TEXT DETAILS 979
The drawString Method 980
Fonts 980

Chapter Summary 985
Answers to Self-Test Questions 985
Programming Exercises 988

GRAPHICS OBJECTS

> *Say, boys! if you give me another whiskey I'll be glad.*
> *And I'll draw right here a picture of the face that drove me mad.*
> *Give me that piece of chalk with which you mark the baseball score,*
> *You shall see the lovely Madeleine upon the bar-room floor.*
>
> **Hugh Antoine D'Arcy, The Face Upon The Floor**

The GUIs you have already seen, such as those made with `JOptionPane` or those in Chapters 12-14, are examples of graphics. They use graphical elements, like windows and buttons to communicate with the user. In fact, The G in GUI stands for *Graphical*. However, the first thing that comes to mind when people hear about computer graphics is not windows, but drawing pictures with a computer. In this chapter we introduce you to some of the Java libraries you can use to draw pictures. The tools we will present create very simple figures, like ovals and rectangles. Even the complete pictures in this chapter are simple. That is because we are concerned with presenting the tools, not giving an art lesson. (That is an exciting story but is another story.) This chapter will give you some tools, but you are the artist. With an artistic flair you can use these simple tools to produce very elaborate pictures.

In addition to exploring drawing graphics, we also introduce you to more details about color and text, including how to create your own colors and how to use fonts.

Objectives

Learn to use the class `Graphics` to draw simple figures such as lines, ovals, and rectangles.

Find out how to create and use new colors with the classes `Color` and `JColorChooser`.

Practice designing Swing GUIs that change their displayed graphics and colors.

Find out how to display text in different fonts using the method `drawString` of the class `Graphics`.

Prerequisites

Before covering this chapter, you need to have covered Chapter 12 which introduces you to Swing. You do not need to have covered Chapters 13 or 14 which cover applets and more advanced features of Swing.

The sections 15.1, 15.2, and 15.3 are independent of each other. You may choose any subset of the three sections to read and may read them in any order.

The subsection ***Polygons (Alternative Ordering)*** requires that you also first cover Chapter 6 on arrays. If you have not yet covered Chapter 6, simply skip that subsection.

15.1 | Basic Figures

> *You can't put a round peg in a square hole.*
>
> ***Common saying***

In this section, you will learn how to draw basic figures such as lines, ovals, and rectangles to produce simple pictures.

Size and Coordinate System for Screen Objects

As in previous work on GUIs, the size of an object on the screen is measured in *pixels*. Recall that a **pixel** is the smallest unit of space on which your screen can write.

pixel

When drawing objects on the screen, Java uses the coordinate system shown in Display 15.1 The **origin** point $(0, 0)$ is the upper left-hand corner of the screen area

origin

Display 15.1 Screen Coordinate System

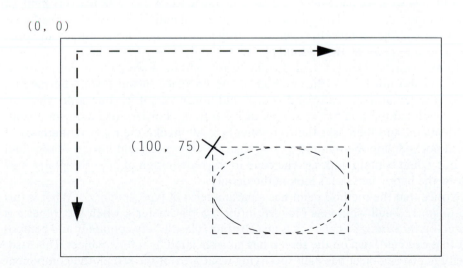

$(0, 0)$

$(100, 75)$

used for drawing (usually a `JFrame` or `JPanel`). The x-coordinate, or horizontal coordinate, is positive and increasing to the right. The y-coordinate, or vertical coordinate, is positive and increasing in the downward direction. Thus, all coordinates are normally positive. Units are in pixels.

(x, y)

When placing a rectangle on the screen, Java will often use a coordinate like (100, 75) to specify where the rectangle is located. The first number is the x-coordinate and the second number is the y-coordinate. Note that the coordinates do not indicate the center of the rectangle, but instead indicate the location of the upper left-hand corner of the rectangle. In Display 15.1, the X marks the location of the point (100, 75) and the rectangle shown is at location (100, 75).

When placing a figure other than a rectangle on the screen, Java encloses the figure in an imaginary tightly fitting rectangle, and positions the upper left-hand corner of the imaginary rectangle. So, in Display 15.1, the oval displayed is located at point (100, 75).

Programming Example
A Happy Face

Display 15.2 shows a GUI program that displays a `JFrame` with a happy face drawn inside of it. The code for drawing the face is given in the method `paint`. We will explain the method `paint` and how the program draws the happy face in the next few subsections.

The `Graphics` Class and the Method `paint`

paint

Almost all Swing and Swing related components and containers have a method named `paint`. The method `paint` draws the component or container on the screen. Up until now, we have had no need to redefine the method `paint` or to even mention it. The method `paint` is defined for you and is called automatically when the figure is displayed on the screen. However, to draw geometric figures, like circles and boxes, you need to redefine the method `paint`.

Look again at Display 15.2. In that class definition we gave a definition of `paint` but did not invoke the method `paint` anyplace in our code. The method `paint` is called automatically, and you should not invoke it in your code. The normal, predefined method `paint` simply draws a frame border, title, and other standard features, and then asks the components to all invoke their `paint` methods. If we did not redefine the method `paint`, then the `JFrame` would have a border and title but would contain nothing. The code in the redefinition of `paint` explains how to draw the happy face. Let's look at the details.

Graphics

Notice that the method paint has a parameter g of type `Graphics`. What is this type `Graphics` and what gets plugged in for the parameter g when the `JFrame` is painted on the screen? `Graphics` is an (abstract) class. Every container and component that can be drawn on the screen has an associated `Graphics` object. This associated `Graphics` object has data specifying what area of the screen the component or container covers. The `Graphics` object g also has all the methods that we will use to draw figures, such as circles and boxes, on the screen. Almost the entire definition of the `paint` method in Display 15.2 consists of invocations of various drawing methods with the parameter g as the calling object. When this `paint` method is (automatically) invoked, the parameter g will be replaced by the `Graphics` object associated with the `JFrame`, and so the figures drawn will be inside the `JFrame`. Let's look at the code in this method `paint`.

Notice the first line in the definition of `paint` in Display 15.2:

super

```
super.paint(g);
```

Recall that, when it is used in this way, s*uper* is a name for the parent class of a derived class. The class in Display 15.2 is derived from the class `JFrame`, and so `super.paint` is the `paint` method for the class `JFrame`. Whenever you redefine the method `paint`, you should start with this invocation of `super.paint`. This ensures that your definition of `paint` will do all the things the standard `paint` methods does, such as draw the title and border for the `JFrame`. (This lesson applies even if the class is derived from some class other than `JFrame`.)

The next few subsections explain the details of how the happy face is drawn by method invocations within the definition of the method `paint` in Display 15.2.

The `Graphics` Class is in the AWT Library

The `Graphics` class is in the awt package (library), and so you should include the following import statement when using this class:

```
import java.awt.*;
```

Drawing Lines, Rectangles, and Ovals

The class `Graphics` has a number of methods that draw various forms of lines, rectangles, and ovals. The program in Display 15.2 illustrates a few of the methods that draw lines, ovals, and arcs.

The left eyebrow is drawn with the following method from the definition of `paint` in Display 15.2. (In this case, *left* means the left side for the viewer not for the face.)

drawLine

```
g.drawLine(X1_LEFT_BROW, Y1_LEFT_BROW,
           X2_LEFT_BROW, Y2_LEFT_BROW);
```

which is equivalent to:

```
g.drawLine(155, 88, 75, 90);
```

This draws a line from the point $(155, 88)$ to the point $(120, 90)$.

An oval is specified by giving the width, height, and location of the (smallest) rectangle that encloses the oval. For example, the following line from the definition of `paint` in Display 15.2 draws the eye of the happy face on the left side of the screen:

fillOval

```
g.fillOval(X_LEFT_EYE, Y_LEFT_EYE, EYE_WIDTH, EYE_HEIGHT);
```

which is equivalent to:

```
g.fillOval(155, 95, 20, 10);
```

Display 15.2 Drawing a Happy Face *(Part 1 of 2)*

```
import javax.swing.*;
import java.awt.*;

/****************************************************
 *Simple demonstration of drawing a face in a JFrame.
 ****************************************************/
public class Madeleine extends JFrame
{
    public static final int FRAME_WIDTH = 400;
    public static final int FRAME_HEIGHT = 400;
    public static final int FACE_DIAMETER = 200;
    public static final int X_FACE = 100;
    public static final int Y_FACE = 50;
    public static final int NOSE_DIAMETER = 10;
    public static final int X_NOSE = X_FACE + 95;
    public static final int Y_NOSE = Y_FACE + 95;
    public static final int EYE_WIDTH = 20;
    public static final int EYE_HEIGHT = 10;
    public static final int X_LEFT_EYE = X_FACE + 55;
    public static final int Y_LEFT_EYE = Y_FACE + 45;
    public static final int X_RIGHT_EYE = X_FACE + 130;
    public static final int Y_RIGHT_EYE = Y_FACE + 45;
    public static final int X1_LEFT_BROW = X_FACE + 55;
    public static final int Y1_LEFT_BROW = Y_FACE + 38;
    public static final int X2_LEFT_BROW = X1_LEFT_BROW + 20;
    public static final int Y2_LEFT_BROW = Y1_LEFT_BROW + 2;
    public static final int X1_RIGHT_BROW = X_FACE + 130;
    public static final int Y1_RIGHT_BROW = Y2_LEFT_BROW;
    public static final int X2_RIGHT_BROW = X1_RIGHT_BROW + 20;
    public static final int Y2_RIGHT_BROW = Y1_LEFT_BROW;
    public static final int MOUTH_WIDTH = 100;
    public static final int MOUTH_HEIGHT = 50;
    public static final int X_MOUTH = X_FACE + 50;
    public static final int Y_MOUTH = Y_FACE + 125;
    public static final int MOUTH_START_ANGLE = 180;
    public static final int MOUTH_ARC_SWEEP = 180;
    public static final int X_TEXT = X_FACE;
    public static final int Y_TEXT = Y_FACE + 250;

    public static void main(String[] args)
    {
        Madeleine picture = new Madeleine();
        picture.setVisible(true);
    }
```

Display 15.2 Drawing a Happy Face *(Part 2 of 2)*

```java
    public Madeleine()
    {
        setSize(FRAME_WIDTH, FRAME_HEIGHT);
        addWindowListener(new WindowDestroyer());
        setTitle("Madeleine by Java");
        getContentPane().setBackground(Color.white);
    }

    public void paint(Graphics g)
    {
        super.paint(g);
        g.drawOval(X_FACE, Y_FACE, FACE_DIAMETER, FACE_DIAMETER);
        //Draw Nose:
        g.fillOval(X_NOSE, Y_NOSE, NOSE_DIAMETER, NOSE_DIAMETER);
        //Draw Eyes:
        g.fillOval(X_LEFT_EYE, Y_LEFT_EYE, EYE_WIDTH, EYE_HEIGHT);
        g.fillOval(X_RIGHT_EYE, Y_RIGHT_EYE, EYE_WIDTH, EYE_HEIGHT);
        //Draw eyebrows:
        g.drawLine(X1_LEFT_BROW, Y1_LEFT_BROW,
                    X2_LEFT_BROW, Y2_LEFT_BROW);
        g.drawLine(X1_RIGHT_BROW, Y1_RIGHT_BROW,
                    X2_RIGHT_BROW, Y2_RIGHT_BROW);
        //Draw Mouth:
        g.drawArc(X_MOUTH, Y_MOUTH, MOUTH_WIDTH, MOUTH_HEIGHT,
                    MOUTH_START_ANGLE, MOUTH_ARC_SWEEP);

    }
}
```

Resulting GUI

This draws an oval that just fits into an invisible rectangle whose upper left-hand corner is at coordinates (155, 95) and that has a width of 20 pixels and a height of 10 pixels. Note that the point that is used to place the oval on the screen is not the center of the oval or anything like the center, but is something like the upper left-hand corner of the oval.

circle

drawOval

Note that a circle is a special case of an oval in which the width and height of the rectangle are equal. For example, the following line from the definition of `paint` in Display 15.2 draws the outline of the happy face.

```
g.drawOval(X_FACE, Y_FACE, FACE_DIAMETER, FACE_DIAMETER);
```

which is equivalent to:

```
g.drawOval(100, 50, 200, 200);
```

Since the enclosing rectangle has both width and height of 200 pixels, this produces a circle of diameter 200 pixels.

Some of the methods you can use to draw simple figures are shown in Display 15.3. Note that most methods come in pairs, one whose name starts with `draw` and one whose name starts with `fill`, such as `drawOval` and `fillOval`. The one that starts with `draw` will draw the outline of the specified figure. The one that starts with `fill` will draw a solid figure obtained by coloring the inside of the specified figure. (We say more about colors in Section 15.2. In this section we are only using the default color, which is black.)

Drawing Arcs

Arcs, such as the smile on the happy face in Display 15.2/page 954, are described by giving an oval and then specifying what portion of the oval that will be used for the arc. For example, the following statement from Display 15.2 draws the smile on the happy face:

drawArc

```
g.drawArc(X_MOUTH, Y_MOUTH, MOUTH_WIDTH, MOUTH_HEIGHT,
          MOUTH_START_ANGLE, MOUTH_ARC_SWEEP);
```

which is equivalent to

```
g.drawArc(X_MOUTH, Y_MOUTH, MOUTH_WIDTH, MOUTH_HEIGHT,
          180, 180);
```

The arguments `MOUTH_WIDTH` and `MOUTH_HEIGHT` determine the size of an invisible rectangle. The arguments `X_MOUTH` and `Y_MOUTH` determine the location of the rectangle. The upper left-hand corner of the rectangle is located at the point (`X_MOUTH`, `Y_MOUTH`). Inside this invisible rectangle, envision an invisible oval that just fits inside the invisible rectangle. The last two arguments specify what portion of this invisible oval is made visible.

Display 15.4 illustrates how these last two arguments specify an arc of the invisible oval that will be made visible. The next to last argument specifies a start angle in degrees. The last argument specifies how many degrees of the oval's arc will be made visible. If the last argument is 360 (degrees), then the full oval is made visible.

The angles are numbered with zero degrees as shown in Display 15.4. In the first figure, the start angle is zero degrees. The counterclockwise direction is pos-

Display 15.3 Some Methods in the Class Graphics

Method	Description
drawLine(*int* x1, *int* y1, *int* x2, *int* y2)	Draws a line between points (x1, y1) and (x2, y2).
drawRect(*int* x, *int* y, *int* width, *int* height)	Draws the outline of the specified rectangle. (x, y) is the location of the upper left-hand corner.
fillRect(*int* x, *int* y, *int* width, *int* height)	Fills the specified rectangle (with color). (x, y) is the location of the upper left-hand corner of the rectangle.
draw3DRect(*int* x, *int* y, *int* width, *int* height, *boolean* raised)	Draws the outline of the specified rectangle. (x, y) is the location of the upper left-hand corner. The rectangle is highlighted to look like it has thickness. If raised is *true*, the highlight makes the rectangle appear to stand out from the background. If raised is *false*, the highlight makes the rectangle appear to be sunken into the background.
fill3DRect(*int* x, *int* y, *int* width, *int* height, *boolean* raised)	Fills (with color) the rectangle specified by draw3DRec(x,y,width, height, raised)
drawRoundRect(*int* x, *int* y, *int* width, *int* height, *int* arcWidth, *int* arcHeight)	Draws the outline of the specified round cornered rectangle. (x, y) is the location of the upper left-hand corner of the enclosing regular rectangle. arcWidth and arcHeight specify the shape of the round corners.
fillRoundRect(*int* x, *int* y, *int* width, *int* height, *int* arcWidth, *int* arcHeight)	Fills (with color) the round rectangle specified by drawRoundRec(x,y, width, height, arcWidth, arcHeight)

Display 15.3 Some Methods in the Class Graphics
••

`drawOval(int x, int y,` `        int width, int height)`	Draws the outline of the oval with smallest enclosing rectangle that has the specified `width` and `height`. The (imagined) rectangle has its upper left-hand corner located at (x, y).
`fillOval(int x, int y,` `        int width, int height)`	Fills (with color) the oval specified by `drawOval(x, y,` `            width, height)`

`drawArc(int x, int y,`
`        int width, int height,`
`        int startAngle, int arcSweep)`
	Draws part of an oval that just fits into an invisible rectangle described by the first four arguments. The portion of the oval drawn is given by the last two arguments.

`fillArc(int x, int y,`
`        int width, int height,`
`        int startAngle, int arcSweep)`
	Fills (with color) the oval specified by `drawArc(x, y,`
	`        width, height,`
	`        startAngle, arcSweep)`

itive. So a start angle of 90 degrees would start at the top of the oval. A start angle of –90 degrees would start at the bottom of the oval. If you study Display 15.4, the way of specifying arcs should become clear. For example, the smile on the happy face in Display 15.2 has a start angle of 180 degrees. So it starts on the left end of the invisible oval. The last argument is also 180, so the arc is made visible through a counterclockwise direction of 180 degrees, or halfway around the oval in the counter clockwise direction. So the smile is the lower half of the oval.

? Self-Test Questions
•••

1. Give an invocation of a method to draw a horizontal line of length 100 starting at position (20, 30) and extending to the right. The calling object of type Graphics is named g.

2. Give an invocation of a method that draws a vertical line of length 100 starting at position (20, 30) and extending downward. Use graphicsObject (of type Graphic) as the calling object.

3. Give an invocation of a method to draw a solid box of width 100 and height 75 with the upper left-hand corner at position (20, 30). The calling object of type Graphics is named g.

Display 15.4 Specifying an Arc

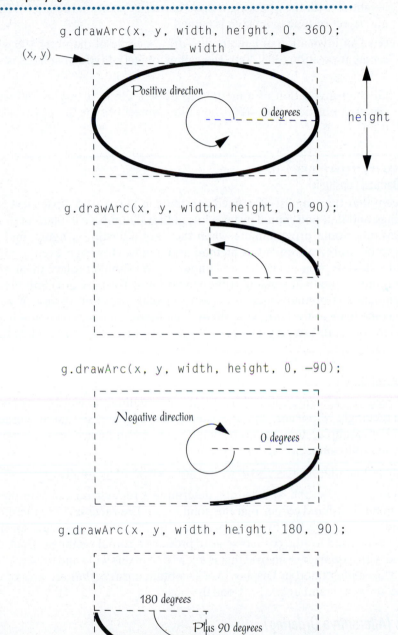

g.drawArc(x, y, width, height, 0, 360);

g.drawArc(x, y, width, height, 0, 90);

g.drawArc(x, y, width, height, 0, -90);

g.drawArc(x, y, width, height, 180, 90);

4. Give an invocation of a method to draw a solid box of width 100 and height 75 with the upper *right-hand* corner at position (200, 300). The calling object of type `Graphics` is named g.

5. Give an invocation of a method to draw a circle of diameter 100 with the *center* at position (300, 400). The calling object of type `Graphics` is named g.

6. Give an invocation of a method to draw a circle of *radius* 100 with the *center* at position (300, 400). The calling object of type `Graphics` is named g.

■ *Programming Tip*
Use Defined Constants

It may seem that the long list of defined constants in Display 15.2/page 954 is over-doing things, and that you should just use lots of literal numbers in place of those de-fined constants. Some programmers, when they are adjusting a figure, find literal numbers to be more convenient as method arguments. However, even if your first version of a class or program uses literal numbers, you should replace them with de-fined constants in the final version. Although you may (or may not) find that using literal numbers as arguments makes it easier to tweak your first version, if you wait and then come back to the code, you will find the literal numbers incomprehensible. But, defined constants are very easy to deal with if you want to change code that has "grown cold."

Round Rectangles

round rectangle

A *round rectangle*? Seems impossible, unless you redefine the words. A **round rect-angle** is a rectangle whose corners have been replaced by arcs so that the corners are rounded. For example, suppose g is of type `Graphics` and consider what would be drawn by the following:

```
g.drawRoundRect(x, y, width, height, arcWidth, arcHeight)
```

The arguments x, y, `width`, and `height` determine a regular rectangle in the usual way. The upper-left-hand corner is at the point (x, y). The rectangle has the specified `width` and `height`. The last two arguments, `arcWidth` and `arcHeight`, specify the arcs that will be used for the corners so as to produce a round rectangle. Each corner is replaced with a quarter of an oval that is `arcWidth` pixels wide and `arcHeight` pix-els high. This is illustrated in Display 15.5. To obtain corners that are arcs of circles just make `arcWidth` and `arcHeight` equal.

Polygons *(Alternative Ordering)*

You need to read Chapter 6 on arrays before covering this subsection.

We have discussed methods to draw rectangles and ovals, but what if you want other shapes, like a triangle or a hexagon? For more complicated figures, you can use the graphics methods that draw various kinds of polygons. A **polygon** is a figure with multiple sides, like a triangle or hexagon. A rectangle is also a polygon, but

polygon

Display 15.5 A Round Rectangle

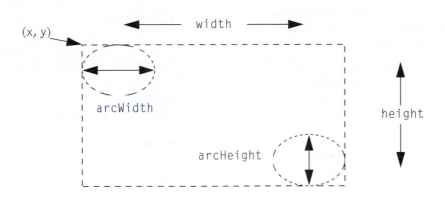

So,

```
g.drawRoundRect(x, y, width, height, arcWidth, arcHeight);
```
produces:

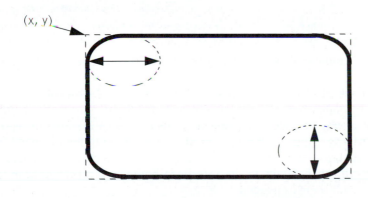

you can draw a rectangle more easily using drawRect. The polygon methods are primarily intended to draw more complicated shapes than rectangles. Display 15.6 gives some methods for drawing various kinds of polygons.

■ Java Tip
Use paintComponent for Panels

You can draw figures on a JPanel and place the JPanel in a JFrame. When defining a JPanel class that contains a graphics drawing, you use the method paintComponent instead of the method paint, but otherwise the details are similar to what we have seen for JFrames. JFrames use the method paint. However, JPanels—and in fact all JComponents—use the method paintComponent.

Display 15.6 Polygon Methods in the Class Graphics

Method	Description
public void drawPolygon(int[] x, int[] y, int points)	Draws a polygon through the point (x[0], y[0]), (x[1], y[1]), ..., (x[points − 1], y[points − 1]). Always draws a closed polygon. If the first and last points are not equal, it draws a line from the last to the first point.
public void drawPolyline(int[] x, int[] y, int points)	Draws a polygon through the point (x[0], y[0]), (x[1], y[1]), ..., (x[points − 1], y[points − 1]). If the first and last points are not equal, the polygon will not be closed.
public void fillPolygon(int[] x, int[] y, int points)	Fills (with color) the polygon specified by drawPolygon(x,y,points)

A very simple example of using paintComponent with a JPanel is given in Display 15.7.

If you look back at Display 12.14/page 810 in Chapter 12, you will see that a JPanel is a JComponent, but a JFrame is not a JComponent. A JFrame is only a Component. That is why they use different methods to paint the screen. It is difficult, and perhaps close to impossible, to keep this level of detail in your head. You can simply note that a JPanel uses paintComponent where a JFrame would use paint, and leave all other details to the reference books and reference web sites where you can consult them as needed.

Action Drawings and repaint

The program in Display 15.8 is similar to the program in Display 15.2/page 954. It draws a face similar to the face given in Display 15.2, but with two differences. When the GUI first comes on the screen, the face is frowning instead of smiling and is near the bottom of the frame. There is a button at the bottom of the GUI that says Click for a Smile. When you click that button, the frowning face changes to a smiling face and moves up closer to the top of the frame. Let's see how you get this graphics to change.

The program in Display 15.8 has a private instance variable smile of type boolean. When the value of smile is true, the paint method draws a smiling face. When the value of smile is false, the paint method draws a frowning face. The variable smile is initialized to false, so when the GUI first appears on the screen, the face is frowning. (We'll look at how you draw a frowning versus a smiling face shortly, but take that detail on faith for a minute.) When the button labeled Click

Display 15.7 `paintComponent` **Demonstration** *(Part 1 of 2)*

```java
import javax.swing.*;
import java.awt.*;

/*********************************************************
 *A toy program to demonstrate the paintComponent method.
 *********************************************************/
public class PaintComponentDemo extends JFrame
{
    public static final int FRAME_WIDTH = 400;
    public static final int FRAME_HEIGHT = 400;

    public static void main(String[] args)
    {
        PaintComponentDemo w = new PaintComponentDemo();
        w.setVisible(true);
    }

    public PaintComponentDemo()
    {
        setSize(FRAME_WIDTH, FRAME_HEIGHT);
        addWindowListener(new WindowDestroyer());
        setTitle("The Oval Is in a Panel");
        Container contentPane = getContentPane();
        contentPane.setLayout(new BorderLayout());
        SamplePanel p = new SamplePanel();
        contentPane.add(p, BorderLayout.CENTER);
    }


    private class SamplePanel extends JPanel
    {
        public SamplePanel()
        {
            //Does nothing except create a JPanel.
        }

        public void paintComponent(Graphics g)
        {
            super.paintComponent(g);
            g.drawOval(FRAME_WIDTH/4, FRAME_HEIGHT/4,
                       FRAME_WIDTH/2, FRAME_HEIGHT/3);
        }

    }

}
```

Display 15.7 `paintComponent` Demonstration *(Part 2 of 2)*

Resulting GUI

for a `Smile` is clicked, this sends an action event to the method `actionPerformed`. The method `actionPerformed` then changes the value of the variable `smile` to *true* and invokes the method `repaint`. This use of the method `repaint` is new, so let's discuss it a bit.

Every `JFrame` (in fact every `Component` and every `Container`) has a method named `repaint`. The method `repaint` will repaint the screen so that any changes to the graphics being displayed will show on the screen. If you omit the invocation of `repaint` from the method `actionPerformed`, then the variable `smile` will change to *true*, but the screen will not change. Without an invocation of `repaint`, the face will still have a frowning face. This is because the method `paint` must be called again with the new value of `smile` before the change takes effect. The method `repaint` does a few standard things, and most importantly, will also invoke the method `paint`, which redraws the screen. Be sure to note that you should invoke `repaint` and not `paint`.

Now we explain why, when `smile` has the value *true*, the method `paint` draws a smiling face, but when `smile` has the value *false*, `paint` draws a frowning face. The relevant part of the code is the following, which draws the smile:

```
if (smile)
    g.drawArc(xMouth, yMouth, MOUTH_WIDTH, MOUTH_HEIGHT,
            MOUTH_START_ANGLE, MOUTH_ARC_SWEEP);
else //Note minus sign:
    g.drawArc(xMouth, yMouth, MOUTH_WIDTH, MOUTH_HEIGHT,
            MOUTH_START_ANGLE, -MOUTH_ARC_SWEEP);
```

Display 15.8 An Action Drawing (Part 1 of 4)

```
import javax.swing.*;
import java.awt.*;
import java.awt.event.*;

/******************************************************
 *Simple demonstration of a face with action (in a JFrame).
 ******************************************************/
public class SadMadeleine extends JFrame implements ActionListener
{
    public static final int FRAME_WIDTH = 400;
    public static final int FRAME_HEIGHT = 400;
    public static final int FACE_DIAMETER = 200;
    public static final int EYE_WIDTH = 20;
    public static final int EYE_HEIGHT = 10;
    public static final int NOSE_DIAMETER = 10;
    public static final int MOUTH_WIDTH = 100;
    public static final int MOUTH_HEIGHT = 50;
    public static final int X_SAD_FACE = 190;
    public static final int Y_SAD_FACE = 150;
    public static final int X_HAPPY_FACE = 100;
    public static final int Y_HAPPY_FACE = 50;
    public static final int MOUTH_START_ANGLE = 180;
    public static final int MOUTH_ARC_SWEEP = 180;

    private boolean smile = false;
    private int xFace = X_SAD_FACE;
    private int yFace = Y_SAD_FACE;
    private int xNose = xFace + 95;
    private int yNose = yFace + 95;
    private int xLeftEye = xFace + 55;
    private int yLeftEye = yFace + 45;
    private int xRightEye = xFace + 130;
    private int yRightEye = yFace + 45;
    private int x1LeftBrow = xFace + 55;
    private int y1LeftBrow = yFace + 38;
    private int x2LeftBrow = x1LeftBrow + 20;
    private int y2LeftBrow = y1LeftBrow + 2;
    private int x1RightBrow = xFace + 130;
    private int y1RightBrow = y2LeftBrow;
    private int x2RightBrow = x1RightBrow + 20;
    private int y2RightBrow = y1LeftBrow;
    private int xMouth = xFace + 50;
    private int yMouth = yFace + 125;
```

Display 15.8 An Action Drawing (Part 2 of 4)

```java
public static void main(String[] args)
{
    SadMadeleine picture = new SadMadeleine();
    picture.setVisible(true);
}

public SadMadeleine()
{
    setSize(FRAME_WIDTH, FRAME_HEIGHT);
    addWindowListener(new WindowDestroyer());
    setTitle("Sad Madeleine");
    Container contentPane = getContentPane();
    contentPane.setLayout(new BorderLayout());
    contentPane.setBackground(Color.white);

    JButton smileButton = new JButton("Click for a Smile.");
    smileButton.addActionListener(this);
    contentPane.add(smileButton, BorderLayout.SOUTH);
}

public void actionPerformed(ActionEvent e)
{
    if (e.getActionCommand().equals("Click for a Smile."))
        smile = true;
    else
        System.out.println("Error in button interface.");
    repaint();
}

public void paint(Graphics g)
{
    super.paint(g);
    if (smile)
    {
        xFace = X_HAPPY_FACE;
        yFace = Y_HAPPY_FACE;
    }
    else
    {
        xFace = X_SAD_FACE;
        yFace = Y_SAD_FACE;
    }
```

Display 15.8 An Action Drawing *(Part 3 of 4)*

```java
            xNose = xFace + 95;
            yNose = yFace + 95;
            xLeftEye = xFace + 55;
            yLeftEye = yFace + 45;
            xRightEye = xFace + 130;
            yRightEye = yFace + 45;
            x1LeftBrow = xFace + 55;
            y1LeftBrow = yFace + 38;
            x2LeftBrow = x1LeftBrow + 20;
            y2LeftBrow = y1LeftBrow + 2;
            x1RightBrow = xFace + 130;
            y1RightBrow = y2LeftBrow;
            x2RightBrow = x1RightBrow + 20;
            y2RightBrow = y1LeftBrow;
            xMouth = xFace + 50;
            yMouth = yFace + 125;

            g.drawOval(xFace, yFace, FACE_DIAMETER, FACE_DIAMETER);
            //Draw Nose:
            g.fillOval(xNose, yNose, NOSE_DIAMETER, NOSE_DIAMETER);
            //Draw Eyes:
            g.fillOval(xLeftEye, yLeftEye, EYE_WIDTH, EYE_HEIGHT);
            g.fillOval(xRightEye, yRightEye, EYE_WIDTH, EYE_HEIGHT);
            //Draw eyebrows:
            g.drawLine(x1LeftBrow, y1LeftBrow,
                        x2LeftBrow, y2LeftBrow);
            g.drawLine(x1RightBrow, y1RightBrow,
                        x2RightBrow, y2RightBrow);
            //Draw Mouth:
            if (smile)
                g.drawArc(xMouth, yMouth, MOUTH_WIDTH, MOUTH_HEIGHT,
                        MOUTH_START_ANGLE, MOUTH_ARC_SWEEP);
            else //Note minus sign:
                g.drawArc(xMouth, yMouth, MOUTH_WIDTH, MOUTH_HEIGHT,
                        MOUTH_START_ANGLE, -MOUTH_ARC_SWEEP);

        }
    }
```

Display 15.8   An Action Drawing *(Part 4 of 4)*

Resulting GUI (when program starts)

Resulting GUI (after clicking button)

If `smile` has the value *true*, then the first version of `g.drawArc` is executed. This first version of `g.drawArc` is exactly the same as the one in Display 15.2/page 954, which we know draws a smile. On the other hand, if the variable `smile` has the value *false*, the second version of `g.drawArc` is executed. This second version of `g.drawArc` is the same as the first version, except that there is a minus sign in front of `MOUTH_ARC_SWEEP`. That means that the line of the smile goes clockwise instead of counterclockwise. So it draws:

MOUTH_START_ANGLE

instead of:

MOUTH_START_ANGLE

`repaint` and `paint`

repaint

The method `repaint` is used for repainting the screen. It takes care of some overhead details and calls the method `paint`. If the method `paint` is defined correctly, then the method `repaint` will work correctly. Note that you need only define the `paint`; you do *not* normally define `repaint`. Normally, you define `paint` but do *not* call `paint`. On the other hand, normally you do *not* define `repaint`, but you do sometimes call `repaint`.

Although this may seem strange at first, it makes perfectly good sense. The duties of `repaint` almost never change. The method `repaint` does a few standard things and calls the method `paint`. So you normally do not need to redefine `repaint`. The duties of the `paint` method depend on what you want the window to look like. So you often do need to define `paint`.

The `repaint` and `paint` Methods

When you change the graphics contents in a window and want to update the window so that the new contents show on the screen, do not call `paint`; call `repaint`. The `repaint` method takes care of some overhead and then calls the `paint` method. Normally, you do not define `repaint`. As long as you define the `paint` method correctly, the `repaint` method should work correctly. Note that you often define `paint`, but you normally do not call `paint`. On the other hand, normally, you do not define `repaint`, but you do sometimes call `repaint`.

15.2 | Colors

> *One ordinary picture is worth a thousand words,
> and one colored picture is worth a million.*
>
> **Variation on a Chinese proverb**

You can specify the color for each figure you draw with the graphics methods and you can define your own colors using the class `Color`.

Specifying a Drawing Color

setColor

extra code
on CD

When drawing shapes with methods such as `drawRect` inside of the definition of the `paint` method, you can think of your drawing as being done with a pen that can change colors. The method `setColor` will change the color of your pen.

For example, consider the happy face that is drawn by the GUI in Display 15.2/ page 954. If you change the definition of the `paint` method to the version shown in Display 15.9, then the eyes will be blue and the mouth will be red. (The file `MadeleineColor.java` on the accompanying CD contains a version of the changed program. It consists of the program in Display 15.9/page 971 with the definition of the `paint` replaced by the one in Display 15.2 and with the class name changed from `Madeleine` to `MadeleineColor`.)

The `setColor` Method

When you are doing drawings with an object of the class `Graphics`, you can set the color of the drawing with an invocation of `setColor`. The color specified can later be changed with another invocation of `setColor`, so a single drawing can have multiple colors.

Syntax:

    Graphics_Object.setColor(Color_Object);

Example:

    g.setColor(Color.blue);

Defining Colors

RGB color
system

Display 12.7/page 778 lists the predefined colors in the class `Color`. If that table does not have the colors you want, you can use the class `Color` to define your own colors. To understand how this is done, you need to first know a few basic facts about colors. By mixing red, green, and blue light in varying amounts, the human eye can be given the sensation of seeing any color the eye is capable of seeing. This is what an ordinary television set does to produce all the colors it displays. The television mixes red, green, and blue light and shines these lights on the screen in differing amounts. This is often called the **RGB color system**, for obvious reasons. Since a computer monitor is basically the same thing as a television set, colors for computer monitors can be

Display 15.9 Adding Color

```
public void paint(Graphics g)
{
    super.paint(g);
    //Default is equivalent to: g.setColor(Color.black);
    g.drawOval(X_FACE, Y_FACE, FACE_DIAMETER, FACE_DIAMETER);
    //Draw Nose:
    g.fillOval(X_NOSE, Y_NOSE, NOSE_DIAMETER, NOSE_DIAMETER);
    //Draw Eyes:
    g.setColor(Color.blue);
    g.fillOval(X_LEFT_EYE, Y_LEFT_EYE, EYE_WIDTH, EYE_HEIGHT);
    g.fillOval(X_RIGHT_EYE, Y_RIGHT_EYE, EYE_WIDTH, EYE_HEIGHT);
    //Draw eyebrows:
    g.setColor(Color.black);
    g.drawLine(X1_LEFT_BROW, Y1_LEFT_BROW,
               X2_LEFT_BROW, Y2_LEFT_BROW);
    g.drawLine(X1_RIGHT_BROW, Y1_RIGHT_BROW,
               X2_RIGHT_BROW, Y2_RIGHT_BROW);
    //Draw Mouth:
    g.setColor(Color.red);
    g.drawArc(X_MOUTH, Y_MOUTH, MOUTH_WIDTH, MOUTH_HEIGHT,
              MOUTH_START_ANGLE, MOUTH_ARC_SWEEP);
}
```

If you replace the method paint in Display 15.2/page 954, with this version of paint, then the face will have blue eyes and red lips.

produced in the same way. The Java `Color` class mixes amounts of red, green, and blue to produce any new color you might want.

Color constructors

When specifying the amount of each of the colors red, green, and blue, you can either use integers in the range 0 to 255 (inclusive), or *float* values in the range 0.0 to 1.0 (inclusive). For example, brown is formed by mixing red and green. So the following defines a color called `brown` that will look like a light shade of brown:

```
Color brown = new Color(204, 102, 0);
```

This color `brown` will have a 204.0/255 fraction of the maximum amount of red possible, a 102.0/255 fraction of the maximum amount of green possible, and no blue. If you want to use fractions to express the color, you can. The following is an equivalent way of defining the same color `brown`:

```
Color brown =
new Color((float)(204.0/255), (float)(102.0/255), (float)0.0);
```

You need the type casts (*float*) because the constructors for the class `Color` only accepts *int*s or *float*s as arguments, and numbers like 204.0/255 and 0.0 are considered to be of type *double*, not of type *float*.

(In a final version of your code, the expression (*float*)(204.0/255) and similar constant expressions should be replaced by defined constants. At this point we are just learning and trying out some details.)

Some constructors for the class `Color` and some of the commonly used methods for the class `Color` are summarized in Display 15.10.

Why Have Exactly 255 Shades of Red?

You should not be surprised to find that the amount of red in a RGB color is specified as a *float* number between 0.0 and 1.0 (and the same for green and blue). But, when specifying the amount of red (or green or blue) as an integer you use an integer between 0 and 255. What is special about 255? The answer is that 256 is a power of 2 (specifically 2^8), and computers work more efficiently with powers of 2. But, then why stop at 255, instead of 256? Because we start at 0. There are 256 numbers in the range 0 to 255. (So counting the case of no red at all, there are actually 256 shades of red, not 255 shades, in the Java RGB color system.)

RGB Colors

The class `Color` uses the RGB method of creating colors. That means that every color is a combination of the three colors red, green, and blue.

■ Gotcha

Using *double*s to Define a Color

Suppose you want to make a color that is made of half the possible amount of red, half the possible amount of blue, and no green. The following seems reasonable:

```
Color purple = new Color(0.5, 0.0, 0.5);
```

This will however produce a compiler error. The numbers 0.5 and 0.0 are considered to be of type *double*, and this construct requires arguments of type *float* (or of type *int*). So, an explicit type cast is required, as follows:

```
Color purple = new Color((float)0.5, (float)0.0, (float)0.5);
```

Java does allow the following method of specifying that a number is of type *float*, and this can be simpler than the previous line of code:

```
Color purple = new Color(0.5f, 0.0f, 0.5f);
```

An even easier way to avoid these problems is to simply use *int* arguments, as in the following:

```
Color purple = new Color(127, 0, 127);
```

Display 15.10 Some Methods in The Class Color
••

Method	Description
public Color(int r, int g, int b)	Constructor that creates a new Color with the specified RGB values. The parameters r, g, and b must each be in the range 0 to 255 (inclusive).
public Color(float r, float g, float b)	Constructor that creates a new Color with the specified RGB values. The parameters r, g, and b must each be in the range 0.0 to 1.0 (inclusive).
public int getRed()	Returns the red component of the calling object. The returned value is in the range 0 to 255 (inclusive).
public int getGreen()	Returns the green component of the calling object. The returned value is in the range 0 to 255 (inclusive).
public int getBlue()	Returns the blue component of the calling object. The returned value is in the range 0 to 255 (inclusive).
public Color brighter()	Returns a brighter version of the calling object.
public Color darker()	Returns a darker version of the calling object.
public boolean equals(Object c)	Returns *true* if c is equal to the calling object; otherwise, returns *false*.

(You may feel that the values of 127 should be replaced by 128, but that is a minor point. You are not likely to even notice the difference in color between say 127 red and 128 red.)

In any final code produced, these numbers should normally be replaced by defined constants, such as

```
public static final float redValue = (float)0.5;
public static final float greenValue = (float)0.0;
public static final float blueValue = (float)0.5;
```

Note that even though the defined constant are specified to be of type *float*, you still need a type cast.

Display 15.11 Color Changes *(Part 1 of 2)*

```java
import javax.swing.*;
import java.awt.*;
import java.awt.event.*;

public class ColorChangeDemo extends JFrame implements ActionListener
{
    public static final int WIDTH = 400;
    public static final int HEIGHT = 200;

    private JPanel colorPanel;
    private Color panelColor;
    private int redValue = 0;
    private int greenValue = 0;
    private int blueValue = 0;

    public static void main(String[] args)
    {
        ColorChangeDemo gui = new ColorChangeDemo();
        gui.setVisible(true);
    }

    public ColorChangeDemo()
    {
        Container contentPane = getContentPane();
        contentPane.setLayout(new BorderLayout());
        setTitle("Color Change Demo");
        setSize(WIDTH, HEIGHT);
        addWindowListener(new WindowDestroyer());

        colorPanel = new JPanel();
        panelColor = new Color(0, 0, 0);
        colorPanel.setBackground(panelColor);
        contentPane.add(colorPanel, BorderLayout.CENTER);

        JPanel buttonPanel = new JPanel();
        buttonPanel.setBackground(Color.white);
        buttonPanel.setLayout(new FlowLayout());

        JButton redButton = new JButton("More Red");
        redButton.setBackground(Color.red);
        redButton.addActionListener(this);
        buttonPanel.add(redButton);
        JButton greenButton = new JButton("More Green");
        greenButton.setBackground(Color.green);
        greenButton.addActionListener(this);
        buttonPanel.add(greenButton);
```

Display 15.11 Color Changes *(Part 2 of 2)*

```
        JButton blueButton = new JButton("More Blue");
        blueButton.setBackground(Color.blue);
        blueButton.addActionListener(this);
        buttonPanel.add(blueButton);
        contentPane.add(buttonPanel, BorderLayout.SOUTH);
    }

    public void actionPerformed(ActionEvent e)
    {
        String actionCommand = e.getActionCommand();

        if (actionCommand.equals("More Red"))
        {
            if (redValue <= 250)
                redValue = redValue + 5;
        }
        else if (actionCommand.equals("More Green"))
        {
            if (greenValue <= 250)
                greenValue = greenValue + 5;
        }
        else if (actionCommand.equals("More Blue"))
        {
            if (blueValue <= 250)
                blueValue = blueValue + 5;
        }
        else
            System.out.println("Unexplained Error");

        panelColor = new Color(redValue, greenValue, blueValue);
        colorPanel.setBackground(panelColor);
    }
}
```

You need to run this program to see how it mixes colors.

Resulting GUI

Dynamically Changing Colors

Colors need not be static. Your GUI can change colors while it is running. In fact, we had examples of this in Chapter 12 (Display 12.13/page 804). With the Color class you can even make fine changes in color after a GUI is running. An example is given in Display 15.11/page 974.

Black and White in RGB

You might be interested to know what RGB values the colors black and white have. You may (or may not) be surprised to find out that black is no red, no green, and no blue, while white is maximum red, maximum green, and maximum blue. If you do not believe this, test it by running and playing with the program in Display 15.11/page 974. The reason that black and white are defined this way in the RGB system is because the RGB system is used for mixing light, not for mixing paint. Black is no light. White is all possible colors of light. If you were mixing paints, the results would be approximately the other way around. Mixing red, green, and blue paint will produce (more or less) black paint.

The JColorChooser Dialog

The program in Display 15.11 is a good exercise, but there is a predefined Java tool that will allow you the programmer, or even the user, to choose a color as easily as you choose a color in a paint store. The JColorChooser dialog window allows you to choose a color by looking at color samples or by choosing RGB values.

The static method showDialog in the class JColorChooser produces a window that allows the user to choose a color. A sample program using this method is given in Display 15.12. The statement that launches the JColorChooser dialog window is the following:

```
changingColor = JColorChooser.showDialog(
                this, "JColorChooser", changingColor);
```

When this statement is executed, the window shown in the second GUI picture in Display 15.12 is displayed for the user to choose a color. Once the user has chosen a color and clicked the OK button, the window goes away, and the chosen color is returned as the value of the JColorChooser.showDialog method invocation. So, in this example, the Color object returned is assigned to the variable changingColor. If the user clicks the Cancel button, then the method invocation returns *null* rather than a color.

The method JColorChooser.showDialog takes three arguments. The first argument is the parent component, which is the component from which it was launched. In most simple cases it is likely to be *this*, as in this example. The second argument is a title for the color chooser window. The third argument is the initial color for the color chooser window. The window shows the user samples of what the that color she or he chooses will look like. The user can chose many colors, and each will be displayed in turn, until the user clicks the OK button. The color displayed when the color chooser window first appears is that third argument.

The color chooser window has three tabs at the top labeled Swatches, HSB, and RGB. This gives the user three different ways to choose colors. If the Swatches tab is

Display 15.12 JColorChooser **Dialog** *(Part 1 of 2)*

```java
import javax.swing.*;
import java.awt.*;
import java.awt.event.*;

public class JColorChooserDemo extends JFrame
                                    implements ActionListener
{
    public static final int WIDTH = 400;
    public static final int HEIGHT = 200;

    private Container contentPane;
    private Color changingColor = Color.lightGray;

    public static void main(String[] args)
    {
        JColorChooserDemo gui = new JColorChooserDemo();
        gui.setVisible(true);
    }

    public JColorChooserDemo()
    {
        contentPane = getContentPane();
        contentPane.setBackground(changingColor);
        contentPane.setLayout(new BorderLayout());
        setTitle("JColorChooser Demo");
        setSize(WIDTH, HEIGHT);
        addWindowListener(new WindowDestroyer());

        JPanel buttonPanel = new JPanel();
        buttonPanel.setBackground(Color.white);
        buttonPanel.setLayout(new FlowLayout());
        JButton changeButton = new JButton("Choose a Color");
        changeButton.addActionListener(this);
        buttonPanel.add(changeButton);
        contentPane.add(buttonPanel, BorderLayout.SOUTH);
    }
```

Display 15.12 JColorChooser **Dialog** *(Part 2 of 2)*

```
public void actionPerformed(ActionEvent e)
{
    if (e.getActionCommand().equals("Choose a Color"))
    {
        changingColor = JColorChooser.showDialog(
                          this, "JColorChooser", changingColor);
        if (changingColor != null)//If a color was chosen
            contentPane.setBackground(changingColor);
    }
    else
        System.out.println("Unexplained Error");
}
}
```

You need to run this program to see how it makes colors.

Resulting GUI (Three views of one GUI.)

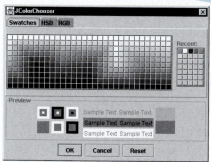

Start view. This first window does not go away until the program ends, but it will probably be covered by other windows at times.

After clicking Choose a Color.

After clicking the RGB tab.

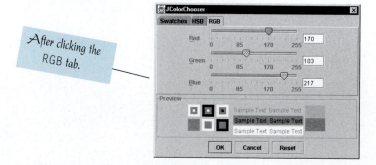

clicked, the window displays color samples for the user to choose from. This is the way the window first comes up. So, if the user clicks no tab, it is the same as clicking the `Swatches` tab. The `RGB` tab allows the user to chose a color by specifying the red, green, and blue values. The `HSB` tab gives the user a chance to choose colors in a way we will not discuss. (Hey, two out of three is not bad.)

The class `JColorChooser` is in the Swing package (library) and so requires the following import statement:

```
import javax.swing.*;
```

Locating the Color Tools

The class `Color` is in the AWT package (library). The method `setColor` is in the class `Graphics` and the class `Graphics` is in the AWT package. So, when using these color tools, you need the following import statement:

```
import java.awt.*;
```

The class `JColorChooser` is in the Swing package. So when using a `JColorChooser` dialog, you need the following import statement:

```
import javax.swing.*;
```

? Self-Test Questions

7. Suppose you want to change the happy face in Display 15.2/page 954 so that it not only has blue eyes and a red mouth, but also has pink skin. How would you change the method `paint`?

8. Suppose you want to change the happy face in Display 15.2/page 954 so that it not only has blue eyes and a red mouth, but also has brown skin. How would you change the method `paint`?

15.3 | Fonts and Other Text Details

> *He who first shortened the labor of copyists by device of movable types was disbanding hired armies, and cashiering most kings and senates, and creating a whole new democratic world: he had invented the art of printing.*
>
> **Thomas Carlyle, Sartor Resartus**

Java has facilities to add text to drawings and to modify the font of the text. **A font** is simply a style of text. Designers have created an almost unlimited collection of fonts. Java guarantees that you will have a few available for your Java programs, and your particular system is almost certain to make more fonts available to you. We will show you enough to allow you to do most things you might want to do with text and fonts, but this will not be a complete introduction to font management. Keep in mind

font

that there are entire books written on fonts, and so this will serve as only an introduction to the topic.

The drawString Method

The program in Display 15.13 is an example of using the method drawString. The GUI starts out displaying the string "Push a button!". When the user clicks a button, the string is changed to either "How are you." or "It was good talking with you.", whichever is appropriate. The strings are written with the method drawString.

The method drawString is similar to the other methods in the class Graphics, but it displays a string of text rather than a drawing. The following line writes the string stored in the variable theText starting at the *x* and *y* coordinates X_START and Y_START:

```
g.drawString(theText, X_START, Y_START);
```

The string is written in the current font. If no font is specified, a default font is used. In the program in Display 15.13 a font is specified. The details are discussed in the next subsection.

Fonts

The way that a program sets the font for the method drawString is illustrated by the program in Display 15.13. That program sets the font for the method drawString with the following two lines in the definition of the method paint:

```
Font f =
     new Font("Serif", Font.BOLD|Font.ITALIC, POINT_SIZE);
g.setFont(f);
```

The constructor for the class Font creates a font in a given style and size. The first argument, in this case "Serif", is a string that gives the name of the font. Some typical font names are "Times", "Courier", and "Helvetica". You may use any font currently available on your system, but Java guarantees that you will have at least the three fonts "Monospaced", "SansSerif", and "Serif". To see what these fonts look like on your system, run the program FontSampler.java on the accompanying CD. It will produce the window shown in Display 15.14.

extra code on CD

Fonts can be expressed in different style modifications and sizes. The second and third arguments to the constructor Font specify the style modifications and size for the font, as in the following from the previous three lines of code:

```
new Font("Serif", Font.BOLD|Font.ITALIC, POINT_SIZE);
```

The second argument specifies style modifications. Note that you can specify multiple style modifications by connecting them with the symbol | as in

Display 15.14 Result of Running `FontSampler.java`

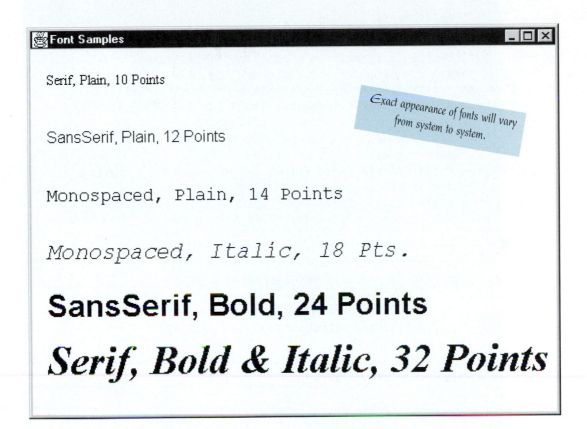

Font.BOLD|Font.ITALIC.[1] The last argument specifies the size of the letters in the version of the font created.

Letter sizes are specified in units known as *points*, and so the size of the letters is called a **point size**. One **point** is 1/72 of an inch, but measurements of font sizes are not as precise as might be ideal; two different fonts of the same point size may be slightly different in size.

---

1. The symbol | is sometimes called the "pipe symbol." In this case it produces a "bitwise or of the numbers", but that detail need not concern you. You need not even know what is meant by a "bitwise or of the numbers." Just think of | as a special way to connect style specifications.

```java
import javax.swing.*;
import java.awt.*;
import java.awt.event.*;

/***********************************************************
 *Simple demonstration of using drawString to display text.
 ***********************************************************/
public class DrawStringDemo extends JFrame
                                    implements ActionListener
{
    public static final int WIDTH = 350;
    public static final int HEIGHT = 200;
    public static final int X_START = 20;
    public static final int Y_START = 100;
    public static final int POINT_SIZE = 24;

    private String theText = "Push a button!";

    public static void main(String[] args)
    {
        DrawStringDemo w = new DrawStringDemo();
        w.setVisible(true);
    }

    public DrawStringDemo()
    {
        setSize(WIDTH, HEIGHT);
        Container contentPane = getContentPane();

        addWindowListener(new WindowDestroyer());
        setTitle("drawString Demonstration");
        contentPane.setBackground(Color.white);
        contentPane.setLayout(new BorderLayout());

        JPanel buttonPanel = new JPanel();
        Button helloButton = new Button("Hello");
        helloButton.addActionListener(this);
        buttonPanel.add(helloButton);
        Button byeButton = new Button("Goodbye");
        byeButton.addActionListener(this);
        buttonPanel.add(byeButton);
        contentPane.add(buttonPanel, BorderLayout.SOUTH);
    }
```

The method setFont sets the font for the Graphics object, which is named g in the case under discussion. The font remains in effect until it is changed. If you do not specify any font, then a default font will be used.

There is no way to change the properties of the current font, such as making it italic. Every change in a font requires that you define a new Font object and use it as an argument to setFont.

Some useful details of the class Font are summarized in Display 15.15.

The drawString Method

The drawString method writes the *String_Of_Text* at the point (*X_Coordinate*, *Y_Coordinate*) of the *Graphics_Object*. The *String_Of_Text* is written in the current font and color and in the current font size.

Syntax:

Graphics_Object.drawString(*String_Of_Text*, *X_Coordinate*, *Y_Coordinate*);

Example:

g.drawString("Surf's Up", X_START, Y_START);

What Does "Serif" Mean?

Serifs are those small lines that sometimes finish off the ends of the lines in letters. For example, S has serifs (at the two ends of the curved line), but S does not have serifs. So, the "Serif" font will always have these decorative little lines. *Sans* means without. So the "SansSerif" font will not have these decorative little lines.

? Self-Test Questions

9. Give code to write the string "Hello Mom!" at position (20, 30) using the method drawString. The object of type Graphics is named g.

10. Give code to write the string "Hello Mom!" two times, at positions (20, 30) and (20, 100), using the method drawString. The first time it is written in Serif bold and the second time in SansSerif italic. The object of type Graphics is named g.

11. Give code to write the string "R2D2 Reporting!" at positions (50, 30) using the method drawString. The string is written in Monospaced bold and italic. The point size is 18. The object of type Graphics is named gObject.

Display 15.15 Some Details About The Class Font

Method or Constant in the Class Font	Description
`public Font(String fontName, int style, int size)`	Constructor that creates a version of the font named by `fontName` in the specified `style` and `size`.
`Font.BOLD`	Specifies bold style.
`Font.ITALIC`	Specifies italic style.
`Font.PLAIN`	Specifies plain style—that is, not bold and not italic.
`public abstract void setFont(Font f)` (This method is in the class `Graphics`.)	Sets the current font to `f`.

Names of Fonts. (These three are guaranteed by Java. Your system will probably have others as well as these.)

Font Name	Sample (Appearance may vary some from system to system.)
`"Monospaced"`	Monospaced
`"SansSerif"`	SansSerif
`"Serif"`	Serif

CHAPTER SUMMARY

- You can draw figures such as lines, ovals, and rectangles using methods in the class `Graphics`.

- You can specify the color of each figure drawn using the method `setColor`.

- You can define your own colors using the class `Color`.

- Colors are defined using the RGB (Red/Green/Blue) system.

- You can add text to a graphics drawing using the `Graphics` method `drawString`.

- You can set the font and point size for a text written with `drawString` by using the `Graphics` method `setFont`.

? ANSWERS to Self-Test Questions

1. `g.drawLine(20, 30, 120, 30);`
   The following will also work:
   `g.drawLine(120, 30, 20, 30);`
2. `graphicsObject.drawLine(20, 30, 20, 130);`
   The following will also work
   `graphicsObject.drawLine(20, 130, 20, 30);`
3. `g.fillRect(20, 30, 100, 75);`
4. `g.fillRect(100, 300, 100, 75);`
5. `g.drawOval(250, 350, 100, 100);`
6. `g.drawOval(200, 300, 200, 200);`
7. The code that is added to the version of paint in Display 15.9/page 971 is shown in color.

Display 15.13 Using `drawString` *(Part 2 of 2)*

```
    public void paint(Graphics g)
    {
        super.paint(g);
        Font f =
            new Font("Serif", Font.BOLD|Font.ITALIC, POINT_SIZE);
        g.setFont(f);
        g.drawString(theText, X_START, Y_START);
    }

    public void actionPerformed(ActionEvent e)
    {
        if (e.getActionCommand().equals("Hello"))
            theText = "How are you.";
        else if (e.getActionCommand().equals("Goodbye"))
            theText = "It was good talking with you.";
        else
            theText = "Error in button interface.";

        repaint();
    }
}
```

Resulting GUI (Three views of one GUI.)

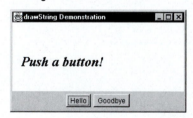

Start view.

After clicking
`Hello`.

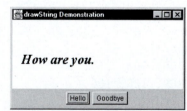

After clicking
`Goodbye`.

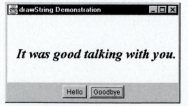

```
public void paint(Graphics g)
{
    super.paint(g);
    g.setColor(Color.pink);
    g.fillOval(X_FACE, Y_FACE, FACE_DIAMETER, FACE_DIAMETER);
    g.setColor(Color.black);
    g.drawOval(X_FACE, Y_FACE, FACE_DIAMETER, FACE_DIAMETER);
    //Draw Nose:
    g.fillOval(X_NOSE, Y_NOSE, NOSE_DIAMETER, NOSE_DIAMETER);
    //Draw Eyes:
    g.setColor(Color.blue);
    g.fillOval(X_LEFT_EYE, Y_LEFT_EYE, EYE_WIDTH, EYE_HEIGHT);
    g.fillOval(X_RIGHT_EYE, Y_RIGHT_EYE, EYE_WIDTH, EYE_HEIGHT);
    //Draw eyebrows:
    g.setColor(Color.black);
    g.drawLine(X1_LEFT_BROW, Y1_LEFT_BROW,
            X2_LEFT_BROW, Y2_LEFT_BROW);
    g.drawLine(X1_RIGHT_BROW, Y1_RIGHT_BROW,
            X2_RIGHT_BROW, Y2_RIGHT_BROW);
    //Draw Mouth:
    g.setColor(Color.red);
    g.drawArc(X_MOUTH, Y_MOUTH, MOUTH_WIDTH, MOUTH_HEIGHT,
            MOUTH_START_ANGLE, MOUTH_ARC_SWEEP);

}
```

8. You cannot simply replace the following (in the answer to Self-Test Question 7):

```
g.setColor(Color.pink);
```

with

```
g.setColor(Color.brown);
```

because there is no predefined `Color` constant for `brown`. This will give a compiler error. You must define the color `brown` yourself.

You can get a brown face by replacing

```
g.setColor(Color.pink);
```

with

```
Color brown =
        new Color(204, 102, 0);
g.setColor(brown);
```

Note that you use an ordinary identifier, like `brown`, not something like `Color.brown` when naming a defined color. You may prefer some other arguments instead of `(204, 102, 0)` so that you get a different shade of brown that is more to your liking. You might use the class `JColor-Chooser` to find the values you want.

9. `g.drawString("Hello Mom!", 20, 30);`

10.

```
Font f = new Font("Serif", Font.BOLD, 24);
g.setFont(f);
g.drawString("Hello Mom!", 20, 30);

Font f = new Font("SansSerif", Font.ITALIC, 24);
g.setFont(f);
g.drawString("Hello Mom!", 20, 100);
```

The following is also correct:

```
g.setFont(new Font("Serif", Font.BOLD, 24));
g.drawString("Hello Mom!", 20, 30);

g.setFont(new Font("SansSerif", Font.ITALIC, 24));
g.drawString("Hello Mom!", 20, 100);
```

You can use any font size. The font size need not be 24 as shown in these answers.

11.

```
Font f = new Font("MonoSpaced", Font.BOLD|Font.ITALIC,
18);
gObject.setFont(f);
gObject.drawString("R2D2 Reporting!", 50, 30);
```

The following is also correct:

```
gObject.setFont(
        new Font("MonoSpaced", Font.BOLD|Font.ITALIC, 18));
gObject.drawString("R2D2 Reporting!", 50, 30);
```

? PROGRAMMING EXERCISES

1. Modify SadMadeleine (Display 15.8/page 965) to MakeMadeleineMad that starts with her happy face and has a button labeled "Make me mad!" that changes her color to red and smile to a frown.

2. Use simple graphics objects such as triangles, lines, circles, ovals, etc. to draw a cat's face with whiskers, eyes, nose, mouth, and ears, similar to that shown below. Make the face black, the nose pink, and the eyes yellow. Display the face in a JFrame.

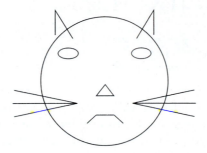

3. Create a GUI for drawing circles with a menu to select one of three sizes, small, medium or large; another menu to select any of four positions, top, bottom, left, or right; and a third menu to select any of three fill colors (your choice). Make the diameter of the small size = 25, medium = 50, and large = 100 and center the circles approximately in the middle of which-ever location is chosen. The user will use be given menus to choose the circle parameters. The circle will be displayed in the content pane of the JFrame. Include a Clear option to erase the current circle. The user can then choose another circle.

4. Redo Programming Exercise 3 except that this time you will use JColor-Chooser to let the user select a color.

5. Redo Programming Exercise 4 except that this time there are three pan-els each of which can contain a circle choice as discussed in Exercise 3. Note that your menu choices must be expanded so the user can choose a panel for the user's circle choice and so that the user can choose to clear either all three panels or any one specified panel.

6. Write a program with a GUI interface that asks user to enter a sentence then echo the sentence, but puts each word on a separate line and increase the font size for each word, starting with 8-point font and incre-menting by 2 points each line.

7. Write a program to demonstrate the three fonts and three styles listed in Display 15.15/page 984. Ask the user to enter a line of text, then each time a Next button is clicked the style or font changes until all combinations have been shown. Start with plain Monospaced, then change it to bold, then italics. Another click on Next will change the font to plain SansSerif, then bold SansSerif, etc., with the last one being Italic Serif. Include a message that states which style and font is used each time.

Appendix 1
RESERVED WORDS

Reserved words are also called *keywords*. You may not redefine any of these reserved words. Their meanings are determined by the Java language and cannot be changed. In particular, you cannot use any of these reserved words for variable names, method names, or class names.

abstract	generic	rest
	goto	return
boolean		
break	if	short
byte	implements	static
	import	super
case	inner	switch
catch	instanceof	synchronized
char	int	
class	interface	this
const		throw
continue	long	throws
		transient
default	native	try
do	new	
double	null	var
		void
else	operator	volatile
extends	outer	
		while
final	package	
finally	private	
float	protected	
for	public	
future		

Appendix 2
PRECEDENCE RULES

Operators on the same line are of equal precedence. As you move down the list, each line is of lower precedence. When the computer is deciding which of two operators to perform first and the order is not dictated by parentheses, then it does the operator of higher precedence before the operator of lower precedence. Some operators have equal precedence, and then the order of operations is determined by the left-to-right order of the operators. Binary operators of equal precedence are performed in left-to-right order. Unary operators of equal precedence are performed in right-to-left order.

Highest Precedence

The unary operators: +, −, ++, − −, !, and type casts (*Type*)

The binary operators: *, /, %

The binary operators: +, −

The binary operators (shift operators)[1] <<, >> , >>>>

The binary operators: <, >, <=, >=

The binary operators: ==, !=

The binary operator &

The unary operator (xor)[1] ^

The binary operator |

The binary operator &&

The binary operator ||

The ternary operator (conditional operator) ? :

Assignment operators =, *=, /=, %=, +=, −=, <<=, >>=, >>>>=, &=, ^=, |=

Lowest Precedence

---

1. Not discussed in this book.

Appendix 3
UNICODE CHARACTER SET

Character number 32 is the blank. Only the printable characters are shown in the table. (The characters shown are a subset of the Unicode character set known as the ASCII character set. The numbering is the same whether the characters are considered to be members of the Unicode character set or members of the ASCII character set.)

32		56	8	80	P	104	h
33	!	57	9	81	Q	105	i
34	"	58	:	82	R	106	j
35	#	59	;	83	S	107	k
36	$	60	<	84	T	108	l
37	%	61	=	85	U	109	m
38	&	62	>	86	V	110	n
39	'	63	?	87	W	111	o
40	(	64	@	88	X	112	p
41	)	65	A	89	Y	113	q
42	*	66	B	90	Z	114	r
43	+	67	C	91	[	115	s
44	,	68	D	92	\	116	t
45	–	69	E	93	]	117	u
46	.	70	F	94	^	118	v
47	/	71	G	95	_	119	w
48	0	72	H	96	`	120	x
49	1	73	I	97	a	121	y
50	2	74	J	98	b	122	z
51	3	75	K	99	c	123	{
52	4	76	L	100	d	124	|
53	5	77	M	101	e	125	}
54	6	78	N	102	f	126	~
55	7	79	O	103	g		

Appendix 4
SAVITCHIN

```java
import java.io.*;
import java.util.*;

/***********************************************************
 *Class for simple console input.
 *A class designed primarily for simple keyboard input of the form
 *one input value per line. If the user enters an improper input,
 *i.e., an input of the wrong type or a blank line, then the user
 *is prompted to reenter the input and given a brief explanation
 *of what is required. Also includes some additional methods to
 *input single numbers, words, and characters, without going to
 *the next line.
 ***********************************************************/
public class SavitchIn
{

    /***********************************************************
     *Reads a line of text and returns that line as a String value.
     *The end of a line must be indicated either by a new-line
     *character '\n' or by a carriage return '\r' followed by a
     *new-line character '\n'. (Almost all systems do this
     *automatically. So, you need not worry about this detail.)
     *Neither the '\n', nor the '\r' if present, are part of the
     *string returned. This will read the rest of a line if the
     *line is already partially read.
     ***********************************************************/
    public static String readLine()
    {
        char nextChar;
        String result = "";
        boolean done = false;

        while (!done)
        {
            nextChar = readChar();
            if (nextChar == '\n')
                done = true;
            else if (nextChar == '\r')
```

```
                {
                    //Do nothing.
                    //Next loop iteration will detect '\n'
                }
            else
                result = result + nextChar;
        }

        return result;
    }


    /*******************************************************
     *Reads the first string of nonwhite characters on a line and
     *returns that string. The rest of the line is discarded. If
     *the line contains only whitespace, then the user is asked
     *to reenter the line.
     *******************************************************/
    public static String readLineWord()
    {
        String inputString = null,
                result = null;
        boolean done = false;

        while(!done)
        {
            inputString = readLine();
            StringTokenizer wordSource =
                                new StringTokenizer(inputString);
            if (wordSource.hasMoreTokens())
            {
                result = wordSource.nextToken();
                done = true;
            }
            else
            {
                System.out.println(
                        "Your input is not correct. Your input must");
                System.out.println(
                    "contain at least one nonwhitespace character.");
                System.out.println(
                                "Please, try again. Enter input:");
            }
        }

        return result;
    }
```

```
/************************************************************
 *Precondition: The user has entered a number of type int on
 *a line by itself, except that there may be whitespace before
 *and/or after the number.
 *Action: Reads and returns the number as a value of type int.
 *The rest of the line is discarded. If the input is not
 *entered correctly, then in most cases, the user will be
 *asked to reenter the input. In particular, this applies to
 *incorrect number formats and blank lines.
 ************************************************************/
public static int readLineInt()
{
    String inputString = null;
    int number = -9999;//To keep the compiler happy.
                       //Designed to look like a garbage value.
    boolean done = false;

    while (! done)
    {
        try
        {
            inputString = readLine();
            inputString = inputString.trim();
            number = Integer.parseInt(inputString);
            done = true;
        }
        catch (NumberFormatException e)
        {
            System.out.println(
                        "Your input number is not correct.");
            System.out.println("Your input number must be");
            System.out.println("a whole number written as an");
            System.out.println("ordinary numeral, such as 42");
            System.out.println("Minus signs are OK,"
                        + "but do not use a plus sign.");
            System.out.println("Please, try again.");
            System.out.println("Enter a whole number:");
        }
    }

    return number;
}
```

```
/************************************************************
 *Precondition: The user has entered a number of type long on
 *a line by itself, except that there may be whitespace
 *before and/or after the number.
 *Action: Reads and returns the number as a value of type
 *long. The rest of the line is discarded. If the input is not
 *entered correctly, then in most cases, the user will be asked
 *to reenter the input. In particular, this applies to
 *incorrect number formats and blank lines.
 ************************************************************/
public static long readLineLong()
{
    String inputString = null;
    long number = -9999;//To keep the compiler happy.
                        //Designed to look like a garbage value.
    boolean done = false;

    while (! done)
    {
        try
        {
            inputString = readLine();
            inputString = inputString.trim();
            number = Long.parseLong(inputString);
            done = true;
        }
        catch (NumberFormatException e)
        {
            System.out.println(
                          "Your input number is not correct.");
            System.out.println("Your input number must be");
            System.out.println("a whole number written as an");
            System.out.println("ordinary numeral, such as 42");
            System.out.println("Minus signs are OK,"
                           + "but do not use a plus sign.");
            System.out.println("Please, try again.");
            System.out.println("Enter a whole number:");
        }
    }

    return number;
}
```

```
/******************************************************
 * Precondition: The user has entered a number of type double
 * on a line by itself, except that there may be whitespace
 * before and/or after the number.
 * Action: Reads and returns the number as a value of type
 * double. The rest of the line is discarded. If the input is
 * not entered correctly, then in most cases, the user will be
 * asked to reenter the input. In particular, this applies to
 * incorrect number formats and blank lines.
 ******************************************************/
public static double readLineDouble()
{
    String inputString = null;
    double number = -9999;//To keep the compiler happy.
                          //Designed to look like a garbage value.
    boolean done = false;

    while (! done)
    {
        try
        {
            inputString = readLine();
            inputString = inputString.trim();
            number = Double.parseDouble(inputString);
            done = true;
        }
        catch (NumberFormatException e)
        {
            System.out.println(
                        "Your input number is not correct.");
            System.out.println("Your input number must be");
            System.out.println("an ordinary number either
            with");
            System.out.println("or without a decimal point,");
            System.out.println("such as 42 or 9.99");
            System.out.println("Please, try again.");
            System.out.println("Enter the number:");
        }
    }

    return number;
}
```

```
/******************************************************
 *Precondition: The user has entered a number of type float
 *on a line by itself, except that there may be whitespace
 *before and/or after the number.
 *Action: Reads and returns the number as a value of type
 *float. The rest of the line is discarded. If the input is
 *not entered correctly, then in most cases, the user will
 *be asked to reenter the input. In particular,
 *this applies to incorrect number formats and blank lines.
 ******************************************************/
public static float readLineFloat()
{
    String inputString = null;
    float number = -9999;//To keep the compiler happy.
                        //Designed to look like a garbage value.
    boolean done = false;

    while (! done)
    {
        try
        {
            inputString = readLine();
            inputString = inputString.trim();
            number = Float.parseFloat(inputString);
            done = true;
        }
        catch (NumberFormatException e)
        {
            System.out.println(
                            "Your input number is not correct.");
            System.out.println("Your input number must be");
            System.out.println("an ordinary number either
            with");
            System.out.println("or without a decimal point,");
            System.out.println("such as 42 or 9.99");
            System.out.println("Please, try again.");
            System.out.println("Enter the number:");
        }
    }

    return number;
}
```

```
/************************************************
 *Reads the first nonwhite character on a line and returns
 *that character. The rest of the line is discarded. If the
 *line contains only whitespace, then the user is asked to
 *reenter the line.
 ************************************************/
public static char readLineNonwhiteChar()
{
    boolean done = false;
    String inputString = null;
    char nonWhite = ' ';//To keep the compiler happy.

    while (! done)
    {
        inputString = readLine();
        inputString = inputString.trim();
        if (inputString.length() == 0)
        {
            System.out.println(
                            "Your input is not correct.");
            System.out.println("Your input must contain at");
            System.out.println(
                        "least one nonwhitespace character.");
            System.out.println("Please, try again.");
            System.out.println("Enter input:");
        }
        else
        {
            nonWhite = (inputString.charAt(0));
            done = true;
        }
    }

    return nonWhite;
}

/************************************************
 *Input should consist of a single word on a line, possibly
 *surrounded by whitespace. The line is read and discarded.
 *If the input word is "true" or "t", then true is returned.
 *If the input word is "false" or "f", then false is returned.
 *Uppercase and lowercase letters are considered equal. If the
 *user enters anything else (e.g., multiple words or different
 *words), then the user is asked to reenter the input.
 ************************************************/
public static boolean readLineBoolean()
```

```
{
    boolean done = false;
    String inputString = null;
    boolean result = false;//To keep the compiler happy.

    while (! done)
    {
        inputString = readLine();
        inputString = inputString.trim();
        if (inputString.equalsIgnoreCase("true")
                || inputString.equalsIgnoreCase("t"))
        {
            result = true;
            done = true;
        }
        else if (inputString.equalsIgnoreCase("false")
                    || inputString.equalsIgnoreCase("f"))
        {
            result = false;
            done = true;
        }
        else
        {
            System.out.println(
                        "Your input number is not correct.");
            System.out.println("Your input must be");
            System.out.println("one of the following:");
            System.out.println("the word true,");
            System.out.println("the word false,");
            System.out.println("the letter T,");
            System.out.println("or the letter F.");
            System.out.println("You may use either upper-");
            System.out.println("or lowercase letters.");
            System.out.println("Please, try again.");
            System.out.println("Enter input:");
        }
    }

    return result;
}

/*****************************************************
 *Reads the next input character and returns that character. The
 *next read takes place on the same line where this one left off.
 *****************************************************/
public static char readChar()
```

```
{
    int charAsInt = -1; //To keep the compiler happy
    try
    {
        charAsInt = System.in.read();
    }
    catch(IOException e)
    {
        System.out.println(e.getMessage());
        System.out.println("Fatal error. Ending Program.");
        System.exit(0);
    }

    return (char)charAsInt;
}


/**************************************************
 *Reads the next nonwhite input character and returns that
 *character. The next read takes place immediately after
 *the character read.
 **************************************************/
public static char readNonwhiteChar()
{
    char next;

    next = readChar();
    while (Character.isWhitespace(next))
        next = readChar();

    return next;
}


/***************************************************
 *The following methods are not used in the text, except for
 *a brief reference in Chapter 2. No program code uses them.
 *However, some programmers may want to use them.
 ***************************************************/
```

```
/*******************************************************
 *Precondition: The next input in the stream consists of an
 *int value, possibly preceded by whitespace, but definitely
 *followed by whitespace.
 *Action: Reads the first string of nonwhite characters
 *and returns the int value it represents. Discards the first
 *whitespace character after the word. The next read takes
 *place immediately after the discarded whitespace.
 *In particular, if the word is at the end of a line, the
 *next reading will take place starting on the next line.
 *If the next word does not represent an int value,
 *a NumberFormatException is thrown.
 *******************************************************/
public static int readInt() throws NumberFormatException
{
    String inputString = null;
    inputString = readWord();
    return Integer.parseInt(inputString);
}


/*******************************************************
 *Precondition: The next input consists of a long value,
 *possibly preceded by whitespace, but definitely
 *followed by whitespace.
 *Action: Reads the first string of nonwhite characters and
 *returns the long value it represents. Discards the first
 *whitespace character after the string read. The next read
 *takes place immediately after the discarded whitespace.
 *In particular, if the string read is at the end of a line,
 *the next reading will take place starting on the next line.
 *If the next word does not represent a long value,
 *a NumberFormatException is thrown.
 *******************************************************/
public static long readLong()
                    throws NumberFormatException
{
    String inputString = null;
    inputString = readWord();
    return Long.parseLong(inputString);
}


/*******************************************************
 *Precondition: The next input consists of a double value,
 *possibly preceded by whitespace, but definitely
 *followed by whitespace.
 *Action: Reads the first string of nonwhitespace characters
```

```
    *and returns the double value it represents. Discards the
    *first whitespace character after the string read. The next
    *read takes place immediately after the discarded whitespace.
    *In particular, if the string read is at the end of a line,
    *the next reading will take place starting on the next line.
    *If the next word does not represent a double value,
    *a NumberFormatException is thrown.
    *************************************************************/
public static double readDouble()
                    throws NumberFormatException
{
    String inputString = null;
    inputString = readWord();
    return Double.parseDouble(inputString);
}


/*************************************************************
  *Precondition: The next input consists of a float value,
  *possibly preceded by whitespace, but definitely
  *followed by whitespace.
  *Action: Reads the first string of nonwhite characters and
  *returns the float value it represents. Discards the first
  *whitespace character after the string read. The next read
  *takes place immediately after the discarded whitespace.
  *In particular, if the string read is at the end of a line,
  *the next reading will take place starting on the next line.
  *If the next word does not represent a float value,
  *a NumberFormatException is thrown.
  *************************************************************/
public static float readFloat() throws NumberFormatException
{
    String inputString = null;
    inputString = readWord();
    return Float.parseFloat(inputString);
}


/*************************************************************
  *Reads the first string of nonwhite characters and returns
  *that string. Discards the first whitespace character after
  *the string read. The next read takes place immediately after
  *the discarded whitespace. In particular, if the string
  *read is at the end of a line, the next reading will take
  *place starting on the next line. Note, that if it receives
  *blank lines, it will wait until it gets a nonwhitespace
  *character.
  *************************************************************/
```

```
public static String readWord()
{
    String result = "";
    char next;

    next = readChar();
    while (Character.isWhitespace(next))
        next = readChar();

    while (!(Character.isWhitespace(next)))
    {
        result = result + next;
        next = readChar();
    }

    if (next == '\r')
    {
        next = readChar();
        if (next != '\n')
        {
            System.out.println(
                "Fatal Error in method readWord of class SavitchIn.");
            System.exit(1);
        }
    }

    return result;
}

/************************************************************
 *Precondition: The user has entered a number of type byte on
 *a line by itself, except that there may be whitespace before
 *and/or after the number.
 *Action: Reads and returns the number as a value of type byte.
 *The rest of the line is discarded. If the input is not
 *entered correctly, then in most cases, the user will be
 *asked to reenter the input. In particular, this applies to
 *incorrect number formats and blank lines.
 ************************************************************/
public static byte readLineByte()
{
    String inputString = null;
    byte number = -123;//To keep the compiler happy.
                        //Designed to look like a garbage value.
    boolean done = false;
```

```
    while (! done)
    {
        try
        {
            inputString = readLine();
            inputString = inputString.trim();
            number = Byte.parseByte(inputString);
            done = true;
        }
        catch (NumberFormatException e)
        {
            System.out.println(
                          "Your input number is not correct.");
            System.out.println("Your input number must be a");
            System.out.println("whole number in the range");
            System.out.println("-128 to 127, written as");
            System.out.println("an ordinary numeral, such as
            42.");
            System.out.println("Minus signs are OK,"
                          + "but do not use a plus sign.");
            System.out.println("Please, try again.");
            System.out.println("Enter a whole number:");
        }
    }

    return number;
}


/**********************************************************
 *Precondition: The user has entered a number of type short on
 *a line by itself, except that there may be whitespace before
 *and/or after the number.
 *Action: Reads and returns the number as a value of type short.
 *The rest of the line is discarded. If the input is not
 *entered correctly, then in most cases, the user will be
 *asked to reenter the input. In particular, this applies to
 *incorrect number formats and blank lines.
 **********************************************************/
public static short readLineShort()
{
    String inputString = null;
    short number = -9999;//To keep the compiler happy.
                    //Designed to look like a garbage value.
    boolean done = false;
```

```
        while (! done)
        {
            try
            {
                inputString = readLine();
                inputString = inputString.trim();
                number = Short.parseShort(inputString);
                done = true;
            }
            catch (NumberFormatException e)
            {
                System.out.println(
                                "Your input number is not correct.");
                System.out.println("Your input number must be a");
                System.out.println("whole number in the range");
                System.out.println("-32768 to 32767, written as");
                System.out.println("an ordinary numeral, such as 42.");
                System.out.println("Minus signs are OK,"
                                + "but do not use a plus sign.");
                System.out.println("Please, try again.");
                System.out.println("Enter a whole number:");
            }
        }

        return number;
    }

    public static byte readByte() throws NumberFormatException
    {
        String inputString = null;
        inputString = readWord();
        return Byte.parseByte(inputString);
    }

    public static short readShort() throws NumberFormatException
    {
        String inputString = null;
        inputString = readWord();
        return Short.parseShort(inputString);
    }


    //The following was intentionally not used in the code for
    //other methods so that somebody reading the code could more
    //quickly see what was being used.
```

```
/***********************************************************
 *Reads the first byte in the input stream and returns that
 *byte as an int. The next read takes place where this one
 *left off. This read is the same as System.in.read(),
 *except that it catches IOExceptions.
 ***********************************************************/
public static int read()
{
    int result = -1; //To keep the compiler happy
    try
    {
        result = System.in.read();
    }
    catch(IOException e)
    {
        System.out.println(e.getMessage());
        System.out.println("Fatal error. Ending Program.");
        System.exit(0);
    }
    return result;
}
}
```

Appendix 5
PROTECTED AND PACKAGE MODIFIERS

We have always used one of the modifiers *public* and *private* before instance variables and before method definitions. Normally, those are the only modifiers you need, but there are two other possibilities that give restrictions whose severity is in between the two extremes of *public* and *private*. In this appendix, we discuss the modifier *protected* as well as the restriction that applies when you use no modifier at all.

If a method or instance variable is modified by *protected* (rather than *public* or *private*), then it can be directly accessed inside of its own class definition, and it can be directly accessed inside of any class derived from it. If an instance variable or method definition is marked *protected*, then not only can it be accessed directly in the definition of any derived class, but it can also be accessed directly in any method definition for any class in the same package. That is the extent of the access. The *protected* method or instance variable cannot be directly accessed in any other classes. Thus, if a method is marked *protected* in class A and class B is derived from class A, then the method can be used inside any method definition in class B. However, in a class that is not in the same package as A and is not derived from A, it is as if the *protected* method were *private*.

The modifier *protected* is a peculiar sort of restriction, since it allows direct access to any programmer who is willing to go through the bother of defining a suitable derived class. Thus, it is like saying, "I'll make it difficult for you to use this, but I will not forbid you to use this." In practice, instance variables should never be marked *protected*. On very rare occasions, you may want to have a method marked *protected*. If you want an access intermediate between *public* and *private*, then the access described in the next paragraph is often a preferable alternative.

You may have noticed that if you forget to place one of the modifiers *public* or *private* before an instance variable or method definition, then your class definition will still compile. If you do not place any of the modifiers *public*, *private*, or *protected* before an instance variable or method definition, then the instance variable or method can be directly accessed inside the definition of any class in the same package, but not outside of the package. This is called **package access**, or **default access.** You use package access in situations where you have a package of cooperating classes that act as a single encapsulated unit. Note that package access is more restricted than *protected*, and that package access gives more control to the programmer defining the classes. If you control the package directory, then you control who is allowed package access.

Appendix 6
DecimalFormat CLASS

An object of the class `DecimalFormat` has a number of different methods that can be used to produce numeral strings in various formats. In this appendix we describe some uses of one of these methods that is named `format`. The general approach to using the `DecimalFormat` class is as follows:

Create an object of the class `DecimalFormat` using a `String` pattern:

Syntax:

    DecimalFormat Variable_Name = DecimalFormat(Pattern);

Example: .

    DecimalFormat formattingObject = new DecimalFormat("000.000");

The method `format` of the class `DecimalFormat` can then be used to convert a number of type *double* to a corresponding numeral `String`.

Syntax:

Decimal_Format_Object. `format` (*Double_Expression*)
produces a numeral string corresponding to the *Double_Expression*.
The *Decimal_Format_Object* is typically a *Variable_Name*.

Examples: .

    System.out.println(formattingObject.format(12.3456789));
    String numeral = formattingObject.format(12.3456789);

Assuming that the object `formattingObject` is created as above, The output produced by the above `println` is:

    012.346

The format of the string produced is determined by the *Pattern* string that was used as the argument to the constructor that created the object of the class `DecimalFormat`.

For example, the pattern `"00.000"` means that there will be two digits before the decimal point and three digits after the decimal point. Note that the result is rounded when the number of digits is less than the number of digits available. If the format pattern is not consistent with the value of the number, such as a pattern that asks for two digits before the decimal point for a number like `123.456`, then extra digits will be added.

When writing patterns, such as `"#0.##0"`, the character '0' stands for a compulsory digit, the character '#' stands for an optional digit. Examples of patterns are shown in Display A6.1

Display A6.1 DecimalFormat **Class** *(Part 1 of 2)*

```java
import java.text.*;

public class DecimalFormatDemo
{
    public static void main(String[] x)
    {
        DecimalFormat twoDigitsPastPoint = new DecimalFormat("0.00");
        DecimalFormat threeDigitsPastPoint =
                            new DecimalFormat("00.000");

        double d = 12.3456789;
        System.out.println(twoDigitsPastPoint.format(d));
        System.out.println(threeDigitsPastPoint.format(d));

        double money = 12.8;
        System.out.println("$" + twoDigitsPastPoint.format(money));
        String numberString = twoDigitsPastPoint.format(money);
        System.out.println(numberString);

        DecimalFormat percent = new DecimalFormat("0.00%");

        double fraction = 0.734;
        System.out.println(percent.format(fraction));

        DecimalFormat eNotation1 =
            new DecimalFormat("#0.###E0");//1 or 2 digits before point
        DecimalFormat eNotation2 =
            new DecimalFormat("00.###E0");//2 digits before point

        double number = 123.456;
        System.out.println(eNotation1.format(number));
        System.out.println(eNotation2.format(number));

        double small = 0.0000123456;
        System.out.println(eNotation1.format(small));
        System.out.println(eNotation2.format(small));
    }
}
```

Display A6.1 DecimalFormat **Class** *(Part 2 of 2)*

Sample Screen Dialogue

```
12.35
12.346
$12.80
12.80
73.40%
1.2346E2
12.346E1
12.346E−6
12.346E−6
```

Percent Notation

The character '%' placed at the end of a pattern indicates that the number is to be expressed as a percent. The '%' causes the number to be multiplied by 100 and appends a percent sign '%'.

Scientific Notation (E-Notation)

E-notation is specified by including an 'E' in the pattern string. For example, the pattern "00.###E0" is an approximation to specifying two digits before the decimal point, three or fewer digits after the decimal point, and at least one digits after the 'E', as in 12.346E1. As you can see by the examples of E-notating in Display A6.1, the exact details of what E-notation string is produced can be a bit more involved than our explanation so far. Here are a couple more details:

> The number of digits indicated after the 'E' is the minimum number of digits used for the exponent. As many more digits as are needed will be used.

> The **mantissa** is the decimal number before the 'E'. The minimum number of significant digits in the mantissa (that is, the sum of the number of digits before and after the decimal point) is the *minimum* of the number of digits indicated before the decimal point plus the *maximum* of the number of digits indicated for after the decimal point. For example, 12345 formatted with "##0.##E0" is "12.3E3".

To see how E-notation patterns work it would pay to play with a few cases, and in any event, do not count on a very precisely specified number of significant digits.

Appendix 7
INTERFACES

In Chapter 12 we used the `ActionListener` interface, in Chapter 14 we used the `WindowListener` interface. So, you should have some idea of how to use an interface. In this appenddix we review what an interface is and how you use it, and we also show you how to define your own interfaces.

An interface specifies the headings for methods that must be defined in any class that implements the interface. For example, the `ActionListener` interface specifies that any class that implements the `ActionListener` interface must implement the following method:

```
public void actionPerformed(ActionEvent e)
```

Chapter 14 contains a number of examples of classes that implement the `Action-Listener` interface.

An interface is a type. This allows you to write a method with a parameter of an interface type, such as a parameter of type `ActionListener`, and that method will apply to any class you later define which implements the interface. An interface serves a function similar to a base class, but it is important to note that it is not a base class. (In fact, it is not a class of any kind). Some programming languages allow one class to be a derived class of two different base classes. That is not allowed in Java. In Java a derived class can have only one base class. However, in addition to any base class a Java class may have, it can also implement any number of interfaces. This gives Java an approximation to allowing multiple base classes, without the complication that arise with multiple base classes.

It is very easy to define your own interfaces. An example is given in Display A7.1. Note that the beginning of the definition starts with

```
public interface Interface_Name
```

rather than

```
public class Class_Name
```

which you would use when defining a class.

The definition of an interface then contains any number of method headings, each followed by a semicolon. And that is all there is to an interface definition. It contains no instance variables. It contains nothing but method headings. Out example has only one method heading, but an interface can contain any number of method headings.

An interface definition is stored in a `.java` file and compiled just like a class definition is compiled.

```
public interface Comparable
{
    public boolean comesBefore(Object otherObject);
}
```

Let's return to our example of an interface, which is shown in Display A7.1. Any class that implements this Comparable interface will have a method named comesBefore which can be used to compare two objects to see if one object "comes before" another. For example, if the method comesBefore is implemented so that it defines an ordering on objects, then an array of objects could be sorted according to the comesBefore ordering. Moreover the sorting method could be written to apply to any class that implements the Comparable interface (and implements it in such as to yield an ordering on its objects).

A class that implements an interface must do two things:

1. It must include the phrase
   implements Interface_Name
   at the start of the class definition. In order to implement more than one interface, just list all the interface names, separate by commas, as in
   implements ActionListener, Comparable

2. The class must implement all the method headings listed in the definition(s) of the interface(s).

Display A7.2 shows an example of a class that implements the Comparable interface given in Display A7.1. (This is a redefinition of the class PetRecord from Display 5.19/page 351.)

There is at least one complication to using interfaces. Consider the method heading for the method comesBefore in the interface defined in Display A7.1, which we reproduce below:

```
public boolean comesBefore(Object otherObject);
```

We want the parameter to be of the same type as the calling object, but the type of the calling object is not specified until we define a class that implements the interface. Thus, we had to settle for making the parameter of type Object. That means that in any class that implements the interface, the parameter in the comesBefore method must be of type Object. This often requires a type cast in the body of the definition of the method, as in Display A7.2.

Display A7.2 **An Implementation of the** Comparable **Interface**

```java
public class PetRecord implements Comparable
{
    private String name;
    private int age;//in years
    private double weight;//in pounds

    //Just a demo main.
    public static void main(String[] args)
    {
        PetRecord dog = new PetRecord("Fido", 5, 55.6);
        PetRecord cat = new PetRecord("Fluffy", 6, 10.3);
        System.out.println("Dog record:");
        dog.writeOutput();
        System.out.println("Cat record:");
        cat.writeOutput();

        if (dog.comesBefore(cat))
            System.out.println("Dog weighs less than cat.");
        else
            System.out.println("Cat weighs less than dog.");
    }

    public boolean comesBefore(Object otherPet)
    {
        return (this.weight < ((PetRecord)otherPet).weight);
    }
```

<Other methods are the same as in Display 5.19/page 351.>

```java
}
```

Sample Screen Dialogue

```
Dog record:
Name: Fido
Age: 5 years
Weight: 55.6 pounds
Cat record:
Name: Fluffy
Age: 6 years
Weight: 10.3 pounds
Cat weighs less than dog.
```

Appendix 8
The Iterator Interface

The `Iterator` interface is designed to be implemented in conjunction with classes whose objects are collections of elements. In a good implementation, repeated execution of the method `next` would produce all elements in the collection. The `Iterator` interface might be implemented by the collection class itself or by another class whose objects are iterators for the collection class. The `Iterator` interface specifies the following three methods:

```
/*************************************************
 *Returns the next element. Throws a
 *NoSuchElementException if there is no next element.
 *************************************************/
public Object next();

/******************************************************
 *Returns true if there is an element left for next to return.
 ******************************************************/
public boolean hasNext();

/*************************************************
 *Removes the last element that was returned by next.
 *Throws an UnsupportedOperationException, if the remove
 *method is not supported by this Iterator. Throws an
 *IllegalStateException, if the next method has not yet
 *been called, or if the remove method has already been
 *called after the last call to the next method.
 *************************************************/
public void remove();
```

All the exception classes mentioned are derived classes of `RunTimeException` and so an object of any of these exception classes need not be caught or declared in a throws clause.

The `Iterator` interface is in that package `java.util`. So, when defining a class that implements the `Iterator` interface, the file should contain

```
import java.util.*;
```

A sample implementation of the Iterator interface is given in the answer to Self-Test Question 19 in Chapter 10 (page 715).

Appendix 9
CLONING

A **clone** of an object is (or at least should be) an exact copy of an object. The emphasis here is on both *exact* and *copy*. A clone should look like it has the exact same data values as the object being copied, and the clone should be a true copy and not simply another name for the object being copied. In Chapter 5 in Section 5.6 entitled ***Information Hiding Revisited,*** we discussed some of the problems involved in making copies of an object. You should read that section before reading this appendix.

A clone is made by invoking the method named `clone`. The method `clone` is invoked, just like any other method. The heading for the method `clone` is as follows:

```
public Object clone()
```

Although, the method `clone` returns a copy of an object of some class, it always returns it as an object of type `Object`. So, you normally need a type cast. For example, consider the class `PetRecord` in Display 5.19/page 351 of Chapter 5. After you make suitable additions to the class definition, you can make a copy of an object of type `PetRecord` as follows:

```
PetRecord original = new PetRecord("Fido", 2, 5.6);
PetRecord extraCopy = (PetRecord)original.clone();
```

Be sure to notice the type cast `(PetRecord)`.

The above invocation of `clone` (or any invocation of `clone`) will not work unless the class implements the `Cloneable` interface. Thus, in order to make the preceding code work, you must do two things. First, you must change the beginning of the class definition for `PetRecord` to the following:

```
public class PetRecord implements Cloneable
```

Second, you must add a definition of the method `clone` to the class definition. In the case of the class `PetRecord`, the method `clone` would be defined as shown in Display A9.1.

If the instance variables are all of types whose objects cannot be changed by its methods, such as the primitive types and the type `String`, then the above definition of `clone` shown in Display A9.1 will work fine. In that definition of `clone`, the method `clone` invokes the version of `clone` in the class `Object`[1], which simply makes a bit-by-bit copy of the memory used to store the calling object's instance variables. The *try-catch* blocks are required because the method `clone` can throw the exception `CloneNotSupportedException`, if the class does not implement the `Cloneable` interface. Of course, in these classes, we are implementing the `Clone-`

Display A9.1 Implementation of the Method `clone` (Simple Case)

```
public Object clone()
{
    try
    {
        return super.clone();//Invocation of clone in class Object
    }
    catch(CloneNotSupportedException e)
    {//This should not happen
        return null; //To keep the compiler happy.
    }
}
```

Works correctly if each instance variables is of a primitive type or of the type `String`. Does not work correctly in most other cases.

`able` interface so the exception will never be thrown, but the compiler will still insist on the `try-catch` blocks. There is a bit of detail to worry about here, but as long as each instance variable is either of a primitive type or of type `String`, then the definition of `clone` in Display A9.1 will work just fine and can simply be copied unchanged into your class definition.

If your class has instance variables of a class type (other than a class like `String` whose objects cannot change), then the definition of `clone` in Display A9.1 is legal, but it probably does not do what you want a `clone` method to do. If the class contains instance variables of some class type, then the clone produced will have a copy of the instance variable's memory address, rather than a copy of the instance variable's data. For a class like `String` that cannot be changed, this is not a problem. For most other classes, this would allow access to private data in the way we described in Chapter 5 in Section 5.6 entitled **Information Hiding Revisited**. When defining a `clone` method for a class that has instance variables of a class type (other than the type `String` or similar unchangeable class types), your definition of `clone` should make a clone of each instance variable of a changeable class type. Of course, this requires that those class types for the instance variables do themselves have a suitable `clone` method. The way to define such a `clone` method is illustrated

---

[1] If your class is a derived class of some class (other than `Object`), then we are assuming the base class has a well-defined `clone` method, since *super*.`clone` will then refer to the base class.

Display A9.2 Outline of a Class with Cloning

```
public class Neighbor implements Cloneable
{
    private String name;
    private int numberOfChildren;
    private PetRecord pet;

    public Object clone()
    {
        try
        {
            Neighbor copy = (Neighbor)super.clone();
            copy.pet = (PetRecord)pet.clone();
            return copy;
        }
        catch(CloneNotSupportedException e)
        {//This should not happen
            return null; //To keep the compiler happy.
        }
    }

        <There are presumably other methods that are not shown.>

}
```

in Display A9.2. Let's go over some of the details in that definition of that `clone` method.

The following line makes a bit-by-bit copy of the memory used to store the calling object's instance variables:

```
Neighbor copy = (Neighbor)super.clone();
```

That sort of copy works fine for the instance variable `numberOfChildren`, which is of the primitive type `int`. It is also satisfactory for the instance variable `name` of type `String`. However, the value it gives to the instance variable `copy.pet` is the address of the `pet` instance variable of the calling object. It does not, as yet, give `copy.pet` the address of a *copy* of the calling object's `pet` instance variable. To change the value of `copy.pet` so that it names a copy of the calling object's `pet` instance variable, the `clone` method definition goes on to do the following:

```
copy.pet = (PetRecord)pet.clone();
```

Appendix 10
javadoc

The Java language comes with a program named `javadoc` that will automatically generate HTML documents that describe your classes. This documentation tells somebody who uses your program or class what she or he needs to know in order to use it, but omits all the implementation details, such as the bodies of all method definitions (both public and private), all information about private methods, and all private instance variables.

In order to use `javadoc` to generate documentation for some classes, the classes must be in a package or packages. Packages are discussed in Chapter 5. You also need to have access to an HTML browser (a web browser) so that you can view the documents produced by `javadoc`. However, you do not need to know very much HTML in order to use `javadoc`. Chapter 13 contains more HTML than you need to know in order to use `javadoc`.

In this appendix, we will first discuss how you should comment your classes so that you can get the most value out of `javadoc`. We will then discus the details of how you run the `javadoc` program.

Commenting Classes for Use with javadoc

To get a more useful `javadoc` document, you must give your comments in a particular way. All the classes in this book have been commented for use with `javadoc`.

The program `javadoc` will extract the heading for your class as well as the headings for all public methods, and if the comments are done correctly, certain comments. No method bodies and no private items are extracted.

For `javadoc` to extract a comment, the comment must satisfy three conditions:

1. The comment must be *immediately preceding* a public class definition or a public method definition (or other public item).

2. The comment must be given by a /* and */ style comment and the opening /* must contain an extra *. So, the comment must be marked by /** at the beginning and */ at the end.

3. Each line of the comment must begin with an *.

Placing extra *'s is both allowed and common. Using a boxlike arrangement, as we have done in this book, will produce comments of the correct form. For example, if `javadoc` is run on the class `SavitchIn` in Appendix 4, the resulting HTML document can be viewed on a browser and will contain all the text shown in color in Appendix 4. None of the black text will be in the HTML document. The layout of the text will be a bit different than it is in the class definition file, but it will be similar.

You can insert HTML commands in your comments so that you gain more control over `javadoc`, but that is not necessary and may not even be desirable. The

HTML commands in comments can clutter the comments when you look at the source file that contains the complete class definition.

Running `javadoc`

You run `javadoc` on an entire package. However, if you want to run it on a single class, you can make the class into a package simply by inserting the following at the start of the `.java` file for the class:

> `package` *Package_Name*;

Remember that the *Package_Name* should describe a relative path name for the directory containing the `.java` file for the class(es). The details on directory placement and package names are given in Section 5.7 of Chapter 5. (Directories are called *folders* in some operating systems. If your system has folders, they are the same as what we are calling *directories*.)

To run `javadoc`, you must be in the directory that *contains* the package directory, not in the package directory itself. To phrase it another way, you must be one directory above the directory that contains the class (or classes) for which you want to generate documentation. Then, all you need to do is give the following command:

> `javadoc -d` *Document_Directory* *Package_Name*

The *Document_Directory* is the name of the directory in which you want `javadoc` to place the HTML documents it produces. For example, *Document_Directory* can simply be the name of a subdirectory of where you are when you run the preceding command. The directory must already exist; `javadoc` will not create the directory for you.

For example, suppose you want to generate documentation for the class `SavitchIn` using `javadoc`. First, go to a directory on your CLASSPATH. (CLASSPATH is discussed in the subsection **Package Names and Directories** on page 365 of Chapter 5.) Create a subdirectory to hold a package; for example, you might call the subdirectory `ExtraSavitchStuff`. Place the file `SavitchIn.java` in the directory `ExtraSavitchStuff`, and place the following at the start of the file `SavitchIn.java`:

> `package` `ExtraSavitchStuff`;

You have now set up the package `ExtraSavitchStuff` so that it contains the class `SavitchIn`.

Next, create a directory to receive the HTML documents. For example, you might call this directory `SavitchDocs`. Make the directory a subdirectory of the same directory as the one *containing* `ExtraSavitchStuff`. (Do not make it a subdirectory of `ExtraSavitchStuff`.)

Finally, be sure you are in the directory such that both `ExtraSavitchStuff` and `SavitchDocs` are subdirectories of where you are, and give the following command:

> `javadoc -d SavitchDocs ExtraSavitchStuff`

If you then look in the subdirectory `SavitchDocs`, you will see a number of HTML documents (files ending in `.html`). You can view these files using your browser. The

HTML documents will describe the package ExtraSavitchStuff, including the class SavitchIn, which is probably all you have in the package.

If you wish, you can use the directory ExtraSavitchStuff in place of SavitchDocs so that both the source file SavitchIn.java and the HTML documents end up in the same directory.

This may seem like a lot of work just to get documentation consisting of the source file with some stuff deleted. However, if you are setting up the package as a library that can be imported into any class or program definition, then you need to do most of this work anyway. Moreover, once you get used to it, it's pretty easy, and best of all, it produces great documentation.

Adding the Icon Pictures

If you generate HTML documents the way we outlined, then you may find that your browser indicates that some art is missing. These are some standard icons used in the documentation for the predefined Java classes. If you can view the HTML documentation for predefined Java classes and there is no art missing, then you have these images. Look for them in a directory whose path name ends with

```
...\java\api\images
```

or

```
.../java/api/images
```

(depending on how your operating system writes path names).

The HTML documents generated by javadoc expects to find these pictures in a subdirectory called images. You can create a suitable subdirectory called images and copy all the picture files into this subdirectory.

Appendix 11
DIFFERENCES BETWEEN C++ AND JAVA

This appendix is for readers who have had some significant programming experience with either C or C++. Other readers should simply ignore this appendix.

Java and C++ appear to be very similar, but have more differences than you might be lead to believe by a casual examination of the two languages. We will not describe all of the differences in this appendix, but will go over a few similarities and differences so as to help you make the transition from C++ (or C) to Java.

Primitive Types

Java has most of the same basic primitive types as C and C++ (*int*, *short*, *long*, *float*, *double*, and *char*), but Java adds the types *byte* and *boolean*. (Recent versions of C++ have the type *bool*, which corresponds to the Java type *boolean*.) Java has no type named *long double*. Unlike C and C++, the size in bytes of a value for some specific primitive type is fully specified in Java, and is not implementation dependent. (See Display 2.2/page 57 for details.)

Strings

Unlike some versions of C and C++, strings in Java are not special kinds of arrays of characters. There is a predefined type *String* in Java. (See the section entitles **String Constants and Variables**, starting on page 80 of Chapter 2, for more details.)

Flow of Control

Control structure (*if-else*, *switch*, *while*, *do-while*, *for*) are the same in Java as in C and C++. However, there are some other differences that can affect your use of control structures in Java. Specifically, Java has no comma operator, the type *boolean* in Java neither is nor can it's values be type cast to a numeric type, and the assignment operator is better behaved in Java than in C and C++.

Java does not have the comma operator. However, the *for*-statement in Java has been defined so as to allow use of the comma, as in the following:

```
for (n = 1, product = 1; n <= 10; n++)
    product = product*n;
```

But, this "comma operator" can only be used in a *for*-statement.

The type *boolean* has the two values *true* and *false*, which cannot be interpreted as numeric values even with a type cast.

A classic error in C and C++ is to use = in place of ==, as in the following:

```
if (n = 42)
    . . .
```

In C and C++ the expression n = 42 returns the value 42, which either is or will be converted to a boolean value depending on what version of C or C++ you are using. In Java, n = 42 does not return a value, and in any event, 42 is not of type *boolean* nor will it convert to type *boolean*. So, in Java, this mistake will produce a compiler error message. (See page 168 for more details.)

Testing for Equality

Testing objects of a class type for equality can be troublesome in Java. With values of a primitive type, the == operator test for equality as you might expect. However, when you compare two objects of a class type with ==, the objects are tested for being in the same memory location, not tested for having the same data. Java classes often define a method called equals to test objects for our intuitive idea of being equal. You cannot overload the == operator (or any operator) in Java.

main Method (Function) and Other Methods

Functions are called **methods** in Java. The main method (function) serves the same purpose in Java as in C and C++. In Java, the main method headings is always:

```
public static void main(String[] args)
```

In Java, all methods, indeed all code of any kind, are defined inside of a class.

Files and Including Files

Java does not have a #include directive. Java does have an *import* statement that allows you to import an entire package (library) for use in a class (file).

The general layout of a Java program consists of a number of classes, each in a file by itself. If all the classes are in the same directory (folder), then Java will automatically find the class (file) it needs when it needs it. Using the *import* statement, it is also possible to combine classes (files) in different directories. (See Section 5.7 in Chapter 5 for more details.)

In Java a class must be in a file that has the same name as the class but with the suffix .java. For example, a class named MyClass must be in a file named MyClass.java. The compiled version of the class is automatically placed in a file named MyClass.class.

Class and Method (Function) Definitions

Java makes no distinctions between defining a method and declaring it (or as some authors phrase it: between a method prototype and a method definition). All methods (functions) have only their definition and no forward references. There is no "heading" or "signature or" "prototype" independent of the method definition.

All methods must be defined in some class.

All class definitions similarly are fully defined in one file and do not have any kind of forward reference or interface file. In particular, all method definitions are given in their entirety in their class definition. (See Chapter 4 for more details.)

No Pointers in Java

There are no pointer types in Java. Java does have pointers. All objects are named by means of pointers. However, the pointers are called *references* and they are handled automatically. A variable of type `String` will contain a reference (pointer) to a string, but there is no type for a pointer to a `String`. (See Section 4.3 of Chapter 4 for more details.)

Method (Function) Parameters

Strictly speaking, Java has only one mechanism for parameter passing, namely call-by-value. However, in practice Java is usually viewed as having two kinds of parameter passing mechanisms, one for primitive types (such as `int`, `double`, and `char`) and one for class types.

For primitive types, the only parameter passing mechanism is call-by-value.

For class type, the parameter passing mechanism is call-by-value, but it is a reference (pointer) to the class object that is passed. This allows a method (function) to change the data in the object, and so some people consider this to be call-by-reference. It does not satisfy the most common definition of *call-by-reference*, but for doing most simple things it behaves very much like call-by-reference. (To see that Java does not really have call-by-reference, just note that in Java you cannot define a method that would swap the values of two variables.) (See Chapters 4 and 5 for more details.)

Arrays

Java arrays are very much like C or C++ arrays, but there are some differences and Java arrays are better behaved. An array in Java knows its range. If `a` is an array, then the instance variable `a.length` contains an integer equal to the number of elements that the array can hold. Java array indexes are checked for being out of range and an exception is thrown if your code attempts to use an array index (subscript) that is out of range. (See Chapter 6 for more details.)

Garbage Collection

Memory management and garbage collection are automatic in Java. Java uses the `new` operator to create a new object of a class type (and so this is a form of memory allocation), but there is no other form of memory allocation. Java has no facility that the programmer can use to do garbage collection. Garbage collection is automatic.

Other Comparisons

Comments in Java and C++ are essentially the same.

There are no global variables in Java.

Java has no enumerated types.

Java has no `typedef`.

Java has no structures or unions.

You can overload method (function) names in Java as in C++, but you cannot overload operators in Java.

Java has no multiple inheritance, but does recover much of the functionality of multiple inheritance via something called an *interface*. (See Appendix 7 for more details on interfaces.)

Java has no templates, but does recover much of the functionality of templates via something called an *interface*.

In Java, a class can have a constructor with a parameter of the same type as the class, but this constructor has no special status as is true of a copy constructor in C++.

Appendix 12
USING JBUILDER

The CD that accompanies this book includes a version of JBuilder from the Inprise/Borland Corporation. JBuilder is a powerful environment that provides many tools to write, compile, run, and debug your Java programs. It is very powerful and so rather complicated. If you are a new programmer, it might be easier to first write your classes and programs using any simple editor you know how to use, and to compile and run your programs with the one line commands discussed in Chapter 1. (This will require that you down load a Java compiler from the Sun website, as discussed in the preface, or obtain a Java compiler in some other way.) Alternatively, if you are on a Windows machine, you can install the simpler environment TextPad which is also included on the CD that comes with this book. (This also requires that you down load a Java compiler from the Sun website or obtain a Java compiler in some other way.) JBuilder does not require you to obtain a compiler or any software beyond what is on the CD, but if you are a true novice, it still might be safest and easiest to use one of the other alternatives for your first few programs.

After you become a little more familiar with Java and your computer, you can install JBuilder and start learning to use it. Be patient when first running JBuilder. A lot can go right, but a lot can also go wrong. A small mistake can make it look like it is not working. It you get into trouble, just exit JBuilder and start all over again. After a good deal of patient practice it will become a powerful tool that you will enjoy using. (As a bit of encouragement we will tell you that, although JBuilder takes some effort to learn, it is easier to learn than most professional programming environments.)

Installing JBuilder

Windows Users:
On the accompanying CD, locate the folder `windows`, in that folder locate the subfolder `foundation` and in the `foundation` folder find the program `setup.exe`. Start the program by clicking on `setup.exe`. (Do not be concerned if you just see `setup` without the `exe`.) Follow the directions on your screen. To install the documentation, which you should do, similarly run another program named `setup.exe` that is in the `docs` subfolder of the `windows` folder on the CD.

UNIX (Solaris and Linux) Users:
Look for a file named `index.html` (or `readme.txt`) on the CD that accompanies this text. Follow the directions in the file. If there is no such file or if you cannot find the file, check the authors's website for this book, given below under *Problems?*.

Mac Users:

At the time this book went to press there was not a version of JBuilder for the Mac. One was due out soon. You may want to check the following website to see if it is available. If it is, you can download it from there.

```
http://www.borland.com/jbuilder/foundation/download/
```

First Use:

The first time you use JBuilder, you will see a dialog box that asks you for a serial number and an installation key. (If the fields for these two entries are not visible, click the Add button.) Before you can use JBuilder, you must enter the two numbers given below in these two fields:

Serial Number: xa32-?5n6h-5398g

Installation Key: zd4-?7a

Problems:

Solutions to known problems will be posted on the author's website for this book:

```
http://www-cse.ucsd.edu/users/savitch/books/cs1.java/
```

Questionnaire:

In exchange for your free copy of JBuilder, Inprise/Borland, the producers of JBuilder, ask that you fill out a questionnaire that you will find at the following website:

```
http://www.borland.com/jbuilder/foundation/download/
```

Running Your First Program

Since the JBuilder environment is designed for organizing and writing professional software packages that involve many classes, it can seem like a lot of work to run a simple program using JBuilder. It is a bit like washing your car with a fire hose, but remember two things: (1) You can wash your car with a fire hose, even if it is overkill. (2) If you use an fire hose to wash your car, then you will know how to use a fire hose when you need to use a fire hose. Now let's learn some details about this fire hose.

To run a Java program in JBuilder you must form a project. A project contains all the classes your program will use. Let's say you want to run the program First-Program in Display 1.5/page 27, then your project will include the classes First-Program and SavitchIn. In outline the details are as follows:

Create and name a project

Set the project properties.

Add the files to the project (FirstProgram.java and SavitchIn.java).

Make the project (that is, compile things).

Run the project.

Let's go through the details step by step.

The following details are for JBuilder under Windows. The details will be similar under other operating systems, but might show some minor variations.

Before you start move the files `FirstProgram.java` and `SavitchIn.java` from the CD to some convenient directory (folder) on out computer.

Start the JBuilder environment.

Close any open projects by repeatedly choosing `Close project ...` on the file menu until all open projects have been closed.

Choose `New project` on the `File` menu and then click the `Browse` button in the resulting dialog box. A new dialog box will appear.

In the new dialog box, choose a directory (folder) for your project and a name for your project, such as `FirstProject.jpr`. The project name should end in `.jpr`. (For now choose the same directory (folder) as the one containing the files `First-Program.java` and `SavitchIn.java`. Later you can try a different directory (folder).) After making these choices, Click the `Save` button and you will be returned to the previous dialog box. In this dialog box click `Next`.

The next dialog box asks you for some information as documentation for your project. This information is optional, but it is a good idea to fill it in. Then click the `Finish` button (even if that is not your nationality).

Choose `Project properties` on the `Project` menu. Be sure the `Paths` tab is activated (it should be automatically). Click the `Add` button, and add the path to the directory (folder) that contains `FirstProgram.java` and `SavitchIn.java`. End this dialog with the `OK` button.

Choose `Add to project` from the `Project` menu. You will then be asked if you want to `Add file` or `Add class/package`. Choose `Add file` and then add the files `FirstProgram.java` and `SavitchIn.java`. You add the files one at a time.

Choose `Make FirstProject` (or `Make` whatever-your-project-is-named) on the `Project` menu to compile your classes.

Next you need to tell JBuilder which class has the `main` method you want to run. (At first your projects will probably have only one class with a `main` method, but later there may be more than one. But in any event, you must always tell JBuilder which class `main` you want to run.) With this in mind, choose `Project properties` on the `Project` menu. Click the `Run` tab. In the resulting dialog box, click the `Application` tab. (It will probably already be clicked, but clicking it again will do no harm.) Then click the `Set` (Main class) button. In the resulting dialog box, set the `main` class to `FirstProgram`. Click `OK` buttons until the dialog boxes all go away,

To run the program, choose `Run project` on the `Run` menu. The dialog window for the program will be at the bottom of the JBuilder display.

You should save and close the project if you plan to return to it later. To save the project choose `Save project` on the `File` menu and then choose `Close project` on the `File` menu. You can later reopen the project using the `Reopen` command on the `File` menu. If you do not wish to save the project, then you should still close the project. If you close the project without saving, a dialog box will appear asking you what files you want to save. If you do not want to save the project, click `Select None` and then click `OK`.

After making and running your first project, you should explore the directory (folder) for your first project to see what files and directories (folders) JBuilder creates. That way you will know what to remove when you no longer want the project and wish to get rid of unused files.

We showed you how to run a program consisting of files that already exist. When you write your own programs, you will need to write these files yourself. To add a new file, you choose the name just as you choose the name of an existing file. When JBuilder asks if you want to create the file, answer yes. To write in the file, just double click the file name in the window on the left side of the JBuilder display. That will place you in the editor. The editor works similarly to most editors. Boxes will appear on the screen as you type. Eventually, you will learn how to use these boxes to save yourself some typing. At first, just ignore them. When you have typed in your class (program), save it.

This should get you started. There are many shortcuts and tools in JBuilder. Once you get started, take the tutorial, check the documentation, play with the environment, and learn some of the "tricks" you can do.

Running a Swing Program

Good news: A swing program is run just like any other application program.

Running an Applet

You run an applet the same way you run an application, except for one detail. When you set the `main` class, you choose the `Applet` tab rather than the `Application` tab. For applets, the applet class is the `main` class (even though it probably has no `main` method.)

Problems

Unfortunately, I will not be able to run an E-mail consulting service for JBuilder. I will place answers to some frequently asked questions on the website for this book. You can submit questions for possible inclusion, but I will not be able to answer individual questions about JBuilder and cannot guarantee that all submitted questions will be answered on the website. The website for these frequently asked questions is:

`http://www-cse.ucsd.edu/users/savitch/books/cs1.java/`

But before you ask questions, take the tutorial provided with JBuilder and try to find the answer in the JBuilder documentation.

Index

Symbols

-- *see* decrement operator 135
!= 133
" 80
% 70
&& 133
    quick reference 134
* 59
*/ 99
    quick reference 102
+
    with strings 80
    used in `System.out.println` 61
++ *see* increment operator
/ 70
/* 99
    quick reference 102
// 99
    comment
        quick reference 102
< 133
<= 133
=
    with arrays 405
    see assignment statement
== 30, 133
    with arrays 405
    dangers of 187
    with strings 135
    with class variables 270
> 133
>= 133
[] *see* array
\" 88
\\
    escape character 88
\' 88
\n 88
\r 88
\t 88
{ 100
| 981
|| 134
    quick reference 135
} 100

A

`A HREF` 850
`abs` 317
`Abstract Button` 939–940
Abstract class 494–496, 939
Abstract data type *see* ADT
Abstract Windows Toolkit *see* AWT
`AbstractButton` 810
    in class hierarchy 856
Abstraction 41
Accessor method 248
Action command 800
    for a `JMenuItem` 880
Action event *see* event, action
Action listener *see* listener, action
`ActionEvent`
    see also `actionPerformed`
`ActionEvent` *see* event, action
`ActionListener` 795
    see also listener, action
`actionPerformed` 795–796
    parameter list 797
    quick reference 799
`add` 764
    quick reference 775, 807
    see also container class
    see also layout manager
    to a `JFrame` 808
    to a panel 806
`addActionListener` 795
`addElement` 670, 672
    quick reference 667, 671
Adder applet 858

Adding machine GUI 823–829
    source code 826
    with exception handling 831
<ADDRESS> 850
Address 6, 8
addWindowListener 765
    quick reference 782
ADT 259
Aiken, Howard 4
Algorithm 21–22
    quick reference 22, 41
Alphabetical order 136–139
Analytical engine 3
Ancestor 475, 477
And *see* &&, &
Anonymous object 779
API 41, 258
Apple 9
Applet 26, 37, 855–869
    adding icons 864–866
    converting a Swing application
            861–864
    ending 40
    init 858
    main 855
    no constructor 858
    placing in HTML document 861
        quick reference 864
    preview examples 37–40
    quick reference 42
    running 858–861
    security 868
    sizing 864
    viewer *see* appletviewer 858
Applet 855, 867–868
    import statement 868
    in class hierarchy 856
    quick reference 868
Applet tag 861
Applet viewer 40
appletviewer 40, 861
Application 26
    quick reference 42
Arc *see* drawArc
Argument 29, 233
    automatic type change 237

correspondence with parameters
        238
    primitive type 232–238
    see also parameter
Arithmetic expression 69–72
    parentheses in 71
    spacing in 72
    type of value returned 69
Arithmetic operators 69–72
ARPANET 14
Array 380–447
    with = and == 405–408
    argument 400–403
        quick reference 402, 404
    in assignment statement 405–407
    base type 383
    in a class 392–400, 412–416
    creating 382–383
        quick reference 386
    declaring 382
        quick reference 386
    element 382, 386
    equality 407–408
    index 382, 388–391
        out of bounds 390–391, 527
    indexed variable *see* variable,
            indexed
    initializing 391
    as instance variable 392, 412
    instance variable
        returning 420–422
    length 383, 386, 388
    multidimensional 429–446
        declaring 430–431
        employee time record example
                440–446
        implementation 435–438
        indexed variable 431–434
        parameter 434
            quick reference 437
        ragged *see* array, ragged
        returned by method 435
            quick reference 437
    as an object 409
    parameter *see* array, argument
    partially full 416–420

ragged 438–440
as reference type 408
returned by method 409–410
    quick reference 409
searching 420
size *see* array, length 383
sorting *see* sorting
square brackets 383
    see also array, creating;
        variable, indexed
subscript 382
terminology *quick reference* 387
`ArrayIndexOutOfBoundsException`
  527
ASCII 88, 613
  see also file, ASCII 613
  table of characters 992
Assignment compatibility 63–64
  of derived class 479
  quick reference 64
Assignment statement 58–60
  with an operator 60
  quick reference 60
  with class variables 265, 270
  with quoted string 80
Augusta, Ada 3, 4
AWT 42, 758

B

Babbage, Charles 3
Backslash 86
`BankAccount` class
  source code 230
Base case *see* recursion, stopping
Base class 461
  constructor *see* `super`
  private instance variable 466–468
  private method 468
  quick reference 465
Basie, Count 154
Beeton, Isabella Mary 423
Berra, Yogi 105, 128
`BevelBorder` 898
Binary operator 72
Binary search 741–749

Binary tree 710
Bit 6
  quick reference 42
Block 231
  quick reference 231
  see also compound statement
`<BODY>` 850
Boole, George 131
`boolean` 57
Boolean expression 131–139, 190–195
  parentheses in 134
Boolean input and output 195
`boolean` type 189–199
Boolean variable *see* variable, boolean
Border 893–900
Border classes summary 899
`BorderLayout` 785, 787
  quick reference 788
`BorderLayout.CENTER` 786
`BorderLayout.EAST` 786
`BorderLayout.NORTH` 786
`BorderLayout.SOUTH` 786
`BorderLayout.WEST` 786
Box 487, 914–917
`BoxLayout` 908–912
`<BR>` 848
brace *see* curly brackets
brackets
  curly *see* curly brackets
Branching statement 128–154
`break`
  in loops 175
    quick reference 175
  in `switch` 148
`brighter` 973
Brooke, Rupert 579
Browser 26, 846, 850, 861
  book mark 850
  not handling applets 867
Bubble sort 454
Buck 538
  passing *see* `throws`-clause
`BufferedReader` 590–629
  end of file 599–628
    quick reference 599
  methods 593

opening a file 592
    quick reference 592
reading numbers 593
Bug 23
Bug infestation example *see* roach
    infestation example
Button 760
Byte 6
    quick reference 8, 42
`byte` 57
Byte code 10–12, 26
    interpreter 11
    quick reference 11, 42
    why it is called that 13

C

C language
    difference from Java 1023–1026
C++ 21
    difference from Java 1023–1026
Calculator
    see also line oriented calculator
Call-by-reference 280
Call-by-value 236
Calling a method *see* method,
    invocation
Calling object 42, 216
    omitting
        quick reference 302
`canRead` 651
    quick reference 652
`canWrite` 652
`capacity`
    vector method 676
        quick reference 669
`CardLayout` 917–922
    methods 922
    quick reference 922
Carlyle, Thomas 979
Carroll, Lewis 16, 98, 128, 264, 604,
    665, 758
Casablanca 154
Case sensitive 33, 34
Casting *see* type casting
`catch` 518–524

`catch`-block parameter 518
    quick reference 520
    multiple 543–546
        order of 543
`catch`-block *see* `catch`
`ceil` 317, 318
`<CENTER>` 848
`"Center"` 787
Central Processing Unit *see* processor
Change program
    see vending machine program
    with windows 115–118
`char` 57
Character
    ASCII *see* ASCII
    special 86–88
    Unicode *see* Unicode
`Character` 320, 321
    static methods 322
Character graphics 482–492
`charValue` 320
Circle *see* `drawOval`
`.class` file 36
Class 17
    abstract 768
        quick reference 808
    abstract *see* abstract class
    base *see* base class
    child 475
    Compiling
        see compiling, Java program
    derived *see* derived class
    inner 367–369, 923
    intuitive view 211–212
    parent 475
    quick reference 42
    wrapper *see* wrapper class
`ClassNotFoundException` 526
`CLASSPATH` 366–367
`clone` 1017
    vector method 677
        quick reference 670
Cloning 1017
Close-window button 762, 767
    not a regular button 792

programming 930–934
>   *quick reference* 934
Code 10, 42
>   byte *see* byte code
>   object *see* object code
>   source *see* source code
Color 970–979
>   black and white in RGB 976
>   RGB 970
Color 778, 970–976
>   import needed 979
>   methods 973
Color in GUI 776–778
>   predefined 778
Comma operator 168–170
Comment 99–100
>   for javadoc 1020–1021
>   *quick reference* 102
Compilation
>   separate 212
Compiler 9–10
>   *quick reference* 10, 42
Compiling
>   Java class *see* compiling, Java
>   program
>   Java program 34–36, 212–213
Complete evaluation 195
Component 807
Compound statement 141
>   *see also* block
Concatenation 80
Conditional operator 152
Confucius 178
Constant 59
>   naming 102–105
>   *quick reference* 103
Constructor 350–359
>   default 354–359
>   omitting 358
>   *quick reference* 359
>   in base class *see* this,
>   as method 470
>   in derived class *see* derived class,
>   constructor
>   invocations through ancestor
>   hierarchy 472

quick reference 357
>   what it returns 359
Container 807–808
Container class 802–808
>   *quick reference* 807
contains vector method 668
Content pane 764, 778
Cookie 16
>   *quick reference* 42
Coordinate system 951
countTokens 598
Cowley, Abraham 802
CPU *see* processor
Crash 110
createHorizontalBox 914
createVerticalBox 914
Curly brackets 100
Cyan 779

D

darker 973
Data 8
Data hiding 42
Data structure
>   linked *see* linked data structure
DataInputStream 615–618
>   closing a file 618
>   methods 616
>   opening a file 617
>   *quick reference* 618
DataOutputStream 605–615
>   appending to a file
>   *quick reference* 614
>   614–615
>   closing a file 585
>   methods 610
>   opening a file 609
Debugging 23
>   loops 186–188
DecimalFormat 1009
Decrement Operator 77–79
default 148
default access 1008
Default constructor *see* constructor,
>   default
delete 652

Derived class 461–464
    assignment compatibility 479
    constructor 469–471
    quick reference 465
    type of 476–478
Descendent 475
Digits to words case study 723–727
Dimension 889
Directory 7, 365
Disk 6
Diskette 6
dispose 927
    quick reference 927
Divide and conquer *see* top-down
    design
DivideByZeroException 529
Division 70
    integer 70–71
DOS 9
Dot 28
Double 320
double 58
    range 57
Double equal sign *see* ==
doubleValue 320
do-while 159, 161
    quick reference 161
draw3DRect 957
drawArc 956–958
    quick reference 958
Drawing *see* Graphics *and* paint
drawLine 953
    quick reference 957
drawOval 956
    quick reference 958
drawPolygon 962
drawPolyline 962
drawRect 957
drawRoundRect 960
    quick reference 957
drawString
    quick reference 983
Driver program 326, 328, 331
Dynamic binding 496–497
    and type checking 498

E

E 317
e in numbers 63
"East" 787
Ecclesiastes 333
EDSAC 5
Einstein, Albert 923
elementAt 670
    quick reference 667
Ellington, Duke 761
else
    omitting 129
    see if-else
Empty statement 173
Empty string 815
EmptyBorder 898
Encapsulation 18–19, 252–263
    implementation 255
    quick reference 19, 42, 259
    user interface 252
Encryption 16
End of file
    binary file 625
    text file 599
ENIAC 4
ensureCapacity 669
EOFException 625
    quick reference 628
Equal sign 29
    see also double equal sign 29
equals
    for Color 973
    example with out *this* 277
    example with *this* 272
    method 270–274
    method in String 82
    String method 136
        quick reference 138
Equals *see* == *and* equals
equalsIgnoreCase
    method in String 82
136
    quick reference 138
Error
    logic *see* logic error

run-time *see* run-time error
syntax *see* syntax error
Error message 24
Escape character *see* character
    special
Escape sequence
    see character, special
EtchedBorder 900
Event 760
    action 792–797
        quick reference 798
    firing 760
    handler 760
Event driven programming 760–761
Exception 512–562
    declaring *see* throws -clause
    defining exception classes 528–533
        quick reference 534
        when to 537–538, 549
    handling 513
    overuse of 549
    predefined classes 526–527
    rethrowing 552
    that need not be caught 542–543
    throwing 513
    uncaught 542
    what it is 521
    when to throw 549
        quick reference 551
Exception 527
    quick reference 527
Execute 8
exists 648
    quick reference 652
exit 110, 112, 177
    quick reference 177
Expression
    boolean *see* boolean expression
    spacing in 72
extends 462

F

Factorial 752
Fibonacci number 754
Field 213
Fields, W. C. 306

Figure 484
File 6
    ASCII 580, 613
    binary
        appending to a file 614–615
        end of 625
        I/O 604–648
        input *see* DataInputStream
        output *see* DataOutputStream
    binary versus text 580
    check for existence *see* exist
    check for readable *see* canRead
    check for writable *see* canWrite
    closing 585, 608
        why do it 587
    deleting *see* delete
    end of 625
    for a Java program 35
    names 582, 584, 608, 609
        reading from keyboard 594,
            619
    opening a binary file 607
    opening a text files 582
    path name *see* path name 651
    text 581–602
        closing 585
        end of 599
        reading from *see*
            BufferedReader
        writing to *see* PrintWriter
File class 648–653
    methods 652
File of records 631–643
    case study 638
FileInputStream 618, 629–653
    quick reference 602, 630
FileNotFoundException 526, 623
    quick reference 625
FileOutputStream 599–602, 629–653
    quick reference 602, 630
FileReader 592, 599–602
fill3DRect 957
fillArc 958
fillOval 953, 958
fillPolygon 962
fillRect 957

fillRoundRect 957
final 102, 466
    quick reference 587, 611
finally 551–552
Firing *see* event, firing
first method in CardLayout 921
firstElement vector method 669
Float 320
float 57, 58
Floating point notation 63
Floating point number 57, 63
    imprecision in 67
floatValue 320
floor 317, 318
Flow of control 128
FlowLayout 787
    quick reference 788
flush 586
    quick reference 611
Folder *see* directory
Font 979–983
    point size 981
    samples 981
Font 980–983
    methods and constants 984
Font.BOLD 984
Font.ITALIC 984
Font.PLAIN 984
for 167–170
    comma used with 168
    extra semicolon 172
    local variable 232
    quick reference 172
    with arrays 390
Fully qualified class name 903
    list of 903
Function 21, 224

G

Garbage collection 687, 696
Geometric progression, 753
getActionCommand 797
    quick reference 801
getBlue 973
getContentPane 38, 764, 768, 808
    when to use 809

getGreen 973
getMessage 519–524, 533
    quick reference 520
getName 652
getPath 652
getRed 973
getText 815
    quick reference 816
GIF 882
Giga- 43
Glue 913, 914
Gosling, James 25
Gotcha 24
Graphical user interface *see* GUI
Graphics
    coordinate system 951
Graphics 952–969
    import needed 979, 953
Greater than or equal *see* >=
Greater than *see* >
GridLayout 788
    quick reference 788
GUI 38, 105, 759
    quick reference 760
    quick reference 43

H

<H1> 847
<H2> 847
Hamlet 392
Hardware 3–7
    quick reference 43
Harmonic progression 753
"Has a" relationship 479
hasMoreTokens 598
<HEAD> 850
Head node 681
    quick reference 680
Heavyweight 904
Heraclitus 664
Heywood, John 874
Hollerith, Herman 4
Home page 847
HotJava 26
    quick reference 43
HREF 850, 853

`<HTML>` 850
HTML 847–854
    break command 848
    center command 848
    comments 849
    file name 848
    heading commands 847
    inserting a hyperlink 850–852
        quick reference 853
    inserting a picture 854
    line break 848
    paragraph command 848
    uppercase versus lowercase 848
`.html` 848
HTML document 40
`http` 853
Hugh Antoine, D'Arcy 950
Hyperlink 847, 850–852
Hypertext 847
Hypertext Markup Language
       see HTML 847

I

I/O 89
IBM 4
Icon 40, 882–886
    in applet 864
    on button 883
    on label 883
    on menu 887
    quick reference 883
Identifier 33
    quick reference 34
    spelling rules 33
    upper- and lowercase in 33
`if-else` 129–131
    multiway 143–144
        quick reference 145
    nested 143–144
`ImageIcon` 39, 883–886
    quick reference 883
    use in applets 866
`IMG SRC` 854
`implements` 795
`import` 108, 365
    quick reference 366

Import statements
    for borders 893
    for Swing and AWT 781
Increment Operator 77–79
Indenting 100–102
Index
    in a string 85
`indexOf`
    method in `String` 83
`indexOf` vector method 668
Infinite Loop *see* loop, infinite
Infinite recursion *see* recursion, infinite
Information hiding 19, 241–263
    quick reference 43
Inheritance 20, 458–507
    quick reference 20, 43
`init` 37
`init` *see* applet, `init`
Input
    echoing 96
    keyboard 61, 91–97
        see also `SavitchIn`
`insertElementAt` 668, 672
Insertion sort 455
`Inset` 889
Instance variables *see* variable, instance
`int` 55
    range 57
Integer 57
`Integer` 320
Interface 795, 799, 1012
Internet 13–16, 26, 846
    quick reference 43
Internet browser *see* browser
Internet Explorer 846
Interpreter 11
    quick reference 43
`intValue` 320
Invocation *see* method, invocation
`IOException` 526, 605, 623
"Is a" relationship 479
`isDigit` 322
`isEmpty` vector method 669
`isLetter` 322
`isLowerCase` 322
`isUpperCase` 322

isWhitespace 322
Iterative version 734
Iterator 691–697
    external 696
    internal 696
    quick reference 694
Iterator interface 1015
Iterator interface 706

J

JApplet 37, 855
    import statements 855
    in class hierarchy 856
    quick reference 858
    see also applet 855
.java file 35
Java
    history of 25
    how named 26
.java 36
Java Beans 43
Java Foundation Classes 758
Java Virtual Machine 10
    quick reference 44
Java web site 852
java.applet 856, 867
java.awt 767
java.awt.event 767
java.io 582, 606
java.util 597, 666
Java 2 43
javac 35
javadoc 263, 854, 1020–1022
JavaScript 44
javax.swing 762
javax.swing.border 893
JBuilder 1027–1030
JButton 791–792
    methods 888
    quick reference 792
    resizing 886
JColorChooser 976–979
    import needed 979
JComponent 807, 810, 856
JDK 44

JFC *see* Java Foundation Classes
JFrame 764
    adding to 808
    methods 781
    quick reference 776
JLabel 38, 764
    methods 888
    quick reference 765
JMenu 875–881
    adding to a JFrame 881
    quick reference 880
JMenuBar 879
    adding to a JFrame 881
    quick reference 880
JMenuItem 879
    methods 940
JOptionPane 105–118
    quick reference 111
JPanel 803–806
    quick reference 806
JPEG 882
JScrollPane 890–892
    add 890
    methods 893
    quick reference 892
JTextArea 812
    quick reference 816
    read only 817
    see also text area
    size of 816
JTextComponent 810, 856
JTextField 815
    quick reference 816
    read only 817
    see also text field
    size of 816
JVM *see* Java Virtual Machine 10

K

Key word *see* reserved word
Khayyam, Omar 412
Kilo- 44

L

Label 38, 764

Language
    assembly 9
    high level 9–10
        quick reference 43
    intermediate 25
    low-level 9–10
        quick reference 44
    machine 9
        quick reference 44
`last` method in `CardLayout` 922
`lastElement` vector method 669
`lastIndexOf` vector method 669
Late binding *see* dynamic binding.
Layout manager 783–788, 808
    default 789
    quick reference 786
Lazy evaluation 194
Leibniz, Gottfried von 3
`length`
    method in class `File` 652
    see also array, length
    method in `String` 82
Less than or equal *see* <=
Less than *see* <
Lexicographic ordering 136
Lightweight 906
Lincoln, Abraham 790
Line oriented calculator 553–567
Line wrapping 817
`LineBorder` 899
Link 679
`link` 681
Linked data structure 679–710
Linked list 679–709
    adding to 685
    doubly linked 709
    empty 681
    exception handling 697–706
    quick reference 680
    removing a node 686
    stepping through 685
    variations on 708
Linker 13
    quick reference 44
Linking 13
Linux 9

List
    linked *see* linked list
Listener 760, 764–765
    action 792–797
        quick reference 798
    registering 765, 795
    window 765
`ListNode` 682
Literal 60
Local variable *see* variable, local
Logic error 24
`Long` 320
`long` 57
`longValue` 320
Look and feel 900–904
    changing 901
    default 901
        changing 904
    quick reference 901
Loop 154–188
    body 154, 179
    count controlled 181
    debugging 186–188
    designing 178–183
    do-while *see* do-while
    ending 181–183
    for *see* for
    infinite 165–166, 186
    initializing statements 180–181
    iteration 154
        zero times 157
    nested 183
    off-by-one error 187
    sentinel value 182
    statement 128
    what kind to use 174–175
    while *see* while
Lovelace, Ada *see* Augusta, Ada

M

Macintosh 9
MacOS 9
Magenta 779
`main` 56, 311–312
Mark I 4
`Math` class 316–318

MatteBorder 900
max 317
Mega- 44
Member 213
Memory 5–8
    auxiliary 6
    main 6
    secondary *see* memory, auxiliary
Memory address 268, 269
Memory location 6
    quick reference 8
Menu 760
    Adding *quick reference* 881
    bar 879
    bar see also JMenuBar
    item *see* JMenuItem
    nested 880
    see also JMenu 875
MERIT 15
Message 32
    error *see* error message
Metal look and feel 901
Method 17, 29, 215–224
    accessor 248
    body 220
    boolean valued 275–278
    call to overridden 471
        quick reference 471
    calling method 297–303
    class 306
        see also method, static 306
    definition 219–228
        overriding *see* overriding
            method definition
        quick reference 226
        syntax summary 239–240
    heading 220
    helping 303
    invocation 29, 215–219
        quick reference 32, 44, 219
    main 221
    mutator 248
    naming 224
    private
        in base class *see* base class,
            private method

    private 303
    recursive *see* recursion
    static 306–312
        quick reference 311
    testing 331–332
    that returns a value 216–218
        quick reference 226
    void 218–219
        quick reference 216, 226
Microcomputer 15
Microsoft's Internet Explorer 846
min 317
Money output case study 324–329
"Monospaced" 984
Motif look and feel 901
m-space 816
Multidimensional array *see*
        array, multidimensional
Multiplication 59
Mutator method 248

N

Name *see* identifier
Naughton, Patrick 26
NegativeNumberException 546
Net browser *see* browser
Netscape 26
Netscape Navigator 846
new 265
    in argument 779
        quick reference 779
    why need
        quick reference 216
    with arrays *see* array, creating
next method in CardLayout 921
nextToken 597–598
    quick reference 598
Node
    deleted
        garbage collection 696
    inner class 690
        quick reference 691
    root 710
"North" 787
NoSuchElementException 598
Not equal *see* !=

Not *see* !
null 304
    in `showMessageDialog` 115
    quick reference 304
Null statement *see* empty statement
`NullPointerException` 689
Number constant *see* constant
`NumberFormatException` 830–834
Numbers 62

O

Object 17, 29
    anonymous 779
    calling *see* calling object
    creation 265
        see also `new`
`Object` 478
    quick reference 478
Object code 10
    quick reference 44
Object program *see* object code
Object-oriented programming
        17–20, 500
Off-by-one error 187
`OneWayNoRepeatsList` 412–416
OOP *see* object-oriented programming
Operating system 9
Operator
    arithmetic *see* arithmetic operator
    binary *see* binary operator 72
    conditional 152
    ternary 152
    unary *see* unary operator 72
Or *see* `|`, `||`
Output
    screen 61, 89–91
        windowing *see* `JOptionPane`
`OutputFormat` class 332
    source code 373
Overloading 333–336
    compared to overriding 466, 475
    interaction with automatic type
        conversion 336
        quick reference 341
    not on type returned 341
    quick reference 336

Overriding method definition 465–466
    compared to overloading 466, 475
    indirectly 498
    quick reference 465
Ovid 241

P

`<P>` 848
`pack` 938
Package 108, 364–367
    name 365–367
        quick reference 366
    quick reference 365
package access 1008
`paint` 952–969
    versus `repaint` 969
`paintComponent` 961–962
Palindrome 454, 753
Panel 803
    in a panel 806
    see also `JPanel` 806
Parameter
    actual 233
        see also argument
    as local variable 236
    class 279–281
        quick reference 281
    comparing class and primitive
        type 281
    formal 233
    names
        choosing 243
    primitive type 232–238
    quick reference 238
    see also argument 238
Parentheses
    in arithmetic expressions 71
`parseByte` 114
`parseDouble` 114, 320, 821
`parseFloat` 114, 321
`parseInt` 108, 114, 321, 818
`parseLong` 114, 321
`parseShort` 114
Pascal programming language 21
Pascal, Blaise 3, 53
Password 16

Path name 651–653
    quick reference 594, 615
Payne, Jonathan 26
Peace, Warren 380
Peer 904
Peirce, Charles Sanders 2
Person class 460
PI 317
Pixel 769, 951
    quick reference 770
Point size 981
Polygon 960–961
Polymorphism 19, 500–501
    quick reference 45, 500
Postcondition 243–244
pow 317
Precedence rule 71, 72, 192, 194
Precedence rules
    complete list 991
Precondition 243–244
previous method in CardLayout 922
print
    method of PrintWriter 584
        quick reference 586
print *see* System.out.print 90
println
    method of PrintWriter 584
        quick reference 586
println *see* System.out.println
PrintWriter 581–585
    closing a file 585, 608
    methods 586, 610
    opening a file 582–584
        quick reference 584
    opening a file for appending
        quick reference 589
Privacy Leak 689
private 244–248
    in base class *see* base class, private
        quick reference 247
Procedure 21
Processor 5
Program 8
Programmer 28
projectedPopulation,   alternative
    implementation 242

protected 1008
Pseudocode 22
    quick reference 22, 180
public 244–247
    quick reference 247
Punch 875
Punched card 4
Purchase class 252–256
    alternative implementation 260
    source code 253

Q

Quotes *see* string

R

read method of BufferedReader 593, 594
readBoolean 617
readChar 96, 617
readDouble 95, 617
    quick reference 616
readFloat 617
readInt 94, 617
    quick reference 616
readLine 93
    method of BufferedReader 593
        quick reference 593
readLineDouble 93
readLineFloat 93
readLineInt 61, 92
readLineLong 93
readLineNonwhiteChar 93
readLong 616
readNonwhiteChar 95
readUTF 617
Recursion 52–118, 722–749
    base cases *see* recursion, stopping case
    compared to overloading 738
    general technique outline 730
    infinite 729
    quick reference 723
    returning a value 734–738
    stopping cases 728, 730, 734
    version iterative 734

Recursive method *see* recursion
Reference 264–281
Reference type 269
　　array 408
removeAllElements 668
removeElement 668
removeElementAt 668
repaint 938, 962–969
　　versus paint 969
Repaint manager 938
Reserved word 34
　　list of 990
return 223–225
　　in *void*-method 225
　　quick reference 227
Returned value 61
　　quick reference 62
Returned value *see* value returned
RGB color system 970
Roach infestation example 161–165
round 317, 318
Round rectangle 960
Running
　　applet 40
　　Java program 12, 36
　　program 8
Run-time error 24

S

Sales report case study 393–400
"SansSerif" 984
SavitchIn 29, 35, 61, 91–96
　　code explained 603–604
　　quick reference 95
　　source code 993–1007
　　static methods 307
Screen 5
Scroll bar *see* JScrollPane 890
SDK 45
Search
　　binary *see* binary search 741
Secondary memory *see* memory,
　　　　secondary
Selection sort 423–427
SelectionSort
　　vector version 673

Self-documenting 99
　　quick reference 99
Semicolon
　　extra in loop 172
Sentinel value 182
"Serif" 984
Serif
　　meaning of 983
setActionCommand 800
　　quick reference 801
setBackground 778, 782
setBorder 898–899
　　quick reference 900
setColor 970
　　quick reference 970
setDefaultCloseOperation 930
setEditable 817
setElementAt 666
　　quick reference 667
setFont
　　quick reference 984
setForeground 782
setHorizontalScrollBarPolicy 891
　　quick reference 893
setHorizontalTextPosition 889
setIcon 39, 883
　　in applet 866
　　quick reference 887, 888
setLayout 783
　　quick reference 786
setLookAndFeel 902
setMargin 886, 888
setMaximumSize
　　for buttons and labels 889
setMinimumSize
　　for buttons and labels 889
setPreferredSize
　　for buttons and labels 889
setSize 677, 764
　　quick reference 669, 782
　　size units 770
setText
　　for buttons and labels 886
　　　　quick reference 887, 888
　　for text component 815
　　　　quick reference 816

setTitle 776
    quick reference 782
setVerticalScrollBarPolicy 891
    quick reference 893
setVerticalTextPosition 889
setVisible 765, 770–771, 935–938
    quick reference 771, 782
Shakespeare, William 13, 79, 364, 381,
    392, 578, 812, 925
Sheridan, Richard Brinsley 847
short 57
Short-circuit evaluation 194
show
    method in CardLayout 921
showInputDialog 108–109
    inputting numbers 114
    quick reference 111
showMessageDialog 110
    multiline output 115
    outputting numbers 113
size
    vector method 670, 676
        quick reference 669, 671
Size units for GUIs 769
Smalltalk 21
Software 3, 8–9
    quick reference 9, 45
Sorting 423–427
Source code 10
    quick reference 45
Source program *see* source code
"South" 787
Spam 15
Species class 275
    source code 276
SpeciesFirstTry class
    source code 214
SpeciesFourthTry class
    source code 249
SpeciesSecondTry class
    source code 234
SpeciesThirdTry class
    source code 246
Spinoza, Benedict 189
sqrt 317
Stack 710

Stack overflow 732
Statement 31
    assignment *see* assignment
        statement
    branching *see* branching statement
    compound *see* compound
        statement
    empty *see* empty statement
    loop *see* loop, statement
    nested 140–141
static 102
    see also method, static
stepwise refinement
    see top-down design
Stream 579
    quick reference 579
String 79–88
string
    quoted 80
    see also String
StringLinkedList 683
StringLinkedListSelfcontained
    692
StringLinkedListWithIterator 698
stringToDouble 822, 833
stringToInt 821
StringTokenizer 597–598
    methods 598
Strut 912–913, 914
stub 332
Student class 463
Style 98–105
substring 83
Sun Microsystems 25
super 469, 472
    calling object 471
        multiple 476
    calling object *quick reference* 470
Swift, Jonathan 581
Swing 758
    class hierarchy 810, 856
    JOptionPane 105
    number I/O 818–823
    number input *quick reference* 822
    number output *quick reference* 823
    quick reference 45

switch 148–150
    break 148
    controlling expression 148
    quick reference 151
Syntax 24
    error 23
    quick reference 24
`System.exit` 767
`System.exit` *see* `exit`
`System.out.print` 90–91
    quick reference 92
`System.out.println` 61, 89–91
    quick reference 91

T

Tera- 45
Ternary operator 152
Testing
    bottom up 331
    see also loop, testing
    see also method, testing
Text area 812–817
    line wrapping 817
    see also `JTextArea`
    see also text component
Text component 812–818
    read only 817
Text field
    labeling 817
    see text component
Text file
    appending to 588–590
    reading numbers from 593
Text file *see* file, text
TextPad
    compiling 35
    running a Java program 36
    running an applet 40
this 225–228
    as method 470
        quick reference 471
    omitting 300–301
        quick reference 302
    quick reference 228

throw 517–518, 519
    multiple 543
    quick reference 518
Throwing an exception *see* *throw*
throws-clause 538–539
    in derived classes 543
    quick reference 542
throw-statement *see* *throw*
`<TITLE>` 850
Token 597
`toLowerCase` 82, 322
Top-down design 329
`toString` 321, 480–481
    as example of dynamic binding 499
`toUpperCase` 82, 322
Toy program 303
Tracing
    loop *see* variable, tracing
    variable 188
Tree 710
    Binary *see* binary tree
`Triangle` 490
`trim` 83
`trimToSize` 677
    quick reference 669
Truman, Harry 538
Truth tables 193
try 514–518
try-block
    variables declared in 585
try-block *see* *try*
try-throw-catch
    nested 551
    quick reference 525
    see also *try*; *throw*; *catch* 525
Turbo Pascal 21
Turing, Alan *footnote* 4
Type 55
    class 56
    primitive 56, 57–58
    reference 269
Type cast
    precedence of 991
Type casting 64–66
    quick reference 66

Type checking
   and dynamic binding 498

U

`UIManager` 902
Unary operator 72
`UnderGraduate` class 473
Unicode 88
   table of characters 992
UNIX 9
`UnknownOpException` 558
`updateComponentTreeUI` 903
URL 853
   quick reference 45
User 26
UTF 613

V

`validate` 935
   quick reference 938
Value returned 218
Variable 29, 53
   boolean 190–191
      ending a loop 196–197
   class 314
      see also variable, static 314
   class type 265–270
      quick reference 269
   declaration 53–56
      location of 56
      quick reference 55
   global 231
   indexed 382
      as method argument 400
   initializing in declaration 67, 68
      quick reference 68
   instance 213–215
   local 229–231
      in `for`-statement 232
      quick reference 231
   as memory location 53
   names 55
   static 314
   subscripted *see* variable, indexed

uninitialized 67, 304
   value 53
Variable, static
Vector 665–678
   accessing at an index 666–670
      quick reference 670
   add element 667
   adding element to 672
   base type 671, 674
      quick reference 674
   capacity 666
   compared to array 674
   constructor
      quick reference 667
   creating 666
   make a copy 670
   memory management 669
   remove element 668
   search methods 668
   size *see* `size`, vector method 670
`Vector` 666
   methods 667–670
Vending machine program 73–77
view port 890
Virus 16
   quick reference 45
Von Neumann, John 4

W

Web browser
   quick reference 45
   see browser
Web browser *see* browser
Web Page 45
`"West"` 787
`while` 155–157
   quick reference 157
Whitehead, Alfred North 297
Whitespace 95, 322
Wilde, Oscar 882
Window 760
   listener 768–769
Window interface 761
   quick guide to designing 809–811
   see also `JFrame`

windowActivated 769, 926
WindowAdapter 766, 768–769
    methods 769
windowClosed 769, 926
windowClosing 766, 769, 926
windowDeactivated 769, 926
windowDeiconified 769, 926
WindowDestroyer 764, 765–767
    source code 766
windowIconified 769, 926

WindowListener 925–927
    methods 926
    quick reference 929
windowOpened 769, 926
Windows 9
Windows look and feel 901
Word
    reserved *see* reserved word
World Wide Web 13–16, 26, 45
    see also Internet
Wrapper class 319–323
    quick reference 320
writeBoolean 611
    quick reference 611
writeChar 611
    quick reference 610
writeDouble 609
    quick reference 610
writeFloat 609, 610
writeInt 608–609
    quick reference 610
writeLong 610
writeUTF 612–613
    quick reference 611

X

X Files 189